G000044194

Published by
Time Out Guides Limited
Universal House
251 Tottenham Court Road
London W1T 7AB
Tel +44 (0)20 7813 3000
Fax +44 (0)20 7813 6001
email guides@timeout.com
www.timeout.com

Editorial
Editor Jenni Muir
Deputy Editor Phil Harriss
Group Food & Drink Editor Guy Dimond
Listings Editors Cathy Limb, Alex Brown
Researchers Shane Armstrong, Gemma Pritchard, Charlotte Middlehurst, Meryl O'Rourke
Proofreader John Pym
Indexer Jacqueline Brind

Managing Director Peter Fiennes
Financial Director Gareth Garner
Editorial Director Sarah Guy
Series Editor Cath Phillips
Editorial Manager Holly Pick
Assistant Management Accountant Ija Krasnikova

Design
Art Director Scott Moore
Art Editor Pinelope Kourmouzoglou
Senior Designer Henry Elphick
Graphic Designers Gemma Doyle, Kei Ishimaru
Advertising Designer Jodi Sher

Picture Desk
Picture Editor Jael Marschner
Deputy Picture Editor Katie Morris
Picture Researcher Gemma Walters
Picture Desk Assistant Marzena Zoladz

Advertising
Commercial Director Mark Phillips
Sales Manager Alison Wallen
Advertising Sales Ben Holt, Alex Matthews, Jason Trotman
Advertising Assistant Kate Staddon
Display Production Manager Sally Webb
Copy Control Alison Bourke, Chris Pastfield

Marketing
Marketing Manager Yvonne Poon
Sales & Marketing Director, North America Lisa Levinson
Marketing Designers Anthony Huggins, Nicola Wilson

Production
Group Production Director Mark Lamond
Production Manager Brendan McKeown
Production Controller Damian Bennett
Production Coordinator Julie Pallot

Time Out Group
Chairman Tony Elliott
Group General Manager/Director Nichola Coulthard
Time Out Communications Ltd MD David Pepper
Time Out International Ltd MD Cathy Runciman
Group IT Director Simon Chappell
Circulation Director Polly Knewstub
Head of Marketing Catherine Demajo

Sections in this guide were written by
African Tamara Gausi, Michela Wrong; **The Americas** (North American) Will Fulford-Jones, Emily Kerrigan; (Latin American) Ramona Andrews, Chris Moss; **Brasseries** Ramona Andrews, Fuchsia Dunlop, Jan Fuscoe, Roopa Gulati, Ronnie Haydon, Cathy Limb, Jenni Muir, Cath Phillips, Natasha Polyviou, Nick Rider, Cyrus Shahrad, Veronica Simpson, Eleanor Smallwood, Peter Watts, Elizabeth Winding; **British** Will Fulford-Jones, Sarah Guy, Martin Horsfield, Ruth Jarvis, Susan Low; **Caribbean** Chris Moss, Amanda Smith; **Chinese** Antonia Bruce, Fuchsia Dunlop, Terry Durack, Phil Harriss, Jennifer Joan Lee, Charmaine Mok, Sally Peck; **East European** Simone Baird, Eleanor Smallwood, Janet Zromczek; **Fish** Terry Durack, Cath Phillips, Yolanda Zappaterra; **French** Richard Ehrlich, Ruth Jarvis, Sally Peck, Nick Rider, Ethel Rimmer, Eleanor Smallwood, Simon Tillotson; **Gastropubs** Tom de Castella, Viv Groskop, Sarah Guy, Patrick Marmion, Jenni Muir, Cath Phillips, Andrew Staffell, Nick Rider, Ethel Rimmer, Veronica Simpson; **Greek** Emma Howarth; **Hotels & Haute Cuisine** Helen Barnard, Roopa Gulati, Jenni Muir, Jeff Ng; **International** Claire Fogg, Jan Fuscoe; **Italian** Elena Berton, Richard Ehrlich, Lewis Esson, Ronnie Haydon, Susan Low, Andrea McGinniss, Jenni Muir; **Japanese** Terry Durack, Tim Jackson, Kei Kikuchi, Jennifer Joan Lee, Susan Low, Jenni Muir, Sally Peck; **Jewish** Judy Jackson; **Korean** Joe Bindloss; **Malaysian, Indonesian & Singaporean** Jenni Muir, Jeff Ng; **Middle Eastern** Ros Sales, Cyrus Shahrad, Eleanor Smallwood, Caroline Stacey; **Modern European** Fuchsia Dunlop, Terry Durack, Richard Ehrlich, Ruth Jarvis, Susan Low, Cath Phillips, Nick Rider, Ethel Rimmer, Cyrus Shahrad, Caroline Stacey, Andrew Turvil; **North African** Eleanor Smallwood, Janet Zromczek; **Oriental** Joe Bindloss, Jennifer Joan Lee; **Portuguese** Amanda Smith; **Spanish** Caroline Hire, Susan Low, Andrew Staffell; **Thai** Ramona Andrews, Sally Peck, Andrew Staffell; **Turkish** Ken Olende; **Vegetarian** Simone Baird, Natasha Polyviou; **Vietnamese** Charmaine Mok; **Budget** Martin Horsfield, Jenni Muir, Holly Pick, Cyrus Shahrad, Amanda Smith, Peter Watts; **Cafés** Simone Baird, Roopa Gulati, Ronnie Haydon, Charmaine Mok, Jenni Muir, Anna Norman, Natasha Polyviou; **Fish & Chips** Martin Horsfield, Jenni Muir, Anna Norman; **Pizza & Pasta** Emily Kerrigan, Andrea McGinniss, Holly Pick, Cyrus Shahrad, Amanda Smith; **Wine Bars** James Aufenast, Susan Low, Sally Peck; **Eating & Entertainment** Gemma Pritchard.

Additional reviews by Ramona Andrews, Alex Brown, Antonia Bruce, Deborah Buzan, Tom de Castella, Claire Fogg, Guy Dimond, Terry Durack, Lewis Esson, Peter Fiennes, Will Fulford-Jones, Jan Fuscoe, Viv Groskop, Roopa Gulati, Sarah Guy, Elaine Hallgarten, Phil Harriss, Ronnie Haydon, Jane Hutcheon, Judy Jackson, Ruth Jarvis, Emily Kerrigan, Tom Lamont, Alice Lascelles, Cathy Limb, Tim Luard, Andrea McGinniss, Patrick Marmion, Charmaine Mok, Chris Moss, Jenni Muir, Anna Norman, Cath Phillips, Holly Pick, Natasha Polyviou, Nick Rider, Ethel Rimmer, Ros Sales, Cyrus Shahrad, Veronica Simpson, Eleanor Smallwood, Amanda Smith, Caroline Stacey, Emma Sturgess, Simon Tillotson, Peter Watts, Elizabeth Winding, Yolanda Zappaterra, Janet Zromczek.
Interviews Jenni Muir. **Shelf Life boxes** Jenni Muir, Lewis Esson. **The Dish boxes** Jenni Muir.

The Editors would like to thank Jessica Cargill-Thompson, Guy Dimond, Lewis Esson, Valerie Fong, Roopa Gulati, Alice Lascelles, Susan Low, Charmaine Mok, Cyrus Shahrad, Gordon Thomson.

Maps JS Graphics (john@jsgraphics.co.uk). Maps 1-18 & 24 are bsed on material supplied by Alan Collinson and Julie Snook through Copyright Exchange. London Underground map supplied by Transport for London.

Cover illustration by Neighbour.

Photography by pages 15, 55, 74, 200, 239, 347 Rob Greig; pages 18, 25 (bottom left), 28, 46, 75, 104, 105, 108, 125, 137, 148, 152, 174, 184, 185, 192, 205, 244, 246, 247, 306, 312, 320, 346 Ming-Tang Evans; pages 21, 31, 59, 64, 85, 122, 140, 141, 145, 179, 240, 335 Michael Franke; pages 25 (right), 126, 127, 234 Alys Tomlinson; page 199 Christina Theisen; pages 25 (top left), 325 David Axelbank; pages 27, 230, 308, 326, 327 Jitka Hynkova; pages 38, 41, 67, 77, 82, 171, 175, 189, 196, 227, 228, 307, 353, 356 Michelle Grant; page 47 Jael Marschner; pages 62, 65, 73, 78, 79, 99, 102, 107, 113, 116, 142, 206, 238, 331 Britta Jaschinski; pages 63, 121 Marzena Zoladz; page 103 Jean Cazals; pages 118, 119, 157, 194, 202, 245, 337 Jonathan Perugia; pages 124, 161, 163 Tricia de Courcy Ling; page 198 Gemma Day; page 338 Nerida Howard; page 350 Hayley Harrison.

The following images were provided by the featured establishments/artists: pages 143, 144, 153, 233, 243, 311.

Printer Pindar Graphics, Shannon Way, Tewkesbury Industrial Centre, Tewkesbury, Gloucestershire GL20 8HB.
Time Out Group uses paper products that are environmentally friendly, from well managed forests and mills that use certified (PEFC) Chain of Custody pulp in their production.

ISBN 978-1-905042-28-9
ISSN 1750-4643
Distribution by Seymour Ltd +44 (0)20 7429 4000.
For further distribution details, see www.timeout.com.

Welcome to the new edition of *Time Out London Eating & Drinking*, the most authoritative and comprehensive guide to good restaurants, gastropubs, cafés, bars and pubs in the capital. All the establishments featured here are selected by our editors as the best of their type. Restaurants do not pay to be included in the guide and can exert no pressure on us as to the content of their reviews.

We take pains to ensure that our reviewers remain totally objective on your behalf. They always visit restaurants anonymously and Time Out always pays the bill. We are proud of our insistence on undercover reporting – it means that, although many of our reviewers are experts in their field, their experience of each establishment is much more likely to reflect those of the average diner. Well-known critics often receive preferential treatment: photos of critics from newspapers and other magazines are pinned up in many restaurant kitchens to ensure that they will not go unrecognised. We, however, want our readers to know just what the experience of eating at each restaurant might be like for them.

Time Out reviewers are writers with a great passion for food, and for finding the best places to eat and drink in London, and many also have extraordinary expertise in specialist areas. Several are trained cooks or former chefs, others are well-established food and/or wine authors, and some are simply dedicated enthusiasts who have lived in foreign countries and learned much about that region's cuisine.

For the weekly *Time Out* magazine alone, our reviewers visit around 200 new places every year. Their better discoveries are then included in this guide. Reviewers also check other new openings, as well as revisiting places included in the previous edition. As a result, at least 2,000 anonymous visits were made in the creation of this guide. We also take in recommendations and feedback from readers and from users of our website. Then we eliminate the also-rans to create the annual list of London's best eateries that this guide represents. We hope you find it useful and entertaining.

Time Out

EDITION **26**

timeout.com/restaurants

Restaurants

Cheap Eats

Drinking

Eating & Drinking 2009

Contents

Maps & Indexes

Features

100% INDEPENDENT
The reviews in the *Time Out Eating & Drinking Guide* are based on the experiences of Time Out restaurant reviewers. All restaurants, bars, gastropubs and cafés are visited anonymously, and Time Out pays the bill. No payment of any kind has secured or influenced a review.

About the guide

ABOUT THE GUIDE

LISTED BY AREA

The restaurants in this guide are listed by cuisine type: British, Chinese, Indian etc. Then, within each of chapter, they are listed by geographical area: ten main areas (in this example, North), then by neighbourhood (Kentish Town). If you are not sure where to look for a restaurant, there are two indexes at the back of the guide to help: an **A-Z Index** (starting on p417) listing restaurants by name, and an **Area Index** (starting on p398), where you can see all the places we list in a specific neighbourhood.

STARS

A red star ★ means that a restaurant is, of its type, very good indeed. A green star ★ identifies budget-conscious eateries – expect to pay an average of £20 (for a three-course meal or its equivalent, *not* including drinks or service).

AWARD NOMINEES

Winners and runners-up in Time Out's Eating & Drinking Awards 2008. For more information on the awards, *see p24*.

OPENING HOURS

Times given are for *last orders* rather than closing times (except in cafés and bars).

MAP REFERENCE

All restaurants that appear on our street maps (starting on p358) are given a reference to the map and grid square on which they can found.

North
Kentish Town

★ ★ **Dunroamin** (100) NEW
2008 RUNNER-UP BEST GASTROPUB
Tally Up Quarter, NW5 6JJ (9876 4321).
Kentish Town tube/rail. **Lunch served**
noon-3pm, **dinner served** 6-11pm daily.
Main courses £8-£13. **Set meal** (6-8pm
Mon-Sat) £12 2 courses, £16 3 courses.
Cover £1. **Credit** AmEx, DC, MC, V.
Kentish Town didn't need another gastropub, but that hasn't deterred TV chef Martin Simon, star of the DIY Channel's *Shed in the Sun*, who has transposed his hit Lincolnshire eaterie lock, stock and composter to the capital. Set in the cellar of a new glass-and-brick property development on the site of a former pub, Dunroamin eschews gastropub clichés in favour of astro turf and rusting garden furniture from B&Q's 1972 range. Simon earned his culinary stripes supplying radishes and rock-hard salad toms to Skegness hotspots, and his experience shows in salads combining Dartmouth Park's finest weeds, seeds and fungi with a juicy wedge of iceberg. Pigeon potluck with dehydrated cucumber and some killer own-made pickled onions typifies the produce-led approach. Seasonal desserts include apple crumble, apple and pear crumble, apple crumble with blackberries and, to brighten winter days, bramley apple and sultana crumble. Wines from Simon's mates in East Anglia are sold on tap instead of beer; cheerful waiters in leather aprons and wellies abring thermoses of strong tea. Simon's latest book is added to each bill at the discount price of £25, but while that may be a bargain, it does steepen the 15 per cent service charge.
Babies and children welcome: high chairs;
buckets and spades. Disabled: toilet. Tables
outdoors (10, cabbage plot). **Map 26 L3**.

NEW ENTRIES

The NEW symbol means new to this edition of the Eating & Drinking Guide. In most cases, these are brand-new establishments; in some other instances we've included an existing restaurant for the first time.

TIME OUT HOT 100

The (100) symbol means the venue is among what we consider to be London's top 100 iconic eating and drinking experiences. For details of the complete 100, *see p22*.

PRICES

We have listed the cheapest and most expensive main courses available in each restaurant. In the case of many oriental restaurants, prices may seem lower – but remember that you often need to order several such dishes to have a full meal.

COVER CHARGE

An old-fashioned fixed charge may be imposed by the restaurateur to cover the cost of rolls and butter, crudités, cleaning table linen and similar extras.

SERVICES

These are listed below the review.

Babies and children We've tried to reflect the degree of welcome extended to babies and children in restaurants. If you find no mention of either, take it that the restaurant is unsuitable.

Disabled: toilet means the restaurant has a specially adapted toilet, which implies that customers with walking disabilities or wheelchairs can get into the restaurant. However, we recommend phoning to double-check.

Vegetarian menu Most restaurants claim to have a vegetarian dish on the menu. We've highlighted those that have made a more concerted effort to attract and cater for vegetarian (and vegan) diners.

Anonymous, unbiased reviews

The reviews in the Eating & Drinking Guide are based on the experiences of Time Out restaurant reviewers. Restaurants, pubs, bars and cafés are always visited anonymously, and Time Out pays the bill. No payment or PR invitation of any kind has secured or influenced a review. The editors select which places are listed in this guide, and are not influenced in any way by the wishes of the restaurants themselves. Restaurants cannot volunteer or pay to be listed; we list only those we consider to be worthy of inclusion. Advertising and sponsorship has no effect whatsoever on the editorial content of the Eating & Drinking Guide. An advertiser may receive a bad review, or no review at all.

So what do you think?

We've long suspected that *Time Out Eating & Drinking Guide* readers are an intelligent, cosmopolitan bunch, but what are their thoughts on eating out in the capital? **ILLUSTRATIONS** DANNY ALLISON

L et's talk about you. We know you like to eat out and that you have bought this guide to help you make the most of the restaurant and bar scene in London – the city that even US magazine *Gourmet* has declared is the world's best place to eat. But what are your feelings about dining and drinking in the capital? What's good, and what needs improvement? To find out, we posted a questionnaire on the Time Out website and invited reader feedback. This is what you told us.

The variety of cuisines on offer is by far the most exciting aspect of eating out in the capital – according to 82 per cent of respondents (as well as many of the restaurateurs and chefs featured in the interviews in this guide). And you should know, because you eat out a lot: 83 per cent of respondents do so more than three times a month, and of those over 30 per cent eat out more than twice a week.

You're not impressed by eating at the restaurants of famous chefs or keeping up with the latest openings (fewer than 3 per cent checked each of these options). A noteworthy 11 per cent of readers think the quality of food available is the most exciting thing about London dining, but a similar number think mediocre food is one of the most annoying. Most are frustrated by the cost of eating out and bad service, but other things get your goat too: notably service charges (8.3 per cent), expensive bottled water (7.5 per cent) and having to book ahead (6.7 per cent).

FAVE RAVES & DISAPPOINTMENTS

Last year Chez Bruce in Wandsworth was respondents' favourite restaurant; this year it didn't even make the top three. When *Time Out* magazine's critics named their 50 top restaurants in the capital in January 2008, Hakkasan was voted number one. It has performed very well with our survey respondents too, coming in a tantalisingly close second place. But what nabbed the top spot? A venue not too far away: Japanese restaurant Roka on Charlotte Street. Here, a robata grill producing healthy dishes takes centre stage; floor-to-ceiling windows make it a great see-and-be-seen destination; and downstairs is the fun Shochu Lounge, Time Out's Best Bar award winner in 2005.

So with two very stylish oriental restaurants taking gold and silver, which took bronze? Somewhere quite different: flagship of the British food revival, St John. The ornate styling and dainty presentation of Hakkasan and Roka are anathema to chef-proprietor Fergus Henderson and his team, but this Farringdon stalwart is still clearly very much in fashion with Londoners.

We also couldn't help notice that all your top three restaurants feature excellent bars that are worthy destinations in their own right. Of course, this might indicate a collective fondness for liquor, but it also suggests that a well-rounded eating and drinking package is what you are looking for on a night out – or at least when it comes to considering your favourite places to go.

We couldn't resist asking you about your dining disappointments either. For two years in a row now our respondents have named the Ivy as London's most overrated restaurant. And for two years in a row it has been followed by Nobu. We'd argue that the celebrity-obsessed corners of the media have done so much to hype these places that it's almost impossible for them not to disappoint on some level. Jamie Oliver's Fifteen was third in the rankings last time we surveyed readers, but has been edged out of the running for this dubious honour by Harvey Nichols' Oxo Tower Restaurant, Bar & Brasserie .

ON THE MENU

With Japanese, Chinese and British venues currently top of the capital's leader board, we could assume that Japanese, Chinese and British cuisines are your favourite choice when dining out, but not so. Japanese restaurants have, overall, taken a bit of a dive compared to our last survey, with Thai cuisine kick-boxing it from fourth into fifth place.

Italian is winner here and, while it's not by a huge margin, it has come in indisputed first place two years in a row. And, just as with our last survey, Modern European cuisine comes in second, with the generally more rustic gastropub dining in third place.

In some ways, this is to be expected, as Italian, Modern European and Gastropubs have long been three of this guide's largest chapters, suggesting London has a proliferation of successful quality eateries in these categories. However, it's the opportunity for more – and better – Thai restaurants in the capital that some in the trade will find intriguing: it accounts for only four-and-a-half pages in this edition.

EASIER BEING GREEN

This year we felt the environment had become such a key issue in the restaurant world that it was time for us to introduce a Best Sustainable Restaurant category to our Eating & Drinking Awards. We also thought it important to ask what you felt about eating out and environmental concerns. Most respondents feel that restaurants should be rated on 'eco-friendliness' but, significantly, a quarter do not think they should and another 18-19 per cent have not yet made up their mind on the subject.

Furthermore, while 74 per cent of readers said they would be 'quite likely, likely or extremely likely' to choose a restaurant rated as 'eco-friendly' over one that was not rated at all, a sizeable 26 per cent were of the (admirably candid) opinion that they would be unlikely to visit a restaurant on this basis. With just under 14 per cent 'extremely likely' to favour an 'eco-friendly restaurant', the message many proprietors will be taking from this is that adopting a sustainable policy purely for PR effect is not worthwhile.

Nevertheless, restaurants have to realise that the days of pressing customers to order 'still or sparkling?' are over. Around 90 per cent of respondents have never been refused tap water in a restaurant. However, a significant proportion – over 41 per cent – have been made to feel embarrassed when asking for tap water. We asked those people who have been refused tap water where it happened and the responses were highly varied: from fashionable foodie establishments attracting a celebrity crowd, to well-known chains and a few small, unlicensed places where presumably sales of non-alcoholic drinks are a much-needed contribution to the profits. One place (we know who they are and will test them on this ourselves on our next visit) even told a customer that their tap water was unsafe for drinking.

A few respondents used the comments box on our website to indicate that they think charging for filtered water, in the manner of Yo! Sushi, is taking the mickey – no way forward for those unlicensed eateries there, unfortunately. Perhaps most revealing, however, was the tendency of people to blame themselves when they were refused tap water. 'My own fault for going somewhere rubbish,' was a typical response, indicating that in future anywhere that does refuse a request for tap water, or attempt to charge for it, could well be perceived as being a bit rubbish too.

HEALTH CLAIMS A GO-GO

The health labelling of restaurant menus is a cause of ongoing debate in the trade. Government health advisers suggest it could help tackle obesity in the population now that consumers spend more money on eating out than they do on meals cooked at home. In New York food labelling has become compulsory for chain restaurants and takeaways; part of the concern here is that such a scheme might be pushed on to other types of restaurant as well.

Yo! Sushi is already using the Food Standard Agency's traffic light system, where dishes are marked with red, amber or green dots to signify high, medium or low levels of fat, sugar, salt and saturates, but some nutritionists argue this system is too simplistic. What do our readers think? Half said they would like to see more restaurants adopting the traffic light system. A significant number, yes, but at 40 per cent so too is the number of people giving the idea a clear thumbs-down.

YOUR DAILY BREAK

At Time Out we're just as concerned with the quality of budget eateries and everyday eating places as we are with fancier gourmet establishments (that's why this guide features a Cheap Eats section), so we were keen to know more about your lunchtime spending.

Despite the extraordinary proliferation of designer sandwich bars and coffee shops in the centre of London, the vast majority of our respondents claim they spend less than £5 on a typical lunch during the week, with an astonishing one-third of readers reporting they spend £3.50 or less – surely, good news for the supermarkets. Considering most of the sandwiches at Pret A Manger cost over £2.40 and a tall latte at Starbucks is £2.05, most of you seem to be doing a good job of keeping a tight rein on workday eating expenses.

It's all too easy to spend £5-£9.99 on lunch in the capital, especially in the City and Docklands, yet only 18 per cent of respondents put themselves in this bracket. Fewer than 3 per cent spend £10-£14.99, which suggests a limited number like to sit down to a hot meal rather than grab a takeaway. It will be interesting to see how the sandwich and coffee chains fare over the next few years of economic downturn – and we'll be back, with more questions (and answers) to track this and other trends. Until then, enjoy making the most of London's vibrant eating and drinking scene.

CANARY WHARF
SHOPPING

famous for business
fabulous
with friends

OVER 200 SHOPS, CAFÉS, BARS AND RESTAURANTS, ONE GREAT LOCATION
www.mycanarywharf.com

The greening

of London's restaurants

Guy Dimond looks behind the recycling bins to find out what makes a restaurant eco-friendly. **ILLUSTRATIONS** DANNY ALLISON

Food shortages, food waste and the environment have all been grabbing the headlines over the last year, yet these – and dozens of related issues, from animal welfare to food miles – are not new discoveries, or even new problems. Since ancient times, feeding, fasting and quaffing have caused angst to moralisers and the thinking diner. The recent resurgence of interest in what, and how, we should eat has merely come into greater prominence because of numerous TV shows (especially those by Jamie Oliver and Hugh Fearnley-Whittingstall), and newspaper and magazine articles waxing lyrical about everything from allotments to happy chickens. This concern about our food supply has even been picked up by world leaders such as Gordon Brown, who have been making increasingly grave comments about food security and even advising us to waste less and tighten our belts. Not since World War II have Londoners been exhorted to waste less food and be careful with resources – the plate of the nation seems to be causing as many furrowed brows as those caused by the current economic downturn, and the two are connected. In times of plenty,

we feast; in times of perceived famine, we become more concerned about our food supply[1].

For gourmets and especially restaurants, the greening of our attitudes towards food could sound like bad news, as restaurants have been inexorably wrapped up with notions of excess, indulgence and celebration. In contrast, people who have given serious thought to environmental issues have come to the inconvenient but inescapable conclusions that we should all drastically reduce our consumption of meat and fish; eat a lot more vegetables; and – when health is also factored in – drink a lot less alcohol than we currently do. The danger is that eating out could become a joyless affair if eco-warriors alone were to decide what's on the menu. Clearly, what is needed is a third way: one where diners can eat well without endangering fish stocks or drinking bottled water shipped from the other side of the world or where a long chain of exploitation and environmental degradation leads to your after-dinner espresso.

This quest for the third way – mindful of environmental and ethical considerations, but also producing wonderful meals, in fun restaurants – is something that

many ethically-minded restaurateurs, from Copenhagen to California, Hammersmith to Vauxhall, have tried to achieve, with varying degrees of success. For some, fish and meat are out: animals are too intensively reared, and fish stocks are too depleted to make fishing sustainable (in the UK, vegans and vegetarians have been making this point since the days of Bertrand Russell). But for most of us, eating out is a treat, and in the UK – with our predominantly Christian heritage with its subordination of the animal kingdom – that still means a meal with meat or fish.

Unable to address every environmental consideration at once, some restaurateurs have chosen to focus on a specific issue. One very well-publicised example of this is Konstam at the Prince Albert (*see p59*), which attempts to use only food produced in the Greater London area, thereby taking the 'local' food argument to an extreme. An earlier pioneer, the Duke of Cambridge gastropub (est. 1998), initially focused on making all its food organic – and became the UK's first certified organic restaurant, adding many other sustainable practices as time went on. And long before this, since the 1960s, there have been vegetarian cafés that have done their bit for both the community and the environment, before 'green' was anything other than a colour. In the early '80s, for example, the Bonnington Centre Café was operating in a squatted building in Vauxhall and using surplus vegetables salvaged from nearby New Covent Garden Market to feed the local community.

Where the Duke of Cambridge has led in organic certification, others have followed and developed or refined other aspects of what we might call 'sustainable' catering. The highest-profile of these has been Acorn House in King's Cross (*see p49*), and then its sibling, Water House in Dalston. Although not fully organic, not vegetarian and with many other inconsistencies in their overall approach to sustainability, their PR campaign has helped make many Londoners more conscious of the myriad issues that need to be considered to make a restaurant more sustainable – ranging from reducing food waste and cutting electricity use to glass recycling and food miles accumulated.

Critics of the new wave of eco-restaurants argue that what they are doing is mere good housekeeping – what any well-managed restaurant ought to be doing. Which is true, but with pressures of time, budget and the complexity of researching sustainable suppliers in a world where everyone from BP to gourmet coffee suppliers is shouting about their eco-credentials, where can they turn for advice?

The eco-wise London Food Link (LFL, www.londonfood link.org) is a small, independent environmentalist outfit that is mostly grant funded. It is part of the food charity Sustain, which, in its own words, 'advocates food and agriculture policies and practices that enhance the health and welfare of people and animals, improve the working and living environment, promote equity and enrich society and culture.' Part of LFL's work involves coaching restaurants that express an interest in how to reduce their environmental impact. This work is also part of Greener Food, a joint project with a number of organisations, with LLF looking specifically at the food aspect of sustainability.

The idea is to get restaurateurs to consider all parts of the environmental equation, as even the best-intentioned people tend to have selective myopia. LFL's team is very small, but one of the ways it gives guidance to restaurateurs is with an environmental audit. This requires one of LFL's self-taught experts – currently Charlotte Jarman – to visit and inspect the premises, sit down with the restaurateur and go through a two-hour discussion of what they do and how they do it, and then present an action plan that details steps that could be taken to further reduce the business's carbon footprint and other environmental costs.

At Time Out, we were thrilled to hear about this new scheme (started in 2007), as we had been keen to introduce a new Best Sustainable Restaurant category to our annual ▶

I ♥ STREET**SMART**
HELPING THE HOMELESS

"All it takes is one well-fed quid next time you're dining at any of the damned fine establishments taking part in this glorious campaign, and that tiny extra sum will go straight to an excellently worthwhile cause. Go on, it'll make you feel good about that expanding waistband"
Ian Rankin, author

STREETSMART
HELPING THE HOMELESS

Supported by

For a full list of participating restaurants and for information on how to take part visit our website:
www.streetsmart.org.uk

Deutsche Bank

Best Sustainable Restaurant: award winner

CLERKENWELL KITCHEN
Review p305.

Helen Gray and Emma Miles first opened their canteen and catering company in 2002, but things didn't really step up a gear until June 2006 when they moved into larger, better premises. Their business is part of Clerkenwell Workshops (a small office development), and is now a licensed café-restaurant open in the daytime only, Monday to Friday. In the words of Miles, it 'serves good food to ordinary people'.

The food isn't all organic as this would push the prices up, though organic produce is used – for example, Rookery Farm eggs, which are organic but misshapen, and so cost £2 instead of £3 per dozen. The milk, eggs and some of the beef is organic – 'sometimes the lamb isn't', manager Ciaran Jones told us – but free range chickens are always used. Instead of being all-organic, Clerkenwell Kitchen is more interested in local sourcing, and deals with a lot of farmers, such as Wild Forest Foods in Mill Hill and Kingcup Farms in Buckinghamshire, using what Miles describes as 'traditional' (ie non-intensive) farming methods, but the farmers don't have the resources needed to go fully organic.

The food is very fresh, cooked every day using seasonal ingredients that are nearly all from the UK (though not coffee, wine, lemons, vanilla pods and so on). There is always a good selection of vegetarian dishes on the daily-changing blackboard menu – perhaps a tortilla with mint and caper mayonnaise and tomato, or an Italian-style tomato, olive and bread salad. The dishes are affordable, with most main courses under £10, puddings around £4. The policy on seafood is to use only what is plentiful: mackerel, sardines, squid, undyed smoked haddock (often line-caught), pollack, crab. Many dry goods are Fairtrade, such as the organic Fairtrade coffee from Union.

So far, so good. But where can CK improve? A recent carbon footprint report by consultancy dcarbon8 concluded that electricity use is the restaurant's most significant source of greenhouse-gas emissions (57 per cent), with gas used for cooking in second place (34 per cent); all other forms of waste combined came to a mere nine per cent. However, the kitchen cooks mainly with gas, as this is what the site was already equipped with. And CK has no control over who its electricity supplier is, as this is determined by its landlord, Workspace (though Workspace is currently in the process of greening its electricity). Other carbon footprint issues have been addressed in some detail by CK already. The London Food Link audit showed that bottled water is on sale, but much to their credit, staff offer 'tap, still or sparkling'. They 'try to minimise waste': paper, glass, plastic and cans

Eating & Drinking Awards for some time, but lacked the technical expertise to judge the category.

Therefore, for the first time this year, we have collaborated with London Food Link to pick a shortlist and a winner. This proved to be a difficult task, as there were around a dozen good restaurants making serious efforts to improve their sustainability, and we had to narrow them down to a mere five; tough decisions had to be made. Also, was the category to be judged purely on green credentials – or did we also have to consider what the restaurants are like to a paying customer, taking into account the service, ambience and, of course, the culinary prowess of the kitchen? We decided on the latter: a compromise, but a compromise that we felt that you, the diner, would agree with. Green credentials aren't worth much if the cooking's not up to scratch, or the prices are too high. Below, we summarise the environmental audits for our five finalists; for the culinary judgements, see the reviews elsewhere in the guide.

Eco champs

are all recycled, via two specialist recyclers, one of which recycles an astonishingly effective 97 per cent of waste.

London Food Link verdict: 'London needs more places like the Clerkenwell Kitchen. Delicious food, very carefully sourced, and at prices which show that being sustainable needn't cost the earth.'

Time Out verdict: 'Brilliant, affordable food, pretension-free place and a great atmosphere – and it ticks most of the green boxes, with more ticks on the way. The winner.'

Runners-up

DUKE OF CAMBRIDGE

Review p126.

For eco-credentials and heritage, the Duke takes some beating. Opened in December 1998, this gastropub was organic from the start, and is Soil Association-certified (the highest possible organic 'qualification'); even the beers are organic. Local, sustainable Marine Stewardship Council (MSC)-certified fish is used whenever possible. Air freight is never used, and most food is sourced locally. Bottled water has never been served, only (filtered) tap water. Only Fairtrade coffee, tea and sugar is used. Although almost all electricity in London comes off the national grid, the Duke pays its electricity bills to a company called Good Energy, which ensures the payments go to renewable wind and solar sources; however, the kitchen cooks on gas, as most restaurants do. There is great attention to detail in cutting waste to a minimum.

In 2008 the Duke won three awards, and partly because of its pioneering nature and the persuasive nature of its founder Geetie Singh, it has won more green trophies and plaudits over the last decade than every other sustainable restaurant put together. At one time the Duke was part of a three-strong chain in the same ownership, but the Duke is the only one to have stood the test of time.

London Food Link verdict: 'Geetie Singh's total commitment to running her business in an ethical and sustainable way is an inspiration. The Duke's green stance is not a marketing gimmick – it reflects what she genuinely believes in.'

Time Out verdict: 'A lovely neighbourhood pub with great beer and a good atmosphere. As a destination eaterie, though, it didn't quite make the mark; prices are high, and both cooking and service variable, at times amateurish. It's perfect for a nice pint, though.'

SAF

Review p291.

Saf has clear advantages over the other restaurants on this shortlist: as it's a vegan restaurant, concerns about animal welfare, factory farming and fish supplies are dealt with in one swift blow. And to top that, much of the food on the menu isn't even cooked – it's served either raw or having been heated to low temperatures – so energy use is a fraction of what it might be. Which sounds terribly worthy, but does that make the dining experience dull? Not at all, as the food is imaginative, colourful and beautifully presented, with surprising flavour and texture combinations. The room is a looker too. Examining in more detail the sourcing of ingredients, however, reveals less seasonality than we had hoped for, with a lot of unnecessarily imported ingredients (Himalayan sea salt, for example); and the water sold is mostly bottled. Saf mostly does a good job, but more work could still be done in implementing its noble aspirations.

London Food Link verdict: 'Cutting down the amount of meat and dairy products we eat is one of the most important   changes we can make to our diets in terms of combating climate change, as well as improving our own health. Saf does a fantastic job at showing that this needn't be a hardship.'

Time Out verdict: 'Saf dispels the stereotypes about vegan and raw food being worthy or boring. The food is amazing, the place has a real buzz, and the cocktail bar is a real treat.' ▶

Busaba Eathai

106–110 Wardour Street
Phone 020-7255 8686
London W1T 0TR

22 Store Street
Phone 020-7299 7900
London WC1E 7DF
Pre-booking available
for groups of 12+
Take away available

8–13 Bird Street
Phone 020-7518 8080
London W1U 1BU
Take away available

TOM'S PLACE

Review p316.

Tom Aikens' fish restaurant – a posh chippie, really – opened at the start of 2008 in a blaze of well-orchestrated publicity, the third (and cheapest) of superstar chef Aikens' restaurants in Chelsea. Even sceptics couldn't fail to be impressed by the efforts Aikens has made to ensure the fish served in the restaurant is from sustainable sources; videos looping endlessly in the dining room show the serious-faced chef travelling out to sea with fisherman all over the country to watch them at work. Only the less endangered species of fish are on the menu, and Aikens' relationships with his suppliers ensure the fish are caught with the minimum environmental impact. There's also great attention to detail inside the dining room, with tables made of recycled materials and cutlery made of cornstarch – though some details, such as tea bags from a grower in Cornwall, do seem gimmicky.

A few months after opening, environmental health officers from the local council started legal proceedings against the restaurant, following a bitter dispute with its neighbours over the problem of chip fat smells emanating from the kitchen. Unfortunately, the issue was not resolved amicably: just days before this guide went to press, Tom's Place closed.

London Food Link verdict: 'Sustainable fish is one of the most complicated issues for a restaurateur to tackle, and Tom Aikens' recent work in this area is very impressive – he has researched his subject incredibly thoroughly. Room for improvement in some other areas, but no other restaurant we know puts this much work into its fish sourcing.'

Time Out verdict: 'The success of Tom's Place shows that fish and chip shops don't have to rely on those endangered mainstays of the British chippie, namely cod, haddock and plaice.'

WATER HOUSE

Review p52.

Spring 2008 saw the opening of this sibling of Acorn House, created along the same lines – that is, with sustainability near the top of the agenda, only more so. With the benefit of a couple of years' more experience in this niche area, manager Arthur Potts Dawson was able to install some state-of-the-art kitchen equipment designed to reduce waste. The electric hobs are induction models, so only use power when a pot is placed on them; the electricity is all Scottish hydro-electric. The dishwasher uses ozone to clean dishes instead of the usual damaging chemicals; the water filters clean the tap water to make it more palatable for customers (there's no bottled mineral water here); a crusher makes waste glass more compact for transport to recycling plants. The menu is not fully organic, though, Potts Dawson preferring to put faith in his suppliers to make sure high standards are adhered to. And many of the early claims made about the restaurant – some of them propagated by Water House's own PR – proved to be unfounded (for example, the heat exchanger built into the canal hasn't yet materialised; the solar panels don't yet work properly).

London Food Link verdict: 'Water House really stands out on its impressive waste minimisation and energy conservation measures. Some effort has also been made to source sustainable ingredients, but Arthur Potts Dawson, like many restaurateurs, depends on his suppliers for information rather than verifying the details himself. One very straightforward improvement would be to switch to certified Fairtrade coffee.'

Time Out verdict: 'Top marks for working through all the details of the design and engineering of the kitchen and building, even if not all the plans came to fruition. More work could be done on the sourcing of ingredients, however, and for a restaurant that isn't cheap, the standard of cooking may be disappointing for some.'

Footnote 1

This phenomenon of worrying about the 'purity' of our food supply, and avoiding 'pollution', particularly in economically lean periods, is not confined to the UK, or present times. It is well documented by social anthropologists in other cultures and eras, and has been studied and described in depth by anthropologist Mary Douglas (*Purity and Danger*, published 1966), and more recently by food writer Bee Wilson in her book *Swindled* (2008).

The year that was

Jenni Muir reports on 12 months of moving and shaking in the London restaurant scene.

As Time Out approaches its third decade of combing London for the best and best-value eating and drinking, the dining-out boom of the 1990s has matured into a sophisticated and diverse restaurant scene catering for all tastes and all pockets. Tire of eating out in London and you really are tired of life. We certainly aren't – every week our team of expert chowhounds assesses everything from budget caffs and diners to the finest gastronomy and cuisines from every corner of the globe. We also look for the most welcoming and original bars and pubs. Since the publication of our last *Eating & Drinking Guide* 12 months ago, we've seen plenty of new developments that are worth attention. Here are some of the best.

2007

AUGUST

Renowned front-of-house and wine expert Thierry Tomasin surprises the industry when he turns his back on the formality of haute cuisine to open a brasserie and lounge by the Lancaster Gate one-way system. The prices at **Angelus** are more accessible than at Tomasin's previous employers Aubergine and Le Gavroche, though we wouldn't say the same of the parking. Still, as a classy local eaterie, it counts among London's best and the ebullient Tomasin has the satisfaction of truly running his own show.

Meanwhile, Fortnum & Mason continues its steady programme of refurbishment and launches London's most expensive ice-cream parlour, called **Parlour**. Designed by David Collins, it's a mix of chocolate swirls and candy colours before you even look in the display cabinet. Premium ingredients, including Amedei chocolate and Ivy House Farm milk, are noted on the menu. Ice-cream cocktails and sundaes cost £9-£12 (the children's menu starts at £4), so it's probably more of a treat for adults than families. Either way, it's guilty pleasures all round.

SEPTEMBER

Two émigrés, a chef and a sommelier, from Raymond Blanc's Oxfordshire restaurant Le Manoir aux Quat' Saisons open **Texture** on Portman Square. It's a brave move for Agnar Sverisson and Xavier Rousset – not

just in trying their luck in the big city, but in siting their haute cuisine restaurant and champagne bar a short walk from Marble Arch.

Over in Mayfair, the folk behind House in Canonbury and the Bull in Highgate reopen the **Only Running Footman** after giving the old boy an extensive refurb. The upstairs dining room produces a conservative British menu at eye-watering prices (£19.50 for our steak), though the bar food is cheaper and, compared to nearby Claridges, the full english breakfast is an outright bargain.

Another burgeoning gastropub group launches the **Duke of Sussex** in the part of Chiswick that a lot of Londoners call Acton. The gorgeous refurb does the place proud, but this is not a typical Realpubs venture, like the Oxford in

Baozi Inn. See p21.

ronnie scott's
JAZZ CLUB

THE WORLDS BEST JAZZ SINCE 1959

Ronnie Scott's is a historic jazz club that has hosted some of the worlds most celebrated musicians for almost 50 years. After an extensive refurbishment the club offers fine food and wine in addition to a fabulous cocktail bar above the club.

Ronnie's Bar has always been a well kept secret, a simple walk up the staircase will lead you to one of the most intimate yet highly sophisticated cocktail bars in Soho. Whether it's a much needed after work cocktail, a boogie during the jazz jam sessions or a unique venue to celebrate a party in style with friends, the bar suits all occasions.

Please see website www.ronniescotts.co.uk or call our bookings line on 0207 439 0747 for full band listings

We are open 7 days a week!
Monday-Saturday from 6pm-3am.
Sundays, 6pm until 12 midnight
Bank Holidays operate on Sunday opening hours
Upstairs Ronnie's Bar open from 6pm Monday to Saturday – free before 9pm

Ronnie Scott's Jazz Club
47 Frith Street
Soho
London
W1D 4HT
020 7439 0740
www.ronniescotts.co.uk

Kentish Town or Crouch Hill's Old Dairy. Instead, chef Chris Payne and manager Mike Buurman are able to set their own style, resulting in a more sophisticated wine list, a more grown-up crowd and a menu that darts between Spain and Britain like easyJet cabin crew.

The City has the chance to rock the kasbah at **Kenza**, a venture from Tony Kitous, owner of Levant in Marylebone and Gloucester Road's Pasha. All sumptuous fabrics, low lighting, intimate alcoves and chill-out music, it couldn't be further from the City's crusty old haunts. The menu of built-for-sharing Lebanese starters, fragrant Moroccan mains and exotic cocktails might even be suited to a date.

Having spent lavishly to redecorate the site of the Pourcel Brothers' failed W'Sens restaurant in St James's, modern Ukrainian restaurant **Divo** opens to almost universal ridicule – although there are those who appreciate the waitresses' corset-tight, burlesque-style folk costumes. Some of the decor's excesses (such as gilt-framed plasma screens playing tourist films) quietly disappear, but Divo doesn't and, on a second visit for this guide, we find much to like.

OCTOBER

After months of delays, Tom Pemberton's **Hereford Road** finally opens in Notting Hill. The former head chef of St John Bread & Wine produces a seasonal British menu that in the opening weeks includes lambs' tongues, whole oxtail, mallard, sand eels, cockles and laverbread. It is some of the most assured, delicious cooking in the capital and gives the original St John in Farringdon a run for its money. When *Time Out* compiles its list of London's Top 50 restaurants a few months later, Hereford Road makes it to number three.

Gordon Ramsay Holdings opens a gastropub in Chiswick, the **Devonshire**, and as with the company's high-end restaurants, booking is immediately a palaver. Is that what Londoners want from a gastropub? It seems many people like the reassurance of a famous name, for several months later getting a table is just as difficult as it was in the early days.

One of Ramsay's main rivals, Claude Bosi, moves his restaurant **Hibiscus** from Ludlow to Mayfair. Originally scheduled to open in August, it is delayed by two months. Sadly, this means inspectors for Michelin's annual guide only have a couple of weeks to make their assessment before their book goes to press; they decide to downgrade Hibiscus from two-star to one 'rising' star status, a surprise to Bosi's fellow chefs, who believe he's destined for the very top. But consolation is found when *Time Out* magazine awards the restaurant its first-ever six-star (maximum points) rating.

NOVEMBER

It's all about haute cuisine in the capital this autumn. While critics and food lovers are still making their pilgrimages to Hibiscus, one of the world's most famous chefs, **Alain Ducasse**, opens a London outpost in the Dorchester Hotel. Bosi need not worry – most critics find Ducasse's venture an expensive yawn. But then **L'Autre Pied** opens in Marylebone. This off-shoot of Charlotte Street favourite Pied à Terre offers similarly inventive high-end food at (slightly) more accessible prices, and the decor is a dream. Why pay a premium for the honour of sitting in a hotel?

There's plenty that's new for Londoners on more restricted budgets too. With the opening of **Harrison's**, Sam Harrison introduces Balham to the smart-casual brasserie style that made his Chiswick spot Sam's *Time Out*'s Best Local

Goodbye

We bid farewell to those restaurants that have changed hands or shut since the last edition of the guide.

@Japan
Lunch @ this Mayfair sushi pitstop no longer.

Brian Turner Mayfair
Ready, steady, go off and do something else.

Cleveland Kitchen
Arriverderci to a cosy budget Italian in Fitzrovia.

The Coyote
Another Southwestern US eaterie shuts, doggone it.

Drones
Antony Worall Thompson and Marco Pierre White have both been involved in this Belgravia restaurant over the years, but let's not drone on about it.

Fook Sing
Sad to see a Fujianese specialist go, but it has made way for Baozi Inn.

Jaan
The Howard's high-end fusion dining room has been replaced by a British concept.

Jo Shmo's
Turned into a schmuck.

Lundum's
Smörgåsbord no more.

Morel
Business didn't mushroom for this Modern European restaurant in Clapham.

Niksons
Battersea restaurant and bar that will reopen as the Bolingbroke.

La Noisette
Was Bjorn van der Horst nuts to join Ramsay?

Old China Hand
Dim sum pub gets the karate chop.

Quiet Revolution
Perhaps a bit too quiet.

Raviolo
Pasta chain concept that never made it to a second branch.

Redmonds
Mortlake has lost some of its sheen.

Rosmarino
St John's Wood Italian, now a St John's Wood Italian.

Safir
We loved the tagines at this Hampstead Moroccan, but there's no point stewing over it.

The Sequel
One was enough – but it will be reopening as a bar.

Shipp's Tearooms
Sunken treasure.

Six-13
Innovative Jewish fine dining restaurant.

Tobia
Sophie Sirak-Kebede hopes to be serving authentic Ethiopian food at a new venue shortly.

Turquoise
Short-lived Holborn Turkish turned into a turkey.

Upper Glas
This smart Swedish outfit just couldn't cut it in Islington.

Restaurant of 2006. **Northbank** brings some much-needed class and witty Timorous Beasties wallpaper to the tourist thoroughfare by the Millennium Bridge. And we discover some terrific Persian cooking in Sheen, at BYO restaurant **Faanoos** – one of this year's Best Cheap Eats finalists.

But it's the champagne lifestyle London apparently yearns for, as the hottest ticket in town this month is the **Champagne Bar at St Pancras**, right by the platform. It's the longest champagne bar in Europe but, this being Britain, we still love to queue to get in.

Also popular – initially, at least – is **Le Café Anglais**, launched by former Kensington Place chef Rowley Leigh. Plugs in his *Financial Times* column, and plenty from friends elsewhere in the media, help his devoted fans overcome any reticence they might have had about dining in a rather dull

Bayswater shopping centre. However, the restaurant is just one part of Whiteley's plans to make the building a food-lovers destination: 2008 also sees the opening of Food Inc, a series of elegant stalls running through the concourse. Any comparison with Harvey Nichols is un-coincidental; the man who created Food Inc, Dominic Ford, also launched the Knightsbridge department store's food hall.

DECEMBER

Another shock six-star review from *Time Out* magazine, this time for Alan Yau's new Japanese restaurant **Sake No Hana** in the modernist building at 23 St James's Street. Renowned as something of an unlucky site (Shumi and Che have failed here in recent years), Yau and architect Kengo Kuma have transformed it into a stunning cedar temple, with staff in Ninja-style outfits serving home-style and modern Japanese dishes. The cooking is wonderful, but prohibitive prices make us worry that it will go the way of its predecessors. Even the downstairs sushi bar, when it opens later in 2008, is no friendlier to the bank balance.

Another unlucky site to receive a makeover this month is 123 Queenstown Road (formerly home to the Food Room, the Stepping Stone, and L'Arlequin). Serbian-born **Tom Ilic**, a well-regarded chef from his days at hotels Addendum and Bonds in the City, has decided to go it alone and opens a restaurant serving elegant yet robust Modern European dishes with a Baltic edge. He, perhaps better than anyone, knows the challenges of this particular address for, ten years previously, he was head chef at the Stepping Stone. Ilic's East European heritage influences rather than directs his menus, but at the **Knaypa**, which Polish émigrée Monika Milcarz opens in Hammersmith, the menu of sour rye flour soup, bigos, golabki, buckwheat and cheesecake is designed to appeal to London's increasing number of Polish residents.

North of Oxford Street, the Langham Hotel, having poached Andrew Turner from rugby players' favourite

The Botanist. See p21.

Pennyhill Park Hotel & Spa in Surrey, opens the **Landau** after months of building work and the installation of a stunning David Collins interior. Sensibly priced set and pre-theatre menus mean shoppers, tourists and BBC staff from Broadcasting House opposite have nothing to fear, while gastronauts can revel in à la carte and tasting menus.

2008

JANUARY

Time Out magazine names its 50 best restaurants in London and places Alan Yau's Hakkasan and Busaba Eathai in the number one and two spots respectively, confirming Yau's position as the capital's most innovative and influential restaurateur. At the same time, Hakkasan and its sister restaurant Yauatcha are sold to the property arm of the Abu Dhabi Investment Authority for a reported £30.5 million, though Yau maintains shares in the business.

January sees other successful operators expanding ambitiously. Among them, the team at Salt Yard, which serves tapas-style Spanish and Italian dishes, launches **Dehesa** near Carnaby Street with a similar menu. In Notting Hill, Vineet Bhatia tries something a little different from his upmarket Chelsea kitchen, opening **Urban Turban** to serve Indian snack bar fare in a lounge setting. South of the river, the people behind Brixton's Plan B bar open the **Loft** in Clapham, a late-night cocktail bar with first-rate mixologists, bar food and an impressive DJ set-up.

Down in Croydon, Malcolm John (who achieved some notoriety when his opening of Chiswick's Le Vacherin was featured on television's *Who Wants to be a Restaurateur*) opens **Le Cassoulet** to wide acclaim – and much discussion of Croydon's emerging sophistication. Good food has been even slower coming to North Finchley, although Vietnamese restaurateur Vin Do's excellent branch of **Khoai Café** immediately sets a new standard for N12.

FEBRUARY

The empire-building continues into February with Tom Aiken's much-delayed opening of **Tom's Place**, an eco-friendly fish and chip restaurant a stone's throw from his other Chelsea Green establishments. His PR machine, already in overdrive with various colour magazines embarrassingly declaring it open well before it was, works the sustainability angle successfully, but the general feeling from critics is that the place is too expensive, even considering the careful sourcing from Marine Stewardship Council-approved boats.

It's not February's only green opening, however: Arthur Potts Dawson and Jamie Grainger-Smith launch the **Water House** by the Regent's Canal in Dalston, a follow-up to their hit King's Cross eaterie Acorn House. Owned by the charitable regeneration agency Shoreditch Trust, any profit from the restaurant goes back into improving the local area. The stated aims are admirable: no air-freighted produce, fish from sustainable stocks, organic wines and various low-carbon-emission structural features. However, we wonder if the location (on an isolated side street) is viable.

Conservation of a different type is on order in Maida Vale as Gordon Ramsay Holdings opens its third gastropub, the **Warrington**. Locals feared the character of the 19th-century pub would die under the new ownership, but the lounge bar's Grade II listing made careful refurbishment essential. Marble pillars, art nouveau friezes, stained glass

The Gallery at sketch

a gastro-brasserie with an edge

Hello

As the guide goes to press, scores of new restaurant openings were being planned. Here, *Time Out* magazine's food and drink editor **Guy Dimond** gives us a peep at his current to-do list.

2008 SEPTEMBER

Murano
20-22 Queen Street, W1J 5PR.
Angela Hartnett's new fine-dining Italian restaurant will open with the usual blaze of publicity you can expect from a venue launched by Gordon Ramsay Holdings.

Andaman
St James's Hotel & Club, 7-8 Park Place, SW1A 1LP (7629 7688).
Chef Dieter Müller (who holds three Michelin stars in Germany) is running this new restaurant inside the revamped St James's Hotel & Club. The theme is 'Marco Polo and the spice routes from the Middle East to China'.

Bob Bob Ricard
1 Upper St James Street, W1.
An open-all-day brasserie serving 'English comfort food' on the Soho site that used to be Circus.

Broome & Delancey
35-37 Battersea Rise, SW11 1HG (www.broomeanddelancey.com).
A new cocktail bar and restaurant in Battersea from the people behind the Establishment, one of our Best Bar finalists this year.

Osteria dell'Angolo
Westminster.
This Italian eaterie from restaurateur Claudio Pulze has Michele Broge as head chef, who worked at Zafferano, Aubergine and the three-Michelin-starred Enoteca Pinchiorri in Florence.

OCTOBER

Westfield London
White City, W10.
The new Westfield London shopping mall will also have 40 places to eat and drink, including Croque Gascon, from the people behind Club Gascon.

Avista
Millennium Hotel Mayfair, 44 Grosvenor Square, W1K 2HP (7596 3399).
An Italian restaurant with cooking by ex-Zafferano chef Michel Granziera, who hails from the Veneto region. Many dishes suitable for sharing are planned.

Trishna London
15-17 Blandford Street, W1.
A branch of the well-regarded Indian seafood restaurant in Mumbai.

King's Place
King's Place, York Way, N1.
A new development near King's Cross station that will include a café, bar and restaurant (called Rotunda).

Mirabelle
56 Curzon Street, W1J 8PA.
Mirabelle shut in summer 2008, but is to reopen under new owners, including fashion designer Joseph Ettedgui.

Love Life Stories
Brick Lane, E1.
Chef Maria Elia (formerly of Delfina) plans to open this fine-dining vegetarian restaurant in the Old Truman Brewery.

END OF 2008/EARLY 2009

J Sheekey Oyster Bar
St Martin's Court, WC2.
J Sheekey fish restaurant is to open a more casual, no-bookings seafood bar next door in the 'late autumn'.

Paramount
Centrepoint, 103 New Oxford Street, WC1 (www.paramount.uk.net).
Chef Pierre Condue, formerly of L'Odéon restaurant, is planning a fine-dining restaurant and bar on the 32nd floor of the landmark Centrepoint building. The project was originally planned for 2007.

Bel Canto
1 Minster Court, Mark Lane, EC3R 7AA (7444 0004/www.lebelcanto.com).
A Parisian opera restaurant – the staff also sing – which promises to do both the opera and the food well.

Cinnamon Kitchen
9 Devonshire Square, EC2M 4YL (www.cinnamonkitchen.co.uk).
A second branch of the excellent Cinnamon Club Indian restaurant, this time in the City.

The Luxe
109 Commercial Street, E1 6BG.
A new café-bar from John Torode on the site of the Spitz music bar in Old Spitalfields Market. The first-floor dining room will specialise in game and poultry.

Boundary
2-4 Boundary Street, E2 7JE (7729 1051/www.theboundary.co.uk).
Sir Terence Conran isn't ready for retirement yet. His Boundary Project in Shoreditch venture will incorporate a café, restaurant and rooftop cocktail bar, together with some hotel rooms.

Megu
17 Bruton Street, W1 (www.megunyc.com).
A Mayfair townhouse is being converted into a branch of New York's Megu, a modern Japanese restaurant.

---

lamps, horseshoe-shaped bar, mosaic tiling, lairy carpet – all are still there, as are all manner of punters enjoying the excellent beer list, which is expertly served.

MARCH

It's a very different story at the **Clissold Arms** in Muswell Hill. Opposite Denmark Terrace, where Kinks founders Ray and Dave Davies grew up, the pub that was scene of their first gig is converted into a gastropub. Fans were campaigning for new owners Jobo Developments to retain the pub's collection of Kinks memorabilia. 'Have they [the tenants] lost their dignity, sense of local history and English heritage?,' Dave Davies asked readers of the *Muswell Hill Journal*. But on opening, the Kinks 'shrine' was reduced to a few photographs near the men's loo. Unfortunately for the group's fans, it's a great gastropub, immediately embraced by locals and shortlisted for our Best Gastropub award.

London's wide range of world cuisines is one of the things food lovers enjoy most about the city, and March sees us enjoying a mouth-watering array of openings: Turkish food in an unusually smart Chelsea setting at **Iznik Kaftan**; South Indian vegetarian cooking at **Shilpa** in Hammersmith;

home-style Japanese kastsu curries and sushi at **Tsuru**, a new lunchspot in Bankside; and the second branch of Vietnamese soup-noodle bar **Pho**. But British food is not forgotten either, as **Jimmy's** opens in Chelsea serving macaroni cheese, beef wellington and knickerbocker glories.

APRIL

While always pricey, hotel dining is no longer the prissy, French-focused affair it used to be, and to prove it Gordon Ramsay Holdings adds an upscale steakhouse to its Maze operations at the Marriott Hotel on Grosvenor Square. We weren't wowed by the cooking at **Maze Grill**, and even less impressed by the prices; for that sort of money we'd rather eat at Jason Atherton's original Maze restaurant.

Meanwhile, the Lanesborough clocks the success of Theo Randall at the Intercontinental just a 30-second limo ride away, and, suffering an embarrassing lack of imagination, opens **Apsley's**, a restaurant serving rustic Italian food. As me-too restaurants go, it's a bit of a so-what, but celebrity custom is helping to get the Apsley's name about.

Stefano Stecca is not above serving simple Italian food at teeth-sucking prices – he did it for a few years at the Baglioni

Hotel in Kensington. But in April he makes a welcome return to his former St John's Wood stomping ground to open **Osteria Stecca**. We find the food superb and the bill reasonable. But you don't have to spend like a Ferrari owner to eat like a Tuscan peasant in London: the true spirit of Italian cooking can be found at **Franco Manca** in Brixton Market. Winner of our 2008 Best Cheap Eats award, this pizzeria's ingredients include sourdough bases made from organic flour, and superb mozzarella produced in Somerset by a cheesemaker specially trained by an Italian artisan.

MAY

A month of opposites. On the one hand, London acquires two new high-end vegetarian restaurants. **Vanilla Black** transfers to the City from Leeds, and international group **Saf** (which is not only vegan, but has a high raw content to its really rather delicious menu) opens in Shoreditch. Yet we also witness the resurrection of 1980s hit the **Chicago Rib Shack**, and the traditional British delights of the chop house when Mark Hix, former chef-director of Caprice Holdings (the Ivy, J Sheekey, Scott's and Daphne's are among the restaurants he's overseen) opens **Hix Oyster & Chop House**. Initial reviews are enthusiastic, but Hix is such a well liked personality in the industry we can't help feeling there is a lot of goodwill smoothing over the rough patches – something our return visit confirms.

Over in Soho, Alan Yau and brother Gary go head to head with two very different oriental operations, **Aaya** and **Cha Cha Moon**. Both have design aesthetics pretty high on the agenda, but while Cha Cha Moon sees Alan revisiting Wagamama noodle bar territory and offering dishes for as little as £3.50, Gary's Aaya is a comparatively high-end Japanese restaurant (with, er, plastic cups and bamboo chopsticks) serving very good food and luscious cocktails for something more in the region of £35-£40 per head.

Other brothers hard at work, this time together, are gastropub maestros Tom and Ed Martin, who launch their first grown-up restaurant, the **Botanist**. It's an elegant but not fusty dining room with French windows opening on to Sloane Square, and English-accented menus that are available virtually all day – making the Botanist a strong contender in our Best Breakfast award this year.

The Connaught Hotel opens the **Coburg Bar**, which immediately becomes our favourite place to drink in central London. India Mahdavi's decor has a modern sophistication that enhances the historic character of the room, and we think the cocktails, at £12 each, are worth every penny.

JUNE

Inspired by the success of the Howard de Walden Estate in making Marylebone Village a destination for food fans, the Grosvenor Estate has been steadily transforming Motcomb Street. In spring, new branches of chocolate shop Rococo and café-traiteur-bakery **Ottolenghi** open, as does the **Pantechnicon Rooms**, in a listed building that was the Turk's Head pub. There is a smart ground-floor bar that seems to have been packed from day one, some appealing pavement tables and an elegant upstairs dining room, but with small bowls of nuts charged at £3, and a meal for two with drinks costing around £90, it's either a restaurant, or a local pub for local (Belgravia) people.

The same can't be said of the **Princess Victoria** in Shepherd's Bush, however. Formerly a gin palace (and registered as a pub in 1872) this spacious and sensitively refurbished property has been smartened up but still welcomes all-comers, from beer drinkers looking for a quiet pint to dating couples wanting accomplished cooking. It's worth a special trip for wine lovers, who'll find one of the best lists in the capital, served by expert sommeliers.

Also this month: Shoreditch acquires a smart Italian restaurant and bar in **L'Anima**; the owners of Bar Shu open **Baozi Inn**, a humble pit stop for Sichuanese noodle dishes and Beijing street snacks; the Hart Brothers, best known for Spanish restaurants Fino and Barrafina, relaunch **Quo Vadis** as a Modern British grill room and members' club; and Australian chef Paul Merrony opens **Giaconda Dining Room** with the folk behind Soho's Flat White coffee bar.

JULY

The Connaught takes the lead in the on-going race between London's grand hotels to update their image and attract new customers. In July, French chef **Hélène Darroze** garners plenty of advance publicity and receives a much warmer welcome from critics at the Connaught than her compatriot Alain Ducasse did earlier in the year at the Dorchester. The same month, another esteemed French chef, Jean-Christophe Ansanay-Alex, decides to open a London restaurant without the safety net of a hotel. Instead he opens **L'Ambassade de l'Ile** on the former site of Lundum's on Old Brompton Road. There's much to like about the food here too, even if the decor has an embarrassingly suburban-disco feel to it.

Meanwhile, Paul Merrett, sometime TV chef, sets out to prove that good food can reside happily in the suburbs by taking over the **Victoria** in downtown Sheen.

As we go to press in mid August 2008, there are many exciting openings to look forward to – you'll find these in the **Hello** box to the left. For all the latest restaurant and bar reviews, log on to www.timeout.com/restaurants, where our expert critics assess each new venue and fellow Londoners add their own feedback.

L'Anima

Time Out's Hot 100

The editors of the *Time Out Eating & Drinking Guide* have picked 100 places, entirely subjectively, that we believe offer some of London's most interesting eating and drinking experiences. We're not saying these venues have the best food and drink in the capital, but we believe each adds something life-enhancing to our city. Here they are, in alphabetical order. Each review is marked with a (100) in the relevant chapter of the guide.

Adam's Café
North African p251.
Neighbourhood Tunisian restaurant serving bargain-priced egg briks and grills.

Amaya
Indian p148.
Haute Indian grill in highly stylish surrounds.

Ambassador
Modern European p230.
Imaginative all-day dining and good wines in Exmouth Market.

Anchor & Hope
Gastropubs p119.
Punters happily wait in line (it's no-bookings) for the rustic, Brit-Mediterranean dishes.

Arbutus
Modern European p237.
Grown-up cooking and fair prices make this a reliable Soho favourite.

Assaggi
Italian p185.
Relaxed Bayswater spot delivering high-end food with prices to match.

Baltic
East European p87.
You won't find a more glamorous eaterie in which to sample cuisine from Europe's east.

Baozi Inn
Chinese p69.
Authentic hand-made noodles and street food.

Bar Shu
Chinese p77.
This spicy Sichuanese guarantees a wake-up call to the taste buds.

Barrafina
Spanish p261.
Sam and Eddie Hart's hugely popular, laid-back tapas bar in Soho.

Bentley's Oyster Bar & Grill
Fish p92.
Premium molluscs and superior fish pies just off Piccadilly.

Bistrotheque
French p108; Bars p337.
Dinner and dance the east London way, with cabaret and high camp on the menu.

Blue Bar
Bars p331.
Serious cocktails vie for attention with flashy celebrities in this bar in the Berkeley hotel.

Breads Etcetera
Cafés p310.
Top-quality breakfasts and artisanal breads you toast at the table.

Brew House
Cafés p314.
Bag a garden table to make the most of this idyllic cafeteria on Hampstead Heath.

Busaba Eathai
Thai p269.
Shared tables create a buzzy atmosphere at this mini chain now branching out across the UK.

Cah Chi
Korean p217.
Canteen-like Korean with super-friendly service, and cooking that's a cut above its New Malden competitors.

Chez Bruce
French p107.
Dishes worthy of a high-profile city-centre restaurant, plus a notable wine list.

China Tang
Chinese p76.
Cantonese cooking in a lavishly decorated space that's in keeping with its Park Lane location.

Clarke's
Modern European p239.
A place that values substance over style with simple, well-sourced dishes served in an unpretentious setting.

Club Gascon
French p101.
Exquisite small dishes for sharing, drawn from the culinary traditions of south-west France.

Coach & Horses
Gastropubs p111.
Proper beers, friendly service and great food, just off Farringdon Road.

Coburg
Bars p332.
A hip hotel bar serving the greatest cocktail hits of the last two centuries.

Cow
Gastropubs p116.
Pleasing pub with convivial bar and small first-floor dining room that's big on oysters.

Czechoslovak Restaurant
East European p86.
Unapologetically retro institution that's a genuine one-off – it's the city's only Czech restaurant and bar.

Dukes Hotel
Bars p332.
The comfortably elegant surrounds are mere accents to this bar's true raison d'être: crafting the perfect martini.

Eyre Brothers
Global p132.
An Iberian-via-Mozambique menu presented in a truly sleek Shoreditch restaurant and bar.

Fish Club
Fish & Chips p317.
Contemporary chippie dedicated to showcasing lesser-seen seafood as well as delivering the traditional goods.

Food for Thought
Vegetarian p288.
A subterranean veggie spot that draws lengthy queues with its wholesome eats.

Franco Manca
Pizza & Pasta p323.
Unassuming Brixton pizza parlour that fires up some of the best ingredients in town.

La Fromagerie
Cafés p306.
Top-notch café, deli and cheese room in genteel Marylebone.

Le Gavroche
Hotels & Haute Cuisine p141.
Professionalism (both in the kitchen and front of house) is taken *très* seriously at Michel Roux Jr's very special establishment.

Geales
Fish p95.
It's fish and chips, but not as you know it, at this gentrified Notting Hill spot run by chef Gary Hollihead.

Golden Hind
Fish & Chips p315.
Unpretentious, nonagenarian chippie, plating up great grub at pleasing prices.

Gun
Gastropubs p123.
Upscale Docklands gastropub that does a cracking line in proper beers and pork pies.

Hakkasan
Chinese p75; Bars p330.
This ultra-glam destination is hard to beat for modern Chinese and exceptional dim sum.

Hawksmoor
The Americas p37; Bars p330.
The cocktail's the thing at this Spitalfields steakhouse.

Hélène Darroze at the Connaught
Hotels & Haute Cuisine p143.
The lady of Landes leads a French revolution in Britain's grandest old dining room.

Hereford Road
British p63.
Bold British food served with assurance and undeniable skill in Notting Hill.

Hibiscus
Hotels & Haute Cuisine p143.
A temple to gastronomy moved down wholesale from its original Ludlow location to wow London.

Hix Oyster & Chop House
British p55.
Old-school dishes from one of the UK's most admired Britfood exponents, served in an austere retro setting.

Hummus Bros
Budget p299.
It's just bowls of houmous with imaginative toppings, but boy, it's done well.

Jerusalem Tavern
Pubs p339.
The organic St Peter's Brewery in Suffolk keeps this cosy tavern supplied with great ales.

LAB
Bars p332.
The mix-masters at this Soho bar throw together some fine drinks.

Landau
Hotels & Haute Cuisine p136.
David Collins' other-worldly interior is the appropriate setting for Andrew Turner's out-of-this-world cooking.

Lobby Bar
Bars p330.
One Aldwych hotel's ground-floor bar is like a Mad Hatter's cocktail party for grown-ups.

Locanda Locatelli
Italian p182.
Glamorous, upscale dining with prices to match.

Lola Rojo
Spanish p265.
'Sheep air' and vegetable lollipops: contemporary tapas in Battersea.

Loungelover
Bars p338.
The standard-bearer for Les Trois Garçons stable is a decadent cocktail bar with a strict bookings policy.

Macaron
Cafés p310.
Fine teas and cutting-edge pâtisserie in endearingly old-fashioned environs by Clapham Common.

Madhu's
Indian p170.
Sleek Indian-African dining in Southall.

Mandalay
Global p131.
The decor is nothing to shout about, but the authentic Burmese dishes are a sensation.

M Manze
Budget p301.
Vintage pie and mash gaff near Tower Bridge.

Marquess Tavern
Gastropubs p127.
Proper pub serving princely roast fore-ribs and other prime English ingredients.

Masa
Global p129.
Flamboyant Afghan restaurant on the fringes of the city.

Maze
Hotels & Haute Cuisine p143.
Jason Atherton elevates the tapas concept to gastronomic heights.

Milk & Honey
Bars p332.
Discreet Soho cocktail bar that feels like a secret club (non-members can ring in advance to get in).

Momo
North African p250.
Sexy decor and a party atmosphere draw the good-time crowds to this veteran Moroccan restaurant.

Moro
Spanish p258.
An eminently edible menu that stretches from Spain right along the Mediterranean.

Nahm
Thai p269.
High-end Thai cuisine elevated by thrilling touches and a glittering dining room.

National Dining Rooms
British p62.
Exemplary eaterie befitting its enviably grand location in the National Gallery.

Nauroz
Indian p167.
Basic local joint serving fabulous Pakistani karahi feasts.

Nobu
Japanese p199.
Internationally celebrated fusion cooking that still attracts the celebs.

Ottolenghi
International p176.
Fresh, vibrant fare makes brunchtime seats

at the flagship Islington branch (our favourite) highly prized.

E Pellicci
Budget p301.
Much-loved Bethnal Green greasy spoon, serving hangover-curing fry-ups and home-style Italian cooking.

Petersham Nurseries Café
Modern European p248.
Bold dishes of harmonious flavours served in a chi-chi garden shed.

Princess Victoria
Gastropubs p116.
Elegantly restored Victorian gin palace now peddling an expert wine list and satisfying gastropub plates.

The Providores & Tapa Room
International p173.
Buzzing Marylebone fusion food destination that does a great line in breakfasts.

Racine
French p102.
Classy and excellent French fare in a 1930s-style atmosphere.

Ram's
Indian p168.
Delectable Gujarati vegetarian specialities in Harrow.

Ranoush Juice
Middle Eastern p223.
Lebanese meze, wraps and fresh juice served late into the (Arabian) nights.

Rasa Samudra
Indian p148.
Authentic Keralan fish cookery on Charlotte Street – and you haven't worked in the West End until you've had the lunchtime takeaway boxes sold out back.

Riva
Italian p187.
Deservedly popular place for classy evenings in Barnes.

The River Café
Italian p185.
Numerous cookbooks have made it a household name, and the kitchen continues to turn out exceptional Italian food.

Roast
British p64.
A meat-eater's paradise at a prime location in Borough Market.

Roka
Japanese p193.
Charlotte Street's best place for people-watching serves inspired Japanese food.

Royal Oak
Pubs p342.
Unshowy Harveys brewery outpost.

S&M Café
Budget p303.
Umpteen varieties of sausages and mash served in a vintage caff setting.

Saf
Vegetarian p291.
Raw vegan food with an haute cuisine edge.

Sagar
Indian p155.
Simple, tasteful decor puts the focus on the unusual vegetarian cuisine of Udupi in South India.

St Alban
Global p131.
Spankingly modern surrounds and a mouth-watering Mediterranean menu.

St John
British p58.
Famous for its nose-to-tail treatment of meats, dining here is a highly satisfying experience.

Sake No Hana
Japanese p199.
Alan Yau's convention-challenging Japanese fine dining eaterie.

Sakonis
Indian p172.
Lip-smacking South Indian vegetarian snacks in Wembley.

Satay House
Malaysian p221.
A stylishly relaxed place in which to enjoy some of the capital's best Malaysian food.

Sketch: The Gallery
International p173.
Pierre Gagnaire's frilly French dishes are flanked by equally outré interior design.

Smiths of Smithfield
Modern European p230.
John Torode's beast of a bar and restaurant complex in Farringdon.

Song Que
Vietnamese p294.
It ain't pretty, and the constant stream of customers makes for

a rushed atmosphere, but the affordable dishes are authentically Vietnamese.

Sushi-Hiro
Japanese p202.
Great-value sushi exquisitely prepared – in Ealing – and it's as authentic as it gets.

Sweetings
Fish p91.
The gentleman's choice for a civilised City lunch, specialising in fish.

The Table
Budget p301.
Cheap yet stylish Bankside canteen.

Tapas Brindisa
Spanish p265.
Recuperate from a trawl round Borough Market at this comfortable tapas spot.

Tiroler Hut
Eating & Entertainment p354.
An Austrian theme restaurant complete with accordion music and cowbell shows.

Tre Viet
Vietnamese p295.
Authentic dishes made with hard-to-find ingredients.

Les Trois Garçons
French p109.
Camp as Christmas but with far better (French) food.

Veeraswamy
Indian p150.
A couple of facelifts from the Panjabi sisters have made this octogenarian Indian one of London's sexiest restaurants.

Vinoteca
Wine Bars p346.
An oenophile's dream, combining wine bar, shop and seasonal menu.

Wapping Food
Modern European p247.
Converted pumping station sending out elegant Modern European fare amid contemporary art exhibitions.

White Horse
Pubs p341.
Plush Parsons Green pub with a stupendous choice of well-kept ales.

The Wolseley
Brasseries p49.
The grand, art deco ambience is perfect for breakfast, high tea and brasserie-style dining.

Time Out's 19th annual Eating & Drinking

Awards

2008

Time Out has an unrivalled reputation for promoting the best of London's eating and drinking places – something of which we are very proud. It not just those with the grandest credentials that we champion, either, but the little places that are, in their own field, worthy of note. This is the ethos behind our broad coverage of London's gastronomic delights – from weekly reviews in *Time Out* magazine to our numerous guides. And this is why our annual Eating & Drinking Awards take in not only London's restaurant élite, but also representatives from neighbourhood restaurants, gastropubs, cafés and other bargain eateries, as independently selected by a panel of Time Out judges.

With a fresh crop of reviews appearing each week in *Time Out* magazine (and on our website, www.timeout. com/restaurants), the list of potential candidates can seem dauntingly long, but our panel of independent (and anonymous) reviewers is able to whittle them down to a shortlist of 50: five nominations in each of ten categories. We ask readers of the magazine and website for their feedback, which helps inform our judges' choices.

The award categories, which vary each year, reflect the diverse needs and tastes of London's diners and drinkers: this year we have included new categories for Best Breakfast and Best Tea Room. Also, in order to reflect the emphasis we have placed on sustainability, provenance, organic food and other green issues in this year's guide, we have also instituted awards for Best Local Market and Best Sustainable Restaurant.

Finally, the judges revisit every shortlisted venue as normal paying punters (we never accept PR invitations or freebies), so that a final decision can be reached.

And the winners are... in alphabetical order.

BEST BAR
Winner
The Loft (Bars) *See p336.*

Runners-up
Amuse Bouche (Wine Bars) *See p348.*
Coburg (Bars) *See p332.*
The Establishment (Bars) *See p335.*
Westbourne House (Bars) *See p335.*

BEST CHEAP EATS
Winner
Franco Manca (Pizza & Pasta) *See p323.*

Runners-up
Baozi Inn (Chinese) *See p69.*
Faanoos (Middle Eastern) *See p228.*
Little Lamb (Chinese) *See p72.*
Teachi (Chinese) *See p83.*

BEST BREAKFAST
Winner
Tom's Kitchen (Brasseries) *See p51.*

Runners-up
The Botanist (Modern European) *See p241.*
Breads Etc (Cafés) *See p310.*
The Providores & Tapa Room (International) *See p308.*
Rivington Bar & Grill (British) *See p64.*

BEST DESIGN
Winner
Saké No Hana (Japanese) *See p199.*

Runners-up
L'Autre Pied (Modern European) *See p233.*
Le Café Anglais (Modern European) *See p238.*
Cha Cha Moon (Chinese) *See p78.*
Landau (Hotels & Haute Cuisine) *See p136.*

Franco Manca

Clerkenwell Kitchen

Le Cassoulet

This year's judges: Jessica Cargill Thompson, Guy Dimond, Roopa Gulati, Alice Lascelles, Susan Low, Charmaine Mok, Jenni Muir, Cath Phillips, Cyrus Shahrad, Gordon Thomson – and thanks to Charlotte Jarman and London Food Link.

BEST GASTROPUB

Winner
Princess Victoria (Gastropubs) *See p116.*

Runners-up
Carpenter's Arms (Gastropubs) *See p115.*
Clissold Arms (Gastropubs) *See p127.*
Duke of Wellington (Gastropubs) *See p112.*
Warrington (Gastropubs) *See p128.*

BEST LOCAL FOOD MARKET

Winner
Alexandra Palace Farmers' Market

Runners-up
Broadway Market
Pimlico Road Farmers' Market
Swiss Cottage Farmers' Market
Wimbledon Park Farmers' Market
For details of all, see p57.

BEST LOCAL RESTAURANT

Winner
Le Cassoulet (French) *See p110.*

Runners-up
Angelus (French) *See p104.*
Le Café Anglais (Modern European) *See p238.*
Osteria Stecca (Italian) *See p192.*
Tom Ilic (Modern European) *See p244.*

BEST NEW RESTAURANT

Winner
L'Autre Pied (Modern European) *See p233.*

Runners-up
Dehesa (Spanish) *See p261.*
Hereford Road (British) *See p63.*
Hibiscus (Hotels & Haute Cuisine) *See p143.*
Hix Oyster & Chop House (British) *See p55.*

BEST SUSTAINABLE RESTAURANT

Winner
Clerkenwell Kitchen (Cafés) *See p305.*

Runners-up
Duke of Cambridge (Gastropubs) *See p126.*
Saf (Vegetarian) *See p291.*
Tom's Place (Fish & Chips) *See p316.*
Water House (Brasseries) *See p52.*

BEST TEA ROOM

Winner
Orange Pekoe (Cafés) *See p309.*

Runners-up
Chaiwalla (Cafés) *See p310.*
Postcard Teas (Cafés) *See p306.*
Tea Palace (Cafés) *See p309.*
Tea Smith (Cafés) *See p312.*

ISLAND
RESTAURANT & BAR

Island Restaurant & Bar is a super-chic dining space located in a prominent site overlooking the Italian Gardens of Hyde Park.

Stiff + Trevillion, the designers behind St Alban, Wagamama and Fakhreldine, have created a sophisticated look for Island. With its white limestone exterior and large glass entrance doors, Island Restaurant & Bar creates visual impact on arrival. Guests enter the restaurant up a wide slate-floored staircase.

Since opening in September 2004, Island has become one of London's most on-trend places to dine. The modern European cuisine is created by Island's Head Chef, Jean-Claude Vydelingum, whose impressive experience has seen him work alongside some of the capital's leading chefs such as: Philip Howard at the Michelin two-star restaurant, The Square; and Bruce Poole at the Michelin starred Chez Bruce.

Jean-Claude is passionate about using the finest ingredients and changes the menu seasonally. Island Bar also uses fresh produce in its extensive list of cocktails.

The menu at Island includes: Seared scallops with warm tomato, chorizo and coriander dressing; and Beef carpaccio with wild rocket, truffle oil and parmesan. While diners can expect to choose from main courses such as: Pot roast pork belly with braised cheek, black pudding, apple and parsnip puree; and Steamed fillet of bream with brown shrimp risotto, spring onion and dill. Desserts are not to be missed and feature delectable delights including: Sticky toffee pudding with sweet stem ginger ice-cream; Hazelnut parfait with chocolate mousse and frosted pistachio nuts; and Vanilla and orange pannacotta with roast fig and shortbread.

The restaurant is open from Noon until 10.30pm from Monday to Saturday, and Noon until 10.15pm on Sundays.

Island Restaurant & Bar, Lancaster Terrace, London W2 2TY
Reservations on 020 7551 6070 or visit www.islandrestaurant.co.uk

Where to...

Got the hunger, the people, the occasion, but not the venue? These suggestions will help you find the perfect spot to eat, drink and be merry.

Looking for something more specific? Then consult the **Subject Index**, starting on p392.

GO FOR BREAKFAST

Breakfast is offered every day unless stated otherwise. *See also* **Cafés** and **Brasseries**.

Acorn House Brasseries p49
Ambassador (Mon-Fri) Modern European p230
Automat The Americas p39
Le Bouchon Bordelais French p107
Butlers Wharf Chop House British p64
Café Strudel Global p130
Canteen British p54
The Capital Hotels & Haute Cuisine p139
Cinnamon Club (Mon-Fri) Indian p153
Le Coq d'Argent (Mon-Fri) French p99
Curve Fish p96
The Diner The Americas p39
Dorchester Grill Room British p61
Eagle Bar Diner The Americas p39
Empress of India British p65
Engineer Gastropubs p124
Fifteen (Trattoria) Italian p191
Fifth Floor (Café, Mon-Sat) Modern European p233
Fox & Anchor Pubs p339
Franco's (Mon-Sat) Italian p184
Gastro French p107
Gazette Brasseries p51
Harry Morgan's Jewish p212
Inn The Park British p61
Lansdowne Gastropubs p124
The Mercer British p54
Mulberry Street (Fri, Sat) Pizza & Pasta p322
Nicole's (Mon-Sat) Modern European p234
1 Lombard Street Brasserie (Mon-Fri) French p99
Only Running Footman Gastropubs p113
Prism (Mon-Fri) Modern European p229
The Providores & Tapa Room International p173
Roast (Mon-Sat) British p64

St John Bread & Wine British p55
Sakonis (Sat, Sun) Indian p172
S&M Café Budget p303
Simpson's-in-the-Strand (Mon-Fri) British p62
Smiths of Smithfield Modern European p230
Sotheby's Café (Mon-Fri) Modern European p235
Suka Oriental p252
Tapas Brindisa (Fri, Sat) Spanish p265
The Terrace (Holborn) (Mon-Fri) Modern European p231
Prince Arthur (Sat, Sun) Gastropubs p124

EAT/DRINK BY THE WATERSIDE

See also the Southbank Centre branches of Giraffe, Strada and Wagamama; and **Dining afloat** section on p351.

Bincho Japanese p206
Blueprint Café Modern European p246
Butlers Wharf Chop House British p64
Curve Fish p96
Gaucho (Tower Bridge and Richmond branches) The Americas p45
Glistening Waters Caribbean p68
Grapes Pubs p343
Gun Gastropubs p123
Kwan Thai Thai p275
Marco Polo Italian p188
The Narrow Gastropubs p123
Northbank Modern European p229

Royal China (Docklands branch) Chinese p81
Oxo Tower Restaurant, Bar & Brasserie Modern European p245
Le Pont de la Tour Modern European p246
Saran Rom Thai p271
Skylon Modern European p245
Stein's Budget p303
Thai Square Thai p272
Waterfront Gastropubs p118
Water House Brasseries p52
Wild Cherry Vegetarian p291
Ubon Japanese p207

TAKE THE KIDS

See also **Cafés**, **Brasseries**, **Fish & Chips**, **Pizza & Pasta** and the **Chain reaction** box on p42.

Ambassador Modern European p230
Babylon Modern European p239
Benihana Japanese p208
Blue Elephant Thai p271
Big Easy The Americas p43
Le Cercle French p98
Chez Kristof French p105
The Depot Brasseries p51
Engineer Gastropubs p124
fish! Fish p95
Harrison's Modern European p243
House Gastropubs p126
Inn The Park British p61
Marco Polo Italian p188
Marine Ices Budget p303
Masala Zone Indian p166
Namo Vietnamese p295
National Dining Rooms British p62
Pacific Bar & Grill The Americas p41
Perry Hill Gastropubs p121
Ping Pong Chinese p81
Rainforest Café Eating & Entertainment p354
Rousillon French p98
S&M Café Budget p303
Tamarind Indian p150
Victoria Modern European p241
Wagamama Oriental p252

ENJOY THE VIEW

Babylon Modern European p239
Bincho Japanese p206
Blueprint Café Modern European p246
Butlers Wharf Chop House British p64
Le Coq d'Argent French p99
Galvin at Windows Hotels & Haute
  Cuisine p141
National Dining Rooms British p62
Northbank Modern European p229
Oxo Tower Restaurant, Bar & Brasserie
  Modern European p245
Ozu Japanese p206
Plateau Modern European p247
Roast British p64
Rhodes Twenty Four British p54
Skylon Modern European p245
Tamesa@oxo Brasseries p52
Thai Square Thai p272
Tate Modern Café Brasseries p52
Top Floor at Smiths British p58
Ubon Japanese p207
Vertigo 42 Champagne Bar
  Eating & Entertainment p356

TRY UNUSUAL DISHES

See also **Global**.

Abeno Too Japanese p197
Adulis African p35
Archipelago International p173
Asadal Korean p214
Baozi Inn Chinese p69
Bar Shu Chinese p77
Biazo African p36
Divo East European p90
Esarn Kheaw Thai p271
Faanoos Middle Eastern p228
Hélène Darroze at The Connaught
  Hotels & Haute Cuisine p143
Hereford Road British p63
Hibiscus Hotels & Haute Cuisine p143
Hunan Chinese p69
Lola Rojo Spanish p265
Little Lamb Chinese p72
The Modern Pantry International p173
Nahm Thai p269
The Providores & Tapa Room
  International p173
Red Sea African p34
Saf Vegetarian p291
Saké No Hana Japanese p199

Snazz Sichuan Chinese p75
Song Que Vietnamese p294
Tbilisi East European p87
Texture Hotels & Haute Cuisine p140
Umu Japanese p199

DO BRUNCH

See also **Cafés** and **Brasseries**.

Ambassador (Sat, Sun)
  Modern European p230
Bermondsey Kitchen (Sat, Sun)
  Modern European p246
Brackenbury (Sun) Modern European p241
Bord'eaux French p103
Bumpkin (Sat, Sun) Modern European p240
Christopher's (Sat, Sun)
  The Americas p37
Le Comptoir Gascon (Sat) French p101
The Farm (Sat, Sun)
  Modern European p241
Fifth Floor (Sun) Modern European p233
Flâneur Food Hall Brasseries p48
Joe Allen (Sat, Sun) The Americas p38
Maze Grill The Americas p39
Ottolenghi International p176
Penk's (Sat) Global p132
Ransome's Dock (Sat, Sun)
  Modern European p244
Roast (Sat) British p64
Sabor (Sat, Sun) Latin American p47
Sam's Brasserie & Bar
  Modern European p238
The Terrace (Kensington) (Sat, Sun)
  Modern European p239
Wapping Food (Sat, Sun)
  Modern European p247
Waterloo Brasserie French p108

DINE ALFRESCO

See also **Park cafés** on p313.

Babylon Modern European p239
Back to Basics Fish p91
Bank Westminster Modern European p237
Bull Gastropubs p126
Cantina del Ponte Italian p189
Chez Kristof French p105
Clerkenwell Kitchen Cafés p305
Clissold Arms Gastropubs p127
Le Coq d'Argent French p99
Curve Fish p96
Daylesford Organic Café Cafés p307
Deep Fish p95
The Dolphin Gastropubs p121
Duke of Sussex Gastropubs p115
Ealing Park Tavern Gastropubs p115
The Engineer Gastropubs p124
Franklins British p64
Geales Fish p95
Greek Affair Greek p133
Gun Gastropubs p123
High Road Brasserie Brasseries p50
Hoxton Apprentice Modern European p247
House Gastropubs p126
Inn The Park British p61
Lemonia Greek p134
Manicomio Italian p188

The Narrow Gastropubs p123
Northbank Modern European p229
El Parador Spanish p268
Paternoster Chop House British p54
Perry Hill Gastropubs p121
Rootmaster Vegetarian p291
Petersham Nurseries Café
  Modern European p248
Phoenix Bar & Grill
  Modern European p243
Plateau Modern European p247
Le Pont de la Tour Modern European p246
RIBA Café Brasseries p49
The River Café Italian p185
Royal China (Docklands branch)
  Chinese p81
Saran Rom Thai p271
Scott's Fish p93
Stein's Budget p303
Suka Oriental p252
The Terrace (Holborn)
  Modern European p231
The Terrace (Kensington)
  Modern European p239
La Trouvaille French p104
Waterfront Gastropubs p118
Yakitoria Japanese p202

PEOPLE-WATCH

Blue Bar Bars p331
Le Café Anglais Modern European p238
Champagne Bar at St Pancras
  Wine Bars p347
Embassy Modern European p234
Eyre Brothers Global p132
Fifth Floor Modern European p233
Hix Oyster & Chop House British p55
The Ivy Modern European p231
Kensington Place
  Modern European p239
Loungelover Bars p338
Mahiki Bars p332
Mr Chow Chinese p75
Obika Italian p179
Papillon French p107
Quo Vadis British p61
St Alban Global p131
Scott's Fish p93
Sketch: The Gallery International p174
Tate Modern Café Brasseries p52
The Wolseley Brasseries p49
Zuma Japanese p194

YOU'VE GOT THE FUNCTION, WE'VE GOT THE SPACE

East Wing • Orchid Lounge • Bar Area • Thai House • Mezzanine • Thai Huts

Weddings • Birthdays • Anniversaries • Christmas Parties

Our award winning Thai restaurant can cater for any event.

187 Stoke Newington High Street, London, N16 0LH 020 7254 6751 www.yumyum.co.uk

The Wet Fish Café

contemporary comfort food

"terrific setting in an old fish shop, well thought-out menu (and not, in fact, particularly fishy)"
Hardens Guide 2009

brunch – martini time – dinner

Reservations 020 7443-9222
⊖ West Hampstead, Jubilee Line + 5 mins walk
242 West End Lane
West Hampstead
London NW6 1LG

www.thewetfishcafe.co.uk

TAKE A DATE

Almeida French p109
Amaya Indian p148
Andrew Edmunds Modern European p237
Angelus French p104
L'Anima Italian p177
Assaggi Italian p185
L'Autre Pied Modern European p233
Bistroteque French p108
The Botanist Modern European p241
Brickhouse Eating & Entertainment p351
Le Café Anglais Modern European p238
Le Cassoulet French p110
Empress of India British p65
Eyre Brothers Global p132
Fifteen Italian p191
Hakkasan Chinese p75
Harrison's Modern European p243
Kenza Middle Eastern p223
Lamberts Modern European p243
Locanda Locatelli Italian p182
Lost Society Bars p336
Magdalen British p64
Maze Hotels & Haute Cuisine p143
Odette's Modern European p247
Osteria Emilia Italian p192
Pasha North African p249
Penk's Global p132
Plateau Modern European p247
Roka Japanese p193
Rosemary Lane French p99
Saké No Hana Japanese p199
Sardo Italian p178
J Sheekey Fish p91
Singapore Garden Malaysian, Indonesian & Singaporean p222
Theo Randall at the Intercontinental Italian p182
Le Trois Garçons French p109
Upstairs Modern European p244
Wapping Food Modern European p247
Wild Honey Modern European p235

EAT AT THE BAR

Anchor & Hope Gastropubs p119
Arbutus Modern European p237
Barrafina Spanish p261
Bentley's Oyster Bar & Grill Fish p93
Le Caprice Modern European p237
Dehesa Spanish p261
Eyre Brothers Global p132
Maze Hotels & Haute Cuisine p143
Moro Spanish p258
Roka Japanese p193
Salt Yard Spanish p258
J Sheekey Fish p91
Tapas Brindisa Spanish p265
Wild Honey Modern European p235
Wright Brothers Oyster & Porter House Fish p96
Zetter Brasseries p48

GRAB A MEAL PRE-THEATRE

Almeida French p109
Anchor & Hope Gastropubs p119
Axis Modern European p231

The Botanist Modern European p241
Canteen (South Bank) British p54
Christopher's The Americas p37
Gaucho (Piccadilly) The Americas p45
Le Mercury Budget p303
Manicomio Italian p188
Ottolenghi International p176
Veeraswamy Indian p150
Waterloo Brasserie French p108

BOOK A PRIVATE ROOM

Alloro Italian p182
Almeida French p109
Amaya Indian p148
Baltic East European p87

Bam-Bou Oriental p252
Chez Bruce French p107
Fish Central Fish & Chips p315
Marquess Tavern Gastropubs p127
Mildred's Vegetarian p289
Osteria dell'Arancio Italian p188
Pasha Turkish p284
Pearl Liang Chinese p77
Phoenix Palace Chinese p75
Rasa Samudra Indian p148
The River Café Italian p185
Sketch Hotels & Haute Cuisine p144, International p174, Cafés p307
Smiths of Smithfield Modern European p230
Tom's Kitchen Brasseries p51
Via Condotti Italian p184
Zetter Brasseries p48

EAT LATE

Artesian Bars p331
Asia de Cuba International p173
Balans Brasseries p49
Camino Spanish p260
Ed's Easy Diner The Americas p39
Fish in a Tie Budget p300
Floridita The Americas p46
Gilgamesh Oriental p254
Hoxton Grille Brasseries p52
Joe Allen The Americas p38
Kenza Middle Eastern p223
Mangal II Turkish p281
Le Mercury Budget p303
Meza Spanish p261
New Mayflower Chinese p73

PJ's Grill The Americas p40
Planet Hollywood The Americas p42
Sariyer Balik Turkish p282
Tinseltown Eating & Entertainment p356
Vingt-Quatre Eating & Entertainment p356
The Wolseley Brasseries p49

LOVE THE LOOK

Amaya Indian p148
L'Anima Italian p177
Apsleys Italian p182
L'Autre Pied Modern European p233
Asia de Cuba International p173
L'Atelier de Joël Robuchon Modern European p231
Baltic East European p87
Benares Indian p150
Le Cercle French p98
China Tang Chinese p76
Cocoon Oriental p253
Dinings Japanese p197
Fifth Floor Modern European p233
Gilgamesh Oriental p254
Hakkasan Chinese p75
Jerusalem Tavern Pubs p339
Kenza Middle Eastern p223
Ladurée Cafés p310
Landau Hotels & Haute Cuisine p136
Lost Society Bars p336
Loungelover Bars p338
Meals Cafés p306
Nobu Berkeley Street Japanese p199
Pearl Bar & Restaurant Hotels & Haute Cuisine p137
Pearl Liang Chinese p77
E Pellicci Budget p301
Petersham Nurseries Café Modern European p248
Rhodes W1 Hotels & Haute Cuisine p139
Roka Japanese p193
Saké No Hana Japanese p199
Saran Rom Thai p271
Shanghai Blues Chinese p75
Sketch: The Lecture Room Hotels & Haute Cuisine p144
Skylon Modern European p245
Trailer Happiness Bars p335
Les Trois Garçons French p109
Wapping Food Modern European p247
Yauatcha Chinese p78
Zuma Japanese p194

Restaurants

African

Although it has certainly not yet reached the ubiquity attained by Chinese or Indian restaurants in London, African food is showing all the signs of being the next 'ethnic' cuisine on the up. We've qualms about using the term 'African cuisine'. It's a terribly lazy way to describe the cooking styles of 52 countries, not to mention the food of the many different cultures found within those national boundaries. Injera (Ethiopia and Eritrea's sour, pancake-like starch staple) has about as much in common with waatse (west African rice and beans) as yorkshire pudding has with Russian golubtsy.

But considering the fact that ten years ago most Londoners would struggle to name any dishes from the continent, knowledge and availability of the food is growing fast. You no longer have to schlep to the furthest reaches of Tottenham or Peckham to get a fix of jollof rice or palm-nut soup. In King's Cross (**Addis**), Westbourne Park (**Mosob**) and South Norwood (**Gold Coast Bar & Restaurant**), you can now try the rich, spicy flavours of the continent (chilli peppers are almost guaranteed, whichever African cuisine you sample). Although west African restaurants still dominate in London, Ethiopian and Eritrean cuisine is increasingly available, as is the food of the city's more numerous expat African communities such as Congolese, Kenyan and South African (for the latter, *see p132* **Chakalaka**). Peckham's **805** remains a firm favourite for lovers of Nigerian cooking, while **Mosob** will give you a warm heart and a full belly.

North African restaurants (Morocco and Tunisia) have their own chapter, starting on p249.

Central

King's Cross

★ Addis
42 Caledonian Road, N1 9DT (7278 0679/ www.addisrestaurant.co.uk). King's Cross tube/rail/17, 91, 259 bus. **Meals served** noon-midnight Mon-Fri; 1pm-midnight Sat, Sun. **Main courses** £6.50-£8.50. **Credit** AmEx, MC, V.
With walls the colour of an African sunset and the sounds of uptempo Ethio-pop mingling with the buzz of expat and local diners, Addis brings more than a ray of light to King's Cross. It is the only Ethiopian restaurant in central London, and offers a generous selection of meat, fish and vegetarian dishes. Diners are seated at western-style tables or traditional *mesobs* (woven tables with near-floor seating; if you fail to book at weekends, you may have no option but to sit at the latter. Service is friendly but slow, giving you more than enough time between ordering and eating to have a couple of Batis (Ethiopian beer). The charcoal-grilled lamb kebab was delicately spiced and tender, while yetesom beyaynetu (chickpeas, cabbage and carrots, served with fresh injera or pitta) was a delicious mini-platter perfect for vegetarians. We suggest you take advantage of the weekday lunch offer (£1 off any dish) to try something a bit different, such as the Horn of Africa favourite fuul (fava beans with feta and falafel), or for the intrepid, dulet (spiced lamb innards).
Babies and children welcome: high chairs. Booking advisable. Takeaway service. **Map 4 L2.**

★ New Merkato
196 Caledonian Road, N1 0SL (7713 8952). King's Cross tube/rail/17, 91, 259 bus. **Meals served** 11am-midnight Mon-Fri; noon-midnight Sat; 1pm-midnight Sun. **Main courses** £6-£10. **Set meal** £17-£22 per person (minimum 2). **Credit** AmEx, MC, V.
Named after Addis Ababa's bustling Merkato, the city's main trading area, this unpretentious restaurant does its best to remain loyal to its Ethiopian roots despite being located on a bleak stretch of the Caledonian Road. The simple red-and-white interior is suffused with the aroma of incense, the walls hung with Amharic tapestries and Ethiopian portraits. This is very much a venue for dinner, rather than lunch. The food, all served on the traditional round tray of injera, can be hit and miss. Lega tibs (lamb cubes cooked in green pepper and onion) was a delight, meltingly tender in the mouth. But the sweetish mix of spices simply swamped any fish flavour in the assa wot (fish curry), and the ayib begomen – a blend of spinach and cottage cheese – was far too salty. On the plus side, it's rare to find own-made tej (tangy honey wine, served in a round-bottomed flask) in London. And you can't fault Merkato's prices.
Babies and children welcome: high chairs. Booking advisable Fri, Sat. Tables outdoors (4, pavement). Takeaway service. **Map 4 M1.**

West

Shepherd's Bush

★ Red Sea NEW
382 Uxbridge Road, W12 7LL (8749 6888). Shepherd's Bush tube. **Meals served** 11am-11pm Mon-Thur, Sun; 11am-midnight Fri, Sat. **Main courses** £5-£7. **Unlicensed. Credit** MC, V.
The charming, family friendly Red Sea cheerfully makes no attempt at urban sophistication. Plastic table covers and an eccentric decor embracing Eritrean peasant scenes, the legendary Sanaa skyline and a giant view of Westminster bridge make it feel like an African transport café. The owners are Eritrean, the cooks Yemeni, the muzak Ethiopian. Service is somewhat absent-minded and for those who don't know their way around the dishes of the region, there's not a great deal of explanation. But the food makes its own case, ranging confidently over the classics of Horn of Africa and Middle Eastern cuisine. Our choice of awaze tibs (lamb cooked in a spicy tomato sauce), shiro (puréed chickpeas), and a range of vegetarian orthodox 'fasting foods' – spinach, potato and lentils – all up-ended as tradition dictates on a springy bed of injera dough. That food of such pleasing delicacy can be found at these modest prices makes Red Sea an unexpected delight. Note that it's unlicensed, and you can no longer bring in your own alcohol.
Babies and children welcome: high chair. Disabled: toilet. Tables outdoors (2, pavement). Takeaway service. Vegetarian menu. **Map 20 B1.**

Westbourne Park

★ ★ Mosob
339 Harrow Road, W9 3RB (7266 2012/ www.mosob.co.uk). Westbourne Park tube. **Meals served** 6pm-midnight Mon-Fri; 3pm-midnight Sat, Sun. **Main courses** £6-£11. **Credit** AmEx, MC, V.
Less than five minutes' walk from Westbourne Park tube lies this fabulous family-owned restaurant serving arguably the best Eritrean food around. Mosob is bedecked in Afro-chic furnishings and has the friendliest waiters in west London. It is also blessed with good, simple cooking (made by mum, served by her son and nephew) that provides both a great introduction for newcomers to the cuisine, and a welcome reminder to fans of Horn of Africa food. We started with some tasty mini-sambusas (samosas), golden crisp pastry stuffed with fresh meat and tangy vegetables. Next up, the mains: after some advice, we chose zigni, a beef stew with a nutty flavour, which nicely complemented the sourdough taste of the injera. Bebe'ainetu was a fantastic choice for vegetarians, consisting of taster-sized portions of dishes like alicha (stewed cabbage, potatoes and carrots) and shiro (spicy ground chickpeas). Desserts are of the rich European gateaux and ice cream variety – a chocolate torte, a parfait of mango sorbet, meringue and fresh fruit. Regrettably, there are no African drinks on the menu either, but when your waiter gives you a stunning Asmaran travel guide to read between courses, who needs suwa?
Babies and children welcome: high chairs. Booking advisable. Separate room for parties, seats 22. Takeaway service. **Map 1 A4.**

South

Brixton

Asmara
386 Coldharbour Lane, SW9 8LF (7737 4144). Brixton tube/rail. **Dinner served** 5.30pm-midnight daily. **Main courses** £4.50-£8. **Set meals** £26 per person (minimum 2) 7 courses (vegetarian), £28 per person (minimum 2) 7 courses (meat). **Credit** MC, V.
It is Coldharbour Lane's most inconspicuous establishment, but inside, with its delicate coffee and incense fragrance and mellow decor, Asmara provides an oasis of east African calm. Simple seating and efficient service underpin a solid menu of traditional Eritrean cuisine. The spicy lentil soup looked very tempting, but we started with Eritrean black tea before lunging into main courses of zigni (spicy beef stew) and spinach cooked with chilli and oil, which we shared on a tasty injera platter that proved ample for two. Of all the injera we've sampled across London's Ethiopian and Eritrean restaurants, this was the best – moist, delicately tangy and barley-hued. The traditional coffee ceremony was a wonderful pageant; diners are given freshly roasted beans to savour before the coffee is served with warm

RESTAURANTS

popcorn. Asmara offers a great alternative to the Japanese, Thai and Caribbean restaurants so loved in this part of Brixton; it's ideal for a good meal before sampling the area's nightlife.

Babies and children welcome: high chairs. Booking advisable. Separate room for parties, seats 35. Takeaway service. Vegan dishes. Vegetarian menu. **Map 22 E2.**

Kennington

★ Adulis

44-46 Brixton Road, SW9 6BT (7587 0055/ www.adulis.co.uk). Brixton tube/rail. **Meals served** 5pm-midnight Mon-Thur; 1pm-midnight Fri-Sun. **Main courses** £7.95-£9.95. **Credit** MC, V.

The uninitiated can sometimes get their Horn of Africa restaurants confused, but this is never likely to happen with Adulis, which positively flaunts its Eritrean nationality. The light and airy restaurant is decorated with framed photographs of Eritrea's old Italian railway, a plaque to the camel (the national emblem), and a mounted pair of the simple rubber sandals worn by Eritrean rebels during their war of independence. For diners with strong nerves, goe s'nigh (green chillies stuffed with onion) makes for a bracing starter. To follow, a classic range of meat stews and pulses, served on an injera base, competes with fish and seafood from the Red Sea. Adulis also offers kitfo (beef in ghee butter, either lightly cooked or raw, according to taste). There's plenty of Asmara beer to cool hot mouths and the bar also serves honey wine and zibib, Eritrea's version of absinthe. Adulis's speedy service, contemporary surroundings and fresh ingredients make it one of London's best Horn of Africa restaurants, which may explain the steady stream of both Eritrean and western customers through its doors, even midweek.

Babies and children welcome: high chairs; nappy-changing facilities. Entertainment: live band 10pm-2.30am Sat. Separate room for parties, seats 150. Takeaway service. **Map 16 M13.**

South East
Peckham

★ 805 Bar Restaurant

805 Old Kent Road, SE15 1NX (7639 0808/ www.805restaurant.com). Elephant & Castle tube/ rail then 53 bus. **Meals served** 2pm-12.30am daily. **Main courses** £7-£15. **Credit** MC, V.

Out of the concrete expanse of the Tustin Housing Estate on Old Kent Road grows something of a culinary rose. Judge the 805 Bar Restaurant not by its humble exterior, nor by its simple white decor (of similar hue to the praise garments worn by members of the Nigerian Celestial Church of Christ). The fact that late on a Sunday night its two spacious dining rooms were heaving with well-to-do Nigerians tells you all you need to know. Since 2001, 805 has been serving up southern Nigerian staples with the odd European flourish to customers from far and wide. On the menu, you'll find a varied selection of west African favourites such as jollof rice, moyin moyin and egusi (ground melon seeds, served with spinach), alongside the restaurant's signature dish, monika (marinated grilled fish with chilli sauce). The asaro – a mashed yam pottage cooked with seasoned tomato and onion – was gorgeous, served with tilapia and plantain. Ewa aganyin (lightly spiced smoked beans, also accompanied by fried plantain) was laudable too. Service comes with a smile, and the portions are as hearty as the atmosphere.

Babies and children admitted. Disabled: toilet. Separate room for parties, seats 55. Tables outdoors (6, pavement). Takeaway service.

South Norwood

Gold Coast Bar
& Restaurant **NEW**

224 Portland Road, SE25 4QB (8676 1919/ www.thegoldcoastbar.com). Norwood Junction rail/Woodside tramlink.

Bar **Open/snacks served** noon-midnight Mon-Thur, Sun; noon-2am Fri, Sat.
Restaurant **Dinner served** 6-10.30pm Mon-Fri. **Meals served** 1-10.30pm Sat, Sun. **Main courses** £7-£11.
Both **Credit** MC, V.

In what used to be the rough-as-anything, and deceptively named, Pleasant Pheasant, lies one of the capital's most successful Afro-gastropubs. On the ground floor at the Gold Coast you can get kelewele (spicy, cubed plantain), posena (bite-sized fried squid) and yam balls as bar snacks alongside Star beers and Apio (rum) from Ghana, while upstairs a split-level restaurant serves a wide choice of solid west African favourites. As with most African eateries, the portions are as generous as the warm service is leisurely. Our snapper stew with jollof rice and plantain was appetising if a little uninspired, as was the hearty stewed beef. But with alternatives like goat soup with fufu on the menu, there are more exciting dishes to be sampled. The Sunday afternoon of our visit saw the restaurant packed with an eclectic mix of expats and locals having their Sunday lunch, while downstairs, football fans of all nationalities watched the latest Premier League nail-biter, followed by a fun evening of live music and dancing.

Babies and children welcome: high chairs (restaurant). Entertainment (bar): DJs 8.30pm-2am Fri, Sat; band 6-10.30pm Sun. Restaurant/ bar available for hire. Separate rooms for parties, seating 15-80. Tables outdoors (7, patio). Takeaway service.

North East
Dalston

★ Suya Obalende

523 Kingsland Road, E8 4AR (7275 0171/ www.obalendesuya.com). Dalston Kingsland rail/38, 67, 76, 149 bus. **Meals served** noon-midnight Mon-Thur, Sun; noon-1am Fri-Sat. **Main courses** £7.95-£8.95. **Set buffet** (Sun) £9.95. **Credit** MC, V.

In the heart of Dalston lies this popular Naija chop shop (for which read 'Nigerian fast-food outlet'), affectionately known as the 'African McDonald's'. Don't be put off: the name is only a reflection of the price and speed at which the food is served – lightning fast by Africa's generally more relaxed standards. Specialising in suya (charcoal-grilled seasoned meat or fish), the restaurant behind the open-front grill in the takeaway section provides a fair menu of meat grills and other west African favourites. Options range from chicken to gizzards (popular offal in Africa), to the more adventurous

crocodile. Our chicken suya was tender and plentiful, although the yams in the vegetarian asaro could have been softer. The handwash point is a great idea, as is the cheeky 'plate tax' (a £2.50 surcharge – donated to charity – for those not clearing their plate during the Sunday buffet). If you're looking for 'good food fast' as the slogan says, this is worth a try.

Babies and children welcome: high chairs. Takeaway service. **Map 25 B5.**
For branch (Suya Express) see index.

North
Kentish Town

★ Queen of Sheba

12 Fortess Road, NW5 2EU (7284 3947/ www.thequeenofsheba.co.uk). Kentish Town tube/rail. **Meals served** 1pm-Mon-Sat; 1-10.30pm Sun. **Main courses** £5-£10.50. **Credit** MC, V.

The strong aroma of incense billows up to greet you on entering this restaurant's dark, cosy interior. With its Amharic crucifixes on the walls and a pair of high-booted, wild-haired waitresses in the Amazonian mould, the Queen of Sheba is a funky juxtaposition of ancient and modern. The exotic combination has succeeded in winning it an enthusiastic western, rather than Ethiopian, following. The menu features modestly priced classics – spicy stews and puréed pulses served on injera – a few in-house inventions, and a range of raw meat dishes (kitfo is the Ethiopian equivalent of steak tartare) for those wanting something more adventurous. There's also a choice of Ethiopian beers; St George's turns out to be a light, if unremarkable, lager. Space in this one-room restaurant is restricted and tables small, so the decibel level soars as numbers rise. With a small kitchen handling what tends to be a heavy flood of orders, this isn't the place for a snappy meal and a quick get-away. Arrive intending to savour the experience, get your orders in smartish, and linger over your food.

Babies and children welcome: high chairs. Booking advisable Fri, Sat. Restaurant available for hire. Tables outdoors (2, patio). Takeaway service. Vegetarian menu. **Map 26 B4.**

Tufnell Park

★ Lalibela

137 Fortess Road, NW5 2HR (7284 0600). Tufnell Park tube/134 bus. **Dinner served** 6pm-midnight daily. **Main courses** £8.50-£9.95. **Credit** MC, V.

RESTAURANTS

Mosob

One of London's older Ethiopian restaurants, the thoroughly enjoyable Lalibela has long been a fixture on the map for Ethiopian expats and Europeans who appreciate the Horn of Africa's traditional cuisine. The decor – embracing old photographs of Emperor Haile Selassie, examples of national costume and wall friezes of the Queen of Sheba story – errs on the heavy side; this can feel more like an ethnographic museum than a restaurant. But the food holds its own. Our awaze tibs (sautéed lamb) and tsom bayentu (a melange of vegetarian food), ritually deposited in small piles on a sourdough base, were fresh, tasty and promptly served. Made from a mix of grains, rather than the classic, hard-to-locate tef, the injera is less sour in flavour than it should be, but that's par for the course in London. Food is served on traditional low tables, and diners ordering coffee at the end can luxuriate in the extended Ethiopian ceremony. Set across two storeys, Lalibela offers a quieter and more relaxed experience than some of its smaller rivals. A ground-floor alcove allows privacy for larger groups.
Babies and children welcome: high chair. Booking advisable. Takeaway service. Vegan dishes. Vegetarian menu. **Map 26 B3**.

North West

Kilburn

Abyssinia

9 Cricklewood Broadway, NW2 3JX (8208 0110). Kilburn tube. **Meals served** noon-midnight Mon-Fri; 2pm-midnight Sat, Sun. **Main courses** £4.50-£10. **Credit** MC, V.
It may look as though it was furnished back in the days when sub-Saharan Africa's oldest state was also called Abyssinia, but don't let that put you off. The friendly welcome and beautiful smell of frankincense that greets diners entering this well-established Ethiopian eaterie soon helps you forget its rather dark, drab surroundings. After considering such delicacies as kitfo (spicy, raw mince beef) and doro wot, we settled on the assa wot (fish stew), which had a similar texture to mince but lacked the spice for which Ethiopian food is famed. However, the dish worked well with the injera with which almost all main courses are served. The tej (honey wine, similar to mead) was tasty and not too sweet, although the highlight of the meal was undoubtedly the Ethiopian coffee at the end, served following an elaborate roasting ceremony. Our food choices were a little

disappointing, but the many Ethiopian diners who ate their tilapia while listening to the latest sounds from Addis looked very happy.
Babies and children admitted: high chairs. Booking advisable. Separate room for parties, seats 30. Tables outdoors (6, garden). Takeaway service.

Outer London

Edgware, Middlesex

Biazo **NEW**

307 Hale Lane, Edgware, Middx HA8 7AX (8958 8826/www.biazo.co.uk). Edgware tube. **Meals served** noon-11pm Tue-Fri; 1-11pm Sat; 1-10pm Sun. **Main courses** £3.50-£14.50. **Set lunch** (1-4pm Sun) £13.99 2 courses. **Unlicensed. Credit** MC, V.
If you're new to west African cooking and want to ease yourself into a world of cow foot, snails and chicken gizzards, then Biazo is a good place to start. With its stylish, Afropean decor and friendly,

Biazo

efficient service, it's a welcome addition to the area's parade of Asian and European restaurants. The extensive menu offers mostly Nigerian food, but also Ghanaian and Kenyan dishes. We ordered the fried yam (preceded by a tasty bowl of crunchy deep-fried chin-chin biscuits), which was followed by some hearty mains: an elegantly spiced efo egusi (spinach with ground melon seeds), waakye (rice and beans) and a portion of stewed tilapia that was ample for our hungry twosome. Die-hard fans of traditional Nigerian cuisine may find the rice not quite moist enough, and the spicing a little too mild. The mocktails on the entirely non-alcoholic drinks menu seem tooth-achingly sweet, so stick to the Nigerian soft drinks. We get the impression that Biazo is still fine-tuning what could in time be a winning menu.
Babies and children welcome: children's menu; high chairs; nappy-changing facilities. Disabled: toilet. Restaurant available for hire. Takeaway service; delivery service (over £20 within 3-mile radius).

Menu

Accra or **akara**: bean fritters.
Aloco: fried plantain with hot tomato sauce.
Asaro: yam and sweet potato porridge.
Ayeb or **iab**: fresh yoghurt cheese made from strained yoghurt.
Berbere: an Ethiopian spice mix made with many hot and aromatic spices.
Cassava, manioc or **yuca**: a family of coarse roots that are boiled and pounded to make bread and various other farinaceous dishes. There are bitter and sweet varieties (note that the bitter variety is poisonous until cooked).
Egusi: ground melon seeds, added to stews and soups as a thickening agent.
Froi: fish and shrimp aubergine stew.
Fufu: a stiff pudding of maize or cassava (qv) flour, or pounded yam (qv).
Gari: a solid, heavy pudding made from ground fermented cassava (qv), served with thick soups.
Ground rice: a kind of stiff rice pudding served to accompany soup.
injera, enjera or **enjerra**: a soft, spongy

Ethiopian and Eritrean flatbread made with teff/tef (a grain originally from Ethiopia), wheat, barley, oats or cornmeal. Fermented with yeast, it should have a distinct sour tang.
Jollof rice: like a hot, spicy risotto, with tomatoes, onions and (usually) chicken.
Kanyah: a sweet snack from Sierra Leone made from rice, peanuts and sugar.
Kelewele or **do-do**: fried plantain.
Kenkey: a starchy pudding that's prepared by pounding dried maize and water into a paste, then steaming inside plantain leaves. Usually eaten with meat, fish or vegetable stews.
Moi-moi, moin-moin or **moyin moyin**: steamed beancake, served with meat or fish.
Ogbono: a large seed similar to egusi (qv). Although it doesn't thicken as much, it is used in a similar way.
Pepper soup: a light, peppery soup made with either fish or meat.
Shito: a dark red-hot pepper paste from

Ghana, made from dried shrimps blended with onions and tomatoes.
Suya: a spicy Nigerian meat kebab.
Teff or **tef**: an indigenous gluten-free Ethiopian grain used for making the injera flatbread (qv).
Tuo or **tuwo**: a stiff rice pudding, sometimes served as rice balls to accompany soup.
Ugali: a Swahili word for bread made from cornmeal and water.
Ugba: Nigerian soy beans; also called oil beans.
Waakye: a dish of rice and black-eyed beans mixed with meat or chicken in gravy.
Waatse: rice and black-eyed beans cooked together.
Wot: a thick, dark sauce made from slowly cooked onions, garlic, butter and spices – an essential component in the aromatic stews of East Africa.
Doro wot, a stew containing chicken and hard-boiled eggs, is a particularly common dish (qv).

The Americas

NORTH AMERICAN

Whether you're hoping for steaks and martinis in a smart setting, heart-stopping burgers, crab cakes and chowder, or authentic barbecue, London has a North American restaurant to suit your mood. This year the reopening of **Chicago Rib Shack** on the former site of Mocotó generated plenty of media coverage, but we found the food disappointing: the owners seemed not to have clocked that **Bodean's** (now with five branches in the capital) had already raised the bar for barbecue in London, while keeping prices keen. **Hawksmoor** made the steakhouse hip, and even Gordon Ramsay Holdings wants a (medium-rare?) cut of the steakhouse action, opening **Maze Grill** in spring 2008. The further expansion of the **Diner**, now with a spacious outlet in Camden, shows that London's passion for burgers and shakes shows no sign of diminishing either. For London's burgeoning collection of gourmet burger bars, *see p303.*

Central
City

Green Door Bar & Grill NEW
33 Cornhill, EC3 (7929 1378/www.greendoor steakhouse.co.uk). Bank tube/DLR. **Meals served** 11am-11pm daily. **Main courses** £9-£30. **Set meal** £41-£58 3 courses. **Credit** AmEx, DC, MC, V.
Sierra Nevada, Anchor Steam, Brooklyn… you'd think an American-inspired bar and grill would attempt to serve some of the better US beers available in London, but no, not at Green Door. The absence encapsulates nicely that this spot is about style (conservative, frumpy) rather than substance. The wine list is another missed opportunity, with a mere three bottles from the USA. And the cocktails? We enjoyed the quintessentially British flavour of the elderflower collins, certainly. Our steaks (sirloin, ribeye and fillet are available in a choice of sizes) were fine specimens, and better accompanied by onion rings and creamed spinach than by the leathery-crusted chips. The menu also proffers venison and veal chops, corn-fed chicken, glazed duck and sea bass; there are a few pasta dishes for vegetarians. But you have to worry about any place trying to sell 'Our Famous Melted Camembert'. For dessert, the cheesecake tasted nice enough, but its low-rise filling would have been laughed out of the Big Apple. Charming staff were a bright spot in the dark wood, mezzanine-level restaurant, which retains some of the grandeur of the old City.
Babies and children welcome: high chairs. Booking essential (lunch). Disabled: toilet. **Map 12 Q6**. **For branch see index.**

★ Hawksmoor (100)
157 Commercial Street, E1 6BJ (7247 7392/ www.thehawksmoor.com). Liverpool Street tube/ rail. **Lunch served** noon-2.30pm Mon-Fri. **Dinner served** 6-10.30pm Mon-Sat. **Main courses** £16-£26. **Credit** AmEx, MC, V.
We know that Christ Church Spitalfields is down the road, but even so, the owners of this cocktail bar/steakhouse were cheeky in naming it after such a celebrated London architect. It's hard to imagine a more undistinguished exterior, a flat-fronted office block with no character or charm. Inside, the design is nothing special either; the unsubtle lighting and whitewashed walls only emphasise the low ceilings, while the open-plan layout draws attention to the uneasy way that drinkers mix with diners. Happily, the food transcends its surroundings. You won't go away hungry: the portion of ribs served as a starter was bigger than a main course in some American eateries we could name, and the pork chop was positively immense. What's more, the quality matches the quantity. The meat is sourced from the Ginger Pig and the kitchen seems happy to let the animals do the talking, delivering a sturdy menu free of unnecessary complication. Supplement the refreshingly unshowy cooking with the fabulous cocktail list (great value too), terrific service and the 'go on, you know you want to' range of desserts, and you have a very impressive operation. Now, about that room…
Babies and children admitted. Disabled: toilet. Separate room for parties, seats 12. Wireless internet (free). **Map 6 R5.**

Missouri Grill
76 Aldgate High Street, EC3N 1BD (7481 4010/ www.missourigrill.com). Aldgate or Aldgate East tube. **Lunch served** noon-3pm, **dinner served** 5-10pm Mon-Fri. **Main courses** £10-£19.50. **Set dinner** £12 2 courses, £16 3 courses. **Credit** AmEx, MC, V.
Unbecomingly located on a busy one-way system opposite Aldgate tube station, Missouri Grill wears its theming lightly. The 40-capacity room has been straightforwardly done out as a penny-plain urban bistro, the music is not distinctive and the wine list contains fewer than half a dozen US options. Only the food menu gives the American game away, but on the quietish night we visited, the kitchen appeared to be cutting corners. A crab cake starter didn't taste especially fresh, while the New England clam chowder was too thin, and the cut of ribeye used for our main course wasn't really up to snuff. Served with a flavourful salad of aubergine, courgettes and peppers, the grilled mahi-mahi was better, as was the light and handsome baked cheesecake. But although we appreciated the efforts of the waiter, who didn't put a foot wrong despite having been left short-handed by absent colleagues, we can't help wondering if the management has turned its attention to the newer sister operation around the corner towards the Tower of London.

Babies and children welcome: children's portions; high chairs. Booking essential lunch. Separate room for parties, seats 14. Wireless internet (free). **Map 12 R6**. **For branch see index**.

Clerkenwell & Farringdon

Dollar Grills & Martinis
2 Exmouth Market, EC1R 4PX (7278 0077/ www.dollargrillsandmartinis.com). Farringdon tube/rail/19, 38, 341 bus.
Bar **Open** 6pm-1am Mon-Sat; 6pm-midnight Sun. **Meals served** 6-11.30pm Mon-Sat; 6-10pm Sun. **Main courses** £4.50-£9.
Restaurant **Lunch served** noon-5pm daily. **Dinner served** 6-11pm Mon-Sat; 6-10pm Sun. **Main courses** £8.50-£22.50. **Set lunch** (Mon-Fri) £9.95 2 courses.
Both **Credit** AmEx, MC, V.
Dramatically located in a huge old corner pub, its bare-brick walls covered in eye-catching Vegas imagery beneath almost theatrical lighting, Dollar isn't really interested in subtlety. This is a brash place, but it's hard not to admire its commitment to the party-hearty aesthetic. While the smart-ish American-slanted comfort cooking won't win any awards, it's better than you might expect given that the ambience seems to favour drinking over eating (there's a separate cocktail bar in the basement). Our weakest dish was a starter of chicken liver parfait, its blandness only partially disguised by a tasty fig chutney. In contrast, grilled scallops, tidily served atop small chunks of potato with a caper butter, were delectable. A dish of chicken served over butternut squash, pancetta and cabbage was fine, if a little greasy, but in general you're better off sticking to the red meat. Our sirloin steak, served with full-flavoured potato gratin, was very decent, and the burgers remain both popular and reliable. Not exactly date material, but a good bet for groups.
Babies and children admitted. Bar available for hire. Entertainment: DJs 8pm Fri, Sat. Tables outdoors (10, pavement). Takeaway service. **Map 5 N4.**

Smithfield Bar & Grill
2-3 West Smithfield, EC1A 9JX (7246 0900/ www.blackhousegrills.com). Farringdon tube/rail. **Meals served** noon-10pm daily. **Main courses** £9.95-£17.50. **Credit** AmEx, MC, V.
Part of the Cheshire-based Blackstone Grills group, the Smithfield Bar & Grill has carved out a tidy niche as a smaller and less frenetic alternative to Smiths of Smithfield across the market. The scene in the slick bar area can be pretty kinetic, but its separation from the attractive restaurant at the back is such that you should be able to hear yourself think. However, the pleasing quasi-sophistication of the design isn't matched by the kitchen. Seared carpaccio of beef was a fair rendition, if under-salted, but clam chowder was pretty indifferent and our 11oz (300g), medium-rare ribeye steak (served with scrumptious horseradish mash) was too tough. While the service could hardly have been more friendly or efficient, on occasions it exuded the unpleasant aroma of head-office hard-sell. The instant our menus were delivered, we were casually offered 'bread and olives for the table'. Just as casually, we said 'yes', only to find that we'd been charged £2.75 for an ashtray-sized helping of stoned olives and, breathtakingly, the same again for a solitary unremarkable roll.
Babies and children welcome: high chairs. Booking advisable. Disabled: toilet. Restaurant available for hire. **Map 11 O5.**

Covent Garden

Christopher's
18 Wellington Street, WC2E 7DD (7240 4222/ www.christophersgrill.com). Covent Garden tube.
Bar **Open/snacks served** noon-1am Mon-Thur; noon-1am Fri; 11.30am-1am Sat; 11.30am-10.30pm Sun.
Restaurant **Brunch served** 11.30am-3.30pm Sat, Sun. **Lunch served** noon-3pm Mon-Fri.

Lucky 7. See p43.

Dinner served 5-11.30pm Mon-Sat; 5-10.30pm Sun. **Main courses** £14-£35.50. **Set brunch** £16.75 2 courses, £19.50 3 courses. **Set meal** (5.30-7pm, 10-11.15pm Mon-Sat) £15.75 2 courses, £19.50 3 courses.
Both **Credit** AmEx, DC, MC, V.
The greatest asset of this Covent Garden favourite has always been the building in which it is housed. A handsome Victorian pile, the structure is reputed to have served as a papier-mâché factory, a casino, a whorehouse and a bank before Christopher Gilmour converted it into a restaurant at the start of the 1990s. From the lovely, buzzy downstairs cocktail bar up the sweeping staircase to the cultured first-floor restaurant (offering precious views across Waterloo Bridge), this is bona fide destination dining. Unfortunately, though we've eaten well here in the past, the quality of the dining is currently failing to match the eye-catching destination. The food's not awful: it's just bland, slightly tired and entirely overpriced. After an above-par cobb salad, californian black bean soup didn't hold the interest, meat loaf fell far short of its £17 price-

tag, and a salmon fish cake was nothing out of the ordinary. You're probably on safer ground with the long-venerated range of steaks. Still, at £34 for surf 'n' turf, you'll almost certainly get more culinary bang for your bucks elsewhere.
Babies and children welcome: children's menu; high chairs. Booking advisable. Separate room for parties, seats 40. Wireless internet (free). **Map 18 F4.**

Joe Allen
13 Exeter Street, WC2E 7DT (7836 0651/ www.joeallen.co.uk). Covent Garden tube.
Breakfast served 8-11.30am Mon-Fri.
Brunch served 11.30am-4.30pm Sat, Sun.
Meals served noon-12.30am Mon-Fri; 11.30am-12.30am Sat; 11.30am-11.30pm Sun. **Main courses** £8-£18. **Set brunch** £18.50 2 courses, £20.50 3 courses incl drink. **Set meal** (noon-3pm Mon-Fri, 5-6.45pm Mon-Sat) £15 2 courses, £17 3 courses. **Credit** AmEx, MC, V.
The London branch of Joe Allen opened in this basement back in 1977, a dozen years after the Manhattan original. It can't have changed much in the intervening 32 years. Sure, the theatre-industry

crowd who flooded here in the 1980s have been supplemented by the inevitable tourists, but the dimly lit room – its brick and wood walls lined with yellowing posters for long-forgotten shows – remains incomparably atmospheric. The place bustles with activity and buzzes with conversation but, miraculously, is never hurried and never loud. Service too is an old-fashioned treat. The team of white-shirted, black-tied waiters and waitresses patrol the room with the quietly competent assurance of dancers who've found their calling in the chorus line. The comfort cooking is carefully unreconstructed, quietly expensive and fairly hit and miss. That said, the positives (caesar salad that was crisp, fresh and entirely as it should be; a tender pan-fried pork fillet with sweet-potato fries that tasted better than its dreary appearance) just about cancelled out the negatives (rubbery mushrooms, a very wan quesadilla). It ain't broke, so they didn't fix it.
Babies and children welcome: booster seats; high chairs. Booking advisable. Entertainment: pianist 9pm-1am Mon-Sat. Takeaway service. Wireless internet (free). **Map 18 E4.**

Fitzrovia

Eagle Bar Diner

3-5 Rathbone Place, W1T 1HJ (7637 1418/
www.eaglebardiner.com). Tottenham Court Road
tube. **Open** noon-11pm Mon-Wed; noon-1am
Thur, Fri; 10am-1am Sat; 11am-6pm Sun.
Main courses £5.95-£14.50. **Credit** MC, V.
The level of cultural interchange between New
York and London these days is such that the Eagle
Bar Diner feels more generically urban than
specifically American. There's no memorabilia and
no fancy-dressed staff: just a long, plainly
decorated and ever so slightly careworn room lined
with smart booths and plain tables. As the name
suggests, the Eagle leads a double life. It's
essentially a drinking den at night, but things are
calmer during the day, when the stereo is
mercifully turned down and the menu of diner
staples becomes a more appealing prospect. The
best bets remain the burgers; the Eagle was among
the first of London's nouveau burger joints, and
the house speciality matches that of any local rival.
Elsewhere on the menu, the barbecue ribs won't
give Bodean's any cause for concern, while the
sausage and mash is below gastropub standard.
On the other hand, the breakfasts are reliable, while
the unsubtle but generous desserts and the terrific
malts (try the Elvis-esque peanut butter and
banana variety) sate the sweet of tooth. Service
varies from over-enthusiastic to diffident, but
sometimes strikes the right note.
Babies and children admitted (until 9pm if
dining): children's menu. Disabled: toilet.
Entertainment: DJs 7.30pm Wed-Sat.
Takeaway service. Wireless internet (free).
Map 17 B2.

Knightsbridge

Chicago Rib Shack [NEW]

145 Knightsbridge, SW1X 7PA (7591 4664/
www.thechicagoribshack.co.uk). Knightsbridge
tube. **Meals served** noon-midnight Mon-Sat;
noon-11.30pm Sun. **Main courses** £8.95-£34.95.
Credit AmEx, MC, V.
The original Chicago Rib Shack closed in 1999, but
2008 saw the relaunch of this icon of 1980s London
(and symbol of its kitschest excesses). The location
is a hitherto rather unlucky Knightsbridge site
once occupied by short-lived Brazilian bar-eaterie
Mocotó, and before that Oliver Peyton's Isola. The
spacious, two-floor set-up is rather grand in a jokey
diner-ish way, with high-backed booths, bare brick
walls and modish lighting. It's probably best suited
for parties and group dining, as the food rarely
rises above reasonable. Our baby-back ribs were
decent, as was a fillet steak, but the beef brisket
and the tender pulled pork were totally
overwhelmed by the gratingly sweet sauce in
which they'd been drowned. Starters of chicken
wings and stuffed potato skins were little better.
Portions are huge. If you make it to dessert, expect
the likes of chocolate sundae with brownies and
aerated cream, and mississippi mud pie. Despite
all this, booking is in our experience essential –
though some tables are set aside for walk-ins.
Babies and children welcome: children's menu,
crayons; high chairs; nappy-changing facilities.
Booking advisable. Disabled: lift; toilet.
Takeaway service. Wireless internet (free).
Map 8 F9.

Marylebone

Black & Blue

90-92 Wigmore Street, W1V 3RD (7486 1912/
www.blackandblue.biz). Bond Street tube. **Meals**
served noon-11pm daily. **Main courses** £9-£26.
Credit AmEx, MC, V.
There's little difference between the five
restaurants in this small, London-only chain. The
ambience at each branch is quite smart yet
approachable, the walls are either whitewashed or
stripped-back brick, and the menu is dominated –
and we mean dominated – by meat. If you're going
to make beef your speciality, the strength of the
current competition means you'd better do it well.
And given the prices charged here, Black & Blue

doesn't do it well enough. The burgers are reliable,
but they're also pricier and less impressive than
anything you'll find at the more relaxed likes of
Gourmet Burger Kitchen (*see p304*). The steaks
are by no means poor, yet they're nonetheless left
in the shade by those of the Gaucho restaurants
(*see p45*), another chain but one with a more
impressive pedigree. Once you move away from
the meat, things get even iffier. A starter of
chargrilled king prawns was unpleasant, its
accompanying garlic butter a nasty gloop, while
the chips that arrived with the fillet steak were
pretty poor, and the salad was of supermarket
standard. Not great.
Babies and children admitted. Bookings not
accepted (under 6). **Map 9 G6**.
For branches see index.

Mayfair

Automat

33 Dover Street, W1S 4NF (7499 3033/
www.automat-london.com). Green Park tube.
Breakfast served 7-11am Mon-Fri. **Meals**
served noon-midnight Mon-Fri; 11am-midnight
Sat; 11am-10pm Sun. **Main courses** £13-£26.
Credit AmEx, MC, V.
Forgoing the 'don't ask don't tell' approach of the
Ivy, this self-described 'American brasserie' is
happy to talk up its celebrity clientele. Its website
is lined with cuttings documenting visits from the
likes of David Beckham, Elijah Wood and the
Duchess of York. Head here at noon, though, and
you'll eat alongside a less starry crowd of
businessfolk, fashion-industry refugees and a few
ladies who lunch. The handsome, low-lit diner-
style section is perfect for an evening meal, while
the airy, tiled back room is at its best during the
day. Regardless of the time, the straightforward
food will be unspectacular yet reliable, served at
prices reflecting the elevated postcode. We didn't
resent the expense for the lovely, tender crab cake
served with faintly peppery guacamole, or for the
perfect pecan pie. But £22 is plainly too much for
an agreeable if unmemorable dish of roast cod
with shrimp hash; and a generous yet slightly
tough rump steak was also priced above its
station. Still, this isn't the kind of place where
people worry about the size of the bill. Also the
service was lunch-hour efficient, it was also devoid
of charm and enthusiasm.
Babies and children admitted. Booking advisable.
Disabled: toilet. Takeaway service.
Map 9 H7.

Maze Grill [NEW]

13-15 Grosvenor Square, W1K 6PJ (7495
2211/www.gordonramsay.com/mazegrill).
Bond Street tube. **Breakfast served** 7am-
10.30am, **dinner served** 6-10.30pm daily.
Lunch served noon-3pm Mon-Fri; noon-4pm
Sat, Sun. **Main courses** £13.50-£28. **Set lunch**
£15 2 courses, £18 3 courses. **Credit** AmEx,
DC, MC, V.
Gifted chef Jason Atherton's new venture is a
steak restaurant adjacent to haute cuisine
establishment Maze (*see p143*) and, like it, boasts
the beefy backing of Gordon Ramsay Holdings.
It's a handsome, if slightly sterile, set-up, kitted
out with inoffensive blond-wood floors, chrome
lampshades and olive green banquettes. Service is
smooth and professional, as it should be in an
establishment serving £120-a-head wagyu steak.
There's even a chef's table near the kitchen. More
modest spenders can choose from a carnivore's
paradise of steak varieties, as well as ribs, chops
and a handful of fish dishes. The steak cuts are
variable in quality; we hit upon a tender ribeye,
but found the Aberdeen Angus sirloin inedibly
tough. As it turned out, that left us with room for
the well-executed desserts. Eton mess with
mascarpone ice-cream is recommended, and
typical of the classic-with-a-twist options that
also include cider apple trifle and yoghurt
cheesecake. Portions are small for the price,
however, and steep wine mark-ups, side dishes
and mineral water quickly send the bill soaring.
Babies and children welcome: children's
portions; high chairs; nappy-changing
facilities. Booking essential. Disabled: toilet.
Map 9 G6.

Soho

★ Bodean's

10 Poland Street, W1F 8PZ (7287 7575/
www.bodeansbbq.com). Oxford Circus or
Piccadilly Circus tube.
Deli **Open** noon-11pm Mon-Sat; noon-10.30pm
Sun.
Restaurant **Lunch served** noon-3pm, **dinner**
served 6-11pm Mon-Fri. **Meals served** noon-
11pm Sat; noon-10.30pm Sun. **Main courses**
£8-£16.
Both **Credit** AmEx, MC, V.
What looked to be a wafer-thin gap in the market
turned out to be a mile-wide chasm. Five years
after its speculative Soho opening, Bodean's now
has five branches across London, and more seem
likely to follow. Although prices have risen since
this original branch was launched, the schtick
remains unchanged: Kansas City-style barbecue,
served in a fairly smart basement restaurant
(where steaks are also available) and in an
agreeably egalitarian street-level 'deli' (laid out
with barstools and long, high tables). Wherever
you sit, American sport will flicker on overhead
screens, Creedence will echo from the speakers,
and the food will be decent, generous and very,
very meaty. The strengths remain the flavourful
spare ribs, the mouth-watering pulled pork, the
tender chicken and the side dishes, which include
spicy beans and top-notch fries. The best value is
offered by the filling sandwiches. We're less keen
on the burgers, the dull beef back ribs and the
lamentable beer selection (a bafflingly dreary
range of bottles supplemented by insipid Coors
Light on tap). Still, quibbles aside, this remains a
fine, reliable operation. Bring an appetite.
Babies and children welcome: children's menu;
high chairs; nappy-changing facilities. Booking
advisable (restaurant). Restaurant/deli available
for hire. Tables outdoors (10, pavement).
Takeaway service. **Map 17 A3**.
For branches see index.

★ The Diner

16-18 Ganton Street, W1F 7BU (7287 8962/
www.thedinersoho.com). Oxford Circus or
Piccadilly Circus tube. **Meals served** 10am-
12.30am Mon-Sat; 10am-midnight Sun. **Main**
courses £5-£9. **Credit** AmEx, MC, V.
The accents are bright red rather than dark green,
and there's a little more nostalgia-inducing
Americana around the place. However, from the
contents of the menu to the layout of the room
(stools along a bar, booths and tables raised up to
the right), the Diner offers a virtual echo of the
Eagle Bar Diner over in Fitzrovia (*see above*). The
choice of food here is lengthy, but not suspiciously
so, taking in a variety of fast-food favourites. The
Eagle might have the edge in the burger stakes, but
the Diner wins for its all-day breakfasts: moist,
mouth-watering pancakes, hearty omelettes and a
broad Mexican spread (comprising eggs with
chunks of spicy chorizo, gloopy black beans, salsa,
fresh guacamole and a couple of flour tortillas).
Milkshakes are only as good as their ingredients,
and the five scoops of ice-cream that went into our
generous pistachio shake were sub-standard. Still,
for the most part, this is a likeable little place that
does exactly what it says on the tin.
Babies and children welcome: booster seats;
children's menu; crayons. Booking advisable.
Tables outdoors (6, pavement). Takeaway service.
Vegetarian menu. Wireless internet (free).
Map 17 A4.

★ Ed's Easy Diner

12 Moor Street, W1V 5LH (7434 4439/
www.edseasydiner.co.uk). Leicester Square or
Tottenham Court Road tube. **Meals served**
noon-midnight daily. **Main courses** £4.95-
£7.95. **Minimum** (6pm-midnight Fri-Sun) £4.95.
Credit MC, V.
'That's the way we've been doing it since 1987,'
reads the blurb on the menu – and who can
disagree? From the hyper-efficient staff to the 21
barstools around the bright red counter (plus four
more by the door), and from the counter-top
jukeboxes to the frill-free menu, this ersatz
American diner hasn't changed a jot since it

opened on this prominent corner site two decades ago. The decor may have been a cheering novelty in the garish 1980s, but it's pretty gauche these days. The real problem, however, is the food, which does its ostensible country of origin few favours. The fairly flavourless burgers are embarrassed by the slew of bourgeois burger joints elsewhere in Soho. The fries are ordinary, and the onion rings taste as if they've been dropped in a puddle. OK, so the butterscotch malts are fine, but how wrong can you go with ice-cream, malted milk powder and butterscotch sauce? Don't be surprised if Ed's is still here two decades from now, however; in its own way, it's becoming as much a Soho fixture as Bar Italia and the Sunset Strip.
Babies and children welcome: children's menu. Tables outdoors (2, pavement). Takeaway service. **Map 17 C3.**
For branch see index.

South Kensington

PJ's Grill
52 Fulham Road, SW3 6HH (7581 0025/ www.pjsgrill.net). South Kensington tube. **Meals served** noon-11.45pm Mon-Fri; 10am-11.45pm Sat; 10am-11.15pm Sun. **Main courses** £10.95-£27.95. **Credit** AmEx, MC, V.
Veteran restaurateur Brian Stein has built his empire on the principle that if you're never in vogue, you'll never go out of fashion. Named, apparently, after the long-forgotten 1930s movie *Polo Joe* (the theme even extends to copies of the doubtless-scintillating *Polo Quarterly International* on the bar), PJ's carries an ambience of classic yet approachable sophistication. The sturdy old fittings are given added appeal by a conversation-friendly acoustic, nicely picked music and highly efficient staff. Food quality, though, is mixed. Thumbs-up for the half-dozen pan-seared scallops, served with a gentle fennel purée and tissue-thin slices of smoked pork belly. A cautious welcome too for a fresh if slightly underpowered tuna tartare. Ribeye steak and chips (seemingly oven-cooked) were nothing special though, and the 'lobster risotto' was just risotto with a couple of pieces of lobster on top; worse, the dish contained a staggering amount of olive oil that rendered it almost inedible. The near-full house on a chilly Tuesday was testament to Stein's skill at atmospherics (the place is also packed for weekend brunches with bloody marys), but the kitchen needs a prod.
Babies and children welcome: children's portions; high chairs. Booking advisable. Separate room for parties, seating 20-82. Tables outdoors (3, pavement). **Map 14 E11.**
For branch see index.

West

Hammersmith

Pacific Bar & Grill
320 Goldhawk Road, W6 0XF (8741 1994). Stamford Brook tube. **Meals served** noon-11pm Mon-Fri; 11am-midnight Sat, Sun. **Main courses** £7.95-£17.50. **Credit** AmEx, MC, V.
Unexpected in these environs, the Pacific aims to bring some Stateside sunshine to dreary Goldhawk Road. The bar is to the right, a comfortable if not exactly charismatic space leading to a lovely little terrace. To the left, a touch larger, is the restaurant. The food is best when the kitchen has confidence in its ingredients, and less impressive when created on something approaching auto-pilot. Our 8oz (227g) ribeye steak was very good, cooked the rare side of medium-rare, but the accompanying skinny chips (a huge bowlful) were limp and lifeless. We were quite taken by a dish of tender and subtly spiced chicken breast, yet the avocado and mango salad beneath it was poor and the side of chive mash was dry and stodgy. For bookends, we enjoyed a pleasing butternut squash and mascarpone soup, yet endured a strawberry cheesecake blighted by the artificiality of its sauce. A mixed experience, then, and we could have done without the cranked-up bar-friendly

soundtrack echoing through the eaterie. Still, prices are fair (starters cost around £5-£7, non-steak mains £9-£14), the service is winning and the margaritas are perfectly agreeable.
Babies and children welcome: children's menu; crayons; high chairs; magician (1-3pm Sun). Booking essential weekends. Tables outdoors (12, terrace). Wireless internet (free). **Map 20 A3.**

Kensington

Sticky Fingers
1A Phillimore Gardens, W8 7QG (7938 5338/ www.stickyfingers.co.uk). High Street Kensington tube.
Bar **Open/snack served** noon-11pm Mon-Sat; noon-10.30pm Sun.

Restaurant **Meals served** noon-11pm Mon-Sat; noon-10.30pm Sun. **Main courses** £9.45-£17.95. *Both* **Credit** AmEx, MC, V.
Bill Wyman may have sold his controlling interest to Maxwell's owner Brian Stein several years ago, but his sticky fingerprints are still all over this squat little space just off Kensington High Street. Wyman's name remains on the branding, the walls are caked in Stones memorabilia (much of it postdating the group's glory years), and the front of the menu is a chips-cheap imitation of the *Sticky Fingers* album cover. From the dated mock-American decor to the efficient service, this is in essence a Stones-themed Hard Rock Café – or, perhaps, a TGI Friday with better music. The similarities extend to the so-so food, prepared by a kitchen that seems to prioritise quantity over quality for the benefit of diners tickled by the

Bodean's. See p39.

RESTAURANTS

Chain reaction

Whether international groups or founded in the UK, these biggun's ain't no ma and pa operations, but they can be useful places to take kids and teenagers, or enjoy an evening with workmates.

Cheers

72 Regent Street, W1R 6EL (7494 3322/www.cheersbarlondon.com). Piccadilly Circus tube.
Bar Open/snacks served noon-3am Mon-Sat; noon-12.30am Sun. **Snacks** £6-£8.
Restaurant Meals served noon-10pm daily. **Main courses** £6.95-£12.90. **Minimum** £10.
Both **Credit** AmEx, MC, V.
The lesser of the US chains, Cheers is a dimly lit, warehouse-sized space, loosely based on the TV show of the same name. Dedicated fans can buy souvenir T-shirts and mugs bearing the familiar *Cheers* logo. The menu borrows heavily from the show, but for somewhere pushing such a strong sense of identity, it's all rather characterless. During the day, the central bar fills with local office workers, enticed by the cheap lunch deal (burgers and salads for under a fiver), and tourists who've emerged from Piccadilly Circus tube and opted for the first watering hole in sight. The atmosphere is more blokey than family-oriented, so it's during major sporting events that the place comes to life, as supporters pack in to watch the big game on the legion of big-screen TVs. Service is speedy, but Cheers isn't a big-hitter in the food stakes – burgers are thin and greasy, and salads lack much punch.
Babies and children welcome (until 5.30pm): children's menu; high chairs; nappy-changing facilities. Booking advisable. Disabled: toilet. Entertainment: DJ 10.30pm daily. Vegetarian menu. **Map 17 J7**.

Dexters Grill & Bar

20 Bellevue Road, SW17 7EB (8767 1858/www.tootsiesrestaurants.co.uk). Wandsworth Common rail/319 bus.
Meals served 11am-11pm Mon-Fri; 10am-11pm Sat, Sun. **Main courses** £6.95-£27.95. **Credit** AmEx, MC, V.
Part of the Tootsies corporate family, Dexters shares a similarly child-friendly ethic and almost identical menu. High chair for high chair, burger for burger, there's very little to distinguish between the two. No matter – families with young children can't get enough of one, or the other. Like Tootsies, restaurants in the Dexters chain are bright and spacious, with large windows, pine furniture and plenty of space to park the pushchair. Both provide colouring books and crayons and feature Annabel Karmel's popular kids' menu. Try the children on macaroni cheese and ham, or beef bolognese blended with five 'hidden' vegetables, with strawberry and rhubarb crumble for afters. Burgers are every bit as pleasing as the versions at Tootsies. Our classic burger of smoked back bacon with melted monterey

jack cheese was fresh and perfectly executed: the best we've tasted at an American chain. Our only quibble in such a family-friendly establishment is the lack of kids' cutlery (although this didn't deter the little ones from clearing their plates on our last visit). Applause all round for Ms Karmel's menu.
Babies and children welcome: children's menu; crayons; high chairs; nappy-changing facilities. Booking advisable weekends. Disabled: toilet. Separate room for parties, seats 40. Tables outdoors (9, patio). Takeaway service.

Hard Rock Café

150 Old Park Lane, W1K 1QZ (7629 0382/www.hardrock.com). Green Park or Hyde Park Corner tube. **Meals served** 11.30am-midnight Mon-Thur, Sun; 11.30am-1am Fri, Sat. **Main courses** £8.50-£15. **Credit** AmEx, MC, V.
Arguably the most famous of the American chains, the top-of-the-pop-tastic Hard Rock has always polled highly in the burger charts. As you'd expect, the walls drip with rock memorabilia, music blares from TV screens and speakers, and sometimes the waitresses themselves grab the mic – oodles of fun for the kids, although you might wish you'd brought earplugs for the tiniest among them. For tourists, the Café is an attraction in itself, for Londoners the draw is the big, succulent burgers, which arrive nicely pink in the middle (you'll pay a couple of quid over the odds for the privilege). Nachos are gooey and spicy, the salads enormous and fresh, and the sandwiches huge and creative. Waitresses are eager to please and efficient (perhaps a little too quick to clear when the queue of tourists out front starts to snake down Park Lane). Ring ahead if you want to bypass this waiting system, which can be notoriously painful at busy times. The link between rock 'n' roll and the waitresses' cutsey white uniforms (somewhere between dental hygienist and old-school tennis kit) has always eluded us.
Babies and children welcome: children's menu; high chairs; toys. Disabled: toilet. Bookings not accepted for groups under 20; call for queue jump service. Entertainment: monthly live music events, call for details; free tour of Vault music museum. Restaurant available for hire. Tables outdoors (18, pavement). **Map 9 H8**.

Planet Hollywood

Trocadero, 13 Coventry Street, W1D 7DH (7287 1000/www.planethollywood.co.uk). Piccadilly Circus tube. **Meals served** 11.30am-1am Mon-Sat; 11.30am-12.30am Sun. **Main courses** £8.95-£21.95. **Credit** AmEx, DC, MC, V.
The Tinseltown version of the Hard Rock, Planet Hollywood was famously launched by Bruce Willis, Sylvester Stallone and Arnold Schwarzenegger. Flashing lights simulate the red-carpet experience, movie memorabilia hangs from every wall, and blasting film soundtracks compete for your attention with clips on high-volume big-screen TVs. There's an extended licence allowing punters to

catch late-night sporting events like the big fight in Vegas, over midnight beers and burgers, but this is predominantly the domain of families; we counted three cakes with candles and all-staff renditions of 'Happy Birthday' on our last visit. Food is hardly of gourmet quality. The 'world famous' chicken crunch won't be winning a foodie Oscar any time soon – but the burgers are fine, the menu is slightly more adventurous than some of the chains, and service is swift and smiley. Bear in mind that all those speakers may be a bit of an ear-ache for tots.
Babies and children welcome: children's menu; crayons; high chairs; nappy-changing facilities. Booking advisable. Disabled: toilet. Entertainment: DJ 6pm Mon-Fri; all day Sat, Sun. Separate room for parties, seats 80. **Map 17 K7**.

Smollensky's on the Strand

105 Strand, WC2R 0AA (7497 2101/www.smollenskys.co.uk). Covent Garden, Embankment or Temple tube/Charing Cross tube/rail.
Bar Open noon-11pm Mon-Thur; noon-1am Fri, Sat; noon-10.30pm Sun.
Restaurant Meals served noon-11pm Mon-Sat; noon-4pm, 6.30-10pm Sun.
Both **Main courses** £8.95-£21.95. **Set meal** (noon-6.30pm Mon-Fri) £10.95 2 courses, £12.95 3 courses. **Credit** AmEx, DC, MC, V.
Chicago-style chain Smollensky's may have launched a sister restaurant at Canary Wharf and mini Metro offspring outlets across half of outer London, but this flagship basement steakhouse remains the daddy. The look is modern and the service slick but the place still seems to be in the grip of a minor identity crisis. With its live band and cocktails, it wants to attract groups of twentysomethings and the pre-theatre crowd, while still keeping its core family diners happy. Luckily, it's a cavernous space, so the kiddies, cake and balloons can commandeer one end while the DINKS have a drink at the other. The emphasis is on steaks: any size, any way. Ours were big, juicy, cooked to order – and, at £14.95 for an 8oz (227g) Scottish rump, fair value. Diners have the option of either 21-day aged Aberdeen Angus or 35-day aged South American, both from welfare-assured producers. Starters can be hit and miss, but desserts are enticing and the wine list not bad.
Babies and children welcome: booster seats; children's menu; entertainment (noon-3pm Sat, Sun); high chairs; toys. Booking advisable. Disabled: toilet. Entertainment: DJ 9.30pm Thur-Sat. Wireless internet (free). **Map 18 L7**.
For branches see index.

TGI Friday's

6 Bedford Street, WC2E 9HZ (7379 0585/www.tgifridays.co.uk). Covent Garden tube/Charing Cross tube/rail.
Bar Open noon-11pm Mon-Sat; noon-10.30pm Sun.
Restaurant Meals served noon-11.30pm Mon-Sat; noon-11pm Sun. **Main courses** £7.95-£17.95.
Both **Credit** AmEx, MC, V.

With a name like TGI Friday's you'd expect this determinedly cheerful chain to be most suited to an end-of-the-week, down-the-tools knees-up – but in practice, Friday's is doing it for the kids. Yes, there are plenty of candy-coloured cocktails and a big central bar, but the focus is on big, noisy parties for those in short trousers, not suits. Enthusiastic staff welcome kids with a goodie bag of puzzles and stickers. The children's menu gets a big thumbs-up from little diners. Carrot sticks and cucumber may be an option with the cheeseburger or fish fingers, but this is more of a 'smiley-face potato waffle and wriggly worms with ice-cream' kind of place. For parents, there's a comparatively varied menu of Tex-Mex, sticky barbecue choices and steaks, although the inevitable burgers and fries are a safe bet.
Babies and children welcome: children's menu; crayons; face painting (1pm Sat); high chairs. Booking advisable. Disabled: lift; toilet. Takeaway service.
Map 18 L7.
For branches see index.

Tootsies Grill

48 High Street, SW19 5AX (8946 4135/www.tootsiesrestaurants.com). Wimbledon tube/rail. **Meals served** 11am-10pm Mon-Thur; 11am-10.30pm Fri; 9am-10.30pm Sat, Sun. **Main courses** £7.50-£22. **Credit** AmEx, MC, V.
Last time we visited Tootsies, four diners at the table next to us were in tears. Not that this collective misery had anything to do with the restaurant; parents aside, the party must have racked up a combined age of no more than three years between them. Tootsies – bastion of lunching yummy mummies and youngsters – has always taken tots, tantrums and teddies in its stride. Staff are smiley, efficient and only too happy to help stash buggies and set up high chairs. The chain has drafted in author and children's nutritional expert Annabel Karmel to devise a kiddies' menu of mini burgers, plus fish and cottage pies: as good as homemade. Her fruit smoothies get the thumbs up as healthy 'milkshakes'; the strawberry version has become an unintentional hit with expectant mums. The adult menu is varied and includes filling super-food salads and steak sandwiches. But Tootsies' biggest draw is its first-rate burgers. Served with crisp, golden fries, an army of sauces and plenty of crowd-pleasing toppings, they arrive juicy and with a nice charcoal tinge, in a toasted sesame seed bun.
Babies and children welcome: children's menu; crayons; high chairs. Tables outdoors (4, pavement). Takeaway service.
For branches see index.

challenge of clearing their plates. Buffalo wings come slathered in a fairly unbecoming hot sauce; the burgers are unremarkable in all but size ('The Mess' is a half-pounder piled high with chilli, sour cream and pretty decent guacamole); and the chips are entirely forgettable. Ah, well. You can't always get what you want.
Babies and children welcome: children's menu; entertainment (face-painting & magician 1.30-3.30pm Sat, Sun); high chairs. Booking advisable. Takeaway service. **Map 7 A9.**

Westbourne Park

Lucky 7

127 Westbourne Park Road, W2 5QL (7727 6771/www.lucky7london.co.uk). Royal Oak or Westbourne Park tube. **Meals served** 10am-10.30pm Mon-Thur; 9am-11pm Fri, Sat; 9am-10pm Sun. **Main courses** £6.50-£13.75. **Credit** MC, V.
Of all London's quasi-American diners, Tom Conran's cosy operation feels the most convincing and, though the word is fraught with difficulties, the most authentic. It's not so much the menu, which contains few surprises. Nor is it the decor, with six green Naugahyde booths set off by an ersatz tin ceiling, vintage rock posters and a funky Pepsi clock. It's more that Lucky 7 doesn't wear its theming with pomposity. With regulars dropping by, waiting staff bantering with locals, and the Arcade Fire's first album playing at a conversation-friendly level – this simply feels like a neighbourhood hangout. Though there are a few salads and sandwiches on the menu, the choice is basically between breakfasts and burgers. In the former category lie such temptations as buttermilk pancakes and huevos rancheros, served until 5pm. In the latter sit hearty, meaty patties caked in supplementary goodies; our fine 'Kalifornian' came ladled with cheese, bacon (crispy but not frazzled), sour cream, a roasted half-tomato and fabulous guacamole. The fries and the shakes are only so-so; a short but pleasing list of US beers (Anchor Steam and Brooklyn Lager among them) compensates. You'd want one in your district.
Babies and children welcome: children's menu. Bookings not accepted. Separate room for parties, seats 35. Takeaway service. Wireless internet (free). **Map 7 A5.**

South West

Chelsea

Big Easy

332-334 King's Road, SW3 5UR (7352 4071/ www.bigeasy.uk.com). Sloane Square tube then 11, 19, 22 bus. **Bar Open/meals served** noon-11pm Mon-Sat; noon-10pm Sun. **Main courses** £9.95-£49.50. **Restaurant Meals served** noon-11.15pm Mon-Thur, Sun; noon-12.15am Fri; noon-12.15am Sat. **Main courses** £9.95-£49.50. **Set lunch** (noon-5pm Mon-Fri) £7.95 2 courses. **Both Credit** AmEx, DC, MC, V.
This immensely popular Chelsea party palace is modelled on the kind of cheerfully ramshackle old crabshack you can still find along the Gulf Coast if you know where to look. However, the Big Easy really has more in common with another American culinary tradition: the slick, corporate and altogether fairly wearying road-food chains that dot suburban strip-malls and the theme-park paradise of your average Las Vegas casino. The atmosphere is fresh, friendly and agreeably raucous. A TV upstairs screens US sport, while a guitar-toting duo rattles out bar-band covers in the basement. The food, though, is another matter. Everything is served in massive portions and at pretty outlandish prices, but flavour is conspicuous by its absence. Calamares was soggy and bland, and a crab-claw starter forgettable. The much-heralded lobster was unpleasantly watery and the accompanying fries no better than adequate. Meat dishes are better, but the ribs that formed part of our surf-and-turf combo weren't a patch on those at Bodean's. Despite the best efforts of the excellent staff, this is a dispiriting place.

Babies and children welcome: children's menu; crayons; high chairs. Entertainment: musicians 8.30pm Mon-Thur; 9.30pm Fri-Sun. Tables outdoors (5, pavement). Takeaway service. **Map 14 D12.**

Fulham

Sophie's Steakhouse & Bar

311-313 Fulham Road, SW10 9QH (7352 0088/ www.sophiessteakhouse.com). South Kensington tube then 14, 211, 414 bus. **Meals served** noon-11.45pm Mon-Fri; 11am-11.45pm Sat; 11am-11.15pm Sun. **Main courses** £6.95-£49. **Set meal** (noon-6pm Mon-Fri) £11.95 2 courses. **Credit** AmEx, MC, V.
The 'New York warehouse feel' promised by the website is a little fanciful. Despite having opened in 2002, Sophie's appears wedded to a very 1990s idea of Manhattan chic: all brick walls and exposed piping. The most archetypically American part of our visit was the harsh-voiced blonde on the next table braying loudly about her ski lodge in Wyoming. Still, we're quibbling: by and large, this is a perfectly agreeable operation, boosted by an efficient team of table staff who didn't put a foot wrong. Co-owners Sophie Mogford and Rupert Power previously worked for Smollensky's and the Conran Group; the approachably buzzy, accessibly upscale ambience of both those chains is much in evidence here. Like the diners, the menu is smart but uncomplicated: chicken liver parfait (likeable); dressed crab salad with coriander mayo (unexpectedly flavourless); rotisserie chicken (tender, generous); and, of course, an array of steaks, reasonably priced and of decent if by no means knockout quality. All told, Sophie's is perhaps not worth a special trip, but it's a good option if you're in the area. Certainly, the locals think so: by 7.30pm on the Wednesday we visited, every table was taken.
Babies and children welcome: children's menu; high chairs. Bookings not accepted. Disabled: toilet. **Map 14 D12.**

East

Wapping

Prohibition NEW

Tower Bridge House, St Katharine Docks, E1W 1AA (0844 800 4153/www.prohibition.uk.com). Tower Gateway DLR or Tower Hill tube. **Bar Open/food served** noon-midnight Mon-Fri; noon-11pm Sat, Sun. **Restaurant Meals served** noon-10.30pm daily. **Both Main courses** £4.95-£10.95. **Credit** AmEx, MC, V.
Enacted in 1920 and repealed 13 years later, the American Constitution's 18th Amendment would, in the right hands, make an intriguing theme for a bar-restaurant. Sadly, this loud, slick import from the provinces isn't it. The prohibition theming doesn't extend to much more than a mocked-up newspaper clipping on the menu, and there's nothing secretive about the glass-walled box by St Katharine Docks that houses the mini-chain's second London branch. The menu is a baffling, undiscriminating mix of American bar fare (chicken wings, steak and eggs), globetrotting snacks (crispy duck spring rolls, fish and chips) and resistible novelties (falafel fritters!), and the food is about as good as you might expect from a kitchen so reluctant to commit to a speciality. You're best off sticking to the dishes that seem the hardest to screw up: the spare-rib starter, for example, or the burgers (a little under-seasoned but otherwise fine). Service is enthusiastic and efficient; the clientele, at least during the week, seems to consist of post-Tower tourists and young City boys drinking to forget the sub-prime mortgage crisis.
Babies and children admitted (until 6pm on weekdays; all day weekends). Bar available for hire. Booking advisable. Dress code: smart casual, no sports trainers. Entertainment: DJ 8pm Thur, Fri; live acts 6pm Wed, Thur. Tables outdoors (20, decking). Wireless internet (free). **Map 12 S7.**

RESTAURANTS

Missouri Angel

Missouri Angel was open on Thanksgiving Day in 2007. The old Angel Pub has been transformed into a fine dining restaurant with two dining rooms and a bar, plus private rooms for meetings and exclusive dining.

Missouri Angel serves the best of Modern American Cuisine but also keeping some of the popular classic dishes.

The whole building is light and elegant, as we are owner run we can be completely flexible in our approach, with service being of the utmost importance along with delicious food and wine

Missouri Angel
America Square
14 Crosswall EC3N 2LJ
Phone: 0207 481 8422
www.missourigrill.com

Bar
El Paso is one of Hoxton's oldest bar restaurants, offering a large selection of wines, beers and cocktails. In our bar you can find drinks you know and some you may not.

Restaurant
Air conditioned restaurant area which can seat up to 40 covers with a menu that includes some of Mexico's most famous dishes.

Basement Bar
Throughout the week El Paso has Djs and live bands playing in our basement bar, music ranging from Electro to Indie Rock (for details check press). Along with our regular promotions, the basement bar is also available for hire and comes fully equipped, perfect for private parties as well as promotional nights.

350-354 Old Street, London, EC1V 9NQ
T: 020 7739 4202   E:info@elpasohoxton.com
W: www.elpasohoxton.com

LET THE PARTY BEGIN...

Belushi's
www.belushis.com

Belushi's - it's a lifestyle choice, not just a place to drink. Nowhere else can you find award winning burgers (**The Daily Telegraph** - **Top Ten Burgers on the Planet**) coupled with a fantastic variety of drinks and the best entertainment in London (**Best Small Comedy Venue – Chortle Awards 2008**).

Belushi's has seven fantastic venues all over London (**London Bridge, Camden, Shepherd's Bush, Covent Garden, Hammersmith, Fulham** and **Greenwich**) plus venues in **Bath, Brighton, Newquay, Edinburgh, Paris, Berlin, Bruges** and **Amsterdam**. Our sister brand - St Christopher's Inns also won the **Best London Hostel 2007 award** for our London Bridge site, so if you want to see what all the fuss is about, come and join us.

Just to make you even happier and whet your appetite a little more – we're giving you a 10% discount on all food and drinks, in all of our bars when you present this advert!

visit LONDON GOLD WINNER AWARDS 2007

Chortle
St. Christopher's Inns
live your life

LATIN AMERICAN

It's only in the past year or so that London's Latin American restaurant scene has moved beyond music, dancing and drinking to focus on the intricacies of the continent's cuisines. The capital's Argentinian restaurants have quietly gone from strength to strength. The success of **Gaucho** (three new branches this year and counting) proves that big wallets are still readily opened for big steak dinners. This year we also welcome the **Buenos Aires Café** in Blackheath. New-wave Mexican eateries such as **Mestizo**, **Wahaca** and **Taqueria** may be slicker than the outdoor shacks where commuters wolf down tacos and burritos in Mexico, but their authenticity is a welcome improvement on what was the usual London Tex-Mex and tacos experience. If you still hunger for a party atmosphere, head to **Rodizio Rico** to enjoy buffet-and-meat fare in the style of a Brazilian churrasqueria.

Argentinian

South West
Chelsea

El Gaucho
Chelsea Farmers' Market, 125 Sydney Street, SW3 6NR (7376 8514/www.elgaucho.co.uk).
Sloane Square or South Kensington tube. **Meals served** noon-8pm daily. **Main courses** £7.90-£14.90. **Credit** AmEx, MC, V.
This fun Chelsea Market restaurant occupies a plain rustic building not unlike the traditional *quinchos* (shacks) where Argentinians eat their steaks semi-alfresco when in the country. You can see the grill from your bench and when the handful of tables fill up – as they do quickly, especially if it rains – there's a warm, buzzy atmosphere. The two waiters dash around while a maître d' coordinates the grill chef and deliveries. It's noisy and chaotic, but it works. Our steaks weren't super-thick but they were lean and tasty: delicious when accompanied with a generous crisp salad and a portion of fries. The wine list is limited, but for lunch a straightforward malbec hits the spot. *Babies and children admitted. Tables outdoors (14, pavement). Takeaway service.* **Map 14 E12**. **For branch see index.**

South
Battersea

La Pampa Grill
60 Battersea Rise, SW11 1EG (7924 4774).
Clapham Junction rail. **Dinner served** 6-11pm Mon-Fri; 6-11.30pm Sat. **Main courses** £7.95-£15.50. **Credit** MC, V.
Buenos Aires has been through a foodie revolution these past ten years. Meanwhile, the menu here hasn't changed in years because 'if it's not broken, don't mend it', claims the Colombian owner. He accepts empanadas and chorizo are not in the typical Argentinian style, but adds that he gets enough traffic to suggest customers like them as they are. Our sirloin and rump steaks were delicious, the salads simple and fresh, the chips thick and beefy – and service was friendly. It's all pretty faultless, but there's not much ambition here; the menu has none of the offal or other extras you get in a real Argentinian steakhouse. The wine list is extensive and reasonably priced: a bottle of Terrazas malbec costs £17.50. La Pampa shouldn't promote itself as an Argentine restaurant: rather as a steakhouse that sells Argentinian steak. *Babies and children welcome: high chair. Booking advisable; essential Sat. Separate area for parties, seats 25. Tables outdoors (2, pavement).* **For branch see index.**

★ Santa Maria del Sur
129 Queenstown Road, SW8 3RH (7622 2088/ www.santamariadelsur.co.uk). Queenstown Road rail. **Dinner served** 6.30-10.30pm Mon-Fri. **Meals served** noon-10.30pm Sat, Sun. **Main courses** £8-£19. **Credit** AmEx, MC, V.
When Alberto Abbate opened this steakhouse in December 2006 (originally as a sister to Buen Ayre, *see right*), it looked like a high-risk investment: the block he chose had a history of prompt closures. But this rather swish, romantic venue has become a hit with locals and draws punters from all over London. The main strengths are the sausages, black pudding and steaks – tender, carefully grilled, sourced in Argentina – and the wonderful all-Argentinian staff. Regulars get a hug from the mildly flirtatious, warm-hearted waiters, while the *parrillero* (grill chef) may wander round to say hello and check customer satisfaction at the end of an evening. Other than meat, the menu offers chargrilled red pepper, butter beans with garlic and parsley, and chargrilled mushroom with pesto, as well as tuna steaks. The wines are well chosen, and Don Pedro (ice-cream, nuts and whiskey) makes the perfect finale, though there are some fancy Mendozan licores to try. *Babies and children welcome: children's portions; high chairs. Booking advisable weekends.*

South East
Blackheath

Buenos Aires Café [NEW]
17 Royal Parade, SE3 0TL (8318 5333/ www.buenosairesltd.com). Blackheath rail. **Lunch served** noon-3pm Mon-Fri; noon-4pm Sat, Sun. **Dinner served** 6-10.30pm daily. **Main courses** £8.50-£24.55. **Credit** MC, V.
Reinaldo Vargas was once a paparazzo and the high walls of his parrilla (grill) restaurant are decked with shots of *Hello!* stars, as well as photos of his beloved home city. Starters of juicy meat empanadas and fantastically tasty grilled provolone cheese fired the taste buds without sating them. Chips were chunky and golden. Desserts are baked in-house, and both the flan (crème caramel) with dulce de leche and cream, and trifle were delectable. But the main draw is meat. Steaks, sourced in Argentina, are huge, tender and packed with clover-perfumed flavour. Vargas has trained his Ecuadorean chef to char them like the best Argentinian *parrillero*. The 400g (14oz) bife de chorizo had the classic grassy quality of rump; it's the gaucho's favourite cut. The menu also features melt-in-the-mouth milanesa (breaded calf's meat): a skinny cut, but enough for lunch for two. *Babies and children welcome: boosters seats. Booking advisable; essential Fri, Sat. Tables outdoors (4, pavement).* **For branch see index.**

Tower Bridge

★ Gaucho Tower Bridge
2 More London Riverside, SE1 2AP (7407 5222/ www.gauchorestaurants.co.uk). London Bridge tube/rail. **Meals served** noon-11pm Mon-Sat; noon-10.30pm Sun. **Main courses** £12.25-£37. **Credit** AmEx, MC, V.
Having already given London it's smartest steakhouse in W1, Gaucho naturally had to have a restaurant among the glass towers near London Bridge and the view as you pass on to the second floor is stunning. Gaucho boasts the UK's widest range of Argentinian wines and, after a chat with Yanina, the Venezuelan sommelier, we were given a fruity malbec to accompany delicious starters of one meat and two cheese-and-ham empanadas (pricey at more than £4 each). The steaks were impeccable, the chorizo smoky and generously flavoured, the ribeye more subtle and perfectly marbled. Skinny chips and a dip of chimichurri sauce completed the experience. Most desserts are quite heavy, so we tried a couple of dessert wines before tango-ing off along the riverside. *Babies and children welcome: booster seats. Disabled: toilet. Separate rooms for parties, seating 8-30. Takeaway service.* **Map 12 R8**. **For branches see index.**

North East
Hackney

★ Buen Ayre
50 Broadway Market, E8 4QJ (7275 9900/ www.buenayre.co.uk). London Fields rail/26, 48, 55, 106, 236 bus. **Lunch served** noon-3.30pm Sat, Sun. **Dinner served** 6-10.30pm daily. **Main courses** £7.50-£22. **Credit** MC, V.
Other Argentina-themed steakhouses might have more clichés and cowhide on the wall, but Buen Ayre is the only restaurant that has the spirit of an authentic neighbourhood parrilla (grill). Hiberno-Argentinian chef-owner John Rattagan is a mean griller – and his sous chefs are almost as good. He spoils regulars with extra-big portions, wines to sample, and after-dinner licores. The perfect meal here is the parrillada or classic mixed grill (minimum two diners). These hefty portions arrive on a hot mini barbecue. The deluxe version (£44 for two) includes a 14oz (390g) sirloin steak, a 10oz (280g) fillet, two chorizo sausages, a nutty black pudding and a slab of smoky provolone cheese, but the house grill (£40 for two), which comes with sweetbreads and kidneys, is equally lavish. All the meats are carefully sourced, and even herbs for the chimichurri dressing come from the home country. A party bustle is routine when this small venue is full – and it usually is for both evening sittings. *Babies and children welcome: high chairs. Booking advisable. Disabled: toilet. Tables outdoors (5, garden).*

Brazilian

North
Finchley

★ Casa Brasil
289 Regents Park Road, N3 3JY (8371 1999). Finchley Central tube. **Meals served** 11am-6pm Tue-Thur, Sun; 11am-9.30pm Fri, Sat. **Main courses** £7.50-£10.60. **Unlicensed. Corkage** £1/person. **No credit cards.**
Casa Basil is a labour of love. Owner Roy, who lived in São Paulo for four years, has kitted out the small, immaculate interior with just six tables – each covered with a green-and-white checked cloth – to create a family-friendly atmosphere. Shelving units displaying Brazilian food products evoke a local Carioca shop. Roy talks customers through the dishes (all prepared in-house), and your selection is then heated up in a microwave, snack-bar style. Classics such as feijoada (pork and bean stew), coxinha (a chicken-filled croquette), empanadas (filled savoury pastries) and Bahian

RESTAURANTS

moqueca (fish stew) are usually available. While the cooking might not blow you away, it's authentic, carefully prepared and a good introduction to Brazilian cuisine. Highlights were the pão de queijo (cheese manioc-flour rolls) and a heavenly passion-fruit mousse. Casa Brasil is unlicensed, but do try the tasty Guaraná soft drink.
Babies and children welcome: high chairs. Booking advisable Fri-Sun. Tables outdoors (8, patio).

Islington

Rodizio Rico
77-78 Upper Street, N1 0NU (7354 1076/ www.rodiziorico.com). Angel tube. **Dinner served** 6pm-midnight Mon-Fri. **Meals served** noon-midnight Sat, Sun. **Buffet** £14 vegetarian, £20.50 meat, £26.90 seafood. **Credit** AmEx, DC, MC, V.
On a Friday night, Rodizio Rico is the culinary equivalent of the Rio carnival. Heaving bodies clog the entrance, hungry diners chill over Brahma beers at the bar, gangs samba up to the buffet to grab some rice, beans and farofa (manioc flour), and the meat waiters dash about serving cuts from their swords. It's surprisingly fun; the staff keep coming with newly grilled bites, and even find time to chat. The buffet is easy to overdo. As well as the aforementioned staples, there are salads, pickles and croquettes filled with imprecise vegetable matter. Better to wait for the delicious prime ribeye, chicken hearts, sweet and spicy sausage and the roast lamb. Desserts are sugary and superfluous. At a fixed, eat-all-you-can £20.50 it's no bargain, but for a lively feast Rodizio Rico is hard to beat.
Babies and children welcome: booster seats; high chairs. Booking advisable. Disabled: toilet. Vegetarian menu. **Map 5 O2.**
For branches see index.

Cuban

Central

Soho

Floridita
100 Wardour Street, W1F 0TN (7314 4000/ www.floriditalondon.com). Tottenham Court Road tube. **Bar Open** 5.30pm-2am Mon-Wed; 5.30pm-3am Thur-Sat. *Restaurant* **Dinner served** 5.30pm-midnight Mon-Wed; 5.30pm-1am Thur-Sat. **Main courses** £11-£35. **Admission** (after 7.30pm Fri, Sat) £15. **Credit** AmEx, DC, MC, V.

Vaguely modelled on the Havana original, Floridita London is a combination of theme park and expensive restaurant, frequented by after-work drinkers, parties and anyone else the parading transvestites can draw in. Once inside, there are some nice dark spaces for an intimate dinner. Food is well-sourced and prepared with care – but pricey. For a special occasion, try a lobster (£30-£34); the wonderful l'armoricaine comes sautéed with tomatoes, tarragon and cognac. Tangy, refreshing snapper ceviche is doused in coconut and lime, making it a heavenly with minty mojitos. The Brazilian-style picanha (top of the rump) steak is delicious, and at £19 much better value than the chateaubriand (served, unnecessarily we thought, with béarnaise and potato gratin). The menu also offers Mexican dishes, baked duck egg, and tasty moros y cristianos (rice and beans).
Booking advisable. Disabled: toilet. Entertainment: Cuban band, DJ 8pm Mon-Sat. Dress: funky/glam. Separate rooms for parties, seating 52-72. **Map 17 B3.**

West

Kensington

La Bodeguita del Medio
47 Kensington Court, W8 5DA (7938 4147/ www.bdelmlondon.com). High Street Kensington tube. **Meals served** noon-11pm Mon-Sat; noon-10.30pm Sun. **Main courses** £9.50-£14. **Credit** AmEx, DC, MC, V.
Havana's La Bodeguita del Medio is credited with creating the mojito cocktail. This franchise falls far short of replicating the boho buzz of the original. Instead, its clean wooden interior, neat alcoves and packed-in office parties exude the vibe of a Hard Rock Café. The menu is eclectic, featuring such Latin standards as swordfish ceviche (so-so); fresh but not flavourful tiger prawns with chilli (too little) and garlic (too much); and thick succulent Argentinian ribeye with herby chimichurri dressing. The classic Cuban staples of black beans, rice, pork and fried bananas go particularly well with the scrumptious but fatty chicharrones con pimientos (crisp lardons of bacon with peppers) and the even tastier ropa vieja (smoky sheets of spiced stewed beef). Hamburgers are excellent too, emphasising that La Bodeguita is better suited to a post-pub or pre-club hour or so, than a lengthy linger. Argentinian reds and Chilean whites are the best-value wines; the Don David Reserve malbec 2005 is a steal at £21.50.
Babies and children welcome: high chairs. Booking advisable (Fri, Sat). Tables outdoors (3, pavement). **Map 7 B8/9.**

Mexican & Tex-Mex

Central

Covent Garden

★ Wahaca
66 Chandos Place, WC2N 4HG (7240 1883/ www.wahaca.co.uk). Covent Garden or Leicester Square tube. **Meals served** noon-11pm Mon-Sat; noon-10.30pm Sun. **Main courses** £5.75-£10. **Set meal** £9.75 per person (minimum 2). **Credit** AmEx, MC, V.
Queues snake into this colourful canteen daily, but it's just about worth the wait. Wahaca has a look as cheery as its staff, created from lamps made out of tomatillo cans dotted with bottle tops, wooden crates packed with fruit, and tubs of chilli plants. Choose one of the large plato fuertes (enchiladas, burritos or grilled dishes) if you don't feel like sharing, or go for the selection of kindly priced tacos, tostadas and quesadillas. Pork pibil tacos marinated in achiote (a spice) and orange, and served with pickled red onions were faultless. Quesadillas with chestnut mushrooms, cheese and huitlacoche (a fungus that grows on corn, considered a delicacy in Mexico) were an earthy treat. The salmon ceviche salad looked dramatic served in its puffy tortilla 'bowl', but was laden with lettuce and a dressing that detracted from the distinctive flavour of the raw fish slices 'cooked' in lime. Tamarind margarita worked well, the tangy fruit-cum-spice balanced by the salt rim.
Babies and children welcome: high chairs. Bookings not accepted. Disabled: lift; toilet. **Map 18 D5.**

Fitzrovia

Mestizo
103 Hampstead Road, NW1 3EL (7387 4064/ www.mestizomx.com). Warren Street tube/Euston tube/rail. **Lunch served** noon-4pm daily. **Dinner served** 6-11.30pm Mon-Sat; 6-10.30pm Sun. **Main courses** £9.50-£14.50. **Credit** MC, V.
Mestizo isn't far from the kind of sleek hotel restaurant you might find in Cancun, with neon Aztec artwork and backlit shelves displaying colourful bottles of more than a hundred tequilas. Cheery Mexican staff serve hearty portions of dishes accompanied by creamy black beans, crumbly queso fresco and a multitude of salsas. To start, there's a choice of taco-stand snacks, such as cactus leaf, poblana pepper and shredded meat; the cochinita pibil tacos (with marinated pork) are fabulous. Nourishing tomatoey tortilla soup, like nearly everything here, comes with assorted goodies to sprinkle over it: smoky pasilla chilli strips, sour cream, cheese and chunks of avocado. Poussin mole verde has a tangy tomatillo and coriander sauce speckled with pumpkin seeds, while a fine dish of filete arriero (beef medallions piled over thick slabs of potatoes and ribbons of courgette and carrot) featured a confidently garlicky sauce. Also worth a mention is the house speciality, molcajete, a traditional stone mortar overflowing with spiced chicken, beef or vegetables, served with cheese, chorizo and avocado.
Babies and children welcome: high chairs. Booking advisable weekends. Disabled: toilet. Separate room for parties, seats 80. Takeaway service (lunch).

West

Notting Hill

★ ★ Taqueria
139-143 Westbourne Grove, W11 2RS (7229 4734/www.coolchiletaqueria.co.uk). Notting Hill Gate tube. **Meals served** noon-11pm Mon-Thur; noon-11.30pm Fri; 10am-11.30pm Sat; noon-10.30pm Sun. **Main courses** £3.50-£7.50. **Set lunch** (noon-4.30pm Mon-Fri) £5.50 1 course. **Credit** MC, V.
With its real-deal tortilla-making machine from Guadalajara, this place shows what Mexican street food is about. The menu explores the versatility of

Sabor

masa (maize dough), flattened into soft tortillas for tacos, fried crisp for tostadas and shaped into thick patties for griddled sopes. Masks, movie posters and gorgeous staff make Taqueria easy on the eye, as well as the taste buds. There's a commendable list of tequilas, many aged, and Mexican beer that can be served with lime, salt and chilli for a refreshing summer drink. Aguas frescas (flavoured waters) include cucumber, hibiscus, guava and creamy horchata, made from soaked rice and cinnamon: a great foil for chilli. As for the tacos, chicken tinga (with fabulous chipotle sauce) was too liquid, and the garlic prawns could have coped with more garlic. In contrast, the crumbly chorizo sopes were impeccable, and the zingy sea bass ceviche tasted as if straight from the sea.
Babies and children welcome: high chairs.
Bookings not accepted (Sat, Sun). Takeaway service. **Map 7 A6**.

South

Clapham

Café Sol

54-56 Clapham High Street, SW4 7UL (7498 8558/www.cafesol.net). Clapham Common or Clapham North tube. **Meals served** noon-midnight Mon-Thur, Sun; noon-1am Fri, Sat. **Main courses** £5.95-£11.95. **Credit** AmEx, DC, MC, V.
This cavernous restaurant with its Latin beats, bold multicoloured mosaics and black-and-white movie pictures is always packed with Claphamites. Locally it's known for serving alligator alongside bar snacks such as sticky barbecued ribs, chicken wings, nachos, quesadillas and potato skins. We went for 'armadillo eggs': stubby super-hot chillies stuffed with refried beans and melting cheese, barely tempered by soured cream, but delectable. Cajun sole dotted with tiny prawns was sound too, while pollo pueblo (a log of tortilla-crumbed chicken oozing with cheese, bacon and cream) was offset by seriously smooth fresh tomato sauce. Ask for yours to come with chunky potato wedges. The cocktail list is full of surprises; Mexican Breakfast, a sour-sweet orange margarita, went down nicely, though it didn't come with the advertised flamed orange zest. Still, with its attentive staff, it's easy to see why Café Sol remains so popular.
Babies and children welcome: high chairs. Booking essential dinner Fri, Sat. Disabled: toilet. Tables outdoors (6, pavement). Takeaway service.
Map 22 B1.

East

Shoreditch

Green & Red

51 Bethnal Green Road, E1 6LA (7749 9670/ www.greenred.co.uk). Liverpool Street or Old Street tube/rail.
Bar **Open** 6.30pm-midnight Thur; 6.30pm-1am Fri, Sat.
Restaurant **Dinner served** 6-11pm Mon-Sat; 6-10.30pm Sun. **Main courses** £10.50-£14.50.
Both **Credit** AmEx, MC, V.
Tequila bar Green & Red is miles away from the world of studenty tequila slammers. The staff's knowledge may be patchy, but only 100% agave tequila is served. Curious cocktails include the Pancho (a deliciously spicy tequila-sour type of tipple made with egg whites) which deserved to be served in a decent martini glass, especially at £9.20 a pop. The menu offers a limited selection of tapas. We enjoyed the crisp yam-bean salad with sheep's cheese and roasted peanuts; and a lime-drenched octopus ceviche. Mains-sized 'platos fuertes' include the likes of stuffed chayote, crisp pork belly with ribs, and roasted hake with a rather disappointing pasilla chilli sauce. The decor is all wooden floorboards and panelling, with the odd mini-shrine of crucifixes and icons, and a wall of Mexican photography. Music is loud. A Day of the Dead mural leads to a clubbier basement.
Babies and children welcome: high chairs. Disabled: toilet. Entertainment (bar): DJs 9pm Fri, Sat. Tables outdoors (1, terrace). **Map 6 S4**.

North

Stoke Newington

Mercado Bar & Cantina NEW

26-30 Stoke Newington Church Street, N16 0LU (7923 0555/www.mercado-cantina.co.uk). Stoke Newington rail/73, 476 bus. **Dinner served** 6-11pm Mon-Fri. **Meals served** noon-11pm Sat, Sun. **Main courses** £8-£14. **Credit** AmEx, MC, V.
Mercado is adorned in bright floral oil cloths, plastic bags, paper cuttings and fairy lights. Cheery all-Hispanic staff dispense fresh-fruit cocktails, a couple of piscos and about 20 tequilas by the glass. Genuine Mexican flavours vie with Tex-Mex regulars on the menu. The crisp corn tortilla tostadas are giant, and we had to eat our monster tacos with a knife and fork. Monkfish taco in a light beer batter contained super-fresh fish. A veracruz tuna steak missed its olive and tomato sauce. Beef steak was tasty, but burnt onion dotted its fried potatoes. Hits and misses then.
Babies and children welcome: high chairs. Restaurant available for hire. Takeaway service.
Map 25 B1.

Pan-American

North

Camden Town & Chalk Farm

Guanabana NEW

85 Kentish Town Road, NW1 8NY(7485 1166/ www.guanabanarestaurant.com). Camden Town tube. **Lunch served** noon-3pm Wed-Fri. **Dinner served** 5-11.30pm daily. **Meals served** noon-11.30pm Sat, Sun. **Main courses** £7.85-£12.75. **Set meal** (5.30-7.30pm) £9.50 3 courses. **Unlicensed. Corkage** £2/bottle. **Credit** MC, V.
Guanabana is a fun fusion restaurant with a lovely bamboo-ceilinged garden-cum-terrace at rear. The menu of Mexican, Caribbean, Argentinian and Colombian dishes is punctuated with wild cards such as jasmine-perfumed Thai rice, beer-battered onion rings and 'slaw. Try starters of red jalapeños stuffed with cream cheese, glazed chicken wings, or cassava chips with tomato salsa. Pan-fried bass came as a tower of succulent fillets between layers of crisp greens and a delicious feta cheese mash. Desserts include sweet potato and banana fritters with coconut ice-cream. Bring your own booze, or stick with a fresh fruit mocktail.
Babies and children welcome: high chairs. Booking advisable weekends. Separate room for parties, Tables outdoors (14, garden). Takeaway service.
Map 27 D1.

Islington

Sabor

108 Essex Road, N1 8LX (7226 5551/ www.sabor.co.uk). Angel tube/Essex Road rail/ 38, 73 bus. **Dinner served** 6-10pm Tue, Wed; 6-11pm Thur, Fri. **Meals served** noon-11pm Sat, Sun. **Main courses** £8-£19.50. **Set lunch** £10 2 courses, £12.50 3 courses. **Credit** MC, V.
Sabor offers 'Nuevo Latino' cuisine, mixing styles from across Latin America. The decor is bright, with primary-coloured tables, disco balls, and multicoloured masks. Start with cocktails made from exotic fruits such as the gooseberry-like lulo, or sample the impressive New World wine list. The focus, however, is on food. Robust own-made chorizo came with a vibrant green spinach and yuca hash, while chive-topped duck quesadillas were lifted by pungent ancho chillies. To follow, rabo encendido from Cuba was slow-cooked Rioja-soaked oxtail balanced by a sweet eggy plantain flan. Brazilian moqueca, the luscious seafood stew, came packed with lime and dried coconut strips. Dessert was sublime: poached tamarillo with sweet lulo coulis and intense rum and raisin ice-cream.
Babies and children welcome: high chairs. Booking advisable. **Map 5 P1**.

Interview
JOHN RATTAGAN

Who are you?
Chef and patron of **Buen Ayre** Argentinian restaurant (*see p45*) in Broadway Market.
What's the best thing about running a restaurant in London?
The London restaurant scene has only taken off over the last 15 years or so, but already dining out has become almost a way of life. Londoners are curious, eager to experiment with new things and there is still room for innovations. It is a really exciting time.
What's the worst thing?
From the perspective of a small business like mine, the constant flux of new regulations we have to comply with is outrageous. Only the big chains and the very successful are able to survive in this environment. If a recession is indeed nigh, then very many independent restaurants will bite the dust.
Which are your favourite London restaurants?
Through *Time Out* I found out about **Dragon Castle** (*see p81*) in Elephant & Castle, near where I live. The quality of both the food and the service is absolutely marvellous, with dim sum to die for. I also often go to **Bistrotheque** (*see p108*), which is a good-quality – and fun – place near my restaurant, and to the Cat & Mutton pub on Broadway Market.
How green are you?
Green issues are extremely important to me, although, unfortunately, to be green in this city is quite expensive. Cheaper schemes should be in place; I'm sure many small businesses would like to recycle more but can't afford it. We pay high prices to get our bottles and oil recycled.
What is missing from London's restaurant scene?
The new grill restaurant I am dreaming of opening soon! I hope nobody beats me to it, though…

RESTAURANTS

Brasseries

A fter a relatively late start on the brasserie scene, London seems to be catching on to the attraction of a form of dining that's long been a favourite with our continental cousins. Brasseries are good all-rounders, generally staying open all day for breakfast, lunches that go on into the afternoon and dinners that often cater to diners with a disposition for starting later than the norm (in the case of **Balans** you can eat into the early hours of the morning). Families are well catered for, sometimes with a dedicated children's menu, and menus tend to be designed around confirmed crowd-pleasers rather than challenging flavours. Fresh contenders this year are Dalston's **Water House**, the sister operation to eco-eaterie **Acorn House**; and inviting French-style bistro **Gazette**. For leisurely weekend lunches with the family or easy evenings with groups of friends, the restaurants in this section are a safe bet.

Central
Belgravia

Chelsea Brasserie
7-12 Sloane Square, SW1W 8EG (7881 5999/ www.sloanesquarehotel.co.uk). Sloane Square tube. **Lunch served** noon-3pm Mon-Sat. **Brunch served** 11am-4pm Sun. **Dinner served** 6-10.30pm Mon-Sat. **Main courses** £13-£21.50. **Set dinner** (6-7.30pm) £17.50 2 courses, £20.50 3 courses. **Credit** MC, V.
It may be attached to the Sloane Square Hotel, but this smart bar-restaurant doesn't feel like a fusty corporate appendage. The vibe is buzzy and the room upbeat, with colourful abstract paintings setting off white-painted and bare brick walls, and a striking copper-sided bar. Service was attentive; tablecloths were starched to perfection. The food (courtesy of head chef David Karlsson Moller, formerly of exemplary French restaurant Racine) was pretty impressive too. Influences are wide-ranging – British, Italian, French, Scandinavian, Japanese, North African – but a Mediterranean mood dominates. The menu isn't short, and many starters are available as main courses too: a useful ploy that other restaurants could adopt. Octopus can be chewy and tasteless, but not this wafer-thin carpaccio version with smoked paprika oil; equally delicate in texture and taste were large, yellow ravioli stuffed with pumpkin and sprinkled with amaretti. No complaints about mains of peppered yellow-fin tuna with pak choi and ginger and lemon grass dressing, or pan-fried calves' liver with caramelised onions and pancetta. A salad of melon, blood orange and mint made a refreshing, zingy dessert. Bar snacks, Sunday brunch and a short pre-theatre menu are available too.
Babies and children welcome: high chairs. Booking advisable. Disabled: toilet. Separate room for parties, seats 12. **Map 15 G10.**

City

Royal Exchange Grand Café & Bar
The Royal Exchange, EC3V 3LR (7618 2480/ www.danddlondon.co.uk). Bank tube/DLR. **Breakfast served** 8-11am, **meals served** noon-10pm Mon-Fri. **Main courses** £6.50-£19. **Credit** AmEx, DC, MC, V.
The grand, Grade I-listed Royal Exchange has always been a temple to London's wealth – so its modern reinvention, as a luxury boutique-lined shopping precinct with a smart brasserie at its centre, is perfectly apt. In the soaring atrium, tables cluster around a gleaming bar and seafood counter, manned by scurrying waiters. For a quieter table overlooking the action, head for the first-floor gallery. Serving food all day, it's most atmospheric at lunchtime, as bankers strike deals over lobster sandwiches and steaks, and shoppers stop for champagne and oysters. In the evening, after a post-work peak, it quietens down – and without the buzz, loses some lustre. On our last visit, hurried, perfunctory service and constant wine refills made for a less than relaxing evening. A dropped langoustine was retrieved from the floor then returned to our table. Mains arrived as we were midway through our starters, then were left to cool on a nearby table. The food itself was also hit and miss; pork belly with lentils packed a flavourful punch, but plump salmon fish cakes were bland. Safer, perhaps, to stick to the upmarket bar snacks and chunky, fluffy-centred chips.
Babies and children admitted (restaurant). Bookings not accepted. Disabled: toilet. Dress: smart casual. Separate room for parties, seats 26. **Map 12 Q6.**

Clerkenwell & Farringdon

Brasserie de Malmaison
Malmaison, 18-21 Charterhouse Square, EC1M 6AH (7012 3700/www.malmaison-london.com). Barbican tube/Farringdon tube/rail. **Breakfast served** 7-10am Mon-Fri; 8-10.30am Sat, Sun. **Brunch served** 11am-3pm Sun. **Lunch served** noon-2.30pm Mon-Sat. **Dinner served** 6-10pm daily. **Main courses** £12-£20. **Set meal** £15.50 2 courses, £17.50 3 courses. **Credit** AmEx, DC, MC, V.
Out-of-office diners form the natural clientele of this self-consciously plush restaurant in a boutique hotel converted from a mansion block. In contrast to the slightly glitzy bar with which it shares the basement, the dining room is intimate, with low lighting, dark colours, tables for two in secluded corners and very comfy high-backed chairs. To go with this setting there's a rather opulent mod-Euro menu, plus an ambitious 'Home-grown and Local' list featuring dishes such as Maldon grilled mackerel based entirely on the goods of small-scale producers in London and the South-east. This is probably the one to go for, as our dishes from the main menu were decent, but lacked any of the sparkle that would make them stand out from the crowd. A lobster omelette was overcooked and dry; fish of the day (halibut), was bland, despite being shadowed by masses of red cabbage, greens and tomatoes; steak-frites with truffle butter was a little more interesting, but with the meat strangely thin-cut, so that much of its quality had got lost in the cooking. Service is anonymously correct.
Babies and children welcome: high chairs. Booking advisable. Disabled: toilet. Separate rooms for parties, seating 6, 14 and 30. Wireless internet (£5). **Map 5 O5.**

★ Flâneur Food Hall
41 Farringdon Road, EC1M 3JB (7404 4422/ www.flaneur.com). Farringdon tube/rail. **Breakfast served** 8.30-10.30am, **dinner served** 6-10pm Mon-Sat. **Lunch served** noon-3pm Mon-Fri. **Brunch served** 10am-4pm Sat. **Main courses** £12-£14.50. **Set lunch** (12-12.45pm) £15 2 courses. **Set meal** £21 2 courses, £26 3 courses. **Credit** AmEx, DC, MC, V.
Set amid a foodie shopper's paradise of library-style shelves full of everything from Seasoned Pioneers spices to Irish tea and Tuscan pasta, this Farringdon food hall incorporates a very pleasing restaurant. Casually elegant customers dine in a classily muted atmosphere created with clever, subtle lighting and a refreshing lack of music. The high-backed chairs and blonde-wood decor might have produced an Ikea vibe, but a deft decorating hand means they seem chic. Brunch here is a strong point, while at lunch and dinner the daily changing menu offers the option of two courses for £21 or three for £26, and the quality of the food makes this good value. A salad of watercress, fennel, manchego and pear provided a crunchy, considered match of ingredients that whet the appetite for a hearty haddock chowder with clams, corn and bacon. A slightly soupy risotto of ceps, shallots and parsley disappointed, but a baked cheesecake with an indulgent layer of lemon curd redeemed our meal. Service is professional and attentive without being intrusive; things can get a little awkward, however, when shop customers need to reach over diners to pick their groceries.
Babies and children admitted. Booking advisable. Separate room for parties, seats 20. Takeaway service. Wireless internet (free). **Map 5 N5.**

The Larder
91-93 St John Street, EC1M 4NU (7608 1558/ www.thelarderrestaurant.com). Barbican tube/ Farringdon tube/rail. **Breakfast served** 8-11am, **lunch served** noon-3pm Mon-Fri. **Dinner served** 6-10.30pm Mon-Sat. **Main courses** £9-£17.90. **Credit** MC, V.
Though it's only been going since 2007, the Larder's look could be a model for a more '90s-ish archetype of a 'trendy modern restaurant': a warehouse-style space with exposed pipes, hard surfaces (so lots of noise), international wines, chirpy if forgetful staff and (a special feature) acres of room receding into dark corners. It includes a shop, bakery and bar, and much emphasis is placed on its use of ingredients from British small-scale producers; menu descriptions are often ornate but seem interesting. It was disappointing, then, to find the results distinctly underwhelming. In a salad of mozzarella and four varieties of tomato, two of the latter (black and green) were tasteless; in honey-crumbed squid with lemon aioli, there was little taste of honey or garlic. Things didn't improve much with the mains: a sirloin steak, supposedly a Larder strongpoint, was nondescript, and the absurdly labelled 'heritage potato chips' with it were not cooked through. Lemon and thyme marinated pork fillet was better, but the parmesan croquettes served alongside had no detectable cheese flavour. A place that should try much harder to justify its pretty ambitious claims.
Babies and children welcome: high chairs. Disabled: toilet. Separate room for parties, seats 18. Takeaway service (Mon-Fri). **Map 5 O4.**

★ Zetter
86-88 Clerkenwell Road, EC1M 5RJ (7324 4455/ www.thezetter.com). Farringdon tube/rail. **Breakfast served** 7-10.30am Mon-Fri; 7-11am Sat, Sun. **Brunch served** 11am-3pm Sat; 11am-4pm Sun. **Lunch served** noon-2.30pm Mon-Fri.

RESTAURANTS

Dinner served 6-10.30pm Mon-Wed, Sun; 6-11pm Thur-Sat. **Main courses** £12.50-£18.50. **Credit** AmEx, MC, V.

The restaurant at Clerkenwell's foremost boutique hotel (a converted warehouse) is appropriately stylish: a lofty, airy space of subtle dark woods and deep maroons, giant hanging lampshades, splashes of vaguely Miró-inspired paintwork and floor-to-ceiling windows. The result is comfortable rather than affected. Zetter is open all day every day, and so makes a relaxing spot for local loft-living singles to sit back over the papers at weekends, or network more intensively midweek. Service is charming as well as sharp, and the mainly Mediterranean, monthly changing menus have a lively, inventive style strong on flavour. Celeriac and pear soup with crème fraîche was a lovely, delicate blend, while an impressively fresh salad was made special by delicious roasted squash – a simple touch very well carried off. Linguini with rabbit confit and pesto was less distinctive, but still offered plenty to enjoy. The wine list is ambitious, with high-quality (and pricey) bottles as wines of the month. For breakfast or weekend brunches you can head back home with substantial full english or veggie brekkies, brunch classics, bagels, juices and smoothies. There's also a retro-plush cocktail bar, making Zetter a very complete package.
Babies and children welcome: children's portions; crayons; high chairs. Disabled: toilet. Separate rooms for parties, seating 8 and 46. Tables outdoors (14, pavement). Wireless internet (£2.50). **Map 5 O4**.

Fitzrovia

RIBA Café

66 Portland Place, W1B 1AD (7307 3888/ www.riba.org). Great Portland Street or Oxford Circus tube. **Meals served** 9am-3pm Sat. **Main courses** £8.50-£19.50. **Set meal** £23.50 3 courses. **Credit** AmEx, DC, MC, V.

A meal here is more likely to be memorable for the location than the food – a shame as a more inspired menu combined with the headquarters of the Royal Institute of British Architects would make a stunning destination. The airy, high-ceilinged, first-floor hall that the restaurant occupies boasts intricately carved stone pillars, a central exhibition space and smart, plant-dotted outdoor terrace. Suited diners take advantage of the 45-minute express lunch, while less stuffy patrons choose from a shorter menu available in the area just outside the main restaurant (by the grand stairs leading down to the ground floor). The menu included, on our visit, steak sandwich, confit duck and blood orange salad, and wild mushroom filo tart. Sensitively cooked halibut on orzo pasta came with mussels instead of cockles as listed, but was none the worse for it. Smoked tofu salad with pickled ginger and yoghurt dressing, on the other hand, didn't have much foil for the strong-tasting root and was left mostly uneaten. The crisply dressed waiters are stiff and proper.
Babies and children welcome: high chairs. Booking advisable. Disabled: lift; toilet. Tables outdoors (20, terrace). Separate rooms for parties, seating 6-270. **Map 3 H4**.

King's Cross

★ Acorn House

69 Swinton Street, WC1X 9NT (7812 1842/ www.acornhouserestaurant.com). King's Cross tube/rail. **Breakfast served** 8-11am Mon-Fri; 10am-noon Sat. **Lunch served** noon-3pm, **dinner served** 6-10pm Mon-Sat. **Main courses** £12-£22. **Credit** AmEx, MC, V.

Nespole, or loquat, is a summer fruit, when it fruits in the UK at all. The Mediterranean climate is more its thing, so we were puzzled to find it sitting (along with buffalo mozzarella, bresaola, balsamic vinegar and various speciality olive oils) on the May menu at this so-called 'sustainable' eaterie. Once you've overcome the disappointment that the produce is not all from England, let alone born within the sound of Bow bells, there's much to like about this bright, sassy establishment. Meat is

well-sourced, impressively cooked and generously portioned. Roast rack of lamb with dragoncello (a sauce of herbs and anchovies), and pork belly with 'Sao Paolo' feijoada (low on beans), were just fabulous, and we didn't regret ordering a side of succulent cauliflower with almonds and chilli. Acorn House is a training establishment for local youngsters. While staff may occasionally struggle with placement of cutlery, they've certainly grasped the techniques of upselling, meeting a request for tap water with the suggestion we try a hazelnut bellini (£7). Would we like bread and olives? Not when they're £2 and £4 respectively. Earlier in the day, drop by for salads, soups, sandwiches, juices, muffins and pastries.
Babies and children welcome: high chairs; nappy-changing facilities. Disabled: lift; toilet. Takeaway service (lunch). **Map 4 M3**.

Mayfair

Truc Vert

42 North Audley Street, W1K 6ZR (7491 9988/ www.trucvert.co.uk). Bond Street tube. **Meals served** 7.30am-10pm Mon-Fri; 9am-10pm Sat; 9am-3pm Sun. **Main courses** £14.95-£17.50. **Credit** AmEx, MC, V.

Styling itself as a 'traiteur' – a deli, café, restaurant and new bar (scheduled to open in September 2008) rolled into one – Truc Vert offers a pleasingly rustic detour from the Oxford Street scrum. Lunchtimes are buzzing with local workers nipping in to take away French food such as smoked ham and leek quiche, chicken and butter bean salad, or tranches of orange and almond cake. In the evening, the pale wood decor is gently romanticised with crisp tablecloths and flickering candles. You can eat light with a cheese or charcuterie plate, or plump for one of the huge dishes from the broadly Mediterranean menu. A classy mozzarella, artichoke and beetroot salad was followed by competently cooked sea bass served with mangetout and spicy tomato salsa. Richer dishes on the changing menu could include roast duck breast on polenta, venison with blue cheese, mustard-spiked ribeye steak, or chicken livers and bacon. Desserts are a high point, so save room for a happy ending of apple crumble with vanilla-specked ice-cream, lemon crème caramel, or own-made pineapple sorbet.
Babies and children welcome: high chairs. Booking advisable. Tables outdoors (6, pavement). Takeaway service. **Map 9 G6**.

Piccadilly

★ The Wolseley (100)

160 Piccadilly, W1J 9EB (7499 6996/ www.thewolseley.com). Green Park tube. **Breakfast served** 7-11.30am Mon-Fri; 8-11.30am Sat, Sun. **Lunch served** noon-2.30pm daily. **Tea served** 3.30-5.30pm

BEST BRASSERIES

Brilliant breakfasts

Start the day like a king by filling up at **Flâneur** (*see p48*), **High Road Brasserie** (*see p50*), **Pick More Daisies** (*see p53*), **Tom's Kitchen** (*see p51*), the **Wolseley** (*see above*) and **Zetter** (*see p48*).

For taking the kids

Brasseries are generally a sensible option for families, but the **Depot** (*see p51*), **Gazette** (*see p51*), **Giraffe** (*see p51*), **Hugo's** (*see p53*) and **Tate Modern Café: Level 2** (*see p52*) are particularly child-friendly.

For a taste of France

Pretend you're in Paris at **Gazette** (*see p51*), **High Road Brasserie** (*see p50*), **Newtons** (*see p51*) and **Truc Vert** (*see above*).

Mon-Sat; 3.30-6.30pm Sun. **Dinner served** 5.30pm-midnight Mon-Sat; 5.30-11pm Sun. **Main courses** £6.75-£29.50. **Set tea** £8.25-£19.50. **Cover** £2. **Credit** AmEx, DC, JCB, MC, V.

The atmosphere in the Wolseley shimmers with glamour and excitement. Iron chandeliers hang from vaulted ceilings like in a central European castle; the gilded chinoiserie of the wall panels and fittings adds fun and lightness; and the dining room is filled with a lively social energy. It's a sought-after venue at any time of day: breakfast, brunch, lunch, tea or dinner. Waiting staff are warm and professional, and the tables are laid out with good linen and silverware, as you'd expect. The quality of the food ranges from humdrum to excellent. On our last visit, the chopped chicken livers with dill pickles and cream crackers were simple and delicious, and a salad of fresh broad beans and peas with asparagus, radish and herbs just right for the season. The pièce de résistance was an astonishingly good piece of halibut, smoky from the grill and perfectly succulent, served with a fine béarnaise sauce. A dessert of butter-roasted pineapple seemed a little sad and soggy, though the rum and raisin ice-cream with it was lovely. Strangely, the one poor dish was a house classic: a wiener schnitzel they'd apparently forgotten to season. If you haven't got a booking the friendly greeters may well be able to find you a place to eat in the cosy bar or cute café area, where a tempting display of cakes commands centre stage.
Babies and children welcome: crayons; high chairs; nappy-changing facilities. Booking advisable. Disabled: toilet. **Map 9 J7**.

Soho

Balans

60 Old Compton Street, W1D 4UG (7437 5212/ www.balans.co.uk). Leicester Square or Piccadilly Circus tube. **Meals served** 8am-5am Mon-Sat; 8am-2am Sun. **Main courses** £8.50-£22.95. **Credit** AmEx, MC, V.

Located in the middle of Soho's most hectic strip, Balans is all things to all people. It functions as a first-stop breakfast café, a pleasant lunchtime brasserie, a buzzy evening restaurant and an after-pub (or even after-club) restaurant-bar. Such adaptability should be applauded, even if the food can be a bit hit and miss. The space is large, with a big open front bar and a more secluded area out back. The menu is impressively – perhaps even worryingly – varied. We started with so-so seared scallops and black pudding and some cracking enchiladas, before moving on to a pleasant and extremely filling fish pie crammed with cod, pollack and prawns. The catch of the day, salmon, was served with a slightly over-tart salsa verde. But Balans isn't really a place for eating, it's somewhere to be seen eating. The pavement and window tables are rarely free of poseurs until the early hours. There's also a weekday cocktail happy two hours beginning at 4pm for those who want to get the party started early.
Babies and children admitted (until 6pm). Bookings not accepted Fri, Sat. **Map 17 B4**. **For branches see index.**

Trafalgar Square

National Café

East Wing, National Gallery, Trafalgar Square, WC2N 5DN (7747 2525/www.thenational cafe.com). Charing Cross tube/rail. **Breakfast served** 8am-11.30am, **lunch served** noon-5pm, **dinner served** 5.30-11pm Mon-Sat. **Tea served** 3-5.30pm daily. **Meals served** 10am-6pm Sun. **Main courses** £8.50-£16.50. **Set dinner** (5.30-7pm) £14.50 2 courses, £17.50 3 courses. **Credit** MC, V.

If you want a more casual alternative to Oliver Peyton's National Dining Rooms (*see p62*) on the other side of the National Gallery, try this, its younger sibling. It's certainly a looker (thanks to designer David Collins), with soaring ceilings, glossy black woodwork and red leather seating, and the opening hours are friendlier too. A long, marble-topped bar runs down one side and in the back is a self-service daytime canteen. Whether you want to have breakfast before work, lunch or

Gazette

afternoon tea during a gallery visit, dinner with friends or an after-cinema cocktail, it can deliver. Pastries, eggs, granola and smoothies are served until noon, followed by classic brasserie fare such as steaks, pastas, burgers and boards of terrines, charcuterie or cheese. Recent highlights have included excellent Colston Bassett stilton, a textbook smoked haddock fish cake with poached egg, and creamy smoked mackerel pâté served with silverskin onions, tiny gherkins and toast. A few specials (chateaubriand, côte de boeuf) appear for the evening, and kids get their own menu – though they'd probably prefer the ice-cream sundaes (something of a speciality), especially the absurdly extravagant 'National Catastrophe'. A welcome sanctuary from the tourist throngs. *Babies and children welcome: high chairs. Booking advisable. Disabled: toilet. Separate room for parties, seats 30. Restaurant available for hire.* **Map 10 K7**.

West

Chiswick

★ High Road Brasserie

162-166 Chiswick High Road, W4 1PR (8742 7474/www.highroadhouse.co.uk). Turnham Green tube. **Breakfast served** 7am-noon Mon-Fri; 8am-noon Sat, Sun. **Brunch served** noon-5pm Sat, Sun. **Dinner served** 5pm-midnight Sat; 5-10pm Sun. **Meals served** noon-11pm Mon-Thur; noon-midnight Fri. **Main courses** £10-£22. **Set lunch** £13 2 courses, £16 3 courses. **Credit** AmEx, MC, V.
This good looking place on Chiswick High Road is a social chameleon. At breakfast the menu sports everything from the 'full English' to generous stacks of buttermilk pancakes. Come in the evening and expect killer cocktails and no-nonsense brasserie mains. We visited for weekend brunch when the place was clattering with trendy west Londoners and young families were spilling out onto the street to enjoy the good weather. Inside there is dark wood furniture, green-grey banquettes

and striking coloured floor tiles, all centred around a busy bar area. Waiters in starched white aprons and black waistcoats deliver faultless service despite the crowds. Our 'pig sandwich' was a delight – shreds of succulent pork mounded into bread with Bramley apple sauce. Giant burgers are served on wooden boards and top-notch shoestring chips come in galvanised pots. You certainly won't leave hungry. Less exciting was a pear crumble with custard, but this place (part of the Soho House group, and with accommodation available) is more about the buzzing atmosphere than cutting-edge cuisine. Whatever the time of day, you are sure to be seduced by the slickness of the operation. *Babies and children welcome: children's menu; crayons; high chairs; nappy-changing facilities; toys. Booking advisable. Disabled: toilet. Tables outdoors (9, terrace).*

Notting Hill

Electric Brasserie

191 Portobello Road, W11 2ED (7908 9696/ www.the-electric.co.uk). Ladbroke Grove tube. **Meals served** 8am-11pm Mon-Fri; 8am-5pm, 6-11pm Sat; 8am-5pm, 6-10pm Sun. **Main courses** £10-£28. **Set lunch** (noon-4.45pm Mon-Fri) £13 2 courses, £16 3 courses. **Credit** AmEx, DC, MC, V.
A stalwart of Portobello's slick media dining scene, the Electric delivers quality retro cooking throughout the day and much of the night. On the first floor is the members' club run by the team behind Soho House. Downstairs, the brasserie has an upmarket hotel feel, with smartly pressed staff wheeling a dome-topped trolley, and a decor of brown leather banquettes and chrome tables. Lighting is appropriately low. Bursting-at-the-seams burgers on wooden boards, pots of fat chips, seafood platters and chateaubriand to share are served alongside tapas-style 'small plates'. On a blustery winter evening, the partridge with crackling bacon, game chips and creamy bread sauce was a welcome filler, though a limply presented Dorset crab salad with over-salted fennel disappointed. A starter of vitello tonnato (the

Piedmont dish of cold veal slices served with a tuna sauce) used top-notch meat. Perfectly squidgy scallops came with an unctuous buttery sauce. There's a worldwide selection of wines (with 14 offered by the glass), a cocktail list to be proud of, and a range of desserts that extends from comfort nursery puddings like jam roly poly with custard to classic French favourites. *Babies and children welcome: high chairs. Disabled: toilet. Tables outdoors (8, pavement).* **Map 19 B3**.

Westbourne Grove

Raoul's Café

105-107 Talbot Road, W11 2AT (7229 2400/ www.raoulsgourmet.com). Westbourne Park or Ladbroke Grove tube. **Meals served** 8.30am-10.15pm daily. **Main courses** £8.50-£16. **Credit** AmEx, MC, V.
Raoul's ever-popular original in Maida Vale may be the more established of this sibling pair but far from letting big sis garner all the attention, this branch attracts its own glossy customer set. Boho model-types fill shaded pavement tables on sunny days; the bright interior features stylish lighting and huge mirrors, chic leather banquettes and an intimate basement bar. The all-day brunch menu goes down a storm with the weekend Portobello Market crowds refuelling on baguettes, pancakes and shakes, but we recommend getting in most of your recommended five-a-day with the huge and fruit-packed smoothies and wonderful fresh salads. Well-sourced, quality ingredients are the key here: bright yellow eggs from Mugello in Italy make for flavoursome, fluffy omelettes and fantastic eggs Florentine; chorizo tortilla, with top-notch, non-fatty sausage and spring onion, was the best we've had. It's not cheap, with prices reflecting the W11 postcode, but the food's good and swift and professional service is an additional draw. *Babies and children welcome: high chairs. Disabled: toilet. Separate room for parties, seats 30. Takeaway service.* **Map 19 C3**.
For branches (Raoul's, Raoul's Deli) see index.

South West

Barnes

The Depot

Tideway Yard, 125 Mortlake High Street, SW14 8SN (8878 9462/www.depotbrasserie.co.uk). Barnes, Barnes Bridge or Mortlake rail/209 bus. **Brunch served** 9.30am-12.30pm Sat. **Lunch served** noon-3pm Mon-Fri; noon-4pm Sat, Sun. **Dinner served** 6-11pm Mon-Sat; 6-10.30pm Sun. **Main courses** £9.95-£17.95. **Set meal** (noon-7.30pm Mon-Fri) £13.50 2 courses, £15.50 3 courses; (Oct-Nov, Jan-Feb) £10 2 courses. **Credit** AmEx, DC, MC, V.

This long-lived bar-restaurant is a polished affair, where gleaming wood meets sleek service and accomplished cooking. Its popularity is partly down to the setting – an attractive Victorian conversion, with riverside windows along one side that are perfect for viewing sunsets and the Boat Race – but it's raised its game in the past year. The bar has more of a buzz (and good cocktails) and the cooking makes deft use of top-notch, seasonal ingredients. Fish and seafood are a forte: grilled Manx kipper appeared among the starters, while a main of succulent grilled mackerel was perfectly matched with tomato and olive salsa, fennel and samphire. Or how about roast pork belly with shiitake broth and steamed chinese greens? And it's hard to turn down a side order of broccoli zinged up with ginger, garlic and chilli. Oh, and the wine list is a winner too. A shame there are no outside tables next to the Thames, but there is a sunny patio in the cobbled front courtyard instead. With Saturday brunch and Sunday roasts, they've got every angle covered.
Babies and children welcome: children's menu; crayons; high chairs; nappy-changing facilities. Booking advisable. Restaurant available for hire. Tables outdoors (8, patio).

Chelsea

Napket

342 King's Road, SW3 5UR (7352 9832/www.napket.com). Sloane Square tube then 11, 19, 22 bus. **Meals served** 8am-8pm daily. **Main courses** £2.95-£5.85. **Credit** AmEx, MC, V.

Looks are everything at this stylish café in Sloane central that goes by the tag-line 'snob food'. The interior is all chic black gloss and space-age perspex, accessorised with iPods on tables and baffling photos of decadent, emaciated models. Seating consists of a corner perching area and two communal tables in front of a long counter laden with the offerings: salads, sandwiches and an array of cakes presented in muffin cases. Steer away from the latter; tempting as orange and marzipan or Nutella cake sounds, those we tried were dry. The savoury stuff is much better: terrific bread generously filled with high-quality ingredients like the meal-in-itself club sandwich layered with roast chicken, ham, bacon and emmental, or more virtuous smoked salmon on wholegrain baguette. Salads come in pots of two sizes, but you can't mix them as they're all priced differently. Unwisely we chose a sickly avocado and artichoke combo that lacked enough lemon to cut through its richness. The space feels cramped, which isn't helped by too many staff members hovering in the tiny area between the tables and serving counter.
Babies and children admitted. Takeaway service; delivery service (over £25 within SW3).
Map 14 D12.
For branches see index.

★ Tom's Kitchen

2008 WINNER BEST BREAKFAST
27 Cale Street, SW3 3QP (7349 0202/www.tomskitchen.co.uk). South Kensington or Sloane Square tube. **Breakfast served** 7-10am, **lunch served** noon-3pm Mon-Fri. **Brunch served** 10am-3pm Sat; Sun. **Dinner served** 6pm-11pm daily. **Main courses** £12.50-£29. **Credit** AmEx, MC, V.

Tom Aitkens' Tom's Kitchen is a home from home for Chelsea's super rich set. But don't let that put you off. A warm, welcoming room framed in gleaming white tiles and homespun prints, it feels as if it was set up simply to make you happy. The menu is formidable, covering much of what you might want to eat from early morning until night. The breakfast and brunch menus include everything from brioches and croissant au beurre to bagels, Belgium waffles and bacon and sausage sarnies, or rather 'bacon sandwich with buttermilk bread and homemade tomato ketchup'. This was a dream of a concoction, the bacon plentiful and beautifully crisp; the egg running majestically through the crevices of the buttermilk bread. We followed with vanilla belgium waffles with blueberry compote, the waffles so crisp and good we barely touched the compote. A breathtaking breakfast experience. The lunch and dinner menu ranges wide – from the down-home (macaroni cheese) through brasserie classics (moules and steak and chips), into Sunday lunch territory with roast beef, horseradish cream and yorkshire pudding, along with robust country cooking, with the likes off slow roast pork belly with buttered lentils and grain mustard mash.
Babies and children welcome: high chairs; nappy-changing facilities. Disabled: toilet. Separate room for parties, seats 22. **Map 14 E11.**

South

Balham

Gazette NEW

1 Ramsden Road, SW12 8QX (8772 1232/www.gazettebrasserie.co.uk). Balham tube/rail. **Meals served** 7am-11pm daily. **Main courses** £8-£25. **Credit** AmEx, DC, MC, V.

More stylish than the local French village cafés by which it is inspired, this brasserie (and its SW11 sister) captures the feel of authentic French eateries better than many other aspiring London establishments. A roll-call of Franco-favourites is served all day, some in cast-iron casseroles for that little *je ne sais quoi*. Think croque-monsieur, grilled goat's cheese salad, crêpes, filled baguettes and hot food such as moules marinière and provençal-style calamares risotto. The breakfast menu features oeufs cocotte meurette (eggs with pancetta, mushroom and red wine sauce) as well as croissants, pain au chocolat, and a soft fresh cheese with fruit option. There's a short children's menu too. We were impressed by the drinks list which runs from freshly squeezed juices and smoothies through cider, beers and a wide choice of French wine at keen prices. Chalk is provided for doodling on the slate tabletops. With windows offering views of passers-by, this is a great place to spend a morning or afternoon.
Babies and children admitted. Booking advisable Thur-Sun. Disabled: toilet. Tables outdoors (5, terrace). Takeaway service. Wireless internet (free).
For branch see index.

Battersea

Butcher & Grill

39-41 Parkgate Road, SW11 4NP (7924 3999/www.thebutcherandgrill.com). Clapham Junction or Queenstown Road rail/49, 319, 345 bus. *Bar* **Open** 8.30am-11pm Mon-Sat; 8.30am-4pm Sun. **Breakfast served** 8.30-11am Mon-Sat; 8.30am-noon Sun. *Restaurant* **Lunch served** noon-3.30pm Mon-Sat; noon-4pm Sun. **Dinner served** 6-11pm Mon-Sat. **Main courses** £9.50-£25. **Set lunch** (Mon-Fri) £12.50 2 courses, £15 3 courses. *Both* **Credit** AmEx, MC, V.

A well-stocked butcher's counter meets the eye as you enter a restaurant focusing on competently cooked, high-quality meat. Large prints of abstract images of old Smithfield market and monochrome photographs of animals grace the high walls of this large, roomy bar and dining space. Butcher & Grill feels like a modern, urban brasserie yet also seems closely connected to the countryside. On our visit, service was erratic; our wine glasses remained empty throughout the main course with no offer to replenish them, while at other times attentiveness crossed into over-familiarity. Starters are less meat-focused than mains, including the likes of seared scallops, and aubergine salad. The second courses offer only one vegetarian dish. Steak and kidney pie was flavoursome and juicy. Tender, succulent roast rump of lamb came with creamed flageolet beans that were salty and very rich. Our desserts – mango crème brûlée, and chocolate fondant with strawberry ice-cream – were enjoyable but too rich to finish. A nice touch is the menu for children, containing the likes of pasta with grated cheddar, parmesan and butter. The wine list has a varied selection by the glass, and there's a short but inventive list of cocktails.
Babies and children welcome: children's menu; high chairs. Booking advisable weekends. Disabled: toilet. Tables outdoors (5, pavement; 6, terrace).
Map 21 C1.
For branch see index.

Clapham

Newtons

33-35 Abbeville Road, SW4 9LA (8673 0977/www.newtonsrestaurants.co.uk). Clapham South tube. **Lunch served** noon-4pm daily. **Dinner served** 6-11pm Mon-Sat; 6-10.30pm Sun. **Main courses** £9.50-£16. **Set lunch** (noon-4pm Mon-Sat) £8 2 courses, £10.50 3 courses; (Sun) £18.50 3 courses. **Set dinner** (Mon-Sat) £15 2 courses, £18.50 3 courses. **Credit** AmEx, MC, V.

The star of Abbeville Road's hamlet of eateries, Newtons has delivered Modern European dishes interspersed with the odd Asian classic to the Clapham crowd for more than a decade. The dining room's exposed white brickwork, French-bistro chairs, crisp white tablecloths and glossy Indian photographs produce an uncluttered yet cosy feel, and the outdoor terrace is a prime spot for people-watching in summer. On our most recent visit, steamed aubergine, though slightly overcooked, had a chilli kick to contrast with some crunchy calamares served with an ectoplasmically green parsley sauce. The creamy chicken liver parfait with sour red onion marmalade was another commendable starter. We went à la carte, though the specials menu with two dinner courses for £15 (or three for £18.50; and cheaper at lunch) offer good value. The bacon and cheese burgers with skinny chips and an array of relishes were also tempting. Top-quality tuna steak arrived with a tart ratatouille sauce and crisp courgette fritters, while comforting lamb casserole provided melt-in-the-mouth meat with mint mash and a splendid mix of warming vegetables. A trio of own-made coconut, passion-fruit and green apple sorbets ended the meal on a light and flavoursome note.
Babies and children welcome: children's portions; crayons; high chairs. Booking advisable. Tables outdoors (8, terrace). **Map 22 A3.**

Waterloo

Giraffe

Riverside Level 1, Royal Festival Hall, Belvedere Road, SE1 8XX (7928 2004/www.giraffe.net). Embankment tube/Waterloo tube/rail. **Meals served** 8am-10.45pm Mon-Fri; 9am-10.45pm Sat; 9am-10.30pm Sun. **Main courses** £6.95-£12.95. **Set meal** (5-7pm Mon-Fri) £6.95 2 courses. **Credit** AmEx, MC, V.

A warm blast of camaraderie envelops you on entering this popular branch of the worldly wise chain. At lunchtimes Giraffe pulls in a substantial family crowd; children are given balloons and baby-cinos, proper food and plenty of attention. With popularity come the usual drawbacks, however. Having to wait for a table is a common occurrence, and the high customer turnover often results in inadequate clean-ups between sittings. Nonetheless, the staff are clearly chosen for their sunny ways and the food is gratifying: in terms of both value and taste. Meals are large, colourful ensembles. Our favourite is the vegetarian meze plate, starring falafel, houmous, beetroot, tabouleh, Tunisian ratatouille and warm pitta. Next we sampled a brace of burgers – one Aberdeen Angus and one lamb kofta – both juicy and delicious. Salads are imaginative, the 'sunshine powerfood' version is bursting with nuts, seeds, and edamame beans alongside the usual leaves. Brunch stuff (such as stacked pancakes, waffles, and eggs and

RESTAURANTS

bacon) is often praised too, as is the Union Roasters coffee. Don't leave without ordering pudding; the apple, rhubarb and ginger crumble is fab but this time we tried a warm pecan, walnut and cranberry pie and weren't disappointed.
Babies and children welcome: children's menu; crayons; high chairs; nappy-changing facilities. Disabled: toilet. Tables outdoors (60, terrace). Takeaway service. **Map 10 M8.**
For branches see index.

Tamesa@oxo
2nd floor, Oxo Tower Wharf, Bargehouse Street, SE1 9PH (7633 0088/www.oxotower.co.uk). Blackfriars or Waterloo tube/rail. **Lunch served** noon-3.30pm, **dinner served** 5.30-10.30pm Mon-Fri. **Meals served** noon-10.30pm Sat; noon-5.30pm Sun. **Main courses** £12-£17.50. **Set meal** (lunch, 5.30-7pm, 10-11.30pm Mon-Sat) £14.50 2 courses, £17.50 3 courses. **Credit** AmEx, MC, V.
A few levels down from the upmarket eateries on the eighth floor in more ways than one, this elongated space on the second floor of the Oxo Tower has seen more than its fair share of restaurants come and go. Tamesa's aquatic interior features retro pod seating and a space-age metal bar set against electric-blue walls undulating in waves, and pillars painted with arty seaweed shapes. The river views through the windows are delightful but can't excuse the food. A starter of Scottish lobster soup with brandy was a thick, flavourless fish broth, but a culinary masterpiece compared to a plate of 'pan fried' (yet somehow stone cold) tiger prawns propped against an elaborate confection of cucumber and rocket, so dry and tasteless and presented so swiftly after ordering it seemed like it had been prepared hours earlier and refrigerated. Workmanlike mains of roasted pork belly and confit of lamb were both tender and accompanied by decent mash, but too small of portion and lacking in anything like the culinary verve to justify the price tag of almost £15. Needless to say, we were the only diners there.
Babies and children welcome: children's menu; crayons; high chairs. Booking advisable. Disabled: lift; toilet. Separate room for parties, seats 28. **Map 11 N7.**

South East
Bankside

★ Tate Modern Café: Level 2
2nd floor, Tate Modern, Sumner Street, SE1 9TG (7401 5014/www.tate.org.uk). Southwark tube/London Bridge tube/rail. **Breakfast served** 10-11.30am, **lunch served** 11.30am-3pm, **tea served** 3-5.30pm daily. **Dinner served** 6.30-9.30pm Fri. **Main courses** £10.50. **Credit** AmEx, DC, MC, V.
Whether you're looking at the art or just the river views, Tate Modern's Level 2 eaterie is a fantastic place for a quick bite or a longer lunch. Glass walls on three sides give the bustling space a wonderfully light feel, enjoyed by everyone from sharp-looking graphic designers, to retirees relishing their freedom and frazzled families with hungry toddlers to appease. Admirably, kids aren't treated with condescension; child-sized portions of all the main dishes are available. This is first-rate food, from a starter of leeks vinaigrette topped with an oozing poached egg, to the day's catch fresh off Cornish fishing boats. On a recent occasion the fish was a splendid piece of pollack on white bean purée with cherry tomatoes and aubergine. The changing menu incorporates seasonal British ingredients as well as more international flavours. Shropshire fidget pie filled with bacon and apples is listed alongside dressed Dorset crab and an Iberian meat plate with catalan tomato bread. The puddings display confident sophistication without being too flashy; rhubarb compote and custard was prettily layered in a tumbler. Breakfast options include mushrooms on toast with spinach and fried duck egg, and Sillfield Farm treacle-cured bacon sarnies. Service is efficient and accommodating, too. Overall, this is an unpretentious, deftly executed gallery café.

Babies and children welcome: children's menu; crayons; high chairs; nappy-changing facilities. Bookings not accepted Sat, Sun. Disabled: toilet. **Map 11 O7.**

Crystal Palace

★ Joanna's
56 Westow Hill, SE19 1RX (8670 4052/ www.joannas.uk.com). Crystal Palace or Gipsy Hill rail. **Meals served** 10am-noon Mon-Sat. **Meals served** noon-11pm Mon-Sat; noon-10.30pm Sun. **Main courses** £9-£16. **Credit** AmEx, MC, V.
Sometimes London's longest serving eateries are the safest bets, and so it proves with this New York speakeasy-styled brasserie founded by the Ellner family in 1978. The dark wood panelling, ceiling fans, wall mirrors, nicotine-tinted interior and 1950s diva soundtrack may be somewhat stagey, but the entire operation rarely falters. The affable, cosmopolitan staff, crisp tablecloths and atmosphere of relaxed sophistication place Joanna's beyond the norm for a suburban eaterie – as does the food. A chicken satay starter was chargrilled to perfection; caramelised onion and parmesan pie had the lightest, crisp pastry casing with a tangy filling; a fish pie main course was a fragrant slab of creamy, piscine goo, studded with garden peas and crowned with crisped potato. Desserts proved a hit with the sweet-toothed. A six-year-old in our party declared herself 'in love' with the sticky toffee pudding, so heavenly was the combination of dense, warm sponge, treacly caramel sauce and vanilla ice-cream. Wines are well-chosen, with a French bias. Crystal Palace may seem an odd place to find a slice of the Lower East Side, but not a single bum note was struck.
Babies and children welcome (before 6pm): high chairs. Separate room for parties, seats 6. Tables outdoors (4, patio).

East
Shoreditch

Hoxton Grille
81 Great Eastern Street, EC2A 3HU (7739 9111/ www.grillerestaurants.com). Old Street tube/rail/ 55 bus. **Meals served** 7am-11pm daily. **Main courses** £7-£20. **Credit** AmEx, MC, V.
The restaurant attached to the hip Hoxton Hotel is stylish and the food surprisingly good. This being Shoreditch, open brickwork, screen prints, brown leather, and exposed ducts come as standard, but the glass wall looking on to a courtyard is a nice touch, as is the fire at the front of the restaurant. The open kitchen serves simple but well-rendered comfort food: steaks, burgers, and big salads (grilled swordfish niçoise, for example). Service is brisk and efficient. Grilled rump steak (on a wooden board) au poivre (in a jug) with chips and roasted vine tomatoes was excellent. Our other choice, roast duck, arrived wonderfully pink and tender, with buttery savoy cabbage and a suitably tart blackberry and sage jus. The cheeseboard is better than many, with sizeable chunks of applewood, camembert and stilton, and plenty of biscuits, fruited bread and chutney. From the long wine list, our mid-priced, full-bodied Dom Martinho (£24.50) went down a treat. It's worth checking the website for special offers; you can get as much as 50% off meals before 7pm.
Babies and children welcome: children's menu; high chairs; nappy-changing facilities. Disabled: toilet. Entertainment: DJ 7pm Sat, Sun. Separate rooms for parties, seating up to 25. Tables outdoors (20, courtyard). Wireless internet (free). **Map 6 Q4.**

Water House NEW
2008 RUNNER-UP BEST
SUSTAINABLE RESTAURANT
10 Orsman Road, N1 5QJ (7033 0123/ www.waterhouserestaurant.co.uk). Liverpool Street/Old Street tube then 67, 149, 242, 243, 394 bus. **Breakfast served** 8-11am, **lunch served** noon-4pm daily. **Brunch served** 10am-4pm Sat, Sun. **Dinner served** 6-10pm Mon-Sat. **Main courses** £13.50-£18.50. **Credit** AmEx, MC, V.

Water House, the new branch of the equally lauded Acorn House (see *p49*), has garnered huge publicity on the back of the efforts it makes towards sustainability. Being down a side street in a dreary part of Dalston means it needs to be a destination eaterie, as it won't attract much passing trade – yet as a dining experience, it needs improvement and prices are on the high side. An unremarkable potato and leek soup was £6; filtered tap water is charged at £2 per bottle. We enjoyed a special of pappardelle with lamb, and duck confit (served on a generous portion of parsnip mash) was also satisfying. Many of the salads are bettered in London's good vegetarian caffs but desserts such as plum jelly and lavender panna cotta show ambition. Even months after opening, there is an amateurishness about some aspects of Water House; on our most recent visit, plates were covered in smudged fingerprints from the kitchen.
Babies and children welcome: high chairs; nappy-changing facilities. Booking advisable Fri-Sun. Disabled: toilet. Restaurant available for hire. Tables outdoors (8, terrace). **Map 6 R2.**

Camden Town & Chalk Farm

★ The Roundhouse
The Roundhouse, Chalk Farm Road, NW1 8EH (0870 389 9920/www.roundhouse.org.uk). Chalk Farm tube. **Meals served** 11am-6pm daily (late openings on gig days; check website for details). **Main courses** £8-£10. **Credit** MC, V.
Free tables may be rarer than hens' teeth during a pre-performance dinner scrum, but swing by for a lazy midweek lunch and you'll find the ground-floor brasserie of this landmark venue a glorious place to while away the afternoon. The bold red and yellow walls lend an angular modernism bolstered by minimalist white tables and chairs; it's like dining in a three-dimensional Mondrian. Big windows offer limitless potential for people-watching on colourful Chalk Farm Road. Food is a cut above the average. Chicken and lentil stew featured large chunks of meat and a hearty, delicately spiced sauce. Venison burger – thick and juicy and served with an intoxicating slab of stilton – was let down only by a rather grim port and cream sauce (served, mercifully, in a separate pot). Sides were equally satisfying: thick-cut chips perfectly fluffy and with crisp, jacket-scarred casings; green-leaf salads fresh and enormous; and chunky coleslaw big on vegetables and laudably low on mayo. Desserts (from double-chocolate brownies to apple pie with saffron and anise) come with either clotted cream or vanilla ice-cream from neighbouring Marine Ices; prices are bargainous beyond belief.
Babies and children welcome: high chairs. Booking advisable. Disabled: toilet. Separate room for parties, seats 40. Tables outdoors (10, terrace). **Map 27 B1.**

Crouch End

Banners
21 Park Road, N8 8TE (8348 2930/ www.bannersrestaurant.co.uk). Finsbury Park tube/rail then W7 bus. **Meals served** 9am-11.30pm Mon-Thur; 9am-midnight Fri; 10am-4pm, 5pm-midnight Sat; 10am-4pm, 5-11pm Sun. **Main courses** £10-£15. **Credit** MC, V.
Many trends have come and gone since Banners opened, but its place in Crouch End life remains unassailable. There's a vaguely Caribbean beach-bar look here, with rainbow colours, battered tables, flags, posters, other junk and a very cool photo of Joe Strummer, producing an unchanging boho feel. A noticeboard offers info on nannies, lost cats, homeopathy and 'metamorphosis'. Local parents come in droves because they can still feel groovy, while their nippers are bound to find something they like from the vast, globe-wandering menu. Dishes come in various sizes and range from chicken fajitas or meze to noodles, burgers, crayfish parcels, Malay curries and loads

of vegetarian choices. The drinks list is also a something-for-everyone mix: an array of coffees and standard to exotic teas; shakes, juices and floats for the kids; a huge choice of cocktails; and an exotic beer and booze range. Grumbles are heard about service at times, and cooking can be slapdash. Jerk chicken (a Banners' standard) was undercooked, even if the zippy peanut sauce covered it up a bit. These faults don't seem to matter, though, to the restaurant's devoted throngs. *Babies and children welcome: high chairs. Booking advisable.*

Pick More Daisies

12 Crouch End Hill, N8 8AA (8340 2288/ www.pickmoredaisies.com). Finsbury Park tube/rail then W7 bus. **Meals served** 9am-10pm Mon-Thur; 10am-10.30pm Sat; 10am-9pm Sun. **Main courses** £6.50-£18.50. **Credit** MC, V.
The 'hello flowers' name of this affable establishment is emphasised with a miniature zen garden on each of the well-spaced tables, and a food-issues newsletter tucked into each menu promoting the suitability of its organic wines for vegetarians. Lest all this seems too touchy-feely, rest assured the menu's focus is on burgers – free range Charolais, kobe beef (from Wales), and bison included. They come between soft flatbreads that taste good but make eating with knife and fork essential. Requests for medium-rare brought a daisy beef burger a little too pink in the centre and a kobe beef burger that was cooked right through. Nor were we impressed with the add-ins demanding a 75p surcharge, such as the derisory spoonful of fried sliced mushrooms, and heavily seeded chipotle chilli pieces that someone had forgotten to turn into sauce. In other respects, however, this is a great local when you want to keep things casual. There are generous salads and grills for those not wanting burgers, and the desserts (chocolaty, sticky, fudgey, creamy) are guaranteed to end the meal on a sugar high. Mornings see the likes of french toast, buttermilk pancakes, 'green eggs and ham' (with basil oil), and huevos rancheros on the menu.
Babies and children welcome: children's menu; crayons; high chairs; nappy-changing facilities; toys. Booking advisable.

Hornsey

Pumphouse Dining Bar

1 New River Avenue, N8 7QD (8340 0400/ www.phn8.co.uk). Turnpike Lane tube/Hornsey rail. *Bar* **Open** 4-11.30pm Tue-Fri; noon-11.30pm Sat, Sun. *Restaurant* **Dinner served** 6-10pm Tue-Fri; noon-10.30pm Sat, Sun. **Main courses** £10-£16. *Both* **Credit** AmEx, DC, MC, V.
This huge barn of a place – once a grand pumping station – was pretty quiet on our lunchtime visit, with only a few couples and families in evidence. If the weather is sunny, take advantage of the outdoor deck. There's a short menu majoring in Italian standards, including pizzas from £5. Our starter of calamares with aïoli was disappointing; the portion was generous, the batter had the requisite crunch, but it was strangely lacking in flavour. Mains include brasserie favourites such as sea bass fillets with Mediterranean vegetables. Our request for garlic mash rather than the advertised new potatoes raised not an eyebrow from the sweet staff, and the entire dish was well-executed. In contrast, sirloin steak, served with a garlic and herb butter, rocket and fries, was a little tough, and haddock, peas and fries was merely adequate (the portion of peas was minuscule and the fries were skinny). Wines come from across the globe, but tend towards recognisable brands such as Stormy Cape and Marlborough. A perfectly decent house merlot or muscadet costs £12.95. Car-drivers must visit the bar to collect keys to the underground car park. Also note that the opening hours have been reduced, but the Pumphouse is open all day from noon on weekends.
Babies and children welcome (restaurant and patio only): children's menu; high chairs; nappy-changing facilities. Booking advisable weekends. Disabled: toilet. Tables outdoors (10, patio).

Water House

North West

Queen's Park

Hugo's

21-25 Lonsdale Road, NW6 6RA (7372 1232). Queen's Park tube/rail. **Meals served** 9.30am-11pm daily. **Main courses** £11.50-£15.80. **Credit** MC, V.
A quirky spot, popular with families and the buggy brigade, Hugo's is situated on a cobbled backstreet, sharing the locale with an unlikely mix of industrial manufacturing units and workshops. Decor is eclectic – sparkly fairy lights, maroon walls, sturdy pine furniture and occasional church pews. Cooking, like the interior, offers something for everyone: all-day brunches, burgers and sandwiches, daily specials, weekend roasts, home-made cakes and hearty puds. These guys are big on organics (the place used to be called the Organic Café), but although our beef stroganoff was made with high-quality ingredients, its sauce needed a meaty boost to lift it from mediocrity. Roast duck breast was a shade overcooked, yet redeemed by a side dish of deliciously delicate cauliflower cream. Desserts restored our faith; we were bowled over by sticky toffee pudding, delectable for its dark, moist sponge and creamy caramel sauce. Drink options include organic wines and beers. Staff, although occasionally harried, managed to stay on top of orders, just about. The mood mellows in the evenings with regular jazz nights creating a more grown-up appeal. The best bet is to order simple substantial snacks here, and if you're treating the kids, we recommend a relaxing weekend brunch: the eggs benedict is a reliable favourite.
Babies and children welcome: high chairs. Booking advisable. Entertainment: musicians 8pm Wed, Thur, Sun. Tables outdoors (7, pavement). Takeaway service (lunch). **Map 1 A1.**

British

The great British food revival shows no sign of slowing; in this edition we welcome some newcomers who are spreading home-grown style beyond the centre of the city, including **Market** in the north, and **Jimmy's** and **Hereford Road** to the west. Not that there's been a lack of action in central London, with **Hix Oyster & Chop House** joining the meat club clustered around Smithfield, the **Mercer** enhancing dining options near the Bank of England, and the **Pantechnicon Rooms** adding some hitherto scant British interest to the Knightsbridge end of Belgravia. Surprise of the year, however, must be the Hart brothers' makeover of **Quo Vadis** – their first venture beyond our Spanish chapter, where the duo's **Fino** and **Barrafina** are established hits. As the Time Out website's 'most viewed restaurant' list has suggested for several months, London has taken last year's newcomer, Holborn's **Great Queen Street**, to its heart. We love its laid-back style, but are not averse to grander and more genteel establishments either, such as the **Goring Hotel**, the **Dorchester Grill Room** and Brown's Hotel's new **Albemarle**.

Central
Belgravia

The Pantechnicon Rooms NEW
*10 Motcomb Street, SW1X 8LA (7730 6074/
www.thepantechnicon.com). Hyde Park Corner
or Knightsbridge tube.*
Bar Meals served noon-10pm Mon-Sat;
noon-9pm Sun. **Main courses** £8.50-£15.50.
Dining room **Lunch served** noon-3pm Mon-
Fri. **Dinner served** 6-9.30pm Mon-Sat. **Main
courses** £8.50-£27.
Both **Credit** AmEx, MC, V.
This Belgravia bar and dining room is centred on
Brit-focused gastropub staples, but stepped up a
posh notch or two and executed with a lot more
polish. The ground-floor bar – decked in swish
marble, expensive leather and polished panelling
– attracts the sort of couture-suited customer more
accustomed to crisp G&Ts than solid pints of ale.
You can't book in the bar but it serves a similar
menu to that offered in the quieter, sympathetically
restored first-floor dining room of the listed
building. The menu comprises winning classics
such as well-prepared steak with great chips and
a choice of sauces – fresh and zingy béarnaise, for
instance. Other choices include wiener schnitzel
made with ethically sound rose veal, and a variety
of expense-account caviar and oysters. Prices are
in keeping with this refined corner of town: side
orders will set you back around £4 and desserts
can reach almost double that. The small pavement
tables make an elegant spot to enjoyably while
away a summer evening.
*Babies and children welcome: high chairs; nappy-
changing facilities. Booking advisable (not accepted
in bar). Separate room for parties, seats 12.
Tables outdoors (4, pavement).* **Map 9 G9**.

City

Canteen
*2 Crispin Place, off Brushfield Street, E1 6DW
(0845 686 1122/www.canteen.co.uk). Liverpool
Street tube/rail.* **Meals served** 8am-11pm
Mon-Fri; 9am-11pm Sat, Sun. **Main courses**
£7.50-£16. **Credit** AmEx, MC, V.
A neat, modern box on restaurant row on the
western side of Spitalfields Market, Canteen is

equally simple inside, furnished with utilitarian
but warm plain oak tables and benches. From
these, diners either watch the world walk by, or
peer into the open kitchen. From here come dishes
ranging from a bacon sandwich (good meaty
bacon, but otherwise a little dry) and afternoon
scones with jam and cream, to full roasts. Classic
breakfast dishes (eggs benedict, welsh rarebit) are
served all day. From lunchtime, the likes of
macaroni cheese or sausage and mash with onion
gravy, or the special pie or stew of the day become
available. Service seems to have improved since
last year, and there were more than enough waiters
to cope when the room filled up. At weekends this
is a good place to bring children – staff talk to them
rather than over them, and kids will love the
chocolate brownie caramel sundae (adults may
prefer the slightly more refined steamed syrup
sponge with custard). An extensive drinks list
contains ciders and stouts as well as wines from
all corners. The Royal Festival Hall branch is
worth remembering if you're on the South Bank.
An unpretentious and welcome addition to
London's British brigade.
*Babies and children welcome: children's portions;
high chairs. Disabled: toilet. Tables outdoors
(10, plaza).* **Map 12 R5**.
For branch see index.

The Mercer NEW
*34 Threadneedle Street, EC2R 8AY (7628
0001/www.themercer.co.uk). Bank tube/DLR.*
Breakfast served 7.30-10am, **lunch served**
noon-3pm, **dinner served** 5.30-9.30pm daily.
Main courses £13-£26.50. **Credit** AmEx,
DC, MC, V.
Black pillars and white napery set the scene, and
British food is the star (handmade ravioli
notwithstanding). Hoorah for Yorkshire ham,
Scottish beef, eccles cakes and British cheeses.
Excellent cullen skink with generous chunks of
smoked haddock started our lunch. The daily
special was chicken pie, but the Mercer pie won the
toss. A light-as-air pastry lid covered an adequate
amount of rump steak and mushrooms in London
Porter Ale; a side dish of spinach was needed as
accompaniment. Though grilled calf's liver, the
pieces elegantly draped over tiny specks of kale
and cauliflower, wasn't as pink as promised, the
accompanying rich, sweet onion sauce saved the

day. So did the patriotic puddings. Pimm's jelly,
studded with appropriate fruit and veg, and
tangy summer pudding sundae, amply made up
for earlier minor disappointments. Staff keep
glasses filled and dispense rather boring bread.
The drinks of choice seem to be the selection of
Meantime beers, but there's an extensive wine list
with many by the glass. This City restaurant is
ideal for eavesdropping on the chattering bankers;
it also offers a great chance to show off delicious
British food to overseas guests.
*Babies and children welcome: high chairs. Booking
advisable. Disabled: toilet. Restaurant available for
hire.* **Map 12 Q6**.

Paternoster Chop House
*Warwick Court, Paternoster Square, EC4M 7DX
(7029 9400/www.danddlondon.co.uk). St Paul's
tube.* **Lunch served** noon-3.30pm Mon-Fri;
11am-5pm Sun. **Dinner served** 5.30-10.30pm
Mon-Fri. **Main courses** £11.50-£20. **Set lunch**
(noon-4pm Sun) £16.50 2 courses, £20 3 courses.
Credit AmEx, DC, MC, V.
A British representative of the D&D restaurant
group, there's no doubt that Paternoster Chop
House is a City restaurant (hefty prices and a
sizeable wine list, not to mention lots of chaps in
suits), but its relaxed atmosphere and bright, light
interior have wider appeal – and it is close enough
to St Paul's to be on the tourist trail. The seasonally
changing menu is positively slavish in its devotion
to British produce: oysters are Colchester rocks,
Falmouth Bay natives and West Mersea natives;
pork sausage comes from Somerset and beef from
Galloway and Dumfries. National recipes are
embraced too: cambridge burnt cream with roast
rhubarb, or bakewell tart with pouring cream for
dessert; hot-water crust veal pie with tomato
chutney to start; and faggot, mash and onion gravy
as a main. We find it hard to resist 'beast of the
day', a changing roast with accompaniments – it's
always good, and a big portion. There's more than
a nod to English fare on the drinks list: not only
white and sparkling wines, but also lagers, ciders
and ales. A mellow time to come here is for Sunday
lunch; the set meal is a good deal, and no one has
a BlackBerry out.
*Babies and children welcome: children's portions;
games; high chairs. Booking advisable. Disabled:
toilet. Restaurant available for hire. Tables
outdoors (25, courtyard).* **Map 11 O6**.

★ Rhodes Twenty Four
*24th floor, Tower 42, Old Broad Street, EC2N
1HQ (7877 7703/www.rhodes24.co.uk). Bank
tube/DLR/Liverpool Street tube/rail.* **Lunch**

BEST BRITISH

Generation game
Dine the family way at **Canteen**
(see left), **Empress of India** (see p65),
Inn The Park (see p61), **National
Dining Rooms** (see p62), **Paternoster
Chop House** (see above), **Rivington
Bar & Grill** (see p64), **Roast** (see p64)
and **Rules** (see p59).

Smart settings
You'll enjoy dressing up for a meal at
the **Albemarle** (see p61), **Dorchester
Grill Room** (see p61), **Goring Hotel**
(see p63), **Lindsay House** (see p61),
The Pantechnicon Rooms (see left),
Quo Vadis (see p61), or **Top Floor
at Smiths** (see p58).

Great food, no fuss
Enjoy the pared-back style of **Hereford
Road** (see p63), **Great Queen Street**
(see p59), **Hix Oyster & Chop House**
(see right), **Market** (see p65), **Medcalf**
(see p57) and **Quality Chop House** (see
p57), plus **St John** (see p58) and its
Bread & Wine offshoot (see right).

served noon-2.15pm, **dinner served** 6-8.30pm Mon-Fri. **Main courses** £16.50-£27. **Credit** AmEx, DC, MC, V.

It's difficult to say which aspect of this Gary establishment is most impressive: the view or the grub. The first is a feast for the eyes, without doubt: best at night, when the Gherkin wears its jolly red belt and the city is a twinkling ocean as far as the eye can see. But the food – and service – are equally stunning. Everything is presented with ceremony, from the amuse-gueule butternut soup with tiny tapenade pinwheel that began our meal, to the petits fours that finished it (neither charged for). In between, the food was precise, delicious and of immaculate quality and seasonality. Dishes such as crisply based cep tart on a fan of jerusalem artichoke; a perfectly textured mutton and onion suet pud with swede; and a celeriac cheese with roasted shallots, sprouts and chestnuts – all provided imaginative employment for earthy English roots and shoots on our February visit. Pricing is interesting, with starters not far behind mains, perhaps reflecting their luxurious ingredients and complex styles. The wine list has slim pickings at the low end, particularly for reds, but if our pure-tasting Côtes du Rhone rosé was any guide, the buyers know what they're doing. *Babies and children welcome: high chair. Booking essential, 2-4 wks in advance. Disabled: toilet. Dress: smart casual.* **Map 12 Q6**.

St John Bread & Wine

94-96 Commercial Street, E1 6LZ (7251 0848/ www.stjohnbreadandwine.com). Liverpool Street tube/rail. **Breakfast served** 9-11am Mon-Fri; 10-11am Sat, Sun. **Lunch served** noon-4pm daily. **Dinner served** 5-10.30pm Mon-Sat; 5-9pm Sun. **Main courses** £11-£16. **Credit** AmEx, MC, V.

We confess – we're fans of the St John take on Brit cuisine. We love the food, like the lack of fuss and pretension in both menu and decor, and welcome the casual but well-informed service. Yet we're also aware the white, bare room won't suit all tastes, and the pared-down dishes won't please those who like lots of everything on their plates. This branch is slightly more casual than the original Smithfield restaurant, but the basic style is the same, and there's plenty of dish-crossover. The distinction between starters and mains is a little blurred: skate and fennel salad was substantial and flavourful; roast quail was succulent; cold mallard, watercress and pickled walnut just-so; and beetroot with curd and sorrel was comfortingly good. Even the green salad is a treat – minty, refreshing, we think it's just about the best in town. Puddings can be hefty (eccles cake and lancashire cheese) or light and palate-cleansing (apple sorbet and russian vodka went down a treat). Coffee is excellent. Bread, cakes and wine are sold from a counter by the semi-open kitchen. If you like this you'll also appreciate St John (*see p58*) and Rochelle Canteen (*see p65*). *Babies and children welcome: high chairs. Booking advisable. Takeaway service.* **Map 12 S5**.

Clerkenwell & Farringdon

Hix Oyster & Chop House NEW (100)

2008 RUNNER-UP BEST NEW RESTAURANT

36-37 Greenhill Rents, off Cowcross Street, EC1M 6BN (7017 1930/www.restaurantsetcltd. co.uk). Farringdon tube/rail. **Lunch served** noon-3pm Mon-Fri; noon-5pm Sun (single seating at 2pm). **Dinner served** 6-11pm Mon-Sat. **Main courses** £10.75-£54.50. **Credit** AmEx, MC, V.

Renowned for innovative updates of British food, Mark Hix now has free rein to indulge us with his passion, in this his first independent project after leaving Caprice Holdings. The menu is a roll-call for local, seasonal produce, the farmers and growers duly name-checked. Hix's food is set against a simple, pared-down decor that recalls postwar village halls. A Scottish granny would have approved our starter, 'Hix cure' smoked salmon – a medium cure with subtle smokiness, served unadorned. Grilled cod, cooked on the bone until opalescent and still moist, arrived with sea purslane, a salt marsh plant with a briny seafront flavour. Not so successful was the Dickensian-

The Mercer

sounding beef and oyster pie. Its burnished crust, which held a single oyster, was hard, and the filling overcooked to the point of dryness. Crunchy chips were fabulous yet bubble and squeak was cold at its heart. The flavours of drop scones served with honeycomb ice-cream and honey worked a treat, but were spoilt by burnt bits hidden at the bottom. Service, though willing, can be a bit clumsy, giving a sense of amateurishness to an otherwise professional operation. The drinks list contains an imaginative choice of Brit-brews.
Babies and children admitted. Booking essential, 2 wks in advance. Tables outdoors (4, pavement). Vegan dishes. Wireless internet (free). **Map 5 O5**.

Medcalf
38-40 Exmouth Market, EC1R 4QE (7833 3533/ www.medcalfbar.co.uk). Farringdon tube/rail/19, 38, 341 bus. **Lunch served** noon-3pm Mon-Fri; noon-4pm Sat, Sun. **Dinner served** 6-10pm Mon-Wed; 5.30-10.30pm Thur-Sat. **Main courses** £10.50-£17.50. **Credit** MC, V.

This ex-butcher's shop has been a big hit since opening, its scruffy-chic looks, robust cooking, relaxed staff and unpretentious vibe attracting steady custom. Medcalf is fashionable, yes, but fortunately without the attitude. The original sign and butcher's block bar-top give a hint of the former incarnation, but otherwise the long, thin main room, with its naked light bulbs, regularly changing artworks and battered metal and wooden furniture, is bang up to the minute. The tables by the bar are cramped; the best space in which to unwind and enjoy the food here is at the back, by the small decked conservatory. There's also an adjoining room, used as a gallery and for overspill. And it is enjoyable food; the daily-changing menu marries quality ingredients with unfussy execution. Potted shrimps, oysters, welsh rarebit and simple, tasty salads (Cumbrian ham, Somerset blue cheese and leaves, say) are typical starters. Shepherd's pie and pork belly with colcannon and black pudding set the tone for the mains. Smoked haddock – fat white flakes, served with creamed leeks, fluffy mash and a perfectly poached egg in crispy casing – was exemplary. British cheeses, seasonal fruit and tarts follow. Top marks for the good range of drinks too, including Paulaner, Erdinger, Old Speckled Hen and Meantime beers on draught, and nicely priced wines, all from France and Spain.
Babies and children admitted (until 7pm). Disabled: toilet. Separate room for parties, seats 18. Tables outdoors (5, garden; 4, pavement). **Map 5 N4**.

Quality Chop House
92-94 Farringdon Road, EC1R 3EA (7837 5093/ www.qualitychophouse.co.uk). Farringdon tube/ rail/19, 38 bus. **Lunch served** noon-3pm Mon-Fri; noon-4pm Sun. **Dinner served** 6-11pm Mon-Fri; 6-11.30pm Sat; 6-10pm Sun. **Main courses** £6.95- £19.95. **Set meal** (lunch Mon-Fri, 6-7.45pm Mon-Sat; Sun) £9.95 2 courses. **Credit** AmEx, MC, V.

Best local markets

There is no better place to buy fresh, local, seasonal ingredients than at a good market, but doing the weekly food shop shouldn't demand trekking to the other side of the city. We launched this new award to celebrate the capital's best neighbourhood food markets operating in residential areas. Our finalists are all places where locals can buy a good range of prime ingredients to cook at home, where the emphasis is on farmers and other producers based in or near London, though the markets may also offer produce from further away and non-food items such as clothing, homeware and books.

Alexandra Palace Farmers' Market
2008 WINNER BEST LOCAL MARKET
Alexandra Palace, Hornsey Gate entrance, off Muswell Hill, N22 7AY (0169 860 840). Alexandra Palace rail then W3 bus.
Open 10am-3pm Sun.
Stalls Around 25.
Be it fresh fruit and vegetables, seafood, cheese, bread, juices or delicious, freshly prepared grub – Ally Pally really does have it all. Created by City & Country Farmers' Markets, most producers come from within a stone's throw of London (including Kent, Surrey and Sussex), with plenty of other local English producers as well. On a hot sunny day, there is no better market to while away the hours – barbecues grill everything from juicy Giggly Pig sausages to coconut milk-basted Mozambican chicken from Zambeziana. Refreshments range from mint tea (from Algerian sweet stall Idli) to Edgebank Organics' strawberry smoothies, to the coffee stall selling chai lattes and cappuccinos. When there are big events on at the palace, the market shifts to Campsbourne School (Nightingale Lane, off Priory Rd, N8 7AF).
Highlight Lots of interesting hot and cold food to take away.
Lowlight A good website is needed to keep regulars and new visitors informed, especially on weeks when the market relocates.

Broadway Market
2008 RUNNER-UP BEST LOCAL MARKET
Broadway Market, E8 4QJ (www.broadwaymarket.co.uk). Bethnal Green tube/London Fields rail/236, 394 bus.
Open 9am-5pm Sat.
Stalls Around 20.
Quaint cafés, pubs, world food shops, indie bookshops and DVD stores line this once bleak Hackney street, making it the food-loving hipster's latest weekend hangout of choice. Sprawl out on the pavement with a freshly grilled burger (from Northfield Farm) in one hand and a chilled Vietnamese coffee (from Ca Phe VN) in the other. Stalls range from organic farmers' produce and local food manufacturers to exotic spices, cheeses and olives. There's plenty of non-foodie stuff too: new and vintage clothing, crafts, bookstalls and the like, giving visitors a total of almost 120 pitches to browse.
Highlight The east London atmosphere.
Lowlight There's not a wide choice of fresh produce.

Pimlico Road Farmers' Market
2008 RUNNER-UP BEST LOCAL MARKET
Orange Square, corner of Pimlico Road and Ebury Street, SW1W ONZ (7833 0338/www.lfm.org.uk). Sloane Square tube/Victoria tube/rail.
Open 10am-2pm Sat.
Stalls Around 27.
This London Farmers' Market operation caters for the chichi residents of Belgravia, Chelsea, Battersea and Pimlico. Opened in June 2002, it's claimed to be one of the city's largest farmers' markets, its concentration of stalls boasting an impressive range of produce. We loved Kingcup Farm, with its range of edible flowers and unusual vegetables and herbs (leek flowers, radish pods); Popina for its seasonal tarts (gooseberry and elderflower); and EFJ Gould's Marmite cheddar.
Highlight A pleasant leafy setting with plenty of benches for resting.
Lowlight There are few hot food options.

Swiss Cottage Farmers' Market
2008 RUNNER-UP BEST LOCAL MARKET
Eton Avenue, opposite Hampstead Theatre, NW3 3EU (7833 0338/ www.lfm.org.uk). Swiss Cottage tube.
Open 10am-4pm Wed.
Stalls Around 15.
Though doubled in size since its days pitching up at the O2 Centre car park in Finchley, this charming market is still rather modest. We found large, juicy padron peppers sold at Wild Country Organics, sand dabs at £1 a piece and organic buttermilk sourdough at Celtic Bakers, and rich, decadent cakes from Cupboard Love. Hot food comes in the form of grilled 'hetties' (Leicestershire slang for patties) at March House or rustic Italian food from Isabella Burino.
Highlight Friendly, knowledgeable stallholders selling prime ingredients.
Lowlight It's on Wednesday.

Wimbledon Park Farmers' Market
2008 RUNNER-UP BEST LOCAL MARKET
Wimbledon Park First School, Havana Road, SW19 8EJ (7833 0338/ www.lfm.org.uk). Wimbledon Park tube/bus 156.
Open 10am-1pm Sat.
Stalls Around 15.
There's always something intruiging for sale here; on a recent visit, the Hand Picked Shellfish Company was wowing the locals with shark meat, while Alham Wood Cheeses does a brisk trade in unpasteurised milk, though it's not available every week. It's worth checking the website to see when producers are visiting so you don't miss the fresh and preserved products from the Garlic Farm, Ladywell Organics meat or Norbury Blue cheeses. Veg-wise, Horti Halycon always has some great seasonal produce, such as delicate bags of bright organic rocket, or fresh crunchy turnips.
Highlight There's little repetition between stalls and the range is comprehensive.
Lowlight The more interesting stallholders turn up only sporadically.

RESTAURANTS

Quality Chop House currently seems to be on a roll. After the odd menu glitch last year, this time around every dish was worth ordering. Spinach, bacon, avocado and roquefort salad was good (especially the bacon), but was outclassed by a fabulous fish soup with rouille and croûtons – and both cost less than £6. We approve too of anchovy and beetroot salad replacing anchovy and tomato as a menu staple. However, the real lipsmacker came next: grilled lamb chops with chips; four little chops with huge taste. Almost as fine were a huge steak and kidney pie (a special), and melt-in-the-mouth grilled calf's liver and bacon with mash and onion. Spinach and savoy cabbage side dishes also won praise. All this meant we had no room for creamed rice pudding with apricot jam, but we did manage some generously scooped ice-creams and sorbets. A nice little wine list and on-the-ball efficient service are further pluses. We love the surroundings too; this is an original 1870s chop house, revamped but not ruined. In fact, the only reason not to stay all night is the realisation that the handsome wooden bench seating is never going to be comfortable.
Babies and children admitted: high chair. Booking advisable. Separate room for parties, seats 40. **Map 5 N4**.

★ St John (100)

26 St John Street, EC1M 4AY (7251 0848/4998/ www.stjohnrestaurant.com). Barbican tube/ Farringdon tube/rail. **Lunch served** noon-5pm Mon-Fri. **Dinner served** 6pm-midnight Mon-Sat. **Main courses** £13.50-£22.50. **Credit** AmEx, DC, MC, V.
St John closed for a spring clean in summer 2008, but apart from a good scrub behind the ears, it's business as usual at this leading light of the British revival movement. Considering the heaps of praise it receives, the restaurant is a remarkably austere-looking and modest place, opened in the shell of a former Smithfield smokehouse by architect and chef-patron Fergus Henderson. Its spirit hasn't changed since the start in 2004. The

focus is entirely on seasonal and unusual British ingredients, simply cooked and presented. Some dishes, such as roast bone marrow with parsley, have become classics; the eccles cake with lancashire cheese also has a cult following. Others, such as pig's head and radishes, or chitterlings and carrots, are more challenging. Despite St John's reputation for offal, there are usually some interesting meat-free dishes, even if they're simple pairings such as fennel and berkswell cheese, or a starter simply named 'kohl rabi'. Puddings are terribly old-fashioned English: treacle toffee and ice-cream, or bread pudding and butterscotch sauce. If you find the dining room too formal (or expensive), try eating in the no-reservations bar, which pares down the menu and is more convivial (aka noisier).
Babies and children welcome: high chairs. Disabled: toilet (bar). Separate room for parties, seats 18. **Map 5 O5**.

Top Floor at Smiths

Smiths of Smithfield, 67-77 Charterhouse Street, EC1M 6HJ (7251 7950/www.smithsof smithfield. co.uk). Barbican tube/Farringdon tube/rail. **Lunch served** noon-2.45pm Mon-Fri; 12.30-3.45pm Sun. **Dinner served** 6.30-10.45pm Mon-Sat; 7-10.15pm Sun. **Main courses** £16-£30. **Credit** AmEx, DC, MC, V.
After ascending in the cramped, blood-red lift, it's a relief to emerge into the mannered surrounds of the Top Floor. In contrast to the lofty dining room and bar below, with their stripped-down aesthetic, it's an intimate, elegant space. Pristine tablecloths, muted lighting and brown leather chairs are smart without being stuffy. Sliding floor-to-ceiling glass doors open on to the terrace, with its well-spaced tables and magnificent views across the rooftops to St Paul's. The best dishes on the concise menu are often the most simple, showcasing unimpeachable seasonal ingredients: English asparagus with a fried egg and parmesan, say, or deliciously fresh, parsley-studded Dorset crab on toast. The steaks are justly famed, with a

daily-changing list of organic and rare-breed meats from listed suppliers; our 29-day-aged Longhorn rump, accompanied by a silky béarnaise sauce, was marvellously tender and full of flavour. Other dishes proved less successful; overly dry salt and pepper squid came drizzled with an artificial-tasting chilli sauce, while a juicy slab of roast monkfish was accompanied by violently over-salted spinach and cloying, orange-infused pickled fennel. Charming, attentive service partially made up for such faults, but next time we think we'll stick to the steaks.
Babies and children welcome: high chairs. Booking advisable. Disabled: lift; toilet. Separate rooms for parties, seating 6-24. Tables outdoors (8, terrace). **Map 11 O5**.

Covent Garden

Rules

35 Maiden Lane, WC2E 7LB (7836 5314/ www.rules.co.uk). Covent Garden tube. **Meals served** noon-11.30pm Mon-Sat; noon-10.30pm Sun. **Main courses** £17.95-£24.50. **Credit** AmEx, MC, V.
Rules, established in 1798, is London's oldest restaurant, and it's doing a good job of growing old gracefully, managing to stay relevant rather than turning into a museum piece. The main, horseshoe-shaped dining room is a symphony of burgundy leather. The walls are decorated with old cartoons, and seating is generously spaced, including some capacious booths. There's also a spiffingly presented bar. The menu treads a delicate path between generational staples such as liver and bacon and chicken curry, simple potted dishes and cold cuts, and more knowing nods to current Modern British food trends. Service and presentation were impeccable when we visited, yet quality was slightly variable: an asparagus soup was velvety, but a risotto too blobby; a duckling with black cherry sauce was delicious, but a steak and kidney pudding featured a leaden suet casing – poor for a signature dish, however traditional.

Opening Times:	Monday to Sunday	07:00 - 10:30
		12:00 - 14:30
		18:00 - 22:30

Restaurant bookings: 0207 616 5930
Group bookings: 0207 479 3895
Email: Brasserie@RhodesW1.com
Website: www.RhodesW1.com

Based at the Cumberland Hotel
Great Cumberland Place, Marble Arch
London
W1H 7DL

Opening Times:
Closed Sundays and Mondays

Lunch • *Dinner*
Tuesday to Friday • *Tuesday to Saturday*
12:00 - 14:30 • *19:00 - 22:30*

Restaurant bookings: 0207 616 5930
Group bookings: 0207 479 3895
Email: Restaurant@RhodesW1.com
Website: www.RhodesW1.com

Based at the Cumberland Hotel
Great Cumberland Place, Marble Arch
London
W1H 7DL

Hix Oyster & Chop House. See p55.

Still, provenance of the ingredients is impeccable: venison from the Highlands, lobster from the Scilly Isles – Rules even has its own game estate in the Pennines. As you might suspect, desserts are thoroughly British: golden treacle sponge pudding; and, in summer, gooseberry fool with elderflower. *Babies and children welcome: children's portions; high chairs. Booking advisable. Dress: smart casual.* **Map 18 E5.**

Holborn

Great Queen Street

32 Great Queen Street, WC2B 5AA (7242 0622). Covent Garden or Holborn tube. **Lunch served** noon-2.30pm Tue-Sat; 2pm sitting Sun. **Dinner served** 6-10.30pm Mon-Sat. **Main courses** £10-£26. **Set lunch** (Sun) £30 4 courses. **Credit** MC, V.

Right from the start, Great Queen Street has been highly popular. Booking is essential and at dinner you may be given a time slot: a notion that fights

with the relaxed, pub-like surroundings. It's also galling, at these prices, to be told there's no English mustard, and that the ale is off. But disregard such irritations, as the robust food is worth it. After several meals here in the past few months we've yet to find something we didn't like. The biggest disappointment we can muster was a blood-orange pot that was slightly spoiled by the great dollops of cream accompanying it. Highlights include hare ragù (a rich, savoury delight), braised Hereford beef with carrots and dumplings (a surefire winner on a cold night) and custard tart with prunes (marvellous, especially the silky-smooth custard). Service is young and personable, and there's generally a happy buzz about the place. New this year: a Sunday lunch session, just like at sister establishment Anchor & Hope (*see p119*), where diners sit and are served together, and the Dive bar which has opened in the basement, serving snacks as well as drinks.
Babies and children admitted. Booking advisable. Disabled: toilet. **Map 18 E3.**

King's Cross

Konstam at the Prince Albert

2 Acton Street, WC1X 9NA (7833 5040/ www.konstam.co.uk). King's Cross tube/rail. **Lunch served** 12.30-3pm Mon-Fri. **Dinner served** 6.30-10.30pm Mon-Sat. **Main courses** £10.50-£17. **Credit** AmEx, MC, V.

The USP at this eco-conscious restaurant is that 'over 85% of the produce used… is grown or reared within the area covered by the London Underground network'. Which is not to say that owner/chef Oliver Rowe's menu is limited or unimaginative. Soft boiled egg and blue cheese salad, ballasted by some good bread, just pipped a sprat, beetroot, diced potato, dill and sour cream combo for best starter – the latter sounding better than it tasted. All was well with main courses of sea bass with almond sauce and purple sprouting broccoli, and lamb chops with barley and braised chard (good ingredients, well handled), and a side

temple place 12
restaurant

12 Temple Place Restaurant • Temple Place • London • WC2R 2PR
T: 020 7836 3555 • www.12templeplacerestaurant.co.uk

12 Temple Place Restaurant is a modern British cuisine restaurant and has been labelled as the 'new home of modern British cuisine'

Modern British cuisine which concentrates on only regional local ingredients. The dishes combine traditional British recipes with modern innovations which will change seasonally.

A capacity to sit 50 guests inside and another 50 outside in the Garden Courtyard where you can enjoy al-fresco dining surrounded by waterfalls and plant life to create a serene dining experience.

of fried potatoes was home-cooked heaven. Try the unusual ice-creams, such as quince, for dessert. The short wine list roams as far as Italy, but contains several bottles from England; there's cider, plus beer from Meantime in Greenwich. Service is attentive and the cutely designed room is attractive, but it's pretty small and tables are snug. This doesn't matter if you're a party of four or more, but couples might think twice; we ended up knowing far too much about Rupert and Caroline at the next table.
Babies and children admitted. Booking advisable. Disabled: toilet. Separate room for parties, seats 18. Tables outdoors (2, pavement). **Map 4 M3.**

Mayfair

The Albemarle NEW

Brown's Hotel, 33-34 Albemarle Street, W1S 4BP (7493 6020/www.roccofortehotels.com). Green Park tube. **Lunch served** noon-3pm Mon-Sat; 12.30-3pm Sun. **Tea served** 3-6pm Mon-Fri; 1-6pm Sat, Sun. **Dinner** served 6-10.30pm Mon-Sat; 7-10.30pm Sun. **Main courses** £14.25-£29.75. **Set lunch** (Sun) £25 2 courses, £30 3 courses. **Set tea** £35 (£44 incl glass of champagne). **Credit** AmEx, DC, MC, V.
Full to bursting on a Tuesday lunchtime, bubbling with relaxed chatter, the Albemarle (formerly Brown's Grill) has emerged swan-like from a lengthy refurb, establishing itself as an exceptional watering hole. The building's period grandeur is decked with subtle contemporary furnishings, inviting folk to dress up or down – everything from Ascot hats to jeans and Uggs were on parade. The menu of British classics is immensely appealing: potted shrimps and baked razor clams, through 'dish of the day', meaty roasts, braises and stews, whole dover sole, and haddock in beer batter with chips and mushy peas – all were going down a storm. Rabbit braised in cider, along with a side order of sweet lettuce hearts, was a dish of truly inspiring simplicity and perfection; generous in quantity, the soft, long-cooked flesh departed from its bones without hesitation, the sauce delicately, gently flavoured yet of satisfying depth and unctuousness. Puddings are traditional: treacle tart and vanilla ice-cream; rice pudding and rhubarb; chocolate and pear cake with custard. Frills are limited to fresh, chewy-crusted bread and good butter, which sums up the whole place: all the fine dining glamour you could desire, deboned of the irritating prickly bits.
Children over 12 yrs admitted (lunch). Disabled: toilet (in hotel). **Map 9 J7.**

★ Dorchester Grill Room

The Dorchester, 53 Park Lane, W1K 1QA (7629 8888/www.thedorchester.com). Hyde Park Corner tube. **Breakfast served** 7-10.30am Mon-Fri; 8-11am Sat, Sun. **Lunch served** noon-2.30pm Mon-Sat; 12.30-3pm Sun. **Dinner served** 6.30-11pm Mon-Sat; 7-10.30pm Sun. **Main courses** £19.50-£42. **Set lunch** (Mon-Sat) £25 2 courses incl coffee, £27.50 3 courses incl coffee; (Sun) £35 3 courses. **Set meal** £50-£70 tasting menu. **Credit** AmEx, DC, MC, V.
There's no ignoring the decor – the Scottish theme in this grand room is inescapable, from oversize murals of tousled Highland folk to a zoomed-in tartan carpet. It may or may not be to your taste, but it's a distraction from some excellent creative cooking from noted chef Aiden Byrne, and superb service from the front-of-house team. The menu describes dishes sparely and at first glance seems to offer predictable hotel fare: summer starters included foie gras terrine, poached salmon, a lobster salad; mains the usual list of meats-plus-accompaniment. But such understatement is blown away on the plate, where spectrums of taste and texture are explored joyously yet with discipline. Smoked eel soup comprises three eel and apple confections including elver beignets, each with a different taste register; beetroot gazpacho contains dollops of avocado and lime sorbet and vodka jelly that get up and party when asked to mix. Chicken with truffle macaroni is deconstructed into shapes on the plate, but saved from pretension by rich flavours. Without imposing, staff and sommelier interpreted the

meal throughout, pacing courses carefully and making dinner an enjoyably immersive experience. It headed towards haute, but nothing felt stuffy.
Babies and children welcome (Sat, Sun): high chairs. Booking advisable; essential weekends. Disabled: toilet. Dress: smart casual. **Map 9 G7.**

St James's

Inn The Park

St James's Park, SW1A 2BJ (7451 9999/ www.innthepark.com). St James's Park tube. **Breakfast served** 8-11am Mon-Fri; 9-11am Sat, Sun. **Lunch served** noon-3pm Mon-Sat; noon-4pm Sun. **Tea served** 3-5pm Mon-Fri. **Dinner served** 5-9pm daily. **Main courses** £12.50-£22.50. **Set lunch** (Sat, Sun) £25.50 2 courses, £29.50 3 courses. **Credit** AmEx, MC, V.
The English class system is alive and well here, where self-service customers fight over tables at the back, while the front terrace overlooking the lake is reserved for the fatter of wallet. The restaurant is open from (build your own) breakfast to dinner, with the accent on local, in-season ingredients and rare breeds. Our booking was lost, and we were sent away for half an hour as the kitchen recovered from a fire. The waiters took our order, only to return with news that the kitchen would be closed for a further 20 minutes: not an auspicious start. A new menu was offered – complete with spelling mistakes; were they rushing to salvage the day's takings? We ordered halibut on samphire in sorrel sauce (firm and buttery), and a wellington of wild mushrooms, smoked cheese and spinach (more of a slice, and not as flavoursome as we'd hoped). Both these dishes from the £25.50 set lunch came without potatoes or vegetables. The decision to serve roasts with chips rather than all the trimmings suggests laziness in the kitchen. Desserts of treacle tart with clotted cream, and eton mess, were sweet and glutinous. Frankly, we didn't sample anything to match the spectacular setting.
Babies and children welcome: children's menu; high chairs. Booking advisable. Disabled: toilet. Tables outdoors (23, terrace). Takeaway service. **Map 10 K8.**

Wiltons

55 Jermyn Street, SW1Y 6LX (7629 9955/www. wiltons.co.uk). Green Park or Piccadilly Circus tube. **Lunch served** noon-2.30pm, **dinner served** 6-10.30pm Mon-Fri. **Main courses** £15-£35. **Credit** AmEx, DC, MC, V.
Prole-proof, recession-proof and frankly critic-proof, Wiltons has been trading in St James's for 260 years, settling into this location in the 1980s. It now, horror of horrors, has a website; but otherwise, from the unalloyed simplicity of the menu to the part-deferential, part-nannyish and wholly ritualistic service, it remains resolutely traditional. As suggested by the restaurant's logo (a lobster in a top hat), seafood is the thing. White-clothed tables come ready-set with fish knives, and the menu features several types of marine life (dover sole, plaice, lobster) offered a variety of ways. Having always found these excellent, we diversified this year, and were impressed if not quite bowled over. To start, the maple-coloured cold beef consommé was as delicate, in its way, as a half-avocado topped with slightly wan crab meat. Of the mains, we enjoyed a subtle omelette made with lobster, crab and specks of truffle, and a decent mixed grill highlighted by tender kidneys and a skinny steak. It's all preposterously expensive (bottled water's a fiver, desserts are twice that), but if you're worried about the prices, you probably shouldn't have come here in the first place. An institution.
Babies and children admitted. Booking advisable. Disabled: lift; toilet. Dress: smart; jacket required. Separate room for parties, seats 20. **Map 17 B5.**

Soho

★ Lindsay House

21 Romilly Street, W1D 5AF (7439 0450/ www.lindsayhouse.co.uk). Leicester Square tube. **Lunch served** noon-2.30pm Mon-Fri. **Dinner served** 6-11pm Mon-Sat. **Set dinner** (6-6.30pm)

£27 3 courses; £56 3 courses, £68 tasting menu (£110 incl wine). **Credit** AmEx, DC, MC, V.
It's not quite flavour of the month any more, but don't be deterred. Richard Corrigan's 11-year-old Lindsay House remains one of Soho's most cultured, impressive and likeable restaurants. Discreetly tucked away in an 18th-century townhouse (ring the bell), it could hardly be more intimate. Each of the two dining rooms holds fewer than 30 covers, and each retains a hushed and respectful atmosphere. The decor in both is smart and appealing, but by no means stuffy: a description that could just as easily be applied to the cooking. Corrigan's menu reads like a mix of the restrained and the earthy, but the food (essentially British with a passport) is unfailingly subtle: a winsome dish of white gazpacho served with potted crab and crunchy toast; a gentle pea risotto with jabugo ham; even a comparatively hearty pork chop with potato gratin and mustard-fruit. Amuse-gueules and petits fours provide wonderful bookends. Service is every bit as gracious as you'd hope. You'll pay for the privilege (lunch is cheaper, when the menu is broadly similar, but a privilege it will be.
Babies and children admitted. Booking advisable. Dress: smart casual. Separate rooms for parties, seating 6, 12 and 18. **Map 17 C4.**

Quo Vadis NEW

26-29 Dean Street, W1D 3LL (7437 9585/ www.quovadissoho.co.uk). Leicester Square, Piccadilly Circus or Tottenham Court Road tube. **Lunch served** noon-2.30pm, **dinner served** 5.30-10.30pm Mon-Sat. **Main courses** £12-£27. **Set meal** (5.30-6pm) £17.50 courses, £19.50 3 courses. £2 cover charge. **Credit** AmEx, DC, MC, V.
This Soho stalwart (in situ since 1926) has recently been reinvented with an agreeably slick hand by brothers Eddie and Sam Hart, the pair responsible for top-quality Spanish eateries Fino (*see p258*) and Barrafina (*see p261*). The dishes here have a British/ Modern European bent – a couple of flavours nodding towards Spain excepted (garlic and chilli razor clams). Dover sole and Colchester oysters vie for space with grill-restaurant classics including steaks, rack of lamb and relatively ethically sound rose veal. Sharing plates include a whole roast chicken and a seafood platter, or you could go on a slightly unusual route and sample the squab pigeon. Alternatives that hit the spot include fresh, well-made crab tagliatelle, which you could accompany with a vibrant, virtuous heritage tomato salad. Puddings are a high point, occupying the well-trodden ground of lemon tart and decadent profiteroles. The £2 cover charge for bread, olives and water irked us, but the quality of the food is decent. Besides, if you can afford the £500 annual fee to the members' club upstairs, two quid won't hurt.
Babies and children admitted. Booking advisable. Separate rooms for parties, seating 12 and 24. **Map 17 B3.**

Stanza

93-107 Shaftesbury Avenue, W1D 5DY (7494 3020/www.stanzalondon.co.uk). Leicester Square tube.
Bar Open 5pm-3am, **meals served** 5-11pm Mon-Sat. **Main courses** £5.50-£8.50. *Restaurant* **Lunch served** noon-3pm, **dinner served** 5.30-11pm Mon-Sat. **Main courses** £9-£16.50. **Set lunch** £11.50 2 courses, £13.50 3 courses. **Set dinner** (5.30-7.30pm) £14.50 2 courses, £16.50 3 courses. *Both* **Admission** £5-£10 after 10pm Fri, Sat. **Credit** MC, V.
On paper, the address seems a plum one: yards from Cambridge Circus, on the cusp of Soho, perfect for a working lunch or a pre-theatre dinner. The reality is different. Stanza is housed in the first-floor space once occupied by starry members' club Teatro (which remains, albeit in reduced form). While the decor is tidy and the views on to Shaftesbury Avenue are almost voyeuristic, it's simply not a very inviting room. Worse, the restaurant has virtually no presence at street level: great for imbuing exclusivity, but terrible for attracting the passing trade that Stanza needs to

survive. On the forlorn Wednesday lunchtime we visited, no other table was occupied. Perhaps understandably, the kitchen was running at half-speed when dealing with the pleasingly straightforward British menu. The results were best with dishes that required little special preparation (tangy prawn and crayfish cocktail, decent fish pie), less impressive with the trickier stuff (a lifeless pork belly served with greasy roast potatoes, wildly overcooked broccoli). We wish Stanza well, not least for its unfailingly pleasant staff, but we fear the main problem – location, location, location – may prove insurmountable.
Babies and children admitted. Booking advisable. Entertainment: DJs 10pm Wed-Sat. Separate room for parties, seats 100. **Map 17 C4.**

Strand

Simpson's-in-the-Strand

100 Strand, WC2R 0EW (7836 9112/ www.simpsons-in-the-strand.com). Embankment tube/Charing Cross tube/rail. **Breakfast served** 7.15-10.30am Mon-Fri. **Lunch served** 12.15-2.45pm Mon-Sat; noon-3pm Sun. **Dinner served** 5.45-10.45pm Mon-Sat; (Grand Divan) 6-9pm Sun. **Main courses** £15.50-£32.50. **Set meal** (5.45-6.45pm) £24.50 2 courses, £29.50 3 courses. **Credit** AmEx, DC, MC, V.
This icon of roast beef, and by extension Englishness itself, has rather fallen from greatness. Service is uncoordinated and uninterested (on the evening we visited, at least), the clientele comprised too great a proportion of tourists for any native character to emerge. Upstairs, the bar speaks more of faded than grandeur, with threadbare sofas. That said, there was a distinct spark of life where it counts: in the kitchen. The food is lighter and more imaginative than Simpson's lengthy heritage might suggest, particularly the specials. A pea and leek tart was crispy and delectable; chicken with seasonal turnip and swede pleasingly subtle. The beef processes down the aisles on its silver-domed trolley accompanied by white-hatted chefs in a Heath Robinson-esque pageant. It was delicious, but swamped by its own gravy and accompanied by bullet-hard roast potatoes. The room – more of a hall, with extravagant mouldings and panelled ceiling – is gorgeous, but the glories of the past don't compensate for the inadequacies of the present, especially given the prices. The Savoy Group should look to its laurels.
Babies and children welcome: high chairs. Booking advisable. Disabled: toilet. Dress: smart casual; no jeans, T-shirts or sportswear. Separate rooms for parties, seating 50 and 120. **Map 18 E5.**

Trafalgar Square

★ National Dining Rooms ⑩

Sainsbury Wing, National Gallery, Trafalgar Square, WC2N 5DN (7747 2525/www.the nationaldiningrooms.co.uk). Charing Cross tube/rail. **Bakery Snacks served** 10am-5.30pm Mon, Tue, Thur-Sun; 10am-8.30pm Wed. *Restaurant* **Lunch served** noon-3.30pm daily. **Dinner served** 5-7.15pm Wed. **Set meal** £17.50 1 course, £24.50 2 courses, £29.50 3 courses. **Credit** AmEx, MC, V.
The death of Shaun Gilmore in a motorcycle accident in March 2008 deprived London of one of its brightest young chefs. However, the restaurant over which he presided, winner of the 2007 Best British Restaurant gong at the *Time Out* Eating & Drinking Awards, remains in fine shape. Housed in the National Gallery's Sainsbury Wing, the Oliver Peyton-run operation offers a variety of eating options. You can choose from a bar menu, sample an array of tempting baked goods, or even (a real Peytonian touch, this) a cultured, cheeky afternoon tea. But the real attraction remains the main menu, which offers an enlightened update of British staples and delivers them with skill and efficiency. Chilled cucumber and ginger soup came with subtle Dorset crab and a hint of melon; a chicken liver mousse was a one-note starter tuned to a pitch-perfect concerto. Mains were just as impressive: gently poached trout served with spring greens; and a wonderful melt-in-the-mouth ox cheek, braised with great patience, making a lovely match for a side of creamed spinach. Desserts remain a weakness, but this is otherwise excellent cooking, far more impressive than its institutional location might suggest.
Babies and children welcome: children's menu; high chairs. Booking advisable. Disabled: lift; toilet. **Map 17 C5.**

Victoria

Boisdale of Belgravia

13-15 Eccleston Street, SW1W 9LX (7730 6922/www.boisdale.co.uk). Victoria tube/rail. **Bar Open** noon-1am Mon-Fri. *Restaurant* **Lunch served** noon-2.30pm Mon-Fri. **Dinner served** 7-11.15pm Mon-Sat. **Main courses** £15-£49. **Set meal** £18.70 2 courses. *Both* **Credit** AmEx, DC, MC, V.
We've never met Boisdale's owner, Ranald McDonald, but we imagine him to be an ebullient likeable fellow. Certainly, his imprimatur is all over this agreeably preposterous operation. Occupying a labyrinthine Belgravia townhouse, it's a triumph of one man's old-fashioned self-assurance over modern-day focus-group fudgery. The Scottish theme includes haggis on the menu, 'McCondoms' in the gents, and tartan virtually everywhere. Unexpectedly, McDonald supplements all this Highlandia with laid-back jazz (the musicians performing on a corner stage), and a range of Cuban cigars (available on a heated cigar terrace). Given the sheer force of the rooms' personality, it'd be easy for the kitchen to lapse into redundance, but the food is pretty impressive. From the flowery menu, we particularly enjoyed a starter of three tender scallops served on saffron mash with delicate roast haggis, and some beautifully tender roast lamb. The steaks are also very good, as of course is the list of whiskies. Indeed, the only off note was some stale-tasting bread. It's all monstrously expensive, but the clientele of exiled Scots, Belgravian toffs, curious Americans and fat-walleted business-folk don't seem to mind.
Children over 10 yrs admitted. Booking advisable. Dress: smart casual. Entertainment: jazz 10pm Mon-Sat. Separate rooms for parties, seating 16-34. **Map 15 H10.**
For branch (Boisdale of Bishopsgate) see index.

Hereford Road

★ Goring Hotel

Beeston Place, Grosvenor Gardens, SW1W 0JW (7396 9000/www.goringhotel.co.uk). Victoria tube/rail. **Breakfast served** 7-10am Mon-Fri; 7-10.30am Sat; 7.30-10.30am Sun. **Lunch served** 12.30-2.30pm Mon-Fri, Sun. **Dinner served** 6-10pm daily. **Set lunch** (Mon-Fri) £35 3 courses; (Sun) £40 3 courses. **Set dinner** (6-6.30pm) £32 2 courses, £47.50 3 courses. **Credit** AmEx, DC, MC, V.

The Goring Hotel's well-judged version of modern Englishness – grand over grandiose, service over servility – suits its restaurant well. It's a gracious, light-filled corner room, decorated by Lord Linley, no less) largely in white, the only showy element the branching modern chandeliers from Swarovski. The menu arranges top-quality British ingredients from Scotland to Cornwall into ostensibly simple combinations. On the plate, things are more complex: each flavour teased out by whatever technique or accompaniment best does the job, including some elusive spicing. Sea bass is steamed then teamed with chive sauce, jerusalem artichokes are roasted in their skins, goat's cheese souffléd. The only slip on our recent visit was in the beef wellington, which was surprisingly soggy. Puddings and British cheeses are wheeled round on a trolley. Everything, wines included, is served with ceremony, by a team led by restaurant manager Stuart Geddes, who deserves mention for his assured conviviality and the atmosphere he fosters, enjoyed by a diverse but uniformly appreciative clientele.
Babies and children welcome: high chairs. Booking essential. Disabled: toilet (in hotel). Dress: smart casual. Separate rooms for parties, seating 6, 12 and 40. Tables outdoors (9, terrace). **Map 15 H9.**

West
Bayswater

★ Hereford Road NEW (100)
2008 RUNNER-UP BEST NEW RESTAURANT
3 Hereford Road, W2 4AB (7727 1144/ www.herefordroad.org). Bayswater tube. **Lunch served** noon-3pm daily. **Dinner served** 6-11pm Mon-Sat; 6-10pm Sun. **Main courses** £8-£16. **Credit** AmEx, MC, V.

Chef Tom Pemberton is a graduate of St John and St John Bread & Wine, and the influence behind his forthright cooking style is clear, from the deep-fried calf's brain starter to the use of laverbread and piccalilli elsewhere. You could only be dining in Britain. Cockles with cider and lovage featured some of the plumpest, juiciest cockles we've eaten. It was an inspired take on moules marinière with the celery-like lovage providing an aroma and flavour that was true Brit. Grilled venison and beetroot came – like the rest of the dishes – utterly plain, with only the perfectly cooked, fine-grained meat and the dressed beetroot and beet-leaves. Such simplicity is daring. We would have preferred our duck livers a bit more rare in the centre, but the generous portion of green beans in a tarragon-mustard dressing was a great foil for the livers' rich flavour. Desserts such as eton mess and raspberry ripple seem designed to appeal to the diner's inner child, but the wines are strictly for grown-ups, with a succinct, Franco-centric list. The room is suitably sparse and there's no music; just the chatter of appreciative diners.
Babies and children welcome: high chairs. Booking advisable. Disabled: toilet. Tables outdoors (3, pavement). **Map 7 B6.**

Olympia

Popeseye Steak House
108 Blythe Road, W14 0HD (7610 4578/ www.popeseye.com). Kensington (Olympia) tube/ rail. **Dinner served** 7-10.30pm Mon-Sat. **Main courses** £10.95-£49. **No credit cards.**

The perfect local – as long as you like steak. The menu lists popeseye (rump), sirloin and fillet, in sizes ranging from 6oz to 30oz (170g to 840g), all of which come with OK chips and a dazzling array of condiments. The only side dish is a mixed salad

that has improved in quality over the years. There are no starters, and just a short list of puddings on a blackboard; we always plump for ice-cream or sorbet and they're always worth ordering. But steak really is the point of this place and luckily it's all good stuff (hung for a minimum of two weeks). A small sirloin served medium rare just melted under the knife. Service is down-to-earth and very competent; the decor (a few paintings and some fairy lights) doesn't seem to have changed since the place opened, but the interior is spotlessly clean. Inevitably the wine list majors on reds. Pay the Popeseye a visit – it's a world away from identikit chain restaurants.
Babies and children admitted. Booking advisable. Restaurant available for hire. **Map 20 C3.**
For branch see index.

South West
Barnes

Barnes Grill
2-3 Rocks Lane, SW13 0DB (8878 4488/ www.awtrestaurants.com). Barnes or Barnes Bridge rail/209, 283 bus. **Lunch** served noon-2.30pm Tue-Fri; noon-4pm Sat. **Dinner served** 6.30-10.30pm Mon-Thur; 6.30-11pm Fri; 6-11pm Sat. **Meals served** noon-10pm Sun. **Main courses** £12.25-£35. **Set lunch** (Tue-Fri) 12.95 2 courses, 14.95 3 courses. **Credit** AmEx, MC, V.

The canopy outside Antony Worrall Thompson's Barnes Grill is showing its age but, once you enter, all's light and airy in this quirky, crescent-shaped room. The staff were relaxed – happy for us to share starters and desserts – offering up five types of bread to munch while we pored over the menu. The accent is on high-quality ingredients prepared simply. Potted shrimp was a lively starter, slivers of zesty gherkin cutting through the paprika-packed shrimp. To follow, a 10oz ribeye came charred on top, pink in the middle and surrendered effortlessly to the knife. Both the thin-cut and chunky chips were winningly crisp. Another main, salmon fish cake, was harder going (it was the size of a small tyre), while 'crusted' tomatoes were the sort of dish Delia Smith might have knocked up on *Swap Shop* in the 1970s. Dessert of pecan pie with chantilly cream was pleasingly brittle; on seeing us struggle with our spoons, the waiter discreetly dropped off a knife. Prices are high; a meal for two can easily top £100 for what's essentially bistro fare. Small wonder, then, that most of our fellow diners seemed to be out on a special treat.
Babies and children welcome: high chairs. Booking advisable, essential weekends.
For branches (Kew Grill, Notting Grill) see index.

Chelsea

Jimmy's NEW
386 King's Road, SW3 5UZ (7351 9997/ www.jimmyschelsea.com). Sloane Square tube. **Lunch served** noon-3pm Mon-Sat, noon-4pm Sun. **Dinner served** 5.30-11pm Mon-Sat; 6-10pm Sun. **Main courses** £13.50-£35. **Set meal** (lunch, 5.30-6.30pm, 10.30-11.30pm) £15 2 courses. **Credit** AmEx, DC, MC, V. **No credit cards.**

A bright, cheerful restaurant on the King's Road, with alfresco seating in good weather: so far, so welcome. Jimmy's weekly-changing menu has a retro British theme that appeals too – salmon fish cake, shepherd's pie, knickerbocker glory (in which both ice-cream and jelly are made in-house) – though the kitchen isn't averse to the likes of parmesan, balsamic vinegar and lemongrass. As Catherine Tate fans will note, there's even soup, tomato, cold (gazpacho). Sunday lunch typically sees roast rib of Aberdeen Angus beef with yorkshire puddings and roast potatoes, and garlic roast chicken with Jersey Royals and curly kale, joining menu staples such as baked sea bream with sauce vierge. We've found the cooking competent, if a little bland. The wine list includes a welcome wider-than-usual choice of champagne, plus over 20 wines offered by the glass. The interior has a feminine twist (creamy leather, chandeliers,

Interview
TOM PEMBERTON

Who are you?
Head chef and co-owner of **Hereford Road** (*see left*).

What's the best thing about running a restaurant in London?
I love the job and get to talk to a lot of the customers, who come from all sorts of backgrounds.

What's the worst thing?
All the bureaucracy: filling in forms, tax. Putting out the rubbish. Parking is quite difficult around here too, so customers having their cars towed away is a problem.

Which are your favourite London restaurants?
Moro (*see p258*) has been going for many years, but the cooking is still very exciting and there is always something new and interesting to eat there, even though the food is very simple. I like **St John Bread & Wine** (*see p55*), where I used to work. It's had a big influence on me. I like it for pioneering British food with real style to it. I don't drink so I don't go to many pubs and bars, but I like the **Anchor & Hope** (*see p119*) which serves tasty food made using good ingredients. I also like to go out to our local tandoori and Thai restaurants, or to various places down the Edgware Road for relaxing, unchallenging meals out.

How green are you?
It's important, but it's a struggle. We recycle as much as we can, but the council seems to be overburdened by it and can't, for example, take all the bottles. We try to buy as much from the UK as we possibly can, and have always given customers a free jug of water on the table.

What is missing from London's restaurant scene?
I have a three-and-a-half-year-old daughter and think we need more local restaurants that are family-friendly, inexpensive and do good-quality, simple food. At Hereford Road we have always tried to be accessible to young families, but for some reason the people around here don't seem to want that so much.

gleaming mirrors, shiny glass bannisters) that makes Jimmy's a pleasant stop-off on the way home from a shopping trip.
Babies and children welcome: high chairs. Booking advisable. Separate rooms for parties, seating 10-24. Tables outdoors (3, pavement). **Map14 D12.**

South

Kennington

Franklins
205-209 Kennington Lane, SE11 5QS (7793 8313/www.franklinsrestaurant.com). Vauxhall tube/rail. **Meals served** 9am-9pm Mon-Sat; 10am-4pm Sun. **Main courses** £8-£16. **Credit** AmEx, MC, V.
Previously seriously meaty, Franklins received some snooty reviews when it opened. Fortunately, the owners have reversed its fortunes with a canny focus on local produce; even the mineral water doesn't have far to travel and comes in recyclable bottles. A deli counter sells fresh vegetables plus some of the meat and cheeses featured in the dishes. Outside, a spacious courtyard (shared with a neighbouring Thai restaurant) makes busy Kennington seem a world away. The short menu changes daily and offers a choice between snacking and a blowout. The cheese on our welsh rarebit had a nice blueish tang and came speckled with worcestershire sauce. For mains, leg of lamb had been diced into fat morsels – delicious, but deserving of a bigger-hitting accompaniment than watery spinach and bland aïoli. The waitress failed to ask how we wanted our ribeye steak; she realised her mistake after a ten-minute hiatus, which may have contributed to our long wait. A dessert of chocolate chilli parfait was cloying, with ginger the dominant spicy note. Still, despite our hit and miss meal, Franklins is a success: and with its daily-changing menu, we hope for better luck next time.
Babies and children welcome: high chairs. Booking advisable. Tables outdoors (15, courtyard). **For branch see index.**

South East

London Bridge & Borough

★ Magdalen
152 Tooley Street, SE1 2TU (7403 1342/www.magdalenrestaurant.co.uk). London Bridge tube/rail. **Lunch served** noon-2.30pm Mon-Fri. **Dinner served** 6.30-10.30pm Mon-Sat. **Main courses** £13.50-£21.50. **Credit** AmEx, MC, V.
Tooley Street with its old warehouses, tacky London Dungeon-style attractions and giant office developments doesn't look quite the place to find a snug and smart modern restaurant, so the Magdalen comes as a very attractive surprise. It's extremely comfortable, with discreetly elegant, understated decor and a slightly hushed atmosphere in its ground- and first-floor dining rooms. The frequently changing seasonal menus are imaginative and notably refined, and show admirable ambition. Duck ham with peas and mint made a lively starter full of freshness; a warm squid and saffron salad was less memorable than our other choices, but still pleasant. Meats seem to be handled exceptionally well, as in a wonderfully tender roast Middle White pork loin with sage and potato gratin, but roast cod was deliciously smooth too, served with potato purée and a perfectly balanced red pepper vinaigrette. This left us happily satisfied, but it was hard to miss the fresh desserts, like an unfeasibly light french toast with apricot jam and vanilla ice. Service is charming, presentation very pretty. The wine list stays close to classic European regions, and could do with more variety in the lower price range.
Babies and children admitted. Disabled: toilet. **Map 12 Q8.**

Roast (100)
The Floral Hall, Borough Market, Stoney Street, SE1 1TL (7940 1300/www.roast-restaurant.com). London Bridge tube/rail. **Breakfast served** 7-9.30am Mon-Thur; 7-10.30pm Fri; 8-11.30am

Sat. **Lunch served** noon-2.30pm Mon-Thur; noon-3pm Fri; noon-3.30pm Sun. **Brunch served** noon-3.30pm Sat. **Dinner served** 5.30-10.30pm Mon-Fri; 6-10.30pm Sat. **Main courses** £12.50-£24. **Set meal** (Sun) £22 2 courses, £26 3 courses. **Credit** AmEx, MC, V.
Perched above Borough Market, Roast celebrates its marvellous location with a menu inspired by British produce, much of it sourced from the stall-holders below. Affluent professionals in smart City suits like to dine here, and they're a boisterous bunch – which wouldn't be a problem if the tables weren't so crammed together. Seasonality and freshness are the buzz words and there's no doubting the quality of the ingredients. It's a pity the kitchen doesn't always do justice to its raw materials. In a variable meal, highlights included six plump rock oysters, glistening with sea freshness and sharpened with the sweet tang of apple vinegar and diced shallots. Main courses weren't as memorable – beautifully cooked whole lemon sole for example was marred by burnt sediment in the browned butter accompaniment. Equally disappointing, sautéed duck breast, although deliciously succulent, was let down by bland jus that betrayed no hint of hoped-for meaty juices. Pear and berry crumble was a serious cock-up: overcooked fruit, lumpen topping and undercooked custard. Service, like the cooking, is uneven. Drop in for breakfast instead and enjoy first-rate fry-ups and steamy pots of tea.
Babies and children welcome: children's menu; high chairs. Booking advisable. Disabled: lift; toilet. Dress: smart casual. **Map 11 P8.**

Tower Bridge

Butlers Wharf Chop House
Butlers Wharf Building, 36E Shad Thames, SE1 2YE (7403 3403/www.danddlondon.co.uk). London Bridge tube/rail/Tower Gateway DLR/ 47, 78, 142, 188 bus.
Bar **Open** 8am-3pm, 6-11pm Mon-Fri; 8am-4pm, 6-11pm Sat; 8am-4pm, 6-10pm Sun. **Breakfast served** 8am-noon daily. **Set meal** (noon-3pm, 6-11pm) £10 2 courses, £12 3 courses.
Restaurant **Lunch served** noon-3pm daily. **Dinner served** 6-11pm Mon-Sat; 6-10pm Sun. **Main courses** £14-£26. **Set lunch** £22 2 courses, £26 3 courses.
Both **Credit** AmEx, DC, MC, V.
After last year's poor review, the Chop House has delivered only a small improvement this time. But – witness the full house on a January evening – the food is only part of the point here, with stunning views of Tower Bridge and a special-occasion buzz (in a 'visiting town' kind of way) contributing to the overall experience. To make the most of the riverside location, the wood-fitted room is long and thin, with french windows to throw back in summer. It's divided into bar and restaurant areas, the latter with added napery and an extra degree of fanciness on the menu. In the bar, we started with a pitcher of flavourless prawns and an oxtail soup that was greasy and seemed to be made from inferior stock. Mains were an improvement, particularly the capably roasted pheasant, but a slightly watery fisherman's pie lacked diversity beyond a couple of rubbery clams. A dessert of rhubarb trifle was delicious, yet its sherry-soaked sponge didn't work. Service was pleasant enough and the wine list well spread. Still, given the high-ish prices and the intensifying competition, the verdict has to be: don't come for the food alone.
Babies and children welcome: high chairs. Booking advisable. Dress: smart casual. Tables outdoors (12, terrace). **Map 12 R8.**

East

Shoreditch

Rivington Bar & Grill
2008 RUNNER-UP BEST BREAKFAST
28-30 Rivington Street, EC2A 3DZ (7729 7053/ www.rivingtongrill.co.uk). Old Street tube/rail.
Bar **Open/snacks served** noon-midnight Mon-Sat; noon-11pm Sun.
Restaurant **Breakfast served** 8-11am, **lunch served** noon-3pm Mon-Fri. **Brunch served**

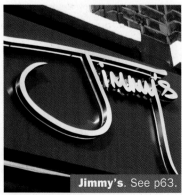

Jimmy's. See p63.

noon-4.30pm Sat, Sun. **Dinner served** 6-11pm daily. **Main courses** £9.75-£27.50. **Set lunch** (Sun) £22.50 3 courses. **Credit** AmEx, DC, MC, V. The easy-going Rivington is one of few Shoreditch restaurants aimed at the over-30s. The look is industrial-conversion, with a bar area near the door leading to a slightly raised restaurant area. It's all plainly decorated: just wood, white walls and white tablecloths, and the odd bright splash of modern art. Mornings are quiet, with noise increasing as the day progresses. We enjoyed breakfast (excellent, very buttery manx kipper, proper leaf tea) despite the amateurish lack of fresh juices (orange and pink grapefruit are claimed on the menu), but dinner remains our favourite. We like the mix and match quality of the menu (there's the possibility of things 'on toast', such as welsh rarebit or devilled kidneys), as well as its tempting dishes. Salt beef and green bean salad or smoked eel with Jersey Royals to start, for example, followed by fish 'fingers' and chips with mushy peas (a winner every time) or the more challenging lamb's heart, kidney and sweetbread with wild cabbage and mustard. Puddings are English cheeses or the likes of chocolate mousse or Yorkshire rhubarb crumble with custard. The Greenwich branch has a similar menu and ethos, but a more family-friendly vibe.
Babies and children welcome: colouring books; crayons; high chairs. Booking advisable. Separate room for parties, seats 27. Vegetarian menu.
Map 6 R4.
For branch (Rivington Greenwich) see index.

Rochelle Canteen

The Canteen, Old School Building, Arnold Circus, E2 7ES (7729 5677/www.arnoldandhenderson. com). Old Street tube/rail. **Breakfast served** 9-11am, **lunch served** noon-3pm Mon-Fri. **Main courses** £9-£12. **Unlicensed. Corkage** £3.50. **Credit** MC, V.
To reach Narnia you went through a wardrobe; here you press the buzzer on the door of this former school to enter another world. Grimy Shoreditch is left outside, and suddenly there are pretty flowerbeds and a lawn with people enjoying coffee and cakes. In the old classrooms, artists and other creatives are at work. The bike shed has been turned into a white, utilitarian restaurant with a large open kitchen. Service is sweet, knowledgeable and professional, so its inefficiency is a surprise. The chefs release dishes far too slowly given this is a lunch venue. It's hard to fault the food, though. The daily-changing menu exhibits the earthiness and simplicity developed by co-owner Margot Henderson with her husband Fergus (of St John, *see p58*). White cabbage, radish and feta salad was creamy, fresh and light: a glamorous take on coleslaw. Warm morel and cep salad featured generous chunks of mushrooms among the vibrant leaves. Mains may include a dish for sharing, such as black bream with grilled fennel and roast tomato. Despite hearty portions, we couldn't refuse the rich, heady piece of trifle. To drink, bring your own wine or stick with ginger beer.
Babies and children admitted: high chairs; nappy-changing facilities. Booking advisable. Disabled: toilet. Tables outdoors (16, courtyard).
Map 6 S4.

Victoria Park

Empress of India

130 Lauriston Road, E9 7LH (8533 5123/ www.theempressofindia.com). Mile End tube then 277 bus. **Breakfast served** 9-11.30am Mon-Fri; 9-11.30am Sat, Sun. **Lunch served** noon-3pm Mon-Sat; noon-4pm Sun. **Tea served** 3-6pm Mon-Sat. **Dinner served** 6-10pm Mon-Fri; 6.30-10pm Sat; 6.30-9.30pm Sun. **Main courses** £9.50-£18.50. **Credit** AmEx, MC, V.
Smart gastropub or upmarket neighbourhood restaurant? We're not quite sure, but at 6.45pm on a Friday, the Empress, despite its mosaic tile floor, lofty ceilings and picture windows, feels like a crèche. Families are soon replaced by unfettered adults, better able to appreciate an impressive drinks list that's heavy on cocktails but doesn't

Market

skimp on draught beers. Starters take in lamb's brain and foie gras parfait alongside a scotch beef broth too close to the tinned stuff for our liking. Mains quality veers from terrific to disappointing. Essex Saddleback pork loin chop looked wan and tasted dry, though the accompanying colcannon and parsley sauce helped alleviate this. Osso buco with white truffle mash, port and garlic jus was as good as it sounds, but a gigantic dollop of pea, mint and crème fraîche risotto looked and tasted like a cloying, savoury rice pudding. Even dessert left us conflicted; raspberry and frangipane tart tasted like mundane bakewell, but sour cream ice-cream was heavenly. Maybe we'll try bar snacks next time; chips and gravy or salt and pepper squid with chilli sauce might offer the simplicity and quality missing from the restaurant.
Babies and children welcome: children's menu; high chairs; nappy-changing facilities. Disabled: toilet. Tables outdoors (15, pavement).

North

Camden Town & Chalk Farm

Market NEW

43 Parkway, NW1 7PN (7267 9700). Camden Town tube. **Lunch served** noon-2.30pm, **dinner served** 6-10.30pm Mon-Sat.

Meals served 1-3.30pm Sun. **Main courses** £9.50-£16. **Set lunch** (Mon-Fri) £10 2 courses. **Credit** AmEx, DC, MC, V.
Camden's other Market is a ulititian British restaurant that opened late in 2007 – and it's very good. Stripped-back hardly covers it: brick walls are ragged and raw; zinc-topped tables are scuffed and marked with innumerable glass-loops; old-fashioned wooden chairs look like they were once used in a classroom at Camden Girls. They probably were. Food is similarly pared down, reliant on the flavours of high-quality seasonal produce. Starter salads made with asparagus and fennel respectively were excellent, the latter set off by flavour-ripe chunks of blue cheese. A main of dover sole, served simply with a wedge of lemon, was moist, delicate and delicious. Ox cheek with mash was richer and less subtle, but no less enjoyable: well complemented by a bottle of grenache from the choice of 20 or so wines of each colour. Our dessert, recommended by a furiously busy waitress who still found time to be chirpy and chatty, was an own-mademascarpone ice-cream – a wonderful finish. Market has been a big hit with locals, who haven't had an exciting restaurant to shout about for a while. It's a big hit with us too.
Babies and children welcome (daytime): high chairs. Booking advisable. Separate room for parties, seats 12. Tables outdoors (2, pavement).
Map 27 C2.

Caribbean

The Caribbean food scene in London is steadily maturing, with an increasing number of mid-market and more sophisticated establishments offering comfortable alternatives to the cheerful urban takeaways that once dominated, while locations stretch from Brentford to Docklands, and Crystal Palace to Chalk Farm. Any evening with a few good cocktails and plates of coconut rundown can be special, but for a date or celebratory occasion you might choose from **Glistening Waters**, **Mango Room**, or **Caribbean Scene**. **Cottons** is the place to explore rums from around the world. Among this year's new openings is **Guanabana** (reviewed in Latin American), which mixes Caribbean dishes with favourites from South America.

Central
Clerkenwell & Farringdon

Cottons
70 Exmouth Market, EC1R 4QP (7833 3332/ www.cottons-restaurant.co.uk). Farringdon tube/rail/19, 38, 341 bus. **Lunch served** noon-4pm Mon-Fri. **Dinner served** 5.30-11pm Mon-Thur; 6.30-11pm Fri, Sat. **Meals served** noon-11pm Sun. **Main courses** £7.50-£8. **Credit** AmEx, MC, V.
Cottons has long set London's benchmark for West Indian cooking. Both branches attract a smart set of Caribbean connoisseurs, although it's this outlet that's currently pulling in the cool crowd. Polished wood, plantation-style shutters and brightly coloured paintings give the venue an updated colonial look. The real head-turner, however, is the long, sleek bar, stocking over 150 rums from around the world. Cottons' menu contains all the usual traditional dishes, from jerked meats and Trinidadian fish curry, to rice and peas and fried plantain. A starter of sweet potato and callaloo tart desperately lacked the help of the sort of spiced-sweet chutney that accompanied the saltfish fritters. Yet any lack of heat was made up for with the mixed jerk meat grill, which packed a serious punch. The traditional goat curry was similarly fiery, paving the way for cans of thirst-quenching ginger beer. Those of sterner stuff should drop by the basement Rhum Jungle Bar: a dining area until 9pm, when it hosts club nights and live music. *Babies and children admitted: high chair. Booking advisable. Disabled: toilet. Entertainment: DJs 9.30pm-2am Fri, Sat. Tables outdoors (5, patio). Takeaway service.* **Map 5 N4**. **For branch see index.**

Soho

★ ★ Jerk City
189 Wardour Street, W1F 8ZD (7287 2878). Tottenham Court Road tube. **Meals served** 10am-10.30pm Mon-Wed; 10am-11pm Thur-Sat; noon-8pm Sun. **Main courses** £6-£8.50. **Credit** MC, V.
This small café is the perfect antidote to the fury and fast pace of nearby Oxford Street. If you're not already a Caribbean convert, Jerk City's welcome of smiling staff, soft reggae music and an uncomplicated menu will quickly win you over. The venue is a popular lunchtime hangout with the area's media types, yet a steady flow of dreadlock-sporting customers gives some reassurance of authenticity. Food is ordered and paid for at the counter, then brought to your table, heaped high. Jamaica's national dish, ackee and saltfish, is a popular choice, as is the jerk chicken. The portions are enormous, so no one minded us splitting a chicken roti, an East Indian-influenced dish of flour pancake wrapped around curried meat and vegetables. As with many meat dishes cooked Caribbean-style, the stewed chicken came richly seasoned: so much so that the peas and rice were a necessary respite. If you're after something lighter, try a takeaway patty – a flaky pastry pocket filled with spiced beef, chicken or vegetables. It's Jamaica's most popular fast food, and best eaten straight out of the paper bag. *Babies and children welcome: high chairs; nappy-changing facilities. Takeaway service.* **Map 17 B3**. **For branch see index.**

★ ★ Mr Jerk
187 Wardour Street, W1F 8ZB (7437 7770/ www.mrjerk.co.uk). Tottenham Court Road tube. **Meals served** 11am-11pm Mon-Sat; noon-8pm Sun. **Main courses** £7-£9. **Credit** MC, V.
It's no coincidence that two Caribbean eateries have set up shop side by side. When business partners split in 2006, Mr Jerk was renamed Jerk City and the original Mr Jerk rocked up next door. Although the two menus are virtually identical, this venue has much more space than its neighbour, with a large dining area and a separate rum-stocked bar – it also has the advantage of being fully licensed. We kicked off with a mutton soup, packed with hefty chunks of meat on the bone. Keen to try another of the one-pot wonders, we opted for the traditional Jamaican stew of oxtail and butter beans, which tasted wonderfully of real stock. Starchy side dishes (fried plantain, peas and rice, macaroni cheese) help you through the gravy-rich main courses, but be warned that the macaroni comes flecked with spicy peppers. If you can't manage dessert (that goes for the majority of customers), finish with a creamy soursop punch. *Babies and children admitted. Bookings not accepted. Takeaway service.* **Map 17 B3**.

South
Battersea

Ace Fusion NEW
110 St John's Hill, SW11 1SJ (7228 5584/ www.acefusion.co.uk). Clapham Junction rail. **Meals served** noon-11pm Mon-Thur; noon-11.30pm Fri; 10am-11.30pm Sat; 10am-10pm Sun. **Main courses** £6.95-£13.50.
A welcome alternative to the straight-down-the-line dining options in the area, Ace is staffed by a friendly and efficient team. The acronym stands for the idea that the restaurant draws on African, Caribbean and English cuisines: so you'll find ingredients like plantain, callaloo (a spinach-like vegetable) and ackee (a fruit cursed with the texture of scrambled egg), residing alongside solid old shepherd's pie and bangers and mash. The fusion element comes into play in dishes such as mango-stuffed, breaded and fried chicken, and 'Creole cod' served with tomato sauce and okra. Succulent jerk-spiced chicken was accompanied by the West Indian staple of saltfish, and very satisfying it was too, especially chased down with refreshing rum punch. Yam balls were a little bland, but side dishes and desserts garnered bonus points. The decor has a breezy feel to it, echoed in the laid-back jazz funk on the stereo. *Babies and children admitted. Restaurant available for hire. Tables outdoors (3, pavement). Takeaway service.* **Map 21 B4**.

Brixton

Bamboula
12 Acre Lane, SW2 5SG (7737 6633). Brixton tube/rail. **Meals served** 8am-11pm Mon-Sat; 1-9pm Sun. **Main courses** £7-£9. **Credit** MC, V.

Mr Jerk

TO MR JERK! DA FOOD IS ALOT! 2007

Menu

Ackee: a red-skinned fruit with yellow flesh that looks and tastes like scrambled eggs when cooked; traditionally served in a Jamaican dish of salt cod, onion and peppers.

Bammy or **bammie:** pancake-shaped, deep-fried cassava bread, commonly served with fried fish.

Breadfruit: this football-sized fruit has sweet creamy flesh that's a cross between sweet potato and chestnut. Eaten as a vegetable.

Bush tea: herbal tea made from cerese (a Jamaican vine plant), mint or fennel.

Callaloo: the spinach-like leaves of either taro or malanga, often used as a base for a thick soup flavoured with pork or crab meat.

Coo-coo: a polenta-like cake of cornmeal and okra.

Cow foot: a stew made from the hoof of the cow, which is boiled with vegetables. The cartilage gives the stew a gummy or gelatinous texture.

Curried (or **curry**) **goat:** usually lamb in London; the meat is marinated and slow-cooked until tender.

Dasheen: a root vegetable with a texture similar to yam (qv).

Escoveitched (or **escovitch**) **fish:** fish fried or grilled then pickled in a tangy sauce with onions, sweet peppers and vinegar; similar to escabèche.

Festival: deep-fried, slightly sweet dumpling often served with fried fish.

Foo-foo: a Barbadian dish of pounded plantains, seasoned, rolled into balls and served hot.

Jerk: chicken or pork marinated in chilli spices, slowly roasted or barbecued.

Patty or **pattie:** a savoury pastry snack, made with turmeric-coloured short-crust pastry, usually filled with beef, saltfish or vegetables.

Peas or **beans:** black-eyed beans, black beans, green peas and red kidney beans.

Pepperpot: traditionally a stew of meat and cassereep, a juice obtained from cassava; in London it's more likely to be a meat or vegetable stew with cassava.

Phoulorie: a Trinidadian snack of fried doughballs often eaten with a sweet tamarind sauce.

Plantain or **plantin:** a savoury variety of banana that is cooked like potato.

Rice and peas: rice cooked with kidney or gungo beans, pepper seasoning and coconut milk.

Roti: Indian flatbread, usually filled with curried fish, meat or vegetables.

Saltfish: salt cod, classically mixed with ackee (qv) or callaloo (qv).

Sorrel: not the herb, but a type of hibiscus with a sour-sweet flavour.

Soursop: a dark green, slightly spiny fruit; the pulp, blended with milk and sugar, is a refreshing drink.

Yam: a large tuber, with a yellow or white flesh and slightly nutty flavour.

a bargain. The experience was like dining at a two-star hotel. On the upside, the jerk chicken was great. If you think you've run the gamut of heat from Mexican to Indian food, try the jerk sauce here: smoky, peppery, deliciously hot. The rice and peas was nutty and perfect, and the fish salty (as is usual in Jamaican cuisine). The wine list is limited, though no bottle costs more than £20. Brown Sugar, like many Caribbean restaurants, feels more of a social hub than a dining venue, so go on a Friday or Saturday when a bar-club atmosphere prevails. *Babies and children admitted. Booking advisable. Disabled: toilet. Tables outdoors (4, pavement). Takeaway service.* **Map 21 B4.**

Brixton

Bamboula

12 Acre Lane, SW2 5SG (7737 6633). Brixton tube/rail. **Meals served** 8am-11pm Mon-Sat; 1-9pm Sun. **Main courses** £7-£9. **Credit** MC, V.
Cheerfully decorated in green, yellow and orange, this popular restaurant-café makes as good a stab at recreating the vibe of a Caribbean beach shack. The old-school reggae soundtrack hits just the right note(s), and the atmosphere is genuinely friendly. It's a shame then that the food and drink no longer match the vibe. The rum punch was shockingly sweet. The batter on the cod fritter was greasy and soft, and the filling bland and stodgy. Much better was the ackee and saltfish with plantain. Mains were equally hit and miss. Curry goat remains an excellent choice, but our accompanying rice and peas was dry. Baked tilapia didn't work at all – the fish overpowered by a heavy okra sauce. It's not just the food that feels a little tired: the credit card machine wasn't working; the Red Stripe had run out; and the sole waitress seemed more than ready to go home when she closed up after us.
Babies and children admitted. Booking advisable Fri, Sat (£5 deposit for more than 4 people). Tables outdoors (2, garden). Takeaway service. **Map 22 D2.**

South East
Crystal Palace

Island Fusion NEW

57B Westow Hill, SE19 1TS (8761 5544/ www.islandfusion.co.uk). Gypsy Hill or Crystal Palace rail. **Dinner served** 5-11pm Mon-Thur; 5-11.30pm Fri, Sat. **Meals served** noon-10.30pm Sun. **Main courses** £9.50-£17.50. **Set lunch** (Sun) £18 2 courses, £22 3 courses incl coffee. **Credit** MC, V.
This small, bamboo-covered dining room creates the right vibe, with two huge murals providing eternal sunsets. Waitresses give a warm greeting, and the barman makes a perfect rum punch. Soul music completes the impression of a chilled tropical refuge. The starter platter is a brilliant way to sample the cooking. You get crispy king prawns doused in coconut, hot jerk chicken wings, rounds of plantain and callaloo, and saltfish fritters; it's just £8.50 for two people. The mains menu comprises Caribbean classics – more jerk chicken, fish stew, fried chicken – plus steak. Mutton curry with rice and peas was delicious: the meat moist but lightly browned. Creole fish stew also verged on the sublime, the bream marinated in a subtly spiced, slightly buttery sauce. To finish, guava cheesecake bettered the crème brûlée.
Babies and children welcome (until 7pm): high chairs. Booking advisable. Disabled: toilet.

East
Docklands

Caribbean Scene

ExCeL Marina, 17 Western Gateway, Royal Victoria Dock, E16 1AQ (7511 2023/ www.caribbeanscene.co.uk). Royal Victoria DLR. **Meals served** noon-10.30pm daily. **Main courses** £11.50-£35.50. **Credit** AmEx, MC,V.
Caribbean Scene has hit the bull's-eye for lucrative locations: three neighbouring hotels, a waterfront view, and both Canary Wharf and the ExCeL

Centre nearby. You might expect customers to be expense-account types, but our visit saw more than half the restaurant filled with immaculately dressed West Indians. The menu showcases top-end Caribbean cuisine, including saltfish fritters, jerk chicken and crab claws. We opted for curried goat and jerk chicken, both notably expensive for relatively low-cost ingredients. After close to an hour, the chicken arrived worryingly undercooked, about which staff were nonchalant and had to be prompted to take it back to the kitchen. The goat curry, however, was perfectly tender, coated in a rich, coconut-flecked sauce. Surrounded as we were by frustrated customers, we didn't dare order dessert, instead trying a couple of sugar-heavy cocktails in the bar on the way out.
Babies and children welcome: high chairs. Booking advisable Fri-Sun. Disabled: toilet. Entertainment: live band 7-10.30pm Fri, Sat. Tables outdoors (18, patio). Takeaway service.

North
Camden Town & Chalk Farm

★ Mango Room

10-12 Kentish Town Road, NW1 8NH (7482 5065/www.mangoroom.co.uk). Camden Town tube. **Meals served** noon-11pm daily. **Main courses** £10-£13. **Credit** AmEx, MC, V.
Of all the places in need of some Caribbean sunshine, the corner by Camden tube is high on the list. Set alongside instant eateries for the loud and lairy, the Mango Room has made its name as the odd one out. Intimate tables dotted with tea lights fill two dining rooms decorated in shabby-chic style. The smiley calm staff are remarkably knowledgeable about the short but imaginative menu, which puts a modern stamp on Caribbean classics. A starter of plantain and sweet-potato fritters with own-made sweet chilli sauce arrived plated like a work by Miró. Mains and desserts were presented with similar pomp, but the combinations of unusual flavours were quite faultless. A honey-and-ginger-seasoned duck breast with juniper berry sauce was delectable, as was a cassava and coconut tart. Clued-up customers largely ignored the substantial wine list, instead opting for beer or cocktails from a sizeable choice. The relaxed atmosphere and delicious food keep the Mango mighty, and booking is a must.
Babies and children welcome: high chairs. Booking advisable weekends. Restaurant available for hire. Separate rooms for parties, seating 10-20. Takeaway service. **Map 27 D2.**

Outer London
Brentford, Middlesex

★ Glistening Waters

5 Ferry Lane, Ferry Quays, High Street, Brentford, Middx TW8 0AT (8758 1616/ www.glisteningwaters.co.uk). Brentford or Kew Bridge rail. **Meals served** 6pm-11.30pm Tue-Fri; 3pm-midnight Sun; 1-10.30pm Sun. **Main courses** £10.95-£50. **Credit** MC, V.
The Thames doesn't glisten much on the dreary riverside walk from Kew Bridge station to the characterless concrete block that houses Glistening Waters. But inside the plain yet colourfully lit interior, there's a cosy vibe. Cool Caribbean and western pop plays quietly so people can chat and chill. Service on our trip was slow but smiley, and the rum punch was, for once, not too sugary. Without doubt, the Caribbean food here is among London's best. Jerk chicken with avocado salad, drizzled with sesame oil, made a lovely starter. Mains of curried goat with basmati rice, and tiger prawns in coconut rundown, were sublime; the former had the full taste of slowly simmered Jamaican home cooking (explaining the slow service?). Portions were big. Dessert was coffee and tropical fruit crumble (perfect), ending what must surely be the best evening-out in Brentford.
Babies and children welcome: high chairs. Bookings advisable. Tables outdoors (2, terrace).

Chinese

Chinatown is dead, long live Chinatown! Even as we were about to announce the demise of Soho's famous Chinese district as a place for serious students of the cuisine, changes were afoot. For years, the area around Soho's Gerrard Street and Lisle Street had failed to attract the best new Chinese restaurants – which instead opened in Bayswater's Queensway (**Royal China**, **Gold Mine**), or as far afield as Harrow (**Golden Palace**), Elephant & Castle (**Dragon Castle**) and Docklands (**China Palace**). But this year, there have been several important new openings in the district, most notably **Baozi Inn**, but also **Leong's Legends** and **Little Lamb**.

It is interesting that none of these three newcomers specialises in Cantonese food, which for long had a near-monopoly in Chinatown due largely to Britain's links with Hong Kong. **Baozi Inn** serves snacks hailing from Beijing and Chengdu, **Little Lamb** has a forte in Mongolian hotpot, while **Leong's Legends** majors in Taiwanese and Sichuan food. This flowering of regional Chinese cooking in London (try also, spice merchants **Snazz Sichuan** and **Bar Shu**) comes at a time when Chinese cuisine as a whole has hit the spotlight. For years we sang the praises of dim sum on these pages, but few westerners took notice until Alan Yau opened the glamorous **Hakkasan** and **Yauatcha**. In 2008 he opened **Cha Cha Moon** in Soho, which is attracting crowds for its modern take on the noodle bar.

So, our city's Chinese dining scene is again thriving, and even Westminster Council's attempts to ban the gas ovens used for cooking aromatic crispy duck (and, in some Korean restaurants, tabletop barbecues) for not meeting carbon monoxide emission levels are unlikely to put a damper on proceedings. London has discovered real Chinese food – and loves it.

Central

Belgravia

Hunan
51 Pimlico Road, SW1W 8NE (7730 5712/ www.hunanlondon.com). Sloane Square tube. **Lunch served** 12.30-2pm, **dinner served** 6.30-11pm Mon-Sat. **Set meal** £38.80-£150 per person (minimum 2). **Credit** AmEx, DC, MC, V.
Hunan can be either a delightful or a frustrating experience, depending on your expectations. For a start, customers are not given a menu. Instead, the Taiwanese owner Mr Peng or his son Michael will bring a number of small dishes until you tell them to stop. The food is neither particularly Hunanese, nor particularly Chinese – we suspect it is genuine, authentic Pengese – although regulars will quite happily ask for their favourite shredded crispy duck, or spicy squid, and it will be brought to the table. In response to a request for more adventurous dishes, we get some undistinguished jellyfish and mooli rolls; a gelatinous pig's ear roll with a satisfying crunch; and wobbly belly pork with sautéed frogs' legs, all of which work well enough. The rest of the 13 courses Mr Peng brings seem to be variations on a theme of rolled and stuffed fish and meat with bland thick sauces, including a somewhat strange turkey roll with lemongrass. Nevertheless, the dining room is comfortable, cosy, and constantly packed with regulars who like Hunan just as it is.
Babies and children admitted. Booking essential. Vegetarian menu. Map 15 G11.

Chinatown

★ ★ Baozi Inn NEW (100)
2008 RUNNER-UP BEST CHEAP EATS
25 Newport Court, WC2H 7JS (7287 6877). Leicester Square tube. **Meals served** 11am-10pm daily. **Main courses** £6.10-£6.50. **No credit cards.**
The decor, inspired by Beijing's hutongs circa 1952, signals kitsch rather than culture, and the backless wooden pews are far from conducive to a lingering lunch, yet the Beijing and Chengdu-style street snacks served here are 100% authentic. The eponymous baozi – steamed bread filled with pork or vegetables typical of northern China – can be accompanied by a bowl of slightly sweet millet porridge for a very inexpensive yet hearty meal. But the real stars are the Sichuanese street snacks. Delicate spicy flowering beancurd is composed of the silkiest own-made tofu, covered in chilli and sesame oils, with deep-fried dough and yellow soybeans (huang dao) lending texture. Don't miss the Chengdu classic, dan dan noodles, which is perfectly prepared here from noodles that are handmade on the premises daily. Soothe the hot and numbing effect of its ground-pork sauce (and that of other dishes laden with Sichuan pepper), with a fresh salad of springy poached peanuts with celery, carrots and tofu skins, or a bowl of spinach flavoured with ginger juice. Service is affable and efficient, provided you can catch the waiters' attention over the roaring Chinese opera.
Babies and children admitted. Bookings not accepted. Takeaway service. Map 17 C4.

Chinese Experience
118 Shaftesbury Avenue, W1D 5EP (7437 0377/www.chineseexperience.com). Leicester Square or Piccadilly Circus tube. **Meals served** noon-11pm Mon-Thur; noon-11.30pm Fri, Sat; noon-10.30pm Sun. **Main courses** £6.50-£22. **Set meal** £16.90-£19.90 per person (minimum 2). **Credit** AmEx, MC, V.
Despite its unpromising name, Chinese Experience has an auspiciously decorated interior (red walls, simple furnishings) and offers surprisingly satisfying, no-fuss dining. The typically long menu includes a page of chef's special recommendations, many of which sound enticing. Braised pork belly in chinese five-spice arrived as a mountain of tender meat cloaked with a savoury, spicy, thick sauce. Steamed chicken with chinese mushrooms and cloud-ear fungus was fragrant with the lotus leaf in which it had been steamed, although the silky-soft mushrooms were let down by the chicken being slightly overcooked. Pea shoots stir-fried with garlic were crisp, crunchy, not too oily and pleasantly spiked with nutty, salty garlic. Our final order, pei pa beancurd, had been stuffed with minced prawns and water-chestnuts, then fried and garnished with enoki and shiitake mushrooms – a pleasing combination of textures and flavours. Savouring competently produced Cantonese food is the Chinese experience you're likely to have here.
Babies and children welcome: high chairs. Booking advisable. Takeaway service. Vegetarian menu. Map 17 C4.

Crispy Duck
27 Wardour Street, W1D 6PR (7287 6578). Leicester Square or Piccadilly Circus tube. **Meals served** 10am-4am daily. **Main courses** £5-£18. **Set meal** £11.50-£12.50 per person (minimum 2). **Credit** MC, V.
With its nondescript exterior and not-so-attractive interior, Crispy Duck wouldn't be a dining destination were it not for word of mouth. The firm operates a sleeker-looking joint in Chinatown's Gerrard Street, but this branch is altogether more modest and carefree. The crispy duck is, as you'd expect, of a high standard, but this old-timer has more to offer. Salt and chilli spare ribs were lip-smackingly good: just the right kick

BEST CHINESE

For pzazz
Glam it up at **China Tang** (see p76), **Hakkasan** (see p75), **Kai Mayfair** (see p76), **Mr Chow** (see p75) and **Pearl Liang** (see p77).

For regional delicacies
For Sichuanese food visit **Bar Shu** (see left) and **Snazz Sichuan** (see p75); sample the delights of Beijing and the north at **Baozi Inn** (see p69) and **North China** (see p78); enjoy Shanghainese cooking at **Shanghai** (see p83) and **Shanghai Blues** (see p75); then head to **Leong's Legends** (see p72) for Taiwanese extras.

For roast meats
Savour the succulence at **Crispy Duck** (see above), **Gold Mine** (see p79), **Green Cottage** (see p84) and **Royal Dragon** (see p74).

For dim sum
Dumplings delight at **China Palace** (see p83), **Hakkasan** (see p75), **Mandarin Palace** (see p84) and **Royal China Club** (see p76 and p84).

For Chinatown's finest
The pick of southern Soho's Sino-sector at **Baozi Inn** (see left), **Golden Dragon** (see p70), **Imperial China** (see p70) and **Leong's Legends** (see p72).

RESTAURANTS

Regional cooking

A basic knowledge of the four 'schools' of Chinese cuisine is helpful when examining restaurant menus. The traditional categories (Cantonese: fresh; western China: fiery and spicy; northern China: stodgy and chilli-hot; eastern China: sweet and oily) may be over-simplistic, but they are not incorrect. Sichuan's rising profile in London has taught diners about western China's penchant for spicy, numbing flavours: from sichuan peppercorns, chillies and zesty tangerine peel, for example.

China's sheer geographical diversity is key to explaining the contrasting approaches to food. The north's blisteringly cold winters have led to a culinary repertoire that includes comforting, filling noodles, buns and breads, aided by chillies and plenty of preserved and pickled meats and vegetables, plus slow-cooked stews and soups. Beef and lamb are more common here than in the inland provinces of the west, where pork is the favoured meat. Both Sichuan and Yunnan are known for their reliance on pork, the latter famed for its air-cured ham – China's answer to parma and serrano.

Also inland is Hunan; its milder climate, fertile land and proximity to lakes and rivers have earned it the nickname 'the land of rice and fish'. Guangdong and Hong Kong's humid, sub-tropical coastal locations lie behind its delicately flavoured seafood dishes and a concentration on simple fresh produce. Similarly, Fujianese cuisine (closely related to Taiwanese cooking) is influenced by its 'shan sui' (mountain, water) landscape. As a result, seafood is one of its most treasured ingredients – succulent oyster omelettes and bouncy fish balls being just two of the most favoured exports.

Shanghai, as one of the country's most cosmopolitan areas, inevitably draws in culinary influences from far and wide; however, its eastern China signature is in the use of alcohol (particularly rice wine; bordering Zhejiang is where the popular drunken chicken originated), as well as the 'red cooking' method (where soy sauce used in slow-cooking imparts a reddish hue to food) also favoured by the western Chinese. With such diversity, it's no wonder the country is so fiercely proud of its culinary traditions.

of chilli, and the meat pulling easily from the bone. We ordered roast belly pork with soy sauce chicken on rice, but were instead presented with a duck and chicken combination, after an uncomfortably long wait. Fortunately, the roast meats (for which Crispy duck is renowned) were very satisfying. Beef congee was less successful, the meat tough and chewy and the congee bland, with only the occasional peppery kick from fresh spring onions. Even though there were few customers on our visit, the service was slow. Our waiters seemed to be in a daydream, but at least they were cheerful.
Babies and children admitted. Separate room for parties, seats 15. Takeaway service. Vegetarian menu. **Map 17 B4.**
For branch see index.

Feng Shui Inn

4-6 Gerrard Street, W1D 5PG (7734 6778/ www.fengshuiinn.co.uk). Leicester Square or Piccadilly Circus tube. **Meals served** noon-11.30pm Mon-Sat; noon-10.30pm Sun. **Main courses** £6.80-£24.80. **Set lunch** (noon-4.30pm) £3.90 1 course incl tea, £5.90-£10.90 2 courses incl tea. **Set meal** £12.80-£33.80 per person (minimum 2). **Credit** AmEx, MC, V.
Right in the heart of Chinatown, Feng Shui Inn has its interior brightly decked out in shades of red, hung with festive decorations and furnished with faux Ming Dynasty furniture, creating a celebratory, if touristy, atmosphere. We didn't order from the untranslated Chinese menu, and found the cooking was geared more to English than Cantonese tastes. Much of what we ate was of a mediocre standard. Wun tun soup featured dumplings that consisted mostly of pork fat, while a plate of minced chicken served with lettuce leaf wrappers was stodgy and oily and lacked the bouncy, crumbly contrast of textures that makes the dish memorable. Salt and pepper deep-fried squid was doughy and chewy, while the 'chef's special' kam sha chicken was dry from being roasted and then deep-fried; it arrived buried in what appeared to be processed garlic chips. Service is curt and quick. An adequate stop for a fast bite, but nothing to write home about.
Babies and children admitted. Booking essential weekends. Entertainment: karaoke (call for details). Separate rooms for parties, seating 12, 20 and 40. Vegetarian menu. **Map 17 C4.**

Golden Dragon

28-29 Gerrard Street, W1D 6JW (7734 2763). Leicester Square or Piccadilly Circus tube. **Meals served** noon-11.30pm Mon-Thur; noon-midnight Fri, Sat; 11am-11pm Sun. **Dim sum served** noon-5pm Mon-Sat; 11am-5pm Sun. **Dim sum** £2.40-£4.30. **Main courses** £6-£25. **Set meal** £13.50-£40 per person (minimum 2). **Credit** AmEx, MC, V.
Further evidence that Chinatown is on the up, Golden Dragon has become a slick operation. Inside the large dining room, tradition reigns: the air-conditioning hums, chairs are metal-framed, the tablecloths pink, and two fierce dragons leap from the rear wall. Staff are plentiful and efficient – ruthlessly so when clearing plates (slurp your sauce before it disappears). Diners, a mix of Chinese couples, office workers and tourists, emit a contented buzz, thanks to food that arrives swiftly, correctly prepared and ultra-fresh. Slips in our dim sum were few and forgettable: a slightly indelicate scallop cheung fun here, a scantily filled mixed meat croquette there. More memorable were the successes: the succulent, texturally varied filling of the stuffed mixed meat dumplings; the tangy gravy and tender flesh of the baby squid in curry sauce; and above all the immaculate freshness of the Chinese broccoli in garlic. Only the failure to translate specials into English disappointed us. The full menu is notable, the vast list ranging from simple meal-in-one noodle dishes to long-simmered hotpots, banquet food (lobster, crab) and the likes of abalone with duck's web.
Babies and children welcome: high chairs. Booking advisable. Separate rooms for parties, seating 20 and 40. Takeaway service. **Map 17 C4.**

Haozhan

8 Gerrard Street, W1D 5PJ (7434 3838/ www.haozhan.co.uk). Leicester Square or Piccadilly Circus tube. **Meals served** noon-11.30pm Mon-Thur; noon-midnight Fri, Sat; noon-10.30pm Sun. **Main courses** £6-£38. **Set lunch** (Mon-Fri) £8 2 courses £10 3 courses. **Credit** AmEx, MC, V.
Haozhan brought a flash of glamour to Chinatown, with its modern decor and its fusion cuisine inspired by Hakkasan (*see p75*). On our early visits we were impressed by the skills of the chefs and the fresh, clean-cut cooking. A year or so later,

standards seem to have slipped. On our most recent visit the chilli quail, which we remembered as thrilling, seemed soggy and over-sweet, and the glamorous house-special doufu (actually tofu made into a kind of custard with eggs) was disappointing, let down by the accompanying scallops that lacked flavour and tenderness. We enjoyed a nicely assembled sichuan hot-and-sour soup, thick with slivered beancurd, cloud-ear fungus, chicken and bamboo shoot. Less exciting (though still quite good) was the taiwanese san pei chicken, stir-fried with sweet basil, chilli and spring onion. Next time we'll be more adventurous and try the Marmite prawns – an extraordinary idea. The restaurant itself is sleek and black, with coloured panels on the walls. Waiting staff seem friendlier than most in Chinatown. We hope the kitchen can recover the verve it displayed in the months after opening.
Babies and children welcome: high chairs. Booking advisable. **Map 17 C4.**

Imperial China

White Bear Yard, 25A Lisle Street, WC2H 7BA (7734 3388/www.imperial-china.co.uk). Leicester Square or Piccadilly Circus tube. **Meals served** noon-11.30pm Mon-Sat; 11.30am-10.30pm Sun. **Dim sum served** noon-5pm daily. **Dim sum** £2.30-£3.60. **Main courses** £5.90-£26.50. **Set meal** £16.50-£31.50 per person (minimum 2). **Minimum** £10. **Credit** AmEx, MC, V.
Visitors to this regal-looking restaurant must first negotiate a curved red wooden footbridge at the front entrance. Thereafter, hospitable staff lead you to tables in a handsome, wood-panelled room with low lighting. At weekends, the place is packed with chatty Chinese families and groups of students, but on a Friday night it was filled with mostly western couples and the type of diner who prefers red wine to tea. We were pleased to find the evening menu as enjoyable as the daytime dim sum. The daily house soup was a clean, savoury broth stewed from chicken bones (with hints of ginseng), served with a plate of appetising poached peanuts and black-eyed beans sprinkled with light soy sauce. Enormous steamed scallops with vermicelli noodles and shiitake mushrooms slid down deliciously, while a stir-fried dish of pork with crunchy lotus roots in nanru (fermented red beancurd) sauce was every bit as flavoursome as expected from a dish rich with this pungent condiment. The only dip in the meal was a salt-baked chicken, which tasted bland in comparison and was messily assembled. Still, there's clearly skill in Imperial China's kitchen.
Babies and children welcome: high chairs. Booking advisable. Disabled: toilet. Entertainment: pianist 7.30-10.30pm Wed-Fri. Separate rooms for parties, seating 10-70. Tables outdoors (5, courtyard). Vegetarian menu. **Map 17 C4.**

Joy King Lau

3 Leicester Street, WC2H 7BL (7437 1132). Leicester Square or Piccadilly Circus tube. **Meals served** noon-11.30pm Mon-Sat; 11am-10.30pm Sun. **Dim sum served** noon-4.45pm Mon-Sun. **Dim sum** £2.10. **Main courses** £6.80-£20. **Set meal** £10-£35 per person (minimum 2). **Credit** AmEx, MC, V.
Despite a vast full menu – taking in lobster, crab, eel and oyster dishes, an immensity of meat and vegetable stir-fries, but no hotpots – Joy King Lau is best known for dim sum. At lunchtime its narrow dark ground floor is full of customers (mostly Chinese) partaking of tea and dumplings. Wall panels, backlit in lime and pink, attempt to brighten a space made mournful by a drab green carpet and little natural light. There are similarly-sized dining rooms on the three upper floors. We found the dim sum well-priced and of impressive variety and reasonable quality. Highlights included tender, long-cooked squid rings in mild curry sauce, juicy char siu croquettes, allium-redolent prawn and chive dumplings, and spongy, slithery fish maw stuffed with springy minced prawn. Even better were the sweet dim sum: feather-light hot sponge cake (butter ma-lai ko) and perfectly crisp, wondrously round, deep-fried custard buns. Less pleasing was the overcooked and untidy 'stuffed chicken with four kinds' (including crabstick and

This is an outpost of fine Guangzhou cuisine in a part of the metropolis, long denigrated but soon to be made new.

This is an oasis of taste fortified with the sure touch to provide pleasures to the palate and satisfaction to the being.

This is the watering hole where dire thirst is quenched by tea and the fermented grape juice intoxicates.

This is where your heart is touched (dim sum) and your spirit is replete.

This is
Dragon Castle

Dragon Castle

100 Walworth Road
Elephant & Castle
London SE17 1JL

020 7277 3388
info@dragoncastle.eu
www.dragoncastle.eu

Café society

Chinatown and surrounding areas of the West End are host to myriad tiny Chinese caffs where you can eat your fill and get change from a tenner. Laid-back and often filled with an eclectic mix of students, adventurous families and Chinese pensioners (who gather for gossip over a cup of tea), these venues do brisk trade in one-plate meals and slurpingly good noodles.

Some excel in particular dishes. Our favourite for roast duck and other barbecued meats is **Canton**, while newcomer **Inn Noodle** impresses with its hand-pulled Shanghainese noodles (la mian). Quintessential Hong Kong-style caffs **HK Diner** and **Café de Hong Kong** are charming places that serve the drink of choice among eastern youth: Taiwanese bubble teas (concoctions with chewy tapioca pearls that are sucked up with extra-wide straws – delightful).

Traditional Chinese desserts are often overlooked, and rarely available in Britain. At **Café TPT** the puddings range from refreshing fruity sago concoctions, to sweet and silky beancurd in syrup – both of which make it worth a visit.

★ Café de Hong Kong
47-49 Charing Cross Road, WC2H 0AN (7534 9898). Leicester Square or Piccadilly Circus tube. **Meals served** 11.30am-11pm Mon-Sat; 11am-10.30pm Sun. **Main courses** £5-£6. **Credit** (over £10) MC, V.
Cheesy Cantonese pop blares constantly, the lighting's garish and the plastic booths can get uncomfortable, but the food here is anything but cringeworthy. All the Hong Kong favourites are present, from unctuous spag bol to creamy condensed milk on thick toast. A big steaming bowl of roast duck noodles is comfort in a bowl, as is the fail-safe option of wok-fried beef ho fun. The long list of bubble teas is formidable, but we rate the thick, aromatic sesame variation – its flavour is ambrosial. *Babies and children admitted. Bookings not accepted. Vegetarian menu.* **Map 17 C4.**

★ Café TPT
21 Wardour Street, W1D 6PN (7734 7980). Leicester Square or Piccadilly Circus tube. **Meals served** noon-1am daily. **Main courses** £6.50-£24. **Set meal** £5.90-£19.50 per person (minimum 2). **Credit** MC, V.
The acronym stands for 'tai pai tong', a type of open-air food stall popular in Hong Kong. Appropriately, the food is fast, cheap and good, but thankfully the surroundings are comfier than the folding tables and stools. Opt for a home-style soup (usually an unctuous pork bone and vegetable broth), a meal-on-a-plate (choose from rice or noodle dishes with roast meats), and one of the phenomenal desserts. The mango and pomelo sago with coconut milk is as good as it gets this side of the Orient, and the silken tofu in ginger syrup is served in a traditional wooden vessel. Service is brusque but well-meaning. *Babies and children admitted. Takeaway service. Vegetarian menu.* **Map 17 B5.**

★ Canton
11 Newport Place, WC2H 7JR (7437 6220). Leicester Square or Piccadilly Circus tube. **Meals served** noon-11.30pm Mon-Thur, Sun; noon-12.30am Fri, Sat. **Main courses** £4.50-£10. **Set meal** £10-£16 per person. **Credit** AmEx, MC, V.
Canton isn't much of a looker. The rack of glistening poultry, slabs of pork belly and neon-orange squid hanging in the window obscures the legion of sated diners within. At lunchtimes, solo diners are likely to be lumped together on a table, but then this is a sit-down and dig-in joint. The roast duck is sensational – a whiff of smokiness, with just the right amount of savoury fat between crisp skin and juicy flesh. Slices of char siu were also delightful, with lean flavourful pork. Both were laid on a bed of fluffy rice, with a silky sauce that was neither too salty nor too sweet. The crowning glory? We got change from a fiver. *Babies and children admitted. Booking advisable. Separate room for parties, seats 22. Takeaway service.* **Map 17 C4.**

★ Hing Loon
25 Lisle Street, WC2H 7BA (7437 3602). Leicester Square or Piccadilly Circus tube. **Meals served** noon-11.30pm Mon-Thur; noon-midnight Fri, Sat; noon-11pm Sun. **Main courses** £3.70-£7.50. **Set lunch** £4.50 2 courses. **Set dinner** £5.80-£9.50 per person (minimum 2). **Credit** AmEx, MC, V.
The two-course set lunch at this tiny, two-floor caff is a bargain at £4.50, but dishes lean towards Anglo-Chinese favourites such as sweet-and-sour pork and sweetcorn soup. Instead, we suggest consulting the 'economic meals' menu pasted on the front window, where larger-than-life bowls of noodles (the beef brisket was particularly tender, though the soup could have been more flavourful) and plates of rice (try the crispy pork belly) are the hidden gems. Vegetarians are catered for surprisingly well; a substantial dish of crunchy bamboo shoots, baby sweetcorn and juicy shiitake mushrooms was a plate-licking delight. *Babies and children admitted. Takeaway service. Vegetarian menu.* **Map 17 C4.**

★ HK Diner
22 Wardour Street, W1D 6QQ (7434 9544). Leicester Square or Piccadilly Circus tube. **Meals served** 11am-4am daily. **Main courses** £5-£25. **Set meal** £10-£30 per person (minimum 2). **Credit** MC, V.
Cosy wooden C-shaped booths provide some intimacy in this fast-moving Hong Kong-style caff. They also give much-needed shelter, post-partying (the Diner is open until an impressive 4am). The best dishes – such as the clay pots – are on the double-sided placard, so ignore the folding menu of typical 'set meals' catering to non-Chinese diners. The melt-in-the-mouth pork belly with preserved vegetables and chinese cabbage was reminiscent of home cooking, whereas chicken chow mein was appropriately crisp and topped with plenty of fresh beansprouts and tender meat: a far cry from the limp, mediocre takeaway version.

flaccid baby sweetcorn), and the unwieldy ovoids of beef and ginger dumplings. Staff zip around purposefully, in a fairly friendly manner. *Babies and children welcome: high chairs. Booking advisable weekends. Takeaway service.* **Map 17 C5.**

Laureate
64 Shaftesbury Avenue, W1D 6LU (7437 5088). Leicester Square or Piccadilly Circus tube. **Meals served** noon-11.30pm Mon-Sat; 11am-10.30pm Sun. **Main courses** £7.90-£25. **Set meal** £12.50-£21.50 per person (minimum 2). **Credit** AmEx, MC, V.
Of all the tourist-geared pit-stops in Chinatown, you could do worse than venture into Laureate. Located on the corner of Shaftesbury Avenue and Wardour Street, it produces a reasonable standard of cooking in a clean, friendly, if rather neon-yellow environment. As well as all the usual Anglo-Chinese choices, the menu has a list of 'Chinese' dishes including classic Cantonese food such as steamed eggs and minced pork with water-chestnuts. We ordered from both lists and were served with friendliness and efficiency. Cold slices of smoked pig's trotter came with jellyfish 'noodles'; both were a little over-seasoned with white pepper,

but otherwise fine. Pork belly with preserved vegetables was soft and savoury yet unremarkable. Of our other choices, king prawns fried with chilli and salt were crisp and bouncy, while french beans stir-fried with yellow bean sauce and minced pork were spicy-hot but too oily and lacking in depth. *Babies and children welcome: high chairs. Booking advisable. Separate rooms for parties, seating 14-30. Takeaway service. Vegetarian menu.* **Map 17 B4.**

Leong's Legends NEW
4 Macclesfield Street, W1D 6AX (7287 0288). Leicester Square or Piccadilly Circus tube. **Meals/dim sum served** noon-11pm daily. **Dim sum** £2.80-£12. **Main courses** £4.50-£18.50. **Credit** (over £12) AmEx, MC, V.
The name of this Taiwanese newcomer refers to a Chinese legend revolving around the rebel Song Jiang and his 108 comrades (sometimes referred to as 'Liang's legends'). Wooden screens and a single low-lying lamp above each table create intimacy. The impressive menu includes plenty of non-Taiwanese food – pork slices with minced garlic and chilli (suan ni bai rou), for example, is a cold appetiser from Sichuan. The translation makes

some dishes sound bog-standard. 'Stir-fried chicken with rice wine, soy sauce and sesame oil' is a famous Taiwanese dish esoterically called 'three cups chicken' (san bei ji), in which a clay pot of tender chicken pieces in rich dark caramel-coloured sauce is spiked with chillies and star anise. 'Fried oysters wrapped with egg', a staple street food of the bustling night markets of Taipei, is a moist omelette filled with succulent, briny baby oysters and stalks of garland chrysanthemum. The short list of dim sum includes delicious xiao long bao (soup-filled dumplings) and pretty pastries of succulent shredded turnip. A service charge is cheekily sneaked on to the bill as 'SC'. Even so, we liked this place – it's different from anything else out there. *Babies and children admitted. Takeaway service.* **Map 17 C4.**

★ Little Lamb NEW
2008 RUNNER-UP BEST CHEAP EATS
72 Shaftesbury Avenue, W1D 6NA (7287 8078). Piccadilly Circus tube. **Meals served** noon-10.30pm Mon-Thur, Sun; noon-11pm Fri, Sat. **Main courses** £2-£6. **Set meal** £20 per person (minimum 2). **Credit** MC, V.

Babies and children welcome: high chairs. Takeaway service. Vegetarian menu. **Map 17 C4**.

★ Jen Café

4-8 Newport Place, WC2H 7JP (no phone). Leicester Square or Piccadilly Circus tube. **Meals served** 10.30am-8.30pm Mon-Wed; 10.30am-9.30pm Thur-Sun. **Main courses** £4-£14. **No credit cards**.

Not the fanciest of caffs, but Jen is certainly homely. There's always at least one nimble-fingered woman manipulating dough by the window to draw in punters, who are rewarded with fresh, home-style pork and vegetable dumplings. Order them steamed or pan-fried. The noodles are worth trying too, with specials such as pork and preserved cabbage. Babies and children admitted. Takeaway service. **Map 17 C4**.

★ Inn Noodle NEW

25 Oxford Street, W1D 2DW (7287 5953/www.innnoodle.co.uk). Tottenham Court Road tube. **Meals/dim sum served** 11.30am-11pm Mon-Wed; 11.30am-midnight Thur-Sat; 11.30am-10.30pm Sun. **Dim sum** £1.80-£4.80. **Main courses** £5-£28. **Set meal** £8 3 courses. **Credit** AmEx, MC, V.

Skilful chefs toss and twirl noodles at the front of Inn Noodle. As they're quick to boast, 'fresh hand-pulled noodles and chinese dumplings' are the speciality. As well as Shanghainese noodle dishes, we were pleased to see other traditional and lesser-known food such as Sichuan dan dan mian (spicy noodles with a peanut and sesame broth), and zhajiang mian (a Beijing dish of noodles with minced pork and mushrooms in a fermented soy bean-based sauce). Supplement the meal with piping-hot xiao long bao, and drink a chilled glass of fresh soy milk. Babies and children admitted. Bookings accepted. Takeaway service. **Map 17 C2**. **For branch see index**.

The image of 13th-century Mongolian soldiers brewing a meaty broth in their helmets before battle is a colourful one, but feels a million miles away from this diminutive restaurant on Shaftesbury Avenue. Here, tables are set with Kenwood hobs, and the decor is a few ethnic prints and paper lanterns away from a greasy spoon. Yet the constant flow of customers (and inquisitive stares from passers-by clocking the craziness through the windows) suggests that the Mongolian hotpot may be a colourful enough image without the legend. Dining is based around an enormous metal pot – filled either with a red chilli broth or a pale herbal tonic, or split down the middle and offering both – into which customers dip meat, fish and vegetables ordered plate by plate. Some were delicious: enormous chunks of squid and thinly sliced lamb absorbed the best of the fiery broth, while needle mushrooms and thick, flat noodles made from mung beans worked well with the herbal brew. Other ingredients, including some flavourless chicken dumplings, were less successful, but all made an enjoyable mess, and the childish amusement of plunging, losing and later finding things in a bubbling broth far outweigh any culinary shortcomings.

Babies and children admitted. Booking advisable (dinner). Takeaway service. Vegetarian menu. **Map 17 C4**.

London Hong Kong

6-7 Lisle Street, WC2H 7BG (7287 0352/ www.london-hk.co.uk). Leicester Square or Piccadilly Circus tube. **Meals served** noon-11.30pm Mon-Thur; noon-midnight Fri, Sat; 11am-11pm Sun. **Dim sum served** noon-5pm daily. **Dim sum** £2-£2.80. **Main courses** £6-£18. **Set meal** £16.80 per person (minimum 2); £18.80 (minimum 4); £20.80 (minimum 6). **Credit** AmEx, MC, V.

One of many Chinese restaurants on Lisle Street, LHK tries a more upmarket approach with smartly dressed waiters, and wine glasses set on tables. Service is often a bit brusque, however, and the configuration of the room means it can be difficult to catch the attention of staff. Dim sum seems to be more popular here than the evening menu, as we've witnessed in the past, but the latter puts on a pretty good show, if you choose well. 'Whole steamed sea bass' tasted fresh and light, though we were perplexed to see the fish pre-sliced with surgical precision into rectangular slabs (hence depriving us of the pleasure of prising apart the whole fish to get at the choice parts – such as the missing tender belly and neck meat). Things improved with a clay pot of fried-then-braised tofu, shaped into round morsels. As the dish's Chinese name (but not the English one) conveyed, each bite revealed milky-soft tofu that emulated the texture of tender scallops. The bill came as soon as we'd finished the meal, though at least it was accompanied by a complimentary plate of fresh seasonal fruits.
Babies and children welcome: high chairs. Booking advisable. Separate room for parties, seats 60. Takeaway service. Vegetarian menu. **Map 17 C4**.

Mr Kong

21 Lisle Street, WC2H 7BA (7437 7341/9679/ www.mrkongrestaurant.com). Leicester Square or Piccadilly Circus tube. **Meals served** noon-2.45am Mon-Sat; noon-1.45am Sun. **Main courses** £6.20-£26. **Set meal** £10 per person (minimum 2); £17.80-£23 per person (minimum 4). **Minimum** £7 after 5pm. **Credit** AmEx, DC, MC, V.

Re-opened in January 2008 after a refurbishment (the second in two years, following a kitchen fire), the long-established Mr Kong now looks spick and span, with yellow tablecloths, catering-contract green chairs and carpet. There are two small dining areas on the ground floor, and one on the first. The restaurant caters well to its (mostly non-Chinese) customers. There's a huge choice of Cantonese food, on three menus: regular, vegetarian specials, and chef's specials. By 8pm on Monday, the ground floor was full. We began with a hotpot of curry crab with glass noodles; parts of the crab were dry, but the curry sauce was appetisingly spicy and the glass noodles absorbed the delicious flavours – an excellent start. Less pleasing was a 'special' of stuffed aubergine, green pepper and beancurd that was heavy on gloopy black bean sauce and low on pork and prawn stuffing. Fried ho fun noodles with beef were also disappointing, with soy sauce the dominant flavour. Monk's vegetables (stir-fried chinese mushrooms, pak choi, broccoli, tofu and cabbage) made a pleasant, subtle contrast to the heaviness of the aubergine and noodles. Service was fast and friendly, with the chatty manager giving a warm reception.
Babies and children welcome: booster seats. Booking advisable. Separate room for parties, seats 30. Takeaway service. Vegetarian menu. **Map 17 C4**.

New Mayflower

68-70 Shaftesbury Avenue, W1D 6LY (7734 9207). Leicester Square or Piccadilly Circus tube. **Meals served** 5pm-4am daily. **Main courses** £7-£48. **Set meal** £11.50-£22 per person (minimum 2). **Minimum** £8. **Credit** MC, V.

For years the strengths and weaknesses of this Chinatown old-stager have been apparent. Its forte? If you order proper Cantonese food (of which there is plenty on the huge menu) and show

Chinese Experience. See p69.

some knowledge of the cuisine, you're likely to be rewarded with well-prepared dishes – such as the gorgeous hotpot of belly pork with preserved vegetables (savour the tender meat, juicy fat, and wine-flavoured gravy), and the vernally fresh gai lan (Chinese broccoli) in oyster sauce. Its drawbacks? The premises are cramped and ill-kept: a series of small rooms furnished in dark-red carpets and light walls. Many of the interesting dishes are on the Chinese menu and aren't translated. Service veers between perfunctory and slapdash, via the odd involuntary spasm of benevolence, from waiters who appear in quick succession then disappear en masse. We had to stand and bellow for our pork, which arrived a full 20 minutes after other dishes. Even more unforgivable was the 'half' peking duck: a measly portion clumsily made to look bigger by resting on crushed prawn crackers made soggy by its juices. Tourists cram in here, but so too do late-night Chinese diners.

Babies and children welcome: high chairs. Booking advisable. Takeaway service. Vegetarian menu. **Map 17 B4.**

New World

1 Gerrard Place, W1D 5PA (7734 0396). Leicester Square or Piccadilly Circus tube. **Meals served** 11am-11.45pm Mon-Sat; 11am-11pm Sun. **Dim sum served** 11am-6pm daily. **Dim sum** £2.40-£4.20. **Main courses** £4.90-£10.50. **Set meal** £10.50-£14.50 per person (minimum 2). **Minimum** (after 6pm) £5. **Credit** AmEx, DC, MC, V.

Time hasn't left this vast dim sum parlour entirely unchanged. The dumplings are now served into the night (almost unheard of before Yauatcha – *see p78*– burst on to the scene) and, come Chinese New Year, red tassels adorn the elaborate chandeliers, and red dragons curl angrily from the ceiling. In other respects, New World remains steadfastly old school. The dull red carpet of antediluvian ancestry, and the metal-framed chairs should probably have been replaced decades ago – yet add to the utilitarian charm. Trolleys still circulate here, full of steamed or deep-fried snacks, pushed by women who can be chatty, but are more often brusque and shaky in English. The dim sum too is variable. Yam croquettes had a juicy minced pork filling covered by smooth yam paste and a coating of crisp fragility. Also highly satisfactory were the char siu pork puffs encased in heavenly pastry and the fresh, crunchy gai lan (Chinese broccoli). But stodginess can raise its stolid head, most evidently in the cold lotus seed buns coated in sesame seeds. Dine here early, before food has spent too long on the trolley; lunchtimes brim with authentic bustle. The full menu has seafood aplenty.

Babies and children welcome: high chairs. Booking advisable Fri, Sat dinner; not accepted Sun lunch. Takeaway service. Vegetarian menu. **Map 17 C4.**

Royal Dragon

30 Gerrard Street, W1D 6JS (7734 1388). Leicester Square or Piccadilly Circus tube. **Dinner served** 5.30pm-3am daily. **Main courses** £7.50-£23. **Set dinner** £14, £17.50, £18.50 per person (minimum 2). **Credit** AmEx, MC, V.

Royal Dragon has a less gaudy interior than a number of its Gerrard Street neighbours. While the neutral, sparse decor may lack attention to detail, the opposite is true of the cuisine, where even carrot slices are served cut into elaborate shapes. The deep-fried squid with pepper salt is particularly tasty; the combination of bouncy tender squid in a light, crisp batter topped with fried chopped garlic, shallot and fresh chilli is hot, salty and addictive. Feeling adventurous, we ordered kung po-style frogs' legs, and stewed sliced abalone with sea cucumber and ducks' feet. The kung po sauce was more sweet-sour than the expected spicy-hot, and the sea cucumber was too tough, but overall both dishes were enjoyable. The star dish was a plate of pei par duck – duck flattened into a 'pei pa' lute shape before seasoning and roasting. Served at room temperature, the

Little Lamb. See p72.

RESTAURANTS

meat was succulent and rich, with crisp lacquered skin and sweet, fruity hoi sin sauce. Another winner is crab steamed in chinese wine – a heady combination of fragrant Shaoxing wine and steaming, sweet crab in the shell.
Babies and children welcome: high chair. Booking advisable weekends. Entertainment: karaoke (7pm daily). Takeaway service. Vegetarian menu. **Map 17 C4.**

Euston

Snazz Sichuan

New China Club, 37 Chalton Street, NW1 1JD (7388 0808/www.newchinaclub.co.uk). Euston tube/rail. **Meals served** 12.30-11.30pm daily. **Main courses** £6.30-£26.80. **Set meal** £14.80-£18.80 per person (minimum 2). **Credit** (over £10) MC, V.
Gastronomic adventurers prick up your ears: 'fragrant and spicy pig tail with shank', 'hot and numbing boiled fish', 'strange-flavour rabbit'. These are just three of many delights found at this yearling restaurant devoted to western Chinese cuisine. The premises, once the Victoria pub, are split into an attractive dining room at the front, bar to the side and a more functional eating area to the rear (with striking Cultural Revolution posters). The basement houses an art gallery. Staff are sweet, yet ill-versed in English. This, coupled with the esoteric menu, can lead to problems. Dishes tend to be oily and fiercely hot – and the menu's chilli-rating system isn't accurate. Boiled rice is an essential antidote, yet ours was overcooked and arrived late. Everything else was a treat: 'fire-exploded kidney flowers' (rubbery offal matched with resilient cloud-ear fungus); 'drifting fragrant king prawns' (dry-fried with copious peanuts, chillies and numbing Sichuan peppercorns); 'white braised pork in hot and garlicky sauce' (bacon-like strips in an intensely savoury sauce); and, above all, 'fish-fragrant fried aubergine' (the trademark Sichuan dish, perfectly prepared giving smoky, sweet and vinegary flavours and a luscious oily texture). We'll be back.
Babies and children welcome: high chairs. Booking advisable dinner. Separate rooms for parties, seating 15 and 50. Takeaway service. Vegetarian menu. **Map 4 K3.**

Fitzrovia

★ Hakkasan (100)

8 Hanway Place, W1T 1HD (7907 1888). Tottenham Court Road tube.
Bar **Open** noon-12.30am Mon-Wed; noon-1.30am Thur-Sat; noon-midnight Sun.
Restaurant **Lunch/dim sum served** noon-3pm Mon-Fri; noon-4pm Sat, Sun. **Dinner served** 6-11pm Mon-Wed, Sun; 6pm-midnight Thur-Sat. **Dim sum** £3-£20. **Main courses** £9.50-£58. *Both* **Credit** AmEx, MC, V.
When Alan Yau opened this glamtastic take on the Shanghai teahouse in 2001, he redefined Chinese dining in the UK. Here was a Cantonese restaurant with the seduction technique and price structure usually reserved for French gastronomy. Today, its dark, moody, nightclub feel, chill-out lounge music, and high-ticket dining (roasted silver cod in champagne, stir-fried lobster, peking duck with caviar) still pull one of the liveliest, monied crowds in town. Hakkasan may not be the world's best Chinese restaurant (as suggested by the 'World's 50 Best Restaurants' list), but we would argue it is the best in London. Chef Tong Chee Hwee's light, modern touch gives a cool twist to the Cantonese food you thought you knew. A crisp, spicy salad of mountain yam and bitter melon in XO sauce is a textural masterclass; stewy Hakka pork ribs with preserved cabbage are rich and homely; and our old friend jasmine tea-smoked chicken has lost none of its smoky allure. A new favourite is the house-made tofu: as rich and creamy as foie gras. Neither food nor wine comes cheap, but you can always sample the brilliant lunchtime dim sum to get the Hakkasan experience for less.
Babies and children admitted (until 7.30pm). Disabled: lift; toilet. Entertainment: DJs 9pm daily. Restaurant available for hire. Separate area for parties, seats 65. **Map 17 C2.**

Holborn

Shanghai Blues

193-197 High Holborn, WC1V 7BD (7404 1668/ www.shanghaiblues.co.uk). Holborn tube.
Bar **Open/dim sum served** noon-11.30pm daily.
Restaurant **Meals served** noon-11.30pm, **dim sum served** noon-5pm daily. **Main courses** £7-£45. **Set lunch** £15 per person (minimum 2, Mon-Fri).
Both **Dim sum** £3.60-£8.60. **Credit** AmEx, MC, V.
The smart, sultry interior of Shanghai Blues makes it ideal for romantic dates – if you can overlook the corporate parties that often take large tables at this popular modern restaurant. Dusty pink screens and powder-blue chairs create a warm, relaxing atmosphere. We began with two unusual dim sum: a steamed Alaskan crab and scallop dumpling, scented with ginger and finished with crunchy flying-fish roe; and a black squid-ink and white rice flour dumpling stuffed with roast duck and earthy preserved vegetables. Both combined soft pastry with juicy fillings full of intriguing flavours and textures. These innovative takes on classic Cantonese dim sum should be the restaurant's main attraction; they are different and fun and it's worth sampling a wide selection. Braised belly pork was served in a sweet-sour sauce that provided a good contrast to the fatty meat, but the pork itself needed longer cooking to reach a meltingly tender consistency. Finally, sea bass with mushrooms and lotus roots was steamed to perfection, if a little more oily than necessary. What Shanghai Blues lacks in technical proficiency and expertise, it makes up for in imagination and enthusiasm.
Babies and children welcome: booster seats. Booking advisable; essential Thur-Sat dinner. Disabled: toilet. Dress: smart casual. Entertainment: jazz 7.30-10.15pm Fri, 7.30-11.30pm Sat. Separate room for parties, seats 30. Takeaway service. Vegetarian menu. **Map 18 E2.**

Knightsbridge

Mr Chow

151 Knightsbridge, SW1X 7PA (7589 7347/ www.mrchow.com). Knightsbridge tube. **Lunch served** 12.30-3pm, **dinner served** 7pm-midnight daily. **Main courses** £12.50-£25. **Set lunch** £25. **Set dinner** £35; £40 per person (minimum 3). **Credit** AmEx, DC, MC, V.
Since it first opened in 1968, Mr Chow has remained one of London's most eccentric, and most expensive, Chinese restaurants. The food may be Chinese, but the black-suited waiters are resolutely European, and the room – with its immaculate leather banquettes, white marble floor and metallic drop lamps suspended over every table – would be at home in Milan or Turin. Many of the people who eat here are rich, or American, or both. Most of them have come for what, at £40 a head, must be London's priciest peking duck. We try the more accessibly priced 'gambler's duck' which turns out to be just another name for good old shredded crispy duck. Better is a subtle shredded velvet chicken with cucumber and chilli. We also enjoyed the delicate prawn dumplings, some baby pak choi with ginger and garlic, and the perfectly crisp shallot pancakes. At 9pm every night, the chef puts on a noodle-making display, which receives rapturous applause, even though most of the audience have seen it many times before.
Babies and children admitted. Booking advisable lunch; essential dinner. Separate rooms for parties, seating 20, 50 and 75. **Map 8 F9.**

Marylebone

Phoenix Palace

5 Glentworth Street, NW1 5PG (7486 3515/ www.phoenixpalace.uk.com). Baker Street tube. **Meals served** noon-11.30pm Mon-Sat; 11am-10.30pm Sun. **Dim sum served** noon-5pm Mon-Sat; 11am-5pm Sun. **Dim sum** £2-£3.80. **Main courses** £6.50-£25. **Set meal** £20 per person (minimum 2). **Credit** AmEx, MC, V.
Dim sum at Phoenix Palace is classic and dependable: har gau were perfectly steamed and prawn and chinese chive dumplings were full of flavour. Hot and sour soup was impressively spicy and packed with prawns, bamboo, chilli and mushroom. Some dishes were faultless: a perfectly simple and flavourful chinese broccoli with ginger, for example. However, a few à la carte offerings promised more than they delivered. A chef's special of whole chicken cooked in Shaoxing wine was bland, as if the seasoning had been overlooked;

Mr Chow

we had to add soy sauce to coax out any taste at all. In contrast, a bitter melon omelette injected a jolt of flavour into proceedings with a truly bitter tang. Regional dishes were sad imitations of the real thing; mapo tofu (beancurd in a minced beef sauce) was gloopy and timidly flavoured. The large multi-level dining room is all mirrors, wood and jigsaw frames, giving a sort of 1980s stylised Chinatown feel. Rudely named shooters on the drinks list – Phoenix Pussy, Blowjob, and Slippery Nipple – suggest that someone here has an odd sense of humour.
Babies and children welcome: high chairs. Booking advisable. Separate rooms for parties, seating 10 and 30. Takeaway service; delivery service (over £10 within 1-mile radius). Vegetarian menu. **Map 2 F4.**

★ Royal China Club

40-42 Baker Street, W1U 7AJ (7486 3898/ www.royalchinagroup.co.uk). Baker Street or Marble Arch tube. **Meals/dim sum served** noon-11pm Mon-Thur; noon-11.30pm Fri, Sat; noon-10.30pm Sun. **Dim sum** £3-£7.50. **Main courses** £8.50-£35. **Credit** AmEx, MC, V.
This sleek establishment may be part of the popular Royal China chain, but the word 'club' – added to imply exclusivity (though membership is not required) – signifies more than just swanky surroundings. The hushed, plush dining room, framed by slatted bamboo walls and gurgling tanks of giant lobsters, is a temple of Cantonese fine dining. Attention to quality and detail is apparent from the first sip of fragrant, premium jasmine tea. Here, dim sum (which translates as 'touch the heart') touches the soul. Traditional and unusual combinations are executed with sublime grace. Both the scallop and the dover sole cheung fun were works of art: the fresh seafood as plump and soft as the slippery pastry that encased them. Deep-fried taro root dumplings were a feat of culinary engineering; the moist, savoury mushroom and chicken filling contrasted beautifully with a case spun from wispy threads

of pastry. Even basic fare such as pan-fried turnip cake was elevated to new heights, with its jiggling, melt-in-the-mouth interior. Other dim sum were equally astounding, including tung choi (water spinach) liberally stir-fried with piquant, fermented bean sauce. Service throughout was swift, professional and knowledgeable.
Babies and children welcome: high chairs. Booking advisable Sat, Sun. Disabled: toilet. Separate room for parties, seats 24. Takeaway service. **Map 9 G5.**

Mayfair

China Tang ⑩⓪

The Dorchester, 53 Park Lane, W1K 1QA (7629 9988/www.thedorchester.com). Hyde Park Corner tube.
Bar **Open/dim sum served** 11am-12.45am Mon-Sat; 11am-11.45pm Sun.
Restaurant **Meals/dim sum served** 11.30am-11.45pm daily.
Both **Dim sum** £4-£22. **Main courses** £12-£48. **Set lunch** £15 2 courses. **Credit** AmEx, DC, MC, V.
Frequented by Kate Moss and other celebrity friends of David Tang (the entrepreneur behind this opulent Cantonese restaurant in the Dorchester Hotel), China Tang was at first renowned more for its clientele than its food. High rollers continue to come here, but the size of the bill is now at least matched by the improved cooking. Roast chicken, served with a soy sauce brewed in-house, was the best we've eaten in London, the skin cooked to a delicate, paper-thin crisp while the meat maintained a melt-in-the-mouth juiciness. Deep-fried salt and pepper beancurd was excellent too: crisp pillows of airy tofu offset by a crunchy sprinkling of garlic chips and chillies. Soft-shell crab battered with duck egg was slightly less impressive, needing more rich, salty yolk for added pungency and texture. A main course of stir-fried pepper beef, however, was pure luxury: plump chunks of top-quality fillet, sautéed to a perfect medium-rare. Even a side dish of

glutinous rice with air-dried sausage was faultless. Service was efficient and courteous, but we were practically the only customers dining at 6pm: the only available slot on a Saturday evening.
Babies and children welcome: high chairs. Booking advisable. Disabled: lift; toilet. Dress: smart casual. Separate rooms for parties, seating 18-50. **Map 9 G7.**

Kai Mayfair

65 South Audley Street, W1K 2QU (7493 8988/ www.kaimayfair.co.uk). Bond Street or Marble Arch tube. **Lunch served** noon-2.15pm Mon-Fri; 12.30-2.45pm Sat, Sun. **Dinner served** 6.30-10.45pm Mon-Sat; 6.30-10.15pm Sun. **Main courses** £16-£53. **Set lunch** £24 3 courses. **Credit** AmEx, DC, MC, V.
This is Mayfair, so don't come looking for wun tun noodle soup in this glossy, upmarket Chinese. Instead, it's all big ticket stuff like 'tan-jia's lobster broth' and 'sea of eight treasures'. The food mostly lives up to the poetry, thanks to seriously talented Cantonese chefs who are smart enough to ameliorate and modify without too much compromise. 'Mermaids in the mist' is (of course) a fillet of juicy, meaty Chilean sea bass in a lovely, light, broad-bean broth. 'A nest of imperial jewels' turns out to be (as you'd expect) a deluxe san choi bau of chopped prawn and mustard greens wrapped in butterhead lettuce. The simplest dish, a platter of gai lan (chinese broccoli) is a joy: exquisitely manicured, soft-crunchy and verdant green. In contrast, 'the drunken phoenix on the scented tree' seems destined to disappoint, the foil-wrapped, roasted pieces of poussin overpowered by raw, spirity mao tai liquor. The high-energy waiting staff know their stuff, although the stepped-up level of service can turn the excitement of table-side dishes like peking duck into innocuous affairs that simply appear and disappear before the seemingly jaded clientele.
Babies and children welcome: high chairs. Booking advisable. Separate rooms for parties, seating 6 and 10. **Map 9 G7.**

Yauatcha. See p78.

Princess Garden

8-10 North Audley Street, W1K 6ZD (7493 3223/ www.princessgardenofmayfair.com). Bond Street tube. **Lunch served** noon-4pm Mon-Fri; noon-4.30pm Sat, Sun. **Dinner served** 6.30-11pm Mon-Sat; 6.30-10.30pm Sun. **Dim sum served** noon-4pm daily. **Dim sum** £2.30-£3.80. **Main courses** £7.50-£12. **Set lunch** £12 per person (minimum 2). **Set dinner** £30-£85 per person (minimum 2). **Credit** AmEx, DC, MC, V.

More than quarter of a century old, Princess Garden has a sleek, serene dining room, very much in keeping with its posh postcode. Local families and couples seeking a quiet meal are shown by friendly, discreet staff through the wood-lined lobby and past the monumental Buddha (who looks serenely down by a fish tank embedded in the glitzy mirrored bar), into the attractive and spacious dining room. The food also reflects the Mayfair address. The offal dishes of Chinatown are absent, though you will find luxury ingredients aplenty: abalone, shark's fin, lobster. Cooking is competent, if not exceptional. Cantonese duck was a classic rendition, salt and pepper veal passable but not very Chinese in flavouring. Sichuanese-style mapo tofu failed to deliver its required spicy

punch. Nevertheless, our mixed dim sum starter was of a high enough quality to suggest that the restaurant might make a pleasant lunch option, and on previous visits we've relished prawn cheung fun, har gau and siu mai. Certainly the calm atmosphere makes a nice break from bustling Oxford Street around the corner, and prices, while not cheap, are reasonable.

Babies and children welcome: high chairs. Booking advisable. Separate rooms for parties, seating 6, 30 and 50. Takeaway service. **Map 9 G6**.

Paddington

Pearl Liang

8 Sheldon Square, W2 6EZ (7289 7000/www. pearlliang.co.uk). Paddington tube/rail. **Meals served** noon-11pm daily. **Main courses** £6.80-£28. **Set meal** £23 per person (minimum 2); £38-£68 per person (minimum 4). **Credit** AmEx, MC, V.

Rich barbecued pork in puff pastry is a perfect example of the delicate touch with dim sum to be found here. Nothing is greasy, and fried dishes are kept light by judicious ratios of batter to filling. The decor is also a highlight; Pearl Liang was a runner-up in the Best Design category at the 2007

Time Out Eating & Drinking Awards. Settling into a fuchsia leather banquette under a blossoming plum branch snaking along a wall, diners can easily escape from the impersonal modern complex outside to a land of stylish and tasty Cantonese snacks. Large xiao long bao (soup dumplings) are superior to many similar offerings in London. A dish of tripe was wonderfully gingery and light – warming and delicate where it can be overly pungent. Whole prawns wrapped in sesame-seed-studded pastry were a study in how to deep-fry: delicate and flavourful, where the Chinatown version is frequently leaden and greasy. Also in contrast to Chinatown, the atmosphere is serene. Come for a leisurely meal.

Babies and children welcome: high chairs. Booking advisable. Separate room for parties, seats 40. Takeaway service. **Map 8 D5**.

Soho

★ Bar Shu ⑩

28 Frith Street, W1D 5LF (7287 6688/www.bar-shu.co.uk). Leicester Square or Tottenham Court Road tube. **Meals served** noon-11pm Mon-Thur, Sun; noon-11.30pm Fri, Sat. **Main courses** £8.50-£28. **Credit** AmEx, MC, V.

Bar Shu is a shining example of a regional Chinese restaurant (in this case Sichuan) that hasn't compromised on authenticity yet is highly successful. Inside, faux Ming Dynasty furniture, dark stone floors and decorative wood carvings convey a classic teahouse atmosphere, while a bar lit in neon-blue adds a modern contrast. The menu contains photos that simplify ordering. Staff are knowledgeable and friendly. We started with 'man and wife offal slices': thinly sliced tripe, heart and tongue, slicked with spicy-hot chilli-oil and sesame sauce, topped with crushed toasted peanuts. Another starter of crunchy ribbons of jellyfish and cucumber, dressed with sweet-sour dark vinegar, formed a perfect accompaniment. Main courses also delighted our taste buds: boiled pork slices in a dense, rich chilli-oil sauce; tenderised beef in a hot, numbing broth of fresh green sichuan pepper; and aubergines glazed with 'fish fragrant' sauce (sweet, vinegary, salty, garlicky, hot). Crushed dried chillies gave the pork a deep, savoury heat – entirely different to the fragrant, almost flowery numbing sensation imparted by green peppers in the beef. Plentiful rice and tea are recommended to ease the spicy assault. This is food for the brave, with great rewards.
Babies and children welcome: high chairs. Booking advisable. Disabled: toilet. Separate room for parties, seats 14. **Map 17 C3.**

★ Cha Cha Moon NEW
2008 RUNNER-UP BEST DESIGN
15-21 Ganton Street, W1F 9BN (7297 9800). Oxford Circus tube. **Meals served** noon-11pm Mon-Thur; noon-11.30pm Fri, Sat; noon-10pm Sun. **Main courses** £3.50. **Credit** AmEx, MC, V.
Attracting queues of diners for weeks after it opened in spring 2008, Alan Yau's venture is in a similar vein to his previous operations catering to the mid market (notably Busaba Eathai, *see p269*). Accessible prices, communal tables and a no-booking policy aim it squarely at on-the-go Soho-ites for use as a quick pit-stop. Noodles are the order of the day, inspired by Hong Kong *mein dong* (noodle stalls), but Yau adds influences that can be traced from across China, as well as Malaysia and Singapore. Wun tun noodle soup fell short of expectations, the pastry wrappers far from delicate and the chicken filling stodgy. Roast duck noodle soup was far better, the stock exuding 'umami' flavour and the exciting scent of red wolfberries, the noodles themselves fresh and pleasingly al dente. You can also try dishes as diverse as zhajiang mian (a northern dry noodle dish with minced pork), Shanghainese fen pi (cold noodles with jasmine tea-smoked chicken), Sichuan dumplings, and Singaporean char kway teow (stir-fried rice noodles with meat and seafood), though we feel the restaurant would benefit from a more focused range of offerings.
Babies and children admitted. Bookings not accepted. Disabled: toilet. Tables outdoors (6, courtyard). **Map 17 A4.**

Yauatcha
15 Broadwick Street, W1F 0DL (7494 8888). Leicester Square, Oxford Circus, Piccadilly Circus or Tottenham Court Road tube.
Tea house **Tea/snacks served** 11am-11.45pm Mon-Sat; 11am-10.45pm Sun. **Set tea** £22.50-£31.50.
Restaurant **Meals served** noon-11.45pm Mon-Sat; noon-10.45pm Sun.
Both **Dim sum served** noon-11.45pm Mon-Sat; noon-10.45pm Sun. **Dim sum** £3.50-£7. **Main courses** £7.80-£38. **Credit** AmEx, MC, V.
Service at Alan Yau's ground-breaking dim sum destination is hit and miss; on this occasion, the three waiting staff at the door were too busy schmoozing with a regular to acknowledge the growing queue of customers. Finally seated in the sultry lounge-like basement den, we could admire the glowing fish tanks and starry ceiling lights. Our fellow diners were a mix of young professionals, Chinese families and suited businessmen. The meal, a succession of freshly prepared dim sum, was highly impressive – in the

main. The kitchen creates magic out of the perennial favourites: har gau have the obligatory al dente skin and crisp, juicy prawns; chicken congee (rice porridge) was luxuriously velvety, given spark with the addition of salty preserved vegetables and fried shredded shallots; sticky rice was appropriately fragrant from being encased in lotus leaf wrappers. A twist on the classics didn't go unnoticed; the venison puffs were even better than the original barbecued pork version. On the other hand, our turnip cake was bland and overloaded with chives, without any of the flavoursome chinese sausage and shiitake mushrooms normally included. It's also a shame that the pots of tea come without leaves, discouraging subsequent brewings.
Babies and children admitted. Booking advisable. Disabled: lift; toilet. Takeaway service (tea house). **Map 17 B3.**

Yming
35-36 Greek Street, W1D 5DL (7734 2721/ www.yminglondon.com). Leicester Square, Piccadilly Circus or Tottenham Court Road tube. **Meals served** noon-11.45pm Mon-Sat. **Main courses** £5.50-£9. **Set lunch** (noon-6pm) £10. **Set meal** £16-£23 per person (minimum 2). **Credit** AmEx, DC, MC, V.
Shaftesbury Avenue has always been a gulf wider than the Yangtze, as far as Yming is concerned. To the south is Cantonese Chinatown with all its bustle. Here, all is serene, with pastel-blue walls, framed artworks, pastel-yellow tablecloths, unspeakably bland muzak, and staff who are models of brisk proficiency and politeness. Chinese diners are a rarity, their place taken by tourists, theatre-going couples and business folk. Given this, food is better than you might expect. Full-flavoured dishes from across China appear on the list: lamb from the north, dry-cooked beans (correctly salty and chilli-hot) from Sichuan, and the classic double-braised pork in hotpot (this version redolent of star anise, with tender belly pork and butter-like fat: exemplary apart from the pork being sliced too thinly). Less appealing was an oily special of emperor's vegetables with scallops and prawns (perked up by shrimp paste and chillies), and an overcooked starter of fried goujons of smoked fish. With bright new restaurants nearby specialising in regional Chinese cooking, Yming needs to up its game.
Babies and children admitted. Booking essential weekends. Separate rooms for parties, seating 10 and 25. Takeaway service. **Map 17 C4.**

West
Acton

North China
305 Uxbridge Road, W3 9QU (8992 9183/ www.northchina.co.uk). Acton Town tube/207 bus. **Lunch served** noon-2.30pm, **dinner served**

Cha Cha Moon

6-11pm daily. **Main courses** £5.50-£12.80. **Set meal** £14.50-£22.50 per person (minimum 2). **Credit** AmEx, MC, V.

As its name implies, North China specialises in the wheat-based food of northern China: dishes rarely found in London. It serves pretty good renditions of this regional cuisine – but first you need to get your hands on the right menu. We had to ask repeatedly for the northern Chinese list to avoid the standard Anglo-Canto dishes offered by the regular menu. Once presented with the hallowed text, you could do far worse than order the boiled dumplings (ten hearty pork and ginger-filled parcels) dipped in vinegar. Cold glass-noodle salad with shredded chicken offered interesting contrasts of texture; gloopy noodles are paired with poached chicken breast and crunchy cucumber sticks for a refreshing summer salad. The house special soup noodle, however, was a disappointment. Its menu description is undoubtedly alluring; typical northern Chinese noodles are supposedly served in a bowl heaped with vegetables, seafood and pork slices. But the advertised soup bore little resemblance to what arrived at our table – a peppery yet bland hot-and-sour stock that didn't pass muster.
Babies and children welcome: high chairs. Booking advisable; essential dinner Fri, Sat. Separate room for parties, seats 36. Takeaway service; delivery service (over £20 within 2-mile radius). Vegetarian menu.

Bayswater

Four Seasons
84 Queensway, W2 3RL (7229 4320). Bayswater tube. **Meals served** noon-11.15pm Mon-Sat; noon-10.30pm Sun. **Main courses** £5.80-£25. **Set meal** £15.50-£20 per person (minimum 2). **Credit** MC, V.

This Queensway veteran has long been cited as having the best roast ducks in the street. But are we the only ones to have noticed their decidedly blackened extremities? The meat is always moist and ducky, with a homely, stewy quality; the skin is consistently glossy and lacquered, but one end is just as consistently burnt. Still, that doesn't seem to stop the queues forming outside, in spite of the superior duck offered at near neighbour Gold Mine (*see below*). Perhaps it's because Four Seasons has the edge in terms of price, or maybe it's the brisk but efficient service. The cramped, nondescript interior is hardly an attraction. Staff couldn't give a hoot if you order sweet-and-sour everything and attack it with a knife and fork, or put together a more subtle banquet of sesame-fragrant, crunchy jellyfish with cucumber; stir-fried crab with ginger and spring onion; and lovely dau miu pea shoots in oil and garlic. The crab in particular is great fun if you like hands-on action food. And honestly, the prices here are so keen only the grumpy would complain that its sauce is too gluggy. So we won't.

Babies and children admitted. Booking advisable. Takeaway service. **Map 7 C6**.

★ Gold Mine
10 Queensway, W2 3RR (7792 8331). Bayswater tube. **Meals served** noon-11.15pm daily. **Main courses** £6.20-£20. **Set meal** £13.50-£18 per person (minimum 2). **Credit** MC V.

Your table may not be ready when you arrive at Gold Mine – the latest addition to Queensway's clutch of reliable workaday Chinese restaurants – but you won't have long to wait, as the mainly Chinese crowd tend to eat and run, and tables turn over at high speed. The food is mainly Cantonese, with a scattering of Malaysian dishes (fish head curry, char kway teow), but the main attraction is Queensway's finest cantonese roast duck: with its crisp, glazed skin and lush, livery flesh served atop soy-braised cabbage. Young Chinese groups tuck into barbecued pork on rice, while older patrons stick to hearty hotpots such as lamb brisket with beancurd. Our chicken, chinese sausage and pig's liver hotpot was honest, big-hearted and homely. sautéed dau miu (mangetout) is a mossy delight, and scallops served in the shell with ginger and spring onion have an appealing sea-sweetness. Waiters are fast but fair, prices are reasonable, and you'll come away feeling better than when you arrived.
Babies and children welcome: high chairs. Booking advisable weekends. Takeaway service. **Map 7 C6**.

Magic Wok
100 Queensway, W2 3RR (7792 9767). Bayswater or Queensway tube. **Meals served** noon-11pm daily. **Main courses** £6-£14. **Set meal** £11.50-£24 per person (minimum 2). **Credit** AmEx, MC, V.

Kitsch and colourful ink paintings of horses and maidens decorate the walls in this old-fashioned but genuine Cantonese restaurant. We've long had a soft spot for Magic Wok, partially due to its generally kindly service, but also because it has for many years translated all its specials list (including several enticing and authentic Cantonese recipes) into English. However, 'magic balls', which promised so much in name, were bland: deep-fried threads of pastry surrounded a minced prawn filling that was overwhelmed by the heavy frying. Pastry-wrapped whole prawns were better, with high-quality seafood. Main courses are off the Anglo-Cantonese piste, and our choices were packed with flavour. We enjoyed some excellent water spinach with two types of preserved egg, the vegetables fresh, and flavour injected via thousand-year-old eggs, dried prawns and smoky mushrooms. A fried cutlet composed of salted fish and ground pork had the richness of the meat but the texture of a fish ball: an intriguing combination. Magic Wok serves a steady stream of locals (plus a fair few tourists) out for a quiet meal.
Babies and children admitted. Booking advisable dinner. Separate room for parties, seats 30. Takeaway service. Vegetarian menu. **Map 7 C6**.

Mandarin Kitchen
14-16 Queensway, W2 3RX (7727 9012). Bayswater or Queensway tube. **Meals served** noon-11.30pm daily. **Main courses** £5.90-£28. **Set meal** £10.90 per person (minimum 2). **Credit** AmEx, DC, MC, V.

If Mandarin Kitchen took every dish off its vast menu except the lobster with noodles, it would still be packed solid every night. Even though the chef defected to the stylish Pearl Liang (*see p77*) last year, lobster after lobster still comes rolling out of the kitchen here. The dish feels a bit heavy-handed, with its rustic chunks of ginger, but still has a messy, get-stuck-in appeal and a fistful of flavour. The booking, greeting and overall service is much more together than it used to be, but the cooking is up and down. A cold salad of jellyfish with shredded chicken and duck lightly touched with sesame oil makes a good starter, but peking ravioli (steamed pork dumplings) were watery, saved only by a spicy chilli sauce. Stir-fried gai lan (chinese broccoli) lacked bounce and crunch, and beware

RESTAURANTS

the 'eight-treasure duck' unless you like your duck covered with stir-fried seafood. 'Oh, you want the traditional eight-treasure duck' said the waitress when we complained that it was not the goody-studded, rice-stuffed duckling we had envisaged. 'This is the *other* eight-treasure duck'. Oh.
Babies and children welcome: high chairs.
Booking essential dinner. Takeaway service.
Map 7 C7.

Ping Pong
74-76 Westbourne Grove, W2 5SH (7313 9832/
www.pingpongdimsum.com). Bayswater tube.
Dim sum served noon-11pm Mon-Wed;
noon-midnight Thur-Sat; noon-10.30pm Sun.
Dim sum £2.99-£3.99. **Set lunch** £10.99-£11.99.
Set meal £11.50; £17.50 (Sun only). **Credit**
AmEx, MC, V.
Riding high on the current popularity of dim sum, Ping Pong is a chain sprouting branches with rapidity. The spacious Notting Hill outlet is decked out with geometric screens, functional wooden tables and unforgiving stools, black flooring and walls, and spotlights. The split-level dining areas soon filled on a midweek night, with a loquacious young crowd eager to try the cocktails. No Chinese were present, either eating or among the waiting staff in their logo-T-shirts (our chirpy, efficient waitress hailed from Ecuador) – a telling warning of the authenticity of the offerings. We liked the spectacle of the flowering amaranth tea, which 'bloomed' in our long glass. We're unable, though, to recommend the food. Char siu bau was plain awful, the interior of the dry bun containing a smudge of indecipherable stew instead of the expected barbecued pork. Pork puffs were indigestible logs of pastry filled with the same stuff. The seaweed, rice and duck wraps, of Japanese ancestry, were almost inedibly dry. Only the fried oysters and the Valrhona chocolate bun dessert (filled with plentiful chocolate sauce) passed muster. Prices are higher than you'd pay for top-class dim sum at nearby Royal China (*see below*), so we find Ping Pong's success baffling.
Babies and children welcome: high chairs.
Bookings accepted for 8 or more only. Vegetarian menu. **Map 7 B6.**
For branches see index.

Royal China
13 Queensway, W2 4QJ (7221 2535/www.royal
chinagroup.co.uk). Bayswater or Queensway tube.
Meals served noon-11pm Mon-Thur; noon-
11.30pm Fri, Sat; 11am-10pm Sun. **Dim sum
served** noon-5pm Mon-Sat; 11am-5pm Sun.
Dim sum £2.30-£5. **Main courses** £7.50-£50.
Set meal £30-£38 per person (minimum 2).
Credit AmEx, MC, V.
The façade of Royal China Group's original branch is inconspicuous among the various Chinese restaurants along Queensway, save for a fluorescent sign announcing 'dim sum daily'. Inside, the large room is decked out in the firm's trademark shiny gold and black lacquer: elegant, if reminiscent of Hong Kong restaurants circa 1955. The dim sum here is renowned; a long list includes lesser-seen varieties such as churros-like strips of crisp fried dough wrapped in cheung fun – a Hong Kong breakfast favourite, best dunked in a sweet soy dipping sauce. The evening menu, while ambitious (with interesting combinations such as stir-fried scallops with strawberries), is less impressive. A cold starter of marinated jellyfish was over-complicated, doused in a chilli sauce that was a touch too sweet. We preferred the chef's special of assorted seafood and meat broth with diced winter melon, which contained generous amounts of prawns, crab meat, and shiitake mushrooms. Another speciality, stewed pork belly with preserved cabbage, was again marred by over-sweetening, though the meat was pleasantly fatty and tender. The evening crowd is eclectic, from lone diners reading Chinese novels to loud punters in football shirts. All seemed to be relishing the food.
Babies and children welcome: booster chairs.
Booking advisable (not accepted lunch Sat, Sun).
Separate rooms for parties, seating 20-40.
Takeaway service. Vegetarian menu. **Map 7 C7.**
For branches see index.

South West
Barnes

Chinoise
190 Castelnau, SW13 9DH (8222 8666).
Hammersmith tube then 33, 72, 209 or 283
bus. **Lunch served** noon-2pm, **dinner served**
6-11pm Mon-Sat. **Meals served** noon-10pm
Sun. **Main courses** £5-£14. **Set meal** £10-
£38 per person (minimum 2). **Credit** AmEx,
MC, V.
The grand interior of this little neighbourhood restaurant – from the elegant dragon-shaped chopstick holders to the shimmering gold napkins, mirrors and framed calligraphy on the walls – stands in stark contrast to the simple unfussiness of the food. Menu-wise, diners should skip the first five or so pages of standard Anglo-Chinese fare and head straight for the dedicated north-eastern specialities at the back. Sanxian ('three flavour') dumplings started off the meal well, with traditional thick and chewy wrappers, but tomato

---

THE DISH

Congee
Congee is perfect food for hangovers, and for any time you feel your body is a temple – or should have been. A simple porridge of rice and water or stock, often eaten for breakfast, it is to many Chinese and other Asians as chicken soup is to Jewish families: not just comfort cooking, but therapeutic too, and recommended for people with colds. The texture of congee should be creamy and silky, the flavour delicate, the aroma mildly fragrant. So far so bland, you may be thinking, but the basic porridge is enlivened with all manner of goodies, from soy sauce and sesame oil, to pickles and peanuts, to a veritable menagerie of meats. In Vietnam, fish sauce is often added, while South Indian versions, known as pongal, may be spiked with curry leaves, ginger, cumin and turmeric.
China Tang offers five varieties of congee, from a simple plain porridge, and a version with minced beef, to the offal-lover's combination of pork meatballs, liver, kidney and tripe. **Imperial China's** congee with firm slivers of white fish and the occasional tiny clam has a very pure, clean flavour that's guaranteed to revitalise. At **Hakkasan**, ask for the elegantly presented century egg congee with spring onion and fried dough sticks cut very finely into rounds – a perfect balance of textures and tastes. On a budget? Head to cheap and cheery **Café TPT** for congee with Chinese mushrooms and frogs' legs.
Traditionally, congee was a clever way for peasants to eke out the amount of rice they had: an inexpensive belly-filler. You'll find it similarly filling, so when choosing congee as part of a Chinese meal, decrease your usual order of rice or noodle dishes. Remember: your body is a temple, your body is a temple…

---

and egg soup was a timid rendition that lacked the essential sweet-sour tang. We were delighted to find tu dou si (a popular Beijing dish of stir-fried shredded potato with green chillies), but were let down by its lack of chilli heat. Still, the crunchy shreds were extremely moreish and lifted by the sharpness of vinegar. The north's penchant for sour flavours continued with our final dish, stewed pork with chinese cabbage and potato noodles, which came steaming in a large clay pot. The meal was enjoyable, but we get the impression that Chinoise favours style over substance.
Babies and children welcome: high chairs. Booking advisable weekend. Tables outdoors (2, pavement). Takeaway service; delivery service (over £10 within 3-mile radius).

Putney

Royal China
3 Chelverton Road, SW15 1RN (8788 0907).
East Putney tube/Putney rail/14, 37, 74 bus.
Lunch served noon-3.30pm Mon-Sat; noon-
4pm Sun. **Dinner served** 6.30-11pm Mon-Sat;
6.30-10pm Sun. **Dim sum served** noon-3.30pm
daily. **Dim sum** £2-£5. **Main courses** £5.50-
£40. **Set meal** £26-£35 per person (minimum 2).
Credit AmEx, DC.
The sight of black lacquer panels, golden waves and flying geese could understandably lead you to assume that this is another of the Royal China Group's successful outposts – but it isn't, having split from the chain many years ago. The first sign of something being amiss is a table-top placard announcing that Diners, AmEx, cash or cheques are accepted, but nothing else. The menu seems no different to what can be found at Royal China Group branches, but the cooking is not quite up to the expected level. Beef cheung fun lacked finesse; the silky texture of the beef filling was broken by tough shreds of leafy greens, and the sauce was too salty. A similarly over-seasoned sauce was served with a quarter of roast duck that lacked the rich unctuousness found in the best renditions of this dish. Chinese broccoli tasted tired from overcooking, while spare ribs with black beans were fine but unimpressive. So, this independent outfit is a decent local, but doesn't match up to the standard set by its namesakes.
Babies and children admitted. Booking advisable. Takeaway service; delivery service (over £15 within 3.5-mile radius).

South East
Elephant & Castle

★ Dragon Castle
100 Walworth Road, SE17 1JL (7277 3388/
www.dragoncastle.eu). Elephant & Castle tube/
rail. **Meals served** noon-11pm Mon-Thur;
noon-11.30pm Fri, Sat; 11.30am-10.30pm Sun.
Main courses £6.80-£22.80. **Set meals**
£14.80-£33.80 per person (minimum 2).
Credit AmEx, MC, V.
Ever since it opened in the unpromising surroundings of the Walworth Road in 2006, this smart restaurant has been wowing the critics and delighting its customers. The menu includes Anglo-Canto stalwarts like lemon chicken, but also a thrilling range of more authentic dishes, deftly cooked. Shortly after the Chinese New Year we ordered a seasonal special with an auspicious Chinese name (rendered in English as 'the whole world is your oyster') – a delicious braise of dried oysters and silky hair moss. From the main menu, the ribbony jellyfish with cucumber was crisp and refreshing, and the green mussels with Thai basil, garlic and chilli turned out to be a piquant oriental version of moules marinière. We also enjoyed a skilful stir-fry of roast duck, fresh lily bulb and celery, and a clay pot of silken beancurd with chicken and salt-fish. Service on our visit wasn't as consistently good as the cooking, and the salubriousness of the dining room was let down somewhat by the stacks of unused chairs near the entrance. Don't let the location put you off, though – this is one of the most enjoyable Cantonese restaurants in London.

RESTAURANTS

The art of dim sum

The Cantonese term 'dim sum' can be translated as 'touch the heart'. It is used to refer to the vast array of dumplings and other titbits that southern Chinese people like to eat with their tea for breakfast or at lunchtime. This eating ritual is simply known as 'yum cha', or 'drinking tea' in Hong Kong. Many of London's Chinese restaurants have a lunchtime dim sum menu, and at weekends you'll find them packed with Cantonese families. A dim sum feast is one of London's most extraordinary gastronomic bargains: how else can you lunch lavishly in one of the capital's premier restaurants for as little as £15 a head?

Dim sum are served as a series of tiny dishes, each bearing two or three dumplings, perhaps, or a small helping of steamed spare ribs or seafood. Think of it as a Chinese version of tapas, served with tea. You can order according to appetite or curiosity; a couple of moderate eaters might be satisfied with half a dozen dishes, while *Time Out's* greedy reviewers always end up with a table laden with little snacks. Some people like to fill up with a plateful of stir-fried noodles, others to complement the meal with stir-fried greens from the main menu. But however wildly you order, if you stick to the dim sum menu and avoid more expensive specials that waiting staff may wave under your nose, the modesty of the bill is sure to come as a pleasant surprise. The low price of individual dishes (most cost between £1.80 and £3) makes eating dim sum the perfect opportunity to try more unusual delicacies: chicken's feet, anyone?

Two of London's Chinese restaurants serve dim sum Hong Kong-style, from circulating trolleys: the cheerful **New World** (*see p74*) and the less-cheerful **Chuen Cheng Ku** (17 Wardour Street, W1D 6PJ, 7437 1398). Some of the snacks are wheeled out from the kitchen after being cooked; others gently steam as they go or are finished on the trolley to order. The trolley system has the great advantage that you see exactly what's offered, but if you go at a quiet lunchtime some of the food may be a little jaded by the time it reaches you. Other places offer snacks à la carte, so everything should be freshly cooked.

Dim sum lunches at the weekend tend to be boisterous occasions, so they are great for children (take care, though, as adventurous toddlers and hot dumpling trolleys are not a happy combination). Strict vegetarians are likely to be very limited in their menu choices, as most snacks contain either meat or seafood – honourable exceptions include **Golden Palace** (*see p84*) which has a generous selections of vegetarian snacks.

HOW TO EAT DIM SUM

Restaurants used to cease serving dim sum at 4pm or 5pm, when the rice-based evening menus took over. These days, however, since dim sum became fashionable outside the Chinese community, several establishments serve them all day and into the night. Dim sum specialists always list the snacks on separate, smaller menus, which are roughly divided into steamed dumplings, deep-fried dumplings, sweet dishes and so on. Try to order a selection of different types of food, with plenty of light steamed dumplings

to counterbalance the heavier deep-fried snacks. If you are lunching with a large group, make sure you order multiples of everything, as most portions consist of about three dumplings.

Tea is the traditional accompaniment. Some restaurants offer a selection of teas, although they may not tell you this unless you ask. Musty bo lay (pu'er in Mandarin Chinese), grassy Dragon Well (long jing) or fragrant Iron Buddha (tie guan yin) are delicious alternatives to the jasmine blossom that is usually served by default to non-Chinese guests. Waiters should keep teapots filled throughout the meal; leave the teapot lid tilted at an angle or upside down to signal that you want a top-up. **Royal China Club** (*see p76* and *p84*) and **Yauatcha** (*see p78*) have the most extensive lists of fine Chinese teas.

WHERE TO EAT DIM SUM

London's best dim sum are found at the **Royal China Club** (*see p76* and *p84*), **Hakkasan** (*see p75*), **Yauatcha** (*see p78*) and **Pearl Liang** (*see p77*), all of which offer delicious dumplings in glamorous settings. The typically Cantonese **Phoenix Palace** (*see p75*), **Dragon Castle** (*see p81*), and any of the **Royal China** (*see p81*) group branches tend to have exciting specials available. If you're eating in Chinatown, **Royal Dragon** (*see p74*) and **Imperial China** (*see p70*) are a cut above the rest. Outside central London, try **Shanghai** (*see right*) in Dalston, **Peninsula** (*see right*) in Greenwich, **Royal China** in Putney (*see p81* – it is not part of the Royal China chain), **Golden Palace** (*see p84*) in Harrow and **Mandarin Palace** (*see p84*) in Gants Hill.

Below is a guide to the basic canon of dim sum served in London:

Char siu bao: fluffy steamed bun stuffed with barbecued pork in a sweet-savoury sauce.

Char siu puff pastry or **roast pork puff:** triangular puff-pastry snack, filled with barbecued pork, scattered with sesame seeds and baked in an oven.

Cheung fun: slithery sheets of steamed rice pasta wrapped around fresh prawns, barbecued pork, deep-fried dough sticks, or other fillings, splashed with a sweet soy-based sauce. For some non-Chinese the texture is an acquired taste.

Chiu chow fun gwor: soft steamed dumpling with a wheat-starch wrapper, filled with pork, vegetables and peanuts. Chiu chow is a regional Chinese cooking style popular in Hong Kong.

Chive dumpling: steamed prawn meat and chinese chives in a translucent wrapper.

Har gau: steamed minced prawn dumpling with a translucent wheat-starch wrapper.

Nor mai gai or **steamed glutinous rice in lotus leaf:** lotus-leaf parcel enclosing moist sticky rice with chicken, mushrooms, salty duck-egg yolks and other bits and pieces, infused with the herby fragrance of the leaf.

Paper-wrapped prawns: tissue-thin rice paper enclosing plump prawn meat, sometimes scattered with sesame seeds, deep-fried.

Sago cream with yam: cool, sweet soup of coconut milk with sago pearls and morsels of taro.

Scallop dumpling: delicate steamed dumpling filled with scallop (sometimes prawn) and vegetables.

Shark's fin dumpling: small steamed dumpling with a wheaten wrapper pinched into a frilly cockscomb shape on top, stuffed with a mix of pork, prawn and slippery strands of shark's fin.

Siu loon bao or **xiao long bao:** Shanghai-style round dumpling with a whirled pattern on top and a juicy minced pork and soup filling.

Siu mai: little dumpling with an open top, a wheat-flour wrapper and a minced pork filling. Traditionally topped with crab coral, although minced carrot and other substitutes are common.

Taro croquette or **yam croquette:** egg-shaped, deep-fried dumpling with a frizzy, melt-in-your mouth outer layer made of mashed taro, and a savoury minced pork filling.

Turnip paste: a heavy slab of creamy paste made from glutinous rice flour and white oriental radishes, studded with fragments of wind-dried pork, sausage and dried shrimps and fried to a golden brown on either side.

Babies and children welcome: high chairs. Booking advisable Fri, Sat. Disabled: toilet. Separate room for parties, seats 60. Takeaway service. Vegetarian menu.

Greenwich

Peninsula

Holiday Inn Express, 85 Bugsby's Way, SE10 0GD (8858 2028/www.mychinesefood.co.uk). North Greenwich tube. **Meals served** noon-11.15pm Mon-Fri; 11am-11.15pm Sat; 11am-10.45pm Sun. **Dim sum** £2-£6. **Main courses** £6.20-£11. **Set meal** £15-£19 per person (minimum 2). **Credit** AmEx, MC, V.

You can smell vinegar and the aroma of steamed buns when approaching this popular dim sum destination. Situated on the ground floor of the Holiday Inn Express, its dedicated entrance is often crammed full of Chinese couples and families clutching little pink numbered tickets denoting their place in the queue. With 450 seats inside, thankfully the wait isn't long, and efficient staff breeze about the room directing people quickly to their tables. The interior is nothing exciting (pale cream and brown colour scheme, linen-topped tables and stackable chairs), so we busied ourselves examining the 70-plus items on the dim sum menu. Steamed tripe with ginger and spring onions was clean and crisp, with hints of tangy garlic; prawn har gau were plump and fresh, though steamed for so long their skins had become unappetisingly gluey. Most dishes were competent renditions – pork-filled siu mai, beancurd rolls in oyster sauce (full of 'umami' flavour), an excellent plate of deeply coloured chickens' feet – but didn't excite. Best was dessert: 'mountain spring water' tofu pudding was appropriately silky, served with lashings of ginger-tinged syrup, ending the meal on a high note.

Babies and children welcome: high chairs; nappy-changing facilities. Booking advisable. Disabled: toilet. Separate rooms for parties, seating 40-100. Takeaway service. Vegetarian menu.

East

Docklands

★ China Palace NEW

2 Western Gateway, Royal Victoria Dock North, E16 1DR (7474 0808/www.chinapalaceexcel.com). Custom House DLR. **Meals served** noon-11pm Mon-Thur; noon-11.30pm Fri, Sat; 11am-11pm Sun. **Main courses** £7.50-£26.80. **Set meal** £13.50-£28.50. **Credit** MC, V.

Formerly known as Superstar, this popular establishment has reinvented itself with a new management and new chefs – but thankfully the food is as good as its predecessor. On a Sunday morning, the venue was abuzz with families and couples, all enjoying their weekly dim sum in bright, spacious and classy surroundings (in a converted warehouse with, sadly, no river view). Chinese murals line the room, broken up by dark, wooden beams. Nearly all the dim sum we tried were faultless: scallop cheung fun was delightfully silky, the flavour of the scallop subtle; turnip cake was perfectly crisp and rich, with plenty of turnip; pork and prawn dumplings were intense with the flavour of shiitake mushrooms, belying a dull exterior. The only anomaly was the siu loon bao – two out of three of our delicate pork dumplings were ripped at the bottom, and thus drained of all their savoury broth (the other, however, was superb). Service was spot-on and attentive. The waiting staff noted our desire for dessert after the meal and came back accordingly to take the order; we left feeling well-catered for, and highly satisfied.

Babies and children welcome: high chairs. Booking advisable. Separate rooms for parties, seating 10-40. Tables outdoors (6, pavement). Takeaway service. Vegetarian menu.

Yi-Ban

London Regatta Centre, Dockside Road, E16 2QT (7473 6699/www.yi-ban.co.uk). Royal Albert DLR. **Meals served** noon-10pm Mon, Sun; noon-10.45pm Tue-Sat. **Dim sum served** noon-4.45pm daily. **Dim sum** £2-£4. **Main courses** £6-£25. **Set meal** £18-£32 per person (minimum 2). **Credit** AmEx, MC, V.

Diners looking for a glad time should head down to this Docklands restaurant on a Friday or Saturday night, when the long, floor-to-ceiling windowed room (with stunning views of London City Airport) is transformed into a convivial hub filled with energetic live jazz. A smart bar at the rear of the restaurant is a popular point for punters, who come for the drink as much as the food. While crispy duck (expertly shredded by dapper waiters) seems to be a mainstay, we suggest trying the chef specials – particularly the 'bay fong tong' crab. This Hong Kong classic has the crustacean served buried under a flurry of boldly flavoured fried garlic and dried chillies. Steamed egg 'three ways' was tame in comparison: the savoury custard curiously bland, even though there were copious amounts of salted egg yolk and chunks of thousand-year-old egg. Stir-fried pea shoots, perfectly rendered, came in generous portions. Service was attentive yet unintrusive, and staff seemed to be having as good a time as the diners. This is a place that is clearly confident in its abilities, not a surprise considering its name: 'yi ban' in Mandarin means first class.

Babies and children welcome: booster seats; high chairs. Disabled: toilet. Takeaway service. Vegetarian menu. Entertainment: jazz (8pm Fri, Sat).

For branch see index.

North East

Dalston

Shanghai

41 Kingsland High Street, E8 2JS (7254 2878). Dalston Kingsland rail/38, 67, 76, 149 bus. **Meals served** noon-11pm, **dim sum served** noon-5pm daily. **Dim sum** £2.10-£4.30. **Main courses** £5.50-£7.80. **Set meal** £13.80-£22.80 per person (minimum 2). **Credit** MC, V.

In its heyday, the building now housing Shanghai was an eel and pie shop. Yet it's amazing how the original fixtures, of green and blue tiles and wrought-metal framed mirrors, have all the feel of 20th-century chinoiserie, along with the worn glamour of a Wong Kar-Wai film – we half expected the waitresses to be wearing cheongsams. After you've settled into one of the handsome dark wooden booths, a glance at the menu will reveal 'modern Shanghainese' dishes (though the offerings include crunchy lotus root sandwiches from Shunde in Guangzhou). A traditional dish of 'lion heads' (minced pork balls with baby pak choi and beancurd sheets) was a joy to find, but the meatballs were too dense and salty. 'Shanghai Lady', an interesting name for a rice dish mixed with diced vegetables, was unlike anything we've ever tried from that city, but was enjoyable in itself with plenty of crunchy greens in the soy-flavoured rice. If you're looking for Chinese food that is slightly different from the more commonly found Cantonese cooking, Shanghai is worth a try.

Babies and children welcome: high chairs. Booking advisable. Disabled: toilet. Separate rooms for parties, both seating 45. Takeaway service. **Map 25 B5.**

North

Camden Town & Chalk Farm

★ Teachi NEW

2008 RUNNER-UP BEST CHEAP EATS

29-31 Parkway, NW1 7PN (7485 9933). Camden Town tube. **Meals/dim sum served** noon-11pm Mon-Sat; noon-10.30pm Sun. **Dim sum** £2.80-£3.20. **Main courses** £6.50-£11. **Set lunch** £6.80 1 course. **Credit** AmEx, MC, V.

Teachi's mix of traditional dim sum and bite-sized Chinese delicacies is well-suited to a city obsessed with downsized oriental dining, and the food has seldom failed to impress since the restaurant's opening in autumn 2007. Flash-fried salt and

RESTAURANTS

SHELF LIFE

While the range of Chinese ingredients available in Britain's supermarkets has improved, stocking up at a specialist store or cash-and-carry is still preferable for the wider choice of authentic brands, unusual ready-made foods and gourmet ingredients. The prices tend to be much cheaper too.

Good Harvest

65 Shaftesbury Avenue, W1D 6LH (7734 4900). Leicester Square or Piccadilly Circus tube.

Want to make steamed fish Teochew-style, or have a go at deep-fried trey chap kampot? This is the place to come for your slapping-fresh pomfret. The closest thing to a Chinese 'wet market' you'll find in London, Good Harvest also sells live eels, lobsters and crab, and has a choice of sea or freshwater prawns.

Hoo Hing

A406 North Circular Road, NW10 7TN (8548 3636/www.hoohing.com). Hangar Lane tube.

Set on a slip-road running alongside the North Circular, Hoo Hing offers a good range of frozen seafood along with every imaginable sauce, curry paste, pickle, noodle and tea. Look out for the duck eggs, sesame candies and tofu powder for making your own tofu at home.

New Loon Moon

9 Gerrard Street, W1D 5PL (7734 3887). Leicester Square or Piccadilly Circus tube.

There are more than 30 brands of soy sauce in this labyrinthine store, which sells all the major Chinese staples, plus fresh gai lan, juicy 'crystal pears', tiny Thai aubergines and hard-to-find herbs. Head to the back room for keenly priced kitchenware.

See Woo Hong

Furlong House, Horn Lane, SE10 0RT (8293 9393/www.seewoo.com). Westcombe Park rail.

A useful Greenwich outpost of the well-known Lisle Street, Chinatown store. You'll find a good selection of fish and shellfish (fresh and live) plus own-made fish balls, roasted and cured meats, and fresh vegetables. The company is a major restaurant supplier and runs the See Café deli in Paddington Basin.

Wing Tai Supermarket

Unit 11a, Aylesham Centre, Rye Lane, SE15 5EW (7635 0714). Peckham Rye rail.

There is a good fresh fish counter at this south-east London gem, which sells a large range of Chinese, Vietnamese and other oriental products. Also worth a visit for seasonal fruit and vegetables, Wing Tai has branches in Brixton and Camberwell too.

pepper squid is light and delicious, despite being served in what looks disarmingly like a wicker dustpan. Marinated salmon bellies are tender enough to arrive virtually falling off the sticks on which they were barbecued; and an interesting take on duck pancakes offers flavoursome chunks of meat coated in an airy batter and cut into quaint triangles. Our only complaint on a recent visit concerned atmosphere; Teachi is pleasantly decorated with a convincing if conventional mix of sculpted rosewood screens, potted bamboo plants and Chinese wall art, but we've seldom seen a restaurant sterilised by such unnecessary brightness. On top of that, service appears to have gone from fawning (at the opening) to frowning. A request for an extra plate was sniffed at, a question about the food laughed at – and so many bottles of wine were unavailable that the next step up from a (rather poor) house red cost almost £20.
Babies and children admitted. Tables outside (2, pavement). Takeaway service. **Map 27 C2.**

North West
St John's Wood

Royal China Club NEW
68 Queen's Grove, NW8 6ER (7586 4280/ www.royalchinagroup.co.uk). St John's Wood tube. **Meals served** noon-11pm Mon-Sat; 11am-10pm Sun. **Dim sum served** noon-5pm daily. **Dim sum** £2.30-£5. **Main courses** £6.50-£36. **Credit** AmEx, MC, V.

Gone are the familiar geese flying across black lacquer walls, as Royal China goes for gold. Aged gold leaf now lines the walls and ceilings, and a handsome stone Buddha peers benignly over the well-heeled local crowd, as the second restaurant in the Royal China Group is elevated to premier status as a Royal China Club. Apart from the classy redesign, a dazzling array of Chinese teas, slim-line black chopsticks and cutting-edge cutlery, this means a concerted if derivative attempt to raise the gastronomic bar. So instead of Chinatown's greatest hits, you get peking duck with caviar, Chilean sea bass with dried shrimp, and stir-fried udon noodles with ostrich. Not everything thrills. Shredded smoked chicken with seaweed was just a gussied-up take on salt-and-pepper squid, and Scottish scallops with black beans were overcooked and under-sauced. Lunchtime dim sum is still a good bet, with its crisp, crumbly spring onion cakes, silky prawn and yellow chive rice rolls and well-crafted shanghai pork and crab dumplings. Staff are watchful and caring, but even the service charge has been upgraded – to 15%.
Babies and children admitted. Booking advisable. Separate rooms for parties, both seating 20. Takeaway service. Vegetarian menu. **Map 2 D1.**

Swiss Cottage

Green Cottage
9 New College Parade, Finchley Road, NW3 5EP (7722 5305/7892). Finchley Road or Swiss Cottage tube. **Meals served** noon-11pm Mon-Sat; noon-10pm Sun. **Main courses** £5.80-£25. **Set meal** £12.50-£25 per person (minimum 2). **Credit** (over £10) AmEx, MC, V.

Green Cottage is a friendly neighbourhood place, with simple utilitarian furnishings on both the ground and first floor. In contrast to such surroundings, it offers a main menu far more exciting than that of your average Chinese restaurant, along with a supplementary list of still more unusual dishes. Cantonese food is the mainstay, and roast meats are a house speciality. Most recently we enjoyed a soup of slivered roast duck with fish, bamboo shoots and shiitake mushrooms. We also grappled with seafood rolls that were crisp and appetising yet fell apart, messily, in our chopsticks. A chicken and beancurd hotpot was robustly seasoned with salt-fish and peppery ginger, while choi sum in a shrimpy Malaysian sauce was a little chewy. Fried rice with slices of chinese broccoli stem, shreds of delicious dried scallop and wisps of egg-white was superb. Many locals have been dining here for years; we'd be happy too, if we lived just up the road.

Babies and children welcome: booster seats. Booking advisable; essential dinner. Restaurant available for hire. Takeaway service. **Map 28 B4.**

Outer London
Harrow, Middlesex

Golden Palace
146-150 Station Road, Harrow, Middx HA1 2RH (8863 2333). Harrow-on-the-Hill tube/rail. **Meals served** noon-11.30pm Mon-Sat; 11am-10.30pm Sun. **Dim sum served** noon-5pm Mon-Sat; 11am-5pm Sun. **Dim sum** £2.30-£3.50. **Main courses** £5.20-£8.50. **Set meal** £18-£26.50 per person (minimum 2). **Credit** AmEx, DC, MC, V.

Fans praise the legendary dim sum here, but the evening menu is becoming more of a reason to visit. Many Chinese people are attracted. Golden Palace is a spacious venue, if mundane in decor and presentation, with the obligatory starched white tablecloths and uncomfortable seats. We couldn't fault the friendly, attentive waitresses, who listened to our preferences and, after consulting the kitchen, returned with a range of dishes that we might like. It's also commendable that the restaurant offers such a wide array of vegetarian food, including rarely seen gluten dishes (vegetarian 'duck', 'pork' and 'roast pork'). Our (non-veggie) braised belly pork, wrapped in thin beancurd sheets then deep-fried, was certainly unusual – the beancurd took on the feel of crisp filo pastry, in stark and enjoyable contrast to the meltingly tender (though greasy) pork belly. Charcoal-roast duck was succulent and flavoursome, but lacked the distinctive smoky aroma of this time-consuming cooking technique. The dining experience ended on a sweet note caused, not by our refreshing mango and pomelo sago dessert, but by the 10% service charge being graciously removed after the card machine broke before we could pay.
Babies and children welcome: high chairs. Booking advisable dinner. Disabled: toilet. Separate rooms for parties, seating 60 and 100. Takeaway service. Vegetarian menu.

Ilford, Essex

★ Mandarin Palace
559-561 Cranbrook Road, Gants Hill, Ilford, Essex IG2 6JZ (8550 7661). Gants Hill tube. **Lunch served** noon-4pm, **dinner served** 6.30-11.30pm Mon-Sat. **Meals served** noon-midnight Sun. **Dim sum served** noon-4pm Mon-Sat; noon-5pm Sun. **Dim sum** £2-£3.80. **Main courses** £7-£15. **Set dinner** £19.50-£39 per person (minimum 2). **Credit** AmEx, DC, MC, V.

You're in for a nice surprise if you assumed a 30-year-old Chinese restaurant on a busy roundabout next to Gants Hill tube would be a desolate takeaway joint with sullen waiter, ordering by numbers, and food thick with MSG. The decor here, it's true, is old fashioned – the myriad screens and lanterns having a slightly faded opulence. And prices are traditionally low. But on a Sunday lunchtime there was a cheerful buzz from a smart, mainly Chinese clientele, as a smiling waitress showed us to a table with crisp white linen, fresh flowers, peanuts and pickled cabbage. A request for meat-free, gluten-free dim sum left her unfazed. There followed a series of exquisite dumplings (prawn and chive a particular highlight) then tender baby squid in a gingery curry sauce, scrumptiously well-filled oyster beancurd rolls, and coriander-specked fish-balls redolent of the sea. Grilled water-chestnut paste and sesame prawn rolls were hits too. The only let-down was the heavy wrapping on the cheung fun. Everything arrived hot, fresh and fragrant, including garlicky choi sum and the scented towels for washing hands after the complimentary oranges.
Babies and children welcome: high chairs. Separate room for parties, seats 50. Takeaway service; delivery service (over £20 within 2-mile radius). Vegetarian menu.
For branch see index.

花坞里桃
庵桃花花庵
桃花仙桃
化仙人种桃
树又摘桃花
换酒钱酒醒
只在花间坐
酒醒还来花
下眠半醉半
醒日复日花
开花落年复
年⑩

Teachi. See p83.

RESTAURANTS

East European

At last the capital's East European restaurants are starting to reflect the number of east Europeans who have come to live and work in London. This year we welcome Polish outfit the **Knaypa**, and **Divo**, which, although widely ridiculed on opening, is turning into a very pleasant restaurant and is one of London's only exponents of Ukrainian food. The capital can also be proud of having three good Georgian restaurants: **Minimo**, **Tbilisi** and **Little Georgia**. The latter is improving year on year, as is upmarket Russian restaurant **Potemkin**.

Czech

North West
West Hampstead

★ Czechoslovak Restaurant (100)
Czech & Slovak House, 74 West End Lane, NW6 2LX (7372 1193/www.czechoslovak-restaurant. co.uk). West Hampstead tube. **Dinner served** 5-10pm Tue-Fri. **Meals served** noon-10pm Sat, Sun. **Main courses** £4-£12. **No credit cards**.
Czech/Slovak food is never going to win prizes for subtlety: think dumplings, potatoes and cream by the bucket-load. Even early in the week, the Czechoslovak Restaurant buzzes with a diverse crowd cocking a snook at healthy eating: young Czechs and Slovaks; older workmen downing a Budva; enthusiastic language-learners trying out their Czech on a patient waiter; and happy diners with no Czech links, just enjoying the charmingly old-fashioned, laid-back vibe. In the communist era, this was a club for exiles. It's now achingly nostalgic, rejoicing in swirly carpets and patriotic paintings. Hearty chicken noodle or creamy sour-cabbage soups set the tone to start. If you're feeling adventurous, try utopenec v octe (pickled sausage) or bramborák se slaninou (potato pancake with extraordinarily fat bacon). Portions are enormous. You'll feel close to explosion if you finish your carp fried in breadcrumbs (which comes with enough potato salad to feed a small family), or crumbly roast lamb in a sea of creamy spinach sauce with knedliky. And you'll need the good Czech beer to wash it all down and make room for... more dumplings, apricot this time, swimming in butter. Retro heaven.
Babies and children welcome: high chairs. Booking advisable weekends. Disabled: toilet. Separate room for parties, seats 25. Tables outdoors (4, terrace). Takeaway service. Vegetarian menu. **Map 28 A3**.

Georgian

West
Kensington

Mimino
197C Kensington High Street, W8 6BA (7937 1551/www.mimino.co.uk). Kensington High Street tube. **Dinner served** 6-11pm Mon-Thur; 6pm-midnight Fri, Sat. **Main courses** £10-£15. **Credit** AmEx, MC, V.
Georgian food, popular all over the former Soviet Union for its breath of spicy exoticism, is enjoyed at Mimino by expats and cosmopolitan locals. Early in the week all is peaceful, with a soundtrack of soulful Russian and Georgian ballads, but we've heard things can hot up at weekends with lively parties trying out the vodka list and the Georgian spirit chacha. A mishmash of dreary retro decor is enlivened by some modernist artwork and an imposing rough-hewn central table – all fittingly post-Soviet. Order mixed meze and you'll receive a variety of scrumptious, fresh veggie salads: adjapsandali and badrijani (both aubergine-based); spinach and leek pkhali; and the highly appetising red-bean lobio. Don't kid yourself they're low-cal; the pounded walnuts put paid to that. The various khachapuri are irresistible; try adjaruli-style with egg. Mains consist of earthy stews and grills; both flattened chicken tabaka with plum sauce, and ojakhuri (spicy fried pork) were tasty but dry. A stellar wine list features over 20 Georgian varieties hard to find in the UK: oaky dry white Vazisubani, fruity Mtatsminda rosé, and the rare semi-sweet red Ojaleshi. An experience to savour.
Babies and children admitted. **Map 7 A9**.

East
Bethnal Green

Little Georgia
87 Goldsmiths Row, E2 8QR (7739 8154). Liverpool Street tube/rail then 26, 48 bus. **Open** 9am-5pm Mon; 9am-11pm Tue-Sat; 10am-11pm Sun. **Main courses** £10-£11. **Unlicensed**. **Corkage** no charge. **Credit** MC, V.
Conjure up a stern auntie lovingly preparing all your favourites in her kitchen in downtown Tbilisi: that's Little Georgia. There's no licence, which means no fabulous Georgian wines, though you can bring in your own alcohol – and for no extra charge, which is a friendly touch. Mossy green paintwork, an ancient gramophone, a wacky 1970s map of Georgia and nostalgic photos, along with soulful/jazzy Georgian sounds, create a homely, laid-back atmosphere. Our friendly waitress was slightly haphazard, stretched to the limit by a party in the basement and a full ground-floor room, but with such a pleasant vibe we didn't mind waiting. The cooking has certainly risen a notch since our last visit and is spicier than at London's other Georgian restaurants. Although khachapuri is hard to resist, try lobiani: scrumptious flatbread stuffed with spicy beans and (optional) smoked pork. Garlicky carrot salad was a good foil to the rich beetroot pkhali. Add barszcz, blini and other delights as meze, or share

Knaypa. See p88.

RESTAURANTS

a hearty main. Chanakhi (lamb, aubergine and potato stew) with pungent ajika spicing (ground red peppers, coriander, and garlic) was rich and comforting, though slightly low on meat. Our evening resulted in an implausibly small bill. *Babies and children welcome: high chairs. Separate room for parties, seats 25. Tables outdoors (2, pavement). Takeaway service.* **Map 6 S3**.

North

Holloway

★ Tbilisi

91 Holloway Road, N7 8LT (7607 2536). Highbury & Islington tube/rail. **Dinner served** 6.30-11pm Mon-Fri daily. **Main courses** £8.95-£9.45. **Credit** AmEx, MC, V.

Tbilisi remains a mystery. Even after years of favourable reviews from us, a well-priced menu, stylish dark-red decor, and a laid-back jazzy soundtrack – it rarely packs in the locals as we'd expect. Service is much improved, with a smiley, chatty waitress on our recent visits. It's great to start a meal with one of the mixed platters named after regions of Georgia. Our kolkheti featured spinach pkhali (a rich, intensely flavoured pâté made with pounded walnuts), beetroot (also in a zingy walnut sauce) and fluffy khachapuri. Robust Georgian stews make ideal comfort food for chill winter nights; Tbilisi's stews include chakapuli (lamb in an intense, tarragon-infused tkemali plum sauce) and chakhokhbili (a rich chicken and tomato stew flavoured with ajika, a Georgian spice-blend). Or try the famous chicken tabaka (here a rather bony spring chicken), flattened under a heavy lid, fried and served with walnut or plum sauce. There are a number of good Georgian wines on the menu (we're Kindzmarauli fans; its unique semi-sweet blackberry flavours are unbeatable with the spicy fare) – we'd visit just to sample them, so the enjoyable, no-nonsense food is a bonus. *Babies and children admitted. Booking advisable Fri, Sat. Restaurant available for hire. Separate room for parties, seats 40. Takeaway service.*

Hungarian

Central

Soho

Gay Hussar

2 Greek Street, W1D 4NB (7437 0973/ www.gayhussar.co.uk). Tottenham Court Road tube. **Lunch served** 12.15-2.30pm, **dinner served** 5.30-10.45pm Mon-Sat. **Main courses** £9.50-£16.50. **Set lunch** £17 2 courses, £19.50 3 courses. **Credit** AmEx, DC, JCB, MC, V.

Despite now being owned by a big hotel group, this venerable Soho institution retains a certain intimacy and old-school charm that's rare in London. From higgledy-piggledy shelves of political biographies to rich wood-panelled walls lovingly laden with caricatures of Westminster worthies, it oozes character. The presiding (Polish, rather than Hungarian) maître d' reminds us of a Bond-style butler; almost lugubriously polite, but with a wry sense of humour, he delights in regaling diners with tales of the restaurant's past glories. Try some lesser-known Hungarian wines (beyond the Tokajis and Bulls Bloods). We loved our crisp white Kemendy zenit. Hungarian friends were full of approval on our most recent visit, with special praise for the authenticity of the cold, outrageously creamy cherry soup, and pancakes stuffed with goulash then breadcrumbed and deep-fried. Delicate fish dumplings in a light sauce spiked with dill (not so typically Hungarian), and a robust main of beef medallions with hot paprika-braised onions and peppers, also went down a treat. Portions are generous, but the sweet-toothed will find it hard to resist walnut pancakes or richly chocolatey dobosz torta. A slice of living history. *Babies and children welcome: children's portions; high chairs. Book dinner. Separate rooms for parties, seating 12 and 24.* **Map 17 C3**.

Pan-East European

South

Waterloo

★ Baltic (100)

74 Blackfriars Road, SE1 8HA (7928 1111/ www.balticrestaurant.co.uk). Southwark tube/ rail. **Lunch served** noon-3.30pm daily. **Dinner served** 6-11.15pm Mon-Sat; 6-10pm Sun. **Main courses** £10.50-£16.50. **Set meal** £14.50 2 courses, £17.50 3 courses. **Credit** AmEx, MC, V.

Baltic's wow factor never wanes. Make your way through the lively bar to the high-ceilinged main room, its stark whiteness punctuated by exposed beams, bare red Gdansk-style brickwork and a stunning chandelier with gleaming amber shards. Though such hard surfaces mean the space sometimes gets a touch noisy for a tête-à-tête, the lively buzz adds to the good-time feel. Baltic remains London's only East European 'destination' restaurant. Nothing in this section rivals its innovative menu, which gives traditional ingredients and cooking styles a subtle modern twist. Try the gravadlax with puréed beetroot spiked with horseradish, plus sour cream and crunchy potato latkes – they're to die for. Our flaky roast cod with nutty kasza risotto swam in slightly insipid cream sauce; better was the roast guinea fowl 'kiev' stuffed with flavoursome herb butter. The restrained portion sizes make one of the delectable puddings possible: a perennial favourite like wódka cherry ice-cream with chocolate sauce, nalesniki with summer berries, or hungarian chocolate torte with honeycomb ice-cream. Add a great cocktail list, a wide choice of vodkas (including own-made infusions like ginger), an eclectic wine list and proper but friendly service, and you have Baltic bliss. *Babies and children admitted. Disabled: toilet. Separate room for parties, seats 30. Tables outdoors (4, terrace).* **Map 11 N8**.

North

Camden Town & Chalk Farm

Zorya NEW

48 Chalk Farm Road, NW1 8AJ (7485 8484/ www.zoryarestaurant.com). Chalk Farm tube. *Bar* **Open** 5pm-midnight Mon-Wed; 5pm-1am Thur, Fri; 1pm-1am Sat; 1pm-midnight Sun. *Restaurant* **Dinner served** 5-10.30pm Mon-Fri. **Meals served** 1-11pm Sat, Sun. **Main courses** £7.50-£11.50. *Both* **Credit** AmEx, MC, V.

With yellow walls, leather chairs and spare decor (save for an incongruous bird-bath affair), Zorya is undoubtedly attractive, but it can get stuffy. A quiet summer evening saw everyone rush to the terrace despite thundering traffic, the odd police siren and music cranked up to disguise the din. Service was very friendly, but many menu choices were unavailable – just like eastern Europe in the old days. Cocktails are awesomely strong; try a yummy Vojito ('v' for vanilla vodka) with fresh mint galore, or Baltika or Zywiec beer. The Hungarian chef's East-Central European fusion cooking works to a point. Shashlik with roasted veg was made from prime steak mince, but seemed more like a posh burger. Pierogi were almost lasagne-like, with mushroom and sour cabbage in tangy sour-cream sauce, and slightly over-the-top spicing. A very tasty but visually unappealing three-meat goulash came on mash with a massive steaming pile of leeks. Having saved room for delectable-sounding walnut pancakes and fruit dumplings, we were dismayed to learn that a 'rethink of the dessert menu' meant only stodgy, tasteless cheesecake was available. Zorya shows promise, but still has a way to go. *Babies and children admitted. Separate rooms for parties, seating 50-60. Tables outdoors (12, roof terrace).* **Map 27 C1**.

SHELF LIFE

Fortune Foods

387-389 Hendon Way, NW4 3LP (8203 9325). Hendon Central tube.
Whether you're looking for Lithuanian, Slovakian, Russian or Polish foods, a trip to this neat store will glean quality smoked fish, caviar, baked goods, fresh sauerkraut and dairy products such as ketyras (drinking yogurt).

Kalinka

35 Queensway, W2 4QP (7243 6125). Queensway or Bayswater tube.
A cheerful and bright Russian shop with a diverse range of authentic products, including cured fish, cheeses and biscuits.

Mleczko

362 Uxbridge Road, W12 7LL (8932 4487). Shepherd's Bush tube.
At first glance, this red-fronted shop looks like a newsagent, but keep walking through to the rear, where a long delicatessen counter holds a terrific range of classic Polish sausages and cured meats.

Polish Specialities

258 Streatham High Road, SW16 1HT (8696 7660/www.polishspecialities. com). Streatham rail.
One of two shops (the other is in Hammersmith) run by the wholesaler of the same name, who is responsible for getting a wide range of Polish foods into corner shops, supermarkets and cash-and-carrys all over the country.

Polsmak

39 Balls Pond Road, N1 4BW (7275 7045/www.polsmak.co.uk). Dalston Kingsland rail/bus 38.
One of London's trendier Polish delis, this well-stocked outfit serves tempting drozdzowka (yeast cake) and doughnuts to enjoy with a cup of coffee.

Red Pig

57 Camden High Street, NW1 7JL (7388 8992) Camden Town or Mornington Crescent tube.
This new shop in Camden offers an extensive charcuterie selection and an international range of cheeses, plus convenience lines for Polish expats, such as instant zurek (sour rye soup).

Polish

Central

Holborn

★ Bar Polski

11 Little Turnstile, WC1V 7DX (7831 9679). Holborn tube. **Meals served** 4-10pm Mon; 12.30-10pm Tue-Fri. **Dinner served** 6-10pm Sat. **Main courses** £5-£8.50. **Credit** MC, V.
Has Bar Polski taken its eye off the ball? This long-time favourite was always primarily a bar, but it was also somewhere you could enjoy decent Polish

Menu

Dishes followed by (Cz) indicate a Czechoslovak dish; (G) Georgian; (H) Hungarian; (P) Polish; (R) Russian; (Uk) Ukrainian. Others have no particular affiliation.

Bigos (P): hunter's stew made with sauerkraut, various meats and sausage, mushrooms and juniper.
Blini: yeast-leavened pancake made from buckwheat flour, traditionally served smothered in butter and sour cream; **blinchiki** are mini blinis.
Borscht: classic beetroot soup. There are many varieties: Ukrainian borscht is thick with vegetables; the Polish version (**barszcz**) is clear. There are also white and green types. Often garnished with sour cream, boiled egg or mini dumplings.
Caviar: fish roe. Most highly prized is that of the sturgeon (**beluga, oscietra** and **sevruga**, in descending order of expense), though **keta** or salmon caviar is underrated.
Chlodnik (P): cold beetroot soup, bright pink in colour, served with sour cream.
Coulebiac (R): see koulebiaka.
Galabki, golabki or **golubtsy:** cabbage parcels, usually stuffed with rice or kasha (qv) and sometimes meat.
Golonka (P): pork knuckle, often cooked in beer.
Goulash or **gulasz (H):** rich beef soup.
Kasha or **kasza:** buckwheat, delicious roasted: fluffy, with a nutty flavour.
Kaszanka (P): blood sausage made with buckwheat.
Khachapuri (G): flatbread; sometimes called Georgian pizza.
Kielbasa (P): sausage; Poland had dozens of widely differing styles.
Knedliky (Cz): bread dumplings.
Kolduny (P): small meat-filled dumplings (scaled-down pierogi, qv)

often served in beetroot soup.
Kotlet schabowy (P): breaded pork chops.
Koulebiaka or **kulebiak (R):** layered salmon or sturgeon pie with eggs, dill, rice and mushrooms.
Krupnik (P): barley soup, and the name of a honey vodka (because of the golden colour of barley).
Latke: grated potato pancakes, fried.
Makowiec or **makietki (P):** poppy seed cake.
Mizeria (P): cucumber salad; very thinly sliced and dressed with sour cream.
Nalesniki (P): cream cheese pancakes.
Paczki (P): doughnuts, often filled with plum jam.
Pelmeni (R): Siberian-style ravioli dumplings.
Pierogi (P): ravioli-style dumplings. Typical fillings are sauerkraut and mushroom, curd cheese or fruit (cherries, apples).
Pirogi (large) or **pirozhki** (small) **(R):** filled pies made with yeasty dough.
Placki (P): potato pancakes.
Shashlik: Caucasian spit-roasted meat.
Shchi (R): soup made from sauerkraut.
Stroganoff (R): beef slices, served in a rich sour cream and mushroom sauce.
Surowka (P): salad made of raw shredded vegetables.
Uszka or **ushka:** small ear-shaped dumplings served in soup.
Vareniki (Uk): Ukrainian version of pierogi (qv).
Zakuski (R) or **zakaski (P):** starters, traditionally covering a whole table. The many dishes can include pickles, marinated vegetables and fish, herring, smoked eel, aspic, mushrooms, radishes with butter, salads and caviar.
Zrazy (P): beef rolls stuffed with bacon, pickled cucumber and mustard.
Zurek (P): sour rye soup.

RESTAURANTS

---

home-style cooking, provided you picked your time carefully. Yet on our last visit, though early in the week, the atmosphere resembled that of a rowdy pub; a large group was braying over thumping music, making it difficult to relax and enjoy the enterprising range of Polish beers (including lesser-known dark brews like Okocim Porter), the chance to have a shot of raspberry syrup in your Zywiec or Tyskie, and the well-organised menu of over 60 vodkas. The range can't be faulted – but Polish drinks are now ubiquitous in London. Vibrant barszcz and tender herring salad went down a treat, but greasy fried pierogi and heavy potato pancakes did little more than mop up the booze. For vodka, try dry Debowa Biala (white oak), sour-sweet Koneser Cranberry or an aromatic Kminkowa (caraway seed). We'll always love the light-wood backdrop to the bold *wycinanki* (traditional paper cut-out designs) of cockerels and other stylised folk motifs, but Bar Polski needs to get its cool vibe back.
Babies and children admitted. Bookings not accepted. Takeaway service. **Map 18 F2.**

Marylebone

Stara Polska
69 Marylebone Lane, W1U 2PH (7486 1333/ www.starapolska.co.uk). Bond Street tube. **Lunch served** noon-3pm, **dinner served** 6-11pm

Mon-Thur. **Meals served** noon-11.30pm Fri, Sat. **Main courses** £8-£13.90. **Credit** MC, V.
Stara Polska is reminiscent of a small-town restaurant somewhere in darkest 1980s Poland, with kitsch decor and uncomfortable cod-rustic pine furniture. Sour zurek got our meal off to a reasonable start, but a so-called rosó (featuring, according to the menu, 'home-style noodles') seemed little more than a chicken stock cube with broken spaghetti. Most dishes come in small or medium sizes, so you can sample a variety. Grilled kielbasa, bigos and a slightly greasy placek (potato pancake) were on the right side of serviceable, but mizeria (cucumber salad with dill and sour cream) came in a thin, watery dressing. Our fellow diners were predominantly elderly locals, who are no doubt relieved just to find something affordable in this now chi-chi area. Stara Polska is authentic, yes, but in a way that some Poles would be happy to forget.
Babies and children admitted. Separate room for parties, seats 9. Takeaway service. **Map 9 G5.**

South Kensington

Daquise
20 Thurloe Street, SW7 2LP (7589 6117). South Kensington tube. **Meals served** 11.30am-11pm daily. **Main courses** £6-£14.50. **Set lunch** (noon-3pm Mon-Fri) £9.50 2 courses. **Credit** MC, V.
What's not to love about Daquise, unless you're an aspiring size zero? This cherished café has clocked

---

up over 50 years of purveying no-nonsense Polish home cooking to students, tourists, impecunious old Polish émigrés and new young arrivals. The place has a cosy, lived-in feel, produced by homely waiting staff, Formica tables, leatherette banquettes and a straightforward menu. It's the real deal, old-Polish style, and is usually abuzz with happy diners. Starters shine: vibrant, beetrooty barszcz with tender uszka; puffy, light and nutty buckwheat blini with smoked salmon or herring and tart apple. To follow, indulge in Russian zrazy (stuffed mincemeat roll) with fluffy kazsa gryczana (baked buckwheat), a creamy mushroom sauce plus a side of piquant beetroot with horseradish. Or go for one of the mammoth calorie-laden platters with potato pancakes, pierogi, galabki and more, plus bigos in the non-veggie version. All is ideally accompanied by Polish beer, and rounded off with vodka (reliable old standards like Zywiec, Zubrówka and Wisniówka). Those with heroic appetites should sample the desserts: a fine selection of traditional pancakes with sweet cheese, cheesecakes, makowiec and so on. There's a great vibe here, and prices are low.
Babies and children admitted. Booking advisable. Separate room for parties, seats 25. **Map 14 D10.**

West
Bayswater

Antony's
54 Porchester Road, W2 6ET (7243 8743/ www.antonysrestaurant.com). Royal Oak tube.
Dinner served 6-11pm Tue-Sun. **Main courses** £10.50-£16. **Cover** 70p. **Credit** MC, V.
The charming owner, warmly greeting newcomers and regulars, has got things just right. Peachy walls, velvet curtains and gilt-framed mirrors make Antony's cosy and intimate. Atmospheric oil paintings, and tables smartly set with starched tablecloths, gleaming cutlery and glassware lend it an air of comfortingly bourgeois Mitteleuropa. Well-rendered Polish choices appear alongside the likes of deep-fried brie, stuffed chicken breasts and steaks on the menu. We rarely resist the good, peppery barszcz with tender uszka and fresh dill, though potato pancakes with creamy mushroom sauce, and steaming pierogi, also go down a treat. You could eschew mains altogether for these excellent starters, but we can also vouch for the zrazy (rolled slices of beef stuffed with pickled cucumbers and bacon), salt beef with horseradish, and thick grilled salmon steak in creamy dill-infused sauce. Accompaniments include tasty sautéed potato, tomatoey cabbage and coarsely grated beetroot. If you've room, try the delectable sweet cheese nalesniki. Older well-heeled locals, young couples and a few stray tourists dine here. We reckon Antony's is ideal for a romantic dinner or an enjoyable catch-up with a friend.
Babies and children welcome: high chairs. Booking advisable weekends. Restaurant available for hire. Separate room for parties, seats 30. **Map 7 C5.**

Hammersmith

Knaypa **NEW**
268 King Street, W6 0SP (8563 2887/ www.theknaypa.co.uk). Hammersmith tube.
Lunch served noon-3pm, **dinner served** 6-10pm Mon-Fri. **Meals served** noon-midnight Sat, Sun. **Main courses** £7.50-£15. **Credit** AmEx, MC, V.
Knaypa certainly makes a design statement, with its rippled purple plastic ceiling, coloured mirrors on the walls, spotlights on the floor and shocking red leather chairs. Piped dance music (even on an otherwise quiet Saturday lunchtime) adds to the half-deserted disco feel. For a calmer meal, head for the basement where the owners have gone for a folksy look, with knotted-wood furniture and soft lighting. The new menu plays to the kitchen's strengths – hearty and authentic Polish cooking. We were brought rich, creamy smalec (seasoned pork fat to be eaten smothered over rye bread) while we waited for our starters of fried smoked cheese with chutneys, and dill-spiked gravadlax. Both these were very salty, but as the Polish

proverb goes 'without salt, the feast is spoiled'. A main course of stuffed rabbit leg with creamy mashed potatoes and sage sauce was expertly prepared, and less of a shock to the British palate. There's an extensive drinks list, served from the neon-lit bar; the choice of vodkas is worth a shot. *Babies and children welcome: high chairs. Takeaway service.* **Map 20 A4.**

★ Polanka

258 King Street, W6 0SP (8741 8268/ http://polanka-rest.com). Ravenscourt Park tube. **Meals served** noon-9.30pm Mon-Sat; noon-7.30pm Sun. **Main courses** £4.90-£11.50. **Unlicensed. Corkage** £3 wine, £6 spirits. **Credit** MC, V.

One window of this deli-restaurant features posters of strapping men advertising the likes of muscle-building powders. At the front is a tiny shop offering a range of Polish cakes, groceries and newspapers. Through the back is the small BYO restaurant: all pine and wicker lampshades, dried flowers and charming staff. A boar skin is pegged on one wall, a mannequin in traditional dress peeks out from an alcove, and 1980s soft rock is on the stereo. On our Saturday night visit, a party of suited elderly Polish men were carefully taking their time over their meals, while some girls about to go out were hurrying through theirs. Polish specialities fill the menu: pierogi, sausages, pork. Clear barszcz was blood-coloured and rich with beef stock. Mains were disappointing. Pork schnitzel 'Polanka' came with rivers of pale melted cheese, mash that tasted more of butter than potato, and sliced raw tomato. A sweet, gelatinous white wine and mushroom sauce overwhelmed the carp it accompanied. We enviously eyed a rich, creamy bigos served in a bread cob. The astonishingly low bill eased any guilt about not finishing our main courses. *Babies and children welcome: high chairs. Booking advisable. Separate room for parties, seats 8. Takeaway service.* **Map 20 A4.**

Kensington

Wódka

12 St Alban's Grove, W8 5PN (7937 6513/ www.wodka.co.uk). High Street Kensington tube. **Lunch served** noon-3pm Tue-Fri, Sun. **Dinner served** 6.30-11.15pm daily. **Main courses** £12.90-£17.50. **Set lunch** £13.50 2 courses, £17 3 courses. **Set meal** £24.50-£28 3 courses. **Credit** AmEx, MC, V.

The less flamboyant, more intimate predecessor of Baltic (*see p87*), Wódka opened in an old dairy in the late 1980s: note the antique tiles. The premises have been brought up to date with sleek woodwork and imaginative lighting. Jan Woroniecki's trademark mixing of traditional eastern European themes and ingredients with modern European style is almost always carried off with great aplomb. We can never resist the warm salad of smoked eel with boczek (fatty bacon), new potato, honey and capers – complex flavours expertly juggled – or nutty organic buckwheat blinis with meltingly tender herring. Mains marry robust flavours with a welcome light touch. We adore the (not very East European) roast cod with earthy butter beans and pesto; and the braised shoulder of lamb, its richness foiled by a sharp apple and pomegranate pilaf. But oh, the service! More than once we've had to wait too long for drinks, been rushed from starter to mains, and so on. Enticing puds include nalesniki with sweet cheese, and sernik (Polish cheesecake) with a white-chocolate twist. Alternatively, opt for one of the fantastic flavoured vodkas; we love the spiced orange and caramel varieties. Just cosset us a little more, please. *Babies and children admitted. Booking advisable. Separate room for parties, seats 30. Tables outdoors (3, pavement).* **Map 7 C9.**

Shepherd's Bush

Patio

5 Goldhawk Road, W12 8QQ (8743 5194). Goldhawk Road tube. **Lunch served** noon-3pm Mon-Fri. **Dinner served** 6-11.30pm daily. **Main**

courses £7-£9.50. **Set meal** £15.99 4 courses incl vodka shot. **Credit** AmEx, DC, MC, V.

The cooking seems to be getting less reliable, but Patio retains a quirky charm. With its £15.99 four-course set menu (including complimentary vodka, pre-dessert fruit and cake), we're inclined to give the place the benefit of the doubt. A meal here reminds us of visiting an elderly Polish aunt's, complete with home cooking, a faded, fin-de-siècle air, piano and velvet drapes. Service this time was complicated by a sweet but uncomprehending and incomprehensible Chinese waitress, who brought very different dishes to the ones we'd ordered. Starters are traditional: potato pancakes, herrings, bigos, barszcz and smoked-salmon blini (a whopping torpedo-shaped affair). Cod in a cloying dill sauce and plain polish sausage à la zamoyski (grilled with onions, mustard and horseradish) were nothing to write home about, and the accompanying vegetables (roast potatoes, green cabbage and carrots) were slightly tired. Our cheesecake was lighter than usual (not typically Polish), but sweet cheese pancakes hit the spot. We've heard gripes about mysterious extras occasionally appearing on the bill, but that could well be due to the confused service. Patio is good value, but there's room for improvement. *Book dinner Fri, Sat. Separate room for parties, seats 45. Takeaway service.* **Map 20 C2.**

Balham

★ Polish White Eagle Club

211 Balham High Road, SW17 7BQ (8672 1723/www.whiteeagleclub.co.uk). Tooting Bec tube/Balham tube/rail/49, 155, 181, 319 bus. *Bar* **Open** 6-11.30pm Mon-Fri; 6pm-midnight Sat; 11am-10pm Sun. *Restaurant* **Lunch served** noon-3pm, **dinner served** 6-10pm Mon-Fri. **Meals served** noon-11pm Sat; noon-10pm Sun. **Main courses** £9.90. **Set lunch** £7 2 courses. **Set dinner** £9.90 2 courses. *Both* **Credit** MC, V.

Across the road from the Polish Kosciol Chrystusa Krola church, this white building hasn't changed much since the 1930s. Inside, it could be any other social club, save for the noticeboards crowded with flyers written in Polish. It's a warren of a place: a ballroom on the right (popular with salsa dancers) runs the length of the building; the main bar has a couple of pool tables and plenty of tables for a chinwag. The restaurant, at the rear, is straight out of a 1970s wedding. Its menu is full of traditional Polish dishes – soups, stews, potato pancakes – which come in generous portions. We liked the sour zurek soup: a shame the accompanying rye bread

Divo. See p90.

was stale. The bigos stew was full of sausage, sauerkraut and chunks of pork. Desserts ranged from the decent (pancakes with curd cheese) to the mediocre (baked cheesecake lacking the necessary cheesiness). Service was friendly enough, but as early sitters we had to go into the bar to order more drinks. Saturday nights feature Polish folk bands and *zabawa* (dance) classes.

Babies and children welcome: high chairs. Booking advisable. Entertainment: musicians, dance classes Sat. Separate rooms for parties, seating 30 and 120. Takeaway service.

Clapham

Café Wanda
153 Clapham High Street, SW4 7SS (7738 8760). Clapham Common tube. **Meals served** noon-11pm Mon-Fri; 11am-11pm Sat, Sun. **Main courses** £6.95-£14.95. **Credit** MC, V.
As we went to press, Café Wanda was closed for refurbishment, which is welcome news as there was more than a whiff of the 1970s at this highly individual café and restaurant. An incongruous small wooden bar tucked away in a back corner offered B52s, sea breezes, and a dozen types of mostly Polish vodka (served as double measures in a frosted glass). On our last visit, the soundtrack of gooey love songs was, thankfully, turned down from pop-concert level to just loud as we were seated. Toulousian cassoulet was off the menu, said our waitress, as the chef couldn't source the right sort of beans. Still, with three menus to choose from, there was no shortage of options.

THE DISH

Pierogi
If you like pasta, you'll love pierogi, the Slavic answer to ravioli. Shaped like half-moons, these dough parcels are filled with a variety of stuffings, from meat to fruit, then boiled. Yes, they take some work to prepare from scratch (most people resort to ready-made frozen varieties), but making them is just the starting point; from then on adding calories seems to be the mission. Often, pierogi will be served with melted butter poured over and dipped in soured cream, or else gently fried in butter or pig fat until browned (a bit like gyoza), maybe scattered with fried onions and the Polish bacon boczek, or crispy golden breadcrumbs. It's the sort of food that has helped generations survive ice-cold Polish winters, so is sure to brighten a foggy day in London town.

Knaypa's pierogi are stuffed with salty-savoury minced veal. At **Baltic** the kitchen favours another classic Polish filling: cream cheese, potato and spring onion; clarified butter is then used for frying. Once sprinkled with herbs and doused in sour cream, these sell in their thousands every week. Come winter, Baltic's pierogi are stuffed with oxtail stew to provide lip-smacking, rib-sticking variety, while over at sister restaurant **Wódka**, chefs offer a sauerkraut and wild mushroom variation in the cold months. It's almost enough to make you look forward to February. Vareniki and pelmeni are the Ukraine's versions, which you can sample at **Divo**.

Traditional bistro fare (schnitzels, sirloin steaks, beef stroganoff) are balanced by Polish dishes like golonka (pork knuckle) and savoury dumplings. Blinis come with pork goulash and are as authentic as you'll find in London. We followed them with a stack of waffle-thick pancakes – propped on the plate with cream, chocolate sauce, sliced banana and a handful of strawberries – which defeated us.
Babies and children admitted. Booking advisable. Entertainment: pianist 8.30-11pm Fri, Sat. Tables outdoors (2, pavement). Takeaway service. Vegetarian menu. **Map 22 B2**.

Romanian

Central
City

32 Old Bailey NEW
32 Old Bailey, EC4M 7HS (7489 1842/ www.32oldbailey.co.uk). St Paul's tube. **Meals served** noon-midnight Mon-Fri, Sun; 6pm-2am Sat. **Main courses** £5-£11. **Credit** MC, V.
By day, this is an old-school Italian eaterie on a baronial scale, decorated by incongruous jazz-themed murals. At weekends, it transforms into a Romanian party venue, with a band, a singer belting out Romanian ballads, and young couples dancing in strict tempo. Later a DJ spins more modern sounds. The place is a magnet for London's young Romanians. On our visit, tables began to fill at around 11pm, mainly with chaps in their twenties. Women (in über-tight microminis) were in short supply. The welcoming staff were happy to guide our choices. A light, fruity village-style red wine, brought by barrel from Romania, slipped down beautifully. Start a meal with one of the chunky soups (ciorba), which come in meatball, chicken, beef or tripe (good for a hangover) versions. Alternatively, try the cascaval pane (fried cheese in breadcrumbs). Meat main courses arrive with piles of potatoes or mamaliga (polenta) accompanied by sour cream and cheese. Mititei (skinless minced pork, lamb and garlic sausages) and garlicky pork tenderloin stuffed with slanina (bacon fat) were simple but tasty. End with a creamy gateau or rum baba from the fabulously retro sweet trolley. A fun, if unusual, experience.
Babies and children admitted. Restaurant available for hire. **Map 11 O6**.

Russian

Central
Clerkenwell & Farringdon

Potemkin
144 Clerkenwell Road, EC1R 5DP (7278 6661/ www.potemkin.co.uk). Farringdon tube/rail. **Meals served** noon-11pm Mon-Fri. **Dinner served** 6-11pm Sat. **Main courses** £9.50-£17. **Set dinner** £20 3 courses. **Credit** AmEx, DC, MC, V.
On occasion we've found Potemkin's ground-floor restaurant over-formal and the food disappointing, but our most recent visit showed it on good form. Service was pretty chaotic on a busy short-staffed Saturday night (though the harassed waitress backed profuse apologies with compensatory drinks). The curved room has opulent padded blue and purple banquettes and gilt-framed niches holding gleaming red, black and gold-lacquered *khokhloma* (papier-mâché ware). Potemkin boasts over 130 vodkas and beers, plus some mean vodka cocktails – which can also be enjoyed in the lively upstairs bar. Our meal began with two immaculate starters: meltingly succulent herring and warm new potatoes sprinkled with fresh dill; and pod shuboy (cured herring layered with juicy beetroot, vegetable salad and mayonnaise) – both ideal companions to a clear vodka like Russkii Standart. If herring's not your thing, try the puffy blinis. Next, chicken shashlik was tender, but not a patch

on pan-fried red mullet in robustly flavoured mustard and shallot sauce. With such light hands at work in the kitchen, you may even have room for a tart cherry pancake. Or just indulge in the seductively sweet flavoured vodkas, such as almond, melon or apple.
Babies and children admitted (lunch). Booking advisable. Takeaway service. **Map 5 N4**.

St James's

Divo NEW
12 Waterloo Place, SW1Y 4AU (7484 1355/ www.divolondon.com). Piccadilly Circus tube. **Meals served** noon-11pm Mon-Fri; 6-11pm Sat. **Main courses** £12-£18. **Set meal** (noon-7pm Mon-Fri) £13.50 2 courses, £15.50 3 courses. **Credit** AmEx, MC, V.
Having opened to some dire reviews, Divo has worked wonders transforming itself from a post-Soviet Ukrainian kitsch temple to a restrained, reasonably priced modern East European restaurant. The surroundings remain ostentatious, with vast chandeliers, heavy drapes and swags galore, yet only a gilt-framed plasma-screen TV (switched off) and the ornate loos betray past excesses. But is it all too late? On a Saturday night things were very quiet (the first floor seemed closed), with little atmosphere and looped muzak. Great sour rye bread accompanied scrumptious starters: a moulded herring, beetroot and potato cake; and meltingly tender smoked salmon with smoked sturgeon and crab. Main courses would have done any of London's best East European eateries proud: potato pancakes (perfectly chewy with a hint of sourness), stuffed with wild mushrooms; and tender chicken shashlik, with buckwheat, spring onions, pine nuts and light mushroom sauce. A very un-Ukrainian iced passion-fruit mousse with banana and thyme made a light and delicious end to an altogether pleasing meal. Some extremely expensive vodkas and champagnes lurk on the drinks list, yet our very quaffable French rosé was £15. Service is charming too.
Babies and children admitted. Disabled: toilet. Separate rooms for parties, seating 12-50. **Map 10 K7**.

North
Camden Town & Chalk Farm

Trojka
101 Regents Park Road, NW1 8UR (7483 3765/ www.troykarestaurant.co.uk). Chalk Farm tube. **Meals served** 9am-10.30pm daily. **Main courses** £6.95-£11.95. **Set lunch** (noon-4pm) £7.95-£11.95 2 courses. **Licensed**. **Corkage** £3 wine, £15 spirits. **Credit** MC, V.
The more we visit Trojka, the more we like its easy-going, cosy atmosphere and good hearty East European food. Where better to repair for a steaming bowl of borscht or hearty bigos after a walk over Primrose Hill on a chilly Sunday afternoon? Service can be hit and miss, but we love the fact you can pop in for coffee and a blueberry pancake, english breakfast or a full East European dinner – whatever takes your fancy. Neighbouring tables may be full of aspiring pop stars recovering from a heavy night out with a black coffee, or family groups enjoying full-on brunch. Dark wooden furniture, ruby-red walls and a massive Chagall-esque painting of a trojka (wooden sleigh drawn by three horses) all add to the authentic homely eastern European vibe. To eat, we adore the herring and the light puffy blinis with smoked salmon, caviar or aubergine purée. For something more substantial, try the succulent roast duck breast. Trojka is good for parties too; by night a violinist or accordion player is sometimes on hand (we defy you not to polka round the tables). Given the chi-chi location, the food is very good value.
Babies and children welcome: high chair. Book dinner Fri, Sat. Entertainment: Russian folk music 8-10.30pm Fri, Sat. Tables outdoors (4, pavement). Takeaway service. **Map 27 A1**.

Fish

Sustainable fishing practices have become a major environmental and food industry concern, yet while one-time staples such as cod and tuna have been under threat, promotion of a wider range of fish and seafoods by organisations such as the Marine Stewardship Council (www.msc.org.uk) is ensuring that the range of species on offer in restaurants across the board is more diverse than ever. Herring, especially, is experiencing a surge in popularity, stocks having recovered from the dark period of the 1970s when it was necessary to ban herring fishing altogether. This year we've eaten pollack, sea trout and gilthead bream at **J Sheekey**, huss, sardines and mackerel at **Fish Hook**, brill, shark and ray at **The Fish Shop**, red snapper at **Curve**, and john dory at **Chez Liline** and **Scott's**.

The restaurants on these pages include resolutely English old-timers as well as specialists in other cuisines such as **Olivomare** (Sardinian), **Deep** (Scandinavian) and **Zilli Fish** (Italian). Also of note is the haute cuisine restaurant **One-O-One** (*see p139*). For budget eateries that specialise in fish and chips, see p315.

Central

Belgravia

★ Olivomare
10 Lower Belgrave Street, SW1W 0LJ (7730 9022). Victoria tube/rail. **Lunch served** noon-2.30pm, **dinner served** 7-11pm Mon-Sat. **Main courses** £14-£26.50. **Credit** AmEx, DC, MC, V.
How brave is this? A seafood restaurant that is perfectly content to be a seafood restaurant without the decorative fishing nets or token meat and poultry options for carnivores. Olivomare's stark minimalist monochrome fish-patterned decor is as single-minded as the menu. On the night we dined at this sibling to fellow Sardinians Olivo (*see p177*) and Olivetto, it was a solely (sorry) seafood affair. Not just seafood, either, but impeccably fresh, intelligently cooked seafood. House-made monkfish ravioli with tomato and bottarga (dried mullet roe) were silky and uplifting, while calamari fritti actually tasted of sweet calamares and not deep-fried cardboard. We also loved sea-sweet, chargrilled sea bass cooked in a salt crust, and a crisp bream fillet sympathetically accompanied by a colourful summery salad of fregola (a couscous-like Sardinian grain). Desserts, including sebada cheese fritters and good sorbetti and gelati are, thankfully, seafood-free but just as much a celebration of freshness. Even the (Italian) waiters are fresh, in a good way.
Booking essential. Children admitted. Disabled: toilet. Tables outdoors (4, terrace). **Map 15 H10.**
For branch (Olivetto) see index.

City

Chamberlain's
23-25 Leadenhall Market, EC3V 1LR (7648 8690/www.chamberlains.org). Bank tube/DLR/ Liverpool Street tube/rail.
Bar **Open** noon-11pm Mon-Fri.
Restaurant **Meals served** noon-9.30pm Mon-Fri. **Main courses** £14.50-£33. **Set dinner** £16.95 2 courses, £18.95 3 courses.
Both **Credit** AmEx, DC, MC, V.
Credit crunch? What's that? There was little sign of belt-tightening in the financial sector among the well-oiled crowds around the bars, shops and eating places that have taken over the Victorian grandeur of Leadenhall Market. Chamberlain's is one of the more individual venues, with a bright ground-floor space with outside terrace, a more sedate dining room above and an oddly modern basement bar. The menu offers plenty of Mod-European combinations, but its centrepiece is fresh fish – lemon sole, halibut, sea bass and more – served plain grilled or in batter (a very geezer-ish indulgence at these lofty prices). Service is zippy. A complimentary little cup of gazpacho was a nice touch, and our grilled sea bass and lemon sole were of a high quality, and very properly cooked. In between, though, a starter of avocado, crab and prawn salad was let down by bog-standard salad ingredients, and any accompaniments to go with the fish (all extra) were downright dull, such as a tiny pot of 'seasonal greens' (mangetout and green beans) for a wildly over the top £4.25. Prices on the refined wine list are also exaggerated, but this seems to go with the territory.
Babies and children admitted. Disabled: toilet. Restaurant available for hire. Tables outdoors (25, pavement). **Map 12 Q7.**

Sweetings (100)
39 Queen Victoria Street, EC4N 4SA (7248 3062). Mansion House tube. **Lunch served** 11.30am-3pm Mon-Fri. **Main courses** £11.50-£27.50. **Credit** AmEx, MC, V.
Get to Sweetings on the right day in April and you could arrive at the same time as the year's first gull's eggs, wild salmon, English asparagus, and Jersey Royal potatoes. In these days of designer makeovers and global menus, Sweetings is that rare and wonderful thing – a traditional British fish restaurant that clings to its traditions as if the Empire depended on it. While the specials board lists soused herring and grilled halibut with lobster sauce, most of the City types who perch on rickety stools at the high white-clothed counters and cram into the communal tables at the back are here for the fried fish of the day, the fish pie and the salmon cakes; leaving room, of course, for the spotted dick pud. We did well with good, briny rock oysters and delicate, lightly oily smoked salmon, but our grilled scampi was relatively flavour-free, and fried plaice was a bit mushy. Sweetings opens only for lunch, takes no bookings, and is full soon after noon, so order a silver pewter mug of Guinness and do what everyone else does: wait.
Babies and children admitted. Bookings not accepted. Restaurant available for hire (dinner only). Takeaway service. **Map 11 P6.**

Covent Garden

Loch Fyne Restaurant
2-4 Catherine Street, WC2B 5JS (7240 4999/ www.lochfyne.com). Covent Garden tube. **Meals served** 10am-11pm daily. **Main courses** £10-£19. **Set meal** (noon-6.30pm, 10-11pm) £12-£15 2 courses. **Credit** AmEx, MC, V.
It's hard to know what to make of Loch Fyne: the staff are lovely, the decor (if you avoid the dark overspill basement) pleasant and airy, and the menu appealing and interesting, featuring a number of reasonably priced dishes. So far, so good. If only the food gave as much pleasure. At times, it does. Loch Fyne oysters (£9 for six) are excellent, not too milky, as fresh as daisies, and with a great texture. The kippers are succulent and meaty without being overpoweringly smoky, and at £7 would make a lovely light supper. But our gravadlax was bland, and soused herring was too strong for its four accompanying marinades. Of our mains, garlic butter king prawns were downright peculiar, their texture mushy and ill-defined – though as soon as we questioned their freshness the waiter was only too happy to replace them. The mussels in moules marinière were belters (plump, fresh and juicy), but the chips in the side order were a travesty: pale, pasty and fat, and an insult to the classic moules frites combo. We left sated by good portions, happy with the prices, impressed by the service, but distinctly unsure about the food.
Babies and children welcome: children's menu; high chairs; nappy-changing facilities. Booking advisable. Disabled: toilet. **Map 18 E4.**
For branches see index.

Fitzrovia

Back to Basics
21A Foley Street, W1W 6DS (7436 2181/ www.backtobasics.uk.com). Goodge Street or Oxford Circus tube. **Lunch served** noon-3pm, **dinner served** 6-10.30pm Mon-Sat. **Main courses** £13.75-£21.75. **Credit** AmEx, DC, MC, V.
This corner restaurant in the backstreets of Fitzrovia was abuzz with bonhomie on a Wednesday night. It's a neighbourhood joint, with homely decor – blond wood tables, cane-backed chairs, hand-painted globe lights, mosaic tiling – and a casual, friendly vibe. A blackboard lists today's catch: 16 options on our visit, from mackerel, cod and skate to tuna and mahi mahi. No wonder fish stocks are waning (though the menu makes no mention of such matters). To start, there are oysters, crab claws, marinated herring, gravadlax or fish soup, plus salads, a few pasta dishes and a couple of meat options (if you must). Cooking is unsophisticated, but the fish is fantastically fresh and portions ample. 'Sea bass with ginger and garlic' featured a mound of beansprouts, carrots and spring onions in a, gingery, chilli-tinted sauce, while a slab of halibut (of impeccable quality) came with an abundance of spinach, avocado and bacon. A side of cauliflower 'salad' was, surprisingly, served hot, with pine nuts – but worked well. Efficient staff and a serviceable wine list (Picpoul de Pinet for a fair £17) keep everything running smoothly. Old-school puddings include bananas baked in foil, bread and butter pud and apple tart.
Babies and children welcome: high chair. Booking advisable. Tables outdoors (10, pavement). Takeaway service. **Map 17 A1.**

Leicester Square

J Sheekey (100)
28-32 St Martin's Court, WC2N 4AL (7240 2565/www.caprice-holdings.co.uk). Leicester Square tube. **Lunch served** noon-3pm Mon-Sat;

olivomare

noon-3.30pm Sun. **Dinner served** 5.30pm-midnight Mon-Sat; 6pm-11pm Sun. **Main courses** £13.75-£39.50. **Set lunch** (Sat, Sun) £24.75 3 courses. **Cover** £2. **Credit** AmEx, DC, MC, V.

Josef Sheekey was a market stall holder given permission by one Lord Salisbury to serve fish and seafood in this 1896 property development, on the proviso that he supply meals to Salisbury's after-theatre dinner parties. Over a century later, the restaurant retains its late-Victorian, theatrical charm, but unlike many of London's period pieces Sheekey's buzzes with fashionable folk and famous faces. Your party of four may be crammed on to a table that other restaurants would allocate to two, but best consider this part of the fun. The menu stretches from comforting favourites (fish pie, dense salmon fish cakes) to accomplished Modern British and European cooking (River Fowey sea trout with wild fennel and sea purslane; chargrilled cuttlefish with braised chickpeas and padrón peppers). Choose carefully and you can eat fairly economically, but mains reach up over £20 and lobster and dover sole further still. Simple salt-baked gilthead bream, shown to the table in its crust before filleting, was stunning; so too the golden, hear-the-crunch battered haddock. Good desserts (honeycomb ice-cream with dark chocolate sauce, black fig tart, elderflower jelly) are a pleasing bi-catch. We've had complaints about rude service here, but staff were pleasant enough on this occasion.
Babies and children welcome: booster seats; colouring books; high chairs. Booking essential. Vegetarian menu. Vegan dishes. **Map 18 D5.**

Mayfair

★ Scott's

20 Mount Street, W1K 2HE (7495 7309/ www.caprice-holdings.co.uk). Bond Street or Green Park tube. **Meals served** noon-midnight Mon-Sat; noon-10pm Sun. **Main courses** £16.50-£39.50. **Cover** £2. **Credit** AmEx, DC, MC, V.

Of all the celebrity hangouts in the capital, Scott's is the one that most justifies the hype: from the greeting by Sean the doorman to the look-at-me contemporary British art on the walls and the glossy Rich List crowd. Yes, tables are like hen's teeth, so snare a perch at the slow curve of onyx bar, where you'll be rewarded by superior, elevated views of all the action. The food here just gets better and better. On our last visit, we thrilled to the hot-cold contrast of sweet, tiny wild boar sausages teamed with chilled Maldon rock oysters, and the single fried duck egg which was bravely undercooked so the yolk became an instant sauce for the strewn duck livers and hearts. A small but whole grilled john dory reminded us of how special fish can be when cooked on the bone, and roast fillet of cod with a spring vegetable risotto was simple and succulent. A high-crusted Bramley apple pie immediately went into our dessert hall of fame. Most of all, we love the fact that Scott's is so much fun, right down to the retro Marie Antoinette champagne glasses.
Babies and children welcome: high chairs. Booking advisable. Separate room for parties, seats 40. Tables outdoors (4, pavement). **Map 9 G7.**

Piccadilly

★ Bentley's Oyster Bar & Grill (100)

11-15 Swallow Street, W1B 4DG (7734 4756/ www.bentleysoysterbarandgrill.co.uk). Piccadilly Circus tube.
Oyster Bar **Meals served** noon-midnight Mon-Sat; noon-10pm Sun. **Main courses** £8.50-£24.
Restaurant **Lunch served** noon-3pm daily. **Dinner served** 6-11pm Mon-Sat; 6-10pm Sun. **Main courses** £16.50-£38.
Both **Credit** AmEx, MC, V.

London certainly knows how to revitalise and reinvent its historic fish restaurants: witness the rise and rise-again of J Sheekey and Scott's. Ever since Irish-born Richard Corrigan (of the Lindsay House, *see p61*) and his partners took over this 92-year-old veteran a couple of years ago, Bentley's

Olivomare. See p91.

has been one of the capital's most charming and consistent performers. While the first-floor dining rooms are more sedate and well-mannered, the downstairs oyster bar is where the action is – and where there's a good chance the ebullient Corrigan himself will be holding forth. The menu crawls all over the place like a mad crab, from the traditional (huge fish and chips, old-fashioned fish pie and a richly endowed shellfish cocktail with pink marie-rose sauce) to the modern (meaty stone-bass fillet with chanterelles, and an inventive steamed Cornish fish with Thai flavours). Best spot is a bar-side stool to watch the oyster-openers shuck and flip like sleight-of-hand magicians. Yes, it's expensive here, but you can't help feeling that your boat has come in.

Booking essential. Disabled: toilet. Dress: smart casual; no shorts. Separate rooms for parties, seating 14 and 60. **Map 17 A5.**

Soho

Zilli Fish

36-40 Brewer Street, W1F 9TA (7734 8649/ www.zillialdo.com). Piccadilly Circus tube. **Meals served** noon-11.30pm Mon-Sat. **Main courses** £9-£29.50. **Set dinner** (5-6.30pm, after 10pm Mon-Sat) £19.50 2 courses, £24 3 courses. **Credit** AmEx, MC, V.

Chef Aldo Zilli may not be as first-name famous as Gordon, Jamie and Nigella, but he's doing his best to boost his celeb status with his Soho mini-empire, TV appearances, cookbooks and cookery classes. This, his flagship operation, benefits from big picture windows on a corner site, though the subdued colour scheme (a symphony in brown) can be a bit of a downer if it's not buzzing. Our food was disappointing. Best were the appetisers: tender crispy squid (though the sweet chilli sauce tasted no better than a supermarket version), mussels and clams in a light broth, and shell-on king prawns in an earthy tomato and olive sauce. We liked the side dish of courgette 'chips' too, but the mains were average. Crab linguine was merely bland, while monkfish medallions wrapped in pancetta (a stingy four for £24) with spring onion mash came with a peculiar-tasting coconut-curry sauce that did the fish no favours. To be fair, the maître d' rushed over as soon as he heard we weren't wowed by the dish to make conciliatory

noises and offer us free glasses of limoncello. Italian bottles dominate the wine list, but there's little choice under £25.

Babies and children welcome: high chairs. Booking advisable. Tables outdoors (2, patio). Takeaway service. **Map 17 B4.**

For branches (Signor Zilli, Zilli Café) **see index.**

South Kensington

Bibendum Oyster Bar

Michelin House, 81 Fulham Road, SW3 6RD (7589 1480/www.bibendum.co.uk). South Kensington tube. **Meals served** noon-10.30pm Mon-Sat; noon-10pm Sun. **Main courses** £8-£15. **Credit** AmEx, DC, MC, V.

This casual café in the lovely tiled foyer of the Michelin building (downstairs from Bibendum, *see p93*) is a consistently reliable operation, much loved by smartly dressed lunching ladies. Who can blame them, with such well-mannered service and an ocean's worth of seafood to enjoy? Seating is at circular, marble-topped tables in a small side space, or in the foyer; the latter is light and airy, but noisy thanks to hard surfaces. The oysters are top-notch, of course (you can buy some for home at the crustacea stall outside). There's also lobster mayonnaise, prawns, crab, potted shrimps and elaborate seafood platters on the standard menu, as well as a short, daily-changing choice of Mediterranean-slanted light dishes, both cold and hot. Options on our visit included chicken breast with piedmontese peppers and pesto, rump of lamb with baba ganoush, lentil and preserved lemon salad, and fillet of sea trout with haricot beans, diced tomatoes and salsa verde (odd-tasting and too strong for the delicate fish). Panna cotta or blackberry cheesecake are typical puddings. The French-focused wine list majors on whites and champagne, with, usefully, all house wines available by the 460ml pot.

Babies and children welcome: high chairs. Bookings not accepted. Disabled: ramp; toilet. Dress: smart casual. **Map 14 E10.**

Poissonnerie de l'Avenue

82 Sloane Avenue, SW3 3DZ (7589 2457/ www.poissonneriedelavenue.co.uk). South Kensington tube. **Lunch served** noon-3pm, **dinner served** 7-11.30pm Mon-Sat. **Main**

courses £14.50-£24. **Set lunch** £14 1 course, £20 2 courses, £24 3 courses. **Cover** £2. **Credit** AmEx, DC, MC, V.

At first glance, this South Kensington veteran looks just like another old-fashioned fish restaurant past its use-by date. Nautically themed oil paintings hang on the walls, the lobster-motif carpet is busier than the fast-moving waiters, and a decidedly senior crowd studies menus filled with coquilles saint jacques with pernod and creole rice, sole veronique and lobster thermidor. But what Poissonnerie de l'Avenue does, it does very well, sourcing impeccably fresh fish from its adjoining fishmonger, and treating this with respect and understanding. Smoked salmon served with boiled quail's eggs and crème fraîche was silky and subtle; a nicely sludgy bouillabaisse was crammed with bits of cod, red mullet, prawns, mussels, and scallops; and an order of crisp, grilled sea bass with artichokes and cherry tomatoes could have happily fed two. Waiters were brusque, but the owner pitches-in when things heat up – and how nice, these days, to be greeted and farewelled in person. Old-fashioned isn't necessarily a bad thing.

Booking advisable dinner. Children admitted (babies admitted lunch only). Dress: smart casual. Separate room for parties, seats 20. Tables outdoors (4, pavement). **Map 14 E10.**

St James's

Green's

36 Duke Street, SW1Y 6DF (7930 4566/ www.greens.org.uk). Green Park or Piccadilly Circus tube. **Lunch served** 11.30am-3pm, **dinner served** 5.30-11pm Mon-Sat. **Main courses** £15.50-£42.50. **Cover** £2. **Credit** AmEx, DC, MC, V.

On one side of Duke Street, an alleyway leads to the White Cube gallery which, on our visit, was showing an exhibition of Hitler watercolours daubed with bright rainbows by the Chapman Brothers. Opposite is Green's, the kind of sturdy English restaurant that would withstand anything Hitler could muster. On a Monday night the leather banquette booths were full of posh English matrons and their portly besuited partners haw-hawing genially and acknowledging each other – and the attentive but nicely unobsequious waiting staff – amicably. Green's may seem a parody of the perfect English establishment, but it serves

Applebee's. See p96.

RESTAURANTS

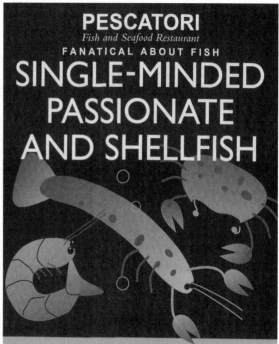

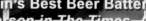

excellent food and the old-school menu is tinged with some interesting modern touches. Lobster salad featured firm but not rubbery crustacean. Mains were cooked to perfection: slivers of lamb's liver melted in the mouth, the crisp deep-fried sage leaves a delicious foil; and a doorstop-thick steak was robust but tender. We'd no room for puddings, though around us the likes of strawberries with black pepper ice-cream went down a treat. Maybe the obviously discerning country set would quite take to the Chapman Brothers after all.
Babies and children admitted. Booking advisable. Dress: smart casual; no trainers. Separate room for parties, seats 36. **Map 9 J7.**

West

Chiswick

Fish Hook
8 Elliott Road, W4 1PE (8742 0766/ www.fishhook.co.uk). Turnham Green tube. **Lunch served** noon-2.30pm Mon-Fri; noon-3.30pm Sat, Sun. **Dinner served** 6-10.30pm Mon-Sat; 6-10pm Sun. **Main courses** £17-£29. **Set lunch** £10 2 courses, £15 3 courses. **Credit** AmEx, MC, V.
With its cream-timbered beach house interior, Fish Hook feels like a cosy seaside cottage that has been inexplicably washed up off the Chiswick High Road. Yet behind its simple, laid-back appearance lies some sophisticated cooking, courtesy of chef-owner Michael Nadra, who has worked with the likes of Stephen Terry, Bruce Poole and Anthony Demetre. There are no clichés on his menu; instead, Nadra likes matching meat with fish, giving a clever, modern twist to 'surf and turf'. So Shetland mussels come with ham hock, grilled sea bream with bayonne ham and wild turbot with alsace bacon. A cassoulet of huss and roast pork belly was a nice idea; sadly it was let down by overcooked pork and undercooked white beans. Better were the deep-fried sardines with Sicilian tomatoes; the dark, intense, bisque studded with mixed seafood; and the delicate three-way dish of mackerel presented as cured, tartare and tempura. Service can be slow, but in an area dominated by 'same as high street' chain restaurants, Fish Hook is a good catch.
Babies and children admitted. Booking advisable (weekends).

Notting Hill

Geales (100)
2 Farmer Street, W8 7SN (7727 7528/ www.geales.com). Notting Hill Gate tube. **Lunch served** noon-2.30pm Tue-Sun. **Dinner served** 6-11pm Mon-Fri; 6-10.30pm Sun. **Meals served** noon-11pm Sat. **Main courses** £8-£17. **Cover** 15p. **Credit** AmEx, MC, V.
In step with its mewsy neighbourhood, Geales has marched upmarket. In 1939 it opened as a chippie, but in recent years – and especially since its 2006 takeover by the team behind the Embassy (see p234), including executive chef Gary Hollihead – it has become the habitat of Notting Hill's casually dressed middle class. The sleek ground and first floors now feature wooden flooring, stylish black-leather armchairs, and grey walls enlivened by old photos of fisher-folk. Service is clued-up and engaging (though part of our order was forgotten). Fish remains the focus of the menu, which states the restaurant is 'dedicated to using sustainable fisheries only'. A starter of creamy moules marinière had plenty of finely chopped shallots and parsley, and tender bivalves: easily enough for two to share. To follow, fish of the day was a handsome, ultra-fresh fried dover sole, served with a tomato and red pepper chutney. Pollack too came perfectly cooked inside its (slightly hard) beer batter. Chips, mushy peas, and excellent sweet-pickled onions all cost extra (and some prices have risen by a third in the past year), but this was a fine meal, rounded off by a luxurious tiramisu.
Babies and children welcome: children's menu; high chairs. Booking advisable. Separate room for parties, seats 12. Tables outdoors (6, pavement). Takeaway service. **Map 7 A7.**

South West

Fulham

Deep
The Boulevard, Imperial Wharf, SW6 2UB (7736 3337/www.deeplondon.co.uk). Fulham Broadway tube then 391, C3 bus. Bar **Open/snacks served** noon-11pm Tue-Sat. **Snacks** £4-£11.50. Restaurant **Lunch served** noon-3pm Tue-Fri; Sun. **Dinner served** 7-11pm Tue-Sat. **Main courses** £13.50-£26.50. Both **Credit** AmEx, MC, V.
Amid the characterless development of Fulham Wharf, Deep lies near the Thames. Yet even with its floor-to-ceiling windows, not a glimpse of water is visible from the chic, airy dining room: only similar sprawl on the other side of the river. The Swedish owners have given the shortish menu a Scandinavian accent, proudly declared by tasty fennel crispbread with the warm rolls, followed by an amuse-gueule of dilled prawns on blinis. For starters, ballotine of gravadlax with fennel salad and crème fraîche was a thick dill-edged tranche of beautifully moist salmon. The selection of herrings was heaven for fans of the fish: little pots of it plain pickled, in mustard sauce, in herbed cream and with chopped egg. Main courses – grilled dover sole with summer greens and pommes du jour; and steamed halibut with eggs, prawns and horseradish – were both exquisitely executed and the fish cooked à point. From an international wine list, a flowery 2004 sauvignon blanc 'petit bourgeois' 2004 measured up to all the flavours with style. A gorgeous orange and black pepper panna cotta with poached rhubarb, and a plate of raspberry and mango sorbets with white chocolate ice-cream, capped a memorable meal.
Babies and children welcome: high chairs. Booking advisable. Disabled: toilet. Dress: smart casual. Entertainment: music 7pm Fri (bar). Tables outdoors (14, terrace). **Map 21 A2.**

South

Kennington

Lobster Pot
3 Kennington Lane, SE11 4RG (7582 5556/ www.lobsterpotrestaurant.co.uk). Kennington tube. **Lunch served** noon-2pm Tue-Fri. **Dinner served** 7-10.45pm Tue-Sat. **Main courses** £16.50-£40. **Minimum** (8-10pm) £23. **Set meal** £39.50-£44.50 tasting menu. **Credit** AmEx, MC, V.
For the past 17 years, London fish-lovers have been coming to Kennington to sit in this wonderfully kitsch room, festooned with fishing nets, lobster pots, lifebuoys, brass portholes and other nautical knick-knacks. The lure was flamboyant Breton chef Hervé Regent. These days however, the Lobster Pot seems to be run by his two sons, who also plan to open a second restaurant, Brasserie Toulouse Lautrec, around the corner in late 2008. Alas, on the night we visited, the cooking was very uneven. Freshly opened No.2 Irish rock oysters were perfectly briny and sweet, but a daily special of gratinated razor clams was both chewy and gritty, and the signature bouillabaisse was a right mess, with a thin, murky broth and undistinguished, over-cooked fish (grouper, rock salmon and conger eel). It was in relief we turned to a generously proportioned skate wing with burnt butter. It may just have been an off night, but it's worth noting that this restaurant is capable of having a very off night.
Babies and children welcome: booster seat. Booking advisable. Dress: smart casual. Separate rooms for parties, seating 20 and 25.

South East

London Bridge & Borough

fish!
Cathedral Street, Borough Market, SE1 9AL (7407 3803/www.fishdiner.co.uk). London Bridge tube/rail. **Meals served** 11.30am-11pm Mon-

Interview
ALDO ZILLI

Who are you?
Owner of Zilli Restaurants, including **Zilli Fish** (see p93).
What's the best thing about running a restaurant in London?
London attracts millions of people from every corner of the world and owning a restaurant means that you get to meet so many of them. Also, the city's diversity means that you can be very adventurous with menus.
What's the worst thing?
Finding and keeping staff. The competition is so fierce. High living costs mean that not enough Italian chefs and waiters are leaving Italy to come to London, and that is becoming more and more of a problem.
Which are your favourite London restaurants?
I love **Zuma** (see p194) for the food and vibrant, buzzing atmosphere. I am also a fan of really good sushi bars and there are quite a few inexpensive and delicious ones tucked away in corners of Soho (see p196). I generally prefer private members' clubs to bars as you always see the same faces, and there is, without fail, a great atmosphere.
How green are you?
In 2008 we were the first London restaurant group to ban all bottled water from our restaurants. I was shocked to find how damaging bottled water is to the environment, with a carbon footprint several hundred times larger than tap water. We offer customers a free carafe of water and they have reacted extremely positively to the change.
What is missing from London's restaurant scene?
Longevity. Nowadays it is all about the latest opening and the trendiest place to be seen. There are fewer and fewer restaurants that last for 30 or 40 years and are real institutions. I think London is missing the point slightly by only ever focusing on the new.

Thur; noon-11pm Fri, Sat; noon-10.30pm Sun. **Main courses** £9.95-£24.95. **Credit** AmEx, DC, MC, V.

A gleaming window on to Southwark Cathedral and Borough Market, fish! continues to reel in a cultured crowd who like to know the provenance of their fish supper. All the glass and chrome makes the restaurant a bright place for lunch on a gloomy winter day, but a bit sweaty in warm weather. The routine hasn't changed much since the (greatly diminished) chain first burst on to the scene. You choose from the list of fish of the day,

SHELF LIFE

You can find fish from the Thames Estuary on sale at farmers' markets in Acton, Blackheath and Walthamstow. At Borough Market, look out for Shellseekers, which dives for scallops off the coast of Dorset, or visit the Applebee's shop, which stocks superior wild and line-caught fish from day-boat fishermen (the quality of scaling and filleting is superb). If you're in wast London, your best source of seafood is Billingsgate Market, open to the public as well as the trade from 5am to 8.30am Tuesday to Saturday.

Cape Clear Fish Shop
319 Railton Road, SE24 0JN (7274 3617). Herne Hill rail.
This new branch of the Brook Green store stocks ethically farmed fish and wild fish from sustainable sources, mostly from boats landing in Devon and Cornwall. They also boast some superb prepared dishes and will cook to order.

James Knight
67 Notting Hill Gate, W11 3JS (7221 6177/www.james-knight.com). Notting Hill Gate tube.
Holder of two royal warrants, this premium-priced fishmonger specialises in fish from sustainable and eco-friendly sources, including ports in England's south-west and the well-managed fisheries of Norway, as well as organic sea trout and salmon from the Shetlands. You'll also find them in Selfridges food hall.

Moxon's
Shop E, Westbury Parade, Nightingale Lane, SW4 9DH (8675 2468). Clapham South tube.
A handy location near the tube, reasonable prices and office-friendly opening hours make this charming shop a must-visit for locals. Look out for treats such as brill, sea trout, live lobsters, samphire and inexpensive mussels and sardines. There is also a branch in East Dulwich.

FC Soper
141 Evelina Road, SE15 3HB (7639 9729). Nunhead rail.
Now into its second century, this well-stocked shop offers competitive prices on fresh fish from Cornwall and Scotland. Unlike most others, it's open on Sundays too.

the way you want it cooked and a sauce. We prefaced our choice with crisp Thai crab cakes served with sweet chilli sauce and a lot of rocket, plus a disappointingly watery fish soup. Organic grilled salmon steak and salsa verde, with a seasonal veg selection of pak choi, carrot and fennel, proved a great choice. As always, the battered (Icelandic) cod and chunky chips with mushy peas was a comforting plateful. Pleasantly not-too-sweet, date-filled sticky toffee pudding and good vanilla ice-cream signed off a decent but unremarkable meal served by friendly, unflurried staff.
Babies and children welcome: children's menu; crayons; high chairs. Booking advisable. Disabled: toilet. Tables outdoors (25, terrace). **Map 11 P8**.

Wright Brothers Oyster & Porter House
11 Stoney Street, SE1 9AD (7403 9554/ www.wrightbros.eu.com). Borough tube/London Bridge tube/rail. **Lunch served** noon-3pm Mon-Fri; noon-4pm Sat. **Dinner served** 6-10pm Mon-Sat. **Main courses** £7.30-£25.50. **Credit** AmEx, MC, V.
When one of the country's most respected oyster wholesalers opens its own restaurant, you'd expect oysters to be taken seriously. And you'd be right. On the night we visited, the blackboard listed natives from West Mersea and the Duchy of Cornwall, and Pacifics from Colchester, Maldon, and Carlingford Lough in Ireland, as well as French spéciales de claires. A mixed platter turned out to be the highlight of a mixed evening. This is an attractive venue, with its wooden counter, exposed bricks and line-up of blackboards. Our night got off to a fine start with a basket of crusty bread, half-pint of good prawns, and lightly smoked salmon. We were less taken by a sludgy beef, Guinness and oyster pie – basically a casserole with pastry lid. Our waiter, none-too-thrilled with a request for tap water, became harder and harder to flag down as the night went on, as the raucous Friday-night crowd started to resemble William Hogarth's 18th-century engravings of hard-drinking City men. Some things never change.
Booking advisable. Disabled: toilet. Tables outdoors (3, pavement). **Map 11 P8**.

East
Docklands

Curve
London Marriott, West India Quay, 22 Hertsmere Road, E14 4ED (7093 1000 ext 2622/ www.marriotthotels.com). Canary Wharf tube/DLR/West India Quay DLR. **Breakfast served** 6.30-11am Mon-Fri; 7-11am Sat, Sun. **Lunch served** noon-2.30pm daily. **Dinner served** 5-10.30pm Mon-Sat; 5-10pm Sun. **Main courses** £10.50-£22. **Credit** AmEx, DC, MC, V.
Although housed in the Marriott's sleek 32-storey tower, Curve doesn't make the most of its location. It is stuck at street level, leaving diners not with dramatic views of the Docklands skyline, but with grounded glimpses of commuters wandering along the quayside. This sounds like a minor frustration, but it downgrades Curve from a destination restaurant to a simple seafood eaterie, and the food alone isn't quite strong enough to warrant a special trip. That said, if you're in the area and your expense account can swallow the bill, you'll eat pretty well. Our crab-cake starter was small yet well-rounded, the gentle crab meat textures set off nicely by cranberries hidden in the accompanying mixed-leaf salad. A special of pan-fried red snapper was daisy-fresh (all the fish comes from nearby Billingsgate Market), and a dish of prawns cooked in coconut and coriander sauce was pricey (£17) but satisfyingly bold in its spicing. Indeed, the only discordant notes were sounded by two simpler dishes: a bland clam chowder and a horribly overcooked side of basmati rice. Good, then. But elevation by a few floors would make a world of difference.
Babies and children welcome: children's menu; crayons; high chairs. Booking advisable. Disabled: toilet (in hotel). Tables outdoors (10, terrace). **Map 24 B1**.

North East
South Woodford

Ark Fish Restaurant
142 Hermon Hill, E18 1QH (8989 5345/ www.arkfishrestaurant.com). South Woodford tube. **Lunch served** noon-2.15pm Tue-Sat. **Dinner served** 5.30-9.45pm Tue-Thur; 5.30-10.15pm Fri, Sat. **Main courses** £9.95-£23.50. **Credit** MC, V.
'If it ain't broke…' might be the motto at this popular local. Every night (bar Monday and Sunday) the Ark starts to fill as soon as its doors open. There's no booking, so arriving early guarantees a table, whereas late-comers must wait at the bar until one becomes free. A daily changing menu is based on whatever the market has to offer, so, together with the main menu, gives plenty of options over which to dither. Dublin rock oysters were a no-brainer: wonderfully fresh and creamy. For mains? Perfectly cooked fried cod and chips, or 'dish of the day': haddock on a pile of champ. Both, with a side of mushy peas, proved to be excellent choices. Desserts are strictly old school: the apple sponge was a delicious combo of sponge, sweet apple and custard; fresh fruit pavlova was a little light on fruit, but what little there was married well with the sweet, crumbly meringue and cream. Drinkers are well catered for too, with beers (bottled and draught) and a short, well-priced wine list – a Battistina Gavi (£15) was a perfectly quaffable choice. Service was friendly and efficient.
Babies and children welcome: children's menu; high chairs. Bookings not accepted.

Wanstead

★ Applebee's
17 Cambridge Park, E11 2PU (8989 1977). Wanstead tube. **Lunch served** noon-3pm Tue-Fri. **Dinner served** 6.30-10.30pm Tue-Sat. **Meals served** noon-9pm Sun. **Main courses** £13.50-£18.50. **Set lunch** £11.50 2 courses, £15.50 3 courses. **Set dinner** £21.50 3 courses. **Credit** AmEx, MC, V.

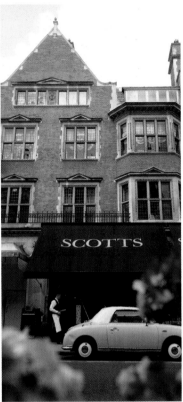

Scott's. See p92.

A great addition to the Wanstead eating scene, Applebee's combines good food with charming service and keen prices. The Mediterranean-influenced interior is a calming combination of beige walls, wooden floors and discreet decorative tiling. Meals here continue to impress; the firm also has a highly regarded fish shop in Borough Market – so sourcing is a strong point. For starters, lovely, creamy scallops were served with crisp bacon and rather too much rocket. Eschewing every other delicious-sounding main course, we dived into a fish and seafood platter for two, comprising appealing chunks of salmon, tuna and halibut, along with octopus, squid and prawns. The meal arrived with a pile of pan-fried new potatoes and lemony tomato and caper dressing. Everything was delicious. To finish, chocolate brownie with chocolate sauce, mascarpone ice-cream and mint went down quickly. The set menus are absolute bargains. Staff were slightly over-enthusiastic on the wine-pouring front, but a South African False Bay sauvignon blanc was a perfectly light, crisp choice from a fairly priced, well-travelled wine list. *Babies and children welcome: children's portions; high chair. Booking advisable dinner. Tables outdoors (5, courtyard).*
For branch (Applebee's Café) see index.

North
Finsbury Park

Chez Liline
101 Stroud Green Road, N4 3PX (7263 6550). Finsbury Park tube/rail. **Dinner served** 6.30-11pm Tue-Sun. **Main courses** £10.95-£17.75. **Set dinner** £15 3 courses. **Credit** AmEx, MC, V.
Owned by a Mauritian family, along with the fishmonger's next door, Chez Liline takes classic seafood recipes then adds its own exotic twist. Bouillon of crab is made with sweet potato; red snapper is doused with spicy, chilli-spiked creole sauce; and the handwritten specials list might include unusual combinations such as john dory with tamarind, coconut and mint. Unexpected

delights abound, such as the beautifully tender, immaculately fresh-tasting slivers of smoked halibut with sliced mango. More conventional dishes are well-handled too, if our impeccable crisp-skinned, salt-flecked sea bass, accompanied by crunchy shredded fennel, is typical. The short, French-influenced dessert menu is less inspired – crêpes, crème brûlée and the like – but, as the owner cheerfully admits, the real focus here is the seafood. It's a shame, then, that Chez Liline is often scantily populated, particularly midweek. Despite the accomplished cooking and charming service, the dowdy decor (utilitarian wooden floors, a few tired-looking bamboo screens and plants, and a stuffed turtle on the wall) is less than inviting on a quiet night. At weekends, when in-the-know regulars descend and a convivial buzz fills the space, it's much more enticing.
Babies and children welcome: high chairs. Booking advisable. Restaurant available for hire.

Islington

The Fish Shop
360-362 St John Street, EC1V 4NR (7837 1199/ www.thefishshop.net). Angel tube/19, 38, 341 bus. **Lunch served** noon-3pm, **dinner served** 5.30-11pm Tue-Sat. **Meals served** noon-8pm Sun. **Main courses** £11-£21. **Set meal** (noon-3pm, 5.30-7pm Tue-Sat; Sun) £17 2 courses, £20 3 courses. **Credit** AmEx, DC, MC, V.
In summer, this spacious three-level fish restaurant comes into its own when the outdoor terrace is hopping and the light streams into the upstairs/ downstairs dining rooms from a pretty internal courtyard. Just as sunny is the bright, can-do attitude of the young serving staff. The menu is a mix of fishy favourites (potted shrimps, fish pie and fish cakes) and more adventurous dishes, including Cornish shark with tomato vinaigrette, and sea trout with samphire and orange beurre blanc. Even so, every second order is for fried fish of the day (haddock, ling or pollock) with chips. A well-made terrine of ray wing in aspic was like an upmarket take on jellied eels, while a platter of

fresh prawns with garlic mayo was a simple, no-frills treat. Best of all was a generous serving of pan-fried brill: the three meaty, crisp-skinned fillets served with crisp pancetta, wilted spring onions and baby onions. The only duff note was the long wait between courses, due to a very large group dining downstairs – simply a case of right place, wrong night.
Babies and children welcome: children's portions. Booking advisable dinner Fri, Sat. Disabled: toilet. Tables outdoors (7, terrace). Map 5 O3.

FishWorks
134 Upper Street, N1 1QP (7354 1279/ www.fishworks.co.uk). Angel tube. **Lunch served** noon-3pm, **dinner served** 6-10.30pm daily. **Main courses** £12-£26 **Set meal** (6-7.30pm) £13.95 2 courses. **Credit** AmEx, MC, V.
The FishWorks formula is simple but successful: a fishmonger's at the front, where plump king prawns and glassy-eyed sea bass recline on beds of crushed ice, and a restaurant at the rear. You can choose a fish from the counter to be baked in salt or roasted, or stick to tried-and-tested classics from the main menu and succinct specials board (skate with black butter and capers; grilled lobster with chips; hearty, saffron-infused fish stew). The food is unpretentious but accomplished. Piping-hot battered calamares, an immense slab of organic grilled salmon, and a rosemary-sprinkled sea bass were all deftly cooked and simply presented, while fish pie was splendidly rich and creamy. Service was affable and efficient. The decor here is pleasant but undemanding, with crisp blue and white paintwork and jaunty maritime paintings – a reminder that you're eating in a chain restaurant, albeit a high-class version. Beware the generous portions and go easy on the bread (served with pungent aïoli and own-made salsa verde) if you want to squeeze-in a dessert. Expect no-nonsense crowd-pleasers such as sticky toffee pudding, lemon tart and baked chocolate pudding.
Babies and children welcome: children's menu; high chairs. Tables outdoors (2, pavement). Takeaway service (after 5.30pm).
Map 5 O1.
For branches see index.

French

Given how influential French cuisine has been to the cooking of Britain, it's perhaps surprising that the establishment claiming to be the 'oldest French restaurant in London', Soho's **Mon Plaisir**, dates back only to the 1950s. The reason lies in our **Hotels & Haute Cuisine** chapter (starting on p136), as it was largely at this exalted level that French restaurant cuisine first came to Britain, with the likes of Escoffier and Ritz. But the Gallic influence has also been felt in more modern times. French Anglophiles – especially the Roux Brothers, who started Le Gavroche (see p141) in 1967 – helped inspire the current restaurant revolution in London. Indeed, in early editions of this guide we called the new style of cooking Anglo-French, before renaming it **Modern European** (starting on p229).

For years, the majority of London's talented young chefs chose to operate within the Mod Euro idiom. During the 1990s, this left London's French restaurant scene somewhat moribund. However, there has been a revival recently, as our city has discovered regional French cuisine (including south-western specialities at **Club Gascon**, **Roussillon** and **Le Cassoulet** and Breton cooking at **Chez Lindsay**), and French dining houses in all their multifarious forms: from simple brasseries (starting on p48) to glamour-puss destinations such as the **Criterion** and **Papillon**, via the innovative excellence of the **Ledbury** and **Rosemary Lane**, and first-rate locals such as **Trinity**. Interestingly, of the new entries this year, one, **Bord'eaux**, is in a grand hotel, and three of the others, **Angelus**, **Côte** and **Waterloo Brasserie**, are the type of French establishment that has always enjoyed most success in Britain: the café/restaurant hybrid.

Central

Belgravia

★ Le Cercle

1 Wilbraham Place, SW1X 9AE (7901 9999/ www.lecercle.co.uk). Sloane Square tube. Bar **Open/snacks served** noon-midnight Tue-Sat. *Restaurant* **Lunch served** noon-3pm, **dinner served** 6-11pm Tue-Sat. **Set lunch** £15 3 dishes incl coffee, £19.50 4 dishes. **Set dinner** (6-7pm, 10-11pm Tue-Sat) £17.50 3 dishes incl coffee, £21.50 4 dishes. **Tapas** £5-£16. **Credit** AmEx, MC, V.

No passing trade here – the entrance, on a side road off Sloane Street, is easily missed. Word gets around, though, and on our visit, this member of the Club Gascon group was full of locals enjoying sublime food in an exciting space. You have to pick your way down two flights of stairs to reach it, but this makes the cavernous basement restaurant all the more dramatic. Long white drapes separate the central area from more intimate surrounding booths and partly conceal a bar along one wall and a wine store on another. The food comes in tapas-style portions (we were advised to choose three or four dishes each from the leather-bound menu: about right), though ours were served in standard French order (salad, fish, then red meat, cheese, pudding). Each small dish was delicious, vividly coloured and intensely flavoured, satisfying through variety rather than quantity. Highlights included mackerel escabeche with a fennel foam; a fantastic combination of barley 'risotto' with spinach and grilled mussels; wood pigeon breasts with a reduced pumpkin purée; and an oxtail coated in creamy blood-orange sauce. With such bijou portions quickly served and cleared, though, it is hard to linger.
Babies and children welcome: children's menu (lunch). Booking advisable. Disabled: toilet.
Map 15 G10.

La Poule au Pot

231 Ebury Street, SW1W 8UT (7730 7763). Sloane Square tube. **Lunch served** 12.30-2.30pm Mon-Fri; 12.30-4pm Sat, Sun. **Dinner served** 6.45-11pm Mon-Sat; 6.45-10pm Sun. **Main courses** £15.50-£21. **Set lunch** £17.75 2 courses, £19.75 3 courses. **Credit** AmEx, DC, MC, V.

The modern outdoor terrace at this Chelsea locals' favourite gives little hint of its cosy interior. Here, a ceiling festooned with wicker baskets and dried flowers over tiny candlelit tables provides such an authentic air of Gallic rusticity that we half expected the waiters to sneer disdainfully when asked what was on the (good value) set menu. Fortunately, instead they rattled off a list of classic French dishes (moules marinière, coq au vin, steak béarnaise) with good-natured patience. With the aid of a good house red (served in a magnum but charged only for what you drink from it), we chose an onion tart and chicken liver pâté. Both were underwhelming; cheese and egg instead of hoped-for sweet onions dominated the tart, and the pâté was supermarket-ordinary. A cassoulet came packed with bland sausages in a sauce that tasted of stock, but none of the pork, goose or duck you'd hope to find. Undeterred, we ploughed on to dessert. Mousse au chocolat looked like Angel Delight but didn't taste quite that bad. Tarte tatin was a game of two halves: the apple and caramel top meltingly good, the base burnt in parts. Around us, diners seemed to be lapping this up; perhaps they spend too much time in Chelsea, not enough in France.
Babies and children welcome: high chairs. Booking essential. Separate room for parties, seats 16. Tables outdoors (12, terrace).
Map 15 G11.

★ Roussillon

16 St Barnabas Street, SW1W 8PE (7730 5550/ www.roussillon.co.uk). Sloane Square tube. **Lunch served** noon-2.30pm Mon-Fri. **Dinner served** 6.30-10.30pm Mon-Sat. **Set lunch** £35 3 courses incl half bottle of wine, £40 4 courses incl half bottle of wine, £48-£58 tasting menu. **Set dinner** £55 3 courses, £60-£70 tasting menu. **Credit** AmEx, MC, V.

Roussillon is both a gastronomic destination and a neighbourhood place. On our visit, the clientele included families with young children, elderly couples, and friends out for a quiet dinner. You have to be well-heeled to treat this as your local, but that's no problem in Pimlico. The decor is subdued, the service solicitous, and the food sublime. Chef Alexis Gauthier refines the richness of south-west France with artful assemblies in pleasingly modest portions. Those sizes are important, making it possible to eat two courses but then have room for dessert. And trust us: you really want to have dessert. Four of us came for dinner, and only one of our 12 dishes failed to elicit gasps of astonishment. Among the stars of the show: perfectly cooked scallops with thin slices of crisp pear and cep marmalade; juicy squab pigeon with a salad made from its liver; lamb served two ways, the shoulder braised and shredded, pink slices of leg with an indecently buttery potato galette. The menu changes with the seasons and vegetarians have their own eight-course tasting menu. On the excellent wine list, the Languedoc and Roussillon will see you through from apéritif to dessert. Prices start at around £20, but £35 will do full justice to the remarkable food.
Booking advisable. Children over 8 years welcome: children's menu. Dress: smart casual. Restaurant available for hire. Separate room for parties, seats 26. Vegetarian menu.
Map 15 G11.

BEST FRENCH

Intime et romantique
Find that *je ne sais quoi* atmosphere at **Almeida** (see p109), **L'Aventure** (see p110), **The Belvedere** (see p105), **Le Cercle** (see left), **Morgan M** (see p109), **Papillon** (see p107) and **Racine** (see p102)

Cuisines du terroir
Explore the classic dishes of the French regions at **Chez Lindsay** (Breton, see p110), **Club Gascon** (south-west France, see p101), **Côte** (Breton, see p107) and **Roussillon** (south-west France, see above).

On peut compter sur
Count on these old favourites to transport you instantly across La Manche: **Le Coq d'Argent** (see right), **Elena's L'Étoile** (see p102), **Mon Plaisir** (see p101) and **La Poule au Pot** (see left).

Cuisine moléculaire
Chefs are pushing the boundaries of French cooking at **Almeida** (see p109), **Le Cercle** (see left), **Club Gascon** (see p101), **The Ledbury** (see p105), **Morgan M** (see p109), **Sauterelle** (see p101) and **Rosemary Lane** (see right).

Racine. See p102.

City

1 Lombard Street

1 Lombard Street, EC3V 9AA (7929 6611/
www.1lombardstreet.com). Bank tube/DLR.
Bar **Open/tapas served** 11am-11pm Mon-Fri.
Tapas £7.50-£14.50.
Brasserie **Breakfast served** 7.30-11am, **meals**
served 11.30am-10pm Mon-Fri. **Main courses**
£16.50-£25.50. **Set meal** £19.50 5 courses.
Restaurant **Lunch served** noon-3pm, **dinner**
served 6-9.45pm Mon-Fri. **Main courses**
£24-£34.50. **Set meal** £32 5 courses.
All **Credit** AmEx, DC, MC, V.
As converted banks go, this Grade II-listed
building (originally home to a forerunner of
NatWest) has a higher interest rate than most
thanks to a central domed glass and stone skylight
that would be a tricky construction today let alone
in 1907. Elsewhere, nearly everything that doesn't
move is marble. In the bar-brasserie area, a large
circular bar with stools for drinkers is surrounded
by tables and semi-circular booths for diners. To
the rear is a highly regarded haute cuisine
restaurant. The kitchen's interest in the latter
impacts profoundly on the brasserie so that all
dishes arrive with unexpectedly overwrought
presentation and in dainty portions, which makes
it all look a bit dated. Still we couldn't fault the
cooking of tender Angus beef fillet with seared
foie gras and a confit shallot, the gorgeously sticky
gravy lightly flavoured with balsamic. Icily
unctuous bloody mary sorbet made a vibrant
topping for a tian of prawns, crab and avocado.
While the attitude may be French, dishes feature
lime, chilli wasabi, coriander – even Colman's
English mustard. A tempting list of specials
makes choosing from the already-long menu

difficult – we finished with a summery gooseberry
crumble. Gracious staff have a terrific knack of
knowing what customers want before they ask for
it. Wines are expectedly priced on the high side but
if you've no loyalty to France, the Argentinian
chardonnay at £21 is a winning budget option.
Booking advisable. Children over 10 years
admitted. Disabled: toilet. Entertainment: pianist
and singer 6.30pm Fri. Restaurant available
for hire. Separate room for parties, seats 40.
Map 12 Q6.

Le Coq d'Argent

No.1 Poultry, EC2R 8EJ (7395 5000/
www.danddlondon.com). Bank tube/DLR.
Brasserie **Lunch served** 11.30am-3pm Mon-Fri.
Main courses £12-£36.
Restaurant **Breakfast served** 7.30-10am Mon-
Fri. **Lunch served** 11.30am-3pm Mon-Fri;
noon-3pm Sun. **Dinner served** 6-10pm Mon-
Fri; 6.30-10pm Sat. **Main courses** £15-£28.50.
Set lunch (Sun) £25 2 courses, £30 3 courses.
Both **Credit** AmEx, DC, MC, V.
In good weather – or if you want to cock a snook
at climate change by sitting under a patio heater –
the terrace here is one of the City's top eating spots.
Even inside is nice, especially if you're near a
window or overlooking the central courtyard. The
restaurant is more formal, more expensive and
more adventurous in its cooking. We ate in the
cheaper brasserie, which was comfortable enough,
apart from our Lilliputian table for two. A starter
of asparagus with tomato and herb dressing, at
the height of the English season, sported only four
spears (over £2 apiece) which were almost devoid
of flavour. Everything else was good if not the
stuff of ecstasy. A chunky terrine was homely,
vegetable tart was cleverly enlivened by chunks of

roquefort. Crustaceans are a strong feature. A top-
notch crab salad arrived perched on tasty avocados
along with a creamy 'bavarois' of brown crab
meat. Some city folk who were eating and drinking
enthusiastically nearby had plates piled high with
meaty dishes that looked appealing. The wine list
pays due respect to the moneyed magnates, but
there are just enough bottles under £30 to keep the
rest of us mirthful. Apart from the one duff dish,
the Coq showed that it's still shining brightly in a
competitive part of town.
Babies and children welcome: high chairs. Booking
advisable. Disabled: lift; toilet. Entertainment:
jazz 12.30-4pm Sun. Restaurant available for hire.
Tables outdoors (14, restaurant terrace; 14,
bar terrace). **Map 11 P6**.

★ Rosemary Lane

61 Royal Mint Street, E1 8LG (7481 2602/
www.rosemarylane.btinternet.co.uk). Tower Hill
tube/Fenchurch Street rail/Tower Gateway DLR.
Lunch served noon-2.30pm Mon-Fri. **Dinner**
served 5.30-10pm Mon-Fri; 6-10pm Sat. **Main**
courses £13-£19. **Set meal** £15 2 courses, £18
3 courses. **Set dinner** (Sat) £30 tasting menu.
Credit AmEx, MC, V.
Despite the bucolic name, you could hardly
imagine a more unlikely site for some of the most
innovative cooking in London: a distinctly unlovely
street with a car rental opposite. Inside, however,
all is bliss. The wood-panelled room was an oasis
of tranquillity on a quiet spring evening, with
quietly competent service adding to the scene.
Most of our food was outstanding. Chef Cristina
Anghelescu loves to fool around with ideas in a
manner that combines elements of France and
California. The menu changes seasonally but
always with an emphasis on highest-quality main

SHELF LIFE

While the range of cheeses on sale in supermarkets can be impressive, local cheesemongers have the edge when it comes to hand-selecting specimens in their prime and giving advice on serving and cooking.

Cheeses

13 Fortis Green Road, N10 3HP (8444 9141/www.cheesesonline.co.uk). Highgate tube then 134 bus.
Vanessa Wiley's olde worlde store may be tiny, but everything in it is of exquisite quality, right down to the carefully chosen pickles. Extremely knowledgeable on her subject, she happily dispenses tips to customers.

La Cave au Fromage

24-25 Cromwell Place, SW7 2LD (0845 10 88 222/www.la-cave.co.uk). South Kensington tube.
Despite the French name, this South Ken outpost is an exciting source of an international range of cheeses, plus artisan-made dairy products and unusual charcuterie.

MacFarlane's

48 Abbeville Road, SW4 9NF (8673 5373). Clapham South tube.
Over 100 farmhouse cheeses from the UK, Ireland and France, all sourced directly from the farm. Angus and Angie Wood reckon they can tell you exactly where anything in the shop comes from; they also stock deli items and organic fruit and veg.

Real Cheese Shop

62 Barnes High Street, SW13 9OF (8878 6676). Barnes or Bridge rail/ 209, 283 bus.
A yellow-fronted shop with cheerful staff selling all manner of British and European cheeses from cashel blue to chaumes, mostly straight from the farm. Since coming under new ownership, the range of cheeses has expanded even further.

Rippon Cheese Stores

26 Upper Tachbrook Street, SW1V 1SW (7931 0628/www.ripponcheese.com). Pimlico tube/Victoria tube/rail.
Owned and run by knowledgeable Compagnons du Guilde des Fromagers, Rippon stocks more than 500 types of European cheese and supplies many eateries in London.

ingredients adorned with complex assemblies of vegetable garnishes. Two exceptional dishes should convey the idea: a startlingly delicious mushroom pâté (roast shiitake and black trumpet) with a salad of leaves and herbs, enoki mushrooms and black truffle shavings; and seven juicy Maine scallops with a ragout of yellow cherry tomatoes, spinach and shallots, and a tian of sweet potatoes and fresh herbs. Belly of pork was perfectly cooked to melting softness and garnished beautifully. The wine and beer lists are exemplary: concise, international, uniformly well chosen and (like the food) very well priced.
Babies and children admitted. Booking advisable (lunch). Dress: smart casual. Restaurant available for hire. **Map 12 S7.**

Sauterelle

Royal Exchange, EC3V 3LR (7618 2483/ www.danddlondon.com). Bank tube/DLR.
Lunch served noon-2.30pm, **dinner served** 6-10pm Mon-Fri. **Main courses** £14-£35.
Set dinner £18 2 courses, £21 3 courses.
Credit AmEx, DC, MC, V.
Situated on the mezzanine level of the Royal Exchange, Sauterelle is a fantastic vantage point over the buzzing Grand Café below. It is set up for City power lunches and after-work dinners, with comfortable blue club chairs and a simple chic look. The owners describe their style as 'bourgeois' French cooking; expect to find classic dishes such as glazed duck in sauce périgord, with modern touches like the accompanying vanilla-flecked parsnip purée. A starter of foie gras ballotine was lovely – rich, dense and melting. However, the trio of apple purées and jellies that went with it was a little too tart and overbearing. A salad of waxy potatoes, cured ham and baby artichokes in a truffle cream also wasn't the best rendition of this dish we've had. Better was the more rustic fare. Rump steak doused with parsley and shallot butter and served with roast vegetables and mushrooms was satisfyingly savoury and meaty – perfect food to set you up for an afternoon back in the office. Staff are relaxed and friendly, and there's a short but interesting wine list.
Babies and children admitted. Booking advisable. Disabled: toilet. **Map 12 Q6.**

Clerkenwell & Farringdon

Café du Marché

22 Charterhouse Square, Charterhouse Mews, EC1M 6AH (7608 1609/www.cafedumarche. co.uk). Barbican tube/Farringdon tube/rail.
Le Café **Lunch served** noon-2.30pm Mon-Fri. **Dinner served** 6-10pm Mon-Sat. **Set meal** £33.85 3 courses.
Le Grenier **Lunch served** noon-2.30pm Mon-Fri. **Dinner served** 7-10pm Mon-Sat. **Set meal** £33.85 3 courses.
Le Rendezvous **Lunch served** noon-2.30pm Mon-Fri. **Main courses** £9-£16.
All **Credit** MC, V.
So French you could bottle it, this compact haven of joie de vivre fills an old Smithfield warehouse. The two main dining rooms, the ground-floor Le Café and Le Grenier in the loft, share similarly cheery rustique decor and the same set-price menu of classic bistro fare (but at a distinctly non-bistro price). The separate Le Rendezvous offers more casual brasserie-style grills. A spiral staircase winds up to Le Grenier, where expert senior waiters direct proceedings with an unmistakably French mix of cranky charm and frenetic zip. There are no great culinary experiments here, but French favourites done very, very well. To start, bayonne ham came with haricot beans and grilled endive in a sweet vinaigrette; a roquefort and leek tartlet exhibited exquisitely crisp-but-powdery pastry. Mains were just as pleasurable: an earthy filet de boeuf with morels; and the plat du jour, wild boar in a rich Calvados sauce. The wine list features some great punchy reds, and there's a superlative *comme il faut* cheeseboard, presented at exactly the right temperature. Very enjoyable, but pricey, especially with the quite whopping 15% charged for service.
Babies and children admitted. Booking advisable (not accepted Le Rendezvous). Entertainment (Le Café): jazz duo 8pm Mon-Thur; pianist 8pm Fri, Sat. Separate rooms for parties, seating 35 and 65. **Map 5 O5.**

Club Gascon (100)

57 West Smithfield, EC1A 9DS (7796 0600/ www.clubgascon.com). Barbican tube/Farringdon tube/rail. **Lunch served** noon-2pm Mon-Fri.
Dinner served 7-10pm Mon-Thur; 7-10.30pm Fri, Sat. **Tapas** £8-£28. **Set lunch** £28 3 courses. **Set meal** £42 5 courses (£65 incl wine). **Credit** AmEx, MC, V.
Club Gascon dazzles just with its extraordinary flower arrangements – in spring, elaborate cherry blossom towers, echoing Japanese touches in the sleekly opulent decor. With Le Comptoir Gascon (*see below*), Le Cercle (*see p98*) and the wine bar

Cellar Gascon (*see p346*), it forms a select group showcasing food and wines from south-west France, but here all expectations of peasanty cassoulets must be let go. Chef Pascal Aussignac uses traditional elements as a springboard from which to create extremely intricate dishes. Divided on the menu by base ingredients – with a whole section of foie gras – they're all starter-sized, so it's recommended you order at least three dishes per person, rather than conventional courses. Some are as impressive as they look, like the hot-cold combination of foie gras with fabulous truffle ice-cream, or richly pleasurable duck magret with lemon, pear and pied bleu mushrooms. Others had more fashionable froth than substance, as in spring tulip with mousseron mushrooms, saffron and broad beans, or a frankly disappointing sole with green tea and salsify. The wine list is a grand but very costly compendium of modern French fine wines (nothing under £22, little under £30); service wavers between utterly charming and bouts of listlessness. Special, certainly, but prices are more to die for here than the food.
Booking essential. Restaurant available for hire. **Map 11 O5.**

Le Comptoir Gascon

61-63 Charterhouse Street, EC1M 6HJ (7608 0851/www.comptoirgascon.com). Farringdon tube/rail. **Lunch served** noon-2pm Tue-Fri. **Brunch served** 10.30am-2.30pm Sat. **Dinner served** 7-10pm Tue, Wed, Sat; 7-10.30pm Thur, Fri. **Main courses** £7.50-£13.50. **Credit** AmEx, MC, V.
Le Comptoir Gascon's modern rustic style (dainty velour chairs and exposed pipes contrast with open brickwork and pottery dishes) exudes class and confidence – as do most of the customers. In one corner is wedged a counter of precise cakes and pastries, shelves of artisan-made breads (the wholemeal sourdough is wonderfully light) and blackboard promoting the three foie gras terrines made on the premises, all of which adds to the posh café vibe. The French staff – unintimidating, practised, hard working, yet relaxed – bring minuscule black olives marinated with herbs. A special of scallop terrine had a delightful buttery flavour, cut with the acid warmth of piquillo sauce. Toulousian cassoulet featured creamy beans and knockout confit duck with lovely crisp skin. Appropriately chewy onglet came with traditional sauce bordelaise; overall the dish was rather so-what – something that can't be said of the sensational chips, which are cooked in duck fat. We finished with an omelette gascon – a meringue bomb of ice-cream, armagnac and prune – and an ornate 'chocolate flower' torte. Dinky, rather close-set tables mean that the comfort factor is not that high, but this is one place that we always look forward to visiting.
Babies and children welcome: high chairs. Bookings advisable. Tables outdoors (4, pavement). **Map 11 O5.**

Covent Garden

Mon Plaisir

19-21 Monmouth Street, WC2H 9DD (7836 7243/www.monplaisir.co.uk). Covent Garden tube. **Meals served** noon-11.15pm Mon-Fri; 5.45-11.15pm Sat. **Main courses** £13.95-£22.
Set lunch £14.50 2 courses, £16.50 3 courses.
Set meal (5.45-7pm Mon-Sat; after 10pm Mon-Thur) £13.50 2 courses, £15.50 3 courses incl glass of wine and coffee. **Credit** AmEx, MC, V.
Proudly claiming to be 'London's oldest French restaurant' (established just after the war), Mon Plaisir is all of its clients' favourite local. A higgledy-piggledy warren of rather homely rooms slathered with French memorabilia, it is a really beguiling one-off. The food is a little more workaday: a surprise-free list of bistro starters and main courses that run from the steak tartare and coq au vin staples, to less predictable dishes of a style that wouldn't be out of place in a Gallic gastropub (if such a thing existed), or even an English one. There's a bit of a disconnect between Mon Plaisir and contemporary French cooking.

Our last couple of meals here have been patchy, with good starters (puy lentil and beetroot salad) and dessert (rhubarb tart) bracketing less ably made mains of a dried-out piglet and good but slightly under-cooked cod. Still, the set lunch is good value, the staff pleasant and the buzz mellow. Ambience and comfort are more the things here than the pushing of any culinary envelopes.
Babies and children admitted. Booking advisable. **Map 18 L6.**

Fitzrovia

Elena's L'Étoile

30 Charlotte Street, W1T 2NG (7636 7189/ www.elenasletoile.co.uk). Goodge Street or Tottenham Court Road tube. **Lunch served** noon-2.30pm Mon-Fri. **Dinner served** 6-10.30pm Mon-Sat. **Main courses** £15.75-£20.25. **Set meal** £19 2 courses, £22 3 courses. **Credit** AmEx, DC, MC, V.

With or without the renowned grande dame of maître d's, Elena Salvoni, offering hospitality, this place has a real buzz. Midweek, it was packed from after work until 9pm, mainly with an over-30 crowd. The main dining room, at street level, is long, with mirrored walls above the red banquettes, the ceilings stained with tobacco and, on every wall, signed photos of great and nearly-great showbiz customers (we were overlooked by Ernie Wise and Bob the Builder). The space at the end, behind a glass screen, is more intimate and there are more rooms on the other floors for private dining. Around us moved a steady flow of long-serving career waiters in suits, generally impeccable, bringing food that was surprisingly good and well-presented. A chicory salad was crisp, fresh and full of impact in a heavy china bowl, while crab, salt-cod and prawn croquettes were enhanced with aïoli and a dusting of paprika. Calf's liver, with bacon, was tender and savoury; a thick sliced entrecôte was, again, tender and the grilled tomato alongside was intensely flavoured. Sure, you pay slightly over the odds on account of the reputation but, on form like this, the reputation is well deserved.
Babies and children admitted. Booking advisable; essential lunch. Separate rooms for parties, seating 10, 16 and 32. **Map 9 J5.**

Knightsbridge

Brasserie St Quentin

243 Brompton Road, SW3 2EP (7589 8005/ www.brasseriestquentin.co.uk). Knightsbridge or South Kensington tube/14, 74 bus. **Lunch served** noon-3pm daily. **Dinner served** 6-10.30pm Mon-Sat; 6-10pm Sun. **Main courses** £12.50-£23.50. **Set lunch** (noon-3pm) £16.50 2 courses, £18.50 3 courses. **Credit** AmEx, MC, V.

Founded in 1980 by food writer Quentin Crewe and friend Hugh O'Neill (now third Baron Rathcavan), Brasserie St Quentin soon became the haunt of Knightsbridge's beau monde. It was sold to the Savoy Group in 1989, then O'Neill bought it back in 2002 with investors that included the chef Anton Edelmann and several titled landowners, who now supply much of its meat, poultry and game. The place feels much as it did when it first opened – all classic tinted mirrors and brass rails – only with a more mature clientele. An early promising sign on our visit was a lady of a certain age dining happily alone at the next table. The meal began with nicely caramelised scallops, and some tasty tiny rings of deep-fried squid on a tomato salad. A main course of grilled ribeye of Buccleuch beef with béarnaise sauce and pommes frites was astoundingly good, despite the rather mean serving of frites; we slowly savoured the incredibly delicious beef, even the little bits of browned fat at the end. Grilled wild sea bass was equally stunning. From a usefully annotated wine list with plenty of labels at reasonable prices and by the glass, a bottle of Château de Belle Garde Bordeaux was almost too tannic, until it met the beef in perfect harmony.
Babies and children welcome: high chairs. Booking advisable. Separate room for parties, seats 20. **Map 14 E10.**

★ Racine (100)

239 Brompton Road, SW3 2EP (7584 4477). Knightsbridge or South Kensington tube/14, 74 bus. **Lunch served** noon-3pm, **dinner served** 6-10.30pm daily. **Main courses** £12.50-£20.75. **Set meal** (lunch, 6-7.30pm) £17.50 2 courses, £19.50 3 courses. **Credit** AmEx, MC, V.

Even on a cold and wet Tuesday evening, Racine was full by 8pm – with neighbouring places, almost as good as this one, nearly empty. What makes the difference? For new customers, the drama: the heavy velvet curtains inside the door allow diners a grand entrance before gracious French waiters in black waistcoats lead them to their white-linen-covered tables. For returning diners, it is all this plus the memories of previous good meals in this warm, vibrant 1930s retro atmosphere. The food, though not cutting edge, has character: picked crab, with salmon roe and mayonnaise, was alluring and bitingly fresh on crunchy toasted pain Poilâne; a veal chop was enhanced with roasted globe artichoke and split baby broad beans; a juicy rabbit fricassee was served with its kidneys. The puddings were fun too. Apple sorbet came with a shot of chilled calvados, while warm cherry clafoutis was pleasantly eggy. The best tables are in the window, depending on who is on your left or right. The tables along the sides, for two, can feel rather small.
Babies and children welcome: high chairs. Booking essential. Dress: smart casual. **Map 14 E10.**

Marylebone

★ Galvin Bistrot de Luxe

66 Baker Street, W1U 7DJ (7935 4007/ www.galvinuk.com). Baker Street tube. **Lunch served** noon-2.30pm Mon-Sat; noon-5pm Sun. **Dinner served** 6-11pm Mon-Sat; 6-9.30pm Sun. **Main courses** £10.50-£21. **Set lunch** £15.50 3 courses. **Set dinner** (6-7pm) £17.50 3 courses. **Credit** AmEx, MC, V.

All credit to the Galvin brothers – not just for setting such high standards for themselves, but also for maintaining and sometimes exceeding them. From the moment we stepped in off this rather impersonal stretch of Baker Street, we were relaxed by the comforting 1930s decor with its nicotine-retro lighting, and by the friendly and efficient staff. As the early-bird diners were leaving after enjoying their fixed-price menus, the place quickly filled with a range of locals in couture, families, friends, colleagues. The cheerful buzz was a sign of reaction to the delightful food, which is consistently better than you might expect at these upper mid-range prices. Fresh ingredients and contrasting textures dominate the menu. A lamb terrine was offset by anchovy sauce; tender slices

Angelus. See p104.

of braised pheasant breast were in perfect partnership with puy lentils and coarse saucisson; rolled slow-cooked lamb belly was a delicious counterpoint to bright pink cutlets with no sign of caramelisation. The high standards continued with desserts, too: apple tarte tatin was chewy but sharp. On such great form, no wonder this place is so popular. Long may it flourish.
Babies and children welcome: high chairs. Booking advisable. Disabled: toilet. **Map 9 G5.**

Le Relais de Venise l'entrecôte
120 Marylebone Lane, W1U 2QG (7486 0878/ www.relaisdevenise.com). Bond Street tube. **Lunch served** noon-2.30pm Mon-Thur; noon-2.45pm Fri; 12.30-3.30pm Sat, Sun. **Dinner served** 6-10.45pm Mon-Fri; 6.30-10.45pm Sat; 6.30-10.30pm Sun. **Set meal** £19 2 courses. **Credit** AmEx, MC, V.
When you're used to menus spanning countries and even continents, to be offered just one dish can be quite a relief. This London cousin serves the same famed formula as the original Parisian brasserie: a small green salad with walnuts, followed by an entrecôte steak with a 'secret' sauce (the recipe is supposedly closely guarded) and own-made frites. The restaurant has also adopted the original's no-reservations policy and its decor, with closely spaced tables, banquette seating, mirrored walls, and attractive waitresses in French maids' outfits (notably, no waiters). With just one dish on the menu, expectations are high, and on our visit we struggled to find fault. The steak (sourced from Donald Russell of Aberdeenshire) came perfectly saignant, boasting great texture and flavour, the frites were crisp and nicely seasoned – both served in two portions for optimal warmth. The sauce didn't disappoint; we noted flavours of tarragon, mustard and butter. The wine list is short and French, the popular choice being the demi-litre of house red. Customer choice is reinstated for dessert; the list includes classic vacherin (meringue with ice-cream), lemon tart and textbook-perfect profiteroles.
Babies and children welcome: high chairs. Bookings not accepted. Disabled: toilet. Tables outdoors (3, pavement). **Map 9 G5.**

The Wallace
Wallace Collection, Hertford House, Manchester Square, W1U 3BN (7563 9505/www.the wallacerestaurant.com). Bond Street tube. Café **Meals served** 10am-4.30pm daily. *Restaurant* **Lunch served** noon-3pm Mon-Fri; noon-3.30pm Sat, Sun. **Dinner served** 5-9.30pm Fri, Sat. *Both* **Main courses** £13.50-£18.50. **Credit** AmEx, DC, MC, V.
The lovely and characterful location of this Oliver Peyton establishment (in the elegant courtyard conservatory of the Georgian townhouse that houses the Wallace Collection of art) wins most customers over before they've even picked up the menu. When they do, they'll find that while there are plenty of small dishes for museum visitors – quiches, cheeses, pâtés, cream teas – you wouldn't come here for quick sustenance (no self-service counter, and prices above impulse level). While extravagant ingredients like foie gras and caviar feature, the main à la carte, along with the atmosphere, is lighter and more modern. To start, good rillettes de porc spoke well of the terrine selection, and sautéed prawns showed the chef's penchant for deeply infused herbal flavourings, though also for butter. Lamb with provençal galette and thyme sauce was well-handled, but the cod with squid, artichoke and ham was very much the star: the fish itself delicate and firm, and the accompanying ingredients all harmonising well. Disappointingly, no one could tell us any details of the cod's provenance (though otherwise staff were pleasant and capable, if occasionally distracted). The Wallace makes a welcome oasis of calm to dive into from manic Oxford Street – though not everyone finds the conservatory-style furniture comfortable.
Babies and children welcome: children's menu, high chairs. Booking advisable. Disabled: lift; toilet. Restaurant available for hire. **Map 9 G5.**

Mayfair

Bord'eaux NEW
Grosvenor House Hotel, 86-90 Park Lane, W1K 7TN (7399 8460/www.bord-eaux.com). Marble Arch tube. **Meals served** 7am-10.30pm Mon-Thur; 7am-11pm Fri, Sat; 7am-10.30pm Sun. **Main courses** £12.50-£21.50. **Set dinner** £16.50 2 courses; £19.50 3 courses (5-7pm). **Credit** AmEx, DC, MC, V.
Situated in the relative Siberia that is the hotel restaurant, where many Londoners and non-hotel guests seldom tread, Bord'eaux nonetheless offers a pleasing, well-crafted dining experience. Taking its cue from the Aquitaine region of south-west France, the brasserie style of the restaurant starts with the smart decor (which hasn't escaped the hotel feel and is a little anodyne and lacking in atmosphere) and extends to the menu. Think familiar French fare in the mould of confit duck, cassoulet, côte de boeuf with béarnaise and a variety of seafood platters. There's even a main course comprised of a combo of croque-monsieur and croque-madame. Joining these classics are a few Basque dishes such as pipérade, an egg and pepper stew. We had few complaints with a competently prepared salad of duck breast topped with poached egg, and also enjoyed pudding, the list of which includes old-fashioned floating islands (meringues bobbing in custard), crème caramel perked up with Sauternes-soaked raisins, and an archetypal death-by-chocolate plate of Valrhona desserts. Overall, the menu and its execution deserve a setting with a little more verve.
Babies and children welcome: high chairs. Disabled: toilet. Separate room for parties, seats 12. **Map 9 G7.**

★ La Petite Maison
54 Brooks Mews, W1K 4EG (7495 4774). Bond Street tube. **Lunch served** noon-2.15pm daily. **Dinner served** 6-10pm Mon-Sat. **Main courses** £9-£35. **Credit** AmEx, MC, V.
Part of the buzz around this place is that it's based on a namesake in Nice and co-owned by venture capitalist Arjun Waney, one of the owners of Roka (*see p193*) and Zuma (*see p194*). It is on a triangular corner plot on a Mayfair backstreet, the windows letting in plenty of daylight without exposing the lack of any view and, from the pavement, you can see every move in the kitchen. Even on a Tuesday, the place was chock-full of locals, financiers, dating couples and socialites, audibly excited by the high standard of the food and the novel way in which it arrives (that is when it is ready to be served, not necessarily when you are). You are encouraged to share the food – a disorienting experience that makes the place seem more informal and allows diners to explore their mutual status ('no, go on, you have the last prawn, darling/ sir/mother'). Among the highlights on our visit: tender calamares with lime and fresh green chillies; anchovies sandwiched between sage leaves; perfectly cooked turbot on the bone with chorizo; and delicate lamb cutlets with caramelised crusts and soft pink centres. You have to be up for novelty to get the most out of this place and, if you are, you can have a memorable time.
Babies and children admitted. Booking advisable. **Map 9 H6.**

Piccadilly

★ Criterion
224 Piccadilly, W1J 9HP (7930 0488/ www.whitestarline.org.uk). Piccadilly Circus tube. **Lunch served** noon-2.30pm Mon-Sat, noon-3.30pm Sun. **Dinner served** 5.30-11.30pm Mon-Sat, 5.30pm-10.30pm Sun. **Main courses** £12.50-£28.50. **Set meal** (lunch, 5.30-7pm Mon-Sat) £14.95 2 courses, £17.95 3 courses. **Credit** AmEx, JCB, MC, V.
The Criterion is a magnificent Victorian bauble. Its 1870s oriental-fantasy decor rarely fails to dazzle, and picking out details in the mosaic ceiling is a pleasure in itself. Nowadays, this relic of old Piccadilly can seem a bit lost amid the dreary tackiness that has long since taken over the Circus, and even boss Marco Pierre White has seemed

Interview
THIERRY TOMASIN

Who are you?
Owner, sommelier and host (I'm your servant of pleasure) at **Angelus** (*see p104*) near Lancaster Gate.
What's the best thing about running a restaurant in London?
The best thing is if you can give customers what they expect – fresh food, lovely service without pomposity – then see them leave smiling. Giving pleasure is the most important thing.
What's the worst thing?
The fact that you can't serve alcohol after 11pm Monday to Thursday. Sometimes, after working late, you want to go out for steak and chips and a glass of wine. and you can't. We're not a pub, we're a restaurant and bar; there are no hooligans here. Of course, you have to be careful in a residential area, but nobody shouts. In France there are no restrictions, if you want to drink at 1am you can.
Which are your favourite London restaurants?
If it's a special occasion I go to **Le Gavroche** (*see p141*), and not just because I used to work there: it is consistent, everything is high quality, and you won't be disappointed. If I want a very good steak tartare, I go to **Papillon** (*see p107*) in Chelsea.
How green are you?
At the moment I'm fighting with the council because it would be nice to recycle more, but there are no facilities, apart from the usual for bottles and papers. It's not easy being green in London – there needs to be more help from government.
What is missing from London's restaurant scene?
Restaurants need to treat customers as customers, not numbers. I'd also like to see more Brits working front of house. Of course, there are guys in the kitchen wanting to be Jamie Oliver, but the British seem to think waiting is something you do as a student.

RESTAURANTS

unsure what to do with it. Lately, though, it has got back on track under chef Gary O'Sullivan, with food to match the setting. The main menu is a traditional but creative mix headlining French classics. Foie gras maison was perfect, with all the proper depth of flavour; smoked salmon came with capers and a deliciously refined horseradish sauce. In a main course, roast monkfish with chorizo and fava beans, the contrasting flavours were finely handled. The Criterion also offers a Sunday lunch menu with English roasts; so does everybody, you might say, but our roast pork was wonderful, a model of how an old favourite can be made fresh. Prices for food and the well-sized wine list are decent by current standards, and service is charming and efficient. Forget the tat outside, and enjoy one of London's special locations.
Babies and children welcome: high chairs. Booking advisable. Dress: smart casual. Separate room for parties, seats 70. **Map 17 B5**.

St James's

Brasserie Roux

Sofitel St James, 8 Pall Mall, SW1Y 5NG (7968 2900/www.sofitelstjames.com). Piccadilly Circus tube. **Lunch served** noon-3pm Mon-Fri; 12.30-3pm Sat, Sun. **Dinner served** 5.30-11pm Mon-Sat; 5.30-10.30pm Sun. **Main courses** £10.50-£30. **Set lunch** (Mon-Fri) £19.50 4 courses. **Set dinner** (5.30-7pm Mon-Sat) £15 3 courses, £20 3 courses incl glass of wine. **Credit** AmEx, DC, MC, V.
Roux is a grand name in the restaurant world, but it doesn't gain much by being attached to this bland venture in a French-owned luxury hotel. Its decor is peculiarly out of whack: a bizarre blend of yellow walls, dark red and green carpets and curtains, monstrously naff giant lampshades and laminated wood tables from an airport bar, which oddly wastes the grand old building's lofty ceilings. Service is more disorganised than we ever expected to see in a big-name French restaurant. The menu is a safe list of grills, salads, old favourites and retro 'brasserie classics'. Starters were the best part of our meal; scrambled eggs with ceps and bacon were deliciously creamy, and a dish of scallops with boudin noir and apple compote was smoothly done. Mains offered less. Grilled tuna, ordered rare, first arrived very well done, and the replacement portion was dinky. A 'classic', braised beef in red wine, was decent but ordinary, and in no way justified a £16 tag, even in Pall Mall. Wines too are extremely expensive. French diners lay great store by the 'quality-price relationship' in restaurants: here it's extremely poor, unless you go for one of the slightly better-value set menus.
Babies and children welcome: children's menu; high chairs. Booking advisable. Disabled: toilet (hotel). Dress: smart casual. **Map 10 K7**.

Soho

L'Escargot Marco Pierre White

48 Greek Street, W1D 4EF (7437 2679/ www.whitestarline.org.uk). Leicester Square or Tottenham Court Road tube.
Ground-floor restaurant **Lunch served** noon-2.15pm Mon-Fri. **Dinner served** 6-11.30pm Mon-Fri; 5.30-11.30pm Sat. **Main courses** £12.95-£14.95. **Set meal** (lunch, 6-7pm Mon-Fri) £15 2 courses, £18 3 courses.
Picasso Room **Lunch served** 12.15-2pm Tue-Fri. **Dinner served** 7-11pm Tue-Sat. **Set lunch** £20.50 2 courses, £25.50 3 courses. **Set meal** £42 3 courses.
Both **Credit** AmEx, DC, MC, V.
It would be hard to imagine Soho without L'Escargot, and hard to imagine L'Escargot without its contingent of theatrical, media-savvy Soho-ites. It looks as good as ever, with its cut-glass mirrors, statement art by Chagall and Miro, and frankly beautiful art nouveau lighting, but times change – even at a snail's pace – and we found the buzz a little quieter, and the kitchen a little less exciting. Upstairs, the lovely Picasso Room still trades in luxury ingredients and anniversary celebrations, while on the ground floor the more

democratic bistro menu results in a livelier crowd of divorce-settlement gossipers and pre-theatre BlackBerry-checkers. As a bastion of Marco Pierre White's empire, we expected more to dazzle us, but it appeared to be running on automatic. At our meal downstairs, the menu was of the season, but not so much of the decade. A terrine of ham hock and foie gras was dry; and smoked salmon paupiette filled with salmon mousse was on the dated side of classic. Crisp-skinned sea bass on crushed potatoes was a treat; but gnocchi with wild mushrooms were little more than fried balls of mashed potato. The service is definitely of the efficient French variety, highly professional but rather aloof.
Babies and children admitted (ground-floor restaurant). Booking essential weekends. Dress: smart casual. Separate rooms for parties, seating 24 and 60. Vegetarian menu. **Map 17 C3**.

La Trouvaille

12A Newburgh Street, W1F 7RR (7287 8488/ www.latrouvaille.co.uk). Oxford Circus tube. **Lunch served** noon-3pm Mon-Fri. **Dinner served** 6-11pm Mon-Sat. **Set lunch** £15.50 2 courses, £20 3 courses. **Set dinner** £29.50 2 courses, £35 3 courses. **Credit** AmEx, MC, V.
On a corner just off Carnaby Street, this upstairs restaurant has sometimes been a favourite of ours and may well be again. However, on this occasion, we pined for the vitality and focus of the packed wine bar on the ground floor, through which you have to walk to reach your table. With few diners except us in the pale dining room, La Trouvaille seemed too self-conscious – the clear perspex chairs needed someone to sit on them to stop them looking odd; the many mirrors lacked people to reflect. In turn, the food seemed more idiosyncratic than before: French food with one too many twists (kumquat, dim sum, cardamom). Sadly, a duck confit crumble was dry and merely crumbly, lacking in texture and flavour, though the dim sum (snail) were tangy, rich and fairly successful. Encouragingly, a main of Herdwick mutton fillet was thoroughly enjoyable (pink, tender and savoury alongside braised lettuce), though a john dory fillet with lentils was just treading water. We would not be put off another visit (this is still usually a good destination, particularly for a date) but would hope for better next time.
Babies and children admitted. Booking advisable. Tables outdoors (8, pavement). **Map 17 A3**.

Strand

The Admiralty

Somerset House, Strand, WC2R 1LA (7845 4646/www.somerset-house.org.uk). Embankment or Temple tube/Charing Cross tube/rail. **Lunch served** noon-2.30pm, **dinner served** 6-10.30pm Mon-Sat. **Main courses** £12.50-£18. **Set meal** (lunch, 6-7pm) £15.50 2 courses, £19.50 3 courses. **Credit** AmEx, DC, MC, V.
One of the strongest attractions of this place is the location. It can be inspiring to wander off the Strand through the arches, across the majestic courtyard with its rising and falling fountains, particularly on a bright, clear day. That is when the dining room looks its best too – the sea-green leather, high arched windows and ship-shaped chandeliers adding to the nautical theme that reminds you of the Thames just out of sight below. On our lunchtime visit, almost every table was taken by groups of colleagues from nearby offices (Inland Revenue, BBC World Service) and we formed the clear and welcome impression that the Admiralty is on better form than before. Each dish, though not overly ambitious, was served in great condition: pan-fried pigeon breast was perfectly tender and pinkish purple; a warm salad of french beans, red onion and sautéed halloumi was well-balanced and fresh. Mains were just as good. The caramelised edges on a rump of English lamb contrasted with the hot pink centre, and a pork fillet remained juicy under a brie and pine nut crust. In warmer months there are tables on the terrace with a different menu.
Babies and children admitted. Booking advisable. Disabled: lift; toilet. Restaurant available for hire. Separate rooms for parties, seating 30-60. **Map 10 M7**.

West

Bayswater

Angelus NEW

2008 RUNNER-UP BEST LOCAL RESTAURANT
4 Bathhurst Street, W2 2SD (7402 0083/ www.angelusrestaurant.co.uk). Lancaster Gate tube. **Meals served** 11am-11pm Tue-Sun. **Main courses** £18-£33. **Set lunch** £36 3 courses incl bottle of wine. **Set dinner** £38 3 courses. **Credit** AmEx, MC, V.
Tucked into the genteel residential area behind the one-way system around Lancaster Gate, this

Gastro. See p107.

brasserie de luxe looks the part: dark wood and white linen, twinkling glassware and chandeliers, burgundy leather banquettes and large mirrors set in art nouveau-style frames. It's owned by Frenchman Thierry Tomasin, who trained as a chef and was also general manager at Aubergine and sommelier at Le Gavroche – so he's certainly got the background to set up his own restaurant. The chef is another Frenchman, Olivier Duret. The food is as polished and demure as the setting. Sometimes flavourings are too subtle: we found it hard to detect any vanilla in a starter of vanilla-marinated salmon with warm asparagus, although the fish was high quality. The addition of preserved lemon lifted a main of pollock, served with a salsa of beans, olives, tomatoes and capers, above the norm. Silky smooth mash came in its own mini saucepan. Pricing is high, with most mains hovering around £25; john dory, served with braised baby fennel and baby artichokes, clocked in at £33. But dishes look beautiful, and service is adept and personable. Drinks and snacks are also available in the atmospheric rear lounge, which resembles a civilised boudoir with its crushed velvet sofas, floral motifs and soft lighting.
Babies and children admitted. Booking advisable. Disabled: lift; toilet. Separate room for parties, seats 22. Tables outdoors (5, terrace). **Map 8 D6.**

Chiswick

La Trompette

5-7 Devonshire Road, W4 2EU (8747 1836/ www.latrompette.co.uk). Turnham Green tube. **Lunch served** noon-2.30pm Mon-Sat; 12.30-3pm Sun. **Dinner served** 6.30-10.30pm Mon-Sat; 7-10pm Sun. **Set lunch** (Mon-Fri) £23.50 3 courses; (Sat) £25 3 courses; (Sun) £29.50 3 courses. **Set dinner** £37.50 3 courses, £45 4 courses. **Credit** AmEx, MC, V.
This jewel of a restaurant, under the same ownership as Chez Bruce (*see p107*) and the Glasshouse (*see p248*), has so much going for it: an attractive dining area that appears bright and spacious; beige walls and taupe banquettes that give a warm glow to the customers; a sommelier who wins awards, not just for his wine knowledge but for his unfailingly kind enthusiasm. When we visited, midweek, it was packed with a wide variety of locals – dates, friends, businessmen on expenses, families – all adding to the friendly feel. We were delighted by our first course. Chicory salad with walnut and roquefort came with quince

poached in red wine: a great combination of colours, textures and flavours. It was almost as impressive as a delicate and fragrant steamed sea bass with (shelled) moules marinière and spinach. Then, unfortunately, there was an unacceptably long delay until our next course. Served with apologies, the duck magret was pink but dry, a side dish of cassoulet-style beans and duck confit barely tepid. Braised lamb shoulder stood up better, but suffered by comparison with how it might have been, if delivered promptly from the kitchen. This has happened to us before, with a similar late sitting (8.30pm) – but maybe we are just unlucky.
Babies and children welcome (lunch): high chairs. Booking essential. Disabled: toilet. Tables outdoors (7, terrace).

Le Vacherin

76-77 South Parade, W4 5LF (8742 2121/ www.levacherin.co.uk). Chiswick Park tube/rail. **Lunch served** noon-3pm Tue-Sun. **Dinner served** 6-10.30pm Mon-Thur; 6-11pm Fri, Sat; 6-10pm Sun. **Main courses** £12.50-£19. **Credit** MC, V.
This place is decked out like the bistro of your dreams, with mirrors, crystal light fittings and plush velvet. Owned by ex-Savoy chef Malcolm John, it's a quintessentially Parisian experience – and all the staff are French. The menu is pleasingly similar: a round-up of French classics from the potted foie gras starter to a dessert of îles flottantes (soft meringues floating on custard). This all goes down well: Le Vacherin was packed with contented well-heeled locals on our Thursday night visit. The execution and lack of attention to detail, however, let things down slightly. A battered basket of mundane bread arrived perched on a doily. Water isn't served in jugs and is clumsily refilled. The food is simply done, hard to fault but not especially memorable. Shallot and gruyère cheese tart was pleasantly cheesy but not exciting. A dish of scallops, black pudding and Alsace bacon was similar – nicely done, but without any flair. The côte de boeuf with béarnaise sauce and matchstick potatoes was very good (especially the frites, which were crisp on the outside and soft inside). Anjou pigeon with beetroot and carrots was presented interestingly, with the liver and heart on a stick, though the breast could have been more tender. With a little extra effort this place could be exquisite.
Babies and children welcome: high chairs. Booking advisable. Separate room for parties, seats 30.

Hammersmith

Chez Kristof

111 Hammersmith Grove, W6 0NQ (8741 1177/www.chezkristof.co.uk). Goldhawk Road or Hammersmith tube. **Deli Open** 8am-7.30pm Mon-Fri; 8.30am-7pm Sat; 9am-6pm Sun. **Restaurant Lunch served** noon-3pm Mon-Fri; noon-4pm Sat, Sun. **Dinner served** 6-11pm Mon-Sat; 6-10.30pm Sun. **Main courses** £12.50-£17.50. **Both Credit** AmEx, MC, V.
Astride a boulevard-wide pavement on a leafy Hammersmith road, Chez Kristof is about as near to a real French local restaurant as you'll find in London. On a summer's evening, pavement tables were packed, but the spacious interior was as cool and relaxed as the service. With the breads came an intriguingly tasty dip – a 'secret recipe', but we managed correctly to guess aubergine, garlic and olive. From an intriguing menu, we plumped for starters of scallops on spinach with cauliflower purée, and soft-shell crab. The former combination was a revelation, the scallops tender but beautifully seared – even their edges. The crab flesh was wonderfully juicy, but marred by a dark-brown exterior just short of burnt. Main courses were swordfish steak on a bed of fennel, chilli and lime, and poached monkfish with chorizo and brown shrimp. These were striking combinations too, although the monkfish could have been poached in a more highly flavoured stock. From a nicely balanced wine list, a marsanne-viognier

2006 (£19.50) was more than a match for the flavoursome seafood. Fresh figs with clotted cream, and white chocolate cheesecake with raspberry sorbet rounded off a very pleasant evening.
Babies and children welcome: children's menu; films; high chairs. Booking advisable. Disabled: toilet. Separate room for parties, seats 45. Tables outdoors (15, terrace). Takeaway service (deli). **Map 20 B3.**

Holland Park

The Belvedere

Holland House, off Abbotsbury Road, in Holland Park, W8 6LU (7602 1238/ www.whitestarline. org.uk). Holland Park tube. **Lunch served** noon-2.30pm Mon-Sat; noon-2pm, 2.30-4pm Sun. **Dinner served** 6-10pm Mon-Sat. **Main courses** £10-£18. **Set lunch** (Mon-Fri) £14.95 2 courses, £17.95 3 courses; (Sat, Sun) £24.95 3 courses. **Credit** AmEx, MC, V.
Arrive around dusk and, with the birds singing in surrounding Holland Park, you see the blue neon sign shining across the car park, tempting you into one of London's most refreshing restaurants. Inside, there are two distinct dining areas: one, up and to the left, is intimate and low-ceilinged while the other, straight ahead, is dramatic with ultra-high ceilings, silk walls, smoked mirrors and hanging silver globes. Both areas have a sense of mystery and occasion and are within earshot of the piano. On our visit, there was a wide range of diners – couples on dates, old friends, families, business people – and the service was professional and friendly. If this all seems too good to be true, the food is not perfect so much as perfectly good. Scallops with diced apple were fresh, light and interesting, while tiger prawns with a heavily corriandered salad were only fresh and light. The strongest dish was a rich, tender piece of venison which, while it lasted, outshone the location. A battered plaice with a mountain of chips was more like upmarket comfort food. A great place to get away from it all, without leaving London.
Babies and children welcome: high chairs. Booking essential. Restaurant available for hire. Tables outdoors (9, terrace).

Westbourne Grove

★ The Ledbury

127 Ledbury Road, W11 2AQ (7792 9090/ www.theledbury.com). Westbourne Park tube. **Lunch served** noon-2pm Mon-Fri; noon-3pm Sat, Sun. **Dinner served** 6.30-10.15pm daily. **Set lunch** (Mon-Sat) £19.50 2 courses, £24.50 3 courses; (Sun) £40 3 courses. **Set dinner** £50 3 courses. **Credit** AmEx, DC, MC, V.
The Ledbury's food is as adventurous and technically accomplished as that of any restaurant in London, but you'll pay 20-30% less. That's reason enough to join the affluent Notting Hillites who flock to this elegant gastronomic gem. Chef Brett Graham worked at the Square (*see p144*), whose owner Nigel Platts-Martin and head chef Philip Howard are partners here. Brett speaks the language of haute cuisine: complicated assemblies on artfully arranged plates. But this is not visual cooking; it's aimed squarely at the palate, with flavours that are intense even when delicate, and often powerfully earthy. Every dish on the mega-bargain weekday lunch was flawless. Mains – halibut with cauliflower beignets, capers, raisins and smoked eel; and loin of Middle White pork with divine pommes purées and a veritable feast of fresh morels – clearly showed the expertise with complementary flavours. Thyme crème brûlée was a miracle of airy lightness. From the carte, a starter of celeriac, rolled in wood-ash, baked in a salt crust, and served with hazelnuts and a 'kromeski' of pork was technically dazzling and one of the best dishes we've ever eaten in London. Service was attentive, formal and friendly. The wine list shows profound knowledge of the world's best producers. Spending £20-£30 is possible, but it's worth pushing the boat out to complement this world-class cooking.
Babies and children admitted. Booking advisable; essential dinner. Disabled: toilet. Tables outdoors (9, pavement). **Map 7 A5/6.**

RESTAURANTS

South West
South Kensington

★ Papillon

96 Draycott Avenue, SW3 3AD (7225 2555/ www.papillonchelsea.co.uk). South Kensington tube. **Lunch served** noon-3pm Mon-Fri; noon-4pm Sat, Sun. **Dinner served** 6-11.30pm Mon-Sat; 6-10pm Sun. **Main courses** £15-£25. **Set lunch** £14.50 2 courses, £16.50 3 courses. **Credit** AmEx, MC, V.

Papillon is the perfect place to play out a fantasy of being a lady-who-lunches, and the French kitchen doesn't miss a note. The menu offers a well-balanced, if expensive, range of fresh, wonderfully paired and perfectly prepared options. Classics are respected; steak tartare was enticingly sharp from capers and a subtle spiciness. A rare flash-fried tuna was contrasted beautifully with tapenade. Portions, like the glamorous customers who frequent the restaurant, are elegant but slim (a crayfish starter was distinctly short on crayfish). Mains of chateaubriand rossini with potato galette had been perfectly cooked; venison with parsnip purée was tender and balanced; pan-fried turbot was sweetened with peas and onions and then accented with a deeper, richer flavour from lardons. The rather sophisticated grey dining room, made sparkling by clever use of mirrors and flattering lighting, is the ideal place to linger with some beautiful friends. Don't be intimidated by the encyclopedic 20-page wine list; the charming sommelier is perfectly able to assist in selections. He tactfully chose for our table a nice crisp £32 chardonnay from the Côtes de Beaune. Papillon is a real (expensive) treat.
Babies and children welcome: high chairs. Booking advisable. Dress: smart casual. Separate room for parties, seats 18. Tables outdoors (6, pavement). **Map 14 E10**.

Wandsworth

★ Chez Bruce (100)

2 Bellevue Road, SW17 7EG (8672 0114/ www.chezbruce.co.uk). Wandsworth Common rail. **Lunch served** noon-2pm Mon-Fri; noon-2.30pm Sat, Sun. **Dinner served** 6.30-10.30pm Mon-Sat; 7-10pm Sun. **Set lunch** (Mon-Fri) £25.50 3 courses; (Sat) £32.50 3 courses; (Sun) £32.50 3 courses. **Set dinner** £40 3 courses. **Credit** AmEx, DC, MC, V.

This Wandsworth institution has an air of exclusivity. We booked several weeks ahead for two and still only managed an early sitting (6.30pm). The first of the eponymous Bruce Poole's three impressive restaurants – the others are La Trompette (*see p105*) and the Glasshouse (*see p248*) – Chez Bruce combines outstanding food with a mildly subdued, reverential feel. It was quietly enjoyed, when we visited, by an almost uniform crowd of young professionals still in their suits. The best seats are near the window, while the main dining area behind can seem slightly airless (not helped by the lack of any focal point). We were delighted with everything the professional staff brought us. Rabbit came in various ways (terrine, rillettes, rolled breast, along with seared prunes and baked shallots): all full of flavour and the whole thing a visual treat. Venison loin (£4 supplement) was deliciously tender, with caramelised and mashed pear, while a pig's trotter, golden as a duck in Chinatown, was stuffed with a pleasingly rich mousse and chopped ham. Vanilla cheesecake came with pink rhubarb strips and mandarin sorbet: sharply impressive. There's a busy, knowledgeable sommelier to help you make the most of the highly regarded wine list. We love the fact that Chez Bruce takes its food so seriously, but we'd prefer a less serious atmosphere.
Babies and children welcome (lunch): high chairs. Booking essential. Separate party room, seats 14.

Wimbledon

Côte NEW

8 High Street, SW19 5DX (8947 7100/www.cote-restaurants.co.uk). Wimbledon tube/rail. **Meals served** noon-11pm Mon-Sat; noon-10.30pm Sun. **Set meal** (noon-7pm, Mon-Fri) £9.95 2 courses, £11.95 3 courses. **Main courses** £8.75-£17. **Credit** AmEx, MC, V.

Wimbledon's popular French restaurant is a busy brasserie with obvious ambitions to be a chain – it has already spawned a branch in Soho. That means blandly tiled floors and mirrored walls extending to the back of a large low-ceilinged venue on the high street. It also means assorted staff with limited knowledge of French cuisine. The food hails from all over France and includes Breton crêpes and cider. Starters range from a decent duck, chicken and pork terrine to some grilled prawns swimming in garlicky butter that seemed mass-produced. Light and predictable mains include the crêpes and tuna niçoise. Our duck confit was dry, albeit moistened by flageolet beans. Or there are various cuts of (ordinary) steak or chicken, both with frites. Desserts are again French staples (crème brûlée, and so on) and there's a range of Gallic wines with all the necessary grape varieties by the glass. Prices vary with time of day or week. Côte is very amenable, but it's also loud, clattery and lacking finesse.
Babies and children welcome: high chairs; nappy-changing facilities. Booking advisable (dinner). Disabled: toilet. Tables outdoors (2, pavement). **For branches see index**.

South
Battersea

Le Bouchon Bordelais

5-9 Battersea Rise, SW11 1HG (7738 0307/ www.lebouchon.co.uk). Clapham Junction rail/ 35, 37 bus.
Bar **Open** 10am-11.30pm Mon-Thur; 10am-midnight Fri, Sat; 10am-11pm Sun. **Breakfast served** 10am-2pm, **meals served** noon-10.30pm daily. **Main courses** £4.75-£16.95. **Set meal** £5.50 1 course.
Restaurant **Lunch served** noon-3pm, **dinner served** 6-11pm Mon-Fri. **Meals served** noon-11pm Sat; 12.30-10.30pm Sun. **Main courses** £14.50-£19.50. **Set meal** (lunch, 6-7pm Mon-Fri) £15 3 courses.
Both **Credit** AmEx, MC, V.

Plenty of French restaurants in London aim to replicate the simple menu, fast service and reliable quality typical of Parisian brasseries. Yet despite a swelling French population in the capital, there is a certain *je ne sais quoi* that eludes them. Le Bouchon Bordelais falls into this category, lacking both style and reliable food. Moules marinière arrived in bland broth that tasted entirely of wine and nearly-raw shallots. A steak was served rare, as requested, and a perfectly respectable green salad was kindly substituted for frites, but the steak tasted as if it had not been seasoned at all. A main of duck confit was fine, but nothing more. Service was friendly but very slow; glasses of wine were not served until well into the first course, and the restaurant has a disappointing policy of serving only large glasses of wine in the dining room (small glasses are available in the bar half of the business). A dining companion told his fiancée on the phone: 'I can't talk; I'm in Café Rouge.' He wasn't far off.
Babies and children welcome: children's menu; crèche (Sun); high chairs. Disabled: toilet. Separate room for parties, seats 30. Tables outdoors (11, terrace). **Map 21 C5**.
For branch (Le Pot Lyonnais) see index.

Clapham

Gastro

67 Venn Street, SW4 0BD (7627 0222). Clapham Common tube. **Breakfast served** 8am-3pm, **meals served** noon-midnight daily. **Main courses** £12.95-£16.75. **Set lunch** (noon-3pm Mon-Fri) £9.95 2 courses incl coffee. **Credit** MC, V.

Almeida. See p109.

Le Cassoulet. See p110.

Nothing much changes at Gastro, Clapham's most venerable bistro. On a recent visit, the service was lackadaisical, the interior musty, and the portions large and rich in animal fat. In other words, it is as French as ever. Soupe de poisson was wonderful: strong in flavour but not too fishy, with a hint of pastis. Scallops were plump and combined well with chorizo and hazelnut. At such a bastion of French traditional cuisine it was hard to overlook the fact that our steak was overcooked, but nevertheless it was tender and juicy. Rabbit in red wine was unattractive in appearance, tasty if a touch gloopy. The standard is not perfect and the food can be erratic but then isn't that the case with many small-town bistros in *La France profonde*? The staff seem to be an all-French team, and little details like the bread evoke proper French flour rather than your supermarket baguette. Perhaps Gastro is a bit overpriced and slightly resting on its laurels, but if you're craving classic bistro food served with a Gallic shrug, it will not disappoint.
Babies and children admitted. Booking advisable. Separate area for parties, seats 25. Tables outdoors (4, pavement). **Map 22 A2**.

★ Trinity

4 The Polygon, SW4 0JG (7622 1199/ www.trinityrestaurant.co.uk). Clapham Common tube. **Lunch served** 12.30-2.30pm Tue-Sun. **Dinner served** 6.30-10.30pm Mon-Sat; 7-10pm Sun. **Main courses** £15-£20. **Set lunch** (Tue-Sat) £15 2 courses, £20 3 courses. (Sun) £20 2 courses, £25 3 courses. **Set dinner** £35 (tasting menu). **Credit** AmEx, MC, V.
Back in 2007 we voted Trinity our Best Local Restaurant, and nothing has changed to blunt our enthusiasm. It's still an outstandingly slick operation, passionately run by chef/proprietor Adam Byatt, who combines top-quality cooking and pristine presentation with some surprisingly easy prices. Dishes on the eclectic but vaguely French menu are listed by their three main ingredients (yes, hence the trinity…). So, you can start with 'pea-mint-crème fraîche' (a mild, chilled soup embellished with pea tendrils) and follow with 'beef-girolles-spinach' (a cluttered landscape of succulent rare beef, mushrooms, marrow and an intense red wine jus). There's no skimping on portions. A risotto of girolles, peas and pecorino was mounded high; a starter of 'sardines-almond-pesto' resembled posh sardines on toast (or wafer

thin tart base), ringed by glorious dollops of thick almond 'soup'. The tasting menu gets you six mini-portions: a good choice if you're not ravenous. 'Chocolate-ice-cream-gru de cacao' is the pick of the puddings. The weighty wine list majors in France, but we tried a delightful Paper Road pinot noir from New Zealand. All this takes place in a cool modern interior, with muted canvases on the walls, fold-back windows, white linen and an eager posse of telepathic French waiting staff.
Babies and children welcome: high chairs. Booking essential. Disabled: toilet. **Map 22 A1**.

Waterloo

★ RSJ

33 Coin Street, SE1 9NR (7928 4554/ www.rsj.uk.com). Waterloo tube/rail. **Lunch served** noon-2pm Mon-Fri. **Dinner served** 5.30-11pm Mon-Sat. **Main courses** £12-£17. **Set meal** £15.95 2 courses, £18.95 3 courses. **Credit** AmEx, DC, MC, V.
RSJ is the place to go in London to learn about Loire wines. Sure, the grey and wood dining room is slightly weathered, but the perennially friendly and polite staff hit just the right note, making this the perfect place for a leisurely meal or a pre-theatre quickie. The great tome of a wine list offers dozens of interesting bottles, or you can choose from the regularly changing wine specials menu, which offers ample by-the-glass options. A 2004 Savenniers Clos de Coulaine and a Château de Villeneuve Saumur Champigny 2005 were interesting and priced at around £20. The seasonal food more than stands up to the fine-wine list. A typical starter of steamed scallops with clams and rocket was fresh, pure and sweet. Roast quail with rocket and endive was perfect. The only time the menu disappoints is when it goes off-piste in a fusion direction, as in a steamed Cornish monkfish in Asian broth. Look out for special wine-tasting/food pairing events and special pre-theatre dinners.
Babies and children admitted. Booking advisable. Separate room for parties, seats 25. **Map 11 N8**.

Waterloo Brasserie NEW

119 Waterloo Road, SE1 8UL (7960 0202/ www.waterloobrasserie.co.uk). Waterloo tube/ rail. **Meals served** 8am-11pm Mon-Fri; 10am-11pm Sat, Sun. **Main courses** £13.50-£24.

Set meal (lunch, 5-7pm) £14.50 2 courses daily. **Credit** AmEx, DC, MC, V.
This place was packed on the Friday evening of our visit, though we suspect the location was responsible (it's across the road from the Old Vic) rather than an inherent allure. The crowd quickly dispersed after the pre-theatre dining slot. The interior is far from relaxing, with an early 1990s-inspired black-and-red colour scheme, vulgar abstract art, space-altering mirrors and irritating background pop music. The feel of contrived flashiness extends to the food, which, although generally flavoursome, did at times fail to match the rather high prices. Starters of brie tatin and seared scallops on puy lentils were tasty, if unmemorable. Whole grilled sea bass was well cooked and of a generous size, putting the other main course – wild halibut en papillote (cooked in paper), small enough to be a child's portion – to shame. A selection of salads and typically fatty sides (gratin dauphinoise, pan-fried green beans) should please dedicated Francophiles; vegetarians might be less satisfied, limited as they are to just two main dishes (a pasta and a risotto). In contrast, the wine list is commendable: extensive, varied, and with many aperitifs. Service was prompt, rehearsed and impersonal.
Babies and children welcome: children's menu; high chairs. Booking advisable. Disabled: toilet. Separate room for parties, seats 55. Tables outdoors (4, patio). **Map 11 N8**.

East

Bethnal Green

Bistrotheque (100)

23-27 Wadeson Street, E2 9DR (8983 7900/ www.bistrotheque.com). Bethnal Green tube/rail/ Cambridge Heath rail/55 bus.
Bar **Open** 6pm-midnight Mon-Sat; 1pm-midnight Sun.
Restaurant **Brunch served** 11am-4pm Sat, Sun. **Dinner served** 6.30-10.30pm Mon-Thur, Sun; 6.30-11pm Fri, Sat. **Main courses** £10-£21. **Set lunch** £21 3 courses. **Set dinner** (6.30-7.30pm Mon-Fri) £14 2 courses, £17.50 3 courses. *Both* **Credit** AmEx, MC, V.
This modish restaurant, bar and cabaret venue is just as popular with regular diners as it is with the fashion crowd, largely thanks to the fact that

everyone is treated to the same cheery service and straightforward bistro food. The place is good-looking in a sort of 'whitewashed warehouse with chandeliers and baby grand piano' kind of way; the cosy Napoleon bar and adjoining cabaret room are on the ground floor, while the first floor holds the restaurant and private dining room. The short, seasonally changing menu is usually reliable: there is the odd duff dish (radish, artichoke, orange and baby watercress salad was so chilled it was almost tasteless, and poor value at £9.50 as a starter), but more typical were smooth seared foie gras with toasted brioche and rhubarb jelly; super-savoury roast cod, chorizo, tomato, fennel and squid stew, and lush lemon posset with shortbread. Fish and chips with pea purée and tartare sauce (a menu staple) is always worth ordering. And occasionally there's a stellar dish – most recently a stupendous starter of crab cakes with saffron hollandaise. Brunch is served at the weekends, and on Sundays it's served to the sound of Xavier at the piano.
Babies and children admitted. Booking advisable. Disabled: toilet. Entertainment: cabaret (check website or phone for details); pianist noon-4pm Sun. Separate room for parties, seats 50.

Brick Lane

Les Trois Garçons (100)

1 Club Row, E1 6JX (7613 1924/ www.lestroisgarcons.com). Liverpool Street tube/rail/8, 388 bus. **Dinner served** 7-10pm Mon-Thur; 7-10.30pm Fri, Sat. **Set dinner** (Mon-Wed) £27 2 courses, £31 3 courses; (Mon-Sat) £42.50 2 courses, £49.50 3 courses, £72 tasting menu. **Credit** AmEx, DC, MC, V.
Although Les Trois Garçons resembles a happy collision between a taxidermist's (it's a toss up between the giraffe's head and the whole swan for the most OTT stuffed item) and an art installation (we particularly love the arrangement of handbags suspended from the ceiling) the owners have also made sure they got all the basics right. Prices are a little overblown – the cheapest starter is soup at £8 and most are well over £10 – but dishes are mostly spot-on. Pumpkin velouté with root vegetable mirepoix and cumin crème fraîche was good, but had been bettered by an amuse bouche of parsnip soup with a dot of vanilla oil. We also liked assiette of Old Spot pork served with braised belly, pork shoulder confit, lentils and cider vinegar jus which followed. The only bargain here is the set menu. From this, salad of chicory and bitter greens with roquefort and toasted hazelnuts was fine but cheese-heavy; better was farmed rainbow trout on braised fennel with caper and olive beurre noisette – crisp and tender in equal measure. Pudding of poached pear with honey and thyme ice-cream had an indifferent pear but wonderful ice-cream. Service matches the decor. A great place for a proper night out, but not to count the pennies.
Booking advisable. Children over 12 admitted. Restaurant available for hire. Separate room for parties, seats 10. **Map 6 S4.**

North
Crouch End

Les Associés

172 Park Road, N8 8JT (8348 8944/ www.lesassocies.co.uk). Finsbury Park tube/rail then W7 bus. **Lunch served** by appointment Wed-Fri; 1-3pm Sun. **Dinner served** 7.30-10pm Tue-Sat. **Main courses** £12.50-£17. **Set lunch** (Sun) £15 3 courses. **Set dinner** (Tue-Fri) £12 2 courses, £15 3 courses. **Credit** AmEx, MC, V.
Hidden away in a quiet residential street, squeezed into the ground floor of one of the terraces, Les Associés is proudly, perfectly French – from the authentically illegible handwritten menu to the chansons playing in the background. Style purists might baulk at the slightly heavy handed, old-fashioned decor (gilt-framed mirrors and starched tablecloths), but the food is impeccable. So, too, is the wine list: a carefully chosen selection of regional AOC wines, sourced from small producers.

Prices are reasonable, and our three-course Sunday lunch was a steal at £15 per head: a dense, garlicky slab of home-made terrine and superb smoked duck salad to start, with bavette of beef and plump, juicy guinea fowl, in a wonderfully subtle plum sauce, to follow. Despite the price, no corners were cut: mains were delivered with side plates of perfectly cooked vegetables, portions were generous, and the artfully-presented trio of desserts was heaven for the sweet-toothed: a scoop of intense lemony mousse, sliver of creamy coffee cake and a sumptuously dark, velvety chocolate mousse.
Babies and children admitted. Booking advisable. Restaurant available for hire. Tables outdoors (8, garden).

Hornsey

Le Bistro

36 High Street, N8 7NX (8340 2116). Turnpike Lane tube/Hornsey rail/41, W3 bus. **Brunch served** 12.30-5pm Sun. **Dinner served** 6.30-11pm Mon-Sat; 5-10pm Sun. **Main courses** £11.95-£18. **Set meal** £12.50 2 courses, £14.50 3 courses. **Credit** MC, V.
This neighbourhood bistro looks as though it might have been scooped off the brassy streets of Montmartre. Charming and kitsch – 1950s French posters line wood-panelled walls, the likes of Alain

---

THE DISH

Brandade

Fish paste: not sexy. But brandade? Ooh la la! This smooth white purée of salt cod, olive oil and milk or cream hails from the south of France (the word comes from the Provençal verb *brandar*, which means to stir). Like every proper French dish, there are variations between towns, so that in Marseille garlic is added, while folk in other regions declare this an aberration. Potato is another very common inclusion, though strictly speaking, it's not authentic – but we say *vive la différence!*

Transport brandade to London and it happily adopts a multicultural edge. At haute cuisine restaurant **Texture** (*see p140*), Agnar Sverisson makes it with cod from his native Iceland, curing the fresh, meaty fish himself in salt, basil and lemon zest, then combining it with desirée potatoes, olive oil, lime juice and herbs. Fortunately, Icelandic cod has the ecological OK, but pollack brandade is a sustainable cod alternative adopted by kitchens in the capital including the **Fox** gastropub (*see p123*), where you might find it served with a soft-boiled duck egg; and **Tom Aikens**' fine-dining restaurant (*see p146*), where poached pollack comes with brandade mousse, cauliflower purée and truffle scrambled eggs, no less.

Islington gastropub the **Charles Lamb** (*see p126*) features brandade made from true-Brit smoked haddock and potatoes, simply served in rustic French style with crunchy toast. For a smarter Mediterranean take, visit Park Lane's **Bord'eaux**, where, in the colder months, Ollie Couillard pairs traditional salt-cod brandade with marinated red peppers and a beurre blanc flavoured with saffron.

Souchon play on repeat, and waiters serve customers with pouting reluctance. The menu is true to stereotype, offering snails, oysters and cassoulets. However, the smart money is on the fixed-price menu, where for less than the price of a main from the carte you can choose two courses from a limited menu. We started with smoked chicken salads that came carefully stacked like a weaver bird's nest, with peppery rocket, sweet cherry tomatoes, and generous pieces of breast. A salmon main was presented with equally lofty precision, the flavour of the fish complemented beautifully by fresh dill butter. The sirloin steak was also a hit, though the frites were soggy and bland. We were lured away from the set menu by a fragrant lavender-infused crème brûlée and a glossy tarte tatin – both well worth the detour.
Babies and children welcome: high chairs. Booking advisable. Tables outdoors (18, garden).

Islington

Almeida

30 Almeida Street, N1 1AD (7354 4777/ www.danddlondon.com). Angel tube/Highbury & Islington tube/rail. **Lunch served** noon-2.30pm, **dinner served** 5.30-10.45pm Mon-Sat. **Meals served** noon-8.30pm Sun. **Set lunch** £20 2 courses, £22 3 courses. **Set dinner** £25 2 courses, £29.50 3 courses. **Set meal** (lunch, 5.30-6.30pm daily; 9.30-10.45pm Mon-Sat) £14.50 2 courses, £17.50 3 courses. **Credit** AmEx, MC, V.
The Almeida is an ex-Conran restaurant that's now part of the D&D group, and for our money one of its best, with prices at the lower end of the scale (in set deals only), and quality at the upper. It's adjacent to the Almedia theatre and offers a pre-theatre menu, but is effectively self-contained as a formal restaurant. The room is spacious and pleasant, in dove-grey with good lighting and graphic flowers and paintings – albeit less cutting-edge in style than its scattering of decor magazines would suggest. The menu is similarly well done, and modern if not innovative, employing British and French ingredients and occasional nuances from other cuisines in pretty, detailed presentations. The website claims chefs use lighter-than-traditional cooking techniques; perhaps that post-dates our visit, when bream and rouget in a langoustine velouté was good but rich, and the vegetables butter-drenched. Other dishes, especially rillettes de lapin from the charcuterie trolley and a starter of truffled and creamed potatoes with asparagus, compensated. Staff are capable and charming (though we've had a couple of unexplained waits for food); the crowd are smart Islingtonians; the atmosphere a low hubbub of engaged conversation.
Babies and children welcome: high chairs. Booking advisable. Disabled: toilet. Restaurant available for hire. Separate room for parties, seats 18. Tables outdoors (8, pavement). **Map 5 O1.**

Morgan M

489 Liverpool Road, N7 8NS (7609 3560/ www.morganm.com). Highbury & Islington tube/rail. **Lunch served** noon-1.30pm Wed-Fri, Sun. **Dinner served** 7-9pm Tue-Sat. **Set lunch** £21.50 2 courses, £25.50 3 courses, £39-£43 tasting menu. **Set dinner** £39 3 courses, £43-£48 tasting menu. **Credit** MC, V.
This very personal operation – Morgan Meunier is the chef patron and the room feels like the dining room of his home – is one to cherish as a bastion of individuality in a corporate world. Not that we like it merely on principle: the food is both good and well-priced. Personal doesn't mean casual: service is formal and black-suited, presentation ritually formal, and the room restrained and simple in decor. The menu (set only) offers three courses with a choice of meat or fish, with amuses-gueules (of which we particularly commend a stunning beetroot velouté with gorgonzola cream). Flavours are intense and ingredients first quality in expertly rendered dishes that are perhaps one twist too far towards the fussy, by current tastes. Stand-outs on our recent visit were a foie gras pâté layered with almonds and jelly, veal with aerosol horseradish

foam, and raspberry soufflé. The restaurant is best suited to couples and quiet groups; with no music and a hushed respectful atmosphere, you can feel a bit self-conscious. Mr Meunier generally comes out of the kitchen to chat with diners, adding to the intimate feel.

Babies and children admitted (lunch).
Booking essential. Dress: smart casual.
Separate room for parties, seats 12.
Vegetarian menu.

Palmers Green

Café Anjou

394 Green Lanes, N13 5PD (8886 7267/ www.cafeanjou.co.uk). Wood Green tube then 329 bus/Palmers Green rail. **Lunch served** noon-3pm, **dinner served** 6.30-10.30pm Tue-Sun. **Main courses** £8.95-£11.75. **Set lunch** (noon-2pm Tue-Sat) £7.45 1 course incl glass of wine and coffee. **Set meal** (Tue-Fri, lunch Sat) £12.95 2 courses, £14.45 3 courses. **Credit** AmEx, MC, V.

Café Anjou is straight out of central casting. The walls, displaying familiar Gallic icons, leave you in no doubt the cuisine is going to be as thoroughly French as the ambience. From the prix fixe, soupe du jour was a workmanlike, if bland, leek and potato. Fish of the day, cod with saffron mashed potatoes, disappointed with lumpy spuds (and we couldn't taste any saffron), but the accompanying red cabbage and mangetout were perfect and plentiful. Our starter and main course from the carte were both hugely successful. A plate piled with high-quality smoked salmon, surrounded by small, succulent pieces of smoked mackerel, haddock, halibut and good mayonnaise formed a distinguished assiette nordique. The generous magret de canard lay on a flavourful bed of plum and ginger sauce. World-class meringue – crisp outside, toffee-like inside – came heaped with raspberries and cream. Decent south of France red and white house wine at £3.75 a glass, an international (but mainly French) wine list from £13.75 and very pleasant service contribute to a valued local bistro which many other areas might well envy.

Babies and children welcome: children's portions; high chairs. Booking essential dinner Fri, Sat. Restaurant available for hire.

North West

St John's Wood

L'Aventure

3 Blenheim Terrace, NW8 0EH (7624 6232). St John's Wood tube/139, 189 bus. **Lunch served** 12.30-2.30pm Mon-Fri. **Dinner served** 7-11pm Mon-Sat. **Set lunch** £15 2 courses, £18.50 3 courses incl coffee. **Set dinner** £28.50 2 courses, £35 3 courses. **Credit** AmEx, MC, V.

Even if you don't want to be seduced by this neighbourhood restaurant, the leafy magical entrance with its twinkling fairy lights, the tapestry drapes, terracotta pots of dried flowers and old oil paintings will make you smile. There's romance – a moneyed, greying charm – to the place and that calmness and hush you get in French country restaurants. Punters with strings of pearls and business accounts keep this institution going. Friendly enough staff make a show of explaining the scrawled French-language menu. The food is well executed, if at times rather too fussy. The kitchen seemed obsessed with baby broad beans and pomegranate seeds as a garnish on our visit. Mains of spiced honey magret de canard, and suprême de volaille with a deep garlicky sauce, were commendable examples of lip-licking indulgence, as was the creamy house foie gras. Later, our 'floating island' came with a host of decorations (forgivable for such a retro dish). L'Aventure is a sound choice for food, befitting the affluence of the area, though perhaps a little stuffy for some.

Babies and children welcome: high chairs. Booking advisable dinner. Tables outdoors (6, terrace).
Map 1 C2.

Outer London

Croydon, Surrey

Le Cassoulet NEW

2008 WINNER BEST LOCAL RESTAURANT
18 Selsdon Road, Croydon, Surrey CR2 6PA (8633 1818/www.lecassoulet.co.uk). South Croydon rail. **Lunch served** noon-3pm Mon-Sat; noon-4pm Sun. **Dinner served** 6-10.30pm Mon-Thur, Sun; 6-11pm Fri, Sat. **Main courses** £12.50-£20. **Set lunch** £16.50 3 courses (Mon-Sat); £19.50 3 courses (Sun). **Credit** AmEx, MC, V.

Although chef-patron Malcolm John's first restaurant, Chiswick's Le Vacherin (*see p104*), is highly regarded, it was always going to be a gamble opening another – especially in the gastronomic desert of South Croydon. But John is a local and knows his market. The place was humming on the Friday night of our visit. The long room is smart if old-fashioned, using shades of dark red and cream, floral wallpaper, velvet-backed chairs and striped banquettes to create a grown-up setting for some grown-up food. Escargots, frogs' legs, châteaubriand and steak tartare all appear on a menu that favours gusty, meaty fare from south-west France (vegetarians, beware). The signature dish was an excellent version: a rich, hearty stew of duck, pork, sausage and beans with a proper crusty top, served in its own mini cast-iron pot. Just as good was fillet of wild sea bass (succulent flesh, crispy skin), with white asparagus and crushed peas. Bread and butter pud with Calvados-soaked prunes provided a rich finish. Add in deft service from French staff clad in black waistcoats and long white aprons, a long, all-French wine list and bargain-priced set lunches and there's little to fault. Maybe the air-con was too efficient.

Babies and children welcome; high chairs. Disabled: toilet.

Kew, Surrey

Ma Cuisine Le Petit Bistrot

9 Station Approach, Kew, Surrey TW9 3QB (8332 1923/www.macuisinekew.co.uk). Kew Gardens tube/rail. **Meals served** 10am-10.30pm daily. **Main courses** £9-£17. **Set lunch** (noon-3pm Mon-Sat) £12.95 2 courses, £15.50 3 courses; (noon-4pm Sun) £15 2 courses, £18 3 courses. **Credit** AmEx, DC, MC, V.

Red gingham tablecloths, chequered tiled floors and belle époque posters make Ma Cuisine an attractive, if slightly kitsch, interpretation of a French bistro in Kew's former post office. During the day, it's a drop-in eatery serving baguettes, salads and quick lunches; in the evening there's a full dinner menu of hearty French classics. Expect the likes of bouillabaisse and onion soup to start, followed by steak, liver or coq au vin. Some components of the dishes were lovely: green beans came with a slick of buttery hollandaise; roast pork belly had a perfect balance of crisp skin and tender meat. However, the chef needs to put fewer elements on the plate. Roast saddle of venison wrapped in bacon would be better served with just confit fennel, gratin dauphinoise and chestnuts. The tear of broad bean purée on the plate and the sharp bursts of redcurrants were unnecessary distractions. Desserts kept things simpler and the indulgent crème brûlée and pear tarte tatin were decent renditions.

Babies and children welcome: children's menu; high chairs. Booking advisable. Tables outdoors (8, pavement).
For branch see index.

Richmond, Surrey

Chez Lindsay

11 Hill Rise, Richmond, Surrey TW10 6UQ (8948 7473/www.chezlindsay.co.uk). Richmond tube/rail.
Crêperie Meals served noon-10.45pm Mon-Sat; noon-9.45pm Sun. **Main courses** £5.50-£10.75.
Restaurant Meals served noon-10.45pm Mon-Sat; noon-9.45pm Sun. **Main courses** £9.25-£18.75. **Set lunch** (noon-3pm Mon-Sat) £14.50

2 courses, £17.50 3 courses. **Set dinner** (after 6pm) £18.50 2 courses, £21.50 3 courses. *Both* **Credit** MC, V.

Lindsay Wooton's lively restaurant has been serving rustic French fare for years and is still as popular as ever. On a recent Sunday lunchtime we found it bustling with customers, mostly families enjoying a day out. You'd think the management would increase staff numbers and try and turn tables, but service was frustratingly slow. Luckily, the sunny atmosphere and view over the Thames kept us happy enough while we waited. Authentic Breton cooking is the speciality, but you'll need to order carefully to pick the gems from the long menu. While seafood is a forte, top billing goes to the nutty buckwheat galettes, which come with a huge choice of fillings. Simple cheese, ham and spinach was perfect, but other more adventurous options include chitterlings, onions and mustard sauce. Pancakes also lord it over the puddings: we chose a frangipane crêpe that was sweet, buttery and divine. Bistro classics were less memorable: onion soup lacked depth of flavour, and the apple tart failed to excite. Stick with the specialities and order a refreshing Brittany cider alongside.

Babies and children welcome: high chairs. Booking advisable. Separate room for parties, seats 38.

Surbiton, Surrey

The French Table

85 Maple Road, Surbiton, Surrey KT6 4AW (8399 2365/www.thefrenchtable.co.uk). Surbiton rail. **Lunch served** noon-2.30pm Tue-Sun. **Dinner served** 7-10.30pm Tue-Sat. **Main courses** £10.50-£15.50. **Set lunch** (Tue-Sat) £15.50 2 courses, £18.50 3 courses; (Sun) £22.50 3 courses. **Credit** MC, V.

There is a certain 'home makeover' feel to this Surbiton eatery, with its pale lilac walls, pine chairs, decorative vases and starched white tablecloths. Fortunately, the crisp, clean look is complemented by a warm, laid-back atmosphere. The menu is a mixture of French dishes and those with a Mediterranean touch. Deep-fried eggs seem to be the chef's latest trick; there were a couple offered and they were indeed very good, with crisp breadcrumb crust and perfectly soft interior. We also enjoyed the meltingly tender suckling pig with apple mousseline and sweet confit onions, though it was rich enough to be a meal in itself. Sea bass with quinoa and scallop risotto was less exciting and the 'tartare' of vegetables lent little to the dish. Staff are attentive and check if customers are there for a special occasion, and made a thoughtful effort for the birthday party at the next table.

Babies and children welcome: high chairs. Booking advisable; essential weekends.

Twickenham, Middlesex

Brula

43 Crown Road, Twickenham, Middx TW1 3EJ (8892 0602/www.brula.co.uk). St Margaret's rail. **Lunch served** noon-3pm, **dinner served** 6-10.30pm daily. **Main courses** £15-£18. **Credit** AmEx, MC, V.

This unpretentious neighbourhood bistro has charm, with its large stained-glass windows, worn parquet floor and lively atmosphere. The church pew seats are just uncomfortable enough to keep you from lingering too long, but otherwise Brula will make you feel right at home. The kitchen combines French classics with Modern European dishes, so the menu is full of tempting choices. Some lived up to expectations better than others. A salad of feta, aubergine and pea shoots scattered with pistachios and a sweet-sour honey dressing was a lovely marriage. Foie gras with toasted brioche and Madeira jelly was also a winner. But red gurnard with jerusalem artichokes, clams, mussels and aïoli was underwhelming, and sea bass overcooked. Roast chicken tagliatelle with morels, broad beans and tarragon was better. There are sister restaurants in East Sheen and Richmond.

Babies and children admitted. Booking advisable. Separate rooms for parties, seating 8, 10 and 24. Tables outdoors (6, pavement).
For branches (La Buvette, La Saveur) see index.

Gastropubs

If you think gastropubs are opening at an alarming rate, you're probably right. Here we've cherry-picked only the best and handiest of this year's many openings – and we've still got 17 brand new ventures for you. The pub trade is in the doldrums, with customers nationwide consuming less beer, and smokers, post-ban, less inclined to spend an evening in the boozer. If pubs are unable to beef up their food side, they become vulnerable to closure and property development. Much as we love gastropubs – one or two would still be a godsend in some barren areas of the capital – no one wants to see the demise of the great British pub. Antony Worrall Thompson (who always has an eye on the major trends) was among the first to say enough is enough. He has even talked of switching his own Henley gastropub back to a more traditional model.

On the following pages you'll find gastropubs in all their variations: small bars that happen to serve very good food, pubs with dining rooms attached, and a few aspirational establishments that really seem to wish they were a restaurant. Among the most welcome of this year's new crop is the **Princess Victoria** in Shepherd's Bush, winner of the Best Gastropub category of the 2008 Time Out Eating & Drinking Awards. We were also impressed by newcomers the **Perry Hill** and the **Clissold Arms**. Interestingly, the raft of new openings hasn't necessarily meant a general raising of the bar (so to speak). Some of our current favourites are established acts, such as the **Marquess Tavern** (a former Time Out award winner that founders Huw Gott and Will Beckett have recently sold), the **Peasant**, the **Princess**, the **Charles Lamb** and Jamie Prudom's **Pig's Ear**.

Central

Belgravia

Ebury
11 Pimlico Road, SW1W 8NA (7730 6784/ www.theebury.co.uk). Sloane Square tube/ Victoria tube/rail/11, 211, 239 bus.
Brasserie Open noon-11pm Mon-Sat; noon-10.30pm Sun. **Lunch served** noon-3.30pm Mon-Fri, Sun. **Dinner served** 6-10.30pm Mon-Sat; 6-10pm Sun. **Set lunch** £11.50 1 course, £16.50 2 courses, £19.50 3 courses.
Dining room **Dinner served** 7-10.30pm Tue-Sat. *Both* **Main courses** £10.50-£18.50. **Credit** AmEx, MC, V.
Like some of its customers, the Ebury tries a bit too hard. A long dining space, with low chairs and sofas illuminated by huge halo lights, adjoins an area of padded stools where drinks can be taken beside a curved bar. The open plan gives the place the feel of a hip airport business lounge, but generates a noisy din that makes the bland house music all the more irritating. On our visit, the service was unfriendly and supercilious. Once we were seated at the table, tap water was hard to come by. The food can be impressive, but too often betrays a lack of confidence by being overdressed. A starter of succulent, delicate lamb sweetbreads was overpowered by smoked bacon in the savoy cabbage accompaniment, while a main of pollock with mussels, gnocchi and kale tasted like moules marinière. On the other hand, a starter of sea trout was glorious (unfishy, rare and melt-in-the-mouth), and a lamb main was full of flavour. Yet looking at the scene around us, it all felt a little depressing. *Babies and children admitted. Disabled: toilets. Separate room for parties, seats 60.* **Map 15 G11**.

Bloomsbury

Norfolk Arms
28 Leigh Street, WC1H 9EP (7388 3937/ www.norfolkarms.co.uk). Euston tube/rail.
Open 11am-11pm Mon-Sat; 11am-10.30pm Sun. **Lunch served** noon-3pm, **dinner served** 6.30-10.15pm daily. **Main courses** £8.50-£14.50. **Credit** AmEx, MC, V.
Everything changed a few years back at this once down-at-heel Victorian backstreet boozer. A glossy gastropub reinvention means that while the tiled exterior, ornate ceiling and magnificent etched-glass windows remain, a businesslike charcuterie slicer now takes pride of place behind the stately mahogany bar, with lomo, chorizo and salchichon hanging overhead. Dining, not drinking, is the focus, but the Norfolk Arms is far from formal; its white-painted antique tables have a rickety charm, and black-clad waiters operate at a leisurely pace. Half the menu is given over to starters and mains, half to an eclectic tapas list, where tortilla and pickled guindilla peppers rub shoulders with baba ganoush, stuffed vine leaves, scotch eggs and mozzarella-style cheese stuffed with white truffle cream. Chorizo in cider, artichoke hearts and a glossy heap of boquerones were simple yet perfectly executed; best of all was the rich chicken liver pâté, served with chunky, aniseed-infused apple and sultana chutney. The wine list offers telegrammatic tasting notes ('crisp flint lively'; 'affable apricot hazelnut') and some interesting

choices. The house red lives up to its billing – 'bouncy juicy redcurrant' – and costs a mere £12.50. Theakston XB and Greene King IPA are on draught, and several sherries are available by the glass or bottle.
Babies and children admitted. Booking advisable. Separate room for parties, seats 25. Tables outdoors (15, pavement). **Map 4 L3**.

Clerkenwell & Farringdon

Coach & Horses (100)
26-28 Ray Street, EC1R 3DJ (7278 8990/ www.thecoachandhorses.com). Farringdon tube/ rail. **Open** noon-11pm Mon-Fri; 5-11pm Sat; noon-4pm Sun. **Lunch served** noon-3pm Mon-Fri, Sun. **Dinner served** 6-10pm Mon-Sat. **Main courses** £9.50-£14. **Credit** AmEx, MC, V.
A handsome pub (apart from the dingy 'outside' room sandwiched between bar and beer garden), the Coach & Horses does its best to appeal to drinkers and diners. There are several real ales, and the wood-panelled and etched-glass interior isn't too jazzed up, but there's also a great wine list (with many by the glass) and a dab hand in the kitchen. Don't expect a restaurant setting – plenty of tables are occupied by drinkers, a crowd gathers by the pavement tables in warm weather, and service comes in jeans and T-shirt. Portions are big; order a bar snack, such as chips and aïoli and some of the fabulous bread, and you may decide that's enough. Which would be a shame: squid salad with rocket and baby plum tomatoes stuffed with chorizo was a delightfully inventive and satisfying take on familiar ingredients. Confit duck leg with lentils and morcilla, with a side of buttery greens, was similarly enjoyable: so too a pair of haddock fish cakes. Typical last courses are English cheeses or Valrhona chocolate cake with rhubarb compote. Though not a venue for that special date, the Coach & Horses does its own thing very competently.
Babies and children welcome: high chairs. Tables outdoors (9, garden). **Map 5 N4**.

Eagle
159 Farringdon Road, EC1R 3AL (7837 1353). Farringdon tube/rail. **Open** noon-11pm Mon-Sat; noon-5pm Sun. **Lunch served** 12.30-3pm Mon-Fri; 12.30-3.30pm Sat, Sun. **Dinner served** 6.30-10.30pm Mon-Sat. **Main courses** £5-£17. **Credit** MC, V.
The Eagle still doesn't have a blue plaque outside, but probably merits one, as it is widely credited with being the first London gastropub (opened in its present incarnation in 1991). While many gastros have gone down the chic-cuisine and designer-decor route, this is still recognisably a pub with quality food: noisy, often crowded, with no-frills service and dominated by a giant open range where T-shirted cooks toss earthy grills amid theatrical bursts of flame. The Iberian/Med-influenced menu (chalked-up, of course) has stayed true to its original idea of 'big flavours', with hefty mains like napoli sausages with polenta and red onions, ribeye steak with Italian tomato sauce, or cod with lentils and aïoli. The house red, Borsao, is a punchy Spanish garnacha to match. As smaller options, there are a few simple starters (fresh soups, risotto) and tapas. With this straightforward style, quality depends on well-sourced ingredients, and awareness in the cooking: the sausages and ribeye were spot on, but an Eagle steak sandwich was poor, the meat a drab grey. Still, blips aside, this is always a convivial spot.
Babies and children admitted. Tables outdoors (4, pavement). **Map 5 N4**.

Easton
22 Easton Street, WC1X 0DS (7278 7608). Farringdon tube/rail. **Open** noon-11pm Mon-Thur; noon-1am Fri; 5.30pm-1am Sat; noon-10.30pm Sun. **Lunch served** 12.30-3pm Mon-Fri; 1-4pm Sun. **Dinner served** 6.30-10pm Mon-Sat; 6.30-9.30pm Sun. **Main courses** £8.95-£13.50. **Credit** MC, V.
Hearty is the obvious word to use about the Easton's full-on food. A lamb and rosemary pie with beans, mash and gravy featured deliciously

BEST GASTROPUBS

Bountiful brews
For interesting and varied real ales, visit the **Charles Lamb** (see p126), **Duke of Sussex** (see p115), **Junction Tavern** (see p127), **Marquess Tavern** (see p127), **Palmerston** (see p121), **Peasant** (see right) and **Warrington** (see p128).

Fine wines
Indulge a love of the grape at the **Greyhound** (see p119), **Princess Victoria** (see p116) and **Rosendale** (see p121).

Gardens of delight
Nab a place in the sun (or shade), at the **Devonshire** (see p115), **Dolphin** (see p121), **Duke of Sussex** (see p115), **Ealing Park Tavern** (see p115), **Engineer** (see p124), **Herne Tavern** (see p121) and **Perry Hill** (see p121).

City slickers
Catch up with the business crowd at the **Coach & Horses** (see p111), **Duke of Wellington** (see right), **Eagle** (see p111), **Easton** (see p111), **Fox** (see p123), **Hat & Feathers** (see below), **Only Running Footman** (see p115), **Princess** (see p123, and **White Swan Pub & Dining Room** (see right).

No bookings
Just rock up at the **Anchor & Hope** (see p119), **Charles Lamb** (see p126) and **Earl Spencer** (see p119).

---

crisp pastry, and could have fed two; braised rabbit, tomato and chicken stew came on top of a plateful of pumpkin and polenta. Best of all was roast lamb with herb and vegetable couscous, harissa and yoghurt, which ideally combined generosity with fresh minty natural flavours. The blackboard menu focuses on main courses, with not much that's smaller and (on our visit) only a salad and a risotto for vegetarians. There's a decent wine selection, but nothing special for beer-drinkers beyond now-standard lagers and one ale (Timothy Taylor Landlord). The bar-room with its archetypical stripped wooden floors and battered tables is broad and open, and so best when there's some warm sunlight to flow in through the big windows. On gloomier nights, it can feel quite chilly. Service seems especially casual even by gastropub standards, and so can be very friendly or annoying, depending on who's on that day. *Babies and children admitted (until 9pm). Tables outdoors (4, pavement).* **Map 5 N4.**

Hat & Feathers
2 Clerkenwell Road, EC1M 5PQ (7490 2244/ www.hatandfeathers.com). Barbican tube/ Farringdon tube/rail. **Open** noon-midnight Mon-Sat. **Lunch served** noon-2.30pm Mon-Fri. **Dinner served** 6-10pm Mon-Sat. **Main courses** £13.50-£18.95. **Credit** AmEx, MC, V.
Hats off to this refurbished City corner pub for avoiding the clichés of gastropub furniture. Instead, the spacious ground-floor bar has some rather smart ostrich-leather chairs in brown and beige; the 1970s vibe continues with curvy plastic Panton chairs on the decked outdoor area, while the first-floor restaurant has the sort of high-backed padded numbers you'd expect to see in a proper restaurant (which this is). The bar menu isn't just a list of nibbles either, with hearty dishes like tempura-style fish and chips with aïoli, and slow-roast fillet of Aberdeen Angus. A pleasing choice of beers takes in Chiswick bitter, Cruzcampo and even strawberry Früli on draught. We dined on the first floor, with views through tall windows of the traffic below. White linens, a plethora of wine recommendations and silver

service from the bread tray weren't the only haute cuisine aspects to the evening; beetroot risotto came with basil foam, and lamb with fine green beans was tightly wrapped in a crêpe-like crumb crust. Simpler dishes (moist roast guinea fowl, fat chips) scored highly too, as did the responsible service team.
Babies and children admitted. Bar available for hire. Disabled: toilet. Tables outdoors (50, terrace). **Map 5 O4.**

★ Peasant
240 St John Street, EC1V 4PH (7336 7726/ www.thepeasant.co.uk). Angel tube/Farringdon tube/rail/19, 38 bus.
Bar **Open** noon-11pm Mon-Sat; noon-10.30pm Sun. **Meals served** noon-10.45pm Mon-Sat; noon-9.30pm Sun. **Main courses** £8.50-£9.50.
Restaurant **Brunch served** noon-3pm Sun. **Lunch served** noon-3pm Tue-Fri. **Dinner served** 6-11pm Tue-Sat. **Main courses** £9.70-£18.
Both **Credit** AmEx, MC, V.
Although we've had meals of varying quality here in the past, on a recent visit the Peasant launched itself into the upper class. The giant main bar of this old Victorian pub – where you can try own-brand Wat Tyler lager as well as other quality beers – is comfortably spacious, with magnificent original tiling as a touch of grandeur. The first-floor dining room, lined with circus and theatre posters, has an airy relaxed feel and service is charming and alert. There are separate menus upstairs and down, but many dishes are shared. Both lists present the same attractive blend of satisfying flavours and sophisticated, globe-trotting inventiveness; cooking throughout seems to have developed a notable finesse. For Sunday brunch we enjoyed some first-rate fish and chips, with lovely crisp delicately flavoured batter; tomato and goat's cheese tart with rocket and grilled figs was brightly refreshing, and the trad roast beef impressive. Leave space and time for the scrumptious desserts: maybe a light bread and butter pudding with caramel sauce, or the irresistibly intricate 'B-52' chocolate parfait. The wine list is as interesting a read as the menus, and very fairly priced.
Babies and children welcome (until 9pm): high chairs. Booking advisable. Tables outdoors (4, garden terrace; 5, pavement). **Map 5 O4.**

Well
180 St John Street, EC1V 4JY (7251 9363/ www.downthewell.com). Farringdon tube/rail. **Open** 11am-midnight Mon-Thur; 11am-1am Fri; 10.30am-1am Sat; 10.30am-11pm Sun. **Lunch served** noon-3pm Mon-Fri; 10.30am-4pm Sat, Sun. **Dinner served** 6-10.30pm Mon-Sat; 6-10pm Sun. **Main courses** £9.95-£16.50. **Credit** AmEx, MC, V.
Part of Tom and Ed Martin's gastropub group, which includes the Gun in Docklands (see p123), the Well exudes an easy bonhomie and self-assurance, with its exposed brick walls, friendly staff and chunky wooden tables piled with the Sunday papers. To drink, the wine list, ordered by grape variety, is more impressive than the choice of beers (no draught ales, though Leffe, Paulaner and San Miguel are on tap). The menu offers hearty (if pricey) brunches and roasts for the weekend crowd, and an inviting evening menu of upper-end Mod Euro gastropub offerings (pan-fried sardines, foie gras terrine on toasted sourdough, ribeye steaks and the like). On our last visit, though, the kitchen was on erratic form. A generous bowl of rich, creamy celeriac soup and a meltingly tender portion of salt and pepper squid, dabbed with punchy wasabi mayonnaise, made for a promising start, but mains disappointed: ragù of wild mushrooms was accompanied by dry, heavy gnocchi, while some overpowering chorizo and undercooked beans added a jarring note to a cassoulet of confit pork belly. We left feeling that the kitchen wasn't firing on all cylinders – and with upscale prices and plenty of local competition, such complacency could be foolish.
Babies and children welcome: high chairs. Booking advisable. Separate room for parties, seats 70. Tables outdoors (6, pavement). **Map 5 O4.**

Holborn

White Swan Pub & Dining Room
108 Fetter Lane, EC4A 1ES (7242 9696/ www.thewhiteswanlondon.com). Chancery Lane or Holborn tube.
Bar & restaurant **Open** 11am-11pm Mon; 11am-midnight Tue-Thur; 11am-1am Fri. **Lunch served** noon-3pm, **dinner served** 6-10pm Mon-Fri.
Restaurant **Main courses** £13-£18. **Set lunch** £24 2 courses, £29 3 courses. **Set meal** (noon-1pm, Mon-Fri) £15 2 courses.
Bar **Main courses** £9-£16.
Both **Credit** AmEx, MC, V.
Besuited after-work crowds milling across the pavement make it easy to spot this smart City pub, run by the same Martin brothers as the Well in Clerkenwell (see above), the Empress of India (see p65) and other successes. The finely restored wood-panelled bar had enough space to make elbow-rubbing only an optional activity, and there seemed plenty of table-space to sample the superior bar menu. The upstairs dining room is a separate restaurant, with sleek mirrored decor, but the two menus have similar features. We sampled the more elaborate and elegantly presented dining room menu, beginning with a delicate salad of smoked black pudding, quails' eggs and tarragon mustard, and a full-on rich ballotine of foie gras with Sauternes jelly. We were still more impressed by our mains: superior pan-fried scallops with champagne velouté, and Gloucester Old Spot pork belly with perfect crackling and beautifully rounded flavours. The wine list is sophisticated, with many modern labels at reasonable prices. Greene King IPA, London Pride and a guest are the draught ales. Service is zippy and charming; we were immediately asked if we wanted a second bottle of wine, but then, that's a City habit.
Babies and children welcome: high chairs. Booking advisable; essential lunch. Restaurant available for hire. Tables outdoors (2, pavement). **Map 11 N5.**

Marylebone

★ Duke of Wellington NEW
2008 RUNNER-UP BEST GASTROPUB
94A Crawford Street, W1H 2HQ (7723 2790). Baker Street tube/Marylebone tube/rail. **Open** noon-11pm Mon-Sat; noon-10.30pm Sun. **Lunch served** noon-3pm Mon-Sat; 12.30-4pm Sun. **Dinner served** 6.30-10pm Mon-Sat; 7-9pm Sun. **Main courses** £8-£16. **Credit** AmEx, MC, V.
With a smart black frontage opposite a splendid Grade I-listed Georgian church, the revamped Duke of Wellington is a descendant of the Pig's Ear (see p117) and Brown Dog (see p116). Its first-floor dining room, next to the kitchen, is exceedingly cramped, with eight tables squeezed into a former sitting room that retains its magnificent fireplace. A better option might be to eat in the lively – but very noisy – downstairs bar, which has a similar if slightly more rustic menu. The likes of Deuchars IPA, Adnams Broadside and London Pride are supplemented by bottled beers, including Früli, and there's an appealingly concise wine list, from which Puglian Primitivo was a good-value choice. Chargrilled sirloin of 30-day-matured Longhorn beef impressed, but came with pasta gratin, spinach and crumbed chunks of bone marrow which didn't unite harmoniously. Better was the not-quite-hot plate of flakily soft pork cheeks cooked in Pedro Ximénez, with cream-laden pommes mousseline and baby carrots. A cup of layered peanut butter, chocolate and griottines was every bit as decadent as it sounds and cleverly paired with unsweetened milk ice-cream. Staff remained sunny, despite the squeeze.
Babies and children admitted. Tables outdoors (6, pavement). Separate room for parties, seats 25. **Map 2 F5.**

★ Queen's Head & Artichoke
30-32 Albany Street, NW1 4EA (7916 6206/ www.theartichoke.net). Great Portland Street or Regent's Park tube. **Open** 11am-11pm Mon-Sat; noon-10.30pm Sun. **Lunch served** noon-3.30pm

Mon-Fri; 12.30-4pm Sat. **Dinner served** 6.30-10.15pm Mon-Sat. **Meals served** noon-10.15pm Sun. **Main courses** £9.50-£13.50. **Credit** AmEx, MC, V.

No great makeovers were needed to gastro-ise the Queen's Head – the bar's grand original wooden panelling and giant leaded windows provide all the right ambience. You can eat there, or from the same menu in the quieter surroundings of a distinctively chic upstairs dining room; there's also a small pavement terrace and a tiny patio. Tables were at a premium in the bar, even early on a midweek evening. We soon realised why. Diners can choose between a long, pan-Mediterranean list of tapas, or an attractive full menu; portions are very generous, but this is no case of quantity without quality. A platter of mixed tapas made a great starter to share, with excellent tabouleh, grilled mushrooms, houmous, various Spanish meats and other good things. Mains were even better, with every ingredient just right: a huge but sumptuously juicy ribeye with punchy anchovy butter, and a similarly flavour-rich pan-fried salmon with pesto potatoes, beans and cherry tomatoes. The wine list shows the same fine level of care and nous, with superior modern wines at decent prices, such as the Spanish Martín Berdugo red, a snip at £17. A very enjoyable refuge in an under-supplied area.
Babies and children admitted. Separate room for parties, seats 55. Tables outdoors (6, garden; 8, pavement). **Map 3 H4**.

Temperance

74-76 York Street, W1H 1QN (7262 1513/ www.thetemperance.co.uk). Baker Street or Marble Arch tube. **Open** noon-11pm Mon-Sat; noon-10.30pm Sun. **Lunch served** noon-3pm Mon-Sat; noon-4pm Sun. **Dinner served** 6-10pm Mon-Sat. **Main courses** £9.95-£14.95. **Credit** AmEx, MC, V.

Only a year or so after opening, they've downsized at the Temperance, closing the upstairs dining room, but the ground floor remains a decent bet for a bite, pint or glass of wine. The environment is undistinguished – another plain glass fish bowl, with stripped wooden floors – but there is opulent red wallpaper in some corners. Drinks comprise a fair range of intoxicants, with well-kept ales and a seductive selection of wines by the glass that complements pretty much everything on the unambitious menu. Sauvignon and chenin blanc consort nicely with starters of smoked eel and thoroughly deep-fried whitebait. Thereafter a mid-range claret went as well with a thick burger and spindly fries, as did a frisky montepulciano with a pork belly and stodgy mustard mash. Finesse isn't a strong point, and puddings hint that someone here is nostalgic for (high-quality) school dinners, but the service and ambience is far from the puritanism suggested by the pub's name. Indeed, the night of our visit, a frisky foursome of French bankers even danced suggestively on their table. Outré, certainly, but not temperate.
Babies and children admitted. Separate room for parties, seats 30. **Map 2 F5**.

Mayfair

Only Running Footman `NEW`

5 Charles Street, W1J 5DF (7499 2988/ www.therunningfootman.biz). Green Park tube. **Open** 7.30am-midnight daily. **Meals served** 7.30am-10.30pm daily. **Main courses** £5.50-£19.50. **Credit** AmEx, MC, V.

This typically smart Mayfair establishment shares owners with the Bull in Highgate and the House in Islington (for both,*see p126*). In the ground-floor bar where you can also eat, it is loud and brash so as to hurt the head. But there's hearty grub, good wines and fine ales served by staff who act like they're interested in the job. Upstairs, things are more tranquil although not dozy. A light pastel-green carpet tastefully coordinates with wallpaper, table linen and upholstered seats. The menu is a world where foie gras terrine shares space with raw tuna and seaweed salad on the list of starters, and where roast dover sole rubs shoulders with veal T-bone for mains. The results are good if not

Norfolk Arms. See p111.

great. Smoked eel went well with asparagus, and grilled sardines were perfectly fresh, but to follow, sea bass (pan-fried, with shallot and coriander mash) and lamb steak were unexceptional. Posh but populist desserts include chewy jam doughnuts and raspberry ice-cream, and rhubarb and sherry trifle. The wine list is well composed. *Babies and children admitted. Disabled: toilet. Separate rooms for parties, seating 14 and 30. Tables outdoors (6, pavement).* Map 9 H7.

West

Barons Court

Queen's Arms
171 Greyhound Road, W6 8NL (7386 5078). Barons Court tube. **Open** noon-11pm Mon-Thur, Sun; noon-midnight Fri, Sat. **Lunch served** noon-3pm Mon-Fri; noon-3.30pm Sat; 12.30-4pm Sun. **Dinner served** 6.30-10pm Mon-Sat; 6.30-9.30pm Sun. **Main courses** £8.95-£15.95. **Set lunch** (Mon-Fri) £10 2 courses, £14 3 courses. **Credit** MC, V.
Hidden in the backstreets between Barons Court tube and Fulham Palace Road, this maroon-painted corner pub no longer resembles the grubby boozer it once was. Smart wooden furniture, white walls and skylights make the ground floor bright and breezy; upstairs is another space, next to the kitchen, with retractable roof. After an adventurous gastronomic start, drinking has taken over again – especially on Mondays, when diners' conversation is drowned out by the quiz master. Draught beers range from Timothy Taylor Landlord and London Pride, to Petermans, Hoegaarden and Leffe. The menu is pretty standard pub fare: burger with cheese, or sausages, mash and cabbage, with sticky toffee pud or warm chocolate mud cake for afters. Most successful were the sharing platters (houmous, baba ganoush, flatbread, peppers and so on) that require minimal cooking. Little attention is paid to seasonality (there was a surfeit of wintery dishes in late May) or balance (three mains came with red wine jus). Staff weren't very clued up either, with no record of our booking and the previous day's menus still in circulation. The Queen's Arms is a sociable spot, and probably a boon if you live nearby, but there's better food available elsewhere. *Babies and children welcome: high chairs. Booking advisable. Disabled: toilet.*

Chiswick

Devonshire NEW
126 Devonshire Road, W4 2JJ (7592 7962/ www.gordonramsay.com). Turnham Green tube. **Open** noon-11pm Mon-Sat; noon-10pm Sun. **Lunch served** noon-2.45pm daily. **Dinner served** 6-10pm Tue-Sat; 6-9.30pm Sun. **Set meal** (noon-2.45pm; 6-7pm Tue-Sat) £13.50 2 courses, £16.50 3 courses. **Main courses** £11.50-£15. **Credit** AmEx, MC, V.
The Devonshire's modern country styling helps it resemble a rural boutique hotel set up for a glossy photo-shoot. Look how the vintage chairs have been wittily covered in shiny striped fabrics; note the carefully positioned Scrabble sets; coo at the old chap on the cover of the drinks list. If this were in Cumbria or Cork, you'd be angling for a weekend stay. The young crowd (and one Japanese family) on our visit seemed perfectly comfortable, though they didn't look like locals. Most took a drink in the pleasant garden before dining on the likes of pan-fried bream with ratte potatoes, fennel and sauce vierge, and beetroot and ricotta salad with basil cress and candied walnuts. There's a retro British hint to the 'on toast' section of the menu with its herring roes and (rather nice) devilled chicken livers, but not as much as we expected after our first visit – perhaps due to the hot weather. We still enjoyed the cottage porter pie with caerphilly, as well as an exquisite herb-crusted lamb. The wine list starts at a reasonable £13.50 a bottle, and for those preferring a brew, pints of Deuchars IPA are a welcome alternative. *Babies and children welcome. Bar available for hire. Tables outdoors (10, garden; 4, pavement).*

Duke of Sussex NEW
75 South Parade, W4 5LF (8742 8801). Chiswick Park tube. **Open** 5-11pm Mon; noon-11pm Tue-Thur; noon-midnight Fri, Sat; noon-11pm Sun. **Meals served** 5-10.30pm Mon; noon-10.30pm Tue-Sat; noon-9.30pm Sun. **Main courses** £7.50-£15.50. **Credit** MC, V.
A cherub-lined skylight adds a romantic glow to the cheerful dining room of this sensitively refurbished Acton-borders outfit. Light, minerally müller-thurgau – not your typical gastropub wine – features on the Europe-focused wine list, which includes several varieties in 175ml and 375ml measures. But the Duke of Sussex is still very much a pub, with a large bar and enviable designer beer garden. On tap you'll find the well-known names plus a varied selection of ales from smaller breweries – the likes of Kelham Island's Eastern Promise, Cornish Knocker, and Harviestoun Bitter & Twisted. Fish features heavily on the blackboard menu, which mixes British classics (ox tongue and piccalilli) and Spanish dishes (morcilla fritters with piquillo sauce). Waiting staff were efficient, but food didn't come quickly; our midweek meal took over two hours for three courses and the dining room was only half full. But it's hard not to forgive the kitchen when desserts were so thrilling. Santiago (almond) tart with vanilla ice-cream was superb; hot, sugar-dusted churros were perfectly tender-crisp – though surely the chocolate pot that came with them should have been dunking-soft? *Babies and children welcome: high chairs. Booking advisable dinner. Disabled: toilet. Separate room for parties, seats 64. Tables outdoors (34, back garden; 3, front garden).*

Roebuck
122 Chiswick High Road, W4 1PU (8995 4392/ www.theroebuckchiswick.co.uk). Turnham Green tube. **Open** 11am-11pm Mon-Sat; noon-10.30pm Sun. **Meals served** noon-10.30pm Mon-Sat; noon-10pm Sun. **Main courses** £8.50-£17.50. **Credit** AmEx, DC, MC, V.
Part of a growing chain that includes the Queens in Crouch End (see p125), this is a reassuringly slick operation: all stripped wooden floors, chocolate suede banquettes and reclaimed pews. The front half operates strictly as a pub with bar snacks (and no children), the back half is a dining room (families welcome). The whole space is light, airy and appealing, with the back opening on to a charming walled garden – a real suntrap. It attracts young families, romantic couples and young drinkers. An extensive varied menu takes in gastropub classics with some experimentation (including excellent fish dishes) but no gimmicks. The open kitchen gives a relaxed, informal feel, although we did hear the odd Ramsay-esque outburst. Creamy smoked mackerel pâté with own-made bread came in a generous portion. Perched on a potato cake, roast chicken breast with leek and tarragon sauce was robust and simple. Flavours sang even in a straightforward dish of tomato pasta. Nothing was cheap but it was all excellent value. Service was swift and unobtrusive. The wine list is top-notch, yet surprisingly limited for such a cosmopolitan venue. *Babies and children welcome: children's menu, high chairs. Disabled: toilet. Tables outdoors (20, garden; 4, pavement).*

Ealing

★ Ealing Park Tavern
222 South Ealing Road, W5 4RL (8758 1879). South Ealing tube.. **Open** 11am-11pm Mon-Sat; noon-10.30pm Sun. **Lunch served** noon-3pm Mon-Sat; noon-3.45pm Sun. **Dinner served** 6-11pm Mon-Sat; 6-9pm Sun. **Main courses** £9.50-£15. **Credit** AmEx, MC, V.
No doubt the lucky locals here would love to keep the place all to themselves, but some things are too good not to share. Fortunately there's plenty of pub to go around; cathedral-like ceilings add an air of grandeur, mismatched furniture brings it back to earth, while the large landscaped beer garden with long tables made for leisurely lunches is a destination in itself. Though informal, and buzzing with a happy din of families, friends and couples,

the Tavern takes its food seriously. Ingredient provenance is proudly displayed, with good reason – those we tried were uniformly excellent. Plump scallops got our meal off to a luxurious start, duck was fall-off-the bone fabulous, and monkfish marinière with cockles and seasonal greens nothing less than swoon-worthy. Death by chocolate wasn't as heart-stopping as we might have hoped, but at least we lived to tell the tale. Service was excellent throughout, with friendly staff more than willing to help out. An excellent venue for parties of two to 20, with space still left for sprawling. *Babies and children welcome (until 8.30pm): high chairs. Tables outdoors (20, garden).*

Hammersmith

★ Carpenter's Arms NEW
2008 RUNNER-UP BEST GASTROPUB
91 Black Lion Lane, W6 9BG (8741 8386). Stamford Brook tube. **Open** noon-11pm daily. **Lunch served** noon-2.30pm Mon-Fri; 12.30-3pm Sat; 12.30pm-4pm Sun. **Dinner served** 6.30-10pm Mon-Fri; 7-10pm Sat; 7.30-9.30pm Sun. **Main courses** £10.50-£17. **Credit** MC, V.
Good sourcing and clever seasonal-ingredient combinations are at the heart of the Carpenter's menus, but sadly the approach isn't extended to the beer. There's just one real ale – Adnams bitter – plus Amstel, Guinness and Addlestones cider on tap. Wines are available by both glass and carafe, and include an enjoyably fruity chilled gamay. You may have to drink in the sizeable garden, as priority is given to diners at this small corner pub. Sautéed lamb sweetbreads with succulent baby turnips, pickled grapes and dandelions, and a huge mound of fresh crab with radishes, red onion and mixed cress got our meal off to a stunning start. Roast halibut steak was overcooked, but sat on a delicious mound of cider-braised bacon, peas, lettuce and a sweet meaty broth. The kitchen gets details such as oven-hot, rugged bread right, so the McD-style french fries are a letdown. We consoled ourselves with excellent puds, including refreshing passion-fruit and pelargonium (geranium) jelly. The two blokes who turned up in tennis sweats and sat at the bar talking loudly over their pints underlined the clash between restaurant and pub, but also proved that perhaps it doesn't matter here. *Babies and children welcome: high chairs. Tables outdoors (8, garden).* Map 20 A4.

Ladbroke Grove

Fat Badger
310 Portobello Road, W10 5TA (8969 4500/ www.thefatbadger.com). Ladbroke Grove or Westbourne Park tube. **Open** noon-11pm Mon-Thur; 11am-midnight Fri, Sat; noon-10pm Sun. **Lunch served** noon-3pm, **dinner served** 6-10pm Mon-Thur; 6-11pm Fri, Sat. **Meals served** noon-10pm Sun. **Main courses** £10-£15. **Credit** AmEx, DC, MC, V.
It has been a while since badgers, fat or otherwise, populated the northern stretch of the Portobello Road, but you'll still find wild life around here. To fit in with its trustafarian locals, this large pub steers clear of the tarted up. The ground-floor bar may sport bare wooden flooring and sofas, but the floor is scuffed and the sofas bashed. Tongue-in-cheek pink wallpaper depicting street muggings adds a faintly louche air. The first-floor dining room is slightly more formal, with attractive old wooden tables. It's often closed for lunch, but the enticing Mod Euro menu is also served downstairs (on coffee tables impossible to get your feet under). There's an Irish slant to proceedings, with the likes of crubeens with onion marmalade, and a top-notch dish of smoked haddock, brown shrimp colcannon and mustard butter, on the daily changing list. A starter of creamy, bland jerusalem artichoke soup was given some pzazz with chopped hazelnuts. For afters, we've heard great things of the monumental sticky toffee pudding. Bob Marley gets a regular outing on the sound system, as does Timothy Taylor Landlord on the handpumps. Service was friendly but flaky. *Babies and children admitted. Tables outdoors (6, terrace; 2, pavement).* Map 19 B1.

Devonshire. See p115.

Olympia

Cumberland Arms

29 North End Road, W14 8SZ (7371 6806/
www.thecumberlandarmspub.co.uk). West
Kensington tube/Kensington (Olympia) tube/rail.
Open noon-11pm Mon-Sat; noon-10.30pm Sun.
Lunch served noon-3pm, **dinner served**
7-10pm Mon-Sat. **Meals served** 12.30-9.30pm.
Main courses £7-£15.50. **Credit** AmEx, MC, V.
In an age of increasingly poncey gastropubs, this
Olympia stalwart keeps it real, with its well-worn
wooden tables and floorboards, real ales (London
Pride, Timothy Taylor Landlord and Black Sheep
on our visit) atop a lengthy wine list, and a fairly
priced menu of Mediterranean and North African
dishes. Drinkers and diners mingle happily, bar
staff smile and the overflowing hanging baskets
(a riot of colour decorating the blue exterior come
summer) lend rustic charm. Food is hearty rather
than gourmet, as befits the setting. The menu
changes monthly, but typical dishes are roast pork
belly, Tunisian lamb and date tagine, pan-roasted
wild salmon, and spaghetti and meatballs. Plates
come piled high. The cooking (and service) can be
slapdash; our waitress had only a hazy idea of
dishes' contents, and the kitchen had run out of
mustard and dill vinaigrette (how can you run out
of vinaigrette?). Still, we enjoyed two decent main
courses – a hefty slab of well-cooked cod with puy
lentils; and spring-like penne with asparagus, peas
and courgettes – and the relaxed vibe aids digestion.
The outside tables are useful in fine weather.
Babies and children welcome (until 7pm):
high chairs. Tables outdoors (9, pavement).

Shepherd's Bush

Anglesea Arms

35 Wingate Road, W6 0UR (8749 1291).
Goldhawk Road or Ravenscourt Park tube. **Open**
11am-11pm Mon-Sat; noon-10.30pm Sun. **Lunch**
served 12.30-2.45pm Mon-Sat; 12.30-3.30pm Sun.
Dinner served 7-10.30pm Mon-Sat; 7-10pm Sun.
Main courses £12.50-£15.50. **Credit** MC, V.
The very essence of a gastropub, the Anglesea has
a clubby front room with comfy sofas around a
roaring fire in colder weather. The sky-lit back
extension packs in lots of wooden tables alongside
the open kitchen, a blackboard proclaiming the
daily menu. One constant seems to be oysters.
Even in 'R'-less breeding months, the recommended
(and cheapest, £8.95 for six) Irish were plump,
sweet and tasty, simply served with shallot
vinegar, tabasco and lemon wedges – though the
accompanying dense chunk of bread was inedible.
A starter of squid with fennel, garlic and coriander
disappointed; the fennel salad seemed undressed
and the squid had an off-putting hint of grill-rack
residue. Mains were more successful: sea bass with
braised little gem, peas and mash; and roast lamb
with minted aubergine and roast tomatoes. Both
were excellent, with every component perfectly
cooked. Sadly, the range of summery light beers
to accompany the lamb was poor, but the wine list
is lengthy, with quite a few at reasonable prices.
Tinpot Hut Marlborough New Zealand sauvignon
blanc (£5.95 a glass) was perfect with the fish.
Babies and children welcome: high chairs.
Bookings not accepted (dinner). Tables outdoors
(10, pavement). **Map 20 A3**.

★ Princess Victoria NEW (100)

2008 WINNER BEST GASTROPUB
217 Uxbridge Road, W12 9DH (8749 5886/
www.princessvictoria.co.uk). Shepherd's Bush tube.
Open 11.30am-midnight daily. **Lunch served**
noon-3pm Mon-Sat; noon-4.30pm Sun. **Dinner**
served 6.30-10.30pm Mon-Sat; 6.30-9.30pm Sun.
Main courses £10.50-£16.50. **Set lunch** (Mon-
Fri) £10 2 courses, £13.50 3 courses. **Credit** MC, V.
Ruddles County, Summer Lightning, Timothy
Taylor Landlord, and Peroni (among others) on tap
– the beer's not thrown out with the bath water at
this exciting new refurbishment. The Princess
Victoria's sheer size gives it the edge over many
competitors, for there's room to house cheerfully
loud drinkers as well as dining couples and
families. Tables are plentiful in both bar and dining
room – the latter including a long communal set-
up where we ate after enjoying beers by the
impressive horseshoe-shaped, marble-topped bar.
Our waiter, a qualified sommelier, confessed he
knew more about wine than the menu, but worked
conscientiously to ensure everything was just so.
Brawn, the least attractive starter, was successful
thanks to its deep flavour and moist texture.
Terrific triple-cooked chips came with accurately
chargrilled 28-day-matured ribeye (the evening's
most popular order), but the Princess Victoria can
do fancy too, as shown by a delicious hake fillet
with clams, smoked eel, macaroni and vegetable
cream sauce. Desserts featured superb ice-creams:
vanilla with cherry clafoutis, rhubarb with a
jamaican ginger cake and rhubarb compote –
though the latter felt like two separate puds. The
sensational wine list offers a choice of carafe sizes
plus 175ml glasses; diners are encouraged to mix
and match with their food. No persuasion needed.
Babies and children welcome: high chairs. Booking
advisable. Disabled: toilet. Separate room for
parties, seats 60. Tables outdoors (10, garden).
Map 20 A2.

Westbourne Grove

Cow (100)

89 Westbourne Park Road, W2 5QH (7221
0021/www.thecowlondon.co.uk). Royal Oak or
Westbourne Park tube. **Open** noon-11pm Mon-
Sat; noon-10.30pm Sun. **Lunch served** noon-
3.30pm daily. **Dinner served** 6-10.30pm
Mon-Sat; 6-10pm Sun. **Main courses** £9-£19.
Set lunch (Sun) £24 3 courses. **Credit** MC, V.
Although not the only pub to request an email
address for table confirmations, Tom Conran's
highly popular Cow has a ramshackle retro-Irish
vibe at odds with such a booking system.
Downstairs, punters cram in like sardines, happily
standing in the limited space by the bar to drink;
preference for tables is given to diners. In the first-
floor restaurant, up a red linoleum staircase, long-
haired bambis with expensive handbags eat with
doe-eyed boyfriends in tight sweaters. Wherever
you sit the smart order is seafood – say a half
dozen clean creamy Irish natives served with
shallot vinegar, or the platter of fruits de mer.
There's a good range of drinks, from Fuller's ESB
and London Pride on tap, to OK martinis made
with Gordon's, and the occasional novelty such as
Byrrh. The wine list has its heart in France but
flirts elsewhere. We appreciated the careful details
– lovely breads and focaccia, delicious rosemary-
laden dauphinoise, discerningly peppered
chargrilled steak – but there was no excusing the
mean cubes of veal in the blanquette. Service
ranges from sweet to smart-arse; the Cow knows
it's cool and the crowds do nothing to dissuade it.
Babies and children admitted (lunch). Restaurant
available for hire. Tables outdoors (2, pavement).
Map 7 A5.

South West

Barnes

★ Brown Dog

28 Cross Street, SW13 0AP (8392 2200). Barnes
Bridge rail. **Open** noon-11pm Mon-Sat; noon-
10pm Sun. **Lunch served** noon-3pm Mon-Fri;

noon-4pm Sat, Sun. **Dinner served** 7-10pm Mon-Sat; 7-9pm Sun. **Main courses** £10.50-£17. **Credit** AmEx, MC, V.

There's much to cherish about this gastropub tucked among the cute backstreet cottages on the border between Barnes and East Sheen. A handsome space by day, with cream wood panelling and retro metal signs, it positively twinkles by night thanks to the warm wooden furniture, polished red ceiling and copper globe lamps above the central bar. The bar divides the smallish space into drinking and dining areas, and there's also a back courtyard for summer lounging. Prices and clientele are upmarket, but not stuffy, and the food can be very good. Classy ingredients are used in unfussy combinations, whether it's top-notch seafood (dressed Cromer crab or Colchester rock oysters to start, beautifully cooked lemon sole with brown shrimp and parsley beurre noisette to follow), a lavish Sunday roast (Longhorn ribeye or whole poussin with all the trimmings), or comforting puds (rice pudding with damson jam, egg custard tart with raspberries). Attention is paid to seasonality, witness a whole baked vacherin mont d'or as a starter to share. Kids get mini portions of adult dishes. French bottles dominate the wine list, and there's Hepworth Sussex Bitter and a seasonal guest ale on tap. Dogs (of any colour) are welcome.
Babies and children welcome: children's portions; high chairs. Disabled: toilet. Tables outdoors (12, garden).

Chelsea

Lots Road Pub & Dining Room

114 Lots Road, SW10 0RJ (7352 6645/ www.lotsroadpub.com). Fulham Broadway tube then 11 bus/Sloane Square tube then 11, 19, 22 bus. **Open** 11am-11pm Mon-Thur; 11am-midnight Fri, Sat; noon-10.30pm Sun. **Lunch served** noon-4pm, **dinner served** 6-10pm Mon-Fri. **Meals served** noon-10pm Sat, Sun. **Main courses** £6.50-£15.50. **Credit** AmEx, MC, V.

This lively gastropub, part of the small Food & Fuel chain, satisfies on most levels without ever being sensational. There are good ales – Hook Norton, Bombardier and Adnams were featured on our visit – and the service is excellent. The dining room feels a bit dark and is something of an annexe to the noisy front bar where the action is. The menu consists of a range of pub classics and salads with a few smart British dishes, such as dressed Cornish crab, thrown in for good measure. Mostly these are done very well. Côte de boeuf and chips was excellent, albeit bleu rather than rare. We also had a great burger and some enjoyable starters – in which a smoked mackerel pâté stood out. The letdown was an insipid risotto of broad beans and pea shoots, and a sticky toffee pudding that lacked treacly stickiness. Come 11pm it might be just you and the staff left – very sobering.
Babies and children welcome: children's portions; high chairs. Booking advisable. Disabled: toilet. Separate room for parties, seats 30. **Map 13 C13**.

★ Pig's Ear

35 Old Church Street, SW3 5BS (7352 2908). Sloane Square tube. **Open** noon-11pm Mon-Sat; noon-10.30pm Sun. **Lunch served** 12.30-3pm Mon-Fri; 12.30-3.30pm Sat; 12.30-4pm Sun. **Dinner served** 7-10pm Mon-Sat; 7-9.30pm Sun. **Main courses** £10.50-£18.50. **Credit** AmEx, MC, V.

The ground floor at the Pig's Ear is a classic posh boozer, popular with cords-and-tweeds locals (and on the night of our visit, a bunch of well-salaried gents in black tie). In addition to an extensive Europhile wine list, there's the Pig's Ear real ale, a top-notch pint. The barman took the trouble to taste a virgin mary (with a straw) before serving it. The bar menu is good, but it's just as enjoyable to escape up the steep set of stairs to the bare-board and oak-panelled dining room. Starters are highly priced (almost all over £7) and include interesting choices, from potage of new-season's garlic, to smoked halibut, steak tartare and palourde clams (a little over-dressed in chilli, ginger, garlic, lemon and parsley). Mains included a gorgeous confit of pork belly, and lamb with

bean cassoulet, but vegetarians were confined to risotto parmigiana. Puddings were far from boring, with a cappuccino crème brûlée and an intriguing bramley apple sorbet. With an original selection of cheeses also on offer, the Pig's Ear is well worth trotting to.
Babies and children admitted. Booking advisable (dining room). **Map 14 E12**.

Parsons Green

Sands End NEW

135-137 Stephendale Road, SW6 2PR (7731 7823/www.thesandsend.co.uk). Parsons Green tube. **Open** noon-11.30pm Mon-Wed; noon-midnight Thur; 9.30am-midnight Sat; 9.30am-11pm Sun. **Lunch served** noon-3pm Mon-Fri. **Dinner served** 6-10pm Mon-Fri. **Meals served** 10.30am-10pm Sat; 10.30am-9pm Sun. **Main courses** £11.50-£16. **Credit** AmEx, MC, V.

This corner pub was given a facelift by the new owners at the end of 2007. It's now light-filled, with cream-coloured walls, old oak floorboards, candles on the tables and blackboard menus. The staff are enthusiastic and clearly committed to the place, whether they're pouring you a pint of real ale (from the Hook Norton brewery perhaps) or dishing up the British Isles menu, which has a recognisably Irish accent. The bread is good, baked daily on the premises. Scallops were served with discs of black pudding, a pleasing combination and done well. But corned beef and carrot pie disappointed: the hot-water crust was served slightly burnt, yet the filling was lukewarm. Summer pudding was the best dessert, sharp and running with dark juices. There are two wine lists: the regular one, and a version for the kind of people who think nothing of ordering a £65 bottle to go with their pub grub (amazingly, there was no shortage of these on our visit). Even the more modest wine list is packed with well-chosen bottles, with more than a dozen sold by the glass.
Babies and children admitted. Booking advisable. Separate room for parties, seats 26. Tables outdoors (4, pavement).

Putney

Normanby NEW

231 Putney Bridge Road, SW15 2PU (8874 1555/www.thenormanby.co.uk). Putney Bridge tube/Putney rail. **Open** 11am-11pm Mon-Thur; 11am-midnight Fri; 10am-midnight Sat; 10am-11pm Sun. **Lunch served** noon-3pm, **dinner served** 5-10pm Mon-Fri. **Meals served** 10am-10pm Sat, Sun. **Main courses** £9.50-14.50. **Credit** AmEx, MC, V.

With its yellow leather trimmed seats, dark wooden floorboards and inviting sofas, the Normanby is trying very hard to make the most of its airy open space. Although the main dining area is set to the back, it still has a slight wine-bar feel. The menu is vast and feels slightly unfocused: light bites compete with sharing plates, main courses, salads, starters and soups. The £4 lunch specials are popular; the cottage pie was a proper meaty homely version – unglamorous but hearty and generous. The hot platter (cod goujons, mini salmon fish cakes, chicken bites, beef skewers and citrus aïoli) was fine, if uninspiring: the sort of food that seems to exist solely to soak up alcohol. Warm chocolate brownie with pistachio ice-cream had something to it, with a wonderful melted texture to the brownie. Despite strenuous efforts, the Normanby feels like a drinker's eaterie (there's an extensive cocktail menu). It has some good ideas and offers value for money, but compares unfavourably to the nearby Prince of Wales.
Babies and children welcome (until 7pm): high chairs. Disabled: toilet. Tables outdoors (4, garden).

Prince of Wales NEW

138 Upper Richmond Road, SW15 2SP (8788 1552/www.princeofwalesputney.co.uk). East Putney tube/Putney rail. **Open** noon-11pm Mon-Wed; noon-midnight Thur-Sat; noon-10.30pm Sun. **Lunch served** noon-3pm Mon-Fri; noon-4pm Sat, Sun. **Dinner served** 6-10pm daily. **Main courses** £8-£18. **Credit** MC, V.

RESTAURANTS

The Prince is fit for a Duchess, combining the old-school feel of a real pub with high culinary standards. It's a corner building on three levels: the bar at the front, a mid-section dining area and a lower dining area. Popular with all ages and types, it had a friendly raucous vibe on our Saturday-night visit. The menu is temptingly adventurous. Potted crab came on its own breadboard with thick-cut toast, pickles (made in-house) and a salad that was more than a boring garnish; the crab was sublime. Pan-fried sprats with horseradish sauce, simply done, were excellent. Roast pork was tasty, if a little cool, with black pudding and chunks of braised celeriac. Côte de boeuf was accompanied by perfect aromatic béarnaise sauce, packed with fresh tarragon, and thick-cut, triple-cooked chips. Tap water flows freely from jugs without you even having to ask. Desserts are superb: raspberry ripple ice-cream was memorably rich and fruity, while buttermilk pudding (an English panna cotta) with rhubarb and shortbread was bursting with vanilla creaminess. Service is perfect: attentive and unobtrusive. Attention to detail combined with real passion make this a great foodie destination. Although less than a year old at the time of writing, the Prince of Wales already had a sister: the Bull & Last, on Highgate Road in Gospel Oak.
Babies and children welcome: high chairs. Tables outdoors (16, pavement).

Spencer Arms

237 Lower Richmond Road, SW15 1HJ (8788 0640/www.thespencerarms.co.uk). Putney Bridge tube/22, 265, 485 bus. **Open** 11am-midnight Mon-Sat; 11am-11pm Sun. **Lunch served** noon-2.30pm Mon-Fri; noon-3pm Sat; noon-9pm Sun. **Dinner served** 6.30-10pm Mon-Sat; 6.30-9.45pm Sun. **Main courses** £7.50-£18. **Credit** MC, V.
A drab and soulless exterior does this Putney Common boozer a disservice – inside is far more lively and welcoming. The big open-plan room curves around three sides of the central bar, and offers a mix of seating at wooden tables and leather sofas. The decor's a bit more bright and shiny than the gastropub norm, but none the worse for it. A daily-changing menu offers a selection of solidly British recipes and ingredients. To start, a bowl of cauliflower soup was simple and unadorned yet smoothly satisfying. Macaroni cheese also went down well, but was a bit half-hearted as it used penne, and hadn't been baked (so just pasta with a cheese sauce, really). Mains were also fine: a whole roast sea bass with roast tomato and salsa verde; a hunk of pork belly atop a slice of good black pudding and shredded cabbage. Desserts might be crème caramel with rum raisins, or rice pudding with roast plums. Beer and wine lovers are equally well catered for; draught ales include London Pride and Adnams Broadside, while the diligent wine list has a superb choice by the glass. A perfect place to end up after a Sunday stroll by the river.
Babies and children welcome (until 9pm): high chairs; nappy-changing facilities. Disabled: toilet. Entertainment: jazz 8pm, call for details. Tables outdoors (11, pavement).

Wandsworth

Freemasons

2 Wandsworth Common Northside, SW18 2SS (7326 8580/www.freemasonspub.com). Clapham Junction rail. **Open** noon-11pm Mon-Thur; noon-midnight Fri, Sat; noon-10.30pm Sun. **Lunch served** noon-3pm, **dinner served** 6.30-10pm Mon-Fri. **Meals served** 12.30-10pm Sat; 12.30-9pm Sun. **Main courses** £9.50-£12.95. **Credit** AmEx, MC, V.
No funny handshakes or strange rituals were in evidence at this large, maroon-fronted corner pub. Just sundry locals out for a quiet pint (there's Timothy Taylor and Everards Tiger on tap, as well as Leffe, Beck's Vier and other continental lagers) or a plate of hearty, no-nonsense food. Most diners were sitting at the front of the pub, where bare floorboards, stripped pine tables and schoolroom chairs fit the gastropub norm, though there's also a smarter, brick-walled restaurant area at the rear. Outside, a row of long picnic tables curves around the front. The menu is straightforward: burgers and potato wedges, sausages and mash, steak and chips, pan-fried cod with braised lettuce and peas. And portions are huge: we ordered a side of houmous and flatbread, expecting it to be more manageable a size than a proper starter, but the plate that arrived could have easily served a trio. Organic pork belly sat in a pool of intense calvados jus next to a mini mountain of mustardy mash; similarly gargantuan was tuscan spaghetti – a variant of puttanesca, basically, with a lip-smacking sauce of capers, tomatoes and anchovies. The easy-drinking wine list is keenly priced, with a 175ml glass starting at £3.50.
Babies and children welcome: high chairs. Tables outdoors (11, patio). **Map 21 B4.**

Waterfront

Baltimore House, Juniper Drive, SW18 1TZ (7228 4297/www.waterfrontlondon.co.uk). Wandsworth Town rail/295 bus. **Open** 11am-midnight Mon-Sat; 11am-11pm Sun. **Meals served** 11am-10.30pm daily. **Main courses** £6.50-£14.95. **Credit** AmEx, MC, V.
On an anonymous stretch of the Thames, an anonymous set of apartment blocks called Battersea Reach houses an anonymous glass-fronted pub called, rather lamely, the Waterfront. In summer, the beer garden on the towpath must be great. Indoors, the place resembles a hotel restaurant or airport bar, with huge glass windows, high ceiling, and a mixture of brown leather banquettes and dark wood tables. Service is slow, with even our menus taking 15 minutes to arrive. Customers seem to consist of whispering tourists or cliquey girlfriends from the flats above. The menu is divided into bar food and à la carte, with the pretentious formulations 'to begin' and 'to follow' giving the game away. Our waitress informed us that roast beef wasn't going to be pink, and that the pie had run out. When the steak arrived it was neither huge as promised, nor rare as ordered. The food isn't terrible: the steak was juicy and served with a good pepper sauce; fish and chips was workmanlike. But the best thing about this soulless barn is its perfectly kept Young's bitter.
Babies and children admitted. Disabled: toilet. Tables outdoors (35, riverside terrace). **Map 21 A4.**

Wimbledon

Earl Spencer

260-262 Merton Road, SW18 5JL (8870 9244/www.theearlspencer.co.uk). Southfields tube. **Open** 11am-11pm Mon-Thur; 11am-midnight Fri, Sat;

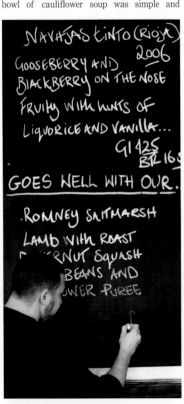

Ealing Park Tavern. See p115.

noon-10.30pm Sun. **Lunch served** 12.30-2.30pm Mon-Sat; 12.30-3pm Sun. **Dinner served** 7-10pm Mon-Sat; 7-9.30pm Sun. **Main courses** £8.50-£14. **Credit** AmEx, MC, V.

Well-used international cookbooks propped above the coffee machine here suggest a fondness for culinary adventure. It's borne out in the menu, where an exemplary just-set pork and chicken-liver terrine might share blackboard space with crisp, grease-free sweet-potato pakoras, or black bean chilli soup. Substitutions are made without compunction or comment, and on our visit the advertised couscous had morphed into boiled potatoes to accompany a main of plaice with a pile of gleaming broad beans and fat cockles. Still, chef Mark Robinson and team know what they're doing, and the laid-back regulars – from pink hair to grey hair – seem to appreciate the good prices, take-us-as-you-find-us vibe and lack of polish in the generously proportioned saloon. Interesting options by the glass are the highlights of a wine list that's fairly priced and, for its length, full of possibilities; beer and cider drinkers won't struggle either, with Hogsback TEA and Aspall's on draught. The own-made bread, which boasts a dark, crackling crust, is cheap at 50p per head and will keep the wolf from the door while you wait for a table. Bookings aren't accepted.
Babies and children welcome: children's portions; high chairs. Bookings not accepted. Separate room for parties, seats 70. Tables outdoors (10, patio).

South

Battersea

Greyhound
136 Battersea High Street, SW11 3JR (7978 7021/www.thegreyhoundatbattersea.co.uk). Clapham Junction rail/49, 319, 344, 345 bus. **Open** noon-11pm Tue-Sat; noon-5pm Sun. **Lunch served** noon-3pm Tue-Sat. **Dinner served** 7-10pm Tue-Sat. **Main courses** £16.50-£19.50. **Set lunch** £18.50 2 courses, £25 3 courses. **Credit** AmEx, MC, V.
From chaos sometimes emerges greatness. A lost booking, an unconvincing amuse-bouche and flavourless frozen pomegranate vodka martini didn't bode well for our meal. Yet thereafter, this out-of-the-way venue proved it is a very fine restaurant. Starters of hare risotto and a stracci pasta with rabbit ragù were both wonderfully meaty. But the highlight was a main course of slow-cooked beef cheek, which oozed and insinuated flavour with every delicious mouthful. Slapstick comedy was never far away during our visit, as a pair of sommeliers crashed around with armfuls of bottles. The wine list is amazing: a vast idiosyncratic selection, featuring hundreds of different bottles, many £500 or more, though wines by the glass are very reasonably priced. The sole pubby thing about the Greyhound is its atmosphere. A linear dining room with a lovely alcove table, exposed brickwork, neutral colours and chandeliers runs into a loud bar area where music plays and comfy banquettes reside (you can also eat here). Only the absence of real ale is disappointing, although staff do serve delicious, cloudy Addlestones cider.
Babies and children welcome: high chairs. Booking advisable. Disabled: toilet. Restaurant available for hire. Separate room for parties, seats 25. Tables outdoors (10, terrace; 6, garden). **Map 21 B2**.

Waterloo

Anchor & Hope (100)
36 The Cut, SE1 8LP (7928 9898). Southwark or Waterloo tube/rail. **Open** 5-11pm Mon; 11am-11pm Tue-Sat; 12.30-5pm Sun. **Lunch served** noon-2.30pm Tue-Sat; 2pm sitting Sun. **Dinner served** 6-10.30pm Mon-Sat. **Main courses** £11-£16. **Set lunch** (Sun) £30 4 courses. **Credit** MC, V.
With the doors pushed back and the weather cooperating, this is a cool, breezy spot that makes The Cut look far more attractive than seems possible when you walk along it. Around half the room was devoted to tables laid for lunch on our weekday visit, and several were free even after 1pm; you're unlikely to be as lucky post-work. Also surprising was the number of pensioners enjoying this favourite destination for food and style mavens. But such folk know the pleasures of dishes like cold roast beef on dripping toast, and brawn: both of which featured on the appealing menu on our visit. British asparagus salad with soft-boiled quail's egg went down a treat, despite its curious garnish of almost-black breadcrumbs. Whole crab – a special – came with a big glass of delicious mayonnaise, but the kitchen seemed to flail when it came to more involved dishes, such as our horribly gluey pot of almond cream topped with preserved cherries. Own-made lemonade was a nice idea, but too sharp. For drinkers, this proper pub has a list of classic cocktails and aperitifs, and a good wine list; beers include Brains, Bombardier, Kirin Ichiban and Erdinger.
Babies and children admitted. Booking essential Sun lunch. Tables outdoors (4, pavement). **Map 11 N8**.

South East

Bermondsey

Garrison
99-101 Bermondsey Street, SE1 3XB (7089 9355/www.thegarrison.co.uk). London Bridge tube/rail. **Open** 8am-11pm Mon-Fri; 9am-11pm Sat; 9am-10.30pm Sun. **Breakfast served** 8-11.30am Mon-Fri; 9-11.30am Sat, Sun. **Lunch served** noon-3.30pm Mon-Fri; 12.30-4pm Sat, Sun. **Dinner served** 6.30-10pm Mon-Sat; 6-9.30pm Sun. **Main courses** £10.30-£15.50. **Credit** AmEx, MC, V.
The Garrison makes an attractive effort to strike out from gastropub clichés. The dominant colours are light greys and whites, and the style of the rickety furniture cramming the bar could be called 'distressed rustic rococo'. It doesn't feel at all precious, though: staff are attentive and friendly, and there's a lively buzz of chat from tablefuls of diners and drinkers. Menus have original touches too, with rather refined, large rye-bread versions of traditional sandwiches (bacon, steak) and some gutsy combinations like excellent Orkney calf's liver with smoked bacon, and some addictive corn dumplings. There's also an attractive range of snacks and starters, such as a warming blue cheese and pecorino risotto, and a refreshing goat's cheese salad with caramelised parsnip. The Garrison opens for hearty breakfasts every day of the week, and also offers its 'Cinema' room in the basement, available for private parties and

RESTAURANTS

If you're looking for a
cool place to party...
Come to Rumi and see what
all the fuss is about.

ALSO AVAILABLE FOR...
CORPORATE EVENTS • LAUNCH PARTIES
LEAVING PARTIES • BIRTHDAYS • REUNIONS
ANNIVERSARIES • CHRISTMAS PARTIES

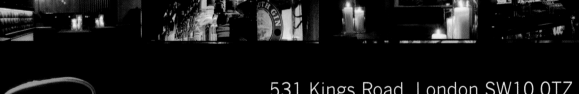

531 Kings Road, London SW10 0TZ
Tel: 020 7823 3362 E-mail: info@rumibar.com

RUMI

www.rumibar.com

(necessarily small-scale) film screenings. The beer range focuses on quality lagers, with only Adnams for ale-drinkers, but there's a competitively priced wine list, with a good choice available by the glass. *Babies and children admitted (lunch Sat, Sun). Booking advisable. Disabled: toilet. Separate room for parties, seats 25.* **Map 12 Q9.**

Catford

Perry Hill NEW

78-80 Perry Hill, SE6 4EY (8699 5076/ www.theperryhill.co.uk). Catford Bridge or Lower Sydenham rail. **Open** noon-3pm Mon-Sat; **dinner served** 6-10pm Mon-Sat. **Meals served** noon-10pm Sun. **Main courses** £8.50-£13.50. **Credit** AmEx, MC, V.

Seasoned restaurant/bar owners Robbie O'Neill and Shaun Wilson have taken the oak-panelled interior of this classic 1930s mock-Tudor pub and turned it into something just the right side of baronial. With freshly swagged curtains, flowery wallpaper and handsome contemporary 'classic' lighting, it embraces all social and demographic divides graciously. The food is generally very good. Chef Andrew Belew has assembled an appetising array of crowd pleasers with a twist, served by friendly and enthusiastic staff. Fish and shellfish are temptingly displayed on the counter of the open kitchen. On one of our recent visits, a scallop starter was tender perfection, accompanied by a fragrant pea and mint blini with a delicious lemon-butter dressing. 'Spring' risotto was creamy, herby and nicely al dente. Roasted aubergine ravioli was spot-on too; and roasted chicken Moroccan-style deliciously crisped and spicy. Presentation often shows aspirations: a vibrant Thai salad arrived on a wooden board lined with a sheet of nori seaweed that slowly absorbed the dressing, making it chewy. The waitress urged us to try the sticky toffee pudding, which turned out to be one of the best we've eaten: a dark, gingery sponge slice, rich with muscovado sugar and dates, drenched in burnt caramel sauce and crème fraîche – a very grown-up pudding. All this, plus very reasonable wines and good ales (London Pride, Bombardier) add up to a covetable package for any neighbourhood: but especially Catford. *Babies and children welcome: high chairs. Restaurant available for hire. Tables outdoors (24, garden).*

Crystal Palace

Dolphin NEW

121 Sydenham Road, SE26 5HB (8778 8101/ www.thedolphinsydenham.com). Sydenham rail. **Open** noon-midnight Mon-Sat; noon-11pm Sun. **Lunch served** noon-3.30pm, **dinner served** 6.30-10pm Mon-Fri. **Meals served** noon-10pm Sat; noon-4pm, 5-9pm Sun. **Main courses** £9-£14.95. **Credit** MC, V.

On a harsh winter night, with Arctic winds blasting Sydenham Road, the Dolphin is an especially welcoming venue: real fires and all. The refurbished 1930s pub interior evokes a classic European brasserie, with its long polished-wood bar, sage-green walls and jellyfish wall lamps. An atmosphere of effortless accommodation pervades the place, from the charming and competent service to the thoughtful menu, which mixes à la carte with dishes designed for sharing. The likes of braised oxtail with aubergine sauce and mash, lamb kofta, smoked salmon tagliatelle, or goat's cheese and pea risotto, may be ordered in small or large portions (the large easily feeding four people as a substantial snack). The kitchen carries off ambitious diversity (Turkish, Asian, Italian, English and Hungarian in one menu) with panache. We sampled exquisite crab cakes with chilli jam. Lamb kofte was spot on too, and the aforementioned oxtail dish was rich, gooey and deeply satisfying. For dessert, a superb rhubarb crumble with vanilla custard. A massive, sun-filled back garden, styled like a mini-Versailles in a pattern of walkways and clipped hedges, comes into its own in summer. *Babies and children welcome (until 8pm): high chairs. Tables outdoors (30, garden).*

Dulwich

Herne Tavern

2 Forest Hill Road, SE22 0RR (8299 9521/ www.theherne.net). East Dulwich or Peckham rail/12, 197 bus. **Open** noon-11pm Mon-Thur; noon-1am Fri, Sat; noon-10.30pm Sun. **Lunch served** noon-2.30pm Mon-Fri; noon-3pm Sat, Sun. **Dinner served** 6.30-9.45pm Mon-Sat; 6.30-9.30pm Sun. **Main courses** £8.50-£12. **Credit** MC, V.

Owned by the same people who run East Dulwich's popular Palmerston, the Herne Tavern is located just around the corner by Peckham Rye, housed in a grand old coaching inn. The boozy front bar is popular with locals – decorators discussing Millwall on the evening we visited – while the more discreet back bar is given over to dining. The big, child-friendly garden makes this a family hotspot at weekends, and there's an unambitious children's menu to entice kids away from the swings. Grown-up food is simple, strong and hearty. A goat's cheese, pear, walnut and endive salad made good use of disparate powerful flavours, while the equally potent marinated herring, potato and apple salad was a trifle salty but exquisitely fresh. Mains were satisfyingly filling. An excellent creamy fish pie was crammed with smoked haddock, prawns and pollock, while the Scottish ribeye steak was very large and very tasty. The understated but appreciated seasonal tone of the menu even extended to the desserts: chestnut parfait, roasted figs and chocolate sauce was just right for a winter's night, and although we didn't really need the hot chocolate fondant, we couldn't resist and didn't regret it. *Babies and children welcome: children's menu; high chairs; nappy-changing facilities. Separate room for parties, seats 60. Tables outdoors (25, garden).*

Palmerston

91 Lordship Lane, SE22 8EP (8693 1629/ www.thepalmerston.net). East Dulwich rail/185, 176, P13 bus. **Open** noon-11pm Mon-Thur; noon-midnight Fri, Sat; noon-10.30pm Sun. **Lunch served** noon-2.30pm Mon-Fri; noon-3pm Sat; noon-3.30pm Sun. **Dinner served** 7-10pm Mon-Sat; 7-9pm Sun. **Main courses** £11-£16. **Set lunch** (Mon-Fri) £11.50 2 courses, £14.50 3 courses. **Credit** MC, V.

The Palmerston attracts East Dulwich trendies and old-timers, treating both with warmth, though many visitors would argue this is largely a dining operation. Our lost booking was sorted out with good cheer and in the meantime there was ample room to stand at the bar admiring the hand-pumped ales – Harveys Best Bitter, Summer Lightning and Copper Ale. Wowser starters produced exclamations of delight: plump, tangy home-cured herring with crème fraîche, mustard and new potatoes; a pretty Thai-style salad of sea trout with fiery nam jim sauce, physalis and the aniseed kick of Thai basil, plus richness from the fried skin of the fish. Then it all went a bit patchy. A majestic plate of Gloucester Old Spot pork chop with creamy tarragon sauce, morels, peas and broad beans arrived at the same time as a smallish, chewy, fatty lamb fillet – though we liked the Middle Eastern accompaniments. Envious looks from fellow diners came with our Chocolate St Emilion and poached cherries, which was enough for two: just as well given the thin, bland custard tart smothered in cinnamon. Such varied standards were a bit of a surprise given that we've rated Jamie Younger's kitchen so highly in the past. The super wine list starts at £12.75 and there are some serious spirits behind the bar, including Janneau armagnac; perhaps the Palmerston is also a drinkers' pub after all. *Babies and children welcome: children's portions; high chairs; nappy-changing facilities. Booking advisable. Tables outdoors (6, pavement).* **Map 23 C4.**

Rosendale

65 Rosendale Road, SE21 8EZ (8670 0812/ www.therosendale.co.uk). East Dulwich or West Dulwich rail.

Interview
CAROLINE JONES & HUGH O'BOYLE

Who are you?
Directors of Jobo Developments, which has a collection of six gastropubs and bars in north London, including the **Clissold Arms** (see p127).
What's the best thing about running gastropubs in London?
The eclectic mix of clientele and the social aspect. Who wouldn't want to own a busy bar in London? It's also great to be part of a more relaxed dining experience. Now you can have everything – great food and wine, premium beers, classic cocktails and great music – all under one roof.
What's the worst thing?
Metering your alcohol intake while all around are having a great time.
Which are your favourite London restaurants, pubs and bars?
The **Commercial Tavern** (142 Commercial Street, 7247 1888) – go see, enough said... **The Wolseley** (see p49) for people-watching. **Galvin at Windows** (see p141) has fantastic views and fabulous food, and **Scott's** fish restaurant (see p82) is a wonderful revival with efficient, approachable service.
How green are you?
We do our best, but it can be a very expensive approach. Our carbon footprint is quite low as we source the majority of our products from the British Isles and as locally as possible.
What is missing from London's restaurant and bar scene?
Central London is missing a greater selection of independent pub/bar companies: chain sites dominate the West End. And for those of us who work late and therefore have to eat out, drink or party late – a better selection of good-quality, late-night eating and drinking establishments so that we can unwind after a hard day's graft.

RESTAURANTS

Princess Victoria. See p116.

Bar **Open** noon-11pm Mon-Thur, Sun; noon-midnight Fri, Sat. **Meals served** noon-10pm daily. **Main courses** £9.50-£16.
Restaurant **Lunch served** noon-3pm Fri, Sat; noon-4pm Sun. **Dinner served** 7-10pm Mon-Sat. **Main courses** £14.50-£29.50.
Both **Credit** MC, V.
When is a gastropub not a gastropub? When it churns its own butter, smokes its own fish and has a wine list of over a dozen closely typed pages, perhaps. The Rosendale, winner of the Best Gastropub gong at the 2007 *Time Out* Eating & Drinking Awards, has so much going for it in terms of inventiveness and ambition, its menu is a far cry from that of your typical gastropub. An ostrich fillet (with sweet-potato purée and beef bobotie) was an appealing, bloody treat: as rich as a good Christmas dinner. Veal shank pie had a perfect puffball of pastry, its rich oozing contents exquisitely flavoured. Yet inconsistency can make a meal here less than the sum of its parts. Cod fillet and asparagus came drowned in hollandaise; a rhubarb and strawberry crumble was tepid and only half cooked; service was distracted and indifferent. The decor is a weird mix of smart upholstery and bad art. Though the bar has its own striking ambience, the dining area's bright lights don't chime well with the high-concept restaurant food. The cavernous ceilings and hard floors make it a very noisy experience too.
Babies and children welcome: high chairs; nappy-changing facilities. Disabled: toilet. Separate rooms for parties, seating 20-100.

Herne Hill

Prince Regent
69 Dulwich Road, SE24 0NJ (7274 1567). Herne Hill rail/3, 196 bus. **Open** noon-11pm Mon-Wed; noon-midnight Thur-Sat; noon-10.30pm Sun. **Lunch served** noon-3pm Mon-Sat; noon-5pm Sun. **Dinner served** 7-10pm Mon-Sat; 6-9pm Sun. **Main courses** £7-£16. **Credit** MC, V.
A favourite with parents who can park their prams by the tables, this cheerful pub occupies an elegantly striped brick building with plenty of original Victorian features lending an atmosphere as warm as the welcome. In the dining room, furniture isn't so much rustic as decrepit – we worried that we'd leave wearing half the stuffing from our chairs. Staff are slightly too unhurried, so our two-course lunch took nearly two hours. At least that gave time to enjoy the excellent beers, including Black Sheep Bitter and, on our visit, guest ales Tinners and Quaff. There's a limited choice of desserts, but they come in generous portions, are wittily presented and incorporate quality ice-creams or custard. Starters tend to be stereotypical: salads, ham terrine and soup. The chips looked good, and the mash and green beans are nicely done. Bread, however, was substandard and main-course portion sizes were variable. Star of the short, hard-to-read blackboard menu was tender chargrilled calf's liver with bubble and squeak. Beef bourguignon was correctly imbued with the taste of red wine. There's an appealing brunch menu too, taking in all the popular ways with eggs, smoked salmon and bacon.
Babies and children welcome (until 7pm): high chairs. Disabled: toilet. Separate room for parties, seats 50. Tables outdoors (12, garden). **Map 22 E3**.

Peckham

Old Nun's Head
15 Nunhead Green, SE15 3QQ (7639 4007). Nunhead rail/78, P12 bus. **Open** noon-midnight Mon-Thur, Sun; noon-1am Fri, Sat. **Lunch served** 12.30-2.15pm, **dinner served** 6.30-10.15pm Mon-Fri. **Meals served** noon-10.15pm Sat; noon-9pm Sun. **Main courses** £6.95-£13. **Credit** AmEx, MC, V.
For years this hostelry was notable for its grisly history. It was built on the site of a convent, whose Mother Superior was beheaded. Since the pub went all gastro, a buzzy, sociable vibe has prevailed and any talk of ghostly nuns has subsided. A busy Friday night saw the friendly proprietors working flat-out serving fabulous bar snacks, cocktails and

RESTAURANTS

pints by Deuchars, Adnams, Brains and distinguished guest breweries. A wait for the table necessitated a sampling of Hector's House signature cocktail, a florid and zingy nectar incorporating tequila, triple sec and raspberries. The food menu is brief, unflashy and alluring. Care in presentation and ingredient sourcing was evident and prices are reasonable for the quality. A huge bowl of spicy vegetable soup would have been sufficient for a simple supper alongside our other starter of goat's cheese bruschetta, topped with caramelised onion slices and surrounded by bright mixed salad leaves. A main of plump cumberland sausage with buttery mash and gravy was textbook winter comfort, a large tuna steak seared with oriental spices was flashed just right to be red inside. Ordering a bowl of fat chips was a shaming display of greed, but a holy treat.
Babies and children welcome (until 9pm): high chairs; nappy-changing facilities. Disabled: toilet. Entertainment: open mic, music Wed 9pm. Separate room for parties, seats 30. Tables outdoors (4, garden).

East
Bow

Morgan Arms
43 Morgan Street, E3 5AA (8980 6389/ www.geronimo-inns.co.uk). Mile End tube. **Open** noon-11pm Mon-Thur, Sun; noon-midnight Fri, Sat. **Lunch served** noon-3pm Mon-Sat; noon-4pm Sun. **Dinner served** 7-10pm Mon-Sat; 6.30-9.30pm Sun. **Main courses** £9.50-£17. **Credit** AmEx, MC, V.
When much of the point of chains is to offer uniform standards, it's curious that this outlet of Geronimo Inns is our favourite by such a margin. It's popular with E3 residents too. The interior features pretty stained glass, a bizarre collection of restaurant chairs and a similarly ragtag library of books. Rolling up for a late Sunday lunch we were promptly and warmly greeted, seated and served. The choice of draught bitters isn't thrilling, but we found consolation in a cheerful bottle of cabernet sauvignon rosé from Chile. High-quality 28-day-hung roast beef came with super yorkshires, but the roast potatoes had been hanging around too long, and the melange of vegetables was overcooked. Still, we were impressed with the 'risotto' (really a pilaff) of quinoa and baby spinach, and the generous fillet of crispy sea bass that came on top of it. Chips were also in fine fettle. A healthier option would have been to start with, say, the carrot and cider soup. We finished with a respectable sticky toffee pudding and a gooseberry crumble that would have been superb save for the burnt flavour lent it by the last-minute use of a blowtorch.
Babies and children admitted (dining room). Disabled: toilet. Tables outdoors (4, pavement; 3, terrace).
For branches (Duchess of Kent, Lord Palmerston, Phoenix) see index.

Docklands

Gun (100)
27 Coldharbour, E14 9NS (7515 5222/ www.thegundocklands.com). Canary Wharf tube/DLR/South Quay DLR. **Open** 11am-midnight Mon-Fri; 11.30am-midnight Sat; 11.30am-11pm Sun. **Lunch served** noon-3pm Mon-Fri; 11.30am-4pm Sat, Sun. **Dinner served** 6-10.30pm Mon-Sat; 6-9.30pm Sun. **Main courses** £11.95-£18. **Credit** AmEx, MC, V.
The Gun takes its name from the cannon fired to celebrate the opening of West India Dock in 1802. The whole building is riddled with history, right down to the toilets, which are labelled Nelson and Emma in memory of Lady Hamilton and her lover, who it is claimed used to rendezvous here. A print by marine painter WL Wyllie towers over the small dining area, which is smartly furnished with dark wood furniture. In addition, there are two bars, two snugs, a private function room and a waterside terrace with a view of the O₂ dome. There are separate menus for the pub and dining room – both quintessentially British and steadfastly seasonal.

From the latter we had beef wellington and a chicken dish with black pudding and rösti. The pastry of the wellington was disappointingly soggy, lacking in crust, but the chicken was exceptional, a delicate cream sauce fusing together the spring-like flavours. We rounded off with a nicely balanced selection of French and English cheeses served with fruity quince jelly. Vigorous construction work around Docklands can make the Gun tricky to reach, but we reckon it's definitely worth the detour.
Babies and children welcome: high chairs. Disabled: toilet. Separate rooms for parties, seating 14 and 22. Tables outdoors (11, terrace). **Map 24 C2.**

Limehouse

★ Narrow
44 Narrow Street, E14 8DQ (7592 7950/ www.gordonramsay.com). Limehouse DLR. **Open** noon-11pm Mon-Sat; noon-10.30pm Sun. **Lunch served** noon-3pm, **dinner served** 6-10pm Mon-Fri. **Meals served** noon-10pm Sat, Sun. **Main courses** £8-£15.50. **Credit** AmEx, MC, V.
With its postcard position smack bang on the Thames, and staff of Gordon Ramsay Holdings at the helm, the Narrow raises diners' hopes understandably high for an unforgettable gastropub experience. It may come as a surprise, then, to find what is essentially an old-fashioned boozer serving the kind of traditional fare that's common throughout the land. The big difference is the quality. Originally a dockmaster's house, the building has retained many charming old features and been given a professional polish. Pleasingly, passers-by can still drop in for a casual pint and some potted shrimps at the bar, while those looking for more can get the Ramsay-brand take on the gastropub experience in the understated dining room. The menu is striking in its simplicity and has mixed results: a starter of scallops and black pudding was sensational, bangers and champ a little boring, and treacle tart with clotted cream warm, rich and gorgeously gooey. Reasonably priced and unpretentious, the Narrow is a great destination for groups of friends, especially if you can nab a prized outdoor table on a sunny afternoon.
Babies and children welcome: high chairs. Booking essential. Disabled: toilet. Separate room for parties, seats 16. Tables outdoors (36, riverside terrace).

Shoreditch

Fox
28 Paul Street, EC2A 4LB (7729 5708/ www.thefoxpublichouse.co.uk). Old Street tube/rail. **Open** noon-11pm Mon-Fri; 6pm-midnight Sat; noon-5pm Sun. **Lunch served** noon-3pm Mon-Fri; noon-4pm Sun. **Dinner served** 6-10pm Mon-Sat. **Main courses** £11.50-£15. **Credit** MC, V.
This pub of two halves sports a spruced-up boozer on the ground floor and a charming dining room above. Tapas-sized snacks and Sunday lunches are served downstairs, which can get boisterous with after-work drinkers. Upstairs feels like another world: calm, relaxing, with attentive service and old-fashioned decor and soft lighting. There's also a small terrace for summer dining – out here it's hard to remember you're in Shoreditch. The short, daily-changing menu makes tempting reading (as does the succinct wine list): grilled sardines on bruschetta with gremolata, or globe artichoke with shallot vinaigrette, say, followed by pan-fried sea bream with salsify, clams, and pea and broad bean broth, or poussin with asparagus and roast tomato. There's cheese from La Fromagerie too. The execution is less reliable, however. We've had some fine feeds here, yet our most recent meal was a letdown, especially a rump steak with chips and béarnaise that looked great but was chewy. On the plus side, pan-fried halibut with lentils and salsa verde was OK, and baked cheesecake with passion-fruit sauce made a good finish. We're hoping the steak was a blip, as we like the Fox's style.
Babies and children admitted. Disabled: toilet. Tables outdoors (5, terrace; 3 pavement). Separate room for parties, seats 12. **Map 6 Q4.**

Princess
76-78 Paul Street, EC2A 4NE (7729 9270). Old Street tube/rail. **Open** noon-11pm Mon-Fri; 6.30-11pm Sat; 12.30-5pm Sun. **Lunch served** 12.30-3pm Mon-Fri; 1-4pm Sun. **Dinner served** 6.30-10pm Mon-Sat. **Main courses** £7-£15.95. **Credit** AmEx, MC, V.
A lazy Sunday is at no risk of turning lively when you wander into the Princess. As though staff know that no one can be arsed climbing the wrought-iron spiral staircase, they don't bother opening the first-floor dining room, and the menu simply comprises Sunday roasts and one pudding. Our laid-back barman, looking as though he'd had a big night, was friendly but entirely unconcerned as he told us both bitters – London Pride and Timothy Taylor Landlord – were unavailable ('someone has to change the keg'). Draught lagers and Guinness are expensive at £3.40 a pint, and the large glasses of Lebanese rosé soon add up. But our food was good: mushroom pie for vegetarians, and a choice of roast rib of beef, leg of lamb, corn-fed chicken and slow-roast pork for omnivores. You're well on your way to five a day with the superb veg (roast squash and carrots, green beans and braised red cabbage), though we'd have liked more potatoes. Bar snacks (served Monday to Saturday) include the likes of grilled chorizo, gambas ajillo (garlic prawns) and plates of charcuterie, along with the usual nuts and olives. Enjoyably shambolic.
Babies and children admitted. Booking advisable. Restaurant available for hire. **Map 6 Q4.**

Royal Oak
73 Columbia Road, E2 7RG (7729 2220/ www.royaloaklondon.com). Bus 26, 48, 55. **Open** 6-11pm Mon; noon-11pm Tue-Sat; noon-10.30pm Sun. **Lunch served** noon-4pm Tue-Sun. **Dinner served** 6-10pm Mon-Sat; 6-9pm Sun. **Main courses** £9-£15. **Credit** AmEx, MC, V.
The upstairs dining room at the Royal Oak has come a long way from its days as a Mexican-themed bar. These days the airy space is all muted Farrow & Ball tones, and on our visit the last light of the evening was streaming through sparklingly clean windows on to mismatched wooden tables and chairs lit by big church candles. From a menu of simple Mediterranean dishes and solid English fare 'with a twist', we opted for cured Italian meats: a generous pile of capocolo toscano (made from the neck of the pig), salami piccante and pancetta coppata, served with melt-in-the-mouth mozzarella and delicious olives doused in marjoram. Roast tomato and garlic soup with basil was wonderfully rich and satisfying. Mains included tender grilled squid that married well with a salad of sweetcorn, roast peppers, chilli and coriander. The only false note was a beautifully presented globe artichoke heart with a softly poached egg nestling inside: the queen-sized bed of peas and broad beans in sage butter that came with it was not a terrific match – but that's to quibble. The food and service are very good indeed and prices incredibly fair – only an Aberdeen Angus ribeye hits £15.50. The broad-based wine list is well priced too, with a decent viognier for £14. Friendly, attentive yet relaxed service is another reason why, on a Thursday evening, the room is packed. A real treat.
Babies and children welcome: high chairs. Booking advisable (dining room). Tables outdoors (3, yard). **Map 6 S3.**

William IV
7 Shepherdess Walk, N1 7QE (3119 3012/ www.williamthefourth.com). Old Street tube/ rail/55 bus. **Open** noon-11pm Mon-Wed; noon-midnight Thur-Sat; noon-10.30pm Sun. **Lunch served** noon-3pm, **dinner served** 6-10pm Mon-Sat. **Meals served** 1-7pm Sun. **Main courses** £6.50-£18. **Credit** MC, V.
While nearby Old Street becomes an increasingly manic party district, this secluded civilised pub is a homely escape for enjoying laid-back drinks or a square meal. The decor is modestly trendy: walls and wooden furniture are painted white and embellished with an assortment of portraits, photographs and stuffed animals. The main bar is a small single room, but clever use of communal

Dolphin. See p121.

Camden Town & Chalk Farm

Engineer
65 Gloucester Avenue, NW1 8JH (7722 0950/ www.the-engineer.com). Chalk Farm tube/31, 168 bus. **Open** 9am-11pm Mon-Sat; 9am-10.30pm Sun. **Breakfast served** 9-11.30am Mon-Fri; 9am-noon Sat, Sun. **Lunch served** noon-3pm Mon-Fri; 12.30-4pm Sat, Sun. **Dinner served** 7-11pm Mon-Sat; 7-10.30pm Sun. **Main courses** £12.50-£17.25. **Credit** MC, V.
Mirrors and wrought-iron chandeliers give this popular Primrose Hill gastropub a cosy retro feel. St Peter's Organic is a highlight among the draught beers, with Bombardier also on tap. The food menu is small but enticing, with a mixture of influences from Asian to Mediterranean. We started with crisp devilled whitebait with a parsley salad that turned out to be predominantly fennel. The whitebait was under-seasoned and tasted of floury batter instead of fish. Another starter, roast mushroom and aubergine tart, also failed to inspire with its oily pastry base and bland chunky vegetable filling. Mains fared slightly better, with a perfectly cooked sea bream full of succulence and flavour. Baked chicken breast was very dry, but the dish was saved by a spicy concoction of chorizo, beans and harissa. Hoping for a big finale, we sampled the lemon posset with blueberries, and a pear and chocolate chimichanga. They were sweet and filling, but lacked that wow factor. Despite our mixed experience, the Engineer has a fine reputation and booking is a must at weekends.
Babies and children welcome: children's menu; high chairs. Disabled: toilet. Separate rooms for parties, seating 20-32. Tables outdoors (15, garden). **Map 27 B2**.

Lansdowne
90 Gloucester Avenue, NW1 8HX (7483 0409/ www.thelansdownepub.co.uk). Chalk Farm tube.
Bar **Open** noon-11pm Mon-Fri; 10am-11pm Sat; 10am-10.30pm Sun. **Brunch served** 10am-noon Sat, Sun. **Lunch served** noon-3pm Mon-Fri; 12.30-3.30pm Sat, Sun. **Dinner served** 6-10pm Mon-Sat; 6-9.30pm Sun.
Restaurant **Lunch served** 1-3pm Sat, Sun. **Dinner served** 7-10pm daily.
Both **Main courses** £10-£16.50. **Credit** MC, V.
Our recent visit to the Lansdowne brought to mind the expression 'jack of all trades, master of none'. It's an appealing venue. Downstairs is a spacious open-plan room with a high black-painted, stuccoed ceiling, wooden tables and big windows, while the first floor is a proper restaurant with neatly laid tables covered in white tablecloths. The same menu is available on both floors, though pizzas are also served downstairs. We ordered one topped with salami, chorizo and fennel and were pleased at its flavour and wafer-thinness, but the oils running from the meats made the crisp dough increasingly soggy. A bowl of squid, tomato and chorizo 'stew' was very tomatoey and quite moreish, but not particularly subtle in flavour. Pork belly with chicory was a solid seasonal offering, yet the meat was bland. We wished we'd ordered simpler fare; our neighbours were tucking into bowls of steaming linguine and clams with gusto. Drinks include a standard selection of pub lagers and a fairly economical list of wines, although the house red wasn't especially notable.
Babies and children admitted. Booking advisable. Disabled: toilet. Tables outdoors (5, pavement). **Map 27 B2**.

Prince Albert NEW
163 Royal College Street, NW1 0SG (7485 0270/ www.princealbertcamden.com). Camden Town tube/ Camden Road rail. **Open** noon-11pm Mon-Thur; noon-midnight Fri, Sat; noon-10.30pm Sun. **Lunch served** noon-3pm; **dinner served** 6-10pm Mon-Sat. **Meals served** 12.30-6pm Sun. **Main courses** £8.95-£15.95. **Credit** AmEx, MC, V.
Up a rather Dickensian wooden staircase, the dining room above this buzzing local features damson walls and swathes of quality fabric. Sterling attempts have been made to provide a leafy view too, but no amount of fairy lights can

---

tables maximises the available space. In good weather there's extra seating outside. Upstairs is a dedicated dining room, though the same menu is available throughout. Food is hearty and filling, but nothing special, and there were some disappointments on a recent visit. The plates were fridge-cold. A burger arrived filled with a big blob of overpowering cheddar, not fully melted, and yet the bun seemed unheated. A slab of pork belly was overdone: the flesh too dry, the skin so caramelised it was almost rock-solid. Less involved starters of mackerel pâté and wild mushrooms on brioche were better. Drinks include draught Black Sheep, London Pride, Hoegaarden, and Leffe, plus a fair selection of inexpensive wines. The cooking could use a boot up the backside, but the pub offers atmosphere in abundance.
Babies and children admitted. Booking advisable. Disabled: toilet. Separate rooms for parties, seating 12 and 40. Tables outdoors (4, yard). **Map 5 P3**.

North East

Hackney

Prince Arthur NEW
95 Forest Road, E8 3BH (7249 9996/ www.theprincearthurlondonfields.com). Hackney Central or London Fields rail. **Open** 4-11pm Mon-Thur; noon-11pm Fri; 10.30am-11pm Sat, Sun. **Lunch served** noon-4.30pm Fri; 10.30am-4.30pm Sat, Sun. **Dinner served** 6-10pm daily. **Main courses** £8-£16. **Credit** MC, V.
After much anticipation, the Prince Arthur – part of Tom and Ed Martin's local gastropub empire – opened in autumn 2007 to show off its bucolic decor. There's a stuffed pheasant in a glass box, fox heads, Anaglypta wall-coverings, dark-green leather seating and a beautiful, traditional and orderly bar topped with vases of fresh flowers. It's certainly aesthetically pleasing, but a true rural vibe is lacking from the rather contrived atmosphere. On our visit, staff weren't quite disarming enough to encourage a relaxed mood. The food is well-prepared from decent ingredients, but paradoxically, it is too focused on impressing to be truly memorable. Dishes are British with French and Mediterranean overtones, with mains featuring the likes of rabbit and hazelnut pasty

with pea and broad bean salad, and breadcrumbed aubergine and mozzarella with tomato chutney and battered courgette flowers. The area reserved for drinkers-only is a pleasant space in which to enjoy a quiet midweek pint of London Pride or Deuchars IPA, and the weekend brunch and lunch menus are admirable (with traditional favourites such as eggs benedict, as well as roast dinners). With less emphasis on trying to impress, this could be a lovely local.
Babies and children admitted. Disabled: toilet. Tables outdoors (4, pavement).

North

Archway

St John's
91 Junction Road, N19 5QU (7272 1587). Archway tube. **Open** 5-11pm Mon-Thur; noon-11pm Fri, Sat; noon-10.30pm Sun. **Lunch served** noon-3.30pm Fri; noon-4pm Sat, Sun. **Dinner served** 6.30-11pm Mon-Sat; 6.30-9.30pm Sun. **Main courses** £9.75-£18.50. **Credit** AmEx, MC, V.
An unpromising location on dreary Junction Road hasn't stopped St John's becoming a hit in the gastropub world. It has the right quirky-artsy look, with an airy stripped-down bar (serving Black Sheep, Timothy Taylor, modish lagers) and touches of grandeur in the cavernous main dining room at the back, lined with an unclassifiable collection of paintings. The chalked-up menu shows ambition and originality, and mostly delivers on its promises. A cheddar and spring onion croquette with squid and chorizo was unusual, the seafood nicely offsetting the cheese. The quality of fresh ingredients is impressive, bringing alive simple choices like an apple, fennel, green bean and manchego salad. Some of our party thought the fish at the centre of seared tuna with chips, rocket and very smooth aïoli could have been more exciting, but a ribeye steak with walnut jus hit all the right notes, and was cooked exactly as requested. In line with house style, the wine list is also above the norm, with carefully picked lesser-known labels at accessible prices. Service can be erratic, but on a good day it's friendly and efficient.
Babies and children welcome: high chairs. Booking essential weekend. Tables outdoors (6, patio). **Map 26 B1**.

detract from the impressive expanse of brickwork at Plumb Centre opposite. The menu aims higher than it should, with most dishes containing one or two ingredients too many. Brixham seafood cocktail contained guacamole as well as crab mayonnaise, caviar, marie rose sauce and saffron crostini. The rhubarb chutney accompanying (seriously overcooked) salmon fillet with foie gras, spicy lentils and crème fraîche was both unsuitable and superfluous. Such 'gourmet' restaurant pretensions extend even to the bread – one modest slice, cut in half, presented on a small square of black slate: gee, thanks. Simpler dishes were the kitchen's best, as shown in guinea fowl with saffron-flavoured crushed potatoes, asparagus and morels, and decent sticky toffee pudding with Baileys ice-cream. Top marks for the welcoming, intelligent staff, in both restaurant and bar, where there's a tempting list of bar snacks (cashews with black pepper and cinnamon, marinated anchovies with gremolata) and a sizeable choice of bottled ciders. *Babies and children welcome: children's menu; high chairs; toys. Disabled: toilet. Separate room for parties, seats 20. Tables outdoors (12, garden). Map 27 D2.*

Crouch End

Queens Pub & Dining Room

26 Broadway Parade, N8 9DE (8340 2031/ www.thequeenscrouchend.co.uk). Finsbury Park tube/rail then W3, W7 bus. **Open** noon-11.30pm Mon-Wed, Sun; noon-midnight Thur-Sat. **Meals served** noon-10pm Mon-Sat; noon-9pm Sun. **Main courses** £5-£16.50. **Credit** MC, V.
Local campaigners helped save this Victorian palace from neglect, and from proposals to knock it about. It reopened with nods to gastropub style (bare wooden tables, no flock wallpaper), but otherwise all its stained glass, wrought iron, elaborate plasterwork and panelling magnificently intact. The Queens is big enough to contain a large pub bar (with imposing wooden island and plenty of comfortable corners) and a spacious dining room beneath an arching ceiling. The menu is an enjoyable mix of gastropub faves and more individual adventures. Satisfying starters on a busy Sunday lunchtime included goat's cheese and grape chutney, deep-fried in hefty batter, and a great bowl of mussels with white wine, garlic and chorizo. To follow, the roast beef was a mixed bag: the meat nicely rare (and the fresh horseradish delicious), but the roast spuds and yorkshire dry. Baked sole with new potatoes and savoy cabbage, on the other hand, was exceptional. The wine list is interesting and well-priced, and friendly staff work hard to keep the customers returning. *Babies and children welcome (until 6pm): children's menu; high chairs. Booking advisable. Disabled: toilet. Tables outdoors (10, garden).*

Finchley

Bald-Faced Stag NEW

69 High Road, N2 8AB (8442 1201/ www.realpubs.co.uk). East Finchley tube. **Open** noon-11.30pm Mon-Wed; noon-midnight Thur; noon-12.30am Fri; 11am-12.30am Sat; noon-10.30pm Sun. **Lunch served** noon-3.30pm Mon-Fri; 11am-4.30pm Sat. **Dinner served** 6-10.30pm Mon-Sat. **Meals served** noon-9.30pm Sun. **Main courses** £7.50-£13.50. **Credit** MC, V.
After watching a film at the lovely old Phoenix, it's just the ticket to slip over the road to the Bald-Faced Stag, reinvented by the Realpubs chain as a smart gastropub. The large dining room is all dark wood, with flower arrangements, an open kitchen and subtle lighting. It buzzes loudly with locals when busy, but friendly staff are on-the-ball, happy to advise and pass on customers' foibles to an adaptable kitchen. There's a laudable range of beers (including three real ales) and eclectic wine choices. All this, plus a modish menu, raises expectations, which, sadly, weren't quite met on our visit. A warm pastry tartlet with chorizo and poached egg was sublime, but deep-fried tuna spring rolls were leaden, saved only by a carrot and celeriac salad with punchy wasabi dressing. Sea bass in tarragon velouté with spinach and saffron

Clissold Arms. See p127.

mash was enormous, yet overcooked and bland. Plain chargrilled seafood (tender squid, juicy scallops, meaty prawns and mussels) tasted fresher and brighter, but didn't make the earth move. Tempting afters included lemon curd and blueberry mess, and English cheeses.
Babies and children welcome: high chairs. Disabled: toilet. Entertainment: jazz 7.30pm last Tue of mth. Tables outdoors (18, garden).
For branch (Oxford Tavern) see index.

Highgate

Bull

13 North Hill, N6 4AB (0845 456 5033/ www.inthebull.biz). Highgate tube. **Open** 5-11pm Mon; noon-11pm Tue-Sat; noon-10.30pm Sun. **Lunch served** noon-2.30pm Tue-Fri; noon-3.30pm Sat; noon-4pm Sun. **Dinner served** 5-9.30pm Mon, Sun; 6-10.30pm Tue-Sat. **Main courses** £12-£20. **Credit** AmEx, MC, V.
In well-heeled Highgate, nobody's expecting a basic boozer with bargain bar food, but the Bull's inflated prices and pretentious take on traditional pub fare can feel annoying. It's a relaxing spot, with creamy walls, artful lighting, a dark wood bar and subtle jazzy music, but service on our visit veered from intrusive to careless. A shepherd's pie summed it all up: served in a dish that made it look like a ready-meal (which of course it wasn't); under the piped mash lurked robustly flavoured, shredded lamb-shank. The pie was rich and satisfying, but rather too uniform without the addition of an expensive side dish of sprouting broccoli. A so-called large caesar salad with (only three) tempura prawns weighed in at a hefty £13.50. Vibrant confit of salmon with beetroot got things off to a better start than heavy butter bean fricassee. Puddings saved the day: a dense and treacly sticky toffee pudding, swimming in rich caramel sauce, and an intense Valrhona fondant pudding. Try one of the guest ales if the wine list seems too pricey.
Babies and children welcome: high chairs. Disabled: toilet. Separate room for parties, seats 70. Tables outdoors (16, terrace).

Islington

Charles Lamb

16 Elia Street, N1 8DE (7837 5040/ www.thecharleslambpub.com). Angel tube. **Open** 4-11pm Mon, Tue; noon-11pm Wed-Sat; noon-10.30pm Sun. **Lunch served** noon-3pm Wed-Sat; noon-6pm Sun. **Dinner served** 6-9.30pm Mon-Sat. **Main courses** £8-£12. **Credit** MC, V.
There's a no-booking policy and few tables at this thriving local, so if you're not ensconced by 7pm forget about ordering anything but a drink. The good news is you'll have plenty of tipples to choose from: frequently-changing ales, bottled beers and a Euro wine list featuring around 12 by the carafe or glass. Swish bar snacks might include goose rillettes, bacon fries and cornish pasties. In the adjacent dining room (order your meal at the bar), a blackboard menu mostly trolls around France, making occasional forays to other parts of Europe and the Med. Vegetarians are welcome, and could be offered red pepper and flageolet casserole with fried polenta, a quail egg and caper salad, or tart of rocamadour cheese with onion and olives. We relished an unusual soup of spinach and preserved lemon with feta before launching into hearty stew-like mains of poulet estragon and provençal daube of beef. Apart from the Portuguese custard tarts, the dessert list brought things back to Blighty.
Babies and children admitted. Bookings not accepted. Tables outdoors (4, pavement).
Map 5 O2.

Duke of Cambridge

2008 RUNNER-UP BEST SUSTAINABLE RESTAURANT
30 St Peter's Street, N1 8JT (7359 3066/ www.dukeorganic.co.uk). Angel tube. **Open** noon-11pm Mon-Sat; noon-10.30pm Sun. **Lunch served** 12.30-3pm Mon-Fri; 12.30-3.30pm Sat, Sun. **Dinner served** 6.30-10.30pm Mon-Sat; 6.30-10pm Sun. **Main courses** £10-£18. **Credit** MC, V.
The UK's first certified organic gastropub chalks up the long list of worthy goals it has achieved on a blackboard, including the buying of phones from a cooperative (go figure). The Duke is also a very

appealing pub, with great beers from Pitfield Brewery, an attractive open room and a friendly mix of green-thinking folk (from dreadlocked cyclists to City suits). As a culinary destination, though, it has some way to go. First: the pricing. When food is this local and seasonal, why so expensive? Mackerel with a stew of black bean, chorizo and tapenade cost a hefty £14.50. Second: too many ingredients recur from dish to dish; on our visit, rocket and beetroot appeared regularly. Most disappointingly: the cooking is amateurish. It is easy to make a decent dhal, but this version contained chunks of carrot and crude spicing; served with brown basmati rice, it was the sort of ballast students might cook at home, not what you'd pay £11 for in a pub. A great place for a beer, but you need more than ethics to run a good kitchen.
Babies and children welcome: children's portions; high chairs. Tables outdoors (4, pavement).
Map 5 O2.

House

63-69 Canonbury Road, N1 2DG (7704 7410/ www.inthehouse.biz). Highbury & Islington tube/rail. **Open** 5-11pm Mon; noon-11pm Tue-Thur; 5pm-1.30am Fri, Sat; noon-10.30pm Sun. **Lunch served** noon-2.30pm Tue-Fri; noon-3.30pm Sat; noon-4pm Sun. **Dinner served** 6-10.30pm Mon-Sat; 6.30-9.30pm Sun. **Main courses** £13.95-£23. **Credit** AmEx, MC, V.
A spacious street-corner terrace is one of the House's prime assets, bringing a touch of café society to Canonbury summers. Inside, the decor is mellow chic: far more restaurant than pub, but with a dining area that can feel distinctly cramped when busy (which seems to be often). Dorset crab spring rolls with ginger and a ketchup dressing were delicate and interesting, if a bit oversweet. We were more impressed by our mains: pan-fried sea bass with ginger and lime dressing; and a perfectly grilled pork chop with spinach, mustard mash and a wonderfully smooth shallot jus. The kitchen seems to have a special way with spuds, making lightly sautéed new potatoes with the fish, for example, a highlight rather than just another pile on the side. Wines are suitably refined but

Prince Arthur. See p124.

RESTAURANTS

pricey, with not much under £20. Adnams is the sole draught ale. The House also opens for breakfast at weekends, so you can sit outside to sample own-baked pastries or a hearty full english. *Babies and children welcome: children's portions; high chairs; nappy-changing facilities. Bar available for hire. Disabled: toilet. Tables outdoors (24, terrace).*

★ Marquess Tavern (100)
32 Canonbury Street, N1 2TB (7354 2975/ www.themarquesstavern.co.uk). Angel tube/ Highbury & Islington tube/rail. **Open** 5-11pm Mon-Thur; 5pm-midnight Fri; noon-midnight Sat; noon-11pm Sun. **Lunch served** noon-4pm Sat; 12.30-5pm Sun. **Dinner served** 6.30-10pm Mon-Sat; 6.30-9pm Sun. **Main courses** £12-£17. **Credit** AmEx, MC, V.

The Marquess is a dining destination, certainly, but unlike so many gastropubs has retained a relaxing, local-pub character. Even if you're planning to feast on the signature joints of 28-day-hung Angus fore-rib chalked up by weight and price on the blackboard (and crossed off as each is nabbed), starters may be necessary as it'll take at least 45 minutes for the beef, yorkshires, greens and roasties to appear. Pan-fried scallops with samphire (£3 each) was the star of our selection: prettily served on the shell and wallowing in garlicky butter sauce; their corals as sweet as the muscle meat. Puds are classic English comforts. All dishes are listed with beer and wine recommendations. In keeping with the policy of sourcing as close to home as possible, the wine list is European, but with a super cab sauv from central Spain at just £14.50 you needn't fear the lack of New World bargains. Froach heather ale and Grozet, both from Scotland, are great accompaniments to food too. The Young's range is on tap, plus the likes of Deuchars IPA. Although we were peeved at having to book via a website, in person the staff are amiable and intelligent. In July 2008, the pub was sold to an independent operator. *Babies and children admitted (until 6pm). Tables outdoors (6, patio). Separate room for parties, seats 14.*

Northgate
113 Southgate Road, N1 3JS (7359 7392). Essex Road rail/38, 73 bus. **Open** 5-11pm Mon; noon-11pm Tue-Thur; noon-midnight Fri, Sat; noon-10.30pm Sun. **Lunch served** noon-3pm Tue-Fri; noon-4pm Sat, Sun. **Dinner served** 6.30-10.30pm Mon-Sat; 6.30-9.30pm Sun. **Main courses** £9.50-£15. **Credit** MC, V.

The favourite local for culture-conscious residents in Islington's eastern fringes, the Northgate still has a comfy real-pub feel in its big bar and front terrace, blended with all the standard gastro features: plain floors and tables, bright lighting, sofas, pale colours. Beers follow a gastropub pattern too: ales like London Pride and Bombardier, Leffe and Czech lagers. Food is served in the bar, but the best place to eat is the more impressive, wood-lined dining room further back, beside the open-range kitchen. Blackboard menus offer a Mediterranean-leaning mix. Lamb kofte with mint yoghurt and pitta was excellent, with first-rate, flavour-rich meat; roast hake was nicely offset by chickpeas and unusually sweet chorizo. Some wrinkles could be ironed out – plump scallops wrapped in pancetta would have been better if the last bits of sand had been properly rinsed out of them; a steak, grilled beautifully red-rare as requested, sat on the range for a while before reaching our table – but they weren't enough to sabotage a relaxing, enjoyable meal, helped along by a user-friendly wine list. *Babies and children admitted (patio, restaurant). Booking advisable weekends. Tables outdoors (15, patio).* **Map 6 Q1.**

Kentish Town

Junction Tavern
101 Fortress Road, NW5 1AG (7485 9400/ www.junctiontavern.co.uk). Kentish Town tube/rail/Tufnell Park tube. **Open** noon-11pm Mon-Sat; noon-10.30pm Sun. **Lunch served** noon-3pm Mon-Fri; noon-4pm Sat, Sun. **Dinner served** 6.30-10.30pm Mon-Sat; 6.30-9.30pm Sun. **Main courses** £10.50-£15. **Set lunch** (Sun) £15 2 courses. **Credit** MC, V.

Chefs have come and gone at this old-timer, but the Junction remains a solid favourite. It's clad in wood panels and deep maroon paint, with big windows overlooking Fortess Road. We prefer the front section, surrounding the open kitchen, to the less atmospheric conservatory at the rear. The menu is seasonal, original and concise, with generally no more than six starters and six mains – never a bad thing. Dishes we've enjoyed recently include a sublime mélange of chicken livers, black pudding, salsify, baby onions and parsley, all swimming in a deliciously rich and meaty jus. Whole roasted sea bass was expertly cooked and served with potatoes, peperonata and sugar-snap peas; a fat dressed Dorset crab was delicious with its robust aïoli. Halloumi with green beans, pomegranate seeds, dukkha (a nutty, spicy Egyptian dip), coriander and hazelnuts was more exciting on paper than on the plate, yet was very fresh. There are decent wines, but the Junction prides itself on its weekly-changing range of real ales from across Britain. *Babies and children admitted (if dining). Booking advisable. Tables outdoors (20, garden).* **Map 26 B4.**

Muswell Hill

★ Clissold Arms `NEW`
2008 RUNNER-UP BEST GASTROPUB
105 Fortis Green, N2 9HR (8444 4224). East Finchley tube. **Open** noon-11pm Mon-Thur; noon-midnight Fri, Sat; noon-10.30pm Sun. **Lunch served** noon-4.30pm, **dinner served** 6-10pm Mon-Sat. **Meals served** noon-9pm Sun. **Main courses** £11-£18.50. **Credit** MC, V.

The scanty Kinks memorabilia (this was the scene of the band's first concert) might be an affront to fans, but while a more characterful decor would be welcome, there's no denying that Muswell Hill needed a great gastropub like this. The Clissold has proved an instant hit with sophisticated local families. Its friendly, enthusiastic staff are keen to promote the wide-ranging wine list, but haven't forgotten their pub status. Timothy Taylor Landlord was poured properly, left to settle then topped up without us having to ask. Chicken and mushroom

pie had a lovely thick, sticky filling and a buttery, tissue-like pastry that should have been a tad thicker. A wide balti-style pan was the unusual receptacle for an accomplished fusion combo of monkfish with chorizo, preserved lemon, new potatoes and spicy sauce. We love the yorkshires-for-all Sunday roasts too. Desserts (a sickly-sweet rhubarb eton mess, maybe) are generally less accomplished, but decent grub nonetheless.
Babies and children welcome: children's menu; high chairs; nappy-changing facilities. Booking essential Thur-Sat dinner, Sun lunch. Disabled: toilet. Tables outdoors (12, terrace).

North West

Hampstead

Horseshoe
28 Heath Street, NW3 6TE (7431 7206). Hampstead tube. **Open** 10am-11pm Mon-Thur; 10-1am Fri, Sat; 10am-10.30pm Sun. **Lunch served** noon-3.30pm Mon-Sat; noon-4.30pm Sun. **Dinner served** 6.30-10pm Mon-Thur; 6.30-

---

THE DISH

Chocolate fondant

Once a posh restaurant special, chocolate fondant (like crème brûlée) has become an all-purpose staple, sold everywhere from gastropubs to Japanese restaurants. Chocolate puds are notoriously difficult to resist, and with theatricality provided by the fondant's hidden sauce centre (revealed when your spoon cuts into the cake), these businesses know that dessert sale is pretty much a done deal.

French chef Michel Bras claims to have invented chocolate fondant in 1981, but his 'chocolate biscuit coulant' recipe relies on a frozen chocolate mixture inserted in the batter. Some restaurants use this technique, but it is rather easy to achieve a hot molten centre and firm exterior with a single cake mix. You are right to be disappointed by any chocolate fondant that arrives at the table still in its baking dish. Not only do you miss the special thrill of watching the hot dark filling ooze out on to the plate, but the residual heat of the vessel will continue cooking the filling, so that by halfway through your pudding it has turned into a rather dry little cake – like the one we've eaten at the **Warrington**.

For a superior take on the can't-refuse pub pud, head to the **Princess**, where the fabulous mixture secretes whole hazelnuts. At former pub **Rosemary Lane** (*see p99*), now a reliable Franco-Californian restaurant, the Venezuelan chocolate fondant has a caramel core. Served with a scoop of Valencia orange ice-cream, it's choc-caramel-citrus heaven. For an oriental twist on the theme, try **Sushi 101** (*see p207*), where the classic dark fondant is partnered by green tea ice-cream. Fancy a night in? There are wonderful physalis-topped chocolate fondants to take away at **Baker & Spice** (*see p310*).

10.30pm Fri, Sat; 6.30-9.30pm Sun. **Main courses** £8-£15. **Set lunch** £7 1 course incl glass of wine. **Credit** MC, V.
A carefully crafted look is the first thing you notice at this elegant gastropub: gleaming woodwork, a bit of bare brick, lofty windows letting in floods of light on to tastefully muted colours. Australian owner Jasper Cuppaidge has given plenty of attention to other details too. A microbrewery in the basement produces distinctive ales. Staff are among the best we've found in any gastropub – quick, aware and attentive, as well as brightly friendly. The refined (but decently priced) wine list is put together with the same care, and ingredients are diligently sourced from farm producers. So it's a pity the cooking doesn't have more flair. A salad of pumpkin, chicory, stilton and spiced walnuts was lovely, but in goat's cheese with Blythburgh ham, beetroot and french beans, the vegetables all lacked flavour. Sunday roast beef (with fabulous yorkshires and horseradish) was fine, but the roast spuds and other veg were lacklustre, while a venison and red wine pie was ordinary. After all the build-up, we expected something more exciting.
Babies and children welcome: high chairs. Booking advisable. **Map 28 B2**.

Wells
30 Well Walk, NW3 1BX (7794 3785/www.the wellshampstead.co.uk). Hampstead tube. **Open** noon-11pm Mon-Sat; noon-10.30pm Sun. **Lunch served** noon-3pm Mon-Fri; noon-4pm Sat, Sun. **Dinner served** 6-10pm Mon-Fri; 7-10pm Sat, Sun. **Main courses** £9.95-£16. **Credit** MC, V.
The interior of this Georgian tavern could feature in *Homes & Gardens*, with a tasteful modern take on old-pub style in chocolate brown in the bar, and elegant, delicately themed dining rooms above: one vaguely Indian in deep terracotta and cerise, another looking further east with pale shades and Chinese vases. With such attention to presentation, we were anxious the food had got left behind, but needn't have worried. The menu mixes gastro-classics and global influences with panache, and the kitchen knows how to handle subtle flavourings. Excellent scallops came with a delicious, original parsley-root purée, and chilli and coriander vinaigrette. Salt-marsh lamb with minted new potatoes and red wine jus was beautifully cooked, the balance of every element hugely impressive. Salmon supreme was just as good, with an irresistible béchamel-like wild garlic sauce. Compared to such pleasures, the dessert menu is ordinary. The wine list contains both grand labels and quality wines at less frightening prices, while there's Addlestones cider, Adnams Broadside, Black Sheep and Leffe on draught. A very comfortable, very Hampstead spot to spend an afternoon: service is charming, and the bar and terrace offer many options for smaller-scale eating.
Babies and children welcome: children's menu; colouring books; high chairs. Disabled: toilet. Entertainment: jazz/acoustic music 8.30pm Mon. Separate room for parties, seats 12. Tables outdoors (8, patio). **Map 28 C2**.

Kilburn

Salusbury
50-52 Salusbury Road, NW6 6NN (7328 3286). Queens Park tube/rail. **Open** 5-11pm Mon; noon-11pm Tue-Thur, Sun; noon-midnight Fri, Sat. **Lunch served** 12.30-3.30pm Tue-Sun. **Dinner served** 7-10.15pm Mon-Sat; 7-10pm Sun. **Main courses** £11.50-£16. **Credit** MC, V.
The Salusbury's trendy drinking area, frequented by smartly dressed regulars, is complemented by a dining room furnished with stripped wood flooring, rustic chairs and a plethora of framed mirrors. Buoyed by genial service, the informal atmosphere is favoured by families during the day and young professionals at suppertime. The kitchen champions seasonal ingredients and hearty flavours – expect plenty of big, bold stews, saucy Mediterranean pastas, and substantial salads. A starter of king prawns fried in garlicky olive oil had a tasty chilli tickle: marvellous for mopping up with the excellent bread. Glistening roast guinea fowl, tender and gamey, made a good

---

match with buttery mash and caramelised fennel, but was marred by splinters of bone. Portions are robust. Our meaty lamb shank, simmered in full-flavoured stock with shallots and carrots, was cooked to succulent perfection, but a juicy ribeye was let down by bitter-tasting béarnaise infused with too much tarragon. Still, the Salusbury offers bonhomie and homely grub, plus a fairly priced wine list, a wide choice of draught lagers (including Eiken), draught Adnams and Aspall cider.
Babies and children welcome (until 7pm): high chairs. Tables outdoors (4, pavement).

Maida Vale

Warrington NEW
2008 RUNNER-UP BEST GASTROPUB
93 Warrington Crescent, W9 1EH (7592 7960/ www.gordonramsay.com). Maida Vale tube. **Open** 11am-11pm Mon-Thur; 11am-midnight Fri, Sat; noon-10.30pm Sun. **Lunch served** noon-2.30pm Mon-Fri; noon-3.30pm Sat, Sun. **Dinner served** 6-10.30pm Mon-Sat; 6-10pm Sun. **Main courses** £12.50-£18.50. **Credit** AmEx, MC, V.
As a pub, we can't fault the beautifully refurbished Warrington since Gordon Ramsay Holdings took over. Staff are plentiful and as convivial as the historic setting, with its marble pillars, art deco lamps, art nouveau stained glass and dark wood. The well-run bar offers four real ales and many intriguing bottled beers, including Wells & Young Banana Bread. But as a gastropub? Well, no one likes being given an inconveniently early (or late) and limited time-slot on booking. The first-floor dining room is disappointing too, after the exquisite bar below. It's decked in restful cream tones, but half is crammed with tiny tables. The menu is surprisingly long, including soups and salads in addition to starters. Portions are modest, so you may need sides, making prices less appealing than they appear. Spelt and pea risotto with devonshire blue cheese was the pick of the enticingly British starters. Roast chicken came with morels and caramelised little gem. Desserts (including an underdone sticky toffee pudding) weren't cooked with the accuracy expected of a Ramsay outfit. We've no complaints about the brief wine list; it starts at £13.50 for a cherry-scented Chilean rosé and contains similarly inexpensive whites.
Babies and children welcome (dining room): high chairs. Booking advisable. Tables outdoors (6, pavement). **Map 1 C3**.

Totteridge

Orange Tree NEW
7 Totteridge Village, N20 8NX (8343 7031/ www.theorangetreetotteridge.co.uk). Totteridge \& Whetstone tube then 251 bus. **Open** noon-11pm daily. **Lunch served** noon-3pm, **dinner served** 6-10pm Mon-Sat. **Meals served** noon-10pm Sun. **Main courses** £10.50-£19. **Credit** AmEx, MC, V.
A favourite of Duncan James and that other guy from Blue – you know, the short one – the Orange Tree by Totteridge village green has been a pub since 1755, but don't come expecting a rustic olde worlde interior. Much of the property functions as a smart-casual restaurant with Asian decorations, including a Buddha's head and feature fireplace. The same menu is served in the bar too. In addition to a nicely written wine list (starting at £13 for South African chenin blanc) there's a sizeable leaflet of soft drinks and tipples, from mulled cider and Ketel One bloody mary to Innis & Gunn oak-aged beers. Food is divided into pastas, grills, pizzas and salads, supplemented by a sheet of specials typically highlighting seafood. Portions are generous, as in a plate of two large sea bass fillets atop a salad of firm new potatoes and fennel. Staff are keen to please; our minor complaint about a plate of pasta saw its cost removed from the bill. Save room for the bodacious desserts. We had no regrets blowing the calorie budget on huge slabs of ginger and toffee pudding, pear and frangipane tart, and rice pud with pineapple and coconut.
Babies and children welcome: high chairs; nappy-changing facilities. Disabled: toilet. Tables outdoors (12, garden).

Global

This small collection of restaurants might seem like the stuff that didn't slot into any other chapter, but it's also one of our favourite sections: a veritable celebration of London's multiculturalism featuring several of our Hot 100 entries. Where else in the world can you visit a German pub one night, enjoy Afghani kebabs or South African kudu steak the next, and still have the home-style cooking of Burma and a sophisticated Iberian-Mozambique restaurant to experience some other time? London's Scandinavian scene has received something of a knock this year with the closure of both Lundum's and Upper Glas, but this is partially compensated by the opening of fun café **Scandinavian Kitchen** (reviewed in the Cafés chapter). **Zeitgeist** and **Café Strudel**, meanwhile, continue the good work of the **Wolseley** (Modern European) in reintroducing Londoners to the joys of central European cooking.

Afghan

North

Islington

★ Afghan Kitchen
35 Islington Green, N1 8DU (7359 8019). Angel tube. **Lunch served** noon-3.30pm, **dinner served** 5.30-11pm Tue-Sat. **Main courses** £5-£6.50. **No credit cards**.
The doorway to Islington's Afghan Kitchen is still occasionally blocked by a baffled gaggle of first-timer visitors struggling to take stock of their surroundings. Initial reactions to the skeletal decor range from bemused horror to full-blown ecstasy. 'Kitchen' is a far more accurate description than 'dining room', both tiny floors embellished with little more than communal wooden tables, and pot plants so gregarious that fronds might need picking from face and food. Make the most of the social benefits of dining elbow-to-elbow with complete strangers, as you're unlikely to get more than a tired smile from staff on busy weekend evenings. The unchanging menu offers a short selection: four meat and four vegetarian dishes. Ghorm-e sabzi (lamb and spinach stew) is as rich and flavoursome as its Iranian equivalent, despite an absence of dried limes. Lavand-e murgh (chicken in yoghurt) subtly combines creamy coolness with a mild chilli kick. Prices are ridiculously low (the most expensive main is less than twice the price of a thick slab of seeded Afghani bread), and the whole operation is so original and invigorating that it's hard not to leave feeling satisfied as well as stuffed.
Babies and children admitted: high chairs. Booking advisable. Takeaway service. **Map 5 O2**.

Outer London

Harrow, Middlesex

★ ★ Masa (100)
24-26 Headstone Drive, Harrow, Middx HA3 5QH (8861 6213). Harrow & Wealdstone tube/rail. **Meals served** 12.30-11pm daily. **Main courses** £4.50-£12. **Set meal** £19.95 (2 people); £30 (2-3 people); £49.95 (4-5 people). **Unlicensed**. **Corkage** no charge. **Credit** AmEx, MC, V.
It may be the commuting equivalent of a long-haul flight for central Londoners, but if you're seeking the capital's most authentic Afghan eating experience, don't think twice about hopping on the overland to Harrow. Masa defies its drab high-street surroundings with an exotic interior blending burgundy walls, engraved wooden furniture and a neon-backlit ceiling dominated by a central chandelier. Not that there's anything formal about a meal here – many local Afghan families eat with one eye on the big screen (tuned to Bollywood station B4U on our last visit). Nor does the food stand on ceremony, with starters like smoky mirza ghasemi (grilled aubergine with garlic, yoghurt and walnuts) and sabzi bourani (steamed spinach, yoghurt and herbs) best tucked into with handfuls of flaky nan fresh from the oven. Ditto the mains, which include various tender lamb and chicken kebabs chargrilled in the open kitchen, and a good range of curries. We plumped for a chicken karahi that was richly flavoursome with just the right level of chilli kick, and a slightly oversalted lamb sabzi that was thick with spinach: both accompanied by glasses of yoghurty dogh flavoured with fresh mint and chunks of cucumber.
Babies and children welcome: high chairs. Disabled: toilet. Takeaway service; delivery service (over £12 within 3-mile radius).

Café Strudel. See p130.

Belgo Noord

RESTAURANTS

Austrian/German

South West

Barnes

Café Strudel NEW

*429 Upper Richmond Road West, SW14 7PJ
(8487 9800/www.cafestrudel.co.uk). Mortlake
rail/33, 337, 493 bus.* **Open** 10am-10.30pm
Tue-Sat; 10am-4pm Sun. **Lunch served** noon-
3pm Tue-Sat; noon-4pm Sun. **Dinner served**
6-10.30pm Tue-Sat. **Main courses** £6-£17.
Credit MC, V.
Orly Kritzman's Austrian brasserie certainly looks
the part with its globe lights, white tablecloths and
tiers of cakes in the window. The kitchen produces

iconic specialities of the Wiener Küche such as
veal schnitzel, rostbraten (steak, served with chips
and paprika-fried onions) and spätzle (gnocchi-like
pasta) using well-sourced British ingredients.
Tasty pork chop from Denham Estate came with
black pudding, roast apple, red cabbage and the
so-called 'napkin dumpling' (a dumpling of
steamed semolina). You could start with a platter
of smoked and cured salmon (from Forman's in
Hackney Wick) or baby beetroots dipped in Stiegel
beer batter and served with horseradish cream.
Come earlier in the day for cheesecake, poppy-seed
cake, sachertorte and, of course, apple strudel –
all made in-house. The range of rich hot chocolates
and flavoured coffees does the Viennese tradition
justice. There's also a varied selection of well-made
Austrian wines and schnapps, and Austrian beers.
A charming place to meet.

*Babies and children welcome: children's portions;
crayons; high chairs; nappy-changing facilities.
Tables outdoors (4, pavement). Takeaway service.
Vegan dishes (on request). Wireless internet (free).*

South

Vauxhall

Zeitgeist NEW

*49-51 Black Prince Road, SE11 6AB (7840
0426/www.zeitgeist-london.com). Lambeth North
tube/Waterloo tube/rail.* **Meals served** noon-
9.30pm Mon-Fri, Sun; 2-9.30pm Sat. **Main
courses** £5.99-£13.99. **Credit** AmEx, DC, MC, V.
The main draw at this revamped Victorian pub
near Lambeth Walk is its range of German beers
– 30 and counting. While most are bottled, those
on draught range from aromatic weiss (white)

130 TIME OUT | EATING & DRINKING

hardly spirit of the age, and suggest the owners are a little unsure of their clientele. But with its inexpensive, warming grub and terrific beers, this venture is unexpected and welcome in Vauxhall. *Babies and children admitted. Booking advisable (Thur-Sat). Tables outdoors (8, pavement; 7, garden). Takeaway service.* **Map 16 M11.**

Belgian

North West

Camden Town & Chalk Farm

Belgo Noord

72 Chalk Farm Road, NW1 8AN (7267 0718/ www.belgo-restaurants.com). Chalk Farm tube. **Lunch served** noon-3pm Mon-Fri. **Dinner served** 5.30-11pm Mon-Thur; 5.30-11.30pm Fri. **Meals served** noon-11.30pm Sat; noon-10.30pm Sun. **Main courses** £9.25-£17.95. **Set lunch** £6.50 1 course. **Credit** AmEx, DC, JCB, MC, V.
Touting the Belgium speciality of moules frites and beer, Belgo Noord attracts a lunchtime crowd of workers and families, while evenings are awash with boozy birthday groups. The restaurant is housed in a roomy industrial-style basement, and has the appearance of a submarine-cum-spaceship. Nonsense words engraved on the walls add to the sense of fun. Kilo pots of mussels are the popular choice, ranging from marinière (white wine and garlic) to Thai green curry. The bivalves are organically farmed, so you don't have to worry whether there's an 'R' in the month. Traditional Belgian dishes, slow-roasted with beer, also make an appearance. We were impressed with the carbonade flamande's tenderness and depth of flavour. As you'd expect, the beer menu is vast, with blonde, brown, red and fruit beers (to name a few), each served in its own quirky branded glass. Such specialisation makes prices higher than you might think; to save cash, try the special offers – and keep count of the schnapps. Helpful, speedy service had us out of the door in less than an hour. *Babies and children welcome: children's menu; colouring books; high chairs. Booking advisable. Tables outdoors (3, pavement).* **Map 27 B1.**
For branches (Belgo Centraal, Bierodrome) see index.

Burmese

Central

Edgware Road

★ ★ Mandalay (100)

444 Edgware Road, W2 1EG (7258 3696/ www.mandalayway.com). Edgware Road tube. **Lunch served** noon-2.30pm, **dinner served** 6-10.30pm Mon-Sat. **Main courses** £4.80-£7.90. **Set lunch** £3.90 1 course, £5.90 3 courses. **Credit** AmEx, DC, MC, V.
Tucked amid the electrical shops and kebab joints of Edgware Road, this tiny restaurant is an unexpected treat. Ten wipe-down tables are squeezed together closely in simple surroundings. Fans of both Indian and Chinese food will be happy, as Burmese cooking fuses them together with the hot-sweet-sour flavours of South-east Asia. Think coconut, cumin, turmeric, dried shrimps, chilli and lemongrass. If you find a menu of unfamiliar dishes daunting, don't worry – the charming owners will guide you through. To start, try tangles of beansprouts deep-fried in batter, with silky tamarind sauce. The thin, hot soups are highly popular in Burma, where often people won't drink wine or even water with their meals. Mains include noodles, curries and rice dishes. Spiced spinach with potatoes was full of flavour, and cumin-spiked meatballs in a rich and savoury tomato sauce were just fabulous. Don't leave without trying the banana fritters. The bill will be

a nice surprise too and set lunches are a bargain, but be sure to book as enthusiastic crowds follow the road to Mandalay. *Babies and children welcome: high chairs. Booking essential dinner. Takeaway service.* **Map 2 D4.**

Mediterranean

Central

Piccadilly

★ St Alban (100)

4-12 Regent Street, SW1Y 4PE (7499 8558/ www.stalban.net). Piccadilly Circus tube. **Lunch served** noon-3pm daily. **Dinner served** 5.30pm-midnight Mon-Sat; 5.30-11pm Sun. **Main courses** £7.75-£29.25. **Credit** AmEx, DC, MC, V.
Apart from Michael Craig-Martin's mural of everyday objects, this 'so modern it's retro' room could have come straight from TV's *Mad Men*. It makes a glamorous backdrop to an accessibly priced occasion that won't disappoint. Low-backed banquettes give an uninterrupted vista of architects Stiff + Trevillion's glorious design and, on our visit, of Harold Pinter – adding gravitas to a restaurant that already oozes class. Here, modern Mediterranean dishes are often stripped of carbs to highlight great ingredients combined with precision and subtlety. Or there are wood-baked pizzas, pastas and a risotto. Juicy gobstopper-sized olives, great breads and terrific olive oil augur well; details are spot on. Dishes like sautéd mussels with chilli, garlic and spring onions, and squeaky green beans with smoked ricotta and black olive dressing, are simple and irreproachable. Pollack 'a la plancha' with deliciously crispy skin, atop a stew of Spanish white beans and piquillo peppers, is one of several dishes featuring sustainable fish. As a final flourish, puddings like perfect blood-orange jelly or a pistachio ice-cream melting into zabaglione, come in martini glasses. Wine by the glass was poured by a Rhys Ifans-lookalike sommelier. This place doesn't miss a beat. *Babies and children welcome: high chairs. Booking advisable. Disabled: toilet.* **Map 10 K7.**

South Kensington

Brompton Quarter Café

223-225 Brompton Road, SW3 2EJ (7225 2107). Knightsbridge or South Kensington tube. **Meals served** 7am-10.30pm Mon-Fri; 8am-10.30pm Sat, Sun. **Main courses** £9.75-£24.95. **Credit** AmEx, MC, V.
Serving breakfast, coffee and cakes as well as a full restaurant menu, and with a grocery next door, this place aspires to food-emporium status. The ground floor is all white paint and bare wooden tables, the basement restaurant has a more rarefied atmosphere. Starters include Middle Eastern meze-style dishes to share 'from the gourmet bar' – the likes of houmous, falafel and moutabal – plus Med-inspired food such as greek salad and scallops. A tabouleh was a high-quality classic Lebanese rendition; camargue red rice salad featured under-flavoured, undercooked rice, redeemed only by the odd broad bean and piece of artichoke, plus an unmistakeably classy olive oil dressing. Main courses have a distinctly traditional Anglo-French bias. Compared to the likes of steak, baked salmon and beef bourguignon, our fish of the day was a lively choice: a vibrant purple mound of beetroot and potato salad topped with slices of pan-fried mackerel. The salty, crispy fish made a great contrast with the bland warmth of the salad. Inconsistency in the food was matched by service that was friendly, yet not especially professional. For this you pay around £15 for main courses. Welcome to Knightsbridge. *Babies and children welcome: children's portions; high chairs; nappy-changing facilities. Disabled: lift; toilet. Takeaway service. Wireless internet (free).* **Map 14 E10.**

beers through light styles such as pilseners to darker, hoppier brews. Bar snacks include Landjäger (dried beef and pork sausage), Frikadelle (meatballs), and wholegrain bread with ham or cheese. At lunchtimes, drop by for sandwiches, soup and grilled sausages served with potato salad. Popular dishes from north and south Germany feature on the dinner menu, which tends towards homely comfort cooking. Himmel und Äd (heaven and earth: cloud-like whipped potatoes with moist black pudding and baked apple), Schweinebraten in Biersosse (roast pork in dark beer sauce with plump bread dumplings and red cabbage), Goulasch mit Semmelknödeln (beef stew with bread dumplings), all cost less than a tenner, and there are also schnitzels in various permutations. Black nightclub-style decor and two wide-screen televisions showing football are

West

Hammersmith

Snows on the Green

166 Shepherd's Bush Road, W6 7PB (7603 2142/ www.snowsonthegreen.co.uk). Hammersmith tube. **Lunch served** noon-3pm Mon-Fri. **Dinner served** 6-11pm Mon-Sat. **Main courses** £11.25-£16. **Set meal** (lunch, 6-8.30pm) £13.25 2 courses, £16.50 3 courses. **Credit** AmEx, DC, MC, V.
In a neighbourhood not known for fine-dining establishments, Snows has always stood out, attracting a steadfast local following since 1991. Now, its star may be fading a little. The place was almost empty on a Thursday night. Though service was fine, the restaurant seemed stuck in an 1980s time warp, from the chichi decor to the soundtrack stuck on a loop of Phil Collins's greatest hits. Breads served with three different dips boded well for the courses to come, but from then things went downhill. Sebastian Snow tries to make the most of seasonal produce, and there's no doubting his three-course set menu is excellent value, but the à la carte can be hit and miss. Haddock tart was tasty yet too cold. Seven-hour braised lamb fell off the bone at the touch of a fork, but came with soggy polenta. Fondant oozed in all the right ways, though was paired with a basil ice-cream that tasted like pesto. Snows needs to tighten up on the finer details to retain its west London fan-base.
Babies and children welcome: high chair. Booking advisable. Separate room for parties, seats 28. Tables outdoors (2, pavement). **Map 20 C3.**

South

Balham

★ ★ Fat Delicatessen

7 Chestnut Grove, SW12 8JA (8675 6174/ www.fatdelicatessen.co.uk). Balham tube/rail. **Meals served** 8am-8pm Mon-Wed; 8am-10pm Thur, Fri; 9am-10pm Sat; 11am-6pm Sun. **Main courses** £3.50-£6.75. **Credit** MC, V.
Renouncing contrived Mediterranean fusion food, Fat Delicatessen serves great tapas and a sprinkling of Italian dishes. The menu is about simple cooking – stews, pasta, cheese, ham and puddings – that's ideal for a lunchtime snack or an evening of sharing among mates. From the street, the place resembles a shop, which it is. Don't be put off. Inside, the simple decor and white shelves holding bottles of oil, boxes and packets, create the air of an apothecary's, but service is friendly and the clientele of mothers, gossiping Sloanes, and young professionals makes for a low-key, convivial vibe. An excellent £14 bottle of Tinta de Toro, olives and pan catalan, were the perfect antidote to a rainy night in Balham. Slivers of nutty jamón serrano put most parma in the shade. Meatballs in tomato sauce and patatas bravas were great comfort food before the fabada (an Asturian stew of beans, belly pork, black pudding and chorizo) and galician chicken really warmed our cockles. With most dishes costing £4-£8, Fat Deli will be more ruinous to your waistline than your wallet.
Babies and children welcome: high chairs. Disabled: toilet. Takeaway service.

South East

Gipsy Hill

Numidie

48 Westow Hill, SE19 1RX (8766 6166/www. numidie.co.uk). Gipsy Hill rail. **Dinner served** 6-10.30pm Tue-Sat. **Meals served** noon-10.30pm Sun. **Main courses** £9.50-£15. **Set meal** (Tue-Thur; Sun) £13 2 courses. **Credit** MC, V.
Stepping into Numidie, you leave behind unromantic Westow Hill for a Parisian-style bistro with mismatched wooden furniture, bright painted walls, a clutter of picture frames and a token chandelier. The venue has a quirky charm to it and would make a great spot for a first date. An interesting mix of French and Algerian cooking is served, though it's the sort of food you could knock up at home. A French classic of duck breast salad looked pitiful and ungenerous on shredded lettuce, but the meat was so tender and smoky we soon forgot its appearance. The house salad had a more North African flavour, containing houmous, falafel, piperade and stuffed artichokes. Saffron-stained seafood couscous was attractive, and a little salt saved the creamy winter vegetable gratin, served with juicy steak. In the basement you'll find an equally characterful wine bar, popular with locals.
Babies and children welcome: booster seats; high chairs. Booking advisable; essential Fri, Sat.

East

Shoreditch

★ Eyre Brothers ⑽⓪

70 Leonard Street, EC2A 4QX (7613 5346/ www.eyrebrothers.co.uk). Old Street tube/rail. **Lunch served** noon-2.45pm Mon-Fri. **Dinner served** 6.30-10.45pm Mon-Fri; 7-11pm Sat. **Main courses** £15-£25. **Credit** AmEx, DC, MC, V.
The news has got around: Eyre Brothers does everything exceptionally well. Hence, it took us three attempts to reserve a table. The interior is framed by dark wood on the floor and ceiling. Clean lines of chic leather furniture, designer lamps and divided dining areas create an aura of sophistication. It's a labour of love for brothers David and Robert, who evidently spend as much time crafting the frequently changing menu as fashioning the decor. Authentic Portuguese dishes reflect the brothers' upbringing in Mozambique, while Spanish and French flavours add range and luxury. Superior duck foie gras came with a sweet port and Madeira reduction, chive oil and crisp toasted almonds. The grilled pigeon breasts couldn't have seen the grill for long, arriving magenta-rare, tender and flavoursome. A main of slow-roasted duck breast was perfectly pink, served with rich garlic mash and an uplifting parsley salad. The wine list is similarly Iberian-slanted, containing fairly priced bottles and a number of wines and sherries by the glass. This is the sort of place that doesn't seem to lack anything, except a second branch.
Babies and children admitted. Booking advisable Thur-Sat. Disabled: toilet. Restaurant available for hire. **Map 6 Q4.**

North West

Queen's Park

★ Penk's

79 Salusbury Road, NW6 6NH (7604 4484/ www.penks.com). Queen's Park tube/rail. **Brunch served** 10.30am-3pm Sat. **Lunch served** noon-3pm Mon-Fri. **Dinner served** 6-11pm Mon-Sat. **Meals served** 10am-10.30pm Sun. **Main courses** £11-£17. **Set meal** (noon-3pm, 6-7.30pm) £13.50 2 courses. **Credit** MC, V.
Queen's Park locals have done well out of this little bistro. Despite its diminutive dimensions, there's a clever use of space by means of strategically placed mirrors, cream wood panelling, and careful table arrangement. Cooking is rustic with a leaning towards Mediterranean sunshine dishes. A first course of coarsely textured duck terrine, flecked with amber-hued apricots and crunchy pistachios, although deliciously succulent, was overshadowed by a dollop of tart chutney: too many flavours on one plate. Main courses were sublime. A steamy mound of spaghetti, tossed with tender chicken pieces, was memorable for its scrumptious white wine and cream sauce, finished with a flurry of chopped parsley. Grilled minute steak, cooked to perfect pinkness, was complemented by a pat of melting herby butter and accompanied with crisp golden chips. Our gold star went to the pud: an outstanding vanilla panna cotta, set to a sexy wobble, and surrounded by tangy passion-fruit pulp. Service is unobtrusive, yet attentive – and like the panna cotta, as smooth as silk. A small but well-chosen wine list caters to various budgets and provides a decent choice by the glass. An ideal location for a romantic tryst.
Babies and children admitted (lunch). Booking advisable. Separate room for parties, seats 20. **Map 1 A2.**

Scandinavian

Central

Marylebone

Garbo's

42 Crawford Street, W1H 1JW (7262 6582). Baker Street or Edgware Road tube/Marylebone tube/rail. **Lunch served** noon-3pm Mon-Fri, Sun. **Dinner served** 6-11pm Mon-Sat. **Main courses** £8.50-£17.95. **Set lunch** (Mon-Fri) £10.95 2 courses, £11.95 3 courses; £12.95 smörgåsbord. **Set buffet lunch** (Sun) £14.95. **Cover** £1 (à la carte only). **Credit** AmEx, MC, V.
On the phone Garbo's seemed astonished that we attempted to book, but just as well we did for this tiny spot was almost full with loyal locals on our Saturday night visit. Photos of Anita Ekberg, Roxette and other Swedish celebrities are displayed on the walls. There's also a virtual gallery of Greta Garbo images, and her face is used on the logo too. Cooking, like the decor, is homely and has a 1970s edge with such dishes as veal oskar and filled savoury crêpes. Highlight of our meal was the Baltic herring salad, with crunchy green apple and gherkins cloaked in a tangy mayonnaise. Also good was a simple grilled halibut steak, but the signature meatballs in cream sauce seemed bland and rubbery. Desserts include rice pudding, apple crumble and chocolate mousse. However, starter and main course portions were so generous we were happy just to nibble the sweet biscuits that came with the bill. There's a brief international wine list, plus Swedish Old Gold pils, Crocodile lager, and pear and apple ciders. Friendly, efficient service was all the more impressive given the challenging dimensions of this busy bolt-hole.
Babies and children welcome: high chair. Booking advisable. Separate room for parties, seats 35. **Map 8 F5.**

South African

South West

Putney

Chakalaka

136 Upper Richmond Road, SW15 2SP (8789 5696/www.chakalakarestaurant.co.uk). East Putney tube. **Dinner served** 6-10.45pm Mon-Fri. **Meals served** noon-10.45pm Sat, Sun. **Main courses** £9.95-£17.95. **Set meal** (dinner Mon-Fri; lunch Sat; lunch & dinner Sun) £15 2 courses. **Credit** AmEx, MC, V.
Subtle isn't the word to describe Chakalaka. Its frontage is a zebra-painted riot, and internal space is given over to tribal shields and dead animal skins. Such an attitude also extends to the menu, most prominently with the £25 challenge: eat a 25oz (700g) steak in 25 minutes and get a free T-shirt. Come here too if you're into competitive artery-blocking; the all-you-can-eat ribs deal at weekends brings out the big boys. The menu is exceptionally meat-heavy, but has an intriguing South African twist. We tried crocodile and weren't disappointed by the taste (something like frogs' legs), and then enjoyed a cracking chargrilled kudu steak (like antelope). Fish also feature, but in general this is a carnivore's paradise. The wine list contains some enticing South African bottles to pair with your meat. Chakalaka was exceptionally busy on our visit, with service occasionally getting a bit frantic, but the odd mistake was dealt with professionally (a complimentary glass of wine easing matters greatly). We left with a big smile and fond memories.
Babies and children welcome: children's portions; high chairs; nappy-changing facilities. Booking advisable. Separate room for parties, seats 60.

Greek

The capital's Greek dining scene seems to be moving in slow motion, with too many restaurateurs trading in identikit dishes and on outdated reputations. Yes, there are great places to sample quality Greek and Greek-Cypriot cuisine, but creativity is in depressingly short supply. Excitement is brewing, though, with rumour that Theodore Kyriakou – the chef who put Greek food on the map with his work at Hoxton's original Real Greek restaurant – is planning a new venture. In the meantime, you'll find impeccably sourced ingredients, quality cooking and masses of charm at both **Retsina** (our pick of the bunch) and **Lemonia**. Stalwarts **Aphrodite** and **Daphne** continue to showcase taverna classics with old-fashioned manners on the side. And for hip environs and seriously good souvláki, kebab fans should make a beeline for buzzy **As Greek As It Gets**, or one of the streamlined branches of the now rather corporate **Real Greek**.

Central

Clerkenwell & Farringdon

★ The Real Greek
140-142 St John Street, EC1V 4UA (7253 7234/ www.therealgreek.com). Farringdon tube/rail. **Meals served** noon-11pm Mon-Sat. **Main courses** £5.25-£9.30. **Set mezédes** £10.50 per person (minimum 2). **Credit** MC, V.
Forget vine-strewn taverna clichés, the Clerkenwell branch of this popular mezédes and souvláki mini-chain (six branches across London; another two in the pipeline for 2008) is stylishly contemporary. A large bar dominates the industrial-chic space – all exposed piping, dark wood and floor-to-ceiling windows – surrounded by bar stools, high benches and small tables for more intimate dining. The chain takes its name from the much-lauded Hoxton Real Greek (itself now pared down in line with its siblings), whose legacy is reflected in the high-quality ingredients and the presence of less ubiquitous Greek specialities (fava, a yellow split-pea purée, for example). Portions are on the small side, but the mezédes are fresh and flavourful. Dishes of creamy white taramosaláta, squeaky saganáki cheese, hot flatbread and tender octopus were real winners, accompanied by Cretan Xerolithia vilana wine. The well-priced souvláki menu provides spot-on sustenance for boozers (this is as much a bar as it is a restaurant) and service is friendly and relaxed. Choose your branch wisely; quality and service have often been known to slip in the Real Greek's more touristy locations.
Babies and children welcome: children's menu; high chairs; nappy-changing facilities. Booking advisable. Disabled: toilet. Tables outdoors (4, pavement). Takeaway service. **Map 5 O4**. **For branches see index**.

West

Bayswater

Aphrodite Taverna
15 Hereford Road, W2 4AB (7229 2206/ www.aphroditerestaurant.co.uk). Bayswater, Notting Hill Gate or Queensway tube. **Meals served** noon-midnight Mon-Sat. **Main courses** £8.50-£28.50. **Set mezédes** £18 vegetarian, £21 meat, £29.50 fish per person (minimum 2). **Cover** £1. **Credit** AmEx, DC, MC, V.
Atmospheric, friendly and unintentionally kitsch (plaster of paris statues, posters of Cyprus and bouzoukis adorn the walls), Aphrodite is a deservedly popular old-stager of the Bayswater Greek scene. The Greek Orthodox Cathedral of Saint Sophia is just around the corner on Moscow Street. Locals flock here for the upbeat, welcoming vibe and quality Greek-Cypriot cooking. The lengthy menu offers mixed mezédes (fish, meat and vegetarian varieties), an array of seafood dishes (monkfish kebabs and giant prawns are house specialities), grills and well-executed taverna staples such as stifádo. Portions are generous, making it tempting to forgo the main courses entirely in favour of a few choice mezédes. Chunky slices of grilled or fried halloumi and own-made dolmádes (vegetarian and meat versions) are cooked to order and served at the table by attentive waiters. Vibrant tabouleh, calamares salad, melitzanosaláta (aubergine purée) and feta-packed greek salad proved equally fine choices. A lengthy wine list with a decent selection of Greek bottles completes a pleasing picture.
Babies and children welcome: high chairs. Booking advisable dinner. Restaurant available for hire (Sun). Tables outdoors (12, terrace). Takeaway service. **Map 7 B6**.

Notting Hill

Greek Affair
1 Hillgate Street, W8 7SP (7792 5226/ www.greekaffair.co.uk). Notting Hill Gate tube. **Lunch served** noon-3pm, **dinner served** 6-11pm Mon-Fri. **Meals served** noon-11pm daily. **Main courses** £7.90-£13.90. **Credit** MC, V.
Greek Affair's tucked away location (just off hectic Notting Hill Gate) and cliché-free interior give it an appealing neighbourhood bistro feel. The crowd on our Tuesday night visit was definitely local: fashionably dishevelled trustafarians ordering 'just one more bottle' for the third time, and suits talking business by candlelight. Service proved slow but helpful – perhaps overly so when the waitress explained the chef had left the garlic out of one of our side dishes to aid romance later in the evening (we weren't on a date). Of our starters, only the spanakópitta (spinach filo pastries) passed muster. So-so melitzanosaláta (aubergine purée), limp calamares and a greek salad that was 90% iceberg lettuce held very little appeal. Mains, however, were much more successful – hearty pasticcio (a lasagne-like dish of layered pasta and minced beef) proved a solid choice, while baked fish cooked with tomatoes and herbs was punchy and flavoursome. Fuss-free decor adds to the appeal (simple wooden tables, vases of lilies dotted about) making this a great place to linger over after-dinner drinks, if not the mezédes.
Babies and children welcome: high chairs. Booking advisable. Tables outdoors (10, roof garden). Takeaway service. Vegetarian menu. **Map 19 C5**.

South West

Earl's Court

★ As Greek As It Gets
233 Earl's Court Road, SW5 9AH (7244 7777/ www.asgreekasitgets.co.uk). Earl's Court tube. **Lunch served** noon-3pm, **dinner served** 5-11pm Mon-Fri. **Meals served** noon-11pm Sat, Sun. **Main courses** £6-£19.50. **Credit** MC, V.
Moody lighting, pumping bass and raucous laughter set the scene at this contemporary kebab joint on our Friday night visit. Both floors (ground and first) were packed with refuelling bar-hoppers, big birthday groups and couples on awkward-looking first dates. But despite the menu's laudable array of Greek wines, bottled beers (Alpha and Mythos) and dishes – classics such as pasticcio (a baked pasta dish) and moussaká sit alongside the lengthy souvláki and gyros (pitta wraps) menu – there was not a Greek in sight. Bar-style seating, overlooking a giant chandelier and Earl's Court

RESTAURANTS

Lemonia

Road, gives the place a hip, fast-paced feel. Smaller table set-ups at the back of the top floor offer more relaxed dining. We opted for the latter and enjoyed expertly grilled pork and chicken souvláki, kritiki saláta (Cretan tomato and cheese salad with large croûtons) and piping-hot spanakópitta (spinach pie): all packed with fresh, tasty ingredients and of far better quality than the sound system's rota of trashy Euro pop.
Babies and children welcome: high chairs. Booking advisable. Tables outdoors (2, pavement). Takeaway service.

North

Camden Town & Chalk Farm

Andy's Taverna
81-81A Bayham Street, NW1 0AG (7485 9718/ www.andystaverna.com). Camden Town or Mornington Crescent tube. **Lunch served** noon-2.30pm, **dinner served** 6pm-midnight Mon-Fri. **Meals served** noon-midnight Sat, Sun. **Main courses** £8.95-£14. **Set mezédes** £13.95 per person (minimum 2). **Credit** AmEx, DC, MC, V.
Tucked next to vine-covered Daphne (*see below*) on Bayham Street, Andy's is another stalwart of the NW1 Greek scene. Our Wednesday night visit saw the memorabilia-strewn, blue-and-white interior all but deserted; there were just two other diners. This was a shame as friendly service and decent-quality mezédes (excellent houmous, tzatzíki and greek salad) got our meal off to a fine start. The main courses, however, proved a real disappointment. A vegetarian platter combined good halloumi, stodgy moussaká, lukewarm chargrilled veg and oily spanakópitta (spinach pie) to uninspiring effect, while grilled Mediterranean prawns looked fantastic but were rather too chewy to be a real success. Weekend nights tend to see more action, with wine-fuelled group dinners and musical accompaniment from the piano by the entrance creating a lively buzz. We suspect Andy's is best approached in this capacity: somewhere to unwind with a gang of mates rather than a place to indulge a passion for Greek cuisine.

Babies and children welcome: high chairs. Booking advisable Fri, Sat. Separate rooms for parties, seating 35 and 45. Tables outdoors (7, garden). Takeaway service. **Map 27 D2**.

Daphne
83 Bayham Street, NW1 0AG (7267 7322). Camden Town or Mornington Crescent tube. **Lunch served** noon-2.30pm, **dinner served** 6-11.30pm Mon-Sat. **Main courses** £9-£14.50. **Set lunch** £7.75 2 courses, £9.25 3 courses. **Set mezédes** £15.50 meat or vegetarian, £19.50 fish per person (minimum 2). **Credit** MC, V.
From the ivy-covered exterior to the charmingly professional service – via some downright comical painted 'windows' depicting classic Mediterranean scenes – Daphne is an unapologetically old-school affair. And its crowd of loyal regulars (loud groups of Greek men sharing bottles of whiskey and mezédes; gossipy Camden mums on first-name terms with the waiters) clearly approve. The place is rammed from 8.30pm every night (though closed Sundays). A blackboard menu is presented with a flourish to the table. It covers all the classics and our waiter was keen to point out that everything was fresh, not frozen. So-so melitzanosaláta (aubergine purée) proved a disappointing start, though a dish of coarsely textured, garlicky houmous was excellent. Mains of chargilled king prawns and swordfish were simply prepared and delicious. Prices are rather high (£14.50 for the swordfish), though when we ordered a third dish of greek salad our waiter immediately offered to include it as a side with the fish. It's all about the service at Daphne.
Babies and children welcome: high chairs. Booking essential Fri, Sat. Disabled: toilet. Separate rooms for parties, seating 18-50. Tables outdoors (8, roof terrace). **Map 27 D2**.

★ Lemonia
89 Regent's Park Road, NW1 8UY (7586 7454). Chalk Farm tube. **Lunch served** noon-3pm Mon-Fri; noon-3.30pm Sun. **Dinner served** 6-11.30pm Mon-Sat. **Main courses** £9-£15. **Set lunch** (Mon-Fri) £8.50 2 courses, £9.75 3 courses. **Set mezédes** £17.75 per person (minimum 2). **Credit** MC, V.
This buzzy Primrose Hill mainstay remains one of London's most highly regarded Greek-Cypriot restaurants – and quite right too. Despite its impressive size, formally attired waiters and bijou Regent's Park Road location, there's a sense of simplicity at Lemonia that's authentically Greek. Service is brisk and decor is pared down (white walls, rustic furniture, hanging baskets and a leafy conservatory), ensuring attention is focused where it should be: on the menu's impeccably sourced ingredients and on having a damned good time. On our Sunday afternoon visit the place was packed with well-to-do local families, Greek ladies-who-lunch and animated thirtysomethings devouring taverna classics like kléftiko and moussaká. From the lengthy mezédes list we plumped for calamares, taramosaláta and gigandes (butter beans baked in tomato sauce) and there wasn't a dud dish among them. Main courses were equally pleasing: flavoursome barbounaki (small red mullet) and tender cinnamon-infused lamb. High prices (par for the course in this part of town) and occasionally brusque service at peak sittings are the only downers – both forgivable with a glass of wine in hand at a pavement table in the sunshine.
Babies and children admitted. Booking advisable, essential weekends. Separate room for parties, seats 40. Tables outdoors (6, pavement). **Map 27 A1**.

Limani
154 Regent's Park Road, NW1 8XN (7483 4492). Chalk Farm tube. **Lunch served** noon-3pm Sat. **Dinner served** 6-11.30pm Tue-Sat; 3.30-10.30pm Sun. **Main courses** £8.75-£16.50. **Set mezédes** £16 meat or vegetarian, £18 fish per person (minimum 2). **Credit** MC, V.
Lemonia's little sister has a laid-back and pleasingly fuss-free feel – pretty setting, simple tables, blue paintwork, the odd decorative plate – but our Wednesday night visit saw the ground floor virtually deserted. We were ushered straight to the over-bright lower level: a shame as part of the fun of Primrose Hill dining is the people-watching potential of a window seat. The mood picked up later in the evening as the crammed-in wooden tables became dotted with moneyed fortysomething couples and gangs of foreign-exchange students trying to make the not-so-generous portions (melitzanes skordaliá consists of three slices of soggy aubergine) stretch

between six. Service proved charming but totally haphazard; our salad failed to arrive, gigandes were replaced with small beans without any warning, and we were billed for a more expensive wine than we ordered (though this was rectified). Still, Limani has an enticing menu (grilled sea bass, an array of kebabs, keftédes, beef stifádo) and a relaxed atmosphere that's hard not to love. Nonetheless, our experience suggests the empty ground floor might have more to do with slipped standards than slow midweek footfall.
Babies and children admitted. Booking advisable, essential weekends. Separate rooms for parties, seating 24-30. Tables outdoors (2, pavement). Map 27 A1.

Wood Green

Vrisaki

73 Myddleton Road, N22 8LZ (8889 8760). Bounds Green or Wood Green tube. **Lunch served** noon-4pm, **dinner served** 6-11.30pm Mon-Sat. **Meals served** noon-9pm Sun. **Main courses** £10-£18. **Set mezédes** £18 per person (minimum 2). **Credit** AmEx, MC, V.
A visit to this enduringly popular north London kebab shop and restaurant is best undertaken following a three-day fast. Check out the skewer-packed fridges (and fantastic aromas) as you make your way through the takeaway joint to the surprisingly expansive taverna at the back. Order the mixed mezédes (£36 for two) and you'll understand why you need a hearty appetite. The first course consists of 16 (we counted) dishes of tzatzíki, tabouleh, octopus salad, olives and the like. These are followed by a mind-boggling array of hot and cold dishes and grills. Our weekday visit saw quantity triumph over quality. Although some dishes were good (salty chunks of halloumi; freshly grilled sea bream), some were very poor (grey melitzanosaláta; flavourless feta; chewy calamares). That said, our previous experiences here were rather more successful (the kebabs are reliably good), and Vrisaki remains a vibrant, buzzing and fun-packed place in which to dine. Come for the vibe, or because it's local, or for the fantastically friendly service – and you shouldn't leave disappointed.
Babies and children welcome: high chairs. Booking advisable, essential weekends. Takeaway service (8881 2920).

North West

Belsize Park

★ Retsina

48-50 Belsize Lane, NW3 5AN (7431 5855/ www.retsina-london.com). Belsize Park or Swiss Cottage tube. **Lunch served** noon-3pm Tue-Sun. **Dinner served** 6-11pm daily. **Main courses** £9-£22.50. **Set mezédes** £18.50 meat, £22.50 fish per person (minimum 2). **Credit** MC, V.
This stylish Belsize Park favourite is packed most evenings with local families and well-bred couples enjoying its candlelit ambience, charming service and fantastically authentic cooking. The enticing menu makes a modest order impossible; we tucked into spinach-packed spanakópitta filos, delicately spiced dolmádes, aubergine purée and hot, salty saganáki (fried Greek cheese) accompanied by a bottle of aromatic moschofilero (one of the wine list's many Greek offerings). Mains proved equally impressive: soúvla was perfectly cooked and tender; lamb kléftiko was the best we've tasted in London. What really sets the place apart, though, is its abundant use of fresh herbs (lots of dill and mint) and high-quality olive oil. Vibrant natural flavours are what good taverna cooking is all about and there's definitely no scrimping here. This is a perfect spot for indulging in every Greek's favourite dining practice, *papara* (the dipping of bread into delicious oils and juices on the plate). Prices reflect the swanky location, but with its upbeat buzz, classy set-up and high-quality food, Retsina is excellent value for money.
Babies and children welcome: high chairs. Booking advisable. Separate room for parties, seats 50. Tables outdoors (5, pavement). Takeaway service. Map 28 B3.

Menu

Dishes followed by (G) indicate a specifically Greek dish; those marked (GC) indicate a Greek-Cypriot speciality; those without an initial have no particular regional affiliation. Spellings often vary.

Afélia (GC): pork cubes, ideally from filleted leg or shoulder, stewed in wine, coriander and other herbs.
Avgolémono (G): a sauce made of lemon, egg yolks and chicken stock. Also a soup made with rice, chicken stock, lemon and whole eggs.
Baklavá: a pan-Middle Eastern sweet made from sheets of filo dough layered with nuts.
Dolmádes (G) or **koupépia (GC):** young vine leaves stuffed with rice, spices and (usually) minced meat.
Fasólia plakí or **pilakí:** white beans in a tomato, oregano, bay, parsley and garlic sauce.
Garídes: prawns (usually king prawns in the UK), fried or grilled.
Gígantes or **gígandes:** white butter beans baked in tomato sauce; pronounced 'yígandes'.
Halloumi (GC) or **hallúmi:** a cheese traditionally made from sheep or goat's milk, but increasingly from cow's milk. Best served fried or grilled.
Horiátiki: Greek 'peasant' salad of tomato, cucumber, onion, feta and sometimes green pepper, dressed with ladolémono (oil and lemon).
Hórta: salad of cooked wild greens.
Houmous, hoúmmous or **húmmus (GC):** a dip of puréed chickpeas, sesame seed paste, lemon juice and garlic, garnished with paprika. Originally an Arabic dish.
Htipití or **khtipití:** tangy purée of matured cheeses, flavoured with red peppers.
Kalamári, kalamarákia or **calamares:** small squid, usually sliced into rings, battered and fried.

Kataïfi or **katayfi:** syrup-soaked 'shredded-wheat' rolls.
Keftédes or **keftedákia (G):** herby meatballs made with minced pork or lamb (rarely beef), egg, breadcrumbs and possibly grated potato.
Kléftiko (GC): slow-roasted lamb on the bone (often shoulder), flavoured with oregano and other herbs.
Kopanistí (G): a cheese dip with a tanginess that traditionally comes from natural fermentation, but is often boosted with chilli.
Koukiá: broad beans.
Loukánika or **lukánika:** spicy coarse-ground sausages, usually pork and heavily herbed.
Loukoumédes: tiny, spongy dough fritters, dipped in honey.
Loukoúmi or **lukúmi:** 'turkish delight' made with syrup, rosewater and pectin, often studded with nuts.
Loúntza (GC): smoked pork loin.
Marídes: picarel, often mistranslated as (or substituted by) 'whitebait' – small fish best coated in flour and flash-fried.
Melitzanosaláta: purée of grilled aubergines.
Meze (plural mezédes, pronounced 'mezédhes'): a selection of either hot or cold appetisers and main dishes.
Moussaká(s) (G): a baked dish of mince (usually lamb), aubergine and potato slices and herbs, topped with béchamel sauce.
Papoutsáki: aubergine 'shoes', slices stuffed with mince, topped with sauce, usually béchamel-like.
Pastourmá(s): dense, dark-tinted garlic sausage, traditionally made from camel meat, but nowadays from beef.
Pourgoúri or **bourgoúri (GC):** a pilaf of cracked wheat, often prepared with stock, onions, crumbled vermicelli and spices.

Saganáki (G): fried cheese, usually kefalotyri; also means anything (mussels, spinach) made in a cheese-based red sauce.
Sheftaliá (GC): little pig-gut skins stuffed with minced pork and lamb, onion, parsley, breadcrumbs and spices, then grilled.
Skordaliá (G): a garlic and breadcrumb or potato-based dip, used as a side dish.
Soutzoukákia or **soutzoúki (G):** baked meat rissoles, often topped with a tomato-based sauce.
Soúvla: large cuts of lamb or pork, slow-roasted on a rotary spit.
Souvláki: chunks of meat quick-grilled on a skewer (known in London takeaways as kebab or shish kebab).
Spanakópitta: small turnovers, traditionally triangular, stuffed with spinach, dill and often feta or some other crumbly tart cheese.
Stifádo: a rich meat stew (often beef or rabbit) with onions, red wine, tomatoes, cinnamon and bay.
Taboúlleh: generic Middle Eastern starter of pourgoúri (qv), chopped parsley, cucumber chunks, tomatoes and spring onions.
Taramá, properly **taramosaláta:** fish roe pâté, originally made of dried, salted grey mullet roe, but now more often smoked cod roe, plus olive oil, lemon juice and breadcrumbs.
Tavás (GC): lamb, onion, tomato and cumin, cooked in earthenware casseroles.
Tsakistés (GC): split green olives marinated in lemon, garlic, coriander seeds and other optional flavours.
Tyrópitta (G): similar to spanakópitta (qv) but usually without spinach and with more feta.
Tzatzíki, dzadzíki (G) or **talatoúra (GC):** a dip of shredded cucumber, yoghurt, garlic, lemon juice and mint.

RESTAURANTS

Hotels & Haute Cuisine

It's been a year of change in the haute cuisine sector, with several new arrivals challenging the established names. We love the fresh faces and fresh thinking at **Texture** and **Hibiscus**, both establishments from people who cut their teeth in the countryside and are now trying their luck (and their inventive menus) in the big city. Also in this category is the creative cooking of Andrew Turner, whose restaurant the **Landau** is now ensconced at the Langham Hotel. Other hotel operators, however, are questioning their commitment to traditional fine dining: this year we've seen the relaunch of the Lanesborough's restaurant as smart Italian eaterie **Apsleys** (*see p182*), and Browns Grill, now known as the **Albemarle** (*see p61*), opt for a slightly more rustic British approach with the help of celebrity chef Mark Hix. Meanwhile, some properties still seem to feel the need to import talent, such as **Hélène Darroze at the Connaught** and **Alain Ducasse at the Dorchester**, but while the former has enhanced London's dining scene, we'd prefer to eat at the **Dorchester Grill Room** (*see p61*) or **China Tang** (*see p76*) in preference to the latter. Joining the French contingent is Jean-Christophe Ansanay-Alex's **Ambassade de l'Ile** on the former site of Lundum's in South Kensington.

Over at the Berkeley, it's largely business as usual. Although the split between Marcus Wareing and Gordon Ramsay made national newspaper headlines, the plan as we went to press was for the two chefs to retain their respective restaurants in the hotel – **Boxwood Café** and **Marcus Wareing at the Berkeley** (formerly Pétrus) – with little alteration. Ramsay is retaining the Pétrus name, so expect it turn up at another site.

Central

City

Addendum

Apex City of London Hotel, 1 Seething Lane, EC3N 4AX (7977 9500/www.addendum restaurant.co.uk). Tower Hill tube. **Lunch served** *noon-2.30pm,* **dinner served** *6-9.30pm Mon-Fri.* **Main courses** *£15-£20.* **Set lunch** *£17.95 2 courses, £21.95 3 courses.* **Credit** AmEx, DC, MC, V.

Apex Hotels is a reliable British chain of business hotels; most of its properties are in Scotland, but another two are planned for London, and this Tower Hill site is being expanded as we go to press. Addendum is divided into three: a central bar, a 'gastro bar' spilling through glass doors on to the pavement, and a more formal restaurant to the rear. Here, orange paintwork is paired with black tiles, white linens, warm wood veneer and unobtrusive abstract art, producing a glossy-brochure atmosphere that's hipper than the City norm. The set lunch is good value, if dull at times with dishes such as bresaola with celeriac remoulade and beetroot, and pollack with seasonal peas, beans and lettuce. The carte isn't excessively priced either, but has little wow-factor. Our linguine with peas, cream and poached egg was lovely, and a good choice for lunchtime, but a mean hand with the truffle made it something we could easily knock up at home. A starter of scallop with crab polenta and shellfish jus read well, but the crescent of mealy, mildly crab-flavoured polenta wasn't special enough to warrant inclusion and the scallop, though perfectly cooked, was small and singular. Shellfish jus comprised a third of the dish, yet staff didn't bring a spoon for it until asked, and seemed to think we should eat the pasta with a knife and fork. Still, they were pleasant and caring. Desserts majored on fruit, with even the chocolate soup and dark chocolate wun tuns featuring fresh cherries. What strawberry and basil risotto lacked in presentation it made up for in summery fragrance and refreshing flavours. Extras were a mixed bag. On the good side: poppy-seed and fennel bread, British farmhouse butter, and a cooling cup of gazpacho served with savoury pastries. Overall Addendum is a restaurant befitting a four-star hotel: good but not up there with the best.
Babies and children welcome: high chairs. Disabled: lift; toilet (in hotel). Separate rooms for parties, seating 10-50. **Map 12 R7.**

Bonds

Threadneedles, 5 Threadneedle Street, EC2R 8AY (7657 8088/www.theetongroup.com). Bank tube/DLR. **Lunch served** *noon-2.30pm,* **dinner served** *6-10pm Mon-Fri.* **Main courses** *£12.95-£25.* **Set lunch** *£19.50 2 courses, £24.50 3 courses.* **Credit** AmEx, DC, MC, V.

From its financial-pun name to its setting in a former banking hall, Bonds is pure City style. Diners are primarily male but range from first-jobbers to chief execs. Satiny brown curtains add a veil of discretion to the closely packed central tables, but even the least portly traders have trouble squeezing between them (there are more spacious tables on the room's outskirts). Early spring saw Barry Tonks' menu incorporating wild garlic leaves, new-season English asparagus and a great deal of slow cooking. There's plenty of meat to satisfy hearty appetites. Butch belly pork featured in two dishes: a starter of 'porchetta' with granny smith apple purée, and a main course with pearl barley, chorizo and cider sauce. We liked the sound of steak tartare with celeriac remoulade, and a sweetcorn risotto with mushrooms and marjoram, but opted for a velvety pea velouté poured table-side over poached egg and pea shoots, and a too-cold smoked salmon terrine from the set menu. Market fish of the day, sea bass, sat in UFO-shaped plates with a verdant sauce featuring chunky beans and pasta. Chocolate fondant – not as dark or as molten as it could be – came with almond milk sorbet, but the show-stopper was a boozy sherry trifle with white chocolate cream and fizzy chocolate space dust; this alone was worth a return visit. The esteemed wine list includes more than 25 by-the-glass choices. Service was disappointing, let down by long waits between courses (something we've not experienced here before). When we were finally able to leave, two staff members were clearly resentful at being handed the coat tickets, taking the shine off an otherwise happy meal. Strange that workers in a City restaurant need to be reminded who's boss.
Disabled: lift; toilet. Dress: smart casual. Separate rooms for parties, seating 9, 12 and 20. **Map 12 Q6.**

Fitzrovia

★ Landau NEW (100)

2008 RUNNER-UP BEST DESIGN
The Langham, Portland Place, W1B 1JA (7965 0165/www.thelandau.com). Oxford Circus tube. **Breakfast served** *7-10.30am Mon-Fri; 7-11am Sat, Sun.* **Lunch served** *12.30-2.30pm,* **tea served** *3-5pm daily.* **Dinner served** *5.30-11pm Mon-Sat; 5.30-10pm Sun.* **Main courses** *£19-£30.* **Set lunch** *£27.50 2 courses, £32.50 3 courses.* **Set dinner** *£57.50-£72.50 tasting menu.* **Credit** AmEx, DC, MC, V.

David Collins' interior, with its otherworldly brass fittings and olde worlde wood panelling, smacks of an HG Wells novel. It perfectly suits a restaurant where chef Andrew Turner presents British ingredients with molecular gastronomy touches. Customers can enjoy a view of Nash's All Souls Church and the BBC's Broadcasting House through regal windows curved around one end of the oval room. Beautiful breads, presented in a silver bowl, included carta di musica smeared with fresh pesto, a baguette glistening with olive oil and nourishing seeded varieties. On the side – a pat of butter and a little pile of pink Himalayan sea salt. Slow-cooked roast chicken had a good crisp skin, which also featured as a decorative shard to garnish pommes purées. This was accompanied by reassuringly seasonal veg including morels and green and white asparagus, plus a lovely mushroom cream sauce. Expect some confident flavour combinations, such as in our sweetly spiced pastry parcel of duck confit with orange segments, green asparagus and sun-dried tomatoes. However, the foie gras terrine with passion-fruit and vanilla sauce was not quite a harmonious match. Desserts are excellent. Most popular are the profiteroles filled with raspberry sorbet and cream and covered with dark Amedei chocolate sauce at the table; their caramel antenna 'allows you to pick up the BBC', staff joke, and the assembly looks like something from *The Jetsons*. A substantial summer pudding came with well-balanced milk and mint sorbet (we doubt there's a better mint ice in London) and a clever blob of vanilla-flavoured milk, formed by dolloping the

Landau

liquid in a seaweed bath. The wine list offers plenty in the £28-£35 bracket but nothing under £25 a bottle. We weren't impressed by the wine waiter pointing us to pricey bins, though the wine he eventually persuaded us to order was delicious. *Babies and children welcome: children's menu; high chairs. Booking advisable; essential weekends. Disabled: toilet. Dress: smart casual. Separate room for parties, seats 16. Wireless internet (£7/hr). Map 9 H5.*

Pied à Terre

34 Charlotte Street, W1T 2NH (7636 1178/ www.pied-a-terre.co.uk). Goodge Street or Tottenham Court Road tube. **Lunch served** 12.15-2.30pm Mon-Fri. **Dinner served** 6.15-10.45pm Mon-Sat. **Set lunch** £24.50 2 courses. **Set dinner** £65 3 courses. **Set meal** £80 tasting menu (£132 incl wine). **Credit** AmEx, MC, V.
A long, low-ceilinged dining room with a skylight and romantically curved banquettes for two give Pied à Terre the feel of a luxury yacht. At the stern are various glass decanters, which sommeliers select according to the wines chosen from the international list. Down in the engine room, chef Shane Osborn doesn't shy away from challenging ingredients – even on the set lunch menu, which offers a choice of just two dishes for each course plus French farmhouse cheese or dessert. You might find Hereford snails, duck hearts with crayfish, or veal sweetbread ravioli. We've enjoyed the most tender slices of lambs' tongues. Meals kick off with exceedingly good canapés, such as foie gras mousse sandwiched between ultra-thin poppy-seed crisps, and a mouthful of potato jelly with sweetcorn foam. On our last visit, lamb fillet came with fennel-flavoured spätzle, meltingly soft roast fennel, whole roast garlic cloves, and sweet cherry tomatoes. A tiny cup of thin, creamy walnut soup with passion-fruit foam was a suitably exciting prelude to the signature bittersweet chocolate tart. More like a rectangular block of mousse, this was divine, served with macadamia foam, the welcome crunch of deep-fried macadamias, grown-up stout ice-cream and a 'bite and it's gone' stout-flavoured candy crisp. Staff are friendly though we've found service slow, especially at lunchtimes, when customers range from besuited businessmen, to in-town-for-the-day couples and (rather surprisingly) gaggles of babes ordering plate after plate of salad. *Babies and children admitted. Booking advisable; essential weekends. Dress: smart casual. Separate room for parties, seats 12. Vegetarian menu.* **Map 17 B1.**

Holborn

Pearl Bar & Restaurant

Chancery Court Hotel, 252 High Holborn, WC1V 7EN (7829 7000/www.pearl-restaurant.com). Holborn tube.
Bar **Open** 11am-11pm Mon-Fri; 6-11pm Sat.
Restaurant **Lunch served** noon-2.30pm Mon-Fri. **Dinner served** 6-10pm Mon-Sat. **Set lunch** £26 2 courses, £29 3 courses. **Set dinner** £52 3 courses, £60 tasting menu (£105 incl wine).
Both **Credit** AmEx, DC, MC, V.
A few yards east of the dreary Holborn crossroads is the Chancery Court Hotel. Its hand-sculpted follies, turrets and general historical loveliness are worth standing back to admire before turning your attention to the other lovely business of eating. Jun Tanaka's modern French food is served in a dauntingly lofty space, which once saw action as the banking hall of the old Pearl Assurance HQ, hence the name and hand-strung crystal beads dripping from every ledge and light fitting. An excellent job has been made of softening the acoustics and machismo of the place by adding warm stretches of walnut veneer and touches of palest pink in the flatware and flowers. Diners now include a decent showing of ladies-who-lunch, along with the suited business folk. Tanaka's background is part Asian, and his approach is only very loosely French: sometimes novel, sometimes classical, sometimes purely British, but always deft, light and seasonal. Main-course partridge – two tender breasts, crisp de-boned legs and ravioli – with chestnut purée, sprouts and mirror-finish jus was a superb example of his art. Vegetarians fare well, and a baked goat's cheese relished the company of baby beetroots, succulent perfumed quince and banana shallots. Spectacular desserts follow the form, as do bread, canapés, many well-cared-for wines by the glass and a new gourmet beer menu. *Babies and children welcome (restaurant): high chairs. Booking advisable. Disabled: toilet. Entertainment: pianist 7.30pm Wed-Sat.* **Map 10 M5.**

Knightsbridge

Boxwood Café

The Berkeley, Wilton Place, SW1X 7RL (7235 1010/www.gordonramsay.com). Hyde Park Corner or Knightsbridge tube. **Lunch served** noon-3pm Mon-Fri; noon-4pm Sat, Sun. **Dinner served** 6pm-12.45am Mon-Fri; 6-10.45pm Sat, Sun. **Main courses** £10.50-£28. **Set lunch** £28 3 courses. **Set meal** £55 tasting menu. **Credit** AmEx, MC, V.
At Boxwood Café they aim for a relaxed alternative to the buttoned-up formality of other hotel dining rooms. Yet despite this, it's still remarkably easy to spend £130 on a meal for two here. Still it attracts many with its approachable menu of ponced-up favourites, such as the signature veal and foie gras burger, and tagliolini with langoustine. Our waiter provided a commentary on every item we ordered before writing it down ('the ceviche contains raw salmon, madam'), then dishes were brought so swiftly it threatened to detract from our enjoyment of the comfortable, silvery-walled split-level room. Smoked salmon and sevruga caviar croque-monsieur was fine but its side salad was low on the promised walnuts and featured cardboard-like apple. Better was the lamb – braised neck and roasted saddle – though the spoonful of girolle and white bean 'cassoulet' was mean. Vegetarians are well catered for and other diners who want extra

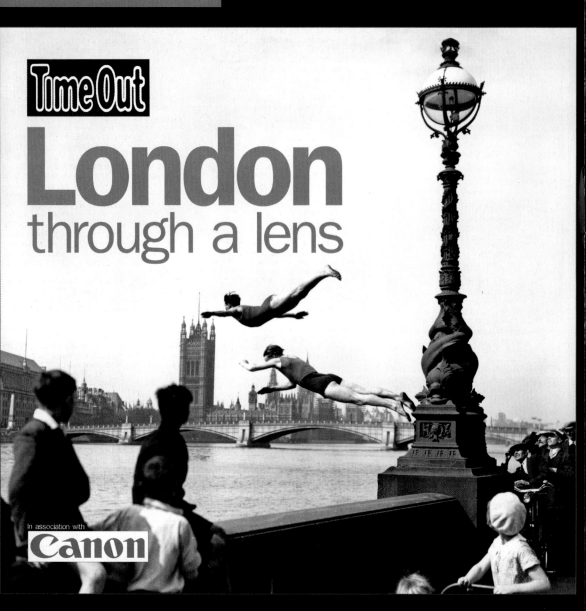

TimeOut

London
through a lens

In association with
Canon

LONDON THROUGH A LENS

The 'London Through a Lens' book brings together a stirring selection of rare and previously unseen images capturing the cultural, social and political history of the capital, all chosen from Getty Images' prestigious archive.

veg will find a choice of three or four sides. A very good dark chocolate fondant came with rock-solid 'iced' almond milk that really should have been churned into ice-cream. The fun of having hot fresh doughnuts with coffee milkshake for pudding was tempered by their blandness – we longed for a hint of cinnamon in the sugar coating. Wines start at £20 a bottle: it was worth paying extra for the smooth bliss of our Argentinian malbec at £28.

Babies and children welcome: children's menu; high chairs. Booking essential. Disabled: toilet (in hotel). Dress: smart casual. Separate room for parties, seats 16. **Map 9 G9.**

The Capital

22-24 Basil Street, SW3 1AT (7589 5171/7591 1202/www.capitalhotel.co.uk). Knightsbridge tube.
Bar **Open** noon-1am, **tea served** 3-5.30pm daily.
Set tea £18.50, £34.50 incl glass of champagne.
Restaurant **Breakfast served** 7-10.30am Mon-Sat; 7.30-10.30am Sun. **Lunch served** noon-2.30pm daily. **Dinner served** 6.45-11pm Mon-Sat; 6.45-10.30pm Sun. **Set breakfast** £14, £18.50. **Set lunch** £29.50 3 courses, £48 tasting menu. **Set dinner** £58 3 courses, £70 tasting menu.
Both **Credit** AmEx, DC, MC, V.
This discreet dining room has only 12-or-so tables, with shiny blue velour chairs, delicate chandeliers, and walls a modern blond take on wood panelling. Were it not for the diverse custom, from bright young things to doddery retirees, the Capital would feel like a secret club; what unites diners is an appreciation of Eric Chavot's carefully crafted cooking. The wine list is predominately French and features three bottles (among them a pleasing rosé) from the hotel's own Levin winery in the Loire. Starting prices are high, which takes the shine off the value of the three-course set menus at lunch and dinner (replete with amuse-this and petit-that). When money's no object, opt for the five-course tasting menu with matching wines. Meats are superb, as shown in our main courses of silky pepper-crusted venison, and pork assiette, though the vegetable content of each dish was low. The pork's partnering pot of creamed cabbage was over-rich in context, but a clear-tasting granny smith sauce brightened plate and palate. We were delighted with an amuse-bouche of lightly curried lentil velouté with tiny beef meatball – not so thrilled that it clashed with our chosen first course of chestnut velouté and foie gras tortellini. A kitchen of this standard should not make such basic menu-planning slips. Deep-fried soft-shell crab gave a well-judged umami-flavour kick to treacle-cured salmon served with a tightly packed summer roll. Desserts, including pear caramel moelleux, were fine, but outshone by the generously proffered petits fours and creamy ganache chocolates. Problems of a slow kitchen were highlighted by one party complaining they would have to leave or would miss a concert nearby. Otherwise, service is efficient and gracious and a meal here is always a treat.
Booking advisable; essential weekends. Children over 12 years admitted. Dress: smart casual. Restaurant available for hire. Separate rooms for parties, seating 10, 12 and 24. **Map 8 F9.**

Foliage

Mandarin Oriental Hyde Park Hotel, 66 Knightsbridge, SW1X 7LA (7201 3723/ www.mandarinoriental.com). Knightsbridge tube.
Lunch served noon-2.30pm, **dinner served** 7-10.30pm Mon-Sat; 7-10pm Sun. **Set lunch** £29 4 courses (£34 incl wine). **Set dinner** £60 4 courses, £75 tasting menu. **Credit** AmEx, DC, MC, V.
Building developments on a grand scale abutting the Mandarin Oriental partly obscured the view of Hyde Park from the aptly named Foliage restaurant for months. By the time you read this, however, the vista will be restored and a terrace added, from which you can sup both view and food. Deft service and refined cooking are still the order of the day, and Chris Staines's innovative, ingredients-focused menu continues to delight. As well as the regular à la carte arrangement, a tasting menu is split into five pick-and-mix style sections.

Within these, dishes are described merely as a brief list of ingredients; for example, our cheese plate was simply listed as stilton / poached pear / honey jelly. Thus the general drift of the dish is readily understood, but the bells and whistles are a delicious bonus – in this instance caramelised walnuts, port reduction and wafer-thin walnut bread. Two further courses demonstrated the kitchen's versatility. Slow-cooked salmon with brown shrimps and horseradish foam was a warm, soft spoonful of comfort. A twist on comparable ingredients from Asia produced a dish of complete contrast; raw tuna on crab, garnished with wasabi ice-cream and tobiko (crunchy flying fish roe) was a triumph of cool flavours and textures.
Babies and children welcome: high chairs. Booking advisable. Disabled: toilet. Dress: smart casual. **Map 8 F9.**

Marcus Wareing at the Berkeley

The Berkeley, Wilton Place, SW1X 7RL (7235 1200/www.the-berkeley.co.uk). Hyde Park Corner or Knightsbridge tube. **Lunch served** noon-2.30pm Mon-Fri. **Dinner served** 6-10.45pm Mon-Sat. **Set lunch** £35 3 courses. **Set dinner** £75 3 courses, **Set meal** £90 tasting menu.
Credit AmEx, DC, MC, V.
Although he has split from the Gordon Ramsay group, Marcus Wareing is continuing to run his own restaurant (formerly called Pétrus) in the Berkeley hotel. The spacious dining room, with its plush claret velvet wall coverings and soft leather, has an air of sophisticated bonhomie. Wareing's menus continually evolve and are given a modern edge with combinations such as scallops and cod confit with cauliflower, macadamia nuts, fourme d'ambert and white chocolate. We chose from the lunch menu which, although more expensive than last year, at £35 still represents good value. Cornish crab arrived with a mirepoix of marinated tuna, celery, apple and avocado. Sticky duck bun, blood orange and toasted cashews created a wonderful juxtaposition of textures to foie gras and sauternes mousse. Next up, a spectacularly good pork belly, which had been slow-cooked then quickly glazed, adding watercress, lemon and almonds for extra dimension. A rump of perfectly roasted Cornish lamb came with braised baby artichokes and asparagus, finished with a hint of fennel pollen. Desserts are especially good. The friable pastry of baked egg custard tart was a blithe companion for the ambrosial filling. Apricot tarte tatin displayed the full spectrum of sweetness and tartness. There are many pleasurable inclusions to meals here – an amuse-bouche of roasted tomato soup with basil crème fraîche; sauternes jelly with apple granita and vanilla cream at the pre-dessert stage; a delectable bon bon trolley. Restraint is needed with the serious and expensive wine list, which is an oenophile's treasure trove with prestige labels from leading producers.
Babies and children welcome: high chairs. Booking essential. Dress: smart; jacket preferred. Separate room for parties, seats 16. Vegetarian menu. **Map 9 G9.**

Mu

The Millennium Knightsbridge, 16-17 Sloane Street, SW1X 9NU (7201 6330/www.millennium hotels.com). Knightsbridge tube. **Lunch served** noon-2.30pm, **dinner served** 6.30-10.30pm Mon-Sat. **Main courses** £18-£26. **Set lunch** £18 2 courses, £22.50 3 courses. **Set dinner** £34.50 3 courses, £50 tasting menu (£100 incl wine). **Credit** AmEx, DC, MC, V.
Mu has all the charm of a conference dining hall, and its first-floor hotel location and dated maroon colour scheme don't help much either. Executive chef Paul Knight recently shifted the kitchen's emphasis from fusion flavours to classic European combinations, with mixed results. Our first course was a throwback to the 1970s; fussy twists of smoked salmon slices doused in dill dressing were accompanied by numerous orange segments and served with a dollop of herby fromage blanc: too many clashing flavours. Chestnut ravioli also missed the mark, with a dense filling and billowing

cloud of basil foam on top. The kitchen team is gung-ho with all things frothy, and the same odd-tasting foam was tipped into a martini glass on top of sautéed mushrooms as part of our amuse-bouche – not a good idea. Main courses were more satisfying, and a superbly roasted chicken breast scored marks for simplicity and succulence. Equally delectable was the calf's liver, seared to perfect pinkness and an excellent match with buttery mashed potato and sweetly caramelised onions. The menu needs to be more accurate with descriptions; neither of our main courses matched expectations, with alternative vegetables substituted without notice or apology. Puddings ranged from drearily dry sticky toffee pudding to a deliciously tangy lemon tartlet encased in thin, crisp pastry: a triumph for the pâtisserie section. Our sulky waitress became increasingly argumentative as the evening progressed. On the positive side, the wine list is extensive and includes fairly priced house recommendations. A noisy bar on the ground floor is popular with business groups. Blustery banter gets funnelled upward into the restaurant after-hours. Mu needs to shake off its coffee-shop appearance, update the menu, and address its service team.
Babies and children welcome: high chairs. Booking advisable. Disabled: lift; toilet. Restaurant available for hire. Separate rooms for parties, seating 8. Wireless internet (£8/hr). **Map 8 F9.**

One-0-One

101 William Street, SW1X 7RN (7290 7101/ www.oneonerestaurant.com). Knightsbridge tube. **Lunch served** noon-2.30pm, **dinner served** 7-10.30pm daily. **Main courses** £13-£15. **Set lunch** £25 3 courses. **Set dinner** £48 5 courses, £79 tasting menu. **Credit** AmEx, DC, MC, V.
You might not twig that this beautifully designed restaurant was inspired by an oyster shell, though the bar's mother-of-pearl-style counter is a clue. The relaxing dining room, shielded from the bustle outside, displays muted sea colours; the oceanic theme extends to seaweed-flavoured butter offered with bread (rather nice, we decided). Chef Pascal Proyart hails from Brittany and makes a feature of Cancale oysters, but also highlights Norwegian seafood, particularly king crab, salmon, scallops, halibut and the seasonal cod, skrei. There are Iberian touches too, such as joselito ham, chorizo and cooking à la planche. The carte (there are also business lunch and 'petits plats' sharing options) is divided into categories such as 'Low tide and wonderful discovery', and 'Delicacies from the shore and beyond'. Combining meat and fish is a Proyart signature: witness the Brittany lobster with a veal sweetbread glazed with spiced honey, saffron carrot compote, vanilla emulsion and citrus. Presentation is accomplished; squid ink pasta arrived as a broad sheet folded to resemble seaweed rising from the sea floor. The wine list starts at £22 and offers a varied international choice including several rieslings. Come dessert there's a sense that Proyart has an espuma machine and is determined to use it. A disappointingly jokey lemon meringue pie combined a scoop each of lemon sorbet and soft canary-yellow meringue, and garnished them with a thin shard of pastry – the best bit was the strip of traditional lemon filling mix. Service expertly blends friendliness with professionalism.
Babies and children welcome: high chairs. Booking advisable Thur-Sun. Disabled: toilet. Dress: smart casual. **Map 8 F9.**

Marble Arch

Rhodes W1

The Cumberland, Great Cumberland Place, W1A 4RF (7616 5930/www.rhodesw1.com). Marble Arch tube.
Bar **Open** 6.30am-midnight daily.
Brasserie **Breakfast served** 6.30-10am Mon-Fri; 7-10.30am Sat, Sun. **Lunch served** noon-2.30pm, **dinner served** 6-10.30pm daily.
Restaurant **Lunch served** noon-2.30pm Tue-Fri. **Dinner served** 7-10.30pm Tue-Sat. **Set lunch** £28 2 courses, £32 3 courses. **Set meal** £52 2 courses, £60 3 courses.
All **Credit** AmEx, MC, V.

RESTAURANTS

An enormous black Fort Knox of a door forbiddingly heaves ajar, allowing entry to Rhodes W1 from the street, unless you choose to go through the Cumberland hotel's main entrance. Inside, a greeter and skinny hallway meet you, and from there it's through to a smallish, windowless den beautifully designed by Kelly Hoppen in her signature black and taupe colours, brought to glittering life by contemporary chandeliers (dripping thousands of crystals), pearlised walls and crisp white linen. Menus sparkle too, dotted with gutsy French, Italian and British specialities such as frogs' legs boudin, smoked eel soup – which was fabulous, flavour-packed and served with steaming hot morsels of deep-fried eel – an amazing cheese trolley and perfectly presented desserts. However, the 30% price hike is not so welcome; a three-course dinner is now £60, and there are £7-£10 supplements on dishes such as beef, veal and cheese. Nonetheless, foie gras terrine with roasted pigeon breast, unctuous date coulis and toasted brioche was faultlessly lovely and generously proportioned. Halibut with crab tortellini, buttered leeks and bacon was again generous and finely cooked, although dominated by its shellfish broth. Saddle of Welsh lamb consisted of just three small roundels, albeit sumptuously flavoured and served with ideally crisp-on-the-outside, soft-in-the-middle goat's cheese gnocchi and caramelised sweetbreads. The international wine list of master sommelier Yves Desmaris offers 250 bins. Though there was no sign of the celebrated Gary Rhodes on our visit, his restaurant remains one to relish.
Babies and children admitted. Booking advisable. Disabled: toilet. Dress: smart casual. **Map 9 G6.**

Marylebone

★ Texture NEW

34 Portman Street, W1H 7BY (7224 0028/ www.texture-restaurant.co.uk). Marble Arch tube. Bar **Open/snacks served** noon-midnight Tue-Sat.
Restaurant **Lunch served** noon-2.30pm, **dinner served** 6.30-11pm Tue-Sat. **Main courses** £21.50-£29.50. **Set lunch** £18.50 2 courses.
Set meal £59 tasting menu.
Both **Credit** AmEx, MC, V.
Texture's relaxed, modern design with comfortable brown leather and plush gold velvet seating sits harmoniously in a grand old room with original plasterwork. At front is a champagne bar that combines the fun of fizz with the seriousness of discernment – co-owner Xavier Rousset is a highly regarded sommelier. Like business partner chef Agnar Sverisson, his CV includes Raymond Blanc's Le Manoir, but here you don't have to pay top whack to enjoy a superb meal. At £18.50 for two courses, the set lunch is the best value on these pages. Also tempting at £49 was the four-course Icelandic menu, a tribute to Sverisson's background, featuring lamb from Skagafjördur in northern Iceland. But first comes London's most intriguing range of nibbles: a long, crisp-like shard of fish skin, mousse-like wasabi dip and a hearty yet vibrant combination of barley, herbs, lemon and yoghurt. Sourdough breads were offered to dunk into lush tapenade or olive oil, then appeared a little glass of pea mousse and mint granita: delightful. Showing world class, Sverisson confidently combined Scandinavia, the tropics and the Mediterranean in a main course of succulent roast Cornish skate with barley risotto, passion-fruit sauce, artichokes and almonds. Lending a personal touch, Rousset recommended a bold pinot gris from Ortago, New Zealand to complement the meal. Dessert of skyr (a dense yoghurt-like cheese) with iced strawberry compote, granita, juice and olive oil was as refreshing as glacier water, the simple list of ingredients belying its intense flavours: stunning. Our only criticisms concern the repetition of flavours, and the (rare) unnecessary ingredient. Seaweed and cardamom flavoured truffles, and coffee and anise macaroons, showed the kitchen's determination to end on a high note. Business dining formed most custom on our visit, but Texture will appeal to anyone looking for light, healthy gourmet cooking.
Babies and children admitted. Booking essential. Vegetarian menu. **Map 9 G6.**

Mayfair

Alain Ducasse at the Dorchester NEW

The Dorchester, 53 Park Lane, W1K 1QA (7629 8866/www.alainducasse-dorchester.com). Hyde Park Corner tube. **Lunch served** noon-2pm Tue-Fri. **Dinner served** 6.30-10pm Tue-Sat. **Set lunch** £35 3 courses.
Set dinner £75 3 courses, £95 4 courses.
Set meal £115 tasting menu. **Credit** AmEx, DC, MC, V.
Alain Ducasse runs a global empire but has only just opened a London restaurant bearing his own name. Surprisingly, he has chosen a subdued space to showcase his culinary ambitions: a contemporary dining room decorated in a beige schema, with wooden panelling and stylish leather chairs. At the centre, a private room cloaked in voile looks odd

during the day, but the embedded fibre optics provide a sparkling focal point at night. Like everything here, entry to this room comes at a hefty price. The main menu starts at £75, the tasting menu is £115, although the lunch menu costs £35. This menu isn't meant to be challenging, as indicated by classics like duck à la orange. Excellent breads were followed by a superb royale of broccoli paired with crunchy radish and black olives. For the first course, gently simmered duck foie gras played wonderfully against tangy mango and was elevated by a dolce-forte (Italian-style sweet and pungent) sauce. Supple Scottish langoustines were rapidly roasted and served with a primavera vegetable garnish. Flavours are clearly pronounced but never too assertive; the technical skill is unquestionable. However, the kitchen tends to be conservative, and cooking lacks individuality given the prices. The best is left to last; Ducasse's desserts could grace any top table. Pink grapefruit soufflé with grapefruit sorbet, and the rum baba, shouldn't be missed. We found the sycophantic service hard to fault, but the wine list, tightly focused on France, is fearsomely expensive; prices start at £25, with limited choice under £100. *Booking advisable. Children over 10 years admitted. Disabled: toilet (in hotel). Dress: smart casual. Separate rooms for parties, seating 10-24.* **Map 9 G7**.

Galvin at Windows

28th floor, The London Hilton, Park Lane, W1K 1BE (7208 4021/www.galvinatwindows. com). Green Park or Hyde Park Corner tube. **Breakfast served** 7-10am Tue-Fri; 7-10.30am Sat, Sun. **Lunch served** noon-3pm Mon-Fri; noon-4pm Sun. **Dinner served** 6-11pm Mon-Fri; 5-11pm Sat. **Set lunch** £29 3 courses

Texture

(£45 incl half bottle of wine, mineral water, coffee). **Set dinner** £58 3 courses. **Set meal** £75 tasting menu. **Credit** AmEx, DC, MC, V. Although the decor here is an appreciably elegant palate of pale pistachio leather, milky walls and glossy dark wood, most diners just ogle the mesmerising views from the Hilton's 28th floor. Galvin and a slick bar have the entire floor to themselves, away from the more pedestrian hotel comings and goings. With all London spread out like a laden table below and the wind whipping against the floor-to-ceiling glass, this is one of the most sensorially exciting places to eat in the capital. And there's good food too. The set lunch menu has shifted up a gear since our last visit, the simpler bistro-fare eschewed in favour of a more classical haute-cuisine approach typical of the evening à la carte and gourmand tasting menus. Expect the likes of poché-rôti Anjou pigeon and pommes écrasées, plus a host of other extravagantly labelled but still-delicious dishes such as slow-cooked mackerel with smoked eel beignets and hollandaise, and wild forest mushroom risotto with aged parmesan. Prices are up too, with the advertised £29 three-course lunch in reality £45 with water, house wine and coffee included (£50 with service). *Babies and children welcome: high chairs. Booking advisable. Disabled: lift; toilet (in hotel). Dress: smart casual.* **Map 9 G8**.

Le Gavroche ⑩⓪

43 Upper Brook Street, W1K 7QR (7408 0881/ www.le-gavroche.co.uk). Marble Arch tube. **Lunch served** noon-2pm Mon-Fri. **Dinner served** 6.30-11pm Mon-Sat. **Main courses** £27-£60. **Set lunch** £48 3 courses incl half bottle of wine, mineral water, coffee. **Set dinner** £95 tasting menu (£150 incl wine). **Credit** AmEx, DC, MC, V.
Named after the street urchin from *Les Misérables*, the 42-year-old Le Gavroche made its founders, the Roux Brothers, internationally famous. Today it lies in the hands of chef-patron Michel Roux Jr, and head chef Rachel Humphrey who joined the establishment as an apprentice in 1996. Despite such modern ideas as women in the kitchen, the decor and service are reassuringly traditional. A first-floor bar with red leather and tartan seating is lined with red moire fabric walls; the basement restaurant is clad in dark green, with Picasso drawings among the unobtrusive modern art. Waiters and porters go about their much-practised business with urgent confidence, announcing dishes with a flourish of silver domes. Sommeliers happily talk customers through possibilities from the wine tome which, though starting under £20, naturally includes some mind-boggling extravagances. The nine-course menu exceptionnel can be ordered with or without matching wines; its most tempting dishes also appear on the lengthy à la carte. The classic soufflé suissesse that helped make the restaurant so famous when it first opened on Lower Sloane Street in 1967 (the dish then cost 19 shillings and served two) doesn't disappoint, floating pertly on its double-cream sauce. More contemporary was a dish of very thinly sliced braised octopus, crowned with a deep-fried soft-shell crab and surrounded by a chopped tomato and coriander salad; its lime and oil dressing prompted us to pick up the sauce spoon to catch every last drop. Baked veal sweetbread came with a deliciously sticky sauce of the teensiest diced apple and calvados. Desserts can hit the price of main courses, but we'd no regrets about ordering the sugar rush of hot passion-fruit soufflé with white chocolate ice-cream. This is one school boy for which it's worth dressing up and splashing out. *Babies and children admitted. Booking essential. Dress: jacket; no jeans or trainers. Restaurant available for hire.* **Map 9 G7**.

★ Gordon Ramsay at Claridge's

Claridge's, 55 Brook Street, W1K 4HR (7499 0099/www.gordonramsay.com). Bond Street tube. **Lunch served** noon-2.45pm Mon-Fri; noon-3pm Sat, Sun. **Dinner served** 5.45-11pm Mon-Sat;

RESTAURANTS

RESTAURANTS

Hibiscus

6-11pm Sun. **Set lunch** £30 3 courses. **Set dinner** £70 3 courses, £80 6 courses. **Credit** AmEx, DC, MC, V.

Set in the stately surrounds of Claridge's hotel, this is one of London's leading culinary attractions, and with good reason. Although Gordon Ramsay is the drawcard, it's his right-hand man Mark Sargeant who is credited with maintaining outstanding quality and excellence in the kitchen. The beautiful interior reflects the building's art deco heritage with gracious restraint; soft warm colours, abundant flower displays, weighty drapes and crisp table-linen set the scene for surprisingly relaxed dining. On a bustling Saturday afternoon every table was filled with diners: romancing couples, celebrating families and well-heeled food lovers. Not once did the service miss a beat – professional, formal and suitably friendly throughout. Of the first courses, we were especially taken with a salad of purple-hued pata negra ham tossed with herby micro leaves (great for bursts of intense flavour). What really scored was the addition of just enough orange segments, dabs of goat's curd, and crunchy hazelnuts to harmonise flavours. Poached salmon fillet had an alluring melt-in-the-mouth texture, and was classically paired with lemon butter sauce. Impeccably cooked guinea fowl breast was another winner; although simply presented, it was complemented by a delicious, indulgent helping of smoked potato purée, and a small ladleful of creamy, thyme-scented sauce. A crisp-skinned fillet of sea trout made a fabulous partner with tender-grained barley and cep risotto, its richness cut with sweet braised red cabbage on the side. Top marks to desserts: splendid passion-fruit crème brûlée sat on a crumbly pistachio biscuit, crowned with darkly inviting chocolate sorbet. It's easy to be daunted by the sizeable wine list, and as the selections don't come cheap, it's worth asking for guidance. This is a world-class restaurant that lives up to its reputation.
Babies and children welcome: high chairs. Booking essential. Disabled: toilet. Dress: smart; jacket preferred; no jeans or trainers. Separate rooms for parties, seating 6, 10, 12 and 24. **Map 9 H6**.

Greenhouse

27A Hay's Mews, W1J 5NY (7499 3331/ www.greenhouserestaurant.co.uk). Green Park tube. **Lunch served** noon-2.30pm Mon-Fri. **Dinner served** 6.45-11pm Mon-Sat. **Set lunch** £25 2 courses, £29 3 courses. **Set meal** £65 3 courses, £65-£80 tasting menu. **Credit** AmEx, DC, MC, V.

We've come to expect great things from the Greenhouse. You'll discover it tucked-away down swish Hay's Mews; the unexpectedly verdant approach between two tall buildings lined with arching bamboos, ferns and gurgling water-features never fails to build anticipation. Inside, a smooth, dark reception and serenely smiling staff bode well. The main restaurant has been refitted in silvery shades of taupe so elegantly restrained as barely to cause a ripple. Service flows with equal tranquillity. Champagne, water, menus and playful appetisers slipped by in a few fluent moves designed not to interrupt conversation, followed by starters from both set lunch and à la carte menus. The former menu is less than half the price of the latter, with no discernible difference in quality or quantity. A 'crispy' (it wasn't) baton of polenta with roasted red pepper was naturally less expensive to produce than the pan-fried foie gras of the à la carte, but both dishes were predictably flavoured and failed to ignite real passion. The rest of the meal followed suit. Slow-cooked paprika-dusted brill was meaty and good, but unexciting; honey-glazed rabbit suffered the same shortcoming; and two mousse-like chocolate millefeuilles were gorgeous but virtually identical, despite different descriptions. Chef Antonin Bonnet was in-house, so this was a disturbing performance from a restaurant on which we (and others) have previously lavished praise.
Babies and children admitted. Booking essential. Dress: smart casual. Separate room for parties, seats 10. Vegetarian menu. **Map 9 H7**.

★ Hélène Darroze at the Connaught NEW (100)

The Connaught, Carlos Place, W1K 2AL (3147 7200/www.the-connaught.co.uk). Bond Street tube. **Lunch served** noon-2.30pm; **dinner served** 6.30-10.15pm Mon-Fri. **Set lunch** £39-£75 3 courses. **Set dinner** £75 3 courses, £95 7 courses. **Credit** AmEx, MC, V.

Despite the Connaught's attempts to get down with the kids in recent years, it has taken the arrival of esteemed French chef Hélène Darroze in the historic dining room to bring real personality, attention to detail and culinary verve. Darroze is a native of Landes, and the flavours of south-west France (Périgord truffles, beaufort cheese, pink garlic, lavender) are well-represented, but there's also a passion for exotic spices with lampong pepper, sichuan peppercorns, galangal and ras el hanout. 'Limited series' dishes and signatures – such as Aquitaine caviar in black jelly with Gillardeau oyster tartare and velouté of fresh haricots maïs from Béarn – are highlighted. The amuse-bouches, inter-course appetisers and chocolates are so many and so memorable, they often eclipse the larger courses. A tiny gazpacho of liquefied almond with garlic was sensational, simpler and more impressive than a risotto laden with chargrilled squid and chorizo topped by a parmesan foam spooned by the waiter. Another main course revealed the same fondness for strong flavours: three perfect cubes of tuna, lightly seared yet juicy and tasting strongly of smoke, served on silver skewers with a mash that was more butter than potato. Desserts were outstanding. Bay-flavoured panna cotta featured a layer of lemon jelly, marinated strawberries and strawberry sorbet. Service was urbane, if over-attentive. The wine list is extravagantly priced; it would be more customer-friendly to increase the number of wines offered by the glass.
Booking essential. Disabled: toilet. Dress: smart; no jeans or trainers. **Map 9 H7**.

★ Hibiscus NEW (100)

2008 RUNNER-UP BEST NEW RESTAURANT
29 Maddox Street, W1S 2PA (7629 2999/ www.hibiscusrestaurant.co.uk). Oxford Circus tube. **Lunch served** noon-2.30pm, **dinner served** 6.30-10pm Mon-Fri. **Set lunch** £25 3 courses; £70 6 courses. **Set dinner** £60 3 courses, £62.50 tasting menu, £75 7 courses. **Credit** AmEx, MC, V.

Having made the move from Ludlow in Shropshire to Mayfair, Claude and Claire Bosi have continued to gain plaudits at their small, intimate venue. The service and food hit their stride right from the start, quickly establishing Hibiscus as one of the most exciting places to eat in the capital. Claude Bosi is a kitchen magician; he plays with texture and flavour in ways that challenge and excite, but stop short of making diners feel they're taking part in a weird science experiment. We experienced a fizzy cucumber and melon concoction as an amuse-bouche, a sharp-tasting lime 'gel' that enlivened an inspired pudding of beurre noisette parfait, and a purée of pea and ginger served with a rosy-pink, crisp-skinned and intensely flavoured piece of Goosnargh duck breast. The menu also lists iced morels, tamarillo powder and seaweed vinaigrette. In general, the chemistry works. Cornish sea bream, stuffed under the skin with finely chopped morels and served with a fricassee of broad beans and whole morels, was given a bitter counterpoint by an intense coffee sauce. Inevitably, not every flavour combination works; we weren't convinced by mixing tiny sharp-sweet wild strawberries with wasabi and honey sauce to go with a starter of mackerel tartare. A meal here doesn't come cheap, but it's bound to be memorable.
Babies and children welcome: children's portions. Booking essential. Disabled: toilet. Separate room for parties, seats 18. Vegetarian menu. **Map 9 J6**.

★ Maze (100)

13-15 Grosvenor Square, W1K 6JP (7107 0000/ www.gordonramsay.com). Bond Street tube. **Lunch served** noon-2.30pm, **dinner served** 6-11pm daily. **Main courses** £16.50-£29.50. **Set lunch** £28.50 4 courses, £42.50 6 courses. **Credit** AmEx, DC, MC, V.

Interview
JASON ATHERTON

Who are you?
Chef-partner of Maze Restaurants (part of the Gordon Ramsay Group), which includes **Maze** (*see left*) and **Maze Grill** (*see p39*), and author of *Maze the Cookbook* (Quadrille).
What's the best thing about running a restaurant in London?
The competition is so hot. It's fierce. You've really got to be on your toes all the time.
What's the worst thing?
Nothing. I love London. I'm not from here, but I consider myself a Londoner. I've worked in Dubai, France and Spain, and unless someone offers me a million pounds a week to live in New York, I'm staying here.
Which are your favourite London restaurants?
My wife is oriental so when we want a relaxed option we go to places like **Yauatcha** (*see p78*) and **Zuma** (*see p194*). For fine dining, I love **Pied à Terre** (*see p136*) and the **Square** (*see p144*). When I'm on a break from work or want some me-time, I go to **Busaba Eathai** (*see p269*) on Bird Street, which is better than the branch on Wardour Street. To drink, it's the Groucho Club.
How green are you?
We make sure we run things efficiently. The waste is recycled, the vegetable oil goes to the right places. We've tried to ban second deliveries except in absolute emergencies, which saves on vans coming into central London. It's very important and everyone's duty to do what they can.
What is missing from London's restaurant scene?
Absolutely nothing, though I do think it's a shame that we only have one three-star Michelin restaurant. I eat in starred restaurants in Paris two or three times each year, and I believe we have restaurants here that are definitely worthy of three stars, but for some reason they are not given them. It's the same with two-star places.

RESTAURANTS

Although part of Gordon Ramsay's stable of restaurants, Maze owes its success to rising star Jason Atherton. Over the past two years he has earned accolades for his line-up of sophisticated morsels, miniature main courses, and awe-inspiring desserts. This is a modern, spacious set-up, furnished in shades of coffee and cream, with a glamorous cocktail bar by the entrance, buff-hued banquettes and groovy coloured glass panels in the dining area. Even though the restaurant is located in embassy heartland, there's nothing stuffy about the atmosphere, the young service team, or the food. The menu takes some negotiating, though; diners can either take their pick from around 30 tapas-style dishes, or opt (as we did) for structured meals. Our lunch was a faultless feast of contrasting, complementary flavours, with occasional forays into the blending of Asian influences with classic European cooking. Beautifully presented slices of yellow-fin tuna provided a rich foil to tart tomato salsa, which worked well with peppery radish salad and black olive purée. Boned, rolled and roasted lamb, sticky with meaty juices, glistened with goodness and admirably partnered a buttery spring onion risotto. Good news continued with the roast pork belly, its fat melding with succulent meat and absorbing caramel-like notes from the richness of Madeira sauce. Head here if mash is your thing, as Maze elevates it to an art form: silken, butter-laden and creamy. Desserts too are top class. Rhubarb and passion-fruit trifle provided a medley of fruity jelly, with vanilla-flecked custard and a flurry of lemonade granité. Seasonal Indian mangoes were transformed into a sublime parfait and served on a sheet of orange and star-anise jelly. The wine list accommodates most budgets and tastes; a friendly, knowledgeable sommelier offers sound advice. *Babies and children welcome: high chairs. Booking advisable. Disabled: toilet. Dress: smart casual. Separate room for parties, seats 10.* **Map 9 G6**.

Sketch: The Lecture Room
9 Conduit Street, W1S 2XZ (7659 4500/ www.sketch.uk.com). Oxford Circus tube. **Lunch served** noon-2.30pm Tue-Fri. **Dinner served** 7-10.30pm Tue-Sat. **Main courses** £21-£52. **Set lunch** £30 2 courses, £35 3 courses. **Set meal** £65-£90 tasting menu. **Credit** AmEx, DC, MC, V.
Theatrical, quirky and fabulously indulgent, the Lecture Room is famed for its stupendous prices and glamorous guests. It occupies the first floor of a Georgian house: high ceilings, mirrors, and sunshine colours combining to celebrate eccentric good taste. There's flamboyance and flights of fancy in the kitchen too and you won't always have to blow the milk money to dine here. At lunchtime, the 'gourmet rapide' menu is a bargain and is served within an hour. On our visit, it featured a procession of miniature morsels made from such curiosities as torrefied sesame seeds, yuzu butter, and agria (a variety of potato, we later discovered). Our favourite, from a spread of four dinky starters, was a tiny portion of creamy cod served with tangy tomato and star anise coulis. We weren't convinced by our soupçon of pumpkin soup (served at room temperature) with its blue potato ice-cream garnish – too weird for its own good. Of the main courses, we loved the roasted sea bream fillet and its citrus-dressed oriental salad with crunchy beansprouts and toasted sesame seeds. Wafer-thin slices of roast lamb didn't quite deliver; the meat wasn't as tender as we'd hoped, and the rice-like pasta accompaniment was short on herby flavour. Pierre Gagnaire's innovative cooking style is commendable and often complex, but it was his simple fresh fruit salad that had us hankering for more. Shredded apple, chunks of exotic fruit, and the chill of floral-scented jelly, were all bathed in heavenly syrup: a fitting finale. Service was a memorable, well-orchestrated, faultless performance. Unsurprisingly, the wine list is weighty – expect to pay big bucks for the price of high living.

Babies and children admitted: high chairs. Booking advisable. Dress: smart casual. Restaurant available for hire. **Map 9 J6**.

The Square
6-10 Bruton Street, W1J 6PU (7495 7100/ www.squarerestaurant.com). Bond Street or Green Park tube. **Lunch served** noon-2.45pm Mon-Fri. **Dinner served** 6.30-10.45pm Mon-Sat; 6.30-9.45pm Sun. **Set lunch** £25 2 courses, £30 3 courses. **Set dinner** £65 3 courses. **Set meal** £90 tasting menu. **Credit** AmEx, DC, MC, V.
Despite gold curtains and mottled gold walls, the Square ain't blingin'; tables are well-spaced and conversation subdued, even from the many American diners. This is one of few haute restaurants to open on Sunday evening, so perhaps it's unsurprising to find it then busy. The three-course menu at £65 includes plenty of add-ons – canapés, amuse-bouches, pre-desserts, spectacular petits fours, superb bread. Wines start at £18 for arneis, a white rarely seen outside Italian restaurants. Many burgundies are included, of course, but the list has a varied choice of German and Austrian wines, and lots served by the glass, including several sherries. The carte is strong on fish and, rather bizarrely, beignets, which chef Phil Howard uses as frequently as his rivals reach for the chervil. A black truffle purée served with halibut was delicious, but the combination was unbalanced; it went better with the wild mushroom cake that sat underneath the gleaming white fish. Another main course, smoked loin of fallow deer, was also swamped, this time by sweet beetroot purée, though the meat and tiny roast root vegetables that also accompanied it were excellent. A promised coconut flavour was lacking from the meringues, but otherwise passion-fruit soufflé with lime ice-cream was an ideal dessert; chocophiles will be delighted with the assiette of bitter, milk and white chocolate served hot, warm and cold. Service from French-accented waiters was slick,

Hotel teas

Afternoon tea at a smart hotel is largely the preserve of visitors to London, but it's a quintessentially English ritual that locals should experience too, at least once. You'll have to dress up, of course, and book well in advance.

The Berkeley

The Bentley
27-33 Harrington Gardens, SW7 4JX (7244 5555/www.thebentley-hotel.com). Gloucester Road tube. **Tea served** 3-6pm daily. **Set tea** £24, £30 incl glass of champagne. **Credit** AmEx, DC, MC, V. *Babies and children admitted. Booking advisable. Dress: smart casual.* **Map 13 C10**.

The Berkeley
Wilton Place, SW1X 7RL (7235 6000/ www.the-berkeley.co.uk). Knightsbridge tube. **Tea served** 2-6pm daily. **Set tea** £34, £42-£49 incl glass of champagne. **Credit** AmEx, DC, MC, V. *Babies and children welcome: high chairs. Booking essential. Disabled: toilet. Dress: smart casual.* **Map 9 G9**.

The Capital
22-24 Basil Street, SW3 1AT (7589 5171/ 7591 1202/www.capitalhotel.co.uk). Knightsbridge tube. **Tea served** 3-5.30pm daily. **Set tea** £18.50, £34.50 incl glass of champagne. **Credit** AmEx, DC, MC, V. *Booking advisable; essential weekends. Children over 12 years admitted. Dress: smart casual.* **Map 8 F9**.

Claridge's
55 Brook Street, W1K 4HA (7409 6307/ www.claridges.co.uk). Bond Street tube.

Tea served 3-5.30pm daily. **Set tea** £31.50; £39.50 incl glass of champagne. **Cover** (if not taking set tea) £3.50. **Credit** AmEx, DC, MC, V. *Babies and children welcome: high chairs. Booking essential. Disabled: toilet. Dress: smart casual. Entertainment: musicians 3-9.30pm daily.* **Map 9 H6**.

The Connaught
16 Carlos Place, W1K 2AL (7499 7070/ www.theconnaught.com). Bond Street or Green Park tube. **Tea served** 2.30-5.30pm daily. **Set tea** £28, £38 incl glass of champagne. **Credit** AmEx, DC, MC, V. *Babies and children welcome: high chairs. Booking essential (Fri-Sun). Disabled: toilet.* **Map 9 H7**.

The Dorchester
53 Park Lane, W1K 1QA (7629 8888/ www.thedorchester.com). Hyde Park Corner tube. **Tea served** 2.30pm, 4.45pm daily.

Set tea £31.50, £40 incl glass of champagne, £46 high tea. **Credit** AmEx, DC, MC, V. *Babies and children welcome: high chairs. Booking essential. Disabled: toilet. Dress: smart casual. Entertainment: pianist 2.30-11pm daily.* **Map 9 G7**.

The Lanesborough
1 Lanesborough Place, Hyde Park Corner, SW1X 7TA (7259 5599/ www.lanesborough.com). Hyde Park Corner tube. **Tea served** 3.45-6pm daily. **Set tea** £31, £39 incl glass of champagne. **Credit** AmEx, DC, MC, V. *Babies and children welcome: high chairs. Booking essential. Disabled: toilet. Dress: smart casual. Entertainment: pianist 3.45-6pm daily.* **Map 9 G8**.

The Ritz
150 Piccadilly, W1J 9BR (7493 8181/ www.theritzhotel.co.uk). Green Park tube. **Tea served** (reserved sittings) 11.30am, 1.30pm, 3.30pm, 5.30pm, 7.30pm daily. **Set tea** £37. **Credit** AmEx, MC, V. *Babies and children welcome: children's menu; high chairs. Disabled: toilet. Booking advisable restaurant; essential afternoon tea. Dress: jacket and tie; no jeans or trainers.* **Map 9 J7**.

The Soho Hotel
4 Richmond Mews, W1D 3DH (7559 3007/ www.firmdale.com). Tottenham Court Road tube. **Tea served** noon-6pm daily. **Set tea** £7.50, £25 incl glass of champagne. **Credit** AmEx, DC, MC, V. *Babies and children welcome: high chairs. Booking advisable. Disabled: toilet. Dress: smart casual.* **Map 17 B3**.

Hélène Darroze at the Connaught. See p143.

professional yet friendly. In all, an accomplished performance from a restaurant rightfully seen as an industry stalwart.

Babies and children admitted. Booking advisable. Disabled: toilet. Dress: smart, no jeans, trainers preferred. Restaurant available for hire. Separate room for parties, seats 18. **Map 9 H7**.

Piccadilly

The Ritz

150 Piccadilly, W1J 9BR (7493 8181/ www.theritzhotel.co.uk). Green Park tube.
Bar **Open** 11.30am-midnight Mon-Sat; noon-11pm Sun.
Restaurant **Breakfast served** 7-10am Mon-Sat; 8-10am Sun. **Lunch served** 12.30-2.30pm daily. **Tea served** (reserved sittings) 11.30am, 1.30pm, 3.30pm, 5.30pm, 7.30pm daily. **Dinner served** 6-10pm Mon-Sat; 7-10pm Sun. **Main courses** £25-£40. **Set lunch** £36 3 courses. **Set tea** £37. **Set dinner** (6-7pm, 10-10.30pm) £45 3 courses; (Mon-Thur, Sun) £65 4 courses; (Fri, Sat) £85 4 courses.
Both **Credit** AmEx, MC, V.
In contrast to the art deco embellishments of the Ritz's Rivoli Bar (the hotel façade was modelled on Paris's Rue de Rivoli), the restaurant looks like one

of the more overblown rooms in the Palace of Versailles: at least four types of marble for the walls and columns, floral carpets, frescoes and a trompe l'oeil sky. Yet for all the French touches, the kitchen takes its sourcing of British produce seriously and is one of the few restaurants certified by the Soil Association. The dining room attracts a diverse crowd treating themselves to a meal at what is (thanks to Irving Berlin) arguably the most famous hotel in the world. Expect cameras to come out, and the musical quartet to burst into 'Happy Birthday', adding to the sense of fun. The various menus include a list of 'Ritz traditions' (double chicken consommé, dover sole meunière) and dishes from the rotisserie (duck with grelot onions). The wine list starts high at £42, but offers several bottles at that price point; we opted for the house chablis ('Why not?' said the sommelier. 'I'm crazy about it.') It went well with celeriac panna cotta piled in a martini glass with duck confit and bright red madeira jelly. Roast pigeon with date purée, braised lettuce and tiny beetroot was a clever flavour combination. For dessert, a fresh, tart apple delice easily outclassed the bland chocolate parfait.
Babies and children welcome: children's menu; high chairs. Disabled: toilet. Booking advisable restaurant; essential afternoon tea. Dress:

jacket and tie; no jeans or trainers. Entertainment: dinner dance Fri, Sat (restaurant); pianist daily. Separate rooms for parties, seating 22 and 55. Tables outdoors (8, terrace). **Map 9 J7**.

St James's

L'Oranger

5 St James's Street, SW1A 1EF (7839 3774/ www.loranger.co.uk). Green Park tube. **Lunch served** noon-2.30pm Mon-Fri. **Dinner served** 6.30-10.30pm Mon-Sat. **Main courses** £26-£28. **Set lunch** £28 2 courses, £34 3 courses. **Set dinner** £45 3 courses, £75 tasting menu. **Credit** AmEx, DC, MC, V.
An olde worlde shop frontage on St James's hints at the romantic delights within. Though a private dining area in the basement points to times past, the spacious ground-floor restaurant is a seamless blend of classic style and lustrous, modern allure. A quirky etched-glass window conceals the kitchen of chef Laurent Michel. His à la carte features all the hallmarks of classic French fare – truffles and girolles, blue and goat's cheeses, lobster and dover sole – but is not set in aspic thanks to keen exploration of the spice box and

inventive combinations such as foie gras with green-apple granita. We chose from the business lunch menu, its generous portions rightfully earning it a title more impressive than set lunch. There were slip-ups: confusion over the wine ordered; an amuse-bouche of tepid soup; and tiny roast chicken wings atop mascarpone risotto that were fridge-cold near the bone (though otherwise the dish was superb). Evoking sophisticated summer holidays around Nice, stalk of bamboo cut a stylish swathe through a main course kebab of grilled tuna and Mediterranean vegetables, while another main of à point pork chop with a terracotta side dish of artichoke-laden gratin was better suited to the Mistral-like winds outside. Pick of the puds was a pretty diced apple millefeuille with cider jus and rosemary and caramel ice-cream. We finished with excellent coffee, mint tea and tiny friands. Sweet staff are attentive and more welcoming than usually found across the Channel. *Babies and children admitted. Booking essential. Dress: smart casual; no trainers. Separate rooms for parties, seating 15 and 36. Tables outdoors (6, courtyard).* **Map 9 J8**.

South Kensington

Ambassade de l'Ile NEW

117-119 Old Brompton Road, SW7 3RN (7373 7774/www.ambassadedelile.com). Gloucester Road or South Kensington tube. **Lunch served** noon-2pm; **dinner served** 7pm-10.30pm Mon-Sat. **Main courses** £28-£38. **Set lunch** £30 3 courses. **Set meal** £65 5 courses, £90 7 courses. **Credit** AmEx, MC, V.
A £2.2 million revamp has failed to make chic this one-time library (former site of Lundum's). Wall-to-wall shag-pile carpet, buttoned white upholstery and mirrored walls give it an unfortunate disco vibe at odds with the sombre quiet often found in aspiring temples of gastronomy. Chef Jean-Christophe Ansanay-Alex, former personal chef to Christina Onassis, has a highly regarded restaurant called l'Auberge de l'Ile just outside Lyon and had been looking for a London outpost for some time; he apparently fell in love with this building, conveniently situated at the heart of London's French expat community. The two-floor premises feature both a chef's table for six and a host's table for eight to 12. It offers many of the dishes that helped earn the mothership two Michelin stars. Prices start at £30 for the three-course set lunch and rise to £90 per head for a seven-course affair. The carte is not outlandishly expensive for the sector and includes a few dishes for sharing (stuffed pigeon with mild spices, turnips and sweet and sour tomatoes, say). We found much to like, from an intensely flavoured morel cappuccino soup to rosemary-flavoured fried apricots with a sablé biscuit. While there are modern touches (line-caught cod with marmalade ravioli and almond milk), an abundance of foie gras, frogs' legs, sweetbreads and classic sauces will keep traditionalists happy. The wine list features over 500 bins, some stupendously priced, but the house wine costs £22.
Babies and children admitted. Booking advisable. Disabled: toilet. Separate room for parties, seats 12. **Map 14 D11**.

★ Tom Aikens

43 Elystan Street, SW3 3NT (7584 2003/www.tomaikens.co.uk). South Kensington tube. **Lunch served** noon-2.15pm, **dinner served** 6.45-10.45pm Mon-Fri. **Set lunch** £29 3 courses incl coffee. **Set meal** £65 3 courses, £80-£100 tasting menu. **Credit** AmEx, MC, V.
Now boasting a luxe brasserie (*see p61*), fish and chip shop (*see p316*) and sizeable concession in Selfridges food hall, Tom Aikens' empire and rather handsome profile is expanding quickly. While he hasn't cornered the market à la Gordon Ramsay Holdings, he's certainly marked out this villagey corner of SW3 as his turf. Fortunately the flagship fine-dining restaurant, with its dark brown pinstripe carpets, black leather and wood chairs and pale walls, is not as Chelseaesque as you might expect, attracting an intelligent food-loving crowd as well as the grown-up ladies who take

luncheon. From a batch of four menus, the £29 set lunch is a wise choice, offering much of the razzmatazz yet less of the faff of pricier options. Portion sizes are tightly controlled, especially with the mains, but flavours are so succinct and presentation so lush that this barely registers. In any case you'll want belly room to enjoy the bounteous madeleines, chocolates, inventive tuiles and myriad creamy, spicy, fruity things that come with coffee, and are all included in the set menu. For starters, a balloon glass of pea velouté was generously punctuated with fresh morels and the meat of frogs' legs – delicious, if a little fiddly to scoop out. Green asparagus with chervil and asparagus mousses, truffle and lemon emulsion was a celebration of spring on a smart, curvaceous plate. Silky beetroot gratin provided an elegant, harmonious pedestal for tender venison loin with hazelnut crumb crust. It's not all spot-on: langoustine risotto overpowered our poached brill, and its pinky-grey foam sauce looked like old bathwater. Cold, flabby pineapple ravioli was just a bad idea, though the coconut and cream elements of the dessert were delectable. On balance, Tom Aikens deserves its status as one of the capital's top foodie destinations.
Booking essential. Children over 7 years admitted. Disabled: toilet. Dress: smart; no jeans. Separate room for parties, seats 10. **Map 14 E11**.

Strand

12 Temple Place NEW

12 Temple Place, WC2R 2PR (7300 1700/www.swissotel.com). Temple tube. **Lunch served** noon-2.30pm Mon-Fri. **Dinner served** 5.45-10.30pm Mon-Sat. **Main courses** £17-£21. **Set lunch** £19.75 2 courses, £23.75 3 courses. **Set meal** £54 5 courses. **Credit** AmEx, DC, MC, V.
We were fans of Jaan, the fusion restaurant at this high-end business hotel, but chef Simon Duff has moved on and the site has been refurbished and relaunched with a British haute cuisine theme under executive chef Brian Spark. The decor retains a few oriental touches, such as the ornate wooden door frame, but dark, bare tables and grey fabric seating bring a relaxed businesslike air softened by pretty patterned teapots used as vases. Outside, the smart courtyard dining area is one of London's best-kept secrets. We visited soon after the new menu was introduced and found performance patchy but promising. Intrigues such as coltsfoot, borage and spring lovage were woven through the dishes, and in common with the restaurant's more rustic British competitors, names such as Denham Estate venison and Elwy lamb are specified. Turnip and bay leaf tortellini seemed the essential starter, but the pasta parcels were bland, so the accompanying wild mushrooms and herb salad dominated. However, a generous bowl of watercress soup with truffled crème fraîche couldn't be faulted. Pork tenderloin roll was let down by a too-salty stack of potato and black pudding, yet we enjoyed sea trout with crisp golden skin, dill tagliatelle and a slightly bitter cumin and cauliflower purée. No complaints about the bountiful cheeseboard: five large pieces including smoked gubbeen, devon blue and flower marie, plus fig and almond roll and plenty of walnuts and crackers. The dessert course offers determined twists on classics: beetroot panna cotta; caramelised pear and tarragon rice pudding; earl grey chocolate fondant with marmalade ice-cream. Buttoned-up service was formal yet unpretentious, but frustratingly slow: lunch took two hours. With a little more finesse, 12 Temple Place could prove a breath of fresh country air in the City.
Babies and children welcome: children's menu; high chairs. Disabled: toilet. Dress: smart casual. Separate room for parties, seats 160. Tables outdoors (40, garden). **Map 10 M7**.

South West
Chelsea

Aubergine

11 Park Walk, SW10 0AJ (7352 3449/www.auberginerestaurant.co.uk). Bus 14, 345,

414. **Lunch served** noon-2.15pm Mon-Fri. **Dinner served** 7-11pm Mon-Sat. **Set lunch** £29 3 courses (£34 incl half bottle of wine). **Set dinner** £64 3 courses, £77 tasting menu (£132 incl wine). **Credit** AmEx, DC, MC, V.
Comfortable sofas, plump cushions and sumptuous flower arrangements make for an impressive entrance at this establishment. Although decor in the main dining area isn't quite as distinctive, the dimmed lighting and eye-catching skylight help produce a romantic setting. Aubergine's serious (and seriously expensive) selection of Old and New World wines reads like an encyclopedia. Prices on the carte are steep too, with the restaurant attracting conservatively dressed Chelsea residents and corporate diners. The set lunch menu promises better value. William Drabble has run kitchen affairs for more than a decade, earning an enviable reputation for his classic French cooking and clever use of seasonal British produce. Vegetarians have a dearth of choice; Drabble is big on meat and fish. A miniature puff-pastry pie was a treat, its beautifully glazed crust yielding a juicy crab-meat filling flecked with sweetened carrot shreds and summery tarragon – our favourite dish of the meal. Fried red mullet fillet and braised jerusalem artichokes would have made a marvellous marriage, were they not so very salty. To follow, golden-hued roast guinea fowl brought the food back on track; especially tasty were the chopped chanterelle mushrooms simmered in cream: a lovely complement to the tender meat. In a meal of hits and misses, sautéed halibut fillet, although perfectly cooked, was paired with a bland cream sauce. Desserts didn't tickle our fancy either. A starchy hot clementine soufflé was further let down by a thick skin over its accompanying chocolate sauce. Slick and attentive service takes the edge off any inconsistencies in the kitchen.
Children over 5 years admitted. Booking advisable; essential weekends. Dress: smart casual. **Map 14 D12**.

Gordon Ramsay

68 Royal Hospital Road, SW3 4HP (7352 4441/www.gordonramsay.com). Sloane Square tube. **Lunch served** noon-2.30pm, **dinner served** 6.30-11pm Mon-Fri. **Set lunch** £45 3 courses. **Set meal** £90 3 courses, £120 tasting menu. **Credit** AmEx, DC, MC, V.
Left to run the most high-profile haute cuisine restaurant in the country, staff handle their roles as ambassadors for fine dining with admirable aplomb. They make no secret of the fact that Gordon Ramsay is not here, talking openly about what head chef Clare Smyth has devised for customers' delectation each day and offering tours of the kitchen. Menus (à la carte, prestige and set lunch) are presented in an elegantly democratic fashion, no matter whether guests are first-timers or familiar faces in the pearl-toned dining room. A special occasion that's expected to stretch the bank balance? This is the right choice; your challenge will be to go easy on the champagne and digestifs – it all adds up. While theatrical elements are incorporated in amuses and petits fours (say, jacket-potato consommé served from a glass teapot, and white chocolate-coated strawberry ice-cream presented in a steaming silver pot of dry ice), the classical French dishes are more *zzzzz* than zeitgeist, but there's no denying the technical precision. Herbs bring a little sparkle. Camomile in a sauternes jelly that accompanied foie gras terrine, and a couple of Asian kicks in a salad served with pretty pigeon and wild mushroom pithiviers, were more successful than the freshly laundered scent of crystallised lavender buds decorating the chocolate tart. Wines start at a tolerable £20 and run to the likes of 1947 Château Latour at £2,900. If you're looking for something to match disparate orders of fish and meat, the unfortunately titled Misery grenache-shiraz at £29 is a good choice, though the friendly sommelier will happily advise on other options.
Booking essential. Children admitted. Dress: smart; jacket preferred; no jeans or trainers. **Map 14 F12**.

Indian

No other city matches London for the diversity of its South Asian restaurant scene. Within our capital, you'll find scores of homely cafés serving earthy dishes that compare favourably with those 'back home' in India, Pakistan, Bangladesh and Sri Lanka. It is the best of these that we've included here, rather than the formulaic curry houses that are found on any British high street. But London also excels at the other end of the South Asian culinary spectrum, with fine-dining venues that set trends for the rest of the world to follow. Cooking at this rarefied level has introduced regional Indian dishes to a new audience, and top chefs at **Amaya**, **Cinnamon Club** and **Veeraswamy** have adapted traditional recipes to suit contemporary tastes without compromising on quality. Watercress and fig patties, honey-steeped tandoori salmon, and whipped yoghurt soups: these are just a few of the dishes that showcase the European/South Asian fusion style that we now call Modern Indian.

If you're looking for an inexpensive and authentic taste of regional cooking, you're spoilt for choice. The best examples are basic cafés sited close to South Asian communities. It's here that you'll find excellent comfort food served without any frills: piping hot rotis, own-made masalas and chilled pitchers of freshly churned lassi. Visit Tooting for South Indian meals (especially at **Radha Krishna Bhavan**), Wembley for Gujarati specialities (**Sakonis**), and Southall and the surrounding area for Punjabi and Pakistani staples (**New Asian Tandoori Centre** and **Nauroz**). **Lahore Kebab House** and **Tayyabs** in the East End outshine curry houses on Brick Lane and are especially noted for their fiery masalas, smoky grills, and stacks of rotis. Noisy and boisterous caffs, both venues are as popular with City suits as with Asian families.

Closer to the heart of London, the **Masala Zone** chain delivers top-quality choices from across South Asia for a fraction of the price charged by its more celebrated peers. If you're looking for a vegetarian feast, try the **Sagar** mini chain, which has a fine selection of dosas (rice and lentil pancakes). Even tea, the kind served on Indian railway platforms, gets a look in – check out the plump samosas and steamy masala brew at Hampstead's **Chaiwalla** (see p313).

As ever, this section of our guide is bursting with vitality; London's culinary love affair with all things Indian remains as hot as ever.

Central
Covent Garden

Mela
152-156 Shaftesbury Avenue, WC2H 8HL (7836 8635/www.melarestaurant.co.uk). Leicester Square tube. **Meals served** noon-11.30pm Mon-Thur; noon-11.45pm Fri; 1.30-11.45pm Sat; noon-10.30pm Sun. **Main courses** £8.95-£14.95. **Set lunch** £2.95-£5.95 1 course. **Set dinner** (vegetarian) £15 per person, (non-vegetarian) £18.50 per person, minimum 2. **Set meal** (5.30-7pm, 10-11pm) £10.95 3 courses. **Credit** AmEx, MC, V. Pan-Indian
There's a pleasing bustle here, helped along by the troupe of tandoori chefs in the open kitchen, plentiful and efficient, prompt waiting staff, cool background beats from the sound system, colourful textile wall-hangings, and the location just off Cambridge Circus. Mela ('festival') attracts a youngish crowd of celebrants, enticed by its alluring menu of pan-Indian dishes. Tandoori food is well-represented, both in non-veg and vegetarian (paneer tikka, grilled with vegetables) form. Our meal began well with tuna ke paarchey (a piccata of tenderised tuna steak marinated in a highly savoury mix of lime, ginger, garlic, yoghurt, chilli and honey), and some crisp lesuni (garlic) whitebait served on a popadom with pickled vegetable and salad garnish. Next, khatta khargosh, rabbit in a thick tangy sauce of yoghurt and mango powder, was a mouth-watering treat. Less successful were the arhar dal kairi ki (supposedly raw mango with toor lentils, but barely discernible from mundane dhal) and a bland curry of watery soft-shell crabs. Variable, then, but the appealing buzz and several well-attended details (first-rate breads and rice) mean Mela merits consideration.
Babies and children welcome: children's menu; high chairs. Booking advisable. Restaurant available for hire. Separate room for parties, seats 40. Takeaway service; delivery service (over £30 within 1.5-mile radius). Vegetarian menu. **Map 18 K6**.

★ Moti Mahal
45 Great Queen Street, WC2B 5AA (7240 9329/www.motimahal-uk.com). Covent Garden or Holborn tube. **Lunch served** noon-3pm, **dinner served** 5.30-11.30pm Mon-Sat. **Main courses** £14-£23.50. **Set lunch** £15 2 courses incl glass of wine. **Credit** AmEx, MC, V. Modern Indian
The London branch of Delhi's long-standing Moti Mahal chain sighs with restrained elegance. Its interior is furnished in muted colours, with dimmed lighting and candles on tables producing an intimate atmosphere good for romancing and special-occasion treats; it seems to be working, the restaurant is popular with expense-account diners, well-heeled young couples and occasional tourists. Modern interpretations of traditional cooking styles pepper the menu. Kebabs are show-stoppers, notable for their imaginative marinades and smoky succulence. Tandoori salmon was cloaked in a light crust of lemony cream cheese, mixed with fresh dill and sweetened with a drizzle of honey. Main courses were distinctive and diverse; Goan sorpotel (a new-wave spin on an Indo-Portuguese stew) worked well with tender, gamey chunks of wild boar. Its masala was a beauty: silken sauce, sharpened with vinegary chilli paste, toasted garlic, and the subtle warming notes of cinnamon, pounded peppercorns and astringent ginger. In contrast, there were no modish twiddles with hyderabad biriani; this superb rendition was resplendent with fragrant rice grains steamed with cardamom and mace-marinated chicken morsels: the best we've had this year. Dining here isn't cheap, but the set lunch is great value.
Babies and children welcome: children's portions; high chairs. Booking advisable dinner. Dress: smart casual. Restaurant available for hire. Vegetarian menu. **Map 18 E3**.

Sitaaray
167 Drury Lane, WC2B 5PG (7269 6422/www.sitaaray.com). Covent Garden or Holborn tube. **Lunch served** noon-3pm, **dinner served** 5.30-11pm Mon-Sat. **Set lunch** £9 2 courses. **Set dinner** £12.50 2 courses (5.30-7pm); £19.50 buffet. **Credit** AmEx, MC, V. Pan-Indian
Glitzy Sitaaray is adorned, nay overwhelmed, with Bollywood memorabilia. Screens play flamboyant dance routines, the deep-red walls are crammed with film star photos, and posters festooned with baubles are visible from both ground-floor and mezzanine. Cocktails (alcoholic and not) are named after key films. It's all good over-the-top fun, but it's also a look that suggests the food might not be up to scratch, so we were pleasantly surprised by its high quality. Tandooris are the speciality, outnumbering curries ten to two on the lunchtime menu. At night, there's an eat-all-you-want format. Choose between vegetarian and non-veg, then you're assailed by dishes, served with unnerving velocity by the congenial staff. A sweetcorn patty, a zesty sea bass fillet, and a juicy lamb chop were the best of our nine (yes, nine) kebabs, but all came well-seared. These were preceded by salad, chutneys, popadoms and nuts, and accompanied by nan and dhal. Then came the curries: creamy chicken, and potato and spinach, with rice. We struggled to finish these and couldn't manage seconds, or one of the standard desserts. Puzzlingly, other diners weren't vast-bellied trenchermen, but Indian couples of modest proportions. Sitaaray was nearly empty midweek – a pity. Trenchermen are missing a treat.
Babies and children admitted. Booking advisable evenings. Disabled: toilet. Takeaway service. **Map 18 E3**.

Urban Turban. See p153.

Fitzrovia

Rasa Samudra ⓘ⁰⁰

*5 Charlotte Street, W1T 1RE (7637 0222/
www.rasarestaurants.com). Goodge Street tube.*
Lunch served noon-3pm Mon-Sat. **Dinner
served** 6-10.45pm daily. **Main courses** £6.25-
£12.95. **Set meal** (vegetarian) £22.50, (seafood)
£30. **Credit** AmEx, JCB, MC, V. South Indian
Forgive the kitsch interior of this upmarket
Keralite seafood restaurant, its pink walls decorated
with saris and wooden sculptures. You might also,
on occasion, have to pardon the service, which
during our visit was gruff and a little grumpy. Ask
for a table by the window or on the first floor, for
more gentle surroundings, and indulge in the
tempting menu. Though there's a long list of
Rasa's vegetarian dishes, seafood is the obvious
choice here, as evidenced by our enjoyable starter,
crab thoran: a light stir-fry of crab meat, chunks
of coconut and mustard seeds. Unfortunately, a
main course of konju manga curry (king prawns
cooked with turmeric, chillies, green mango and
coconut) didn't live up to its elaborate description;
it seemed watered down. In contrast, varutharacha
meen curry was evocative of houseboat meals on
the backwaters of Kerala: delicate tilapia steeped
in a thick, buttery sauce of coconut, tomatoes,
tamarind and chillies. As the menu recommends,
team this dish with lemon rice, or try an appam (a
bowl-shaped pancake made from fermented rice
flour). We've had great meals here in the past, but
there were too many shortcomings this time.
*Babies and children welcome. Booking advisable.
Separate rooms for parties, seating 12, 15 and
25. Takeaway service. Vegetarian menu.*
Map 9 J5.
For branches see index.

Knightsbridge

★ Amaya ⓘ⁰⁰

*19 Motcomb Street, 15 Halkin Arcade, SW1X
8JT (7823 1166/www.realindianfood.com).
Knightsbridge tube.* **Lunch served** 12.30-2.30pm
Mon-Sat; 12.45-2.45pm Sun. **Dinner served**
6.30-11.30pm Mon-Sat; 6.30-10.30pm Sun. **Main
courses** £8.50-£25. **Set lunch** £25. **Set dinner**
£37.50 tasting menu. **Credit** AmEx, DC, JCB,
MC, V. Modern Indian
Glamorous, stylish and seductive, Amaya is
sleekly appointed with sparkly chandeliers,
splashes of modern art and a groovy bar. This
restaurant's calling card is its sophisticated Indian
creations from a menu that cleverly links dressed-
up street food with regal specialities. If you fancy
a table with a view, bag one by the open kitchen
and watch the chefs wield laden skewers and slap
rotis against the walls of the tandoor. Of our
selections, we loved a meltingly tender chicken
tikka for its smoky, lemony flavour and subtle
marinade of rose-scented gingery yoghurt. Good
news continued with a gigantic Madagascan
prawn steeped in chilli-spiked lime juice and
cooked to perfect pinkness; the robust juices were
gratefully mopped up with hot nans. An earthy
rich staple of creamy spinach paste spiced with
ginger and green chillies was elevated to fine-
dining status and sensibly served without any
experimental flourish. Service was faultless. Only
mango tiramisu (piped on to a sponge finger) was
less than outstanding – a little too close to home
cooking to win accolades. Amaya is a magnet for
deep-pocketed Knightsbridge suits as well as
romancing couples.
*Babies and children admitted (until 8pm). Booking
advisable. Disabled: toilet. Dress: smart casual.
Separate room for parties, seats 14.* **Map 9 G9**.

Haandi

*7 Cheval Place, SW3 1HY (7823 7373/
www.haandi-restaurants.com). Knightsbridge tube.*
Lunch served noon-3pm daily. **Dinner served**
5.30-11pm Mon-Thur, Sun; 5.30-11.30pm Fri, Sat.
Main courses £6-£16. **Set lunch** £8-£12 incl
soft drink. **Credit** MC, V. East African Punjabi
Try and get a seat close to the cooks here; the
glass-fronted kitchen allows diners to watch all
manner of culinary theatrics. Besides, the rest of

RESTAURANTS

the restaurant is a bit beige, though not entirely bland. A lush edge is lent by towering potted palms. Pots of spices in the kitchen underline Haandi's North Indian (by way of Africa) cuisine. The cooking might not be extremely sophisticated, but it is seriously satisfying. The Punjabi classic of chole masaledar (curried chickpeas) was perfection: on a par with that served in Indian homes, the chickpeas cooked to melting gingery creaminess. The business has branches in east Africa, and the faultless jeera (cumin) chicken is an authentic Kenyan favourite. Speedy lunch specials have been introduced, and seemed to be going down well with a mixed Knightsbridge crowd of tourists, office workers and lone diners. A succulent lamb masala from this express menu was a cut above the conventional curry-house standard, as were the prices. Haandi is superb value given its location and fresh, fragrant food.
Babies and children welcome: high chairs. Booking advisable. Restaurant available for hire. Separate room for parties, seats 30. Takeaway service; delivery service (within 1-mile radius). **Map 14 E9.**
For branch see index.

★ Salloos
62-64 Kinnerton Street, SW1X 8ER (7235 4444). Hyde Park Corner or Knightsbridge tube. **Lunch served** noon-2.15pm, **dinner served** 7-11pm Mon-Sat. **Main courses** £13.50-£16.50. **Credit** AmEx, DC, MC, V. Pakistani
You'd be forgiven for thinking you've walked into an elaborate living room after climbing the stairs into this family-owned, first-floor restaurant. The clean, crisp tablecloths, intricately carved trellises and exquisite works of art on the wall create an intimate, old-school setting suitable for special occasions, from birthdays and romantic meals to important business lunches. Service is equally traditional – efficient, formal and delivered with a poker face. The head chef has worked with the Salloo family since 1966 and was trained by its matriarch. Salloos is famous for its kebabs, but nothing exemplifies the chef's expertise more than the extraordinary haleem akbari. Long strands of tender lamb are slowly cooked along with lentils, whole wheatgerm, ghee (clarified butter), ginger, garlic and various spices for up to eight hours. The result is a dish luxurious in flavour and aroma, and of a thick, porridge-like texture. The haleem is best eaten garnished with the diced ginger and chillies, browned onions and garam masala powder that accompany it, as well as a simple roti. If you order this high-calorie dish, opt for a light starter. We had yakhni, a simple, flavourful lamb consommé, spiced with fresh herbs, cardamom and fennel seeds.
Booking advisable. Children over 8 years admitted. Takeaway service. **Map 9 G9.**

Marylebone

Woodlands
77 Marylebone Lane, W1U 2PS (7486 3862/ www.woodlandsrestaurant.co.uk). **Lunch served** noon-3pm, dinner served 6-11pm Mon-Thur. **Meals served** noon-11pm Fri-Sun. **Main courses** £4.75-£7.25. **Set lunch thali** £7.50. **Set thali** £15.95-£17.95. **Credit** AmEx, MC, V. South Indian vegetarian
The flagship restaurant of a burgeoning group, Woodlands has been a popular destination for office workers and occasional tourist groups for more than 25 years. Its dining room is lent modernity by twinkling lights, a light wooden floor, and mirrors across the walls. The menu is based on South Indian vegetarian cookery, though incorporates a few North Indian stalwarts. Our meal was of a variable standard. Rasam, a tart tomato broth spiked with red chillies and fried flecks of ginger, impressed us with its peppery kick. Toasted wheat uppama, simmered with crunchy fried lentils, curry leaves, and split cashew nuts, also won approval for its deliciously creamy texture and delicate flavour. Good news over. Our uthappam, billed as a lentil pizza with vegetable toppings, proved unyieldingly dense and overcooked. Dosas are much-trumpeted here, and

fillings for these rice and lentil pancakes are diverse, ranging from classic crushed potatoes to stir-fried mushrooms. Our dosa was badly let down by lacklustre sambar and bland coconut chutney. Service matches the inconsistent cooking and needs to be more attentive. We've had better meals at lower prices in community caffs.
Babies and children welcome: high chairs. Booking advisable weekends. Restaurant available for hire. Takeaway service. Vegan dishes. Vegetarian menu. **Map 9 G5.**
For branches see index.

Mayfair

Benares
12A Berkeley Square House, Berkeley Square, W1J 6BS (7629 8886/www.benaresrestaurant. com). Green Park tube. **Lunch served** noon-2.30pm daily. **Dinner served** 5.30-10.30pm Mon-Sat; 6-10pm Sun. **Main courses** £15-£40. **Set meal** (lunch, 5.30-6.30pm) £24.99 2 courses, £29.99 3 courses. **Credit** AmEx, DC, MC, V. Modern Indian
A magnet for moneyed media moguls and wealthy tourists, Benares is buoyed by celebrity chef Atul Kochhar's TV appearances. It's a stylish set-up – a flight of stairs leading from the discreet entrance to a seductive, dimly lit bar, furnished in black granite, opening on to a spacious dining area. A starter of beautifully presented seared scallops, coated in crunchy spices and a minted sweet grape dressing, was a triumph for fusion cooking. Crisp-fried soft-shell crab was equally impressive; deliciously sweet, its paper-thin crust was seasoned with warming cinnamon. Although tandoori chicken was succulent, mouth-wateringly garlicky, and cooked on the bone (as it should be), it needed an accompaniment to add interest and justify the high price. Roast lamb with rosemary and chickpeas was a lost cause: marred by tough meat and bland chickpeas (we couldn't taste rosemary). Traditional Indian staples of creamy black dhal and piping hot breads are top notch, western desserts need more attention if they are to hit the sweet spot. Our white chocolate mousse was overly gelatinous and its sidekick – an uninspiring passion fruit and banana sorbet – did it no favours. Smooth-as-silk service helps make up for culinary glitches and high prices.
Booking advisable. Disabled: toilet. Dress: smart casual. Entertainment: live music noon Sun. Restaurant available for hire. Separate rooms for parties, seating 14, 22 and 30. Takeaway service. **Map 9 H7.**

Tamarind
20-22 Queen Street, W1J 5PR (7629 3561/ www.tamarindrestaurant.com). Green Park tube. **Lunch served** noon-2.45pm Mon-Fri, Sun. **Dinner served** 6-11.15pm Mon-Sat; 6-10.30pm Sun. **Main courses** £16-£28. **Set lunch** £18.95 2 courses, £21.50 3 courses. **Set dinner** £42-£72 3-4 courses. **Credit** AmEx, MC, V. Pan-Indian
Alfred Prasad has maintained Tamarind in the top rank of Indian restaurants since taking over the cheffing from Atul Kochhar in 2002. Behind an unassuming frontage, this capacious basement has a grandiose demeanour, helped by burnished gold pillars and walls, polished wooden flooring and equally polished (if slightly overbearing) service. Pity that the refurb a few years back robbed diners of a view into the kitchen. Prasad relies on innovative spicing, expert presentation and a lightness of touch to make his mark; most dishes are based on classic North Indian cuisine. A special two-for-one deal on the summer tasting menu was hard to resist (consult the website for such bargains). To this we added two dishes: a seafood salad starter (a tired, fridge-cold assembly), and baingan bharta (a wonderfully smoky aubergine mush). From the tasting menu, rich dhal makhani and luxurious saag paneer were exemplary, and a simple chicken curry sang of fowl and fenugreek. Most original were the appetisers, including a salmon fish cake heavily laced with kaffir lime leaves, and a salad of black-eyed beans with cantaloupe melon. Fruit sorbet made a fitting finale to a lunch that was competently rendered, if a little short on sparkle.

Babies and children welcome (before 7pm): high chair. Booking advisable. Dress: smart casual. Takeaway service; delivery service (£4 charge, within 1-mile radius). **Map 9 H7.**

★ Veeraswamy (100)
Mezzanine, Victory House, 99-101 Regent Street, W1B 4RS (7734 1401/www.realindianfood.com). Piccadilly Circus tube. **Lunch served** noon-2.30pm Mon-Fri; 12.30-2.45pm Sat, Sun. **Dinner served** 5.30-10.45pm Mon-Sat; 6-10.15pm Sun. **Main courses** £14-£29.50. **Set meal** (lunch, 5.30-6.30pm, after 10pm Mon-Sat) £16.50 2 courses, £19.50 3 courses; (Sun) £22 3 courses. **Credit** AmEx, DC, MC, V. Pan-Indian
London's oldest Indian restaurant (established 1926) has been modernised twice since being taken over in 1997 by the Masala World group. You might not realise this from the decor, which features a chintzy chandelier and pink carpet of uncertain ancestry, both of which jar with the more modish silver upholstery on chairs and banquettes. Still, once you've ascended the lift to the airy first-floor dining room, it's the large windows looking down on Regent Street that provide the panache, along with the faultless table service and the food, which is of the highest order. Dishes from across India fill the exciting, oft-changing menu. Crab and ginger soup was a revelation: wisps of shredded ginger and chunks of white crab meat, on to which was poured a consommé that sang sweetly of both. It was questionable whether the following coconutty pineapple curry (one of several enticing side dishes) was a perfect match for the rich sauce and tender breast of the white chicken curry, but the quality of ingredients and the spicing (ground fresh each day, it is claimed) was beyond reproach. Also excellent: the flaky ajwain lacha bread and the khubuli rice with lentils, fragrant with star anise. Desserts include novel kulfis (rich chocolate, caramelised banana). The wine list is one of Indian London's best too.
Babies and children admitted (lunch). Booking advisable weekends. Disabled: lift. Dress: smart casual. Separate room for parties, seats 36. **Map 17 J7.**

St James's

Quilon
41 Buckingham Gate, SW1E 6AF (7821 1899/ www.thequilonrestaurant.com). St James's Park tube. **Lunch served** noon-2.30pm Mon-Fri; 12.30-3.30pm Sun. **Dinner served** 6-11pm Mon-Sat; 6-10.30pm Sun. **Main courses** £9-£23. **Set lunch** £17 2 courses, £20 3 courses. **Credit** AmEx, MC, V. South Indian

BEST INDIAN

Best Modern Indian
Creative cuisine, perfectly presentated at high-fliers **Amaya** (see p148), **Chutney Mary** (see p157), **Cinnamon Club** (see p153), **Moti Mahal** (see p147) and **Veeraswamy** (see above).

Best bargains
Proper 'Indian' cookery for less at **Dosa n Chutny** (see p161), **Five Hot Chillies** (see p171), **Ram's** (see p168), and **Sagar** (see p155).

Around South Asia
Savour the best of Sri Lanka at **Apollo Banana Leaf** (see p161), the Punjab at **Brilliant** (see p168) and **Five Hot Chillies** (see p171), Bangladesh at **Kolapata** (see p165), Karnataka at **Sagar** (see p155), and Pakistan at **Salloos** (see left).

Best meatless meals
Peerless vegetarian delicacies at **Dosa n Chutny** (see p161), **Ram's** (see p168), **Rasa** (see p165) and **Sagar** (see p155).

LONDON'S MOST GLAMOROUS
INDIAN RESTAURANTS

AMAYA

This award winning Indian grill presents an unmistakable experience for lunch and dinner in Belgravia.

Private room seats 14

Halkin Arcade, Motcomb Street Knightsbridge, London SW1

Telephone: 020 7823 1166

CHUTNEY MARY

The rich setting, interesting art and romantic candle lighting are secondary details in London's temple of great Indian food.

Sunday lunch £22 for 3 courses

Private room seats 24

535 Kings Road Chelsea, London SW10

Telephone: 020 7351 3113

VEERASWAMY

Divine dishes, lovingly prepared and beautifully served in sumptuous surroundings overlooking Regent Street.

Sunday lunch £22 for 3 courses

Private room seats 32

Mezzanine Floor, Victory House 99 Regent Street, London W1

Telephone: 020 7734 1401

For outside catering, please contact our Head Office on 020 7724 2525

 MasalaWorld

Benares. See p150.

The Taj Group of hotels runs numerous excellent restaurants in India, and has trained several of London's top Indian chefs. At this St James's hotel restaurant, the firm has rolled out a familiar formula. If success is to be measured by accolade, Quilon is doing well, having been awarded a Michelin star in 2008, but if ambience matters, this place is a failure. Despite use of colour in an bid to give the dining room vibrancy, it feels drab and institutional. Luckily the menu is more exciting. Beautifully cooked South Indian favourites are joined by refined dishes such as guinea fowl supreme braised in coconut milk, or out-of-season asparagus with crunchy mustard seeds. All the food tastes light and healthy, and the spices are subtly balanced: though sometimes a little too subtle (the chilli heat of some Keralite dishes has been toned down, perhaps for the clientele of tourists and businessmen). The lunchtime menu is good value, but prices are high in the evening. You could keep costs down by skipping dessert – both we tried (a mango rice pudding, and a far-from-delightful 'almond delight') were unexciting. *Babies and children welcome: high chair. Booking advisable. Takeaway service. Vegetarian menu.* **Map 15 J9.**

Soho

Chowki

2-3 Denman Street, W1D 7HA (7439 1330/ www.chowki.com). Piccadilly Circus tube. **Meals served** noon-11.30pm Mon-Sat; noon-10.30pm Sun. **Main courses** £7.95-£11.95. **Set meal** (vegetarian) £15.95 3 courses, (non-vegetarian) £18.95 3 courses. **Credit** AmEx, DC, MC, V.
Pan-Indian
Devised by chef-proprietor Kuldeep Singh – of Mela (*see p147*) fame – Chowki's format is alluring: a monthly changing menu of authentic regional cooking at fair prices. On a recent visit, we found the delivery a marked improvement on last year. With its soundtrack of chilled beats, its communal seating (at long wooden tables) and its low-lit interior (in two large rooms), Chowki is ideal for a low-cost dinner with chums. In the afternoon it's somewhat gloomy, though the lunch menu of meal-in-one dishes is a bargain. Food from Lucknow, Goa and the North-West Frontier featured in April, with each region providing three starters and mains plus a dessert (the Goan multi-layered cake, bebinca, say). Tender coils of just-cooked squid came coated with a zesty tomato and carom-seed masala and superfluous coriander relish in an otherwise well-judged Goan starter. Next, the North-West Frontier provided our lamb kofta: flavour-packed meatballs peeping from a pond of tangy yoghurt curry. As with other mains, this came with chickpea curry, nan and rice:

high marks to all three. Within a chapati-fling of Piccadilly Circus, Chowki is worth knowing about.
Babies and children welcome: high chairs. Booking advisable. Separate room for parties, seats 40. Vegetarian menu. **Map 17 K7.**

★ Imli

167-169 Wardour Street, W1F 8WR (7287 4243/ www.imli.co.uk). Tottenham Court Road tube. **Meals served** noon-11pm daily. **Tapas** £3.95-£6.95. **Set lunch** £5-£7.50 1 course. **Credit** AmEx, MC, V. Pan-Indian

Indian tapas is the hook here, but Imli is no passing fad. Cut-price brethren of the classy Tamarind, this vibrant restaurant has culinary zip aplenty. Deep orange and pale-green walls are further brightened by colourful photos of Indian folk and foodstuffs, the front space leading on to a larger back area. We sat by bowls of perfect red capsicums: a stylish touch. Tiled flooring and bare wooden furniture discourage dallying; Imli is somewhere to relish then relinquish. Standard dishes are rendered well – the gingery tang and tender meat of the Goan pork; the comforting dhal; the smoky, mushy aubergine masala – but the innovative food is even better. Don't miss the seared slices of masala grilled beef, served atop mild cumin and turmeric mash with (a mouth-watering masterstroke) a coriander and avocado dip. Almost as good is the Imli risotto, featuring crunchy spiced veg over a creamy mix of mushrooms and arborio rice. Three dishes amount to a substantial two-course meal: great value for food of such quality. If you've never tried Modern Indian cuisine, come here first.
Babies and children welcome: children's menu; high chairs. Disabled: toilet. Separate room for parties, seats 45. Takeaway service; delivery service (over £15 within half-mile radius).
Map 17 J6.

Red Fort

77 Dean Street, W1D 3SH (7437 2115/ www.redfort.co.uk). Leicester Square or Tottenham Court Road tube. **Lunch served** noon-2pm Mon-Fri. **Dinner served** 5.45-11pm Mon-Sat; 5.30-10pm Sun. **Main courses** £15-£29. **Set lunch** £12 2 courses. **Set meal** (5.45-7pm) £16 2 courses incl tea or coffee. **Credit** AmEx, MC, V. North Indian

The epitome of elegance, the Red Fort has a calming, restrained demeanour. Lighting is low (apart from spotlights on the pristine white tablecloths), artefacts are reassuringly expensive (a capacious copper urn here, a grand water feature there), and the smartly garbed staff (the brisk side of brusque) are proficiency incarnate. Multinational media types in their 30s and 40s dine here. Food is classic Moghul (especially from regal Lucknow), rather than innovative, so don't expect surprises – save, perhaps, for the frightening bill. Starters lacked lustre: monkfish tikka looked lovely, but was mushy and overcooked; in contrast hara kebabs (two spinach and fenugreek patties) seemed measly in appearance, but had a soft, luscious filling. To follow, dum pukht biriani was exemplary: the lamb tender, the rice moist with meat juices, fragrant with cardamom pods and cinnamon bark. Equally faultless were the kaddu chana (nicely resilient white pumpkin with chana dhal) and the four little discs of perfectly weighted rotis. Raspberry shrikhand is the eye-catcher among the desserts. As with the Red Fort in its entirety, the wine list can't fail to impress business clients.
Babies and children admitted. Booking advisable. Dress: smart casual. Entertainment: DJ 8pm Thur-Sat (bar). Vegetarian menu. Vegan dishes. **Map 17 K6.**

Victoria

Sekara

3 Lower Grosvenor Place, SW1W 0EJ (7834 0722/www.sekara.co.uk). Victoria tube/rail. **Lunch served** noon-3pm, **dinner served** 6-10pm daily. **Main courses** £7.95-£14.95. **Set lunch** (Mon-Sat) £5 1 course. **Set buffet** (Sun) £12. **Credit** MC, V. Sri Lankan

A cosy restaurant, Sekara offers a serene retreat from the busy street outside. It's not much to look at, but don't let that dissuade you. Dated photos of

Sri Lankan bigwigs and large framed paintings provide a reminder of the owners' heritage, but it's the cooking that does the talking. Expatriates and well-travelled diners of all ages come here for homely, authentic and keenly priced island cooking. We recommend ordering Sri Lankan specialities rather than the ubiquitous North Indian options. Of the starters, vadai (deep-fried lentil patties) were pleasingly crunchy with bursts of crisp curry leaves and toasted cumin. Yet main courses were the stars. Chicken lamprais, a rich biriani of Sri Lankan Dutch extraction, had gorgeous, bold flavours absorbed from cardamom-infused meat stock. The glistening rice was studded with chicken pieces and accompanied by a marvellous russet-hued curry made from a raunchy caramelised-onion masala. On-bone chunks of seer fish, simmered in coconut and tamarind broth, needed an extra dollop of tamarind to lift them from blandness. Service on this occasion was slow and decidedly dour, which detracted from our overall enjoyment.
Booking advisable. Restaurant available for hire. Separate room for parties, seats 25. Takeaway service. Vegetarian menu. **Map 15 H9.**

Westminster

★ Cinnamon Club

The Old Westminster Library, 30-32 Great Smith Street, SW1P 3BU (7222 2555/ www.cinnamonclub.com). St James's Park or Westminster tube. Restaurant **Breakfast served** 7.30-9.30am Mon-Fri. **Lunch served** noon-2.30pm, **dinner served** 6-10.45pm Mon-Sat. **Main courses** £11-£29. **Set meal** £19 2 courses, £22 3 courses. **Credit** AmEx, DC, MC, V. Modern Indian

Housed in a former Victorian library, the Cinnamon Club is a grand affair with high ceilings, a gallery of bookshelves and elegant leather chairs, which all help create a colonial atmosphere. On our visit, staff were having a bad day – we witnessed an argument among two hostesses, were gruffly told to wait in the bar even though we had a reservation, then our order was botched. Chef Vivek Singh, thankfully, seems to be running a tighter ship in the kitchen. The food is exemplary. We started off with boti kebab: four tender pieces of grilled lamb infused with garlic, ginger and cardamom, and served with sweetened yoghurt garnished with cumin. A sharp sorbet arrived mid-course as a palate cleanser. Our main course, an organic rare-breed pork loin, was served with quinoa and a selection of vegetables. The pork's intense flavours of cumin, chilli, dates and tamarind flooded our mouths with each bite. Not to be outdone, the tilapia in a tangy lentil crust was moist and light. Served with chilled yoghurt rice and an exhilarating pea relish that tasted like wasabi, this unassuming fish was transformed into a gourmet marvel. Great food, shame about the service. A new branch, Cinnamon Kitchen, is being planned in the City for November 2008.
Babies and children welcome: high chairs. Bars available for hire. Booking advisable. Disabled: lift, toilet. Separate rooms for parties, seating 30 and 60. **Map 16 K9.**

West
Bayswater

Urban Turban NEW

98 Westbourne Grove, W2 5RU (7243 4200/ www.urbanturban.uk.com). Bayswater or Notting Hill Gate tube. **Lunch served** noon-4pm Sat, Sun. **Dinner served** 6-11pm daily. **Main courses** £6-£12. **Thalis** £5.50-£6. **Set lunch** £9.95. **Credit** AmEx, MC, V. Modern Indian

This younger sister to fine-dining restaurant Rasoi Vineet Bhatia (*see p159*) is a trendy lounge bar themed around stylised Indian tapas and cool cocktails. The venue's low-slung banquettes, high bar stools and salkin cushions have already been bagged by fashionistas. When we made our reservation, staff demanded to know how long we'd take to vacate the table; we've had warmer welcomes at motorway service stations. On a

Interview
VIVEK SINGH

Who are you?
Executive chef of the **Cinnamon Club** (*see left*).
What's the best thing about running a restaurant in London?
London is uniquely multicultural in every sense, which makes it easy to find a variety of high-quality ingredients from all over the world. Also, guests are so open to trying new things, and so well aware of world cuisines, that it makes for a really fun and engaging dialogue with them – much more so than in any other city.
What's the worst thing?
Finding and keeping good workers. There are not enough people working in this industry out of choice; it seems to be something one does to make money on the side. It's a shame because, properly done, a career in this industry is immensely rewarding.
Which are your favourite London restaurants?
My choices vary from the ubiquitous **Mirch Masala** (*see p161*) to **Roka** (*see p193*), to **Barrafina** (*see p261*), to the **Capital** (*see pXXX*). I guess what makes each of these places special is that they achieve excellence in the space they operate in – and believe me, that's not always easy to achieve.
How green are you?
It's one of the hottest subjects and, understandably, on everyone's mind. I also feel anything taken out of context is dangerous and futile, and therefore scaremongering on environmental issues is pointless. What's needed is a commitment to making a difference every day, however small it may be.
What is missing from London's restaurant scene?
The capital does not have a culture of street food that you find in cities like Hong Kong, Bangkok and Mumbai. There is space for a concept that celebrates street food from Britain and around the world.

brighter note, once we'd arrived the sommelier and waiters were quick to soothe away rough edges with charm and warmth. We're not convinced that the cooking here measures up to expectations; we'd hoped for innovation and were disappointed. Out of five choices, only seared 'gunpowder' prawns were noteworthy: for their juicy freshness and lemony flavour, though we couldn't detect any chilli kick. Tandoori chicken, radioactive-red in hue, was served with what tasted depressingly like spicy cream of tomato soup: the lowest ebb of an undistinguished meal. Even the samosas were let down by a pasty, ground-mince filling. The menu indicates that dishes are served as they are prepared: shame that our five orders arrived, like London buses, all at once.

Babies and children welcome: high chairs.
Booking advisable Tue-Sat. Disabled: toilet.
Restaurant available for hire. Separate rooms for
parties, seating 20 and 30. Vegetarian menu.
Map 7 B6.

Hammersmith

★ ★ **Sagar** ⓾⓪⓪
157 King Street, W6 9JT (8741 8563).
Hammersmith tube. **Lunch served** noon-2.45pm Mon-Fri. **Dinner served** 5.30-10.45pm Mon-Thur; 5.30-11.30pm Fri. **Meals served**

noon-11.30pm Sat; noon-10.45pm Sun. **Main courses** £5-£13. **Thalis** £9.95-£12.45. **Credit** AmEx, DC, JCB, MC, V. South Indian vegetarian
One of the few restaurants in London to serve Udupi vegetarian dishes from Karnataka, Sagar now has three branches stretching from the West End to Twickenham. This original Hammersmith site has smooth blond-wood walls dotted with elegant brass figurines that are beautifully lit at night. The place gets packed during the evenings, and can bustle at lunchtimes too, as students, shoppers, workers and families stop by for a fix of spice, and myriad variations on rice. Puffy, spongy idlis soaked up our freshly made sambar and fiery coconut chutney: a highly satisfying combination. Uthappam was just the right side of searingly hot, and was made livelier still with a topping of fresh tomato. A cooling contrast came from the vegetable kootu (spinach cooked with yoghurt and coconut) – faultlessly done. The dosas are excellent too, with delicately spiced fillings from potato to paneer. A slightly stodgy samosa was the one duff note among our meal's many highs. What's more, the prices are pretty much as low as you can get in London for South Indian food of this quality.
Babies and children welcome: high chair. Booking
advisable. Takeaway service. Vegetarian menu.
Vegan dishes. **Map 20 B4.**
For branches see index.

Shilpa NEW
206 King Street, W6 0RA (8741 3127/
www.shilparestaurant.co.uk). Hammersmith
tube. **Lunch served** noon-3pm daily. **Dinner served** 6-11pm Mon-Wed, Sun; 6-12pm Thur-Sat. **Main courses** £2.92-£10.50. **Set lunch** £3.99 (vegetarian). £4.99 (non-vegetarian). **Credit** MC, V. South Indian
The design and decor of this unassuming modern restaurant (brightly painted lilac walls, starched white tablecloths and plasma screens showing Bollywood movies) won't set your pulse racing. No matter, as the fiery Keralite food surely will. Shilpa celebrates southern coastal cooking with a seafood-heavy menu. Expect rich coconut masalas, an abundance of curry leaves, and spicy-hot flavours that pack a punch. Dense and crunchy vadai (lentil fritters with a creamy coconut chutney) were a lovely way to start the meal. A large bowl of rasam broth was also top-notch – rich and warming with a sour hit of tamarind and fresh coriander. To follow, king fish curry with green chillies and coconut milk was a little overcooked, but the masala dosa brought things back on track, the spiced potatoes encased in a perfectly light and crisp pancake. Friendly staff warned us when we were ordering too much, but it was hard to believe portions would be so

RESTAURANTS

Pan-Indian menu

Spellings of Indian dishes vary widely; dishes such as gosht may appear in several versions on different menus as the word is transliterated from (in this case) Hindi. There are umpteen languages and several scripts in the Indian subcontinent, the most commonly seen on London menus being Punjabi, Hindi, Bengali and Gujarati. For the sake of consistency, however, we have tried to adhere to uniform spellings. The following are common throughout the subcontinent.

Aloo: potato.
Ayre: a white fish much used in Bengali cuisine.
Baingan: aubergine.
Balti: West Midlands cooking term for karahi cooking (qv, North Indian menu), which became all the rage a decade ago. Unfortunately, many inferior curry houses now apply the name to dishes that bear little resemblance to real karahi-cooked dishes.
Bateira, batera or **bater:** quail.
Bengali: Bengal, before Partition in 1947, was a large province covering Calcutta (now in India's West Bengal) and modern-day Bangladesh. 'Bengali' and 'Bangladeshi' cooking is quite different, and the term 'Bengali' is often misused in London's Indian restaurants.
Bhajee: vegetables cooked with spices, usually 'dry' rather than sauced.
Bhajia or **bhaji:** vegetables dipped in chickpea-flour batter and deep-fried; also called pakoras.
Bhatura: deep-fried doughy discs.
Bhindi: okra.
Brinjal: aubergine.
Bulchao or **balchao:** a Goan vinegary pickle made with small dried prawns (with shells) and lots of garlic.
Chana or **channa:** chickpeas.

Chapati: a flat wholewheat griddle bread.
Chat or **chaat:** various savoury snacks featuring combinations of pooris (qv), diced onion and potato, chickpeas, crumbled samosas and pakoras, chutneys and spices.
Dahi: yoghurt.
Dahl or **dal:** a lentil curry similar to thick lentil soup. Countless regional variations exist.
Dhansak: a Parsi (qv) casserole of meat, lentils and vegetables, with a mix of hot and tangy flavours.
Dhaniya: coriander.
Ghee: clarified butter used for frying.
Gobi: cauliflower.
Gosht, josh or **ghosh:** meat, usually lamb.
Gram flour: chickpea flour.
Kachori: crisp pastry rounds with spiced mung dahl or pea filling.
Lassi: a yoghurt drink, ordered with salt or sugar, sometimes with fruit. Ideal to quench a fiery palate.
Machi or **machli:** fish.
Masala or **masaladar:** mixed spices.
Methi: fenugreek, either dried (seeds) or fresh (green leaves).
Murgh or **murg:** chicken.
Mutter, muter or **mattar:** peas.
Nan or **naan:** teardrop-shaped flatbread cooked in a tandoor (qv, North Indian menu).
Palak or **paalak:** spinach; also called saag.
Paan or **pan:** betel leaf stuffed with chopped 'betel nuts', coconut and spices such as fennel seeds, and folded into a triangle. Available sweet or salty, and eaten at the end of a meal as a digestive.
Paneer or **panir:** Indian cheese, a bit like tofu in texture and taste.
Paratha: a large griddle-fried bread that is sometimes stuffed (with spicy mashed potato or minced lamb, for instance).

Parsi or **Parsee:** a religious minority based in Mumbai, but originally from Persia, renowned for its cooking.
Pilau, pillau or **pullao:** flavoured rice cooked with meat or vegetables. In most British Indian restaurants, pilau rice is simply rice flavoured and coloured with turmeric or (rarely) saffron.
Poori or **puri:** a disc of deep-fried wholewheat bread; the frying makes it puff up like an air-filled cushion.
Popadom, poppadom, papadum or **papad:** large thin wafers made with lentil paste, and flavoured with pepper, garlic or chilli. Eaten in the UK with pickles and relishes as a starter while waiting for the meal to arrive.
Raita: a yoghurt mix, usually with cucumber.
Roti: a round, sometimes unleavened, bread, thicker than a chapati and cooked in a tandoor or griddle. Roomali roti is a very thin, soft disc of roti.
Saag or **sag:** spinach; also called palak.
Tamarind: the pods of this East African tree, grown in India, are made into a paste that imparts a sour, fruity taste – popular in some regional cuisines, including Gujarati and South Indian.
Thali: literally 'metal plate'. A large plate with rice, bread, metal containers of dahl and vegetable curries, pickles and yoghurt.
Vadai or **wada:** a spicy vegetable or lentil fritter; dahi wada are lentil fritters soaked in yoghurt, topped with tamarind and date chutneys.
Vindaloo: originally, a hot and spicy pork curry from Goa that should authentically be soured with vinegar and cooked with garlic. In London restaurants, the term is usually misused to signify simply very hot dishes.
Xacuti: a Goan dish made with lamb or chicken pieces, coconut and a complex mix of roasted then ground spices.

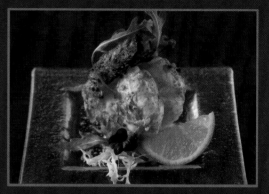

generous with prices so reasonable. In particular, the set lunches under a fiver are a bargain. *Babies and children welcome: high chairs. Booking advisable. Restaurant available for hire. Takeaway service; delivery service (over £15 within 3-mile radius). Vegetarian menu.* **Map 20 B4.**

Kensington

Zaika
1 Kensington High Street, W8 5NP (7795 6533/ www.zaika-restaurant.co.uk). High Street Kensington tube. **Lunch served** noon-2.45pm Mon-Fri, Sun. **Dinner served** 6.30-10.45pm Mon-Sat; 6.30-9.45pm Sun. **Main courses** £14.50-£21.50. **Set lunch** £19.50 4 courses. **Set meal** £39-£89 tasting menu. **Credit** AmEx, DC, MC, V. Modern Indian
Opposite Kensington Palace, in a former bank, Zaika occupies the upper echelons of fine Indian dining. Wood-panelled walls are offset with vast stone Hindu sculptures and swathes of silk. The food is fun – taking concepts from here, there and everywhere to produce mostly happy fusions. Smoked salmon, mildly marinated with tandoori spicing, married successfully with the gravadlax-style cure of mustard, honey and dill, helped by avocado raita and a lentil pancake in place of a blini. Seared tuna also worked well, with its 'caviar' of popped mustard seeds, a chutney of crab cocktail and an understated version of dhokla (hot, savoury gram-flour cake). The high standard of starters was best exhibited in a mixed platter: each dish a hit,

from a tender, subtly spiced morsel of blackened chicken, and a more assertive duck seekh kebab flecked with red chilli, to a delicate small samosa rich with creamy cheese and cashews. Mains were less happy melanges; tender tandoori guinea fowl came with a vibrant chilli consommé, but both suffered from the sweet swampiness of the 'upma'-style asparagus polenta. Yes, Zaika has a tendency to over-elaborate, but generally, this elegant outfit scores highly – helped by skilful service.
Babies and children welcome: high chair. Booking advisable; essential weekends. Dress: smart casual. Restaurant available for hire. Vegetarian menu. **Map 7 C8**.

South West
Barnes

Mango & Silk NEW
199 Upper Richmond Road West, SW14 8QT (8876 6220/www.mangoandsilk.co.uk). Mortlake rail/33, 337 bus. **Lunch served** noon-2.30pm Sat, noon-3pm Sun. **Dinner served** 6-10pm Tue-Thur, Sun; 6-10.30pm Fri, Sat. **Main courses** £5.50-£9.95. **Set buffet lunch** (Sun) £11.95. **Credit** AmEx, MC, V. Pan-Indian
Udit Sarkhel, long a major influence on Indian food in London, closed his own Earlsfield restaurant in 2007, but he's now head chef here. A beige and white colour scheme and wooden flooring create seemly environs for embarking on the menu's tour

of India's home kitchens. Parsi classics, Moghul stalwarts, southern coconut masalas and Punjabi comfort food are all here. We began with a Goan squid balchao from the daily specials list: succulent seafood in a vinegary masala, cut with sweet cinnamon and fiery red chillies. We'd have given it top marks if there'd been less sauce. Crisp samosas, with a lemon-drenched potato filling, were delectable too. Standards were maintained by the mains. Malai fish curry delivered perfectly cooked cod in a creamy coconut-milk broth, punctuated by chillies and mustard seeds. Murgh makhani, the Punjabi precursor to tikka masala, produced tender chicken in a buttery tomato sauce. Weekday 'express' lunches cost just £5.50, and the Sunday buffet is a mere £11.95. Judging from the full house on a Friday night, Sarkhel's cooking attracts well-heeled aficionados. Much is owed to owner Radhika Jerath's charm at front of house. This good-value, amiable restaurant is doing East Sheen proud.
Babies and children welcome: booster seats. Booking advisable weekends. Disabled: toilet. Restaurant available for hire. Tables outdoors (2, decking). Takeaway service.

Chelsea

★ Chutney Mary
535 King's Road, SW10 0SZ (7351 3113/ www.chutneymary.com). Fulham Broadway tube/11, 22 bus. **Lunch served** 12.30-2.30pm

Sagar. See p155.

PRITHI RESTAURANT

'The quality of cooking is very high'
Bloomberg.com

Recommended as the best Indian Restaurant in London
Itchy London

'I have been to Preem Restaurant with my friends, I like the food and service. I hope to visit again soon.'
Readers rating ★ ★ ★ ★
thisislondon /Evening Standard

'We were more than impressed with the quality of the food and in spite of enjoying every mouthful; we could not eat all of the generous portions. We would recommend Preem to lovers of good food.'
www.restaurant-guide.com

'If you're in the East End and want a curry that's low in fat and splendid to taste then head down to Preem. At £7.50 per head its a tasty bargain.'
Exceptional ★ ★ ★ ★
visitbricklane

118-126 Brick Lane, London E1 6RL
Tel: 020 7377 5252   Fax: 020 7247 0397
www.preembricklane.com

North Indian menu

Under the blanket term 'North Indian', we have included dishes originating in the Punjab (the region separating India and Pakistan), Kashmir and all points down to Hyderabad. Southall has some of London's best Punjabi restaurants, where breads cooked in the tandoor oven are often preferred to rice, marinated meat kebabs are popular, and dahls are thick and buttery.

Bhuna gosht: a dry, spicy dish of lamb.
Biriani or **biryani:** a royal Moghul (qv) version of pilau rice, in which meat or vegetables are cooked together with basmati rice, spices and saffron. It's difficult to find an authentic biriani in London restaurants.
Dopiaza or **do pyaza:** cooked with onions.
Dum: a Kashmiri cooking technique where food is simmered in a casserole (typically a clay pot sealed with dough), allowing spices to permeate.
Gurda: kidneys.
Haandi: an earthenware or metal cooking pot, with handles on either side and a lid.
Jalfrezi: chicken or vegetable dishes cooked with fresh green chillies – a popular cooking style in Mumbai.
Jhingri, jhinga or **chingri:** prawns.
Kaleji or **kalezi:** liver.
Karahi or **karai:** a small iron or metal wok-like cooking dish. Similar to the 'balti' dish made famous in Birmingham.
Kheema or **keema:** minced lamb, as in kheema nan (stuffed nan).
Kofta: meatballs or vegetable dumplings.
Korma: braised in yoghurt and/or cream and nuts. Often mild, but rich.
Magaz: brain.
Makhani: cooked with butter (makhan) and sometimes tomatoes, as in murgh makhani.
Massalam: marinated, then casseroled chicken dish, originating in Muslim areas.

Moghul, Mogul or **Moglai:** from the Moghul period of Indian history, used in the culinary sense to describe typical North Indian Muslim dishes.
Nihari or **nehari:** there are many recipes on the subcontinent for this long-simmered meat stew, using goat, beef, mutton or sometimes chicken. Hyderabadi nihari is flavoured with sandalwood powder and rose petals. North Indian nihari uses nutmeg, cloves, dried ginger and tomato. In London, however, the dish is made with lamb shank (served on the bone).
Pasanda: thin fillets of lamb cut from the leg and flattened with a mallet. In British curry houses, the term usually applies to a creamy sauce virtually identical to a korma (qv).
Paya: lamb's feet, usually served on the bone as paya curry (long-cooked and with copious gravy); seldom found outside Southall.
Punjabi: Since Partition, the Punjab has been two adjoining states, one in India, one in Pakistan. Lahore is the main town on the Pakistani side, which is predominantly Muslim; Amritsar on the Indian side is the Sikh capital. Punjabi dishes tend to be thick stews or cooked in a tandoor (qv).
Roghan gosht or **rogan josh:** lamb cooked in spicy sauce, a Kashmiri speciality.
Seekh kebab: ground lamb, skewered and grilled.
Tak-a-tak: a cooking method – ingredients (usually meat or vegetables) are chopped and flipped as they cook on a griddle.
Tandoor: clay oven originating in north-west India in which food is cooked without oil.
Tarka: spices and flavourings are cooked separately, then added to dahl at a final stage.
Tikka: meat, fish or paneer cut into cubes, then marinated in spicy yoghurt and baked in a tandoor (qv).

the liver been a slender strip, it would have been the latter, but the hefty hunk of meat detracted from the gloriously fragrant spicing, which was nicely offset by apple and grape chaat. Lemon sole, wrapped around smoked salmon stuffed in turn with sour potatoes, worked beautifully. But mains were mixed. Blackened seared sea bass with masala mash was another brilliant combination, though the accompanying curry sauce was indistinguishable from the sweetish tomato and cream combination in which the mundane chicken tikka was cooked. A trio of chutneys (garlic, beetroot and coconut) served with popadoms were absolute perfection. The Painted Heron itself doesn't quite maintain this standard, but comes close when the creative combinations work.
Babies and children admitted. Booking advisable weekends. Separate room for parties, seats 35. Tables outdoors (5, garden). Vegetarian menu. Vegan dishes. Map 14 **D13**.

Rasoi Vineet Bhatia

10 Lincoln Street, SW3 2TS (7225 1881/ www.rasoirestaurant.co.uk). Sloane Square tube. **Lunch served** noon-2.30pm Mon-Fri. **Dinner served** 6-11pm Mon-Sat. **Set meal** £45 2 courses, £55 3 courses, £75 tasting menu. **Credit** AmEx, DC, MC, V. Modern Indian
Located within a smart Chelsea townhouse, Vineet Bhatia's much lauded restaurant sighs with hushed elegance. The chocolate-hued interior is complemented by sweeping silk drapes, occasional artefacts, tribal masks and colourful artwork across the walls. On our visit, dishes were marred by an overdose of salt – unacceptable in a restaurant of this stature. That aside, chilli-dusted scallops were juicy, well-cooked, and made a good partner with nutty-tasting cauliflower purée and fried droplets of cauli coated in gram-flour batter. Main courses didn't score as highly. Perfectly sautéed fillet of sea bass was let down by a cloying, coconut-based sauce and tandoori potatoes that lacked any hoped-for smokiness. Disappointments continued with slow-cooked lamb shank, which although tender, was spoilt by a stodgy onion masala. We'd like to see less experimentation with the likes of foie gras and spiced cocoa powder and more attention given to cooking techniques. Prices are eye-wateringly high, and although the service team was superb, we're not convinced that the cooking matches expectations. Bhatia is one of London's best-known Indian chefs; let's hope our recent experience was a hiccup.
Babies and children admitted. Booking essential (£45 deposit per person for groups over 6). Dress: smart casual. Separate rooms for parties, seating 8 and 12. Vegetarian menu. Map 14 **F11**.

Vama

438 King's Road, SW10 0LJ (7351 4118/ www.vama.co.uk). Sloane Square tube, then 11, 22 bus. **Lunch served** noon-3pm Sat, Sun. **Dinner served** 6.30-11pm Mon-Sat; 6.30-10.30pm Sun. **Main courses** £9.50-£15.50. **Set buffet** (noon-3pm Sun) £14.99. **Credit** AmEx, MC, V. North Indian
Andy Varma's becoming little restaurant has long been a favourite with well-off Chelsea folk. Its light but ornate interior is replete with oil paintings and carved teak chairs. The kitchen offers some excellent dishes derived from the culinary traditions of India's north-west frontier, but while Vama has won awards and acclaim aplenty, there was nothing warm about our recent evening here. The room was chilly and rather empty, lacking the warm buzz of conversation. Among the best dishes were the adraki gosht (tender lamb laced just so with ginger) and scallop masala (where the spicing perfectly offset the sweetness of the scallops). Bhindi bhojpuri (battered, deep-fried slivers of okra dusted with tangy mango powder) was delightful too, and the dessert of ras malai (curd dumplings poached in a saffron-infused syrup) also elicited sighs of pleasure. But a refined and primly plated starter platter of Indian street snacks (including sev puri, a fairly flavourless aloo tiki, and a little heap of small black chickpeas) was not the strong gutsy

Sat; 12.30-3pm Sun. **Dinner served** 6.30-11pm Mon-Sat; 6.30-10.30pm Sun. **Main courses** £14.50-£26. **Set lunch** £22 3 courses. **Credit** AmEx, DC, MC, V. Pan-Indian
When Chutney Mary opened in 1991 it was the smartest and most ambitious Indian restaurant in the UK, serving proper regional cooking from across India. It continues to update the menu regularly and introduce innovative dishes, as well as keeping the look fresh. The most recent makeover has added wall hangings studded with crystals, glamorising an otherwise slightly fuddy-duddy conservatory, and etchings evocative of the Raj era. Service is smoother than a moghul's turban, but the dishes remain the main attraction. Halibut in mustard sauce is inspired by a Bengali dish, chingri malai, with a cross-section of meaty halibut replacing the traditional shrimps; the coconut cream and mustard seeds are a perfect blend, while a garnish of shiso cress helps produce a western-style presentation. Many dishes show off the skills of the kitchen staff, such as the duck galouti. This dish, usually of finely minced lamb patties, should be very tender; here they've pulled it off despite using tougher duck meat, unusually pairing it with blueberry chutney. Not every dish

has the same wow-factor (there's chicken tikka masala on the menu, after all), but at Chutney Mary you're guaranteed an excellent, memorable meal.
Babies and children welcome: booster seats. Booking advisable dinner; essential Thur-Sat. Dress: smart casual. Entertainment: jazz 1pm Sun. Separate room for parties, seats 34. Map 13 **C13**.

Painted Heron

112 Cheyne Walk, SW10 0DJ (7351 5232/ www.thepaintedheron.com). Sloane Square tube/11, 19, 22, 319 bus. **Lunch served** noon-2.30pm Mon-Fri. **Dinner served** 6-10.30pm Mon-Sat; 6-9.30pm Sun . **Main courses** £13-£18. **Thalis** £15-£17. **Credit** AmEx, MC, V. Modern Indian
A contemporary, unconventional venue tucked in a corner of Chelsea, the Painted Heron has won awards aplenty. It's certainly chic, with white walls and modern paintings lending an art-gallery vibe to the crisp, cool interior. It's also a favourite with locals, drawn back regularly by a set menu that changes daily and an inventive carte that's updated seasonally. The cooking is inspirational, if a little inconsistent. Starters were innovative. Spiced calf's liver with rose petals: a mad dream or genius? Had

RESTAURANTS

affair it should have been. In the end, there was something vapid about the Vama experience: the place just lacked oomph. Pricing is very high too. *Babies and children welcome: high chairs. Booking essential weekends. Separate room for parties, seats 30. Tables outdoors (2, patio). Takeaway service.* Map 14 D12.

Putney

Ma Goa

242-244 Upper Richmond Road, SW15 6TG (8780 1767/www.ma-goa.com). East Putney tube/Putney rail/Putney tube, 337 bus. **Lunch served** noon-2.30pm Tue-Fri; 1-3.30pm Sun. **Dinner served** 6.30-11pm Mon-Sat; 6-10pm Sun. **Main courses** £7.50-£12. **Set dinner** (6.30-8pm) £10 2 courses. **Set buffet** (Sun lunch) £10. **Credit** AmEx, DC, MC, V. Goan
Ma Goa used to pride itself on its Goan home cooking, but although it still offers many Goan dishes, the menu has been infiltrated by several non-Goan recipes. Punjabi chickpea masala and chicken tikka masala have replaced the offal dishes (such as sorpotel) and other more challenging options. But choose carefully and you can still enjoy a taste of the coastal state. The pork vindaloo, perhaps the best-known Goan dish, is a good rendition – correctly sour-sweet, a happy marriage of the Portuguese influence (vinegar, pork consumption) with Indian spicing. Shrimp balchao was also a fine version, with the chilli-heat of the masala the dominant flavour (it was Portuguese settlers who brought chillies from the New World to Goa). This was accompanied by sanna, little Goan steamed rice cakes with an appealing fermented-coconut tang. But some dishes were lacklustre. The fish caldin was bland; this stew should have a kick, and needed more of the smoky kokum (fish tamarind) spice. Ma Goa remains a good neighbourhood restaurant, but we're not sure that it's still the standard-bearer for Goan food in London it once was.
Babies and children welcome: children's menu; high chairs. Booking advisable; essential weekends. Dress: smart casual. Restaurant available for hire. Separate room for parties, seats 35. Takeaway service; delivery service (within 3-mile radius).

South

Tooting

Tooting has been a destination for cheap South Indian meals since the **Sree Krishna** (192-194 Tooting High Street, SW17 0SF, 8672 4250) opened in 1973. It now has an unusual diversity of 'Indian' restaurants, from East African Asian to Sri Lankan and Pakistani. Standards tend to be good, but rarely outstanding; old stalwarts such as **Kastoori** (*see below*) appear to be surviving on past fame, while Tanzanian Punjabi restaurant **Masaledar** (121 Upper Tooting Road, SW17 7TJ, 8767 7676) still cooks great dishes, but now prioritises takeaway orders over restaurant service. Of the two newest South Indian/Sri Lankan Tamil restaurants, **Sarashwathy Bhavans** (70 Tooting High Street, SW17 0RN, 8682 4242) is refreshingly low-priced and serves good food, but having paid several visits to both over the past year, we've found the service and ambience of **Dosa n Chutny** (*see below*) slightly the better of the two.

Although Tooting and Colliers Wood have a mixed Asian community with a majority of Sri Lankan Tamils (some estimates put the community at 30,000), the growth in the Moslem population has been pronounced over the past few years. New halal butchers and cafés are appearing all the time in the stretch between Tooting Bec and Broadway, and the area now has one sizeable mosque, several madrasahs (colleges) and a couple of small Islamic bookshops. Of the halal

restaurants, we rate the Tooting branch of the karahi joint, **Mirch Masala** (213 Upper Tooting Road, SW17 7TG, 8672 7500) as the best, with a varied selection of hearty, warming Punjabi dishes that you can also find at the Norbury original.

★ Apollo Banana Leaf

190 Tooting High Street, SW17 0SF (8696 1423). Tooting Broadway tube. **Meals served** noon-11pm daily. **Main courses** £3.50-£6.25. **Unlicensed**. **Corkage** no charge. **Credit** MC, V. Sri Lankan
The stretch between Tooting and Colliers Wood has a few low-rent Tamil caffs, but Apollo Banana Leaf makes that little extra effort and succeeds in being a proper restaurant. It's true that the decor isn't a strong point, unless junk art of Sahara scenes and Ikea mirrors are to your taste; but the staff are solicitous and smiling, the prices very low, and – most importantly – the Sri Lankan dishes are some of the best you'll find in London. The tastes of the Tamil north of the island are expressed in dishes such as mutton string-hopper fry: the rice vermicelli cut into chunks and fried with hot, full-flavoured mutton curry (the dark-brown colour a clue that the spices have been roasted, in the Sri Lankan way). Pay close heed to the menu's chilli-heat warnings; the squid curry is also fiery. The menu is extensive, incorporating many South Indian and Sri Lankan dishes, rice dishes and the like. One generically subcontinental dish brilliantly executed here is the prawn puri: a huge crisp, puffed bread the size of a small pillow, with a rich gravy dense with prawns. The BYO policy is a bonus.
Babies and children welcome: high chairs. Booking advisable weekends. Takeaway service.

★ Dosa n Chutny NEW

68 Tooting High Street, SW17 0RN (8767 9200/ www.dosa-chutny.com). Tooting Broadway tube. **Meals served** 10am-10.30pm daily. **Main courses** £3-£6. **Set buffet** (noon-10.30pm) £5.95 daily. **Credit** MC, V. South Indian vegetarian
Tooting's old guard of South Indian restaurants caters mainly for non-Asian diners, but the new wave is aimed firmly at the many recent Tamil immigrants who have moved to the area. The look of Dosa n Chutny is as uncompromising as the menu descriptions are terse: bright lighting, orange furniture the colour of traffic cones, a flat-screen TV droning overhead. Classic breakfast and snack dishes are beautifully prepared, such as the wafer-thin, crisp dosas or the idlis with perfect sponge-like texture and bite. For somewhere with 'chutny' in the name, the chutneys are a little repetitive: standard coconut dips, green or red. The sambar is rich and sweet, in the Chennai style. Other food,

such as the chicken 65, is far less impressive, and the Sri Lankan string-hopper dishes aren't a strong point, but at prices this low – idli sambar £2.99, masala dosa £2.50 – it's churlish to complain. Do try the tea and masala tea; they're as close to Indian chai as you'll find in Tooting. On several visits, we have consistently been the only table with non-Asian diners present; it's time the rest of Tooting gave this place a try.
Babies and children welcome: high chairs. Takeaway service.

Kastoori

188 Upper Tooting Road, SW17 7EJ (8767 7027). Tooting Bec or Tooting Broadway tube. **Lunch served** 12.30-2.30pm Wed-Sun. **Dinner served** 6-10.30pm daily. **Main courses** £5.25-£6.25. **Thalis** £8.95-£16.50. **Minimum** £7. **Credit** MC, V. East African Gujarati vegetarian
We can't help thinking standards have slipped here – or maybe they've improved everywhere else. On our recent visits, service was indifferent and inattentive. As neither the room (decorated with a few bas-reliefs of temple dancers) nor the menu has changed for what seems like decades, it's perhaps not surprising the staff seem bored. But the East African Gujarati dishes redeem Kastoori. The various bhel poori are tantalising explosions of sour-sweet flavours, with interesting mixes of crunchy and soft textures. Sev poori, for example, are spilling over with crisp orange sev (deep-fried gram-flour vermicelli), but undercut with the sour tang of tamarind. So far, so Mumbai. But it's the 'Thanki family specials' that are most unusual, using African ingredients such as matoki (plantain) and kasodi (sweetcorn) prepared in Gujarati-style vegetable dishes. It's a shame that so few of the dishes listed are ever available: rarely more than a couple are. Still, the tomato curry is a good alternative, mouth-wateringly spicy and sweet in the style of Kathiawar (the Gujarati peninsula renowned for its cooking). Visit on a Sunday if you want to try the Kathiawadi specialities, millet loaf, khichdi or kadhi.
Babies and children admitted. Booking advisable. Takeaway service. Vegan dishes.

★ Radha Krishna Bhavan

86 Tooting High Street, SW17 0RN (8682 0969). Tooting Broadway tube. **Lunch served** noon-3pm daily. **Dinner served** 6-11pm Mon-Thur, Sun; 6pm-midnight Fri, Sat. **Main courses** £1.95-£6.95. **Minimum** £5. **Credit** AmEx, MC, V. South Indian
This established Keralite restaurant knows its (mainly non-Asian) customers well, and offers a mix of South Indian snacks and breakfast fare, seafood and meat dishes, plus a few Keralite specialities to keep them all happy. We recommend

Shilpa. See p155.

sticking to the specialities such as the avial ('mixture' vegetable stew), vellappams (large frisbee-shaped crumpets), thorans (vegetable stir-fries including finely diced beetroot or grated cabbage), and lemon rice. The dosas, idlis and vadai are also fine, but several restaurants in Tooting now do these better, and cheaper. Recently we've found RKB inconsistent; sometimes the food is faultless, but on our last visit, one of the dishes – a mango and yoghurt curry called kalan – contained yoghurt that had curdled, giving the dish an unappealing lumpy texture. Mostly, though, we don't find much to pick fault with, and the interior here is particularly memorable, inducing enjoyable getaway reveries. The walls are covered with bold photographic wallpaper depicting coconut-fronded beaches and sunsets; a full kathakali dance costume sits imposingly in one corner; and statues of blue boy Krishna and his favourite girlfriend, Radha, adorn the counter. *Babies and children admitted. Booking advisable. Takeaway service; delivery service (over £20 within 3-mile radius). Vegetarian menu.* **For branch (Sree Krishna Inn) see index.**

South East
Herne Hill

Mela
136-140 Herne Hill, SE24 9QH (7738 5500/ www.melarestaurant.co.uk). Herne Hill rail/3, 37, 68 bus. **Lunch served** noon-2.30pm, **dinner served** 6-11pm Mon-Sat. **Meals served** noon-10.30pm Sun. **Main courses** £6.95-£9.95. **Set lunch** (Mon-Fri) £7.95 2 courses, £10.95 3 courses. **Buffet lunch** (Sun) £6.95. **Set dinner** £12.95 2 courses. **Credit** AmEx, DC, MC, V. Pan-Indian
Branch of the West End Mela (*see p147*) and Chowki (*see p152*), this restaurant changed its name from 3 Monkeys in summer 2008. It's an upmarket neighbourhood local, offering a taste of

mainly North Indian cooking at fair prices. The spacious ground floor and basement could do with freshening up: let down by a musty atmosphere, wilting flowers, and an ad hoc arrangement of 'modern' artwork. In contrast, the noisy open kitchen hits the spot with judiciously spiced, homely cooking. Methi chicken was our favourite for its tender morsels of meat, and caramelised onion and tomato masala, flecked with peppery mustard greens – a homage to hearty Punjabi cooking. Makhani dhal, made with slow-cooked black lentils, provided buttery, cream-laden indulgence: a tasty partner to hot nans. Vegetarian food matches the quality of the meat dishes; dry-cooked cauliflower with potatoes, a 'mum's-own' delectation, was notable for its fried tomato masala, toasted cumin spicing, and shredded ginger garnish. Service, although pleasant, needs to be more confident. We were miffed to be directed to a duff table behind a pillar, despite the restaurant being virtually empty (and this has happened several times before). Good-value meal deals abound; check out the Sunday buffet spreads and weekday set lunches.
Babies and children welcome: high chairs. Booking advisable. Disabled: toilet. Separate rooms for parties, seating 30 and 60. Takeaway service; delivery service (within 3-mile radius). **Map 23 A5.**

East

Whitechapel is a predominantly Bangladeshi neighbourhood, though you'll look hard for much evidence of this on the menus at the northern 'tourist' end of Brick Lane. Yet many low-budget caffs in Whitechapel do serve Bangladeshi specialities alongside the more usual pan-Indian dishes – either advertised in Bengali script only, or not written down but available if you ask.

Among our favourites are **Ruchi** (303 Whitechapel Road, E1 1BY, 7247 6666),

which looks like a generic fast-food place selling fried chicken and formula curries, but the dining room is concealed up stairs at the back. **Sabuj Bangla** (102 Brick Lane, E1 6RL, 7247 6222) also gets the flavours right, but it's a basic, absolutely no-frills venue with a point-and-order display cabinet of unlabelled dishes. If you prefer a slightly more upmarket dining experience – table service and a menu in English – then try **Kolapata** (*see p165*). And if you're looking for a more conventional approach to good and cheap 'Indian' food, try the Pakistani-run **Tayyabs** (*see p165*) or **Lahore Kebab House** (*see p165*).

Bethnal Green

★ **Mai'da** NEW
148-150 Bethnal Green Road, E2 6DG (7739 2645/www.maida-restaurant.co.uk). Bethnal Green tube/Liverpool Street tube/rail. **Meals served** noon-11pm daily. **Main courses** £4.25-£9.50. **Credit** AmEx, MC, V. Pan-Indian
Surrounded by the regulation urban kebab and tikka takeaways, Mai'da – with its cream walls, calligraphic paintings, mood lighting and dark-wood furniture – has upmarket aspirations. The name is Arabic for dining table; in Urdu it means flour. The extensive menu is ambitious, incorporating North Indian, Pakistani, Parsi and Indo-Chinese influences. Alcohol isn't allowed, so we ordered sweet lassi. Starters of lamb chops and kachay aam ka murgh tikka (tangy chicken tikka wrapped around a green-mango and coriander filling), were melt-in-the-mouth and worthy of London's best Indian restaurants. Main courses were variable. Nimbu aur hare dhaniye ka murgh was a chicken curry supposedly flavoured with lemon and coriander, but tasting like weak soup. Seafood tawa biriani was bland too, with none of the sharpness of tomatoes and onion that

Mango & Silk. See p157.

distinguishes good seafood biriani (nor any hint that a tawa grill had been used). Dinner was redeemed by khade masala ka gosht, lamb flavoured with crushed spices (black peppercorns, cumin, cardamom, cloves and bay leaf), and the roomali roti. We ended the meal with the satisfying sugar buzz of falooda. Mai'da has all the ingredients for greatness – but should pare down its menu and focus on its strengths.
Babies and children welcome: children's menu; high chairs. Disabled: toilet. Separate rooms for parties, seating 8-24. Takeaway service; delivery service (free over £15 within 3-mile radius).
Map 6 S4.

Brick Lane

You may be surprised that this guide doesn't carry reviews of any Brick Lane restaurants. The reason is simple: we have tried many, year after year, but in recent times none has been of a sufficient standard.

Despite this, Brick Lane touts still make claims to be recommended by *Time Out*. In 2006 Tower Hamlets Council introduced a byelaw that banned restaurateurs from touting for customers. Brick Lane touting

waned for a while, but on our recent visits, it seemed to have returned to the previous level. The salesman's patter might offer a free bottle of wine, two-for-one pricing, or other special deals. The clincher, for many, seems to be 'recommended by *Time Out*'. Maybe their restaurant was – five, ten, or more years ago. Ask to see proof, as we did. The only evidence they could summon up was favourable reviews that were several years old, some with the dates conveniently removed. A review that old is, of course, no recommendation at all.

Whitechapel

Café Spice Namaste
16 Prescot Street, E1 8AZ (7488 9242/ www.cafespice.co.uk). Aldgate East or Tower Hill tube/Tower Gateway DLR. **Lunch served** noon-3pm Mon-Fri. **Dinner served** 6.15-10.30pm Mon-Fri; 6.30-10.30pm Sat. **Main courses** £12.50-£18.55. **Set meal** £30 3 courses, £40 4 courses, £60 tasting menu. **Credit** AmEx, DC, MC, V. Pan-Indian
Given that Café Spice Namaste is a chef-owned restaurant (the chef being the acclaimed Cyrus

Todiwala), the decor at its bright, spacious premises is short on warmth and imagination: think Nando's meets Urban Outfitters. Thankfully, what this stiff, corporate-friendly Parsi eaterie lacks in ambience it makes up for in friendly service and inventive food. The menu has detailed descriptions under each dish – perfect for newcomers to Parsi cuisine. The Indian Parsi community are Zoroastrians whose ancestors arrived in the subcontinent over 1,000 years ago. They pride themselves on a cuisine that bridges the gap between Persia and the Indian state of Gujarat. Savour the traditional dhansak, an intricate blend of lentils, ginger, garlic, cumin, vegetables and tender pieces of lamb. Less enjoyable was the shockingly insipid patra ni machchi: pomfret fillets layered with a mint and coconut chutney and steamed in a banana leaf. The fish was dry, the flavours dull and the portion small. Better instead to opt for the delectable guisado de chouriço javali, an ingenious fusion dish made of soft wild-boar chipolatas tossed in a powerful, tangy vindaloo masala and served with crisp pitta bread.
Babies and children welcome: high chairs. Booking advisable. Disabled: toilet. Tables outdoors (8, garden). Takeaway service; delivery service (within 2-mile radius). **Map 12 S7**.

The best guides to enjoying London life

(but don't just take our word for it)

'A treasure trove of treats that lists the best the capital has to offer'

The People

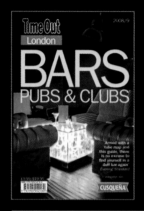

'Armed with a tube map and this guide there is no excuse to find yourself in a duff bar again'

Evening Standard

'I'm always asked how up to date with shoppi and services in a city a as London. This guide the answer'

Red Magazine

'Get the inside track on the capital's neighbouhoods'

Independent on Sunday

'You will never again be stuck for interesting things to do and places to visit in the capital'

Independent on Sunday

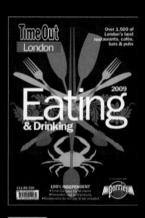

Rated 'Best Restaurant Guide

Sunday Times

TIME OUT GUIDES WRITTEN BY LOCAL EXPERTS

timeout.com/shop

★ Kolapata

*222 Whitechapel Road, E1 1BJ (7377 1200).
Whitechapel tube.* **Meals served** noon-11.30pm
daily. **Main courses** £3.95-£8.95. **Set buffet**
(12.30-3pm Mon-Fri) £4.95. **Unlicensed.**
Corkage no charge. **No credit cards.**
Bangladeshi

In recent years Kolapata – 'banana leaf' in Bengali
– has been the leading destination to experience
Bangladeshi cooking in London. The restaurant
is modest, cheap and very popular with local
Bangladeshis. Here they rediscover the tastes of
home, more often than not, with dishes such as
haleem (a stew of lentils and lamb still on the
bone); or with bony Bengali river fish such as
fillets of rui in a spicy gravy. Pedestrian lamb
madras and chicken tikka masala dishes make up
the bulk of the menu, so ask the waiters to guide
you towards traditional Bangladeshi food like
labra (a mixed vegetable stir-fry with mustard
seeds) or the extraordinary borhani: a yoghurt
drink with the distinctive sulphurous aroma of the
spice called kala namak (black salt). On our three
visits over the last year, we've found standards
highly variable. When the food is freshly cooked
and the full complement of chefs from Dhaka is
in the kitchen, the flavours and freshness sing; but
visit off-peak and you may find birianis and other
dishes reheated, and other corners cut.
*Babies and children welcome: high chairs. Booking
advisable. Takeaway service.*

★ Lahore Kebab House

*2 Umberston Street, E1 1PY (7488 2551/
www.lahore-kebabhouse.com). Aldgate East
or Whitechapel tube.* **Meals served** noon-
midnight daily. **Main courses** £5.50-£9.50.
Unlicensed. Corkage no charge. **Credit**
MC, V. Pakistani

Over 40 years old, Lahore Kebab House has never
had it so good. As noisy and boisterous as a school
canteen, it appeals to a diverse group of curry
lovers, including brash City suits, families, and
young office workers. Functional tables and a
gleaming open kitchen are the setting for hearty,
earthy cooking with plenty of smoky grills, onion-
ginger-garlic masalas, and hot, buttery breads. At
weekends, keep an eye out for specials such as
trotter curry, and haleem (unusually made with
chicken rather than lamb, simmered with cracked
wheat). Our dhal gosht (lentils simmered with
browned lamb in a fried onion masala) was tender
and robustly flavoured with garlic and ginger, a
marvellous match with tandoori roti. Vegetarians
are well-catered for, and we loved the homely spin
on paneer curry flecked with peas – especially the
soft curd cheese cubes, cloaked in cumin-scented
tomato masala. Our neighbours on the next table
were devouring tandoori lamb chops with so much
relish that we know what we'll be ordering on our
next visit. Despite the cacophony around us,
service is prompt and efficient. This is no place to
linger over kulfis; chances are there'll be a queue
of takers for your table.
*Babies and children welcome: high chairs.
Disabled: toilet. Takeaway service; delivery
service (by taxi).*

★ Tayyabs

*83 Fieldgate Street, E1 1JU (7247 9543/
www.tayyabs.co.uk). Aldgate East or Whitechapel
tube.* **Meals served** noon-11.30pm daily. **Main
courses** £6-£10. **Unlicensed. Corkage**
no charge. **Credit** AmEx, MC, V. Pakistani

If you're expecting refined Indian cooking, best
move on – Tayyabs is the East End equivalent of
the caffs favoured by truckers in South Asia.
Affected flourishes, new-wave flavours, and
adaptations for western palates have no place here.
This canteen has been around since the 1970s, and
although the interior has been refurbished and
extended to embrace three separate dining areas,
it's still a challenge to bag a table. On most nights,
a serpentine queue of City folk, young couples and
office types winds out of the door. Cooking is big,
bold and sassy. Deliciously sticky nihari made
with lamb shanks simmered in cardamom and
clove-scented broth showed melt-in-the-mouth
tenderness. Dhals are a highlight, especially an
unsung gem of grainy white urad lentils,
sharpened with lime juice and crowned with a
tangle of crisp-fried onions. Chicken karahi was
the only disappointment for its oily masala. Yes,
the place is crowded and noisy, but service is swift,
and dishes are pegged at very low prices. We've
had uneven meals here in the past, but recent
experiences have convinced us to return Tayyabs
to our address book.
*Babies and children welcome; high chairs. Booking
advisable. Separate room for parties, seats 35.
Tables outdoors (8, garden). Takeaway service.*

North East

Stoke Newington

Rasa

*55 Stoke Newington Church Street, N16 0AR
(7249 0344/www.rasarestaurants.com). Stoke
Newington rail/73, 393, 476 bus.* **Lunch
served** noon-3pm Sat, Sun. **Dinner served**
6-10.45pm Mon-Thur, Sun; 6-11.30pm Fri, Sat.
Main courses £3.95-£5.95. **Set meal** £16
4 courses. **Credit** AmEx, DC, MC, V.
South Indian vegetarian

This, the original branch of the Rasa chain, caused
a stir when it opened in 1997. The vegetarian home
cooking of the Nair caste of Kerala had never
before been so successfully reproduced in the UK,
and both locals and the critics were bowled over
by the vibrancy, inventiveness and novelty of the
dishes. More than a decade on, the central London
seafood restaurant Rasa Samudra (*see p148*) and
even a meaty restaurant, Rasa Travancore, have
been added to the Rasa empire. Nowadays this
pioneer may not create quite the same excitement
as when it opened, but the dishes are excellent
and the execution still good, if not quite as precise
as the early years. Cabbage thoran is still a
surprise; this delicate stir-fry sings with the
flavours of popped mustard seed and cumin, plus
the subtle aroma of curry leaves and the texture
of shredded coconut. Moru kachiathu is another
signature dish, the turmeric-stained yoghurt
bathing large pieces of orange mango, the sweetly
spicy dish tasting as exotic as it looks. The appam
pancakes on our recent visit were disappointingly
scorched on the outside, but the own-made pickles
were of such magnificence that we quickly forgave
this sloppy detail.
*Babies and children welcome: high chairs. Booking
essential weekends. Takeaway service. Vegetarian
menu. Vegan dishes.* **Map 25 B1.**
For branches see index.

South Indian menu

Much South Indian food consists
of rice, lentil- and semolina-based
dishes (semolina being small grains
of crushed wheat). Fish features
strongly in non-vegetarian restaurants,
and coconut, mustard seeds, curry
leaves and red chillies are widely
used as flavourings.

If you want to try South Indian snacks
like dosas, idlis or uppama, it's best
to visit restaurants at lunchtime, which
is when these dishes are traditionally
eaten, and they're more likely to be
cooked fresh to order. In the evening,
we recommend you try the thalis and
rice- and curry-based meals, including
South Indian vegetable stir-fries like
thorans and pachadis. For the tastiest
Tamil food, try **Sanghamam** (*see p172*)
in Wembley. **Satya** (*see p171*) in
Uxbridge offers some of the liveliest,
most colourful Keralite specialities.
Sagar (*see p155*) in Hammersmith
is best for Udupi vegetarian cooking
from Karnataka.

Adai: fermented rice and lentil pancakes,
with a nuttier flavour than dosais (qv).
Avial: a mixed vegetable curry from
Kerala with a coconut and yoghurt
sauce. Literally, 'mixture' in Malayalam
(the language of Kerala).
Bonda: spiced mashed potatoes,
dipped in chickpea-flour batter and
deep-fried.
Dosai or **dosa:** thin, shallow-fried
pancake, often sculpted into interesting
shapes; the very thin ones are called
paper dosai. Most dosais are made
with fermented rice and lentil batter,
but variants include **rava dosai,** made
with 'cream of wheat' semolina.
Masala dosais come with a spicy
potato filling. All variations are
traditionally served with sambar
(qv) and coconut chutney.
Gobi 65: cauliflower marinated in spices,
then dipped in chickpea-flour batter
and deep-fried. It is usually lurid pink
due to the addition of food colouring.
Idli: steamed sponges of ground rice
and lentil batter. Eaten with sambar
(qv) and coconut chutney.
Kadala: black chickpea curry.
Kalan: a thin curry from the southern
states made from yoghurt, coconut
and mangoes.
Kancheepuram idli: idli (qv) flavoured
with whole black peppercorns and
other spices.
Kappa: cassava root traditionally
served with kadala (qv).
Kootu: mild vegetable curry in a
creamy coconut and yoghurt sauce.
Kozhi varutha: usually consists of
pieces of chicken served in a medium-
hot curry sauce based on garlic and
coconut; it is very rich.
Moilee: Keralite fish curry.
Pachadi: spicy vegetable side dish
cooked with yoghurt.
Rasam: consommé made with
lentils; it tastes both peppery-hot
and tamarind-sour, but there are
many regional variations.
Sambar or **sambhar:** a variation on
dahl made with a specific hot blend
of spices, plus coconut, tamarind and
vegetables – particularly drumsticks
(a pod-like vegetable, like a longer,
woodier version of okra; you strip out
the edible interior with your teeth).
Thoran: vegetables stir-fried with
mustard seeds, curry leaves, chillies
and fresh grated coconut.
Uppama: a popular breakfast dish in
which onions, spices and, occasionally,
vegetables are cooked with semolina
using a risotto-like technique.
Uthappam: a spicy, crisp pancake/
pizza made with lentil- and rice-flour
batter, usually topped with tomato,
onions and chillies.
Vellappam: a bowl-shaped, crumpet-
like rice pancake (same as appam
or hoppers, qv, Sri Lankan menu).

Gujarati menu

Most Gujarati restaurants are located in north-west London, mainly in Wembley, Sudbury, Kingsbury, Kenton, Harrow, Rayners Lane and Hendon, and they tend to be no-frills, family-run eateries.

Unlike North Indian food, Gujarati dishes are not normally cooked in a base sauce of onions, garlic, tomatoes and spices. Instead they're tempered; whole spices such as cumin, red chillies, mustard seeds, ajwain (carom) seeds, asafoetida powder and curry leaves are sizzled in hot oil for a few seconds. The tempering is added at the start or the end of cooking, depending on the dish. Commonplace items like grains, beans and flours – transformed into various shapes by boiling, steaming and frying – are the basis of many dishes. Coriander, coconut, yoghurt, jaggery (cane sugar), tamarind, sesame seeds, chickpea flour and cocum (a sun-dried, sour, plum-like fruit) are also widely used.

Each region has its own cooking style. Kathiyawad, a humid area in western Gujarat, and Kutch, a desert in the north-west, have spawned styles that are less reliant on fresh produce. Kathiyawadi food is rich with dairy products and grains such as dark millet, and is pepped up with chilli powder. Kutchis make liberal use of chickpea flour (as do Kathiyawadis) and their staple diet is based on khichadi. In central Gujarat towns such as Baroda and Ahmedabad, grains are widely used; they appear in snacks that are the backbone of menus in London's Gujarati restaurants.

The gourmet heartland, however, is Surat – one of the few regions with heavy rainfall and lush vegetation.

Surat boasts an abundance of green vegetables like papadi (a type of broad bean) and ponk (fresh green millet). A must-try Surti speciality is undhiyu. Surti food uses 'green masala' (fresh coriander, coconut, green chillies and ginger), as opposed to the 'red masala' (red chilli powder, crushed coriander, cumin and turmeric) more commonly used in western and central regions.

The standard of Gujarati food available in restaurants has improved in recent years. Authentic Surti food is now available at **Ram's** (see p168); and **Sakonis** (see p172) offers good Kenyan-Gujarati versions of Mumbai street snacks. The best time to visit Gujarati restaurants is for Sunday lunch, which is when you'll find little-seen regional specialities on the menu – but you will almost certainly need to book.

Bhakarvadi: pastry spirals stuffed with whole spices and, occasionally, potatoes.

Bhel poori: a snack originating from street stalls in Mumbai, which contains crisp, deep-fried pooris, puffed rice, sev (qv), chopped onion, tomato, potato and more, plus chutneys (chilli, mint and tamarind).

Dhokla: a steamed savoury gram-flour cake.

Farsan: Gujarati snacks.

Ganthia: Gujarati name for crisply fried savoury confections made from chickpea flour; they come in all shapes.

Ghughara: sweet or savoury pasties.

Kadhi: yoghurt and chickpea flour curry, often cooked with dumplings or vegetables.

Khandvi: tight rolls of 'pasta' sheets

(made from gram flour and curds) tempered with sesame and mustard seeds.

Khichadi or **khichdi:** rice and lentils mixed with ghee and spices.

Mithi roti: round griddle-cooked bread stuffed with a cardamom-and-saffron-flavoured lentil paste. Also called puran poli.

Mogo: deep-fried cassava, often served as chips together with a sweet and sour tamarind chutney. An East African Asian dish.

Pani poori: bite-sized pooris that are filled with sprouted beans, chickpeas, potato, onion, chutneys, sev (qv) and a thin, spiced watery sauce.

Patra: a savoury snack made of the arvi leaf (colocasia) stuffed with spiced chickpea-flour batter, steamed, then cut into slices in the style of a swiss roll. The slices are then shallow-fried with sesame and mustard seeds.

Pau bhajee: a robustly spiced dish of mashed potatoes and vegetables, served with a shallow-fried white bread roll.

Puran poli: see mithi roti.

Ragda pattice or **ragada patties:** mashed potato patties covered with a chickpea or dried-pea sauce, topped with onions, sev (qv) and spicy chutney.

Sev: deep-fried chickpea-flour vermicelli.

Thepla: savoury flatbread.

Tindora: ivy gourd, a vegetable resembling baby gherkins.

Undhiyu: a casserole of purple yam, sweet potatoes, ordinary potatoes, green beans, Indian broad beans, other vegetables and fenugreek-leaf dumplings cooked with fresh coconut, coriander and green chilli. A speciality of Surat.

North

Camden Town & Chalk Farm

★ ★ **Masala Zone** NEW
25 Parkway, NW1 7PG (7267 4422/www. masalazone.com). Camden Town tube. **Lunch served** 12.30-3pm, **dinner served** 5.30-11pm Mon-Fri. **Meals served** 12.30-11pm Sat; 12.30-10.30pm Sun. **Main courses** £7-£15. **Thalis** £7.80-£10.70. **Credit** MC, V.
Pan-Indian

This recent addition to the Masala Zone chain is especially popular with hip youngsters who come for the buzzy vibe, reasonable prices and decent pan-Indian and regional Indian food. Distinctive in looks, the place has an eye-catching decor themed around colourful 1930s-style posters, retro artefacts and colourful lampshades. The menu is notable for its earthy curries, thalis and zesty street snacks, but also offers spicy burgers and chilli-flecked noodles – a sample of modern Indian tastes. Opting for traditional dishes, we gave our gold star to gol guppas: puffed pastry globes filled with delicious tart tamarind water spiked with black salt. A main course of smoky lamb korma had tender morsels of meat in a robust onion masala. Equally memorable, chicken lazeez, the meat simmered in a broth-like curry, had been delicately infused with fragrant floral notes and citrussy cardamom: a great rendition of royal palace cooking. Always a safe bet are the thalis,

which take the stress out of ordering and include daily specials of dhals and side dishes. Backed by the Panjabi sisters – who also run the fine-dining Amaya (see p148), Veeraswamy (see p150) and Chutney Mary (p159) – this chain looks destined for continued expansion.
Babies and children welcome: children's menu; high chairs. Bookings not accepted (under 10). Separate room for parties, seats 30. Takeaway service. **Map 3 H1.**
For branches see index.

North West

Mill Hill

Atithi NEW
418-422 Watford Way, NW7 2QJ (8203 6573/ www.atithi.co.uk). Mill Hill Broadway rail. **Lunch served** noon-2pm Mon-Thur, Sat, Sun. **Dinner served** 6-11pm daily. **Main courses** £7.95-£13.95. **Credit** AmEx, MC, V. Pan-Indian

Backed by cookery writer Mridula Baljekar, Atithi is a capacious new venue on a dull parade by the roaring A1. Inside, money has been lavished on black floor tiles, linen tablecloths and logoed white crockery. Modern art decorates the cream walls. It's attractive, but was deserted throughout our midweek dinner. Food includes the usual tandooris, bhunas and jalfrezis, but there's plenty more – notably vegetarian food, incorporating the likes of Kashmiri lotus root kebabs. Our starter, kadhai mogo, had cubes of cassava bathed in a sweet-sour sauce boosted by garlic, black pepper

and spring onions. Service is well-meaning, but can be clueless. Orders were muddled, and a waiter described kedgeree as 'sauce'. His blushes were spared when the venison with shiitake kedgeree ('Mridula's signature dish') turned out to be unavailable. Instead we enjoyed a Keralite dish of meen moiley: flavoursome king prawns in creamy coconut sauce pepped up with curry leaves and chilli. Puddings are alluring, especially in the summer mango season, though whether the perfect fruit was enhanced by crème anglaise is questionable. We wish Atithi well: it's handsome and the kitchen has talent, but the bill can mount up, and some staff training wouldn't go amiss.
Babies and children welcome. Booking advisable.

Swiss Cottage

Atma
106C Finchley Road, NW3 5JJ (7431 9487/ www.atmarestaurants.com). Finchley Road or Swiss Cottage tube. **Lunch served** noon-3pm, **dinner served** 6-11pm Tue-Sun. **Main courses** £12.50-£14.50. **Set meal** £22.50 tasting menu. **Credit** AmEx, MC, V.
Modern Indian

Striding purposefully into its second year, Atma ('soul') has an assuredness born of skill and training. The smart waiters are models of quiet efficiency, and the kitchen staff (with experience at Zaika among others) know their Modern Indian onions. Amuses bouches, perhaps an exquisite espresso cup of dhal soup, emphasise the culinary ambitions. A seafood platter starter maintained the standard: dense salmon fish cakes, tender tubes of

squid in the lightest batter, and, best of all, ajwain-garlic tandoori king prawn, the blackened but juicy crustacean on a pungent garlicky relish. The menu embraces Kashmiri and South Indian food, so as well as tandooris you'll find chettinad chicken, zinging with coconut and spiced (a little meekly) with warming black pepper, and lemon rice boosted with mustard seeds and curry leaves. Neither should you miss the mixed bread basket, featuring the best of north and south. Two caveats: 'smoked chicken' was too much like tikka masala despite its highfalutin description; and blinds to banish the worst outrages of the Finchley Road would greatly improve this otherwise serene, terracotta-hued restaurant. In all, though, Atma deserves to succeed.
Babies and children admitted: high chair. Booking advisable weekends. Takeaway service. **Map 28 B3**.

Eriki
4-6 Northways Parade, Finchley Road, NW3 5EN (7722 0606/www.eriki.co.uk). Swiss Cottage tube. **Lunch served** noon-3pm Mon-Fri, Sun. **Dinner served** 6-11pm daily. **Main courses** £7.95-£11.95. **Set lunch** £12.95 2 courses. **Credit** AmEx, MC, V. Pan-Indian
With ambient red hues and tasteful wooden furniture, it's hard to find fault with the decor at this warm, inviting restaurant. Take a seat by the bar from where you can gaze at the intricately carved screens. Notably pleasant staff enhance Eriki's relaxing atmosphere, proving helpful and efficient without being overbearing. Our only complaint concerns the slightly misleading menu, which forsakes straightforward dish names for pretentious descriptions. The subji shingora sounded intriguing, but turned out to be nothing more than a plate of samosas. Otherwise, the food here is impressive and fairly priced. We highly recommend the divine handi gosht dum biriani, which rivals anything you can get on a Delhi dinner table. Luscious, plentiful pieces of lamb are mixed with flavoursome basmati rice steeped in

saffron, cardamom and cloves and served in a handi (a small copper wok-like vessel). The biriani arrives with cucumber raita, but it's worth ordering something saucy in addition. We opted for a well-prepared and creamy shahi paneer makhani (generous chunks of paneer cheese with tomatoes, butter and fenugreek); this North Indian favourite is best soaked up with a crispy nan.
Babies and children admitted. Booking advisable. Restaurant available for hire. Takeaway service; delivery service (6-9.45pm, over £15 within 4-mile radius). Vegetarian menu. **Map 28 B4**.

Outer London

Eastcote, Middlesex

★ ★ **Nauroz** (100)
219 Field End Road, Eastcote, Middx HA5 1QZ (8868 0900). Eastcote tube. **Meals served** noon-midnight Tue-Sun. **Main courses** £3.50-£9. **Set lunch** £5 2 courses. **Licensed. Corkage** no charge. **Credit** MC, V. Pakistani
Eastcote's best known community caff is a magnet for curry aficionados from across London, as well as local Pakistani and North Indian families. In a brightly lit interior on functional seating, expect succulent kebabs, rustic dhal, and full-flavoured curries. On our last visit, we shared a fish tikka starter of juicy cod chunks, cooked to perfection and cloaked in a smoky crust of gingery yoghurt. Nihari, a meltingly tender lamb stew, scored bonus points for its sticky spicy stock infused with fennel seeds and sweet cardamom. Vegetable choices don't quite reach the standards of meat main courses, but we've never been let down by slow-cooked butter beans simmered in tangy tomato masala with peppery fenugreek leaves – a marvellous match with hot, buttery nan. When the kitchen gets busy, service can be erratic, but there's plenty of Punjabi banter from boisterous families to keep entertainment levels high. Save space for the creamy rice pudding topped with a flurry of

pistachio nuts: it's divine. Family-run Nauroz excels at producing down-to earth meals, pegged at prices that wouldn't be out of place in India.
Babies and children welcome: high chairs. Booking advisable Fri, Sat. Takeaway service; delivery service (over £15 within 3-mile radius). Vegetarian menu.

Harrow, Middlesex

Blue Ginger
383 Kenton Road, Harrow, Middx HA3 0XS (8909 0100/www.bgrestaurant.com). Kenton tube/rail. **Lunch served** noon-3pm Tue-Sat. **Dinner served** 6-11pm Mon-Sat. **Meals served** 1-10.30pm Sun. **Main courses** £5.25-£10.95. **Credit** AmEx, MC, V. North Indian
Blue Ginger is clearly popular with Kenton's well-to-do Asian families. Porsches and Mercedes crowd the car park, and flat-screen TVs and black leather couches dot the interior. Don't let this put you off the food, though. The menu is split into 'Indian specials' and 'Chinese specials', though several dishes are a fusion of both cuisines, thus brilliantly capturing Delhi's thriving Punjabi-Chinese food scene (which largely entails adding more chilli and Indian herbs and spices to classics like spring rolls). So, a meal could start with pan-fried masala fish in a delicious ginger, red chilli, coriander and peppercorn crust; or masala mogo, consisting of deep-fried cassava patties tossed in a distinct sweet and sour sauce. Cultural purists might prefer paneer bhurji, a favourite brunch dish among Delhites and one often eaten in place of scrambled eggs, shredded paneer is cooked with onions, tomatoes and coriander. Or, as recommended by our charming waiter, try the fish masala: a generous helping of tilapia fillets in a light, tomato broth infused with ginger and garlic and topped with roasted mustard seeds and fresh coriander.
Babies and children welcome: high chairs. Booking essential. Disabled: toilet. Dress: smart casual. Separate rooms for parties, seating 40 and 50. Tables outdoors (7, terrace). Takeaway service.

RESTAURANTS

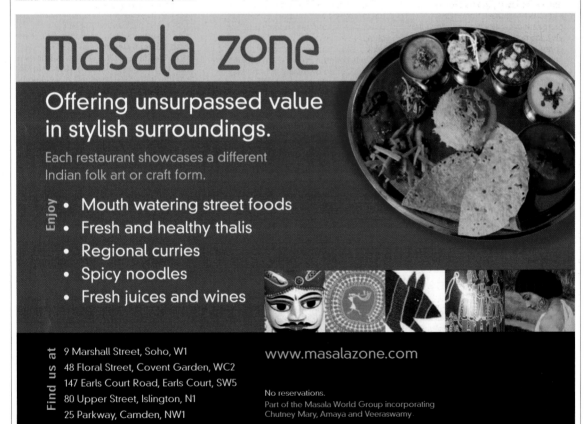

★ ★ Ram's (100)

203 Kenton Road, Harrow, Middx HA3 0HD (8907 2022). Kenton tube/rail. **Lunch served** noon-3pm, **dinner served** 6-11pm daily. **Main courses** £4-£5. **Thalis** £4.99-£8.99. **Set meal** £16.50 (unlimited food and soft drinks). **Credit** AmEx, MC, V. Gujarati vegetarian

This small café, simply furnished with wipe-clean tables and framed images of Hindu deities, champions the best of Gujarati vegetarian cooking. It duly attracts a loyal audience of locals (family groups and others). These guys are big on authenticity – there's even polished steel tableware to showcase mum's-own cooking. We reckon Ram's spiced street snacks are the best in town. Top marks went to the pani puri (crisp puffed pastry discs filled with diced onions and chickpeas): a perfect match with minted chilli-speckled tamarind water. Pau bhaji was equally satisfying; buttery potato mash simmered with onions, tomatoes and peppers made a surprisingly good marriage with toasted bread rolls: the ultimate Indian fast food. We moved on to the more substantial main courses. Kadhi (gram flour simmered with whipped yoghurt, popped mustard seeds and crisped curry leaves) was deliciously soupy and tart with tamarind. Our only gripe concerned the overdose of green peppers in virtually every main course. Breads are tip-top, especially puffed pooris served straight from the pan, and piping hot chapatis. For a taste of sunshine, order the fresh lime sodas seasoned with black salt and toasted cumin. Ram's is undoubtedly the jewel in Kenton's crown.
Babies and children welcome: high chairs. Booking advisable weekends. Disabled: toilet. Restaurant available for hire. Takeaway service.

Southall, Middlesex

As 'authentic' as markets in North India, the shops and stalls on Southall's Broadway and surrounding roads bring the flavours of Punjabi street life to Middlesex. There's little you can't pick up here – from crisp samosas and smoky kebabs, to sequinned salwar suits, glittering gold jewellery, and swathes of brightly hued silk.

Visit **Kwality Foods** (47-61 South Road, UB1 1SQ, 8917 9188) for its vibrant display of exotic vegetables, fragrant seasonal mangoes, and aisles crammed with pickles.

Southall is best enjoyed at the weekend when its thoroughfares are jammed with noisy vendors and bargain hunters haggling over prices. Arrive just after 10am when shops open for business and you'll be greeted by the soothing melodic refrain of devotional music. Decibel levels increase as the morning progresses, the earthy tones of Punjabi vernacular a backdrop to noisy traffic and bhangra beats.

Join the jostling crowds around pavement kiosks as they tuck into creamy kulfis and hot jalebis (crisp-fried whirls of batter) coated in sticky, rose-scented syrup. Sample alfresco sweet treats at **Moti Mahal** (94 The Broadway, UB1 1QF, 8571 9443), but don't confuse this venue with the identically named ('pearl palace'), but unrelated restaurant in Covent Garden (*see p147*). For fudge-like blocks of barfi, and patisa (wispy, honeycomb-like squares of sweetened gram flour fried in ghee), **Ambala** (107 The Broadway, UB1 1LN, 8843 9049) offers consistently good quality. If milky puds are your weakness, head for **Royal Sweets** (92 The Broadway, UB1 1QF, 8570 0832), which has excellent ras malai (curd-like dumplings simmered in sweetened spiced milk).

Southall's Punjabi community – which hails from the Sikh heartlands on the Indian side of the border, as well as from Pakistan and East Africa – has improved its financial lot in recent years. Flashy cars, glitzy shop fronts and redecorated restaurants are a testament to the newly acquired wealth. Cooking, however, remains homely and true to its rustic subcontinental roots.

For hearty feasts, make for the **New Asian Tandoori Centre** (*see p170*). It's well worth the brisk walk away from Broadway and down South Street. Our current favourite meal here (available at weekends) is kadhi and rice (toasted gram-flour curry spiked with tart yoghurt, ginger flecks and fried curry leaves). If you're looking for low-fat spins on crunchy snacks, curries and buttery breads, there's not much to choose from, although **Brilliant** (*see below*) makes some attempt to address healthy cooking.

Most Southall cafés have pan (pronounced 'parn') on the menu. These tasty mouth-fresheners are served at the end of a meal and are made by wrapping astringent betel nut leaves around a usually sweetish filling of dates, cardamom, coconut and a sliver of betel nut.

If you're driving, take the car to the main car park behind The Broadway's Himalaya Centre to be assured of a place. Better still, take the train or bus; shops are close by and there's plenty to see on the way. Although standards of cooking at the multifarious caffs might vary, the street life of Southall is incomparable.

★ Brilliant

72-76 Western Road, Southall, Middx UB2 5DZ (8574 1928/www.brilliantrestaurant.com). Southall rail. **Lunch served** noon-3pm Tue-Fri. **Dinner served** 6-11.30pm Tue-Sun. **Main courses** £4.50-£14. **Credit** AmEx, DC, MC, V. East African Punjabi

There's plenty to take in here, even before being seated. Wafts of incense shroud a Ganesh figurine by the front door, next to a glass wall in which water and lights swirl, opposite statues of Masai

---

Sri Lankan menu

Sri Lanka has three main groups: Sinhalese, Tamil and Muslim. Although there are variations in the cooking styles of each community and every region, rice and curry form the basis of most meals, and curries are usually hot and spicy. The cuisine has evolved by absorbing South Indian, Portuguese, Dutch, Arabic, Malaysian and Chinese flavours over the years. Aromatic herbs and spices like cinnamon, cloves, curry leaves, nutmeg, and fresh coriander are combined with South-east Asian ingredients such as lemongrass, pandan leaves, sesame oil, dried fish and rice noodles. Fresh coconut, onions, green chillies and lime juice (or vinegar) are also used liberally, and there are around two dozen types of rice – from short-grained white varieties to several long-grained, burgundy-hued kinds.

Curries come in three main varieties: white (cooked in coconut milk), yellow (with turmeric and mild curry powder) and black (with roasted curry powder, normally used with meat). Hoppers (saucer-shaped pancakes) are generally eaten for breakfast with kithul palm syrup and buffalo-milk yoghurt, while string hoppers (steamed, rice-flour noodles formed into flat discs) usually accompany fiery curries and sambols (relishes).

Sri Lankan cafés in Tooting, Southall, Wembley and Harrow are becoming increasingly popular.

Ambul thiyal: sour fish curry cooked dry with spices.
Appam or **appa:** *see* Hoppers.
Badun: black. 'Black' curries are fried; they're dry and usually very hot.
Devilled: meat, seafood or vegetable dishes fried with onions in a sweetish sauce; usually served as starters.
Godamba roti: flaky, thin Sri Lankan bread, sometimes wrapped around egg or potato.
Hoppers: confusingly, hoppers come in two forms, either as saucer-shaped, rice-flour pancakes (try the sweet and delectable milk hopper) or as string hoppers (qv). Hoppers are also known as appam.
Idiappa: see string hoppers.
Katta sambol: onion, lemon and chilli relish; fearsomely hot.
Kiri: white. 'White' curries are based on coconut milk and are usually mild.
Kiri hodi: coconut milk curry with onions and turmeric; a soothing gravy.
Kuttu roti, kottu or **kothu roti:** strips of thin bread (loosely resembling pasta), mixed with mutton, chicken, prawns or vegetables to form a 'bread biriani'; very filling.
Lamprais or **lumprice:** a biriani-style dish where meat and rice are cooked together, often by baking in banana leaves.
Lunnu miris: a relish of ground onion, chilli and maldives fish (qv).
Maldives fish: small, dried fish with a very intense flavour; an ingredient used in sambols (qv).
Pittu: rice flour and coconut steamed in bamboo to make a 'log'; an alternative to rice.
Pol: coconut.
Pol kiri: see kiri hodi.
Pol sambol: a mix of coconut, chilli, onions, maldives fish (qv) and lemon juice.
Sambols: strongly flavoured relishes, often served hot; they are usually chilli-hot too.
Seeni sambol: sweet and spicy, caramelised onion relish.
Sothy or **sothi:** another name for kiri hodi.
String hoppers: fine rice-flour noodles formed into flat discs. Usually served steamed (in which case they're dry, making them ideal partners for the gravy-like kiri hodi, qv).
Vellappam: appam (qv) served with vegetable curry.
Wattalappan or **vattilapan:** a version of crème caramel made with kithul palm syrup.

warriors. A screen belts out Bollywood pop. Add the happy chatter of a full house – extended families, groups of friends, couples – and it's hard not to enjoy the chaotic buzz. The food is robust: a Kenyan/Punjabi take on Indian cuisine that's full of uncomplicated, concentrated flavour. From the first bite of the own-made pickles (including the sharp lemon with mustard seed served in many Punjabi homes), to the last morsel of soft, thin roomali (handkerchief) roti, every dish packed a punch. Starters included the Kenyan favourite nyama choma ('roast meat', in this case grilled lamb chops: succulent, salty, lemony, with a good hit of chilli). Silky seekh kebabs of ground lamb with fresh green chilli and coriander, and fried tilapia fillets in spicy gram-flour batter, were superb, as was a main course of chicken redolent with cumin. There are dishes marked as healthy options, but restraint wasn't on the menu during our visit, when so many diners were having way too much fun to consider restraint.
Babies and children welcome: high chairs. Booking advisable weekends. Separate room for parties, seats 120. Takeaway service. Vegetarian menu.

Madhu's (100)
39 South Road, Southall, Middx UB1 1SW (8574 1897/www.madhusonline.com). Southall rail. **Lunch served** 12.30-3pm Mon, Wed-Fri. **Dinner served** 6-11.30pm Mon, Wed-Sun. **Main courses** £6-£12. **Set meal** £17.50-£20 per person (minimum 6) 16 dishes incl tea or coffee. **Credit** AmEx, MC, V. East African Punjabi
Gleaming glass panels, glossy black tiles and crisp table linen set the scene for upmarket dining at Southall's smartest restaurant. Although the dishes are mainly North Indian, the owners (the Anand family) introduce an African twist in menu specialities that reflect their own Indo-Kenyan heritage. The most distinctive of these is nyama choma – smoky lamb ribs, much-loved for their lemony zing. On this occasion, we opted for northern Indian stalwarts, with mixed results. Deep-fried mini patties of grated paneer, pounded

peas and chopped fenugreek had a tangy tease of peppery flavour that worked well with the sweetness of tamarind chutney. Portions are sizeable and there's enough for two people in a single starter. Main courses were disappointing. Chicken curry simmered with slivers of bitter gourd was let down by an oily, ginger-laden masala that overpowered the astringent gourd. The same spice base appeared in the chickpea curry: another downer. Breads were excellent but an exception, almost everything else fell short of expectation. Service, although well meaning, needs to be more confident and less obsequious. We've had much better meals at Madhu's in the past.
Babies and children welcome: high chairs. Booking advisable. Disabled: toilet. Separate room for parties, seats 35. Takeaway service. Vegan dishes.

★ New Asian Tandoori Centre (Roxy)
114-118 The Green, Southall, Middx UB2 4BQ (8574 2597). Southall rail. **Meals served** 8am-11pm Mon-Thur; 8am-midnight Fri-Sun. **Main courses** £5-£7. **Credit** MC, V. Punjabi
This Southall institution has been a family-run business for more than 30 years. Over time it has expanded from takeaway joint to an expansive 'tandoori centre'. The entrance remains a canteen-style hall with Indian sweets, bhajias and curries to take away, while a functional central room is brightly lit with frosted-glass windows, tiled floors and long communal tables. The menu is largely Punjabi, characterised by rich and earthy flavours, but there are a few good South Indian dishes too. We started with pakoras which, although a little dense and doughy, were lifted by fresh coriander. Chana dhal, an Indian truck drivers' favourite, was thick, buttery and tempered with toasted cumin seeds – just right. The chickpeas in the chana bhatura were fragrant and judiciously spiced, but the accompanying rounds of bhatura (deep-fried dough) had deflated and were heavy with oil. Nan, on the other hand, was sweet, light and flaky.

Painfully slow service meant we eventually resorted to stacking our dirty plates to get them cleared away. In spite of this, we'll be returning for well-priced food in generous portions.
Babies and children welcome: high chairs. Booking advisable. Disabled: toilet. Separate room for parties, seats 60. Takeaway service. Vegetarian menu.

Stanmore, Middlesex

Papaji's Lounge
865 Honeypot Lane, Stanmore, Middx HA7 1AR (8905 6966/www.papajis.com). Cannons Park tube. **Lunch served** noon-3pm Fri-Sun. **Dinner served** 6-11pm Mon-Fri, Sun; 6pm-midnight Sat. **Main courses** £4.95-£12.95. **Credit** DC, MC, V. Punjabi
Smartly furnished, this long narrow restaurant boasts a brightly lit 1970s-style bar at its centre and a couple of flatscreen TVs pulsating to contemporary Bollywood beats. Cooking is mainly old-school Punjabi with occasional curry-house diversions (chicken madras, chicken tikka masala). In a meal of hits and misses, it was the staples that reassured – dark-hued makhani dhal simmered with butter and tomatoes, delectable for its creamy texture and rustic appeal. Breads are top drawer too: light, fluffy and served straight from the tandoor. Sadly, a sizzling tandoori platter lacked distinctive spicing, and the salmon tikka, tandoori prawns, and chicken tikka were too salty. Only the seekh kebab (a skewered, minced lamb 'sausage', scented with ginger) restored our faith with its succulence and judicious spicing. A main course of butter chicken delivered the goods with a saucy tomato masala flecked with toasted fenugreek leaves: great comfort food. Service is helpful and attentive, but on a Saturday night, only a few tables were occupied. Standards need to be raised for Papaji's to meet expectations.
Babies and children welcome: high chairs. Booking advisable. Disabled: toilet. Takeaway service. Vegetarian menu.

Sudbury, Middlesex

★ ★ Five Hot Chillies

875 Harrow Road, Sudbury, Middx HA0 2RH (8908 5900). Sudbury Town or Sudbury Hill tube. **Meals served** noon-midnight daily. **Main courses** £3.50-£9. **Unlicensed. Corkage** no charge. **Credit** MC, V. Punjabi

If you can't grab the attention of one of the friendly but busy waiters, simply walk up to the counter of this clean, no-frills café to place your order. Contrary to its name, Five Hot Chillies offers authentic Punjabi cooking that doesn't scorch your taste buds. Yet even though your mouth won't need cooling during the meal, your tastebuds will definitely appreciate a fresh passion-fruit juice while reading the extensive menu. We started with juicy lamb kebabs and a zesty plate of chilli paneer. For mains, choose one of the dishes made in a karahi, an iron wok used to prepare food in Punjabi households. The karahi gosht in particular is scrumptious. Made of tender mutton pieces in a thick tomato, ginger, garlic and chilli sauce, it is rather heavy on the stomach (and arteries), so order plenty of nan, roti, or rice to help soak up the oil. Sadly, karahi saag paneer – a blend of spinach and cream dotted with lumps of shallow-fried paneer – wasn't as impressive. Finish with a refreshing almond kulfi.

Babies and children welcome: high chairs. Booking advisable. Takeaway service. Vegetarian menu.

Twickenham, Middlesex

Tangawizi

406 Richmond Road, Richmond Bridge, East Twickenham, Middx TW1 2EB (8891 3737/ www.tangawizi.co.uk). St Margaret's rail. **Dinner served** 6.30-11pm Mon-Sat. **Main courses** £6.95-£12.95. **Credit** AmEx, MC, V. North Indian

Perhaps Tangawizi has come up with a blueprint for a new type of suburban curry house. It's obviously a success, attracting young local diners (including the occasional British Asian couple), yet it serves properly prepared North Indian food. The surroundings doubtlessly help. This is a relaxed, hip enterprise with attractive staff, a backlit bar and tables inlaid with sari fabric; background beats and purple lighting lend a chilled nightclub vibe. Though the owners hail from Uganda and Tanzania, the African influence on the menu is slight (tilapia might be fish of the day), and there's always chicken tikka masala for the unenterprising. Yet everything we sampled spoke of a dab hand in the kitchen. To start, try the mixed non-veg starters (minimum two diners): a variety of juicy seared tandoori meats and a dense potato patty. Next, we can vouch for the 'tanghai' lamb: tender chunks in a sublime mild gravy based on coconut juice, mustard seeds and curry leaves, served in a green coconut shell. Flavourful too was the methi 'wala' (*sic*) chicken, where fenugreek leaves were matched by a rich tomato sauce. For dessert, wizi samosas (filled with almond and coconut) were dryish, but overall this was a fine meal.

Babies and children welcome: high chairs. Booking advisable Fri, Sat. Restaurant available for hire. Takeaway service; delivery service (over £15 within 3-mile radius). Vegetarian menu.

Uxbridge, Middlesex

★ Satya

33 Rockingham Road, Uxbridge, Middx UB8 2TZ (01895 274250). Uxbridge tube. **Lunch served** noon-3pm, **dinner served** 6-11pm daily. **Main courses** £5.50-£9.50. **Set buffet** (noon-3pm Mon-Fri) £6.50. **Credit** AmEx, MC, V. South Indian

A shocking fuchsia façade belies the stylish interior of this neighbourhood restaurant. Once past it, taupe and deep-red walls, crisp white tablecloths, soft lighting and wooden floors make an inviting setting for the colourful South Indian cooking. On past visits Satya has been busy, but during a recent lunchtime we were the only customers. A line of waiters greeted us warmly, eager to recommend dishes from their native

Brilliant. See p168.

Kerala. All the favourites are here – uthappam, idlis, adai with avial – as well as more unusual snacks such as methi bhajia (dense, deep-fried balls made from fenugreek leaves and banana). Speciality of the house is chicken cooked with shreds of fresh ginger, onion and green chilli: perfect with the coconut-flecked rice. Chutneys are fresh and tangy, making ideal accompaniments. Some of the dishes lacked texture; the spiced potato filing of the masala dosas, for example, would have benefited from being less vigorously mashed, as would the pumpkin cooked with black-eyed beans. Nonetheless, flavours here are generally clean and light, and all the food was thoughtfully spiced.
Babies and children welcome: high chair. Booking advisable. Disabled: toilet. Separate room for parties, seats 10. Takeaway service.

Wembley, Middlesex

Karahi King
213 East Lane, North Wembley, Middx HA0 3NG (8904 2760). North Wembley tube/245 bus. **Meals served** noon-midnight daily. **Main courses** £4-£12. **Unlicensed. Corkage** no charge. **Credit** AmEx, DC, MC, V. Punjabi
This popular little neighbourhood eaterie attracts an eclectic following. On our visit, we spotted a large Punjabi family dressed in all their finery; canoodling couples tucked away in the back; and several weary men in search of a hangover cure. If you're in the mood for greasy, cheap Punjabi food, cooked before you in the open kitchen, this is the place for you. Don't expect anything too healthy – to prepare most of its dishes, Karahi King uses the karahi (a wok-like cooking vessel), and lots of oil. Nevertheless, there's also a wide choice of vegetarian food here, such as karahi chana (chickpeas), bhindi (okra) and paneer. We were drawn towards the meat dishes and opted

for a karahi saag gosht, which arrived as an uninspired green mush of lamb pieces, cardamom shells and spinach. Karahi chicken tikka renewed our hope, however; the sauce's simple ingredients of onion, garlic, tomato and coriander were fresh, and each bite ended with a tangy burst of lemon. We recommend skipping the starters – although the chilli bhajia (battered, deep-fried whole chillies) is mouth-wateringly delicious – because the main courses are so large.
Babies and children welcome: high chairs. Separate room for parties, seats 60. Takeaway service. Vegetarian menu.

★ Sakonis (100)
129 Ealing Road, Wembley, Middx HA0 4BP (8903 9601). Alperton tube/183 bus. **Breakfast served** 9-11am Sat, Sun. **Meals served** noon-10pm daily. **Main courses** £2-£7. **Set buffet** (breakfast) £4.99; (noon-4pm) £7.99; (7-9.30pm) £10.99. **Credit** MC, V. Gujarati vegetarian
This flagship branch of a vegetarian chain is a no-frills destination popular with local residents. Turnover is fast, service efficient but abrupt, and the food keeps you coming back for more. As well as the hugely popular buffet, a wide menu includes Indo-Chinese dishes, South Indian specialities, and snacks with an East African influence – all seasoned to suit the Gujarati sweet tooth. We opted for the traditional Mumbai-style street snacks. Pani puri (puffed pastries filled with potatoes and tamarind water) were light and crisp enough to hold the thin, spiced sauce, while crunchy aloo bhajia (potato slices fried in coriander-flecked batter) were so delicious that almost every table had wisely ordered a plate. There were some disappointments, including the bhel poori, which was too sweet and lacked tang, but then aloo papadi chat (crushed popadoms, potatoes and spikes of raw onion smothered with sweet yoghurt and herby chutney) was spot on. Fresh juices and

iced lassis cut through the richness of the fried food perfectly. Expect a lively throng of customers at weekends and remember to pick up some tooth-achingly sweets and savouries from the snack counter on the way out.
Babies and children welcome: high chairs. Takeaway service.
For branch see index.

★ Sanghamam
531-533 High Road, Wembley, Middx HA0 2DJ (8900 0777). Wembley Central tube. **Meals served** 8am-11pm daily. **Main courses** £4.25-£6.95. **Set lunch** (11am-4pm) £3.95 3 dishes. **Thalis** £4.95-£6.95. **Credit** MC, V. Pan-Indian vegetarian
Sanghamam may claim to serve Gujarati, North and South Indian, and Chinese food, but a step inside soon establishes its antecedents: strictly Tamil. Most of the customers and all the staff speak rapid Tamil or thick Tamil-accented English, and Tamil songs are played in the background. Our tomato-and-onion uthappam (a fluffy South Indian pancake made of fermented rice and lentil batter) was fresh from the pan, filling and tasty. The accompanying coconut, coriander and turmeric chutneys were full-flavoured too. Eating the sambar, however, was like playing a game of Russian roulette: the first helping was lukewarm and bland, the second surprisingly hot, spicy and delicious. Sanghamam's utilitarian atmosphere – heavy steel cutlery, a one-page laminated menu card, and fast, no-frills service – doesn't make for a fine-dining experience, but if you're looking for quick, wholesome, value-for-money South Indian food (a meal for two is around £10) this restaurant is a safe bet.
Babies and children welcome: high chairs. Separate room for parties, seats 80. Tables outdoors (4, pavement). Takeaway service. Vegetarian.

Sweets menu

Even though there isn't a tradition of serving puddings at everyday meals in South Asia, there is much ceremony associated with distributing sweetmeats at auspicious events – especially weddings and religious festivals. Many of these delicacies are rarely found in the West: shahi tukra (nursery-like bread and butter pudding); nimesh (rose-scented creamy froth, scooped into clay pots); and misti dhoi (jaggery-flavoured set yoghurt from Bengal).

Desserts served at many Indian restaurants in London include the likes of gulab jamun, cardamom-scented rice pudding, creamy kulfi, and soft, syrup-drenched cheese dumplings. In the home, family meals don't often include a dessert; you're more likely to be treated to a platter of seasonal fruit. Even in Britain, thousands of miles away from mango groves, the onset of India's mango season in May is a date for the calendar. To appreciate this lush fruit at its best, look for boxes of alphonso mangoes in Asian stores.

Winter warmers also have their place, including comforting, fudge-like carrot halwa, a Punjabi favourite and popular street snack. In Punjabi villages, a communal cauldron is often simmered for hours on end, sending out wafts of aromatic cardamom and caramelised carrots as the halwa cooks down into an indulgent treat. Winter is also the season for weddings, where other

halwas, made with wholewheat flour, semolina, lentils and pumpkin, might be served. Most 'sweets' take a long time to make, which is why people prefer to visit sweetmeat shops, the best known of which is **Ambala**'s flagship store near Euston station (112 Drummond Street, NW1 2HN, 7387 3521). Here, an impressive array of eye candy for the seriously sweet-toothed includes soft cheese-based dumplings immersed in rose-scented syrup, cashew-nut fudgy blocks, toasted gram-flour balls, and marzipan-like rolls. Expect floral flavours, shed-loads of sugar and a good whack of calorie-laden ghee (clarified butter). It's hard to believe that with all the varieties offered, specialist sweet-makers (known as halwais) cook with so few ingredients; milk products, dried fruit, sugar and ghee are the key constituents.
Barfi: sweetmeat usually made with reduced milk, and flavoured with nuts, fruit, sweet spices or coconut.
Bibenca or **bibinca**: soft, layered cake from Goa made with eggs, coconut milk and jaggery.
Falooda or **faluda**: thick milky drink (originally from the Middle East), resembling a cross between a milkshake and a sundae. It's flavoured with either rose syrup or saffron, and also contains agar-agar, vermicelli, nuts and ice-cream. Very popular with Gujarati families, faloodas make perfect partners to deep-fried snacks.

Gajar halwa: grated carrots, cooked in sweetened cardamom milk until soft, then fried in ghee until almost caramelised; usually served warm.
Gulab jamun: brown dumplings (made from dried milk and flour), deep-fried and drenched in rose-flavoured sugar syrup, best served warm. A traditional Bengali sweet, now ubiquitous in Indian restaurants.
Halwa: a fudge-like sweet, made with semolina, wholewheat flour or ground pulses cooked with syrup or reduced milk, and flavoured with nuts, saffron or sweet spices.
Jalebis: spirals of batter, deep-fried and dipped in syrup, best eaten warm.
Kheer: milky rice pudding, flavoured with cardamom and nuts. Popular throughout India (there are many regional variations).
Kulfi: ice-cream made from reduced milk, flavoured with nuts, saffron or fruit.
Payasam: a South Indian pudding made of reduced coconut or cow's milk with sago, nuts and cardamom. Semiya payasam is made with added vermicelli.
Rasgullas: soft paneer cheese balls, simmered and dipped in rose-scented syrup, served cold.
Ras malai: soft paneer cheese patties in sweet and thickened milk, served cold.
Shrikhand: hung (concentrated) sweet yoghurt with saffron, nuts and cardamom, sometimes with fruit added. A traditional Gujarati favourite, eaten with pooris.

RESTAURANTS

International

The revolution in the London restaurant scene over the past two decades has transformed its international restaurants. Until the late 1980s, the term generally referred to eating houses that mixed cuisines on the same menu; now it denotes those that do so on the same plate. Where once chefs might have offered moussaká, lasagne and curry among their culinary repertoire, today's gastronomic adventurers have broken down international barriers and regularly dip into London's global larder of ingredients. This year we've encountered tempura with risotto at **Hadley House**, lobster in a rum-coconut red curry at **Asia de Cuba** and a meze platter placing chinese beans alongside falafel at **Shish**. Some dishes work wondrously, others are plain gruesome, but there's no denying the excitement of encountering a successful experiment.

This year we were especially impressed with the pan-Asian flavours created at **Champor-Champor**, but fusion-meister Peter Gordon's innovations at the **Providores & Tapa Room** are usually worth experiencing. Modern European, Oriental, Pacific Rim and New Indian cuisines have been forged in the kitchens of such pioneers, and London is still the best place to sample these mould-breaking restaurants. Be adventurous and try one – it's what our city is all about.

Central
Clerkenwell & Farringdon

The Modern Pantry NEW
47-48 St John's Square, EC1V 4JJ (7250 0833/ www.themodernpantry.co.uk). Farringdon tube/rail.
Café **Meals served** 8am-11pm Mon-Fri; 9am-11pm Sat; 9am-10pm Sun. **Main courses** £10-£15.50.
Restaurant **Lunch served** noon-3pm Mon-Sat; noon-4pm Sun. **Dinner served** 6-10.30pm Mon-Sat. **Main courses** £12-£19.
Deli **Open** 7.30am-7.30pm Mon-Sat.
All **Credit** AmEx, MC, V.
Anna Hansen worked together with Peter Gordon at the Sugar Club, then at Providores (*see right*), before striking out on her own with this much-delayed project inside a handsome, Grade II-listed Georgian building facing a traffic-free square. When complete, it will feature a café, deli and first-floor dining room, but when we visited soon after opening in August 2007, the ground floor was in use as the dining room. Hansen's style of food resembles Providores': a genre-bending fusion of ingredients and cooking styles from around the world, with no affiliation to any region. For example, a sugar-cured prawn omelette initially resembled the Vietnamese dish banh xeo, but had been given a Kiwi makeover with a spicy sambal dressing and Thai basil on top. A main course of onglet steak (an inexpensive French cut) had been marinated in miso, and was served with cassava chips instead of the more usual potato. Not every dish was a success – one described as chorizo, date and feta fritters resembled onion bhajis – but the originality of them won us over. This is best demonstrated in the desserts, which included a chocolate liquorice mousse in a tiny espresso cup, served with half a tamarillo and a bitter-tasting wafer of caramelised cocoa and chilli.
Babies and children welcome: high chairs. Disabled: toilet. Separate room for parties, seats 30. Tables outdoors (9, square). Takeaway service (deli). **Map 5 O4**.

Covent Garden

Asia de Cuba
45 St Martin's Lane, WC2N 4HX (7300 5588/ www.morganshotelgroup.com). Leicester Square tube. **Breakfast served** 6.30-11am Mon-Fri; 7-11am Sat, Sun. **Lunch served** noon-2.30pm daily. **Dinner served** 5pm-midnight Mon-Sat; 5-10.30pm Sun. **Main courses** £22.50-£48. **Set meal** (noon-7pm daily) £22.50-£28 bento box. **Credit** AmEx, MC, V.
Hidden behind the anonymous, office-like façade of St Martin's Lane Hotel is the chi chi Asia de Cuba, where beatific staff ply you with Hollywood smiles against a clubby backbeat. If the white modernist decor doesn't stun you into submission, then Philippe Starck's witty accents of pot plants, higgledy-piggledy photos and vintage books should make an impression. It's mainly dining à deux here – intimacy is encouraged by an Asian-Cuban menu where every dish is for sharing. The spiced cuisine might borrow from the Chino-Latino cafés of Havana and Miami, but that understanding doesn't extend to the pricing, which soars skywards for lobster in a rum-coconut red curry (£62) or wagyu beef with tempura king prawns (£74). Dishes are of a high standard, but can be giddily unbalanced. Thai beef salad brought shredded coconut and orange segments to the hot-and-sour mix, but was light on the seared carpaccio; an otherwise ballsy hoi sin duck proved thin on Asian green salad and tropical salsita. Desserts and drinks are inventive: don't miss the defiantly fluffy asian pear bread-and-butter pudding, or splendid lychee mojito.
Babies and children welcome: children's menu; high chairs. Booking advisable. Disabled: toilet. Separate rooms for parties, seating 48 and 96. Vegetarian menu. **Map 18 D5**.

Le Deuxième
65A Long Acre, WC2E 9JH (7379 0033/ www.ledeuxieme.com). Covent Garden tube.
Lunch served noon-3pm, **dinner served** 5pm-midnight Mon-Fri. **Meals served** noon-midnight Sat; noon-11pm Sun. **Main courses** £14.50-£18.50. **Set meal** (noon-3pm, 5-7pm, 10pm-midnight Mon-Fri; noon-midnight Sat; noon-11pm Sun) £13.50 2 courses, £16.50 3 courses. **Credit** AmEx, MC, V.
Theatregoers find much to applaud at this understated little restaurant, where, as they often desire, service is pacy enough to have you wined, dined and out of the door in record time. Your inner Francophile, though, can emerge thinking '*quelle dommage!*' The French name (it's the second acquisition of the team behind Le Café du Jardin), starched white table linen and courteous staff belie the multifaceted menu, where wild mushroom risotto, Scotch beef and Thai tempura bed down alongside French classics. That said, dishes are sparkier since chef Simon Conboy took over. They taste – and look – more than proficient. The no-nonsense fish soup, served with rouille and a giant 'croûton' on the side, delivered a paprika punch; the crab cake contained a goodly amount of shredded meat; and roast cod with white bean stew added interest with merguez. Such is the variety of mains, though, that they jump around like a greatest-hits medley. Perhaps Le Deuxième needs the confidence to serenade customers with French cuisine from start to finish.
Babies and children admitted. Booking advisable. **Map 18 E3**.

Fitzrovia

Archipelago
110 Whitfield Street, W1T 5ED (7383 3346/ www.archipelago-restaurant.co.uk). Goodge Street or Warren Street tube. **Lunch served** noon-2.30pm Mon-Fri. **Dinner served** 6-10.30pm Mon-Sat. **Main courses** £13.50-£20.50. **Set lunch** (Mon-Fri) £12.50 per person (minimum 2). **Credit** AmEx, DC, MC, V.
Culinary explorers will find new adventures at this niche restaurant. Archipelago is home to the kind of wild creatures seldom seen on a plate. Sitting cheek by jowl with a kooky hodgepodge of golden Buddhas, fertility idols and giant peacock feathers from bazaars the world over, diners choose from such delicacies as marinated kangaroo, wok-seared frogs' legs and seared zebra. While most restaurants revamp their menus to add interest, dishes here are strangers to reinvention – but then again, the wow factor is omnipresent. Gastronomic gadabouts will delight in the juicy seared crocodile fillet (tastes like fish, has the texture of chicken) or savoury slivers of peanut-crusted wildebeest. Favoured as a daring destination by couples in the first bloom of dating, Archipelago is fun and intimate. But despite numerous distractions such as menus tightly rolled into scrolls fit for Indiana Jones, you're likely to notice that service is patchy. Note too that you have to divulge your credit card details at time of booking, as there's a non-refundable deposit for late cancellation.
Babies and children admitted. Booking advisable. Tables outdoors (2, patio).

Marylebone

★ The Providores & Tapa Room (100)
2008 RUNNER-UP BEST BREAKFAST
109 Marylebone High Street, W1U 4RX (7935 6175/www.theprovidores.co.uk). Baker Street or Bond Street tube.
The Providores **Lunch served** noon-2.45pm daily. **Dinner served** 6-10.30pm Mon-Sat; 6-10pm Sun. **Main courses** (lunch) £18-£26. **Set meal** (dinner) £29 2 courses, £42 3 courses, £52 4 courses, £60 5 courses. **Cover** (lunch Sat, Sun) £1.50.
Tapa Room **Breakfast served** 9-11.30am Mon-Fri; 10am-3pm Sat, Sun. **Meals served** noon-10.30pm Mon-Fri; 4-10.30pm Sat; 4-10pm Sun. **Tapas** £2-£14.40.
Both **Credit** AmEx, MC, V.
If the test of a good restaurant is a negative answer to 'could I cook this at home?' then the Pacific Rim fusion at Providores passes with rocketing colours. It's not just that Peter Gordon

dazzles with such epicurean obscurities as barrel-aged Banyuls vinegar, from a French seaside town better known for its fortified wines; it's also that some produce is imported from his native New Zealand and is a rarity in London, as is the case with kumara (a uniquely flavoured sweet potato). Factor-in that dishes – even starters – are so complicated their descriptions snake down several lines of the menu, and you could feel overwhelmed. Fortunately, the flavours work in blissful harmony: witness the robust wild hare fillet, accompanied by a creamy cabbage purée with toasted walnuts, goat's cheese and tangy pomegranate. Cocktails are commendable, the wine list a New Zealand tour de force. In the past, service has been excellent, but this time staff were unsmiling – a small slip, perhaps, yet with mains around £25 and elbow room at a premium, no lapses should be tolerated. The ground-floor Tapa Room, tailored to extravagant breakfasting and exuberant evening drinks, was quieter than usual too.
Babies and children welcome: high chairs. Booking advisable Providores; bookings not accepted Tapa Room. Disabled: toilet. Tables outdoors (2, pavement). **Map 9 G5.**

Mayfair

Sketch: The Gallery (100)
9 Conduit Street, W1S 2XG (7659 4500/ www.sketch.uk.com). Oxford Circus tube. **Dinner served** 7-11pm Mon-Sat. **Main courses** £12-£32. **Credit** AmEx, MC, V.
The Sketch tag-line 'eat music drink art' seems to be arranged in reverse order of importance. It's the art you encounter first – with the theatrically black entrance hall housing a zippy light installation and a statue of a dalmatian standing nose-first in a bin – while the 'eat' bit is forever playing catch-up. There's a touch of Marie Antoinette about the twirly-backed chairs inside the Gallery (the mid-priced restaurant of the three here), but it's not terrifyingly outré. The clubby beats and swirling projected lights are tiresomely distracting if you're serious about your food, but then dishes are smallish and variable. A starter of organic salmon was accompanied by a bland lime and horseradish chantilly; chestnut velouté was better, but had a gimmicky dollop of ice-cream. Mains were OK: the scallops, accompanied by braised turnips, were nice and plump; the chicken and wok-fried vegetables a bit predictable. Sittings are for two-hour slots, with service swift and inevitably swift. It would be hard to justify coming here for the food alone, but the place is endearingly original, and entertainingly try-hard.
Booking essential. Entertainment: DJs 11pm-2am Thur-Sat. Restaurant available for hire. **Map 9 J6.**

Soho

Refuel
The Soho Hotel, 4 Richmond Mews, W1D 3DH (7559 3007/www.refuelsoho.com). Tottenham Court Road tube. **Meals served** 7am-11pm Mon-Sat; 7.30am-11pm Sun. **Main courses** £13.50-£30. **Set meal** (noon-11pm Mon-Sat) £19.95 3 courses; (noon-11pm Sun) £24.95 3 courses. **Credit** AmEx, MC, V.
Residing on the ground floor of the chic Soho Hotel, which is itself tidily tucked into a mews between two of Soho's sooty and sweaty main drags, Refuel boasts one of those swanky 'in the know' addresses. Impressive in some respects, it manages to exude modernity and time-honoured charm in equal measure. Arrive during the early evening lull, however, and you'll wish you were downing a few cheeky shots with the media livewires crushed into the modest adjoining bar. Sadly, the menu is more gastropub than private club, with what ought to be straightforward dishes too-often failing to deliver. A simple starter of seared scallops was modestly portioned and a little oddly paired with roast red and green peppers. 'Onion tarte tatin with goat's cheese glaze' turned out to be a single onion encased in deep pastry and topped with a rollicking round of cheese. Perhaps roast pork rump, cavolo nero, cider and mustard would have been nicer. Here's a tip: get the vibe without expecting any foodie feats by ordering from the basic three-course set menu at £19.95 per person. Or come for traditional afternoon tea or sample from the vast choice of breakfasts.
Babies and children welcome: children's menu; high chairs. Booking advisable. Disabled: toilet. Separate room for parties, seats 45. **Map 17 B3.**

Westminster

The Atrium
4 Millbank, SW1P 3JA (7233 0032/www.atrium restaurant.com). Westminster tube. **Lunch served** noon-3pm, **dinner served** 6-9.45pm Mon-Fri. **Main courses** £9.95-£19.75. **Set meal** £17.95 2 courses. **Credit** AmEx, DC, MC, V.
Politicos are prominent among the Atrium's suited lunchtime clientele, as attested by the magazine rack headed 'Political Intelligence Served Here'. As restaurants go, it's something of a curiosity: set in the sunken central atrium of a large complex that comes complete with health club. You dine many floors below a soaring glass ceiling, bathed in natural light and surrounded by small offices rented by media companies. The menu is a mixed bag of brasserie-style dishes, which, when it came to the chewy starter of Thai chicken patty with sweet chilli dressing, seemed to sacrifice subtlety

for convenience. Much better is the more lovingly prepared traditional fare such as roast duck with braised savoy cabbage, pancetta and sage jus, or ribeye steak with pont neuf potatoes. Nothing here will wow you with originality, but it's serviceable enough, albeit with a two-course set lunch at a not inconsequential £17.95. Officially the restaurant is open till 11pm, but evenings are so quiet that it can close early; best phone ahead to check.
Babies and children admitted. Booking advisable lunch. Disabled: lift; toilet. Separate rooms for parties, seating 12 and 30. **Map 16 L10.**

West
Kensington

Abingdon
54 Abingdon Road, W8 6AP (7937 3339/ www.theabingdonrestaurant.com). High Street Kensington tube. **Lunch served** 12.30-2.30pm Mon-Fri; 12.30-3pm Sat, Sun. **Dinner served** 6.30-11pm Tue-Sat; 6.30-10.30pm Mon; 7-10.30pm Sun. **Main courses** £12.50-£22. **Set lunch** (Mon-Fri) £15.95 2 courses. **Credit** AmEx, MC, V.
Adventurous eclecticism meets classical proficiency in this bar and dining room just off Ken High Street. The decor is in keeping with gastropub norms, and the red leather booths were comfortable. Dinner started well with a trio of perfectly cooked scallops – crisp and caramelised on the outside, melting and sweet within, served with a sorrel sauce that worked and a 'tzatziki' of crème fraîche and cornichons that did not. This unnecessary embellishment was a portent of things to come. Venison carpaccio was fresh and beautifully presented, if swamped with rocket, pine nuts and parmesan. Less garnish and more meat would have made the dish delightful. Mains were disappointing: a salmon fillet served with rubbery, gruyère-topped mussels, in an overly buttery seafood bisque; and overcooked seared tuna surrounded by a watery soup and topped with skewers of octopus that seemed out of place. Sticky toffee pudding, full of dates and cooled with clotted cream, convinced us that Abingdon can excel, providing it keeps things simple.
Babies and children welcome: high chairs. Booking advisable. Tables outdoors (4, pavement). **Map 13 A9.**

South
Waterloo

Laughing Gravy
154 Blackfriars Road, SE1 8EN (7721 7055/ www.thelaughinggravy.co.uk). Southwark tube/ Waterloo tube/rail. **Food served** noon-10pm

The Providores & Tapa Room. See p173.

Mon-Fri; 7-10pm Sat. **Main courses** £9.95-£15.75. **Credit** MC, V.

Jokey monikers on restaurants can be off-putting – this one comes from the name of Laurel and Hardy's dog, star of a movie of the same title – but maybe you have to do something to get attention in such a functional part of SE1. Pictures and little figures of Stan and Ollie feature in the original decor. A cosy bar area leads into a rather romantic all-white dining space, with cool high-backed chairs and eclectic artwork. To eat, there are gastropubby bar snacks, or an often elaborate-sounding main menu, plus daily specials. Dishes don't seem to taste quite as well as they read, and some were misnamed on our visit; smoked salmon came with capers instead of the promised gherkins, and beef medallions turned out to be two small steaks. Our choices were pleasant rather than anything to savour; a chorizo, tomato and pepper risotto was well-flavoured but heavy. Some prices seem high for food of this quality, yet portions are big, and the one waitress worked hard to keep everyone happy. A decent standby in an under-supplied area, but nothing more.
Babies and children admitted. Booking advisable. Disabled: toilet. Restaurant available for hire. Tables outdoors (2, pavement).

South East

London Bridge & Borough

★ Champor-Champor

62-64 Weston Street, SE1 3QJ (7403 4600/). London Bridge tube/rail. **Lunch served** by appointment Mon-Wed; noon-2pm Thur, Fri. **Dinner served** 6-10pm Mon-Sat. **Set meal** £25 2 courses, £29.50 3 courses. **Credit** AmEx, MC, V.
Saturated-red walls and a gentle aroma of incense greet you at this Asian fusion restaurant, modelled on the restaurant-bar founded by the two owners in Malaysia. A handwritten seating card on your table is one gesture of thoughtfulness among many: candles cast a soft light, tactile twigs of pussy-willow perk up place settings, and even drinks coasters are fashioned from delicate embroidered fabric. 'Champor champor' is Malay for 'mix and match', and each dish is a creative blend as well as a course in its own right (there are no side orders). Boneless steamed chicken with sweet mango and chilli salsa was a toothsome starter. A succulent main of sea bream baked in banana leaf was nicely offset by fennel salad and coconut rice, while slithers of roast ostrich were spiced up with sticky soy and served with fragrant Thai basil rice. Softly spoken waiters brought pleasing extras such as tofu-skin bread (wafer thin and sprinkled with cumin powder); they also supplied the occasional 'lost in translation' moment, notably the 'inter-course menu' (exotic, rather than erotic, sorbets). If there's two of you, try to bag the mezzanine table when booking.
Babies and children welcome: high chairs. Booking essential. Separate room for parties, seats 8. **Map 12 Q9**.

East

Shoreditch

Cantaloupe

35-42 Charlotte Road, EC2A 3PD (7613 4411/ www.cantaloupe.co.uk). Old Street tube/rail/55 bus. **Brunch served** noon-6pm Sun. **Lunch served** 11am-3pm Thur, Fri. **Dinner served** 6-11pm Mon-Sat. **Main courses** £9.50-£19.75. **Set meal** (Mon-Wed; noon-7pm Thur, Fri) £12.50 2 courses. **Credit** MC, V.
The granddaddy of London's cool, New York-style bars (bare brick, battered sofas... it all started here), Cantaloupe is as popular as ever. Therein lies the problem. On a Wednesday night the place was packed to its exposed pipework – and as the eating area is only a step away from the drinking denizens, we were in for a noisy night. That said, the menu is simple and, in the main, well-executed. A starter salad of avocado, papaya, palmitos (palm hearts), grapefruit and toasted cashews had a wonderfully tangy lime and chilli dressing, yet a

Laughing Gravy

fish cake tasted odd and unfishy. Tender, juicy Argentinian steak came with good chunky chips. Moqueca (a Brazilian casserole with seafood, tomatoes and cashews) was well-spiced with the right balance of chilli to coconut-milk, but the accompanying moros y cristianos (rice and peas) were dry. The strong Latin wine list contains plenty of low-end bottles, though our waitress served us with a more expensive malbec than we'd chosen, and we were charged for it. Despite this, we reckon Cantaloupe to be a fine destination for stomach-fillers. Check the website for special offers.
Bar available for hire. Disabled: toilet. Entertainment: DJ 8pm Thur-Sun. Restaurant available for hire. **Map 6 R4**.

Shish

313-319 Old Street, EC1V 9LE (7749 0990/ www.shish.com). Liverpool Street or Old Street tube/rail. **Meals served** 11.30am-11.30pm Mon-Fri; noon-11.30pm Sat; noon-10.30pm Sun. **Main courses** £6.95-£10. **Set meal** (until 7pm Mon-Fri) £6.95-£8.45 2 courses. **Credit** AmEx, DC, MC, V.
At 7pm we were the only people in this spacious, clean-lined branch of the mini-chain. By 8pm almost all the tables were full. It's easy to see why Shish packs out nightly: food is fresh, well sourced and fairly priced; staff are friendly and efficient. Mixed meze makes a fine start to a meal. Ours were indeed mixed: chinese beans with soy, ginger and garlic were crisp, fresh and zingy; falafel were delicious; spinach borek were a bit soggy, but the smoked aubergine dip was sublime. For mains, choose a kebab (beef, chicken, fish or halloumi cheese), then select an accompaniment of rice, couscous, chips or salad. Satay chicken (thigh meat marinated in coconut milk, lemongrass and coriander) was perfectly tender and well flavoured. In contrast, the halloumi, flavoured with peppers, red onion and rosemary, was a little underdone, and the king prawns (garlic, lemon and chilli) slightly overcooked. Gripes aside, we were looked after well and will return. Drinks comprise decent

bottled beers, many smoothies, juices and lassis, and inexpensive wines, including a crisp, fresh 2007 South African Boland chenin blanc (£13.95). *Babies and children welcome: children's menu; high chairs. Bookings not accepted for parties of fewer than 8 (restaurant). Disabled: toilet. Entertainment: DJs 8.30pm Fri, Sat Tables outdoors (6, pavement). Takeaway service. Vegetarian menu. Vegan dishes.* **Map 6 R4**. **For branch see index**.

North East

Wanstead

Hadley House

27 High Street, E11 2AA (8989 8855). Snaresbrook or Wanstead tube. **Breakfast served** 10-11.30am Sat, Sun. **Lunch served** noon-3pm; dinner served 6-10pm daily. **Main courses** £11-£16. **Set lunch** (Mon-Sat) £14.95 2 courses, £19.95 3 courses. **Credit** MC, V.
Hadley House is looking a little tired. The view of the green opposite, through huge glass windows, is pleasant, but the lilac walls are scuffed. On our visit, chair cushions were crumby, the table needed wiping, and there was an overwhelming smell of frying. A blackboard of specials augments the extensive menu. Service, while friendly and well intentioned, was confused. Three staff offered to take our order without answering questions about specials. Our wine, a reasonable montepulciano from a well-chosen list, was opened away from the table and not offered for tasting. As for the food, we found the simplest dishes worked best. Prawn tempura was perfectly cooked, but didn't need to be on a pile of risotto with peas, mussels and crayfish. A special of skate was well rendered; a fish cake, full of chunky fish, benefited from its simple sorrel sauce and fresh spinach. Our worst dish was the steak: tough, gristly and accompanied by overcooked 'parmentier' potatoes that tasted strangely of cinnamon, plus a pile of chard that had seen better days. Yes, the cheeseboard was

pleasing – five sizeable chunks including well-kept goat's cheese, cheddar and dolcelatte – but the prices here are hard to justify.
Babies and children welcome (lunch; Sun): high chairs. Booking advisable. Tables outdoors (7, patio). Takeaway service (lunch).

North

Islington

Ottolenghi (100)

287 Upper Street, N1 2TZ (7288 1454/ www.ottolenghi.co.uk). Angel tube/Highbury & Islington tube/rail. **Meals served** 8am-10.30pm Mon-Sat; 9am-7pm Sun. **Main courses** £9.50-£14.50. **Meze** (dinner) £7-£13. **Credit** AmEx, MC, V.
Towering stacks of snowy meringues, reckless plates of crisp chocolate tarts and lavish deep-dish cheesecakes all practically scream 'eat me' at passers-by. But this is more than an inviting bakery. Behind the pastries piled in the window is a comparatively prim deli counter with lush salads, available day and evening, eat-in or take away. As a stylish daytime café, Ottolenghi is undeniably brilliant, thanks not only to those pastries, but also to the inventive array of cold dishes oozing vitality, such as french beans and mangetout with red onions, chervil and hazelnuts, or roasted sweet potatoes with avocado, rocket and pistachios in an orange cumin dressing. For dinner, the menu adds starter-sized hot dishes to mix and match, but the long canteen-style central table, slow-footed service and bright white decor are not for special occasions. Nipping in for a sprightly supper of mouth-watering pan-fried guinea fowl breast with sweetcorn risotto cake, well-seasoned roast lamb rack with spiced aubergine, and simple grilled halibut with confit baby fennel, was pleasant, but the cost soared before appetites were sated.
Babies and children welcome: high chairs. Booking advisable dinner; not accepted lunch. Takeaway service. **Map 5 O1**. **For branches see index**.

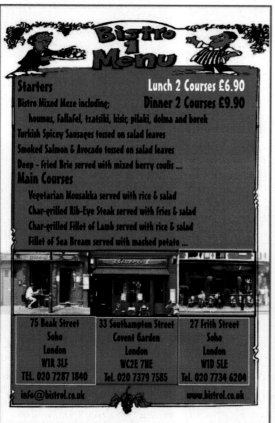

Italian

After being polarised for years between joints serving simple, regional fare and high-end central London venues with prices to match, Italian restaurateurs realised it was time to fill the mid-market gap. This shift has happened thanks to the increasing sophistication of the capital's diners, who have long moved on from the safety of linguine with pesto, followed by panna cotta, and are now hungry to discover lesser known dishes and ingredients. On the other hand, there's a growing community of professional Italian expats in London who can't be satisfied with mamma's home-style cooking when eating out, but who are equally unimpressed with fashionable venues that lack substance. Having first-rate ingredients airlifted daily from Italy doesn't cut it anymore, you also have to do something ingenious with them.

Hence the growing popularity of restaurants set in trendy neighbourhoods, where inventive chefs come up with classy takes on traditional dishes without the matching expense-account-only price tags. **Osteria Stecca** and **Osteria Emilia** are two newcomers that are running with this trend, while well-established **Assaggi** and **Tentazioni** have grown from strength to strength and become destination venues in their own right. And for diners with plenty of funds, there's an increasing number of glamorous Italian restaurants attached to hotels. Joining **Locanda Locatelli** and **Theo Randall at the Intercontinental** in the West End this year is **Apsleys** at the Lanesborough. Then there's glossy new **L'Anima**, bringing Italian sophistication to Shoreditch. Sardinian cooking, with its crisp, rustic flavours and earthy fare, continues to be the most popular regional Italian cuisine in London, as shown by the successful launch of **Mediterranea** and **Terra Nostra** in the past year, and the continued popularity of **Sardo** and **Olivo**. Also of note is the success of **Olivomare** (see p91), the Belgravia fish restaurant from the owner of Olivo.

Central

Belgravia

Il Convivio

143 Ebury Street, SW1W 9QN (7730 4099/ www.etruscagroup.co.uk). Sloane Square tube/ Victoria tube/rail. **Lunch served** noon-3pm, **dinner served** 7-11pm Mon-Sat. **Main courses** £16.50-£22. **Set lunch** £17.50 2 courses, £21.50 3 courses. **Credit** AmEx, MC, V.
Generally regarded as one of the best restaurants in the Etrusca group, Il Convivio has been serving a faithful Belgravia clientele for over a decade. The room is lovely, long and spacious, and service is attentive. Presentation is taken as seriously as in any palace of French haute cuisine, and every plate looked ravishing. Sometimes flavours followed through on looks, as in a creamy saffron and mussel soup garnished with heavenly croûtons of brown bread, and a hefty portion of veal scaloppine with capers and raisins. In other dishes, refinement won out over fireworks: a lovely presentation of marinated fish was inventive and adventurous, but in flavour merely adequate. Minor shortcomings in cooking would have been no problem were it not for the prices: most mains came with little green accompaniment, and side dishes would have pushed the spend uncomfortably higher. The wine list, mostly Italian, has a number of outstanding bottles and the sommelier gave excellent advice; £30 is the effective minimum. In this area, customers probably don't care, which is fine for them, but the expense and uneven cooking make Il Convivio a riskier proposition for others.
Babies and children admitted. Booking advisable dinner. Restaurant available for hire. Separate room for parties, seats 14. Map 15 G10.

Olivo

21 Eccleston Street, SW1W 9LX (7730 2505/ www.olivorestaurant.com). Sloane Square tube/Victoria tube/rail. **Lunch served** noon-2.30pm Mon-Fri. **Dinner served** 7-11pm Mon-Sat; 7-10.30pm Sun. **Main courses** £14.50-£19. **Set lunch** £19.50 2 courses, £22.50 3 courses. **Credit** AmEx, DC, MC, V.
Perennially busy, Olivo remains a key destination for local office workers and well-heeled residents, who flock here to sample reasonably priced (by Belgravia standards), authentic Sardinian food in a Mediterranean-inspired setting. Any visit should include at least one dish featuring bottarga, the dried mullet roe that imparts a rich and intensely savoury flavour to the dishes to which it's added. It can be found grated on a classic dish of spaghetti, but also in more modern variations, such as grilled courgettes sprinkled with slivers of this marine delicacy. Simple, rustic main courses, such as chargrilled chicken escalope with fresh herbs, are pleasantly executed, but no match for Olivo's excellent pasta dishes. Chocoholics are almost guaranteed to become addicted to the delectable chocolate and almond cake, while oenophiles will be pleased by the excellent selection of Sardinian bins (also available by the glass) that make up the lion's share of the wine list. Staff are competent, if not overly friendly, but can become easily distracted as the restaurant gets deservedly busy.
Children admitted. Booking advisable. **Map 15 H10.**

Volt

17 Hobart Place, SW1W 0HH (7235 9696/ www.voltlounge.com). Victoria tube/rail. **Lunch served** noon-3pm Mon-Fri. **Dinner served** 6-11pm Mon-Sat. **Main courses** £10-£16. **Credit** AmEx, DC, MC, V.
The room has a capsule-like feel that smacks of amateurish over-design, with violet neon strip lights and red crushed-velvet pillars. A DJ booth pounds out throbbing house music that just about allows loud conversation. The owners are also involved with Noura, the Lebanese restaurant next door, so it's understandably that while the cooking is competent, it is not always authentically Italian. Risotto of asparagus and peas took a promising 20 minutes to cook, and indeed the rice was al dente; however, the seasoning was bland and the dish lukewarm, causing a skin to form over the rice. Pan-fried scallops with baby fennel were likewise cooked well enough, but lacked seasoning and taste. In contrast, a sea bass fillet, served with clams and an artichoke and potato gratin, was far too salty, though otherwise fine. Our most disappointing dish was lobster spaghetti, which featured overcooked shreds of lobster meat, a tomato sauce that lacked depth and supermarket-standard spaghetti. Chocolate soufflé – really more of a chocolate fondant served with pistachio ice-cream – was unremarkable. Staff are generally friendly and helpful.
Babies and children welcome: booster seat. Booking advisable. Separate rooms for parties, seating 14, 18 and 30. Tables outdoors (4, pavement). **Map 15 H9.**

City

L'Anima NEW

1 Snowden Street, EC2A 2DQ (7422 7000/ www.lanima.co.uk). Liverpool Street tube/rail. *Bar* **Meals served** 8.30am-11.45pm Mon-Fri. **Main courses** £7.50-£20.
Restaurant **Breakfast served** 7-10.30am, **lunch served** 11.45am-3pm, **dinner served** 5.30-10.30pm Mon-Fri. **Main courses** £12.50-£25.50.
Both **Set lunch** £20.50 2 courses, 23.50 3 courses. **Credit** AmEx, DC, MC, V.
It may be located on the frontier of Shoreditch and the City, but the ushers at the door of this swish new venue immediately clarify which side of the border it belongs to. The minimalist interior is all clean lines, floor-to-ceiling glass, stark white linen and modernist leather chairs. Calabrian chef Francesco Mazzei heads up the kitchen with a pan-Italian menu served brasserie-style throughout the day. Specialities include a faultless fritto misto, the Venetian fried seafood favourite, while southern influences are apparent in the use of ingredients such as Sardinian fregola (couscous-like pasta) and burrata cheese from Apulia. Our mains, including an unremarkable fish stew, did not quite live up to the expectation created by the high prices. Desserts – such as an imaginative combination of baked peach scented with passion-fruit and lavender – are a stronger point and also beautifully presented. Not an everyday dining destination then, unless you have the deep pockets or expense account that doesn't demand dazzling food for these prizes.
Babies and children welcome: high chairs. Booking advisable. Disabled toilet. Separate room for parties, seats 14. **Map 6 R5.**

Refettorio

*Crowne Plaza Hotel, 19 New Bridge Street,
EC4V 6DB (7438 8052/www.refettorio.com).
Blackfriars tube/rail.* **Lunch served** noon-
2.30pm Mon-Fri. **Dinner served** 6-10.30pm
Mon-Sat. **Main courses** £11.50-£22. **Credit**
AmEx, MC, V.
This hotel restaurant (part of the Crowne Plaza)
has become deservedly popular among the City
slickers who flock here at lunchtime for cheese and
charcuterie platters featuring lesser-known
specialties imported from all over Italy. Thanks to
its mostly business clientele, Refettorio seems to
get away with steep prices, since only those on
expense accounts wouldn't flinch at the £3.60
charge for the (admittedly scrumptious) bread
basket. Pasta and risotto are the kitchen's main
strengths. Traditional dishes like orecchiette, the
traditional ear-shaped pasta from Apulia, are given
a contemporary twist with simple sauces like peas,
pancetta and cherry tomato confit. Those wishing
to sample more classic Italian fare might choose
from own-made egg tagliatelle with ragù or
summery spaghetti al crudo, where fresh tomatoes,
black olives and anchovies are added to just-
drained pasta. Main dishes can be underwhelming
and are no match for the pasta. For dessert, try
Sicilian cannoli filled with ricotta and topped with
hazelnut ice-cream. The Italian staff are full of
smiles and remain charming even at busy times.
Some Italian products are available to purchase
from the deli at the entrance.
*Babies and children admitted. Booking
advisable. Separate room for parties, seats 30.*
Map 11 O6.

Terra Nostra NEW

*27 Old Bailey, EC4M 7HS (3201 0077/
www.terranostrafood.co.uk). St Paul's tube.*
Lunch served noon-3pm Mon-Fri. **Dinner
served** 6-10pm Mon-Sat. **Main courses**
£8.90-£16.90. **Credit** AmEx, MC, V.
Urbane yet informal – with wooden tables, art on
the walls, a bar at the back (for serving rather
than sitting), and terrace dining in summer –
Terra Nostra is not the kind of restaurant you
expect to find in the City. The warm spirit of the

surroundings extends to the food, which has a
Sardinian bent. A meal starts with good bread,
olives and oil ready and waiting on the tables. A
first course of swordfish carpaccio with rocket was
elevated by drops of superlative olive oil and
judiciously sprinkled grains of rock salt. Calamari
ripieni (tender grilled baby squid filled with a
smooth, dense sauce of calamari meat, tomatoes
and herbs) packed layers of flavours to make
another winner. Mains were nearly as successful:
an aromatic, robust Sardinian sausage, grilled with
spikes of rosemary; and lorighittas (Sardinian
ring-shaped pasta) with pesto, aubergine and
scallops. The latter featured a brilliantly fresh,
herby pesto, though the scallops got lost in the
flavour-fest. But this, and the fact our white wine
wasn't quite cold enough, were our only quibbles
in a meal that delivered great flavours and a real
feel-good factor.
*Babies and children admitted. Disabled: toilet.
Tables outdoors (10, pavement).* **Map 11 O6.**

Covent Garden

Orso

*27 Wellington Street, WC2E 7DB (7240 5269/
www.orsorestaurant.co.uk). Covent Garden tube.*
Meals served noon-midnight daily. **Main
courses** £8.50-£17. **Set meal** (5-6.45pm Mon-
Sat) £16 2 courses, £18 3 courses incl coffee.
Credit AmEx, MC, V.
Occupying a spacious basement in a prime Covent
Garden location, Orso's underground bunker is
cosy rather than oppressive, lifted with warm
lighting and the friendly clamour of relaxed get-
togethers over a gratifying Italian meal. Slick,
smiley waiters flit between large family groups,
men discussing shares and couples en route to the
theatre. Service was a little inattentive on our
midweek visit but they did had a full house. Food
is served on country-style ceramic plates: the drill
here is hearty pastas and big pizza pies laden with
toppings like a sea of homemade pesto and meaty
wild mushrooms. Roast venison medallions in a
flavour-packed gravy were sprinkled with
pomegranate seeds whose sweet-sour flavour was
a good foil to the gameyness of the meat, but the
texture didn't quite gel with the accompanying
mashed potatoes. Desserts are great – a flourless
chocolate cake was rich, moussey and decadent
under a crisp top and served with creamy
mascarpone. In another welcome touch, wine is
also available by the carafe.
*Babies and children welcome: booster seats.
Booking advisable.* **Map 18 E4.**

Fitzrovia

Latium

*21 Berners Street, W1T 3LP (7323 9123/
www.latiumrestaurant.com). Oxford Circus tube.*
Lunch served noon-3pm Mon-Fri. **Dinner
served** 6.30-10.30pm Mon-Fri; 6.30-11pm Sat.
Main courses £12.50-£16. **Set lunch** £15.50
2 courses, £19.50 3 courses. **Set meal** £24.50
2 courses, £28.50 3 courses. **Credit** AmEx, MC, V.
Latium, purveyor of modern Italian cooking,
resides in a comfortable space that has a dimly lit,
romantic glow at dinnertime. What's more, prices
are reasonable. On our most recent visit, we
enjoyed some eye-poppingly wonderful dishes. Of
the main courses, roast Gressingham duck with
lentils, endive timbale and spinach, and slow-
roasted belly of pork with Savoy cabbage, baby
leeks and balsamic vinegar showed ambition and
delivered on flavour. Sadly, our choice from the
special list of ravioli dishes was terrible: leathery
pasta stuffed with wild mushrooms, served with
tasteless snails and a tomato sauce. When the
waiter enquired about our uneaten dish, our
feedback was handled ungraciously, casting a pall
over what would otherwise have been a great meal,
competently served. The succinct wine list is of
high quality, with plenty of choice between £20
and £30. On that basis, we're happy to recommend
Latium – as long as you have some good luck
choosing the dishes.
*Babies and children welcome: high chairs. Booking
advisable weekends.* **Map 17 A2.**

Passione

*10 Charlotte Street, W1T 2LT (7636 2833/
www.passione.co.uk). Goodge Street tube.* **Lunch
served** 12.30-2.15pm Mon-Fri. **Dinner served**
7-10.15pm Mon-Sat. **Main courses** £14-£22.
Credit AmEx, DC, MC, V.
Gennaro Contaldo has become a familiar face
through his television appearances, and his
restaurant's rustic-chic food and ambience ensure
a full house of well-heeled customers who don't
mind the rather steep prices and increasingly
distracted service as Passione gets busier. The
kitchen has lost most of the contrivance it
sometimes displayed on previous visits, returning
to well-executed home-style cooking using
impeccable ingredients. Sadly, at the same time,
prices have crept up – main dishes now start at
£22.50. Still, there's plenty to choose from on the
appealing, daily-changing menu if money is no
object. Main courses are Passione's strength with
robust, flavourful classics like lamb cutlets in
barolo wine, or moreish Ligurian-style rabbit,
roasted on the bone with a glossy black olive sauce.
If you don't have £550 to spare on a special bottle
of Brunello di Montalcino, there are several more
affordable bins available by the glass or in half
bottles. Those with a sweet tooth may feel let down
by the unadventurous dessert list.
*Babies and children admitted. Booking advisable.
Restaurant available for hire. Tables outdoors
(2, patio; 1, pavement).* **Map 17 B1.**

★ Sardo

*45 Grafton Way, W1T 5DQ (7387 2521/
www.sardo-restaurant.com). Warren Street tube.*
Lunch served noon-3pm Mon-Fri. **Dinner
served** 6-11pm Mon-Sat. **Main courses** £8.90-
£18. **Credit** AmEx, MC, V.
Sardo serves amazing Sardinian food at
exceptionally reasonable prices. Set on the ground
floor of a Fitzrovia townhouse, it is simply and
comfortably decorated, with a buzzier front end
and more intimate tables at the back. Service is
warm, charming and nigh-on flawless – they
apologised for a few minutes' lapse between
ordering and receiving a bottle of wine. The food?
On our visit, uniformly spectacular. Tartar of tuna
with balsamic dressing and rocket salad, and a
special of vegetable soup with scallops, both
showed an artful ability to combine rusticity with
urban sophistication. A flavourful nodino di vitello
(veal chop) was perfectly cooked. Another special
of ravioli with buffalo mozzarella and ricotta,
topped with slivers of bottarga (dried mullet roe),
was light and airy but dense with the pungency of
exceptional ingredients. Even the perfectly cooked
spinach took our breath away. For wine, you could
spend no more than £20 to £25 when choosing
from the outstanding Sardinian list. Sardo is a gem
of a restaurant.
*Babies and children admitted. Booking advisable.
Separate area for parties, seats 30. Tables
outdoors (3, patio).* **Map 3 J4.**
For branch (Sardo Canale) see index.

Knightsbridge

San Lorenzo

*22 Beauchamp Place, SW3 1NH (7584 1074).
Knightsbridge tube.* **Lunch served** 12.30-3pm,
dinner served 7.30-11.30pm Mon-Sat. **Main
courses** £15.50-£28.50. **Cover** £2.50. **Credit**
AmEx, MC, V.
San Lorenzo has been a celebrity haunt since the
'60s, with an equally lengthy reputation for
indifferent food and service. A cheery welcome
was, therefore, a pleasant surprise, and the menu
wasn't as dull as anticipated. To start we had a
satisfying platter of finocchiona (Tuscan fennel
salami), and grilled sardines, a mean pair of
smallish fish but admittedly fresh and well cooked.
Wine choices under £25 are scarce though the
waiter recommended a delicious Scalabrone rosato
under that price. About this point, everything
changed – a glossy throng came down the staircase,
heads turned to watch them and service went
haywire. We got the wrong wine and our waiter
disappeared. Eventually the main courses arrived,
saltimbocca alla romana and calf's liver, both as

they should be, although the liver was spoiled by gluey mash. On leaving, we had to struggle past an intimidating cordon of grim paparazzi. So if you like to pay heftily for ho-hum food, have your evening descend into chaos due to an unseen celebrity presence and fight your way past the living dead to get out, this is the place.
Babies and children welcome: children's portions; high chairs. Booking advisable Fri, Sat. Dress: smart casual. Restaurant available for hire. Separate rooms for parties, seats 20 and 40. **Map 14 F9.**
For branch see index.

Zafferano

15 Lowndes Street, SW1X 9EY (7235 5800/ www.zafferanorestaurant.com). Knightsbridge tube. **Lunch served** noon-2.30pm Mon-Fri; 12.30-3pm Sat, Sun. **Dinner served** 7-11pm Mon-Sat; 7-10.30pm Sun. **Set lunch** £29.50 2 courses, £34.50 3 courses, £39.50 4 courses. **Set dinner** £34.50 2 courses, £44.50 3 courses, £54.50 4 courses. **Credit** AmEx, DC, MC, V.
Plan ahead and book early if you want to snatch a table for dinner. The Knightsbridge locals and wealthy Italian expats who frequent this upscale restaurant can't seem to get enough of its classy cooking, impeccable service and luxuriously understated, yet slightly cramped dining area. There's no à la carte menu, but a seasonal set dinner starting at £34.50 for two courses. The food, which has won accolades for its flawless execution, ranges from simple dishes that highlight the flavour of their superior ingredients to more complex creations that don't stray too far from classical Italian cuisine. Team a simple starter, such as creamy burrata cheese adorned with wedges of artichoke, with one of the robustly flavoured and imaginative main courses. The only, albeit minor, disappointment on our visit was the handmade tagliolini pasta with crab, courgettes and sweet chilli, which looked good but lacked pzazz. Zafferano's attention to detail shines with desserts. We recommend the elegant torta caprese, a flourless almond torte that originated on Capri, which comes adorned with a scoop of almond ice-cream. A sommelier is on hand to help with the remarkably good and fairly priced wine list.
Babies and children welcome: high chairs. Booking essential. Dress: smart casual; no shorts (dinner). Separate room for parties, seats 20. **Map 15 G9.**

Marble Arch

Obika

2nd floor, Selfridges, 400 Oxford Street, W1A 1AB (7318 3620/www.obika.co.uk). Bond Street tube. **Meals served** 11.30am-7.30pm Mon-Wed, Fri, Sat; 11.30am-8.30pm Thur; noon-5.30pm Sun. **Main courses** £12-£18. **Credit** AmEx, DC, MC, V.
Prices seem to have come down a notch at Obika, the 'mozzarella bar' in Selfridges, but so has the quality of the degustation platters that are its main draw. Gone are the rare, regional delicacies such as lardo and wild boar ham, replaced with such commonplace ingredients as smoked salmon and prosciutto cotto (despite the exotic Italian name, it's just plain cooked ham). Still, some more appealing, less obvious choices remain, so it's possible to indulge in a delicate, creamy ball of mozzarella from a choice of three varieties, along with smoked tuna and finocchiona (Tuscan fennel salami) for £11. Starters include a delectable selection of crostini topped with creamy stracchino cheese or spicy Calabrian sausage, while there are a few trattoria-like pasta dishes available for those willing to opt for a more substantial meal. The bread basket is £1.75 extra, but it's nothing to write home about. Much better are the scrumptious desserts, notably a feather-light aniseed-scented panna cotta. The friendly Italian staff didn't miss a beat during our packed Saturday lunchtime seating, competently dealing with homesick Italian expats and well-heeled tourists alike.
Babies and children welcome: high chairs. Disabled: lift; toilet (in Selfridges). Takeaway service. **Map 9 G6.**
For branch see index.

★ Trenta

30 Connaught Street, W2 2AF (7262 9623). Marble Arch tube. **Lunch served** 12.30-2.30pm Tue-Fri. **Dinner served** 6.30-10.30pm Mon-Sat. **Main courses** £13.50-£17.50. **Set lunch** £17.50 2 courses. **Set dinner** £25 2 courses. **Credit** AmEx, MC, V.
Since its 2006 opening, Trenta's elegant cooking has gone from strength to strength, but has remained faithful to well-chosen seasonal ingredients and a daily changing menu. It has turned this tiny neighbourhood spot just off Edgware Road into a destination restaurant. The set-menu formula with supplements for some dishes remains, but there are now a few nice touches, such as no extra charge for the moreish stuzzichini titbits and the scrumptious bread basket, which is perhaps a good reason to splurge on an aperitif. In addition to a few signature dishes, such as the exquisite grilled baby squid with fresh chilli and garlic, the menu has been beefed up with an even more appealing choice of starters. Marinated grilled vegetables nesting beside a snow-white ball of unctuous burrata (a mozzarella-like cheese filled with cream) is the most remarkable, its unbelievable freshness guaranteed via daily deliveries from the southern Italian region of Apulia. From the enticing main course list, we found the roasted rabbit leg with olives and pan-fried swordfish escalopes livened up with punchy Sicilian caponata outstanding. Dessert is essential, especially the delicate tiramisu and delectable own-made chocolate panna cotta.
Babies and children admitted. Booking essential weekends, advisable weekdays. Separate room for parties, seats 12. **Map 8 E/F6.**

Marylebone

2 Veneti

10 Wigmore Street, W1U 2RD (7637 0789). Bond Street or Oxford Circus tube. **Lunch served** noon-3pm Mon-Fri. **Dinner served** 6.30-10.30pm Mon-Sat. **Set meals** £16 1 course, £25 2 courses, £29 3 courses, £33 4 courses. **Credit** AmEx, MC, V.
Tucked behind the mayhem of Oxford Street, 2 Veneti specialises in the cuisine of Venice and the Veneto, its surrounding region. Well-heeled regulars and local office workers flock to the somewhat dated dining room, but don't expect to find many homesick Venetians dining here, since the cooking is uneven at best. While a rustic, countryside dish of pan-fried slices of soppressa (a fatty, coarse-grained sausage) over grilled radicchio bowled us over, other typical dishes fared less spectacularly. Fritto misto (deep-fried mixed seafood) is one of the pillars of Venetian cuisine and won plaudits on a previous visit, but unfortunately not this time, when it arrived as a plateful of chewy calamari rings and a few woolly-textured prawns. Since Venetian cooks don't bother preparing fritto misto if they can't find perfectly

L'Anima. See p177.

RESTAURANTS

Grana Padano – a taste of Italy

Grana Padano cheese is perfect for any occasion.

The very best of authentic Italian cuisine is now within your reach. Grana Padano owes its name to its grainy consistency ('grana') and to its beautiful birthplace in the Padana Valley in Italy. However, it is Grana Padano's singular taste that has made it the world's best selling PDO (Protected Designation of Origin) hard cheese. PDO is a sign of quality implemented by the European Union to regulate and protect the production of selected food and drink products across Europe.

This full-bodied taste has the potential to be used in more than just a humble grating over spaghetti. In fact, Grana Padano can be used to enhance a range of hot and cold traditional Italian dishes, from risotto to ice cream, or tagliatelle with chestnut, mushrooms and cream (right). It is also a welcome addition to a cheeseboard, served with nuts, fruit or chutney, or simply as a delicious snack without any accompaniment.

The distinctive taste and grainy texture of Grana Padano is perfectly suited to white wines with enduring bouquets or medium reds and those with greater tannin content. A Brunello from Tuscany or a Piedmontese Bartelo will complement the flavour of the cheese, as will the dried fruit aroma of chilled Sicilian Marsala.

First made by monks, Grana Padano owes its quality to 1,000 years of tradition. Today it is produced in the Lombardy, Piedmont and Veneto regions and in the Trento and Piacenza provinces. Production is overseen by the Consorzio Tutela Grana Padano, ensuring its traceability. As a result, Grana Padano is as nutritious as it is flavoursome. It's packed with calcium and easily digestible protein and uses only semi-skimmed milk, meaning that it's low in fat too.

Grana Padano can be matured to achieve a variety of subtle flavours. Its aging process – anything from 12 months – brings about quite striking differences in taste. The younger cheese is mild and delicate with a milky taste and is perfect for sauces, whilst the mature versions are grainy, strong and full-bodied, so much so that they can be served alone. Grana Padano's premium offering is the Riserva, matured for a minimum of 20 months, the specially selected wheels represent the oldest vintage and are richer and fuller in taste than younger Grana Padano.

Grana Padano can be enjoyed by all ages. Find it in all of its variations at Waitrose, Marks & Spencer, Harvey Nichols and Tesco.

Tagliatelle with Chestnut, Mushrooms and Grana Padano Cream

Serves 4

2 tbsp olive oil
250g chestnut mushrooms, sliced
375g Tagliatelle paglia e fieno
4 shallots, peeled and sliced
splash of Pernod
284ml single cream
75g Grana Padano, grated

1. Heat 1 tbsp of the olive oil in a pan and sauté the mushrooms for 3-4 minutes. Remove with a slotted spoon and set aside.

2. Bring a large pan of water to the boil and add the pasta. Cook for 8-10 minutes, until al dente.

3. Meanwhile, heat the remaining tbsp of olive oil in the pan used for the mushrooms and sauté the chopped shallots for 2-3 minutes. Add a splash of Pernod and boil rapidly for 1-2 minutes to reduce the liquid.

4. Pour in the cream, bring to the boil and simmer for 1 minute before stirring in the grated Grano Padano. Simmer while you drain the pasta.

Return the drained pasta to the pan, pour in the Grana Padano cream and the mushrooms and mix well. Serve immediately with a crisp green salad.

fresh-tasting seafood, perhaps the kitchen at 2 Veneti should try harder. Another Venetian stalwart, risotto with seafood, came in a huge portion, but was greasy and rather indifferent. Sadly the textbook tiramisu, indulgent selection of grappas and prized Veneto wines could barely make up for 2 Veneti's unfulfilled promises.
Babies and children admitted. Booking advisable. Restaurant available for hire. Tables outdoors (4, pavement). **Map 9 H5.**

Caffè Caldesi
118 Marylebone Lane, W1U 2QF (7935 1144/ www.caldesi.com). Bond Street tube.
Bar **Meals served** noon-10.30pm Mon-Sat. **Main courses** £9-£19.
Restaurant **Lunch served** noon-3pm Mon-Fri. **Dinner served** 6-10.30pm Mon-Sat. **Main courses** £16-£20.
Both **Credit** AmEx, MC, V.
Bereft when the Italian family sitting beside us moved downstairs to this establishment's more caffè-like area, we stuck with the starched-linen restaurant and the sophisticated (and therefore expensive) menu. Below us, the evening buzz seemed alluring. Nonetheless we wallowed in attentive service, despite an unwonted Monday evening rush that saw all the tables filled by 9pm. Pea and broad bean soup was a pungent legume and garlic blast that disappeared quickly. Carpaccio of selected fish – swordfish wrapped around rocket, salmon marinated in beetroot, sea bass and tuna – was fresh and tangy. Ravioli stuffed with a rich mix of minced swordfish and garlic, with a buttery, lemony sauce, needed only a mixed salad as a side. This, simply dressed at the table, was a happy tumble of frilly leaves, pea shoots, tomatoes and fennel – delicious. The meat-eater in our party was disappointed with a pricey main of saltimbocca alla romana, which was offputtingly salty and accompanied by overcooked broccoli. The pudding list caused a ripple of excitement – we plumped for a vanilla-rich panna cotta, with a too-small puddle of gorgeous rhubarb sauce on the side.
Babies and children welcome: high chairs; nappy-changing facilities. Booking advisable (restaurant). Disabled: toilet. Restaurant and bar available for hire. Tables outside (3, pavement). **Map 9 G5.**
For branch (Caldesi Tuscan) see index.

★ Locanda Locatelli (100)
8 Seymour Street, W1H 7JZ (7935 9088/ www.locandalocatelli.com). Marble Arch tube.
Lunch served noon-3pm Mon-Sat; noon-3.30pm Sun. **Dinner served** 6.45-11pm Mon-Thur; 6.45-11.30pm Fri, Sat; 6.45-10pm Sun. **Main courses** £11-£31.50. **Credit** AmEx, MC, V.
Locanda Locatelli has 'It' status. Chef-owner Giorgio Locatelli is one of the most recognised and well regarded Italian chefs in the capital, and the loungey, sexy dining room is a celeb magnet. If that makes you think 'high prices and lengthy waiting lists', you'd be right. Yet once through the hallowed portals, diners are treated like royalty regardless of rank – although the two-hour slots for a table are strictly adhered to. Locatelli takes seasonal ingredients seriously; peas, artichokes and broad beans appeared in several guises on our spring visit and we couldn't resist a pasta dish of borage parcels with walnut sauce, which delivered a gorgeous interplay of gently bitter flavours. A starter of deep-fried calf's foot 'salad' with mostarda was far more delicate than the name would imply. Locatelli may hail from near Lake Maggiore on the Swiss-Italian border, but he's a dab hand with southern Italian flavours, as in the well-rendered Sicilian dish of sardines beccafico – butterflied sardines stuffed and rolled and served on a salad of fennel and orange. This is cooking with a real sense of style and attention to detail. Service is appropriately solicitous and professional. The mostly Italian wine list is impressive, if not cheap, with some good, food-friendly wines by the glass.
Babies and children welcome: high chairs. Booking essential. Disabled: toilet (in hotel). Dress: smart casual. **Map 9 G6.**

Mayfair

★ Alloro
19-20 Dover Street, W1S 4LU (7495 4768/ www.alloro-restaurant.co.uk). Green Park tube.
Bar **Open** noon-10pm Mon-Fri; 7-10pm Sat. **Main courses** £12-£16.
Restaurant **Lunch served** noon-2.30pm Mon-Fri. **Dinner served** 7-10.30pm Mon-Sat. **Set lunch** £27 2 courses, £32 3 courses. **Set dinner** £29.50 2 courses, £35 3 courses, £39 4 courses.
Both **Credit** AmEx, DC, MC, V.
The reason for Alloro's popularity and wide appeal lies on the plate: it remains one of London's prime venues for high-end Italian cooking, confidently sparked with contemporary influences from France and even modern British touches. Echt-Italian featured in starters of taglierini with tender calamari and sweet chilli, and two ravioli dishes, one with ricotta and Swiss chard and the other with shreds of juicy rabbit. More far-ranging influences came in heavenly fillet steak served on a towering disc of crushed potatoes, and in the perfectly balanced jus that formed the basis of poached guinea fowl with roast potatoes. There was a slight letdown in the somewhat bland, dry confit leg of rabbit, though its border-crossing accompaniment of crushed peas with mint was a revelation. Those responsible for the wine list know their business exceptionally well. While £40 is the point at which the fun really starts, you can find a handful of good things between £30 and £35. Service was near faultless. Despite the minor flaws in our meal, Alloro's outstanding dishes are utterly winning.
Babies and children admitted. Booking advisable. Restaurant and bar available for hire. Separate room for parties, seats 16. **Map 9 J7.**

Apsleys NEW
The Lanesborough, 1 Lanesborough Place, SW1X 7TA (7333 7254/www.lanesborough.com). Hyde Park Corner tube. **Breakfast served** 7-11.30am daily. **Lunch served** noon-2.30pm daily. **Tea served** 4pm, 4.30pm daily. **Dinner served** 7-10.30pm Mon-Sat; 7-10pm Sun. **Main courses** £12.50-£30. **Set lunch** £24 3 courses. **Set tea** £31-£39. **Credit** AmEx, DC, MC, V.
Just across Hyde Park Corner from Theo Randall at the Intercontinental (*below*) is the Lanesborough, whose switch to serving overpriced cucina rustica seems like blatant copying. Gone is the Conservatory's kitsch colonial charm (it was great for afternoon tea); in its place is Apsleys, expensively decorated like a smart box of chocolates, with not much rustica about it. Chef Nick Bell's CV includes some of London's most prestigious Italian restaurants, and his shopping list contains ingredients from top Italian producers. But when you're using great- tasting deli foods such as culatello (a premium ham from Parma), burrata, bottarga and smoked tuna, not much effort is required from the kitchen. We were impressed with basics like breads, olive oil and balsamic dips (though at these prices, we should be), but also more complex dishes such as fat pasta strands with sea urchin and sweet chilli, and Sicilian cannoli with orange sauce – an old favourite of Bell's from Zafferano (*see p179*). Smart modern dishes might include veal sweetbreads with peas and mint, and new-season lamb with wild garlic, lamb sweetbreads and tongue. Bell also attempts retro classics such as veal saltimbocca, chicken cacciatora and the ubiquitous tiramisu. The wine list is not so Italian though, with around 500 bins from around the world and a particularly strong showing from esteemed French regions.
Babies and children welcome: high chairs. Booking advisable; essential tea. Disabled: toilet. Dress: smart, no jeans dinner. Separate rooms for parties, seating 10-12.

Ristorante Semplice
9-10 Blenheim Street, W1S 1LJ (7495 1509/ www.ristorantesemplice.com). Bond Street tube.
Lunch served noon-2.30pm Mon-Fri. **Dinner served** 7-10.30pm Mon-Sat. **Main courses** £16-£22. **Set lunch** £16 2 courses, £19 3 courses. **Credit** AmEx, MC, V.

Upscale Italian restaurants are by no means a rarity in Mayfair, but Ristorante Semplice lays fair claim to a ranking in the very top echelons. Expensively clothed patrons are drawn to the seriously good cooking in a clean-lined, dark-panelled space. What's more, despite the location it won't make you worry about bankruptcy. A set lunch offers very good value, and even ordering from the carte, as we did, prices are not exorbitant. Our food was mostly of the very highest standard, especially two profoundly flavourful pasta dishes of linguine with rabbit ragù and ravioli with oxtail sauce. On the minus side, grilled octopus lacked sparkle and came on an inappropriate bed of grated carrot. But the flaws were minor, and more than offset by a selection of wines by the glass or carafe that made us wish every high-class restaurant offered something similar. Starting at £13, the carafes made it unnecessary to stray further into the list – though you won't be sorry if you do, because the all-Italian selection is very strong. Service was quiet, unobtrusive, and perfectly paced even when the restaurant was at its busiest.
Babies and children admitted. Booking advisable. Disabled: toilet. Tables outdoors (4, pavement). **Map 9 H6.**

Sartoria
20 Savile Row, W1S 3PR (7534 7000/ www.danddlondon.com). Oxford Circus or Piccadilly Circus tube.
Bar **Open/snacks served** 9am-11pm Mon-Fri; noon-11pm Sat.
Restaurant **Lunch served** noon-3pm Mon-Fri. **Dinner served** 5.30-11pm Mon-Fri. **Meals served** 3-11pm Sat. **Main courses** £17-£25. **Set meal** £20 2 courses, £25 3 courses.
Both **Credit** AmEx, MC, V.
Sartoria has taken a leaf out of Savile Row tailoring to inspire its understated elegant decor with just a slight nod to modernity. The kitchen, meanwhile, has looked to Milan to borrow the comforting classical fare favoured by the city's business people. Northern Italian stalwarts such as beef carpaccio, risotto with mushroom and veal milanese appear on the menu along with southern specialties like burrata, a fresh mozzarella-like cheese, and gutsier meat dishes with an Anglo-Saxon bent. The safe selection seems to appeal to the mainly corporate clientele, but never manages to reach the wow factor you would expect from a sophisticated establishment charging steep prices. The dessert list spans interesting concoctions like poached pear in red wine with cinnamon ice-cream, to Italian cheeses or traditional tiramisu. Japanese-style screens separate two private dining rooms from the main area, presumably to enable privacy-seeking power-brokers to ink that elusive deal away from prying eyes.
Babies and children welcome: high chairs. Booking advisable; essential lunch. Disabled: toilet. Entertainment: pianist 7-10pm Thur-Sat. Restaurant available for hire. Separate rooms for parties, seating 22 and 48. **Map 9 J7.**

★ Theo Randall at the Intercontinental
1 Hamilton Place, Park Lane, W1J 7QY (7409 3131/www.theorandall.com). Hyde Park Corner tube. **Lunch served** noon-3pm Mon-Fri. **Dinner served** 6-11pm Mon-Sat. **Main courses** £20-£28. **Set lunch** £21 2 courses, £25 3 courses. **Credit** AmEx, DC, MC, V.
More luxe than the River Café, while not as salacious as Locanda Locatelli, the decor at Theo Randall's hotel-restaurant is comfortably glamorous with thick Frette linens, large vases of bow-headed sunflowers, and simple modern artwork. The set lunch menu offers superb value and little sense of compromise on the à la carte. Complimentary bruschetta was the apotheosis of tomatoes on toast, with soft, ripe fruit, chargrilled sourdough and judicious use of fresh herbs and olive oil. Anchovy sauce and parmesan flakes gave bright-green English asparagus a one-two 'umami' flavour punch that threatened to knock out the delicate seasonal spears. Pasta dishes are freshly appealing and even a slow-cooked ragù of beef

Fratelli la Bufala

If you have been brought up and taught right, the benefits will always shine through. There's no better example of this than Mimo Rimoli, owner of South End Green's popular Fratelli la Bufala. Born in Pozzuoli, Naples (birthplace of Sofia Loren), the Italian was destined to make his mark in the restaurant world. While Mimo was growing into the man he is today, his family restaurant business was continuing to grow.

We have once again been nominated for the 'Archant Food and Drink Awards 2008' Nominations and Shortlists have been received from 'The Evening Standard London Restaurant Awards'.

Fratelli la Bufala is a brand that showcases the gastronomic heritage of Naples, using bufalo meat and mozzarella cheese. The bufalo meat is healthy, low in fat and beautifully tender. Whilst the acclaimed Fratelli la Bufala were springing up all over Italy, the rest of the world was taking notice. Mimo decided he would be the first to bring the family business to England.

Showing the same passion he has had for art and motorcycles, Mimo threw himself into creating a menu that showcased what Fratelli la Bufala was all about.

Lip-smacking bufalo fillets, sausages, mozzarella and authentic pizzas, all cooked in a traditional rural Italian way, with the emaphasis on quality and freshness.

We now have a daily fish special with a list of seasonal fish dishes which are proving to be extremely popular. Choose from fresh sea bass and sea bream baked in the wood oven, king prawns, scallops and seared tuna or halibut steaks. Our fish menu sells quickly so booking is essential at the weekends and evenings.

Northwest London has some fantastic restaurants and it is places like Fratelli la Bufala that bring something different.

45a South End Road, NW3
www.fratellilabufala.com
020 7435 7814

Via Condotti

fillet and Chianti served with golden tagliatelle was a suitably summery affair on the hot day of our visit. We liked the idea of a main course frittata (organic eggs, ricotta and courgette) too. A spoonful of crème fraîche was the perfect acidic contrast to crumbly, buttery apricot and almond tart; opt for the likes of white peach sorbet if you need something lighter. The wine list starts at £20 a bottle; go by-the-glass and you'll find intriguing options from Greece and Austria complementing the Italian staples.

Babies and children welcome: high chairs. Booking advisable. Disabled: lift; toilet. Dress: smart casual. Separate room for parties, seats 24. Map 9 G8.

★ Via Condotti

23 Conduit Street, W1S 2XS (7493 7050/ www.viacondotti.co.uk). Oxford Circus tube. **Lunch served** noon-3pm Mon-Fri; 12.30-3pm Sat. **Dinner served** 5.45-10.30pm Mon-Sat. **Set lunch/dinner** £22.50 2 courses, £27.50 3 courses, £52.50 4 courses. **Set meal** (lunch, 5.45-7pm) £14.50 2 courses, £18.50 3 courses. **Credit** AmEx, MC, V.

Wedged between the Queen's corsetier, Rigby & Peller, and an upscale Italian fashion boutique, Via Condotti has none of the stuffiness that its prime location would suggest. The understated, chic ambience feels almost cocooning. Service is warm and attentive without being intrusive, never missing a beat as the dining room gets busy. But what brings Via Condotti on a par with similar establishments on Italian soil are the simple, superlative ingredients and the almost maniacal attention to the tiniest details. This starts with the scrumptious bread basket, generously filled with crisp Sardinian pane carasau, rustic breadsticks and fragrant ciabatta. On our visit, we spotted prized Italian specialties like culatello ham, which has a mellower, more delicate flavour than prosciutto. Other treats included a platter of Tuscan ham topped with a grilled chunk of smoked scamorza, a mozzarella-like cheese with a saltier, firmer texture. The daily-changing menu features a selection of imaginative, own-made pasta dishes and well-executed mains that put a twist on tradition. Among these, chargrilled lamb cutlets with wild mushrooms was the highlight of the meal. The all-Italian wine list ranges from the affordable to the extravagant, but several bins are available by the glass and the knowledgeable staff are happy to make suggestions (not necessarily the most expensive options).

Babies and children admitted. Booking advisable. Separate rooms for parties, seating 18 and 35. Map 9 J6.

Piccadilly

Brumus

Haymarket Hotel, 1 Suffolk Place, SW1Y 4BP (7470 4000/www.haymarkethotel.com). Piccadilly Circus tube. **Meals served** 7am-11.45pm Mon-Sat; 8am-11pm Sun. **Main courses** £16-£35. **Set meal** £14.99 2 courses, £19.95 3 courses. **Credit** AmEx, DC, MC, V.

While the louche, cerise-and-magenta dining room has stayed the same, the food at Brumus has moved away from the northern Italian slant that marked its opening last year, settling for Anglo-Italian brasserie-style fare that's more likely to please its theatre-going and touristic clientele. As a result, the menu now lists steak and kidney pudding alongside rigatoni pasta with beef ragù, but also features competently executed first-rate seafood. If available, the Dorset crab with saffron aïoli sauce and the gargantuan grilled seafood platter, dressed in a simple lemon butter sauce, shouldn't be missed. The scrumptious bread baskets, filled to the brim with pane carasau, the Sardinian crispbread, and focaccia morsels could easily tempt the most inveterate carbohydrate phobics. The dessert list will please the sweet-toothed with sugary concoctions like steamed syrup pudding with custard, chocolate fondant and crème brûlée. There is a better-than-usual list of wine by the glass, but the steeper-than-usual prices can easily bulk up the final bill. Brumus offers pre- and post-theatre menus, in addition to breakfast and afternoon tea.

Babies and children welcome: high chairs. Booking advisable. Disabled: toilet. Separate rooms for parties, seating 15-100. Map 10 K7.

St James's

Al Duca

4-5 Duke of York Street, SW1Y 6LA (7839 3090/www.alduca-restaurant.co.uk). Piccadilly Circus tube. **Lunch served** noon-3pm Mon-Fri; 12.30-3pm Sat. **Dinner served** 6-11pm Mon-Sat. **Set lunch** £22.50 2 courses, £26.50 3 courses, £29.50 4 courses. **Set dinner** £25.50 2 courses, £32.50 4 courses. **Credit** AmEx, MC, V.

While it may not set culinary standards, Al Duca remains a perennial favourite thanks to its affordable Mediterranean-inspired fare and wine list, a boon given its St James's location. Affluent locals and theatregoers flock to its modern, simple dining room decked in pale wood and terracotta tiles to sample the reasonably priced set dinners, which start at £25.50 for two courses and rise to £32.50 for four, with some dishes attracting supplements. Pleasant, imaginative starters include grilled smoked scamorza cheese with chargrilled aubergines and black olives, as well as the signature warm poached egg topped with a tangy parmesan cheese wafer and crispy bacon. There is a good selection of adequately prepared classic pasta dishes, with an eye to pleasing vegetarians, and one daily changing risotto. The extensive all-Italian wine list features lesser-known wines from South Tyrol and an amazing selection of 17 grappa varieties. Italian waiting staff try their best to remain charming and pleasant despite the busy seatings, but on our visit became increasingly distracted as the venue got busier.

Babies and children welcome: high chair. Booking advisable. Dress: smart casual. Restaurant available for hire (Sun). Map 9 J7.

Franco's

61 Jermyn Street, SW1Y 6LX (7499 2211/ www.francoslondon.com). Green Park tube. **Breakfast served** 7.30-10.30am, **lunch served** noon-2.30pm Mon-Sat. **Tapas served** 2.30-11pm Mon-Thur; 2.30pm-midnight Fri, Sat. **Dinner served** 5.30-11pm Mon-Thur; 5.30pm-midnight Fri, Sat. **Tapas** £7.50-£16. **Main courses** £15-£26. **Set lunch** £25 2 courses, £30 3 courses, £35 4 courses. **Credit** AmEx, MC, V.

Lunch at this all-day operation left us beaming: sated with uniformly good food; cheered by skilled, smiling service; and not very much poorer. Franco's succeeds not by putting fireworks on the plate but by getting dozens of small details exactly right: excellent bread and petits fours; rich, buttery but not overpowering stock in an onion and leek soup; an ultra-fresh, sensitively dressed salad of tender leaves, fine beans and pomegranate seeds. Though situated in the heart of affluent St James's and filled with mostly very posh customers, it feels more like a continental café than a smart London restaurant. The set lunch is a bargain but dinner is pricier with grills, simply presented meat and fish, plus enticing pasta dishes vying for attention. Wine is on the expensive side: £30 the real starting point. One word of warning: the small entrance room was quiet even when full, but the larger room on the side, also jam-packed, was uncomfortably noisy. Book in the smaller room if you like to dine without din.

Babies and children admitted. Disabled: toilet. Dress: smart casual. Separate rooms for parties, seating 18 and 50. Tables outdoors (4, pavement). Map 9 J7.

Luciano

72-73 St James's Street, SW1A 1PH (7408 1440/ www.lucianorestaurant.co.uk). Green Park tube. **Lunch served** noon-3pm Mon-Fri; noon-2.30pm Sat. **Dinner served** 6-11pm Mon-Sat. **Main courses** £16.50-£28.95. **Credit** AmEx, MC, V.

The late photographer Bob Carlos Clarke was best known for work that some people would call erotica and others would call softcore porn. He was also a close friend of Marco Pierre White, who has mounted a permanent exhibition of Clarke's work at Luciano, his mainly Italian restaurant in St James's. Luciano has some talent in the kitchen and an amiable waiting staff. We ate one dish, a starter of scallops with bottarga and roasted pumpkin, that was wonderful. Others were marred by jarring faults. Gazpacho was dull in flavour and oddly chewy in texture, and grilled calamari salad had too much carbon-bitterness and not nearly enough acidity to balance its oily dressing. Spaghetti with lobster and tomato sauce featuring leathery pasta and bland lobster was inexcusable. The meaty ensembles making their way to other tables – occupied mostly by men in suits – looked appealing. On the wine list we counted four bottles under £20 and not much under £30: the scope is international, strong on France. If you're looking for hearty, meaty fare, and don't mind PVC-clad women on the walls, Luciano may appeal.

Babies and children admitted. Booking advisable. Disabled: toilet. **Map 9 J8**.

Soho

Vasco & Piero's Pavilion

15 Poland Street, W1F 8QE (7437 8774/ www.vascosfood.com). Oxford Circus or Tottenham Court Road tube. **Lunch served** noon-3pm Mon-Fri. **Dinner served** 5.30-10.30pm Mon-Sat. **Main courses** £9.50-£20. **Set dinner** £24.50 2 courses, £28.50 3 courses. **Credit** AmEx, MC, V.

Even celebrated restaurants can have their off nights, so we hope our recent experience at this old Soho favourite was a temporary blot on its well-earned reputation for earthy Umbrian dishes and first-rate ingredients showcased in twice-daily changing menus. Tables at Vasco & Piero's Pavilion are usually packed close together, and on our visit the place felt as if it was bursting at the seams. Unsurprisingly, service was rushed: waiting staff remained friendly despite the manic pace, but the food seemed to have been prepared in haste. The pork filet scaloppine that landed, literally, on our table, displayed a rosy tinge, indicating it hadn't been thoroughly cooked. Own-made pasta dishes, such as spinach and ricotta tortelloni in butter-and-sage sauce, and plump parcels of guinea fowl, didn't suffer as much as the main courses, but weren't on a par with the assiduously prepared fare we've sampled in the past. Imaginative desserts (try the carpaccio of pineapple, ginger, saffron and vanilla ice-cream, if available) and the good-value wine list were meagre consolation for such disappointments.
Booking advisable. Children over 6 years admitted. Separate room for parties, seats 36. **Map 17 A3**.

South Kensington

Daphne's

112 Draycott Avenue, SW3 3AE (7589 4257/ www.daphnes-restaurant.co.uk). South Kensington tube. **Lunch served** noon-3pm Mon-Fri; noon-3.30pm Sat; noon-4pm Sun. **Dinner served** 5.30-11.30pm Mon-Sat; 5.30-10.30pm Sun. **Main courses** £12.75-£26.50. **Set lunch** £16.75 2 courses, £18.75 3 courses. **Credit** AmEx, DC, MC, V.

Daphne's has an inviting interior with touches that make it feel grand, such as the impressive ratio of attentive staff. They weren't put out when asked for tap water. Starters included a beetroot salad with goat's cheese, and a red and white endive salad with pear, pecorino and roasted walnuts. Both were excellent combinations and beautifully dressed, but there just wasn't enough of them. Bream, the fish of the day, was excellent. Ordering 'pan-fried' calf's liver with Italian bacon and baby onions and asked for cooking preference, we requested pink on the inside and crisp outside. What came, though, was a sort of stew with lots of fairly small strips of liver and bacon morsels paddling in gravy. The liver was indeed pinkish inside, but far from crisp. To add insult to disappointment, the bread disappeared from the table too soon to be used for mopping up the gravy. But Daphne's ended the meal on a high note with well-judged puddings of panna cotta with fresh orange sauce and a deeply scrummy chocolate pot.
Babies and children welcome: high chairs. Booking advisable. Separate room for parties, seats 40. **Map 14 E10**.

Westminster

Quirinale

North Court, 1 Great Peter Street, SW1P 3LL (7222 7080/www.quirinale.co.uk). St James's Park or Westminster tube. **Lunch served** noon-2.30pm, **dinner served** 6-10.30pm Mon-Fri. **Main courses** £12.50-£19. **Credit** AmEx, DC, MC, V.

Quirinale pulls off its basement location with impressive elegance, with subtle decor and attractive lighting. It's a small space, giving the opportunity for intimacy which must suit the parliamentarians working a few minutes away, as well as the local businessmen and couples it attracts. Ordering from the seasonally changing, modern Italian menu posed a challenge: we wanted everything. Our choices proved a mixed bag: crab salad featured one of the best tomato sauces ever served in London, with pesto adding a contrast of flavours. Cold courgette soup, beautifully presented, was delicate and refined. But there was a certain lack of sparkle in asparagus tips served with a poached egg and beetroot. Roast rabbit stuffed with apricots and porcini mushrooms didn't have the intensity you'd expect from such a bold assembly. A mixed salad with too many bland leaves (can someone please ban lollo rosso?), was spoiled by grittiness. Service was sweetly attentive, and the carefully chosen wine list reaps generous rewards if you can throw £35 to £40 at a single bottle. If Quirinale's amply talented chef paid just a little more attention to detail, this restaurant could rank among the capital's best Italians.
Babies and children admitted. Booking advisable. **Map 16 L10**.

West

Bayswater

★ Assaggi ⑽

1st floor, 39 Chepstow Place, W2 4TS (7792 5501). Bayswater, Queensway or Notting Hill Gate tube. **Lunch served** 12.30-2.30pm Mon-Fri; 1-2.30pm Sat. **Dinner served** 7.30-11pm Mon-Sat. **Main courses** £18-£24. **Credit** MC, V.

Don't be fooled by the unassuming gastropub look of Assaggi. Despite the informal, pared-down dining room with scrubbed wooden floorboards and paper table mats, it is one of those rare places in London where prime ingredients marry culinary artistry at reasonable prices. The compact menu is written in Italian, but there's no need to brush up your language skills before visiting: the warm, friendly and knowledgeable staff are on hand to explain the dishes and eagerly offer suggestions if you are still undecided, especially when choosing from the remarkable all-Italian wine list. We couldn't fault any of our dishes. The elegantly presented deep-fried courgette flowers must have been inspired by Cadbury Creme Eggs, hiding a surprise creamy filling of egg yolk and courgette purée. Fritto misto, the Venetian speciality of mixed deep fried seafood, was a towering pile of superbly fresh seafood cooked to perfection. If ordering just one dessert, go for the flourless chocolate cake with white chocolate ice-cream. Booking is imperative.
Babies and children welcome: high chair. Booking essential. **Map 7 B6**.

Hammersmith

Bianco Nero

206-208 Hammersmith Road, W6 7DP (8748 0212/www.bianconerorestaurants.com). Hammersmith tube. **Lunch served** noon-3pm Mon-Fri. **Dinner served** 6-10pm Mon-Sat. **Main courses** £11-£18. **Credit** AmEx, MC, V.

Bianco Nero's black-and-white decor is smart but lacks atmosphere, rather like a branch of a pizza chain. Tables for four are small, but service was attentive and patient when asked to repeat specials, which were about the only things of interest given the brief and predictable menu. A starter of thinly sliced rabbit stuffed with rabbit liver was delicious, and the gnocchi was obviously homemade, but swamped with red onion. Main courses ranged from just acceptable to inedible. Best was roast turbot: slightly overcooked, but the accompanying crushed potatoes and beurre blanc worked well. Pasta with spicy sausage was workmanlike. However the pork loin was awful: not just pink, but totally uncooked in parts, with too sharp mustard mash and an overpowering sauce. A carafe of pinot grigio wasn't cold enough either. We shared a portion of white chocolate and raspberry cheesecake, which was excellent. Bianco Nero needs to up its consistency, so that the food is more in line with the prices.
Babies and children welcome: high chairs. Booking advisable lunch. Disabled: toilet. Separate room for parties, seats 20. **Map 20 C4**.

★ The River Café ⑽

Thames Wharf, Rainville Road, W6 9HA (7386 4200/www.rivercafe.co.uk). Hammersmith tube. **Lunch served** 12.30-3pm daily. **Dinner served** 7-9.30pm Mon-Sat. **Main courses** £23-£32. **Credit** AmEx, DC, MC, V.

West Londoners and fans from further afield have just endured an entire summer without their favourite alfresco spot – the legendary River Café has been shut for (another) refit. As we went to press, the already delayed reopening was scheduled for September. The open kitchen was being renovated, a private dining room and cheese room were being added, and some changes made to the reception, but the dining room is to be more or less the same. No doubt Chris and Gwynnie, Amanda Wakeley and the rest will rush back for – ooh, well, in the autumn the wood-roast fish could be dover sole with lemon and capers, fine green beans and parsley. Or you could opt for wild sea bass cooked in a sea salt crust and served at room temperature with fennel, courgette, swiss chard and aïoli. Seasonal starters and pastas always prompt a bit of negotiation over who will have the

Osteria Emilia. See p192.

RESTAURANTS

buffalo mozzarella with black figs, purple basil and purslane; the bruschetta of Devon crab; or the fresh tagliatelle with girolles, garlic and parmesan. But the produce-based menu changes twice daily, so there are no guarantees. The sensible wine list (try a chilled red) and the riverside setting are two more of the River Café's many charms.
Babies and children welcome; high chairs. Booking essential. Disabled: toilet. Dress: smart casual. Tables outdoors (15, terrace). **Map 20 C5.**

Holland Park

Edera

148 Holland Park Avenue, W11 4UE (7221 6090). Holland Park tube. **Lunch served** 12.30-2.30pm Mon-Fri; 12.30-3pm Sun. **Dinner served** 6.30-11pm Mon-Sat. **Meals served** 12.30-10pm Sun. **Main courses** £11-£18. **Credit** AmEx, MC, V.
Subtly chic decor and clever subdued lighting give Edera ('ivy') a most inviting atmosphere. From a rather predictable antipasti list, with none of the Sardinian flair of the rest of the menu, we chose calamari and a mozzarella salad. The former was beautifully cooked in a delicate batter; the latter an elaborate assembly of half a dozen thin slices of large tomato and three large basil leaves arranged like petals around a whole mozzarella – the dressing a simple sprinkling of oil from the waiter. It was totally delicious and every speck was mopped up. The day's special, a guazzetto of just-cooked prawns and moist red mullet in garlicky tomato sauce, delivered transporting Mediterranean flavours. Calf's liver was cooked exactly as requested, still melting and pink inside but with a nicely seared exterior. From a vast list of intriguing Sardinian wines, a £25 Cannonau di Sardegna was one of the few reds whose price didn't venture into the stratosphere, but it was a revelation.
Babies and children admitted. Booking advisable dinner. Restaurant available for hire. Separate room for parties, seats 15. Tables outdoors (4, pavement). **Map 19 B5.**

Kensington

★ Timo

343 Kensington High Street, W8 6NW (7603 3888/www.timorestaurant.net). High Street Kensington tube. **Lunch served** noon-2.30pm, d**inner served** 7-11pm Mon-Sat. **Main courses** £14.90-£21.95. **Credit** AmEx, MC, V.
An unusually charming greeting from proprietor Piero Amodio set the tone for our visit. Ushered into the serene, elegant dining room, with large tables well spaced, the effect is of being welcomed into someone's gracious home. Service is attentive without being fussy, and with the breads come little bruschettini topped with forceful Italian ham. The smallish menu is well composed and includes intriguing specialities, like wild venison bresaola with celeriac and horseradish, and ravioloni filled with oxtail and beetroot butter. Maltagliati (flat pasta pieces) with duck ragù was bursting with flavour. Timo's elegant version of buffalo mozzarella salad has marinated tomatoes, basil pesto and tasty chopped black olives. Meat eaters should look no further than the tagliata di manzo, Angus fillet perfectly cooked to order, piled with rocket and parmesan shavings on a bed of rosemary roast potatoes. A special of plaice fillets in basil crust on a bed of young artichoke sounds unlikely but was delicious and perfectly cooked. To continue the basil theme we shared a panna cotta dusted with basil powder and served with melon sorbet. Exquisite little petits fours with the fresh mint tea and coffee rounded off a memorable evening. We look forward to revisiting.
Babies and children admitted. Booking advisable. Restaurant available for hire. Separate room for parties, seats 18. **Map 13 A9.**

Ladbroke Grove

Essenza

210 Kensington Park Road, W11 1NR (7792 1066/www.essenza.co.uk). Ladbroke Grove tube. **Meals served** 12.30-11.30pm daily.

Main courses £15.50-£17.50. **Set lunch** £12.50 2 courses. **Credit** AmEx, MC, V.
Tucked away from the buzzy parts of Notting Hill, this intimate little restaurant could be a bit too much so: given a table by the coats (while the place was only 25 per cent full), even staff managed to kick our seat on every pass. The evening began badly with a classic error: a bowl was filled with oil and vinegar and then many hungry minutes later we had to ask for the bread. Gnocchi with four cheeses was tasty but the portion was too large for a starter. Perfectly cooked calamari came with a clever chilli jam. All but two of the meat dishes were of veal and when asked if the veal was ethical, all the maître d' could say was that it was 'very tasty'. Spiedini (skewers) of 'char-grilled monkfish, squids and scallops' were nicely cooked but patently had never been on a skewer and lacked the expected barbecue flavour. Whole sea bass with broccoli was fine but a tad dull. Fortunately, prompted by the waiter, we also shared some deliciously crisp zucchini fritti. A bottle of lemony and floral Rocca di Montemassi Vermentino made the perfect accompaniment.
Babies and children welcome: high chairs. Booking essential Fri, Sat. Tables outdoors (2, pavement). **Map 19 B3.**
For branch (Osteria Basilico) see index.

Mediterraneo

37 Kensington Park Road, W11 2EU (7792 3131/www.mediterraneo-restaurant.co.uk). Ladbroke Grove tube. **Lunch served** 12.30-3pm Mon-Fri; 12.30-6pm Sat; 12.30-3.45pm Sun. **Dinner served** 6.30-11.30pm Mon-Sat; 6.30-10.30pm Sun. **Main courses** £8-£16.50. **Credit** MC, V.
Our first impressions weren't auspicious: 'We can let you have a table at 7pm, but you'll have to be up by 9.15.' Get over yourselves, guys. Mediterraneo's a decent, mid-range Italian serving quite good Italian food (particularly pasta) but Mr Ramsay needn't lose sleep just yet. The look is '90s-style Tuscan farmhouse chic, with rustic earthy tones. We were served great bread, the focaccia still warm, the brown sourdough very fresh, which set things on to a better footing. A starter of squidgy smoked scamorza cheese melted over sliced mushrooms sautéed with tomato and onion, topped with rocket, was simple and generous. A red, white and green main course of halved cherry tomatoes, tender grilled squid bodies and more vivid-green rocket, was punchily dressed with quality olive oil and lemon – simple but good. Spaghetti with a tomato and lobster sauce was perhaps a bit oversauced (the way Brits like it), but was cooked properly al dente. There's plenty of competition in the area, but this place is always busy – a popular local spot.
Babies and children welcome: high chairs. Bookings advisable weekends. Tables outdoors (4, pavement). **Map 19 B3.**

Olympia

Cibo

3 Russell Gardens, W14 8EZ (7371 6271/2085/ www.ciborestaurant.co.uk). Shepherd's Bush tube/Kensington (Olympia) tube/rail. **Lunch served** noon-2.30pm Mon-Fri, Sun. **Dinner served** 7-11pm Mon-Sat. **Main courses** £10.50-£23.50. **Set lunch** (Mon-Fri) £16.50 2 courses; (Sun) £18.95 2 courses, £24.95 3 courses. **Credit** AmEx, MC, V.
The awkward, cramped, but engagingly arty-shabby interior was pulsing with the arrival of two large parties so we remained unnoticed until we were seated. That said all subsequent service was prompt and attentive. The clientele is mostly local regulars – Notting Hill Gaters and Holland Parkers who flocked there in the '80s, now greying and with grown-up kids. Lovely platters of fat olives and mini pizza were already on table, plus a nice mix of breads. A swordfish and sea bream carpaccio starter was disastrous: it tasted like it had been prepared many hours before, was too cold and the fish had lost all texture, but the fish-stuffed black pasta with clam sauce was delicious. A main course of monkfish was disappointing, consisting of three oddly shaped bits, mainly bone. La

Nostra Grigliata di Mare (a whopping but worthwhile £26.50) was, however, a tour de force: a vast array of the very freshest baby squid, mussels, clams and other assorted crustaceans with a seared swordfish fillet and thick sea bream steak; all grilled to perfection.
Babies and children welcome: high chair. Booking advisable dinner. Dress: smart casual. Restaurant available for hire. Separate rooms for parties, seating 12 and 16. Tables outdoors (4, pavement).

South West

Barnes

★ Riva (100)

169 Church Road, SW13 9HR (8748 0434). Barnes or Barnes Bridge rail/33, 209, 283 bus. **Lunch served** 12.15-2.15pm Mon-Fri, Sun. **Dinner served** 7-10.30pm Mon-Sat; 7-9pm Sun. **Main courses** £12-£21. **Credit** AmEx, MC, V.
Despite spectacular arrays of fresh flowers at either end of the room, Riva's decor is a tad gloomy. Deep colours and high ambient lighting produce a Magritte-ish dimness at table level that cries out for candles. Service was immensely charming and informative; the menu inviting and dotted with classic dishes and unusual specialities

---

THE DISH

Carpaccio

Carpaccio's wide popularity belies the fact that it was invented just 59 years ago, at Harry's Bar in Venice. Thinly sliced raw beef rubbed with olive oil and crosshatched with creamy mustard dressing, it was named after the Italian Renaissance painter because of its striking colours. The word carpaccio quickly came to mean thinly sliced food, and now you're as likely to find carpaccios of fish, mushrooms and fruit on menus as you are meat.

The **River Café** favours Longhorn beef fillet for carpaccio; through the year, dressings and toppings vary from rocket and Sardinian pecorino to fresh horseradish and crème fraîche. Sometimes its chefs don't serve the beef raw at all, but seared with a crust of thyme and pepper. River Café alumnus **Theo Randall** uses Aberdeen Angus fillet, and in season serves it with wet (juicy, unripe) walnuts, red chicory and gorgonzola.

Petersham Nurseries Café (*see p248*) keeps an Italian sensibility with its simple carpaccio of wild sea bass, shaved fennel and chilli, while the **Landau** (*see p136*) cranks it up several notches, serving raw milk-fed veal with (among other things) hazelnut and salt crumble, iberico ham, baby artichokes, white balsamic jelly and parmesan foam. Pineapple carpaccio makes a refreshing dessert, whether steeped in saffron syrup, as at the **Clissold Arms** (*see p127*), or combined with coconut sorbet, malibu lime jelly and seaweed croquette, as at **Maze** (*see p143*). No, that's not very authentic, but then carpaccio's not so much an Italian export these days as an Italian expat.

of Lombardy, homeland of owner, Andrea Riva. We began with the unmissable antipasto for two (£20): a dazzling platter of San Daniele ham and pears, bresaola, coppa, speck and fegato d'oca (goose liver) dressed with syrupy balsamic, delicious fruit mostarda, cornmeal pancakes with speck and asiago cheese, and pickled vegetables (pickled celeriac was a novel delight). All the ingredients were fresh and flavoursome – there was even a basket of unbrowned toast as the perfect foil for the goose liver. Mains of roast lamb cutlets with roast potatoes and peppers, and roast rabbit and artichokes with mashed potatoes were faultless and filling, but we still felt forced to sample their splendid desserts – prunes and blackberries in grappa with cinnamon ice-cream, and panna cotta with fig compote. Wonderful.
Babies and children welcome (lunch): high chairs. Booking essential dinner. Tables outdoors (3, pavement).

Chelsea

Manicomio

85 Duke of York Square, SW3 4LY (7730 3366/ www.manicomio.co.uk). Sloane Square tube. **Deli Open** 8am-7pm Mon-Fri; 10am-7pm Sat; 10am-6pm Sun. **Restaurant Lunch served** noon-3pm Mon-Fri; noon-5pm Sat, Sun. **Dinner served** 6.30-10.30pm Mon-Sat; 6.30-10pm Sun. **Main courses** £12-£24. *Both* **Credit** AmEx, MC, V.
Located in the redevelopment of the Duke of York's barracks on the King's Road, Manicomio's set-up includes an Italian deli and large terrace – although sadly (or blessedly, according to taste) this doesn't front on the road. Inside, red leather banquettes against exposed brick walls give a chic but cosy atmosphere. Service is a mix of pleasant and slightly aloof. The menu is shortish, but full of interesting ingredients, like puntarella (a wild dandelion/chicory cross) and cime di rapa (turnip greens). Starters include intriguing twists on standards, like buffalo mozzarella salad with roasted peppers and grilled aubergine, a quite superb warm octopus salad with potatoes, lime leaves, chilli and capers, and a generous platter of delicious Parma ham with pears and ubriaco – the sweet-spicy unpasteurised cheese from Lombardy a revelation. Main courses were along more familiar lines, but did make a feature of incorporating some of the novel veg – a practice many Italian restaurants could do with adopting. Gutsy tarragon-stuffed guinea fowl wrapped in prosciutto was served with cime de rapa, and meltingly tender lamb shanks with spinach and chickpea purée.
Babies and children welcome: booster seats. Booking advisable. Separate room for parties, seats 30. Tables outdoors (30, terrace). **Map 14 F11.**
For branch see index.

Osteria dell'Arancio

383 King's Road, SW10 0LP (7349 8111/ www.osteriadellarancio.co.uk). Fulham Broadway or Sloane Square tube. **Lunch served** noon-2.30pm Mon-Fri; noon-3pm Sat, Sun. **Dinner served** 6.30-11pm Mon-Sat; 6.30-10pm Sun. **Main courses** £12-£18. **Credit** AmEx, DC, MC, V.
This unusual and lively restaurant is the sister of one in Grottammare in the Marche. The London branch luxuriates in that Italian joy of mixing art and food, with practically every surface, tabletops included, colourfully decorated, and statues climbing into recesses in the ceiling. The atmosphere is warm and the staff even exhibit a Dada-esque sense of humour – extra bread for our starters came in a white paper bag with the announcement 'bag of toffees!' The menu is an exciting mix of regional specialities and adventurous dishes such as octopus carpaccio with walnut pesto, and rack of lamb stuffed with liver pâté, braised artichoke and blueberry sauce. For starters we had scallops wrapped in lardo with beetroot coulis, and chargrilled squid with aubergine caponata and anchovy vinaigrette – both well conceived and beautifully executed. Main

courses of swordfish rolls stuffed with aromatic bread and pecorino, braised escarole and anchovy sauce, and turbot wrapped in savoy cabbage with pecorino, lardo and jerusalem artichoke coulis, again lived up to our growing expectations, although the jury is still out on the artichoke coulis.
Babies and children welcome: high chairs; nappy-changing facilities. Disabled: toilet. Separate room for parties, seats 35. Tables outdoors (12, terrace). **Map 14 D12.**

Fulham

La Famiglia

7 Langton Street, SW10 0JL (7351 0761/ 7352 6095/www.lafamiglia.co.uk). Sloane Square tube then 11, 22 bus/31 bus. **Lunch served** noon-3pm, **dinner served** 7-11.30pm daily. **Main courses** £8.50-£26. **Cover** £1.85. **Minimum** £18.50 dinner. **Credit** AmEx, MC, V.
A lovely old place that has been a World's End institution since 1975, La Famiglia is run by Alvaro Maccioni and his family. It has a charmingly authentic Tuscan feel, with half-tiled walls and family photographs everywhere. Even the immaculate service from the waiters in their whites is pleasingly faithful to Italian tradition. Seasonal menus feature classic dishes like fiori di zucca and vitello tonnato, as well as less well-known specialties 'alla campagna', such as stuffed pheasant with wild boar, garlic and fennel. Our starters included good old mozzarella in carrozza with a fine tomato sauce and satisfying full flavour to the cheese. Deep-fried baby artichoke came with an intense basil coulis. Main course choices were a satisfying gramigna (curled strand pasta) with pancetta and pecorino and agnello in padella, a superb, moist leg steak of salt-marsh lamb imbued with garlic and rosemary. This, like the veal – indeed, most of the meat – was organic. Little in this engaging time capsule has changed since its early days, expect perhaps the clientele: the colourful bohemians of old Chelsea have been firmly replaced by hedge-fund Henrys.
Babies and children welcome: high chairs. Booking advisable dinner and Sun. Tables outdoors (30, garden). **Map 13 C13.**

Putney

Enoteca Turi

28 Putney High Street, SW15 1SQ (8785 4449/ www.enotecaturi.com). Putney Bridge tube/Putney rail/14, 74, 220, 270 bus. **Lunch served** noon-2.30pm, **dinner served** 7-11pm Mon-Sat. **Main courses** £14.50-£22.50. **Set lunch** £14.50 2 courses, £17.50 3 courses. **Credit** AmEx, DC, MC, V.
With its Tuscan earth-toned colour scheme, Enoteca Turi has a comfortable, well-padded tastefulness about – a bit like the customers it attracts. The daily specials on a menu which keeps an eye on the season are particularly appealing, like a main course of turbot ravioli with potato and fennel sauce. The pasta itself was perhaps a bit thick, but tender enough, with delicately flavoured stuffing and a gently creamy sauce. Sicilian-style rabbit was a gutsy counterpoint, the boned loin stuffed with the liver, breadcrumbs, pine nuts and raisins, served with sautéed red pepper, onion and celery. There's real skill at work in the kitchen – and in the wine cellar. The owner is a learned aficionado of Italian wines and the list here is one of the best in the capital, a masterpiece of clear tasting notes and carefully curated (mostly Italian) bottles, ranging in price from frugal to blow-the-budget. Wines by the glass are recommended with each dish on the menu and the staff seem capable of making sensible wine suggestions too: there's no excuse for ordering a mere glass of pinot grigio.
Babies and children admitted. Booking advisable. Disabled: toilet. Separate rooms for parties, seating 20-30.

Marco Polo

6-7 Riverside Quarter, Eastfields Avenue, SW18 1LP (8874 6800/www.marcopolo.uk.net). East Putney tube. **Meals served** noon-11pm Mon-Thur; noon-11.30pm Fri, Sat; noon-10.30pm

Sun. **Main courses** £12.50-£22.50. **Set lunch** £7.95 1 course, £9.95 2 courses, £11.95 3 courses. **Credit** MC, V.
The setting, hard by the river in a development of high-rise 'luxury flats' (as the estate agents would have it), is hard to beat. On sunny summer days and on warmer evenings, the outdoor tables are a sea of eating, drinking, convivial humanity – with children much in evidence. Inside, it's sleek and modern, but comfortable. Marco Polo doesn't serve up the best Italian food this side of the Eternal City; it's little more than adequate, but the surroundings and service, by Italian waiters straight from Central Casting, make up for it. The pan-Italian menu takes in pizza and pasta plus lots of fish and a few veal-based dishes. Our spicy prawns with tomato and chickpeas was competent enough, but we found the base of our goat's cheese, walnut and caramelised onion a bit on the tough side. A halibut steak served with butter and capers was moist and nicely cooked. Desserts such as chocolate and hazelnut cake and tiramisu are in the traditional mould. Wines don't stray too far from pinot grigio and chianti but are reasonably priced.
Babies and children welcome: high chairs. Booking advisable. Disabled: toilet. Separate room for parties, seats 30. Tables outdoors (60, riverside terrace).

South

Clapham

Mooli

36A Old Town, SW4 0LB (7627 1166/ www.moolirestaurant.com). Clapham Common tube. **Lunch served** noon-3.30pm, **dinner served** 6.30-11pm Mon-Fri. **Tea served** 3-6pm Mon-Sat. **Meals served** noon-11pm Sat; 1-11pm Sun. **Main courses** £12.95-£14.50 **Credit** AmEx, MC, V.
Mooli's menu lists dishes from Veneto to Sardinia, each marked with its region of provenance. Unusually for better Italian restaurants, seasonality wasn't such a strong point on our visit. Our starter of crostini di melanzane was nicely presented in a tower arrangement, but the aubergine was undercooked and the (unexpected) tomato slices under-ripe. Main courses were better executed. 'Sardinian veal' was thinly sliced grilled veal wrapped around parmesan slivers and a handful of rocket leaves, topped with a creamy gorgonzola sauce; gutsy and full-flavoured. We like a good pun so had to try arancini 'Moolinese'. A freeform interpretation, the meat was formed into little cups upon which sat the rice balls – clever; tasty too. Mooli is a casual place that doesn't take itself too seriously. The decor is easy on the eye and service is keen to make diners feel at home. Cocktail fans should be aware that drinks supremo Douglas Ankrah can sometimes be found behind the small bar.
Babies and children welcome: high chairs. Booking advisable. **Map 22 A1.**

South East

Bermondsey

Arancia

52 Southwark Park Road, SE16 3RS (7394 1751/www.arancia-london.co.uk). Bermondsey tube/Elephant & Castle tube/rail then 1, 53 bus. **Lunch served** 12.30-2.30pm Tue-Sun. **Dinner served** 7-11pm Tue-Sat. **Main courses** £10-£13.75. **Set lunch** £7.50 2 courses, £10.50 3 courses. **Credit** AmEx, MC, V.
A slightly scuffed splash of orange on a busy grey road, Arancia's bare brick alcoves, worn floorboards, sloping ceilings and old dials and gauges on the walls give it an antique, boiler room air. The changing menu of inexpensive Mediterranean food is distinguished by its simplicity and bold use of bright, fresh market produce. Our visit on a rainy lunchtime was a pleasure from the start, when a request for tap water was answered promptly with a chilled bottle of 'Bermondsey Spa', together with a bowl of

fresh, juicy olives and preserved lemons. The inexpensive set lunch (£7.50) began with a superb bowl of delicate pale green zuppa di stagione, with peas, fennel, baby spinach and potatoes served with garlicky bruschetta and parmesan. This was followed by richly sauced linguine with aubergines and peppers. Crespelle (pancakes) had a tempting filling of chard and fontina cheese, although the stalky veg rather dominated the plate. The accompanying mixed leaves, tomato sauce and green lentils were more nutritious than delicious. Glasses of light, cooling prosecco made a fine partner to the meal. We regretted our ineffectual coffee but left happy.

Babies and children welcome: high chair. Booking advisable evenings. Separate room for parties, seats 8.

Crystal Palace

★ Mediterranea NEW

21 Westow Street, SE19 3RY (8771 7327/ www.mediterranealondon.com). Crystal Palace or Gypsy Hill rail. **Lunch served** 12.30-2.30pm, **dinner served** 6.30-10.30pm Tue-Sun. **Main courses** £8.50-£15.90. **Set lunch** (Tue-Sat) £6.90 1 course incl drink, £9.50 2 courses incl drink. **Credit** MC, V.

There's much to like at this charming, canteen-like cheap eat run by Efisio Fronteddu, ex-Olivo staffer and flag-flier for the honest cooking of his native Sardinia. Mediterranea's menu makes good use of seafood (fresh from Billingsgate), and high-quality Sardinian ingredients, namely pork, wild boar, honey, wild herbs and the superb cheeses (from cow and ewe) for which the island is famous. We enjoyed straightforward delights in the shape of grilled fennel dotted with ricotta, and satisfying culurgione (plump pecorino-stuffed pillows of own-made pasta in a simple tomato sauce). Dessert was a nicely moist ricotta cheesecake drizzled with honey. In fact the only let-down was a bland slab of pork with wild boar salami and some tired-looking borlotti beans; it lacked both the choice ingredients and sound cooking that made the other dishes a success. It's a shame that Fronteddu has taken his restaurant's name so literally, allowing diverse tastes of the Med (halloumi cheese, Turkish bread, Andalucian saltfish) to clutter and confuse his Sardinian-inflected menu; a simpler approach might work better.

Babies and children welcome: high chair. Booking advisable weekends.

Tower Bridge

Cantina del Ponte

Butlers Wharf Building, 36C Shad Thames, SE1 2YE (7403 5403/www.danddlondon.com). Tower Hill tube/Tower Gateway DLR/London Bridge tube/rail/47, 78 bus. **Lunch served** noon-3pm daily. **Dinner served** 6-11pm Mon-Sat; 6-10pm Sun. **Main courses** £9.50-£16. **Credit** AmEx, DC, MC, V.

Given its superb location next to Tower Bridge and lower prices than many nearby restaurants, the outside tables at Cantina del Ponte are very popular on sunny summer weekends, when Butlers Wharf assumes the air of a Mediterranean resort. Just don't cexpect to be overwhelmed by culinary wizardry, authentic flavours or pampering service. Instead, follow the example of the regular clientele of continental European expats, who tend to stick to simple Mediterranean fare, like spaghetti with shellfish. More aspirational dishes, like bruschetta with potted duck, feel contrived and are likely to disappoint. There is a good selection of pizzas, cooked in a traditional brick oven, as well as a few enticing desserts, such as a pleasantly crumbly almond and lemon cake. On the plus side, the set lunch menu, which starts at £14.95 for two courses, is good value. Service can verge on the non-existent and lingering at the end of the meal is not encouraged, which guarantees to cut that holiday feeling short.

Babies and children welcome: high chairs. Booking advisable dinner. Dress: smart casual. Restaurant available for hire. Tables outdoors (20, terrace). **Map 12 S8.**

★ Tentazioni

2 Mill Street, SE1 2BD (7237 1100/ www.tentazioni.co.uk). Bermondsey tube/London Bridge tube/rail. **Lunch served** noon-2.45pm Mon-Fri. **Dinner served** 6.30-10.45pm Mon-Sat. **Main courses** £17-£20. **Set dinner** £40 5 course tasting menu (£62 incl wine). **Credit** AmEx, MC, V.

Tucked away on a side street in unglamorous Bermondsey, at first glance Tentazioni feels like a secretive members-only club, with an almost racy decor of plum-and-red walls and edgy artwork. Like the ambience, the food veers away from tradition through spectacularly assembled bold combinations that rarely fail to impress. A simple dish of gnocchi with seafood was given a distinct marine flavour with the addition of sea urchin.

Main courses, whether in the guise of an artistically constructed rack of lamb or simple pan-fried cod, are outstanding and superbly presented. Despite the slick decor, the atmosphere remains unpretentious and relaxed. Staff are professional and friendly, always eager to help finding the perfect match for the food from the well-chosen wine list, which unusually includes several good quality bins available by the glass. There are prix fixe menus as well as an appealing tasting menu for those who feel unable to choose from the options available à la carte. With such decadent surroundings and indulgent food, Tentazioni is the perfect intimate venue to impress that special date.

Babies and children admitted. Booking advisable dinner Fri, Sat. Restaurant available for hire. Separate room for parties, seats 24. **Map 12 S9.**

East

Docklands

Carluccio's Caffè

Reuters Plaza, E14 5AJ (7719 1749/ www.carluccios.com). Canary Wharf tube/DLR. **Meals served** 7am-11.30pm Mon-Fri; 9am-11.30pm Sat; 10am-10.30pm Sun. **Main courses** £8.75-£12.75. **Credit** AmEx, DC, MC, V.

The warmth and clatter, the smell of coffee and baked goods and the shelves of aspirational deli items bring la Repubblica Italiana to the hard lines of Docklands. That's probably why the suited and booted office folk gallop here for lunchtime pasta and salad. The waiting staff are the apotheosis of Italian expansiveness, with lots of *ciao bella!* for the ladies and extra twinkle and charm for the babies. The food is as appealing as the welcome. From the first order of the savoury bread selection with its little pool of fruity olive oil, to the superb cioccolato fondente flavoured with coffee liqueur, a hearty meal is assured. Between those, dishes of sea bass fillets with sautéed potatoes and tomato salsa, penne with courgettes and fried spinach balls, and a huge, businesslike salad of roasted vegetables, pesto, olives and mozzarella made a flavour-filled lunch to linger over, helped along by a bottle of fruity Sicilian fiano from the inexpensive wine list.

Babies and children welcome: children's menu; high chairs; toys. Disabled: toilet. Tables outdoors (30, terrace). Takeaway service. **Map 24 B2.** **For branches see index.**

Arancia

Shoreditch

Fifteen

15 Westland Place, N1 7LP (0871 330 1515/ www.fifteenrestaurant.com). Old Street tube/rail. Trattoria **Breakfast served** 7.30-11am Mon-Sat; 9-11am Sun. **Lunch served** noon-3pm Mon-Sat; noon-3.30pm Sun. **Dinner served** 6-10pm Mon-Sat. **Main courses** £10-£19. *Restaurant* **Lunch served** noon-2.30pm, **dinner served** 6.30-9.15pm daily. **Main courses** £22-£25. **Set lunch** £25 2 courses, £30 3 courses. **Set dinner** £60 tasting menu. *Both* **Credit** AmEx, MC, V.

Although Jamie Oliver's charity venture is housed in a stunning Victorian building, the interior fails to be either grand or cosy, with oddly tatty tables and oversize menus. Worst of all are the unwieldy knives that practically sprain the wrist. An officious maitre d' had one of us waiting unnecessarily by the upstairs bar while the other was already installed at the table downstairs. From then on, however, service was very professional and friendly. As it was Monday lunchtime, we questioned ordering fish and were assured it was fresh that day. The dressed Devonshire crab on bruschetta was, however, disappointing; the pollack special overcooked and dry. 'Wicked' Sicilian fisherman's stew featured nicely cooked salmon and sea bass and a delicious soupy tomato and garlic base, delightful with toasted sourdough bruschetta spread with lemon aïoli. Sadly, the smattering of accompanying seafood around a solitary saffron potato had a high percentage of empty shells, some disguised with squid rings. Desserts, in the form of a caramel panna cotta with poached pears and a quince and pannetone pudding, were by far the best course.
Babies and children welcome: high chairs. Booking essential (restaurant). Disabled: toilet (trattoria). Dress: smart casual. **Map 6 Q3.**

North

Archway

★ 500 Restaurant NEW

782 Holloway Road, N19 3JH (7272 3406/ www.500restaurant.co.uk). Archway tube/Upper Holloway rail. **Meals served** noon-10pm Tue-Sat; 5-10pm Sun. **Main courses** £7.40-£12.90. **Credit** MC, V.

Chef Mario Magli and barman Giorgio Pili met while working at Neal Street restaurant. They subsequently worked at Passione (see p178) before boldly opening their own restaurant here. It's a modest place, with rich red walls, clean-lined blond wood chairs and a few rather clichéd pictures on the walls – perhaps for reassuring a conservative local market. Sensibly, prices have been kept very low (wines start at £2.05 a glass), and the food is several notches above that of an average north London trattoria. A generous bread basket features semolina-dusted rosemary focaccia, tangy tomato pinwheels and simple white rolls, all made on the premises. The likes of red snapper ragù, and a sauce of Italian sausage, fennel seeds and tomatoes, are paired with superb egg pasta or Magli's own whisper-light gnocchi: a refreshing change from the carbonara, bolognese and marinara of lesser establishments. Monkfish rolled in bacon and served with spinach, raisins and pine nuts was every bit as good as similar dishes found in the West End. To finish, a very classy, very classic tiramisu, and tart of the day: a jammy rhubarb number perfectly in tune with the season. *Babies children admitted. Booking advisable (dinner).* **Map 26 C1.**

Camden Town & Chalk Farm

La Collina

17 Princess Road, NW1 8JR (7483 0192). Camden Town or Chalk Farm tube. **Lunch served** noon-3pm Sat, Sun. **Dinner served** 6.30-11pm daily. **Set meal** £14.50 1 course, £19.50 2 courses, £23.50 3 courses. **Credit** MC, V.

La Collina has two significant problems, both a few minutes' walk away: Sardo Canale, the local branch of Fitzrovia's Sardo (see p178) and the Engineer gastropub (see p124). While these more famous names might draw punters away from La Collina, that would be a shame, because it is a serious, authentic Italian local. The small ground-floor room is better than the cramped downstairs, and the garden out back is glorious on a warm day. The menu changes frequently, but the dishes we ate give a good idea of the ambition of the kitchen, which demonstrates a sure hand with seafood: our meal featured a dazzling octopus and cuttlefish salad, excellent gnocchetti neri (little squid-ink gnocchi) with mussels, spaghetti with prawns and langoustines. Braised rabbit with artichoke hearts was beautifully cooked and deeply flavourful. The short, all-Italian wine list could offer more choice under £20 but sound house wines mean you can eat three courses for £40 a head. If there is a complaint, it's the absence of that finishing touch which raises a dish from good to wonderful: the bland, oily dressing on an otherwise impeccable starter of grilled radicchio and endive with young goat's cheese exemplified that failing. But such complaints are minor – La Collina is cherishable.
Babies and children welcome: high chair. Booking advisable. Separate room for parties, seats 16. Tables outdoors (14, garden). **Map 27 B2.**

Islington

Metrogusto

13 Theberton Street, N1 0QY (7226 9400/ www.metrogusto.co.uk). Angel tube. **Brunch served** 10am-5pm Wed-Sun. **Dinner served** 6.30-10.30pm Mon-Thur; 6.30-11pm Fri, Sat; 6-10pm Sun. **Main courses** £11.50-£17.50. **Set meal** (6-9pm Mon-Fri, Sun) £14.50 two courses, £18.50 3 courses. **Credit** AmEx, MC, V.

Almost hidden away off Islington's Upper Street, Metrogusto couldn't be more removed from the tired image of the neighbourhood trattoria that still manages to survive in London. The decor is downright wacky, with surrealist-inspired paintings and curious props scattered around the main dining area. The cooking, which bills itself as 'progressive', is so innovative it verges on the playful, as shown by a starter of Tuscan ham with honey-sweetened grilled banana. Chef Antonio Di Salvo's concoctions may sound unlikely, almost offputting, but they rarely fail to hit the mark. The pan-fried duck breast with plum and Campari sauce shouldn't be missed, if available, along with at least one choice from the remarkable dessert menu, featuring quirky ice-cream flavours like goat's cheese and rosemary. The wine list is equally edgy and features a few lesser-known whites from the Alto Adige region, near the Austrian border, which are worth sampling. Several bins are available by the glass or in half bottles. With its efficient, pleasant service and affordable prices, Metrogusto is a real treasure.
Babies and children welcome: high chairs. Booking advisable; essential weekends. Separate room for parties, seats 38. Tables outdoors (4, pavement). **Map 5 O1.**

Kentish Town

Pane Vino

323 Kentish Town Road, NW5 2TJ (7267 3879). Kentish Town tube/rail. **Lunch served** noon-3pm, **dinner served** 6.30-11pm Mon-Sat. **Main courses** £15-£18. **Credit** MC, V.

Kentish Town dwellers, long deprived of decent dining-out options, can't seem to stop heaping praises on this culinary beacon. On Saturday nights they enthusiastically flock to this understated dining room to sample generous portions of rustic Sardinian fare, or happily queue for a takeaway box of fragrant pizza. Pane Vino's grilled sardines served with pane carasau (the traditional parchment-like bread of Sardinian shepherds) has become one of its signature dishes and shouldn't be missed. Pasta dishes are filled to the brim and feature most stalwarts of Sardinian cuisine. We suggest you visit with several friends

and swap dishes for the chance to sample the excellent malloreddus (maggot-shaped pasta) dressed with a pork sausage and tomato sauce enlivened with lashings of sharp pecorino cheese, linguine with either bottarga (dried grey mullet roe) or sublimely fresh shellfish in a simple tomato sauce. Disappointingly, the dessert menu forsakes the delectable Sardinian sweets, playing it safe with panna cotta and an unremarkable tiramisu. Our only gripe is the brusque, at times even frosty service that mars an otherwise pleasurable dining experience.
Babies and children admitted. Tables outdoors (2, pavement). Takeaway service. **Map 26 B5.**

Osteria Stecca

North West
Belsize Park

Osteria Emilia NEW

85 Fleet Road, NW3 2QY (7433 3317). Belsize Park tube/Hampstead Heath rail. **Lunch served** noon-3pm Tue-Fri. **Dinner served** 6.45-10pm Tue-Sat. **Main courses** £9-£18. **Credit** AmEx, MC, V.

Renate and Raffaele Giacobazzi – owners of Giacobazzi deli, which specialises in made-on-the-premises pasta – have opened this very welcome restaurant across the road from their shop. Behind the smart chocolate and black frontage lies a beach-house-style eaterie with skylight, plywood chairs and white linen: a relaxed setting for dishes from Emilia-Romagna and beyond. The well-balanced menu offers a satisfying mix of the unusual and familiar, pitching the likes of rabbit saltimbocca, and pike with capers, anchovies, parsley and garlic alongside classic grilled calf's liver with balsamic vinegar and onions. Polenta appears in both starters and mains. You can expect three or four dishes of pasta and gnocchi, plus a similar number of sides. A deli-owner's eye for sourcing has resulted in ice-cream from Oddono's, and a sizeable cheeseboard featuring organic Sicilian quince paste. Such delights made the dreary slices of ciabatta (the only disappointment in our meal) all the more surprising. Prices are quite high for this style of restaurant, but perhaps not for this part of town.
Babies and children welcome: high chairs. Booking advisable dinner. Disabled: toilet. Separate room for parties, seats 30. **Map 28 C3**.

Golders Green

Philpott's Mezzaluna

424 Finchley Road, NW2 2HY (7794 0455/ www.philpotts-mezzaluna.com). Golders Green tube. **Lunch served** noon-2.30pm Tue-Fri; noon-3pm Sun. **Dinner served** 7-11pm Tue-Sun. **Set lunch** £12 1 course, £17 2 courses, £20 3 courses, £25 4 courses. **Set dinner** £19.50 1 course, £23 2 courses, £28 3 courses, £33 4 courses. **Credit** MC, V.

This is the kind of warmly welcoming local anyone would love to have nearby. Apart from Warhol-esque oil paintings of Madonna, Al Pacino and other Italianate media stars, the decor is charmingly old-fashioned. There's a similar combination of new and old on the menu, underpinned by technical mastery that often owes as much to France as Italy. Our starters lay mainly in the French camp: leek and potato soup, sautéed scallops with a fennel and orange salad, fish soup, and chicken terrine wrapped in parma ham and served with sauce gribiche. They were classic, and flawless. Fishy main courses were more experimental, and let down only by a tendency to throw too much strength at the delicate piscine flesh. Olives and sun-dried tomatoes just had too much pungency for the star attraction of barramundi with a lovely aubergine purée and sprightly spinach. The wine list is big and international, and dinner prices are very reasonable for cooking of this quality. North Londoners should put this place on their must-visit list.
Babies and children welcome: high chairs. Booking advisable dinner Sat. Restaurant available for hire. Tables outdoors (3, terrace).

Maida Vale

Green Olive

5 Warwick Place, W9 2PX (7289 2469). Warwick Avenue tube/6 bus. **Lunch served** noon-2.30pm Fri, Sat. **Dinner served** 6-10.30pm Mon-Fri; 6.30-11pm Sat. **Main courses** £14-£19. **Credit** AmEx, MC, V.

Tucked in a quiet street among the white stucco houses and lush gardens of Little Venice, the bright and airy dining room at Green Olive almost feels like your own little place, if only for a couple of hours. It doesn't aspire to be a destination restaurant, but can be relied on for fairly executed Italian stalwarts at reasonable prices, and service

is friendly. The rather short menu is supplemented by several specials with a nod to seasonality, such as the summery starter of deep-fried courgette flowers and baby courgettes. An equally mouth-watering, butter-soft ribeye steak served with a simple rocket and tomato salad followed. The only let-down was spaghetti with clams, which came dressed in a butter sauce, rather than the more traditional extra virgin olive oil. Desserts don't veer far from tested classics, but the tiramisu is worthy of a Venetian mamma. If visiting in summer, reserve a table on the tiny back patio.
Babies and children admitted. Booking advisable. Restaurant available for hire. **Map 1 C4**.

St John's Wood

Osteria Stecca NEW

2008 RUNNER-UP BEST LOCAL RESTAURANT
1 Blenheim Terrace, NW8 0EH (7328 5014/ www.osteriastecca.com). St John's Wood tube. **Lunch served** noon-2.30pm Tue-Thur; noon-3pm Fri-Sun. **Dinner served** 6.30-10.30pm Tue-Thur; 6.30-11pm Fri, Sat; 7-10pm Sun. **Main courses** £12.50-£21. **Credit** AmEx, MC, V.

Osteria Stecca's large front terrace, with its big black umbrellas and smart box hedging, is the choice spot for a balmy summer night. But if this is full – as it was on our visit, with an upmarket local crowd, many of them Italian – the adjacent conservatory is almost as nice. Even the back of the restaurant is light and airy, with a simple, modern decor of white walls and linen, and dark-brown chairs and floor. Chef-proprietor Stefano Stecca knows this site well; he was chef of Rosmarino here in 2001 (when it won the Time Out Best Local Restaurant award). The menu offers classic dishes from the north and south of Italy, often with a modern slant. To start, buffalo mozzarella with grilled vegetables, and tuna three-ways (as tartare, seared and sashimi) showed that minimal interference with top-grade ingredients pays off; the tuna was sparklingly fresh. Less so a main of sea bass (a rather meagre fillet), which was mushy and didn't taste fresh enough; the accompanying fennel was overly sweet too. Seafood risotto won points for both taste and texture. Ice-creams and sorbets dominate the dessert list. The all-Italian wine list, about 80-strong, provides ample choice for under £30.
Babies and children welcome: high chairs. Booking advisable dinner Thur-Sun. Restaurant available for hire. Tables outdoors (7, terrace). **Map 1 C2**.

Outer London
Twickenham, Middlesex

A Cena

418 Richmond Road, Twickenham, Middx TW1 2EB (8288 0108). Richmond tube/rail. **Lunch served** noon-3pm Tue-Sun. **Dinner served** 7-10.30pm Mon-Sat. **Main courses** £14-£19. **Set lunch** (Sun) £25 3 courses. **Credit** AmEx, MC, V.

The narrow frontage of A Cena ('to supper') is easily missed, but widens out to a cavernous clubby dining room, offering intimate tables either side of the boxed-off door, well away from larger parties inside. Apart from a gruffish reception when we arrived early for lunch, service was impeccable. Even before it got busy, the place had the pleasantly casual atmosphere of a well-loved local favourite. Some delicious cakey focaccia came immediately and starters arrived in short order. A huge platter of delicious meaty bresaola, dressed with just enough truffle oil and pecorino shavings, snapped the appetite to attention while fat scallops were expertly caramelised and just-cooked inside. The Sunday lunch menu contained sops to British tastes, including pot roast lamb shoulder (wonderfully tender) with mint and roast cauliflower. Corn-fed chicken marinated in chilli and lemon was deliciously moist. Desserts are more Italian in spirit, such as chocolate tartufo with a moist cake base and rich topping that appeared heavy but melted in the mouth, adorned with own-made honeycomb pieces.
Babies and children welcome: high chairs. Booking advisable. Restaurant available for hire.

RESTAURANTS

Japanese

The popularity of Japanese cuisine in London shows no sign of waning. This might be down to the widely acclaimed health benefits (it's generally a low-calorie, omega-rich style of cooking), the affordability of filling noodle dishes, the enthusiasm of celebrities for glamorous restaurants such as **Nobu**, maybe even the highly aesthetic nature of the food presentation – or all of the above. What's important is that right across the city, Londoners have a wider choice of Japanese dining options than ever before, confirming the fact (and not before time) that Japanese food isn't all about sushi. You can now sample cooking styles ranging from grill specialists such as **Tosa** and the recently expanded **Bincho**, right through to shojin kaiseki (Buddhist vegetarian haute cuisine) at **Saki**. Not that sushi should be dismissed, and in the excellent **Sushi-Hiro** and newcomer **Sushi 101**, London has two fine purveyors of Japan's most famous culinary export. The move from the familiar into the slightly esoteric (but highly authentic) areas of the cuisine has been welcomed by the Japanese community as well as other Londoners. Modern takes on the food continue to flourish, as at Soho's **Aaya** where staunchly Japanese ingredients are intertwined with almost European cooking techniques. In contrast, tradition is impressively upheld at elegant **Saké No Hana**, where classic dishes are arranged by cooking method rather than ingredient or courses – just like in Japan.

Central

City

Miyako

ANdAZ, Liverpool Street, EC2M 7QN (7618 7100/www.london.liverpoolstreet.andaz.com). Liverpool Street tube/rail. **Lunch served** noon-2.30pm Mon-Fri. **Dinner served** 6-10.30pm Mon-Fri; 6-10pm Sat. **Main courses** £6.50-£23. **Set lunch** £18-£25. **Credit** AmEx, DC, MC, V.

It has a new name and a fresh look, but little else has changed at this bento box-sized Japanese, formerly known as Miyabi. A reasonable standard of sushi and sashimi, and favourites from pork tonkatsu to salmon teriyaki, continue to draw in City workers, especially at lunch. Prices are higher than those at conveyor-belt chains, but the food is a class above. The selection of sashimi, sushi and maki, while unexciting, is reliably fresh and correctly prepared. More commendable is the excellent prawn tempura, which is perfectly hot, fluffy and crispy. For lunch, the generous bento boxes are a good bet, offering nutrient-packed meals that include sashimi, miso-dressed sunomono, a choice of hot main dishes, as well as miso soup, rice and chunks of fresh fruit. Accompany the food with bottomless cups of green tea. Service is appropriately efficient; in such a cramped space, there's little temptation to linger any longer than an hour.
Babies and children admitted: high chairs; nappy-changing facilities. Booking advisable. Disabled: lift; toilet. Takeaway service. **Map 12 R6.**

Moshi Moshi Sushi

24 upper level, Liverpool Street Station, EC2M 7QH (7247 3227/www.moshimoshi.co.uk). Liverpool Street tube/rail. **Meals served** 11.30am-10pm Mon-Fri. **Dishes** £1.70-£3.50. **Main courses** £8-£11. **Credit** MC, V.

Hidden behind an M&S shop on the upper concourse of Liverpool Street Station, this branch of Moshi Moshi comes as a bit of a surprise – first, that an eaterie of such striking design could lurk in this afterthought of a space; second, that a Japanese chain offering conveyor belt sushi and takeaway meals could also boast such unusual raw and cooked foods as monkfish liver terrine and Cornish crab zosui (a rice dish softened with fish stock). Starters, marketed here as zensai tapas, included a pair of tasty but lukewarm pork and vegetable gyozas, a bland tuna tataki, and a delicately crisped and pillowy agedashidofu. The gourmet sushi set came with a standard array of nigiri and maki, including tuna, salmon and mackerel. The fish were all fresh and of good quality, though their preparation lacked excitement. The tempura selection included a trio of meagre prawns and a few vegetables, nicely fried in a light batter. As was the case wth the sushi, it was a decent but rather predictable dish. Service throughout was friendly, though rushed, as staff hurried to serve impatient City boys on their lunch break.
Babies and children admitted. Disabled: toilet. Takeaway service; delivery service. Vegetarian menu. **Map 12 R5.**
For branches see index.

Clerkenwell & Farringdon

★ Saki

4 West Smithfield, EC1A 9JX (7489 7033/ www.saki-food.com). Barbican tube/Farringdon tube/rail.
Bar **Open** noon-11pm Mon-Wed; noon-midnight Thur, Fri; 6pm-midnight Sat.
Deli **Open** 10am-7pm Mon-Fri.
Restaurant **Lunch served** noon-2.30pm, **dinner served** 6-10.30pm Mon-Sat. **Set lunch** £13.50-£35. **Set dinner** £35-£65.
All **Credit** AmEx, MC, V.

When this Smithfield restaurant and bar first opened in 2006, it caught the headlines with gimmicks such as paperless loos and automatic noodle-makers. But the reason it continues to thrive is no gimmick – just sophisticated, seasonally based Japanese cooking from a very capable kitchen. The moody basement dining room features central communal seating arranged around an eye-catching garden of white pebbles and stalagmite candles, but most eyes are on the sensitively crafted sushi, the miso-marinated black cod, and the lobster tempura in black vinegar. On our visit, service oscillated wildly from on-the-case to lost-the-plot, but the food was consistently good. Slow-grilled iberico pork cubes with teardrops of miso sauce were tender and long-flavoured, and a salad of thinly sliced octopus with gomasu (sesame and garlic sauce) was a textural treat. We adored the simplicity of new season's green asparagus with mizuna, the crisp crunchy nuggets of chicken tatsuta, and the loll-about richness of negi toro (fatty tuna rolls). And if it's true you can tell how good a Japanese restaurant is by the quality of its rice, then this is a good Japanese restaurant.
Babies and children admitted. Booking advisable. Disabled: lift; toilet. Separate room for parties, seats 12. Takeaway service. Vegan dishes. Vegetarian menu. **Map 11 O5.**

Fitzrovia

★ Roka ⓘ (100)

37 Charlotte Street, W1T 1RR (7580 6464/ www.rokarestaurant.com). Goodge Street or Tottenham Court Road tube.
Bar **Open** 6pm-midnight Mon, Sat, Sun; noon-midnight Tue-Fri.

BEST JAPANESE

One-dish wonders
Visit **Abeno Too** (*see p197* **Quick Bites**) for okonomiyaki, **Benihana** (*see p208*) for teppanyaki, **Bincho** for yakitori (*see p206*), **Kushi-Tei** (*see p205*) for kushiyaki and **Sushi-Hiro** (*see p202*) for sushi.

Art moderne
For cutting-edge fusion fare, try **Chisou** (*see p197*), **Dinings** (*see p196*), **Nobu** (*see p199*) – plus siblings **Nobu Berkeley Street** (*see p199*) and **Ubon** (*see p206*) – **Saki** (*see above*), **Tsunami** (*see p205*) and **Yakitoria** (*see p202*).

Take the kids
Families are welcome at **Benihana** (*see p208*), **Chisou** (*see p197*), **Eat Tokyo** (*see p196* **Quick bites**), **Japan Centre** (*see p196* **Quick bites**), **Jin Kichi** (*see p208*), **Satsuma** (*see p196* **Quick bites**), **Wow Simply Japanese** (*see p207*), **Yakitoria** (*see p202*) and **Yo! Sushi** (*see p197* **Quick bites**)

Belt up for a fast ride
Your food glides by on the conveyer belts at **Kulu Kulu**, **Yo! Sushi** (for both, *see p197* **Quick bites**), **Moshi Moshi Sushi** (*see left*) and **Sushi Hiroba** (*see p194*).

Flash some cash
For a special night on the town, head to **Nobu** (*see p199*), **Roka** (*see above*), **Tsunami** (*see p205*), **Saké No Hana** (*see p199*), **Umu** (*see p199*), and **Zuma** (*see p194*).

Park and riverside
Rooms with a view include **Bincho** (*see p194*), **Nobu** (*see p199*), **Ozu** (*see p206*) and **Ubon** (*see p207*).

RESTAURANTS

Restaurant **Lunch served** noon-3pm Mon-Fri;
12.30-3pm Sat. **Dinner served** 5.30-11.30pm
Mon-Sat; 5.30-10.30pm Sun. **Main courses**
£3.60-£39.90. **Set meal** £50-£75 per person
(minimum 2) tasting menu.
Both **Credit** AmEx, DC, MC, V.
Roka, sister to Zuma (*see below*), is where to come
for restaurant theatre at its best. Smack-bang in
the middle of the dining room is the sushi bar and
robata grill, putting the chefs centre stage. The air
fills with the fragrant smoke that rises from the
grill. The well-lit room is warm and elegant,
constructed from smooth brown wood and slate.
For the wide of wallet, there are tasting menus
costing £50 and £75 per person, but if you eat à
la carte you can keep the price down. A gorgeously
savoury rice hotpot with king crab, wasabi and
tobiko (flying fish roe) was served in an ohitsu (a
wooden rice tub), with the condiments arranged on
top and stirred in at table. The flavours in our
Korean-style roast pork, kimchi and shiso maki
rolls were equally inspired. A contemporary
interpretation of tuna tataki featured the tataki
slices gently seared and arranged like jewels
around the plate, with sharp mustard and apple
dressing. Baby back ribs with 'master stock' were
tender, gently smoky, burnished a deep walnut,
and had a slightly sticky finish. There's a great
saké list, and a dedicated basement shochu bar.
Believe the hype.
Babies and children welcome: high chairs.
Booking essential. Disabled: toilet. Tables outdoors
(10, pavement). **Map 17 B1.**

Holborn

★ Aki
182 Gray's Inn Road, WC1X 8EW (7837 9281/
www.akidemae.com). Chancery Lane tube. **Lunch**
served noon-2.30pm Mon-Fri. **Dinner served**
6-11pm Mon-Sat. **Main courses** £4.50-£11.50.
Set lunch £5.10-£17. **Set dinner** £20.50-£46.50.
Credit AmEx, MC, V.
Aficionados of Japanese food know that it's the
cooking, not the unassuming and rather worn
decor, that counts here. The multitude of small
dishes are made to be enjoyed with the sakés and
shochus listed at the back of the menu. The chef's
recommendations make a good diving-in point, or
there's also a more predictable selection of izakaya-
style skewered foods such as yakitori or kushiage
(battered and deep-fried morsels on a stick). We
went for a range of flavours, from the delicate
(chazuke: tender raw sea bream on hot rice, over
which hot green tea is poured) to the punchy (a
whole head of garlic with miso paste, simply
steamed – a real drinking-session dish, best
enjoyed with shochu). Most were spot-on. A
warming braised beef dish, nikujaga, had a sweet
and savoury flavour and was unusual for
containing konnyaku jelly along with more
familiar western ingredients such as carrot and
potato. Sautéed shimeji mushrooms were robustly
meaty, and deep-fried oyster hot and juicy. Only a
dish of slightly overcooked sardines disappointed.
Aki is a humble but deservedly popular spot.
Babies and children admitted. Booking advisable.
Separate room for parties, seats 30. Takeaway
service. **Map 4 M4.**

★ Matsuri
71 High Holborn, WC1V 6EA (7430 1970/
www.matsuri-restaurant.com). Chancery Lane
or Holborn tube. **Lunch served** noon-2.30pm,
dinner served 6-10pm Mon-Sat. **Main courses**
£8.50-£30 lunch; £18-£36.50 dinner. **Set lunch**
£16-£47. **Set dinner** £25; £35-£70.
Credit AmEx, DC, MC, V.
Large floor-to-ceiling windows at Matsuri's corner
site keep the lively Holborn surroundings in view,
but at bay. Interior furnishings consist of subtle
wooden tables and chairs, and elegant partially-
revealing blinds that separate the sushi counter
from the main dining room. The serving staff are
friendly and knowledgeable, helping customers
navigate the wine and saké menus. Traditional
Japanese food is the primary attraction. Excellent
tokkurimushi soup was served in a cunning three-
layered bowl, allowing for the dipping of pickled
and steamed vegetables, prawn and tofu (which

came floating in a rich miso broth), in the more
pungent daikon-laden dipping sauce. Semi-firm
tofu, deep-fried, was topped with robustly
flavoured fish flakes in a sweet soy sauce, creating
a perfect balance. A mixed sushi boat included
some high-quality fatty salmon and lean tuna, plus
a roll of salmon and avocado topped with roe.
Black cod arrived in a generous portion. Book a
grill-side table in the lower-ground dining room for
a teppanyaki cooking display while you eat.
Babies and children admitted. Booking advisable.
Disabled: toilet. Separate rooms for parties,
seating 10 and 32. **Map 10 M5.**
For branch see index.

Sushi Hiroba
50-54 Kingsway, WC2B 6EP (7430 1888/
www.sushihiroba.co.uk). Holborn tube. **Lunch**
served noon-3pm Mon-Fri. **Dinner served**
6-11pm Mon-Sat; 5-10pm Sun. **Main courses**
£7.50-£9. **Set lunch** £13-£15. **Set meal** £50.
Credit MC, V.
Roll up, roll up. This is a two-ring sushi circus
where every act is a dazzler, every dish has crunch
and colour, and the two-lane conveyor belt goes
round and round – where it stops, nobody knows.
Adding to the festive atmosphere is a dramatic red
and black colour scheme, bright Japanese lanterns
and filigree screens. We can't help but be worried
by a sign that offers to reheat your food if it's not
hot enough. If we wanted reheated, microwaved
food we could have stayed at home. The nigiri
sushi here is the best bet, if a bit fridge-cold. Other
dishes are more problematic. Our gyoza dumplings
were oily and lacklustre, chicken yakitori was on
the small side, and an off-the-belt order of udon
noodles with fried tofu and boiled fish cake came
without the promised fish cake. Handy, perhaps,
for time-pressed office workers and sushi ingénues
who don't mind the lack of spontaneity or the
surfeit of mayonnaise.
Babies and children admitted. Takeaway service.
Map 18 F2.

Knightsbridge

★ Zuma
5 Raphael Street, SW7 1DL (7584 1010/
www.zumarestaurant.com). Knightsbridge tube.
Bar **Open** noon-11pm Mon-Fri; 12.30-11pm Sat;
noon-10pm Sun.

Saké No Hana. See p199.

Restaurant **Lunch served** noon-2.15pm Mon-Fri;
12.30-3.15pm Sat; 12.30-2.45pm Sun. **Dinner**
served 6-10.45pm Mon-Sat; 6-10.15pm Sun.
Main courses £14.80-£70.
Both **Credit** AmEx, DC, MC, V.
Even on weekday evenings, the Mercs idling
outside and the bar crammed with beautiful people
testify to Zuma's staying power among London's
smartest top restaurants. But there's more to this
'contemporary izakaya' than a striking wood-and-
stone interior and a stylish wine and saké list. The
surprise is that the mix of Japanese and fusion
food on the long menu fully justifies the high
prices. Highlights include starters of sea bass
sashimi heady with truffle oil and yuzu (a
grapefruit-like citrus fruit), three sticks of spicy
grilled quail, and a wooden box of cool fresh tofu,
eaten with wooden spoons and six condiments.
Mains are also worth a trip across town. From the
robata, salt-grilled fish had the crispest of skins
and was moistly delicious inside; seared foie gras
(oddly, priced lower than lemon sole) was perfectly
offset by a pickled plum compote – both dishes
came in unexpectedly big portions. Rice, miso soup
and vegetable tempura (eight different types) made
fine side plates. Advance warning of the 15-minute
wait for an excellent hot chocolate soufflé with
hazelnut ice-cream would have been nice, but
service was otherwise totally professional.
Babies and children welcome: high chairs. Booking
essential. Disabled: toilet. Separate rooms for
parties, seating 12 and 14. Tables outdoors
(4, garden). **Map 8 F9.**

Marylebone

CoCoRo
31 Marylebone Lane, W1U 2NH (7935 2931/
www.cocororestaurant.co.uk). Bond Street tube.
Lunch served noon-2.30pm Mon-Fri. **Dinner**
served 6-10.30pm Mon-Fri; 6-10pm Sat, Sun.
Main courses £7-£12. **Set lunch** £8-£30. **Set**
dinner £17.50-£40. **Credit** AmEx, DC, MC, V.
The background music straight out of the 1950s
('I'll Be Seeing You' and 'People Will Say We're In
Love'), and the extremely good-looking sushi chef,
mark this quirky, homely Marylebone Japanese as
something a bit outside the norm. The food is
equally individual, with some of the more eye-
catching items including duck carpaccio with

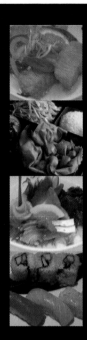

Quick bites

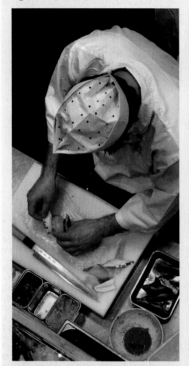

Japan Centre (Toku)

When you want something quick, healthy and cheap to eat, London's Japanese canteens, diners and takeaways are ideal. Select your own sushi and salads from a conveyor belt, watch okonomiyaki being cooked to order on your table, or enjoy a steaming bowl of soup noodles or katsu curry. The eateries here are suitable for lone diners or for visiting with friends. Worth noting too is the new West End branch of **Eat Tokyo** (*see p208*) on the former site of Kyoto, at 27 Romilly Street, W1D 5AL (7437 2262).

THE ALL-ROUNDERS

Centrepoint Sushi (Hana)
20-21 St Giles High Street, WC2H 8JE (7240 6147/www.cpfs.co.uk). Tottenham Court Road tube. **Lunch served** noon-3pm, dinner served 6-11pm Mon-Sat. **Main courses** £8-£17. **Set lunch** £8-£14.50. **Credit** MC, V.
A soothing oasis above St Giles Circus, Hana is a welcoming mix of plush booths, etched glass and Kirin beer posters. Its wide choice of bento boxes includes a hearty special comprising deep-fried chicken, pork cutlet, mixed sashimi, rice, soup and pickles. The jasmine tea is lovely.
Babies and children admitted. Booking advisable. Takeaway service. Vegetarian menu. Map 17 C2.

Japan Centre (Toku)
212 Piccadilly, W1J 9HG (7255 8255/www.japancentre.com). Piccadilly Circus tube. **Shops Open** 10am-9pm Mon-Sat; 11am-7pm Sun. *Restaurant* **Meals** served noon-10pm Mon-Sat; noon-9pm Sun. **Main courses** £5-£14. **Set meal** £9.60-£27.80. **Credit** MC, V.

Many of the dishes at this big, bustling, red-walled eaterie are priced over £10, but check the front of the menu for daily discounts. Char siu pork ramen is one of the good-looking cheaper dishes, or splash out on tuna don: raw tuna cloaked in sesame sauce over rice. Takeaway sushi is available from the basement and the new shop next door.
Babies and children welcome: high chairs. Booking advisable. Takeaway service. Map 17 B5.

Ramen Seto
19 Kingly Street, W1B 5PY (7434 0309). Oxford Circus tube. **Meals served** noon-9.30pm Mon, Tue; noon-10pm Wed-Sat; 1-8pm Sun. **Main courses** £5.70-£8. **Set meal** £6-£9.60. **Credit** MC, V.
A home-from-home for Japanese expats and a popular lunch spot for west Soho office staff, this friendly spot has an almost-permanent queue of folk ordering a takeaway or waiting to pay. Herby salmon gyoza come juicy, plump and well-browned from the pan; order them in a set meal with stir-fried veg, white miso soup and a bowl of rice. Ramen, naturally, are also a favourite; try the negi (spring onion) ramen with chicken.
Babies and children welcome: high chairs. Booking advisable weekends. Takeaway service. Map 17 J6.

Satsuma
56 Wardour Street, W1D 3HN (7437 8338/www.osatsuma.com). Piccadilly Circus tube. **Meals served** noon-11pm Mon, Tue; noon-11.30pm Wed, Thur; noon-midnight Fri, Sat; noon-10.30pm Sun. **Main courses** £5.90-£16.50. **Credit** AmEx, DC, MC, V.
This long-time favourite of Soho's media crowd looks as fresh as when it opened.

The bentos and curries offer reliable value but check the seasonal specials card for grown-up treats such as saba shioyaki (salt-grilled mackerel). Our agedashi dofu arrived with a crisp tempura of shiso leaf and mushroom on top. The bright fresh strawberry juice is a popular drink.
Babies and children welcome: high chairs. Bookings not accepted. Disabled: toilet. Takeaway service. Map 17 K6.

Soho Japan
52 Wells Street, W1T 3PR (7323 4661/www.sohojapan.co.uk). Oxford Circus tube. **Lunch served** noon-2.30pm Mon-Fri. **Dinner served** 6-10.30pm Mon-Sat. **Main courses** £5-£15 dinner. **Set lunch** £8-£30. **Set dinner** £27 3 courses. **Credit** AmEx, MC, V.
Pinewood pub decor and piped accordion music give this friendly spot the feel of an Alsatian café, but the wide-ranging menu is thoroughly Japanese. Lunch dishes such as chirasushi (mixed raw fish over rice) are quite pricey, though come with decent miso soup. In the evening, options expand to include the likes of chilled tofu with spicy garlic sauce, and grilled smelt.
Babies and children admitted. Booking advisable. Tables outdoors (3, pavement). Takeaway service. Map 17 A2.

Taro
10 Old Compton Street, W1D 4TF (7439 2275). Leicester Square or Tottenham Court Road tube. **Lunch served** noon-2.50pm Mon-Fri; 12.30-3.15pm Sat, Sun. **Dinner served** 5.30-10.30pm Mon-Sat; 5.30-9.30pm Sun. **Main courses** £5.90-£8.80. **Set meal** £8.50-£14. **Credit** MC, V.
A pinewood basement refectory with entertaining views through the street-level window of legs walking past. Taro's menu is at the cheaper end of the canteen spectrum, offering various don (meals on rice), bento, popular gyoza, sushi, sashimi, katsu and more. Our generous bowl of yakiudon (thick wheat noodles in soup) came with succulent deep-fried chicken thigh, fine strips of seaweed, and a smile.
Babies and children welcome: high chairs. Booking advisable. Separate room for parties, seats 30. Takeaway service. Map 17 C3.
For branch see index.

Tokyo Diner
2 Newport Place, WC2H 7JP (7287 8777/www.tokyodiner.com). Leicester Square tube. **Meals served** noon-midnight daily. **Main courses** £6.60-13.20. **Set lunch** (noon-6pm Mon-Fri) £4.90-£9.70. **Credit** MC, V.
A corner of Chinatown that's been Japanese since 1992, Tokyo Diner may not be the trend-setter it once was, but it has acquired a patina of homely authenticity. The inexpensive set meals are even cheaper between 3pm and 6pm. We love the cool aubergine agé bitashi topped with a thick slice of lotus root.
Babies and children admitted. Bookings not accepted Fri, Sat. Takeaway service. Map 17 K7.

RESTAURANTS

Zipangu

8 Little Newport Street, WC2H 7JJ (7437 5042). Leicester Square tube. **Meals served** noon-11pm Mon-Sat; noon-10.30pm Sun. **Main courses** £4.50-£14.90. **Set lunch** (noon-5.30pm) £6.50-£12.50. **Set dinner** £8.90 bento box; £14.90 5 dishes. **Credit** AmEx, MC, V.

A tiny, intimate spot with caring staff and keen prices. Tempting set meals include a generous, nicely cooked tempura featuring three large prawns and a mix of succulent vegetable slices. With a small dish of summery soba, salmon sashimi with crisp mooli salad, a sizeable bowl of sticky rice and miso soup all included, you won't be hungry again for hours.

Bookings not accepted Fri, Sat. Separate room for parties, seats 6. Takeaway service. Map 17 K7.

THE SPECIALISTS

Abeno Too

17-18 Great Newport Street, WC2H 7JE (7379 1160/www.abeno.co.uk). Leicester Square tube. **Meals served** noon-11pm Mon-Sat; noon-10.30pm Sun. **Main courses** £7.80-£25.80. **Set lunch** £7.80-£12.80. **Credit** AmEx, MC, V.

Okonomiyaki (hearty pancakes with nuggets of veg, seafood, pork and other titbits) are cooked to order on hot-plates set into Abeno's tables and counter. Don't dismiss the desserts: own-made matcha ice-cream, rice dumpling pancake, whipped cream, aduki beans and maple syrup make a sensational combination.

Babies and children admitted: high chairs. Bookings not accepted. Disabled: toilet. Takeaway service. Map 18 K6. For branches (Abeno, Abeno San) see index.

Feng Sushi

101 Notting Hill Gate, W11 3JZ (7727 1123/www.fengsushi.co.uk). Notting Hill Gate tube. **Meals served** 11.30am-10pm Mon-Wed; 11.30am-11pm Thur-Sat; noon-10.30pm Sun. **Main courses** £5-£15. **Set meal** £8-£15 bento box. **Credit** AmEx, DC, MC, V.

The tiny Notting Hill Gate outlet of Feng Sushi is cramped, but this cheerful chain also has larger branches by Royal Festival Hall and Chalk Farm. Our bento lunch (no box) contained excellent vegetable tempura plus serviceable salmon and tuna sashimi and nigiri. Hand-rolls were fine too, but brown-rice mackerel maki, which had a strong, fresh flavour, fell apart too easily. The menu also includes interesting fusion dishes such as noodle salads.

Babies and children admitted. Bookings not accepted. Takeaway service; delivery service (over £10 within 2-mile radius). Map 7 A7. For branches see index.

Kulu Kulu

51-53 Shelton Street, WC2H 9HE (7240 5687). Covent Garden tube. **Lunch served** noon-2.30pm Mon-Fri; noon-3.30pm Sat. **Dinner served** 5-10pm Mon-Sat. **Dishes** £1.20-£3.60. **Credit** MC, V.

You may be squeezed into a small section of counter that your neighbours feel you shouldn't take, but once you're settled this conveyor-belt operation is a friendly spot. Service was nonexistent on our visit, so it was cheeky to ask for gratuities on the card machine. Still, we loved the crispy salmon-skin hand-rolls and deep-fried aubergine with ginger and soy sauce.

Babies and children admitted. Bookings not accepted. Takeaway service. Map 18 D3. For branches see index.

Ryo

84 Brewer Street, W1F 9UB (7287 1318). Piccadilly Circus tube. **Meals served** 11.30am-midnight Mon-Wed, Sun; 11.30am-1am Thur-Sat. **Main courses** £5-£14. **Set meal** £5.50-£10. **No credit cards.**

For newbies, perusing the menu of ramen, rice dishes, gyoza and sushi is a little awkward. You need to order and pay at the front counter before taking a seat. Friendly staff then bring steaming bowls of springy ramen with crisp veg promptly. With re-runs of *Diagnosis Murder* and the like on TV, Ryo is a cosy choice for a quiet lunch in winter, or late-night fillers.

Babies and children admitted. Separate rooms for parties, seats 25 and 40. Takeaway service. Map 17 J7.

Tsuru NEW

4 Canvey Street, SE1 8AN (7928 2228/ www.tsuru-sushi.co.uk). London Bridge or Southwark tube. **Meals served** 11am-6pm Mon-Fri. **Tapas served** 6-9pm Thur, Fri. **Main courses** £4.95-£7.25. **Credit** MC, V.

Eat in or take away at this new Bankside spot, which seems to have all the right ingredients to become a hit chain. Organically farmed cod, Cornish crab and salmon skin feature on the sushi menu, but there are also salads (such as octopus, cucumber and ginger), teriyaki bentos, and good katsu curries.

Babies and children admitted. Disabled: toilet. Restaurant available for hire. Tables outdoors (5, pavement). Takeaway service. Map 11 O8.

Yo! Sushi

52 Poland Street, W1V 3DF (7287 0443/ www.yosushi.com). Oxford Circus tube. **Meals served** noon-11pm Mon-Sat; noon-10.30pm Sun. **Main courses** £7.50-£10. **Credit** AmEx, DC, MC, V.

St Pancras Station is among the new branches of this now-international chain (Dublin, Moscow, Dubai...). Yo!'s flagship Soho outlet has a darkened nightclub vibe and attracts a media-friendly crowd. The pumpkin koroke (croquette) is delicious whether served hot by the kindly chefs or left to wind its way around the trademark conveyor belt. Watch out for the cheeky charge on filtered water.

Babies and children welcome: high chairs. Bookings accepted (minimum 4 people). Disabled: toilet. Takeaway service. Vegetarian menu. Map 17 A3. For branches see index.

ponzu, foie gras in Japanese custard, rape blossoms with tofu and miso paste, and snazzily named sushi rolls such as spiderman roll (salmon), superman roll (tuna) and Buckingham Palace roll (inside-out salmon and avocado). Cooking is haphazard: rolled pork belly with crisp leeks and mustard was clumsy, while the miso cod was coated in glug, and an oily, floury chicken kariage lacked the deep crunch that makes this deep-fried dish a universal favourite. Well-made inside-out tuna and avocado roll, and a fresh simple sashimi salad were more successful. We were also taken by the sheer, single-minded authenticity of slippery squid guts pickled in salt, and by draught Kirin served in tall, frosted glasses.

Babies and children admitted. Separate rooms for parties, seating 10 and 12. Takeaway service; delivery service (over £20 within 2-mile radius). Map 9 G6.

★ Dinings

22 Harcourt Street, W1H 4HH (7723 0666). Marylebone tube/rail. **Lunch served** noon-2.30pm **Dinner served** 6-10.30pm Mon-Sat. **Main courses** £6.50-£16. **Set lunch** £10-£15. **Credit** AmEx, MC, V.

You'll find some of London's best contemporary Japanese cuisine here. A meal consists of a series of perfectly formed 'tapas' that stand out for their clear, bold flavours. The chef-proprietor is a Nobu alumnus and the influence shows in the house special of 'tar-tar chips' (crunchy potato shells filled with salmon and sweet shrimp), or tobiko-topped crab (recalling Nobu's now-classic tacos). Elsewhere, miso is mingled with truffle, and soy sauce with raspberry. Don't mistake innovation for reckless rule-breaking though. Crisp-skinned duck breast tataki, with a salsa made from finely chopped shiso and shallot, was difficult to fault, as was squid and natto inside-out maki roll. Pork kakuni, slow-cooked, meltingly soft pork belly in a sweetish soy-based sauce, a riff on Chinese tungpo pork, was stunning. A simple salad of kelp, cucumber, red onion and pea shoots had an unexpected depth of flavours, helped by a smoky, sharp dressing. Western-style puddings are given an eastern twist in desserts such as green tea crème brûlée. Service is sweet and helpful and the surroundings are as surprising as the food. Housed in a genteel townhouse, the tiny basement is full-on modernist.

Babies and children admitted. Takeaway service. Map 8 F5.

Mayfair

★ Chisou

4 Princes Street, W1B 2LE (7629 3931/ www.chisou.co.uk). Oxford Circus tube. **Lunch served** noon-2.30pm, **dinner served** 6-10.15pm Mon-Sat. **Main courses** £12-£20. **Set lunch** £12.50-£18.50. **Credit** AmEx, MC, V.

The smiling sushi chef looks so overjoyed to see you when you walk into this smart, well-run restaurant, that you'd swear he has mistaken you for a long-lost friend. Or a particularly fresh sea bass. In spite of the black-clad staff, plain wooden tables, smart blond chairs and black slate floor, Chisou has a friendly izakaya tavern-style atmosphere that lures its regulars back time and again. It looks like a restaurant that means business, and here that business is putting a bright contemporary spin on Japanese classics. Highly recommended is the chef's speciality of anikimo ponzu (lightly pressed monkfish liver with ponzu sauce), which tastes deliciously like fishy foie gras. We also loved a bubbly scorched salted sea bass fillet classically served with lemon and grated daikon; an exemplary inside-out tempura prawn roll; and a crispy-crunchy seaweed salad. The generously proportioned nigiri sushi was all good, from the three types of tuna (fatty, fattier, fattiest) to the shimmering, sea-sweet salmon. A highlight is the tamago (Japanese omelette), which is just as it should be – soft and freshly cooked, with the tang of rice vinegar and the lilting sweetness of mirin.

Babies and children welcome: high chairs. Booking advisable. Separate rooms for parties, seating 6-12. Takeaway service. Map 9 J6.

Atami. See p200.

★ Nobu (100)

1st floor, The Metropolitan, 19 Old Park Lane, W1K 1LB (7447 4747/www.nobu restaurants.com). Hyde Park Corner tube. **Lunch served** noon-2.15pm Mon-Fri; 12.30-2.30pm Sat, Sun. **Dinner served** 6-10.15pm Mon-Thur; 6-11pm Fri, Sat; 6-9.30pm Sun. **Dishes** £3.50-£29.50. **Set lunch** £26 bento box; £50, £60. **Set dinner** £70, £90. **Credit** AmEx, DC, MC, V.
There's so much hype surrounding the Michelin-starred Nobu that you'd be forgiven for coming here weighed down with prejudice – but excellent, efficient service and the elegant setting should seduce you into changing your mind. Celebrity sightings are less frequent these days, which means you can concentrate on the expertly prepared and exquisitely plated food. Luxury ingredients are of top quality: a lobster salad with spicy dressing was expensive (£20), but generous with the well-prepared meat; a salmon skin salad was rich and wonderfully fishy. Flavours aren't edited for a western audience, and remain sharp and bright. Rock shrimp tempura has been much copied around London, but Nobo's version puts other attempts to shame – the shrimps were fresh and the tempura light. This is one of the best places in town to try creative, modern Japanese cuisine, as the unconventional pairings genuinely work. The wine list offers interesting accompaniments too. The elegant first-floor dining rooms lined with floor-to-ceiling windows overlooking Hyde Park make the perfect spot for a romantic meal à deux.
Babies and children welcome: high chairs. Booking essential. Disabled: lift; toilet. Dress: smart casual. Separate room for parties, seats 14-40. **Map 9 H8**.

Nobu Berkeley Street

15 Berkeley Street, W1J 8DY (7290 9222/ www.noburestaurants.com). Green Park tube.
Bar **Open** noon-1am Mon-Wed; 1pm-2am Thur, Fri; 6pm-2am Sat; 6-9pm Sun.
Restaurant **Lunch served** noon-2.15pm Mon-Fri. **Dinner served** 6-11pm Mon-Wed; 6pm-midnight Thur-Sat; 6-9pm Sun. **Dishes** £11.50-£27.
Both **Credit** AmEx, MC, V.
Three years after opening, the third London branch of Nobu Matsuhisa's international chain is finally more accessible. The no-bookings policy has been dropped and, surprisingly, tables are available even with a day's notice, albeit at more unpopular hours. Still, the cocktail bar and upstairs restaurant and sushi bar continue to buzz with celeb-studded glamour, and the cooking remains brilliant. Signature dishes like yellowtail sashimi with jalapeño are reassuringly thrilling, with thick, expertly cut slabs of the freshest fish enlivened by slivers of pepper. Ever-popular new-style sashimi (raw fish drizzled with hot oil) is especially sublime when made with scallops: a melt-in-the-mouth sensation of contrasting flavours, textures and temperatures. Black cod with miso – the dish that launched a thousand imitations – remains top league. Unlike others, the marinade here is infused throughout the smooth white flesh. A rare disappointment was the toban yaki beef. It looked dramatic, simmering in a stone dish, but the taste was anti-climactic: the weak sauce doing no favours for the cubes of nicely cooked beef. Tempura dishes were of standard quality. A fragrant, creamy yuzu tart rounded off the meal cleanly. Unlike the food, service throughout was unremarkable.
Babies and children welcome: high chairs. Bookings advisable. Disabled: toilet. Dress: smart casual. Entertainment: DJ 9pm Wed-Sat. Vegan dishes. **Map 9 H7**.

Umu

14-16 Bruton Place, W1J 6LX (7499 8881/ www.umurestaurant.com). Bond Street or Green Park tube. **Lunch served** noon-2.30pm Mon-Fri. **Dinner served** 6-11pm Mon-Sat. **Main courses** £11-£55. **Set lunch** £21-£45. **Set dinner** £60-£135. **Credit** AmEx, DC, MC, V.
Umu's relaxed glamour gives it an edge over many kaiseki establishments in Japan. It's secreted behind a push-button sliding door straight out of Blofeld's volcano lair at Kagoshima. Inside, the welcome is as warm as the brown tones of the chic wooden walls, flooring and furniture. Chef Ichiro Kubota and his team work diligently behind the sushi bar; service is efficient and knowledgeable, which it needs to be when so many unusual dishes are offered. There's a choice of kaiseki menus (a series of small, exquisitely presented seasonal dishes), plus à la carte and set lunch options. Both saké and wine lists are formidable. In the past we've recommended Umu highly, yet two visits this year left us disappointed. Outré ingredients don't impress when you can't get the basics right. Watery tofu (made in-house) had a strong flavour of dried soybeans, and the tempura was chewy, though sashimi and miso soup were of a high standard. We noticed other customers leaving food uneaten – quite an achievement when portions are so small. Curiously it was the desserts and 'chocolates' that shone, especially the well-balanced black bean ice-cream, topped with a multiseed tuile and candied butter bean.
Babies and children welcome. Booking advisable dinner. Disabled: toilet. Dress: smart casual. **Map 9 H7**.

Piccadilly

Yoshino

3 Piccadilly Place, W1J 0DB (7287 6622/ www.yoshino.net). Piccadilly Circus tube. **Meals served** noon-9pm Mon-Sat. **Dishes** £2.80-£5.80. **Set meal** £5.80-£19.80 bento box. **Credit** AmEx, MC, V.
Yoshino used to be the preserve of Japanese diners on expense-account lunches or business dinners. The atmosphere was formal, and the menu incomprehensible to those not fluent in Japanese, though the quality of the sushi and sashimi was always superb. Things have changed. Gone are the discreet aproned servers, replaced by smiling, eager-to-please young folk, and the menu's now fully bilingual. The sashimi, including exquisitely fresh sea bream and top-quality chutoro (medium fatty tuna), is as good as we remember, and our grilled eel in a sweet sauce was succulent and tender. Oshinko maki rolls, made with large pieces of pickled daikon, however, were inexpertly constructed and fell apart when we ate them; some of the other dishes disappointed too. We couldn't quibble about the quality of the simply grilled crisp-skinned mackerel from our 'mini Yoshino' set menu, but an accompanying side dish, spinach with sesame sauce, lacked flavour and seemed like an afterthought. Mixed tempura more closely resembled stir-fried battered vegetables with the odd prawn thrown in. Prices, once prohibitive, have come down, making Yoshino a decent mid-range venue with great sashimi.
Babies and children admitted. Booking advisable. Takeaway service. **Map 17 A5**.

St James's

★ Saké No Hana NEW (100)

2008 WINNER BEST DESIGN
23 St James's Street, SW1A 1HA (7925 8988). Green Park tube. **Lunch served** noon-2.30pm Mon-Sat. **Dinner served** 6-11pm Mon-Thur; 6-11.30pm Fri, Sat. Main courses £4-£40. **Credit** AmEx, DC, MC, V.
With a glittering track record (Wagamama, Busaba Eathai, Hakkasan, Yauatcha), Alan Yau had much to live up to when opening his first Japanese fine-dining restaurant in 2007. Situated on a street where you can buy cigars, guns and yachts – all far more prominently signed – Saké No Hana is coolly designed inside but may be too discreet for its own good. On the first floor, Japanese-cedar tables with foot-wells sit amid some acreage of tatami (there's western-style seating too), while narrow tilted screens provide shade from, and add elegance to, ceiling-high, wraparound windows. Slick-mannered staff deliver attentive table service. Some of the food is modern and playful, much of it orthodox and simple. If you dine on Chilean sea bass or wagyu beef accompanied by top-dollar Krug, Saké No Hana can be hideously expensive. But lunch bentos (£25 and £30) or wise à la carte selections for dinner (including

Interview
AYAKO WATANABE

Who are you?
Managing director of **Saki** bar and food emporium (*see p193*).
What's the best thing about running a restaurant in London?
Although the awareness of Japanese cuisine has improved in the last ten years, it is still a novelty for many diners. Ensuring that their first encounter with our cuisine is a delight, and seeing many happy returns, is the best thing to see on a daily basis.
What's the worst thing?
Running a restaurant is like riding a rollercoaster – there are as many moments you think of as the worst as those in which you encounter nice surprises. The worst moments tend to happen when we fail to manage the customers' expectations and have them completely satisfied. In the very early days, our ignorance let us stretch beyond what we could deliver, but we learnt the lesson.
Which are your favourite London restaurants?
If I am after gastronomic delights, I like **L'Atelier de Joël Robuchon** (*see p231*). For cafés, I like one with a garden or river view, such as **Kensington Palace Orangery** (*see p313*).
How green are you?
We try to use as much local produce as possible, (organic soy sauce from Wales, fish from European seas, Japanese mushroom varieties from Kent). However, there are things that are simply not available. We receive fresh produce from Japan a few times a week, but our food sourcing is much more localised than that of our peers in the United States.
What is missing from London's restaurant scene?
In France or Japan, where consumers are known to be demanding, no restaurant can survive long if it hasn't got the food right, no matter how high it scores on ambience and customer service. Some restaurants here take advantage of customers who don't complain or are simply not discerning about the quality of food served.

moderately priced sashimi and tempura) yield a much better-value meal than the restaurant's reputation might suggest. The tempura is superb: slightly elastic, incredibly well-drained; when in season, courgette flowers are a must. The drinks list emphasises saké: a lengthy selection subdivided by flavour rather than grade.
Babies and children admitted (lunch). Booking advisable. Disabled: lift; toilet. Restaurant available for hire. Separate room for parties, seats 10. **Map 9 J8.**

Soho

Aaya NEW
66-70 Brewer Street, W1F 9UP (7319 3888). Piccadilly Circus tube. **Lunch served** noon-3pm daily. **Dinner served** 6pm-12.30am Mon-Sat; 6-10pm Sun. **Main courses** £5-£13.50. **Credit** AmEx, MC, V.
Star restaurateur Alan Yau isn't the only member of his family to enter the business; sister Tina Juengsoongneum co-opened Thai eaterie Isarn (*see p276*) in 2005, while younger brother Gary launched this new spot in 2008. Apart from a general leaning towards eastern cuisines, the familial marker seems to be eye-catching, often inventive, interior design. Here we have a sleek, nightclubby decor, billowing staff uniforms and a high-ticket wine list juxtaposed with cheap bamboo chopsticks and plastic mugs. We found it incongruous. The kitchen, however, works seamlessly: exquisite presentation and impressive modern takes on traditional combinations, such as king crab with ponzu jelly, blue swimmer crab in red miso soup, and grilled apple miso salmon. Soft-shell crab maki was excellent – in fact the meal's only duff note was a bland tai chazuke (sea bream with rice submerged in tea). Desserts boldly marry traditional Japanese ingredients with European techniques – we loved the shiso panna cotta. A waitress diligently refilled our cups of tap water throughout the meal. This is a large, two-floor operation, which means it can feel embarrassing when not busy. Given the cheap, thoroughly cheerful Japanese diners nearby, we wonder whether enough people will appreciate Aaya's superior food to keep it going.
Babies and children admitted. Booking advisable. Separate room for parties, seats 50. **Map 17 A4.**

Donzoko
15 Kingly Street, W1B 5PS (7734 1974). Oxford Circus or Piccadilly Circus tube. **Lunch served** noon-2.30pm Mon-Fri. **Dinner served** 6-10.15pm Mon-Sat. **Main courses** £6.50-£28. **Set lunch** £6.50-£30. **Credit** AmEx, DC, MC, V.
This buzzing izakaya continues to attract a cross-section of Japanese salarymen, young Japanese student types and Japano-phile Londoners. The menu has some classic but challenging dishes, such as fermented raw squid and grilled chicken gizzards, among the long list of raw, fried, grilled, simmered and skewered food. Don't miss the garlic dishes, for which Donzoko is known; they're ideal accompaniments to the impressive list of sakés and shochus. Look out too for seasonal dishes such as a wintry hotpot special of hanpen (white fish and yam cake), a spongy triangular cake with a mild flavour and soft texture, served with an enlivening smear of hot mustard. Small dishes include konnyaku dengaku (gelatinous translucent triangles made from the root of the devil's tongue plant) skewered and brushed with shiro (white) miso and sprinkled with sesame seeds. Fried aubergine with minced chicken was a bit oily and slightly over-fried, but highly savoury. The range of maki (our squid and cod's roe roll was nicely spicy) and nigiri is super-fresh. There are plenty of dishes that will satisfy, and service is smiling and keen to advise.
Babies and children admitted. Booking advisable. Takeaway service. **Map 17 A4.**

So Japanese
3-4 Warwick Street, W1B 5LS (7292 0760/ www.sorestaurant.com). Piccadilly Circus tube. **Lunch served** noon-3pm Mon-Fri. **Dinner**

Aaya

served 5-10.30pm Mon-Thur; 6-11pm Fri. **Meals served** noon-11pm Sat. **Main courses** £12-£40. **Set lunch** £8-£16. **Set dinner** £25-£70. **Credit** AmEx, MC, V.
This contemporary Soho Japanese is serious about saké. So serious. You walk in past display cases of premium saké on glass plinths, illuminated like precious museum artefacts. Two large saké dispensers sit on the bar, and the walls hold shelves with more bottles and barrels of the stuff. Beginners are even invited to try a flight of four specially chosen sakés presented on a wooden tray. So you'd better eat something, then. Luckily the intriguingly contemporary take on Japanese cooking runs to an impressive salad of plump, lightly caramelised scallops with sashimi-like centres, and a French-style salad of duck confit and walnuts that is richly lingering on the palate – and very saké-friendly. Sushi, from the ground-floor sushi bar, is generously proportioned and always impeccably fresh. We particularly liked a tempura prawn temake handroll, which showed that the kitchen here really knows the secret of light, crunchy tempura. The only downside was a somewhat soggy

chicken teriyaki incongruously served with potato and cold broccoli. So not exciting.
Babies and children welcome. Separate room for parties, seats 4. Takeaway service. **Map 17 A5.**

Westminster

Atami
37 Monck Street, SW1P 2BL (7222 2218/ www.atamirestaurant.co.uk). St James's Park tube. **Lunch served** noon-2.30pm Mon-Fri. **Dinner served** 5.30-10.30pm Mon-Sat. **Main courses** £12.50-£21.50. **Set lunch** £8.50-£18. **Credit** AmEx, MC, V.
Dramatic ceiling orbs and flickering candles send light ricocheting off the mirrors and the fine glassware that adorns the tables in this elegant corner restaurant. Atami's impressive wine list adds to the feeling that this is a place for splurges. You'd do well to steer a course through the lengthy menu past the strange fusion dishes and head straight to the traditional sushi: well-rendered classics prepared by Japanese sushi chefs. While someone just off the plane from Tokyo might quibble that the sushi rice is

Kappa

under-seasoned with sugar and vinegar, no-one could doubt that the fish is of top quality and comes draped in generous portions over the rice. Nothing, however, explains the need for foie gras sushi (perfectly respectable liver that clashes with nori and is wasted on a lump of rice). Other fusion offerings like lobster tempura with potato truffle sauce appeared to be an unnecessary gilding of the lily. Deep-fried soft-shell crab was enjoyable, but though the raw marble beef with chive tempura was OK, the beef had been overpowered by ponzu dressing, and seemed overpriced for its size.
Babies and children welcome: high chairs. Takeaway service. **Map 16 K10.**

West

Ealing

★ ★ Sushi-Hiro ⑩⑩
1 Station Parade, Uxbridge Road, W5 3LD (8896 3175). Ealing Common tube. **Lunch served** 11am-1.30pm, **dinner served** 4.30-9pm Tue-Sun. **Sushi** 60p-£2.40. **Set meal** £8-£18. **No credit cards.**
There are a few things you need to know about Sushi-Hiro. For a start, all it does is sushi and sashimi: no noodles, no tempura, no teppanyaki. Furthermore, it takes no credit cards, and there's no wine – just saké, beer and tea. The restaurant is tiny, with just five tables and ten seats at the sushi bar, and the atmosphere is sober. Service can be slow, especially when the owner mans the sushi bar alone. The opening hours are distinctly odd, with no orders taken after 1.30pm or 9pm. (We once watched, astounded, as the Fat Duck's Heston Blumenthal was refused service at 1.32pm.) So why on earth would you want to go here? Because Sushi-Hiro produces some of the best, freshest, most deftly handled sushi you're liable to find. Every piece of tuna glistens; every scallop astounds with its sweetness; every translucent sliver of sea bream thrills with its clarity of flavour; and every grain of rice feels as if it has been gently pampered into position. The menu is great value too, with prices not much higher than you'd pay for conveyor belt sushi. As for everything else about this place, you can't say you weren't warned.
Babies and children welcome: high chair. Booking advisable (Fri, Sat). Takeaway service.

Hammersmith

★ Tosa
332 King Street, W6 0RR (8748 0002/ www.tosatosa.net). Ravenscourt Park or Stamford Brook tube. **Lunch served** 12.30-2.30pm daily. **Dinner served** 6-11pm Mon-Sat; 6-10.30pm Sun. **Main courses** £5.30-£12. **Set meal** £20-£25. **Credit** MC, V.
That might seem like a sushi counter in the front room of this popular split-level, low-key local, but take a closer look at the refrigerated cabinet. Instead of fish, it is jam-packed with meaty skewers ready for the grill: pork loin, chicken livers, duck breast, ox tongue and more. Behind the counter, a robata chef tends two smoulderingly hot grills, which are kept working overtime by the mainly local crowd. Sushi appears from an out-of-sight kitchen and is not bad at all, especially the silky salmon, buttery tuna, and sweet, sticky eel. We also loved the firmly packed, scorchy-bottomed gyoza dumplings. But you're really here for the grills. Don't miss the asparamaki (thinly sliced belly pork wrapped around asparagus spears), the beefy, lightly chewy ox-tongue, and the crisp and sticky chicken wings (so good we immediately ordered more). Salt-grilling is also done well, turning mackerel into a crisp and smoky delight. Tosa's not fancy, but with an Asahi beer in your hand and the smell of barbecue in the air, we can think of many worse places to while away the evening.
Babies and children admitted. Booking advisable. Tables outdoors (3, terrace). Takeaway service. Vegetarian menu. **Map 20 A4.**

Paddington

Yakitoria
25 Sheldon Square, W2 6EY (3214 3000/ www.yakitoria.co.uk). Paddington tube/rail. **Lunch served** noon-3pm Mon-Fri. **Dinner served** 6-11pm Mon-Sat. **Main courses** £13.50-£30. **Set lunch** £12.50-£20. **Credit** AmEx, DC, MC, V.
You really want Yakitoria to be as good as the eager, charming eastern European staff obviously think it is. Yet in spite of their best intentions and the restaurant's industrial-chic, nightclub feel, our dinner here was a soulless, up-and-down affair marred by a slow kitchen and uneven cooking. We're still not sure what 'white tuna' is, except for the fact that it doesn't make for very good sushi. Assuming that grills would be a strong point of a restaurant called Yakitoria, we were disappointed with chicken skewers that were practically uncooked at one end, and quail kushi that was close to cremated. Plump, deep-fried gyoza dumplings were well put-together, a sashimi salad was prettily presented, and 'rare' beef teriyaki had good meaty flavour, even if the beef was too well done. Yakitoria seems to function more as a bar with food than a restaurant, which suits the young Paddington Basin crowd just fine. Downstairs, the loungier Mizu bar revs up as the night rolls on.
Babies and children welcome: high chairs. Booking advisable. Disabled: lift; toilet. Dress: smart casual. Tables outdoors (15, terrace). Takeaway service. **Map 7 C6.**

South West

Earl's Court

Kappa NEW
139 Earl's Court Road, SW5 9RH (7244 9196/ www.kapparestaurant.co.uk). Earl's Court tube. **Lunch served** noon-3pm Tue-Sun. **Dinner served** 6-11pm daily. **Main courses** £6.90-£12.80. **Set lunch** £4.90-£12.90. **Credit** MC, V.
A relative newcomer to Earl's Court's restaurant row, Kappa is a top pick of the neighbourhood. It's a low-key place, but has a certain stylishness, with gold-toned walls, candles and black tables. The owner is a Korean-born sushi chef and there's a clear Korean influence on many dishes here, such as grilled scallops with gochujang (a Korean spicy bean paste). Three scallops, cut through the middle into discs and sandwiching finely chopped vegetables, were topped with a frazzle of deep-fried sliced leek and zigzagged with the spicy red paste; they looked gorgeous on their rectangular plate and were just as pleasing on the palate. A temaki (cone-shaped hand roll) containing stir-fried pork belly, rice and the well-loved Korean condiment kimchi, may have been difficult to eat, but was spicy and savoury nonetheless. Dry-fried pieces of baby squid, spiced with powdered chilli, were crisp outside, tender inside. Nigiri sushi is well-turned-out too; our sea bass nigiri was quite delicate and superbly fresh, as was nori-wrapped salmon roe. Black cod with miso, at the ungrasping price of £10.90, couldn't be faulted. In all, a cut above average.
Babies and children welcome: high chairs. Booking advisable dinner. Takeaway service. **Map 13 B10.**

Fulham

Yumenoki
204 Fulham Road, SW10 9PJ (7351 2777/ www.yumenoki.co.uk). Fulham Broadway or South Kensington tube then 14 bus. **Lunch served** noon-3pm, **dinner served** 5.30-10.30pm daily. **Main courses** £7.80-£28. **Set lunch** £8-£15 bento box. **Credit** AmEx, MC, V.
The look at this relative newcomer is whimsical, done out in colourful fabric wall-hangings and a collection of bright paper goldfish. Like its neighbour Feng Sushi (*see p197*), Yumenoki ('dream tree') does a brisk takeaway trade, although here the emphasis is more on dining-in. The menu's an odd read with a number of vaguely 'Asian'-sounding dishes including the likes of

Menu

For further reference, Richard Hosking's *A Dictionary of Japanese Food: Ingredients & Culture* (Tuttle) is highly recommended.

Agedashidofu: tofu (qv) coated with katakuriko (potato starch), deep-fried, sprinkled with dried fish and served in a broth based on shoyu (qv), with grated ginger and daikon (qv).

Amaebi: sweet shrimps.

Anago: saltwater conger eel.

Bento: a meal served in a compartmentalised box.

Chawan mushi: savoury egg custard served in a tea tumbler (chawan).

Chutoro: medium fatty tuna from the upper belly.

Daikon: a long, white radish (aka mooli), often grated or cut into fine strips.

Dashi: the basic stock for Japanese soups and simmered dishes. It's often made from flakes of dried bonito (a type of tuna) and konbu (kelp).

Dobin mushi: a variety of morsels (prawn, fish, chicken, shiitake, ginkgo nuts) in a gently flavoured dashi-based soup, steamed (mushi) and served in a clay teapot (dobin).

Donburi: a bowl of boiled rice with various toppings, such as beef, chicken or egg.

Dorayaki: mini pancakes sandwiched around azuki bean paste.

Edamame: fresh soy beans boiled in their pods and sprinkled with salt.

Gari: pickled ginger, usually pink and thinly sliced; served with sushi to cleanse the palate between courses.

Gyoza: soft rice pastry cases stuffed with minced pork and herbs; northern Chinese in origin, cooked by a combination of frying and steaming.

Hamachi: young yellowtail or Japanese amberjack fish, commonly used for sashimi (qv) and also very good grilled.

Hashi: chopsticks.

Hiyashi chuka: Chinese-style ramen (qv noodles) served cold (hiyashi) in tsuyu (qv) with a mixed topping that usually includes shredded ham, chicken, cucumber, egg and sweetcorn.

Ikura: salmon roe.

Izakaya: 'a place where there is saké'; an after-work drinking den frequented by Japanese businessmen, usually serving a wide range of reasonably priced food.

Kaiseki ryori: a multi-course meal of Japanese haute cuisine.

Kaiten-zushi: conveyor-belt sushi.

Karaage: deep-fried

Katsu: breaded and deep-fried meat, hence **tonkatsu** (pork katsu) and **katsu curry** (tonkatsu or chicken katsu with mild vegetable curry).

Kushiage: skewered morsels battered then deep-fried.

Maki: the word means 'roll' and this is a style of sushi (qv) where the rice and filling are rolled inside a sheet of nori (qv).

Mirin: a sweetened rice spirit used in many Japanese sauces and dressings.

Miso: a thick paste of fermented soy beans, used in miso soup and some dressings. Miso comes in a wide variety of styles, ranging from 'white' to 'red', slightly sweet to very salty and earthy, crunchy or smooth.

Miso shiru: classic miso soup, most often containing tofu and wakame (qv).

Nabemono: a class of dishes cooked at the table and served directly from the earthenware pot or metal pan.

Natto: fermented soy beans of stringy, mucous consistency.

Nimono: food simmered in a stock, often presented 'dry'.

Noodles: second only to rice as Japan's favourite staple. Served hot or cold, dry or in soup, and sometimes fried. There are many types, but the most common are **ramen** (Chinese-style egg noodles), **udon** (thick white wheat-flour noodles), **soba** (buckwheat noodles), and **somen** (thin white wheat-flour noodles, usually served cold as a summer dish – hiyashi somen – with a chilled dipping broth).

Nori: sheets of dried seaweed.

Okonomiyaki: the Japanese equivalent of filled pancakes or a Spanish omelette, whereby various ingredients are added to a batter mix and cooked on a hotplate, usually in front of diners.

Ponzu: usually short for ponzu joyu, a mixture of the juice of a Japanese citrus fruit (ponzu) and soy sauce. Used as a dip, especially with seafood and chicken or fish nabemono (qv).

Robatayaki: a kind of grilled food, generally cooked in front of customers, who make their selection from a large counter display.

Saké: rice wine, around 15% alcohol. Usually served hot, but may be chilled.

Sashimi: raw sliced fish.

Shabu shabu: a pan of stock is heated at the table and plates of thinly sliced raw beef and vegetables are cooked in it piece by piece ('shabu-shabu' is onomatopoeic for the sound of washing a cloth in water). The broth is then portioned out and drunk.

Shiso: perilla or beefsteak plant. A nettle-like leaf of the mint family that is often served with sashimi (qv).

Shochu: Japan's colourless answer to vodka is distilled from raw materials such as wheat, rice and potatoes.

Shoyu: Japanese soy sauce.

Sukiyaki: pieces of thinly sliced beef and vegetables are simmered in a sweet shoyu-based sauce at the table on a portable stove. Then they are taken out and dipped in raw egg (which semi-cooks on the hot food) to cool them for eating.

Sunomono: seafood or vegetables marinated (but not pickled) in rice vinegar.

Sushi: a combination of raw fish, shellfish or vegetables with rice – usually with a touch of wasabi (qv). Vinegar mixed with sugar and salt is added to the rice, which is then cooled before use. There are different sushi formats: **nigiri** (lozenge-shaped), **hosomaki** (thin-rolled), **futomaki** (thick-rolled), **temaki** (hand-rolled), **gunkan maki** (nigiri with a nori wrap), **chirashi** (scattered on top of a bowl of rice), and **uramaki** or **ISO maki** (more recently coined terms for inside-out rolls).

Tare: a general term for shoyu-based cooking marinades, typically on yakitori (qv) and unagi (qv).

Tataki: meat or fish quickly seared, then marinated in vinegar, sliced thinly, and seasoned with ginger.

Tatami: a heavy straw mat – traditional Japanese flooring. A tatami room in a restaurant is usually a private room where you remove your shoes and sit on the floor to eat.

Tea: black tea is fermented, while green tea (**ocha**) is heat-treated by steam to prevent the leaves fermenting. **Matcha** is powdered green tea, and has a high caffeine content. **Bancha** is the coarsest grade of green tea, which has been roasted; it contains the stems or twigs of the plant as well as the leaves, and is usually served free of charge with a meal. **Hojicha** is lightly roasted bancha. **Mugicha** is roast barley tea, served iced in summer.

Tempura: fish, shellfish or vegetables dipped in a light batter and deep-fried. Served with tsuyu (qv) to which you add finely grated daikon (qv) and fresh ginger.

Teppanyaki: 'grilled on an iron plate. In modern Japanese restaurants, a chef standing at a hotplate (teppan) is surrounded by several diners. Slivers of beef, fish and vegetables are cooked with a dazzling display of knifework and deposited on your plate.

Teriyaki: cooking method by which meat or fish – often marinated in shoyu (qv) and rice wine – is grilled and served in a tare (qv) made of a thick reduction of shoyu (qv), saké (qv), sugar and spice.

Tofu: soy beancurd used fresh in simmered or grilled dishes, or deep-fried (agedashidofu), or eaten cold (hiyayakko).

Tokkuri: saké flask – usually ceramic, but sometimes made of bamboo.

Tonkatsu: see above katsu.

Tsuyu: a general term for shoyu/mirin-based dips, served both warm and cold with various dishes ranging from tempura (qv) to cold noodles.

Umami: the nearest word in English is tastiness. After sweet, sour, salty and bitter, umami is considered the fifth primary taste in Japan, but not all food scientists in the West accept its existence as a basic flavour.

Unagi: freshwater eel.

Uni: sea urchin roe.

Wakame: a type of young seaweed most commonly used in miso (qv) soup and kaiso (seaweed) salad.

Wasabi: a fiery green paste made from the root of an aquatic plant that belongs to the same family as horseradish. It is eaten in minute quantities (tucked inside sushi, qv), or diluted into shoyu (qv) for dipping sashimi (qv).

Yakimono: literally 'grilled things'.

Yakitori: grilled chicken (breast, wings, liver, gizzard, heart) served on skewers.

Zarusoba: soba noodles served cold, usually on a bamboo draining mat, with a dipping broth.

Zensai: appetisers.

diced tofu in red curry sauce, and tuna steak with ginger sauce. We stuck with the more distinctively Japanese offerings, such as an escabeche (nanbanzuke): thin slices of fried fish marinated in vinegar, a bit of dashi and thinly sliced carrot, onion and pepper – pleasingly sharp, if slightly chewy. Nigiri of mackerel was tender and fresh, and yellowtail sashimi exemplary, but uni (sea urchin) lacked the fresh whiff of the sea. The custard in our chawan mushi was rather firm, but good-quality dashi gave it a deep smokiness. Boneless grilled unagi (eel), basted in a thick, soy-based sauce and served on rice, was richly flavoured. Service on our visit was amateurish and forgetful. Saké prices are high (£12 for 180ml of mid-range saké) so stick with beer or tea.
Babies and children admitted: high chairs. Separate room for parties, seats 25. Takeaway service; delivery service (within 2-mile radius). **Map 13 C12.**

Putney

Chosan
292 Upper Richmond Road, SW15 6TH (8788 9626). East Putney tube. **Lunch served** noon-2.30pm, **dinner served** 6.30-10.30pm daily. **Main courses** £3.30-£25. **Set lunch** £7.90-£13.90. **Set dinner** £18.90-£20.90; £19.90-£24.90 bento box. **Credit** MC, V.
Chosan has an unpretentious, homespun quality. Inside there's a plethora of knick-knacks and coverlets; a meal here feels like eating at your granny's house – provided your granny is Japanese, a great cook and happens to have a sushi bar in her front room. The sizeable menu comes in two versions (one with pictures, one without) bolstered by daily specials. Either way, it's an enticing read, with fish dishes (raw or cooked) a strong point. Our raw aji (horse mackerel) and seaweed with ponzu was a generous portion, nicely sharp and refreshing, with properly fresh fish. Small vegetable dishes, such as sweet-savoury simmered radish and dried beancurd, are another strong point. A varied choice of fish featured in the mixed sushi set; the fish was of good quality but some pieces were less than expertly cut (the usual chef wasn't behind the bar). Since our visit last year, we were pleased to see that an expanded saké list now contains some interesting brews at decent prices. Chosan has a loyal local following, and service is usually friendly.
Babies and children admitted. Separate area for parties, seats 30. Takeaway service.

Wimbledon

Kushi-Tei
264 The Broadway, SW19 1SB (8543 1188/ www.kushi-tei.com). Wimbledon tube/rail. **Meals served** 6-11.30pm daily. **Dishes** 75p-£8.65. **Set meal** £9.95-£26.95. **Credit** MC, V.
This charming little spot specialises in grilled things on sticks ('kushi' is Japanese for skewer). There's yakitori, naturally, but the skewered offerings go much further than chicken, including various vegetables, fish and meat. Some are skewered and cooked over a charcoal grill, others coated with egg and crisp breadcrumbs and deep-fried. Kushiyaki-ya in Japanese cities cater for drinkers; Kushi-Tei is a more sedate affair, with subtle decor, a calm atmosphere and a modest drinks list, yet it still feels properly 'Japanese'. Some dishes are more successful than others. Our maguro (tuna) skewer looked and tasted gorgeous, deeply savoury and zigzagged with wasabi mayonnaise. Niko-shiitake, mushroom caps filled with light, juicy spheres of minced chicken flavoured with black sesame seeds, was subtle and delicious, and tori-shoso (succulent pinwheels of chicken and shiso leaf) did credit to the free-range bird. Less successful was a bland ebi-koro (deep-fried shrimp croquette), and dry half-moons of aubergine with miso. Non-skewered food includes a deliciously gummy-textured starter of raw, sliced okra topped with paper-thin shavings of bonito, as well as maki and rice dishes. A great neighbourhood venue that deserves more custom.
Babies and children welcome: high chairs. Booking advisable weekends.

Tsunami

South

Battersea

Tokiya
74 Battersea Rise, SW11 1EH (7223 5989/ www.tokiya.co.uk). Clapham Junction rail. **Lunch served** 12.30-3pm Sat, Sun. **Dinner served** 6.30-10.30pm Tue-Sun. **Main courses** £8-£18. **Set lunch** £7-£15 2 courses. **Set dinner** £16-£28 3 courses. **Credit** AmEx, MC, V.
With just a dozen tables, Tokiya is a bijou place with a sombre, monochrome look. Tables are painted black, the floor and walls off-white. The sushi chef works behind a small bar at the back, turning out a varied array. On our visit, the nigiri options were somewhat limited and the toro (tuna belly), despite being that day's recommended fish, was tough and fibrous. In contrast, yellowtail sashimi was exemplary. We had difficulty choosing from the long list of enticing maki, finally settling for the neat, umami-rich natto (fermented soybean) rolls. Classics such as agedashidofu and seaweed salad are competently done and portions are quite generous. Daily specials are chalked on a board. We noticed that the now-ubiquitous black cod with miso was offered, at the Mayfair price of £18 – cheeky for such humble surroundings. Service is polite and helpful, but the drinks list (a

small selection of uninspiring beer, wine and saké) could do with a boost. Opening times can be erratic, so ring ahead first.
Babies and children admitted. Booking advisable; essential weekends (dinner). Takeaway service; delivery service (over £20). **Map 21 C4.**

Clapham

★ Tsunami
5-7 Voltaire Road, SW4 6DQ (7978 1610/ www.tsunamirestaurant.co.uk). Clapham North tube. **Lunch served** 1-4pm Sat, Sun. **Dinner served** 6-10.30pm Mon-Fri; 6-11pm Sat, Sun. **Main courses** £7.50-£17.50. **Set lunch** (Sat, Sun) £10.50. **Credit** MC, V.
Now something of a Clapham institution, Tsunami is located down a dreary-looking road near a railway line, but its warm atmosphere and good looks (white walls warmed up with dark wood, flickering candles, orchids) put any initial doubts to rest. The menu's a confident-sounding read, from sushi and sashimi to tempura, rice and noodle dishes; the modern-Japanese specials are the most indicative of the chefs' skills. Korean and western influences mark dishes such as kimchi lamb skewers, and yellowtail sashimi with jalapeño peppers. Our skewers sang with the spicy, gutsy flavours of chilli, sesame and garlic. Another Korean-inspired dish, spicy gyoza soup,

RESTAURANTS

was deep and intense: spicy, fermented flavours contrasting with the delicate minced chicken dumplings. Steamed sea bass, artfully arranged on a white plate festooned with enoki mushrooms and steamed pak choi, featured tender, flaky fish spiked with rice vinegar. The only let-down was dessert – an intriguing-sounding steamed pudding for which we were happy to wait the advertised 20 minutes, but which arrived, fridge-cold and disappointing, five minutes later. Stick to savoury food and you'll see why Tsunami's appeal extends far beyond that lucky man on the Clapham omnibus.
Babies and children admitted. Booking advisable; essential weekends. Takeaway service. **Map 22 B1**.

Waterloo

★ Bincho

2nd floor, Oxo Tower Wharf, Barge House Street, SE1 9PH (7803 0858/www.bincho.co.uk). Blackfriars or Waterloo tube/rail. **Lunch served** noon-3pm Mon-Fri; 12.30-3.30pm Sat, Sun. **Dinner served** 5-11.30pm Mon-Fri; 5.30pm-11.30pm Sat; 5.30-10.30pm Sun. **Dishes** £1.20-£11. **Credit** AmEx, DC, MC, V.
Many London restaurants boast impressive views, but Bincho, with its glorious Thames-side vista, has one of the best. Add to this the excellent yakitori (grilled meat, fish and veg), and you have a prime spot for a romantic date. Electronic beat music pulses, keeping the energy of the chic young crowd high, as they absorb St Paul's, saké (there's a wide choice, hot or cold) and the beautiful scent of the barbecue. Start your meal with motsunikomi: rich, earthy miso broth with pig's intestine, carrots, daikon and cabbage. While the full fragrance of the offal is somewhat subdued here, the balance of the soup is divine – sweet, rich, soothing, with just a hint of the pungency of innards. Then move on to the barbecue. The menu lists many yakitori options, but we noted with glee that diners are invited to ask for any part of the chicken not on the menu. Chicken oysters were particularly tender. Grilled fish was crisp, and the spring onion wonderfully sweet. After dinner, head upstairs in the Oxo Tower and continue the romance with a view-enhanced cocktail.
Babies and children welcome: high chairs. Booking advisable. Disabled: lift, toilet. Takeaway service. **Map 11 N7**.
For branch see index.

Ozu

County Hall, Westminster Bridge Road, SE1 7PB (7928 7766/www.ozulondon.com). Embankment tube/Charing Cross or Waterloo tube/rail. **Lunch served** noon-2.30pm, **dinner served** 6-10pm daily. **Main courses** £18-£27. **Set meal** £22-£35 lunch; £55 dinner. **Credit** MC, V.
Because Ozu is such a study in awkward contrasts and bizarre juxtapositions, you might wonder whether the owner has ever visited the restaurant. Set in the spectacular wood-lined County Hall building (which, presumably, along with superior ingredients, is supposed to justify the astronomical prices), Ozu serves good food but lacks identity. Illogical floor design has placed a sushi preparation bar and a hot food prep island in key spots, blocking prime views of the Houses of Parliament. The clientele, largely tourists and men in suits, come to nibble on tempura, but we found it far too heavy. Instead, order sushi and sashimi, which is made from high-quality fish, though the range is limited; our sashimi selection included lean cuts (hence not the most expensive) of tuna, salmon, sea bass and yellowtail. Waiting staff are mostly European; they're friendly, helpful and discreet, but our queries about the food were met with blank looks. We're also puzzled by the choice of music here. Why bore diners with the Bangles' 'Eternal Flame'? Still, given the stunning location, Ozu makes a good spot for a business lunch.
Babies and children welcome: high chairs. Booking advisable. Disabled: toilet (in County Hall). Vegetarian menu. **Map 10 M9**.

Bincho

East

Docklands

Kombu NEW
2 Western Gateway, Royal Victoria Dock, E14 1DR (7474 1459). Custom House DLR. **Meals served** noon-10.30pm daily. **Main courses** £7-£16.25. **Credit** AmEX, MC, V.
Kombu could be described as 'Japanese-lite'. On our first visit, soon after it opened, we were taken with the range of enticing options. Six months later, the likes of tempura sea urchin had been replaced by a more anodyne menu. The choice of sushi was limited to the usual finny suspects (tuna, salmon, sea bass) while main courses such as fillet steak with ginger, garlic and basil seemed more suited to business diners than food enthusiasts. As the restaurant is near the massive ExCeL exhibition centre, the switch to a conservative approach may have proved necessary. Silken tofu with sesame and miso dressing was pleasant enough, but tuna tataki, quickly seared and seasoned heavily with black pepper, had none of the advertised matsuhisa dressing. 'Hand-pulled' noodles with Japanese sausage, prawn, fish cake and chilli paste was so characterless it could have come from a Chinese takeaway. Some effort has gone into giving the interior a stylish look, but service could do with a polish. We were brought the wrong wine (three times) and no effort was made to pace the dishes, which all arrived within five minutes of ordering.
Babies and children welcome: booster seats. Disabled: toilet. Separate rooms for parties, seats 12-14. Tables outdoors (3, pavement). Takeaway.

★ Ubon
34 Westferry Circus, Canary Wharf, E14 8RR (7719 7800/www.noburestaurants.com). Canary Wharf tube/DLR/Westferry DLR. **Lunch served** noon-2.15pm Mon-Fri. **Dinner served** 6-10.15pm Mon-Sat. **Main courses** £7-£32.50. **Set meal** £55-£90. **Credit** AmEX, DC, MC, V.
If it annoys you to witness groups of business-suited executives bonding over magnums of Billecart-Salmon rosé and £70 per person omakase (chef's choice) set menus – at lunch – then stay away from Ubon, the Canary Wharf offshoot of the mighty Nobu (*see p199*). On the other hand, Ubon offers a more flexible introduction to the big-hit dishes Nobu Matsuhisa made famous. You can share the same views of the Thames over a more modest lunchtime 'Ubon In and Out' bento box, a rather glamorous two-box affair that showcases the master's classics of black cod in miso, crisp and golden rock shrimp tempura, assorted sushi, a refreshing sashimi salad and lightly spiced vegetables with rice. The room feels blandly corporate, but the food is good enough to continue this city's love affair with all things Nobu. At night, the restaurant is less businesslike as the full à la carte menu kicks in, and there are fewer discussions about mezzanine credit schemes and my-watch-is-bigger-than-yours.
Babies and children welcome: high chairs. Booking essential. Disabled: lift; toilet. Dress: smart casual. Takeaway service. Vegetarian menu. **Map 24 A2.**

North

Camden Town & Chalk Farm

★ Asakusa
265 Eversholt Street, NW1 1BA (7388 8533/8399). Camden Town or Mornington Crescent tube. **Dinner served** 6-11.30pm Mon-Fri; 6-11pm Sat. **Main courses** £5.20-£9.80. **Set dinner** £5.20-£13. **Credit** MC, V.
Asakusa is crammed every evening. The young Camden crowd, Japanese and otherwise, don't come for the frankly rather dingy, 'squat-chic' decor; they come for the low prices and the food, which is generally very good. Relentlessly cheerful servers bear constant smiles and a willingness to help decipher the menu. This makes few concessions to readability, but lists a staggering array of inviting victuals. Teishoku (set meals)

make a decent starting point. Our mixed tempura (fat prawns and various veg) was hot and crisp. Sushi (juicy eel maki) and sashimi (yellowtail) are of a high standard and there's a varied range. Small dishes are difficult to resist; our beef tataki wasn't the most tender meat in town, but had plenty of flavour and was nicely presented. Buta kakuni, a slow-cooked pork belly dish, was rich and warming with an appetisingly sweet undertone, but we'd have liked it cooked a bit more, until it fell apart under the pressure of chopsticks. Most customers stick to large-format bottles of beer or tea, but there's saké on the drinks list too. Book ahead if you're after a ground-floor table; otherwise, it's down to the basement.
Babies and children admitted. Booking advisable Thur-Sat. Takeaway service. Vegetarian menu. **Map 27 D3.**

Crouch End

Wow Simply Japanese
18 Crouch End Hill, N8 8AA (8340 4539). Finsbury Park tube/rail then W3 bus/Crouch Hill rail. **Lunch served** noon-2.30pm Wed-Sun. **Dinner served** 6-10.30pm Mon-Sat; 6-10pm Sun. **Main courses** £7.80-£40. **Set lunch** £5.90-£8.80. **Credit** MC, V.
The first Japanese restaurant to open its doors in Crouch End, in autumn 2006, didn't actually wow us, but it was an instant hit in the neighbourhood. You're still wise to reserve a table on a Friday or Saturday evening, when this neat, square room of pale walls and dark tables (set a little too closely together) is filled, predominantly with couples and pairs of friends. Service by the busy waitresses is unfailingly polite, punctuated by friendly smiles. The menu seems truer to its 'simply' tag these days, apparently eschewing previous 'modern' dishes such as foie gras or seared tuna and asparagus in favour of straightforward sushi, noodles, bentos and traditional side orders. Even the blackboard specials kept things basic on our last visit, with sweet potato tempura and seared salmon sashimi. We couldn't get enough of the tasty garlic egg fried rice and moist, warm spider roll (soft-shell crab futomaki), but could have done without the agedashidofu, its light, crisp coating let down by stodgy, greyish beancurd. In between were fine renderings of chicken gyoza, nigiri sushi and nabeyaki udon (seafood noodle hotpot) – so Wow is still a safe bet for decent Japanese dining.
Babies and children welcome: high chairs. Booking advisable. Takeaway service.

Hornsey

Matsu NEW
50 Topsfield Parade, N8 8PT (8340 7773/www.matsu-restaurant.com). Archway or Finsbury tube. **Dinner served** 6-11pm Tue-Sat; 6-10pm Sun. **Set meal** £8.50-£15. **Main courses** £5-£12. **Credit** MC, V.
Despite seeming less busy than Wow (*see above*), Matsu celebrated its first year in business in May 2008 with a free bottle of Asahi for every customer over the anniversary weekend – a gesture indicative of the welcoming attitude you'll find here. The cuisine is even homelier than that of its 'simply' named compatriot at the other end of Crouch End Broadway, never straying beyond trad sushi, donburi, noodles and tempura. Well, there's no need to, when high-quality ingredients are combined with skill. The setting is equally uncomplicated: just cream walls bearing a few pieces of embroidery artwork, neutral-toned tiles and two lines of tables in a long room. We like the cut of chef-owner Shigeki Matsushima's sashimi, but particularly recommend the luscious unagidon (freshwater eel on a bowl of rice) and juicy chicken gyoza. Matsu also offers a rare chance to roll your own sushi, complete with personal *shamoji* (wooden spatula) and bamboo mat. There may not be any high chairs, but accommodating staff and plenty of space between tables make this a pleasantly relaxed, family-friendly venue.
Babies and children admitted. Booking advisable. Takeaway service.

Islington

Sa Sa Sushi
422 St John Street, EC1V 4NJ (7837 1155/www.sasasushi.co.uk). Angel tube. **Lunch served** noon-2.30pm Mon-Sat. **Dinner served** 5.30-10pm Mon-Thur; 5.30-11pm Fri, Sat. **Main courses** £3.50-£18. **Sushi** £1.20-£2.50. **Set dinner** £22.50-£27.50. **Credit** AmEx, MC, V.
Behind a cheery green shop-front a few doors from the Angel tube traffic junction, this well-lit spot combines restful design with good food. It's less busy than it deserves, and so is a perfect daytime venue to gather your thoughts or chat with a friend. What makes it unusual is that the sushi chef, from Vietnam, produces dishes that a neighbourhood joint in Tokyo would be proud of. Flagship of the sushi plates is the Sa Sa deluxe, which combines a tasting of salmon and tuna sashimi with an enticing set of nigiri – in which the tai (sea bream) and hamachi stood out as particularly fresh and clean – and a skilfully made maki of warm deep-fried soft-shell crab. The umami taste rang through an excellent nasu dengaku (grilled aubergine with miso sauce), while salmon teriyaki comprised two good slices, grilled just right. Though desserts were uninspiring, green tea was of a high quality, and service was prompt and helpful.
Babies and children admitted: high chairs. Booking advisable. Disabled: toilet. Takeaway service; delivery service (over £15 within 2-mile radius). **Map 5 N3.**

Muswell Hill

Sushi 101 NEW
Raglan Hotel, 8-12 Queens Avenue, N10 3NR (8883 6274/www.sushi101.co.uk). Highgate tube then 43, 134 bus or Finsbury Park tube then W7 bus. **Meals served** 11am-10.30pm daily. **Dishes** £1.75-£7. **Sushi platters** £19-£45. **Set lunch** £6-£7. **Credit** MC, V.

SHELF LIFE

Other good places to buy authentic Japanese ingredients are **Saki** (*see p193*), **Centrepoint Sushi** and the **Japan Centre** (for both, *see p196*).

Fuji Foods
167 Priory Road, N8 8NB (8347 9177). W7 bus.
A charming Japanese deli with several organic lines. Pick up home-made sushi and miso-marinated black cod, green tea and black sesame ice-creams, plus staple groceries such as haiga rice, sea urchin pasta and kimchee base.

Natural Natural
20 Station Parade, Uxbridge Road, W5 3LD (8992 0770/www.natural-natural.co.uk). Ealing Common tube.
On the same parade as Sushi-Hiro, this colourful little food store favours organic foods. As well as fresh fish, sushi, sashimi and noodles, it sells vegetables, breads, snacks and a wide range of Japanese seasonings.

Rice Wine Shop
82 Brewer Street, W1F 9UA (7439 3705/www.ricewineshop.com). Leicester Square or Piccadilly Circus tube.
You'll find many types of rice wine, plus Japanese beers and other drinks. For the cook, there is mirin (cooking wine) and different kinds of soy, teriyaki and tamari sauces.

Like neighbouring Crouch End, Muswell Hill had to wait a long time for a Japanese restaurant to come along. Then there were two. Neither is outstanding, but behind the Victorian features of the Raglan Hall Hotel, Sushi 101 favours modernity. It purveys an appetising line in new-style Japanese: mains such as miso-smeared lamb cutlets; desserts like green tea ice-cream paired with still-hot mango tempura. However, the basics don't always pass muster. Chutoro (medium fatty tuna sashimi) was off-colour and -flavour on our most recent visit. Fancier items concocted by an ex-Nobu chef work well. Mango and crabmeat maki are satisfyingly soft, fresh and skilfully constructed. The L-shaped restaurant provides table and counter dining and is smart – though shiny black surfaces, white vinyl cuboid seating and red accents plus a 1980s pop soundtrack make for an oddly retro experience. The illuminated fish tank set into one wall must be a child-pleaser, but couples and groups of business people appear to be the norm at lunchtime.
Babies and children welcome: high chairs. Booking advisable for groups over 6. Tables outdoors (10, garden). Takeaway service; delivery service (free over £15, within 2-mile radius).

North West
Golders Green

Café Japan
626 Finchley Road, NW11 7RR (8455 6854). Golders Green tube/13, 82 bus. **Lunch served** noon-2pm Sat, Sun. **Dinner served** 6-10pm Wed-Sat; 6-9.30pm Sun. **Main courses** £8-£9. **Set lunch** £8.50. **Set dinner** £12-£17. **Credit** MC, V.
Brightly lit yellow-walled Café Japan is always buzzing. Portions are large, prices reasonable and service friendly: a good formula and one that seems to keep loyal locals coming back. The daily specials caught our eye. Pirikara sashimi – big pieces of tuna, salmon and sea bream, marinated in wasabi and ginger – was sinus-searingly hot, a real wake-up call. Seldom-seen king crab tempura was delicately flavoured, but the crisp cloak of batter quickly went soggy. The sushi and sashimi, turned out by white-hatted chefs at the front of the restaurant, shouldn't be missed. Our inside-out maki with fried butterfish and a spicy mayonnaise sauce (another unusual dish) worked well. Nigiri of tender toro (tuna belly), sea urchin and razor clam all sang with freshness. Café Japan isn't the only Japanese restaurant in the neighbourhood – Eat Tokyo (*see below*) is just around the corner – but it's deservedly popular, so book ahead.
Babies and children admitted. Booking advisable. Takeaway service.

Eat Tokyo
14 North End Road, NW11 7PH (8209 0079). Golders Green tube. **Lunch served** 11.30am-3pm, **dinner served** 5.30-11pm daily. **Main courses** £2.50-£10 lunch; £7-£18 dinner. **Set lunch** £4.80-£13. **Set dinner** £7-£25. **Credit** MC, V.
This restaurant's interior is more comfortable and inviting than you'd expect from its dowdy shop-front. But stylish it isn't: pink-red chairs and pine tables compete with Japanese wall-hangings and an assortment of knick-knacks. Though the feeling may be authentically Japanese, this is very much small-town Japan. The menu matches the mood, offering a wide range of well-priced bento and set meals that combine all the old favourites. On our visit, things didn't look promising at first. The deep-fried tofu in one of our bento boxes was soggy, and the avocado in the accompanying maki was an unappealing brown. Things looked up with a solid sashimi set lunch, including tasty if poorly cut salmon, tai (sea bream), hirame (halibut) and tuna. And the unaji was terrific: precisely cooked, generous eel fillets slathered with the traditional salty-sweet sauce, and served on sticky rice. Eat Tokyo is great value, as the large number of Japanese customers has noticed. Friendly service, though leisurely, makes it a pleasant place to visit.
Babies and children welcome: high chairs. Booking advisable dinner. Takeaway service.

Hampstead
★ Jin Kichi
73 Heath Street, NW3 6UG (7794 6158/ www.jinkichi.com). Hampstead tube. **Lunch served** 12.30-2pm Sat, Sun. **Dinner served** 6-11pm Tue-Sat; 6-10pm Sun. **Main courses** £4.90-£14.80. **Set lunch** £8.80-£15.90. **Credit** AmEx, DC, MC, V.
This might be Hampstead, but there's no need to dress up for a meal here. Jin Kichi is very much a come-as-you-are, neighbourly dinner spot with an unpretentious and cottagey feel. The premises seem very lived-in, with its charming rice paper lanterns, noren curtains, and tables poked-in every which way. In the middle of the action is an island bar where a young chef expertly manhandles skewers of chicken wings, shiitake mushrooms, and shiso leaf and pork rolls. But there's plenty more to choose from. If it is Japanese and you can eat it, then you'll probably find it on the vast menu: from noodles to rice dishes, to simmered dishes, to grills, sushi and sashimi. Remarkably, it's all of a decent standard. Highlights included succulent tsukune (grilled chicken balls with yakitori sauce); skewered chicken livers that taste like lush pâté; juicy, scorchy chicken wings; and the best agedashidofu we've had in London. Deep-fried squid legs were chewy yet full of flavour, and an inside-out yellowtail and avocado roll was all freshness and light. This is party food Japanese-style: a continuous line-up of delicious things to nibble on while you're having a drink.
Babies and children welcome: high chairs. Booking advisable Fri-Sun. Takeaway service. **Map 28 B2.**

Swiss Cottage
Benihana
100 Avenue Road, NW3 3HF (7586 9508/ www.benihana.co.uk). Swiss Cottage tube. **Lunch served** noon-3pm daily. **Dinner served** 5.30-10.30pm Mon-Sat; 5-10pm Sun. **Main courses** £11.75-£52. **Set lunch** £13.50-37.50. **Set dinner** £47-£57 tasting menu. **Credit** AmEx, DC, MC, V.
From a glance at its abstract wall designs and spot-lit basement tables set around big teppan (flat steel griddles), you might think this place is as modern as the new buildings above it on the Swiss Cottage roundabout. In fact, it's a dinosaur of restaurant history. Founded in 1964, the Benihana chain popularised 'Japanese-style' for Americans, where the teppan is used to cook steak and seafood, which are served with side-orders of beansprouts, fried rice and mushrooms. Our set meals began with a routine iceberg and cherry-tomato salad. California rolls were heavy on the mayo, with under-ripe avocado. Cubed griddled steak was tasty, the chicken tolerable, egg-fried rice greasy but OK, and lemon sorbet palatable – but food plays second fiddle to showmanship at Benihana. In an otherwise deserted restaurant on a weekday lunchtime, our chef did cool tricks with eggs, salt cellars, onion rings, and bowls of rice: though with a heavy heart that was more North Korean than Japanese. Not even a generous tip raised a smile. Perhaps the chain needs to motivate its staff better; a rowdy Thursday-night party on expenses might have better luck.
Babies and children welcome: children's menu (Sun); high chairs. Booking advisable; essential weekends. Entertainment: clown, Sun lunch. Tables outdoors (4, garden). Takeaway service. **Map 28 B4.**
For branches see index.

Wakaba
122A Finchley Road, NW3 5HT (7443 5609). Finchley Road tube. **Lunch served** noon-2.30pm, **dinner served** 6.30-11pm Mon-Sat. **Main courses** £4.50-£19.80. **Set lunch** £7.30. **Set dinner** £22.50-£34. **Credit** AmEx, DC, MC, V.
Wakaba is housed in a John Pawson-designed building fronted by a frosted curve of glass. Inside, the bright lighting reveals a rather scuffed, less than pristine interior. Careful reading of the extensive menu can be rewarding (particularly the list of daily specials), as there are some unusual – and generally well-executed – dishes. We decided

to brave the toriwasa: rare-cooked chicken breast, seared, sliced and served with soy sauce, topped with thinly sliced nori. It had a delicate taste and appealing texture (raw most of the way through, but we suffered no ill effects). Turbot-fringe nigiri, looking like a piece of white frilly knickers laid atop a finger of rice, was firm and chewy. Another winning dish was sliced cuttlefish mixed with cod's roe, combining an appealing texture with a richly savoury flavour. Kureson goma ae (watercress in sesame sauce) is less common than its spinach-based relation; the savoury, slightly bitter sauce contrasted beautifully with the pepperiness of the watercress – full marks. The only disappointment was spicy prawn maki, which had an unpleasant vinegary flavour. Be adventurous and you can eat very well here, aided by friendly service.
Babies and children admitted. Booking advisable Fri, Sat. Restaurant available for hire. Takeaway service. **Map 28 B3.**

Willesden
★ Sushi-Say
33B Walm Lane, NW2 5SH (8459 2971). Willesden Green tube. **Lunch served** noon-2pm Tue-Fri; 1-3pm Sat, Sun. **Dinner served** 6.30-10pm Tue-Fri; 6-10.30pm Sat; 6-9.30pm Sun. **Main courses** £6.60-£13.20. **Set dinner** £21-£35. **Credit** MC, V.
If you come here expecting a dowdy interior and cutesy cat collection, you're in for a surprise. In their place is a cool modern look of dark slatted wood, translucent green glass and discreet spotlights. Sushi Say serves an eclectic mix of north-west London professionals and artsy Japanese, often the sushi chef's friends. Despite a long menu covering everything from noodles and yakitori to sushi and tempura, the food is very reliable. One night in late spring, for instance, standout starters were beef tataki in a vinegary sauce with onions, and poached pumpkin with mangetout slices. Vegetable tempura was varied and startlingly fresh, while the sashimi moriawase boasted buttery mackerel and generous doorsteps of skilfully-cut salmon. Only the fresh tofu was unexciting. The sushi is worth crossing town for, particularly the amaebi (raw sweet shrimp), chutoro (medium fatty tuna), and scallop in the toku set dinner. Even with all seats taken, service is friendly, swift and professional. For the prices, this quality of food is thoroughly good value.
Babies and children welcome: high chairs. Booking advisable dinner. Takeaway service.

Outer London
Richmond, Surrey

Matsuba
10 Red Lion Street, Richmond, Surrey TW9 1RW (8605 3513). Richmond tube/rail. **Lunch served** noon-3pm, **dinner served** 6-11pm Mon-Sat. **Main courses** £10-£30. **Set lunch** £10-£20. **Set dinner** £40-£45. **Credit** AmEx, MC, V.
Sleek as a box of designer chocolates and almost as bijou, Matsuba's look is easy on the eye, with low lighting and slate floors. The restaurant is Korean-run, so you'll find a number of chilli-spiked and barbecued Korean-style dishes here, scattered among the more strictly Japanese offerings. From the sushi bar comes a variety of creative combinations, both maki and temaki (cone-shaped hand rolls), such as the 'bagel' maki, made with salmon, cream cheese and chives, plus a decent selection of nigiri and sashimi. Our maguro (tuna) and suzuki (sea bass) nigiri were fine, but tako (octopus) nigiri wasn't as fresh as we'd have liked. Mixed tempura came cloaked in an overly thick batter, so the food isn't without its faults. On the positive side, tori kariage – plump, juicy balls of deep-fried chicken – put a slightly guilty smile on our faces. Wine, such as the lively Aussie verdelho from Tempus Two, is better value than saké. Best book ahead or you'll risk having to queue.
Babies and children admitted. Booking advisable. Takeaway service.

RESTAURANTS

Jewish

Unlike French cuisine, where home cooks rarely attempt to make a baguette or croissant, the best Jewish food has always been found at home. If you want a slow-cooked sabbath cholent (a hearty, bean-based stew) or the best matzah balls and roast chicken, you need to find a Jewish mamma. There was a time when food in a Jewish restaurant meant a salt beef sandwich and lockshen pudding. But today, London's kosher venues have diversified. You might find a taste of Tel Aviv, or food full of memories for those who once lived in Iran or Egypt. You'll certainly find Moroccan cigars (rolls of filo pastry with a sweet or savoury filling), American burgers and, with new places opening every few months, Indian curries, Japanese sushi and Chinese crispy duck. All but one of the restaurants below follow the laws regarding permitted animals and fish, and the rules about the separation of meat and dairy products. Jewish diners might also like to try newcomer **Chicago Rib Shack** (*see p39*), where the kosher steaks and burgers are cooked in a special pan, though the menu includes far-from-kosher spare ribs.

Surprisingly – given supervision costs – kosher restaurants are generally not expensive. You will never leave hungry; plates are abundantly filled and appetising. For good value, look for set menus and main-course prices that include vegetables. Four establishments stand out: **Eighty-Six Bistro Bar** has an inventive menu, featuring top-class meat; **Novellino** still triumphs for the best fish and pasta, with seriously good bread and pâtisserie; of the Israeli-style grills, **Dizengoff's** is the leader, with its meze starters and chargrilled meats; and top of the list for elegance and service is **Bevis Marks Restaurant**, with its enchanting location beside an 18th-century synagogue. Unlike at most other meat restaurants, where desserts are limited and often include pale imitations of cream, the chef at Bevis Marks conjures up imaginative non-dairy sweets that taste as good as they look.

Central

City

★ Bevis Marks Restaurant

4 Heneage Lane, EC3A 5DQ (7283 2220/ www.bevismarkstherestaurant.com). Aldgate tube/Liverpool Street tube/rail. **Lunch served** noon-2.15pm Mon-Fri. **Dinner served** 5.30-8.30pm Mon-Thur. **Main courses** £14.95-£22.95. **Credit** AmEx, MC, V.

From Bevis Marks' tables, set with fine linen and glassware, there are two views: modern paintings on one wall and, opposite, a glimpse into the adjoining 18th-century synagogue (well worth a visit before lunch). The chef offers a seasonal menu – unique in London kosher restaurants – catering to the demanding clientele. The stylish presentation, well-executed dishes and inventive desserts make non-Jewish guests unaware of the restrictions of kashrut. Chopped liver comes as a pâté, the smooth meatiness contrasting with a sweet fig compote. Butternut squash soup was silky, but less flavoursome than last summer's trio of soups. Chargrilled rib steak and rack of lamb were both juicy: the steak served with salsa verde and crisp, dark chips; the lamb covered in a deep, rich sauce with pommes anna that were bland, but also beans redolent of a slow-cooked cassoulet.

There's plenty of meat-free food too, such as wild mushroom risotto, smoked haddock chowder and sea bass with oriental noodles. Sweets are appealing: melting chocolate fondant, frangipane tarts with lemon sorbet, fruit crumbles with crème anglaise. Service is smooth and unobtrusive. An extensive wine list completes the experience: an elegant meal in great surroundings.
Babies and children admitted. Booking advisable lunch. Disabled: toilet. Kosher supervised (Sephardi). Restaurant available for hire. Tables outdoors (3, courtyard). Takeaway service. **Map 12 R6**.

Marylebone

Reuben's

79 Baker Street, W1U 6RG (7486 0035/ www.reubensrestaurant.co.uk). Baker Street tube. Deli/café **Open** 11.30am-4pm, 5.30-10pm Mon-Thur; 11.30am-3pm Fri; 11.30am-10pm Sun. *Restaurant* **Meals served** 11.30am-4pm, 5.30-10pm Mon-Thur; 11.30am-3pm Fri; 11.30am-10pm Sun. **Main courses** £9-£23. **Minimum** £10. **Credit** MC, V.

Since the closure of the only other kosher restaurant in the West End (Six-13 in Wigmore Street), Reuben's has been enjoying its monopoly. It's not a stylish venue (bright blue walls and linen tablecloths) and there's little finesse to the service,

although staff are pleasant enough. More expensive than kosher restaurants in the suburbs, Reuben's boasts a wide variety of dishes including chicken stuffed with fresh mango, magret of duck, and beef wellington. Yet most customers seem to prefer the traditional fare: tender salt beef, chicken soup rich with lockshen and knaidlach, pâté with a choice of chicken or calf's liver. We were hoping to see someone tackle the mixed grill: lamb chop, steak, chicken strips, salt beef, viennas, beef burger, tomato, mushroom and chips. The lamb and steak would undoubtedly be first rate, as meat here tends to be chargrilled to perfection. There's a good choice of fish too, ranging from gefilte fish with chrain to more elegant dover sole. If you can manage dessert after the generous portions, sorbets and chocolate mousse look more promising than the traditional lockshen pudding or strudel.
Babies and children welcome: high chairs. Booking advisable (restaurant). Kosher supervised (Sephardi). Tables outdoors (3, pavement). Takeaway service. **Map 3 G5**.

North

Finchley

★ The Burger Bar

110 Regents Park Road, N3 3JG (8371 1555). Finchley Central tube. **Meals served** noon-midnight Mon-Thur; noon-11pm Sun. **Main courses** £5.40-£6.95. **No credit cards.**

Photos of 1960s America hang above the plain tables. Outside there are dark wooden benches, but opt for a takeaway and you might park overlooking a field of buttercups: part of the farm opposite the restaurant. Portions are huge: 300g (11oz) of meat in a burger, wraps that come in twos, and a big mound of chips. The burgers are of juicy beef, and buns are filled with an array of extras like aubergine or peppers, fried egg or, for the more adventurous, beetroot or sweet potato. The wraps are thin and chargrilled, with a filling of sliced minute steak or chicken, anointed with a sweet chilli sauce. To appreciate the taste of the meat, it might be better to avoid the pot of guacamole. For vegetarians there's a portobello mushroom burger and a side salad of mixed leaves with avocado, red onions and pine nuts. Children can choose from chicken wings or nuggets, or a small burger and a faux milkshake. Unlike adults, who will be stuffed, kids may also want to try a dessert of apple pie or warm chocolate pudding.
Babies and children welcome: children's menu. Booking advisable. Kosher supervised (Federation). Tables outdoors (8, pavement). Takeaway service.

Olive Restaurant

224 Regents Park Road, N3 3HP (8343 3188/ www.olivekosherrestaurant.co.uk). Finchley Central tube. **Meals served** 10am-11pm Mon-Thur, Sun; 10am-5pm Fri. **Main courses** £10-£18. **Set meal** £20 2 courses (minimum 2). **Credit** AmEx, MC, V.

This kosher Iranian restaurant has been revamped, with the space being expanded and walls hung with tapestry and beaten trays. Persian music plays gently and unintrusively in the background. The tables (quiet at lunchtime) are laid with crisp white linen and fresh roses. The menu is authentic, though for Persian tastes there are some lapses; ash-e-reshteh (a hearty soup with beans, spinach, lentils and freshly made noodles) was rich but too peppery. Ghormeh sabzi (a lamb stew) was short on the advertised lime, consisting of little meat in a soupy liquid. Kebabs – minced or flattened lamb, beef or chicken – came with perfect shirin polo, a sweet rice dish with saffron, orange and slivers of nuts. The beef wasn't the most tender, but the portion was almost big enough to feed two. Rice is certainly a strong point, with another version, tahdig, featuring the crisp crust from the pan base. It came covered with okra and tomato sauce, which might have been better served on the side. Complimentary juicy clementines from Iran are offered for dessert. Even if you've no room for them, order

Olive Restaurant. See p209.

mint tea with pistachio baklava; staff bring eight triangles, which are easily enough to take home a sweet memory of Persian cuisine.
Babies and children welcome: children's menu; high chairs. Booking advisable. Disabled: toilet. Kosher supervised (Sephardi). Restaurant available for hire. Tables outdoors (3, pavement). Takeaway service.

Orli

108 Regents Park Road, N3 3JG (8371 9222). Finchley Central tube. **Meals served** 8am-11pm Mon-Thur, Sun; 8am-4pm Fri. **Main courses** £6.95-£13.95. **Unlicensed**. **No credit cards**.
The three Orli cafés serving fish and dairy food are under the same ownership as Eighty-Six (*see p212*), the Burger Bar (*see p209*) and an excellent bakery. The decor here is unremarkable: photos of the USA with plain dark tables and chairs, and unsubtle lighting. What brings in the punters is the all-day menu: omelettes, borekas and danish pastries for breakfast, through to full evening dinner. In between there's freshly squeezed orange juice or coffee, with an inviting selection of cakes. The cooking is at its best when simple: grilled salmon or sea bass (rather than the fish in cream sauce); or deep bowls of gutsy soup with fresh challah rolls. Salads are towering, literally – topped with tuna or palm hearts and fried halloumi cheese; needing little attention from a chef. In a starter salad called 'bebe' creamy houmous with pickles and hard-boiled egg covered a vast plate (imagine the size of a 'grown-up'). The young staff are amiable: agreeing to turn down the music, and apologising for the lack of a ripe avocado. All very pleasant, but variety of dishes and sheer quantity seem more evident than memorable flavours.
Babies and children welcome: children's menu; high chairs. Booking advisable. Kosher supervised (Federation). Tables outdoors (4, pavement). Takeaway service. Vegetarian menu.
For branches see index.

North West
Golders Green

Armando

252 Golders Green Road, NW11 9NN (8455 8159). Brent Cross tube. **Lunch served** noon-3pm, **dinner served** 6-11pm Mon-Thur, Sun. **Main courses** £8-£16. **Sushi** £3.50-£6. **Credit** MC, V.
Away from the bustling end of Golders Green, this unusual little restaurant hides behind a dark exterior. Inside, there's seating for barely two dozen. Tables are set with large metallic plates and candles, adding to the glow from woven foil wall lights. Armando, the chef-proprietor, is passionate about Japanese and Italian cuisines and creates adventurous fusion cooking. Half his menu is devoted to sushi and sashimi, but instead of dairy dishes, he now specialises in meat. We tried a starter of edamame (soy beans in pods) with crunchy sea salt while we chose between aged entrecôte steak, chicken or pasta, opting for conchiglie (shells) with a pleasantly spiced chicken liver and tomato sauce. From the Japanese menu there was no tuna or yellowtail, but the salmon and sea bass nigiri sushi was adequately prepared. An American influence can be seen in the maki, with california and other inside-out rolls offered. Armando is perfect for Orthodox diners wanting raw fish while their companion tucks into bistecca or chicken cacciatore. For dessert there's a choice between pear, chocolate or lemon tart. It's not cheap (lemon tea, £3.50), but it's worth visiting. Next time we'll try more meat.
Babies and children admitted. Booking advisable. Kosher supervised (Beth Din). Tables outdoors (2, pavement). Takeaway service.

Bloom's

130 Golders Green Road, NW11 8HB (8455 1338/www.blooms-restaurant.co.uk). Golders Green tube. **Lunch served** noon-3pm Fri. **Meals served** noon-10.30pm Mon-Thur, Sun. **Main courses** £15-£25. **Credit** AmEx, MC, V.
Things aren't what they used to be at Bloom's. The East End photographic mural has been replaced with a garish depiction of Moses at the Red Sea.

More important, Leon, a waiter at Bloom's for 40 years, has left. Instead of his cheery banter ('you want water? I'll ask my secretary to get it for you') a young waiter will set down an expanded menu by the square crockery and heavy new cutlery. Curries and grills have been added to the old favourites of chopped herring, chicken soup and tongue. With competition all along the road, the owners have astutely judged that increasing prices as well as variety brings in customers. Now they even offer veggie burgers and main course salads. Yet looking around, most people are spreading unctuous chopped liver on rye bread, or tucking into soup and knaidlach. Apart from pickled cucumbers, there's little that's green on the plates that follow. A wise choice would be schnitzel or goulash. Warm salt beef still comes in vast portions, sadly without the fat that used to make it extra succulent. Don't bother with apple crumble and faux custard, have a glass of lemon tea instead and dream of the old days.
Babies and children welcome: children's menu; high chairs. Kosher supervised (Beth Din). Takeaway service.
For branch see index.

★ Chopstick NEW
119 Golders Green Road, NW11 8HR (8455 7766). Golders Green tube. **Meals served** 11am-2am Mon-Thur, Sun; 11am-5am Sat. **Main courses** £6-£9. **Set meal** £12 1 course incl soft drink. **No credit cards.**
A new addition in the kosher restaurant mile of London, Chopstick has Chinese staff, red lanterns and – apart from the absence of pork – a menu typical of many Soho noodle bars. Advertised in the window are the lunch specials and the fact that no MSG is used in the cooking. There's a strong emphasis on the deep fryer. Most starters and many of the chicken dishes arrive in batter, though the fried dishes aren't really crisp, as many are immersed in sweet, bright sauces. Well-flavoured noodles or rice form the base for the meat dishes. Thinly sliced steak comes in a peppery sauce. Sticky lamb ribs or duck are alternatives for meat-lovers. Vegetarians will be pleased to find curried and stir-fried vegetables here, as well as crispy seaweed and edamame (soy beans in their pods). There's a large choice, and the set menus are popular with hungry teenagers. More discerning parents might avoid the potato wedges and caramelised chicken wings, and might prefer a pot of green tea to the slightly insipid sorbets. But the fried chocolate is something to be tried: two plump fritters filled with melting chocolate.
Babies and children welcome: high chairs. Booking advisable. Kosher supervised (Sephardi). Restaurant available for hire. Tables outdoors (2, pavement). Takeaway service.

★ Dizengoff's
118 Golders Green Road, NW11 8HB (8458 7003/www.dizengoffkosherrestaurant.co.uk). Golders Green tube. **Meals served** Summer 11am-11.30pm Mon-Thur, Sun; noon-3.30pm Fri. Winter 11am-11.30pm Mon-Thur, Sun; noon-3.30pm Fri; 7pm-1am Sat. **Main courses** £12-£18. **Credit** AmEx, MC, V.
Under low-voltage lights and canvas photos of Tel Aviv's coastline, Dizengoff's can offer a casual meal or a Middle Eastern feast. Our lunch was a lively affair, despite only a pair of occupied tables. A waiter, ancient and smiling, arrived with a plate of green olives, pickled carrot, spiced cauliflower and the menu. Compliments on the lemony Yemenite soup, kooba, flew across the restaurant in Hebrew; another customer campaigned for the chicken soup. We opted instead for meze favourites, such as houmous and a slightly smoky aubergine pâté: creamy, gutsy and authentically Israeli. Charcoal grilled meats are Dizengoff's speciality (chips or rice and salad included, not extra). We were tempted by a juicy steak at another table, but it was hard to resist the lamb shwarma. This comes generously packed in pitta bread, topped with crunchy salad. Chips (cut in-house) are crisp and sumptuous. The extensive menu caters for the kosher palate yearning for classics (such as schnitzel, moussaka and tandoori chicken) that

would otherwise be inaccessible. For dessert, baklava wasn't up to the usual standard, but fresh mint tea was sweet and refreshing.
Babies and children welcome: children's menu; high chairs. Booking essential weekends. Kosher supervised (Sephardi). Tables outdoors (3, pavement). Takeaway service.

★ Entrecote NEW
102 Golders Green Road NW11 8HB (8455 3862). Golders Green tube. **Meals served** 10.30am-midnight Mon-Fri, Sun. **Main courses** £4.50-£9.50. **No credit cards.**
Yet another new venue is jostling for space amid the dozen or so kosher restaurants on Golders Green Road. This is a 'bar', decked out in striking silver, black and red decor, with stools at the counter overlooking the cooking or facing out towards the bustle of the street. 'Entrecôte' conjures up a juicy French steak-frites, but here the beef is given the Israeli treatment: beaten thin, deftly seared and flipped on a grill, then chopped and scooped into freshly made flat pancakes. The production on our visit (five weeks after opening) was smooth and fast. Three staff try to deliver chunky chips, onion rings and drinks, while the chef smooths guacamole and a range of salads into the pancakes to roll up with the beef. The menu is sensibly short. Apart from the steak there's chicken or chorizo – good value pick-up-and-go food for families or teenagers. The owners made a wise decision: no fake milkshakes, but fruit shakes with the refreshing taste of berries, mango or passion fruit.
Babies and children admitted. Restaurant available for hire. Tables outdoors (3, pavement). Takeaway service.

La Fiesta
235 Golders Green Road, NW11 9ES (8458 0444/www.lafiestauk.com). Brent Cross tube. **Meals served** noon-11pm Mon-Thur, Sun. **Main courses** £8.75-£26.50. **Set lunch** £15.50 3 courses. **Credit** MC, V.
The front area of this Argentinean-style steak house – overlooking the charcoal grill, with a display of mouth-watering steaks – is for snacks and takeaway burgers. The restaurant is at the back, with ponchos and photos of Argentina on the walls, and solid pine tables. Avoid the tables near the open kitchen door, as the view is not of rolling South American pastureland, but of bins and ladders. Starters arrive on chunky white china: meat or mushroom empanadas or chorizo. Soups are filling; we found the tomato and roasted pepper more flavourful than the chicken, which we suspect had seen little of the bird. Locals praise the meat: lamb cutlets, entrecôte steak, brochettes and the asado ribs on the bone. This is usually excellent, but cooking can be variable, with lapses of attention resulting in uneven grilling (though the flavour is invariably good). Reserve your appetite for main courses; a salad is brought before the sizzling grills. The portions of meat (sadly served on cold plates on our visit) are generous, as are the chunky chips. Desserts (crêpes or bananas topped with faux cream and ice-cream) aren't a strong point. Come here with hungry friends – and not vegetarians.
Babies and children admitted. Booking advisable dinner. Kosher supervised (Beth Din). Takeaway service.

Mattancherry
109A Golders Green Road, NW11 8HR (8209 3060/www.mattancherry.net). Golders Green tube. **Lunch served** noon-2.30pm Mon-Fri, Sun. **Dinner served** 6-10.45pm Mon-Fri, Sun. **Main courses** £10.90-£17.95. **Set lunch** (Mon-Fri) £12.95 2 courses. **Credit** MC, V.
Mattancherry takes its name from a town in India's southern state of Kerala, though the style of food here is mainly North Indian. At lunchtime it's comparatively quiet and there's a good-value set menu at £12.95 for two courses including rice or bread. The main menu lists ample curries and birianis, and explains the differences between korma, bhuna and ghosht. Apart from the lamb, chicken and beef dishes, there are many vegetarian choices. From the buffet, dhal soup was thin and

lemony, but nan bread, red tandoori chicken and chickpea chana masala had authentic flavours. From the main menu, both the beef in the vindaloo and the lamb in the bhuna was well-spiced yet hardly tender, though golden kashmiri rice with saffron, raisins, cashews and apple made a good foil for the beef. With so much choice, a meal here is a bit hit and miss. Fruit salad was refreshing, but pistachio kulfi was a pale imitation of the authentic creamy version made with real milk. The pleasant Indian waiters are happy to elaborate on the menu. Yet there's something unrelaxing about the bright-orange surroundings.
Babies and children admitted. Booking advisable dinner. Kosher supervised (Kedassia). Takeaway service. Vegetarian menu.

Met Su Yan
134 Golders Green Road, NW11 8HB (8458 8088/www.metsuyan.co.uk). Golders Green tube. **Lunch served** noon-2.30pm, **dinner served** 6-11pm Mon-Thur, Sun. **Main courses** £12.95-£15.95. **Set lunch** £12.95 2 courses. **Set meal** £25 3 courses, £30 4 courses. **Credit** AmEx, MC, V.
The name comes from the Hebrew word for excellence and Met Su Yan is certainly one of the most elegant and attractive of London's kosher restaurants. White walls are hung with calming photographs of water and mountains; gentle music plays. Lunchtimes tend to be quiet, in spite of the enticing, good-value special menu. The food is oriental fusion: Japanese sushi and steamed or pan-fried fish, plus an array of Chinese poultry and meat dishes. Although the menu is short on vegetarian main courses, there are numerous vegetable starters and side dishes. Crisp iceberg leaves are served next to chopped, fried ingredients (choose from mixed veg, chicken, or crispy lamb) in the 'lettuce wraps'. Popular dishes include sesame chicken toast and barbecued lamb ribs. Sizzling chicken with black bean sauce or ginger and spring onions is a better bet than the costly aromatic duck. Beef and lamb come in many guises, and coconut rice or fried noodles make great accompaniments to the sauces, which some may find over-salted. Service is unobtrusive, but staff have to remember to wipe the tables between courses. There are fruit fritters and an intriguing chocolate volcano to finish.
Babies and children welcome: high chairs. Booking advisable. Kosher supervised (Federation). Takeaway service; delivery service (over £30 within 2-mile radius).

★ Novellino
103 Golders Green Road, NW11 8EN (8458 7273). Golders Green tube. **Meals served** 8.30am-11.30pm Mon-Thur, Sun; 8.30am-4pm Fri. **Main courses** £9-£18. **Credit** MC, V.
A basket of country breads with butter or olive oil and tapenade signals the theme at this Italian kosher restaurant and bakery: freshly cooked food with wide appeal. One of the busiest lunchtime haunts in a street full of restaurants, Novellino packs in customers for a full meal or an appetising snack. Starters and salads are bracketed together, but our plate of antipasto with roasted vegetables, smoked salmon and camembert was large enough for a main course. Vegetarians enjoy a wide choice: roast beetroot, aubergine parmigiana, mushroom bruschetta or baked butternut squash with cheese. Pastas include the usual spaghetti with tomato and garlic sauce, but also appealing variations such as wide strips of fettuccine with mushroom, with salmon or with the more inventive cod and green vegetables. A bland asparagus risotto with too-firm rice was less successful. From the fish selection, apart from the popular salmon and crispy tempura, there's sea bream with orange and broad bean sauce. Best of all was the pavé of tuna: two thick, generous rounds with a sesame crust, perfectly cooked leaving a rare centre. The dessert counter contains professionally made pâtisserie, including chocolate delicacies and coffee macaroons with a sumptuous mocha filling.
Babies and children welcome: children's menu; high chairs. Booking advisable. Disabled: toilet. Kosher supervised (Beth Din). Tables outdoors (5, pavement). Takeaway service.

Solly's

148A Golders Green Road, NW11 8HE (ground floor & takeaway 8455 2121/first floor 8455 0004). Golders Green tube. **Ground floor Lunch served** 11.30am-5pm Fri. **Meals served** 11.30am-11pm Mon-Thur, Sun. *Winter* 1hr after sabbath-1am Sat. **First floor Lunch served** 12.30-4.30pm Sun. **Dinner served** 6.30-11pm Mon-Thur, Sun. *Winter* 1hr after sabbath-midnight Sat. *Both* **Main courses** £10-£15. **Set dinner** £26 3 courses. **No credit cards**.

After fire destroyed Solly's first-floor restaurant, the building was still under reconstruction at the time of our visit. Downstairs, the wipe-clean tables are closely packed, making it noisy at busy times (most evenings). Service is friendly but sometimes hurried; main courses might arrive before starter plates are cleared. The Middle Eastern food is consistent: great houmous and aubergine dishes, spicy cigars and a lemony, if soupy, fuul medames, served with perfect laffa cooked in the pitta oven at the back. Main courses are mostly grills, served in large portions; the 'special' consists of boned chicken, kebabs, chops and steaks. Happily, crunchy chips and Iraqi-type rice with vermicelli are included with main courses, as is a shredded salad with no dressing. For traditionalists, there's chicken or goulash soup and salt beef, though most customers seem to choose Israeli food, with falafel and shwarma top takeaway favourites. Apart from the varied vegetable starters, vegetarians don't fare well. It will be interesting to see what the refurbished 'exclusive' restaurant will offer. To live up to that description it will need some refinements and careful service. Meanwhile, order a mint tea and baklava and dream.
Babies and children welcome: high chairs. Disabled: toilet. Kosher supervised (Beth Din). Takeaway service.

Hendon

Beit Hamadras NEW

105 Brent Street, NW4 2DX (8203 4567/ www.beithamadras.co.uk). Hendon Central tube. **Dinner served** 5.30-11pm Mon-Thur. **Meals served** noon-3pm, 5.30-11pm Sun. **Main courses** £17.50-£25.50. **Set meal** £12.95 3 courses. **Credit** AmEx, MC, V.

The name means Madras House and is a Hebrew pun for those in the know (being similar to Beit Midrash: 'place of learning'). The blue awning outside and elegant maroon walls inside look typically Indian. In the first week after the restaurant's opening, waiters, wearing matching maroon silk, were eager to please, bringing complimentary popadoms. Tables are a little too close together and not quite large enough to accommodate the many dishes that follow – some time after the arrival of heated plates, in our case. Vegetable samosas were crisp, with a dominant cinnamon flavour; the onion bhajis were crisp too, but slightly mealy inside. Main courses were more successful: tender marinated lamb chops, tandoori chicken (sizzling and pleasantly spiced), and a lamb korma that, in spite of the necessary substitution for cream, was mild and rich with coconut and almonds. Birianis come with saffron-streaked rice; okra is sautéed with onions and tomatoes. The curries and grills include several fish options, but prices are high. We finished with a refreshing pistachio kheer (rice pudding); sadly, the fresh mango or fruit salad versions weren't available. We hope the proprietors will iron out the early teething troubles.
Babies and children welcome: children's menu; high chairs. Booking advisable. Kosher supervised (Federation). Takeaway service.

La Dorada

134 Brent Street, NW4 2DR (8202 1339). Hendon Central tube. **Meals served** noon-10pm Mon-Thur, Sun. **Main courses** £10.95-£18.95. **Set meal** (until 6.30pm) £11.95 2 courses; (6.30-10pm) £15.95 2 courses. **Credit** MC, V.

Fried fish was reputedly brought to England by Portuguese Marranos in the 16th century. Serving it cold was certainly a Jewish tradition, much admired by English gourmets years later, so it's no surprise that a kosher fish restaurant should thrive in Hendon. The pictures on the walls are reminiscent of open-air art shows, but they brighten up an otherwise plain interior. Tables are wipe-clean and set with vinegar and ketchup – essential additions for fried fish. This is what La Dorada does well: cod, haddock, plaice on the bone or even dover sole, crisp fried in matzo meal with a flaky, fresh inside. Chips are faultless. In the evening the place is busy with takeaway orders, but if you decide to eat-in there's a choice of starters that involve no cooking (egg mayonnaise, avocado, and the like) and the usual salad and pasta options. More expensive are the grills: thick portions of fish with a wine or pesto sauce. For these prices you'd expect staff who can talk about the food, and a generally higher standard of management and care. So our advice is to stick to the fried fish and forget about starters or dessert.
Babies and children welcome: children's menu; high chairs. Kosher supervised (Beth Din). Takeaway service.

★ Eighty-Six Bistro Bar

86 Brent Street, NW4 2ES (8202 5575). Hendon Central tube. **Lunch served** noon-3pm Sun. **Dinner served** 5.30-11pm Mon-Thur, Sun. **Main courses** £9.95-£22.95. **Credit** MC, V.

The decor isn't particularly French and the charming waiter is Hungarian, but the cuisine at Eighty-Six is studied and careful, using top-class meat. Crudités and tomato-topped crostini are brought with the menu, and balloon glasses are filled with Israeli or French wine. This is a haven for meat-eaters, with a changing menu offering food that's rarely available in kosher restaurants: a sweet-sauced foie gras with apples and calvados, carpaccio of beef, and veal chops, for example – all quite pricey. Less expensive are the salads and burgers. Starters of chicken liver pâté and herb-crusted lamb were perfectly executed: the pâté smooth and rich and the lamb schnitzel pink in the middle. Main courses come with rice or potatoes (baby roast or fried). We can't recommend the duck, which arrives with a concoction of jammy fruit. We can, however, vouch for the whole, freshly cooked sea bass. Portions are huge so you won't have room for cake or pie to finish. The problem here is pricing. Only one side dish was offered between three of us (a stack of roasted aubergine, carrots, peppers and courgettes), and even without dessert the bill was the highest we were charged in kosher London.
Babies and children welcome: children's portions; high chairs. Booking advisable. Kosher supervised (Federation). Takeaway service.

★ Fernando's Chicken Grill Bar NEW

56 The Burroughs, NW4 2DX (8203 5313). Hendon Central tube.. **Meals served** noon-midnight Mon-Thur, Sun. **Main courses** £5-£25. **Credit** MC, V.

Claiming to be Europe's first kosher gastropub, Fernando's is proving enormously popular with a young Jewish crowd. Long tables and an L-shaped bar accommodate those who come to play on the machines and watch football on the large screen. It's like a party, where food is only part of the story. The Israeli owners have sensibly decided to offer simply chicken – grilled or served in pitta or burger buns, in generous portions. For those who can tear themselves away from the music throbbing from the sound system, there are bottomless soft drinks (fill your glass as often as you like) to accompany the chicken. No one will go hungry: the barbecued chicken wings are big and plump; a large portion of chips is enough for two. To start, there's a salad bar and some Mediterranean meze, including cigars and falafel, plus onion rings. For vegetarians there are standard veggie burgers or schnitzels. It will be interesting to see how the locals react: whether they choose a takeaway or prefer the lively, hot atmosphere. Either way, the staff need to be more attentive to get the orders right, and out on time.
Babies and children welcome: children's menu; high chairs. Kosher supervised (Beth Din). Tables outdoors (12, garden). Takeaway service.

Kavanna

60 Vivian Avenue, NW4 3XH (8202 9449/ www.kavanna.co.uk). Hendon Central tube. **Dinner served** 5.30-11pm Mon-Thur, Sun. **Main courses** £9.50-£15.50. **Set meal** £22 per person (minimum 2), £20 per person (minimum 4). **Credit** MC, V.

From the outside, Kavanna looks like a small white temple; inside there are linen-topped tables with elegant high-backed chairs. Service comes with a smile, though at times can be slow. Indian food is the speciality: baltis, birianis and meat grilled in a clay oven (appetisingly sizzling), plus more than 20 vegetarian dishes. The menu resembles that of a standard British curry house, but here spicing is mild and creamy sauces are created from soya milk. The chef blends almonds with onions and tomatoes; ginger and garlic with peppers, though only a few dishes merit the red chilli symbol denoting intense heat. Starters are filling. Anglo-Indian mulligatawny soup ('pepper water' in Tamil) is a smooth, silky blend. Lamb samosas are crisp and satisfying, and a portion of tandoori chicken is enough for two. As a main course, chicken massala delivered tomato creaminess over tender leg portions, but lamb in a similar sauce was more sparing and tough. Rice and potatoes come in various fragrant guises; peshwari nan (leavened bread stuffed with coconut, sultanas and almonds) is a must. To finish, pass up the apple-dominant fruit salad or faux-cream desserts in favour of Indian honey cake or halva.
Babies and children welcome: children's portions; high chairs. Booking advisable. Kosher supervised (Beth Din and Sephardi). Takeaway service. Vegetarian menu.

Sami's Kosher Restaurant

157 Brent Street, NW4 4DJ (8203 8088). Hendon Central tube. **Meals served** noon-11pm Mon-Thur, Sun. **Main courses** £11.95-£14.50. **Set lunch** (Mon-Thur) £9.95-£12.95 2 courses. **Credit** MC, V.

The combination of hard surfaces – stone floor, mirrors and a wall of glass – makes the noise reverberate at Sami's, so if tables are full, attempting conversation can be frustrating. Staff are pleasant and efficient, bringing a menu that's more varied than you'd expect from a small neighbourhood restaurant. They offer three types of cuisine here: 'A taste of India', charcoal grills and homely Iraqi dishes. You'd encounter starters like houmous, tabouleh and aubergines in Israel, but Sami's also has dishes that you'd find in an Iraqi home, such as deep-fried cigars or kooba. The home-cooked theme continues with stuffed peppers, and a beetroot-sauced shwandar of chicken in a rice and semolina dough. Tabeet, the sabbath chicken and rice dish, was tasty but didn't seem to have undergone the required slow cooking that gives deep flavour and melting texture. Perhaps this type of food can't succeed in a restaurant, so an option is to choose chargrilled meat or fish. Lamb cutlets are especially good and there are 15 'snacks' which can be stuffed into the freshly made Iraqi pitta bread. With portions generous, we didn't have space for the desserts, though were tempted by the hot chocolate cake and baklava.
Babies and children welcome: children's menu; high chairs. Kosher supervised (Federation). Takeaway service.

St John's Wood

Harry Morgan's

31 St John's Wood High Street, NW8 7NH (7722 1869/www.harryms.co.uk). St John's Wood tube. **Breakfast served** 8.30-10.30am Mon-Fri. **Meals served** 11.30am-10pm Mon-Fri; noon-10pm Sat, Sun. **Main courses** £9.95-£12.95. **Credit** AmEx, MC, V. **Not kosher**.

Set in the middle of boutique land, this old-established eaterie still pulls in the punters. The awning outside advertises what's on offer: salt beef, chopped liver, chicken soup, blintzes, borscht. Inside, the decor is simple and functional: mirrors and a wall trumpeting the restaurant's reviews ('best chicken soup in London'). At the back is a bar with bottles that seem to have been arranged by an interior decorator, yet few people drink wine here with their hefty portions of Jewish-style food. The menu caters to the lunch-and-shop crowd, with houmous and falafel, as well as salads. Our sautéed chicken with peppers and mushrooms on a bed of mixed leaves didn't have the *heimishe* (home-made) taste of salt beef or tongue. Fish also comes in trendy versions: even the fried haddock is served hot (unlike the authentic cold fish served in England since Spanish Jews brought the dish here). Since Harry's doesn't follow rules of kashrut, patrons can choose dairy desserts after their meat. We found these hit and miss; lockshen pudding and blintzes weren't as good as Grandma made, but the cheesecake and the warm almond tart were of professional pâtisserie standard.

Babies and children welcome: children's portions; high chairs. Booking advisable (not accepted Sat, Sun). Tables outdoors (5, pavement). Takeaway service. **Map 2 E2**.
For branch see index.

Outer London

Edgware, Middlesex

★ **Aviv**

87-89 High Street, Edgware, Middx HA8 7DB (8952 2484/www.avivrestaurant.com). Edgware tube. **Lunch served** noon-2.30pm, **dinner served** 5.30-10.30pm Mon-Thur, Sun.

Main courses £10.95-£16.95. **Set lunch** (noon-2.30pm Mon-Thur) £9.95 2 courses. **Set meal** £16.95-£20.95 3 courses. **Credit** AmEx, MC, V.

Aviv is expanding: taking over other restaurants (Met Su Yan – *see p211*) and enlarging its own space. The expansion has meant more space for more dinner tables and a private room for parties, but it's still packed to the gills with diners most evenings. The reason? Not amazing food, but a great selection of dishes and competitive prices. Even the set menus offer eight choices for each course. The traditional Ashkenazi soups or chopped liver are fine, but it's best to go for the Israeli starters: kooba with a crisp shell and meat filling, or houmous with lamb and pine nuts which is almost a meal in itself. Grills are competent (if occasionally overcooked) and the kebabs and rib steaks are flavourful. Less appealing was a vivid chicken escalope or half a barbecued chicken with an oversweet sauce. Chips and rice are perfect, and the mixed vegetables (courgette, carrot and mangetout) arrive crisply sautéd. For dessert there are more decent choices: a hot chocolate 'volcano', sticky toffee pudding with an even stickier toffee sauce, and a good fruit salad. Ice-cream is the parev equivalent. Service is swift and pleasant, with waiters bringing large plates that, unlike in classier places, are filled to capacity.

Babies and children welcome: children's portions; high chairs. Booking essential. Kosher supervised (Federation). Tables outdoors (14, patio). Takeaway service.

Ralphy's New York Grill

32-34 Station Road, Edgware, Middx HA8 7AB (8952 6036/www.ralphys.com). Edgware tube. **Lunch served** noon-3pm, **dinner served** 6-11pm Mon-Thur, Sun. **Main courses** £5.95-£15.95. **Set lunch** (Mon-Thur) £8.50 1 course incl soft drink. **Set meal** £19.95 3 courses. **Credit** AmEx, MC, V.

Away from the cluster of Jewish shops and delis at the other end of Station Road, Ralphy's emulates a New York diner, but somehow without the bustle and style. The food is named after famous landmarks (Empire State, Central Park, Staten Island and so on), but the ambitious claim of 'bringing the Big Apple to Edgware' doesn't quite succeed. There are photos of baseball players and New York bridges on the walls. The corned beef comes thinly sliced, rather than in thick chunks like the salt beef in the UK, and it lacks flavour. Perhaps a burger or pastrami sandwich would be a better bet. Starters include vegetable egg roll (crisp and tasty, though a bit oily) and 'fire poppers' (boneless chicken pieces in spicy barbecue sauce, served with a small pot of rice like a mini main course). The steak salad – juicy slivers of beef tossed with capers and tomatoes – could have done with a less overpowering dressing. That said, the three-course set menu is good value, and in the evenings Ralphy's is heaving with families enjoying the deli-style food. The desserts are surprisingly good; the chocolate fondant is a wow.

Babies and children welcome: children's menu; high chairs. Booking advisable. Kosher supervised (Beth Din). Takeaway service.

Menu

There are two main strands of cooking: Ashkenazi from Russia and eastern Europe; and Sephardi, originating in Spain and Portugal. After the Inquisition, Sephardi Jews settled throughout the Mediterranean, in Iraq and further east. London used to contain mainly Ashkenazi restaurants, but now Hendon and Golders Green are full of Sephardi bakeries and cafés, specialising in the Middle Eastern food you might find in Jerusalem. You can still get traditional chicken soup and knaidlach or fried latkes, but these are never as good as you'll find in the home. Nor will you find the succulent, slow-cooked Sabbath dishes that are made in many homes every Friday. The Israeli-type restaurants are strong on grilled meats and offer a range of fried or vegetable starters.

Since most kosher restaurants serve meat (and therefore can't serve dairy products), desserts are not a strong point. Rather than non-dairy ice-cream, it's better to choose baklava or chocolate pudding. Though, by the time you've got through the generous portions served in most places, you may not have room for anything more than a glass of mint or lemon tea.

Bagels or **beigels**: heavy, ring-shaped rolls. The dough is first boiled then glazed and baked. The classic filling is smoked salmon and cream cheese.
Baklava: filo pastry layered with almonds or pistachios and soaked in scented syrup.
Blintzes: pancakes, most commonly filled with cream cheese, but also with sweet or savoury fillings.
Borekas: triangles of filo pastry with savoury fillings like cheese or spinach.
Borscht: a classic beetroot soup served either hot or cold, often with sour cream.
Challah or **cholla**: egg-rich, slightly sweet plaited bread for the Sabbath.
Chicken soup: a clear, golden broth made from chicken and vegetables.
Cholent: a hearty, long-simmered bean, vegetable and (sometimes) meat stew, traditionally served for the sabbath.
Chopped liver: chicken or calf's liver fried with onions, finely chopped and mixed with hard-boiled egg and chicken fat. Served cold, often with extra egg and onions.
Chrane or **chrain**: a pungent sauce made from grated horseradish and beetroot, served with cold fish.
Cigars: rolls of filo pastry with a sweet or savoury filling.
Falafel: spicy, deep-fried balls of ground chickpeas, served with houmous and tahina (sesame paste).
Gefilte fish: white fish minced with onions and seasoning, made into balls and poached or fried; served cold. The sweetened version is Polish.
Houmous: chickpeas puréed with sesame paste, lemon juice, garlic and oil, served cold.
Kataifi or **konafa**: shredded filo pastry wrapped around a nut or cheese filling, soaked in syrup.
Kibbe, kuba, kooba, kubbeh or **kobeiba**: oval patties, handmade from a shell of crushed wheat (bulgar) filled with minced meat, pine nuts and spices. Shaping and filling the shells before frying is the skill.
Knaidlach or **kneidlach**: dumplings made from matzo (qv) meal and eggs, poached until they float 'like clouds' in chicken soup. Also called matzo balls.
Kreplach: pockets of noodle dough filled with meat and served in soup, or with sweet fillings and eaten with sour cream.
Laffa: large puffy pitta bread used to enclose falafel or shwarma (qv).
Latkes: grated potato mixed with egg and fried into crisp pancakes.
Lockshen: egg noodles boiled and served in soup. When cold, they can be mixed with egg, sugar and cinnamon and baked into a pudding.
Matzo or **matzah**: flat squares of unleavened bread. When ground into meal, it is used to make a crisp coating for fish or schnitzel.
Parev or **parve**: a term describing food that is neither meat nor dairy.
Rugelach: crescent-shaped biscuits made from a rich, cream cheese pastry, filled with nuts, jam or chocolate. Popular in Israel and the US.
Salt beef: pickled brisket, with a layer of fat, poached and served in slices.
Schnitzel: thin slices of chicken, turkey or veal, dipped in egg and matzo meal and fried.
Shwarma: layers of lamb or turkey, cooked on a spit, served with pitta.
Strudel: wafer-thin pastry wrapped around an apple or soft cheese filling.
Tabouleh: cracked wheat (bulgar) mixed with ample amounts of fresh herbs, tomato and lemon juice, served as a starter or salad.
Viennas: boiled frankfurter sausages, served with chips and salt beef.
Worsht: beef salami, sliced thinly to eat raw, but usually cut in thick pieces and fried when served with eggs or chips.

Korean

Korean food is the little-known gem of Asian dining in London. The capital has the largest expat Korean population in Europe; at last count, there were 20,000 Korean citizens living in the city. Given such a large customer base, you might expect these restaurants to crop up all over town, but Korean food is mainly found in two well-defined enclaves – Soho and New Malden, on the south-west edge of the city. If you want to sample this famously healthy cuisine, you'll have to make a trip to one of these two areas, or try the smattering of Korean establishments in Mayfair and Golders Green.

The core ingredients of Korean food are denjang (fermented soy-bean paste, like a stronger version of miso) and kimchi (fermented vegetable pickle, usually including chinese leaf, with chilli and garlic). Most Korean dishes include at least one of these two ingredients, and many include both. Several Korean restaurants in London are kalbi houses, specialising in table-top barbecues. Thin slices of marinated beef, pork, chicken and seafood are cooked on a gas-fired grill, then wrapped in lettuce leaves with denjang paste. The name kalbi (also spelled galbi) comes from the most popular cut of beef in Korea – a thin slice taken from the front of the rib. Whatever you order, expect the meal to come with a selection of panch'an (small dishes), including kimchi and a selection of namul (vegetable side dishes).

Some of the best Korean cooking can be found at **Jee Cee Neh** in New Malden and **Cah Chi** in Raynes Park. In the West End, **Asadal**, **Kaya** and **Jin** offer top-notch dishes for the after-office crowd, while laid-back **Nara**, **Jindalle**, **Myung Ga** and **Bi Won** provide authentic food at more accessible prices. **Palace, Sorabol** and **Yami** have swelled the ranks of Korean eateries on New Malden High Street. To beat the credit crunch, take advantage of the cheap set menus offered by most of these restaurants at lunchtime.

Central
Bloomsbury

★ ★ Bi Won
24 Coptic Street, WC1A 1NT (7580 2660).
Holborn or Tottenham Court Road tube. **Meals served** noon-11pm daily. **Main courses** £5-£8.
Set lunch £6.50. **Set meal** £17-£25 per person (minimum 2). **Credit** MC, V.
The kimchi chigae at Bi Won is one of the best quick lunches in the West End. Served bubbling in a hot stone bowl, the stew is packed with thin slices of belly pork, green onions, tofu and fermented cabbage, with a chilli kick that almost lifts off the top of your head. This is one of half a dozen dishes you can try as part of the bargain set lunch, which comes with rice, soup and a selection of panch'an. Over the past few years, we've enjoyed every dish we've tried here, and the bright, wood-lined dining room is a great place to retreat from shopping on Oxford Street or trawling around the British Museum. As well as the chigae, we recommend the tolsot bibimbap (rice, meat and vegetables cooked in a stone pot – here enlivened by the addition of pine nuts) and the jajangmyun (thin, Chinese-style noodles rolled in sweet soy sauce). The menu also runs to sashimi and Japanese bento-style box meals, but for our money, the Korean food wins every time.
Babies and children admitted. Separate room for parties, seats 30. Tables outdoors (2, pavement).
Map 18 D2.

Chinatown

★ Corean Chilli
51 Charing Cross Road, WC2H 0NE (7734 6737). Leicester Square tube. **Meals served** noon-midnight daily. **Main courses** £6.50-£15.
Set lunch £5-£6. **Credit** (over £15) MC, V.
Corean Chilli looks like the kind of place where the teenage heroes of Korean martial arts cartoons hang out. The ceilings are low, the walls are covered in chipped granite or mock concrete blocks, and diners sit at bench seats beneath oversized red lampshades. It feels a little like dining in an underground car park, which won't appeal to everyone; the most inviting spot is at the front, facing Charing Cross Road. When we visited, the place was full of Korean and Chinese students taking advantage of the cheap lunch specials (served until 5pm), many happy to dine alone while reading a book. The menu covers the full spectrum of Korean cooking, but some dishes are definitely better than others. Dried pollock soup was a pleasant surprise – a light broth full of sliced radish, tofu and flavoursome strips of the sustainable white fish – but jeyuk deopbap (spicy fried belly pork) was flat and lacking in flavour. The handy location within sight of Leicester Square tube makes this a good choice for a weekday lunch or a quick bite after work.
Babies and children welcome: high chairs. Booking advisable dinner Fri, Sat. Restaurant available for hire. Takeaway service.
Map 17 C4.

Covent Garden

★ Woo Jung
59 St Giles High Street, WC2H 8LH (7836 3103). Tottenham Court Road tube. **Meals served** noon-1am Mon-Sat; 5pm-midnight Sun.
Main courses £6-£8. **Set lunch** £5.90-£7.90.
Set meal £17-£23. **Credit** MC, V.
Most people come to Woo Jung for the prices rather than the atmosphere. The faded dining room looks like a fish and chip shop in a down-on-its-luck seaside town, but the menu covers all the usual Korean favourites and the low prices attract crowds of Asian students. If you can, sit in the small dining room at the front instead of the rather isolated seating area on the first floor. As on previous visits, our meal was a little hit and miss. We liked the beef and dumpling soup, which was packed with beef strips, egg threads, wun tun-like dumplings and chewy tteok (rice cakes), but the accompanying mung bean pancake was heavy and oily. In Woo Jung's favour, the food arrived quickly and we left with change from a tenner per head, but there are better Korean meals available at similar prices in more appealing surroundings in neighbouring Soho.
Babies and children admitted. Takeaway service.
Map 18 C2.

Holborn

★ Asadal
227 High Holborn, WC1V 7DA (7430 9006/ www.asadal.co.uk). Holborn tube. **Lunch served** noon-3pm Mon-Sat. **Dinner served** 6-11pm Mon-Sat; 5-10.30pm Sun. **Main courses** £6-£20.
Set lunch £8.50-£15.80. **Set dinner** £17.50-£30.
Credit AmEx, MC, V.
Korean food and romantic dining rarely go hand in hand, so this elegant basement restaurant next to Holborn tube is something to be treasured. The dining room is dark and moody, with glass and stone partitions, and barbecue tables illuminated by small pools of light. One wall is entirely covered by an abstract mural of wooden blocks, giving the place a vaguely Frank Lloyd Wright feel. Service can be a bit touch and go, and you can expect a long wait for a table if you arrive without a reservation, but the menu is extensive and the food excellent. We got a kick from the spicy heat of the yukkaejang (beef soup) and the meaty bite of the kalbi (rib-cut beef), cooked on the table-top barbecue. Bibimbap and light tofu jeon (silken tofu in a delicate batter) provided a nice counterpoint to the strong flavours from the grill. All in all, not far off perfection.
Babies and children welcome: high chairs. Booking advisable. Disabled: toilet. Separate rooms for parties, seating 6 and 12. Takeaway service.
Map 18 E2.

Leicester Square

★ Jindalle
6 Panton Street, SW1Y 4DL (7930 8881). Piccadilly Circus tube. **Meals served** noon-11pm daily. **Main courses** £6.90-£17.90. **Set lunch** £4.50-£7.50. **Set dinner** (5-9pm) £8.90.
Credit AmEx, MC, V.
Tucked away off the Haymarket in the heart of Theatreland, Jindalle is a delight. While most Korean restaurants go for the modernist look that was all the rage in the 1980s, Jindalle has bare brick walls and exposed chrome ducts that dangle from the ceiling like the vents of a 1950s airship (it's rather eccentric, but we like it). The menu covers everything you would expect to find in a British Korean restaurant, with a handful of exotic specials to appeal to expat diners. The three-course set lunch is astonishingly good value – £7.50 gets you Korean miso soup, kimchi and namul, rice and a choice of starters and main courses, including proper barbecue dishes, prepared at the table on the gas grill. We began with a fluffy tofu pancake, followed by deliciously tender kalbi (beef rib barbecue), which was grilled on the bone then chopped into bite-sized morsels with scissors. Service doesn't exactly zip along,

Jee Cee Neh. See p217.

RESTAURANTS

but then you would struggle to find a more satisfying meal for less in the West End.
Babies and children welcome: high chairs. Booking advisable. Takeaway service. **Map 17 C5.**

Mayfair

Kaya
42 Albemarle Street, W1S 4JH (7499 0622/ 0633/www.kayarestaurant.co.uk). Green Park tube. **Lunch served** noon-3pm, **dinner served** 6-11pm Mon-Sat. **Main courses** £9-£20. **Set lunch** £10-£15. **Credit** AmEx, MC, V.
Kaya is like a Soho Korean restaurant upgraded for a Mayfair clientele. Waitresses wear graceful embroidered gowns and even the cheapest house white wine is served from an ice bucket. The sleek dining room is a mock-up of a Korean *gung* (palace), with bottle-green roof tiles, painted beams and a wall of framed Korean objets d'art, including a gorgeous print of a deranged tiger. For an elegant dining experience, book the paper-screen banquet room at the back of the restaurant. The menu has plenty of barbecue and hotpot dishes, but we ordered the bossam – steamed pork, wrapped in cabbage leaves with sweet pickles, raw garlic, chilli and a pungent seafood sauce. It was an interesting combination of flavours but bettered by a dish of sweet-marinated beef ribs barbecued and wrapped in lettuce leaf parcels with ssam jang (fermented bean paste) and tangy shredded spring onion. A 15% service charge is included on the bill, but the attentive staff deserve every penny.
Babies and children admitted. Booking advisable. Separate rooms for parties, seating 8 and 12. **Map 9 J7.**

Soho

Jin
16 Bateman Street, W1D 3AH (7734 0908). Leicester Square or Tottenham Court Road tube. **Lunch served** noon-3pm, **dinner served** 6-10.30pm Mon-Sat. **Main courses** £8-£15. **Set lunch** £7.50-£10. **Set dinner** £30-£35. **Credit** AmEx, MC, V.
Jin is hidden behind a sleek rendered façade on a side-street just south of Soho Square. Inside, groups of friends and couples on dates talk animatedly while slices of bulgogi sizzle on the square grills set into the tops of the granite tables. This is definitely the sophisticated end of the Soho Korean spectrum; the menu extends well beyond the usual stews, barbecues and hotpots to rare and expensive dishes containing sea cucumber, abalone and pine mushrooms. Even familiar dishes come with a twist. Our hot battered chicken was served in a refreshingly savoury chilli sauce with black-ear fungus, bamboo shoots and sliced shiitake mushrooms. For the barbecue, we mixed dak bulgogi (marinated chicken) and beef tenderloin, rolled into lettuce leaf parcels with some of the tastiest pa muchim (tangy shredded spring onions) we've found in London. The service also marks Jin out from the competition; the black-clad waitresses are constantly communicating with each other to ensure that nothing on the barbecue singes and nobody waits too long for a table.
Babies and children admitted. Booking advisable weekends. Separate room for parties, seats 10. Takeaway service. **Map 17 C3.**

★ Myung Ga
1 Kingly Street, W1B 5PA (7734 82200/ www.myungga.co.uk). Oxford Circus or Piccadilly Circus tube. **Lunch served** noon-3pm Mon-Sat. **Dinner served** 5.30-11pm Mon-Sat; 5-10.30pm Sun. **Set lunch** £9.50-£12.50. **Set dinner** £25-£35. **Credit** AmEx, MC, V.
We like Myung Ga. It could be something to do with the laid-back, post-work, pre-theatre vibe or the zippy service provided by the young, enthusiastic waiting staff. The restaurant is hemmed in by pubs and bars on Kingly Street and Beak Street, so it gets extremely busy in the evenings; make a booking for dinner or face a long wait. We came straight from work and our starter – kimchi and a basket of fried goonmandu (beef dumplings) – arrived at the table within seconds. This was rapidly followed by an enjoyable beef

Su La. See p218.

sirloin barbecue, cooked fresh at the table and served with a sesame oil, salt and pepper dip, and a sizzling platter of dak bulgogi (spicy chicken barbecue), prepared in the kitchen to avoid overloading the extractor fans. The menu includes plenty of soups, stews and hotpots but most people come for the grills. Make a meal of it by ordering four or five cuts of beef, pork or chicken for the barbecue. Another plus point: the toilets are probably the cleanest in Soho.
Babies and children welcome: high chairs. Booking advisable. Separate room for parties, seats 12. **Map 17 A4.**

★ Nara
9 D'Arblay Street, W1F 8DR (7287 2224). Oxford Circus or Tottenham Court Road tube. **Lunch served** noon-3.30pm Mon-Sat. **Dinner served** 5.30-11pm daily. **Main courses** £6.50-£30. **Set lunch** £6.50. **Set dinner** £7.50. **Credit** AmEx, MC, V.
Nara is typical of Korean restaurants in Soho – a narrow dining room lined with wooden barbecue tables, matching high-backed chairs and framed prints on the walls. Most lunchtimes, every table is full, so come early or watch someone else eating the lunch that could have been yours. In the evenings, most people order à la carte, but the service can leave something to be desired. We always look forward to ordering the tolsot bibimbap – rice, beef, vegetables and chilli sauce, folded together at the table in a hot stone bowl. At the sides of the bowl, the rice cooks into a delicious caramelised crust. Bibimbap is one of half a dozen dishes you can sample as part of the excellent-value set lunch, which comes with Korean miso soup, kimchi and several types of namul. Another hit was the sogogee dop bap, a full-flavoured stir-fry of beef and vegetables in a bulgogi-style sauce, served with an earthenware cup of fragrant green tea. If you feel like mixing cuisines, try some of the decent Japanese food also offered here.
Babies and children admitted. Bookings not accepted for fewer than five people Fri, Sat. Takeaway service (lunch only). **Map 17 B3.**

RESTAURANTS

★ Ran

*58-59 Great Marlborough Street, W1F 7JY
(7434 1650/www.ranrestaurant.com). Oxford
Circus tube.* **Lunch served** noon-3pm Mon-Sat.
Dinner served 6-11pm daily. **Main courses**
£5.90-£12. **Set lunch** £7-£10. **Set dinner**
£23-£69. **Credit** AmEx, MC, V.
A great all-rounder, Ran feels like a restaurant
from the boom years of the 1980s. Diners waiting
for tables sip drinks at the front bar, while coils of
steam rise up to the air-conditioners from the table-
top barbecues in the dining room behind. The
upmarket vibe is reinforced by a convincing wine
list with plenty of prestige labels. There's a subtle
Japanese influence here – hence the udon and soba
noodle dishes on the menu – but the Korean food
is entirely authentic. Don't miss the Korean-style
tempura: thin vegetable threads in a deliciously
light batter, served in a wicker basket. We followed
this with 'hot battered chicken' fried in a tongue-
tingling red and green chilli sauce. Barbecues are
the house speciality; a selection of beef (bulgogi,
kalbi and sirloin) arrived at the table in a black
lacquer box. Waiting staff cooked the meat to
perfection, though we have had to keep an eye on
the barbecue on previous visits. Nonetheless, this
is one of our favourite downtown Koreans.
*Babies and children welcome: high chairs. Booking
advisable. Separate room for parties, seats 12.
Takeaway service. Map 17 A3.*

South West

Raynes Park

★ Cah Chi ⑩

*34 Durham Road, SW20 0TW (8947 1081/
www.cahchi.com). Raynes Park rail/57, 131 bus.*
Lunch served noon-3pm, **dinner served** 5-
11pm Tue-Fri. **Meals served** noon-10.30pm Sat,
Sun. **Main courses** £6-£14. **Set dinner** £18.
Corkage 10% of bill. **Credit** MC, V.
Families love Cah Chi. It may have something to
do with the bright, friendly decor and the children's
drawings plastered all over the walls, or the way
the waiters automatically bring over learner
chopsticks for younger diners. At first glance, the
interior looks more like a kindergarten than a
restaurant, but don't let that fool you. The food is
delicious and extremely authentic. We strongly
recommend the £18 set menu: four courses, plus
Korean red rice and a huge spread of panch'an
(including tangy sweet pickled radish and some
deliciously nutty soy beans in syrup). We loved the
variety of flavours and textures – the soft bite of
the pork and vegetable dumplings, the slip and
slide of the stir-fried glass noodles, the chilli zing
of the spicy fried squid, and the fresh crunch of
lettuce leaves wrapped around perfectly cooked
beef bulgogi. We also rate the service; although
most diners are regulars, staff make a real effort
to make newcomers feel at home. Now that credit
cards are accepted, we really can't fault this place.
*Babies and children welcome: high chairs. Booking
essential. Separate room for parties, seats 18.
Takeaway service.*
For branch see index.

North West

Golders Green

Kimchee

*887 Finchley Road, NW11 8RR (8455 1035).
Golders Green tube.* **Lunch served** noon-3pm
Tue-Fri; noon-4pm Sat, Sun. **Dinner served**
6-11pm Tue-Sun. **Main courses** £5.90-£8.50.
Set lunch £5.90-£6.90. **Credit** MC, V.
Most of London's Korean restaurants are grouped
together in Soho or New Malden, so Kimchee is a
surprising find in the middle of Golders Green.
This is one of the capital's most atmospheric
Korean eateries. The dining room is styled like a
traditional yeogwan (Korean inn) with gas
barbecues mounted into aged wooden tables and
light spilling from mock screen windows along the
walls. The attentive waitresses wear traditional
costume, mirroring the prints of Korean village
scenes on the wallpaper. The menu is short and

predictable, but every dish we tried was well
prepared. The house kimchi had real fire, and we
enjoyed the smooth yolky flavour of the bibimbap
(rice in a hot bowl). Another pleasant surprise was
the tangsuyuk – hunks of tender battered beef,
served in a sweet-and-sour sauce with fresh
pineapple, providing a lovely counterpoint to the
tartness of the kimchi. If you order a barbecue, it
may be cooked on a portable gas grill at the next
table, as the fixed grills take up a lot of space.
*Babies and children welcome: high chairs. Booking
essential Fri-Sun. Takeaway service.*

Outer London
New Malden, Surrey

Hankook

*Ground floor, Falcon House, 257 Burlington Road,
New Malden, Surrey KT3 4NE (8942 1188).
Motspur Park rail.* **Lunch served** noon-3pm
Mon, Tue, Thur, Fri. **Dinner served** 6-11pm
Mon-Fri. **Meals served** noon-11pm Sat, Sun.
Main courses £6.50-£50. **Credit** MC, V.
Hankook has an unpromising location, tucked
between an accountancy firm and an air-
conditioner dealer in a New Malden industrial
complex. But while it doesn't look much from the
outside, step through the doors and you'll find a
surprisingly cosy wood-lined dining hall and a row
of traditional banquet rooms, complete with low
tables and sliding paper screens. The decor doesn't
quite disguise the fact that this used to be an
industrial unit, but waiting staff aim to please and
the menu includes some interesting dishes
imported from Korea by way of Los Angeles. Our
favourite dish here is the LA-style ribs, cut into thin
slices across the bone to add extra flavour on the
barbecue; order the ribs as a stand-alone dish or
with a bubbling bowl of seafood chigae. You'll
need deep pockets to sample the house speciality:
fresh turbot and lobster sashimi. Live lobsters and
turbots splash around in an aquarium at the back
of the restaurant, seemingly unaware of their fate.
Because of the location, Hankook tends to be fairly
quiet for lunch, but gets busier in the evenings.
*Babies and children welcome: high chairs. Booking
essential dinner Fri-Sun.*

★ Jee Cee Neh

*74 Burlington Road, New Malden, Surrey KT3
4NU (8942 0682). New Malden rail.* **Lunch
served** noon-3pm, **dinner served** 6-11pm Tue-
Fri. **Meals served** 11.30am-10.30pm Sat, Sun.
Main courses £7-£13. **Credit** (over £20) MC, V.
Jee Cee Neh is surprisingly sophisticated given its
suburban location, set among grocers and
hairdressers on a residential New Malden street.
The owners have quite a flair for interior design;
the long dining hall is lined with dark-wood
barbecue tables, and a modernist mural of green
stripes runs along one wall. It's upbeat, bright and
inviting – accordingly, it is packed with Korean
families most lunchtimes. Prices seem high, but
portions are huge. Our bowl of yukkaejang (a rich,
chilli-infused broth of beef shreds, egg and green
onions, with a kick that a mule would be proud of)
could easily have fed two. We barely had space for
the main course: tender belly pork fried with chilli
and ssam jang (fermented bean paste). Enormous
jeongol stews, served bubbling at the table, seem
the dish of choice for locals. Korean barley tea
comes free with your meal, but the drinks menu
runs to wine, beer, and lemon and cucumber soju
(rice wine). Highly recommended.
*Babies and children welcome: high chairs.
Takeaway service.*

★ Palace NEW

*183-185 High Street, New Malden, Surrey
KT3 4BH (8949 3737). New Malden rail.*
Meals served noon-11pm daily. **Main courses**
£6-£25. **Credit** MC, V.
There are half a dozen Korean canteens dotted
around New Malden High Street, offering almost
identical menus of barbecues, spicy stews, stir-
fries and hotpot rice. Palace sits at the bottom end
of the price spectrum and the handy location
attracts plenty of shoppers looking for a quick bite

on the hoof. From outside, the restaurant looks
upmarket, but inside, you'll find the same relaxed
café vibe offered by most other local Korean
restaurants. That said, the friendly couple who run
the place have made an effort to inject some
character: the walls are covered with Korean bric-
a-brac, and barbecues are cooked on cute '50s-style
chrome gas burners. For lunch, we settled for a
quick bowl of fish and kimchi chigae – a warming
stew of green onions, fermented cabbage leaves,
chilli and mackerel, with a smouldering chilli heat
– which came with half a dozen small plates of
namul and pickles (the garlic stems in sweet chilli
sauce were particularly tasty). Our conclusion? We
like the relaxed mood, but Palace is probably better
for a quick lunch than a lingering dinner.
*Babies and children welcome: high chairs. Booking
advisable Fri, Sat. Restaurant available for hire.
Takeaway service.*

Sorabol NEW

*180 New Malden High Street, KT3 4ES (8942
2334/www.sorabol.co.uk). New Malden rail.* **Lunch
served** noon-3pm, **dinner served** 6-11pm Mon-
Fri. **Meals served** noon-11pm Sat. **Main courses**
£6-£9.50. **Set meal** £18 4 courses. **Credit** MC, V.
This welcoming spot has appeared on the site of
the original Asadal. Come on Saturday lunchtime
and you'll find many Korean families here, whiling
away the afternoon sharing dishes, their well-
behaved children silently entertained by electronic
games. Each table has a barbecue set in the centre,
though the menu also offers an extensive choice of
casseroles, stir-fries, jeon (pancakes), noodles and
raw meat and seafood dishes. Wholesome plates
of golden-fried mung bean pancake and steamed
tofu with soy sauce and chillies got our meal off to

THE DISH

Naengmyun

Korea's super-skinny buckwheat
noodles have a springy chewiness
that knicker elastic would envy and
for this dish (which literally means
'cold noodles') waiters will use
scissors to snip them down to a
more manageable, indeed edible,
length. There are a few different
varieties, served year-round in North
Korea and popular in summer in
the south. In mul naengmyun the
noodles swim in cold vinegary beef
broth with cucumber, nashi pear,
hard-boiled egg and a few slices
of cooked beef – you add mustard
and extra vinegar to taste. Bibim
('mixed') naengmyun is an altogether
drier but more fiery affair, with the
noodles cloaked in a red sauce
dominated by gochujang (Korean red
chilli paste) – sometimes it arrives
with ice cubes, which provide a
thrilling contrast to the hot sauce.

At Leicester Square canteen and
karaoke spot **Corean Chilli** the menu
gives it a deserved maximum two-
chilli rating, though the sesame oil
dressing on the complimentary
namul will help soothe the tastebuds
a little. Still, don't forget your hankie.
Corean Chilli, like **Ran**, uses wheat
noodles instead of buckwheat. Head
to **Myung Ga** in Soho or **Sorabol**
in New Malden for naengmyun
featuring raw skate. The cross-
section strips of wing (yes, cartilage
and flesh) add a crunchy-chewy
element to an otherwise highly
slippery gastronomic adventure.

a pleasing start, along with bottles of refreshing OB and Hite lagers. Chicken bulgogi – one of some 15 barbecue options – can come with a mild or spicy marinade. Order lettuce in which to wrap it, and maybe some mixed vegetables (green pepper, prettily carved mushrooms, onions and large slices of garlic) to barbecue alongside the poultry and further boost the nutrient content. 'Garlic is good for the heart,' the friendly waitress informed us as she turned the ingredients on the hotplate with dainty metal tongs. Walls are soothingly decorated with calligraphy, while a couple of etched-glass screens add intimacy, making Sorabol somewhere to explore Korean cuisine in comfort.
Babies and children welcome: high chairs. Booking advisable (Fri, Sat). Disabled: toilet. Takeaway service.

Su La

79-81 Kingston Road, New Malden, Surrey KT3 3PB (8336 0121). New Malden rail. **Lunch served** noon-3pm, **dinner served** 6-11pm Mon-Fri. **Meals served** noon-11pm Sat. **Main courses** £7.50-£11. **Set lunch** £5-£7. **Set dinner** £12.50 per person (minimum 2). **Credit** MC, V.
One of the better Korean restaurants in the New Malden area, Su La has a bright, spacious dining room, an extensive menu, fast and friendly service, and food that's well above average. Don't be put off by the slightly dated exterior – inside, everything is clean and modern. Crazy chrome extractor fans dangle from the ceiling like the tentacles of a giant robot octopus. We came at lunchtime and were impressed by the speed with which our food arrived. The searing heat of the beef and chilli broth, which came bubbling in a hot stone bowl, was enjoyable accompanied by a selection of

panch'an. Korean families are drawn here by the seafood; the menu includes half a dozen kinds of fish, served dozens of different ways. If you're in a group, book one of the traditional banquet rooms, hidden away behind paper screens. One criticism: it can be a little hard to know what you're ordering from the translations on the menu.
Babies and children welcome: high chairs. Booking advisable Fri, Sat. Restaurant available for hire. Separate rooms for parties, seating 4-40. Takeaway service.

Yami NEW

69 High Street, New Malden, Surrey KT3 4BT (8949 0096). New Malden rail. **Lunch served** noon-3pm, **dinner served** 6-11pm Mon-Sat. **Set lunch** £5. **Main courses** £6-£11. **Credit** MC, V.
Yami is a casual, welcoming little place with enough style to put it in a class above canteen. The interior is decorated in a mixture of woods including pretty table inlays; partitions create intimate nooks. It's an authentic spot, with a partly untranslated menu, a young Korean clientele and some fiery cooking – especially in the good-value lunch hotpots. 'Yami' translates as 'wild taste', but waiters will obligingly point diners with dainty palates towards the tamer offerings: kimchi pancake, for instance, a generous appetiser and better, we thought, than the bland pan-fried dumplings. Soups are listed at the back with drinks. Don't miss the fun of table-barbecued meats, especially beef. Ox tongue comes with a delicate pepper sesame oil dip. Alternatively, try pyun galbi: sweet (perhaps too sweet) marinated rib of beef with a miso-chilli dip. Three types of very moreish kimchi accompany main dishes, and a little fruit tray comes at the end. Drink beer or

barley tea. And don't push the bicycle bell-shaped device by your table unless you need a waiter.
Babies and children welcome: high chairs. Booking advisable (dinner). Disabled: toilet. Separate rooms for parties, seating 8 and 10. Takeaway service (lunch).

★ You-Me

96 Burlington Road, New Malden, Surrey KT3 4NT (8715 1079). New Malden rail. **Meals served** noon-11pm Mon, Wed-Sun. **Main courses** £4.90-£20. **Set meal** £17.90-£19.90. **Credit** MC, V.
Imagine a Korean restaurant combined with a traditional English tea shop and you'll have some idea of the aura of You-Me. Set on a quiet row of neighbourhood shops, the restaurant is small, homely and slightly chaotic, which somehow adds to its charm. Tables are divided by wood and paper screens and the walls are covered in posters advertising special dishes in rounded Korean letters – but how many restaurants in Korea have pink doily tablecloths? We rate this place as much for its friendly demeanour as its food; the genial owners are always keen to explain the rules of Korean dining to novices, and the menu has useful photos of every dish to help you choose. We liked the home-made taste of the wangmandu – steamed rice dumplings stuffed with meat and vegetables, a little like Chinese bao buns. Khan pung gi (garlic chicken) wasn't quite so impressive; the batter was a little stodgy and the flavours muted. Based on past experience, the soups, stews and barbecues are better than the fried dishes.
Babies and children welcome: high chairs. Separate room for parties, seats 10. Takeaway service.

Menu

Chilli appears at every opportunity on Korean menus. Other common ingredients include soy sauce (different to both the Chinese and Japanese varieties), sesame oil, sugar, sesame seeds, garlic, ginger and various fermented soy bean pastes. Until the late 1970s eating meat was a luxury in Korea, so the quality of vegetarian dishes is high.

Given the spicy nature and overall flavour of Korean food, drinks such as chilled lager or vodka-like soju/shoju are the best matches. A wonderful non-alcoholic alternative that's always available, although not always listed on the menu, is barley tea (porich'a). Often served free of charge, it has a light dry taste that works perfectly with the food. Korean restaurants don't usually offer desserts (some serve orange or some watermelon with the bill). Spellings on menus vary hugely; we have given the most common.

Bibimbap or **pibimbap:** rice, vegetables and meat with a raw/fried egg dropped on top, often served on a hot stone.
Bindaedok, bindaedoek or **pindaetteok:** a mung bean pancake.
Bokum: a stir-fried dish, usually including chilli.
Bulgogi or **pulgogi:** thin slices of beef marinated in pear sap (or a similar sweet dressing) and barbecued at the table; often eaten rolled in a lettuce leaf with shredded spring onion and fermented bean paste.
Chang, jang or **denjang:** various fermented soy bean pastes.

Chapch'ae or **chap chee:** mixed vegetables and beef cooked with transparent vermicelli or noodles.
Cheon, jeon or **jon:** the literal meaning of the word is 'something flat'; this can range from a pancake containing vegetables, meat or seafood, to thinly sliced vegetables, beancurd, or other ingredients, in a light batter.
Cheyuk: pork.
Chigae or **jigae:** a hot stew containing fermented bean paste and chillies.
Gim or **kim:** dried seaweed, toasted and seasoned with salt and sesame oil.
Gu shul pan: a traditional lacquered tray with nine compartments containing individual appetisers.
Hobak chun or **hobak jun:** sliced marrow in a light egg batter.
Japch'ae or **jap chee:** alternative spellings for chapch'ae (qv).
Jjim: fish or meat stewed for a long time in soy sauce, sugar and garlic.
Jeongol: casserole.
Kalbi, galbi or **kalbee:** beef spare ribs, marinated and barbecued.
Kimchi, kim chee or **kimch'i:** fermented pickled vegetables, usually chinese cabbage, white radishes, cucumber or greens, served in a small bowl with a spicy chilli sauce.
Kkaktugi or **kkakttugi:** pickled radish.
Koch'ujang: a hot, red bean paste.
Kook, gook, kuk or **guk:** soup. Koreans have an enormous variety of soups, from consommé-like liquid to meaty broths of noodles, dumplings, meat or fish.
Ko sari na mool or **gosari namul:** cooked bracken stalks dressed with some sesame seeds.

Mandu kuk or **man doo kook:** clear soup with steamed meat dumplings.
Namul or **na mool:** vegetable side dishes.
Ojingeo: squid.
P'ajeon or **pa jun:** flour pancake with spring onions and (usually) seafood.
Panch'an: side dishes; they usually include pickled vegetables, but possibly also tofu, fish, seaweed or beans.
Pap, bap, bab or **pahb:** cooked rice.
Pokkeum or **pokkm:** stir-fry; for example, **cheyuk pokkeum** (pork), **ojingeo pokkeum** (squid).
Porich'a: barley tea.
Shinseollo, shinsonro, shinsulro or **sin sollo:** 'royal casserole'; a meat soup with seaweed, seafood, eggs and vegetables, all cooked at the table.
Soju or **shoju:** a strong Korean vodka, often drunk as an aperitif.
Teoppap or **toppap:** 'on top of rice'; for example, **ojingeo teoppap** is squid served on rice.
Toenjang: seasoned (usually with chilli) soy bean paste.
Tolsot bibimbap: tolsot is a sizzling hot stone bowl that makes the bibimbap (qv) a little crunchy on the sides.
Tteokpokki: bars of compressed rice (tteok is a rice cake) fried on a hotplate with veg and sausages, in a chilli sauce.
Twaeji gogi: pork.
T'wigim, twigim or **tuigim:** fish, prawns or vegetables dipped in batter and deep-fried until golden brown.
Yach'ae: vegetables.
Yuk hwe, yukhoe or **yukhwoe:** shredded raw beef, strips of pear and egg yolk, served chilled.
Yukkaejang: spicy beef soup.

Malaysian, Indonesian & Singaporean

Given Britain's historical links with Malaysia and Singapore, the cuisine of the region has been under-represented in London. The occasional Chinese restaurateur offers Malaysian specialities, but there are relatively few places that serve only Malaysian food, and fewer still that specialise in Indonesian or Singaporean dishes. It's absurd, though, to get too hung up about purity and authenticity where this region's cooking is concerned. Like the countries themselves, the cuisine is a glorious amalgam of cultures, showing influences from India, China and Thailand, as well as from the indigenous Malays; Indonesia also throws its Dutch colonial heritage into the mix. New to the guide this year are **Jom Makan** (specialising in Malaysian street food), **54** (with a chef from Penang) and **Bugis Street Brasserie** (with a Singaporean slant), though our favourites remain two old-stagers: **Satay House** and **Singapore Garden**.

Central

City

54 NEW

54 Farringdon Road, EC1R 3BL (7336 0603/ www.54farringdon.com). Farringdon tube/rail. **Lunch served** noon-3pm Mon-Fri. **Dinner served** 6-10.45pm Mon-Sat. **Main courses** £9.50-£15. **Set lunch** £9.95 2 courses. **Set dinner** (6-7pm) £11.95 2 courses. **Credit** AmEx, MC, V.

Furnishings are inexpensive but stylish in this small dining room: simple wood furniture, multi-coloured seat covers, batik prints, carved screen, and small mirrors arranged like mosaic. Unusually, 54 serves Malaysian and British dishes, but not fusion-style – the cuisines are kept distinct. The kitchen claims to favour organic, free-range and local produce. Flaky roti canai came with a tasty dhal curry dip, pickled onion and sambal. Masak lemak udang featured fresh prawns but a bland turmeric and coconut-milk sauce, so we were grateful for the deep-fried shallots that gave the steamed rice extra kick. From the specials, asam laksa, a Penang speciality, transported us to that tropical island. Chopped lettuce, cucumber, pineapple and fresh mint are served in a piquant hot fish soup with thick white rice noodles; tamarind provides sourness while umami-flavour comes from a pungent, dark gooey shrimp paste. It was certainly authentic, so we weren't surprised to find the chef hails from Penang. Desserts such as cherry custard tart are entirely West facing. To drink, there's an inventive selection of wines. We liked 54's laid-back feel, and staff were friendly. At lunch there's a steady flow of local office workers. *Babies and children welcome: highchairs. Booking essential (Fri, Sat). Tables outdoors (2, pavement).* **Map 5 N5**.

Soho

New Fook Lam Moon

10 Gerrard Street, W1D 5PW (7734 7615/ www.newfooklammoon.com). Leicester Square tube. **Meals served** noon-11.30pm Mon-Sat; noon-10.30pm Sun. **Main courses** £6.90-£11. **Set meal** £11.50-£19.50 per person (minimum 2). **Credit** AmEx, MC, V.

Roast meats hang in the window of this titchy restaurant, which is indistinguishable from many in Chinatown, but New Fook Lam Moon is notable for offering a dozen Chinese-Malaysian specialities amid its menu of Cantonese dishes. Business can be hectic in the rather basic, cramped dining room. Staff, dressed in bright T-shirts, are occasionally brusque but never rude; it was nice to see the manager politely showing some tourists how to get the most out of a crispy duck. We were pleased to find bak kut teh, a popular soup of pork and herbs that in Malaysia is normally eaten at breakfast by the menfolk. Fried asam baby squid, coated with tamarind and chillies, got our meal off to a good start. Fillet of venison with a black pepper sauce was a touch salty, and more Chinese than Straits cuisine. Best was a tender belly of pork, braised in dark soy sauce with piquant rice vinegar offsetting the richness. Big flavours dominate the cooking – some might call it unrefined – but more worrying is the uniformity of flavours and textures, making it difficult to differentiate the dishes. There are no Malaysian desserts, but complimentary fresh oranges are offered. *Babies and children welcome: high chairs. Booking advisable. Takeaway service.* **Map 17 C4**.

South Kensington

Awana

85 Sloane Avenue, SW3 3DX (7584 8880/ www.awana.co.uk). South Kensington tube. *Bar* **Open** noon-11pm Mon-Fri; noon-11.30pm Sat; noon-10.30pm Sun. *Restaurant* **Lunch served** noon-3pm daily. **Dinner served** 6-11pm Mon-Fri; 6-11.30pm Sat; 6-11pm Sun. **Main courses** £12-£25. **Set lunch** £12.50 2 courses, £15 3 courses. **Set dinner** £40 tasting menu. *Both* **Credit** AmEx, DC, MC, V.

Satay House. See p221.

Framed covers of *OK!* magazine, a collage of famous faces and a signed photograph of Pierce Brosnan in the foyer suggest the kind of customer this restaurant is used to serving, but the welcome was warm for us too. Part of an international chain, Awana has a relaxed glamour more in keeping with Asia's luxury hotels than hawker centres, but flatscreen TVs showing the roti chefs slapping, filling and folding their thin circles of dough add an element of epicurean showmanship. Menus in brown silk, and black napkins decorated with dried orange slices, add to the luxe vibe. Staff have a tendency to hover during quiet spells. The long menu is confusing to read, with 'Malaysian favourites' main courses, a tasting menu, satay and chef's specials, then more starters and mains. We couldn't resist perfectly juicy satay scallops, and eventually settled on asam kari lautan, a peppery mixed seafood curry with okra and tomato. Fragrant chicken murtabak (filled bread), smooth curry sauce and crunchy pickled cabbage and onion made a perfect marriage, but coconut rice lacked coconut flavour. We finished with deliciously smoky chocolate and lemongrass ice-cream. Wines start at a pricey £19; alternatives include superior cocktails.
Babies and children welcome: high chairs. Booking essential Thur, advisable Fri, Sat. Takeaway service. **Map 14 E10.**

Bugis Street Brasserie NEW

Millennium Gloucester Hotel & Conference Centre, 4-18 Harrington Gardens, SW7 4LH (7373 6030/www.millenniumhotels.co.uk). South Kensington tube. **Food served** noon-10.30pm daily. **Main courses** £6.95-£11.25. **Set lunch** (noon-4pm) £5.95 2 courses. **Set meal** £15.50 3 courses (minimum 2 people). **Credit** AmEx, MC, V.
Until the 1980s, Bugis Street was a tourist nightspot in Singapore renowned for its parade of transsexual women. Today the area has been sanitised and the sex industry closed down. The atmosphere at this hotel brasserie, on a corner plot with a petite alfresco area at the front, is equally sterile, with tourists the only diners on our visit. The place seems to have been designed to resemble a Singaporean coffee shop, with gold ceiling fans, marble table-tops, bird cages, a mosaic floor, black and white photos of street stalls, and irritating pop muzak. The menu has a Chinese and Singaporean slant. Chicken satay, not chargrilled but worryingly pan-fried then skewered, was very poor. Stir-fried king prawns with tamarind sauce was bland. Better was the seafood ho fun, which featured fresh seafood and reasonable flat rice noodles. Our sago dessert seemed to be made with ordinary brown sugar rather than palm sugar. Next time we'll stick with the noodle dishes. Unfortunately, the service was just as dozy and uncaring as the kitchen, and things weren't redeemed by the rather high prices charged for cooking of this standard.
Babies and children admitted: high chairs. Disabled: toilet. Tables outdoors (3, pavement). Takeaway service. **Map 13 C10.**

Trafalgar Square

Jom Makan NEW

5-7 Pall Mall East, SW1Y 5BA (7925 2402/ www.jommakan.co.uk). Charing Cross tube/ rail. **Meals served** 11am-11pm Mon-Sat; noon-10pm Sun. **Main courses** £6.50-£8.50. **Credit** MC, V.
In a somewhat incongruous location – an imposing building just off Pall Mall – Jom Makan breaks the mould of nearby Trafalgar Square's boring grills, bog-standard cafés, cheesy bars and other tourist spots. The menu is an impressive log of Malaysian street foods. From roti canai to kway teow goreng and gado-gado, you'll find many of the classics here. The problem mainly lies in execution; we did not, for example, expect to find thick Japanese udon noodles in our asam laksa. The restaurant claims to serve 'tasty Malaysian cuisine, fresh every day!' but our lamb satay tasted old and dry, enlivened only by the own-made peanut dipping sauce. A rendition of nasi lemak was not better

than the sum of its parts. We liked the tender cubes of coconut-fragrant beef rendang and crisp-fried anchovies, but the squid sambal was lukewarm both in temperature and chilli heat. So, the cooking tends to be timid, but Jom Makan partially makes up for this in its genuine service and modern (though culturally anonymous) surroundings.
Babies and children welcome: high chairs. Disabled: toilet. Separate room for parties, seats 40. **Map 10 K7.**

West

Bayswater

★ Kiasu

48 Queensway, W2 3RY (7727 8810). Bayswater or Queensway tube. **Meals served** noon-11pm daily. **Main courses** £4.90-£7.50. **Set meal** (noon-3pm) £8.90 2 courses. **Credit** (minimum £10) MC, V.
Since Kiasu won the Best Cheap Eats category at the 2007 Time Out Eating & Drinking Awards, we've had mixed experiences dining here. It's a cheerful, all-day restaurant with walls featuring graphic twists on the logo in confident tones of blue and grey. On our last visit, most customers were of South-east Asian descent, dining in couples, groups of colleagues, or solo. Kueh pai tee got the meal off to an excellent start with correctly crisp pastry cups and distinct flavours of bamboo shoot, prawn and coriander, however the acar was too watery. Kangkong belacan (water spinach with shrimp paste) came swamped in sauce, though we appreciated its fragrant fishy aromas. Soft-shell crabs, cooked in the Singapore chilli crab style, were sweetly succulent and served with feather-light mantou (Chinese buns). Portions were generous, leaving us too full for desserts of cendol or pulut hitam (black rice pudding), though they were tempting. Glass mugs of sweet teh tarik, Malaysia's favourite blend of tea and condensed milk, helped soothe the chilli heat of dishes. Alternatively, you could opt for slushies (mango or honeydew melon, perhaps), house-made iced lemon tea, a Chinese lager, or something from the inexpensive wine list.
Babies and children welcome: high chairs. Booking advisable dinner. Separate room for parties, seats 60. Takeaway service. **Map 7 C6.**

Notting Hill

Nyonya

2A Kensington Park Road, W11 3BU (7243 1800/www.nyonya.co.uk). Notting Hill Gate tube. **Lunch served** 11.30am-2.45pm, **dinner served** 6-10.30pm Mon-Fri. **Meals served** 11.30am-10.30pm Sat, Sun. **Main courses** £5.50-£8.50. **Set lunch** (Mon-Fri) £8 2 courses. **Credit** AmEx, DC, MC, V.
Nyonya (which means 'Straits Chinese lady') sits on a corner plot, its prime location close to Portobello Market ensuring a bustling trade from locals and visitors. It is reminiscent of the *kopi tiams* (coffee shops) of the Straits; dining takes place in small rooms spread over two floors, with Formica benches on the ground and tables upstairs. On our latest visit, the complacent service seemed to be in 'out-of-office' mode, seldom moving above first gear. Peranakan cooking should be flavoursome, but our chicken satay was tame, and golden deep-fried belacan chicken could have done with more shrimp paste. The chefs (the Khoo family) used to run a respected Peranakan restaurant in Singapore, and their best dishes set the benchmark for this cuisine. Penang-style char kway teow is the real deal, pungent and garlicky. Sour and spicy flavours, a common thread with this cuisine, show up best in a curry tumis of sea bream and okra, laced with tamarind. Daughter Purdey is an expert on kueh (vividly coloured cakes, usually made with coconut and rice flour), so the tasting plate is worth exploring, particularly kueh tai tai (purple glutinous rice with coconut jam).
Babies and children welcome: high chairs. Booking advisable. Separate room for parties, seats 40. Takeaway service. **Map 7 A7.**

Paddington

★ ★ Satay House (100)

13 Sale Place, W2 1PX (7723 6763/www.satay-house.co.uk). Edgware Road tube/Paddington tube/rail. **Lunch served** noon-3pm, **dinner served** 6-11pm daily. **Main courses** £5-£18.50. **Set meal** £15.50-£26.50 per person (minimum 2). **Credit** AmEx, MC, V.
Satay House attracts a happy mix of expats, locals and fans of Malaysian food, who clearly make a special journey. We arrived at 7.30pm on a Thursday to find the ground floor full and just a few tables left in the cosy yet sleekly designed basement. We waited well over half an hour for our starters. Still, the standard of cooking rewards patience. Buttery squares of roti canai came with chunky dalca (lentil and vegetable curry). The satay were imbued with a lovely lemongrass scent, but slightly tough chicken indicated they'd been grilled too long. No complaints about the luscious begedil (spiced lamb and potato cutlets) however – or the generous, juicy pineapple curry. The nutty scent of curry leaves wafted from a plate of tender sotong berempah (stir-fried squid with peppers). Satay House's list of soft drinks (rose syrup and lime, watermelon juice, Milo) is fun; beer lovers can choose from four eastern lagers. Banana fritters – meltingly tender fruit inside, crisp without – came with maple syrup

RESTAURANTS

and devilishly good chocolate ice-cream. Another bonus: the bill was under £50 for two.
Babies and children welcome: high chairs. Booking advisable. Separate room for parties, seats 35. Takeaway service. Vegetarian menu. **Map 8 E5.**

Westbourne Grove

★ C&R Restaurant

52 Westbourne Grove, W2 5SH (7221 7979). Bayswater or Queensway tube. **Meals served** noon-11pm daily. **Main courses** £6-£15. **Set meal** (vegetarian) £14.50, (meat) £17 per person (minimum 2). **Credit** MC, V.
Faded menus on front windows aren't usually a good sign, but C&R's dining room is spick and span, with stone floors, blond-wood chairs, comfy rippled banquettes, white tablecloths, magnolia walls and splashes of red from modern artwork. Named after Chong and Rosa, the owners, it is popular with students, so ringtones and mobile chat are the order of the day. Service is pleasant and efficient. Crispy vegetarian spring rolls were a fair rendition. Also respectable was Indian mee goreng (fried noodles) with tomatoes, egg, prawns and beancurd, though we would have preferred a

spicier flavour. Best was the Malaysian chicken curry with potatoes: good enough to grace most homes in the East. It featured great rempah (curry paste) with coconut milk, and the bird was cooked on the bone for extra flavour. Dessert was a lacklustre chendol, which had too much coconut milk and shaved ice, and too little gula melaka (palm sugar). Still, we enjoy the lively atmosphere here, which is enhanced by a brisk takeaway trade.
Babies and children welcome: high chairs. Takeaway service. **Map 7 B6.**
For branch (C&R Café) see index.

North West
Swiss Cottage

★ Singapore Garden

83A Fairfax Road, NW6 4DY (7624 8233/ www.singaporegarden.co.uk). Swiss Cottage tube. **Lunch served** noon-3pm Mon-Sat; noon-4pm Sun. **Dinner served** 6-10pm Mon-Thur, Sun; 6-11pm Fri, Sat. **Main courses** £7.50-£29. **Set meal** £28-£38.50 per person (minimum 2). **Minimum charge** £15 per person. **Credit** AmEx, MC, V.

Malaysian expats, who travel across town to visit this swanky restaurant, tend to be amazed by the number of well-heeled locals who consistently order the standard Anglo-Chinese dishes, rarely venturing past the satay chicken. But a sense of adventure is rewarding. The list of more than 20 Singaporean and Malaysian dishes is supplemented by seasonal specials, such as terrific sambal udang okra: plump king prawns and crunchy okra stir-fried with the region's characteristic chilli paste-cum-sauce. Mee goreng was delectable, with full-flavoured pieces of tender beef and perfectly cooked egg noodles. Ho jien, a glistening omelette filled with oysters, could convert anyone who claims not to like that particular bivalve. To accompany these, you need look no further than the choice of house wines, which includes a pleasing Chilean sauvignon blanc at £18. Mango pudding, reminiscent of blancmange, was a pleasant rather than special. Elegantly dressed staff make every effort to be friendly, as do customers, who are rather used to others trying to squeeze between the closely packed tables for two.
Babies and children admitted. Booking advisable. Takeaway service; delivery service (within 1-mile radius). **Map 28 A4.**

Menu

Here are some common terms and dishes. Spellings can vary.
Acar: assorted pickled vegetables such as carrots, beans and onions, often spiced with turmeric and pepper.
Ayam: chicken.
Bergedel: a spiced potato cake.
Blachan, belacan or blacan: dried fermented shrimp paste; it adds a piquant fishy taste to dishes.
Char kway teow or char kwai teow: a stir-fry of rice noodles with meat and/or seafood with dark soy sauce and beansprouts. A Hakka Chinese-derived speciality of Singapore.
Chilli crab: fresh crab, stir-fried in a sweet, mild chilli sauce.
Daging: meat.
Ebi: shrimps.
Gado gado: a salad of blanched vegetables with a peanut-based sauce.
Galangal: also called yellow ginger, Laos root or blue ginger, this spice gives a distinctive flavour to many South-east Asian dishes.
Goreng: wok-fried.
Hainanese chicken rice: poached chicken served with rice cooked in chicken stock, a bowl of light chicken broth and a chilli-ginger dipping sauce.
Ho jien: oyster omelette, flavoured with garlic and chilli.
Ikan: fish.
Ikan bilis or ikan teri: tiny whitebait-like fish, often fried and made into a dry sambal (qv) with peanuts.
Kambing: actually goat, but in practice lamb is the usual substitute.
Kangkong or kangkung: water convolvulus, often called water spinach or swamp cabbage – an aquatic plant often steamed and used in salads with a spicy sauce.
Kecap manis: sweet dark soy sauce.
Kelapa: coconut.
Kemiri: waxy-textured candlenuts, used to enrich Indonesian and Malaysian curry pastes.
Keropok or kerupuk: prawn crackers.
Laksa: a noodle dish with either coconut milk or (as with penang laksa) tamarind

as the stock base.
Lemang: sticky Indonesian rice that is cooked in bamboo segments.
Lengkuas or lenkuas: Malaysian name for galangal (qv).
Lumpia: deep-fried spring rolls filled with meat or vegetables.
Masak lemak: anything cooked in a rich, red spice paste with coconut milk.
Mee: noodles.
Mee goreng: fried egg noodles with meat, prawns and vegetables.
Mee hoon: rice vermicelli noodles.
Murtabak: an Indian-Malaysian pancake fried on a griddle and served with a savoury filling.
Nasi ayam: rice cooked in chicken broth, served with roast or steamed chicken and a light soup.
Nasi goreng: fried rice with shrimp paste, garlic, onions, chillies and soy sauce.
Nasi lemak: coconut rice on a plate with a selection of curries and fish dishes topped with ikan bilis (qv).
Nonya or Nyonya: the name referring to both the women and the dishes of the Straits Chinese community.
Otak otak: a Nonya (qv) speciality made from eggs, fish and coconut milk.
Pandan leaves: a variety of the screwpine plant; used to add colour and fragrance to both savoury and sweet dishes.
Panggang: grilled or barbecued.
Peranakan: refers to the descendants of Chinese settlers who first came to Malacca (now Melaka), a seaport on the Malaysian west coast, in the 17th century. It is generally applied to those born of Sino-Malay extraction who adopted Malay customs, costume and cuisine, the community being known as 'Straits Chinese'. The cuisine is also known as Nonya (qv).
Petai: a pungent, flat green bean used in Malaysian cooking.
Poh pia or popiah: spring rolls. Nonya or Penang popiah are not deep-fried and consist of egg or rice paper wrappers filled with a vegetable and prawn medley.
Rempah: generic term for the fresh curry pastes used in Malaysian cookery.

Rendang: meat cooked in coconut milk, a 'dry' curry.
Rojak: raw fruit and vegetables in a sweet spicy sauce.
Roti canai: a South Indian/Malaysian breakfast dish of fried unleavened bread served with a dip of either chicken curry or dal.
Sambal: there are several types of sambal, often made of fiery chilli sauce, onions and coconut oil; it can be served as a side dish or used as a relish. The suffix 'sambal' means 'cooked with chilli'.
Satay: there are two types – terkan (minced and moulded to the skewer) and chochok ('shish', more common in London). Beef or chicken are the traditional choices, though prawn is now often available too. Satay is served with a rich spicy sauce made from onions, lemongrass, galangal (qv), and chillies in tamarind sauce; it is sweetened and thickened with ground peanuts.
Sayur: vegetables.
Soto ayam: a classic spicy chicken soup, often with noodles.
Sotong: squid.
Tauhu goreng: deep-fried beancurd and beansprouts tossed in a spicy peanut sauce, served cold.
Udang: prawns.

DESSERTS
Ais or es: ice; a prefix for the multitude of desserts made with combinations of fruit salad, agar jelly cubes, palm syrup, condensed milk and crushed ice.
Ais (or es) kacang: shaved ice and syrup mixed with jellies, red beans and sweetcorn.
Bubur pulut hitam: black glutinous rice served in coconut milk and palm sugar.
Cendol or chendol: mung bean flour pasta, coloured and perfumed with essence of pandan leaf (qv) and served in a chilled coconut milk and palm sugar syrup.
Gula melaka: *see p221* **The Dish**.
Kueh or kuih: literally, 'cakes', but used as a general term for many desserts.
Pisang goreng: banana fritters.

Middle Eastern

The raw and distinctly unsavoury vagaries of geopolitics have helped shape the London experience of Middle Eastern food over the past 30 years. It is no accident that the two main types of cuisine to be found here are Lebanese and Iranian. The human fall-out from the Lebanese civil war and the Iranian revolution, both of which began in the late 1970s, has helped enrich London's restaurant scene enormously. It is generally held that the Lebanon is the cradle of Arabian food, like France is for western cuisine. The venerable **Al Hamra** in Shepherd Market proudly emblazons its website with 'Authentic Lebanese cuisine – established in 1984' and indeed, in atmosphere, it seems firmly lodged there (if not 1894). Fortunately, Londoners can now sample Arabic cuisines from places as diverse as Iraq (**Mesopotamia**), Egypt (**Ali Baba**) and Syria (**Abu Zaad**).

Iranian cooking is quite distinct from all these, being based on the courtly, subtly spiced and fruit-sauced food of the various dynasties that constituted the Persian Empire. Although experts claim that what we can sample at places like **Alounak** and **Mohsen** is very much everyday fare in Iran, the food has an unrivalled richness and subtlety.

Generally, most of the capital's Middle Eastern restaurants are to be found in central London (especially along the southern stretch of Edgware Road), although the Iranians showed an early fondness for West Kensington and Hammersmith. However, two of this year's new establishments are in rather uncharted territory: **Faanoos** in East Sheen is Iranian, and **Hiba** at the 'wrong' end of Borough High Street is Lebanese. Both have avoided romanticising their roots and instead try to give an up-to-date flavour of the cooking in their native lands.

Central

City

Kenza NEW
10 Devonshire Square, EC2M 4YP (7929 5533/www.kenza-restaurant.com). Liverpool Street tube/rail.
Lounge **Open** noon-2.30am Mon-Wed; noon-3.30am Thur-Sat.
Restaurant **Meals served** noon-10pm Mon-Wed; noon-11.30pm Thur, Fri; 6-11.30pm Sat. **Main courses** £13-£22. **Set lunch** £12.50 2 courses. **Set meal** £32 3 courses, £70 4 courses. **Credit** AmEx, MC, V. Lebanese & Moroccan
The mysterious East begins at Kenza's front door. Diners make their way down a series of lamp-lit corridors, before emerging into an orientalist's opium dream of carved wooden screens, cushions in jewel-bright colours, ornate glass lamps, and calligraphy-inspired murals. Most striking of all, a large carved metal grille hung with Hand of Fatima charms adorns the bar. Over the top, some might say, but beautiful. The look is similar to that of Moroccan sister restaurant Pasha (*see p249*). Here the food is best summed up as Lebanese with a twist. There are two set menus, but we ordered from the carte. Overall, the food failed to live up to its ambitions. A dish of artichoke and broad beans was overpowered by added lemon juice; a classic moujadara hamra was mellow if a little bland, but suffered from an ill-matched topping of cucumber sticks in yoghurt. Falafel kreidis (with prawns) was more successful. A main course samak tagine was

not a tagine but two boring pieces of grilled fish, partly redeemed by the accompanying fragrant rice. Kenza's target market is City folk who want to party; the rather inflated prices reflect this. Belly dancers sway every night too.
Booking advisable. Disabled: toilet. Entertainment: belly dancer .Separate rooms for parties, seating 15 and 50. Takeaway service. **Map 12 R6**.

Edgware Road

Maroush Gardens
1-3 Connaught Street, W2 2DH (7262 0222/www.maroush.com). Marble Arch tube. **Meals served** noon-midnight daily. **Main courses** £13-£16. **Set lunch** £16 2 courses. **Set dinner** £45 per person (minimum 2) 3 courses. **Credit** AmEx, DC, MC, V. Lebanese
One of several incarnations of Maroush around London, this branch is just a few doors from the company flagship, which has dedicated itself to nightly entertainment, with musicians, belly-dancers and a hefty cover charge. Maroush Gardens aims at sophistication, with black marble flooring stretching across the wide expanse of the dining area, ceiling spotlights and a water feature. It was chilly the evening we visited, and the joint was quite certainly not jumping. The absence of warmth (both temperature and ambience) was matched by food that sometimes lacked gusto: an insipid beige falafel with no crunch, halloumi cheese cut too thick (giving a rubbery texture). Other dishes were much better. We loved the sawda dajaj (butter-soft chicken livers in a much richer, browner, more fruity sauce than is usual for this

dish); dense, garlicky houmous; and tabouleh, made with the fine chopping and delicate combination of herbs and lemon juice that we expect of Maroush. A bottle of Lebanese Ksara Blanc de l'Observatoire made an equally refined accompaniment. Good food, then, but not quite as consistent as this chain usually produces. And the atmosphere-free zone made us think wistfully of the belly dancers and musicians down the road.
Babies and children welcome: high chairs. Booking advisable. **Map 8 F6**.
For branches (Maroush) see index.

★ Patogh
8 Crawford Place, W1H 5NE (7262 4015). Edgware Road tube. **Meals served** 12.30-11pm daily. **Main courses** £6-£12. **Unlicensed. Corkage** no charge. **No credit cards.** Iranian
'Dahaati' is a word used by Iran's urban elite to describe people and places they consider rural or low-rent. Such snobs wouldn't be seen dead in Patogh, which forsakes the forced orientalism of many Middle Eastern restaurants in favour of almost bare mud-coloured walls. Its crew of paper-hat-wearing, Farsi-speaking staff weave effortlessly between a handful of shared tables spread over two tiny floors (ground and first). Nor does the plastic laminated menu stand on ceremony, with a complete absence of the subtle soups and stews that fuel Iran's upmarket dinner parties. Instead you'll find workmanlike starters of masto khiar, masto musir and houmous, along with freshly baked persian bread. Mains are served, like the starters, on grim metal plates, and consist of lamb and chicken kebabs – both tender and delicious, although the latter needed longer in the traditional lemon and saffron marinade – accompanied either with buttered rice or wrapped in bread. It's all so authentic that you could easily believe you were in a cheap café in Tehran's central bazaar, if it weren't for the bottles of bring-your-own booze.
Booking advisable weekends. Takeaway service. **Map 8 E5**.

Ranoush Juice (100)
43 Edgware Road, W2 2JE (7723 5929/www.maroush.com). Marble Arch tube. **Meals served** 8am-3am daily. **Main courses** £3-£10. **No credit cards.** Lebanese
Ranoush, part of the Maroush empire, has been squeezing juices and churning out shawarmas for decades. Behind the busy counter where the juice-squeezers and shawarma-makers toil, a modest selection of meze is displayed. Many dishes here, like falafel, can also be wrapped in shami bread – along with pickles and garlicky tahini sauce – to take away. Or you can order your food 'on a plate' and eat at one of the café's marble-topped tables or at the counter facing the mirrored wall. We were impressed with our plateful recently. It may have been fast food, but everything was very carefully garnished and well presented. While some of the dishes didn't have the finesse you might expect of the pricey Maroushes down the road, flavours were big and bold. Batata hara contained big chunks of pepper, and slices of garlic the size of 1p pieces; falafel were crunchy and spicy; tabouleh arrived a little coarsely chopped, but with a lively citrussy zing. With a generous pile of warmed bread, this all made an honest, satisfying lunch. A great place to call in, day or night (and it's open until the small hours): just don't expect peace and quiet.
Babies and children admitted. Takeaway service. **Map 8 F6**.
For branches (Ranoush Juice, Beirut Express) see index.

Marylebone

Ali Baba
32 Ivor Place, NW1 6DA (7723 7474/5805). Baker Street tube/Marylebone tube/rail. **Meals served** noon-midnight daily. **Main courses** £7-£10. **Unlicensed. Corkage** no charge. **No credit cards.** Egyptian
On a quiet sidestreet, Ali Baba functions largely as a takeaway with a restaurant at the back. It seems a desultory spot, but its unique selling point is

Egyptian food. You'll find the full repertoire here, from molokhia to koshari, via fuul and tamaya (falafel). We were big fans of the fuul on a recent visit, which was mashed into a coarse paste with lashings of olive oil and plenty of spicy flavouring – very different from Lebanese versions. Koshari (a mix of rice, vermicelli and lentils topped with caramelised onions) was too plain, needing more oil and onion. We also tried grilled lamb and chicken (both well-cooked, tender cubes of meat), and the Egyptian national dish, molokhia: a soupy stew with a distinctive slimy texture, served with rice and, in this case, chunks of lamb; it's an acquired taste, but this was a good, robust version. Ali Baba is a family affair. It's not licensed, but you can bring your own. After a couple of beers, some good food, and a chat with the owner's daughter, the place didn't seem so desultory after all.
Babies and children welcome: high chairs.
Booking advisable. Takeaway service; delivery service. **Map 2 F4.**

Fairuz
3 Blandford Street, W1U 3DA (7486 8108/ 8182/www.fairuz.uk.com). Baker Street or Bond Street tube. **Meals served** noon-11.30pm Mon-Sat; noon-11pm Sun. **Main courses** £11.95-£19.95. **Set meze** £19.95. **Set meal** £26.95 3 courses. **Cover** £1.50. **Credit** AmEx, MC, V. Lebanese
Middle Eastern country kitchen – bare bricks, swags of dried chillies and aubergine skins, a threateningly large vase beside one table – may not make it into an interior decorator's top-ten looks, but it sure makes Fairuz a one-off. Rough hewn can be charming, but not when it extends to the service, as it did the tremendously bustling night of our visit. With what appeared to be one wine list for the entire restaurant to share, the somewhat testy staff scuttled ungraciously between the tightly packed tables. The room was filled with youngish westerners, attracted by the relatively low prices at this singularly rustic and well-regarded Lebanese. Moutabal passed muster; fuul medames, houmous prettily decorated with a diamond of red pepper, and delicate fatayer, made up a fine meze selection. Staff forgot the kibbeh we'd ordered. If Fairuz was slightly off colour that night (like the slightly brown edge of the iceberg lettuce included with lemony olives, bread and an onion, carrot and tomato salad in the cover charge), the makloobeh, a terrific stew of aubergine, rice, lamb and almonds, left a lastingly good impression that explains the restaurant's popularity.
Babies and children welcome: high chairs. Booking essential dinner. Separate room for parties, seats 25. Takeaway service; delivery service (within 3-mile radius). **Map 9 G5.**

Levant
Jason Court, 76 Wigmore Street, W1U 2SJ (7224 1111/www.levant.co.uk). Bond Street tube. **Bar Open** noon-12.30am Mon-Wed, Sun; noon-2.30am Thur-Sat. *Restaurant* **Meals served** noon-11.30pm daily. **Main courses** £12.50-£26. **Set lunch** (noon-5.30pm Mon-Fri) £8-£15 2 courses. **Set dinner** (Wed-Sat) £37-£60 per person (minimum 2) 3 courses; £60 per person (minimum 8) kharuf feast.
Both **Credit** AmEx, DC, MC, V. Lebanese
Down a lamp-lit and petal-strewn staircase, through a heavy wooden door and into a louche basement bar with low seats, Levant pans out into a Marrakech-ish mishmash of furniture. Dappled light is cast on the earthy-toned walls by filigree lanterns, and frantic music plays. There are some surprises. Least welcome, if not that unexpected, are the belly dancers. Fizzy water and sickly-sounding cocktails are given a hard sell by staff in black T-shirts, but the cooking is home-style, the Lebanese flair for hospitality wins through, and there are some delightfully innovative meze. Dull houmous, oily fried aubergine with mint, and a coarse but decent moutabal began a meal of our devising (rather than the over-priced feasts staff tried to steer us towards). D'jaj mohammar (small chicken stewed in heavenly lemony juices with cinnamon and mint) put a too-chunky and chewy lamb meshwi to shame. Our enjoyment of Levant

Menu

See also the menu boxes in **North African** and **Turkish**. Note that spellings can vary. For more information, consult *The Legendary Cuisine of Persia*, by Margaret Shaida, *Lebanese Cuisine* by Anissa Helou (both Grub Street), and *Flavours of the Levant* by Nadeh Saleh (Metro).

MEZE
Baba ganoush: Egyptian name for moutabal (qv).
Basturma: smoked beef.
Batata hara: potatoes fried with peppers and chilli.
Falafel: a mixture of spicy chickpeas or broad beans ground, rolled into balls and deep fried.
Fatayer: a soft pastry, filled with cheese, onions, spinach and pine kernels.
Fattoush: fresh vegetable salad containing shards of toasted pitta bread and sumac (qv).
Fuul or **fuul medames:** brown broad beans that are mashed and seasoned with olive oil, lemon juice and garlic.
Kalaj: halloumi cheese on pastry.
Kibbeh: highly seasoned mixture of minced lamb, cracked wheat and onion, deep-fried in balls. For meze it is often served raw (**kibbeh nayeh**) like steak tartare.
Labneh: Middle Eastern cream cheese made from yoghurt.
Moujadara: lentils, rice and caramelised onions mixed together.
Moutabal: a purée of chargrilled aubergines mixed with sesame sauce, garlic and lemon juice.
Muhamara: dip of crushed mixed nuts with red peppers, spices and pomegranate molasses.
Sambousek: small pastries filled with mince, onion and pine kernels.
Shankleesh: aged yogurt cheese flavoured with thyme.
Sujuk: spicy Lebanese sausages.
Sumac: an astringent and fruity-tasting spice made from dried sumac seeds.
Tabouleh: a salad of chopped parsley, tomatoes, crushed wheat, onions, olive oil and lemon juice.
Torshi: pickled vegetables.
Warak einab: rice-stuffed vine leaves.

MAINS
Shawarma: meat (usually lamb) marinated then grilled on a spit and sliced kebab-style.
Shish kebab: cubes of marinated lamb grilled on a skewer, often with tomatoes, onions and sweet peppers.
Shish taouk: like shish kebab, but with chicken rather than lamb.

DESSERTS
Baklava: filo pastry interleaved with pistachio nuts, almonds or walnuts, and covered in syrup.
Konafa or **kadayif:** cake made from shredded pastry dough, filled with syrup and nuts, or cream.
Ma'amoul: pastries filled with nuts or dates.
Muhallabia or **mohalabia:** a milky ground-rice pudding with almonds and pistachios, flavoured with rosewater or orange blossom.
Om ali: bread pudding, often made with filo pastry, also includes nuts and raisins.

IRANIAN DISHES
Ash-e reshteh: a soup with noodles, spinach, pulses and dried herbs.
Ghorm-e sabzi: lamb with greens, kidney beans and dried limes.
Halim bademjan: mashed chargrilled aubergine with onions and walnuts.
Joojeh or **jujeh:** chicken marinated in saffron, lemon and onion.
Kashk, qurut, quroot: a salty whey.
Kashk-e bademjan: baked aubergines mixed with herbs and whey.
Khoresht-e fesenjan: chicken cooked in walnuts and pomegranate juice.
Kuku-ye sabzi: finely chopped fresh herbs with eggs, baked in the oven.
Masto khiar: yoghurt mixed with finely chopped cucumber and mint.
Masto musir: shallot-flavoured yoghurt.
Mirza ghasemi: crushed baked aubergines, tomatoes, garlic and herbs mixed with egg.
Sabzi: a plate of fresh herb leaves (usually mint and dill) often served with a cube of feta.
Salad olivieh: like a russian salad, includes chopped potatoes, chicken, eggs, peas, gherkins, olive oil and mayonnaise.

had more to do with the memorable crab kibbeh and duck fatayer, plus an extravagant end to our meal of fragrant mint tea and a tiered cake-stand overflowing with sweetmeats, than the overbearing music and 'international nitespot' vibe.
Booking advisable. Entertainment: belly dancer 9pm Mon-Wed, Sun; 8.30pm, 11.30pm Thur-Sat. Separate area for parties, seats 10-14. Takeaway service. **Map 9 G6.**
For branch (Levantine) see index.

Mayfair

Al Hamra
31-33 Shepherd Market, W1J 7PT (7493 1954/ www.alhamrarestaurant.co.uk). Green Park or Hyde Park Corner tube. **Meals served** noon-11.30pm daily. **Main courses** £14-£22.50. **Cover** £2.50. **Minimum** £20. **Credit** AmEx, DC, MC, V. Lebanese

Chintzy ruched viennese blinds, carpets and low ceilings may seem an unlikely look for a Lebanese restaurant, but the slightly kitsch homeliness of the space is matched with the more usual snowy-white starched tablecloths, sparkling glassware and besuited staff. Al Hamra has occupied its Shepherd Market corner site since 1984. Decor has changed very little since, and the cosmopolitan customers seem to love it as much as ever; the place is usually bursting with bonhomie by night. Lunchtimes are quieter, but standards rarely slip and a recent afternoon visit (when we were seated next to some Foreign Office types) was no exception. Fattoush was packed with the freshest chopped salad vegetables. Add a lemony dressing, crunchy chips of toasted pitta and a dusting of warm sumac spice, and you have a summery classic. Muhamara had finely chopped nuts and a subtle, spicy flavour. Silky moutabal and a vibrant,

RESTAURANTS

zesty tabouleh complemented the other dishes well. A main course shish taouk was a sizeable portion of tender chicken, served with garlicky mayonnaise. It was all just right for a summer lunch, especially when accompanied by a Lebanese beer, and followed by turkish coffee with a complimentary selection of fresh little pastries.
Babies and children welcome: high chairs. Booking advisable dinner. Tables outdoors (8, terrace). Takeaway service; delivery service. **Map 9 H8**.

Al Sultan
51-52 Hertford Street, W1J 7ST (7408 1155/ 1166/www.alsultan.co.uk). Green Park or Hyde Park Corner tube. **Meals served** noon-11pm daily. **Main courses** £13-£16. **Minimum** £20. **Cover** £2. **Credit** AmEx, DC, MC, V. Lebanese
Al Sultan just keeps going and going. In Mayfair there are still customers willing to pay top dollar for bright lighting, pastelly decor and a look of dated luxury – or perhaps it's the high-quality food that attracts them. A recent visit, though, revealed a few slips in standards. Sambousek were rather over-baked filo parcels, with a dark, slightly bitter spinach filling. Fuul makala (usually a bright dish of fresh green broad beans with coriander, olive oil and lemon juice) was rather soggy and bland. Meat too, in the form of lahem meshwi, suffered from too much cooking: not the succulent cubes of barbecued lamb we expect from this cuisine (and this price tag). To be fair, other dishes were bang on, like a lively, citrussy batinjan raheb (mashed aubergine salad with tomatoes and parsley), which contrasted nicely with manakeish bizzaatar (pitta bread sprinkled with olive oil and warm spices). A shish taouk was fine too. Staff were professional but not frosty, and Al Sultan's own-label house white made a fine accompaniment.
Babies and children welcome: high chairs. Booking advisable dinner. Tables outdoors (4, pavement). Takeaway service; delivery service (over £35 within 4-mile radius). Vegetarian menu. **Map 9 H8**.

Piccadilly

Fakhreldine
85 Piccadilly, W1J 7NB (7493 3424/ www.fakhreldine.co.uk). Green Park tube. **Meals served** noon-midnight Mon-Sat; noon-11pm Sun. **Main courses** £13-£23. **Set lunch** £17 2 courses, £22 3 courses. **Credit** AmEx, DC, MC, V. Lebanese
Follow the night-lights and *American Beauty*-style red-rose wall up the stairs to this glamorously sleek bar and restaurant, which belies its long-standing prime position on Piccadilly. An inviting lounge area and great drinks list including rose lemonade is reason enough not to go straight to one of the restaurant tables with a view of Green Park. Who knew there were so many wines from the Bekaa Valley? Cooking doesn't consistently do the Lebanon quite as much credit. Inspired meze, including crisp pumpkin and walnut kibbeh and a standout dish of chicken livers with pomegranate molasses, outshone the bland baba ganoush and fatayer. Considering the prices and their relative simplicity, main courses could have had more care and definition. Three little red mullet, spoilt by greasy fried aubergine slices and strips of pitta on the dark side of toasted, left a poor impression. Milk pudding with the texture and aroma of face cream was improved no end by a jug of rose syrup. Service excelled right until the ending of orange blossom and mint teas in see-through teapots, helping make Fakhreldine better as a rendezvous for drinks and meze than as a restaurant.
Babies and children welcome: high chairs. Booking advisable. Takeaway service; delivery service (within 4-mile radius). **Map 9 H8**.

St James's

Noura
122 Jermyn Street, SW1Y 4UJ (7839 2020/ www.noura.co.uk). Piccadilly Circus tube. **Meals served** noon-midnight daily. **Main courses** £14-£22. **Set lunch** £18 2 courses, £25 3 courses. **Set dinner** (6-7pm) £18 3 courses. **Credit** AmEx, DC, MC, V. Lebanese

An oasis of civilisation in chain-reactionary territory. OK, there are four Nouras in London, but each is different and the interior at this branch is exceptionally dramatic, with a two-storey crimson wall dotted with little round mirrors. Silky cushions are scattered with abandon. Hedonism reigns in the evening when a DJ stokes up the decibels, but even at lunchtime there was a birthday party at one table, while business was being done elsewhere. Staff can rise to any occasion – so, generally, does the food, though given the prices of even the quite heavy 'light menu', so it should. Most of the greatest hits (exemplary silky-smooth and smoky moutabal, tabouleh all the more refreshing for parsley outweighing bulgar, crisp falafel, lemony dolmades and tidy little fatayer) were executed with dash, if not perfection. There's nothing outré on the menu, but for a variation on the minced lamb and pine kernel matrix, there's kibbeh bissayniyeh: a slice of minced lamb, cracked wheat and pine kernel layer cake, jauntily accessorised with yoghurt and mint sauce. Kofte was spot on. Service is slick and responsive too. Noura gives eating out in the West End a good name.
Babies and children welcome: high chairs. Disabled: toilet. Dress: smart casual. Entertainment: DJ 8.30pm Wed-Sat. Restaurant and bar available for hire. Separate area for parties, seats 40. **Map 10 K7**.
For branches see index.

West

Bayswater

★ Al Waha
75 Westbourne Grove, W2 4UL (7229 0806/ www.waha-uk.com). Bayswater or Queensway tube. **Meals served** noon-11.30pm. **Main courses** £9.50-£18.50. **Set lunch** £12.50 2 courses. **Set dinner** £21 per person (minimum 2) 3 courses, £25 per person (minimum 2) 4 courses. **Cover** £1.50. **Minimum** £12.50 (dinner). **Credit** MC, V. Lebanese
A recent dinner at Al Waha was as good as it gets. Well, almost. Negatives first: it was Saturday night and the small restaurant was obviously expecting plenty of business. Still, it was galling for three of us to be seated at a table for two in the corner. And the next group who arrived were put right next to us, tables about two inches apart. The place did fill quickly, though, and it's easy to see why. The kitchen seemed to be on a roll. With meze dishes this good you end up with a meal that's way more than the sum of its parts. Perhaps we chose well, complementing textures and tastes: butter-soft chicken livers in a rich gravy with gentle citrus overtones were a good match for earthy moujadara (lentils and rice with caramelised onions); fresh, crunchy fattoush was full of spicy zest, and great with thick, rich houmous. Everything else was enjoyable too: perfectly cooked sambousek parcels, and fuul makala (the broad beans a fresh, young green, delicately flavoured with lemon and coriander). The main course meats were pretty faultless, and a bottle of Gris de Gris rosé made an ideal accompaniment. Definitely a hit.
Babies and children welcome (until 7pm). Booking advisable; essential dinner. Tables outdoors (4, patio). Takeaway service; delivery service (over £20 within 3-mile radius). **Map 7 B6**.

Fresco
25 Westbourne Grove, W2 4UA (7221 2355/ www.frescojuices.co.uk). Bayswater or Royal Oak tube. **Meals served** 8am-11pm daily. **Main courses** £5.95-£7.95. **Set meze** £11.95. **Credit** MC, V. Lebanese
Health and vitality are the names of the game at Fresco, a juice-bar-cum-Lebanese takeaway and caff. Fruit fills the front window; photos of fruit line the seaside-yellow walls; the juicer whirs loudly in the background. The juice menu is extensive, ranging from heavy-duty 'energisers' involving the likes of broccoli and beets, to mixed 'tutti frutti' cocktails and 'milky way' milkshakes, such as the silky banana and strawberry version with honey that we tried on a recent visit. Meze dishes are lined up in bowls behind the counter. Pick what you want from the menu, staff will microwave the dishes to be served hot, and present you with a heaving plateful of three dishes for £4.50 (you can order individually too). We chose a delicately flavoured baba ganoush – nicely served in a swirl, with a well in the middle filled with pomegranate seeds. The full-flavoured fuul was lovely and sloppy. Only a rather bland batata hara wasn't quite up to scratch. At lunchtime, Fresco does a roaring trade in houmous and falafel sandwiches in pitta bread.
Babies and children welcome: high chairs. Bookings not accepted. Takeaway service; delivery service (within 3-mile radius). Vegetarian menu. **Map 7 B6**.
For branches see index.

Hafez
5 Hereford Road, W2 4AB (7221 3167/7229 9398/www.hafez.com). Bayswater tube/328 bus. **Meals served** noon-midnight daily. **Main courses** £6-£14.50. **No credit cards**. Iranian
Smaller and less glamorous than many of its competitors, Hafez is still popular with Iranian expats who relish its immunity to the slings and arrows of passing time. Its single square room has remained virtually unaltered over the years and sports only the most sparing decoration (a framed print here, some artfully exposed bricks there). It's less a restaurant than a communal living room. Everyone seems to be on first-name terms, and our last visit saw staff dividing their time between serving everyone and playing with a diner's three-year-old daughter. However, the cooking can occasionally be rather underwhelming. Portions are relatively paltry, especially for the starters. Masto khiar arrived in a ramekin, kashk-e bademjan in a glorified ashtray. A main course of mixed chelo kebab was less than spectacular: the minced lamb koubideh tender and flavoursome, but the joojeh surprisingly dry. A stew of ghorm-e sabzi (lamb with greens, kidney beans and dried limes) was more successful, packed with meat and with a satisfying bitterness. All told, Hafez is neither London's best Iranian eaterie nor its worst by a long shot.
Babies and children welcome: high chairs. Tables outdoors (4, pavement). Takeaway service. **Map 7 B6**.
For branch see index.

Hammersmith

★ Mahdi
217 King Street, W6 9JT (8563 7007). Hammersmith or Ravenscourt Park tube. **Meals served** noon-11pm daily. **Main courses** £5-£12. **Set lunch** (noon-6pm Mon-Fri) £4.90 1 course. **Unlicensed. Credit** MC, V. Iranian
With an output in plastic doggie bags potentially warranting an offset of its carbon footprint, Mahdi is crowned king when it comes to unnecessarily large portions of lovingly prepared, artfully presented Iranian food. It's not the homeliest of restaurants, its brick walls arching like the inside of a kiln, its waiters unduly serious and its tables cramped together almost uncomfortably. The abundance of decorative Persian trinkets verges on the oppressive – from micro-mosaic framed prints and coloured vases to a stuffed peacock watching forlornly from one corner. But if there's better Iranian food being served in the capital, we've yet to taste it. The list of starters supplements the usual repertoire with rarities like ash-e reshteh, a smoky bean and noodle soup thickened with whey. Marinated chicken and lamb kebabs are succulent, super sized and served with perfectly fluffy rice, but you'd be foolish not to experiment with the more traditional Iranian dishes here, like baghali polo ba mahiche: rice with dill and broad beans accompanied by a melt-in-the-mouth lamb shank – so delicious you'll be only too happy to tuck into the leftovers later at home that same evening, if you've room.
Booking advisable. Disabled: toilet. No alcohol allowed. Takeaway service. **Map 20 B4**.
For branch see index.

Fakhreldine

Kensington

Randa

23 Kensington Church Street, W8 4LF (7937 5363/www.maroush.com). High Street Kensington tube. **Meals served** noon-11.30pm daily. **Main courses** £11.95-£16. **Set lunch** £12 2 courses. **Set dinner** £45 per person (minimum 2) 3 courses. **Credit** MC, V. Lebanese
This outlet of the prolific Maroush empire is aimed at a young and cosmopolitan Kensington crowd. Snappy service and a slick design keep it vibrant, while the menu follows the tried and tested formula of the Edgware Road branches. As one of the longest-established Lebanese chains in London, Maroush has had time to get the food right, and it does. While the menu is strong on chargrilled meats and offal, the meze are undoubtedly the stars. The good-value set menu will give you a taste of all the favourites – among them intensely smoky moutabal, velvety houmous, zippy tabouleh and spicy sausages sautéd in lemon. Sticky chicken wings came with a sauce that positively sang with raw garlic, while the falafels had correctly crisp jackets encasing soft centres. If you're still hungry (which is unlikely given the generous portions), sample the wonderful sweet nutty pastries. Try and get a table on the ground floor, where you can enjoy the buzz of the high street and the drama of the open kitchen.
Separate room for parties, seats 40. Takeaway service; delivery service (over £25 within 1-mile radius). **Map 7 B8.**

Olympia

Alounak

10 Russell Gardens, W14 8EZ (7603 7645). Kensington (Olympia) tube/rail. **Meals served** noon-midnight daily. **Main courses** £6.30-£12.30. **Unlicensed. Corkage** no charge. **Credit** MC, V. Iranian
Perhaps it's a case of good nights and bad nights – nothing has changed on the surface, after all. Alounak's front room remains a temple to the kind of token handicrafts imported ten-a-penny from Tehran, such as colourful blown-glass ornaments and miniature samovars. A clay oven is in one corner and a fake palm tree loiters conspicuously in the other, while the rear room is dominated by fish tanks, a central fountain and an enormous chandelier looming menacingly overhead. It's a pleasant enough setting (albeit an isolated one in terms of public transport), but recent visits have revealed a restaurant satisfying studenty kebab seekers by the dozen, while leaving those seeking more traditional Iranian dishes out in the cold. Grilled sea bass was both miserably small and mercilessly overcooked, while khoresht-e bamieh (lamb and okra stew) consisted of just two pieces of meat (and miniscule ones at that) floating in a barely seasoned tomato broth. Coming as it does from a culture that loves to bitch about others' food, Alounak is treading a thin line.
Babies and children welcome: high chairs. Booking advisable. Takeaway service.
For branch see index.

Mohsen

152 Warwick Road, W14 8PS (7602 9888). Earl's Court tube/Kensington (Olympia) tube/rail. **Meals served** noon-midnight daily. **Main courses** £12-£15. **Unlicensed. Corkage** no charge. **No credit cards.** Iranian
Mohsen may be bracketed by a pair of moribund boozers and opposite a Homebase, but the temptation here is to wind your watch forward three hours and start working on Tehran time. Few places draw so wide a cross-section of London's Iranian community. They are met with hearty handshakes and banter by Mrs Mohsen herself, before being seated at one of the functional tables and furnished with a laminated menu. Like the decor (a handful of Iranian posters in the front room; a gleeful mismatch of coloured lights, potted plants and garden furniture out back), the menu remains unaltered by the passing years. Regulars know the importance of not filling up on starters like kashk-e bademjan (mashed aubergine and whey dip) and sharp masto musir. They also tuck into the dishes of the day – including baghali polo ba mahiche, a lamb shank on a bed of rice with dill and lima beans. Less frequent visitors tend to opt for the legendary chelo kebabs: lamb barg or koobideh (filleted or minced), or chicken joojeh, which come wrapped in hot bread or alongside a mountain of perfectly fluffy persian rice.
Babies and children admitted. Takeaway service. **Map 13 A10.**

Shepherd's Bush

★ Abu Zaad

29 Uxbridge Road, W12 8LH (8749 5107/ www.abuzaad.co.uk). Shepherd's Bush tube. **Meals served** 11am-11pm daily. **Main courses** £5-£11. **Credit** MC, V. Syrian
A landmark on the Shepherd's Bush strip known as 'Little Syria', Abu Zaad is one of London's few Levantine restaurants not to pose as Lebanese. It is usually packed with locals who come to enjoy the reasonably priced Damascene food. Inside, harsh lighting and tiled floors don't make for an intimate atmosphere, but a back room with painted panels on the walls and inlaid marble tables has more charm. Smiling waiters will guide you through the long menu and ensure food is brought out from the kitchen quickly. Most dishes are meat-heavy: lamb kebabs with mounds of spiced rice or various mince-stuffed vegetables baked in yoghurt. However, vegetarians needn't despair. The meze outshone the mains on our visit, and it's tempting to make a meal just of these alone. Highlights include little baby aubergines stuffed with chilli-flecked walnuts, and tamarind lentils with cubes of silky pasta and crisp shards of fried bread. We'll certainly be back again for this slice of the Middle East in W12.
Babies and children welcome: high chairs. Booking advisable weekends. Separate room for parties, seats 30. Takeaway service. **Map 20 B2.**

Sufi

70 Askew Road, W12 9BJ (8834 4888/ www.sufirestaurant.com). Hammersmith tube then bus 266. **Meals served** noon-11pm daily. **Main courses** £6.90-£11.90. **Set lunch** (noon-5pm Mon-Fri) £9.50 3 courses. **Credit** MC, V. Iranian
You know you're dealing with an authentic Iranian restaurant when you find the provincial bean and noodle soup, ash-e reshteh, on the menu: even more so when it's made like grandmother's own, the beans whole instead of pulped and the mixture thickened with creamy whey. Sufi's kitchen is keen on emulating the motherland in more than just token gestures. As such we get starters rarely found in London, including kookoo sabzi, a herb omelette rich with coriander, parsley and dill, and tah dig (crispy rice from the bottom of the dish) seeped in the sauces of different stews – Iranian comfort food at its most comforting. Mains are similarly convincing, the range of perfectly tender kebabs complemented by a mix of superb stews including a rich, bitter khoresht-e fesenjan (chicken cooked in walnuts and pomegranate juice), and a khoresht-e bademjan (lamb with fried aubergines) packed with tender pieces of meat. Surprisingly for an Iranian eatery, there's also a good choice of vegetarian dishes. Unlike the food, the decor's not

especially notable, adorned with the usual mix of Tehran trinkets and Persian ephemera (wrinkled bazaaris, a panoramic view of pre-earthquake Bam). *Babies and children welcome: high chair. Separate room for parties, seats 40. Takeaway service.* **Map 20 A2**.

South West

Barnes

★ ★ Faanoos NEW
2008 RUNNER-UP BEST CHEAP EATS
481 Upper Richmond Road West, SW14 7PU (8878 5738). Mortlake rail. **Meals served** noon-11pm daily. **Main courses** £4.95-£9.95. **Credit** MC, V. Iranian

London's numerous Iranian restaurants seem divided between those attempting to evoke the opulence of ancient Persia and those content to emulate the warm familiarity of bustling Tehran kebab houses. Faanoos is among the latter – its clay walls matted with straw and embellished with occasional sepia prints of pre-revolutionary Iran, its staff on first-name terms with justifiably dedicated locals – but the food is cosmopolitan enough to rival pricier Kensington establishments. A combination starter plate was uniformly excellent, mixing some smoky kashk-e bademjan (mashed aubergine with garlic and whey), zingy masto musir (shallot yoghurt), salad olivieh (shredded chicken salad) and torsh, a Persian pickle packed with chunky vegetables. Mains were similarly satisfying: a tender chicken kebab was yellowed from a long marination in saffron, lemon and onion, while a stew of ghorm-e sabzi (lamb with dried limes, kidney beans and bitter greens) was heavy on the meat and hearty of portion; both were served with mountains of perfectly fluffy, saffron-tinted rice. Plan to save room for a rare Persian dessert; both the faloodeh (frozen rice noodles in rosewater) and bastani (traditional ice-cream) are seldom seen in London.
Babies and children welcome: high chairs. Booking advisable. Dress: smart casual. Tables outdoors (2, pavement). Takeaway service.

South East

London Bridge & Borough

Hiba NEW
Maya House, 134-138 Borough High Street, SE1 1LB (7357 9633/www.hibarestaurant.com). Borough tube. **Meals served** noon-11pm

Mon-Thur; noon-midnight Fri, Sat. **Main courses** £9.75-£13. **Set Lunch** £11.75 2 courses. **Set meal** £39.75 2 courses (minimum 2), £79.75 3 courses incl wine (minimum 4). **Credit** AmEx, DC, MC, V. Lebanese

A Lebanese outpost in previously uncharted Borough High Street, Hiba has stylish, retro furnishings of olive-green and brown. The look may not be classic Lebanese, but the food is. All the favourite meze are here, though a couple of details are absent: warmed pitta was served rather than puffed-up Lebanese bread; and the traditional bowl of fresh salad vegetables was missing. Small points perhaps, but they hindered our enjoyment of an otherwise superb spread. Houmous beiruty was dense and luscious, with a touch of chilli adding an extra dimension; falafel were perfect (crunchy on the outside, soft inside and warmly spiced with cumin); samak harra (little pieces of fish in a hot tomato and chilli sauce) packed a punch; tabouleh was light and lemony; and salty grilled halloumi added to a great mix of strong, fresh flavours. We were rather taken aback to discover there was no fuul (a bit like a fish and chip shop having no fish), but the manager got the kitchen to rustle us up a basic version. Helpful service and great food, then. We just wish Hiba would reinstate those vital elements of the Lebanese dining ritual: bread and veg.
Babies and children admitted (until 3pm). Disabled: toilet. Separate room for parties, seats 30. Tables outdoors (4, pavement). Takeaway service. **Map 11 P8**.

North

Camden Town & Chalk Farm

Le Mignon
98 Arlington Road, NW1 7HD (7387 0600). Camden Town tube. **Lunch served** noon-3pm, **dinner served** 6pm-midnight daily. **Main courses** £9.50-£18.50. **Credit** MC, V. Lebanese

It was Saturday lunchtime and Camden market was heaving, yet a few streets away Le Mignon was empty and the lone waiter was ordering himself a Subway sandwich. Things didn't look promising. Our concerns weren't alleviated by the strange rather old-fashioned decor – salmon-pink tablecloths, bizarre stone-clad walls, the small room dominated by a large candle chandelier with no candles. Luckily, when the food hit the table, all this was forgotten. Silky houmous came topped

with warm broad beans and a generous slick of grassy olive oil: perfect to scoop up with fluffy rounds of flatbread. Doughnut-shaped falafel had a wonderfully light and crunchy crust, encasing herby centres. Buried under a mound of shredded onions and peppers came a decent lamb kebab with a smoky charred crust. Aubergine with tomatoes and chickpeas was too cold and had a disappointing lack of flavour, but on the whole Le Mignon produces good honest Lebanese cooking and deserves to be busier.
Babies and children admitted (daytime). Booking advisable. Tables outdoors (4, pavement). Takeaway service. **Map 27 D3**.

Outer London

Wembley, Middlesex

★ Mesopotamia
115 Wembley Park Drive, Wembley, Middx HA9 8HG (8453 5555/www.mesopotamia.ltd.uk). Wembley Park tube. **Lunch served** noon-2.30pm Mon-Fri. **Dinner served** 6pm-midnight Mon-Sat. **Main courses** £8-£15.50. **Set dinner** £23 3 courses. **Credit** AmEx, DC, MC, V. Iraqi

Holding its own on a street lined with fast-food caffs, family-run Mesopotamia flies the flag for Iraqi home cooking. The place is crammed with a grotto of artefacts, decorative wall friezes and candles, and our friendly host was happy to talk about the history of the various fittings and fixtures. The cooking reflects a range of Middle Eastern flavours and is as diverse as it is delicious. After sipping a chilled Lebanese pilsener, we tucked into warm flatbreads and fabulous houmous, notable for its subtle sesame flavour and lemony tang. This went down a treat with herby tabouleh and garlicky aubergine purée. Of the mains, we were especially impressed by fesenjan – chicken thighs simmered in a creamy covering of pomegranate molasses, crushed walnuts and onions. Dried fruit and meat combos are classic pairings, and slow-cooked lamb shoulder simmered in a cinnamon-infused broth with sweet apricots and tart prunes was marvellously mellow. Sweet-toothed diners should check out the delectable walnut-stuffed dates cooked in spiced syrup. These sticky delights make a great partner to the strong arabic coffee served from a traditional pot. A wonderfully warm, welcoming restaurant with top-class cooking and friendly service.
Babies and children admitted. Booking advisable. Restaurant available for hire. Vegetarian menu.

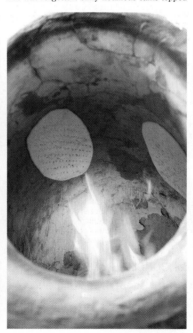

Faanoos

RESTAURANTS

Modern European

A pologies for the term Modern European, but we have found no better way to sum up the contemporary magpie style of cooking that melds British and other European foundations with flavours and techniques from further afield. As the largest chapter in this guide, it is arguably London's favourite cuisine, as suited to a family or working lunch as to a romantic evening or special occasion. One of the most pleasing aspects of the Modern European style is that it sits as happily in a neighbourhood restaurant as it does in the West End, so you won't have to travel far to enjoy it. Here we feature restaurants throughout the capital, from Ham to Greenwich, and Tooting to West Hampstead. You'll find several hardy perennials (**The Ivy**, **Andrew Edmunds**, **Clarke's** and **Blueprint Café**, to name but a few), maturing saplings (**Wild Honey**, **Odette's**, **Fouronine**), plus an exciting number of new blooms. Among our favourites making their debut this year are **L'Autre Pied**, winner of the 2008 Best New Restaurant award, the **Botanist**, **Harrison's**, **Giaconda Dining Room** and **Northbank**.

Central

Bloomsbury

Giaconda Dining Room NEW
9 Denmark Street, WC2H 8LS (7240 3334/ www.giacondadining.com). Tottenham Court Road tube. **Lunch served** noon-2.15pm, **dinner served** 6-9.45pm Mon-Fri. **Main courses** £9.50-£13. **Cover** £1. **Credit** AmEx, MC, V.
Paul and Tracey Merrony's simple black-and-white dining room belies the esteem in which chef Paul is held in his native Australia. Yet, as with many of the best Sydney restaurants, this is a generous egalitarian spot where the unpretentious food is the star. A cover charge is levied, but it seems churlish to complain when a carafe of sparkling water arrives at the table unbidden, along with sliced ciabatta and a dish of olives of all shapes and colours. In her vintage waitress outfit, Tracey relays the specials – on our latest visit, a plate of piedmontese peppers; grill of the day was onglet with chips and salad. Salad of beetroot and leeks vinaigrette with goats' curd appealed. The menu also featured roast chicken and rack of lamb for a cosy twosome. Merrony's take on vitello tonnato is a heaped plate of cold poached veal with radicchio, potato, boiled egg and a generous drizzle of tuna sauce. We loved the hot pillow of ham hock hash with fried egg and lightly dressed mixed leaves. Desserts might be iced nougat parfait, tiramisu or eton mess. Surprisingly, the wine list isn't a tribute to Oz but is Europe-focused with admirably lean mark-ups. Glasses of wine start at £3.75; bottled organic beers from Pitfield Brewery are also available.
Babies and children admitted. Booking advisable. Tables outdoors (2, pavement). **Map 17 C3**.

City

The Don
The Courtyard, 20 St Swithin's Lane, EC4N 8AD (7626 2606/www.thedonrestaurant.com). Bank tube/DLR.
Bistro **Lunch served** noon-3pm, **dinner served** 6-10pm Mon-Fri. **Main courses** £8.95-£14.95.
Restaurant **Lunch served** noon-2.30pm, **dinner served** 6-10pm Mon-Fri. **Main courses** £12.95-£25.50.
Both **Credit** AmEx, DC, MC, V.
There are four compelling reasons to dine at the Don. One is the atmospheric basement bistro, a brick-vaulted space that was formerly the cellars of Sandeman port house, the owners. Second is the wine list, one of London's best – and never a better bargain than on Friday nights, when every bottle over £50 is half price. Third is hunger: the Don will conquer even the most ravenous appetite. And fourth, though slightly less compelling, is the food. The menu sticks to classic ideas, and mostly carries them off with skill. Our starters were pleasing: a straightforward terrine, grilled prawns on tabouleh, poached duck egg on delicious polenta. A 'cappuccino' soup of jerusalem artichokes and wild mushrooms was too creamy given the gargantuan serving, but delicious. Mains were fine, if not perfect. Grilled lamb burgers came cooked as ordered, with the same excellent chips that accompanied a perfectly cooked steak. Confit duck leg with cabbage and mash was as it should have been. Flaws appeared in sloppy presentation; the mangetout accompanying that steak, for instance, shouldn't have been underneath it. Service was somewhat remote and perfunctory: a few more smiles, please. Flaws apart, the Don is good value in this area – and Friday nights, with more of the globe-trotting wine list within striking distance, are a strong attraction.
Booking essential. Dress: smart casual. Separate room for parties, seats 24. **Map 12 Q7**.

Northbank NEW
One Paul's Walk, EC4V 3QH (7329 9299/ www.northbankrestaurant.com). St Paul's tube/ Blackfriars tube/rail. **Lunch served** noon-3pm Mon-Sat; 11am-5pm Sun. **Dinner served** 6-11pm daily. **Main courses** £12.50-£22.50. **Set meal** (lunch, 6-7pm) £13.50 2 courses, £17.50 3 courses. **Credit** AmEx, MC, V.

With its wonderful location on the brink of the Thames, just opposite the Tate Modern, Northbank feels like a place for a special occasion. There's a terrace outside where you can sip cocktails as the sun goes down, and picture windows in the dining room which frame the golden lights of the South Bank at night. The menu is short, straightforward and mainly modern British; ingredients from the West Country are favoured. Our roasted veal marrow bones with caramelised snails on toast were so delicious we almost had to lick the plate, while Brixham mussels cooked in ale with cream, shallots and thyme were delightful. Mains were mixed: a pea and mint risotto was overcooked and seemed completely unsalted. Service was charming but a little chaotic – we had to wait an age between our first and main courses. Still, romantic lighting and the air of bonhomie emanating from the banquetted booths and other tables helped to create a charming evening. And we like the wallpaper: 19th-century toile de jouy at a glance; on closer inspection filled with vignettes of contemporary London life.
Babies and children welcome: high chairs. Booking essential lunch (Mon-Fri). Disabled: toilet. Tables outdoors (11, terrace). **Map 11 O7**.

Prism
147 Leadenhall Street, EC3V 4QT (7256 3875/ www.harveynichols.com). Monument tube/Bank tube/DLR.
Bar **Open** 11am-11pm, **lunch served** 11.30am-3pm Mon-Fri. **Main courses** £10-£14.
Restaurant **Breakfast served** 8-10am, **lunch served** noon-3pm, **dinner served** 6-10pm Mon-Fri. **Main courses** £18-£30.
Both **Credit** AmEx, DC, MC, V.
The façade of the former Bank of New York building, dating from the 1920s, still emanates power and money, with the impression continuing into what is now the huge dining room of this Harvey Nichols-run restaurant. Vast columns soar up to the ornate corniced ceiling, and the room is filled with well-spaced tables and a huge bar down one side. Bright modern art and cool 1960s-style red leather chairs add some colour. There's a narrow 'conservatory', which is not as airy as it sounds. The menu promises strong flavours: roast Anjou pigeon comes with pickled chinese cabbage, pastilla and star anise vinaigrette in a complex starter; the dish featured a good-quality bird and well-made pigeon-stuffed pastry, but a lot of flavours fought for attention. Not every flavour punches its weight, witness the anaemic red wine sauce accompanying a confit sea trout and braised lentils. The gin ice-cream with rhubarb crumble

BEST MODERN EUROPEAN

A room with a view
Survey the surrounds at **Babylon** (*see p239*), **Blueprint Café** (*see p246*), **Northbank** (*see left*), **Oxo Tower Restaurant, Bar & Brasserie** (*see p245*), **Plateau** (*see p247*) and **Skylon** (*see p245*).

Vanity fair
Eat with the in-crowd at **L'Atelier de Joël Robuchon** (*see p231*), **Bumpkin** (*see p240*), **Le Caprice** (*see p237*), **Fifth Floor** (*see p247*) and **Odette's** (*see p231*) and **Villandry** (*see p231*).

Grape expectations
Wine lovers can drink it all in at **Ambassador** (*see p230*), **The Avenue** (*see p235*), **Bibendum** (*see p237*), **The Don** (*see left*), **The Glasshouse** (*see p248*), **Launceston Place** (*see p239*), **Orrery** (*see p233*) and **Ransome's Dock** (*see p244*).

was well-made and delivered a pleasing kick from the alcohol. Service is cheerful and effective, which is no mean feat given the size of the place. As this is the City, most customers wear suits.
Babies and children welcome: high chairs. Booking advisable. Disabled: toilet. Separate rooms for parties, seating 23 and 45. Vegetarian menu. **Map 12 Q6**.

Clerkenwell & Farringdon

★ Ambassador ⓝ

55 Exmouth Market, EC1R 4QL (7837 0009/ www.theambassadorcafe.co.uk). Farringdon tube/rail/19, 38, 341 bus. **Breakfast served** 8.30am-noon, **lunch served** noon-2.30pm Mon-Fri. **Brunch served** 11am-4pm Sat, Sun. **Dinner served** 6-10.15pm Mon-Sat. **Main courses** £9.50-£17. **Set lunch** £12.50 2 courses, £16 3 courses. **Credit** AmEx, MC, V.
Who needs diplomatic relations with France when the Ambassador creates so well the food we hope to find there? A proper all-day café, with wide-open doors and tables outside, it is run with real commitment and devilishly close attention to detail. From the croissants in the morning, through lunch and the perfectly baveuse omelette (so rare this side of the Channel), to the chocolate marquise with spiced red wine syrup and vanilla ice-cream that rounds off dinner, it has never let us down. Don't go expecting all Gallic. Yorkshire tea, bacon sandwich on proper thick slices of crusty white loaf, and the joyously seasonal likes of asparagus tart with mixed-leaf salad or plaice with jersey royals and baby leeks – all come at keen prices. A pudding of mango soufflé with passion-fruit sorbet would have been as at home on a stiff white cloth as on the dark green Formica table tops. Dream drinks include Hendrick's gin and Hereford cider, Noilly Prat and a Manzanilla. Wines with France to the fore, from £14 a bottle and with many by the 50cl or glass (poured from the bottle at your table) are a source of wonder. But where's our favourite aperitif Lillet got to?
Babies and children welcome: children's menu; high chairs; toys. Booking advisable. Disabled: toilet. Tables outdoors (5, pavement). **Map 5 N4**.

Clerkenwell Dining Room

69-73 St John Street, EC1M 4AN (7253 9000/ www.theclerkenwell.com). Barbican tube/ Farringdon tube/rail. **Lunch served** noon-2.30pm Mon-Fri. **Dinner served** 6-11pm Mon-Fri; 7-11pm Sat. **Main courses** £15-£22. **Credit** AmEx, DC, MC, V.
Like a well-tailored beige jacket with slightly out-of-date lapels, CDR is dependable if not at the cutting edge. It looks smart, apart from the 'Bayswater Road railings' artworks. A free hand with the balsamic, veloutés and purées characterise the expansive style of cooking. Tortellini of sweetbread in a creamy cep velouté with mushrooms, tarragon, asparagus and pea shoots had a hint of the ancient aceto. There was inevitably more balsamic in a satisfying salad of artichoke hearts, little red peppers stuffed with ricotta, spinach, pine nuts, parmesan, red pepper purée and nibbed chives. Plenty going on too, in the main course of halibut glazed with a sticky sweet jus paired with a neat little disc of pork belly sporting a thin topping of crackling, plus pea purée, apple purée and rather hard tart cubes of apple. And there were walnuts in there. The kitchen might benefit from choice editing; desserts show a similar reluctance to leave anything out. Rice pudding with cherries and blackcurrant sorbet in a tuile was good but something of a mismatch. Service was friendly and eager, yet we'd have preferred not to be asked for our opinion after every course.
Babies and children welcome: high chairs. Booking advisable. Separate room for parties, seats 40. **Map 5 O4**.

Smiths of Smithfield ⓝ

67-77 Charterhouse Street, EC1M 6HJ (7251 7950/www.smithsofsmithfield.co.uk). Barbican tube/Farringdon tube/rail.
Wine Rooms Lunch served noon-3pm Mon-Fri. **Dinner served** 5.30-10.30pm Mon-Wed; 5.30pm-midnight Thur-Sat. **Main courses** £10-£28.
Dining Room **Lunch served** noon-3pm Mon-Fri. **Dinner served** 6-10.45pm Mon-Sat. **Main courses** £11-£12.50.
Café-bar **Open** 7am-11pm Mon-Wed; 7am-11.30pm Thur, Fri; 10am-11.30pm Sat; 9.30am-10.30pm Sun. **Meals served** 7am-5pm Mon-Fri, 10am-5pm Sat, 9.30am-5pm Sun. **Main courses** £4-£7.50.
All **Credit** AmEx, DC, MC, V.
John Torode's eating and drinking emporium – each floor with a different offer – continues to attract Smithfield socialisers. It's a former warehouse, with brick walls, iron pillars, huge windows and bags of noisy atmosphere. The ground floor is an expansive sofa bar, with breakfasts, sarnies and snacks; next up is a wine bar with snacky mod-Brit food and more global mains, plus Sunday roasts. Segregated from the

Giaconda Dining Room. See p229.

masses, Top Floor is Torode's svelter fine-dining operation (*see p68*). In between is the main dining room, where an open kitchen dispenses a simple menu of grills and modern favourites to a crowd largely comprised of groups (eating here à deux is fun, but scarcely intimate). It's a slick, impressive operation, yet things were a tad tired on this visit. Roast bream and pappardelle with mushrooms was OK, but a plum tomato tart should have been better, and chips were flaccid and not quite hot. The steak was good, though, as it usually is, and the salad leaves worth a mention, with sorrel and baby watercress in the mix. Service was capable if not knowledgeable. Sunlight pouring through the big windows served to expose dusty ledges and scuffed tables.
Babies and children welcome (restaurant): high chairs. Disabled: toilet. Entertainment (ground floor): DJs 7pm Thur-Sat; jazz 4.30pm Sun. Separate rooms for parties, seating 12 and 24. Tables outdoors (4, pavement; 6, terrace). **Map 11 O5.**

Covent Garden

Axis

One Aldwych, 1 Aldwych, WC2B 4RH (7300 0300/www.onealdwych.com). Covent Garden or Embankment tube/Charing Cross tube/rail. **Lunch served** noon-2.30pm Mon-Fri. **Dinner served** 5.45-10.30pm Mon-Fri; 5.45-11.30pm Sat. **Main courses** £15.50-£23. **Set meal** £15.50 2 courses, £17.50 3 courses. **Credit** AmEx, DC, MC, V.
A restaurant situated in the basement of a hotel has to fight for attention. Axis, the subterranean dining room of the grand and imposing One Aldwych hotel, benefits from its own entrance from the street, and another boasting, no less, a sweeping staircase in an airy atrium. The high ceilings of the dining room help reduce that basement feeling, and the new decor brings some texture and colour to what is essentially a large space with soaring columns. The menu is an appealing mix of British and European influences with some creative touches. Thus beautifully smoky eel is combined with super-thin slices of beetroot and a piece of cured pork belly in a starter, while main-course roast duck breast is served pink and comes with the liver, some honey-glazed onions and artfully arranged dandelion leaves. Presentation is good all round, including desserts of peanut and banana parfait, and a light and luxurious steamed treacle sponge. Tables are well-spaced and smartly set, making this a popular business venue. While the service is suitably professional, it manages to stay relaxed.
Babies and children welcome: high chairs. Booking advisable. Disabled: toilet. Restaurant available for hire. Vegetarian menu (book in advance). **Map 18 F4.**

The Ivy

1 West Street, WC2H 9NQ (7836 4751/www.the-ivy.co.uk). Leicester Square tube. **Lunch served** noon-3pm Mon-Sat; noon-3.30pm Sun. **Dinner served** 5.30pm-midnight daily. **Main courses** £9.25-£25.50. **Cover** £2. **Credit** AmEx, DC, MC, V.
That the Ivy continues to be a celeb-magnet is no doubt partly down to the herd mentality of the famous, but also to the fact that it gives them just what they want. Which (minus the staff discretion and a careful seating policy) is pretty much what most people want: an atmospheric room, a sense of occasion, a thrum of staff activity, and good food pitched at various tastes and moods. The long menu is the food equivalent of easy listening: an accumulation of popular world classics from pasta to grills, Thai curry to shepherd's pie, shellfish to fish and chips. But if the kitchen can't claim originality, it does nod to seasonality and, in the main, has quality nailed. When we visited, the caesar salad and steak tartare were near-definitive; white asparagus sensitively handled; lamb sweetbreads unctuous, and chips satisfying. A steak and anticlimactic desserts disappointed – but the celebrity count did not (three: from film, fashion and soap opera). You can generally get a booking here at off-peak times with a month's notice, sometimes less.

Babies and children welcome: high chairs. Booking essential, 4-6 weeks in advance. Separate room for parties, seats 60. Vegetarian menu. Vegan dishes. **Map 18 D4.**

L'Atelier de Joël Robuchon

13-15 West Street, WC2H 9NE (7010 8600/www.joel-robuchon.com). Leicester Square tube. *Bar* **Open** 2.30pm-2am Mon-Sat; 2.30-10.30pm Sun. *Restaurant* **Lunch served** noon-2.30pm, **dinner served** 5.30-10.30pm daily. **Main courses** £15-£55. **Set lunch** £19 2 courses. **Set dinner** (5.30-6.30pm) £19 2 courses, £25 3 courses. **Set meal** £80-£95 9 courses. *Both* **Credit** AmEx, MC, V.
The locations in Joël Robuchon's restaurant empire sound like 007 stopovers – Macau, Hong Kong, Monaco – but Robuchon is no Bond baddie, he's a French super-chef. The Japanese-inspired ground-floor L'Atelier is dimly lit, but the open kitchen makes an impressive focal point, and sitting by the counter brings customers into its drama. Small tasting dishes are the best way to explore the work of this fine chef, though a European-style menu format is available both on the ground floor and in the first-floor dining room, La Cuisine (a brighter, more traditional-looking space). Options range from the simple, where the reliance is on fine ingredients such as Iberian ham served with diced tomato on toasted bread, to the more complex: quail artfully stuffed with foie gras, accompanied by its roasted leg and truffled mash. The quality of the produce was displayed in the freshest, lightest squid, partnered with (but not overwhelmed by) chorizo, artichoke and tomato water. The pig's trotter on parmesan toast is, thankfully, still on the menu and displays the deft touch of a master: rich and light, with just sufficient fat to make you purr. Green Chartreuse soufflé was perfectly risen, light and packed a punch. There's a touch of attitude in the service, but it is efficient. It will come as no surprise that the pricing is high.
Babies and children admitted. Booking advisable. Disabled: access; toilet. Dress: smart casual. Restaurant available for hire. **Map 17 C3.**

Euston

Number Twelve NEW

12 Upper Woburn Place, WC1H 0HX (7693 5425/www.numbertwelverestaurant.co.uk). Euston tube/rail. **Lunch served** noon-3pm Mon-Fri. **Dinner served** 5.30-10.15pm Mon-Sat. **Main courses** £12-£18. **Set lunch** £10.50 1 course, £13.50 2 courses. **Set dinner** (5.30-7pm) £15.50 3 courses, £21.50 3 courses incl glass of prosecco. **Credit** AmEx, MC, V.
A stone's throw from Euston Station, in the Ambassadors Hotel, Number Twelve has attracted affectionate reviews since it opened in 2007. Staff are friendly and attentive, and it feels somehow more personal than your average hotel restaurant. The dining room, with its cool lines and warm colours, is a good place to talk. As for the menu, head chef Santino Busciglio mixes English and Italian influences, using well-sourced and seasonal ingredients, with a splash of tropical fruit here and there. The results are nice but not amazing. Our favourite dish was a marvellous appetiser of smoked duck breast with tiny salad leaves and Sicilian citrus fruits, enlivened by slivers of fresh mint and pickled green peppercorns. In another starter, warm samphire and roasted beetroot confused rather than enhanced the pure appeal of a Pugliese burrata cheese. Mains of guinea fowl with aubergine cream and sautéed turnip tops, and sea trout with crayfish and crushed peas, were decent but didn't quite hit the spot. Puds were mixed: a pleasant panna cotta with rhubarb; an insipid pineapple mousse with coconut sorbet.
Babies and children admitted. Booking essential. Disabled: lift; toilet. Separate rooms for private parties, seating 20-120. **Map 4 K3.**

Fitzrovia

Villandry

170 Great Portland Street, W1W 5QB (7631 3131/www.villandry.com). Great Portland Street tube.

Bar **Open** 8am-11pm Mon-Fri; 9am-11pm Sat. **Breakfast served** 8-11.30am, **meals served** noon-10pm Mon-Sat. **Main courses** £11.50-£22.50. **Set dinner** (6-10pm Sat) £25 3 courses. *Restaurant* **Lunch served** noon-3pm Mon-Fri; 11.30am-3.30pm Sat; noon-4pm Sun. **Dinner served** 6-10.30pm Mon-Sat. **Main courses** £11.50-£32.50.
Both **Credit** AmEx, MC, V.
Villandry's deli area is shrinking, as tables for the charcuterie bar extend into the shop – which shows, perhaps, on what side the firm's bread is buttered these days. The huge premises are divided into a series of high-ceilinged spaces providing plenty of refuelling options: from a plate of excellent meats in the charcuterie, or smoked haddock and cod fish cake in the bar, to the restaurant, where the tables are clothed in white and the monthly-changing menu delivers its version of European brasserie cooking. A concrete floor and high ceiling might conspire against a convivial atmosphere, but to some diners the sound levels add to the buzz. The kitchen is not beyond a little showiness, with a rich and perfectly seasoned red mullet soup arriving in a copper pan to be poured by the waiter into a bowl over some pieces of the fish. Main-course cassoulet delivered less-than-perfect duck confit, but a well-flavoured, tomato-based ragoût. Side orders of vegetables are charged extra. You'll also find daily specials – game pie with parsnip mash, maybe – and desserts such as lemon tart.
Babies and children welcome: children's menu; high chairs. Bar and restaurant available for hire. Booking advisable. Entertainment: jazz 8pm Sat (bar). Tables outdoors (13, pavement). Takeaway service. **Map 3 H5.**

Gloucester Road

★ L'Etranger

36 Gloucester Road, SW7 4QT (7584 1118/www.etranger.co.uk). Gloucester Road tube. **Lunch served** noon-3pm, **dinner served** 6-11pm daily. **Main courses** £16.40-£49. **Set meal** (lunch, 6-6.45pm Mon-Fri) £16.50 2 courses, £19.50 3 courses. **Credit** AmEx, MC, V.
Behind the silky threads that screen the discreetly wealthy clientele from the street, this haute-cuisine haunt, soothingly decorated in shades of lilac and dove grey, generates an appreciative babble bordering on the noisy. Jerome Tauvron's cooking is in danger of giving fusion food a good name, dazzling with Asian flavours gilding mostly French foundations. His repertoire of dishes is bewitching, but the menu doesn't change much. Give a wide berth to the caviar selection, there to pander to the money-no-object tendency. More rewarding starters were Charolais tartare made lip-smartingly tangy with garlic, capers, green chilli and Worcestershire sauce; and a pair of elegant and palate-levitating spring rolls (one tuna, one crab) accessorised with cress and mooli salad and dipping sauces. The concise, unflashy but breathtakingly good main courses of turbot with lemongrass crumbs, and melting lamb with baked aubergine and onion confit, sealed Tauvron's reputation. It deserves to spread beyond London's Francophile neighbourhood. The wine list is daunting but it helps having albariño, viognier and riesling by the glass. Staff didn't make us feel like the cheap date we were, in comparison to the well-coiffed, white-haired, gold-card carrying regulars. Tea in silver pots makes a graceful ending.
Babies and children welcome: high chairs. Booking advisable. Restaurant available for hire. Vegetarian menu. **Map 13 C9.**

Holborn

The Terrace

Lincoln's Inn Fields, WC2A 3LJ (7430 1234/www.theterrace.info). Holborn tube. **Breakfast served** 8-11am, **lunch served** noon-3pm, **dinner served** 5.30-8pm Mon-Fri. **Main courses** £10.50-£17.95. **Set lunch** £15.95 2 courses, £17.95 3 courses. **Credit** AmEx, MC, V.
There can be few more delightful havens for a long summer's lunch or supper and a viognier sundowner than this spot, with its outdoor terrace next to the tennis courts in Lincoln's Inn Fields

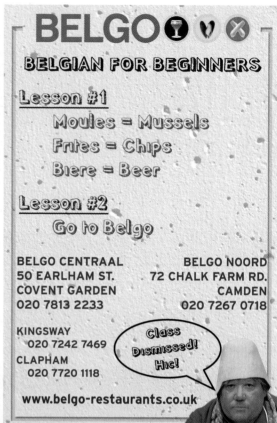
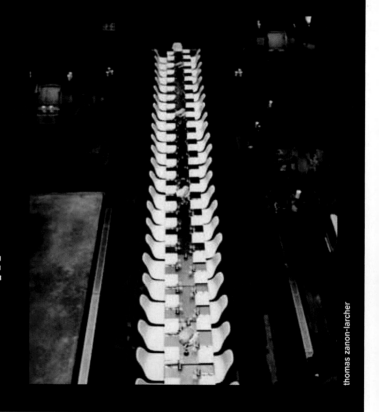

– though the staff might have told us that the kitchen closes at 8pm, the time we'd booked to arrive. Chef Patrick Williams' Afro-Caribbean-accented seasonal menus are another draw and, on our latest visit, included a spirited starter of two large crisp parmesan discs sandwiching asparagus, proper bacon and little leaves. Red mullet with a lemony aubergine caviar, butternut squash and shiso leaves was an eclectic collection of ingredients well-combined. Another vibrant main, jerk chicken salad with a mango and chilli dressing, was made with tastier thigh meat (not the usual breast), the cooked pak choi contrasting a little oddly with crunchy leaves. Pear and raspberry crumble with pistachio ice-cream would have been perfect whatever the weather. Outdoor tables are prime, but eating inside the sauna-style pavilion with its sky-blue tables brightens the dullest day. Pity that no wines are offered by the glass. A final unexpected pleasure is being escorted out of the park after dark by the waiter with a key to the gate.
Babies and children welcome: high chairs. Booking advisable. Disabled: toilet. Restaurant available for hire. Tables outdoors (15, terrace). **Map 10 M6.**

Knightsbridge

Fifth Floor

Harvey Nichols, Knightsbridge, SW1X 7RJ (7235 5250/www.harveynichols.com). Knightsbridge tube.
Café **Breakfast served** 8am-noon, **lunch served** noon-3.30pm, **dinner served** 6-10.30pm Mon-Sat. **Brunch served** 11am-5pm Sun. **Tea served** 3.30-6pm Mon-Sat; 3.30-5pm Sun. **Main courses** £9.50-£15.
Restaurant **Brunch served** noon-4pm Sat, Sun. **Lunch served** noon-3pm Mon-Fri. **Dinner served** 6-11pm Mon-Sat. **Main courses** £15-£24. **Set dinner** £19.50 3 courses.
Both **Credit** AmEx, DC, MC, V.
The white-on-white room off Harvey Nichols food hall takes monochrome to clinical extremes; but while staff from the beauty counters downstairs wouldn't look out of place here, it's priced beyond their means. Lunch is the raison d'être of the restaurant, and when everyone's gone home it can feel a little out of hours, with some dishes looking distinctly dainty for dinner. Consolation comes from terrific springy bread insistently flavoured with apricot, fennel seeds and rosemary, and nice nutty chocolate truffles. Jonas Karlsson's daily-changing menu, featuring charcuterie terrine, loin of wild boar and a ragout of cannellini beans on our visit, sounded earthy but the execution was deft. An 'assiette' of milk-fed goat consisted of tiny cutlets, a kidney, cherry tomatoes stuffed with goat's cheese, tiny shallots, baby leeks and green beans – beautiful, but an itty-bitty collection of size 0 parts. Monkfish with baby leeks, chickpeas and chorizo was put together with flair. For somewhere so ladylike, puddings aren't especially tempting and a lemon millefeuille with lemon sorbet and jelly proved rather pursed-lipped. Perfect perhaps during daylight, but a little lacking in soul and substance at night.
Babies and children welcome: children's menu; high chairs; nappy-changing facilities. Disabled: lift; toilet. Tables outdoors (15, café terrace). **Map 8 F9.**

Marylebone

★ L'Autre Pied NEW

2008 WINNER BEST NEW RESTAURANT
2008 RUNNER-UP BEST DESIGN
5-7 Blandford Street, W1U 3DB (7486 9696/ www.lautrepied.co.uk). Baker Street tube. **Lunch served** noon-2.45pm Mon-Sat; noon-3pm Sun. **Dinner served** 6-10.30pm Mon-Sat; 6.30-9.30pm Sun. **Main courses** £19.95-£22.95. **Set lunch** £19.95 3 courses. **Set dinner** (6-7pm Mon-Sat) £26.95 3 courses. **Credit** AmEx, MC, V.
This sister restaurant to the fabled Pied à Terre (*see p137*) made its debut in autumn 2007 with talented chef Marcus Eaves at the helm. Prices are at a level that suggests diffusion range rather than haute couture, though they've snuck up a little since opening. The cooking is accomplished and

precise, with imaginative yet well-considered flavour combinations. The food looks stunning too. A translucent poached egg sat upon a vibrant green bed of crushed peas and broad beans; the flavours were brought together by a smoked butter emulsion. Best end of lamb and boned, rolled breast of lamb evoked the Med with oven-dried tomatoes, a sticky black olive jus and a side of (slightly over-salted) soft polenta. An inspired pud of strawberry crumble, served in a martini glass and topped with a quenelle each of strawberry and basil ice-creams, was like summer in a glass. The surroundings have a vaguely oriental feel, with cloisonné-like screens and dark wood. A Euro-centric wine list contains some good bottles, but there are no tasting notes or style designations (by-the-glass offerings are excellent). Eaves has evidently hit his stride; this is one of the best places to dine in the capital.
Babies and children welcome: high chairs. Booking advisable. Separate room for parties, seats 18. Tables outdoors (3, pavement). **Map 9 G5.**

Orrery

55 Marylebone High Street, W1U 5RB (7616 8000/www.danddlondon.com). Baker Street tube.
Bar **Open** 11am-11pm daily.
Restaurant **Lunch served** noon-2.30pm, **dinner served** 6.30-10.30pm daily. **Main courses** £36-£50. **Set lunch** £26 3 courses (£40 incl wine). **Set dinner** £59 tasting menu (£97 incl wine).
Both **Credit** AmEx, DC, MC, V.

Compared to the heady days when it was the Michelin-starred darling of the Conran Restaurant empire and Chris Galvin ruled the stoves, Orrery was in danger of becoming no more than a pleasant but pricey corporate diner. D&D London subsequently installed a polished new service team and talented, ex-Mirabelle head chef, Igor Tymchyshyn. Now, once again, Orrery feels like a restaurant with something to prove. Every detail has been polished to a high gloss – even a request for tap water brings a handsome carafe carried to the table on a silver salver. Tymchyshyn's food flies high, with simple-sounding dishes of asparagus with truffles, and smoked Scottish salmon, both dazzlingly presented. Just thinking about the work that has gone into a breast of truffled guinea fowl, presented with spring vegetables and a plug of boned thigh meat filled with a chicken and foie gras farce, could leave you too exhausted to eat it. Halibut fillet teamed with langoustine ravioli and morels also showed culinary skill. Regrettably, blips in timing left the halibut overcooked and the guinea fowl undercooked. Still, anyone that can make such a perfect prune and armagnac soufflé deserves the benefit of the doubt. Orrery's 45-page wine list offers plenty to savour, including an extensive choice of riesling, pinot noir and sweet wines, plus a house carafe of the day.
Babies and children welcome: high chairs. Booking essential. Disabled: toilet. Tables outside (12, bar roof terrace). Vegetarian menu. **Map 3 G4.**

Northbank. See p229.

RESTAURANTS

Number Twelve. See p231.

Mayfair

Embassy

29 Old Burlington Street, W1S 3AN (7851 0956/www.embassylondon.com). Green Park or Piccadilly Circus tube. **Lunch served** noon-3pm Tue-Fri. **Dinner served** 6-11.30pm Tue-Sat. **Main courses** £15-£25. **Credit** AmEx, MC, V.
Behind the chic pavement terrace, the restaurant's white leather chairs, fake stuccoed ceiling and chandeliers seem a touch glitzy for daytime. Loos bearing the scars of the club's night life give away Embassy's real identity. The dark woody bar at the back was deserted on our visit, and without the WAG-ish crowd the whole place seemed somewhat abandoned at midday. But we joined a couple of businessmen and a dowager with her granddaughter, and Embassy came up trumps. Rather than frothy, fashionable club food, Garry Hollihead produces assured, classical dishes at considerate prices for Mayfair. We enjoyed two very fine creations: lobster tagliatelle with sauce américaine, a rich cream and tomato bisque with plenty of shellfish; and beautifully cooked rump of lamb on a sumptuous smoked aubergine purée with melting shallots. You could downsize price-wise to a burger with optional scarmoza (an Italian smoked cheese) or go upscale with grilled lobster. Puddings look beautiful. Panna cotta with gingerbread crumb topping, rhubarb and pink rhubarb granita was the bee's knees. The staff, however, seemed to be more concerned with straightening cutlery than responding to customers. *Booking advisable. Dress: smart casual. Restaurant available for hire. Tables outdoors (6, terrace).* **Map 9 J7**.

Langan's Brasserie

Stratton Street, W1J 8LB (7491 8822/ www.langansrestaurants.co.uk). Green Park tube. **Meals served** 12.15-11pm Mon-Thur; 12.15-11.30pm Fri, Sat. **Main courses** £13.50-£18.50. **Cover** £1.50. **Credit** AmEx, MC, V.
Langan's was refurbished in March 2008, but don't panic, don't reach for a brandy to calm your nerves – it looks pretty much the same. There's a new wooden floor, new ceiling, new kitchen, but the same yellow-washed walls and copious paintings and photographs of Peter Langan with glass in hand. The menu is the same too, and still sports the sketch of the three founders, Michael Caine defiantly hanging on to his cigar. The combination of European brasserie classics and British comfort food means escalope of veal Holstein sits alongside grilled dover sole with parsley butter. Even the bread is decidedly old-school white and brown rolls, the butter provided in heart-stopping portions. A starter of snails with garlic butter, bacon, onions and mushrooms served in a lightly toasted brioche was well-executed, and roast duck made a hearty main course. Desserts remain as comforting as ever: treacle tart, chocolate pie and sticky toffee pudding with custard, or there's fresh fruit salad (for the ladies, perhaps?). The £1.50 cover charge is an anachronism, and vegetables cost extra, albeit properly cooked and generous in volume. Service runs smoothly and staff coped well with a rowdy bunch of gents during our visit. *Babies and children welcome: booster seats. Booking advisable; essential dinner. Entertainment: jazz 10.30pm Thur-Sat. Separate room for parties, seats 80.* **Map 9 H7**.
For branches see index.

Nicole's

158 New Bond Street, W1S 2UB (7499 8408/ www.nicolefarhi.com). Green Park tube.
Bar **Open** 10am-6pm Mon-Sat. **Meals served** 10am-5.30pm Mon-Sat. **Main courses** £9-£13.50.
Restaurant **Breakfast served** 10am-noon Mon-Sat. **Lunch served** noon-3.30pm Mon-Fri; noon-4pm Sat. **Tea served** 3.30-6pm Mon-Sat. **Main courses** £15.50-£25. **Cover** (noon-4pm Mon-Sat) £1.
Both **Credit** AmEx, DC, MC, V.
The Bond Street fashion store's basement restaurant aspires to higher culture by covering the walls with a collection of black-and-white photographic portraits, including one of designer

Nicole Farhi's playwright husband David Hare. So don't go thinking this is just a light lunch spot for footsore Manolo-wearing shoppers. Most customers are men escaping from nearby offices and service is paced to get them back to work sharpish. Dishes are metrosexual, evidenced by crab and avocado salad – the crustacean, guacamole and half a sliced avocado, with pea shoots, watercress and flatbread. Precision-cooked scallops with long slices of chorizo on a pillow of butternut squash purée shot through with lime and chilli was let down by a thin, tough leek astride the plate. These fairly unremarkable ensembles were redeemed by exceptional accessories: side orders of tomato salad featuring all sorts, shapes and shades; and fat chips in their skins. Puddings lacked conviction. Inedibly hard pink stalks let down a rhubarb tart, and lemon surprise pudding was like sweet scrambled egg. The bill seemed too much to pay for the quality; we'd rather have spent the money shopping than eating.
Babies and children admitted. Booking advisable. Restaurant available for hire. **Map 9 H7.**

★ Patterson's

4 Mill Street, W1S 2AX (7499 1308/ www.pattersonsrestaurant.co.uk). Bond Street or Oxford Circus tube. **Lunch served** noon-3pm Mon-Fri. **Dinner served** 6-11pm Mon-Fri; 5-11pm Sat. **Main courses** £20. **Set lunch** £20 2 courses, £25 3 courses. **Credit** AmEx, MC, V.
Since opening in 2003, this sleek, family-run venture has garnered a following of customers discussing business over an impeccable lunch, or dining peacefully in refined surroundings come evening. Maria Patterson runs front-of-house with a knowledgeable personal touch. The evening's specials were explained in enough detail to set mouths watering, keen advice was proffered on food-and-wine matching, and queries answered on the spot. Behind the scenes, husband Raymond specialises in sourcing British meat, while langoustine, lobster and crabs arrive from his hometown of Eyemouth, Scotland. Each course is charged at a flat rate and you almost wish they weren't – that way, at least, you would have some way to choose from a menu where everything delights. Squab breast on potato and apple parmentier paired with foie gras parfait was an accomplished starter, while the assiette of suckling pig teased us with the tastes and textures of crisp bacon, tender confit of shoulder, and three dainty cutlets. Puddings (£10) include glammed-up versions of favourites such as chocolate brownie and crème brûlée, while the international wine list (which starts at £22) has a French bias. If we were to look for fault, the halibut wrapped in prosciutto was a touch dry – but overall, this place is a joy.
Babies and children welcome: high chairs. Booking essential. Separate room for parties, seats 20. **Map 9 H/J6.**

★ Sotheby's Café

Sotheby's, 34-35 New Bond Street, W1A 2AA (7293 5077). Bond Street or Oxford Circus tube. **Breakfast served** 9.30-11.30am, **lunch served** noon-3pm, **tea served** 3-4.45pm Mon-Fri. **Main courses** £12.50-£17. **Set tea** £5.75. **Credit** AmEx, DC, MC, V.
'You can never get in here without a booking,' said the beautifully suited man at the next table. 'And you know, it has never even been in a guide book,' replied the other. Oops, sorry, gentlemen. We loved striding through the Sotheby's doorway as if about to bid for an Old Master, only to duck into this clubby, tastefully decorated dining room for lunch instead. The clientele is distinctly Bond Street: people who appreciate details like the fragrant lilac roses in dappled vases on each table, the mirrored walls and the cheery service. Chef Laura Greenfield posts a short but sweet menu of artful, seasonal food that is pretty and pleasing rather than robust and filling. A free-form prawn cocktail came as three very good king prawns on lettuce leaves with a splodge of marie rose sauce, while crisp golden parmesan beignets with nicely squidgy centres worked well with a fennel, artichoke and asparagus salad. A rosemary-marinated spatchcocked chicken with mustard

and lemon coleslaw was a fitting prequel to the English cheese of the day – in this case, stichelton, a buttery, unpasteurised blue cheese modelled on the original recipe for stilton.
Babies and children admitted. Booking essential lunch. Disabled: toilet. **Map 9 H6.**

★ Wild Honey

12 St George Street, W1S 2FB (7758 9160/ www.wildhoneyrestaurant.co.uk). Oxford Circus or Bond Street tube. **Lunch served** noon-2.30pm Mon-Sat; noon-3pm Sun. **Dinner served** 5.30-10.30pm daily. **Set lunch** £16.95 3 courses. **Set dinner** (5.30-7pm) £18.95 3 courses. **Credit** AmEx, MC, V.
It only takes a few seconds after crossing the threshold of this sister of Arbutus (*see p237*) to be won over by the charm and professionalism of the place. The oak-panelled walls could be a little stifling, but modern artworks banish thoughts of the old world order. Wild Honey's popularity means a happy buzz is inevitable, and even the seats at the bar counter are much in demand. The reasonably priced menu demonstrates a desire to pick and choose the best the UK and mainland Europe has to offer: Cornish gurnard alongside Limousin veal, and lamb from the Pyrenees or Elwy Valley. A starter of warm smoked eel was a fabulous piece of fish, served with small sweet-and-sour turnips, a delectable conference-pear purée and small pieces of crisp-fried eel, each packing a punch. Belly of pork was cooked long and slow; it came with a top-drawer barbecue-style sauce, pearl barley and chorizo in the form of risotto, the smokiness emphasised further by the use of smoked olive oil. Desserts like treacle tart are equally well-made, and the cheeseboard from La Fromagerie (*see p306*) sits on a table in the middle of the room. Service is just right (effective, friendly), the wine list gives the option of 250ml carafes, and the coffee is damn fine.
Babies and children admitted. Booking essential. **Map 9 H6.**

Pimlico

Rex Whistler Restaurant at Tate Britain

Tate Britain, Millbank, SW1P 4RG (7887 8825/ www.tate.org.uk). Pimlico tube/87 bus. **Breakfast served** 10-11.30am Sat, Sun. **Lunch served** 11.30am-3pm, **tea served** 3.15-5pm daily. **Main courses** £15.95-£19.95. **Credit** AmEx, DC, MC, V.
With the captivating Rex Whistler mural, *In Pursuit of Rare Meats*, around its walls, the restaurant next to Tate Britain's cavernous café presents an inviting prospect. But the ugly false ceiling, waiter station and slightly inept service (two of our courses were carried past us and offered to other diners) give it an institutional air. While the clientele look distinguished (at one table was a group from the Royal Academy), the food is less so. The menu's ingredients are well-chosen, but inconsistent execution let them down. Devilled kidneys on sourdough toast were nicely piquant with mustard. An anaemic leek and pea quiche was improved by a purple and green cress salad. But green tagliatelle with griddled artichokes, fennel and lemon was unforgivably overcooked and oily – costly, too, as the vegetarian choice on a set price menu. Still, the desserts shone. Chilled rice pudding with blueberry compote in a little kilner jar, and a buttery almond sponge with gooseberries and an elderflower sorbet were English summer heaven. The British cheese trolley is enticing and the wine list another redeeming feature.
Babies and children welcome: high chairs. Booking advisable. Disabled: toilet. Tables outdoors (8, terrace). **Map 16 L11.**

St James's

The Avenue

7-9 St James's Street, SW1A 1EE (7321 2111/ www.danddlondon.com). Green Park tube. **Bar Open** noon-11pm Mon-Fri; 6-11pm Sat. *Restaurant* **Lunch served** noon-3pm Mon-Fri. **Dinner served** 5.45pm-11pm Mon-Sat.

Main courses £12.50-£18. **Set meal** £19.95
2 courses, £21.95 3 courses.
Both **Credit** AmEx, DC, MC, V.
The glass wall frontage brings a touch of metropolitan modernism to this old-school street, and the cavernous space remains a temple to hard-edged simplicity. The Avenue's whiteness is broken only by a touch of colour from red banquettes and the bottles behind the long bar; even the pictures on the walls share a muted palette. Waiting staff, smartly attired in white shirts and long black aprons, are well-drilled, and the white-clothed tables are well-spaced, so business can be done. Prices aren't as scary as the St James's location might suggest, and the menu has more than a little 'brasserie' about it. Smoked duck and foie gras salad was an assembly of good ingredients and complementary textures, with chicory, watercress and walnut dressing. Main courses can be as robust as barnsley chop with fresh pea and broad bean purée, or as distinguished as gilthead bream, with good crisp skin, moist and tender flesh, and a tarragon-heavy herb nage; the accompanying jerusalem artichokes, however, would have been declared too firm by the Crown Prince of Al Dente himself. Desserts are a European tour, from bramleys and coxes in a crumble to crème brûlée.
Babies and children welcome: high chairs. Booking advisable. Disabled: toilet. **Map 9 J8.**

Le Caprice
Arlington House, Arlington Street, SW1A 1RJ (7629 2239/www.caprice-holdings.co.uk). Green Park tube. **Lunch served** noon-3pm Mon-Sat; noon-5pm Sun. **Dinner served** 5.30pm-midnight Mon-Sat; 6-11pm Sun. **Main courses** £12.75-£28. **Cover** £2. **Credit** AmEx, DC, MC, V.
The Caprice's status has long passed from that of 1980s hot-ticket to uptown institution, so you come here nowadays for its unchanging qualities. Above all, there's the service: charming, unsnooty, utterly professional and genuinely of the nothing-is-too-much-trouble kind, making everyone feel enjoyably cared for. The premises are quite small (one of the staff's great skills is in negotiating tight spaces); the celebs of yore may not call in so often now, but tables are still hard to come by, and there's still an urbane buzz. Menus stick to a classic modern-brasserie style, with a few interesting novelties – especially among the vegetarian options. Nettle and wild garlic soup with a Keen's cheddar scone, one of the week's specials, was original and deliciously refreshing; san daniele ham with grilled squash and pecorino was also very nicely done. Our mains too struck all the right chords: fine-quality squid chargrilled with bacon, and a very superior prime-beef burger elegantly dressed up as 'chopped steak américaine'. The wine list has an admirable balance of quality and price. Prices overall are, of course, not particularly low, but have risen less than those of many of the Caprice's competitors.
Babies and children welcome: high chairs. Booking essential, two weeks in advance. Entertainment: pianist (6.30pm-midnight Mon-Sat; 7-11pm Sun). Vegetarian menu. **Map 9 J8.**

Quaglino's
16 Bury Street, SW1Y 6AJ (7930 6767/ www.danddlondon.co.uk). Green Park tube. **Bar Open** 11.30am-1am Mon-Thur; 11.30am-2am Fri, Sat; noon-11pm Sun.
Restaurant **Lunch served** noon-3pm daily.
Dinner served 5.30-11.30pm Mon-Thur; 5.30pm-12.30am Fri, Sat; 5.30-10.30pm Sun.
Main courses £12.50-£25. **Set meal** (noon-3pm, 5.30-7.30pm) £14.50 2 courses, £17.50 3 courses.
Both **Credit** AmEx, DC, MC, V.
Hangar-sized and glamorous, Quaglino's was the epicentre of exciting dining-out when Terence Conran relaunched this 1930s icon 15-odd years ago. Descending the sweeping staircase into the vast expanse of restaurant still gives a frisson, but otherwise most of the thrill has gone, along with the cigarette girls – leaving ashtrays filled with salt and pepper, a bar full of suits, and efficient but impersonal Australian service. Like a proper French brasserie, it's not offering an exclusive experience, and lunch is a fair price. Mushrooms on toast were poshed up with black pepper, brioche

and truffle oil. A generous seafood cocktail billed as prawn turned out to be inferior crayfish, and a smaller serving with fewer, tastier prawns would have been preferable. Pork belly with perfect pillowy butter beans infused with spicy tomato sauce, chorizo and crackling hit the (Gloucester Old) spot. The larger menu is very standard and its retro-ness looks dated. Though Quaglino's hasn't aged too badly, you might wish for a bit more sparkle if you were splashing out on seafood on a night out.
Babies and children welcome: children's menu; high chairs. Booking advisable. Disabled: toilet. Entertainment: musicians 7pm daily. Separate rooms for parties, seating 20 and 44. **Map 9 J7.**

Soho

Alastair Little
49 Frith Street, W1D 4SG (7734 5183). Leicester Square or Tottenham Court Road tube. **Lunch served** noon-3pm Mon-Fri. **Dinner served** 6-11.30pm Mon-Sat. **Main courses** £22 (lunch); £23 (dinner). **Set meal** £18-£35 2 courses, £23-£40 3 courses. **Credit** AmEx, DC, MC, V.
One of Modern European cooking's earliest exponents, Alastair Little is no longer involved here, but Juliet Peston who worked with him for years carries the torch. The restaurant was always almost shockingly stark and never cheap. Its small plain room now has tablecloths and feels a little dated, but prices aren't retro. The smattering of Soho media lunchers seemed like regulars and that's what our exceptionally welcoming and knowledgeable waiter made us want to be. Does cooking cut the mustard? Yes. Thrilling enough for the price? Not quite. The enticing, cliché-free menu includes some Middle Eastern and Italian dishes. Potato pancakes with smoked eel, beetroot and dill and mustard sauce was deliciously forthright. A surprisingly skimpy plaice fillet with minty crushed peas, own-made tartare sauce and potato cakes stopped just short of exceptional. Onion and tomato tart flavoured with black olives and thyme with a green bean, leaf and mi-cuit tomato salad – fine though it was – didn't give vegetarians great value from the set price menu. But we guessed even the flaky pastry was made on the premises, as were the lovely shortbread biscuits served with lemon posset and strawberries.
Babies and children admitted. Booking advisable. Separate room for parties, seats 25. Tables outdoors (2, pavement). **Map 17 C3.**

Andrew Edmunds
46 Lexington Street, W1F 0LW (7437 5708). Leicester Square, Oxford Circus or Piccadilly Circus tube. **Lunch served** 12.30-3pm Mon-Fri; 1-3pm Sat; 1-3.30pm Sun. **Dinner served** 6-10.45pm Mon-Sat; 6-10.30pm Sun. **Main courses** £10-£17. **Credit** MC, V.
Andrew Edmunds' refusal to play the Soho fashion game has won it a network of friends that Facebook would envy. Over the years it has become something of a private non-members' club, with an intimate mood fostered by proprietorial staff and its resemblance to a spruce, charming country cottage. The short menu kicks off with a thoughtful aperitif list, including good-value sherries, and moves into seasonal, flavoursome Mod Euro fare. The cooking is generally pleasing and adroit, with a light touch. Typical dishes could be artichoke salad with goat's cheese crotin balanced by a delicate olive oil, salt-cod with black-eyed beans, or monkfish with chive mash perked up by sauce vierge. We've heard talk of inconsistency here, but have suffered only one misfire ourselves, an over-elaborate scallop dish. Downstairs, the basement is cosy for winter; the ground floor is cuter and full-on Soho, with a pretty conservatory that, combined with country garden floral displays, make it lovely in summer.
Babies and children admitted. Booking essential. Tables outdoors (2, pavement). **Map 17 A4.**

Arbutus (100)
63-64 Frith Street, W1D 3JW (7734 4545/ www.arbutusrestaurant.co.uk). Tottenham Court Road tube. **Lunch served** noon-2.30pm Mon-Sat; noon-3.30pm Sun. **Dinner served** 5-11pm Mon-

Sat; 5.30-9.30pm Sun. **Main courses** £14-£19.95. **Set lunch** £15.50 3 courses. **Set dinner** (5-7pm) £17.50 3 courses. **Credit** AmEx, MC, V.
Chef and co-owner Anthony Demetre oversees a consistent kitchen and an enticing menu strong on hearty British fare, accented with continental flavours. Seasonality matters here. Our visit in early spring featured some of the first English asparagus and wild garlic leaves in a dish of roast organic chicken and a risotto of garlic leaves, spring onion and courgette. The risotto, however, had only the merest whisper of said garlic. A starter of squid and mackerel 'burger', surrounded by pieces of succulent, sea-scented razor clams and scatterings of parsley, was the star of the show. The Spanish-influenced main course of pollock featured macaroni, chorizo and octopus, piquillo peppers, capers and tomato sauce. A former winner of our Best New Restaurant award, Arbutus is very popular, and its renown is likely to spread further with the publication of Demetre's first book. Be sure to book ahead and expect the place to be full to bursting at dinner (service may be rushed as a consequence). Prices at dinner are not a bargain in the way that lunchtime set menus are, but value is ably delivered by the wine list. It's not too long and there are plenty of good bottles, all of which are available by 250ml carafe, which are not marked up from bottle price.
Babies and children welcome: high chairs. Booking advisable. **Map 17 B3.**

South Kensington

★ Bibendum
Michelin House, 81 Fulham Road, SW3 6RD (7581 5817/www.bibendum.co.uk). South Kensington tube. **Lunch served** noon-2.30pm Mon-Fri; 12.30-3pm Sat, Sun. **Dinner served** 7-11pm Mon-Sat; 7-10.30pm Sun. **Main courses** £16-£25. **Set lunch** (Mon-Fri) £25 2 courses, £29.50 3 courses. **Set dinner** (Sun) £29.50 3 courses. **Credit** AmEx, DC, MC, V.
You can't beat the Michelin building for charm, with those Michelin men brandishing bicycle tyres in the stained-glass windows, lying in mosaic form on the floor and smiling out of vintage posters on the walls. The interior design of the restaurant is neither classic nor contemporary, but clean-cut and comfortable. What really impresses here, though, is the food. Our seared scallops, just-cooked and perfectly fresh, came atop an impeccable risotto, flavoured zestily with lemon and thyme. Sautéed rabbit, stuffed with sage and onion and partly wrapped in ventrèche bacon, was served with a splendid mustard sauce; a nice piece of veal, infused with smoky rosemary, was accompanied by anchovies and some baked aubergine that made us sigh with pleasure. After all this magnificence, we had little room for pudding, but managed to share a light champagne clafoutis with little madeleines, fresh from the oven, and some startlingly delicious petits fours. Service struck just the right balance too: efficient and friendly without being obsequious.
Babies and children welcome: high chair. Booking essential; 1 week in advance for dinner. Bookings not accepted for parties of more than 10. **Map 14 E10.**

Westminster

Bank Westminster
45 Buckingham Gate, SW1E 6BS (7379 9797/ www.bankrestaurants.com). St James's Park tube. **Bar Open** 11am-11pm Mon-Wed; 11am-1am Thur-Fri; 5pm-1am Sat.
Restaurant **Meals served** noon-11pm Mon-Fri.
Main courses £10.50-£30.
Both **Credit** AmEx, MC, V.
Bank Westminster is set in the St James's Park Hotel, which also houses Zander bar. The restaurant's setting is gorgeous, particularly in the summer months when the conservatory-style glass walls open on to an ornate Italianate garden complete with burbling fountain. The dining room gleams with white linen and polished glasses. Diners are a combination of tourists, expense-account business diners and lone hotel guests. The brasserie-style menu has a 'greatest hits' feel, as it

RESTAURANTS

wends its way from Euro-classics such as fish cakes and steak and chips, to Asian-lite faves like Thai green curry and crispy duck with pak choi. Prices are on the steep side for cooking that is competent but unexciting (a couple of the fish dishes are just shy of £20). Our deep-fried crispy duck rolls were packed with duck and spiked with ginger, but served with an overly sweet dipping sauce. The flavours in a starter of smoked haddock with hash browns, spinach and a poached egg were nicely judged, but fried calf's liver, requested medium-rare, was overcooked and a bit tough. By-the-glass wine offerings are run of the mill, but the short 'fine wine' section is notable.
Babies and children welcome: children's menu; high chairs. Booking advisable. Disabled: toilet. Separate room for parties, seats 40. Tables outdoors (15, courtyard). Map 15 J9.

West

Bayswater

★ Le Café Anglais NEW

2008 RUNNER-UP BEST LOCAL RESTAURANT
2008 RUNNER-UP BEST DESIGN

8 Porchester Gardens, W2 4DB (7221 1415/ www.lecafeanglais.co.uk). Bayswater tube. **Lunch served** noon-3pm daily. **Dinner served** 6.30-11.30pm Mon-Sat; 6.30-10pm Sun. **Main**

courses £8-£27.50. **Set lunch** (Mon-Fri) £16.50 2 courses, £19.50 3 courses. **Cover** £1.50. **Credit** AmEx, MC, V.
Chef-proprietor Rowley Leigh's new restaurant opened to great acclaim at the end of 2007. There have been grumbles since, but we found little to complain about on a midsummer night. It's situated, rather unglamorously, on the first floor of Whiteley's shopping centre – though you wouldn't realise if you enter by the door (and lift) on Porchester Gardens. The white, art deco-style room is very big, with floor-to-ceiling leaded windows on one side, the open kitchen, rotisserie grill and bar opposite. Tables are mixed with booth seating, so diners retain a sense of intimacy while being able to check out new arrivals: it's definitely a see-and-be-seen kind of place. The long menu is a mix-and-match delight, divided into first courses (grilled kipper, omelette, pan tomate), fish (fish pie, mackerel with gooseberry sauce), roasts, vegetables (mains and sides listed together) and desserts (fruits, tarts, ice-creams, cheeses). Particularly inspired are the hors d'oeuvres at £3 a pop; two or three are a great alternative to a standard starter (don't miss the anchovy toasts with parmesan custard). Ingredients are first-rate: the wafer-thin smoked eel in a starter salad with bacon was the best we've ever had. Professional service, a lengthy wine list divided by region and a buzzy, West End vibe add to the satisfaction.

Babies and children welcome: high chairs. Bookings advisable dinner. Disabled: toilet. Separate room for parties, seats 26. Map 7 C6.

Island Restaurant & Bar

Royal Lancaster Hotel, Lancaster Terrace, W2 2TY (7551 6070/www.islandrestaurant.co.uk). Lancaster Gate tube. **Bar/Restaurant Open/meals served** noon-11pm daily. **Main courses** £8.50-£22.50. **Set meal** (noon-5pm) £12.50 1 course incl glass of wine. Both **Credit** AmEx, MC, V.
The rather unprepossessing tower block that is the Royal Lancaster Hotel looms large over the northern edge of Hyde Park. The views must be fantastic as you work your way up the building, but, sadly, the Island Restaurant & Bar is on the raised ground floor. It has its own entrance from the street and the space has had to incorporate large pillars into the design, but with a kitchen visible through a wide hatch, and large floor-to-ceiling windows, it is all very contemporary. The mood lighting in the evening is all a little night-clubby. The bar area of the large open-plan space does good cocktails, and the menu sports a broad range of British and European-inspired ideas. It can be as classic as caesar salad, and fish and chips with tartare sauce, or as ambitious as steamed fillet of bream (nicely timed) with brown shrimp risotto with spring onions and dill. The balance of flavours is sometimes a little awry, but a starter of seared scallops with warm tomato, chorizo and coriander dressing did show skill. Service is friendly and surprisingly enthusiastic.
Babies and children welcome: children's menu; high chairs. Bar/restaurant available for hire. Booking advisable. Disabled toilet. Map 8 D6.

Chiswick

Sam's Brasserie & Bar

11 Barley Mow Passage, W4 4PH (8987 0555/ www.samsbrasserie.co.uk). Chiswick Park or Turnham Green tube. **Bar Open** 9am-midnight Mon-Wed, Sun; 9am-12.30am Thur-Sat. **Brunch served** 9am-noon, **lunch served** noon-3pm, **dinner served** 6.30-10.30pm daily. **Main courses** £4.75-£9.50. **Restaurant Brunch served** 9am-4pm Sat, Sun. **Lunch served** noon-3pm Mon-Fri; 9am-4pm Sat, Sun. **Dinner served** 6.30-10.30pm Mon-Sat; 6.30-10pm Sun. **Main courses** £9.50-£17.50. **Set lunch** (Mon-Fri) £12 2 courses, £15 3 courses; (Sun) £21 3 courses. Both **Credit** AmEx, MC, V.
This surprisingly spacious split-level restaurant, tucked down a pretty passage off Chiswick High Road, looks rather like an upmarket Slug & Lettuce. The art on the wall is inconsequential, there's no music and the decor is low-key neo-industrial – suitable for a building that used to be a paper factory. Your place-mat is your menu, with the date posted above, as some dishes are changed daily. First comes the free bread, and it comes all the time and is excellent: airy, fresh, in three different flavours. The wine list is outstanding, ranging from £13.50 to £125; the Finca Las Paredes malbec, at £18.50, was exceptional value. From 12 starters, the mozzarella with vine-ripened tomatoes, and the feta, pea and lettuce salad, featured cheeses that were creamy and full of taste, and subtle vinaigrettes. A crisp cod main course was also delicately flavoured, served with a parsley-based salsa verde that could have been a bit punchier. Our steak came undercooked and, once sent back, was delivered anew slightly overcooked: a pity as the meat was of a high standard. For dessert, the truffles were enough – four little balls of gooey chocolate, which worked well with ice-cream.
Babies and children welcome: children's menu; high chairs; toys. Booking advisable Thur-Sat. Disabled: toilet.

Kensington

11 Abingdon Road

11 Abingdon Road, W8 6AH (7937 0120/ www.abingdonroad.co.uk). High Street Kensington tube. **Lunch served** 12.30-2.30pm Mon-Sat;

Le Café Anglais

noon-3pm Sun. **Dinner served** 6.30-10.30pm Mon-Thur; 6.30-11pm Fri, Sat; 6.30-9.30pm Sun. **Main courses** £11.95-£18.50. **Set meal** £17.50 2 courses. **Credit** MC, V.

Everything you could wish for in a local restaurant is present and correct here. Pistachio-painted rooms are furnished with minimalist flair and some remarkable modern and contemporary artworks – Giacometti? Hockney? – from a collection that circulates between stablemates Sonny's (*see p241*) and the Phoenix (*see p243*). In contrast, rococo rules in the pretty bar area where you can sit softly on brightly upholstered gold-legged chairs and give the global wine list the attention it deserves. The jaunty seasonal menu is equally compelling. Asparagus soup made a pleasing partner for the good chewy bread. Mango, shrimp and broad bean salad dressed with chilli (the most outré dish offered) was wonderfully zesty. Deftly cooked rabbit with tarragon stuffing wrapped in crisp parma ham came on a herby butternut-squash purée: flavoursome, but not too filling for people who eat out regularly (as the Kensington patrons probably do). Crème brûlée was textbook-smooth and yolky. We felt the waiting staff could have been a little more attentive. Even though on this occasion the impression wasn't of a restaurant going the extra mile, prices are very reasonable for the locality.
Babies and children welcome: children's portions; high chairs. Booking advisable. Disabled: toilet. Separate rooms for parties, seating 20-60.
Map 7 A9.

Babylon

7th floor, The Roof Gardens, 99 Kensington High Street, W8 5SA (7368 3993/www.roofgardens. com). High Street Kensington tube. **Lunch served** noon-2.30pm daily. **Dinner served** 7-10.30pm Mon-Sat. **Main courses** £18.50-£24. **Set lunch** (Mon-Sat) £16.50 2 courses, £19.50 3 courses; (Sun) £22 2 courses, £25 3 courses. **Credit** AmEx, DC, MC, V.

By the time the elevator doors open on to the seventh floor, you'd be forgiven for expecting magnificence on a biblical scale, but Richard Branson's Babylon is an understated affair: a long room in neutral colours and clean lines; candles flickering in sand; rose heads floating in miniature fish-bowls. The famous Roof Gardens, one floor down, charms drinkers silly in the summer months, and the views from Babylon's perimeter terrace are stunning – although come nightfall you'll need 20:20 vision to make out the capital's central landmarks. Service is impeccable, as you'd expect at these prices, and the food seldom fails to impress. A starter posing the business end of a Scottish langoustine on a bed of Cornish crab meat tasted sea fresh. Flavoursome ham hock terrine suffered only slightly from too little time out of the refrigerator. Main courses benefit from an ability to bring out the best in red meats; the richness of a roast saddle of venison was complemented by a sweet Madeira jus, while the 28-day-hung sirloin of Irish beef displayed a depth and darkness to put prime fillet steaks in the shade.
Babies and children welcome: children's menu; entertainer (Sun); high chairs. Booking advisable. Disabled: lift; toilet. Entertainment: musicians dinner Thur. Separate room for parties, seats 12. Tables outdoors (15, balcony). **Map 7 B9.**

Clarke's (100)

124 Kensington Church Street, W8 4BH (7221 9225/www.sallyclarke.com). Notting Hill Gate tube. **Lunch served** 12.30-2pm Mon-Fri; noon-2pm Sat. **Dinner served** 7-10pm Mon-Sat. **Main courses** (lunch) £14-£16. **Set dinner** £49 3 courses incl coffee. **Credit** AmEx, DC, MC, V.

It was the mid 1980s when Sally Clarke, inspired by her experiences dining at Chez Panisse in California, brought something fresh, light and sunny to a dour and grey London. A trailblazer she certainly was, but the road she travels today now seems familiar. The parquet floor, cane chairs and white tablecloths don't make for a cutting-edge environment, but it is a pleasing one – civilised, bright and calm. There's a basement area too, which is often in. The waiting staff have a way of making

everyone feel like a regular. Ingredients have always been at the heart of things here, and a fine chargrilled Welsh lamb chump chop was as good as it gets ('proper' flavour, full of depth, tender), and served with a rich wine gravy and mash. The preceding buffalo mozzarella, chive and chervil risotto balls were accomplished and the dessert (soft pistachio meringue with spring rhubarb), although overloaded with cream, showed a good balance of sweet and sharp. Incidentals are spot-on, such as the fantastic bread: as you'd expect, as it comes from Clarke's own highly successful bakery. The wine list contains many Californian gems, but doesn't ignore the rest of the world.
Babies and children welcome: high chair. Booking advisable; essential weekends. Restaurant available for hire. **Map 7 B7.**

★ Kensington Place

201-209 Kensington Church Street, W8 7LX (7727 3184/www.kensingtonplace-restaurant. co.uk). Notting Hill Gate tube. **Lunch served** noon-3pm Mon-Fri; noon-3.30pm Sat, Sun. **Dinner served** 6.30-10.30pm Mon-Thur; 6.30-11pm Fri, Sat; 6.30-10pm Sun. **Main courses** £14-£25. **Set lunch** (Mon-Fri) £19.50 3 courses; (Sun) £24.50 3 courses. **Set dinner** £24.50 3 courses (£39.50 incl wine). **Credit** AmEx, MC, V.

When Rowley Leigh left KP after 20 years as chef in 2006, the doom-sayers predicted it was the end of the line for this Notting Hill pioneer. That didn't stop D&D London (the Conran Restaurant group, under new ownership) from adding the venue to its collection last year and installing chef Henry Vigar from Bjorn van der Horst's La Noisette in the kitchen. The room has been freshened up, without losing any of its 1980s London vibe, and while lunch remains a more casual Brit/French mix, things step up at night with a quite special French-driven menu. Grilled red mullet with braised beef and carrot and caper emulsion was a neat take on surf'n'turf; suckling pork belly was a wobbly sticky delight; and a salad of labne, pistachio nuts and herbs was a breath of fresh spring air. To finish, an apple tarte fine with beurre noisette ice-cream was textbook stuff. With such light-hearted flavour-packed and seasonally driven cooking, it would seem that rumours of Kensington Place's demise have been greatly exaggerated.
Babies and children welcome: high chairs. Booking advisable; essential weekends. Disabled: toilet. Separate room for parties, seats 45. **Map 7 B7.**

★ Launceston Place

1A Launceston Place, W8 5RL (7937 6912/ www.danddlondon.com). Gloucester Road or High Street Kensington tube. **Lunch served** 12.30-2.30pm Tue-Sat; noon-3pm Sun. **Dinner served** 6.30-10.30pm daily. **Set lunch** £18 3 courses; (Sun) £24 3 courses. **Set dinner** £38 3 courses, £48 6 courses. **Credit** AmEx, DC, MC, V.

In autumn 2007, Launceston Place was acquired by D&D London, owners of Coq d'Argent, Plateau, Sartoria, Le Pont de la Tour and numerous other top-end establishments. It's undergone a full refurb, shedding its former dowdiness for a sultry, chic elegance, all chocolate-brown and sexy low lighting. At the stoves is Tristan Welch, former head chef for Marcus Wareing at Pétrus (*see p139*), who's also undergone something of a transformation, swapping French classicism for British modernity. The cooking is superb. A food stylist couldn't have made a starter of scallops in their shells, balanced on a piece of olive wood and strewn with wild flowers look more deliciously glamorous, but the straight-from-the-sea flavour was what really impressed. Deep velvety green nettle soup was served with a little mound of frozen horseradish 'snow' – on our visit, the only over-embellishment encountered. Mains of suckling pig with creamed onions and warm potato salad and Cornish mackerel bring English classics bang up-to-date with an evident feel for flavours. The £38 three-course prix-fixe menu delivers all the bells and whistles – amuse-bouche, pre-dessert and petits fours, all at a leisurely pace and without fussiness. The wine list is long and priced with the surroundings but the sting of 12.5% service charge is mitigated by the professionalism of staff,

L'Autre Pied. See p233.

who combine just the right mix of solicitousness and humour. Traditionalists take note: Sunday roasts are served here too.
Babies and children welcome: high chair. Booking advisable. Separate room for parties, seats 10.
Map 7 C9.

The Terrace

33C Holland Street, W8 4LX (7937 3224/ www.theterracerestaurant.co.uk). High Street Kensington tube. **Brunch served** noon-3pm Sat; noon-3.30pm Sun. **Lunch served** noon-2.30pm Mon-Fri. **Dinner served** 6.30-11pm Mon-Sat. **Main courses** £14.50-£18.50. **Set brunch** (Sat, Sun) £17.50 2 courses, £21.50 3 courses. **Set lunch** £14.50 2 courses. **Credit** AmEx, MC, V.

The Terrace sits off Kensington Church Street on a picture-postcard side street that could have come straight out of a Richard Curtis film. It's popular with plummy locals (most of whom could also have come out of a Richard Curtis film), though was quiet on the midweek night we visited. The interior is neat but small; if you can, get a seat at one of the outdoor tables that gives the restaurant its name. They're protected from the street by an array of shrubs. Husband-and-wife team Nadene and Maga Ayacouty run the show; she's the manager, he's in the kitchen. The menu is short and quite old-fashioned; the execution of all our dishes was competent, but nothing thrilled the taste buds. A starter of seared scallops with asparagus was

RESTAURANTS

as it sounds, while a main of monkfish fillet, although nicely cooked, was not enhanced by its insipid trimmings of cauliflower purée, courgette salad and avocado salsa. The crust of a peach and mango crème brûlée was properly burnt and the interior suitably creamy, but it was hard to detect any fruit. The wine list is short, with not much choice by the glass, and the coffee was weak. Could do better, we say.

Babies and children welcome: high chairs. Booking advisable. Restaurant available for hire. Tables outdoors (8, terrace). **Map 7 B8**.

Whits

21 Abingdon Road, W8 6AH (7938 1122/ www.whits.co.uk). High Street Kensington tube.
Bar **Open** 5.30-11pm Tue-Sat.
Restaurant **Lunch served** 12.30-2.30pm Mon-Fri; 12.30-3pm Sun. **Dinner served** 6.30-10.30pm Tue-Sat. **Main courses** £13.50-£19.50. **Set lunch** £14.95 2 courses, £17.95 3 courses. **Set dinner** £14.95 2 courses, £23.50 3 courses. **Credit** AmEx, MC, V.
Whits occupies an awkwardly shaped, two-level space with an over-large bar at the front (evidence of its previous incarnation as a wine bar). It has too much twiddly metal furniture and although the

chaise longue we were led too looked pretty, it made an uncomfortable perch for a meal. But such shortcomings are easily ignored thanks to the smartly dressed tables, judicious lighting and utterly charming, unaffected service. Although popular with softly spoken, well-bred Kensington locals, it's often half-empty. The atmosphere was hushed on our Friday night visit – a shame, but competition on this short stretch of road is fierce. The menu leans towards France with the likes of steak tartare and cassoulet, but you could also have Hungarian-style potage with kolbasz sausage, or salmon with wasabi and pickled ginger. The cooking style can be over-rich and a tad fussy, with too many elements competing on the same plate. But meat-eaters do well, as do lovers of rich, indulgent ingredients (foie gras, venison, suckling pig); dieters and plain-food fans should look elsewhere. Mains were good: a luxurious scallop risotto with scallop tempura, and slow-roast duck breast with confit duck leg and honey and cumin jus. But an excess of butter marred our starter of lobster and shellfish ravioli with buttered spinach, and the banana tatin was sickly-sweet.

Babies and children admitted. Booking advisable. Restaurant available for hire. **Map 7 A9**.

Notting Hill

Bumpkin

209 Westbourne Park Road, W11 1EA (7243 9818/www.bumpkinuk.com). Westbourne Park tube.
Brasserie **Lunch served** noon-3.30pm Mon-Fri. **Brunch served** 11am-3.30pm Sat; 12.15-3.30pm Sun. **Dinner served** 6-11pm daily.
Restaurant **Lunch served** 12.15pm-3.30pm Sun. **Dinner served** 6-10.30pm Mon-Sat.
Both **Main courses** £8-£20. **Credit** AmEx, MC, V.
With flowery wallpaper, linen tea towels as napkins and mismatched china, Bumpkin's take on a funky farmhouse kitchen is charming. It's buzzy, fun and one up from a gastropub, with a jolly wine list, farmhouse ciders and a guest ale on draught – hurrah! The emphasis on cocktails is telling; Bumpkin belongs to the bar group that includes Prince Harry's hangout Boujis. Notting Hill's ex-boarding-school crowd appreciates this British comfort food, and the more sedate upstairs dining room should be ideal for entertaining guests from abroad. But visitors might be baffled by the seemingly cheddar-less cauliflower cheese, or miss the point of a dull fish cake. For pudding they might wonder if the crumble topping should be so

Launceston Place. See p239.

crunchy, but enjoy the proper vanilla custard. We couldn't fault starters of butternut squash soup with thyme and almonds, and a glorious spring vegetable salad of baby roots, beans, peas, cherry tomatoes and pea shoots plus bosworth ash goat's cheese. Full marks too for the heritage tomato salad. Weirdly there was no bread available. Service was friendly: too familiar in the case of the waitress who sat at the next table to recount her life story while we waited for our bill.
Babies and children welcome: high chairs. Bookings not accepted in brasserie dinner. Separate rooms for parties, seats 20-30. **Map 7 A5.**

Notting Hill Brasserie

92 Kensington Park Road, W11 2PN (7229 4481/www.nottinghillbrasserie.com). Notting Hill Gate tube. **Lunch served** noon-3pm Wed-Sun. **Dinner served** 7-11pm Mon-Sat; 7-10.30pm Sun. **Main courses** £19.50-£25.50. **Set lunch** (Wed-Sat) £17.50 2 courses, £22.50 3 courses; (Sun) £25 2 courses, £30 3 courses. **Credit** AmEx, MC, V.
Brasserie? Hardly. This restaurant is smart and grown-up, with the comfort that comes from thick table-linen and upholstery: somewhere to talk without being overheard or interrupted. There's a grand piano and jazz combo, and service is grave rather than warm. NHB takes seriously the responsibility of looking after the more mature, less flighty denizens of Notting Hill who dress up to dine out even on a Monday night. The customers, in turn, clearly appreciate it. Starters read like main courses and can take the wind out of an appetite's sails, especially after terrifically light and crusty walnut and raisin rolls, and an appetiser of artichoke soup that (characteristic of the cooking) had more creamy substance than froth. A main course of gloriously compatible cod, mini chorizo, salt-cod croquettes, carrot purée and golden-crisp pont neuf chips, plus a huge side bowl of thick dark buttery spinach leaves, didn't leave much space for panna cotta with a nicely lactic tang joining sweet forces with a poached pear sprinkled with pain d'épice crumbs and a millefeuille of pear compote. Orange choc-chip cantuccini with real mint tea ended a satisfying and substantial meal.
Babies and children welcome: high chairs; supervised crèche (Sun lunch). Booking advisable. Entertainment: jazz/blues musicians (Sun lunch, 7pm daily). Separate rooms for parties, seating 12 and 32. **Map 7 A6.**

Shepherd's Bush

Brackenbury

129-131 Brackenbury Road, W6 0BQ (8748 0107/www.thebrackenbury.co.uk). Goldhawk Road or Hammersmith tube. **Brunch served** 10am-3.30pm Sun. **Lunch served** noon-3pm Mon-Fri. **Dinner served** 7-10.45pm Mon-Sat. **Main courses** £9-£18. **Set lunch** £12.50 2 courses, £14.50 3 courses. **Credit** AmEx, MC, V.
The daily-changing menu was hot off the printer for our early evening booking. Short and to-the-point, it picks up well on the seasonal zeitgeist: in early June, asparagus and mousserons (aka St George's mushrooms) turned up in two dishes, while peas and broad beans featured elsewhere. Our emerald-green (slightly under-seasoned) spinach soup, served chilled, was adorned with tiny crunchy croutons, and grilled mackerel with a summery cucumber salad showed flair for simplicity as well as seasonality. Vegetarians are well catered for here, with mains such as a plate of young Kent vegetables, or salad of tomatoes, tender artichoke hearts and broad beans, with boiled eggs cooked just-so, their yolks still molten. Lunchtime features good value set menus and on Sunday morning you could treat yourself to a croque-monsieur, Stornoway black pudding and fried eggs, or French toast with banana and maple syrup. The Brackenbury is a long-standing neighbourhood favourite; its cosy interior, done up in taupe and brown, has a gracious laid-back feel that's reflected in the casual, friendly service. In summer, the terrace tables are the ones to reserve.
Babies and children welcome: high chairs. Booking advisable. Separate rooms for parties, seating 30-40. Tables outdoors (8, patio). **Map 20 B3.**

South West

Barnes

Sonny's

94 Church Road, SW13 0DQ (8748 0393/ www.sonnys.co.uk). Barnes or Barnes Bridge rail/33, 209, 283 bus.
Café Open 10.30am-5pm Mon, Tue; 10.30am-5.30pm Wed; 10.30am-6pm Thur-Sat. **Lunch served** noon-4pm Mon-Sat. **Main courses** £4.50-£10.25.
Restaurant Lunch served 12.30-2.30pm Mon-Sat; 12.30-3pm Sun. **Dinner served** 7-10.30pm Mon-Thur; 7-11pm Fri, Sat. **Main courses** £10.25-£19.95. **Set lunch** (Mon-Sat) £15.50 2 courses, £17.50 3 courses; (Sun) £22.50 3 courses. **Set dinner** (Mon-Thur) £18.50 2 courses, £21.50 3 courses.
Both **Credit** AmEx, MC, V.
The Barnes faithful have kept Sonny's thriving for almost a quarter of a century. It's part of a trio of neighbourhood restaurants run by Rebecca Mascarenhas, including the Phoenix (*see p238*) and 11 Abingdon Road (*see p243*). The white-painted back room with its glass-brick wall is more relaxed than the brighter front area, though the low ceiling means it can be noisy. The eclectic artworks should provide a talking point if conversation flags. There's much to like: staff are efficient and amenable, the wine list is pleasing, the set menus are nicely priced. But something was amiss with the food on our last visit. The ratio of (overcooked) exterior to interior was awry on our mini double-baked cheese soufflé, and the creamed leeks on the side were cloying. Roast fillet of Atlantic cod was little better, the fish mushy, and the accompanying compote of fennel and pernod too strongly flavoured. Perhaps we'd have fared better with one of the meat dishes: duck confit, rump of lamb, steak tartare (though why, when the menu isn't long, was that offered as both a starter and main course?). Sonny's has always produced good desserts: a wobbly vanilla panna cotta with orange jelly and segments maintained standards. A refurbishment was on the cards as we went to press – perhaps it's time to revamp the kitchen too.
Babies and children welcome: children's menu; high chairs. Booking advisable (restaurant). Restaurant available for hire. Separate room for parties, seats 20.

The Victoria

10 West Temple Sheen, SW14 7RT (8876 4238/ www.thevictoria.net). Mortlake rail. **Meals served** noon-10.30pm Mon-Sat; noon-8pm Sun. **Main courses** £10.50-£16. **Credit** MC, V.
This small hotel and restaurant in a former pub building has been taken over by Paul Merrett, who is familiar to BBC TV audiences through his appearances on shows such as *Ever Wondered About Food*. Long an unpretentious haven of good food for wealthy locals and families, the Victoria still has its huge conservatory dining room and a large outdoor garden, but Merrett and business partner Greg Bellamy have added a barbecue area. The food is often simple, but done well – such as in ribeye steak with triple-cooked chips and béarnaise, ham hock and foie gras terrine, or bread and butter pudding. Among the more adventurous dishes are gravadlax served with beetroot sorbet, and bramley apple samosas with greek yoghurt and chilli ice-cream. The bar could do with a more interesting range of beers; the international wine list, which has been prepared by Olly Smith, another aspiring TV 'personality', features around 35 bottles including three rosés. While concessions should be made for early days, on our visit and on trying to book, staff showed a lack of experience and professionalism.
Babies and children welcome: high chairs. Booking advisable weekends. Tables outdoors (12, garden).

Chelsea

Bluebird

350 King's Road, SW3 5UU (7559 1000/ www.danddlondon.com). Sloane Square tube then 11, 19, 22, 49, 319 bus.
Bar Open noon-midnight Mon-Thur; noon-1am Fri, Sat; noon-11.30pm Sun. **Restaurant Brunch served** noon-3.30pm Sat, Sun. **Lunch served** 12.30-2.30pm Mon-Fri. **Dinner served** 6-10.30pm Mon-Sat; 6-9.30pm Sun. **Main courses** £13.50-£25. **Set meal** (lunch, 6-7.30pm Mon-Fri) £15.50 2 courses £18.50 3 courses.
Both **Credit** AmEx, DC, MC, V.
Complete with café and expensive épicerie, Bluebird is no longer the culinary destination it once aspired to be, but remains a relatively popular meeting place for Chelsea residents. The spacious first-floor interior is nicely decorated in shades of rose and red, offset with modern metallic chandeliers and light structures. The menu is eclectic and please-all, with French accents. Spiced parsnip soup was rich and heady with cumin and coriander, while a périgourdine salad lacked the advertised truffle garnish, replaced bacon lardons with shreds of ham, and paired them with duck gizzards that were too tough to be tasty. A main course of pan-fried sea bass fillet was fine, if a little greasy, while slow-roast glazed duck with cherry brandy and montmorency sauce was a crisp-skinned, tender pair of duck legs served with a slightly sweet, slightly savoury sauce that was otherwise unremarkable. Prices reflect the location. While it may not be a culinary destination, Bluebird remains a perfectly pleasant meeting and drinking place.
Babies and children welcome: high chairs; nappy-changing facilities. Disabled: lift; toilet. Dress: smart casual. Separate rooms for parties, both seating 30. **Map 14 D12.**

★ The Botanist [NEW]

2008 RUNNER-UP BEST BREAKFAST
7 Sloane Square, SW1W 8EE (7730 0077/ www.thebotanistonsloanesquare.com). Sloane Square tube. **Breakfast served** 8-11.30am Mon-Fri; 9-11.30am Sat, Sun. **Lunch served** noon-3.30pm Mon-Sat; noon-4pm Sun. **Tea served** 3.30-6pm Mon-Sat; 4-6pm Sun. **Dinner served** 6-10.30pm daily. **Main courses** £14-£19. **Set lunch** (Mon-Fri) £19 2 courses, £23 3 courses. **Credit** AmEx, MC, V.
Tom and Ed Martin, well-known for their gastropub group including favourites such as the Gun and White Swan, appropriately opened this rather beautiful Sloane Square dining room the week of the Chelsea Flower Show. It was named in tribute to Sir Hans Sloane, and its decor celebrates the natural world; check out the sensational wood-framed chairs and gorgeous botany-flavoured tableau on the back wall. Food (including afternoon tea) is served most of the day and there are majestic roasts on Sundays. Dinner might be poached gull's egg with chorizo, alsace bacon and fresh peas, followed by an assiette of Scottish Blackface lamb. Breakfast comprises all the usual cooked and continental options, perfectly presented. Finish with a rich pudding (cherry and white chocolate panna cotta, whisky crème brûlée), an ice-cream coupe or the monthly-changing selection of British and French cheeses served with chutney, oatcakes and muscatel grapes. For breakfast, kipper on toast with poached egg was perfectly peppery and smoky. The pancakes seemed rather thin, but the maple syrup served with them was the real deal and the blueberries were fresh and juicy. We were equally won over by the service, and generally elegant atmosphere.
Babies and children welcome: high chairs. Booking advisable. Disabled: toilet. Tables outdoors (4, pavement). **Map 15 G10.**

Fulham

The Farm

18 Farm Lane, SW6 1PP (7381 3331/ www.thefarmfulham.co.uk). Fulham Broadway tube/11, 14, 211 bus.
Bar Open noon-midnight daily. **Meals served** noon-11pm daily.
Restaurant Brunch served 10am-4pm Sat; 10am-4.30pm Sun. **Meals served** noon-11pm Mon-Fri. **Dinner served** 5-11pm Sat, Sun. *Both* **Main courses** £9.95-£13.95. **Credit** AmEx, MC, V.

The Farm consists of a smart-casual, pub-like front room with dining rooms behind. Neatly divided into sections, the relaxed space has a feeling of intimacy akin to a living room. You could come here every day of the week, or once a year, and be treated with the same laid-back style of service. We started with a lovely own-made black pudding accompanied by a whole breadcrumbed duck egg, and a fish bouillabaisse with rouille that lacked intensity but was otherwise good. Mains of sea bass with artichokes and cherry tomatoes, and a ribeye steak with béarnaise sauce, were competently executed, as was our apple tarte tatin with crème fraîche. Alternatively, you could finish with a plate of English cheese and a glass of port. Sunday lunchtimes see a full family roast of lamb or beef offered along with bloody marys. The wine list features around 40 bottles, plus champagnes, and a choice of 20 by the glass. Good ingredients, simply served in a welcoming environment – what more could you want from a local?
Babies and children welcome: high chairs. Booking advisable. Disabled: toilet. Tables outdoors (5, pavement; 4, terrace). **Map 13 A13**.

Parsons Green

The Establishment NEW

2008 RUNNER-UP BEST BAR

45-47 Parsons Green Lane, SW6 4HH (7384 2418/www.theestablishment.com). Parsons Green tube. **Lunch served** noon-4pm, **dinner served** 6.30-10.30pm daily. **Main courses** £11-£16.50. **Set lunch** (Mon, Tue) £12 2 courses, £15 3 courses. **Set dinner** (Mon, Tue) £19 2 courses, £24 3 courses, £30 3 courses incl half bottle wine. **Credit** AmEx, MC, V.

Literally a hop, skip and stumble across the road from Parsons Green tube station, this spot has quickly established itself as a super-slick and sophisticated food and drink destination. With its loud 1970s-style wallpaper and cool shades-of-chocolate colour scheme, the decor is retro funk toned down with typical Fulham taste. Two rooms dedicated to dining and a compact glass-walled courtyard suggest the handsome former pub building provides the venue for some serious cooking. One glance at the Modern European menu confirms it. Head chef Karl MacEwan, formerly of the Glasshouse in Kew, is big on seasonal produce and generous portions. Along with succulent slow-cooked pork belly and fillet steak are more adventurous offerings that lift the menu way beyond the mundane. Our broad bean and crab risotto was as good as anything so bright-green in colour can be, while lime and vanilla cheesecake buried in bright purple berries was a sensual treat. Those with a penchant for cocktails might like to sip a chocolate martini for pud instead. Worth hopping off the tube for. *See also p335.*
Babies and children welcome: high chairs. Disabled: toilet. Separate room for parties, seats 25. Tables outside (7, courtyard).

Putney

Phoenix Bar & Grill

162-164 Lower Richmond Road, SW15 1LY (8780 3131/www.sonnys.co.uk). Putney Bridge tube/22, 265 bus. **Lunch served** 12.30-2.30pm Mon-Sat; 12.30-3pm Sun. **Dinner served** 7-11pm Mon-Sat; 7-10pm Sun. **Main courses** £9.50-£18. **Set lunch** (Mon-Sat) £13.50 2 courses, £15.50 3 courses; (Sun) £17.50 2 courses, £19.50 3 courses. **Set dinner** £15.50 2 courses, £17.50 3 courses. **Credit** AmEx, MC, V.

With a sense of style and space, this white-painted corner restaurant has long been a landmark at the quieter end of Putney. The pale interior is decorated with mirrors and modern art and tends to draw an enthusiastic local crowd – though in warmer months you can sit outside, with bamboo screens between you and the traffic. Oddly, on our midweek visit, the Phoenix was quiet and not on its usual good form. It didn't help that some of the Italian-themed dishes, such as monkfish wrapped in prosciutto, reminded us of meals eaten here almost 20 years ago, without any contemporary interpretation; or that scallops were served with a

single cima di rapa that was cooked nearly to an unfashionable mush. Chicken terrine had a salsa that needed more kick to brighten it up. The biggest disappointment, however, was a signature dish, vincisgrassi maceratese. A kind of rich lasagne with chicken livers among the béchamel, it is complicated to make but, here, spoilt by overpowering saltiness. These lapses were all the more frustrating as the Phoenix is usually better than this. Perhaps the faltering service was a clue that the A-team had had the night off.
Babies and children welcome: children's menu; crayons; high chairs. Booking essential summer; advisable winter. Disabled: toilet. Tables outdoors (15, terrace).

South

Balham

★ Harrison's NEW

15-19 Bedford Hill, SW12 9EX (8675 6900/ www.harrisonsbalham.co.uk). **Lunch served** noon-3pm; **dinner served** 6-10.30pm Mon-Fri. **Meals served** 9am-4pm, 6-10.30pm Sat, Sun. **Main courses** £9.50-£17.50. **Set lunch** £11.50 2 courses, £15 3 courses. **Set dinner** £14 2 courses, £17 3 courses. **Credit** AmEx, MC, V.

Harrison's, the latest venture of Sam Harrison (co-owner of Sam's Brasserie in Chiswick), opened in October 2007. Like the west London original, this is a lovely laid-back venue. It has eased snugly into a corner site in the funky part of Balham and makes much of its neighbourhood credentials. Brunch is a particular pleasure – on a hot summer's morning the windows are thrown wide; a jazzy soundtrack accompanies the buzz of happy, white-aproned staff in the central kitchen area; and a mixed Balham clientele slouches on the big, brown banquette. The design is beautifully simple: wood, flowers, metal kitchen, lots of muted light. For brunch, try the house salad of tomatoes, avocado, caramelised onion, lettuce and salty crayfish tails; or an utterly succulent cheeseburger with own-made spicy chutney and frites. The tuna niçoise contains just-boiled eggs, a bouncy bed of leaves, and a slab of barely seared tuna. We envied the stack of buttermilk pancakes on the next table. In the evenings or at lunchtime, the culinary approach is just as simple – cumberland sausages, pan-fried mullet, and so on. There's a separate menu (and face painting) for the kids, jazz on Sunday evenings, and a private bar. In all, just what any neighbourhood needs.
Babies and children welcome: children's menu; high chairs, toys. Booking advisable. Disabled: toilet. Separate room for parties, seats 40. Tables outdoors (6, pavement).

★ Lamberts

2 Station Parade, Balham High Road, SW12 9AZ (8675 2233/www.lambertsrestaurant.com). Balham tube/rail. **Lunch served** noon-3pm Sat. **Dinner served** 7-10.30pm Mon-Sat. **Meals served** noon-9pm Sun. **Main courses** £14-£18. **Set meal** (Mon-Thur) £15 2 courses, £18 3 courses. **Credit** MC, V.

To describe this as Balham's best restaurant doesn't do it justice. Lamberts is more than able to hold its own in any neighbourhood. It is run with mustard-keen enthusiasm and professionalism, which animates the plain mustard-coloured room. The focus is all on what matters most: excellent service, a helpful list of well-chosen wines at decent prices, and great dishes starring fine seasonal ingredients. Everything is own-made and nothing wasted, so bread (with farmhouse butter, a typically thoughtful detail) is an extra, but espresso cups of artichoke soup are automatically given. What followed was plate-lickingly good: steak and kidney pudding with cockle and parsley sauce as a starter; then intensely rewarding main courses of sea bass with masses of wild greens, heritage potatoes and a tangy gribiche-like salsa; and crispy-skinned guinea fowl with roast jerusalem artichokes and smoked bacon united by a tarragon-infused sauce. Only heavy-going, pastry-driven puds had feet of clay. Rhubarb was too resistant and ice-creams indistinguishable. But

Interview
JOHN TORODE

Who are you?
Owner of **Smiths of Smithfield** (*see p230*), which includes **Top Floor at Smiths** (*see p68*). Also co-presenter of BBC1's *Masterchef* and *Celebrity Masterchef*; and author of various books including new release *John Torode's Beef* (Quadrille).

What's the best thing about running a restaurant in London?
The people – the team that work in the restaurants, and the customers. The buzz makes for a great life and happy people make people happy!

What's the worst thing?
The mechanical plant, which is always difficult to maintain and costs a fortune. That, and keeping the pavement clean now that all the smokers just drop their butts on the ground.

Which are your favourite London restaurants and bars?
I love **Hakkasan** (*see p75*) for Chinese food and **J Sheekey** for fish (*see p81*). **Canteen** (*see p64*) is clever. I also like the bar at Claridge's and the Slaughtered Lamb pub on Great Sutton Street.

How green are you?
Smiths of Smithfield now recycles nearly all its waste. We have looked really hard at what we waste and how we can reduce it, making the chefs aware of the issues. We've started sending all our food waste to a plant that turns it into bio-fuel and fertiliser, and we plan to dump Tetrapaks as it seems the only way they can be recycled is to send them back to where they are made. The design of our new café-bar in Spitalfields Market, the **Luxe** (*see p20*), has been pushed by many environmentally friendly ideas too.

What is missing from London's restaurant scene?
Apart from the Luxe? Not much, the town rocks.

RESTAURANTS

with nutty chocolate squares sweetening a bill that seemed very reasonable for such quality, Lamberts left an excellent lasting impression.
Babies and children welcome: children's menu (weekends); high chairs. Booking advisable; essential weekends. Restaurant available for hire.

Battersea

Ransome's Dock

35-37 Parkgate Road, SW11 4NP (7223 1611/ www.ransomesdock.co.uk/restaurant). Battersea Park rail/19, 49, 319, 345 bus. **Brunch served** noon-5pm Sat; noon-3.30pm Sun. **Meals served** noon-11pm Mon-Fri. **Dinner served** 6-11pm Sat. **Main courses** £11.50-£22.50. **Set meal** (noon-5pm Mon-Fri) £15.50 2 courses. **Credit** AmEx, DC, MC, V.

An air of Dickensian mystery hangs about this place overlooking the moored-up barges close to the Thames. The dated decor is a mix of Provence, nautical kitsch and excruciatingly bad 1980s artwork. Together with the geographically promiscuous menu, it suggests an owner desperately seeking distinctiveness but not quite sure how to achieve it. In the event, dining here was a strange, disappointing experience. Neither was it cheap, with 30-day-aged sirloin steak and chips selling at a pricey £22.50, and our bill marked with the surprising and petty addendum of '2 bread and butter £2'. A starter of goat's cheese crostini was bland, 'Elizabeth David's lamb and aubergine casserole' was homely but seemed overpriced at £17, while an otherwise acceptable fish stew was accompanied, bizarrely, with green salad. Only the interesting and good-value wine list, including an excellent Loire house red, and a rustic starter of rabbit terrine, hit the spot. Most damning of all is the fact that on a Friday night the restaurant was only a quarter full.

Babies and children welcome: high chairs. Booking advisable. Disabled: toilet. Tables outdoors (10, terrace). **Map 21 C1**.

Tom Ilic NEW

2008 RUNNER-UP BEST LOCAL RESTAURANT
123 Queenstown Road, SW8 3RH (7622 0555/ www.tomilic.com). Battersea Park or Queenstown Road rail. **Lunch served** noon-2.30pm Wed-Sat; noon-3.30pm Sun. **Dinner served** 6-10.30pm Tue-Sat. **Main courses** £12.95-£14.95. **Set lunch** £12.50 2 courses, £14.95 3 courses; (Sun) £16.50 2 courses, £18.95 3 courses. **Credit** MC, V.

The porker logo gives the game away: Tom Ilic is a man who likes pig. It appears in various forms on the menu at his new Battersea restaurant, including braised pig's cheeks and roast pork belly, alongside other concoctions that will delight the committed carnivore. He's particularly good at hearty, strongly flavoured dishes that are perfect for winter. Fish fans do well too – both blue fin tuna (a starter, as carpaccio and tartare) and halibut fillet (a main) were high quality and deftly cooked – but vegetarians should look elsewhere. Desserts included a a messy-looking but delicious peach gratin that was big enough for two. Ilic is also not prey to superstition, it seems: this is a notoriously unlucky site that has seen many restaurants fail in the past (a decade ago he was head chef here, when it was the Stepping Stone). Terracotta and off-white walls and dark wood furniture provide a calming environment, while the clever use of mirrors amplifies the space – though we'd ditch the scruffy carpet in the inner room. The wine list covers all bases and the set lunch is a bargain, but the service needs work: staff seemed inexperienced, and someone should really stop them from spray-wiping tables while diners are still eating.

Babies and children welcome: high chairs. Booking advisable weekend.

Brixton

Upstairs

89B Acre Lane, entrance on Branksome Road, SW2 5TN (7733 8855/www.upstairslondon.com). Clapham Common tube/Brixton tube/rail. **Dinner served** 6.30-9.30pm Tue-Thur; 6.30-10.30pm Fri, Sat. **Set dinner** £21 2 courses, £25 3 courses. **Credit** MC, V.

Judging by the amount of time we had to wait in the busy bar before being seated, Upstairs is no longer the well-kept Brixton secret it once was. Located on a side street off Acre Lane, it has no entrance sign, just a door with a buzzer to press. Once inside, this three-storey townhouse has the feel of a salon or speakeasy. It's all very intimate, there are only seven tables in the turquoise dining room and diners choose from a nicely minimalist set menu, which at £21 and £25 for two and three courses respectively, is good value. But despite the restaurant's quirky charms, we felt the quality of food had suffered in the past year. 'Rump and leg of lamb' meant a chunk of delicious lamb served with a bowl of shepherd's pie – not the finest combination. Snapper with pine nuts, squid ink and big thick chips was excellent, as was a pudding of lemon posset. But our apple crumble was woeful. While the food isn't what it used to be, this is still a cherished place for the cognoscenti of Brixton.

Babies and children welcome: high chair (call in advance). Booking advisable weekends. **Map 22 C2**.

Clapham

Fouronine

409 Clapham Road, SW9 9BT (7737 0722/ www.fouronine.co.uk). Clapham North tube. **Dinner served** 6-10.30pm daily. **Main courses** £13-£19. **Credit** MC, V.

The Botanist. See p241.

Harrison's. See p243.

At Fouronine you press a buzzer by the front door and (assuming you're not selling encyclopedias) someone lets you in and shows you to your table. Whether this is to bolster the air of exclusivity or keep out randoms from surrounding estates is open to debate, but it makes for an evening akin to dining round at a friend's house – albeit a friend with André Dupin, formerly of Chez Bruce (*see p107*), rattling around in the kitchen. Aesthetics lend a sense of Zen-like calm – from the backlit cocktail bar to the soft play of candlelight on the overhead beams – while the intimacy of the 50-at-a-push seating makes getting the waiter's attention easy. The menu still needs a little fine tuning (a starter of pork belly with savoy cabbage and braised baby onions was paired with a sauce so salty that it rendered the rest of the meal virtually tasteless) but it's more hit than miss. Fish dishes are done with real flair, from a starter of gilthead bream with squid ink risotto, to crispy sea bass with olive oil mash and chunks of grilled courgette. Desserts might be poached English rhubarb with champagne sorbet, or panna cotta with cinnamon-scented oranges, and there are cheeses from Neals Yard Dairy for those who prefer a savoury finish. Despite our minor gripes, we reckon Fouronine may well be replacing that buzzer through over use before the year is out.
Babies and children admitted. Booking advisable.
Map 22 C1.

Tooting

Rick's Café
122 Mitcham Road, SW17 9NH (8767 5219).
Tooting Broadway tube. **Lunch served** noon-3pm, **dinner served** 6-11pm Tue-Sat. **Main courses** £6-£12. **Credit** MC, V.
It would take real culinary verve to tempt out-of-towners away from this rather tawdry stretch of Tooting, but Rick's Café is a sanctuary for locals seeking dinners that don't come served in Styrofoam tubs. Its interior is nothing to scream about, a single room of scrubbed wooden tables and a range of overpowering abstract paintings sitting lopsidedly on the walls – all of which justify the 'Café' part of the equation. But a meal at Rick's is full of surprises. While our goat's cheese and baby beet salad was small and unimaginative, the slice of cheese unpleasantly chilled from the fridge, another starter of chicken liver parfait was smooth and richly satisfying. Mains were flawed but still

pleasing; duck breast came decidedly less pink than promised, but was tender and tempered with an assertive red wine jus and a buttery stack of crushed potatoes. Best of all was bream draped over a startling pink mash of potato and beet; it suffered slightly from some greasy fried mushrooms but tasted twenty times as good as it looked. As the only local enterprise of its kind, Rick's Café can afford to take risks, and they sometimes pay off.
Babies and children welcome: high chairs. Booking advisable dinner and weekends. Disabled: toilet.

Waterloo

Oxo Tower Restaurant, Bar & Brasserie
Eighth floor, Oxo Tower Wharf, Barge House Street, SE1 9PH (7803 3888/www.harveynichols. com). Blackfriars or Waterloo tube/rail.
Bar **Open** 11am-11pm Mon-Wed; 11am-11.30pm Thur-Sat; noon-10.30pm Sun.
Brasserie **Lunch served** noon-3.15pm Mon-Sat; noon-3.45pm Sun. **Dinner served** 5.30-11pm Mon-Sat; 6-10.15pm Sun. **Main courses** £13-£27. **Set meal** (lunch Mon-Sat; 5.30-6pm Mon-Fri) £21.50 2 courses, £24.50 3 courses.
Restaurant **Lunch served** noon-2.30pm Mon-Sat; noon-3pm Sun. **Dinner served** 6-11pm Mon-Sat; 6.30-10pm Sun. **Main courses** £22-£35. **Set lunch** £33 3 courses.
All **Credit** AmEx, DC, MC, V.
If you're tired of the view of London from the eighth floor of Oxo Tower, you're tired of life, to misquote Samuel Johnson. Excellent use is made of the riverside position and the high ceilings of the two large spaces that make up the restaurant and the bar-brasserie. Floor-to-ceiling windows are artfully angled towards the sky, while the long terrace is the favoured position when the weather allows. It would be a crying shame if the food was a disappointment, but the crew at Harvey Nichols know what they're doing. A dinner in the brasserie produced a dish that banished thoughts of the rain pounding the windows; octopus was cooked twice to succulence and combined with a Mediterranean assemblage of black olives, feta cheese and oven-dried tomatoes. It was a journey south for the main course, too: rabbit saltimbocca with a slightly underwhelming truffle pecorino polenta. The restaurant offers a little more comfort – tablecloths no less – and space (tables for two can be painfully close in the brasserie), but prices aren't cheap.

Service is well-drilled and surprisingly friendly, given the over-abundance of expense-account diners staff have to deal with.
Babies and children welcome: children's menu; high chairs. Booking advisable. Disabled: lift; toilet. Entertainment (brasserie): jazz (lunch Sat, Sun; 7.30pm daily). Restaurant and brasserie available for hire. Tables outdoors (50, brasserie terrace; 40, restaurant terrace). Vegetarian menu. Vegan dishes. **Map 11 N7.**

Skylon
Royal Festival Hall, Belvedere Road, SE1 8XX (7654 7800/www.danddlondon.com). Waterloo tube/rail.
Bar **Open/snacks served** noon-1am daily.
Brasserie **Meals served** noon-10.45pm daily. **Main courses** £9.50-£18.50. **Set dinner** (5.30-6.30pm, after 10pm) £17.50 2 courses, £21.50 3 courses.
Restaurant **Lunch served** noon-2.30pm Mon-Sat; noon-3.30pm Sun. **Dinner served** 5.30-10.30pm daily. **Set meal** £39.50 3 courses. **Set dinner** (5.30-6.30pm, after 10pm) £24.50 2 courses, £29.50 3 courses.
All **Credit** AmEx, MC, V.
We went here on a difficult night in the brasserie, when a huge party had arrived late and caused a serious service-jam. The front-of-house crew coped admirably, and couldn't have been nicer, but the other problems we encountered can't be explained away by temporary glitches. For one thing, there was the music. Skylon's huge riverside space in the Royal Festival Hall has unforgiving acoustics, and a totally inappropriate disco thump made shouting a necessity. We asked staff to turn down the volume, which they did happily, but it crept back up. This would have been endurable were it not for the food. Flavoursome lamb shanks with risotto, and eggs 'Skylon' (spinach, crab meat, poached eggs and hollandaise), were both well-executed, but much was slipshod. Two soups were tiny in portion and tinier in flavour. A hamburger – ordered rare, delivered just short of well-done – came with pallid, flabby lukewarm chips. The wine list is good and reasonably priced, and served with care. On the evidence of our visit, however, this lovely room is not doing justice to its awesome view of the Thames. One of our party thought the highlight of the meal was the free packet of toothpicks provided at the end.
Babies and children welcome: children's menu (brasserie); high chairs. Booking advisable. Disabled: lift; toilet. **Map 10 M8.**

South East

Greenwich

Inside

19 Greenwich South Street, SE10 8NW (8265 5060/www.insiderestaurant.co.uk). Greenwich rail/DLR. **Lunch served** noon-2.30pm Tue-Fri; noon-3pm Sun. **Dinner served** 6.30-11pm Tue-Sat. **Main courses** £10.95-£16. **Set lunch** £11.95 2 courses, £15.95 3 courses. **Set dinner** (6.30-8pm) £16.95 2 courses, £20.95 3 courses. **Credit** AmEx, MC, V.

That Inside is a local fine-dining fave is evident by the polite familiarity between owners and patrons. The interior is tastefully done out with white and dark brown walls, bleached tablecloths, wooden floors, framed photos and abstract art; the starkness is softened by the sound of civilised conversation once the small space fills up (which it does on most nights). But it's the food that's the real draw: based on classical Anglo-French traditions, dishes are cooked with flair and creativity, using the freshest ingredients. The set-price dinner menu is popular and excellent value (£16.95 for two courses; £20.95 for three), but you can also opt for à la carte. Cornish mussels with coconut milk, lemongrass and chilli made for a deliciously vibrant starter. Mains of pan-fried halibut with potato purée, steamed leeks, broad beans and chive velouté, and roast duck breast with red cabbage, parsnips, bean and pancetta cassoulet, were perfectly executed and beautifully presented. This is the sort of place where the full flavour and richness of the dishes means that portion sizes are appropriately compact. Own-made bread, a good choice of wine, accomplished desserts, reasonable prices and dedicated owners keep the locals coming back.
Babies and children admitted. Booking advisable. Disabled: toilet.

London Bridge & Borough

Bermondsey Kitchen

194 Bermondsey Street, SE1 3TQ (7407 5719/www.bermondseykitchen.co.uk). Borough tube/London Bridge tube/rail. **Brunch served** 9.30am-3.30pm Sat, Sun. **Lunch served** noon-3pm Mon-Fri. **Dinner served** 6.30-10.30pm Mon-Sat. **Main courses** £10.25-£16. **Credit** AmEx, DC, MC, V.

A classic piece of once-workaday old London, Bermondsey Street has taken on a much more suave look of late, as its former sweatshops are taken over by studios, chic jewellers and places to eat and hang out. The Bermondsey Kitchen was a curtain-raiser to the street's renovation, and has the most laid-back, friendly atmosphere, with an open range, hefty wooden tables and gastropub-style leather sofas near the bar. Its cooking is consistently enterprising, with daily-changing menus based on well-sourced, frequently-organic ingredients. The usual list shows strong Iberian influences, but also offers unusual and original combinations such as pan-fried pigeon breast wrapped in parma ham – a bit tough, but interesting. A more conventional goat's cheese, walnut and pear salad, though, hit all the right spots, and penne with courgettes, blue cheese and pesto made a satisfying vegetarian main course. More typical of the kitchen's inventiveness was roast chicken stuffed with black pudding with swede purée and spinach – potentially over the top, but a beautifully smooth, subtle mix. Our well-priced Navajas Rioja was just as smooth, and staff were likeably welcoming. There are bargain single-course lunch dishes in the week, and a popular weekend brunch.
Babies and children welcome: high chairs. Booking advisable. Disabled: toilet. Restaurant available for hire. **Map 12 Q9.**

Delfina

50 Bermondsey Street, SE1 3UD (7357 0244/www.thedelfina.co.uk). London Bridge tube/rail. **Lunch served** noon-3pm Mon-Fri. **Dinner served** 7-10pm Fri. **Main courses** £13-£16. **Credit** AmEx, DC, MC, V.

This popular Bermondsey lunch spot began life as a canteen for the resident artists of the Delfina Studio. Although no longer run by the Delfina Studio Trust (it was taken over by a catering group in 2007), it retains its light, bright, white gallery feel, with art from the nearby Poussin Gallery. We were almost expecting someone to come round with a tray of sherry, and cubes of cheddar cheese (they didn't, of course). Chef Maria Elia has moved on after ten years, but new chef Richard Simpson's menu has retained the same contemporary bistro feel, right down to the chargrilled Australian fish of the day. The food is polite and pretty, although we found flavours fairly reticent – more watercolours than robust oil paintings. A velvety smooth split-pea purée didn't really need the accompanying oily truffled pastry strips, while a starter of roast quail with goat's cheese cream and cubed beetroot lacked seasoning and oomph. The grilled fillet of barramundi was lacklustre, leaving us pining for the more copious serving of ossobuco at the next table. Coffee was tragic.
Babies and children admitted. Booking advisable. Disabled: toilet. **Map 12 Q9.**

Tower Bridge

Blueprint Café

Design Museum, 28 Shad Thames, SE1 2YD (7378 7031/www.danddlondon.com). Tower Hill tube/Tower Gateway DLR/London Bridge tube/rail/47, 78 bus. **Lunch served** noon-3pm Mon-Sat; noon-4pm Sun. **Dinner served** 6-11pm Mon-Sat. **Main courses** £12.50-£22. **Credit** AmEx, DC, MC, V.

This light-filled, white-painted room above the Design Museum remains one of the best places to dine beside the river. Tables by the (often open) windows are at a premium, but there isn't really a duff spot in the spacious modern room as all tables have City skyline, if not actual water, views. Best dishes on a rather chilly night were just-right brisket with beetroot and horseradish cream, and a delicious, chunky hare pie, both served in generous portions. Starters of baked salsify with parmesan, and smoked eel sandwich with red onion pickle, were pleasing too. A final warming came from poached winter fruits with crème fraîche and pine nuts. The menu, under long-serving head chef Jeremy Lee, changes regularly;

more summery dishes might be feta, tomato, mint and black olive crumbs followed by whole grilled bream with warm potato salad, with lemon posset and blueberries to finish. A wide-ranging wine list has plenty by the glass, and there's advice on hand if you need it. Solicitous service made for a relaxed evening; there's no relentless turning of tables here. Good to see a long-standing restaurant not resting on its laurels.
Babies and children welcome: high chairs. Booking advisable dinner. Disabled: lift; toilet (in museum). Restaurant available for hire. Tables outdoors (4, terrace). **Map 12 S9.**

Le Pont de la Tour

Butlers Wharf Building, 36D Shad Thames, SE1 2YE (7403 8403/www.danddlondon.com). Tower Hill tube/Tower Gateway DLR/London Bridge tube/rail/47, 78 bus. **Bar & grill Lunch served** noon-3pm Mon-Fri; noon-5pm Sat; noon-4pm Sun. **Dinner served** 6-10pm Mon-Sat; 6-11pm Sun. **Main courses** £11.50-£22. **Set lunch** £13.50 2 courses, £17.50 3 courses. *Restaurant* **Lunch served** noon-3pm Mon-Sat; noon-4pm Sun. **Dinner served** 6-11pm daily. **Main courses** £16.50-£35. **Set lunch** £20 2 courses, £25 3 courses. *Both* **Credit** AmEx, DC, MC, V.

On a summer's evening on the terrace, Le Pont has the air of a French Riviera marina. Rather snooty Gallic service and slick tanned clientele add to the effect; there's just that big 'pont', Tower Bridge, reminding you where you are. Magnificent seafood platters are a definite draw, accompanied by something from the wealth (and 'wealth' is the word) of choice from the hardback wine book. Inside, it's all pressed linen tablecloths, live cocktail piano and ink drawings of toffs in top hats. The food could have done with more attention to detail, given the prices. Showy silver service landed us some stale sourdough bread – and where were the advertised pommes pailles to accompany our otherwise faultless beef fillet? Sea bass was nicely cooked, but came with cold caramelised salsify. Top marks went to a well-balanced starter of heady smoked eel with a golf ball of soft poached egg. Generally the food is underwhelming, but if fawning French waiters serving with a flourish make you feel special (and in these surroundings they easily can) this restaurant is for you.

Walnut. See p248.

Babies and children welcome: high chairs. Booking advisable. Entertainment: pianist 7pm daily (bar & grill). Separate room for parties, seats 20. Tables outdoors (22, terrace). **Map 12 S8.**

East

Docklands

Plateau

Canada Place, Canada Square, E14 5ER (7715 7100/www.danddlondon.com). Canary Wharf tube/DLR. ***Bar & grill* Meals served** noon-11pm Mon-Sat. **Main courses** £10-£19.50. ***Restaurant* Lunch served** noon-3pm Mon-Fri. **Dinner served** 6-10.30pm Mon-Sat. **Set meal** £29.50 2 courses, £35 3 courses. *Both* **Credit** AmEx, DC, MC, V.

Plateau is about occasion dining. The occasion in question here is impress-the-client business entertaining, Canary Wharf-style. Which means expense-account prices, a serious wine list, attentive, well-orchestrated staff and a wall of views to gleaming tower blocks. Decor and food both represent safe modern luxury, the former reflecting Plateau's Conran origins (though it is now owned by D&D London). The furniture and lighting are stylish if no longer cutting edge (nor 'futuristic' as the website claims). The restaurant food aims to be fashionable, but in ingredients rather than technique – dishes include tuna with ponzu onions, and pig's trotter with Yukon gold potatoes. The cooking is reliably well-executed, and prettily presented. The bar menu is cheaper and more Mediterranean in character, to an extent that seems distinctly unseasonal in winter, when you can't get a good plum tomato for love nor money. We were disappointed by crab rolls no better than you'd find at a good Vietnamese restaurant for a quarter of the price, though our partridge was excellent, and pork chop with orzo pasta flavour-packed. Plateau is certainly worth considering, at least if someone else is picking up the bill (particularly for the £9.50 bloody marys). *Babies and children welcome: high chairs; nappy-changing facilities. Booking advisable. Disabled: toilet. Dress: smart casual. Separate rooms for parties, seating 15 and 24. Tables outdoors (17, terrace). Vegetarian menu.* **Map 24 B2.**

Shoreditch

Hoxton Apprentice

16 Hoxton Square, N1 6NT (7739 6022/ www.hoxtonapprentice.com). Old Street tube/rail. ***Bar* Open** noon-11pm Mon-Sat; noon-10pm Sun. ***Restaurant* Lunch served** noon-3pm daily. **Dinner served** 6-11pm Mon-Sat; 6-10pm Sun. **Main courses** £9.90-£16.75. **Set lunch** (Mon-Fri) £6.99 1 courses, £9.99 2 courses, £12.99 3 courses. *Both* **Credit** AmEx, MC, V.

We don't want to be too harsh on what is, after all, a training restaurant set up by the Training for Life charity to teach the homeless and jobless a trade in hospitality. Still, it would be nice if the instructors taught the students how to take a booking. The first time we rang, we were asked to wait. And wait. But no one ever did come back. So was it worth waiting for? We like the woody, gastropubbish room with its tall windows and parquetry floor, and the menu reads well enough, but the atmosphere was joyless and staff seemed preoccupied. Little things declared the amateur status: the empty salt grinder, the rock-hard butter, the bread rolls reminiscent of airline fare. A simple linguine with confit tomatoes and marinated artichokes was competent, and miniature fish cakes had good form, but an overly ambitious saddle of Kent rabbit stuffed with black pudding was virtually unchewable. We passed on the cocktail of the day, weirdly called a 'Junge Bag' – Midori, malibu, Sweet & Sour, pineapple juice and mint cream – but the international wine list starts at a tempting £12.95 per bottle. *Babies and children welcome: children's menu; high chairs. Disabled: toilet. Separate room for parties, seats 40. Tables outdoors (9, pavement).* **Map 6 R3.**

Wapping

Wapping Food (100)

Wapping Hydraulic Power Station, Wapping Wall, E1W 3ST (7680 2080/www.thewappingproject. com). Wapping tube/Shadwell DLR. **Brunch served** 10am-12.30pm Sat, Sun. **Lunch served** noon-3.30pm Mon-Fri; 1-4pm Sat, Sun. **Dinner served** 6.30-11pm Mon-Fri; 7-11pm Sat. **Main courses** £11-£22. **Credit** AmEx, MC, V.

Housed in a spectacular Victorian pumping station, often with a backdrop of stimulating contemporary art, Wapping Food should be a wonderful venue for a night out. Sadly a combination of indifferent service, uncomfortable seating and hit-and-miss cooking made our recent visit a disappointment. On our arrival, the front-of-house seemed more interested in her computer screen than showing us to our table. Three types of bread were delivered with no explanation as to what they were. We ordered a £26 bottle of Cascabel tempranillo from the all-Australian wine list (with nothing under £20), but the one our waiter 'opened' at the table was only two-thirds full, and when this was pointed out, he simply mumbled 'Someone in the kitchen…'. Still, a starter of creamy foie gras with toasted almonds and toast was delicious, as was a beautifully tender main of lamb with accompanying pile of potato and parsnip and an anchovy 'parfait'. Purple truffled potatoes served with swordfish looked gorgeous, but were dry and overcooked. Apart from some over-solicitous wine pouring, service was so slow that a two-course meal took almost three hours. Desserts, if we'd wanted them, could have included balsamic ice-cream with berry compote, or Valrhona chocolate fondue. This is a great venue and some of the cooking is very good, but it's not cheap so there's no excuse for laurel resting. *Babies and children welcome: high chairs. Booking essential (Wed-Sun). Disabled: toilet. Entertainment: performances and exhibitions; phone for details. Tables outdoors (20, garden).*

North

Camden Town & Chalk Farm

Odette's

130 Regent's Park Road, NW1 8XL (7586 8569/ www.odettesprimrosehill.com). Chalk Farm tube/ 31, 168, 274 bus. **Lunch served** noon-2.30pm Tue-Fri; noon-3pm Sat; noon-3.30pm Sun. **Dinner served** 6.30-10.30pm Tue-Sat. **Main courses** £11.50-£25. **Set lunch** £17.95 2 courses, £21.95 3 courses. **Set dinner** (6.30-7.30pm Tue-Thur) £21.95 2 courses, £25.95 3 courses. **Credit** AmEx, MC, V.

RESTAURANTS

Under chef Bryn Williams, a representative of Wales in the second *Great British Menu* series, the new-look Odette's has become more than a useful local in a chi-chi enclave. Prices appear high and inflexible, though there are no unexpected extras to pay, and a Mozart piano concerto sets a serious tone. Napkin-fluttering service was irksome; on the plus side 'pollock for madam?' gave us a new catchphrase. Said sustainable fish sprouting squid tentacles was accompanied by concentric rings of baby squid, rather hard chickpeas, chorizo and a pink, chorizo-spiked foam. Artful. Sea trout fell into beautiful thick flakes; freshly podded peas, pea shoots and horseradish cream set it off well. Lamb on asparagus and a pair of cheesy potato croquettes came with a copper pan of peeled broad beans stewed with tomato. So far so lovely. Raspberry jelly with ice-cream and berries appealed more than strawberry cheesecake and peanut butter parfait on a not-very-compelling pudding list. With the front completely open to the street and tables continuing seamlessly from the flamboyantly wallpapered dining room on to the pavement, joining the gregarious throng on the bold yellow chairs can feel like gatecrashing a Primrose Hill party. Outsiders might feel more at home in the contrastingly calm white-painted conservatory at the back.
Babies and children admitted. Booking advisable. Restaurant available for hire. Separate room for parties, seats 25. **Map 27 A2.**

Islington

Frederick's
Camden Passage, N1 8EG (7359 2888/ www.fredericks.co.uk). Angel tube. **Lunch served** noon-2.30pm, **dinner served** 5.45-11pm Mon-Sat. **Main courses** £12-£21. **Set meal** (lunch, 5.45-7pm) £14 2 courses, £17 3 courses. **Credit** MC, V.
Frederick's sets out to dazzle newcomers with visual oomph. From the rather louche-and-glitzy lounge bar you descend into a spacious, dark-brick dining room lined with vibrant contemporary abstract paintings, which leads on to the soaring, glass-vaulted mini-Crystal Palace of the Garden Room, which opens in turn on to a chic terrace garden. This wow-factor gives it a certain flash-the-cash appeal and keeps the restaurant busy, but the food frankly doesn't match the setting or the lofty prices. A starter of scallops with spiced lentil salsa was the best of our choices, with nicely balanced flavours; salt and pepper squid was pretty ordinary, with a slightly peppery batter and a sweet-and-sour sauce on the side. Mains were unmemorable. In rump of lamb with dauphinoise and (really excellent) spinach, the meat was insufficiently tender and lacked flavour; roast cod with butter beans and (really dull) chorizo was blandly pleasant, but surely we should expect a bit more than that nowadays for £17.50? Staff are abundant, but often seem a bit disorganised. The wine list is refined, but, again, pricey.
Babies and children welcome: children's menu; high chairs. Booking advisable weekends. Separate rooms for parties, seating 16 and 30. Tables outdoors (12, garden). **Map 5 O2.**

North West

West Hampstead

The Green Room NEW
182 Broadhurst Gardens, NW6 3AY (7372 8188/ www.thegreenroomnw6.com). West Hampstead tube/rail. **Lunch served** 12.30-3.30pm Sun. **Dinner served** 6.30-11pm Tue-Sat; 6.30-10.30pm Sun. **Main courses** £11-£17. **Set meal** (6.30-7.30pm, Tue-Thur) £20 3 courses. **Credit** MC, V.
Walk into this little place and you feel you've made a friend. The Anglo-French owners are exceptionally welcoming, greeting each arrival and chatting over wines and the day's specials with real – but unpushy – enthusiasm. This charm and warmth clearly helped the Green Room make its mark as a local favourite almost as soon as it opened in late 2007; it is now seen as a real asset to the neighbourhood. The dining room is suitably snug, with a surprisingly up-for-it chic decor mix

of silver-flock wallpaper, pinks and emphatic modern art (but very little that's actually green). Menus are shortish but attractive, oriented to satisfying Italian and French bistro classics with a few modern touches. A starter of cabbage stuffed with soft cheese and mushroom offered an original blend of flavours; goat's cheese soufflé with onion marmalade was a bit dry, but still pleasant. Roast monkfish wrapped in parma ham and a trad beef bourguignon also did everything required (though the beef could have done with more onion and red wine). Desserts (tiramisu, chocolate fondant) are of the delectably indulgent variety. An above-average wine list completes the pleasing picture.
Babies and children welcome: high chair. Booking advisable; essential Fri, Sat. Separate room for parties, seats 16. Takeaway service. **Map 28 3A.**

Walnut
280 West End Lane, NW6 1LJ (7794 7772/ www.walnutwalnut.com). West Hampstead tube/rail. **Dinner served** 6.30-11pm Tue-Sun. **Lunch served** by arrangement. **Main courses** £9.50-£16. **Credit** AmEx, DC, MC, V.
West Hampstead has its share of routine, typical-local pizzerias, tandooris and the like, so Walnut comes as an attractive break from the norm. The dining room is stylish, with chic high-backed chairs leading up, as if in homage, to the raised open kitchen, where you can see chef-owner Aidan Doyle doing his stuff. His cooking is distinctive, and makes much use of locally sourced, rare-breed and organic ingredients; presenting such sophisticated menus all week in a neighbourhood restaurant shows real dedication. Fine-textured seared scallops in sesame and soya dressing were lovely. Another starter, confit of duck with raspberry dressing, was a little overcooked, but still interesting. Steaks seem to be a highlight. A New Forest ribeye was perfect: prime meat grilled just right, with very moreish garlic butter. Braised pork shank was less impressive, but was offset by an unusually subtle little bowl of sauerkraut instead of time-honoured apple sauce. There's plenty to explore too in the wine list, with an above-average choice of half bottles. Prices, however, are also above the local norm, especially since most vegetables come as side dishes, for £3-plus.
Babies and children welcome: high chairs; nappy-changing facilities. Booking advisable weekends. Restaurant available for hire. Tables outdoors (4, pavement). **Map 28 A2.**

Outer London

Kew, Surrey

★ The Glasshouse
14 Station Parade, Kew, Surrey TW9 3PZ (8940 6777/www.glasshouserestaurant.co.uk). Kew Gardens tube/rail. **Lunch served** noon-2.30pm Mon-Sat; 12.30-2.45pm Sun. **Dinner served** 6.30-10.30pm Mon-Sat; 7-10pm Sun. **Set lunch** (Mon-Fri) £23.50 3 courses; (Sat) £25 3 courses; (Sun) £29.50 3 courses. **Set dinner** £32 2 courses, £37.50 3 courses; (Mon-Fri) £50 tasting menu. **Credit** AmEx, MC, V.
A cool sedate restaurant tucked away to one side of the forecourt at Kew's pretty mid-Victorian railway station, the Glasshouse is well worth the readies. Patrons of Chez Bruce (*see p107*) and La Trompette (*see p105*) will already be familiar with the formula of subtle flavours and tasteful design. Here this means plain starched linen and glossy wood floors, with a long wall covered with embossed creamy wallpaper, creating a mirage of depth opposite the plate-glass front. But it's better to focus on the nuanced menu, with starters such as our divine foie gras, guinea fowl and artichoke terrine, or ruby tuna served with clam barigoule. Finely composed fish mains included roast cod with braised celery, fondant leek and mash with garlic velouté, while assiette of pork with apple tarte fine, choucroute and Madeira was tantalisingly sticky. The best of our dishes, though, was a raviolo of chicken, sweetbread and pig's trotter recumbent on a slithery bed of black morels and celeriac. Then, with desserts including a dreamy raspberry and champagne trifle, the

Glasshouse could do no wrong. Service is crisp without being stiff, and a charming sommelier pilots you through the dark waters of the encyclopedic wine list, which starts at a reasonable £15 for a bottle of the house bergerac.
Babies and children welcome: children's menu; high chairs. Booking advisable dinner, Sun lunch.

Kingston, Surrey

Rocksons Restaurant NEW
17 High Street, Kingston-upon-Thames, Surrey KT1 4DA (8977 0402/www.rocksonsrestaurant. co.uk). Kingston rail. **Dinner served** 5.30pm-10.30pm Mon-Thur; 5.30pm-11pm Fri. **Meals served** 10am-11pm Sat; 10am-3.30pm Sun. **Main courses** £9.50-£15.50. **Set dinner** £14.95 2 courses, £17.95 3 courses. **Credit** MC, V.
Small, unshowy and on a heavily trafficked bend on the main road to Kingston Bridge, Rocksons is barely noticeable as you head for the river. But the warm service, good food and general atmosphere make it worth a visit. A starter of seared king scallops was small but exquisitely prepared, while the leek and wild mushroom risotto still had a little nuttiness and came drizzled with porcini oil. For mains, the seared sea bass fillets were also perfectly cooked and came on a bed of crushed new potatoes, along with spring onions, crisp asparagus tips, concassé tomatoes and herb vinaigrette, all drizzled (yes, this is Modern European) with a balsamic and red wine reduction. A steak dish also tasted great, but came a bit cool, suggesting it had had to wait for the fish. A further five minutes in the kitchen and it was returned perfect to eat. The lovely waitress was a smile on legs. Sleepy jazz played all the time, soothing in a suburban kind of way. Of the desserts, the roasted rhubarb and cinnamon crumble – with a dollop of vanilla ice-cream – had a slight edge over the chocolate tart, though this last came laced with anis, which was a nice surprise. It was good to see albariño on the wine list, but it wasn't quite as zesty as it might have been.
Babies and children welcome: children's menu; high chairs. Disabled: toilet.

Richmond, Surrey

Petersham Nurseries Café (100)
Church Lane, off Petersham Road, Petersham, nr Richmond, Surrey TW10 7AG (8605 3627/ www.petershamnurseries.com). Richmond tube/ rail then 30min walk or 65 bus. **Restaurant Lunch served** 12.30-3pm Tue-Sun. **Main courses** £14-£29. **Credit** AmEx, MC, V. *Tea house* **Tea served** 10am-4.30pm daily. **No credit cards.**
Sundry media bigwigs, heiresses, chefs and restaurateurs congregate here, paying top whack (starters are £11-£15, mains £14-£29) to eat amid potted plants, their Gina flip-flops and Ralph Lauren deck shoes scuffing the dusty dirt floor. On a summery weekend, not-in-the-know customers tramp all the way from Richmond station to find the teahouse closes promptly at 4.30pm and restaurant tables have been booked up for weeks. You might be allocated a roomy wooden table, or a battered, dinky metal thing hard to get your legs under. Chef Skye Gyngell and Co hope you'll decide to find the place charming (most do), for Petersham Nurseries is not all as ramshackle as it appears: witness the lavish, centrally heated loos in the shed. Gyngell has a talent for flavour combining, even if the textures aren't always balanced. Our meal suffered from too many similarly creamy dressings, but otherwise was superb, with tepid main courses suiting the hot weather perfectly. Salt-baked turbot with tarragon and chervil dressing and crushed yellow potatoes was memorably harmonious; lean lamb with Indian spices, chickpeas and flatbread was another winner, all making a copy of Gyngell's cookbook hard to resist. Drinks are reasonably priced and include French perry, Hop Back Brewery bottled ale, good provençal rosé and own-made amalfi lemonade.
Babies and children welcome: high chairs; nappy-changing facilities. Booking essential, two weeks in advance (restaurant). Disabled: toilet. Tables outdoors (15, garden).

North African

Moroccan sequinned throw cushions, metallic platters and striped rugs may not be as popular for home interiors as they were a few years ago, but barley couscous, preserved lemons, harissa and rosewater are increasingly common in home kitchens, as more and more people see North African cuisine as a viable part of the midweek supper mix. Such culinary confidence is the result not just of holidays enjoyed in Morocco and Tunisia, but of the appealing dishes eaten at London's sunny collection of Maghrebi restaurants. Whether you're looking for a glamorous night on the town (in which case, see **Momo** or **Pasha**), a romantic meal (try **Original Tagines**) or authentic food at bargain prices (head to **Adam's Café** or **Moroccan Tagine**), you'll find something in this city that appeals.

Central

Covent Garden

Souk Medina

1A Short's Gardens, WC2H 9AT (7240 1796/ www.soukrestaurant.co.uk). Covent Garden tube. **Meals served** noon-midnight daily. **Main courses** £8.50-£12.95. **Set lunch** £16.95 4 courses. **Set dinner** £19.50 4 courses. **Credit** AmEx, DC, MC, V.

Seeking the Moroccan party experience on a budget? Souk Medina may be for you. It attracts large groups of twentysomethings into its warren of cave-like rooms with an all-inclusive party menu. Consequently, it's often a bit cramped and noisy at weekends: not great for a relaxed tête-à-tête. The staff always seem rushed off their feet, so service, while friendly, can be chaotic. That said, we were pleasantly surprised by the standard of cooking on our most recent visit. To start, rich zaalouk was a superior choice to the rather bland chicken briouats. Next, lamb couscous was spot-on: tender meat, a lightly spiced tasty broth with vegetables cooked just right, and harissa brought on request for added heat. Lamb tagine with peas was fine, our one complaint (as ever) being the unsuitability of pitta bread to soak up the juices.

Why don't more Moroccan restaurants serve good bread? The wine list includes some decent Moroccan choices like Siroua rosé and spicy red Siroua Carignan. Drink too much, though, and you'll be shaking your stuff with the glam belly dancer and all those women on hen nights.
Babies and children welcome: high chairs. Booking advisable Fri, Sat. Disabled: toilet. Entertainment: belly dancer 8pm Thur-Sat. Separate rooms available for parties, seating 15-100. Takeaway service. Vegan dishes. Vegetarian menu. **Map 18 D3.**
For branch (Souk Bazaar) see index.

Edgware Road

Sidi Maarouf

56-58 Edgware Road, W2 2JE (7724 0525/ www.maroush.com). Marble Arch tube. **Meals served** noon-12.30pm Mon-Sat; noon-midnight Sun. **Main courses** £14-£18. **Set meal** £30-£35 4 courses. **Credit** AmEx, DC, MC, V.

Sidi Maarouf combines a Moroccan menu and chef from Casa with all we expect from owner Marouf Abouzaki's reliable Maroush chain. Service is old fashioned and slightly starchy, from an all-Lebanese team. Even on quiet days, a cheesy organ player is on hand, massacring songs from Khaled to Fairouz. Still, this is an attractive place, livelier at weekends when belly dancers shimmy around the tables. Red brick walls, dark wood and studded leather upholstery are softened by glowing lamps and billowing silks. With an extensive menu of kemia (Moroccan meze) together with tagines, couscous and grills, plus an impressive list of Lebanese wines, the choice is huge. Light crispy briouats are particularly good. Get the mixed plate and savour eggy minced lamb, prawn and pimento, goat's cheese and spinach, and, our favourite, lemony chicken with ginger. Kemron souirra (king prawns in tomato sauce) weren't thrilling, an olivey zaalouk was miles better. Delicious tagine kefta (garlicky lamb meatballs in a rich cumin-infused tomato sauce with an egg gently poached on top) was generous enough for two. A long wait for strikingly fresh mint tea was assuaged by delicate sweet pastries on the house. We'll be back.
Babies and children admitted. Booking advisable. Entertainment: belly dancer 9.30pm, 10.30pm Thur-Sat. Tables outdoors (6, pavement). **Map 8 F6.**

Gloucester Road

★ Pasha

1 Gloucester Road, SW7 4PP (7589 7969/ www.pasha-restaurant.co.uk). Gloucester Road tube/ 49 bus. **Meals served** noon-11.30pm Mon-Wed, Sun; noon-midnight Thur-Sat. **Main courses** £13-£24. **Set lunch** £20 3 courses incl cocktail. **Set dinner** (4.30-6.30pm, 10pm Mon-Thur, Sun) £20 3 courses. **Credit** AmEx, DC, MC, V.

For sheer oriental opulence, a simmeringly sexy vibe and a winning mix of North African and Middle Eastern classics, plus fab fusion dishes, Gloucester Road's Pasha is hard to beat. Behind a heavily carved wooden door lies a Moroccan wonderland of beaten copper walls, beaded lamps, rose petal-strewn tables and red silk cushions. After being escorted to our table by an unctuous greeter and equipped with slightly stingy but deliciously minty mojitos, we waited an age to order; generally, though, staff are friendly and obliging. Noise levels can be intimidating, yet the lively atmosphere, aided by the arrival of belly dancers, adds to the fun. From the irresistible kemia menu (of meze dishes) we loved the textural treat of very rare tuna with nutty bulgar wheat and crunchy pea-shoots, and seared scallops with sweet potato. A simple chicken, lemon and olive tagine with saffron potatoes was sublime, brought bubbling our table with scrumptious yeasty Moroccan bread to accompany it. Savour sniwat laham meshwi (chargrilled marinated chicken breast, slightly pink lamb and merguez) with zingily

Pasha

THE DISH

Pastilla

Sweet and sour – nice. Sweet and salty – mmmm. But sweet and poultry? North Africa's most courtly, special-occasion pie is, on paper at least, a tricky combination of ingredients: cinnamon, icing sugar, flower water, almonds and pigeon.

Bringing it all together – physically, and in terms of flavour – is the region's traditional ouarka pastry, a blend of flour, vinegar, oil and water that is used for making pastilla (bastilla or b'stilla), as well as briouats and Tunisian briks. Its extraordinary thinness means ouarka is often compared to filo pastry; however, it is really more like a crêpe. Look carefully and you will see a very fine, crêpe-like laciness to the pastry layers, which comes from cooking the ouarka on something rather like an upturned frying pan before use. Some chefs then bake the filled pastilla, others fry it, which adds a delectable richness to the pastry parcel.

Ouarka is available ready-made from North African stores, but one restaurant that takes pride in making its own is **Moro** (see p258). **Original Tagines'** pastilla, cut in thin, dainty squares, is made with shredded chicken, as are many in Morocco today, and the icing sugar is added so judiciously you might not even notice it. At Islington's **Maghreb**, known for its culinary innovation, pastilla fillings include corn-fed chicken, duck, and goat's cheese. Onion, parsley, coriander and saffron help give the correct savoury balance to the spectacular wood pigeon pastilla served at **Momo**, which comes dusted with a star-and-crescent design in icing sugar. Momo also offers a fabulous dessert rendition of pastilla, filled with rice pudding.

---

fresh tomato and coriander salad. Mint tea brought with a stand of pistachios, turkish delight and pastries made a fitting end to this Moroccan magic. *Babies and children admitted (lunch only). Booking advisable; essential weekends. Dress: smart casual. Entertainment: belly dancer 9.15pm Mon-Wed, Sun; 8pm, 10.30pm Thur-Sat. Separate room for parties, seats 18. Vegetarian menu.* **Map 7 C9.**

Leicester Square

Saharaween

3 Panton Street, SW1Y 4DL (7930 2777/ www.saharaween.co.uk). Leicester Square or Piccadilly Circus tube. **Meals served** noon-midnight daily. **Main courses** £8-£14. **Set lunch** (noon-5pm) £14.95 2 courses. **Credit** MC, V. Tucked away in a side street just down from Leicester Square, the entrance to Saharaween isn't very enticing. Yet once you're through the bizarre pastiche columns (reminiscent of the set of a school panto), you'll find a small, cosy room replete with the usual souk-style paraphernalia (berber cushions, brass lamps and so on) as well as books about Morocco. The restaurant changed hands last

year and now has an alcohol licence. Try the decent Moroccan pale rosé, Gris de Guerrouane, with its fresh raspberry flavours. The menu is short and to the point, offering couscous along with a few less common dishes like tagine sfiria (chicken slow-cooked to tender flakiness with fried cinnamon-scented cheesy fritters) and almost-too-sweet lamb mhamar (cooked just to the point of crumbliness with plums and apple, and dotted with toasted almonds). We enjoyed the mixed meze starter; the vegetarian version comes with zaalouk, falafel and rich tomato and pepper stew. This is a reasonably priced haven from the tourist traps of Piccadilly Circus, especially if you opt for the set menu. *Babies and children admitted. Separate room for parties, seats 40. Tables outdoors (2, pavement). Takeaway service.* **Map 17 B5.**

Marylebone

★ Occo

58 Crawford Street, W1H 4NA (7724 4991/ www.occo.co.uk). Edgware Road tube. **Lunch served** noon-3pm Mon-Fri. **Dinner served** 6.30-11pm Mon-Fri; 6.30-10pm Sat. **Credit** AmEx, MC, V.
A labour of love for its young owner Sam Ahmimed, Occo is exquisitely designed – an eclectic multi-level mix of spaces, all featuring clever modern takes on traditional Moroccan craftsmanship. On our weekend visit, a large party was having dinner in the airy downstairs conservatory. The opulent, womb-like red boudoir (a shisha lounge before the smoking ban) was home to an upmarket hen night, and the main bar-dining area was about half full. In the week, the place can be heaving and getting pretty noisy during happy hour. Begin with a great mojito or something wacky like a fig bellini with manuka honey. The food is a happy fusion of traditional Moroccan ingredients and techniques with the best of Modern European cooking. This is one of the few London restaurants to bake its own Moroccan bread: here served with argan oil. Crab cakes with chermoula, coriander and rocket salad made our taste buds (and hearts) sing, as did the daring combination of chicken liver, merguez, beetroot and radish. Earthily spiced cod and prawn brochettes with rough-mashed sweet potato and a rich fig and sweet onion relish was lip-smackingly luscious too. Exciting food in stylish surroundings. *Babies and children admitted (lunch only). Separate rooms for parties, seating 20, 25 and 50. Tables outdoors (6, pavement).* **Map 8 F5.**

Original Tagines

7A Dorset Street, W1U 6QN (7935 1545). Baker Street tube. **Lunch served** noon-3pm Mon-Fri. **Dinner served** 6-11pm Mon-Sat. **Main courses** £10.50-£13. **Set lunch** £9.50 2 courses. **Credit** MC, V.
Tired of the over-the-top *Road to Marrakech* tat beloved of many Moroccan restaurants in London? Original Tagines has an altogether more aesthetically pleasing approach. Sunny yellow walls are decorated with shimmering golden calligraphy, and intricate mosaic and ironwork tables spill on to the front terrace on warm evenings. Starters are imaginative: try gently braised kidneys; broad beans in a garlicky cumin-infused tomato sauce; or briouats filled with cheese or kefta (minced lamb). To follow, you'll find the standard selection of tagines and couscous, but there's a certain lightness here that means you won't end up feeling stuffed. Lamb tagine with almonds and prunes, subtly spiced with cumin and cinnamon, would have benefited from a more robust sauce. In contrast, couscous royale was just as it should be: tasty chicken, lamb and merguez, flavoursome broth, tender veg, and light, fluffy couscous. Rice pudding with orange-flower water, and almond briouat are among the tempting desserts. The wine list is fairly priced and includes Moroccan labels. With its serene decor, high food standards and appealing, laid-back vibe, Original Tagines is a cut above its competitors. *Babies and children welcome: high chairs. Booking advisable. Tables outdoors (5, pavement). Takeaway service.* **Map 3 G5.**

Mayfair

Momo (100)

25 Heddon Street, W1B 4BH (7434 4040/ www.momoresto.com). Piccadilly Circus tube. **Lunch served** noon-2.30pm Mon-Sat. **Dinner served** 6.30-11pm Mon-Sat; 6.30-10.30pm Sun. **Main courses** £11-£22.50. **Set lunch** £14 2 courses, £18 3 courses. **Credit** AmEx, DC, MC, V.
A disappointing night at Momo? We regret it can happen. On our visit an unsmiling waiter and grumpy maître d' stage-whispering malevolently into the ears of the staff failed to create a happy atmosphere. A couple of slips like that and other questions spring to mind. Do the tightly packed tables encourage sociability, or are they a cynical way to cram in more diners? Great cocktails, but why so pricey? Still, the usually high reputation, great Maghrebi soundtrack, cool Marrakech-style decor and some of the best North African food in London keep punters pouring in. Birthdays are celebrated in style: the music is ratcheted up a few notches and the glam young staff get everyone up, clapping and dancing round the room. Starters range from traditional briouats and zaalouk to fusion dishes like scrumptiously sweet sea-fresh scallops with beetroot, and mixed seafood with falafel in a light saffron sauce. The usual tagines and couscous rise to new heights here. Our chicken couscous was fabulous: marinated cumin-infused grilled breast with earthily spiced broth and tender veg; harissa with coriander; and astonishingly light, almost silkily fine couscous. Not infallible, then, but still an experience to savour. *Babies and children admitted. Booking advisable weekends. Disabled: toilet. Tables outdoors (5, terrace). Takeaway service. Vegetarian menu.* **Map 17 A4. For branch (Mô Tea Room) see index.**

West
Bayswater

Couscous Café

7 Porchester Gardens, W2 4DB (7727 6597). Bayswater tube. **Meals served** noon-11pm Mon-Thur, Sun; noon-midnight Fri, Sat. **Main courses** £9.95-£15.95. **Licensed. Corkage** no charge. **Credit** AmEx, MC, V.
This place has put a great deal of effort into its decor, letting the quality of food fall by the wayside. It's an intimate spot with tiled tables tucked closely together, striped rugs on the walls, and lanterns scattered about. On our recent visit, every table was occupied with laughing young people and couples on first dates. The food doesn't stray far beyond tagines, brochettes and the café's namesake dish. Several items were off the menu on our visit, and others didn't live up to their exalted descriptions. Lamb couscous would have benefited from the promised harissa-kick, raisins and chickpeas that failed to materialise. Likewise, vegetable briouats would have been much improved had the flavour of cumin and saffron been perceptible. Our meal had its high spots too, however; perfectly cooked chicken tagine was tangy with preserved lemon, and there are few nicer ways to end a meal than with a pot of mint and orange-blossom tea. Service was achingly slow and inattentive, but no one seemed to mind. People come here to enjoy themselves. *Babies and children admitted. Booking essential. Tables outdoors (2, pavement). Vegetarian menu.* **Map 7 C6.**

Ladbroke Grove

★ Moroccan Tagine

95 Golborne Road, W10 5NL (8968 8055). Ladbroke Grove or Westbourne Park tube/23 bus. **Meals served** 11am-11pm daily. **Main courses** £5.50-£7. **Unlicensed. Credit** MC, V.
In the heartland of London's Moroccan community, this café is a regular haunt for many locals. It attracts both the trendy Portobello Road set and visiting tourists, who come to eat from the budget menu amid scatter cushions and the sound of Maghrebi music. No alcohol is served, so most

Adam's Café

customers drink glasses of sweet mint tea from silver teapots. Our waiter confided in us that he preferred western patrons; Moroccans too often complain the food is not as good as their mothers'. Sadly, we agree with the Moroccans. The starters lacked zing: beetroot salad consisted of undressed cubes of beet on iceberg lettuce, while the zaalouk (aubergine dip) was bitter, and the falafels dry and flavourless. A light, fluffy mound of couscous partially made up for these lapses, but the lamb tagine with artichokes and peas did taste quite overpoweringly meaty and, sadly, lacked the subtle spicing of the best Moroccan food. Even the vegetarian loubia (white beans in tomato sauce) tasted strangely pungent. It's a shame that food standards have slipped here as this is a nice, casual spot that many people regard with affection.
Babies and children welcome: high chairs. Booking advisable. No alcohol allowed. Tables outdoors (4, pavement). Takeaway service. Map 19 B1.

Shepherd's Bush

★ ★ Adam's Café (100)
77 Askew Road, W12 9AH (8743 0572). Hammersmith tube then 266 bus. **Dinner served** 7-11pm Mon-Sat. **Set dinner** £11.50 1 course, £14.50 2 courses, £16.95 3 courses. **Licensed. Corkage** £3. **Credit** AmEx, MC, V.
A Tunisian-British couple set up Adam's Café over 15 years ago and found a winning formula – inexpensive menu, cheery laid-back atmosphere and top-notch food. No wonder the place is so popular with locals. While waiting for our food, staff brought out baby balls of lamb, fiery harissa and spicy pickled vegetables to whet our appetite for the excellent starters that followed. The Tunisian classic, brik à l'oeuf (a still-soft egg encased in a brittle fan of ouarka pastry), was perfect: a rare find in London. A generous bowl of harira soup was thick and warming, and pastry cigars of spicy minced meat were among the best we've tried. For mains, we ordered a large bowl of couscous with cumin-infused meatballs in a satisfyingly rich tomato sauce. Food presentation is a bit dated (think carved lemons and flamboyant use of parsley garnishes) as is the decor. Nevertheless, we hope the owners banish any thought of updating their establishment. We love the café just the way it is.
Babies and children admitted. Booking advisable weekends. Separate room for parties, seats 24. Vegetarian menu. Map 20 A1.

North

Islington

Maghreb
189 Upper Street, N1 1RQ (7226 2305/ www.maghrebrestaurant.co.uk). Highbury & Islington tube/rail. **Meals served** 6-11.30pm daily. **Main courses** £8.50-£13.50. **Set dinner** (Mon-Thur, Sun) £10.95 2 courses, £13.95 3 courses. **Credit** AmEx, MC, V.
Away from the frenetic busier end of Upper Street, chef-owner Mohamed Faraji plays modern riffs on traditional Moroccan dishes. They may not always hit the right note, but the sense that Faraji is putting heart and soul into his labours is palpable. At quiet times, he may even work the front of house too, taking pleasure in explaining the dishes to novice diners. The decor resists cliché with

bright yellow walls, red silk lanterns, and red and blue upholstery. Our crab and prawn tabouleh had fresh, clean accents of parsley and lemon, but the pièce de resistance was smoky grilled merguez, served innovatively with earthy puy lentils. The sauce in the lamb tagine with prunes wasn't sufficiently rich and gloopy, yet was tasty nonetheless. In contrast, rabbit tagine with raisins and pears was not a good mix of flavours. Desserts range from Moroccan pastries and pancakes to dark chocolate and pistachio terrine. A big plus is the wide-ranging Moroccan wine list. You can try bottles rarely found in London – from crisp sauvignon blanc right up to the pricey Les Coteaux de l'Atlas, the first Moroccan premier cru wine: a full-bodied, woody, spicy red.
Babies and children welcome: high chairs. Booking advisable. Restaurant available for hire. Separate areas available for parties, seating 38 and 44. Takeaway service. Map 5 O1.

Menu

North African food has similarities with other cuisines; see the menu boxes in **Middle Eastern** and **Turkish**.
Brik: minced lamb or tuna and a raw egg bound together in paper-thin pastry, then fried.
Briouats, briouettes or briwat: little envelopes of deep-fried, paper-thin ouarka (qv) pastry; these can have a savoury filling of ground meat, rice or cheese, or be served as a sweet, flavoured with almond paste, nuts or honey.
Chermoula: a dry marinade of fragrant herbs and spices.
Chicken kedra: chicken stewed in a stock of onions, lemon juice and spices (ginger, cinnamon), sometimes with raisins and chickpeas.
Couscous: granules of processed durum wheat. The name is also given to a dish where the slow-cooked grains are topped with a meat or vegetable

stew like a tagine (qv); couscous royale usually involves a stew of lamb, chicken and merguez (qv).
Djeja: chicken.
Harira: thick lamb, lentil and chickpea soup.
Harissa: very hot chilli pepper paste flavoured with garlic and spices.
Maakouda: spicy potato fried in breadcrumbs.
Merguez: spicy, paprika-rich lamb sausages.
Ouarka: filo-like pastry.
Pastilla, bastilla or b'stilla: *see left* **The Dish.**
Tagine or tajine: a shallow earthenware dish with a conical lid; it gives its name to a slow-simmered stew of meat (usually lamb or chicken) and vegetables, often cooked with olives, preserved lemon, almonds or prunes.
Zaalouk or zalouk: a cold spicy aubergine, tomato and garlic dip.

Oriental

A grab-bag of flavours and cooking styles from various countries, London's pan-oriental cuisine emerged in the late 1980s, when Chinese restaurateurs clocked the popularity of various other Asian cuisines (from Malaysian to Vietnamese and even Tamil) and began offering versions of these dishes on their menus. Then, in 1992, **Wagamama** opened, inspiring imitators as well as fresh ideas from the competition, and by 1996 there was a sufficient number of 'oriental' restaurants in the capital for us to give the cuisine its own chapter.

Success has come to two distinct segments of the market: the style-conscious restaurants such as those of Will Ricker's empire (**E&O** and **Great Eastern Dining Room** among them) and Caprice Holding's **Bam-Bou**, and budget-conscious noodle bars. The past couple of years have seen a swift expansion of **Itsu** in the West End and City, and even Wagamama founder Alan Yau has been inspired to reinterpret his own hit concept at **Cha Cha Moon** (*see p78*). And who would have thought that some of the best pan-Asian cooking in London could be found at a business hotel on Albert Embankment? **Chino Latino** (which is not Chinese or Latin, or even a blend of the two) is worth seeking out if you've become a fan of this dynamic culinary style.

Central

Bloomsbury

Wagamama

4A Streatham Street, WC1A 1JB (7323 9223/ www.wagamama.com). Holborn or Tottenham Court Road tube. **Meals served** noon-11pm Mon-Sat; noon-10pm Sun. **Main courses** £6.15-£10.35. **Credit** AmEx, DC, MC, V.
This chain of noodle bars has become an international phenomenon, with branches as far afield as Cyprus, Boston and New Zealand. It all kicked off here, in the basement of an office block in Bloomsbury, a hop and a skip from the British Museum. All the UK Wagamamas serve the same menu: rice plate meals and Japanese ramen, soba and udon noodles, cooked teppanyaki-style on a flat griddle or simmered in huge bowls of spicy soup, all served in double-quick time. The Wagamama concept has been widely copied but rarely beaten. For one thing, the use of high-quality ingredients raises the chain above many of its imitators. We were impressed by the cut of the chargrilled steak, served on a bed of soba tossed with pak choi and sweet soy sauce. We also got a kick from the ebi raisukaree: perfectly cooked tiger prawns in a Thai-influenced coconut soup that burst into life with a squeeze of fresh lime. How much you enjoy Wagamama will depend on how much you like canteen-style dining. At this branch, diners share long bench tables in a huge panelled dining room not unlike a school refectory.
Babies and children welcome: children's menu; high chairs. Takeaway service. Vegan dishes. **Map 18 D2.**
For branches see index.

Fitzrovia

Bam-Bou

1 Percy Street, W1T 1DB (7323 9130/ www.bam-bou.co.uk). Goodge Street or Tottenham Court Road tube.
Bar **Open** 6pm-1am Mon-Sat.
Restaurant **Lunch served** noon-3pm Mon-Fri. **Dinner served** 6-11pm Mon-Sat. **Main courses** £9.25-£14.50.
Both **Credit** AmEx, MC, V.
Managed by the group that runs J Sheekey and the Ivy, this charming restaurant offers the same winning mix of good food and buzzy atmosphere that makes the others so popular. The four-storey Georgian townhouse, decorated like an Indo-Chinese colonial manor, boasts two dining rooms, three private rooms and a cocktail bar – each offering a dining experience as different as the cuisines to be had: Vietnamese, Chinese and Thai. A starter of deep-fried soft-shell crab with pomelo and jicama was generous on the perfectly crispy crab but mean with the pomelo. Bo la lot, a Vietnamese starter of ground beef wrapped in wild pepper leaves, lived up to its stellar billing from our friendly, knowledgeable waiter; it was juicy and bursting with complementary flavours. To follow, a whole black bream steamed in a tangy and complex lime chilli sauce was slightly undercooked, but fresh enough to consume anyway. Tender peppered beef fillet with stir-fried chinese greens was another highlight. Desserts didn't disappoint either. Beneath the crackle of the star-anise flavoured crème brûlée, a layer of stem ginger purée added a warm, eastern touch to a French classic.
Babies and children admitted. Booking advisable. Separate rooms for parties, seating 9, 12, 14 and 20. Tables outdoors (4, terrace). **Map 10 K5.**

★ Crazy Bear

26-28 Whitfield Street, W1T 2RG (7631 0088/ www.crazybeargroup.co.uk). Goodge Street or Tottenham Court Road tube.
Bar **Open/dim sum served** noon-10.45pm 'Mon-Fri; 6-10.45pm Sat.
Restaurant **Meals/dim sum served** noon-10.45pm Mon-Fri. **Dim sum** £2.50-£6.50. **Main courses** £10-£28. **Set meal** £30-£40 tasting menu.
Both **Credit** AmEx, DC, MC, V.

Not many restaurants boast of branches in London, Oxford and Beaconsfield, but Crazy Bear is not your average restaurant. Don't be fooled by the pub-style frontage; the London outlet is every inch the gourmet Asian eaterie, attracting a mixed crowd of West End trendies and executives on business lunches. First up, congratulations to the interior designer; the ground-floor dining room swims with Victorian opulence. Black lacquer, ostrich-leather upholstery and patinated mercury mirrors create the backdrop for an upmarket pan-Asian menu dominated by dishes from Thailand and China. We began with the house dim sum: light rice-flour parcels bursting at the seams with prawns. Peking duck salad was another hit: an imaginative fusion of shredded duck, Japanese leaves and pomegranate seeds with a chilli dressing that tingled on the lips. Mains were more mainstream, but still well done. Wok-fried honey-glazed cod was delicately scented with ginger, but let down slightly by the incongruous addition of battered onion rings. In the basement is an extremely slick bar with booths upholstered in studded red leather. The futuristic toilets are like stepping into a looking glass.
Babies and children admitted. Booking advisable. Vegetarian menu. Vegan dishes. **Map 4 K5.**

Suka

The Sanderson, 50 Berners Street, W1P 4AD (7300 1444/www.morganshotelgroup.com). Oxford Circus or Tottenham Court Road tube. **Breakfast served** 6.30-11.30am, **lunch served** noon-2.30pm daily. **Dinner served** 5pm-midnight Mon-Wed; 5pm-12.30am Thur-Sat; 5-10.30pm Sun. **Main courses** £8-£26. **Set lunch** £24.50-£35 3 courses incl glass of wine. **Credit** AmEx, MC, V.
To access Suka, located on the ground floor of the voguish Sanderson hotel, you must shoulder past the loud glam pack thronging the Long Bar. Not the best approach. Then, seated at one of the stylish refectory tables, you discover that the din from the drinkers spills into the restaurant. Not a promising start. You order a selection of dishes from the 'modern' Malaysian menu, and just one minute later, the heaviest main dish arrives. Not a good sign. The remainder of our meal confirmed initial misgivings: Suka gives the feel of being more about style than substance; speed over service. Beef rendang, typically a rich Malaysian stew, appeared as a lonely, braised shank barely veiled in a spiced coconut-milk sauce. Crispy pork belly and papaya salad was more like slabs of fatty meat on slivers of slimy fruit. Some dishes, such as a crispy chicken salad, deserved praise. But accompanied by the woefully incompetent service – we were rushed through our meal despite being practically the only customers in the restaurant – and the fearfully high prices, they still left a bitter taste.
Babies and children welcome: high chairs. Booking advisable Wed-Sat. Tables outdoors (20, garden). **Map 9 J5.**

Mayfair

Haiku

15 New Burlington Place, W1S 2HX (7494 4777/www.haikurestaurant.co.uk). Oxford Circus or Piccadilly Circus tube. **Lunch served** noon-3pm daily. **Dinner served** 6-11pm Mon-Sat; 5-10pm Sun. **Main courses** £10-£24. **Set meal** £40-£70 tasting menu. **Credit** AmEx, MC, V.
The pan-Asian menu of Chinese, Japanese, Thai and Indian dishes is intriguing; the low-lit, dark-wood interior is warm and sleek; the hidden location off Regent Street is exclusive but central. Yet Haiku fails to draw the crowds. It certainly tries hard, but on the details, it fumbles. Japanese green salad with ponzu should have come as a delicate bowl of lightly dressed leaves, but arrived as a mountain of foliage. Spicy chicken xiao long bao tasted fine, but missed the soupiness of authentic dumplings. Spider roll with soft-shell crab would have been great but for the unripened avocado. We've no complaints, however, about the marvellous chicken kali mirch: impossibly succulent kebabs of marinated, tandoor-cooked

chicken. Black cod robata was also chopstick-tender, but could have been elevated by a more experienced hand at the Japanese grill to ensure even charring. Service is similarly well-meaning yet lacking in polish. Dishes came in haphazard order: too slowly, then all at once. When the wrong item arrived at the end of the meal, the manager apologised by topping up a wine glass instead of removing the dish from the bill.
Children admitted. Booking advisable. Disabled: toilet. Separate areas for parties, seating 35 and 40. Map 9 J6.

Piccadilly

Cocoon

65 Regent Street, W1B 4EA (7494 7609/www. cocoon-restaurants.com). Piccadilly Circus tube. **Lunch served** noon-3pm Mon-Fri. **Dinner served** 5.30pm-midnight Mon-Sat. **Main courses** £11.50-£65. **Set meal** £15 bento box noon-3pm, 5.30-6.45pm Mon-Sat. **Credit** AmEx, MC, V.
With a perch overlooking Regent Street, and a highly designed, retro space-age interior, this pan-Asian lounge and restaurant remains a fashionable destination. Cocoon may have lost some of its earlier buzz, but the cooking has kept momentum. The menu – trendy interpretations of Japanese, Thai and Chinese cooking – might seem sacrilegious to purists, yet dishes respect regional flavours and techniques. A starter of beef and foie gras gyoza was nicely rendered, the creamy foie gras giving the dumplings a lovely, musky unctuousness. Tiger prawns with chilli and sichuan sauce were also true to form: spicy enough to jolt the palate without masking the taste of the plump crustaceans. Rock shrimp tempura with yuzu aïoli was fluffy and crisp, though the dip needed an extra squeeze of citrus. One intriguing combination was wasabi lamb, a dish that risked being awful but turned out to be rather good; the meat was cooked to a tender pink, its gamey scent offset by a subtle, mustardy aftertaste. Sadly, service was careless. Two requests for the complimentary gin and tonic to be served without alcohol were blithely forgotten. Happily, the potent drinks were all that remained unconsumed at the end of our meal.
Babies and children welcome: high chairs. Booking advisable. Disabled: toilet. Dress: smart casual. Entertainment: DJs 11pm Thur-Sat. Separate room for parties, seats 14. Map 17 A5.

West

Kensington

★ dim t

154-156 Gloucester Road, SW7 4TD (7370 0070/www.dimt.co.uk). Gloucester Road tube. **Meals served** noon-11pm Mon-Sat; noon-10.30pm Sun. **Dim sum** £2.80. **Main courses** £7.45-£8.95. **Credit** AmEx, MC, V.
Much thought has been given to the dim t concept. While the chain borrows from old-style Chinese restaurants – slightly tongue in cheek, you'll be offered prawn crackers to start and fortune cookies to finish – it also provides a modern take with its slick good looks and accessible pan-Asian menu. Everyone will find something that tempts, whether it is old favourites like Singapore noodles and Thai green curry, or the wide range of dim sum served stacked in bamboo baskets. Choose prawn and lemongrass dumplings, say, or roasted pork steamed buns. Stir-fried broccoli had a generous kick of garlic, and shanghai lemon chicken came crisply coated in breadcrumbs. As with many of the dishes, a saline hit of soy sauce was needed to balance an over-enthusiastic sweetness. Dishes are well-constructed and the price is right, even if you do get the feeling that food quality and service were afterthoughts for the owners. Nonetheless, with five dim t branches in London and others further afield, the formula seems to be working. This large outlet was buzzing on our weekday evening visit.
Babies and children welcome: children's menu; high chairs; nappy-changing facilities. Booking advisable; essential weekends. Disabled: toilet. Takeaway service.
For branches see index.

Bam-Bou

Ladbroke Grove

★ E&O

14 Blenheim Crescent, W11 1NN (7229 5454/ www.rickerrestaurants.com). Ladbroke Grove or Notting Hill Gate tube.
Bar **Open** noon-midnight Mon-Sat; 12.30pm-11pm Sun. **Dim sum served** noon-10.30pm Mon-Sat; noon-10pm Sun. **Dim sum** £2.50-£6.50.
Restaurant **Lunch served** noon-3pm Mon-Fri; noon-4pm Sat; 12.30-4pm Sun. **Dinner served** 6-11pm Mon-Sat; 6-10.30pm Sun. **Main courses** £9.50-£22.50.
Both **Credit** AmEx, DC, MC, V.
It has been some eight years since Will Ricker opened this chic pan-Asian restaurant, but E&O still draws the beau monde. That's not surprising, as the premises (brown-slatted walls, minimalist fittings) remain cosy, dark and stylish, and the cooking is strong as ever. The menu offers creative interpretations of Chinese, Japanese and Thai classics. Unusually, they're often an improvement on the originals. Chilli tofu was the most striking example: deep-fried tofu cubes, coated with chilli powder and salt, sweetened by aubergine sambal, then wrapped in shiso leaf: a delicious blend of flavours, textures and fragrances. Less successful was a watery prawn curry with asparagus and orange, featuring overcooked shellfish. A safer bet is chilli squid, skilfully deep-fried with spring onions and bird's-eye chillies, enhanced by a spicy, tart, sweet dipping sauce. Highly palatable too is the Nobu classic of black cod with miso, roasted to a honey-coloured glow. For dessert, mango and macadamia mochi was a treat: four slabs of high-quality macadamia ice-cream encased in elastic Japanese pastry and drizzled with mango coulis. Service was professional and efficient.
Babies and children welcome: high chairs. Booking essential. Separate room for parties, seats 18. Tables outdoors (5, pavement). Vegan dishes. Map 19 B3

South West

Chelsea

Itsu

118 Draycott Avenue, SW3 3AE (7590 2400/ www.itsu.com). South Kensington tube. **Meals served** 11am-11pm Mon-Sat; 11am-10pm Sun. **Main courses** £4.50-£6.75. **Credit** MC, V.
This trendy sushi chain picked up some unfortunate associations following the death of Victor Litvinenko. But at the Chelsea branch you can concentrate instead on the sushi, sashimi and fusion dishes revolving around the counter-style dining room. Service is as slick as an oiled otter. If no seats are available, diners are dispatched upstairs to the moody lounge bar with an electronic pager. Once you sit down to eat, cold dishes rotate past constantly on a conveyor belt. We were thrilled by the textures of the melt-on-the-tongue seared beef fillet and the full-flavoured duck rolls with hoi sin sauce. Pan-Asian dishes like chicken and coconut soup – rather like Thai tom kha gai but with more lime – were also skilfully prepared. The bill is added up according to the colour of the cold plates, plus the cost of any hot items from the menu (chicken teriyaki, prawn tempura and the like). Keep an eye on the number of plates as the bill can mount up quickly. Around the City and West End, several Itsu outlets skip the conveyor belt and focus on lunchtime takeaways.
Babies and children welcome: booster seats. Bookings not accepted. Takeaway service; delivery service (over £20 within 3-mile radius). Map 14 E10.
For branches see index.

South

Battersea

★ Banana Tree Canteen

75-79 Battersea Rise, SW11 1HN (7228 2828). Clapham Junction rail. **Lunch served** noon-2.30pm, **dinner served** 6-11pm Mon-Fri. **Meals served** 11am-11.30pm Sat, Sun. **Main courses** £5.95-£8.95. **Set dinner** (6-7pm Mon-Fri) £7 2 courses. **Credit** MC, V.

Catering to Clapham Junction twentysomethings who appreciate good food at fair prices, Banana Leaf Canteen takes simple ingredients and throws them together into dishes that are greater than the sum of their parts. In style and presentation, the restaurant owes more than a little to Wagamama – bench seats, shared tables, plain rendered walls and servers in matching casuals – but the menu features dishes from across South-east Asia, and diners queue here seven nights a week, a sure sign that BLC is doing something right. We started with Indonesian gado gado salad, which was heavy on iceberg lettuce but redeemed by a zingy peanut dressing. Mains were more inspired; mamak lamb curry was note perfect, with rich flavours of coconut, lemongrass and lime leaves (there must surely be Malaysian cooks in the kitchen). Vietnamese pork stew was also convincing, with strong aromas of cinnamon and white pepper. Mains can be ordered alone or as part of a set meal, with rice, glass-noodle salad, prawn crackers and (rather ordinary) Thai-style corn fritters. Our summary: some dishes are better than others, but everything is better than you'd expect for the price.
Babies and children welcome: children's menu; high chairs. Bookings accepted for 6 or more. Disabled: toilet. **Map 21 C4**.

Vauxhall

★ Chino Latino NEW
Riverbank Park Plaza Hotel, 18 Albert Embankment, SE1 7TJ (7769 2500/ www.chinolatino.co.uk). Vauxhall tube. **Lunch served** noon-2.30pm. **Dinner served** 6-10.30pm Mon-Sat; 6-10pm Sun. **Main courses** £19-£26. **Set meal** £27-£37 per person (minimum 4). **Credit** AmEx, MC, V.
Located inside a nondescript hotel on a nondescript swathe of waterfront, this restaurant looks more like a pit-stop for business travellers than a gourmet dining destination. The sleek, dark, modern decor is attractive, but the ambience suffers from the room being perpetually half-empty. Endure any lack of atmosphere, though, as Chino Latino serves up some of the best, most innovative pan-Asian and fusion cuisine in London. The menu – divided into starters, sushi/ sashimi, tempura, meats and seafood – is filled with tempting dishes that look and taste even better than they sound. Seared marbled beef with garlic chips and yuzu vinaigrette is a melt-in-the-mouth sensation of flavours and textures; duck and nashi pear dumplings with plum wine jelly and port reduction is a rich, fruity twist on the gyoza. Lobster and lychee rolls were generously stuffed with fresh lobster tail, though the delicate flavour was in danger of being overpowered by the accompanying mango coulis. Don't miss the seafood jungle curry, which boasted hefty cuts of lobster, pan-fried scallops and prawns: each individually cooked to perfection before being lowered into a soupy, yet creamy and spicy sauce. Service throughout was friendly and faultless.
Babies and children welcome: children's menu; high chairs; nappy-changing facilities. Booking advisable. Disabled: toilet. Restaurant available for hire. **Map 16 L11**.

South East

Gipsy Hill

Mangosteen
246 Gipsy Road, SE27 9RB (8670 0333). Gipsy Hill rail/322 bus. **Lunch served** noon-3pm Fri-Sun. **Dinner served** 6-11pm Mon-Sat; 6-10pm Sun. **Main courses** £8.50-£12. **Set lunch** £6.95 2 courses. **Set dinner** (Mon-Thur) £10 2 courses. **Credit** MC, V.
Locals in this quiet, residential neighbourhood would certainly consider Mangosteen a find. This compact, congenial restaurant serves a neat variety of Vietnamese, Thai and other Asian favourites at fair prices. Small wonder the simply furnished dining room was full on a Tuesday night. Dishes are presented on modern white crockery, promising a fresh interpretation of the traditional repertoire. Sadly, some of our food turned out to

be weak variations of Indo-Chinese classics. Tom yam soup was chock-full of fresh prawns, but the flavour of tinned bamboo shoots overwhelmed the watery broth. Red Thai chicken curry was even more disappointing, with its shockingly insipid sauce. Chinese stir-fried black-bean beef, while nicely presented, lacked pungency too, due to the restrained use of the fermented bean. Vietnamese dishes proved more gratifying. Cold vegetarian spring rolls were generously stuffed with noodles and tofu, though hoi sin as a dipping sauce (seemingly from a jar) was a lazy accompaniment. Staff were warm and welcoming, but proved helpful too late. Before we left, the waiter remarked that we'd ordered all the wrong dishes; he suggested the tamarind chicken, pho noodle soup and banh xeo pancakes.
Babies and children welcome: high chairs. Booking advisable weekends. Tables outdoors (5, terrace). Takeaway service.

Herne Hill

Lombok
17 Half Moon Lane, SE24 9JU (7733 7131). Herne Hill rail/37 bus. **Dinner served** 6-10.30pm Tue-Sun. **Main courses** £6-£8. **Credit** MC, V.
There's something for everyone at Lombok, with its pleasing, colonial-lite ambience and a menu that covers almost every interpretation of popular South-east Asian cuisine – from Chinese seafood noodles to Thai green and red curries and Vietnamese lettuce wraps. Thailand dominates, unsurprisingly, as that's where the charming staff and owner hail from. Ingredients are fresh and well-sourced, and the kitchen doesn't use MSG. It's nice to see more unusual dishes listed, like gaeng karee (a yellow, mild Thai curry, similar to massaman). Salt and pepper squid was mouth-wateringly delicious, and we enjoyed nibbling the deep-fried, coconut-and-breadcrumb-coated balls of minced prawn on chewy sugar-cane sticks, served with chilli sauce. Burmese rangoon curry was a real hit: fresh fish cooked in coconut milk flavoured with cumin, lime leaves and star anise. Speciality rices include a flavourful garlic and sweet red pepper combo. To finish, puddings go beyond the usual sorbets and ices. Thai-style custard cooked in palm sugar was a thick, syrupy treat, surrounded by fresh tropical fruit – the perfect conclusion to a mouth-tingling meal.
Babies and children admitted. Booking essential weekends. Takeaway service. **Map 23 A5**.

East

Shoreditch

★ Great Eastern Dining Room
54-56 Great Eastern Street, EC2A 3QR (7613 4545/www.greateasterndining.co.uk). Old Street tube/rail/55 bus.
Below 54 bar **Open/meals served** 7.30pm-1am Fri, Sat. **Main courses** £9-£15.
Ground-floor bar **Open/dim sum served** noon-midnight Mon-Fri; 6pm-midnight Sat. **Dim sum** £5-£6.50.
Restaurant **Lunch served** 12.30-3pm Mon-Fri. **Dinner served** 6.30-10.45pm Mon-Sat. **Main courses** £9-£17.50.
All **Credit** AmEx, DC, MC, V.
With dark wooden flooring, feature wallpaper and a good-looking crowd, the Great Eastern fits neatly among the hip hangouts of Shoreditch. What sets it apart is the quality of the cooking. The pan-Asian menu is short and dishes are simply listed – no need to show off when the food speaks for itself. Butternut squash gyoza was a creative, satisfying interpretation of the Japanese dumpling: the squishy squash studded with mushrooms, garlic and ginger to produce a tasty blend of flavours and textures. Prawn tempura was expertly deep-fried, with light crisp batter and tender prawn. The accompanying jalapeño dipping sauce was overpowering, so we stuck with the citrus-infused ponzu sauce. A beautifully presented penang curry consisted of a neat pile of perfectly cooked chicken and colourful vegetables

surrounded by a pool of velvety, rich sauce – which, alas, lacked the necessary kick. Redemption came with 'eight treasures tofu', a stir-fried Chinese dish bursting with authentic flavours and ingredients, including cloud-ear fungus and a sauce enlivened by pungent fermented tofu. Teetotallers will appreciate the reasonably priced, non-alcoholic cocktails, including a virgin mojito so refreshing you'd barely miss the rum.
Babies and children admitted (restaurant). Bars available for hire. Booking advisable; essential Fri, Sat. Entertainment: DJs 8.30pm Fri, Sat. **Map 6 R4**.

North East

Stoke Newington

★ Itto
226 Stoke Newington High Street, N16 7HU (7275 8827/www.ittolondon.co.uk). Stoke Newington rail/67, 73, 76, 149, 243 bus. **Meals served** noon-11pm daily. **Main courses** £4.20-£6.20. **Credit** AmEx, MC, V.
It's easy to walk by without noticing this unassuming place on the quiet end of Stoke Newington High Street. That would be a pity as Itto offers some enjoyable food at very reasonable prices. Surroundings are rather drab (bare lilac walls, wooden stools, undressed tables), but the service is attentive and friendly. The menu dances around Asia, so you could choose light Japanese tempura followed by Singapore fried rice, or dry-marinated Chinese ribs with flecks of garlic and chilli, then a Thai green curry. The Vietnamese beef pho was the winner – thick noodles, vegetables and thin slices of meat in a heady broth. On the side come rounds of chilli, Thai basil and a wedge of lime, so you can adjust the hot-sweet-sour flavours to your liking. Less exciting were the stir-fries, which came in thick, sweet sauces familiar from Anglo-Chinese takeaways. Generous portions mean you can leave full and satisfied for a tenner.
Babies and children welcome: high chairs. Takeaway service; delivery service (over £10 within 2-mile radius). **Map 25 C1**.

North

Camden Town & Chalk Farm

Gilgamesh
Stables Market, Chalk Farm Road, NW1 8AH (7482 4922/www.gilgameshbar.com). Chalk Farm tube.
Bar **Open/snacks served** 6pm-2.30am Mon-Thur; noon-2.30am Fri-Sun.
Restaurant **Lunch served** noon-3pm, **dinner served** 6pm-midnight daily. **Dim sum** £4-£6. **Main courses** £10-£24.80.
Both **Credit** AmEx, MC, V.
The food at Gilgamesh had always transcended the restaurant's overblown decor of over-sized Babylonian murals and furniture. Cooking was assured, refined, and unlike its surroundings – a strange, vast space, with tea rooms, DJ station, retractable glass roof and long bar – executed with restraint. Alas, on our recent visit those standards seem to have slipped. The meal started off well with a perfectly deep-fried squid showered with chilli, coriander and shallots. Served with a sour apple dipping sauce, it was clean, crisp and tender. In contrast, a previous favourite, son-in-law eggs with chilli jam, was a touch overcooked and under-seasoned, thus losing the dish's delicate texture. Banana and prawn rolls suffered from a hard, thick pastry that overwhelmed the undercooked prawns. The worst offender though was beijing steamed dumplings filled with pork; stale, rubbery pastry rendered the morsels inedible. Traditional dim sum dishes such as turnip cake and steamed rice in banana leaf were comparable to those served in Chinatown: satisfying, but not surprising. During a Saturday lunch, the huge restaurant was empty, which may explain why ingredients weren't at their freshest.

Babies and children admitted: high chairs.
Booking esssential. Disabled: lift; toilet. Dress:
smart casual. Vegetarian menu. **Map 27 C1.**

Outer London

Barnet, Hertfordshire

★ Emchai
78 High Street, Barnet, Herts EN5 5SN
(8364 9993). High Barnet tube. **Lunch**
served noon-2.30pm daily. **Dinner served**
6-11pm Mon-Thur; 6pm-midnight Fri, Sat;
5-10pm Sun. **Main courses** £4.20-£7.90. **Set**
meal £14.50-£18.50 per person (minimum 2).
Credit AmEx, MC, V.
Boldly painted walls, multicoloured paper
lanterns and fairy lights bring a hint of South-east
Asian night markets to this bustling, friendly
joint. Prices are low, yet Emchai is no cheap gaff.
The trendy seating is comfortable, tables are wide
and well spaced (good for sharing dishes), and the
fashionably attired young families and groups of
friends who visit in droves on Friday nights
(leaving other local oriental restaurants practically
empty) give the place a terrific buzz. The menu
takes in dishes from various parts of Asia – from
'Assam' red snapper in a brothy tamarind sauce,
to Chinese crispy duck and Singaporean laksa.
The latter was a tame version, but succulent satay
chicken was enjoyably imbued with sweet,
aromatic lemongrass. Stars of the meal were the
tender pieces of venison stir-fried with black
pepper sauce, and side dishes of the greenest gai
lan and garlicky spinach. The organic brown rice
options are welcome. In fact our only complaint
was with a dish of prawns coated in honey and
oats: a brave idea foiled by leaden, overcooked
shellfish. Freshly squeezed fruit juices supplement
a bargain-priced wine list and Tsing Tsao and
Tiger beers. Desserts include sago pudding, fruity
fritters and ice-creams.
Babies and children welcome: high chairs.
Disabled: toilet. Restaurant available for hire.
Takeaway service.

Kingston, Surrey

★ Cammasan
8 Charter Quay, High Street, Kingston upon
Thames, Surrey KT1 1NB (8549 3510).
Kingston rail.
Meinton noodle bar **Lunch served** noon-3pm,
dinner served 5.30-11pm Mon-Fri. **Meals**
served noon-11pm Sat, Sun. **Main courses**
£5.50-£8.90.
Chaitan restaurant **Lunch served** noon-3pm,
dinner served 5.30-11pm Mon-Fri. **Meals**
served noon-11pm Sat, Sun. **Main courses**
£5.50-£30. **Set meal** £14.90-£20.90 per person
(minimum 2). **Minimum** £15.
Both **Credit** AmEx, MC, V.
Surrounded by famous-name chain restaurants
exploiting the wharf-side location, Cammasan is
refreshingly low key and commendably
independent. In fact, you get two restaurants for
your money here. The first-floor dining room
serves high-quality traditional Chinese food in a
banquet-hall setting, while the informal noodle bar
downstairs offers huge portions of dishes from all
over Asia – Thailand, Indonesia, China, Malaysia,
you name it. When we visited for a late Sunday
lunch, there were just a few diners at the
communal, bench-style tables in the noodle bar, but
the scattering of Asian faces suggested that the
food was going to be authentic. It was. Chilli beef
noodle soup had a fiery heat that complemented
rather than drowned the spices, and the beef was
sliced across the grain and flash-cooked to keep it
tender in the classic mainland Chinese style.
Honey-basted ribs had less of a wow factor but
were still competently prepared. The menu is
divided into 'big' and 'little' plates and bowls – and
here a big bowl of soup is a meal in itself. You can
order grass jelly and other uniquely Asian drinks
as well as wine and beer.
Babies and children welcome: high chairs.
Booking advisable. Disabled: toilet. Restaurant
available for hire. Tables outdoors (12, terrace).
Takeaway service.

Emchai

RESTAURANTS

Portuguese

Portugal is bordered by Spain to the east and the ocean to the west and south, and it's the latter that has had the greatest influence over the country's cuisine. You'll find fish and seafood on every menu, especially bacalhau (salt cod), Portugal's favourite fish. Head to one of the expat family-run restaurants in Vauxhall or Stockwell for traditional seafaring specialities, as well as hearty bean-rich stews and grilled meats dabbed with fiery piri-piri sauce. No Portuguese meal is complete without a dose of football, which is why most of these venues have mounted televisions (and beer on tap). If you're a fan of fado more than footie, try **O Fado**, which has musicians on hand to perform the famed sad folk songs. A sweeter side of Portuguese cuisine can be found in Ladbroke Grove, where two authentic pastelarias, **Lisboa Pâtisserie** and **Café Oporto**, sell time-honoured sweets rich in egg yolks and sugar, and high-quality coffee, whether a bica (espresso) or a galão (milky coffee).

PASTELARIAS

West
Ladbroke Grove

★ Café Oporto
62A Golborne Road, W10 5PS (8968 8839). Ladbroke Grove or Westbourne Park tube/23, 52 bus. **Open** 8am-7pm daily. **No credit cards.**
Against the backdrop of fashion-conscious Portobello Road, Café Oporto looks so dated it's pushing vintage. Yet the tired furniture and faded photos don't seem to faze the thriving community who treat the café as an extension of their home. Just like the football teams from Portugal's two biggest cities, pastelarias Lisboa and Oporto are forever in head-to-head competition. Located on opposite sides of Golborne Road, they sell pretty much the same things at the same prices, so you might as well go for your preference of city or football team – it works for the locals. Oporto has more indoor seating than Lisboa, making it a great pit stop for a cheap lunch. Its warm savoury pastéis are divine; we gorged ourselves on fillings of chicken and cheese, and salty bacalhau. The coffee came strong and honestly priced, and the pastéis de nata (custard tarts) were the very essence of creamy egginess.
Babies and children admitted. Tables outdoors (3, pavement). Takeaway service. **Map 19 B1.**

★ Lisboa Pâtisserie
57 Golborne Road, W10 5NR (8968 5242). Ladbroke Grove or Westbourne Park tube/23, 52 bus. **Open** 8am-7.30pm daily. **Credit** MC, V.
The Ladbroke Grove area is home to London's second largest Portuguese community and Lisboa Pâtisserie is a local hotspot. Here punters willingly wait in the painfully slow queue for nothing more than a quality bica (espresso). Unless you arrive early you'll be lucky to get a table, especially outside where there's now also a crowd of exiled smokers to contend with. Nevertheless, if you want to experience an authentic pastelaria it's worth hanging around – Lisboa is the genuine article. Take the edge off your coffee with one of the renowned cakes or pastries (some of them made from recipes dating back to the Middle Ages). They come in varying shapes and consistencies, but two ingredients are constant: egg yolk and sugar.

Pastéis de nata (custard tarts) remain the favourite with their delicate flaky pastry and rich, gooey centres. We also saw plenty of coconut- and orange-flecked goodies being piled into takeaway boxes, no doubt to provide a sweet end to a long Portuguese dinner.
Babies and children admitted. Tables outdoors (3, pavement). Takeaway service. **Map 19 B1.**
For branches see index.

RESTAURANTS

Central
Clerkenwell & Farringdon

★ Portal
88 St John Street, EC1M 4EH (7253 6950/ www.portalrestaurant.com). Barbican tube/ Farringdon tube/rail. **Lunch served** noon-3pm Mon-Fri. **Dinner served** 6-10.15pm Mon-Sat. **Main courses** £12-£22. **Credit** AmEx, MC, V.
Within swaggering distance of the square mile, Portal serves Portuguese petiscos (tapas) and a full dining menu to City types, tuned-in tourists, and Portuguese football managers. There are few spaces as carefully thought through as Portal's, with its discreet open kitchen, walk-in wine cellar, and industrial-style conservatory housing the main dining room. Finishing touches of voluptuous orchids and tea lights create a relaxed, refined atmosphere. Defying convention, head chef Ricardo Janco digresses from a strictly Portuguese menu, incorporating other cuisines, notably French. The steep prices are reflective of the luxury ingredients, including starters of foie gras and Portuguese crab. Main dishes favour fish but give a nod to hearty slow-cooked meats. We went for the Setúbal favourite: red mullet, teamed with two plump scallops, swimming in a deflated, yet wonderfully rich, leek foam. The house special of braised bisaro, a cross-breed of wild boar and black pig, left our knives redundant and sang of Madeira. The service has been criticised for being slow, and you certainly won't get three courses in an hour, but for savouring innovative Portuguese cuisine at your leisure, Portal stands alone.
Babies and children welcome: high chairs. Disabled: toilet. Separate room for parties, seats 14. **Map 5 O4.**

Knightsbridge

O Fado
49-50 Beauchamp Place, SW3 1NY (7589 3002). Knightsbridge or South Kensington tube. **Lunch served** noon-3pm, **dinner served** 6.30pm-11pm Mon-Sat. **Main courses** £13.95-£17.95. **Credit** AmEx, MC, V.
Beneath the showy streets of Knightsbridge, a snug basement houses London's oldest Portuguese restaurant. Low lighting, intimate tables and the poignant singing of fado musicians make it an instant hit with couples and nostalgic expats. Tiled murals of Portuguese landmarks add to the faded charm. Expect a back-patting welcome at this unpretentious establishment, where waiters make cheeky jokes and a sizeable mother figure toils in the kitchen. Olives and freshly baked bread are on hand to get you through the extensive menu. After careful counsel we were steered towards melon paired with a beautiful, subtly smoked presunto ham (cut from the bone in the restaurant) and three fleshy sardines with a perfect lingering aftertaste. At this point the food took a downward turn. Watery vegetables accompanied a sea bass whose flavour had been sacrificed to heavy garlic sauce. Dessert was also below par, a stodgy crème caramel with the consistency of a flourless cake. We can only hope these mistakes were exceptions to O Fado's usually exemplary food.
Babies and children admitted. Booking advisable; essential dinner weekends. Entertainment: guitarists 8pm Mon-Sat. Separate room for parties, seats 35. Takeaway service. **Map 14 F9.**

South West
Wandsworth

The Algarve Restaurant NEW
314 Trinity Road, SW18 3RG (8875 0313/ www.thealgarverestaurant.co.uk). Wandsworth Common or Earlsfield rail/Tooting Bec tube, then 219 bus. **Meals served** 10am-11pm Tue-Fri; noon-midnight Sat, Sun. **Main courses** £9-£15.50. **Credit** AmEx, MC, V.
Within minutes of our arrival, Vitor, the friendly owner here, was telling us about 'the real Algarve' where fresh fish and seafood dominate and traditional dishes come packed with Arab-influenced flavours. The restaurant is true to its origins, from the typical blue and white tiled mural on the wall to the wine fridge stocked solely with Portuguese bottles. The menu is similarly steadfast with starters of chouriço sausage and presunto ham, and mains centred around fish and varieties of cataplana – a stew for two people, cooked and served in an enclosed copper dish. We tried the bacalhau with potatoes and cream. It looked like a simple fish pie but the taste was in another league: bacalhau bliss. We were also won over by the fluffy molotov dessert, served with a caramel and cinnamon sauce. Given such reasonably priced and delicious food, why was only one other table occupied on our visit? The restaurant's name can't be doing it any favours.
Babies and children welcome: high chairs. Restaurant available for hire. Tables outdoors (2, pavement). Takeaway service.

South
Brixton

The Gallery
256A Brixton Hill, SW2 1HF (8671 8311). Brixton tube/rail/45, 118, 250 bus. **Dinner served** 7-10pm Thur-Sun. **Main courses** £7-£17. **No credit cards.**
Access to The Gallery is via a secure door at the back of a fried chicken takeaway. It's rather like a speakeasy – especially when you realise it is a cash-only set-up. Colourful tiles and painted murals cover the walls, creating an Aladdin's cave-like quality. Seating is split over two levels by a wooden mezzanine balcony on which diners can overlook musicians who often perform below. The

RESTAURANTS

menu favours bacalhau, pork, and seafood dishes. We started with grilled spatchcock quail in a Madeira wine sauce that was mopped up with chunks of high-quality bread. Next followed a sumptuous piece of peixe espada (swordfish): a Madeiran favourite not to be missed. From The Gallery's extensive Portuguese wine list we chose a well-rounded vinho tinto from Alentejo, a region renowned for excellent reds. It was refreshing to see wines with such low mark-ups – another reason this unique restaurant is such good value. *Babies and children welcome: high chairs. Booking advisable. Takeaway service.* **Map 22 D3.**

Stockwell

Bar Estrela

111-115 South Lambeth Road, SW8 1UZ (7793 1051). Stockwell tube/Vauxhall tube/rail. **Meals served** 8am-11pm daily. **Main courses** £7-£13. **Tapas** £2.70-£5.90. **Credit** AmEx, MC, V.
The life of this bar-restaurant revolves around its mounted televisions. Regulars stop by to catch the footie or a homeland soap, and to polish off a plate of steaming clams and a beer. Although all eyes are on the box, you needn't worry; the food is of a consistently high standard. The extremely well-dressed waiters are proud, if not even a little jealous, of the dishes they bring to the tables: traditional favourites made with fresh, high-quality produce. We warmed up with a bowl of delicious caldo verde, then shared a succulent dourada (gilt-head bream), accompanied by the customary combo of boiled potatoes and salad. From the Portuguese-dominated wine list we opted for the white vinho verde (the 'green' refers to its immature grapes), which was slightly sparkling and perfectly tart. Our only disappointment was the painfully fridge-cold bolo de bolacha that should have tasted of creamy coffee. Despite this, the success of the preceding courses means we'll certainly be returning here.
Babies and children welcome: high chairs. Tables outdoors (10, pavement). **Map 16 L13.**

Grelha D'Ouro

151 South Lambeth Road, SW8 1XN (7735 9764). Stockwell tube/Vauxhall tube/rail. **Meals served** 7am-11pm daily. **Main courses** £8.50-£14.50. **Credit** MC, V.

Grelha D'Ouro is more than just a pit stop for the local Portuguese who make up most of its fold. On our visit children were playing table football in the basement, men played cards in the back room, and women with babies were watching Portuguese soaps in the main dining area. Although the place is treated like a home from home, it doesn't look the part, with stark, whitewashed walls, white floor tiles and basic, functional furniture. Daytime orders of coffee and petiscos are eaten at the bar. Our savoury pastéis, chargrilled chicken wings, slices of presunto ham and plump olives were all well-executed, nicely presented and fairly priced. Evenings attract a hungrier, noisier crowd – cue tablecloths, napkins, and the TV volume hitched up to a steady roar. Families order big pots of soupy rice with seafood, skewers of meat and poultry, and Sagres beer. Our only gripe is that the daily specials continue to be written solely in Portuguese, but the menu now comes with photos so a little pointing and nodding should see you through.
Babies and children welcome: children's portions. Booking advisable weekends. Separate room for parties, seats 60. Takeaway service. **Map 16 L13.**

O Moinho

355A Wandsworth Road, SW8 2JH (7498 6333/ www.moinho.co.uk). Stockwell tube/Vauxhall tube/ rail/77, 77A bus. **Meals served** 10am-11pm daily. **Main courses** £6.50-£26.90. **Credit** MC, V.
Smart waiters, pristine tablecloths and elegant wine glasses might seem a little excessive, given O Moinho's location on a grubby stretch of Wandsworth Road. Yet this family-run restaurant's high standards attract well-turned-out families and even a large group of nuns on our visit. The walls are decorated with signed football shirts and other Portuguese paraphernalia, adding charm to an otherwise formal setting. Tables are ready-laid with snacks of olives, bread and fish pâtés, but as in Portugal, you'll be charged for these. The menu is evenly split between meat and fish; there are also pizza and pasta options. Many customers share mains, as portions are massive. We split a seafood and vegetable skewer sporting enormous king prawns, tender squid and sweet peppers. But the smart money was with our neighbours, who took the soupy seafood rice, pitched at two people, and stretched it to feed four. O Moinho offers own-made desserts as well as bought-in ice-creams for kids; we loved 'Mrs Eggy' – in what other cuisine would an egg yolk make it as a cartoon character?
Babies and children admitted. Booking advisable. Tables outdoors (5, pavement). Takeaway service.

Vauxhall

Casa Madeira NEW

46A-46C Albert Embankment, SE1 7TN (7820 1117/www.madeiralondon.co.uk). Vauxhall tube/rail. Café-deli **Open** 6am-9pm daily.
Restaurant **Meals served** 11am-11.30pm daily. **Main courses** £8.95-£13.50. **Tapas** £3-£5.
Both **Credit** (over £10) AmEx, MC, V.
Since a commercial coffee chain arrived within customer-nabbing distance, the Madeira empire has gone into overdrive. The delicatessen remains unchanged, but the café now has a lucrative internet sideline, and the bakery has become a Portuguese restaurant. In a bid to widen appeal, the café has sacrificed its Portuguese dishes for popular, yet predictable, fry-ups, toasted sarnies and omelettes. In fact, the only Portuguese dish cited was chicken piri-piri, and that came with chips. If you're wondering where the Portuguese chef went, look no further than the owners' new restaurant next door, Casa Madeira, which opened in late 2007. It has a spick and span appearance with starched tablecloths, uniformed waiters and a smart bar. To our relief the menu showcased some great Portuguese dishes, including bacalhau, swordfish, and arroz de marisco. We went for pork and clams, which came with well-marinated meat, plenty of baby clams, and a scattering of fresh coriander – spot on. Sadly, Portuguese dishes are outnumbered by pizzas, pastas and burgers.
Babies and children admitted. Booking advisable weekends. Disabled: toilet. Tables outdoors (10, pavement). Takeaway service. **Map 16 L11.**

Menu

If you think the cooking of Portugal is just a poor man's version of Spanish cuisine, you haven't eaten enough Portuguese food. It's true that many of Portugal's dishes share the Spanish love for chorizo-style sausages (chouriço), dry cured ham (presunto) and salt cod (bacalhau), but the Portuguese have developed a cooking style that has a character, a culture and a cachet all its own. Take the famous arroz (rice) dishes that appear on practically every Portuguese menu. While they are often compared to paella, they are, in fact, far soupier, with the rice used almost as a thickening agent.

Portuguese cooking is in essence a peasant cuisine: the food of farmers and fishermen. Pork, sausages and charcuterie figure prominently, as does an abundance of fresh fish, seafood and olive oil (azeite). There's a strong tradition of charcoal-grilled fish and meats. The hearty bean stews from the north and the thick bready soups (açordas) are also worth trying, as is the coastal speciality of caldeirada, Portugal's answer to bouillabaisse. Garlic, lemon juice, wine and wine vinegar are much used in marinades, with favoured spices being piri-piri (hot peppers, often used to flavour oil in which chicken is basted) and, for the cakes, cinnamon – the latter showing the culinary influence of Portugal's colonial past.

To finish, there is always a lush arroz doce (rice pudding), a wobbly pudim flan (crème caramel) or the world's most loved custard tart, the deliciously scorched pastel de nata.

Açorda: a bread stew, using bread that's soaked in stock, then cooked with olive oil, garlic, coriander and an egg. Often combined with shellfish or bacalhau (qv).
Amêijoas à bulhão pato: clams with olive oil, garlic, coriander and lemon.

Arroz de marisco: soupy seafood rice.
Arroz de tamboril: soupy rice with monkfish.
Arroz doce: rice pudding.
Bacalhau: salt cod; soaked before cooking, then boiled, grilled, stewed or baked, and served in myriad variations – Portugal's national dish.
Bifana: pork steak, marinated in garlic, fried and served in a bread roll.
Caldeirada: fish stew, made with potatoes, tomatoes and onions.
Caldo verde: classic green soup of finely sliced spring cabbage in a potato stock, served with a slice of chouriço.
Canela: cinnamon, a favourite spice, used in sweet and savoury dishes.
Caracois: boiled snails, eaten as a snack with Super Bock or Sagres beer.
Carne de porco alentejana: an Alentejo dish of fried pork, clams and potato.
Cataplana: a special copper cooking pan with a curved, rounded bottom and lid; it gives its name to several southern Portuguese lightly simmered seafood dishes.
Chouriço assado: a paprika-flavoured smoked pork sausage cooked on a terracotta dish over burning alcohol.
Cozido à portuguesa: the traditional Sunday lunch – various meats plus three types of sausage, cabbage, carrots, potatoes and sometimes white beans, all boiled together.
Dobrada: tripe stew.
Feijoada: bean stew, cooked with pork and sausages.
Molotov: a fluffy white pudding made from egg whites combined with caramelised sugar, often with custard.
Pastel de bacalhau (plural **pasteis**): salt cod fish cake.
Pastel de nata: a rich egg custard tart made with crisp, thin, filo pastry.
Piri-piri or **peri-peri:** Angolan hot red pepper.
Pudim flan: crème caramel.
Queijo: cheese.
Sardinhas assadas: fresh sardines, roasted or char-grilled.

RESTAURANTS

Spanish

The current Spanish dining scene in London is best described as 'good but could do better'. We are blessed with some excellent restaurants, including such gastro-stars as **Moro** and top-quality establishments like **L Restaurant**, **Cambio de Tercio**, **El Faro** and **Lolo Rojo**, which have started to bring Spain's nueva cocina to our shores. Yet there are still few venues that specialise in regional Spanish food. You may get some Basque dishes at **Pinchito Tapas** and **Mesón Bilbao**, a few Galician recipes at **Galicia**, and a marked Catalan influence at Lola Rojo, but generic tapas bars are still the norm. That's not to say some tapas bars aren't first-rate. Among our favourites this year are **Barrafina**, **El Parador**, **Orford Saloon**, **Tapas Brindisa**, **Tapas y Vino** and **Tendido Cero** (which has an excellent new branch, Tendido Cuatro, at 108-110 New King's Road, SW6 4LY, 7371 5147). **Salt Yard** and its offshoot, newcomer **Dehesa**, also serve excellent tapas that include Italian flavours and dishes alongside Spanish recipes.

Central
Bloomsbury

Cigala
54 Lamb's Conduit Street, WC1N 3LW (7405 1717/www.cigala.co.uk). Holborn or Russell Square tube.
Bar Open/tapas served 5.30-10.45pm Mon-Sat. **Tapas** £2-£8.
Restaurant **Meals served** noon-10.45pm Mon-Fri; 12.30-10.45pm Sat; noon-9.45pm Sun. **Main courses** £11-£18. **Set lunch** (noon-3pm Mon-Fri) £15 2 courses, £18 3 courses. **Set meal** (Sun) £12 1 course.
Both **Credit** AmEx, DC, MC, V.
You'd be unlikely to guess from the Scandinavian-style decor (white walls, blonde furniture, gleaming white-clothed tables), that Cigala's a tapas restaurant. Inauthentic it may appear, but the cooking certainly is not, and it's a rare pleasure to be able to enjoy this kind of food in upmarket, elegant surroundings. The tapas menu ticks off a few classic exports: gambas al pil pil featured three enormous, succulent king prawns in a piquant and not-too-oily sauce; habas y jamón was a simple mix of broad beans and high-quality lardons (perhaps a little too salty). Also offered are grilled sardines, tortilla and the rest, but it's not all that predictable and obvious; three perfectly grilled wings of quail were paired with a tomato and red onion salad, for example. The menu delves into regional specialities with great success too. Txangurro is a Basque dish of baked crab with tomato, brandy and cayenne pepper that's delightfully rendered here. The sense of sophistication is enhanced by the superb all-Spanish wine list, one of London's best. Covering all Spanish regions and varieties (including cava and sherry), it offers bottles from just over a tenner up into the thousands, making Cigala a choice destination for oenophiles.
Babies and children welcome: high chairs. Bar available for hire. Booking advisable. Tables outdoors (11, pavement). **Map 4 M4.**

BEST SPANISH

Ingredients for success
First-rate Iberian dishes at **Camino** (*see p260*), **Dehesa** (*see p261*), **L Restaurant** (*see p262*), **Salt Yard** (*see right*) and **Tapas Brindisa** (*see p265*).

Tip-top tapas
Sublime snacks at **Barrafina** (*see p261*), **El Parador** (*see p267*), **Orford Saloon** (*see p267*), **Tapas Brindisa** (*see p265*), **Tapas y Vino** (*see p267*) and **Tendido Cero** (*see p262*).

Beyond the boundaries
Influences stray over national frontiers to North Africa at **Moro** (*see right*) and to Italy at **Salt Yard** (*see right*) and **Dehesa** (*see p261*).

Bars for the buzz
Sink the sangría with the lively crowds at **Camino** (*see p260*), **Mar i Terra** (*see p265*), **Meza** (*see p261*), **Olé** (*see p263*), and **Pinchito Tapas** (*see p266*).

Clerkenwell & Farringdon

★ Moro (100)
34-36 Exmouth Market, EC1R 4QE (7833 8336/www.moro.co.uk). Farringdon tube/rail/19, 38, 341 bus.
Bar Open/tapas served 12.30-11.45pm Mon-Sat (last entry 10.30pm). **Tapas** £3.50-£14.50.
Restaurant **Lunch served** 12.30-2.30pm, **dinner served** 7-10.30pm Mon-Sat. **Main courses** £14.50-£20.
Both **Credit** AmEx, DC, MC, V.
Now a plucky 11 years old, Moro has an enduring popularity that seems unassailable. It's fully booked night after night, so phone at least 48 hours ahead if you want to sample the reasons for its ongoing popularity; the success has been fuelled by a series of bestselling cookbooks, but it is mainly due to consistently high-quality cooking and a convivial dining space on fashionable Exmouth Market. The inventive menu isn't afraid to incorporate flavours from around the Mediterranean, especially North Africa. Egyptian bottarga (grey mullet roe) was sliced wafer-thin and made a sensational salad with avocado, dill and lemon, while shredded lamb was served slightly crispy with houmous. From seven main courses, we chose wood-roasted pollack with seville orange sauce, white beans and spinach; plus charcoal-grilled bream with grilled leeks and garum (fermented fish) sauce – both intelligent, innovative ensembles cooked to perfection. Meat alternatives included fabada (the Spanish pork and bean stew), and braised oxtail with red wine, chorizo and mash. Wines and sherries are all Spanish and offer excellent value for money, from the respectable house red upwards. The only faults are some dubious acoustics and too few toilets: but that's a small price to pay for an experience of this calibre.
Babies and children welcome: high chairs. Booking essential. Disabled: toilet. Tables outdoors (6, pavement). **Map 5 N4.**

Fitzrovia

Fino
33 Charlotte Street, entrance on Rathbone Street, W1T 1RR (7813 8010/www.finorestaurant.com). Goodge Street or Tottenham Court Road tube.
Lunch served noon-2.30pm Mon-Fri; 12.30-2.30pm Sat. **Dinner served** 6-10.30pm Mon-Sat. **Tapas** £4-£15.50. **Credit** AmEx, MC, V.
Sam and Eddie Hart have an eye for detail. Their modern, bright and surprisingly airy basement restaurant is effortlessly cool, from the minimalist beech and brown decor to the bar-side view of a bustling, steamy kitchen. Reassuringly printed on a daily basis, the menu celebrates Spain's finest ingredients and reflects the country's new wave of fine dining. But if you prefer, you can still enjoy your food traditional-style, from a seat at the bar rather than at one of the booths or tables. From a string of generously portioned tapas, clams with sherry and ham stood out, the sauce necessitating an impromptu order of bread to mop up every last drop. Equally well received was a chickpea, chorizo and spinach stew bathed in rich beef broth, and a creamy Pedro Ximenez ice-cream with plump alcohol-soaked raisins. Efficient yet easy-going staff delivered our meal in waves, allowing time for each dish, and the occasion, to be savoured. Come here for 'posh tapas' – and expect a bill to match. Accordingly, the clientele are a well-heeled bunch, yet the restaurant effortlessly retains a laid-back enjoyable charm, humming with easy conversation.
Babies and children welcome: high chair. Booking advisable. Disabled: lift; toilet. **Map 9 J5.**

★ Salt Yard
54 Goodge Street, W1T 4NA (7637 0657/www.saltyard.co.uk). Goodge Street tube.
Bar Open noon-11pm Mon-Fri; 5-11pm Sat.
Restaurant **Tapas served** noon-3pm, 6-11pm Mon-Fri; 5-11pm Sat. **Tapas** £2.75-£8.50.
Both **Credit** AmEx, DC, MC, V.
After four years of deserved popularity, Salt Yard spawned a second branch (Dehesa, *see p261*) in early 2008. It's a wonder this didn't happen sooner, and just as surprising the culinary concept hasn't been emulated elsewhere. This is tapas, but not as we knew it, bringing Spanish and Italian ideas and ingredients together with brilliant results. The setting is sophisticated, smart, yet relaxed. Fine selections of charcuterie and cheese front the menu. It'd be easy to blow a fortune on the acorn-fed black-foot ham (£17 a plate) before you've started. But best concentrate on the delights emanating from the kitchen. Confit of Gloucester Old Spot with cannellini beans is always a sensation, and one of the only perennials on the frequently changing, always alluring menu. Other recent winners have included cavolo nero with chestnuts and farro (a type of wheat), clams with black rice, and smoked monkfish with apple vinaigrette and pancetta. In several visits we've never had a dud dish, just the odd plate that doesn't quite rival its table-fellows. The wine list follows the food: a connoisseur's choice of Italian and Spanish bottles, including some splendid sherries. Book well ahead, and try to get a table upstairs.
Babies and children admitted. Booking essential. Tables outdoors (3, pavement). **Map 9 J5.**

King's Cross

★ Camino

*3 Varnishers Yard, Regents Quarter, N1 9FD
(7841 7331/www.camino.uk.com). King's Cross
tube/rail.*
Bar **Open/tapas served** noon-midnight
Mon-Wed; noon-1am Thur-Sat. **Tapas**
£3-£7.75.
Restaurant **Breakfast served** 8-11.30am, **lunch
served** noon-3pm, **dinner served** 6.30-11pm
Mon-Fri. **Meals served** 9am-4pm, 7-11pm Sat;
11am-4pm Sun. **Main courses** £10.50-£23.
Both **Credit** AmEx, MC, V.
This huge, costly, Spanish-themed bar-restaurant
in the heart of the King's Cross construction zone
was a big gamble for owner Richard Bigg.
Originally the bar and restaurant sections were
completely segregated (you had to go outside to
move between the two), but they've now been
knocked together, and the original 'concept' menu
(a fiddly, fold-out concertina) has been replaced by
a conventional, linear list. In the bar you can order
good tapas, but it's worth sitting down for a proper
three-course meal in the restaurant, where the
exposed brickwork and natural materials are
married with soft lighting and murals to create a
laid-back ambience.The cooking conveys the
central principle of traditional Spanish food: the
finest ingredients, simply cooked. Fish is always
of a high quality; at a recent meal, pan-roasted sea
trout with tomatoes and rocket, and grilled sea
bass with roasted winter veg, were terrific. Steak
is also a favourite. The wine list is all-Spanish, with
everything available by the glass and many
interesting bottles up for grabs. Also noteworthy
is the little-known, but marvellous, Spanish beer
Ambar. There's still a long way to go before King's
Cross is properly scrubbed up, but Camino is a
shining beacon of things to come.
*Babies and children welcome: high chairs;
nappy-changing facilities. Disabled: toilet.
Booking advisable. Tables outdoors (5, garden).*
Map 4 L3.

Mayfair

El Pirata

*5-6 Down Street, W1J 7AQ (7491 3810/
www.elpirata.co.uk). Green Park or Hyde Park
Corner tube.* **Meals served** noon-11.30pm
Mon-Fri. **Dinner served** 6-11.30pm Sat.
Main courses £10.50-£16. **Tapas** £3.95-£9.
Set lunch (noon-3pm) £9.95 2 dishes incl glass
of wine. **Set meal** £14.95-£19.50 per person
(minimum 2). **Credit** (over £10) AmEx, JCB, MC, V.
As you might expect in Mayfair, this popular tapas
restaurant is filled with a smart yet casual crowd,
which in fine weather spills out on to pavement
tables. El Pirata has an informal, buzzy bistro vibe,
with tightly packed tables and groups huddled in
conversation along the bar. A celebration of
Spain's most popular painters adorns the walls, in
the form of Miró, Picasso and Dalí. The lower floor
is more sparsely populated than the street-level
room and contains cavernous cubby holes that are
definitely worth requesting for a cosy meal with

Goya

RESTAURANTS

friends. The set menus are good value; the cheapest began with a pleasing array of cold meats, stuffed peppers, artichokes and other nibbles. Dishes of fish goujons, garlic prawns and button mushrooms each had their merits. The round of meat-based tapas that followed was less successful, but satisfying nonetheless. Generous quantities meant that dessert was not an option. Food is sound, service is quick and surroundings are relaxed, resulting in a steady stream of custom that makes booking advisable.
Babies and children admitted. Booking advisable dinner. Separate room for parties, seats 65. Tables outdoors (4, pavement). Takeaway service. **Map 9 H8.**

Pimlico

Goya
34 Lupus Street, SW1V 3EB (7976 5309/ www.goyarestaurant.co.uk). Pimlico tube. **Meals served** noon-11.30pm daily. **Main courses** £10.90-£16.95. **Tapas** £1.80-£6.85. **Credit** AmEx, MC, V.
Primary colours and wall-to-wall windows breathe sunshine into the compact ground floor of this slice of Spain in Pimlico. The basement offers more room with less of the dazzle. Impressively, the entire restaurant was booked up at 7pm on a Wednesday evening. Without a reservation, we were happy to take our place along the bar for nevertheless quick and attentive service. From a broad selection of standard tapas and course-by-course meals, our choices were executed competently. Garlicky prawns were big on flavour, hardly requiring the aïoli which instead came to the aid of not-so-crisp, fried artichokes. Pepper-flecked meatballs and tortilla couldn't be faulted, although a neighbouring table's zarzuela fish stew, with an impressive array of seafood, gave rise to much envy. Desserts included the customary flan, tarta de santiago and crema catalana, along with tiramisu and other less-than-typical (but no doubt popular) interlopers. The lively post-work crowd, including a smattering of Spaniards, reflects the overall tone of the restaurant: reliable, inexpensive and a comfortable choice for fans of Spanish food.
Babies and children admitted. Booking advisable. Restaurant available for hire. Tables outdoors (6, pavement). **Map 15 J11.**

Soho

★ Barrafina (100)
54 Frith Street, W1D 4SL (7440 1463/ www.barrafina.co.uk). Leicester Square or Tottenham Court Road tube. **Tapas served** noon-3pm, 5-11pm Mon-Sat; 12.30-3.30pm, 5.30-10.30pm Sun. **Tapas** £1.90-£16.50. **Credit** AmEx, MC, V.
Before you even enter this stylish tapas restaurant, the air is redolent of frying garlic and grilling meat: an enticing aroma made more appealing by the dishes that waiters carry past as you queue for a seat. And you probably will queue, as Barrafina is tiny, popular and doesn't take bookings. This is the second, less formal, venture for the Hart brothers, who also run Fino (*see p258*) and, now, Quo Vadis (*see p61*). It's little more than an open kitchen surrounded by a stainless-steel bar and tall stools. The quality of ingredients, many of them on display, is impeccable. Neither of the brothers was present on our visit, but we could hardly fault the dishes: from tender, succulent octopus sharpened with capers, to plancha-fried chorizo with potato and watercress, to a dome-shaped, properly squidgy-centred tortilla. Coca Mallorquin (Majorcan-style 'pizza' topped with spinach, sultanas and pine nuts) was more flavourful than the ingredients might suggest. Our only quibble was with a special of razor clams that were quite small and hence slightly overcooked. Barrafina takes its drink seriously, providing excellent sherries by the glass and wines from some of Spain's best modern-style producers.
Babies and children admitted. Bookings not accepted. Tables outdoors (4, pavement). **Map 17 C3.**

Dehesa NEW
2008 RUNNER-UP BEST NEW RESTAURANT
25 Ganton Street, W1F 9BP (7494 4170). Oxford Circus tube. **Tapas served** noon-11pm Mon-Sat; noon-5pm Sun. **Tapas** £3.50-£7.25. **Credit** AmEx, MC, V.
The second restaurant for Sanja Morris and Simon Mullins, who also own the highly regarded Salt Yard (*p258*), is a bijou place serving top-rank Spanish-Italian tapas. Expect bicultural bites such as jamón iberico, hand-sliced from a leg on display and intensely flavoured wild boar salami, plus a range of cheeses from the bar snacks and charcuterie. After a 20-minute wait for a table (near-inevitable here, as reservations aren't taken), we pulled up a stool and were served a series of small plates. A sweet-and-savoury Italianate tapas of duck breast was served with mustard fruits, while whole baby courgettes, flowers intact, were stuffed with cheese before being deep-fried and drizzled with honey. Salt cod croquetas were the best we've found in London – hot and crisp, with plenty of firm-textured cod flecked with green herbs, but the accompanying romesco sauce was disappointingly thin. Caramelised yellow peaches with peach and basil ice-cream sounded gloriously summery, but the under-ripe fruit reminded us that we were dining in London, not Madrid. Eight sherries are served by the glass and the wines are an eclectic selection from lesser-known regions of Italy and Spain, including a brooding old-vine red from Spain's Toro and a gorgeous Mallorcan rosé. Service is keen and well-informed, helping to make Dehesa is a deservedly busy spot.
Babies and children admitted. Bookings not accepted. Separate room for parties, seats 12. Tables outdoors (8, pavement). **Map 17 A4.**

Meza
100 Wardour Street, W1F 0TN (7314 4002/ www.danddlondon.com). Leicester Square or Piccadilly Circus tube.
Bar Open noon-2am Mon-Wed; noon-3am Thur-Sat.
Restaurant Lunch served noon-4pm, **dinner served** 5-11.30pm Mon-Sat. **Tapas served** noon-12.30am Mon-Sat. **Main courses** £6.75-£17.50. **Tapas** £3.50-£10. **Set lunch** (noon-2.30pm) £8 2 courses, £10 3 courses. **Credit** AmEx, DC, MC, V.
If you're looking for a great place to drink at the weekend, Meza will certainly deliver. Pumping music, a metre-deep bar and a sequin-clad crowd set the tone for a night on the town. The tapas platters have a Mediterranean rather than Spanish slant, but are easy to pick at and make ideal drinking companions. The 'fish selection' – including swordfish brochettes, devilled whitebait and salt-cod fritters – vied for attention and was strongly seasoned, making a side order of greek salad a welcome contrast. A la carte offers the opportunity for more of a balance, and there are two set menus (though this isn't the cheap option). The impressive drinks list is a draw, with a huge range of cocktails including 'Grande' cocktails to share that contain an entire bottle of champagne. Other attractions are an unpretentious door policy, friendly staff and a huge amount of space right in the centre of Soho. During the day, the venue serves as a quiet haven for anyone wanting to escape the hustle and bustle.
Babies and children admitted (lunch). Booking advisable weekend. Disabled: lift; toilet. Separate room for parties, seats 38. **Map 17 B3.**

South Kensington

★ Cambio de Tercio
163 Old Brompton Road, SW5 0LJ (7244 8970/ www.cambiodetercio.co.uk). Gloucester Road or South Kensington tube. **Lunch served** noon-3pm daily. **Dinner served** 7-11.30pm Mon-Sat; 7-11pm Sun. **Main courses** £13.90-£15.50. **Credit** AmEx, DC, MC, V.
Cambio de Tercio is one of the only genuine nueva cocina fine-dining restaurants in London. Some traditional dishes appear on the menu (garlic prawns, patatas bravas, squid with aïoli), but

---

mostly these are left to sister tapas restaurant Tendido Cero across the road (*see p262*). Best instead to explore starters such as grilled red mullet fillets with scallop, artichoke, basil and pine nuts, or 12-hour caramelised oxtail with a red-wine jus, celeriac purée and foamed carrots. Move on to mains that might include sea bream with seasonal vegetables and manchego foam, or three-hour slow-cooked suckling pig with rosemary potatoes. These were all superb: meat, fish and vegetables handled exceptionally well; flavours nicely balanced (even the combination of fish and cheese in the main course). The decor is suitably spirited – black, yellow and magenta walls and big, bold Spanish canvases – but sophisticated, complemented by low lighting and crsip white tablecloths. The restaurant is a wine destination too; the formidable all-Spanish list offers hundreds of choices covering many regions and budgets.
Babies and children admitted. Booking advisable dinner. Restaurant available for hire. Separate room for parties, seats 20. Tables outdoors (3, pavement). **Map 13 C11.**

★ Tendido Cero

174 Old Brompton Road, SW5 0BA (7370 3685/ www.cambiodetercio.co.uk). Gloucester Road or South Kensington tube. **Tapas served** noon-3pm; 6.30-11pm daily. **Tapas** £4-£14. **Credit** AmEx, MC, V.

Sister restaurant to the equally successful Cambio de Tercio across the road (*see p261*), Tendido Cero is less gastronomically ambitious, offering traditional tapas with the odd flourish. Yet we reckon it occupies the superior venue: a simpler-shaped room (also decorated in atmospheric black and yellow) with a bar running along one side and a semi-open kitchen. It's a fairly formal restaurant, but has a buzzier, more appealing atmosphere. Since our last visit, a two-sitting system has been introduced – irritating, but a testament to the place's popularity. It's worth booking ahead to enjoy dishes that offer originality and quality way above average. Baby eels are heaped on slices of baguette with aïoli, then grilled so the aïoli just sets. Sobrasada sausage is rolled up with pieces of burgos cheese in tiny flutes of fine pastry, which are deep-fried and drizzled with honey. Old favourites are produced with class too; simple fried calamares were perfect. We also indulged in a superb dessert: three little squares of a rich layered orange chocolate cake. Our only gripe is that the wine list offers little choice below £20, but that's par for the course in this neighbourhood.
Babies and children admitted. Booking advisable dinner Tue-Sat. Restaurant available for hire. Tables outdoors (5, pavement). **Map 13 C11**.

West
Hammersmith

Los Molinos

127 Shepherd's Bush Road, W6 7LP (7603 2229/ www.losmolinosuk.com). Hammersmith tube. **Lunch served** noon-3pm Mon-Fri. **Dinner served** 6-10.45pm Mon-Sat. **Tapas** £3.70-£6.50. **Credit** AmEx, DC, MC, V.

Entering Los Molinos is like walking into the house of an eccentric relative. The orange-hued walls are covered with knick-knacks, and the welcome is as warm and cosy as the surroundings. The menu offers plenty of variety, with 80 tapas listed, but it seems that the restaurant's ambitions are well placed. Every dish we chose was a success, both in terms of presentation and taste. Each ingredient could be discerned and savoured in a super-fresh bowl of gazpacho. The same could be said of all our food: soupy fabada came packed with tasty morsels of bacon, chorizo and black pudding; shellfish and other goodies were crammed into a creamy, saffron-spiked paella; and a special of steaming mussels excelled in its chunky, garlic and parsley-flecked tomato sauce. The bill here makes a pleasant surprise too. This local haunt is certainly worth revisiting time and again.
Babies and children welcome: high chairs. Booking advisable dinner Fri, Sat. Separate room for parties, seats 50. **Map 20 C3**.

Kensington

★ L Restaurant & Bar

2 Abingdon Road, W8 6AF (7795 6969/ www.l-restaurant.co.uk). High Street Kensington tube. **Lunch served** noon-2.30pm Tue-Sat. **Dinner served** 6-10.30pm Mon-Sat. **Meals/tapas served** 12.30-8.30pm Sun. **Main courses** £9.50-£17.50. **Tapas** £3.25-£4.95. **Credit** AmEx, MC, V.

We awarded L Restaurant a red star in its debut year, and 12 months later, we're just as impressed. The venue is curious. The main restaurant (reached via a compact bar at the front) occupies a long, thin, back-yardish area, but the use of space is intelligent. A glass roof floods it with light. Some diners like sitting on the mezzanine level, but we much prefer to be downstairs where it feels a little less cramped. Service is professional and sophisticated, perfectly complementing the top-notch modern Iberian cooking. Food consists of generally unfussy combinations of first-rate, super-fresh ingredients cooked with precision and passion. Every dish on our latest visit was fantastic. To start: a big slab of roast butternut squash with cubes of pancetta and salad; and seared scallops with chunks of chorizo. Next came slices of sublimely juicy suckling lamb on a bed of tomato and butter beans; and magnificent cubes of monkfish atop a pile of herb-enriched lentils. The house red wine was great value too. L Restaurant isn't a budget eaterie, but it's one of the best bargains in town.
Babies and children admitted. Booking advisable. Separate room for parties, seats 14. Tables outdoors (2, pavement). **Map 13 A9**.

Ladbroke Grove

Café García

248-250 Portobello Road, W11 1LL (7221 6119/ www.cafegarcia.co.uk). Ladbroke Grove tube. **Tapas served** 9am-5pm daily. **Tapas** £1.50-£5. **Credit** AmEx, MC, V.

In the heart of bustling Portobello Road, this is a café in the traditional sense of the word – pop in for coffee and pastries or a simple bite to eat. It's an easy stop for bands of shoppers or locals, but you can feel equally comfortable alone in these surroundings. On our visit, a selection of empanadas and tortillas was on display in the glass-fronted counter, along with paella, fabada and other cooked dishes, ready to be plated and popped in the microwave. Plump boquerones and salad were also available, but there isn't a vast choice overall, so Garcia isn't somewhere for a special occasion. Decor is simple and functional, with a few sepia photos to pull it together. The main point of interest is the collection of Spanish products on view behind the counter. On our visit, Garcia is certainly worth a visit; R Garcia offers a range of Spanish supermarket favourites, from biscuits to shampoo, and its deli counter has a tempting array of meats and cheeses that's not to be missed.
Babies and children admitted. Disabled: toilet. Takeaway service. **Map 19 B2**.

Dehesa. See p261.

Galicia

*323 Portobello Road, W10 5SY (8969 3539).
Ladbroke Grove tube.* **Lunch served** noon-3pm
Tue-Sun. **Dinner served** 7-11.30pm Tue-Sat;
7-10.30pm Sun. **Main courses** £7.90-£13.95.
Tapas £2.95-£6.50. **Set lunch** £7.50 3 courses;
(Sun) £8.50 3 courses. **Credit** AmEx, DC, MC, V.
Tucked away at the quiet end of Portobello Road,
Galicia nevertheless continues to attract a crowd.
Its narrow corridor of tables and bar quickly
filled up early on a week night. The menu offers
regional and national dishes, including classic
seafood and meat tapas. Gruff but amenable, the
old-school waiting staff ensured professional
service throughout. We opted for a tomato-based
Galician chicken stew, and veal in sherry sauce.
Presentation of the dishes and combination of
their ingredients were both very much from the
traditional school of cooking, but not to their
detriment. The dishes arrived with a huge silver
platter of simply cooked, seasonal vegetables and
chips. Puddings were on display and a quick
inspection tempted us into ordering a rich
caramelly flan and a slice of tarta santiago, doused
in a generous slug of almond liqueur. With a lively
atmosphere, simple decor and solid, dependable
cooking, Galicia is the place to head for an informal
night with friends or an intimate tête-à-tête.

*Babies and children admitted. Booking essential
weekends.* **Map 19 B1**.

Maida Vale

Mesón Bilbao

*33 Malvern Road, NW6 5PS (7328 1744). Maida
Vale tube.* **Lunch served** noon-3pm Mon-Fri.
Dinner served 6-11pm Mon-Thur; 7-11.30pm
Fri; 6-11.30pm Sat. **Main courses** £9.95-£12.95.
Tapas £3.50-£6.95. **Set menu** £12.95 2 courses
and coffee. **Credit** MC, V.
Reasonably priced, tasty food and cosy, taverna-
style charm make Mesón Bilbao a great local
restaurant, but on the night we visited customers
were thin on the ground. According to the helpful
waiting staff, the restaurant is packed on many
nights, but we reckon it might suffer from the out-
of-the-way location, despite a set menu offering
excellent value for £12.95. Juicy meatballs came in
a rich tomato sauce. Sadly, Basque-style chicken
from the same menu had a seemingly identical
sauce, which took the edge off an otherwise well-
executed dish. From the à la carte, grilled prawns
were cooked to perfection, and chorizo busturia –
slices of chorizo sandwiched between layers of
crisp fried aubergine – was a delight. Tortilla de
jamón had a good balance of potato and egg and

was succulent, well-flavoured and fresh. Cosy tables
clustered around the bar are suited to couples or
small groups. This restaurant also welcomes
parties to its spacious lower level.
*Babies and children welcome: high chairs. Booking
advisable dinner Fri, Sat. Tables outdoors
(2, pavement).* **Map 1 A3**.

South West

Putney

Olé

*240 Upper Richmond Road, SW15 6TG
(8788 8009/www.olerestaurants.com). East
Putney tube/Putney rail.*
Bar & restaurant **Open/meals served** noon-
11pm Mon-Thur; noon-11.30pm Fri, Sat; noon-
10pm Sun.
Restaurant **Main courses** £11.95-£15.50. **Set
lunch** (noon-6pm) £8.95 2 tapas; £9.95 2 tapas
& glass of wine. **Set meal** (Sun) £13.50 paella.
Both **Tapas** £3-£6.50. **Credit** AmEx, DC, MC, V.
On Saturday night, Olé is abuzz with lively parties
of diners. Nevertheless, two floors, a generous bar
area and plenty of space between tables mean you
needn't feel overpowered as a couple. A keyboard
player added to the swing of things on our visit,

in a setting that's all white and beech with splashes of primary colour and floor-to-ceiling windows along the back wall. The kitchen offers both tapas and a full menu, in the low to mid-price bracket. From the tapas list, calamares had a delightfully crunchy batter. The creamy melt-in-the-mouth textures of oven-baked aubergine with a cheesy tomato sauce elicited an enthusiastic response too. Simply marinated black olives were outstanding, and we devoured mussels in a soupy tomato sauce to the last morsel. Our main course, a colourful paella valenciana, lacked a discernible saffron taste but made up for it with generous helpings of seafood and chicken. Staff were efficient, whisking away plates, providing finger bowls, hot towels and drinks as required.
Babies and children welcome: high chairs.
Booking advisable weekends. Disabled: toilet.
Restaurant/bar available for hire.

South
Clapham

★ Lola Rojo (100)
78 Northcote Road, SW11 6QL (7350 2262/ www.lolarojo.com). Clapham Junction rail. **Meals served** noon-10.30pm Mon-Fri; 10am-10.30pm Sat; noon-5pm Sun. **Main courses** £7.50-£11. **Credit** AmEx, DC, MC, V.
True to its name, Lola Rojo ('rojo' meaning red) is accessorised in scarlet, from the blood-red candles to the stylish crimson crockery, all set against a clean white background. This is no cliché-riddled tapas bar – it's contemporary cooking as you'd find in Spain. There's a strong Catalan influence in dishes such as grilled asparagus with romesco sauce, tomato-rubbed toasted bread, and Majorcan rice with prawns and vegetables. Flavour combinations are mostly traditional, but execution is stylishly contemporary. There are nods to the modernist cooking for which Spain is now famed, in dishes such as 'apple, beetroot and sheep air'. Ingredients are impeccably sourced. Our cecina (air-dried beef), served with slivers of manchego cheese, rocket and pine nuts was mellow and deeply flavoured. Other tapas such as broad bean stew with mint and spring onions hit the mark too. The aïoli with our squid-ink rice didn't have a tingling garlic kick, but cooking is generally spot-on. The wine list contains excellent bottles from Spain's up-and-coming regions. Space is the only drawback; the place is tiny and tables can be cramped (book ahead). On sunny weekends, tapas are sold from a counter outside.
Babies and children admitted. Booking advisable Thur-Sat. Separate room for parties, seats 15. Tables outdoors (16, terrace). Takeaway service.
Map 21 C5.

Vauxhall

Rebato's
169 South Lambeth Road, SW8 1XW (7735 6388/www.rebatos.com). Stockwell tube. **Tapas bar Open** 5.30-10.45pm Mon-Fri; 7-11pm Sat. **Tapas** £3.25-£5.50. *Restaurant* **Lunch served** noon-2.30pm Mon-Fri. **Dinner served** 7-10.45pm Mon-Sat. **Main courses** £10.95-£15.25. *Both* **Credit** AmEx, MC, V.
Walking into Rebato's feels like entering another world, or at least another part of it. An uninviting exterior shields those inside from passers-by. This may suggest you won't get a warm welcome, but inside you can expect bull-fighting posters, football memorabilia, dim lighting and an old-school taverna, so pull up a stool by the bar or grab one of the velvety benches around it. As is often the case in Spain, tapas were already prepared when we visited. Some were on display and nearly all arrived at the table within microwave minutes. The albóndigas, champiñones al ajillo and pulpo (meatballs, garlic mushrooms, and octopus) were nevertheless very fresh tasting. Grilled sardines arrived later, of course (straight from the grill), and serrano came sliced from a haunch on full and succulent view. Families, couples and friends all happily co-exist in these laid-back surroundings –

Rebato's is a real favourite with locals. Beyond the bar, you'll find a leafy, candlelit restaurant that's perfect for a more intimate evening, with a full menu and dessert trolley to tempt.
Babies and children admitted. Booking essential.
Map 16 L13.

Waterloo

Mar i Terra
14 Gambia Street, SE1 0XH (7928 7628/ www.mariterra.co.uk). Southwark tube/Waterloo tube/rail. **Tapas served** noon-3pm, 6-11pm Mon-Fri; 5-11pm Sat. **Tapas** £3.50-£7.95. **Credit** AmEx, MC, V.
Nestled among the rabbit warren of railway arches near Southwark tube is a small and unassuming beacon of rustic Spanish cooking. Once a British pub, the premises have been transformed. You'll now find a blue, well-lit interior bedecked with Spanish prints, a high-stooled bar and wooden tables. Snappy service saw the arrival of menus, olives and bread within minutes. Our order of fried chorizo delivered both on spice and succulence, with Asturian cider pleasantly cutting through the fat. A meaty rabbit stew with mushrooms and potatoes arrived in a thick herby sauce, ideal for dunking. We also relished the chipirones, the baby squid remaining tender in a tomato and white wine sauce. Mar i Terra's laminated menu indicates an unyielding permanence and, not surprisingly, our out-of-season broad beans didn't live up to their table-mates. However, the menu shows an endearing love for Spanish ingredients with a drinks list to match, including an extensive wine selection, sherries and sangria laced with ponche brandy. Upbeat salsa and other beats provided the soundtrack for a reasonably priced night out that's equally suitable for couples or groups.
Babies and children admitted. Separate room for parties, seats 50. Tables outdoors (15, garden).
Map 11 O8.
For branch see index.

South East
Herne Hill

Number 22
22 Half Moon Lane, SE24 9HU (7095 9922/ www.number-22.com). Herne Hill rail/3, 37, 68 bus. **Tapas served** noon-4pm, 6-11pm Mon-Sat; noon-11pm Sun. **Tapas** £3-£8. **Credit** MC, V.
This year, Number 22 has added a conservatory, which provides welcome space in a hitherto tightly packed restaurant. Flickering candles, dim lighting and dark wood furnishings create an intimate atmosphere that's great for an evening of good conversation. There is much to tempt on the predominantly tapas-based menu, which has a refreshingly modern take on Spanish food. Staff get high marks; our knowledgeable waitress was happy to take us through the subtleties of each dish before we ordered. The humble croqueta has here been given a makeover, and a crunchy plateful stuffed with spinach and goat's cheese hit the spot. Next, succulent chorizo, sliced in half and standing proud, made a welcome change to what can be an oily offering. A mix of rabbit and sobrasada sausage was also a feast for eyes and belly. Much attention is paid to presentation, and dishes stream to the table on angular white plates: elegance epitomised. A creamy wedge of blue-veined picos de europa cheese provided a pleasing end to an above-average meal.
Babies and children admitted. Restaurant available for hire. Tables outdoors (16, patio).
Map 23 A5.

London Bridge & Borough

★ Tapas Brindisa (100)
18-20 Southwark Street, SE1 1TJ (7357 8880/ www.brindisa.com). London Bridge tube/rail. **Breakfast served** 9-11am Fri, Sat. **Lunch served** noon-3pm Mon-Thur; noon-4pm Fri, Sat. **Dinner served** 5.30-11pm Mon-Sat. **Tapas** £3.25-£9. **Credit** AmEx, MC, V.

Interview
RICHARD BIGG

Who are you?
Co-owner and managing director of the Cantaloupe Group, which runs **Camino** (*see p260*), **Market Place** (*see p330*), Cargo, the **Big Chill House** (*see p331*) and the Big Chill Festival.
What's the best thing about running restaurants and bars in London?
The industry is all about socialising and I absolutely love the atmosphere that creates. I'm heavily into booze – wine, beers, mixed drinks – and love looking at how wine and food go together, running tasting sessions for the staff. London is especially exciting, of course, but at the moment all over the country exciting things are happening in this business.
What's the worst thing?
New leases are a headache. Luckily the administrative, behind-the-scenes stuff is not my area so much these days, but I did it when I started out.
Which are your favourite London restaurants?
When I go out I don't want to worry about whether I'm wearing the right shoes or labels, I just want to have fun and relax. **Crazy Bear** (*see p252* and *p330*) is lively downstairs and they pay attention to quality. **Vinoteca** (*see p346*) is a superb wine bar/ shop-restaurant, totally unpretentious. **Green & Red** (*see p47*) is fun. **Shochu Lounge** (*see p330*) has fantastic design and lighting. **J Sheekey** (*see p91*) is impeccable. I used to live in Hackney, and **Buen Ayre** (*see p45*) is great too.
How green are you?
As a group we're never going to be like the Acorn Houses of this world, but we source our fish from Cornwall, the North Sea and Hastings, and at the moment our beef comes from Scotland and Northern Ireland. I've never had a better steak than those I ate in Argentina, but I'd never transport them here.
What is missing from London's restaurant scene?
Not a whole lot, but when I read the trade magazines I often think I'm seeing too many places that are style over substance.

Tapas Brindisa makes its corner of Borough Market seem like a part of Madrid in the heart of London. Eurotravellers (many of them Spanish or South American) and Londoners rub elbows at the invariably packed bar, sipping sherry or one of the rather good wines by the glass. Bookings for the small, cramped tables aren't taken so you're likely to spend at least 30 minutes at the bar admiring the way in which this former warehouse has taken on a Spanish persona. It's now the restaurant incarnation of the well-regarded Spanish food importer, Brindisa, which also has a stall at the market. Many dishes are based on prime ingredients, such as mojama (air-dried tuna loin) with sliced pear and olive oil, and mahón cheese with a sweet tomato jam. Finely sliced, ruby-red Joselito jamón doesn't come cheap, but the quality's outstanding. Likewise, our grilled lamb chops served with aïoli and fresh mint salad were tender and gently smoky. It's pretty hard to go wrong with any dish here. Service does its best to keep smiling, but staff make it plain there are others waiting for your table. A popular place that's lost none of its pulling power.
Babies and children admitted. Bookings not accepted. Disabled: toilet. Tables outdoors (4, pavement). **Map 11 P8.**

East

Docklands

★ El Faro

3 Turnberry Quay, Pepper Street, E14 9RD (7987 5511/www.el-faro.co.uk). Crossharbour DLR. **Meals served** noon-3.30pm, 5-11pm Mon-Sat; noon-3pm Sun. **Main courses** £14-£17.50. **Tapas** £3.50-£14.50. **Credit** AmEx, MC, V.
A relative newcomer, this classy restaurant already has a host of enthusiastic reviews adorning its reception. The interior is sleek and modern, with large windows overlooking a watery view of Crossharbour dock. Arriving without a reservation, we were obligingly squeezed in along the bar. Tables were packed with business types, a few couples breaking up the sea of shirts. The menu is what you might expect of any smart London eaterie, with the necessary salute to fine ingredients, provenance and regionality. To start, a juicy own-made chorizo sausage was beautifully complemented by tart balsamic-dressed rocket. Skilfully prepared seafood paella contained creamy grains of rice and a subtle depth of flavour rarely achieved in the average Spanish restaurant. Our impressive meal ended with a selection of house desserts, visual treats that tasted just as good – cinnamon-spiked arroz con leche; a delicate slab of warm, moist chocolate cake; and silky crema catalana. Despite being busy, staff went out of their way to make us feel welcome. Even if you don't live or work nearby, El Faro is worth the trip.
Babies and children admitted (until 8.30pm). Booking advisable. Disabled: toilet. Separate room for parties, seats 70. Tables outdoors (16, terrace). **Map 24 B3.**

Shoreditch

★ Laxeiro

93 Columbia Road, E2 7RG (7729 1147/ www.laxeiro.co.uk). Bus 26, 48, 55. **Lunch served** noon-3pm, **dinner served** 7-11pm Tue-Sat. **Meals served** 9am-3pm Sun. **Main courses** £3.50-£8.95. **Credit** AmEx, DC, MC, V.
A smattering of Alhambra-style tiling, a terracotta colour scheme and the odd potted plant give Laxeiro a homey, honest feel. This unassuming little restaurant is busy most days. On our visit we found it hard to resist the paella with its immense prawns, but went instead for the classic tapas, which were verging on raciones in portion size and perfect for a large group. An authentic tortilla was potatoey and eggy in all the right places, while skinny-cut calamares were far from rubbery. Cochinillo, irresistibly tender suckling pig, came with a gentle tomato and apple sauce, while salty pimientos de padrón were handled with care. Our only criticism concerns the sad-looking patatas bravas which, though nicely flavoured, had

L Restaurant. See p262.

probably been sitting around too long. The wine (and sherry) list sticks to Spain, and jugs of sangría are available for sharing. Service is at times sketchy, but staff are in general all smiles. Judging by the queues on Columbia flower-market day, this reliable family-run joint is clearly a success.
Babies and children welcome: high chairs. Booking advisable; not accepted Sun. Tables outdoors (4, pavement). Takeaway service. **Map 6 S3.**

★ Pinchito Tapas

32 Featherstone Street, EC1Y 8QX (7490 0121/www.pinchito.co.uk). Old Street tube/rail. **Breakfast served** 10.30am-noon; **Tapas served** noon-11pm Mon-Fri; 5pm-midnight Sat. **Tapas** £2-£12. **Credit** AmEx, MC, V.
Tucked behind Old Street station, this quiet bar is very 'Shoreditch', all exposed brickwork and breeze blocks, low-wattage teardrop lights, magazine-like images of urban stuff and a chill-out corner with leather armchairs. Pinchito Tapas is named after the Basque appetiser of bread piled with various ingredients. It has previously been criticised for its lack of pinchos (or 'pintxos'), but this time pinchos-galore welcomed us at the bar-counter, topped with octopus, esqueixada (salt-cod salad), or chunks of spanish omelette – all a quid each. The wine list is exclusively Spanish and there's a decent selection of sherries, as well as cocktails. For tapas, choose from reliable dishes such as chickpeas and morcilla, garlic mushrooms, or octopus and chorizo. Meltingly moist 'moruno' (chargrilled

skewers of spiced pork tenderloin) were a dream. For dessert, we went for chocolate con churros; it was well-made, but we remembered why the dish is usually served at breakfast – you need the day to burn off the calories. Pinchito does in fact open for late-risers wanting breakfast (like Brighton sibling Pintxo People), with a menu that includes Spanish fry-ups. The food isn't remarkable, but staff lend the place a good vibe.
Babies and children admitted. Takeaway service.
Map 6 Q4.

North East
Walthamstow

★ Orford Saloon
32 Orford Road, E17 9NJ (8503 6542). Walthamstow Central tube/rail. **Tapas served** 6-10.30pm Tue-Fri; noon-3pm, 6-10.30pm Sat; noon-5pm, 6-9.30pm Sun. **Tapas** £3.50-£10.50. **Set meal** £10.50 per person (minimum 2) paella. **Credit** MC, V.
Along this stretch of Orford Road is a quaint little strip of shops and restaurants that forms an oasis in the urban landscape. Among them, Orford Saloon brings a splash of colour to a building that was once a 'Gentlemen's hairdressers' of the same name. Gentle mauves and reds, exposed brick and warm-coloured woods create a cosy, laid-back atmosphere. Locals sit around the tile-topped tables, enjoying a traditional tapas menu that's well above average. The array of specials including crisp, fried cuttlefish with delightfully fresh own-made aïoli. Not seen enough on Spanish menus here, the perky salpicón de marisco was a delight with its contrast of crunchy vegetables and tender seafood hunks. Creamy lentil stew with slivers of chorizo was packed with meaty flavour and proved to be the perfect accompaniment to a bottle of Mahou. Besides Spanish beers, sherries, juices and good coffee, there's an extensive selection of Spanish wines. For seekers of high-quality Spanish food at a fair price, this gem warrants a detour.
Babies and children admitted. Booking advisable. Disabled: toilet.

North
Camden Town & Chalk Farm

★ El Parador
245 Eversholt Street, NW1 1BA (7387 2789). Mornington Crescent tube. **Tapas served** noon-3pm, 6-11pm Mon-Thur; noon-3pm, 6-11.30pm Fri; 6-11.30pm Sat; 6.30-9.30pm Sun. **Tapas** £4-£7.50. **Credit** MC, V.
Year after year we've been delighted to enjoy some of the best tapas in London at this neighbourhood restaurant. In most other respects it's a pretty unremarkable venue: from the forgettable frontage to the plain (though perfectly amenable) decor. Food-wise, though, it's not just the high-quality ingredients and excellent cooking that impress, it's the originality and eclecticism of the menu. In most cases a list of over 40 tapas would be a bad omen; here it's inspirational. From the selection of 16 vegetable tapas, we chose roast beetroot with chestnuts and red onion in a balsamic reduction; Calasparra rice with roasted aubergines, peas and mint; and grilled wild mushrooms with rosemary and confit garlic. All were superb assemblies of flavours and textures, prepared with obvious diligence and passion. Our selections of fish and meat were equally impressive, such as seared scallops served with buttered spinach; or chicken livers fried in sherry with serrano ham. The wine list offers nearly 40 bottles in the £13-£30 bracket, with 16 of them available by the glass. It's rare that a family-run, diminutive diner like this can be called a destination restaurant, but El Parador continues to be worth a trip across town.
Babies and children admitted. Bookings accepted for 3 or more only. Separate room for parties, seats 30. Tables outdoors (10, garden). Vegetarian menu. **Map 27 D3.**

Crouch End

La Bota
31 Broadway Parade, Tottenham Lane, N8 9DB (8340 3082/www.labota.co.uk). Finsbury Park tube/rail then 91, W7 bus. **Lunch served** noon-2.30pm Mon-Fri; noon-3pm Sat. **Dinner served** 6-11pm Mon-Thur; 6-11.30pm Fri, Sat. **Meals served** noon-11pm Sun. **Main courses** £7.50-£12.75. **Tapas** £2.65-£4.50. **Credit** MC, V.
Asking for directions to La Bota resulted in an effusive review of this traditional Spanish restaurant from a local. Once we had sat down to a meal here, it was easy to see why. The waiter arrived at the table with a blackboard full of promising specials to complement an already extensive menu. Padrón or 'russian roulette' peppers, lightly blackened and salted, stimulated the taste buds for the meal to come. Calamares fritos in a light batter were cooked and seasoned to perfection, requiring nothing more than the wedge of lemon provided with them. The rabbit stew, like all the dishes we opted for, was inexpensive, hearty and well-prepared. Diners during Saturday lunch were a comfortable, lively mix of families, friends and couples – all happily enjoying themselves amid the low-key decor of wooden tables, pale walls, posters, prints and mementos. Stools at the bar allow for passers-by who fancy a light bite and a beer. La Bota is a restaurant that doesn't need to try too hard; good food, good prices and comfortable surroundings make a winning combination.
Babies and children welcome: high chairs. Booking advisable dinner Fri, Sat. Takeaway service.

Outer London
Twickenham, Middlesex

★ Tapas y Vino
111 London Road, Twickenham, Middx TW1 1EE (8892 5417/www.tapasyvino.co.uk). Twickenham rail. **Tapas served** noon-2.30pm, 6-10.30pm Mon-Sat. **Tapas** £2-£5. **Credit** MC, V.
This exceptional tapas joint next to Twickenham station is run by chef John McClements, who is already known around south-west London for his French mini-chain, Ma Cuisine Le Petit Bistrot (*see p110*). Tapas y Vino is a humble little place, with a cute Mediterranean decor of terracotta-tiled floor, whitewashed walls and slightly naff provençal tablecloths and trinkets on the walls. Initially the restaurant was called El Vino, but although the wines are good, the main event here is the food, hence the revised name. This isn't tapas in the familiar sense; portions might be small, but the Spanish influence is one of many, and the cooking displays a sophistication uncommon in tapas bars. Most of the magic happens in the 'speciality tapas' section of the menu: witness perfectly pan-fried slabs of monkfish with butter and capers; moreish croquettes of morcilla with quince jam; succulent scallops on a fantastically tar-like squid-ink risotto; or slabs of oxtail in a sticky red-wine reduction with creamed potatoes. And there are many more dishes, updated seasonally.
Babies and children admitted. Booking advisable weekends. Disabled: toilet. Restaurant available for hire.
For branch see index.

Pinchito Tapas

RESTAURANTS

Thai

The similarities are striking. The path along which Thai food has advanced in London has been well trodden by both Indian and Chinese restaurants. Yet after a huge expansion in the 1990s, the cuisine has now reached a crossroads. Are we to get more top-end dining: the imaginative 'Modern Thai' food so brilliantly created at **Nahm**, and the authentic delicacies produced at **Saran Rom** and by Nongyao Thoopchoi at **Nipa**? Or will there be a growth in the proponents of more economic regional Thai cookery: the likes of the excellent north-eastern specialist **Esarn Kheaw** and South Norwood's **Mantanah**? Or will we have to put up with more of the tempered down, sickly sweet version of the cuisine that is now commonly found in our city's high streets, pubs and supermarkets?

Whereas Punjabi chefs in Southall or Cantonese cooks in Chinatown might not need to attract diners from outside their own communities, Thai restaurateurs do not have the benefit of a large Thai population in the city. Initially, this led to a dumbing down of the cuisine, but it might now prompt Thai food's renaissance. Clued-up, 21st-century London diners have been the major impulse behind the soaring standards of cooking found first at Indian and latterly Chinese restaurants. By demanding genuine South-east Asian flavours, such customers could also bring about a similar flowering of Thai cuisine in the capital. News that **Busaba Eathai** has secured funding to expand across Britain is exciting, if quality standards can be maintained.

Central

Belgravia

★ Nahm (100)

The Halkin, Halkin Street, SW1X 7DJ (7333 1234/www.nahm.como.bz). Hyde Park Corner tube. **Lunch served** noon-2.30pm Mon-Fri. **Dinner served** 7-10.45pm Mon-Sat; 7-9.45pm Sun. **Main courses** £11-£16.50. **Set lunch** £26 3 courses. **Set dinner** £55 3 courses. **Credit** AmEx, DC, MC, V.

Truly exceptional food is produced in the chic Halkin Hotel dining room known as Nahm – but at seriously high prices, which limits many fans' visits to special occasions. Knowledgeable staff steer you through the menu, which features traditional Thai dishes as well as updates on the theme using British ingredients. We began an epic feast with sweet coconut cupcakes topped with a fresh and light red crab curry. An outstanding pork salad with fried garlic, mint, coriander, chilli, pomelo and dried shrimp was a perfect example of chef-supremo David Thompson's understanding of the delicate balance of Thai flavours and his dedication to using the finest ingredients (though these days the kitchen is largely run by head chef Matthew Albert). Red minced quail curry had the perfect amount of heat. Sweet yellow bean relish was just savoury enough, and arrived with fried betel leaves, fresh fennel, fresh red pepper, cucumber and starfruit. Fish soup was a triumph; hot and sour flavours competed for attention with rich smoked fish. Our meal was perfectly accompanied by a Schlumberger 2005 riesling grand cru. Sleek, subtle and cool: this is the best Thai restaurant in London. Visit the website for discount menu offers.
Babies and children welcome: high chairs; nappy-changing facilities (hotel). Booking advisable. Disabled: toilet. Dress: smart casual. **Map 9 G9.**

Marylebone

Busaba Eathai (100)

8-13 Bird Street, W1U 1BU (7518 8080). Bond Street tube. **Meals served** noon-11pm Mon-Thur; noon-11.30pm Fri, Sat; noon-10pm Sun. **Main courses** £5.50-£10.90. **Credit** AmEx, MC, V.

Busaba Eathai is in danger of being a bit too cool for school. Incense wafts as you enter the dark wood-lined dining room. Wood so pleased the designers that benches, tables, chopsticks and even menus all shine with the same rich grain motif. The stylish room is populated with chic diners and attractive servers who ask questions like: 'Are you OK with the dried shrimps in the green papaya salad? They're strong.' This makes diners suspect that Alan Yau's fast-food canteen is not designed for Thai purists, but for Europeans who want a nice atmosphere and simple flavours. On the menu, curries and stir-fries sit next to enticing juices (mandarin juice with lemongrass, mint and chilli was refreshing), highlighting the restaurant's nod to health. Tom yam noodle soup was a real sinus-clearer, resplendent with chillies and ample fresh greenery, but with only three rather flavourless prawns – £10.90 seemed a bit steep. Trendy cloth takeaway bags might lead diners to grumble that they are paying to much for design affectations. As we went to press, Yau had secured investment to roll out between 20 and 30 branches of Busaba Eathai across the UK – let's hope they can maintain their hitherto high standards.
Babies and children admitted. Bookings not accepted. Disabled: toilet. Takeaway service. **Map 9 G6.**
For branches see index.

★ Chaopraya Eat-Thai

22 St Christopher's Place, W1U 1NP (7486 0777/www.eatthai.net). Bond Street tube. **Lunch served** noon-3pm, **dinner served** 6-10.30pm

Mon-Fri. **Meals served** noon-10.30pm Sat, Sun. **Main courses** £10.50-£23.95. **Set lunch** £12.95 bento box. **Set dinner** £25-£35 per person (minimum 2-6) 3-4 courses. **Credit** AmEx, MC, V.

Unlike the hectic Bangkok river after which it is named, Chaopraya Eat-Thai is a peaceful dining oasis: an intimate space that mixes trendy western wallpaper with Thai relics, both chic and kitsch. The menu features the usual Thai favourites, but ingredients are of a higher quality than found at many competitors, and several dishes exhibit well-placed creative flair. Steamed dumplings were delicate packages of prawn, pork, pickled vegetables and spices, made sweet with ground peanuts. By contrast, the recommended deep-fried taro and crab cakes were little tastier than bland, bready pub crab cakes – and seemed overpriced at £7.95. A rich star anise-infused massaman lamb curry was excellent; tender flaky meat contrasted texturally with smooth roasted sweet potato, and was perfectly topped with cashews and own-made sweet potato crisps. Chargrilled marinated pork arrived with a sauce of chilli, pungent roasted rice and tamarind. The wine list is short but well-thought-out; however, by-the-glass options are limited to basic vins de pays, which is out of keeping with the high standards maintained here.
Babies and children welcome: high chairs. Takeaway service. Vegetarian menu. **Map 9 G6.**

Mayfair

Patara

3&7 Maddox Street, W1S 2QB (7499 6008/ www.pataralondon.com). Oxford Circus tube. **Lunch served** noon-2.30pm, **dinner served** 6.30-10.30pm daily. **Main courses** £6.75-£19.95. **Set lunch** £11.95-£14.95 2 courses. **Credit** AmEx, DC, MC, V.

This international chain of Thai restaurants has proved popular in London where it has four swanky outposts. The sleek interior, good service, relaxed atmosphere and contemporary food keep well-heeled customers returning. Patara serves modest portions of artfully displayed creative cooking, though some fusion dishes seem aimed at corporate customers rather than genuine Thai aficionados. The menu is littered with trendy ingredients like veal osso buco (here smothered in a northern-style yellow curry) and tuna tartare (which at Patara gets a lime and lemongrass vinaigrette), but also inexplicably boasts of serving New Zealand lamb. Still, the generally high quality of ingredients means that customers are unlikely to be disappointed. Highlight of our meal was a fillet of sea bass chargrilled in a banana leaf and topped with a rich and wonderfully sweet-and-spicy penang curry. The Oxford Circus branch is highly popular, so booking is advisable.
Babies and children admitted. Booking advisable. Separate room for parties, seats 45. **Map 9 J6.**
For branches see index.

West

Bayswater

★ Nipa

Royal Lancaster Hotel, Lancaster Terrace, W2 2TY (7262 6737/www.niparestaurant.co.uk). Lancaster Gate tube. **Bar Open** 8am-midnight daily. *Restaurant* **Lunch served** noon-2pm Mon-Fri. **Dinner served** 6.30-10.30pm Mon-Sat. **Main courses** £7.85-£14. **Set meal** £27-£32 4 courses. **Both Credit** AmEx, DC, MC, V.

Who would guess that the 1960s concrete monolith of the Royal Lancaster Hotel conceals this serene, authentic gem of a Thai restaurant? You'll quickly forget the skyscraper above and the three lanes of heavy traffic below as you gaze over verdant Hyde Park from the compact, wood-panelled, flower-adorned dining room. Head chef (Ms) Nongyao Thoopchoi produces a first-rate menu that incorporates many lesser-known Thai delicacies alongside all the familiar staples. On our recent visit the kitchen was, as usual, in fine fettle, turning

out precisely cooked dishes with super-fresh ingredients. Thai omelette with fresh crab meat made for a delicious start; it went well with khao krieb pak mor (dim sum-like steamed dumplings of minced pork and peanuts). Pork red curry was spot on; we also loved a sweet-sour dish of deep-fried slabs of white fish garnished with shredded chicken, oriental mushrooms and chillies. The long menu gives you plenty of excuses for repeat visits. Service is typically Thai and perfectly dignified. Prices are a little high, but that's customary for hotel dining, and there aren't many London restaurants producing Thai cuisine of this quality.
Babies and children welcome: high chairs; nappy-changing facilities (hotel). Booking essential Fri, Sat. Disabled: toilet (hotel). Dress: smart casual. Restaurant available for hire. Vegetarian menu. **Map 8 D6**.

Tawana

3 Westbourne Grove, W2 4UA (7229 3785/ www.tawana.co.uk). Bayswater tube. **Lunch served** noon-3pm, **dinner served** 6-11pm Mon-Sat. **Meals served** noon-10pm Sun. **Main courses** £5.75-£19.95. **Set meal** £15.95 2 courses. **Minimum** £10 per person (food only). **Credit** MC, V.

Tawana's glass front provides great people-watching opportunities over Westbourne Grove. Inside, the decor is generic Thai: bamboo chairs, wooden panelling and gilded Thai artwork in gold and mahogany. Food is the priority here. All the soups can come as a 'hotpot' for two; we went for poh tak, a fragrant lime-leafy seafood broth packed with fresh mint. Puu nim (salty soft-shell crab) had fresh soft flesh under its crunchy coat, making it a dish worthy of the term 'special'. Spicy duck salad packed a modest chilli punch, while a side of golf-ball aubergine dotted with soy beans came in a dreamy tangy lagoon of ginger, mint and soy sauce. Gaeng massaman neur was all you'd expect of this rich peanut dish: soft chunks of potato and beef adrift in a smooth coconut-milk sauce. We were also pleased to see plenty of vegetarian choices on the menu. Our only complaint concerned the odd lump of raw garlic found in the stir-fried morning glory. The extensive wine list includes a couple of Thai wines by the glass. Definitely worth a stop if you're in the area and crave high-quality Thai food.
Babies and children admitted. Booking advisable. Separate room for parties, seats 50. Takeaway service; delivery service (over £20 within W2). Vegetarian menu. **Map 7 B6**.
For branches (Thai Hut) see index.

Shepherd's Bush

★ ★ Esarn Kheaw

314 Uxbridge Road, W12 7LJ (8743 8930/ www.esarnkheaw.com). Shepherd's Bush tube/ 207, 260, 283 bus. **Lunch served** noon-3pm Mon-Fri. **Dinner served** 6-11pm daily. **Main courses** £5.50-£8.95. **Credit** MC, V.

The mint-green dining room decorated with false exposed beams, photos of the Thai royal family and an excessive seven no-smoking signs, may not win any design prizes, but the food at Esarn Kheaw is deserving of all the accolades heaped upon it. Adventurous diners will revel in the opportunity to sample the earthy 'off' flavours of north-eastern Thai cuisine, and will also appreciate the chance to explore the impressive offal-heavy arsenal of meats available. A papaya salad prepared in the north-eastern style was a fiery medley of firm shredded fruit and carrot, generous chilli and garlic, sharp dried prawns and peanuts smothered in lemon juice and fish sauce; it boldly eschewed the insipid sweetness favoured in versions of this dish at lesser restaurants. The chef's special chicken was a gloriously rich and pungent medley of vegetables and shredded fowl. Nevertheless, you will still find popular favourites such as fried rice with king prawns and pineapple on the menu. And with most main dishes priced below £8, Esarn Kheaw is well worth a trip to Shepherd's Bush for the opportunity to sample such authentic Thai cooking.
Babies and children welcome: high chairs. Booking advisable. Takeaway service. **Map 20 B1**.

South West

Fulham

Blue Elephant

4-6 Fulham Broadway, SW6 1AA (7385 6595/ www.blueelephant.com). Fulham Broadway tube. **Lunch served** noon-2.30pm Mon-Fri; noon-3pm Sun. **Dinner served** 7-11.30pm Mon-Thur; 6.30-11.30pm Fri; 6-11.30 Sat; 6.30-10.30pm Sun. **Main courses** £10.60-£28. **Set meal** £33-£39 3-4 courses. **Set buffet** (lunch Sun) £25. **Credit** AmEx, DC, MC, V.

Can one Thai restaurant be all things to all people? The international chain Blue Elephant is certainly making a valiant attempt. After traipsing over bridges and ducking under hanging vines in the spectacular 'Disney goes oriental' jungle of a dining room, diners are offered a variety of enticing options: discounts on days when Chelsea FC has a home game; face-painting for children at Sunday brunch; and a £21 'herbal lunch' for the dieting set. However, the food is hit and miss. Cod stir-fried with chilli paste and herbs was served in a heavy batter that lacked crispness; it had been smothered in a bland sweet-and-sour sauce that was hardly worthy of the 'three-elephant' chilli warning stamped on the menu. Exotic fruits for dessert were sadly under-ripe. The Blue Elephant's theatrical surroundings make it a perennial favourite with moneyed locals, and the friendly staff were engaging on our visit – but the food seemed tired and predictable. We suggest you order carefully to avoid bland dishes.
Babies and children welcome: crayons; face painting (Sun); high chairs; nappy-changing facilities. Booking advisable. Disabled: toilet. Dress: smart casual; no shorts. Takeaway service; delivery service (over £30 within SW6). Vegetarian menu. **Map 13 B13**.

★ Saran Rom

Waterside Tower, The Boulevard, Imperial Wharf, Townmead Road, SW6 2UB (7751 3111/ www.saranrom.com). Fulham Broadway tube

Nahm. See p269.

Charuwan. See p276.

then 391, C3 bus. **Lunch served** noon-3pm, **dinner served** 6-11pm daily. **Main courses** £13-£19. **Set dinner** £35 per person (minimum 2) 3 courses. **Credit** AmEx, MC, V.

It would be easy to be prejudiced against Saran Rom, hidden as it is in a soulless modern complex along the Thames. Sure, the waterside view, which can be enjoyed alfresco, is attractive, but the restaurant is difficult to get to, and the dining room – all dark wood, elaborate chandeliers and high ceilings – seems the product of bizarre imaginings of a Thai gentlemen's club, and jars with the modern surroundings. Nevertheless, the awkward journey is worth it for some intriguing and well-executed dishes. Classics are confidently and attractively served: fish cakes were pleasantly springy; roast duck in a spicy coconut-milk soup was enlivened by shavings of fresh young coconut and galangal. A lemongrass-infused main dish of minced chicken excellently exhibited the bitter and

sour earthiness typical of northern Thailand. A perfectly tender sirloin steak crusted in pepper and sugar and served in a spicy sauce was a fine example of the kitchen's high-quality ingredients and confident cooking skills. The international wine list includes a Thai white. While not exactly oozing charm, this high-end branch of the Blue Elephant group has much to recommend it.
Babies and children welcome: high chairs. Disabled: lift; toilet. Separate rooms for parties, seating 8, 25, 35 and 110. Tables outdoors (28, riverside patio). Takeaway service. **Map 21 A2**.

Parsons Green

Sukho

855 Fulham Road, SW6 5HJ (7371 7600). Parsons Green tube. **Lunch served** noon-3pm, **dinner served** 6.30-11pm daily. **Main courses**

£9.95-£16.95. **Set lunch** £7.95 1 course, £10.95 2 courses. **Credit** AmEx, MC, V.

Sukho is an intimate, stylish and peaceful retreat from the bustle of London, offering friendly, bright service and aesthetically appealing and subtly flavoured food. The kitchen serves well-executed versions of classic Thai fare, including aromatic grilled pork pepped up with betel nut leaves; chilli-laden sirloin salad; and exquisite flower-shaped dumplings filled with sweet minced chicken and peanuts. A dish of excessively chewy fried squid rings was the only letdown. The overall skill of the kitchen and the quality of the ingredients shine in simple dishes like tender, flaky fried pork fillet flavoured with garlic, pepper and coriander. Alphonso mangoes elegantly splayed over savoury sticky rice with coconut milk, and deep-fried banana with vanilla ice-cream, made the perfect end to a meal. The wine list features some good rieslings that match well with the subtle food. Sukho is perhaps reflecting trends in its pricey neighbourhood, but £2.50 seems a rather inflated price for a meagre portion of steamed rice.
Babies and children admitted. Booking advisable. Takeaway service.
For branch see index.

Putney

Thai Square

Embankment, 2-4 Lower Richmond Road, SW15 1LB (8780 1811/www.thaisq.com). Putney Bridge tube/14, 22 bus.
Bar **Open/snacks served** noon-11pm Mon-Thur; noon-2am Fri, Sat; noon-10.30pm Sun.
Restaurant **Lunch served** noon-3pm daily. **Dinner served** 6.30-11pm Mon-Thur; 6pm-midnight Fri, Sat; 5.30-10.30pm Sun. **Main courses** £7.95-£23. **Set dinner** £35 per person (minimum 2) 3 courses, £40 per person (minimum 2) 4 courses. *Both* **Credit** AmEx, MC, V.

The ship-like copper and granite structure that surveys Putney Bridge from the west makes an architecturally impressive, if unlikely, venue for a branch of this above-average chain. Its two floors (bar downstairs, first-floor restaurant) are spacious, but there were precious few empty tables on our visit. No doubt the high-quality Thai cooking has something to do with that. An extensive menu of appetisers, curries, stir-fries and chef's specials makes choosing hard, but we were rewarded by our selection of 'royal Thai-style' dim sum (a mixture of chicken, prawn and vegetable steamed dumplings) and a superb seafood salad (squid, mussels, scallops and king prawns with glass noodles and a delicious hot-salty-sour dressing). 'Drunken duck' was an unfamiliar but successful stir-fry of Thai aubergine, sweet basil, chillies, bamboo shoots, lemongrass and Thai whisky. A prawn green curry was the only disappointment: far too sweet, the taste of palm sugar obscuring any piquancy or tang. We reckon there's more meat-free choices than any other Thai in town, too. Sweeping river views and efficient, smiling service boost Thai Square's appeal still further.
Babies and children welcome: high chairs. Bar available for hire. Booking advisable Fri, Sat. Disabled: lift; toilet. Takeaway service. Vegetarian menu.
For branches see index.

South East

Blackheath

★ Laicram

1 Blackheath Grove, SE3 0DD (8852 4710). Blackheath rail. **Lunch served** noon-2.30pm, **dinner served** 6-11pm Tue-Sun. **Main courses** £4.00-£13.90. **Credit** MC, V.

Down a side-street close to Blackheath station, Laicram is a great locals' haunt and perennially busy. It has an old-fashioned look with a wooden trellis decorated with fake plastic ivy and flowers; Thai royal family portraits take centre stage. Friendly service adds to the cosy feel. We loved the kitchen's classic spicy seafood tom yum, with salmon among the generous portion of seafood. Equally spicy tom kha gai had a typically aromatic coconut broth to take the edge off the specks of red chilli. Fresh spring rolls filled with pork and

The Thai Restaurant offers delicious food and 1st rate service in a stylish and relaxed atmosphere. The restaurant really does live up to it's reputation of serving some of the

'Best Thai Food in Town'.

Open:

Monday to Friday
11.30am - 3.30pm
6.30pm - 11.30pm

Saturday and Sunday
Open all day
11.30am - 11.30pm

www.thethai.co.uk

The Thai
Restaurant & Bar

Set Lunch £9.95 and £13.95

Private Function Room Available

The Thai Restaurant & Bar
93 Pelham Street,
Chelsea SW7 2NJ
Tel: 020 7584 4788

362 Old York Road,
Wandsworth, SW18
Tel: 020 8877 2725
Fax: 020 8877 2724

THAI THO
Restaurant

We look forward to serving you.

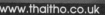
www.thaitho.co.uk

Tennis player Maria Sharapova described Thai Tho as her favourite restaurant during the Wimbledon Championships. Those who have eaten here and return time and time again would certainly agree.

Thai Tho is a stylish restaurant, serving some of the best Thai food outside of Thailand

The Staff are delightful, the food delicious. The ingredients are fresh, many are flown from Thailand each week. It is rare to find a restaurant of such quality at such reasonable prices.

Open : Lunch 11.30am - 3.30pm
Dinner 6.30pm - 11.30pm
Sunday : Open all day

Thai Tho, 20 High Street,
Wimbledon Village,
London SW19 5DX
Tel: 020 8946 1542 / 020 8296 9034

Menu

We've tried to give the most useful Thai food terms here, including variant spellings. However, these are no more than English transliterations of the original Thai script, and so are subject to considerable variation. Word divisions vary as well: thus, kwaitiew, kwai teo and guey teow are all acceptable spellings for noodles.

Thailand abandoned chopsticks in the 19th century in favour of chunky steel spoons and forks. Using your fingers is usually fine, and essential if you order satay sticks or spare ribs.

USEFUL TERMS

Khantoke: originally a north-eastern banquet conducted around a low table while seated on traditional triangular cushions – some restaurants have khantoke seating.
Khing: with ginger.
Op or ob: baked.
Pad, pat or phad: stir-fried.
Pet or ped: hot (spicy).
Prik: chilli.
Tod, tort, tord or taud: deep-fried.
Tom: boiled.

STARTERS

Khanom jeep or ka nom geeb: dim sum. Little dumplings of minced pork, bamboo shoots and water chestnuts, wrapped in an egg and rice (wun tun) pastry, then steamed.
Khanom pang na koong: prawn sesame toast.
Kratong thong: tiny crispy batter cups ('top hats') filled with mixed vegetables and/or minced meat.
Miang: savoury appetisers with a variety of constituents (mince, ginger, peanuts, roasted coconut, for instance), wrapped in betel leaves.
Popia or porpia: spring rolls.
Tod mun pla or tauk manpla: small fried fish cakes (should be lightly rubbery in consistency) with virtually no 'fishy' smell or taste.

SOUPS

Poh tak or tom yam potag: hot and sour mixed seafood soup.
Tom kha gai or gai tom kar: hot and sour chicken soup with coconut milk.
Tom yam or tom yum: a hot and sour soup, smelling of lemongrass. **Tom yam koong** is with prawns; **tom yam gai** with chicken; **tom yam hed** with mushrooms.

RICE

Khao, kow or khow: rice.
Khao nao: sticky rice.
Khao pat: fried rice.
Khao suay: steamed rice.
Pat khai: egg-fried rice.

SALADS

Laab or larb: minced and cooked meat incorporating lime juice and other ingredients like ground rice and herbs.
Som tam: a popular cold salad of grated green papaya.
Yam or yum: refers to any tossed salad, hot or cold, but it is often hot and sour,

flavoured with lemon and chilli. This type of yam is originally from the north-east of Thailand, where the Laotian influence is greatest.
Yam nua: hot and sour beef salad.
Yam talay: hot and sour seafood salad (served cold).

NOODLES

Generally speaking, noodles are eaten in greater quantities in the north of Thailand. There are many types of **kwaitiew** or **guey teow** noodles. Common ones include **sen mee:** rice vermicelli; **sen yai** (river rice noodles): a broad, flat, rice noodle; **sen lek:** a medium flat noodle, used to make pad Thai; **ba mee:** egg noodles; and **woon sen** (cellophane noodle): transparent vermicelli made from soy beans or other pulses. These are often prepared as stir-fries.

The names of the numerous noodle dishes depend on the combination of other ingredients. Common dishes are:
Khao soi: chicken curry soup with egg noodles; a Burmese/Thai dish, referred to as the national dish of Burma.
Mee krob or mee grob: sweet crispy fried vermicelli.
Pad si-ewe or cee eaw: noodles fried with mixed meat in soy sauce.
Pad Thai: stir-fried noodles with shrimps (or chicken and pork), beansprouts and salted turnips, garnished with ground peanuts.

CURRIES

Thai curries differ quite markedly from the Indian varieties. Thais cook them for a shorter time, and use thinner sauces. Flavours and ingredients are different too. There are several common types of curry paste; these are used to name the curry, with the principal ingredients listed thereafter.
Gaeng, kaeng or gang: the generic name for curry. Yellow curry is the mildest; green curry (**gaeng keaw wan** or **kiew warn**) is medium hot and uses green chillies; red curry (**gaeng pet**) is similar, but uses red chillies.
Jungle curry: often the hottest of the curries, made with red curry paste, bamboo shoots and just about anything else to hand, but no coconut cream.
Massaman or mussaman: also known as Muslim curry, because it originates from the area along the border with Malaysia where many Thais are Muslims. For this reason, pork is never used. It's a rich but mild concoction, with coconut, potato and some peanuts.
Penang, panaeng or panang: a dry, aromatic curry made with 'Penang' curry paste, coconut cream and holy basil.

FISH & SEAFOOD

Hoi: shellfish.
Hor mok talay or haw mog talay: steamed egg mousse with seafood.
Koong, goong or kung: prawns.
Maw: dried fish belly.

minced crab came with a tart tamarind sauce dotted with sesame seeds; the rolls were made with pancakes rather than rice wrappers so were slightly gloopy. A delicious Thai version of sweet and sour chicken was similar to the Chinese restaurant classic, but contained less sugar. The house-recommended roast duck red curry could have been spicier and less oily, while plump prawns stir-fried with garlic, ginger and soy sauce were just right. For afters, there are dessert trolley goodies and exotic fruits on offer.
Babies and children admitted. Booking essential Fri, Sat. Takeaway service. Vegetarian menu.

London Bridge & Borough

Kwan Thai

The Riverfront, Hay's Galleria, Tooley Street, SE1 2HD (7403 7373/www.kwanthairestaurant. co.uk). London Bridge tube/rail. **Lunch served** noon-3pm Mon-Fri. **Dinner served** 6-10.30pm Mon-Sat. **Main courses** £9.95-£15. **Set lunch** £7.95-£8.95 2 courses. **Set dinner** £21-£30 per person (minimum 2) 3 courses. **Credit** AmEx, DC, MC, V.
River views and shy waiting staff give Kwan Thai a certain charm, though the pastel decor peppered with Thai art is rather characterless. City types, tourists and passing trade make up the clientele; this is no destination restaurant, but the food is sound and location near London Bridge useful. Fried wun tuns toong tong ('golden bags' in Thai) were well-balanced: the soft filling of minced chicken and prawn encased by crunchy pastry. Tom yam goong was murky and would have benefited from more than just a smattering of button mushrooms and prawns, though the fragrant lemongrass broth was satisfying. Gaeng pet yang, a creamy red curry redolent of lychee, cut through the succulent duck, and was enhanced by sharp pea aubergines. A typical som tam (papaya salad) had the right tangy dressing and chilli kick, while the stir-fry pad graprow provided a luscious covering for prawns with its heady garlic-packed sweet soy sauce. Choose from sorbets, fruit in syrup, banana fritters and crêpes stuffed with pandan leaves for dessert (though we found the latter overly processed).
Babies and children welcome: high chairs. Booking advisable. Tables outdoors (40, riverside terrace). Takeaway service. Vegetarian menu. **Map 12 Q8.**

New Cross

★ Thailand

15 Lewisham Way, SE14 6PP (8691 4040). New Cross or New Cross Gate tube/rail. **Lunch served** noon-2.30pm Mon-Fri. **Dinner served** 5-11.30pm daily. **Main courses** £4.95-£10. **Set meal** (lunch, 5-7pm) £4.45 2 courses. **Credit** MC, V.
A buzzy no-frills eaterie, Thailand is nevertheless much loved by Goldsmiths students who come in droves for its lunchtime deals. The setting is plain: simple wooden tables adorned with plastic flowers, and mandalas hanging from the walls. The menu concentrates on dishes from the north of the country and over the border to Laos. All the staples are here – red, green, yellow, jungle and mussaman curries – but it's worth investigating the regional dishes. We started with bo la lot, tender bundles of chargrilled beef wrapped in pepper leaves, and a selection of hors d'oeuvres that included crisp prawn spring rolls, properly rubbery fish cake, tender chicken satay and Japanese-style tempura. Laotian duck breast cooked over charcoal and garnished with sesame paste hit the spot, as did laab neau e-san (the hot and sour minced beef salad from north-east Thailand).
Babies and children admitted. Booking essential Fri, Sat. Takeaway service; delivery service (over £10 within 3-mile radius). Vegetarian menu.

South Norwood

★ ★ Mantanah

2 Orton Building, Portland Road, SE25 4UD (8771 1148). Norwood Junction rail. **Lunch served** noon-3pm Sat, Sun. **Dinner served**

6-11pm Tue-Sun. **Main courses** £6.95-£13.95.
Set dinner £18 per person (minimum 2)
3 courses, £25 per person (minimum 2) 4 courses.
Set buffet (lunch Sun) £7.95. **Credit** AmEx,
DC, MC, V.

Mantanah revels in bold, contrasting and unmistakably authentic Thai flavours. Our wonderfully delicate glutinous steamed pork dumplings were accented with a well-orchestrated contrast of garlic and peanuts. Rings of deep-fried squid and king prawns arrived at table perfectly light. But the real culinary seduction came with the complex main dishes. A northern Thailand special made from top-quality chicken had an earthy depth and a freshness created by banana blossom, bamboo shoots, a spot of chilli and fresh herbs. The dish was typical of the restaurant's confident preparation of the characteristic bitter and 'off' flavours of north-eastern Thailand. A salad of lemongrass-infused shredded chicken was fiery with chilli. The menu lists dishes by geographical provenance making Mantanah a good place to try regional specialities. Don't be put off by the drab suburban surroundings, or the dining room's bright yellow walls – the food here is excellent and the service friendly and knowledgeable.
Babies and children admitted. Booking advisable. Takeaway service. Vegetarian menu.

North

Archway

Charuwan
110 Junction Road, N19 5LB (7263 1410).
Archway or Tufnell Park tube. **Lunch served**
noon-3pm Mon-Fri. **Dinner served** 6-11pm
daily. **Main courses** £4.95-£8.95. **Set dinner**
£18-£20 per person (minimum 2) 3 courses.
Credit AmEx, MC, V.

Few of London's Thai restaurants boast a decor as evocative as this popular local. Apart from the myriad ethnic trinkets and photographs adorning the walls, a huge wooden Lanna-style roof is suspended above the room. Service is also authentically Thai – calm, efficient and deferential. The cooking might not be the best in town, but it's reliable and economical and disappointments are few. Tod mun pla, the classic thai fish cakes, were spot on and served with a well-balanced sweet-sour chilli sauce. Salad of tender warm grilled pork and spring onions had a typically punchy, hot and tangy dressing. Mains include an extensive range of curries and stir-fries, plus assorted 'chef's specials'. Our very good lamb mussaman had a complex, spicy peanut sauce. Thai-style fried fish with chilli sauce was the weakest link: the fish was fresh, but the sauce was saccharine and unsubtle. Still, with prices that make it easy to return time and again, this kind of blip is easily overlooked.
Booking advisable. Children over 5yrs admitted. Takeaway service. Vegetarian menu.
Map 26 B2.

Islington

Isarn
119 Upper Street, N1 1QP (7424 5153).
Angel tube/Highbury & Islington tube/rail.
Lunch served noon-3pm, **dinner served**
6-11pm Mon-Fri. **Meals served** noon-11pm
Sat; noon-10.30pm Sun. **Main courses** £6.50-
£14.50. **Set lunch** £5.50 3 courses. **Credit**
AmEx, MC, V.

The bustling long narrow dining room of this Upper Street joint is often packed. Judging from our experience, the attraction has more to do with the location than the food. Isarn serves the usual Thai dishes, with a strong emphasis on the sweeter aspect of the cuisine. Starters sounded appealing. Betel nut leaves added a slightly bitter taste to shreds of overly sweet crispy duck and spring onion, but the pomelo accompanying the meat was too weak to stand up to the other strong flavours. Deep-fried soft-shell crab was greasy, though the dish was much enhanced by a refreshing mango salsa. To follow, a beef stir-fry with bamboo shoots and holy basil was a dull assembly, while mussels in yellow bean curry was too sweet a dish for our taste. Although Isarn's launch in 2005 garnered positive reviews, our subsequent visits have been disappointing more often than not.
Babies and children admitted. Tables outdoors (2, garden). Takeaway service.
Map 5 O1.

North West

Kensal

★ Tong Kanom Thai
833 Harrow Road, NW10 5NH (8964 5373).
Kensal Rise tube. **Lunch served** noon-3pm
Mon-Fri. **Dinner served** 6-10pm Mon-Sat.
Main courses £4.20-£6.50. **No credit cards**.
Kensal Rise is on to a good thing. The green sponge-painted walls, the photograph of the Thai king, and the old refrigerator in the corner (topped with a laughing Buddha), may make you feel like you've stumbled into a Thai granny's sitting room. But at Tong Kanom Thai you also get live (and loud) traditional music. The staff's friendly, casual manner, and the simple good flavours of the dishes add to the homely feel of this enticing spot. The menu contains some real gems and is excellent value. Chicken wrapped in pandan leaves was outstanding: the meat infused with lemongrass and steamed to fragrant perfection. Salad of beef with fresh herbs and spring onions showed signs of how prices are kept so low – the iceberg lettuce was a bit dull – but as the dish cost just £4.80, it's hard to complain. A red curry was hearty if not quite spicy enough. We preferred the fresh, flavourful stir-fried morning glory with garlic and chilli. Desserts are specials that change periodically – perhaps alphonso mangoes with sticky coconut rice. On the night of our visit, one local couple arrived with a bottle of champagne. With most dishes costing less than £5, it's quite possible to push the boat out in such a fashion.
Babies and children admitted. Takeaway service; delivery service (over £15 within 2-mile radius). Vegetarian menu.

Turkish

Realisation that Turkish food is one of the world's great cuisines is spreading across our city – as are high-quality Turkish restaurants. Harringay and Dalston in north and north-east London remain the two centres for this style of cooking, and are still the best places to find a wide choice of low-priced Turkish cafés and food shops (along with a mostly Turkish clientele), but in the past few years excellent restaurants have been opening far away from these heartlands. If there has been a trend in the past 12 months, it is for established restaurants to open new branches in affluent districts. Examples include **Pomegranate** (a Richmond branch of **19 Numara Bos Cirrik**), **Gem** (which has opened a branch in Clapham), **Haz** (with a new branch in the City), **İznik Kaftan** (a new Fulham Road branch of **İznik**) and **Kazan** (opening a second branch in the City). Sometimes these closely follow the formula of the original; sometimes they expand on it or aim for a new vibe, such as at İznik Kaftan; and sometimes the intended market is quite different, as is the case with Dalston's 19 Numara and its upmarket Richmond cousin, Pomegranate.

The objectionable habit of charging for pide is still practised by a few, mostly West End restaurants. It leads to the odd experience of ordering a meze such as houmous or cacik and having a waiter ask with a relatively straight face, 'Do you want bread with that?' on the grounds that a charge can't be levied without asking the customer. The nominal charge per person and money saved in not supplying refills can't justify messing about with a good Turkish tradition.

Central

Bloomsbury

Tas

22 Bloomsbury Street, WC1B 3QJ (7637 4555/ www.tasrestaurant.com). Holborn or Tottenham Court Road tube. **Meals served** noon-11.30pm Mon-Sat; noon-10.30pm Sun. **Main courses** £5.95-£14.45. **Set meal** £8.95 2 courses. **Set meze** £8.45-£9.95 per person (minimum 2). **Credit** AmEx, MC, V.

The corner site just by the British Museum allows plenty of light through the large windows of this branch of the Tas chain. There's also a spacious basement dining area and pavement tables. The restaurant was very busy on our visit, and service was blindingly fast. Dishes were brought to the table on enormous trays, accompanied by folding stands. A big portion of patlıcan salatası was a superior starter: very creamy and smoky aubergine, with fresh mint leaves. A main course of pirasali köfte featured minced lamb kebab on a bed of pan-fried leeks, with tomato; the combination worked well and wasn't over-flavoured. Other restaurants in the group are similar and have spread strategically around central London. Rebelling against a long Turkish tradition of combining simple flavours, Tas chefs prefer to blend intense flavours rather than risk blandness. This can occasionally lead them astray, but in general the inventiveness of the menu pays off.
Babies and children welcome: high chairs. Booking advisable Fri, Sat. Disabled: lift, toilet. Separate room for parties, seats 80. Tables outdoors (12, pavement). Takeaway service. **Map 18 D1.** **For branches (Tas, Tas Café, Tas Pide) see index.**

City

Haz

9 Cutler Street, E1 7DJ (7929 7923/ www.hazrestaurant.co.uk). Liverpool Street tube/rail. **Meals served** 11.30am-11.30pm daily. **Main courses** £7-£13. **Set meal** £9.25 2 courses, £18.95 3 courses incl coffee. **Set meze** £6.45. **Credit** AmEx, MC, V.

You're likely to have an interesting but odd dining experience here. Haz is anything but intimate – a smart canteen space serving rather good food to suits squeezed at long tables. The fittings are high quality but impersonal; the decor doesn't encourage folk to linger. A large number of staff float around, and cooks operate behind a counter at the side of the room, opposite the large windows. The menu is neither small nor conservative and the wine list is extensive. Our starter of muhamara paste had a pleasing texture and a walnut flavour, though surprisingly it appeared not to include the usual hot peppers. We also enjoyed a spicy and fresh ezme (crushed chillies with red onions and tomatoes). A main course of kuzu shish kebab was exceptionally tender, arriving with a small neat portion of rice and lightly steamed vegetables. Our other choice, hünkar beğendi, featured stewed lamb that fell apart pleasingly, though the mashed aubergine could have had a smokier flavour. Desserts include kayisi tatlisi (dried apricots stuffed with almond, pistachio and cream) and kazandibi (cinnamon-flavoured milk pudding). Haz gets busy and loud, but the quality of the cooking keeps tempting people back.
Babies and children welcome: high chair. Booking advisable Mon-Fri. Restaurant available for hire. Takeaway service. **Map 12 R6.** **For branch see index.**

Covent Garden

Sofra

36 Tavistock Street, WC2E 7PB (7240 3773/ www.sofra.co.uk). Covent Garden tube. **Meals served** noon-11pm daily. **Main courses** £6.95-£21.95. **Set meal** £9.95-£12.95 1 course incl drink. **Set meze** £9.95-£10.95. **Credit** AmEx, MC, V.

The Sofra chain has a formula for its four London restaurants: well-produced food and quick service. This relatively small branch is hidden in the small streets between Covent Garden and Aldwych. The long thin interior widens at the back, but tables still seem rather crowded together in the middle. Thick white tablecloths are offset by a scarlet wall, and metal vents snake across the ceiling. Incongruous as these are, the only jarring element was a painting of the crucifixion for sale on one wall. The traditional Turkish menu is augmented by steaks and vegetarian dishes, Turkish pizzas and a selection of daily specials. We started with a wonderful börek platter, the leek pastry having an outstanding mix of crisp and soft textures. Equally rich in texture was an exceptionally succulent portion of albanian liver. This was followed by a tender hünkar beğendi – stewed lamb on a bed of smoky mashed aubergine. We also sampled a nicely moist grilled sea bass that was beautifully orange in colour, accompanied by lightly steamed vegetables and mashed potato.
Babies and children welcome: children's portions; high chairs. Booking advisable. Separate room for parties, seats 80. Takeaway service. **For branches see index.** **Map 18 E4.**

Fitzrovia

★ Istanbul Meze

100 Cleveland Street, W1T 6NS (7387 0785/ www.istanbulmeze.co.uk). Great Portland Street or Warren Street tube. **Meals served** noon-11pm Mon-Sat. **Dinner served** 5-11pm Sun. **Main courses** £7-£12. **Set lunch** £8.90 2 courses incl coffee. **Set dinner** £11.90 2 courses. **Set meze** £20. **Credit** AmEx, MC, V.

It might be in the West End, but Istanbul Meze has the feel of a good local restaurant. Oblong kilim mats with rectangular patterns decorate the walls. Starters of grilled halloumi cheese and excellent sautéed albanian liver showed that there's no skimping on quality here, though it's a pity the chef still chooses to accompany meals with ordinary pitta rather than any of a range of pide breads. A main course of chicken beyti was lightly spiced and beautifully grilled, leaving the centre moist. It came with rice cooked in a typically Turkish way with slivers of vermicelli – tasty, but boiled a little too long for perfection. Et sote was a satisfying casserole, with sautéed lamb cubes and lots of tomato and green pepper. As is traditional in this restaurant, chilli sauce is brought to the table in a saucepan. On a busy Saturday night, a stream of young Turkish people made their way to an event in the basement; high-quality singing ensued. Istanbul Meze would be worth visiting for its relaxed atmosphere and warm welcome alone, but the high-quality food makes it doubly attractive.
Babies and children admitted. Booking essential weekends. Separate room for parties, seats 50. Tables outdoors (3, pavement). Takeaway service. Vegetarian menu. **Map 3 J4.**

Özer

5 Langham Place, W1B 3DG (7323 0505/ www.sofra.co.uk). Oxford Circus tube. *Bar* **Open** noon-11pm daily. *Restaurant* **Meals served** noon-midnight daily. **Main courses** £8.95-£23.95. **Set meze** £9.95 (lunch), £12.95 (dinner). *Both* **Credit** AmEx, MC, V.

Entering upmarket Özer you find yourself in a busy bar with low chairs. This offers a range of wine, spirits and beer, but is primarily an antechamber for the large restaurant behind. A scarlet wall dominates the dining area. Service is famously efficient, though businesslike rather than warm. The wine list ranges widely, as does the

Íznik Kaftan

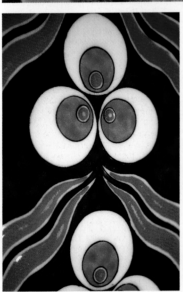

menu, which provides all the expected Turkish grills plus several less traditional creations. The food is excellent. Much thought goes into presentation; mixed meze were laid out in a neat grid pattern on the plate, with one small sample of each perfectly prepared morsel. A basket of good warm pide bread was filled as required. Next, tender grilled lamb chops were served with chips and broccoli, while an exceptional duck-breast salad came with green leaves and sharp, tangy berries. Özer is top dog in the Sofra restaurant group, and avoids the cramped feel common in some branches. We reckon it's the leading Turkish restaurant in the West End.
Babies and children welcome: children's menu; high chairs. Disabled: toilet. Tables outdoors (5, pavement). Takeaway service. **Map 9 H5**.

Marylebone

★ Ishtar
10-12 Crawford Street, W1U 6AZ (7224 2446/ www.ishtarrestaurant.com). Baker Street tube.
Meals served noon-11pm Mon-Thur, Sun; noon-11.30pm Fri, Sat. **Main courses** £7.95-£13.50. **Set lunch** (noon-6pm) £7.95. **Set meal** £17.95. **Set meze** £9.95. **Credit** MC, V.
Ishtar is a modern restaurant, with fancy twisting cutlery, big wine glasses and square plates. It has noisy wooden floors but classy, thick white tablecloths. Both the ground floor and the large basement are on stepped levels dominated by curves – such as the sinuous bar around the cooking area. A wide staircase sweeps downstairs, where there's music and belly dancing at weekends. The venue incorporates space for couples and for large groups. The food is fine too. Mixed meze included outstanding aubergine salad, houmous, cacik and kısır. It was served with high-quality pide bread. A main course of incik arrived with mashed potato and, more unusually, olives and a rich orange sauce. A succulent grilled biftek (sirloin steak) also came on a bed of mashed potato, with a little dish of salad. We rounded off our meal with exemplary baklava. A fine all-round performer, Ishtar is heartily recommended.
Babies and children welcome: high chairs. Booking advisable Thur-Sat. Entertainment: musicians Fri, Sat; belly dancer Fri, Sat. Separate room for parties, seats 120. Tables outdoors (6, pavement). Takeaway service. Vegetarian menu. **Map 2 F5**.

Pimlico

Kazan
93-94 Wilton Road, SW1V 1DW (7233 7100/ www.kazan-restaurant.com). Victoria tube/rail.
Meals served noon-11pm daily. **Main courses** £9.95-£17. **Set meal** (noon-6.30pm) £9.99-£14.95 2 courses. **Credit** MC, V.
Kazan's interior mixes modern trends, like large square plates, with traditional Anatolian and Middle Eastern artefacts including tagine dishes and hookah pipes. The atmosphere is upmarket, with a plentiful supply of staff floating about, and, on the night we visited, a slightly haughty head waiter. The menu offers a range of large mezes as well as starters and main courses, traditional and less usual dishes. We sampled the triangular börek, which had an outstanding texture both in the filo pastry and the filling. Also excellent were the sardines, wrapped in vine leaves and stuffed with pine nuts; dealing with the bones was slightly fiddly, but well worth the effort. Quality was maintained with a main course of parmak kebab, a subtly spiced köfte wrapped in slices of aubergine and then baked. Adana chicken was more typical of the food widely served in London Turkish restaurants and came with beautiful basmati rice. There's a good choice of alcoholic and non-alcoholic cocktails. The sense of luxury is also evident in the splendid toilets. No wonder Kazan is busy and has opened a second branch in the City.
Babies and children welcome: high chairs. Booking advisable dinner. Disabled: toilet. Entertainment: belly dancers; phone for details. Separate rooms for parties, seating 30 and 50. Tables outdoors (3, pavement). Takeaway service. **Map 15 J11**. **For branch see index.**

West
Notting Hill

Manzara

24 Pembridge Road, W11 3HL (7727 3062).
Notting Hill Gate tube. **Meals served** 8am-1am
Mon-Wed; 8am-3am Thur-Sat; 8am-11.30pm Sun.
Main courses £6.75-£9.95. **Credit** MC, V.
Though it could seat 30, the restaurant part of this
operation appears to be very much secondary to
the takeaway. Service was very slow on the night
we visited. Manzara prides itself on using organic
and GM-free ingredients, yet it can seem expensive
for a café, with a dish of houmous costing £4.35.
The interior looks a little worn too, though we
noticed that a fresh flower had been placed on each
table. You'll find a limited range of Turkish grills
here, but there is a good selection of vegetarian
dishes. The choice of pide is impressive, so it's a
shame that the kebabs are served with pitta. Lamb
beyti showed a laudable balance of meat, spice and
herb flavours, and the accompanying salad (of
green leaves and green pepper) was fine, though
the use of dressing was slightly unusual. As the
only establishment serving authentic Turkish food
for some distance, Manzara is well worth visiting.
Babies and children welcome: high chairs. Booking
advisable. Tables outside (2, pavement). Takeaway
service. **Map 7 A7**.

West Kensington

★ Best Mangal

104 North End Road, W14 9EX (7610 1050).
West Kensington tube. **Meals served** noon-
midnight Mon-Thur; noon-1am Fri, Sat. **Main**
courses £8.50-£17.50. **Set meal** £17 2 courses,
£19 3 courses, incl soft drink. **Credit** MC, V.
Primarily, Best Mangal is a very busy takeaway,
but squeezed behind all the carry-out kerfuffle is
a serviceable small restaurant, seating about 30 at
close-set tables with thick cloths. A painting on one
wall shows the magnificent Ottoman Blue Mosque,
but very obviously the work was inspired in 21st-
century Istanbul. It's a good sign that many of the
diners here are Turkish. Service on our last visit
was efficient and remarkably fast. Patlıcan esme
made an excellent starter: both smoky and creamy,
served with a basket of excellent pide and piping-
hot saç bread, which was replenished without us
having to ask. To follow, the yaprak döner kebab
that was placed before us showed the heights to
which this generally maligned dish can aspire. An
enormous pile of sliced meat was accompanied by
a large fresh salad containing finely sliced red
cabbage, carrot and lettuce. Desserts tend to be
high quality too, and in general portions are
generous. Best Mangal has built a deserved
reputation in this Turkish neighbourhood and is
continuing steadily along its chosen path.
Babies and children welcome: high chairs. Booking
advisable. Takeaway service. Vegetarian menu.
For branch see index.

South West
Chelsea

★ İznik Kaftan NEW

99-103 Fulham Road, SW3 6RH (7581 6699/
www.iznik.co.uk). South Kensington tube. **Meals**
served noon-midnight daily. **Main courses**
£12-£14.45. **Credit** AmEx, MC, V.
This elegant new restaurant has a small ground-
floor room and a more spacious basement. Fittings
are plush purple, with metallic blue-grey walls
and glass-screen partitions. A kaftan theme is
ubiquitous throughout the establishment. There
are photos of patterned kaftans on the walls and
a highly decorated kaftan framed over the stairs.
The restaurant is an offshoot of İznik (*see p283*),
an established family-run favourite in Islington,
but has gone for a very different look to the
original's relaxed clutter. Cut-glass, patterned wine
glasses give an exclusive feel that is emphasised
by the prices. The menu is relatively short, but
everything we tried was faultless. A starter of

patlıcan salata had just the right amount of smoky
flavour infused into the aubergine. Etli yaprak
sarma was excellent: dainty vine-leaf parcels
stuffed with ground lamb, bathed in yoghurt. İçli
köfte also came with a yoghurt sauce but the four
large pliant ovals of cracked wheat filled with
mince and flavoured with pine kernels gave the
dish a very different texture. Turkish restaurants
have suffered in upmarket locations in the past.
This one deserves to succeed.
Babies and children admitted. Booking advisable.
Separate room for parties, seats 80. Takeaway
service. **Map 14 E10**.

Earlsfield

★ Kazans

607-609 Garratt Lane, SW18 4SU (8739 0055/
www.kazans.com). Earlsfield rail/44, 77, 270 bus.
Dinner served 6-11pm Mon-Fri. **Meals served**
5-11pm Sat, Sun. **Main courses** £7.50-£14.95.
Credit AmEx, MC, V.
Not to be muddled with the Kazan chain (*see left*),
Kazans comprises a restaurant and adjacent bar.
In summer a couple of tables are placed on a
narrow platform outside. Within, the walls are
decorated with enlarged and fascinating family
photos from 1960s Turkey. We started our meal
with a mixed cold meze featuring enginar,
houmous, tarama, cacik and shaktuka (a creamy
fried aubergine, pepper and yoghurt dip). All were
excellent, and came with good pide. The portions
were big enough to make us fear we wouldn't
complete our main courses (belatedly we noticed
an alternative menu choice of just three meze:
tarama, houmous and cacik). The mains certainly
deserved saving space for. Alinazik was spicy
lamb on aubergine and yoghurt. From the specials
board, a delicious rack of lamb came with gratin
potato, rocket and caramelised onions; the only
problem was cutting through the bones without
tipping the food off the plate. Baklava, ice-cream
and chocolate cake are available to those who want
dessert. In south London you have to go a long way
to find a Turkish restaurant of this standard.
Babies and children welcome: high chairs. Booking
advisable weekends. Disabled: toilet. Separate
rooms for parties, seating 30 and 50. Tables
outdoors (4, decking). Takeaway service.

South
Waterloo

Troia

3F Belvedere Road, SE1 7GQ (7633 9309).
Waterloo tube/rail. **Meals served** noon-midnight
Mon-Sat; noon-10.30pm Sun. **Main courses**
£8.25-£12.95. **Set lunch** £8.75 2 courses. **Set**
meze £9.80 per person (minimum 2). **Credit**
AmEx, MC, V.
There's a somewhat playful atmosphere in Troia
('Troy' in Turkish). A large framed copy of an
Ancient Greek relief shows the Trojan horse, with
warriors looking out of windows in its side as if
riding a bus to work. The restaurant's walls are
bright red and yellow. Two spiral 'chandeliers'
made from collections of coloured Turkish
lanterns dominate the ceiling. Despite all this, the
busy dining room isn't garish. Many of the
customers are tourists, yet this isn't used as an
excuse to make the food inauthentic. The menu
may not be extensive, but it isn't restricted to basic
mezes and grills. A starter of zeytinyağlı bakla
(broad beans with yoghurt) had a light, clean taste
that worked well alongside our mantar izgara
(spicy grilled mushrooms). A main course of incik,
lamb melting off the bone, came with potatoes and
baby sweetcorn. The chicken breast featured in
kuskonmazlı tavuk had been spiced before grilling
and was laid on asparagus spears with lightly
steamed vegetables. Service was unhurried and
chatty. This fine restaurant seems to be thriving,
despite being slightly lost in the space between
Waterloo and the London Eye.
Babies and children welcome: children's menu;
high chairs. Booking advisable. Disabled: toilet.
Tables outdoors (14, pavement). Takeaway
service. Vegetarian menu. **Map 10 M9**.

Interview
ADEM ONER

Who are you?
Founder and director of **İznik** (*see*
p283) and **İznik Kaftan** (*see left*).
What's the best thing about running
a restaurant in London?
London is the centre stage when it
comes to bringing new experiences
to diners. It's a vibrant place. People
want to enjoy themselves; they're
foodies and love trying different
things. I love sharing my culture
and heritage through our cuisine.
What's the worst thing?
Bringing chefs over from Turkey is
a nightmare due to work permit
bureaucracy. The long-term solution
is more investment in training, but in
the short-term it is a big problem.
Which are your favourite London
restaurants?
Eating at **Hakkasan** (*see p75*) is
an experience – they have the food,
service and ambience spot on.
Busaba Eathai (*see p269*) is one
chain that is getting things right.
How green are you?
As we have witnessed over the last
18 months, green issues, thankfully,
appear to be here to stay. Businesses
are having to adapt or they risk falling
foul of ever-increasing customer
expectations. This can only be a good
thing. Where possible, we source
ingredients from local producers. This
is quite hard in some instances; for
example, our cuisine uses a lot of
aubergine, which invariably comes
from abroad. There are plenty of easy
ways to improve too, and we are
focusing on these. We've stopped
selling our very popular bottled
Turkish water in favour of Welsh
mineral water, and we buy from
smaller companies so that the money
goes back directly into a community.
What is missing from London's
restaurant scene?
London desperately needs more
choices when it comes to eating
quality food 24 hours a day.

RESTAURANTS

"Our main courses were both excellent. We shared a perfectly tender 'oven cooked lamb', served on a bed of very smoky grilled aubergine and cheese puree, and a stew like mixed seafood broth"

"It isn't what you'd expect from a traditional Turkish restaurant... it has many adventurous dishes, even oriental ingredients."

"It's beautifully run, thoroughly professional and the inventive modern Turkish food is delicious. imaginative and keenly priced"
- *Time Out Eating & Drinking Guide*

"A simple formula well executed is the consensus on this vibrant Turkish spot in Waterloo that's something of a jewel, with friendly staff serving interesting cooking (including a great vegetarian selection) at reasonable prices. Best of all, despite being very popular, it manages to keep it's feet on the ground"
- *Zagat Survey*

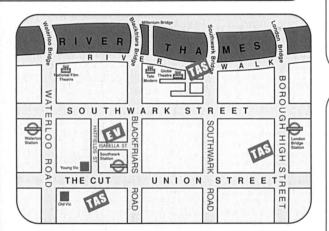

EV Restaurant/Bar/Delicatessen

97/98 Isabella Street
London SE1 8DA

Tel: 020 7620 6191
020 7620 6192
Fax: 020 7620 6193

Tas Restaurant
72 Borough High Street,
SE1 1XF

Tel : 020 7403 7200
Tel : 020 7403 7277
Fax : 020 7403 7022

Tas Restaurant
22 Bloomsbury
WC1 B 3QJ

Tel : 020 7637 4555
Tel : 020 7637 1333
Fax : 020 7637 2226

Tas Café
76 Borough High Street
SE1 1QF

Tel : 020 7403 8557
Fax : 020 7403 8559

Tas Restaurant
33 The Cut, Waterloo
SE1 8LF

Tel : 020 7928 1444
Tel : 020 7928 2111
Fax : 020 7633 9686

Tas Restaurant
37 Farringdon Road
EC1M 3JB

Tel : 020 7430 9721
Tel : 020 7430 9722
Fax : 020 7430 9723

Tas Pide
20-22 New Globe Walk
SE1 9DR

Tel : 020 7928 3300
Tel : 020 7633 977
Fax : 020 7261 1166

South East

Dulwich

Hisar NEW

51 Lordship Lane, SE22 8EP (8299 2948). East Dulwich rail. **Meals served** *Takeaway* noon-midnight daily. *Restaurant* 4pm-midnight daily. **Main courses** £4.95-£10. **Set meze** £14.95 per person (minimum 2). **Credit** MC, V.

Order well and the food at this solid local restaurant can be very good. There's a double glass frontage to the premises, with a takeaway at one entrance. The long cream interior has tiled flooring, uncovered tables, and a bar and ocakbaşı grill down one side; it seats about 60. We started with enormous and flavour-packed tiger prawns in a rich, spicy tomato sauce, along with a portion of mushrooms cooked in white wine – both were excellent. The accompanying pitta bread was warm, but singed at the edges where it had been on the grill a little too long. Grills arrive with a green salad and are served with a choice of bulgur wheat or chips. The enjoyable, slightly gamey taste of bıldırcın made it worth our efforts to take apart the two quails. Altı ezmeli, presented in a metal dish (with a very hot lid), consisted of a luscious tomato sauce covering sizeable chunks of lamb. Hisar is a popular spot in Dulwich and deserves a visit if you're in the district.
Babies and children welcome: high chairs. Separate room for parties, seats 10. Tables outdoors (4, terrace). Vegetarian menu. **Map 23 E4.**

Lewisham

★ Meze Mangal

245 Lewisham Way, SE4 1XF (8694 8099). St John's rail/Lewisham rail/DLR. **Meals served** noon-1am Mon-Thur; noon-2am Fri, Sat; noon-midnight Sun. **Set meze** £4 per person (minimum 4), £5.50 per person (minimum 2). **Credit** MC, V.

Although it is set in the middle of an unusually dilapidated parade, this doesn't seem to put off punters and Meze Mangal remains a popular local destination. Once inside, dining is a very pleasant experience. The restaurant is often busy, full of locals plus staff and students from the college across the road. Pride of place goes to the authentic, traditional ocakbaşı grill, which is responsible for the scorch marks on the floor from falling cinders. The core of the menu is a standard set of Turkish grills, which is not a problem in an area with no other decent source for such food. Meze Mangal also offers vegetarian dishes, a hearty moussaka and a range of Turkish pizzas. We tried a very filling sucuklu yumurtali peynirli pide – a boat-shaped pizza with spicy sausage, egg, cheese and shredded salad. A tasty, well-formed beyti was served with a large salad, but no rice. Still, we cared not, as there was a plentiful supply of good pide to accompany the meal.
Babies and children welcome: high chair. Booking advisable; essential Fri, Sat. Takeaway service. Vegetarian menu.

East

Brick Lane

★ Maedah Grill NEW

42 Fieldgate Street, E1 1ES (7377 0649/ www.maedahgrill.net). Aldgate East tube. **Meals served** noon-11pm daily. **Main courses** £5.95-£16.95. **Set meal** £15-£20 3 courses. **Unlicensed. Credit** AmEx, MC, V.

In the area near Brick Lane, in the heart of London's Bengali community, an interesting new Turkish restaurant has opened. It produces fine Turkish food, but is slanted more to local Bengalis – which is not to say that anyone else is made less welcome. As well as Turkish grills, and steaks, the menu includes shawarma (grilled slices of marinated meat), vegetarian dishes, Turkish pizzas and a range of stews. As with many Turkish restaurants the meat is halal. More unusually, there's a strict no-alcohol policy. The topping on our starter of lahmacun was pleasingly fresh,

including pine kernels in the minced lamb paste. Çöp şiş was a good portion of yielding lamb cubes with nicely cooked rice and green salad. The space here is well used, with a real sense of design. A sheet of glass tops each dark wooden table, with tiny patterned carpets underneath. There are several traditional private booths for modest family eating. The dining area is surrounded by patterned glass in round frames. Doors too are round and the takeaway section is unobtrusive.
Babies and children welcome: high chairs. Booking essential Fri, Sat. Separate rooms for parties, seating 6-20. Takeaway service.

Docklands

Mez

571 Manchester Road, E14 3NZ (7005 0421/ www.mezrestaurant.com). South Quay DLR. **Meals served** noon-midnight daily. **Main courses** £8.95-£12.45. **Set meze** (noon-3pm) £7.45; £9.45 per person (minimum 2). **Credit** MC, V.

The location of Mez is perhaps a little odd for an upmarket restaurant: on the Isle of Dogs, straddling the financial area and the surrounding estates. It boasts big windows running the length of the dining area, but the view is primarily of the housing estate across the road. The decor is pastel, the walls painted with images from Middle Eastern empires. Presentation is very important here. Diners sit at round heavy wooden tables on which large cloth napkins are neatly folded. We were each served an individual pide. Peynirli börek (three pastries with a cheese and parsley filling) were fine, and came with a small dressed salad. To follow, iskender arrived in a pleasingly old-fashioned metal dish with lid, which held slivers of döner and slices of köfte neatly stacked around bread and thick yoghurt. Rice and vegetables can be ordered as side dishes – by no means typical at Turkish restaurants – and overall the food was superb. While we were eating, a belly dancer appeared unannounced, skilfully swinging a sword between the tables. Mez deserves to prosper.
Babies and children welcome: high chairs. Booking advisable. Separate room for parties, seats 100. Takeaway service. Vegetarian menu. **Map 24 C3.**

North East

Between roughly Dalston Kingsland station and Stoke Newington Church Street, you are in the Turkish and Kurdish heart of Hackney. The food available on this strip is more authentic and varied than anywhere else in London. Restaurants, cafés, takeaways, pâtisseries and grocers are constantly appearing and disappearing around a few more permanent landmarks. There's a constant race to provide different services and dishes. As well as the restaurants reviewed in full below, the following would each merit their own write-up if they were anywhere else in London: **Aziziye** (117-119 Stoke Newington Road), an alcohol-free eaterie beneath the tiled mosque; **Café Z Bar** (58 Stoke Newington Road); **Dem** (18 Stoke Newington High Street); **Dervish Bistro** (15 Stoke Newington Church Street); **Evin** (115 Kingsland High Street); **Hasan** (14 Stoke Newington Road); **Istanbul Iskembecisi** (9 Stoke Newington Road); **Sölen** (84 Stoke Newington High Street); **Şhomine** (131 Kingsland High Street); **Tava** (17 Stoke Newington Road); and **Testi** (36 Stoke Newington High Street).

Dalston

★ ★ 19 Numara Bos Cirrik

34 Stoke Newington Road, N16 7XJ (7249 0400). Dalston Kingsland rail/76, 149, 243 bus. **Meals served** noon-midnight daily. **Main courses** £7.50-£10.50. **Unlicensed. Corkage** £5. **Credit** MC, V.

This popular little restaurant, set on the busy main drag, needs to get its door fixed so it stops swinging open – but there isn't much else to criticise here. Izgara soğan, grilled onion with pomegranate sauce, is served as a complimentary starter and remains a house speciality. A plate of onion with chilli also appeared soon after we arrived, and a salad. There's a perfectly decent range of meze available in addition to these dishes, should you be ravenous. Reliefs depicting ancient Mediterranean empires decorate the walls. The small interior was very crowded on our visit, populated by fans of the exceptional grills. The outstanding adana kebab with fresh spices, sumac and cumin, shows what all the fuss is about. Cirrik's success has led to the opening of a number of branches, but this original remains our favourite. Just occasionally dishes have been less than 100% perfect and it's possible that the business may be spreading itself a little thinly, but everything was fine on this visit.
Babies and children admitted. Booking advisable. Separate room for parties, seats 40. Takeaway service. **Map 25 C4.**
For branches see index.

★ Mangal II

4 Stoke Newington Road, N16 8BH (7254 7888/ www.mangal2.com). Dalston Kingsland rail/ 76, 149, 243 bus. **Meals served** noon-1am daily. **Main courses** £7-£12. **Set meal** £16.25 3 courses (minimum 2). **No credit cards.**

A bustling crowd fills Mangal II most evenings, making it one of the most popular Turkish restaurants on a strip that has many. Families like to come here for Sunday lunch. The walls are bright pink and have been decorated with framed prints; white tablecloths are topped with practical blue covers. We were served good bread, which arrived in plastic bowls. For starters böreği were enjoyable, but the filo pastry triangles were a little overdone, with the cheese melting. No complaints, though, about the meltingly tender böbrek (lambs' kidneys). Next, the plump tasty little quails that make up Bıldırcın were accompanied by a well-constructed mixed salad. Iskender came with lots of yoghurt; its sauce was an unusually dark brown and (in a pleasing modification to the traditional recipe) contained mushrooms and other vegetables. The fresh chilli sauce was undeniably hot. To finish, we suggest deviating from the ubiquitous baklava and sampling tulumba (pastry with cream, pistachios and syrup), keskul (milk pudding with ground almonds, pistachios and cinnamon), or firin sutlac (rice pudding). Despite the full house, the atmosphere remains remarkably relaxed.
Babies and children welcome: high chairs. Booking essential weekends. Takeaway service. **Map 25 C4.**

★ ★ Mangal Ocakbaşı

10 Arcola Street, E8 2DJ (7275 8981/ www.mangal1.com). Dalston Kingsland rail/67, 76, 149, 243 bus. **Meals served** noon-midnight daily. **Main courses** £7-£13. **Unlicensed. Corkage** no charge. **No credit cards.**

With its legendary reputation for grills, Mangal doesn't bother with frills. It has started producing a takeaway menu, but diners are asked to choose from the long list of kebabs above the counter before taking their seats (this can occasionally mean queuing). The interior is long, dominated on one side by the counter and the ocakbaşı grill. Tiled walls feature traditional kilim mats preserved in frames of various dimensions. The functional tables have plain wooden tops and metal legs, like old school desks. More starters are now available, including lahmacun, houmous and cacik. That's all to the good, but it's the grills that have earned Mangal a hallowed status – and they're worthy of it. A long lamb beyti hung off the edges of our plate and came with chopped leaf salad and bread (both thick fresh pide and fine saç bread). Fresh herbs and spices could clearly be seen and tasted in the minced lamb after it had been sliced: excellent. The slow evolution of Mangal is commendable, but don't expect the chefs to stray too far from the grill. Nor should they.
Babies and children admitted. Booking essential weekends. Takeaway service. **Map 25 C4.**

Newington Green

★ Sariyer Balik

56 Green Lanes, N16 9NH (7275 7681).
Manor House tube then 141, 341 bus/73 bus.
Meals served 5pm-1am daily. **Main courses**
£6.50-£10. **No credit cards.**
A recent refit has done nothing to change the
essential character of Sariyer Balik, which centres
on the provision of perfect grilled fish. There's a
new sign outside and the interior is a little brighter,
though no less cosy. The tiny dining area now sports
a revised collection of clutter, including oars,
paintings of boats and an exquisite wooden fish
relief. There's more seating in the basement. The
cooking is faultless. Our mixed hot starter included
kalamar marinated in vodka, battered mussels in
beer, and prawns in spicy tomato sauce – all the
starters are available separately too. The restaurant
is dependent on what fish can be sourced fresh on
any given day, so often not everything on the menu
is available, but Sariyer Balik has always relied on
quality rather than range. Our sea bass melted in
the mouth. Steamed anchovies with shards of
carrot, onion and potato were also excellent. Fans
will be pleased to hear that the surreal dried fish
with babies' dummies in their mouths remain,
dangling in nets from the ceiling.
Babies and children welcome: high chairs. Booking
advisable. Separate rooms for parties, seating 30
and 40. Takeaway service. **Map 25 A3.**

North

Finchley

The Ottomans

118 Ballards Lane, N3 2DN (8349 9968/
www.theottomans.co.uk). Finchley Central tube.
Meals served noon-11pm daily. **Main courses**
£5.90-£12.50. **Set lunch** £6.95 2 courses.
Set dinner £14.50-£15.90 3 courses incl coffee.
Credit MC, V.
An enormous mural of Ottoman boating scenes
dominates one wall of this relaxed dining
establishment. Slowly but surely the number of
other decorations and small paintings has been
increasing. Generic café food is served as well as
Turkish meals, and this includes reasonable lunch
deals. The quality of the meze dishes is notable;

houmous kavurma (large chunks of diced fried
lamb in a nest of fresh houmous) was brilliant, as
were large rings of kalamar in a very light batter.
Main courses kept the standard high. Tender
külbastı came with good basmati rice. Adana was
well-spiced and fairly burst with the lively flavour
of fresh herbs. The range of Turkish desserts strays
well beyond baklava to include armut tatlısı
(poached pears, here served with pistachios). Staff
are exceptionally friendly and helpful. This
popular stop for locals is still the best of a
promising clutch of Turkish eateries in the vicinity.
Babies and children welcome: children's portions;
high chairs. Booking essential weekends.
Takeaway service. Vegetarian menu.

Finsbury Park

Petek

96 Stroud Green Road, N4 3EN (7619 3933).
Finsbury Park tube/rail. **Meals served** noon-
midnight daily. **Main courses** £6.45-£14.85.
Set meal £6.85 2 courses. **Set meze** £6.45-£9.85
per person (minimum 2). **Credit** AmEx, MC, V.
The lights at Petek are dim and the atmosphere
favours couples taking an evening out. The
furniture is made of solid wood, and a vase on each
table holds a bamboo shoot. Prints of old Istanbul
decorate the walls. Look up and you'll see lanterns
clustered under the ceiling. The food is excellent
and varied. Little details are never forgotten: like
the warm bread and beautiful olives that were
brought as we browsed the menu. There's a
growing number of fish dishes listed here. A main
course of Petek köfte consisted of four very large
mince patties with thick yoghurt, a dressed salad
and superb rice. The portion was enormous.
Despite being busy, staff were welcoming and took
an interest in our needs. Into its second year of
trading, Petek is already a popular restaurant
that's building a strong local reputation.
Babies and children welcome: high chairs. Booking
advisable. Tables outdoors (2, pavement).
Takeaway service.

★ Yildiz

163 Blackstock Road, N4 2JS (7354 3899/
www.yildizocakbasi.co.uk). Arsenal tube. **Meals**
served noon-midnight daily. **Main courses**
£7.50-£12.50. **Set lunch** £7.50 2 courses incl
soft drink. **Credit** MC, V.

You'll find Yildiz a little away from the main drag
of Finsbury Park, amid a parade of restaurants.
The place has been recently redecorated, and now
has cream walls dotted with decorative plates and
small pictures. The menu contains an enticing
selection of mezes or starters, but as the restaurant
follows the current trend of serving a range of side
dishes in addition to the main course, these will be
unnecessary unless you have the heartiest of
appetites. Our mains were accompanied by extra
grilled onion with pomegranate sauce, chilli onion,
and a terrific salad including sliced gherkin.
Excellent quail came with rice cooked just so, with
slivers of vermicelli – a typical Turkish addition.
Iskender kebab was very tasty too. Vegetarians
have a choice of five mains served with rice, salad
and bread; desserts are limited to baklava and ice-
cream. Swift, unobtrusive staff added to our
enjoyment. All round, the refit has led to an
improvement in what was already a solid local.
Babies and children welcome: high chair.
Takeaway service.

Haringay

With some 20 cafés and restaurants along
the strip, Harringay Green Lanes offers the
most intense concentration of Turkish food
in London. It also features a wide range of
Turkish grocers, pâtisseries, greengrocers
and butchers. The restaurants may lack the
variety of the cluster round Dalston and
Stoke Newington in Hackney, but many of
the ocakbaşı grill cafés are well worth a
visit. Few are licensed for alcohol, but most
will let you bring your own. The menu rarely
strays from the standard grills, guveç and
pide (both bread and pizza), but the food is
high quality, fresh and very cheap.
   The following is a selection of some of
the better choices: **Bingol** (551 Green
Lanes); **Diyarbakir** (69 Grand Parade);
Gaziantep (52 Grand Parade); **Gökyüzü** (27
Grand Parade); **Harran** (399 Green Lanes);
Mangal (443 Green Lanes); **Öz Sofra** (421
Green Lanes); **Tara** (6 Grand Parade), which
has a more Middle Eastern feel; and **Yayla**
(429 Green Lanes).

Mez. See p281.

Selale NEW

2 Salisbury Promenade, Green Lanes, N8 0RX (8800 1636). Turnpike Lane tube/Harringay Green Lanes rail/29, 141 bus. **Open** 6am-2am daily. **Main courses** £5.50-£9.50. **No credit cards.**
This stretch of Green Lanes is solid with Turkish cafés, almost all following a similar pattern. They serve filling daily stews, standard grills, soups and pideler (Turkish pizzas). Everything is freshly prepared, usually in front of the diner. Selale stands out in having a small fountain inside and a covered, fenced-off area on the wide pavement outside with a few more tables. Our pide was of a high standard (the lahmacun is notable here too), but the music on the CD player oozed cheese. Halep in a thick sauce was energetic rather than subtle. Water features aside, these cafés survive on the authentic freshness of their food rather than on any claim to originality, but several thrive on this basis and are worth a visit. The atmosphere at Selale was relaxed and the staff friendly, overcoming an initial confusion over the order.
Babies and children welcome: high chairs. Tables outdoors (4, pavement). Takeaway service.

Harringay

★ Antepliler

46 Grand Parade, Green Lanes, N4 1AG (8802 5588). Manor House tube/29 bus. **Meals served** noon-11.30pm daily. **Main courses** £6-£9.50. **Credit** AmEx, MC, V.
Still the only real restaurant on a street famed for its Turkish cafés, Antepliler stays enormously popular by having a more adventurous menu than any of its neighbours. The cooking is always hearty and vigorous, the clientele mostly Turkish. Chairs have unusually low backs, giving a slightly Ottoman feel to the interior. A line of tiles decorated with complex patterns marches along the wall. Some 70 people can be seated in the noisy and often hectic interior, which is made to appear larger thanks to some large mirrors. The high ceiling is patterned in wood. A starter of fıstık lahmacun set the pace for our meal, smaller than lahmacun offered elsewhere, but with a more powerful flavour, dominated by pistachio. Soğon kebab was served in a hot metal dish – meatballs with shallots grilled unskinned, and pomegranate sauce. It was accompanied by fine pide and a side plate of salad. Staff were helpful, though there simply wasn't enough of them for such a busy venue. Next door is the related pâtisserie that gives the restaurant its name (which means pâtisserie).
Babies and children welcome: high chairs. Takeaway service.

Highbury

İznik

19 Highbury Park, N5 1QJ (7354 5697/ www.iznik.co.uk). Highbury & Islington tube/rail/ 4, 19, 236 bus. **Lunch served** noon-3.30pm Mon-Fri; 11am-4pm Sat, Sun. **Dinner served** 6-11pm daily. **Main courses** £7.50-£12.50. **Credit** MC, V.
A chain mail surcoat and helmet hang just inside İznik's door, preparing visitors for an interior full of fascinating clutter. The restaurant has built a strong reputation through concentrating on Ottoman stews and baked dishes, instead of the grills more commonly found in London. Staff have started serving good pide, but now add a separate charge for the bread. Our mixed meze was first rate and included patasea köftesi (lightly textured potato balls), small triangular meat börek with an interesting dusty pastry texture, houmous, tarator and fried courgette patties. After this excellence, we were surprised the karni yarik was rather bland: never previously a problem here. The rice was slightly overcooked too. Fortunately the grilled chicken İznik was up to the standards we expect. It came with a separate dressed salad featuring lettuce, olives and pomegranate seeds. İznik has recently opened another branch across town (*see p279*). We hope this doesn't mean compromising the high standards of the original.
Babies and children welcome: high chairs. Booking advisable; essential weekends. Takeaway service.

Islington

Bavo

105-107 Southgate Road, N1 3JS (7226 0334/ www.bavo-restaurant.co.uk). Essex Road rail/ 76, 141, 271 bus. **Meals served** noon-11pm daily. **Main courses** £9.50-£16.50. **Set meal** £18 per person (minimum 2) 4 courses. **Credit** MC, V.
Flame-coloured flowers warm Bavo's light, spacious interior. Much of the rest of the decor is in muted greens, though seats at the pleasantly spread-out tables are white and wide. We ordered the mixed meze which displayed many of the restaurant's strengths. It included a faultless selection of houmous, kısır, dolma and sigara börek – each bursting with fresh flavours and each complementing the others. The accompanying pide bread was wonderful too. Next, külbastı was seasoned with just the right amount of oregano. It arrived with a scoop of fine basmati rice, pide bread and a tossed green salad. Our other main course, kléftico, was so tender it dissolved in the mouth; the dish came with a thick sauce, including vegetables. Service was very enthusiastic and helpful, yet staff were slightly too keen in encouraging us to add an extra course or drink. The evening would have been more relaxed had they backed off a bit. That quibble aside, Bavo is a fine restaurant and deserves success.
Babies and children welcome: high chairs. Booking essential weekends. Disabled: toilet. Tables outdoors (4, pavement). Takeaway service.

Gallipoli Again

120 Upper Street, N1 1QP (7359 1578/ www.cafegallipoli.com). Angel tube. **Meals served** noon-11pm Mon-Thur; noon-midnight Fri; 10.30am-midnight Sat; 10.30am-11pm Sun. **Main courses** £6.50-£10. **Set lunch** £12.95 3 courses. **Set dinner** £15.95 3 courses incl coffee. **Set meze** £8.95 lunch, £10.95 dinner. **Credit** MC, V.
Three Gallipoli restaurants are scattered along a hundred yards of Upper Street, and are undoubtedly the most popular Turkish restaurants in Islington. The bill of fare in the first two is identical, but Gallipoli Bazaar also serves Moroccan food. The long, narrow Gallipoli Again is always lively. Aim to sit near the front or out on the pavement rather than towards the back, where it is darker and everyone seems to be crushed together. The very efficient staff wear black; some have the restaurant's name in silver lettering on their T-shirts. For starters, a plate of two meat börek was merely acceptable; the parcels were of good filo pastry, but the filling was unimaginative and bland. To follow, a shish kebab was fine: six large cubes of lamb served with basmati rice, fresh chilli sauce and a dressed green salad. The Gallipoli restaurants retain their popularity with a young crowd; perhaps that's why they haven't felt the need to make their food as consistently first-rate as some other Turkish establishments in the area.

Babies and children welcome: high chairs. Booking advisable. Tables outdoors (6, garden; 5, pavement). Takeaway service. Map 5 O1.
For branches see index.

Gem

265 Upper Street, N1 2UQ (7359 0405/ www.gemrestaurant.org.uk). Angel tube/Highbury & Islington tube/rail. **Meals served** noon-midnight Mon-Sat; noon-10.30pm Sun. **Main courses** £6.95-£9.95. **Set lunch** £6.95 3 courses, £8.95 4 courses. **Set dinner** £9.95 3 courses, £12.95 4 courses, £24.95 5 courses incl house wine or beer. **Credit** MC, V.

This Kurdish restaurant is less pretentious than much of the competition on Upper Street and remains popular. The decoration is agricultural, with authentic Kurdish farm implements suspended from walls and ceiling. Our small portion of complimentary stuffed qatme bread was as outstanding as ever. Starters of moist mücver courgette fritters were tasty, if slightly oily. Kısır was good, but lacked the piquant freshness that we've previously relished here. In contrast, a main course of bıldırcın was above reproach: wonderfully tender and flavoursome grilled quail with a fresh chopped salad. Patlıcan kebab was enjoyable too, if slightly bland. There are six vegetarian main courses, most based on aubergine. A small portion of honeyed baklava with ice-cream made the ideal finish. Gem's local vibe and attentive service are to be cherished, but the cooking this time wasn't as consistently excellent

as it has been on previous visits. The restaurant's generally deserved success, however, has led to it opening a second branch (which has a more contemporary decor) near Clapham Common. Babies and children admitted: high chairs. Booking advisable. Separate room for parties, seats 100. Takeaway service. Vegetarian menu. Map 5 O1.
For branch see index.

★ Pasha

301 Upper Street, N1 2TU (7226 1454/ www.pasharestaurant.co.uk). Angel tube/Highbury & Islington tube/rail. **Meals served** 11am-11.30pm Mon-Sat; 11am-11pm Sun. **Main courses** £7.95-£14.95. **Set meal** £16.95 2 courses, £19.95 3 courses. **Credit** AmEx, MC, V.

Last year Pasha changed its generally traditional look to a slicker, more modern style befitting the Angel location. Rich dark greys and low lighting are now the order of the day, enlivened by cream walls, bright cushions and sections of red and gold textured wallpaper. Wooden flooring and a lack of tablecloths can make the interior noisy. Our meal couldn't be faulted. We started with a first-rate houmous kavurma, and squid in beer batter. A main course of iskender came in a big bowl containing a wide range of meat, both lamb and chicken, shish and köfte, mixed in a rich tomato-based sauce on yoghurt and pide. In cafés, manti (Turkish ravioli) is often served as tiny parcels in a bowl of yoghurt. Here, a bowl of large, tasty pasta envelopes were pleasingly displayed around

a central dollop of thick yoghurt. Of late, the menu has moved beyond providing only traditional Turkish food, branching out to include the likes of roast rack of lamb on a potato gratin. Perhaps as a result, a broader spectrum of diners seems to come here. Good for them: Pasha deservedly remains the top spot for Turkish food in Angel. Babies and children admitted. Booking advisable weekends. Restaurant available for hire. Tables outdoors (2, pavement). Takeaway service. Map 5 O1.

Sedir

4 Theberton Street, N1 0QX (7226 5489/ ww.sedirrestaurant.co.uk). Angel tube/Highbury & Islington tube/rail. **Meals served** 11.30am-11.30pm Mon-Thur, Sun; 11.30am-midnight Fri, Sat. **Main courses** £7.50-£12.95. **Set lunch** (11.30am-5.30pm) £6.95-£7.95 2 courses. **Set meal** £18.95 per person (minimum 2) 3 courses. **Credit** AmEx, MC, V.

You'll find Sedir on a parade of restaurants that spills over from Upper Street. In good weather, staff put tables on the relatively narrow pavement outside. Inside, the dark red walls are dominated by enormous prints of European paintings of the Ottoman bazaars and harems. Recently, Sedir's menu has consciously become less exclusively Turkish and more generically Mediterranean, with several pasta choices. Even many Turkish dishes are now offered with chips or mashed potato. The core of the list, though, is still Turkish, and the dishes we ordered were first rate. We started with

Menu

It's useful to know that in Turkish 'ç' and 'ş' are pronounced 'ch' and 'sh'. So şiş is correct Turkish, shish is English and sis is common on menus. Menu spelling is rarely consistent, so expect wild variations on everything given here. See also the menu boxes in **Middle Eastern** and **North African**.

COOKING EQUIPMENT

Mangal: brazier.
Ocakbaşı: an open grill under an extractor hood. A metal dome is put over the charcoal for making paper-thin bread.

SOUPS

İşkembe: finely chopped tripe soup, an infallible hangover cure.
Mercimek çorbar: red lentil soup.
Yayla: yoghurt and rice soup (usually) with a chicken stock base.

MEZE DISHES

Arnavut ciğeri: 'albanian liver' – cubed or sliced lamb's liver, fried then baked.
Barbunya: spicy kidney bean stew.
Börek or **böreği:** fried or baked filo pastry parcels with a savoury filling, usually cheese, spinach or meat. Commonest are **muska** or **peynirli** (cheese) and **sigara** ('cigarette', so long and thin).
Cacik: diced cucumber with garlic in yoghurt.
Çoban salatası: 'shepherd's' salad of finely diced tomatoes, cucumbers, onions, perhaps green peppers and parsley, sometimes with a little feta cheese.
Dolma: stuffed vegetables (usually with rice and pine kernels).
Enginar: artichokes, usually with vegetables in olive oil.
Haydari: yoghurt, infused with

garlic and mixed with finely chopped mint leaves.
Hellim: Cypriot halloumi cheese.
Houmous: creamy paste of chickpeas, crushed sesame seeds, oil, garlic and lemon juice.
Houmous kavurma: houmous topped with strips of lamb and pine nuts.
Imam bayıldı: literally 'the imam fainted'; aubergine stuffed with onions, tomatoes and garlic in olive oil.
Ispanak: spinach.
Kalamar: fried squid.
Karides: prawns.
Kısır: usually a mix of chopped parsley, tomatoes, onions, crushed wheat, olive oil and lemon juice.
Kizartma: lightly fried vegetables.
Köy ekmeği: literally 'village bread'; another term for saç (qv).
Lahmacun: 'pizza' of minced lamb on thin pide (qv).
Midye tava: mussels in batter, in a garlic sauce.
Mücver: courgette and feta fritters.
Patlıcan: aubergine, variously served.
Patlıcan esme: grilled aubergine puréed with garlic and olive oil.
Pide: a term encompassing many varieties of Turkish flatbread. It also refers to Turkish pizzas (heavier and more filling than lahmacun, qv).
Pilaki: usually haricot beans in olive oil, but the name refers to the method of cooking not the content.
Piyaz: white bean salad with onions.
Saç: paper-thin, chewy bread prepared on a metal dome (also called saç) over a charcoal grill.
Sucuk: spicy sausage, usually beef.
Tarama: cod's roe paste.
Tarator: a bread, garlic and walnut mixture; **havuç tarator** adds carrot;

ıspanak tarator adds spinach.
Yaprak dolması: stuffed vine leaves.
Zeytin: olive.

MAIN COURSES

Alabalik: trout.
Balik: fish.
Güveç: stew, which is traditionally cooked in an earthenware pot.
Hünkar beğendi: cubes of lamb, braised with onions and tomatoes, served on an aubergine and cheese purée.
İçli köfte: balls of cracked bulgar wheat filled with spicy mince.
İncik: knuckle of lamb, slow-roasted in its own juices. Also called kléftico.
Karni yarik: aubergine stuffed with minced lamb and vegetables.
Kléftico: see incik.
Mitite köfte: chilli meatballs.
Sote: meat (usually), sautéed in tomato, onion and pepper (and sometimes wine).
Uskumru: mackerel.

KEBABS

Usually made with grilled lamb (those labelled **tavuk** or **piliç** are chicken), served with bread or rice and salad. Common varieties include:
Adana: spicy mince.
Beyti: usually spicy mince and garlic, but sometimes best-end fillet.
Bıldırcın: quail.
Böbrek: kidneys.
Çöp şiş: small cubes of lamb.
Döner: slices of marinated lamb (sometimes mince) packed tightly with pieces of fat on a vertical rotisserie.
Halep: usually döner (qv) served over bread with a buttery tomato sauce.
İskender: a combination of döner (qv), tomato sauce, yoghurt and melted butter on bread.
Kaburga: spare ribs.

a spinach pancake (rolled thickly, in a rich tomato sauce), and delicately fried albanian liver. To follow, sea bass was grilled in a traditional Turkish manner yet came with mashed potato, broccoli and runner beans which, while not traditional, went well. Mengen (delicious pan-fried chicken with mushrooms and rice) is named after one of Turkey's most famous culinary towns by the Black Sea. Our dining experience was enjoyable, but would have been improved by more space between tables.
Babies and children welcome: children's menu; high chairs. Booking essential dinner. Separate room for parties, seats 50. Tables outdoors (6, pavement). Takeaway service. Vegetarian menu. **Map 5 O1.**

Muswell Hill

Bakko

172-174 Muswell Hill Broadway, N10 3SA (8883 1111/www.bakko.co.uk). Highgate tube then 43, 134 bus. **Meals served** 11.30am-10.30pm daily. **Main courses** £8.90-£16.90. **Set lunch** (11.30am-4pm Mon-Fri) £7.90 3 courses. **Set meal** £16.90 per person (minimum 2) 4 courses. **Credit** MC, V.
'Bakko' is a Kurdish term for 'village elder' and this otherwise modern-looking restaurant has many Kurdish artefacts on its walls. In fine weather, the glass front opens up on to noisy Muswell Hill Broadway. Over recent years the restaurant has tried a couple of new directions – but to our eyes, a new bar-like section at the front, complete with settee and a TV playing music videos, doesn't improve the ambience. Aspects of the menu are

Kanat: chicken wings.
Köfte: mince mixed with spices, eggs and onions.
Külbastı: char-grilled fillet.
Lokma: 'mouthful' (beware, there's a dessert that has a similar name!) – boned fillet of lamb.
Patlıcan: mince and sliced aubergine.
Pirzola: lamb chops.
Şeftali: seasoned mince, wrapped in caul fat.
Şiş: cubes of marinated lamb.
Uykuluk: sweetbread.
Yoğhurtlu: meat over bread and yoghurt.

DESSERTS
Armut tatlısı: baked pears.
Ayva tatlısı: quince in syrup.
Baklava: filo pastry interleaved with minced pistachio nuts, almonds or walnuts, and covered in sugary syrup.
Kadayıf: cake made from shredded pastry dough, filled with syrup and nuts or cream.
Kazandibi: milk pudding, traditionally with very finely chopped chicken breast.
Kemel pasha: small round cakes soaked in honey.
Keşkül: milk pudding with almonds and coconut, topped with pistachios.
Lokum: turkish delight.
Sütlaç: rice pudding.

DRINKS
Ayran: refreshing drink made with yoghurt.
Çay: tea.
Kahve (aka Turkish coffee): a tiny cup half full of sediment, half full of strong, rich, bitter coffee. Offered without sugar, medium or sweet.
Rakı: a spirit with an aniseed flavour.

drifting away from the Kurdish origins, though you'll also find new Kurdish and Turkish dishes among the more general Mediterranean fare. The best of the food here is good. As a starter, three long sigara börek were served with a small dish of houmous. Next, kuzu shish included large chunks of succulent grilled lamb, basmati rice and a pungent chilli sauce. A dessert trolley near the entrance tempted with a range of western puddings as well as such Turkish standards as baklava. Staff were pleasantly chatty and outgoing throughout our meal. Bakko deserves a visit.
Babies and children welcome: high chairs. Booking essential weekends. Vegetarian menu.

North West

Belsize Park

★ Zara

11 South End Road, NW3 2PT (7794 5498). Belsize Park tube/Hampstead Heath rail. **Meals served** noon-11.30pm daily. **Main courses** £7.50-£12. **Credit** MC, V.
There's a relaxed and cosy feel to Zara, and the food is excellent, which makes this an ideal place to stop after a walk on Hampstead Heath. In summer, the glass front opens on to the wide pavement and there are tables outside. Inside, cushioned benches run along the walls, which are decorated with Turkish paintings, patterned tiles and photos. Mixed meze were served with first-rate pide and included handsome sigara böreği, beautifully textured egg-shaped falafel, a rich kısır, cacik and houmous. To follow, the grilled sea bream with salad was superlative. Külbastı – yielding, thin fillets of grilled lamb with oregano – were equally good, accompanied by salad and basmati rice. The menu also includes vegetarian dishes. Zara is the kind of spot where you feel like staying for a leisurely pudding or coffee (and, indeed, syrupy Turkish desserts and Turkish coffee are available). Staff were exceptionally helpful. Highly recommended.
Babies and children welcome: high chairs. Booking essential weekends. Tables outdoors (4, pavement). Takeaway service. Vegetarian menu. **Map 28 C3.**

Golders Green

Beyoglu

1031 Finchley Road, NW11 7ES (8455 4884). Golders Green tube/82, 160, 260 bus. **Meals served** noon-11pm. **Main courses** £6.50-£10. **Set buffet** £10 per person (minimum 2). **Set dinner** £12-£13.75 3 courses incl coffee. **Credit** MC, V.
The grill here has been moved away from the door to make the interior roomier and dispel any chance of Beyoglu being mistaken for a simple takeaway. It's a pity, therefore, that the sign outside has seen much better days. The restaurant has recently introduced a lunch deal for £10 a head, featuring a self-service cold meze bar as well as a main course and coffee or tea. The meze bar contains all the standard dishes, plus beetroot and potato salads. For diners, the danger is in filling up on all the houmous, kısır, cacik and good pide while waiting for main courses. Our chicken shish was excellent: large chunks of poultry served with rice and a fresh salad. However, while the ribs in the kaburga tasted good, they were too chewy at the centre and charcoaly on the outside – quite a disappointment as on previous visits we've found the kitchen's output to be uniformly excellent. Still, the service is very friendly, making Beyoglu a very enjoyable dining venue.
Babies and children welcome: high chairs. Booking advisable weekends. Tables outdoors (2, pavement). Takeaway service. Vegetarian menu.

Outer London

Richmond, Surrey

Pomegranate **NEW**

94 Kew Road, Richmond, Surrey TW9 2PQ (8940 0033). Richmond tube/rail. **Meals served** noon-midnight daily. **Main courses** £8-£14.50. **Credit** MC, V.

Zara

Recently opened, Pomegranate is linked to 19 Numara Bos Cirrik (*see p281*), one of London's best chains of Turkish grill restaurants, but has taken the excellent cooking upmarket. Our courses were served on designer plates, atop tables decorated with tall white candles. The appealing corner site allows large windows on two sides, and tables outside (beneath distinctive bright red sunshades). To start, we sampled excellent kalamar: clothed in a light batter, the seafood had no trace of toughness. Both our main courses were a little out of the ordinary for London Turkish cuisine. Shepherd's fry-up, as the name suggests, was fried rather than grilled, mixing pepper, mushroom and lamb – but it was tasty and certainly not greasy. Lamb beyti came wrapped in fine saç bread with sauce sizzling on top. Extra plates of onion with pomegranate and chilli onion were supplied with these dishes, as was a salad. Pomegranate was quiet on the night we visited, which has never been the case with its relative in Hackney. We hope the word will spread about the exciting food to be had here.
Babies and children admitted. Booking advisable dinner. Tables outdoors (20, garden).

RESTAURANTS

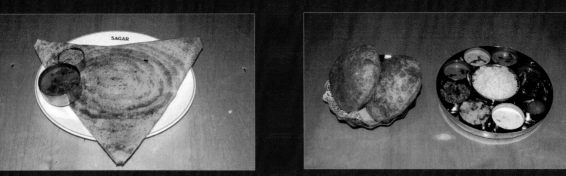

Vegetarian

For the past few years the vegetarian dining scene in the capital has lacked excitement, but wait long enough and, just like the proverbial London buses, three new vegetarian restaurants have come along at once. Welcome raw food restaurant and cocktail bar **Saf** in Shoreditch, the very grown-up **Vanilla Black** in the City, and **Rootmaster**, a vegan café in, er, one of those red London buses. **The Gate**, **Manna** and **Blah Blah Blah** remain favourite places to enjoy good food in pleasant surrounds, but for special occasions don't forget the meat-free menus at fine restaurants such as **Morgan M** and **Roussillon** (both in French). **Middle Eastern** (starting on p223) and **South Indian** (p147) eateries also have plenty to offer those looking to avoid meat, whether for ethical or dietary reasons.

Central

Barbican

Carnevale

135 Whitecross Street, EC1Y 8JL (7250 3452/ www.carnevalerestaurant.co.uk). Barbican tube/ Old Street tube/rail/55 bus. **Lunch served** noon-3.30pm Mon-Fri. **Dinner served** 5.30-10.30pm Mon-Sat. **Main courses** £11.50. **Set meal** (lunch Mon-Fri, 5.30-7pm Mon-Sat) £13.50 2-3 courses. **Credit** MC, V.

A combination of deli, lunchtime takeaway spot and compact restaurant, Carnevale brings a non-corporate feel to its corner on the edges of the City. During the day, fill up on their interesting salads (beetroot, watercress, walnut and honey; tabouleh; penne with capers and pine nuts), imaginative sandwiches (smoked mozzarella and aubergine in piadina, an Italian flatbread) and substantial hot takeaways (how about risotto with plum tomatoes, wild garlic leaves and parmesan?). In the evenings the restaurant is somewhat lacking in atmosphere; gentler lighting might help. A miniature courtyard housing three tables is a nice touch, but in such a tight squeeze we knew everything about our neighbouring diners' work problems by the end. The Med-influenced menu fell quite flat on several counts. Nutty-textured veggie sausages were way too sweet, and the accompanying colcannon wasn't heated through – enough to put anyone off a meal. Simple butternut squash and saffron risotto was better and the portion quite generous. A new delivery service is available to offices in the locality: a good idea, as Carnevale is a better option for lunch than for dinner.

Babies and children admitted. Booking advisable. Tables outdoors (3, conservatory). Takeaway service; delivery service (lunch only, over £25 within 1-mile radius). Vegan dishes. **Map 5 P4.**

City

★ The Place Below

St Mary-le-Bow, Cheapside, EC2V 6AU (7329 0789/www.theplacebelow.co.uk). St Paul's tube/Bank tube/DLR. **Breakfast served** 7.30-11am, **lunch served** 11.30am-2.15pm, **snacks served** 2.30-3pm Mon-Fri. **Main courses** £5.25-£7.75. **Unlicensed. Corkage** no charge. **Credit** MC, V.

Quiches, salads and filling breakfasts are the order of the day in this subterranean café below Bow Bells (St Mary-le-Bow) church in the Square Mile. The menu, dished out canteen-style before you retreat to a pew, varies daily but that old veggie staple the quiche is reliably churned out; scrumptious fillings might include mushroom and smoked cheddar, served with nondescript salad leaves and very good rosemary new potatoes. You can also choose from soups (displaying creative tinkerings like minestrone with Thai flavours); 'healthbowls' of rice and puy lentils in a tamari and sesame dressing; imaginative ciabatta sandwiches (sweet potato, olive tapenade and goat's cheese); and a hot dish such as leek and lentil bake served with patatas bravas. The setting is key here – the cool, cavernous crypt offering a respite to overstretched City folk and older patrons who appreciate the calm atmosphere and simple, satisfying food. Take note, bargain hunters: prices are dropped either side of peak serving times (11.30am-noon and 1.30-2.30pm).

Babies and children admitted. Tables outdoors (20, churchyard). Takeaway service. Vegan dishes. **Map 11 P6.**

Vanilla Black **NEW**

17-18 Tooks Court, off Cursitor Street, EC4A 1LB (7242 2622/www.vanillablack.co.uk). Chancery Lane tube. **Lunch served** noon-2.30pm, **dinner served** 6-10pm Mon-Fri. **Set lunch** £21 2 courses, £26 3 courses. **Set meal** £25 2 courses, £32 3 courses. **Credit** AmEx, MC, V.

RESTAURANTS

Vanilla Black

Originally a York restaurant of some repute, Vanilla Black now attracts the besuited denizens of London's legal quarter. Its look and feel are suitably sober. Presentation of dishes is as tidy as a solicitor's file, with towers, wafers and other tricksy garnishes, as well as the fashionable use of extra hardware such as the tiny preserve jar that held the green olives accompanying our green bean starter. This haute cuisine edge extends to a few up-to-the-minute molecular gastronomy ideas such as a celery meringue crisp used to garnish a galette of baked blue vinny and bramley apples – one of several dishes featuring cheese. Elsewhere the kitchen in inspired by Indian, Japanese and Mediterranean ingredients, but we felt the flavours needed to be bolder. A vindaloo for example was no fiery feast but mildly spiced sweet potato with a moat of saffron risotto. Desserts include the likes of red fruits and jelly with goat's milk and vanilla spread, and rum and raisin curd cake with tomato ripple ice-cream. Service was good and the setting conducive to business, making this an excellent place to take colleagues on special diets. *Babies and children admitted. Booking advisable. Disabled: toilet.* **Map11 N6**.

Covent Garden

★ Food for Thought (100)

31 Neal Street, WC2H 9PR (7836 9072). Covent Garden tube. **Meals served** noon-8.30pm Mon-Sat. **Lunch served** noon-5pm Sun. **Main courses** £4.20-£7. **Minimum** (noon-3pm, 6-7.30pm Mon-Sat) £2.50. **Unlicensed. Corkage** no charge. **No credit cards**.
The menu of this very much-loved Covent Garden stalwart changes daily, though you can expect three or four main courses, a selection of salads and a few desserts. The laid-back restaurant is down a steep, narrow stairway that, during the lunchtime rush, is usually filled with a patient queue. Efficient staff move quickly behind the counter; the seating at wobbly wooden tables is decidedly cosy, but somehow they manage to fit

everyone in. Moussaka was rich, creamy and full of green lentils, the sprightly rocket, broccoli and red pepper salad a welcome light companion. Quiche of the day was pleasingly full of spinach but had rather too much cheese on top. Raspberry and almond scrunch, the most popular dessert, is all decadence: cream, fresh fruit and a yummy crunchy oat base. You may feel like a removal worker getting in and out, especially when laden with shopping bags, but the crowd is friendly; knock against someone's table and all you're likely to receive is an understanding smile. The ground floor offers the same cut-above vegetarian menu to take away for busy office folk on the move. *Babies and children admitted. Bookings not accepted. Takeaway service. Vegan dishes.* **Map 18 D3**.

★ World Food Café

1st floor, 14 Neal's Yard, WC2H 9DP (7379 0298). Covent Garden tube. **Meals served** 11.30am-4.30pm Mon-Fri; 11.30am-5pm Sat. **Main courses** £4.95-£8.45. **Minimum** (noon-2pm daily) £6. **Credit** (over £10) MC, V.
This Covent Garden stalwart in the hippy HQ of Neal's Yard has a homespun feel. Staff assemble platters right in the middle of the first-floor walk-up as if they were catering a church fete. They tend to be either harried or distracted, but that doesn't put off customers, as the joint gets packed at lunchtime. The food is stomach-filling stuff. Root vegetable and chickpea masala with a mound of brown rice was a perfectly fine rendition of a healthy stew, but too heavy for our lunch (the café is not open in the evening). Other appealing options from around the globe include a Turkish meze plate with aubergines, tabouleh and pitta bread; Mexican tortilla with refried beans and guacamole; West African sweet potato stew; and Middle Eastern falafel. We were surprised by a slice of that great vegetarian cliché, carrot cake: unfrosted and dense, it resembled a traditional fruit cake but was very pleasantly spiced. You can eat at the counter around the central food

preparation area, or nab a window-side table to eye-up passers-by in the bustling courtyard below. *Babies and children welcome: children's portions; high chairs. No alcohol allowed. Takeaway service. Vegan dishes.* **Map 18 D3**.

Euston

★ Greens & Beans

131 Drummond Street, NW1 2HL (7380 0857/ www.greensandbeans.biz). Euston Square tube/ Euston tube/rail. **Meals served** 9am-5pm Mon-Fri. **Main courses** £4.25-£6.95. **Set lunch** (noon-3.30pm) £6.50 buffet. **Credit** MC, V.
There's no shortage of vegetarian restaurants on Drummond Street, a stone's throw from Euston station and surrounded by offices. Here they mostly serve Indian-style food, so this modern vegetarian eatery stands out. The ground floor offers a small range of organic groceries and beauty products while the hugely popular takeaway buffet boasts a selection of salads and hot food. A favourite destination for besuited local workers as well as lithe yoga divas in their sportswear, the basement café seems bright and full of summer, no doubt due to the combined forces of clean white walls, wooden tables and a chipper Australian waitress. While our smoothies were cold, thick and divine, the main courses proved disappointing. The nut roast was bland and perched on watery potatoes; the 'now that's a salad' salad was a plateful of delicious sprouts let down by almost tasteless fresh tomatoes that needed more dressing – better to use sun-dried tomatoes instead, we thought. Happily, the 'now that's a pizza' pizza was so good we devoured another, full of creamy feta, spinach and thick flavoursome tomato sauce. There's a great breakfast menu too, with options including millet or quinoa porridge, gluten-free muesli, scrambled eggs, veggie sausages and various wheat and barley grass concoctions.. *Babies and children admitted. Separate room for parties, seats 24. Tables outdoors (1, terrace). Takeaway service. Vegan dishes.* **Map 3 J3**.

Marylebone

Eat & Two Veg

*50 Marylebone High Street, W1U 5HN
(7258 8595/www.eatandtwoveg.com). Baker
Street tube.* **Meals served** 9am-11pm Mon-Sat;
10am-10pm Sun. **Main courses** £8.75-£10.75.
Credit AmEx, MC, V.
With its red vinyl booths, open-plan kitchen,
and 1950s automobile adverts, there's a distinct
feel of an American diner to this Marylebone
establishment – something that extends to the
menu. Many of the main courses feature meat
substitutes: burgers, schnitzels, sausages. Our
adequate starter of fried halloumi with tomato
and chilli relish arrived at the same time as the
mains, and so wasn't finished. The schnitzel
was delicious, but protein-substitutes tend to be
dry and this needed more of its delectable white
wine and watercress sauce. 'Marylebone hotpot'
was warming, with nuggets of soya protein,
beans and a nicely rich red-wine sauce. A
neighbouring table's enormous goat's cheese
salad caused food-envy and so we tried the
successful 'not niçoise' salad, tofu replacing the
tuna. With a huge skylight lending daytime
brightness to the bare brick walls and exposed
steel pipes, this is a cheerful – if sometimes
noisy – spot, but we found it difficult to dine
here during the constraints of an office lunch
break; most other customers were relaxed
shoppers not watching the clock.
*Babies and children welcome: high chairs; nappy-
changing facilities. Booking advisable. Disabled:
toilet. Tables outdoors (2, pavement). Takeaway
service. Vegan dishes.* **Map 3 G4.**
For branch see index.

Soho

★ Beatroot

*92 Berwick Street, W1F 0QD (7437 8591).
Oxford Circus, Piccadilly Circus or Tottenham
Court Road tube.* **Meals served** 9.15am-9pm
Mon-Sat. **Main courses** £3.90-£5.90.
No credit cards.
Beatroot has been providing Sohoites with reliable,
healthy eats for over a decade. Cheerful staff dole
out generous portions of hot dishes and salads
from behind the counter. Grab your choice as a
takeaway, or eat it at one of a handful of acid-
green and sunny-orange wooden tables. Various
salads bursting with interesting veg and dressings
include red-cabbage coleslaw with fresh dill, a
seasonal celeriac and radish number, and greek
salad with feta (one of the few instances of non-
vegan ingredients used). Among the ten hot dishes
were chunky moussaka, lentil shepherd's pie,
gently spiced cauliflower and potato curry, a
gingery tofu stir-fry and sausage rolls (a bit burnt
when we last went, but that's not a regular
occurrence). A raspberry and coconut flapjack was
lip-smackingly sweet and salty but didn't hold
together too well and skimped on the fruit. The
constant stream of customers features all the
characters that Soho attracts: alternative types,
Berwick Street record-store browsers and regulars
from the surrounding offices. A handy spot for a
quick, filling lunch in the centre of town.
*Babies and children admitted. No alcohol allowed.
Tables outdoors (5, pavement). Takeaway service.
Vegan dishes.* **Map 17 B3.**

Mildred's

*45 Lexington Street, W1F 9AN (7494 1634/
www.mildreds.co.uk). Oxford Circus or Piccadilly
Circus tube.* **Meals served** noon-11pm Mon-Sat.
Main courses £6.50-£8.75. **Credit** MC, V.
This perennially popular Soho vegetarian joint is
usually clamorous and cramped. Bookings aren't
taken, so staff suggest you wait at the bar, which
is fair enough as our table was ready faster than
the 40 minutes we'd been quoted. The servers here
are a little indifferent and difficult to attract being
so harried. Inside, a lively vibe is created with
bright lighting, gaudy canvases of fairground
rides and fresh-looking customers. The eclectic
menu is generally decent – a so-called 'light meal'
featured verdant spinach, thick, nicely textured
slices of halloumi, and flavoursome, traffic-light
coloured cherry tomatoes. Mixed mushroom and

Saf. See p291.

RESTAURANTS

ale pie was too tart (someone had overdone the balsamic vinegar), but it arrived encased in lovely light puff pastry sprinkled with poppy seeds. Mushy peas on the side were a healthy delight and the chunky chips non-greasy. For pudding, sickly sweet apple sorbet was trumped by a lush plum tarte tatin with cinnamon ice-cream. Mildred's has the gastropub end of London's vegetarian dining scene all chalked up.
Babies and children welcome: high chair. Bookings not accepted. Separate room for parties, seats 24. Tables outdoors (2, pavement). Takeaway service. Vegan dishes. **Map 17 A4**.

West

Hammersmith

The Gate
51 Queen Caroline Street, W6 9QL (8748 6932/ www.thegate.tv). *Hammersmith tube*. **Lunch served** noon-2.45pm Mon-Fri. **Dinner served** 6-10.45pm Mon-Sat. **Main courses** £8.50-£13.50. **Credit** AmEx, MC, V.
This part of Hammersmith will never be described as salubrious, but, accessed via a pretty courtyard, there are few dining rooms as immediately pleasing as the Gate's. Lush bamboo soars to the ceiling and there's a feeling of Zen-like calm. Much loved by sandal-wearers and meat-eaters alike, London's most famous vegetarian restaurant is a venue to which you would happily trek across town, yet our recent visit was disappointing. We had to bunch our coats on a spare chair. Then the waiter left us with dessert menus and it proved impossible to catch his attention, so we went in search of the correct list ourselves. Nevertheless, most of the food was a success. A shared meze was full of interesting, fresh textures and flavours. Pasta came perfectly al dente, with silky mushrooms and butter adding the illusion of cream. A shame, then, that the forgotten side dish of broccoli finally arrived overcooked and swimming in olive oil. Sticky date pudding was cold and dry, its accompanying toffee sauce lukewarm and meanly portioned. Tables around us were being sprayed and cleaned despite the early hour; the clatter of cutlery dumped into containers hastened our exit.
Babies and children welcome: high chairs. Booking essential. Tables outdoors (15, courtyard). Vegan dishes. **Map 20 B4**.

Shepherd's Bush

★ Blah Blah Blah
78 Goldhawk Road, W12 8HA (8746 1337/ www.gonumber.com/2524). *Goldhawk Road tube/ 94 bus*. **Lunch served** 12.30-2.30pm Mon-Sat. **Dinner served** 6.30-10.30pm Mon-Thur; 6.30-10.45pm Fri, Sat. **Main courses** £9.95. **Unlicensed**. **Corkage** £1.45 per person. **No credit cards**.
The decor of this sprightly 18-year-old aims at fun: strings of silvery Christmas decorations, disco balls, palms laden with fairy lights, wooden carvings and old-school theatre spotlights. Glasses of crayons are on the tables should creative inspiration strike, while the basement has a cosy snug for four near the toilets, together with another dining room full of colourful cushions. The appealing, fresh menu nods to world flavours (India, the Middle East, the Mediterranean), and we had difficulty making a decision. Artichoke salad was a light flavoursome starter; grilled halloumi came orangey-red, thanks to its tikka and yoghurt dressing. Ordering laksa, we expected a steaming bowl of spicy Singaporean soup noodles, but instead received a small amount of thick sauce underneath vegetables, tofu and plain egg noodles, topped with a single wun tun; the potatoes were incongruous and unnecessary. Still, the sweetcorn tostado, a tower of crisp corn tortillas filled with black beans, was a success. Service was efficient and friendly, if a little harried; the bill came as a final scrawled figure with no breakdown of costs – no blah blah blah there! Note that payment is by cash only – though, on the plus side, this is a BYO establishment.
Babies and children admitted. Booking advisable. Restaurant available for hire. Separate room for parties, seats 35. Takeaway service. Vegan dishes. **Map 20 B2**.

West Kensington

222 Veggie Vegan
222 North End Road, W14 9NU (7381 2322/ www.222veggievegan.com). *West Kensington tube/West Brompton tube/rail/28, 391 bus*. **Lunch served** noon-3.30pm, **dinner served** 5.30-10.30pm daily. **Main courses** £7.50-£10.50. **Set lunch** £7.50 buffet. **Credit** MC, V.
Run by the charming Ben Asamani, 222 (as locals call it) offers an all-you-can-eat lunchtime buffet with half a dozen each of hot and cold dishes that will soon have you making lunch the biggest meal of the day. More impressive yet, all the food is vegan. Aubergine parmigiana was a miracle of rich tomato sauce and creamy tofu – no dairy in sight, yet it was impossible not to go back for seconds. Full-flavoured chickpea curry came with nutty, fluffy wholegrain basmati rice, while the house salad was a riot of crunchy shredded veg. Dessert? It would have been rude not to. Carrot and walnut cake was impossibly light and moist, while the vanilla ice-cream delectable. The wine list is very short – comprising just one bottle each of decent organic red and white, but these are also served by the glass. Evenings feature an à la carte menu of stir-fries, pastas and salads, though in the past we've not found the cooking as satisfying at dinner. Despite the busy North End Road outside, the café is a soothing space, small and bright and furnished with blond wood tables and chairs. And it's certainly a popular place, with plenty of young families and singles filling the tables on our visit.
Babies and children welcome: high chairs. Booking advisable. Takeaway service. Vegan dishes. **Map 13 A12**.

East

Bethnal Green

★ Wild Cherry

241-245 Globe Road, E2 0JD (8980 6678). Bethnal Green tube/8 bus. **Meals served** 10.30am-4pm Tue, Thur-Sat; 10.30am-7pm Wed. **Main courses** £3.70-£6.25. **Unlicensed. Corkage** £1. **Credit** MC, V.

Locals love this café run by members of the London Buddhist Centre, and flock here for weekday lunches and the leisurely Saturday all-day breakfast. It's easy to see why the latter is a draw – puffy American-style pancakes are a strong point, whether piled with savoury toppings such as spinach and mixed mushrooms, or with fruit salad and sweet mascarpone. The vegetarian full english is hugely popular and includes scrambled eggs or tofu, sausages (a touch tough on our last visit), baked beans, more 'shrooms and delectably herby tomatoes. Portions are huge and, while you tackle them, there are free filter coffee refills to keep you going. Changing artwork decorates the walls, and there's a plant-strewn courtyard for when the weather cooperates. Staff are amiable and ready with high chairs to accommodate the numerous families who pack the place at weekends.
Babies and children welcome: high chairs. Tables outdoors (9, garden). Takeaway service. Vegan dishes.

Brick Lane

Rootmaster NEW

Old Truman Brewery car park, off Dray Walk, E1 6QI (07912 389314/www.root-master.co.uk). Aldgate East tube/Liverpool Street tube/rail. **Meals served** noon-9.45pm daily. **Main courses** £4-£12. **Credit** MC, V.

This vegan eaterie sited in an old Routemaster bus is just the ticket. It is staffed by an ebullient team and filled with nostalgic details such as wind-down windows and that steep spiral staircase. An evening here is a memorable experience. Diners have the run of the upper deck, where a communal table, three individual tables and a diner-style bar make for a cramped yet convivial vibe. Cooking takes place downstairs. The menu comprises Asian and European dishes, including gyoza bursting with 'umami' flavour, and juicy stuffed mushrooms (life's not too short, apparently). A sweet-potato, marinated tofu, and coconut curry excepted, mains weren't as impressive. The maple rice supporting a mound of sprouting broccoli was watery and insipid, while a lentil money bag was under-seasoned, and its filo pastry not crisp enough. If the sun's shining, take advantage of the tables out front, if it's pouring, don't worry – the steamy windows and clatter of rain on the roof combine to create a lovely atmosphere.
Babies and children admitted. Restaurant available for hire. Tables outdoors (30, courtyard). Takeaway service. **Map 6 S5.**

Shoreditch

★ Saf NEW (100)

2008 RUNNER-UP BEST SUSTAINABLE RESTAURANT

152-154 Curtain Road, EC2A 3AT (7613 0007/www.safrestaurant.co.uk). **Lunch served** noon-3.30pm, **dinner served** 6.30-11pm Mon-Sat. **Main courses** £8.50-£11. **Credit** AmEx, MC, V.

A strikingly good-looking bar and restaurant, Saf is airy and bright, and filled with fashionable Shoreditch folk. It's part of an international chain, and aims to set new standards for the artistry of vegan and raw food. Dishes are so pretty, with their vivid colours, variety of textures and unusual flavours, it's almost a shame to eat them. Lunch offers a range of wraps, salads, noodles and rice dishes, while evenings see the introduction of a five-course chef's menu that focuses on local seasonal ingredients. Mains include a 'buddha bowl' with rice, green-tea-smoked tofu, garlic greens, wakame seaweed and sambal. In addition to the usual absence of animal products, refined sugar is banned even from the desserts – agave syrup is used instead. 'Cheeses' are made from crushed nut-milk and resemble moist halva. The wine list features vegan, organic and biodynamic wines; organic cocktails are available too, so you can indulge with a reasonably clear conscience. With such little energy spent on producing and cooking the food (dishes that experience heat over 48°C/118°F are marked on the menu), it's no surprise that Saf's carbon footprint is very small.
Babies and children welcome: high chairs. Disabled: toilet. Tables outdoors (2, courtyard). Vegan dishes. **Map 6 R4.**

North

Camden Town & Chalk Farm

★ Manna

4 Erskine Road, NW3 3AJ (7722 8028/www.manna-veg.com). Chalk Farm tube/31, 168 bus. **Lunch served** noon-3pm Tue-Sun. **Dinner served** 6.30-10.30pm daily. **Main courses** £10-£13. **Credit** MC, V.

Following a refurb, Manna seems keen to shed any old-fashioned notions of what vegetarianism entails and shift the emphasis to its gourmet credentials. The chic new decor features crisp tablecloths, warm lighting and flock wallpaper in subtle tones of sand, gold and black. Careful thought has gone into the menu, which picks and chooses from a variety of global cuisines. Daily specials make it even more difficult to choose. Thai tempeh falafel with papaya salad sang out with fresh zingy flavours, while breaded ricotta managed to be delicate rather than bland. The seasonal menu could include seaweed and Japanese pickle salad, or halloumi with wild rice and pistachios. The chef's salad is a reliable favourite: an almost overwhelming platter of lemony artichokes, juicy caper berries, crisp marinated tofu, alfalfa sprouts and more. Fajita towers showed that Mexican food can be light if done properly; this rendition featured tomatillo sauce, green mango and smoky pinto beans. Desserts, like cardamom panna cotta, are similarly sophisticated. As a special-occasion venue, Manna is a cut above most other meat-free contenders.
Babies and children welcome: children's portions; high chairs. Booking essential. Tables outdoors (2, pavement; 2, conservatory). Takeaway service. Vegan dishes. **Map 27 A1.**

Outer London

Kingston, Surrey

Riverside Vegetaria

64 High Street, Kingston upon Thames, Surrey KT1 1HN (8546 0609/www.rsveg.plus.com). Kingston rail. **Meals served** noon-11pm daily. **Main courses** £7.60-£8.95. **Credit** MC, V.

It's not a long walk from Kingston train station to this Thames-side terrace restaurant, which opened in 1989 but feels a decade or two older. Never mind: the carnations and wooden chairs with colourful tie-on cushions could be considered delightfully kitsch, and the place is certainly cosy. Organic apple wine came quickly by the glass, but it took repeated requests to receive tap water. Gorgeous complimentary garlic bread was made from a nutty wholemeal loaf. Stuffed avocado was buried under iceberg lettuce, cucumber and french dressing, while a masala dosai (South Indian pancake stuffed with spiced potatoes), aided by a helpful kick of coconut sambal, was delicious. When mains arrived we realised we had over-ordered. Enormous helpings of a rather retro salad accompanied nearly every plate from the kitchen. Jamaican stew was a spicy mix of beans, sweet potato and coconut milk; red lentil and avocado kedgeree was equally flavourful. In all, this was a hugely enjoyable experience.
Babies and children welcome: high chairs. Booking advisable weekends. Separate room for parties, seats 25. Tables outdoors (7, riverside terrace). Takeaway service. Vegan dishes.

Vietnamese

Vietnamese cuisine, characterised by its use of fresh, aromatic herbs and balance of sweet, salty and sour flavours, is an intriguing culinary export unlike any other. As a country that borders Laos and Cambodia, and one that has experienced the influence of French colonialism as well as a period of Chinese rule, Vietnam is both a cultural and gastronomic melting pot. Most of London's Vietnamese restaurants have congregated east of the centre, especially in Shoreditch and Hackney, though recently we have seen tentative openings closer to the City. The arrival in Fitzrovia of the second branch of **Pho** signals the cuisine's move into the mainstream, as more and more Londoners are tempted by the multifaceted flavours of Vietnamese cooking. It is 13 years since we first listed one of the pioneers, **Viet Hoa**, and there is now a new-found confidence growing among Vietnamese restaurateurs, with less reliance on putting Chinese dishes on the menu to attract punters. **Tre Viet** takes the lead with its use of rare Vietnamese herbs and produce, while **Green Papaya** in Hackney and the new **Khoai Café** in Finchley both impress with their classic approaches to recreating the fresh, clean flavours of Vietnam.

Central

Fitzrovia

Pho NEW
3 Great Titchfield Street, W1W 8AX (7436 0111/ www.phocafe.co.uk). Oxford Circus tube. **Meals served** noon-10.30pm Mon-Sat. **Main courses** £5.75-£8.95. **Credit** MC, V.
This second branch of the original Pho in Clerkenwell is already making waves with the Fitzrovian lunchtime crowd. They're attracted to the clean-cut, modern surroundings that are a far cry from the canteens of east London. Here, striking photographs of Vietnam's street culture flank the walls; the grey-red-white colour scheme epitomises minimalist chic. This simplicity extends to the cooking, with a menu offering a basic round-up of Vietnam's best-known dishes. Unlike the original set-up, however, there are no banh mi (Vietnamese baguettes). The laudable aim is to make Vietnamese cooking more accessible, but we found the food a pale imitation of the cuisine. Pho's eponymous dish of beef noodle soup was let down by the broth – it lacked depth, tasting more of carrots than meat and subtle spices. However, we couldn't fault a dish of fresh summer rolls bursting with herbs and juicy prawns, nor did we dismiss a perfectly brewed 'weasel' coffee, rich with sweet condensed milk. Pho offers only a small sampling when it comes to authentic Vietnamese cuisine, but we can't deny it presents a fair introduction – and it's good to find such an option in the West End.
Babies and children admitted. Takeaway service. Vegetarian menu. **Map 17 A2.**
For branch see index.

West

Hammersmith

Saigon Saigon
313-317 King Street, W6 9NH (0870 220 1398/ www.saigon-saigon.co.uk). Ravenscourt Park or Stamford Brook tube.
Bar **Open/snacks served** 6pm-midnight Fri, Sat.
Restaurant **Lunch served** noon-3pm Tue-Sun. **Dinner served** 6-10pm Mon, Sun; 6-11pm Tue-Thur; 6-11.30pm Fri, Sat. **Main courses** £5.50-£13.95.
Both **Credit** MC, V.
An elegant and intimately arranged bar and restaurant, Saigon Saigon is a hub for romantic tête-à-têtes. Couples perch on dark wooden furniture behind bamboo screens, taking languorous sips of wine. Less classy is the laminated menu, with numbers that correspond to nearly 100 dishes – but at least the food looks the part. We loved how tap water was brought unbidden in small glass pitchers, and how the starters arrived beautifully presented on neat, square platters. These were impressive, yet showed restraint: a small mountain of crisp battered frogs' legs had the delicate aroma of rich butter; and chim cut nuong (chargrilled marinated quails) were exquisite, imbued with a light smoky flavour. The generous portions had us sated before a main course of stewed pork in coconut juice with quails' eggs, which was slightly underwhelming in comparison; the dish tasted strongly of star anise, with no discernible coconut flavour, though the belly pork was wonderfully melt-in-the-mouth tender. For west Londoners hoping to wow a date, the combination of 1940s oriental charm and kitchen flair make Saigon Saigon a good bet.
Babies and children welcome: high chairs. Bar available for hire. Booking advisable. Tables outdoors (4, pavement). **Map 20 A4.**

East

Shoreditch

Cây Tre
301 Old Street, EC1V 9LA (7729 8662/ www.vietnamesekitchen.co.uk). Old Street tube/ rail. **Lunch served** noon-3pm Mon-Sat. **Dinner served** 5.30-11pm Mon-Thur; 5.30-11.30pm Fri, Sat. **Meals served** noon-10.30pm Sun. **Credit** AmEx, MC, V.
A haunt of Hoxtonites, Cây Tre veers towards the hip and trendy – separating itself from the homey institutions around the corner on Kingsland Road. Wallpaper is swirling line drawings with Buddhist iconography that wouldn't look out of place in a psychedelic colouring book. Cheerful fairy lights dot the walls leading from the ground-floor dining area to the more intimate basement space. Perhaps what is most appealing to the clientele – mainly non-Vietnamese foodies – are the suggested wine pairings with most dishes. Our starter of Indochine beef (a ceviche of tenderloin doused in lemon juice, herbs and shallots) went very nicely with the Costières de Nîmes red. It soon became clear that Cây Tre excels in meat; the bo luc lac ('shaking' beef) was sensational, rich with the smoky flavour of the wok and a hint of cognac. Stuffed swimming crab was oversalted and drenched in a gloopy sauce, but we ended on a delicious high note with the basa (a type of catfish) grilled with lemongrass and turmeric. Service was efficient, though on a busy Friday night you're likely to feel pressured into leaving as soon as you put down your cutlery.
Babies and children admitted. Booking advisable. Takeaway service. **Map 6 4R.**
For branch (Viet Grill) see index.

★ Hanoi Café
98 Kingsland Road, E2 8DP (7729 5610/ www.hanoicafe.co.uk). 26, 48, 55, 67, 149, 242, 243 bus. **Meals served** noon-11.30pm daily. **Main courses** £4-£6.50. **Set lunch** (Mon-Fri) £3.80. **Credit** (over £10) AmEx, MC, V.
In its owners' own words, Hanoi Café offers 'homemade Vietnamese cuisine in a relaxed atmosphere', which is a pretty accurate description of this charming 'mom and pop' eaterie. There's no fussiness about the easy-wipe tabletops and the black and white photographs of Vietnam on the walls, nor do the dishes come intricately plated. We had plenty of fun with the rustic 'roll your own summer roll' platter, which arrived with personal bamboo mats, circles of rice paper wrappers that had to be soaked in an accompanying bowl of water, and mounds of shredded vegetables, herbs, and vermicelli noodles. Our choice of lime chicken filling, however, was more paltry than poultry – mostly batter rather than anything resembling meat. The menu features pho (noodle soups) and bun (rice noodles), served in massive bowls. Hanoi bun topped with sautéed beef, chicken and king prawns was a satisfying meal in itself, especially when accompanied by a strong Vietnamese iced coffee. Hanoi Café might not be the fanciest joint in town, but the food is honest and comforting.
Babies and children welcome: high chair. Restaurant available for hire. Takeaway service. **Map 6 R3.**

★ Mien Tray NEW
122 Kingsland Road, E2 8DP (7729 3074). Old Street tube/rail/26, 48, 55, 67, 149, 242, 243 bus. **Lunch served** noon-3pm, **dinner served** 5-11pm daily. **Main courses** £4-£7. **Unlicensed. Corkage** no charge. **Credit** MC, V.
On the site of the former Thang Loi, which was notable for its north Vietnamese dishes, Mien Tray conversely prides itself on the fresh, sweet flavours of southern Vietnam, a cuisine characterised by its emphasis on seafood and influences from southern Chinese immigrants. The stunner of our meal was deep-fried sea bass with fish sauce and mango. Presented whole with slivers of the just-ripe fruit, chilli and lashings of fishy nuoc mam, it was a pure harmony of flavours (sweet, salty, sour) and textures (crisp skin, moist fish, slippery mango). Pho dac biet ('special' pho with beefy goodies) contained superb, irregularly shaped beef balls that bounced nicely on the teeth and had clearly been handmade (mass-produced beef balls tend to have a limp, overly processed texture). To finish, the Vietnamese coffee was also excellent – a refreshing, smooth brew and not cloying thanks to a judicious hand with the condensed milk. Alternatively, try the tra sua tran chau (Vietnamese tapioca pearl tea), if available.
Babies and children welcome: high chairs. Restaurant available for hire. Takeaway service. Vegetarian menu. **Map 6 R3.**

Pho

Que Viet NEW

102 Kingsland Road, E2 8DP (7033 0588). Old Street tube/rail/26, 48, 55, 67, 149, 242, 243 bus. **Lunch served** noon-3.30pm, **dinner served** 5-11pm daily. **Main courses** £5-£10. **Credit** MC, V.

Taking over the former site of Au Lac, this newcomer has a completely new look, making it the most elegant Vietnamese restaurant on the block. A heavy, leather-bound menu lists more than 200 dishes, with lots of subheadings. You can choose from several preparations for frogs' legs, scallops, eels and more, and there's a mind-boggling number of noodles, soups and stir-fries. Like its predecessor, Que Viet offers the seldom seen 'fire pot'. For £15-£20 a head you can cook pieces of meat, vegetables or seafood in a bubbling vessel of broth set up at your table – it's a fun experience. Our soft-shell crab with lemongrass was a stodgy rendition, suffering from too much batter and grease, although a limey rare-beef salad was refreshing and showed a good balance of mint and coriander. Bun thit nuong (rice noodles with pork and vegetables) hit the right spot with grilled, juicy pork but was let down by a watery nuoc cham. Service seemed a bit rocky and the waiters lacked confidence, but we'll put that down to opening jitters.
Babies and children admitted: high chair. Takeaway service.

★ ★ Song Que (100)

134 Kingsland Road, E2 8DY (7613 3222). Old Street tube/rail/26, 48, 55, 67, 149, 242, 243 bus. **Lunch served** noon-3pm, **dinner served** 5.30-11pm Mon-Sat. **Meals served** 12.30-11pm Sun. **Main courses** £4.50-£6.20. **Credit** MC, V.

After all this time, Song Que still sets the benchmark for exceptional Vietnamese cooking in London. It's an efficient, canteen-like operation commanding the corner of Kingsland Road and Pearson Street. Diners of all types are attracted (be prepared to share tables at busy times). The beef pho is the best in London – an unmatchable broth that's rich in spices, with a complexity that can only come from hours of simmering beef bones and meat together with star anise, ginger and cinnamon. It is served with a plateful of fresh, verdant herbs: ngo gai (saw-leaf herb), rau que (Asian basil) and mint. The beef la lot (minced beef wrapped in betel leaves) came in generous portions, the juicy meat complemented by the chargrilled, slightly crisp betel leaves. Muc rang ruoi (chilli salted squid) was perfectly battered and seasoned, the squid springy and fresh. Simple stir-fried rau muong (morning glory) surprised us with its crisp texture and smoky wok flavours. The only disappointment was dessert, a tepid che bam au (a parfait-like drink consisting of red beans, green jelly, mung beans and coconut milk) that was sickeningly sweet: easily forgiven considering the rest of the meal.
Babies and children welcome: high chairs. Booking advisable. Takeaway service.
Map 6 R3.

★ Tay Do Café

65 Kingsland Road, E2 8AG (7729 7223). Old Street tube/rail/26, 48, 55, 67, 149, 242, 243 bus. **Lunch served** 11.30am-3pm, **dinner served** 5-11.30pm daily. **Main courses** £5-£12. **Set lunch** £4.30. **Unlicensed. Corkage** £1 per person. **Credit** (over £10) AmEx, MC, V.

The façade of this tiny café does it no favours. The frontage is often obscured by a bus stop directly in front of the doors, and its fluorescent sign speaks more of greasy spoons than restaurant dining. Tay Do's popularity relies mostly on word of mouth. The canteen-style interior fills up quickly at weekends, mostly with East End locals who take full advantage of the BYO policy. To start, our prawn and pork summer rolls came beautifully presented, but, unfortunately, were more style than substance: the rolls mostly filled with vermicelli noodles, with a single sliver of pork and two halves of a prawn. In contrast, we were happy with the banh xeo, with its crisp turmeric-yellow exterior and filling of juicy chicken and crunchy beansprouts. Caramelised mekong catfish in a clay pot was sizzlingly good too. Service seemed a little careless; we had to prise open the burning-hot clay pot with napkin-covered hands ourselves, and when paying, were urged to do so in cash. Only later did we discover that the café does indeed accept credit cards.
Babies and children admitted: high chair. Takeaway service. **Map 6 R3.**
For branch (Tay Do Restaurant) see index.

★ Viet Hoa

70-72 Kingsland Road, E2 8DP (7729 8293). Old Street tube/rail/26, 48, 55, 67, 149, 242, 243 bus. **Lunch served** noon-3.30pm, **dinner served** 5.30-11pm Mon-Fri. **Meals served** 12.30-11.30pm Sat, Sun. **Main courses** £3.50-£8.50. **Credit** AmEx, MC, V.

Once a Kingsland Road institution, often credited with introducing Londoners to authentic Vietnamese cooking in the 1990s, Viet Hoa had become a shadow of its former self, with food that rarely lived up to expectations. Hang on, though: our most recent visit may have reinstated our belief in this family-run joint, where the waitresses have a gentle charm and tap water comes in jugs. The meal began a little shakily; banh xeo, while clearly fragrant with plenty of turmeric and coconut milk, had very little stuffing, and beansprouts were replaced entirely by slippery onions and, curiously, rice. Things looked up when our chao tom (sugar-cane prawns) and fried tilapia fish arrived. The tilapia drew looks of astonishment from neighbouring diners; the fat fish was fried whole, smothered with slivers of mango and generous sloshes of nuoc cham. The slightly under-ripe fruit had a pleasant bite, a perfect accompaniment to the tender fish. A plate of stir-fried morning glory, served with lime for squeezing, rounded off the meal perfectly, leaving us happy and sated (if smelling of pungent garlic).

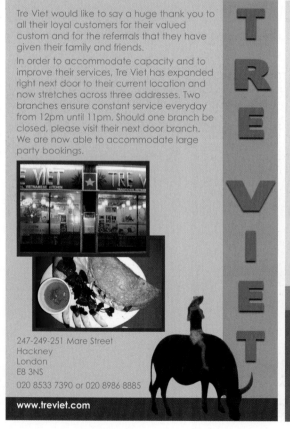
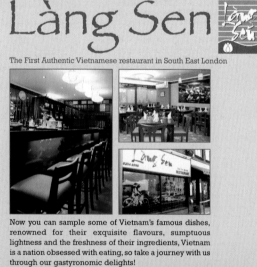

Babies and children welcome: high chairs. Booking advisable; essential dinner. Takeaway service.
Map 6 R3.

Victoria Park

★ Namo

178 Victoria Park Road, E9 7HD (8533 0639/ www.namo.co.uk). Mile End tube then 277 bus. **Lunch served** noon-3.30pm Fri-Sun. **Dinner served** 5.30-11pm Tue-Sun. **Main courses** £6.90-£8.50. **Credit** MC, V.

Charming young waitresses patter around attending to diners at this modest little café, sister to Huong-Viet in Dalston (*see below*). The surroundings are mellow if slightly eccentric, with smiling Buddhist statues, red flocked wallpaper and pale blue lanterns. There's also a tiny outdoor patio for warmer weather. The menu is similar to the Dalston restaurant, with several Chinese dishes cropping up alongside more traditional Vietnamese food. The fish cakes were flavourful, with plenty of lemongrass, though they had a curiously dense texture, and we loved the cha ca la vong (monkfish with turmeric and dill), even if it didn't come sizzling on a hotplate. Our favourite, however, was the bun hue (spicy beef noodle soup) which had appropriately tongue-tingling, complex flavours from its lemongrass and shrimp paste; the beef was tender and the rice noodles al dente too. To drink, there are inexpensive wines from Borough Wines in east London, which add to Namo's attraction. A thoroughly enjoyable, low-key venue that won't break the bank.
Babies and children welcome: children's menu; high chairs. Booking essential weekends. Tables outdoors (5, garden). Takeaway service.

North East
Dalston

★ Huong-Viet

An Viet House, 12-14 Englefield Road, N1 4LS (7249 0877/www.huongviet.co.uk). Dalston Kingsland rail/67, 149, 236, 242, 243 bus. **Lunch served** noon-3.30pm Mon-Sat. **Dinner served** 5.30-11pm Mon-Sat. **Main courses** £4.90-£6.50. **Set lunch** £7 2 courses. **Credit** (over £12) MC, V.

Success seems to have gone to the head of this once-modest little community-centre dining room. Plastered across walls are various newspaper and magazine articles, and nomination forms for 'restaurant of the year' are given out as 'comment cards' by the waiters – sneaky. Set in the run-down building of the An Viet Foundation, the kitchens have gone from serving home-style food to Vietnamese refugees, to attracting praise from the national press (a glowing *Guardian* review is pasted on the back of the drinks list) and winning our hearts too. What a shame, then, that on our most recent visit we were presented with a greasy banh xeo and a beef pho (Huong-Viet's trademark) that arrived without its accompanying fresh herbs and beansprouts. Still, we moved on and saw glimpses of former glories. Strips of tender chargrilled squid with lemongrass and chilli was fragrant and delectable, while cari ga (chicken curry) tasted of the pleasant sweetness of Vietnamese curry powder. A dessert of creamy tofu spiked with ginger syrup and coconut cream made a pleasant end to the meal.
Babies and children welcome: high chairs. Booking advisable; essential weekends. Disabled: toilet. Separate room for parties, seats 30. Takeaway service. Vegetarian menu.

Hackney

★ ★ Green Papaya

191 Mare Street, E8 3QE (8985 5486/ www.greenpapaya.co.uk). London Fields rail/ 48, 55, 253, 277, D6 bus. **Dinner served** 5-11pm Tue-Sun. **Main courses** £5-£8. **Credit** DC, MC, V.

It's refreshing to see a Vietnamese restaurant that proudly highlights its specials. At Green Papaya, dishes of the day are cheerfully splashed across a blackboard behind the bar. This time, though, we

Green Papaya

weren't tempted by the various stir-fries offered. Instead, a delightful salad of thinly shredded banana flowers with coriander and a powerful salty-sour dressing set the pace for the rest of the meal. The pho ga (chicken noodle soup) here is sublime – a far more delicate dish than its cousin pho bo (beef noodle soup). The savoury soup was peppered with juicy shreds of chicken and hints of sweet onion and ginger, elevated with a squeeze of lemon juice. We were also impressed by the (rarely seen) smoked tofu, which had a distinct 'umami' meatiness about it. Staff were amicable and knowledgeable, explaining the provenance of the dried 'Vietnamese olives' in a dish of braised pork belly; these are imported from north Vietnam, where the olives are harvested. Located on a lonely stretch of Mare Street, this joint isn't as lively as its Shoreditch counterparts, but we rate highly the food and mellow atmosphere.

Babies and children welcome: high chairs. Booking advisable. Tables outdoors (5, garden). Takeaway service.

★ Tre Viet ⑩⓪

251 Mare Street, E8 3NS (8533 7390). Hackney Central rail/26, 48, 55, 253, 277, D6 bus. **Meals served** 11.30am-11pm Mon-Thur, Sun; 11.30am-11.30pm Fri, Sat. **Main courses** £4.70-£13. **Unlicensed. Corkage** no charge. **Credit** MC, V.

This veteran café does a brisk trade every night, when Vietnamese families and office workers (many bringing their own alcohol) squeeze into the tables for a feast. The menu seems endless, with all the vital Vietnamese classics alongside such rarities as goat in lemongrass and chilli. We sampled the canh chua ca bong lau, a sweet and sour catfish soup that came chock-full of juicy morsels of fish and pineapple, flavoured with zingy tamarind and the rarely seen bac ha (taro

Although most Vietnamese restaurants in London offer a range of Chinese dishes, it's best to ignore these and head for the Vietnamese specialities. These contain fresh, piquant seasonings and raw vegetables that create entirely different flavours from Chinese cuisine. Vietnamese cookery makes abundant use of fresh, fragrant herbs such as mint and sweet basil; it also utilises refreshing, sweet-sour dipping sauces known generically as nuoc cham. Look out for spices such as chilli, ginger and lemongrass, and crisp root vegetables pickled in sweetened vinegar.

Some dishes are assembled at the table in a way that is distinctively Vietnamese. Order a steaming bowl of pho (rice noodles and beef or chicken in an aromatic broth) and you'll be invited to add raw herbs, chilli and citrus juice as you eat. Crisp pancakes and grilled meats are served with herb sprigs, lettuce leaf wraps and piquant dipping sauces. Toss cold rice vermicelli with salad leaves, herbs and hot meat or seafood fresh from the grill. All these dishes offer an intriguing mix of tastes, temperatures and textures.

Aside from the pronounced Chinese influence on Vietnamese culinary culture, there are hints of the French colonial era (in sweet iced coffee, for example, and the use of beef), along with echoes of neighbouring South-east Asian cuisines. Within Vietnamese cooking itself there are several regional styles; the mix of immigrants in London means you can sample some of the styles here. The food of Hanoi and the north is known for its street snacks and plain, no-nonsense flavours and presentation. The former imperial capital Hue and its surrounding region are famed for a royal cuisine and robustly spicy soups; look out for Hue noodle soups (bun bo hue) on some menus. The food of the south and the former Saigon (now Ho Chi Minh City) is more elegant and colourful, and makes much greater use of fresh herbs (many of these unique to Vietnam), vegetables and fruit.

Below are some specialities and culinary terms; spellings can vary.

Banh cuon: pancake-like steamed rolls of translucent fresh rice pasta, sometimes stuffed with minced pork or shrimp (reminiscent in style of Chinese cheung fun, a dim sum speciality).
Banh pho: flat rice noodles used in soups and stir-fries, usually with beef.
Banh xeo: a large pancake made from a batter of rice flour and coconut milk, coloured bright yellow with turmeric and traditionally filled with prawns, pork, beansprouts and onion. To eat it, tear the pancake apart with your chopsticks, roll the pieces with sprigs of herbs in a lettuce leaf, and dip in nuoc cham (qv).

Bun: rice vermicelli, served in soups and stir-fries. They are also eaten cold, with raw salad vegetables and herbs, with a nuoc cham (qv) sauce poured over, and a topping such as grilled beef or pork – all of which are tossed together at the table.
Cha ca: North Vietnamese dish of fish served sizzling in an iron pan with lashings of dill.
Cha gio: deep-fried spring rolls. Unlike their Chinese counterparts, the wrappers are made from rice paper rather than sheets of wheat pastry, and pucker up deliciously after cooking.
Chao tom: grilled minced prawn on a baton of sugar cane.
Goi: salad; there are many types in Vietnam, but they often contain raw, crunchy vegetables and herbs, perhaps accompanied by chicken or prawns, with a sharp, perky dressing.
Goi cuon (literally 'rolled salad', often translated as 'fresh rolls' or 'salad rolls'): cool, soft, rice-paper rolls usually containing prawns, pork, fresh herbs and rice vermicelli, served with a thick sauce similar to satay sauce but made from hoi sin mixed with peanut butter, scattered with roasted peanuts.
Nem: north Vietnamese name for cha gio (qv).
Nom: north Vietnamese name for goi (qv).
Nuoc cham: the generic name for a wide range of dipping sauces, based on a paste of fresh chillies, sugar and garlic that is diluted with water, lime juice and the ubiquitous fish sauce, nuoc mam (qv).
Nuoc mam: a brown or pale liquid derived from fish that have been salted and left to ferment. It's the essential Vietnamese seasoning, used in dips and as a cooking ingredient.
Pho: the most famous and best-loved of all Vietnamese dishes, a soup of rice noodles and beef or chicken in a rich, clear broth flavoured with aromatics. It is served with a dish of fresh beansprouts, red chilli and herbs, and a squeeze of lime; these are added to the soup at the table.

Though now regarded as quintessentially Vietnamese, pho seems to have developed as late as the 19th century in northern Vietnam, and may owe its origins to French or Chinese influences. Some restaurants, such as **Song Que** (see p294), offer many versions of this delicious, substantial dish.
Rau thom: aromatic herbs, which might include Asian basil (rau que), mint (rau hung), red or purple perilla (rau tia to), lemony Vietnamese balm (rau kinh gioi) or saw-leaf herb (ngo gai).
Tuong: a general term for a thick sauce. One common tuong is a dipping sauce based on fermented soy beans, with hints of sweet and sour, often garnished with crushed roasted peanuts.

stem), a spongy South-east Asian vegetable. Less authentic and enjoyable was a bland mien xao thom thit (rice vermicelli stir-fried with prawns and pork). Fried frogs' legs are usually a wise choice, but on this occasion the otherwise crisp batter was let down by an overpowering flavour of butter – still, we enjoyed the simplicity of the accompanying onions and Vietnamese coriander. Tre Viet excels in using rare and interesting ingredients, though which dishes include them isn't always apparent; your choice of food can make the difference between an extraordinary and a merely average dining experience.
Babies and children welcome: high chairs. Booking advisable weekends. Disabled: toilet. Separate room for parties, seats 30. Takeaway service.
For branch (Lang Huong) see index.

North

Camden Town & Chalk Farm

★ Viet Anh
41 Parkway, NW1 7PN (7284 4082). Camden Town tube. **Lunch served** noon-4pm, **dinner served** 5.30-11pm daily. **Main courses** £4.50-£8. **Credit** MC, V.
With its pale turquoise walls and simple furniture, Viet Anh is a friendly little caff that's popular with the Camden crowd who flock here for quick and easy meals. A photo album holding images of all dishes makes it easier for novices to choose from the 250 or so items. The idea is sound in principle, though our rule of thumb is to go for the dishes marked 'Vietnamese', to avoid mistakenly ordering extraneous Chinese-style fare. Prawns wrapped and fried in betel leaves were good but greasy, a shortcoming remedied by punchy nuoc cham. We were excited to see bun rieu on offer (a northern Vietnamese noodle soup of crab and tomato), but were disappointed by its watery broth, processed crab sticks and the lack of crab or shrimp paste to give it a much-needed flavour boost. The highlight of our meal was a refreshing lotus-stem salad teeming with rau que (Asian basil), shredded chicken and prawns; it came doused with piquant lime and chilli dressing. So, despite our mixed experience, Viet Anh has at least one winning card.
Babies and children admitted. Booking advisable. Tables outdoors (2, pavement). Takeaway service. **Map 27 C2**.

Finchley

★ Khoai Café [NEW]
362 Ballards Lane, N12 0EE (8445 2039). Woodside Park tube/82, 134 bus. **Lunch served** noon-3.30pm, **dinner served** 5.30-11.30pm daily. **Main courses** £5-£9.95. **Set lunch** £4.99 1 course, £7.45 2 courses. **Credit** MC, V.
This outpost of the original Khoai Café in Crouch End is the kind of place that effortlessly brightens up a neighbourhood. The spacious, airy interior is sleek, but not cold; modern, but not pretentious. Most importantly, the food is flawlessly executed. Everything we tried was bursting with fresh flavours and skilful presentation: from the colourful summer rolls that didn't skimp on the prawns, to the fragrant minced beef rolled in betel leaves and chargrilled. Green leaf soup had less of a presence, but the flavour of the broth was clear and sweet. Similarly, the southern-styled hu tiu (a Chinese and South-east Asian noodle soup made with pork broth and without fish sauce) with chicken, prawn, grilled fish cake and chives was delicate and soothing. The tongue-twistingly named bun tom cang nuong goi xoai was the highlight of our meal – fat, butterflied tiger prawns fresh from the grill, topped with slivers of juicy mango and served with vermicelli noodles, crunchy carrot and cucumber, Vietnamese herbs and piquant nuoc cham. All the desserts are outsourced: a shame, as we would have loved to see the same culinary flair applied to the puds.
Babies and children welcome: high chairs. Disabled: toilet. Restaurant available for hire. Takeaway service.
For branch see index.

RESTAURANTS

Cheap Eats

Budget

The cost of eating out in London is a favourite complaint of tourists and some residents, but there are plenty of bargains to be had when you know where to look. This selection of favourites (primarily chosen for their location in otherwise expensive districts of the city) is a good place to start. Here we also celebrate London's pride and joy – traditonal pie and mash shops – and the new wave of gourmet burger joints, where the emphasis is on well-sourced beef and other high quality, fresh fillings.

For budget meals connected to the cuisine of a particular country, consult the relevant chapter elsewhere in this guide (Chinese, Global, Indian, Korean, Thai, Turkish and so on), where you will find low-priced venues indicated by a ★. Time Out's annual *Cheap Eats in London* guide contains an even wider choice of budget eateries: more than 500 places across the capital where you can dine for less than £20 per head – so it certainly pays to pick up a copy.

Central

Bloomsbury

Square Pie
Brunswick Centre, WC1N 1AF (7837 6207/ www.squarepie.com). Russell Square tube. **Open** 11.30am-10.30pm Mon-Sat; 11.30am-10pm Sun. **Main courses** £4.25-£6.96. **Credit** MC, V.
Martin Dewey's small chain has expanded from its origins at Spitalfields Market to take root in a certain kind of London neighbourhood – Canary Wharf, Selfridges, and the Brunswick Centre: the sort of locale where traditional pie and mash shops wouldn't last five minutes. Trendy though the place is, Square Pie's pies are relatively cheap and filling, with good mushy peas and decent Maris Piper mash made with skins included. The pies come in two sizes with a choice of fillings: from the traditional steak and ale or chicken and mushroom, to the more imaginative. Our pie of the month contained lumps of chicken, salty parma ham and bits of lemon, as well as a nice big bay leaf. Very satisfying. Other treats include sausage rolls made with chorizo and, for the sweet of tooth, apple and cherry pies – try one with a strong Antipodean-style flat white coffee. At the smart Brunswick Centre branch, where cartoon illustrations of the baking process decorate the walls, there are tables indoors and out, and an alcohol licence as well.
Babies and children welcome: high chairs. Disabled: toilet. Tables outdoors (10, patio). Takeaway service. **Map 4 L4.**
For branches see index.

City

Grazing
19-21 Great Tower Street, EC3R 5AR (7283 2932/www.grazingfood.com). Monument or Tower Hill tube/Fenchurch Street rail. **Open** 7am-4pm Mon-Fri. **Main courses** £3.95-£5.50. **No credit cards.**
No sooner are we greeted breezily at the door by the aproned staff of this City sandwich bar, than one of them has to race into the kitchen to attend to some burning toast. A plume of acrid smoke threatened to engulf Grazing's white-tiled interior. Sitting on a brushed-steel stool, we sampled an expertly grilled 'Denhay of Dorset' streaky bacon sandwich. There's an unashamedly meaty outlook here, and the company is proud of its products' provenance. This is probably the only place in town where you can pick up a haggis and fried egg

butty on the way to work. A healthier breakfast option comes in the shape of a build-your-own muesli bar. By lunchtime, Donald Russell's Aberdeenshire beef rolls are the big draw, though on our breakfast visit, the prospect of a filled yorkshire pudding special was enough to make us consider a half-day skive. Small wonder, then, that Grazing is as popular with site-workers scanning *The Sun* as City folk spilling ketchup on their ties.
Babies and children admitted. Tables outdoors (2, pavement). Takeaway service; delivery service (over £25 within the City). **Map 12 R7.**

Leon
3 Crispin Place, E1 6DW (7247 4369/ www.leonrestaurants.co.uk). Liverpool Street tube/ rail. **Meals served** 8am-10pm Mon, Tue; 11am-10.30pm Wed-Fri; 9am-10pm Sat; 10am-9pm Sun. **Main courses** £4.20-£11. **Credit** MC, V.
The concept of furnishing the city's time-poor, health-conscious lunch-breakers with a quick-fire menu of Mediterranean superfoods is clearly a hit. Recognition of Leon's righteousness has over the years allowed it to expand into a nine-branch London wonder. The cafés are tiled in primary colours and teem with artfully rustic tat – coffee grinders, wooden crates, empty honey pots. Praise has been heaped on the firm, although our recent visits have hinted that complacency may have crept in. Vegetarian roasted mushroom and plum tomato breakfast baps were satisfyingly rich yet had dry, unappealing bread. Portions of the lunchbox superfood salads seemed rather small when opened in the office. A recent sit-down dinner presented us with a ceaseless stream of let-downs: from an overpoweringly lemony houmous and rubbery sliced chorizo, to a meagre main of moroccan meatballs and another of dried-out Devonshire Red chilli chicken, the latter whipped away by over-eager staff while the last mouthful was still being mulled over. A cracking concept this may be, but more love and attention is needed.
Babies and children welcome: high chairs. Disabled: toilet. Tables outdoors (30, market). Takeaway service. **Map 12 R5.**
For branches see index.

★ Passage Café NEW
12 Jerusalem Passage, EC1V 4JP (3217 0090/ www.thepassagecafe.com). Farringdon tube. **Meals served** 11am-11pm Mon-Fri. **Main courses** £5.50-£10. **Credit** AmEx, MC, V.
You dream of (but rarely get) places like this in provincial France. The Passage is a tiny finger of

a venue with hardly room for 20 diners – though there's a few tables outside. Within, furniture is caff-style, but deep-orange and white walls, wooden flooring and Gallic paintings give a bistro feel. At the rear is a minuscule kitchen, where a clued-up, friendly duo work wonders. There's a menu of savoury and sweet crêpes, an à la carte featuring the likes of bouillabaisse followed by salt-cod with potatoes, egg and hollandaise (£10), and a list of keenly priced specials. From the latter we were treated to luxuriously thick cream of white-asparagus and leek soup (well worth £3.50; garnished with parsley and a twirl of olive oil), then a (barely) baked salmon fillet with chunky sautéed potatoes and a crisp rocket salad (just £6.50). Our only criticism: some bland sliced apples in the otherwise exemplary crêpe normande (flambéed with a sizeable slug of calvados) – though we did eat in apple-impoverished July. Attractive dish presentation and a list of Belgian beers, cidres bouchées and interesting wines, juices and teas further heightened our admiration. High-quality brasserie food at caff prices.
Babies and children admitted. Tables outdoors (2, pavement). Takeaway service. **Map 5 O4.**

Clerkenwell & Farringdon

Little Bay
171 Farringdon Road, EC1R 3AL (7278 1234/ www.little-bay.co.uk). Farringdon tube/rail. **Meals served** noon-midnight Mon-Sat; noon-11pm Sun. **Main courses** £6.45-£8.45. **Credit** MC, V.
Linda Barker would aspire to produce an interior so inventive, but while there's no denying the makeshift *Changing Rooms* vibe here (oh, the crimes that can be performed with a roll of turquoise velour and a staple gun), Little Bay has proved admirably resilient. The wine list starts at £10.50 and nearly all bottles cost less than £25. Our roast vegetable tarte tatin arrived as a pretty pinwheel with rocket and parmesan. Lamb steak was cooked to order and came with a lovely melange of Mediterranean veg and mash. The menu also takes in burgers, duck breast and plenty of fish. Sides aren't necessary but you shouldn't miss the terrific chips fried in goose fat. Desserts are of the hip-sticking variety. Chocolate fondant wasn't molten but it was satisfyingly dark. Staff were kind and cheerful throughout. Little Bay has branches in Fulham, Kilburn, Croydon, Battersea (where live music is offered five nights a week) – and Belgrade. How do they do it for the price? Goodness knows. If you come before 7pm the whole menu is even cheaper.
Babies and children admitted. Booking advisable. Disabled: toilet. Separate room for parties, seats 120. **Map 5 N4.**
For branches see index.

Covent Garden

★ Canela
33 Earlham Street, WC2H 9LS (7240 6926/ www.canelacafe.com). Covent Garden tube. **Meals served** 9.30am-10pm Mon-Thur; 9.30am-11pm Fri, Sat; 10am-8pm Sun. **Main courses** £5.90-£8.90. **Credit** MC, V.
Canela means cinnamon in Portuguese, which explains why you're given a quill of the spice when ordering a coffee here. Stir it in for a subtle Christmassy flavour. It's a charming tradition at an equally charming café-bar, which specialises in Portuguese and Brazilian food. Located just off Seven Dials, Canela has high ceilings, large windows and a grand chandelier that help it achieve an airy feel in a small space. The menu highlights Brazilian favourites including gluey cheese bread and rich feijoada (served with manioc flour). Portuguese cuisine is showcased with bacalhau (salt-cod), and creamy pasteis de nata (custard tarts). On our last visit we tried the vegetarian lasagne, which we deemed a rare hit; it came beautifully laced with stilton and packed with sweet roasted red peppers. We were also lucky enough to get a slice of the smooth, indulgent cheesecake that often sells out before

Grazing

midday. As prices are quite high, many customers only stop by for a drink, but these are drinks worth stopping for – refreshing caipirinhas and mojitos, as well as bright fresh juices, including the grape-coloured Brazilian açai.

Babies and children admitted. Tables outdoors (4, pavement). Takeaway service. **Map 18 D3**.

Ooze

62 Goodge Street, W1T 4NE (7436 9444/ www.ooze.biz). Goodge Street tube. **Meals served** noon-11pm Mon-Sat. **Main courses** £5.25-£9.95. **Credit** AmEx, MC, V.

Opinion remains divided about the name, but this runner-up in the 2007 Cheap Eats category of the *Time Out* Eating and Drinking Awards continues to thrive. Risotto is the USP, though there are plenty of alternatives: tiger prawns (three big juicy fellows) with garlic, chilli and trebbiano to start, say, or fresh pasta of the day, or slow-roast lamb shank with creamed potatoes to follow. On a cold, rainy night, two meaty risottos (ribeye with sweet onions, rocket and montepulciano wine, and pancetta with rosemary, borlotti beans and radicchio) hit the spot – both punchily flavoured and very filling. On balmier evenings you might plump for alle vongole (with clams, trebbiano, chilli and garlic), or funghi (with a mix of dried and fresh mushrooms and rosemary). Most of the risottos come in two sizes: small isn't really that small and costs £6.50-£7.95; large is £8.50-£13.95. Desserts include a nice range of own-made ice-creams alongside traditional favourites like panacotta and tiramisu, a tart of the day and a selection of Italian cheeses. Service is genuinely smiley, and there's a nicely priced wine list. The pared-down, gently-modern decor looks briskly efficient at lunchtimes, while clever lighting makes it seem cosier by night.

Babies and children welcome: children's menu; high chairs. Tables outdoors (2, pavement). Takeaway service. **Map 17 A1**.

Squat & Gobble

69 Charlotte Street, W1T 4RJ (7580 5338/ www.squatandgobble.co.uk). Goodge Street or Warren Street tube. **Meals served** 7am-5pm Mon-Fri; 9am-5pm Sat. **Main courses** £3.95-£7.95. **Credit** AmEx, MC, V.

Treading a well-balanced line between caff-style homeliness, canteen-style effectiveness and bistro-style funkiness, Squat & Gobble has proved to be a palpable hit amid myriad lunching options provided by the restaurant super-highway that is Charlotte Street. Whether you go for a jacket or sarnie, you can choose from basic fodder (fish-finger sandwich, spud with beans, cheese and bacon) or slightly more imaginative fillings (deep-fried brie and cranberry baguette, tarragon chicken filled potato). There are also plentiful breakfasts, salads, soups and mains up for grabs – from fish cakes to falafel. The enterprise occupies two sites, one on Charlotte Street and another just around the corner, but both are small, with few tables for eating-in and long queues of desktop lunchers popping by for takeaways.

Babies and children admitted. Tables outdoors (9, pavement). Takeaway service. **Map 3 J5**.

Leicester Square

Gaby's

30 Charing Cross Road, WC2H 0DB (7836 4233). Leicester Square tube. **Meals served** 11am-midnight Mon-Sat; noon-10pm Sun. **Main courses** £4-£9. **No credit cards**.

Style zealots will find little reassurance in the spartan floor tiles, utilitarian plastic seating and closely packed Formica tables numbered with handwritten stickers, but this New York-style Jewish diner prides itself on function before fashion. A long metal counter by the front door serves as a hectic base of operations, a handful of signed West End posters (and a couple of framed

photos celebrating the custom of Matt Damon) as decoration. A starter of chicken livers fried with onions and mild mustard arrived almost before it was ordered, only to be replaced – five minutes later and barely finished – with a main course of hungarian goulash that was fine if a little fatty. Sandwiches, bagels and pittas occupy a large part of the laminated menu, as do salads from the counter display. Baklava and a crumbly own-made cheesecake share space on the dessert list. As well as local office staff, Gaby's attracts plenty of elderly diners who linger over bottles of Greek wine and gesticulate with a vehemence that would make real New Yorkers proud.

Babies and children admitted. Takeaway service. **Map 18 D5**.

Soho

★ Hummus Bros (100)

88 Wardour Street, W1F 0TJ (7734 1311/ www.hbros.co.uk). Oxford Circus or Tottenham Court Road tube. **Meals served** 11am-10pm Mon-Wed; 11am-11pm Thur, Fri; noon-11pm Sat; noon-10pm Sun. **Main courses** £2.50-£6. **Credit** AmEx, MC, V.

The simple and hugely successful formula at this Soho café/takeaway is to serve houmous as a base for a selection of toppings, which you scoop up with warm, fluffy pitta bread. Super-smooth, creamy, flavoursome houmous comes shaped around the edges of a bowl, filled with a topping of your choice. Decide from fresh-tasting, zingy guacamole, salad, stewed mushrooms, slow-cooked beef and fava beans, or daily specials such as Thai green chicken curry. Portions are satisfying rather than generous, but you can also add extras (feta, jalapeños, toasted pine nuts) and side dishes (barbecued aubergine, tabouleh, grilled vegetables). The concept works, and the food is nutritious and good value – though note that at

Just Falafs

CHEAP EATS

weekends and after 5pm there's a price hike. Gluten-free pitta alternatives (rye bread, carrot sticks) are available too. Round off with a brownie, baklava or malabi (a milk-based dessert with date honey) if you still have room. Staff are patient and helpful and there's free Wi-Fi, but don't expect to linger here; the canteen-style set-up doesn't lend itself to chilling out at peak times.
Babies and children admitted. Bookings not accepted. Takeaway service. Vegan dishes.
Map 17 B3.
For branch see index.

★ Just Falafs NEW
155 Wardour Street, W1F 8WG (7734 1914/ www.justfalafs.com). Tottenham Court Road tube. **Meals served** 10am-10pm Mon-Fri; noon-10pm Sat. **Main courses** £3.45-£6.75. **Credit** MC, V.
While the wrap reigns supreme in this attractive timber-decked refectory, there's more to Simon Davies and Chris Skinner's emerging chain than just falafel. Scrumptiously light Dorset lamb meatballs, for instance, which are rolled up with red cabbage, spinach, tomato sauce, yoghurt and cucumber – or smoked organic chicken complemented by roast sweet potato, spinach, and tahini garlic sauce. Order your own combo from the colourful serving cabinet or opt for one of the menu's suggestions, which are well-judged even if they do suffer from embarrassing 'geddit?' names. The perfectly filling 'regular' size (with two falafels) costs £4.50. Virtuous ingredients such as beansprouts are tempered by lush sauces; the heavenly aubergine sauce is probably a long way from being low-cal, but hey, you'll probably be well on your way to five-a-day here. Drinks-wise, there's the usual range of espresso-style coffees, bottled smoothies and other soft drinks. The larger Soho outlet, unlike the Covent Garden original, is open late and charges a premium to eat-in; you can also drop by for breakfast of 'magic porridge' with rice milk, spices and honey.
Tables outdoors (2, pavement). Takeaway service.
Map 17 B3.
For branch see index.

Mother Mash
26 Ganton Street, W1F 7QZ (7494 9644/ www.mothermash.co.uk). Oxford Circus tube. **Meals served** 8.30am-10pm Mon-Fri; noon-10pm Sat; noon-5pm Sun. **Main courses** £6.95-£7.95. **Credit** AmEx, MC, V.
It's not built for comfort – the high wooden bench seating demands you place your feet on a bar beneath the table, or leave them swinging like a five-year-old – but comfort food is what Mother Mash serves, in big soothing spoonfuls. Read the school dinnery desserts list first, as the puds are delicious and portions are small enough to squeeze one in after a mix-and-match main course. Ordering is easy in theory: you choose your mash, you choose your pie or sausages, you choose your gravy. The hard bit is in deciding what you want from the tempting list. We didn't have horseradish mash, or crème fraîche and lemon, or chopped green olive. Cheesy mustard mash and champ seemed like better accompaniments to our chicken, leek and ham pies and onion gravy. Veg, should you want them, include grilled french beans wrapped in bacon, and mushy or 'garden' peas. Main-course salads are available too (oh please, get real). The beer list is disappointing, with bottles of London Pride the only British option. Why no Innis & Gunn, or Old Hooky? Fentimans soft drinks strike a more appropriate note, and the short wine list is appealing.
Babies and children admitted. Tables outdoors (6, pavement). Takeaway service. **Map 17 A4.**

Stockpot
18 Old Compton Street, W1D 4TN (7287 1066). Leicester Square or Tottenham Court Road tube. **Meals served** 11.30am-11.30pm Mon, Tue; 11.30am-midnight Wed-Sat; noon-11.30pm Sun. **Main courses** £3.40-£5.50. **Set meal** (Mon-Sat) £5.85-£6.45 2 courses; (Sun) £6.50 2 courses.
No credit cards.
An old, old favourite, Stockpot never changes and we wouldn't have it any other way. In the slim chance that you're one of the few people in London who have never been here, the scene is easy to set. The spartan but comfortable ground floor has booth seating at the back and tables for two at the front – those by the window allow you to watch the strutting Old Compton Street peacocks – while the basement is more functional and less popular. The menu is just one sheet of paper offering such ancient delights as gammon with pineapple and other forgotten standards of British mass dining. Little costs over £5, and you can get two courses and a small beaker of red wine for less than a tenner. Omelettes, grills and pasta are your best bets. Keep it simple, enjoy the atmosphere, appreciate the prices and line the stomach for a night of Soho-based roistering. Stockpot has been providing just such a service for years.
Babies and children admitted. Tables outdoors (2, pavement). Takeaway service. **Map 17 C3.**

Westminster

★ Vincent Rooms
Victoria Centre, Vincent Square , SW1P 2PD (7802 8391/www.westking.ac.uk). St James's Park tube/Victoria tube/rail. **Lunch served** noon-1pm Mon-Fri. **Dinner served** 6-7pm Tue, Thur. Closed 2 wks Apr, July-Sept, 2 wks Dec-Jan. **Main courses** £7.25-£10.50. **Set meal** Escoffier Room £22.50 3 courses incl coffee. **Credit** MC, V.
You can't very well complain about the Vincent Rooms – the food's too good and the prices too low. It's where students (waiters and chefs) get to practise their trade at this catering college, whose alumni include Jamie Oliver. Booking is tricky, with odd opening hours during term-time only, but you can eat in the brasserie or the posher Escoffier restaurant. Only more experienced students are unleashed on the public, so standards are consistently high. In the brasserie you may get baked duck egg and spiced tomato cannellini beans, fennel and lemon pot-roasted pork loin, or passion-fruit crème brûlée. In the Escoffier it's a full-blown three-course set menu bookended by exquisite canapés and coffee or tea with petits fours. After starters of seared scallops, and rabbit loin, then mains of john dory with cockle and clam fricassee, and chicken bordelaise, we were impressed. Following on with frangipane cake and raspberry mousse from the dessert trolley (there's also a cheeseboard), we were gorged too. Maybe the artichoke was stringy. Maybe the rooms feel like a school hall. Maybe the wine list (£11-£20) is too short, but at £22.50 this is among the best-value set menus in town.
Babies and children welcome: high chair. Booking advisable. Disabled: toilet. Separate room for parties, seats 30. **Map 15 J10.**

South

Battersea

Fish in a Tie
105 Falcon Road, SW11 2PF (7924 1913). Clapham Junction rail. **Lunch served** noon-3pm, **dinner served** 6pm-midnight Mon-Sat. **Meals served** noon-11pm Sun. **Main courses** £5.95-£10.50. **Set lunch** (Mon-Sat) £7.50 2 courses. **Credit** MC, V.
This friendly spot is a veritable oasis from the noise of buses chugging up Falcon Road. Inside, paper tablecloths and wax-encrusted liqueur bottles cover some rickety plywood tables, but the cluttered, 'art nouveau on the cheap' bistro vibe is part of the charm. A basket of crunchy sesame-seeded bread arrived without our prompting (and, refreshingly, without charge). All main courses and specials come with the same vegetables (shredded cabbage, sautéed potatoes and runner beans, on this occasion). Flash frying and enthusiastically whipped-up sauces are popular here. We spied the chef raiding the bar for wine and whisky, which we hope went in the food. Dishes are hearty – if occasionally eccentric; our jumbo, slightly burnt salmon and cod fish cake came perched on just a few french fries. A complimentary portion of watermelon was proffered when we pleaded we had no room for dessert. You get the impression that Fish in a Tie wants to send all its customers away happy and full. All mains are pegged at about £7, so what it adds to the waistline, it won't take away from the pocket.
Babies and children welcome: children's portions; high chairs. Booking advisable. Separate rooms for parties, seating 25 and 40. **Map 21 C3.**

Galapagos Bistro-Café NEW
169 Battersea High Street, SW11 3JS (8488 4989). Clapham Junction rail. **Meals served** 9am-9.30pm Tue-Fri; 9.30am-9.30pm Sat. **Main courses** £5-£7.50. **Set dinner** (7-9.30pm) £10.50 2 courses, £12.50 3 courses. **Credit** AmEx, MC, V.
It could be the screenplay for a triumph-of-the-little-guy film; cosy little Galapagos (the owner is from Ecuador, the chef Burmese) used to be a deli until the arrival of two supermarket giants on its patch threatened extinction. Unwilling to bow out,

Pie and mash shops

Few London restaurants can match the city's last remaining pie and mash shops for simple authenticity. Their menu has altered little since the mid 19th century: a wedge of glutinous mashed potatoes, pies (minced beef and gravy in a watertight crust), liquor (loosely based on parsley sauce) and eels (jellied and cold, or warm and stewed) – though with the high prices of eels, more shops are now sticking to plain pie and mash. But it's often their remarkably beautiful design that gives punters an exceptional dining experience: in the lettering of their facades, usually pitched somewhere between clean-cut art deco and twirly art nouveau; the austere hygiene of their tiled interiors, complete with moulded ceramic dadoes, backless wooden benches and marble-topped tables; and the spare functionality of their steel counters and cash registers.

From the very beginning, the business was largely dominated by three families – the Cookes, the Kellys and the Manzes – and the decor of some of their first establishments still delights the eye. The **Cookes** came first, apparently. Their oldest existing shop (opening in 1900) is at Broadway Market near London Fields, Hackney. The family's magnificent Kingsland High Street shop, which opened in 1910, was Grade II listed in 1991, the first of its kind in the capital to receive that official seal of approval; it's now a Chinese restaurant, **Shanghai** (see p83), but you can still view its lavishly decorated frontage and interior.

The first of the **Manze's** shops is still the best-looking, on Tower Bridge Road. Opened in 1902, though the building itself is ten years older, it features high-backed benches below long mirrors set into plain white-tiled walls relieved by flower-pattern tiles. The **Kelly** shops are on two famous East End streets, Bethnal Green Road and Roman Road, where they're well patronised by market traders and shoppers. The oldest existing branch, at 284 Bethnal Green Road, opened in 1937. In Tooting, **Harrington's** shop is one of the oldest, dating from the early 20th century. Nearer central London, **Clark's** took over a 1930s Manze operation in Exmouth Market in the late '50s, keeping the original shopfront (though in the '70s the signwriter apparently misspelt their name). All are worth a look, as well as a meal, which would still be cheap at twice the price.

WJ Arment
7 & 9 Westmoreland Road, SE17 2AX (7703 4974). Elephant & Castle tube/rail/12, 35, 40, 45, 68A, 171, 176, 468 bus. **Open** 10.30am-5pm Tue, Wed; 10.30am-4.30pm Thur; 10.30am-5.30pm Fri; 10.30-6pm Sat. **No credit cards.**

Castle's
229 Royal College Street, NW1 9LT (7485 2196). Camden Town tube/Camden Road rail. **Open** 10.30am-3.30pm Tue-Fri; 10.30am-4pm Sat. **No credit cards.**

Clark's
46 Exmouth Market, EC1R 4QE (7837 1974). Farringdon tube/rail/19, 38, 341 bus. **Open** 10.30am-4pm Mon-Thur; 10.30am-5pm Fri, Sat. **No credit cards. Map 5 N4.**

Cockneys Pie & Mash
314 Portobello Road, W10 5RU (8960 9409). Ladbroke Grove tube. **Open** 11.30am-5.30pm Tue-Thur, Sat; 11.30am-6pm Fri. **No credit cards.**

F Cooke
150 Hoxton Street, N1 6SH (7729 7718). Old Street or Liverpool Street tube/rail/ 48, 55, 149, 242, 243 bus. **Open** 10am-7pm Mon-Thur; 9.30am-8pm Fri, Sat. **No credit cards. Map 6 R2.**

F Cooke
9 Broadway Market, E8 4PH (7254 6458). Liverpool Street tube/rail then 26, 48 or 55 bus/London Fields rail. **Open** 10am-7pm Mon-Thur; 10am-8pm Fri, Sat. **No credit cards.**

AJ Goddard
203 Deptford High Street, SE8 3NT (8692 3601). Deptford rail/Deptford Bridge DLR/1, 47 bus. **Open** 9.30am-3pm Mon-Fri; 9am-3pm Sat. **No credit cards.**

Harrington's
3 Selkirk Road, SW17 0ER (8672 1877). Tooting Broadway tube. **Open** 11am-9pm Tue, Thur, Fri; 11am-2pm Wed; 11am-7.30pm Sat. **No credit cards.**

G Kelly
600 Roman Road, E3 2RW (8983 3552/ www.gkellypieandmash.co.uk). Mile End or Bow Road tube/Bow Church DLR/8, 339 bus. **Open** 10am-2.30pm Thur, Fri; 10am-5pm Sat. **No credit cards.**

G Kelly
414 Bethnal Green Road, E2 0DJ (7739 3603). Bethnal Green tube/rail/8 bus. **Open** 10am-3pm Mon-Thur; 10am-6.30pm Fri; 9.30am-4.30pm Sat. **No credit cards.**

S&R Kelly
284 Bethnal Green Road, E2 0AG (7739 8676). Bethnal Green tube/rail/8 bus. **Open** 9am-2.30pm Mon-Thur; 9am-5.30pm Fri; 10am-3.30pm Sat. **No credit cards. Map 6 S4.**

Manze's
204 Deptford High Street, SE8 3PR (8692 2375). Deptford rail/Deptford Bridge DLR/ 1, 47 bus. **Open** 9.30am-1.30pm Mon, Thur; 9.30am-3pm Tue, Wed, Fri, Sat. **No credit cards.**

L Manze
76 Walthamstow High Street, E17 7LD (8520 2855). Walthamstow Central tube/rail. **Open** 10am-4pm Mon-Wed; 10am-5pm Thur-Sat. **No credit cards.**

L Manze
74 Chapel Market, N1 9ER (7837 5270). Angel tube. **Open** 11am-5pm Tue-Sat. **No credit cards.**

M Manze (100)
87 Tower Bridge Road, SE1 4TW (7407 2985/www.manze.co.uk). Bus 1, 42, 188. **Open** 11am-2pm Mon; 10.30am-2pm Tue-Thur; 10am-2.15pm Fri; 10am-2.45pm Sat. **No credit cards.**

M Manze
105 Peckham High Street, SE15 5RS (7277 6181/www.manze.co.uk). Peckham Rye rail. **Open** 11am-2pm Mon; 10.30am-2pm Tue-Thur; 10am-2.15pm Fri; 10am-2.45pm Sat. **No credit cards.**

M Manze
226 High Street, Sutton, Surrey SM1 1NT (8286 8787/www.manze.co.uk). Sutton rail. **Open** 10.30am-3pm Mon; 11am-5pm Tue-Fri; 10.30-5pm Sat. **No credit cards.**

CHEAP EATS

the business adapted, presumably heeding the theory of natural selection hit upon by Darwin while exploring the very islands that give this dining room its name. So, post-reinvention, it's now a very pleasant café-restaurant. Comfy corner sofas, fresh flowers and shelves stacked with boxes of tea and other deli cast-offs make a visit here feel a little like stepping into somebody's front room – an illusion enhanced by the loyal locals who have made the place their home from home, and the incredibly friendly staff. Complimentary olives and canapés are a thoughtful touch on our arrival, thereafter the set dinner menu is short and very sweet, not least for its price – two courses for just £10.50. Mains of fisherman's pie and merguez sausage with spicy rice were both fine examples of cheap-eat fodder. However, it's in puddings that Galapagos excels. Our Mexican pecan pie was nicely spiced with cinnamon, while a chocolate fondant was rich and moist.
Booking advisable. Restaurant available for hire. Tables outdoors (2, pavement). Takeaway service. **Map 21 B2.**

South East

Bankside

The Table (100)
83 Southwark Street, SE1 0HX (7401 2760/ www.thetablecafe.com). Southwark tube/London Bridge tube/rail. **Meals served** 7.30am-5pm Mon-Thur; 7.30am-9.30pm Fri; 9am-3pm Sat. **Main courses** £5-£10. **Credit** AmEx, MC, V. The ground floor of a major architectural firm supplies the location for this innovative food-provider. Artisanal examples of the sandwich can be found wrapped and waiting on a stand by the entrance – the Cuban, for example, containing 16-hour slow-roasted pork. There's also an old-fashioned self-service salad buffet, packed with the likes of roasted vegetable couscous, greek salad and sticky barbecued chicken drumsticks (marinated in muscovado sugar, lime and mango). Diners with time to spare head to the back counter, where smartly dressed staff dispense hot meals from a daily changing menu that includes a soup of the day (garden pea and mint on our last visit), as well as a tart (roast broccoli and gruyère), plus a range of meat and fish dishes chargrilled to order: from organic minute steaks to Billingsgate-fresh monkfish. It's then a case of perching on one of the chunky wooden pews (assuming there's a spare spot) and dining with one eye people-watching through the big windows, and one ear cocked for amusing conversations.
Babies and children admitted. Disabled: toilet. Tables outdoors (8, terrace). Takeaway service. **Map 11 O8.**

East

Bethnal Green

E Pellicci (100)
332 Bethnal Green Road, E2 0AG (7739 4873). Bethnal Green tube/rail/8, 253 bus. **Meals served** 6.15am-5pm Mon-Sat. **Main courses**

£5-£8. **Unlicensed**. **Corkage** no charge. **No credit cards**.

Not just a caff, but a social club, taxi drivers' meeting room and unofficial matchmaking service, E Pellicci has been warmly welcoming customers since 1900. The heritage-listed marquetry-panelled interior is cramped; sharing tables is to be expected, nay relished. As a maître d', Nevio Junior exhibits skills on a par with those of Silvano Giraldin at Le Gavroche. ('Have you met Steve? He's just back from Nepal, climbed the Himalayas. Are you swimming the Channel again this year, Steve?'). An espresso machine customised with the Ferrari logo produces coffee and hot water for mugs of sweet builders' brew. The good-value cooking includes traditional English and Italian dishes, sarnies and classic puds, and of course a roster of glistening fry-ups – everything from a set veggie breakfast to black pudding. Staff are amenable. (To pensioner: 'One poached egg on one toast? You're causing real trouble for the kitchen with that order, young lady.' Pensioner giggles, delighted.) The chips are rightly renowned, though our bubble could have done with more vegetable bits. Some say Pellicci's is now so famous it attracts too many posers, but that wasn't a problem on our last visit.
Babies and children welcome: children's menu.

Brick Lane

Story Deli

3 Dray Walk, The Old Truman Brewery, 91 Brick Lane, E1 6QL (7247 3137). Liverpool Street tube/rail. **Meals served** noon-10pm daily. **Main courses** £6-£11. **Unlicensed**. **Corkage** no charge. **Credit** AmEx, MC, V.

This cosy little pizzeria is ideal for a chat and a chew. Inside you'll find rough-hewn tables, little pod stools, big wax church candles and ambient music (Kruder & Dorfmeister on a loop during our visit), along with a huge plate-glass window through which to gaze at the hectic goings-on of Dray Walk. There's no menu. Everything is chalked up on blackboards hanging on a wall – 'everything' being pizzas, generously topped with well-sourced ingredients. The pizzas are rather like Alsatian tarte flambée: thin crispy oven-baked dough covered in the likes of roast chicken and mushroom, prawn and green pepper, or five-cheese (gorgonzola, feta, parmesan, mozzarella and mascarpone). Our ham and artichoke pizza featured coppa air-dried ham and came on a board with a pile of rocket. With the exception of a margherita (£9), they're all £10. Beers include

Freedom and Canabia; wine is either £4 or £5 a glass or £14-£20 a bottle. There are also plenty of coffees and teas, plus ice-cream (butterscotch, honey and ginger) for afters.
Babies and children welcome: children's portions; toys. Tables outdoors (2, pavement). Takeaway service. Map 6 S5.

Whitechapel

Nando's

9-25 Mile End Road, E1 4TW (7791 2720/ www.nandos.com). Mile End tube. **Meals served** noon-11pm Mon-Sat; noon-10pm Sun. **Main courses** £5.80-£10.60. **Credit** AmEx, MC, V.

How fast does fast food have to be? Dishes come pretty quickly here, but the addition of Mediterranean decor, real crockery, wooden tables and floor-staff puts Nando's a notch above a standard fast-food outlet. The chain's success has been secured by its succulent Portuguese peri peri (chilli-spiced) chicken, which comes flame-grilled and to your own spicy specification: lemon and herb, medium, hot, or extra hot. Many branches also sell halal chicken. Prices vary according to the number of side dishes you add; popular choices of peri peri chips and spicy rice keep palates pulsating. The new vegetarian dish of portobello mushroom with halloumi cheese and chilli jam in a bun or pitta makes a tasty alternative to the chicken choices. We found staff at the Mile End branch friendly and attentive, and despite a high turnover the place was kept clean and tidy. This is fast food done well.
Babies and children welcome: children's menu; high chairs. Disabled: toilet. Takeaway service. **For branches see index.**

North East

Hackney

LMNT

316 Queensbridge Road, E8 3NH (7249 6727/ www.lmnt.co.uk). Dalston Kingsland rail/236 bus. **Meals served** noon-11pm Mon-Sat; noon-10.30pm Sun. **Main courses** £7.95-£9.95, all mains £7.95 before 7pm. **Credit** MC, V.

From the moment you walk in you know you're in for an unusual experience. Your table might be in a huge amphora, or up some steps to a tiny gallery with only enough space for two. Wherever it is you'll be surrounded by drapes, candles, walls covered in Egyptian pharaohs and hieroglyphs, and the sounds of an eccentric, but not unpleasant,

soundtrack. The Mediterranean-tinged menu produced a delicious starter of grilled portobello mushroom, and a puy lentil salad with feta so plentiful we had to leave some to save room for the mains. Breast of duck was beautifully presented and served in wonderfully rich gravy. But the medium-to-well-done ribeye we'd requested was slightly overcooked and a little gristly; celeriac remoulade was watery; and the fondant potato tasted less than fresh – but it seems churlish to complain when prices are so low and service so swift and helpful. Food prices are slightly reduced if you get your order in before 7pm, when starters and desserts are £2.95 and mains £7.95. On Sundays, the menu expands to include roasts for just £7.95. There's a decent choice of wines too, starting at about £10.
Babies and children admitted. Entertainment: opera 8pm Sun. Tables outdoors (3, garden). **Map 25 C5.**

Stoke Newington

Blue Legume

101 Stoke Newington Church Street, N16 0UD (7923 1303). Stoke Newington rail/73 bus. **Open** 9.30am-11pm Mon-Sat; 9.30am-6.30pm Sun. **Main courses** £4.95-£8.95. **Credit** (Mon-Fri) MC, V.

Blue Legume is best known for its sterling brunches, making it a mecca for locals at the weekend. Hungover twenty-somethings dawdle over sticky, maple syrup-drizzled waffles with fruit and yoghurt, eggs benedict or mushrooms on toast with crème fraîche, while families pile into the conservatory area out back; on sunny days, the strip of pavement tables on the street is prime people-watching terrain. In the evening, it morphs from a sunny café into a low-key neighbourhood bistro, with candles flickering on the mosaic tables, jazz playing in the background and an ambitiously extensive menu, encompassing everything from seafood tagliatelle and tapas to moussaka and home-made burgers. Amiable waiters deliver giant plates of food: we barely made a dent in a heaped dish of spicy, saffron-infused paella, while a rack of lamb (slightly fatty but perfectly pink) was accompanied by a mountain of fluffy mashed potato and plump mushrooms covered in Madeira sauce. Desserts, while equally enormous, were disappointing: a baked cheesecake was too bland, and a banofee pie unexceptional.
Babies and children welcome: high chairs. Booking advisable dinner. Tables outdoors (5, pavement). Takeaway service. **Map 25 B1.**

E Pellicci. See p301.

North
Camden Town & Chalk Farm

Marine Ices
8 Haverstock Hill, NW3 2BL (7482 9003/ www.marineices.co.uk). Chalk Farm tube. **Lunch served** noon-3pm, **dinner served** 6-11pm Tue-Fri. **Meals served** noon-11pm Sat; noon-10pm Sun. **Main courses** £6.10-£13.75. **Credit** MC, V.
It's no surprise to find a line of people queueing outside this retro ice-cream parlour for a tub of fresh fruit sorbet (lemon, papaya) or cone of own-made ice-cream (caribbean coconut, toffee crunch). The spacious interior is often packed too. Marine Ices is a great place for families and group get-togethers (staff are more than happy to serenade you with their rendition of 'Happy Birthday'). The happy vibe can border on the noisy, but food is good value and tasty. To start, there's a range of antipasti (including lovely garlicky bruschetta), followed by pizzas, meat dishes (plenty of veal) and many pasta dishes: you pick the pasta shape and the classic Italian sauce to go with it. Alternatively, choose from the more unusual house specialities – how about risotto barbara with Spanish sausage, cream, peas and saffron? The family-run business started in 1928 and the owners are proud of their history. Pictures of family members adorn the walls, along with those of minor celebrities and their scrawled autographs. *Babies and children welcome: children's portions; high chairs. Takeaway service.* **Map 27 B1.**

Islington

Le Mercury
140A Upper Street, N1 1QY (7354 4088/ www.lemercury.co.uk). Angel tube/Highbury & Islington tube/rail. **Meals served** noon-1am Mon-Sat; noon-11.30pm Sun. **Main courses** £6.45. **Credit** AmEx, MC, V.
This sweet French restaurant is an ideal option for a budget meal in a charming setting. The rustic dining area, cosily lit by dripping candles, is frequently packed, but don't assume you can't get a table as there's a second dining room on the first floor. The majority of the menu follows the classic French bistro theme, but there are a few surprise combinations thrown in. Starters (all £3.95) such as chèvre chaud, moules marinière and foie gras are complemented by less Gallic fare such as deep-fried squid. Mains included a pleasing lamb shank with rosemary jus (choose it over the entrecôte grillée which was average by comparison), as well as seared mackerel with beetroot, fennel and lime pickle, and roast pork with black pudding. Desserts might be the ubiquitous crème brûlée, or the more unusual roast rhubarb with basil ice-cream. Anyone on a budget has little to complain about here – an imaginative selection of dishes, cooked to a reasonable standard, at amazing prices, with wine from £10.45.
Babies and children admitted. Booking advisable weekends. Separate room for parties, seats 50. **Map 5 O1.**

S&M Café (100)
4-6 Essex Road, N1 8LN (7359 5361/ www.sandmcafe.co.uk). Angel tube. **Meals served** 7.30am-11pm Mon-Fri; 8.30am-11pm Sat; 8.30am-10.30pm Sun. **Main courses** £6.95-£7.75. **Credit** MC, V.
Friendly, efficient staff handle busy periods well at this Islington stalwart, taking names and honouring tables so customers don't have to queue. Although famously preserved by S&M founder Kevin Finch, the decor of the former Alfredo's café is a mix of periods, with panelling covering a probable multitude of building sins, lairy blue Formica tables and tiny red leather chairs. It's cramped, but mostly jovial. The all-day breakfasts are as popular as the eponymous sausage and mash, while the blackboard promotes Sunday lunch-type meals – say curried parsnip soup, roast lamb shanks, and spotted dick with vanilla

custard. The only problem with our meal was that the rather thin onion gravy and bubble and squeak were simply not hot, unlike the wild boar and calvados sausages they accompanied. But we enjoyed the daily special of chicken and asparagus bangers (toulouse was another option) partnered by tasty potato, parsnip and turnip mash. Super freshly squeezed orange juice, mugs of cappuccino and the floral-medicinal kick of dandelion and burdock went swimmingly with the hearty meal.
Babies and children welcome: children's menu; high chair. Booking advisable; not accepted before 4pm weekends. Tables outdoors (5, pavement). Takeaway service. **Map 5 O1.**
For branches see index.

Outer London
Richmond, Surrey

Stein's
55 Richmond Towpath, west of Richmond Bridge, Richmond, Surrey TW10 6UX (8948 8189/ www.stein-s.com). Richmond tube/rail then 20mins walk or 65 bus. **Meals served** noon-10pm Mon-Fri; 10am-10pm Sat, Sun. **Main courses** £3.90-£14.90. **Credit** MC, V.
Unusual and quirky, Stein's is a family-friendly riverside Bavarian beer-garden a stone's throw from Richmond bridge. It was converted from a ramshackle ice-cream parlour in 2004 and consists of a kiosk with a sizeable kitchen behind, surrounded by benches alongside the river – about half of them under cover. There's a safe, small area where under-fives can play. The menu is 100% German: Wurst, plus Bavarian specialities like roasted pork shoulder with dumplings, and pork meatloaf. The Bavarian cheese and sausage sharing platter was excellent, accompanied by soft, almost sweet bread rolls, and featuring three cheeses, seven cold meats, salad and gherkins. Bratkartoffeln (potatoes sautéed with bacon, onion and spices) was good comfort food, popular with children. Stein's also serves some mean breakfasts and a vast array of strudel desserts. German beer flows freely (obviously) and the Almdudler, an apple-flavoured herbal lemonade from Austria, is lovely. Service is basic – you order and pay at the kiosk then wait for your food – but this is a friendly, authentic place. You can even hear the

chefs singing along to German pop music in the kitchen. Watch out for the weather: at the slightest sign of rain, the place closes.
Babies and children welcome: high chairs. Tables outdoors (28, towpath). Takeaway service.

GOURMET BURGER BARS

Central
Bloomsbury

Ultimate Burger
34 New Oxford Street, WC1A 1AP (7436 6641/ www.ultimateburger.co.uk). Tottenham Court Road tube. **Meals served** noon-11.30pm daily. **Main courses** £5.55-£6.95. **Credit** AmEx, MC, V.
Ouch! Squeeze past the queue, between the densely packed tables, and inch on to one of the angular stools at the window here and you'll still have to watch your head throughout the meal, thanks to some annoyingly dangled light fittings. Ultimate Burger's ergonomic problems don't just apply to the decor. Though its food is visually impressive, with shiny sesame-seed buns, fat slices of tomato and lawns of green leaf, the burgers' sheer girth makes them difficult to eat. A slick of brown fat spurted from our bacon cheeseburger; the over-puffy onion rings left behind blobs of yellow goo. There was one final surprise when a banana milkshake became ice-cream as we reached the bottom of its metal pitcher, rendering it impossible to drink. The menu promises interesting ways with lamb, chicken, and grilled mushrooms and aubergines (for vegetarians) but – state-of-the-art mexican burger served in a folded flour tortilla aside – this was a big, fatty let-down.
Babies and children welcome: high chairs. Disabled: toilet. Takeaway service. **Map 18 D2.**
For branch see index.

Fitzrovia

Hamburger Union
64 Tottenham Court Road, W1C 2ET (7636 0011/www.hamburgerunion.com). Goodge Street or Tottenham Court Road tube. **Meals served**

Ground. See p304.

CHEAP EATS

11.30am-10.30pm Mon-Sat; 11.30am-8pm Sun.
Main courses £5-£8. **Credit** AmEx, MC, V.
With its canteen-like feel and retro-modern
trappings, Hamburger Union's rapidly expanding
chain – six in London, up to ten due to roll out across
the Middle East – seems to have inadvertently set
the template for the recent makeovers at
McDonald's. Despite great claims for the
provenance of its grass-reared beef, this fast-food
feel is carried over to the burgers. Our bacon
cheeseburger was flaccid and tasteless (not least
the bacon, which was practically translucent). On
the other hand, there's an imaginative menu,
including an unctuous, paprika-packed chorizo
sandwich and citrus-marinated halloumi cheese.
Milkshakes come in ice-cold metal buckets, and
there are Chegworth juices and Fentimans soft
drinks too. For the diet-conscious, burgers are
available bread-free, for everyone else, we heartily
recommend a bowl of the fat, golden and fluffy
fries, which always disappear fast on our visits.
Babies and children admitted. Takeaway service.
Map 10 K5.
For branches see index.

Leicester Square

Burger Shack
*147-149 Charing Cross Road, WC2H 0EE
(7287 8728/www.smollenskys.com). Tottenham
Court Road tube.* **Meals served** 11am-midnight
Mon-Sat; noon-midnight Sun. **Main courses**
£5.95-£15.95. **Credit** AmEx, MC, V.
Self-respecting Londoners will probably steer a
wide berth around Burger Shack's location, yet it's
worth asking what this place offers tourists.
Well, northerners will appreciate the unlikely
appearance of chips and gravy on the menu in the
guise of 'wet fries'; Americans will find the spirits
and mixers well-priced; and families will easily get
a seat (on a Saturday lunchtime there were only
three tables occupied, while nearby Hamburger
Union was packed). With pictures of movie stars
on the walls, likeable pop-soul music in the
background, and – unlike most 'gourmet' chains –
table service, the Shack is pleasant enough.
Unusually, staff ask how you want your burgers
done, and relish is considerately put to the side.
Vegetarians have a decent choice too: beanburgers,
quorn burgers, big mushrooms or falafels. Flaky
supermarket-style buns aside, it seems all Burger
Shack is missing is customers.
*Babies and children welcome: children's menu.
Disabled: toilet. Takeaway service.* **Map 17 C3.**

West
Chiswick

★ Ground
*217-221 Chiswick High Road, W4 2DW (8747
9113/www.groundrestaurants.com). Turnham
Green tube.* **Meals served** noon-10pm Mon, Tue;
noon-10.30pm Wed, Thur; noon-11pm Fri; 11am-
11pm Sat; 11am-10pm Sun. **Main courses**
£5.35-£8.95. **Credit** AmEx, MC, V.
With its opulent central pendant light and loft-style
exposed brickwork, this Chiswick independent is
more stylish and spacious than any of its gourmet-
chain rivals. You're led to olive-green leather
booths to order from a menu that offers interesting
beers and soft drinks (Mexican dark lager Negro
Modelo, mint lemonade). All of the burgers – blue
cheese, new york deli, hawaiian – are available
meat-free, with two big beanburger patties.
Vegetarians will be less pleased if the bacon's left
in, as it was with our order. The meat burgers are
noticeably ground more coarsely than at most
chains, producing a truly beefy bite, though the
'artisan' buns could do with beefing up; both our
burgers collapsed into a gloopy mess. Top marks,
though, for perfectly seasoned beer-battered onion
rings. Ground's high prices make it more suitable
for a big blow-out than a fast-food fix, but the
chains could certainly pick up a trick or two here.
*Babies and children welcome: children's menu;
high chairs. Disabled: toilet. Separate room for
parties, seats 52. Tables outdoors (8, pavement).
Takeaway service.*

South
Balham

Fine Burger Company
*37 Bedford Hill, SW12 9EY (8772 0266).
Balham tube/rail.* **Meals served** noon-10pm
Mon-Wed, Sun; noon-11pm Thur-Sat. **Main
courses** £5.60-£14.50. **Credit** AmEx, DC, MC, V.
The Flaming Lips on the stereo, album art on the
walls, and menus like mini newspapers – three
indicators that FBC fancies itself as hipper than
the opposition. It's also going more aggressively
for your wallet, with a loyalty card, two-for-one
nights, and a take on the tasting menu: mini
burgers. The best innovation is the option to
upgrade to a 'combo' with half-portions of two side
dishes (skin-on, hand-cut chips and fiery onion
rings) for £3; that should make a hearty meal for
two cost less than £20, provided you don't care
for a milkshake. Our 'double red hot' burger was
one of the biggest in town, with a hefty slice of
beef tomato the size of a Big Mac and pickled
jalapeños, though proper chilli rather than salsa
would have been preferable. With crayons and
toys for the young 'uns, FBC is a fun place to eat
cheaply, and more spacious than its rivals, who
should be watching with interest.
*Babies and children welcome: children's menu;
high chairs; toys. Booking advisable weekends.
Tables outdoors (2, pavement). Takeaway service.*
For branches see index.

Clapham

Gourmet Burger Kitchen
*44 Northcote Road, SW11 1NZ (7228 3309/
www.gbkinfo.com). Clapham Junction rail/49,
77, 219, 345 bus.* **Meals served** noon-11pm
Mon-Fri; 11am-11pm Sat; 11am-10pm Sun.
Main courses £5.55-£8.95. **Credit** MC, V.
There's an inventive international flavour to the
food here, with imaginative greek, thai and
jamaican burgers joining their beetrooted kiwi
cousin at this well-established New Zealand-
inspired chain. The burgers are picture-perfect,
housed in freshly baked sesame-seed sourdough
buns with acres of lush lettuce and aged cheddar
cheese melting alluringly down the sides. The
robust Aberdeen Angus beef patties certainly put
Burger King's efforts at similarly sourced meat into
perspective (even the kids' burgers seem bigger
than the BK Angus burgers, and are crisply
chargrilled). There are new organic products too,
such as wild boar burgers, albeit at a pricey £8.95
without chips. Vegetarians are kept happy with a
spicy puy lentil burger augmenting the 'big
mushroom'. However, over-eagerness with those
cosmopolitan relishes (on our visit, customers were
pulling their burgers apart and rebuilding),
cramped seating and a long wait for tables will
have to be addressed if the Gourmet Burger
Kitchen is to stay pre-eminent.
*Babies and children welcome: children's portions;
high chairs. Tables outdoors (4, pavement).
Takeaway service.* **Map 21 C4.**
For branches see index.

South West
Fulham

★ Haché
*329-331 Fulham Road, SW10 9QL (7823 3515/
www.hacheburgers.com). South Kensington tube.*
Meals served noon-10.30pm Mon-Fri; noon-
11.15 Sat, Sun. **Main courses** £6.50-£12.50.
Set lunch (noon-3pm Mon-Fri) £7.95 1 course,
£10.95 2 courses. **Credit** AmEx, MC, V.
Haché is derived from the French for 'to chop' but
the only Gallic twist on the great American burger
here is attention to detail. Rather than the now-
ubiquitous underpinning with skewers, Haché's
crisp toasted ciabattas are left ajar for us to admire
the ingredients. Our spanish burger was topped
with a slice of grilled pepper and a generous disc
of goat's cheese. Squashed down, it made for a
mammoth mouthful and held together well. It was
also markedly more meaty than everything else

we sampled for this guide. The thick-cut chips will
divide opinion, though. Yes, they're crisp but
they're also too reminiscent of 3am-kebab-shop
hollow. Haché is, we're told, constantly tweaking
its burgers. So perhaps the chefs could next turn
their attention to their vegetarian patrons. Despite
proud claims of fresh vegetables, chickpeas, cumin
and coriander, the 'au naturel veggie burger' still
has more than a hint of shop-bought frozen veggie
burgers. Given the quality of everything else here,
that's frustrating.
*Babies and children welcome: high chairs.
Disabled: toilet. Tables outdoors (2, pavement).
Takeaway service.* **Map 14 D12.**
For branch see index.

North
Kentish Town

Grand Union
*53-79 Highgate Road, NW5 1TL (7485 1837/
www.gugroup.co.uk). Kentish Town tube/rail.*
Meals served noon-3pm, 5-9pm Mon-Sat;
1-8pm Sun. **Main courses** £3.95-£6.95.
Credit MC, V.
Floral wallpaper, chinese lanterns, sofas aplenty
and a motley collection of lamps and vases lend
this dimly lit spot a youthful gastropub vibe. The
concept, though, is to fuse a gourmet burger bar
with a cocktail lounge. A blackboard advertises
bargain-priced mojitos, while on tap there's Leffe
and Staropramen. The highly seasoned burgers
(£4.95-£6.95) are impressive, arriving precariously
stacked with salad, slathered with condiments like
creamy smoked chilli mayo or satay sauce, and
anchored by a bamboo skewer. Stray from the
beefy norm by choosing greek lamb, or various
chicken options. Alternatively, go veggie with
chargrilled aubergine and goat's cheese, or falafel
combos. Don't miss the fabulous, richly flavoured
chips fried in groundnut oil; there are a couple of
side salads too. Sharing-platters (with mini-
burgers, crostini, dips and more) are available at
an hour's notice. Friendly quiz nights, comedy, live
music and DJs provide entertainment throughout
the week, making Grand Union a welcome twist
on the local.
*Babies and children welcome (before 9pm): high
chairs. Entertainment: quiz 7.30pm Tue; DJs 6pm
Fri, Sat. Disabled: toilet. Restaurant available for
hire. Separate room for parties, seats 75. Tables
outdoors (15, pavement). Takeaway service.*
Map 26 A4.
For branches see index.

North West
St John's Wood

Natural Burger Company
*12 Blenheim Terrace, NW8 0EB (7372 9065).
St John's Wood tube.* **Meals served** noon-11pm
Mon-Sat; noon-10.30pm Sun. **Main courses**
£8.75-£12. **Credit** MC, V.
The party of supersized Americans tucking in
here suggested that Natural Burger Company is
doing something right (though said customers may
have had problems with the hobbit-sized toilet).
But it's telling that everyone requested 'no mayo'
and 'no relish', as NBC tends to load its burgers
with gunk. Fortunately, the toasted ciabatta buns
are up to the job and each burger is pinned upright
with two wooden skewers. Vegetarians will be
impressed by the similarly whopping vegetable
stacks, less so by the fountain of juices that
erupted from our too-rare 'natural burger'. Also,
we'd rather taste blue cheese than 'blue cheese
sauce'. Real fruit in the milkshakes is a bonus,
though, as is the side dish option of chicken wings
in piri piri sauce. With its local bistro atmosphere
(or lack of), we find it difficult to work out who NBC
aims to cater for. Well-heeled locals are unlikely to
crave such basic fare, and the experience is in no
way exciting enough to warrant a tube ride.
*Babies and children welcome: children's menu;
high chairs. Separate room for parties, seats 35.
Tables outdoors (6, pavement). Takeaway service.*
Map 1 C2.

Cafés

L ike its caffeine-fuelled regulars, London's café sector continues to fizz with vitality. It has had a long way to catch up with its European cousins over the past couple of decades, since the law was amended to enable cafés to serve alcohol through the afternoon. We've included several new venues this year, and they help to show the direction that the café scene as a whole is taking. The concentration on first-rate, well-sourced ingredients is plain to see, especially at **Daylesford Organic**, the **Clerkenwell Kitchen** and Hackney's **Pavilion Café**; the focus on excellent ingredients is also apparent at London's new breed of tea rooms, particularly at **Orange Pekoe**. Notable too is the continuing renaissance of the park café, with two new openings this year: the aforementioned Pavilion Café and Fulham Palace's the **Lawn**, the latest venture from Oliver Peyton. Most such establishments are especially child-friendly: places where yummy mummies might take their little treasures for a 'babycino' (frothy warm milk, perhaps topped with a dusting of cocoa).

CAFÉS, PÂTISSERIES & TEA ROOMS

Central

Bloomsbury

★ Bea's of Bloomsbury NEW
44 Theobald Road, WC1X 8NW (7242 8330/ www.beasofbloomsbury.com). Holborn or Chancery Lane tube. **Open** 8am-6pm Mon-Fri; 10.30am-4pm Sat. **Main courses** £3-£7.50. **Credit** MC, V.
Multi-tiered special-occasional cakes make a spectacular window display at Bea Vo's plush café. At the rear, three steps lead up to the open-plan sky-lit kitchen, adding a sense of theatre to the busy chefs' activities. Roast vegetables were made the most of during our visit: as in a couscous and halloumi salad, and a 'flatbread' sandwich. Shredded duck salad with pomegranate and salty 'kim chee' cucumber was savourily satisfying, though the acidic dressing had begun to attack the leaves. All except the moroccan chicken soup was displayed on the counter – and the menu is posted on the website daily. A constant stream of cakes seemed to come from the kitchen: 'killer' brownies with peanut butter, coconut, praline *and* mixed nuts; blood-orange, chocolate or raspberry meringues; swirly-topped cupcakes. The rich gateaux are full of creamy, chocolatey and nutty flavours. Coffee is excellent, teas come from Jing, but best of all is Bea's own recipe chai latte, surely London's best. Service is friendly, though it's confusing to work out whether to order at table or counter.
Babies and children admitted. Tables outdoors (1, pavement). Takeaway service. **Map 4 M4**.

Clerkenwell & Farringdon

★ Clerkenwell Kitchen
2008 WINNER BEST SUSTAINABLE RESTAURANT
27-31 Clerkenwell Close, EC1R 0AT (7101 9959/ www.theclerkenwellkitchen.co.uk). Angel tube/ Farringdon tube/rail. **Open** 8am-5pm Mon-Wed, Fri; 8am-midnight Thur. **Main courses** £4.50-£14. **Credit** MC, V.

This super eaterie, tucked between Farringdon and Clerkenwell Roads, serves delicious, fresh, seasonal food at fair prices. The furnishings are simple: plenty of wood, windows and white walls with architectural seating and lighting. In the warmer months, the outdoor decked terrace comes into play. Before opening the Kitchen, its two owners, Helen Gray and Emma Miles, worked at the Eyre Brothers restaurant in Shoreditch and for Hugh Fearnley-Whittingstall at River Cottage in Dorset, respectively. The open kitchen serves breakfast (anything from a bowl of muesli to big bacon and egg constructions) through to afternoon tea (own-made brownies, muffins, pastries, delicious lemon tarts). At lunchtime you can pick up a takeaway (freshly made soup, perhaps, or a luxuriously creamy courgette and parmesan tart with a lentil, mint and beetroot salad) or sit down for the works. Each day there are six dishes offered, such as honey-roasted gammon, roasted carrots and parsley sauce, or fish stew with squid, mussels, chorizo and croûtons. A decent glass of red or white will cost an additional £3.75. Your fellow diners will likely be as sleek and stylish as the surroundings; many of them hail from nearby architectural practices and workshops.
Babies and children welcome: high chairs. Disabled: toilet. Tables outdoors (8, courtyard). Takeaway service. **Map 5 N4**.

★ Kipferl
70 Long Lane, EC1A 9EJ (7796 2229/ www.kipferl.co.uk). Barbican tube. **Open** 8am-5pm Mon-Fri; 9am-5pm Sat. **Main courses** £3-£6.50. **Credit** MC, V.
Lucky are the folk of Smithfield that they get such a thoroughly modern Austrian café on their doorstep. Somehow this small square gem doesn't feel crowded, every inch of the light, airy space being used well. Pale wooden tables run along inside the shop's glass window. An L-shaped counter juts into the room, displaying freshly made open sandwiches on rye, a gorgeous strudel crammed with wafer-thin slices of apple and almond, stacks of vanilla kipferl (a traditional Austrian biscuit) and a moist doorstopper apfelkuchen (Jewish apple cake). The meat and cheese counter completes the L with wiener, debreziner and käsekrainer sausages. A back corner is given over to shelves full of imported Austrian food and drink – wines, beers, Staud's

pickles, pumpkin-seed oils, baskets of fresh bread. The coffee is outstanding and comes beautifully presented: a double espresso served on a small tray with petite glass of water and piece of chocolate. Lunch specials change daily and might include frittaten soup (fine strips savoury pancakes in clear soup), cold pasta salads and hot sausages.
Babies and children admitted. Takeaway service. **Map 11 O5**.
For branch see index.

Covent Garden

Bullet
3rd floor, Snow & Rock, 4 Mercer Street, WC2H 9QA (7836 4922/www.bullet-coffee.com). Covent Garden tube/Charing Cross tube/rail. **Open** 10am-6pm Mon-Wed, Fri, Sat; 10am-7pm Thur; 10am-4.30pm Sun. **Main courses** £3.50-£6.50. **Credit** MC, V.
Bullet occupies a section of the extreme-sports Snow & Rock shop in Covent Garden, so it's appropriate that you have to climb three flights of stairs to find this gem of a café. There's no lift – that would be cheating – but the trek is worth the effort for the coffee alone. The firm sources its own organic fair-trade beans and roasts them itself (you can buy packets of beans here or online). The result is a dark, rich black coffee (or flavoursome flat white) that put a spring in our step for the schlep down the stairs. The food menu is limited. Of the two main choices (own-made beef lasagne and quiche of the day), the quiche was finished. A selection of baguettes and bagels was available for toasting. We couldn't resist the anzac biscuits (made from oats and golden syrup; such biscuits were sent by Australian women to their men in World War I). They came as big as your hand and were deliciously crunchy. Still, we'd have preferred healthier options. The only real nod to the 'health and fitness' nature of the shop was a big glass bowl full of fresh fruit.
Babies and children admitted: nappy-changing facilities. Disabled: lift, toilet. **Map 18 D4**.

Kastner & Ovens
52 Floral Street, WC2E 9DA (7836 2700). Covent Garden tube. **Open** 8am-5pm Mon-Fri. **Main courses** £3.25-£5.25. **No credit cards**.
A handy spot to grab a bite when you're in Covent Garden, K&O is tucked away just off the main drag on the north end of Floral Street. The compact space is just enough to accommodate two buffet-style tables from which staff serve you with savoury and sweet comestibles (we've experienced both helpful and brusque service). Each day you'll find a variety of substantial, flavour-packed, imaginative salads that let high-quality vegetables shine: raw cauliflower, chunky broccoli, celery and beansprouts; or roasted red pepper, courgette, aubergine and chickpea – accompanied by walnut bread or rosemary-flecked focaccia. Hot dishes could include chilli con carne and chicken pie. The array of mouth-watering cakes might feature delicate lemon layer sponge, tarte au citron, bramley apple pie, treacle tart and giant white chocolate and macadamia cookies. The more interesting dishes tend to sell out speedily, so get here early to beat the lunch-hour rush. Seating is scarce, but arriving back at your desk with a K&O lunch box beats munching a pre-packed sarnie any day.
Babies and children admitted. Takeaway service. **Map 18 E3**.

Euston

Peyton & Byrne
Wellcome Collection, 183 Euston Road, NW1 2BE (7611 2142/www.peytonandbyrne.co.uk). Euston Square tube/Euston tube/rail. **Open** 10am-6pm Mon-Wed, Fri, Sat; 10am-10pm Thur; 11am-6pm Sun. **Lunch served** 11am-3pm daily. **Main courses** £3.50-£9.50. **Credit** MC, V.
A justifiably popular café that attracts Wellcome Collection visitors as well as local office workers having off-site meetings and scanning their laptops. Oliver Peyton's colourful, chic styling is spot-on but keeping floors and tables clean and

turned over at peak times is a challenge. Take a perch by the window for views over Euston Road; tables provide a panorama of the foyer and bookshop. The counter holds a spectacular array of cakes and other treats – cupcakes as high and bright as the Matahorn, fat juicy wedges of pear and almond tart, multi-layered victoria sponge – but there's a goodly range of savoury food too. Opt for salads, pâtés, sausage rolls and pies from the counter, or order the likes of spiced tuna burger with chilli and mango chutney, or Herdwick lamb cutlets from the rear kitchen. Our roast vegetable skewer, lacking the advertised spelt salad, was below the high standard we've come to expect here, but normal service was resumed with a robust gluten-free chocolate and almond cake thickly decorated with frosting and guaranteed to deliver fat grams even for those on special diets.
Babies and children admitted. Disabled: toilet. Takeaway service. **Map 4 K4.**

Fitzrovia

Meals

1st floor, Heal's, 196 Tottenham Court Road, W1T 7LQ (7580 2522/www.heals.co.uk). Goodge Street or Warren Street tube. **Open** 10am-6pm Mon-Wed, Fri; 10am-7.30pm Thur; 9.30am-6.30pm Sat; noon-6pm Sun. **Afternoon tea served** 3-6pm daily. **Main courses** £9-£10.50. **Set lunch** £12.50 2 courses. **Credit** AmEx, DC, MC, V.
Oliver Peyton's restaurant in Heal's furniture store is unexpectedly airy and peaceful, given the anarchy of Tottenham Court Road outside. There's something decidedly childlike about this first-floor eaterie, with its pale oak, white-painted chairs and pastel colours. It was quiet on our midweek visit, with three floor staff looking after eight other tables. We ordered quickly from the short brasserie menu and our bottle of rosé arrived swiftly. It took several more promptings to receive tap water, then we settled in to wait. The wine was finished before the food arrived. A fish cake was moist, full of salmon and delicious: a shame the yolk in the poached egg was solid. Goat's cheese salad came with pear that tasted tinned – the waiter, however, insisted it had been 'slowly poached by the chef'. The chips arrived a full ten minutes later ('we can't make the fryer work any faster,' said the harassed waiter). We had to help ourselves to cutlery from nearby tables; staff seemed to ignore customers' waving hands. Meals is fine for a leisurely lunch when you're furniture shopping, but give it a wide berth if you've anything else to do that day.
Babies and children welcome: high chairs. Booking advisable. Disabled: lift; toilet. Restaurant available for hire. **Map 4 K5.**

Marylebone

★ La Fromagerie (100)

2-6 Moxon Street, W1U 4EW (7935 0341/ www.lafromagerie.co.uk). Baker Street or Bond Street tube. **Open** 10.30am-7.30pm Mon; 8am-7.30pm Tue-Fri; 9am-7pm Sat; 10am-6pm Sun. **Main courses** £6-£12.40. **Credit** AmEx, MC, V.
Famed with foodies for its dedicated cheese room, Patricia Michelson's high-end deli also dishes out freshly cooked café food. Its communal tables are often packed with devotees. La Fromagerie's location, in Marylebone's rarefied shopping enclave, means that punters are polished and in search of high-quality nourishment pre- or mid-spending spree. Go for an indulgent breakfast or late lunch, as the café closes in the early evening. Fromage-o-philes are spoilt with plates of artisan cheese served with great bread. The daily changing kitchen menu could include salmon and pollock fish pie nestled under clouds of mashed potato, or rich terrines of foie gras, duck or rabbit. Meal-in-one salads also feature. Artichoke, beetroot, red cabbage, walnut and speck was over-complicated and bitter, but fat-speared asparagus, pea, broad bean and pearl barley was light and vernal. Desserts are exceptional; try the creamy tarte au citron enlivened with a perfect shot of sharpness, or ditch the calorie counting and savour the great hunks of dense chocolate brownies.
Babies and children admitted. Café available for hire (evenings). Takeaway service. **Map 3 G3. For branch see index.**

Postcard Teas `NEW`

2008 RUNNER-UP BEST TEA ROOM
9 Dering Street, W1S 1AG (7629 3654/ www.postcardteas.com). Bond Street or Oxford Circus tube. **Open** 10.30am-6.30pm Tue-Sat. **Credit** MC, V.
Tim d'Offey lives for tea: so much so, he has spent a decade travelling to far-flung estates across Asia. His simply furnished tea room is a Zen-like sanctuary from the world outside – a reasonably priced spot in which to linger around the communal table sipping some of the world's finest infusions. Although d'Offey suggests tea is best enjoyed without milk and sugar, there are no rigid rules. He'll happily put out the milk jug and sugar bowl if you'd rather not make that leap of faith. In the past, we've enjoyed the boldness of 'big smoke' (black tea leaves smoked over cinnamon wood and blended with darjeeling), which is outstanding for its clarity and warm spicy aroma. Equally notable is blossom tea, made with flowers from coffee bushes (which bloom for a day or so twice a year) blended with a variety of silver-needle white tea, for a supremely delicate brew. There's usually one light sponge cake to whet the appetite, but here it's the tea that does the talking.
Babies and children admitted. **Map 9 H6.**

Scandinavian Kitchen `NEW`

61 Great Titchfield Street, W1W 7PP (7580 7161/www.scandikitchen.co.uk). Oxford Street tube. **Open** 8am-7pm Mon-Fri; 10am-6pm Sat; 10am-4pm Sun. **Main courses** £4.50-£7.50. **Set meal** (from 11.30am) £4.50-£7. **Credit** MC, V.

Ice-cream parlours

The Parlour

In addition to the outlets below, you can find good Italian-style ice-cream at **Marine Ices** (*see p303*), the Sloane Square and Spitalfields branches of **Pâtisserie Valerie** (*see p310*), and at the Morelli's counter in Harrods food hall.

Caffè Deli Paradiso

109 Highgate West Hill, N6 6AP (8340 7818). Bus C2, C11, 214.
Joining standards like pistachio and tartufo are flavours such as watermelon, white coffee, coconut and the lurid blue puffo (a creamy anise variety – not as bad as you might think). Close to Hampstead Heath, this outfit also offers a wide range of Sicilian-style pastries.

Gelateria Danieli

16 Brewers Lane, Richmond, Surrey TW9 1HH (8439 9807/www.gelateria danieli.com). Richmond tube/rail.
This excellent Richmond outfit has been quietly expanding, with kiosks in Bentall's of Kingston, Centre Court Shopping Centre in Wimbledon, a stall by John Lewis on Oxford Street, and a new outlet slated for Battersea. The ever-changing range of flavours includes cinnamon and plum ice-cream and pink grapefruit sorbet.

Gelato Mio

138 Holland Park Avenue, W11 4UE (7727 4117/www.gelatomio.co.uk). Holland Park tube.
A sleek shop with swivel chairs that would look at home in a classy hotel bar. Among the dozen-or-so sorbets are flavours such as pear and papaya. We liked the classic chocolate and pistachio ice-creams.

Oddono's

14 Bute Street, SW7 3EX (7052 0732/www.oddonos.co.uk). South Kensington tube.
Portions are generous at this renowned shop, which also has kiosks in Whiteley's and Selfridges. Try the Venezuelan Araguani single origin dark chocolate ice-cream, which is heaven. Those on special diets can choose from soya-based gelato and no-added-sugar options.

The Parlour

1st floor, Fortnum & Mason, 181 Piccadilly, W1A 1ER (7734 8040/ www.fortnumandmason.co.uk). Green Park or Piccadilly Circus tube.
The Parlour's warm, silky Amedei chocolate sauce is superior to the chocolate ice-cream sold here, so our best recommendation is to order an ice-cream flight – three scoops of, say, marmalade and bergamot, strawberry and balsamic, and lemon curd – with the sauce to pour over it. Prices are on the high side, but cups of coffee come with tiny sample cones, and the David Collins-designed interior is a stunner.

Scoop

40 Shorts Gardens, WC2H 9AB (7240 7086/www.scoopgelato.com). Covent Garden tube.
Long lunchtime queues are a testament to the fact that even the dairy-free health ices (intriguingly made from rice flour) at this Italian artisan's shop are utterly delicious. Flavours we love include fig and ricotta, and nocciola tonda gentile delle langhe (that's a very superior Piedmont hazelnut ice-cream).

Scandinavian Kitchen

While wheat-avoiders are prone to scan the shelves here earnestly for crisp-this and rye-that, this friendly café-grocer's doesn't take itself seriously. The lively multicultural crowd of local office workers is kept entertained by flirty male staff breaking into song (no Abba in our experience) and a self-deprecating sheet of instructions for eating open sandwiches. These are offered aplenty: choose from, say, chicken and green-pepper salad, danish or swedish meatballs, Norwegian smoked salmon, roast beef, and three types of herring. Fancy something hot? There's soup and hot dogs. In today's world, no café could survive without brownies and espresso, but for more Scandinavian treats try the wonderful (if prepackaged) Delicato marzipan nibbles – by royal appointment to the King of Sweden – and Gevalia filter coffee. Order at the counter then take your tray over to the tables. The café's design (cute knob-handled mugs, curvy plywood chairs, bright red walls and Normann light shades) is approachable rather than Arctic cool. Result: a fun spot for a healthy lunch.
Babies and children welcome: high chairs. Tables outdoors (5, pavement). Takeaway service.
Map 9 J5.

Mayfair

Sketch: The Parlour
9 Conduit Street, W1S 2XJ (0870 777 4488/ www.sketch.uk.com). Oxford Circus tube. **Open** 8am-9pm Mon-Fri; 10am-9pm Sat. **Tea served** 3-6.30pm Mon-Sat. **Main courses** £4-£8.50. **Set tea** £9.50-£19.50; £31 incl glass of champagne. **Credit** AmEx, DC, MC, V.
The several eating venues at Sketch share a distinctive visual style that borrows from the listed building's former roles as HQ of the Royal Institute of British Architects and Christian Dior and then thows in a little wit and spectacle all of its own. In the ground floor café Parlour, a creepy chandelier made from black desk-lamps hangs spider-like at the rear. Combined with the Shoreditch-style mix-and-match antiques and black-lacquered, Swarovski crystal-covered loos, it helps produce as edgy a tea room as you're likely to find in the West End. The choice seats are by the enormous windows, looking on to Conduit street. During our visit, staff – fresh faced, sweet and shod in perfectly battered Converse trainers – were easily baffled and excruciatingly slow. A waiter nearly had a meltdown when we asked what was in the wonderfully salty dressing that came with the quiche of the day's side salad. To drink, we ordered a pot of jasmine silver fur tea, which arrived in chintzy china. But the main event here is cake. Little slices of carrot cakes were spicy and appealing; a finger of chocolate eclair was dreamily light. Less pleasing was the chocolate cake, clumsily layered with heavy cream. In all, though, Parlour would be a super destination, were its service sorted out.
Babies and children welcome: high chairs. Café available for hire. Takeaway service. **Map 9 J6.**

Pimlico

Daylesford Organic NEW
44B Pimlico Road, SW1W 8LP (7881 8060/ www.daylesfordorganic.com). Sloane Square tube. **Open** 8am-8pm Mon-Sat; 10am-4pm Sun. **Main courses** £8-£14. **Credit** AmEx, MC, V.
With zhooshy pavement tables, counter seats by the window and a smart communal table down the centre, there is plenty of temptation to stop for a meal while shopping in this elegant white marble food hall. Juices are freshly squeezed, and to them you might add a booster of wheatgrass, macca powder or manuka honey. Alternatively, there's wine from Daylesford's own estate in Provence. The menu's emphasis is on health too. The list includes seasonal restaurant-style salads such as our delightful crab, pea and radish number, which came with a swoosh of pea purée, an exotic shard of crisp, herby bread, and a sprig of edible flowers. For something heartier, try the burger, or roast smoked haddock with poached egg. The cashier was unsurprised that the basket of bread we'd ordered hadn't been delivered, promptly removed it from the bill and offered a discount voucher for the homewares sold upstairs, by way of apology. A common occurrence, then. But with so many pleasant, smartly uniformed staff scuttling about, this, and the slow arrival of dishes, is a surprise.
Babies and children welcome: high chairs. Disabled: toilet. Tables outdoors (7, pavement). Takeaway service. **Map 15 G11.**
For branch see index.

Soho

Amato
14 Old Compton Street, W1D 4TH (7734 5733/ www.amato.co.uk). Leicester Square, Piccadilly Circus or Tottenham Court Road tube. **Open** 8am-10pm Mon-Sat; 10am-8pm Sun. **Main courses** £4.75-£9.50. **Credit** MC, V.
This old-school Italian caff is brimming with charm and character. Colourful art deco posters of dancers adorn the walls, and the tables and chairs are made of a dark, warm wood. The convivial atmosphere is ideal for an afternoon cuppa or a after-dinner cake and coffee with gossip. While the main draw is clearly the astonishing array of sweet delights (which all but fill one long, L-shaped glass display cabinet, as well as the window space), the hot food is surprisingly on a par. Piping-hot smoked salmon fettuccine came in outageously generous portions, with fresh al dente pasta and an artery-clogging amount of cream (our only complaint with it). For dessert, we couldn't fault the millefoglie (the Italian version of millefeuille), a creamy treat paired with paper-thin layers of crisp puff pastry. Yet given Amato's Italian heritage, its cappuccinos could be better made.
Babies and children welcome: high chairs. Takeaway service. **Map 17 C3.**
For branch see index.

Fernandez & Wells
73 Beak Street, W1F 9RS (7287 8124/ www.fernandezandwells.com). Oxford Circus or Piccadilly Circus tube. **Open** 7.30am-7pm Mon-Fri; 8am-7pm Sat; 9am-7pm Sun. **Main courses** £3.50-£6. **Credit** (over £5) MC, V.
If only there were more coffee bars like this in central London, rather than the minefield of mediocre café and sandwich chains. In 2007, Fernandez & Wells won the Best Coffee Bar category at the Time Out Eating and Drinking Awards. At around £5 a pop, its sandwiches aren't cheap, but they are something special. First there's the great bread: chewy panini, crusty half baguettes and hearty baps. The fillings add a mouth-watering sparkle to the working day. We opted for sandwiches: mortadella, rocket, salami, prosciutto, parmesan and aïoli (that's just one filling!); Montgomery cheddar and chutney; and, for something more subtle, an Iberian version of pancetta with creamy egg mayonnaise. There's also a tempting range of cakes (from £1.75). We particularly liked the moist bitter orange and almond cake. The millionaire's slice, with its layer of dark chocolate on caramel, made a perfect complement to F&W's excellent coffee (supplied by Monmouth Coffee Company). At lunchtime, seats are at a premium but worth the wait. Drop by in the morning for, say, a cheese toastie made with sourdough bread, or a breakfast pastry. Sitting amid all that tastiness will put you in a positive frame of mind for the rest of the day.
Babies and children admitted. Takeaway service.
Map 17 A4.
For branch see index.

Flat White

17 Berwick Street, W1F 0PT (7734 0370/ www.flat-white.co.uk). Leicester Square, Oxford Circus or Tottenham Court Road tube. **Open** 8am-7pm Mon-Fri; 9am-6pm Sat, Sun. **Main courses** £3-£6.50. **No credit cards**.

'A flat white', as the definition on the wall here will tell you, is 'an Antipodean-style coffee': a shot of espresso with plenty of milk. It's also the name of this small Soho coffee shop, which has tiny tables running along one wall underneath pictures of beaches. The short blackboard menu includes all-day breakfasts (presented with jars of Vegemite as well as bottles of ketchup), a decent selection of paninis, and salads. Our long black coffee was more than capable of waking the dead, but the green salad with goat's cheese toasted on fluffy baguette was nothing like the crunchy crostini described. A dark single macchiato came in a small glass, reminiscent of Melbourne cafés, but the oat and raisin cookies were dry. Think Australian and Kiwi accents sound the same? The pronunciation guide to 'flat white' on the board is amusing. *Babies and children admitted. Takeaway service.* **Map 17 B3.**

For branch (Milk Bar) see index.

Maison Bertaux

28 Greek Street, W1D 5DQ (7437 6007). Leicester Square, Piccadilly Circus or Tottenham Court Road tube. **Open** 8.30am-11pm Mon-Sat; 8.30am-7pm Sun. **Main courses** £1.50-£4.50. **No credit cards**.

Oozing arty charm, this café dates back to 1871 when Soho was London's little piece of the Continent. Battered old bentwood tables and chairs add to the feeling of being in a pâtisserie in rural France. The window twinkles with an array of croissants, tartlets and other confections – the only difference from France is a dearth of savoury items, just pizza slices and wedges of quiche – no onion tart, say, or mushroom tourtière. However, this is a good place to pass time with friends over a pot of tea and a cream horn. In summer, there are tables outside, each with a little glass filled with unusual fresh flowers, which would be perfect for people-watching were the street not permanently choked with traffic. Despite the high quality of the pastries, Maison Bertaux is often accused of being pricey – a dijon slice (cheese and onion on a flaky pastry base spread with dijon mustard) at £3.90 was steep for its size, while a piece of solid-looking but delicious broccoli quiche was £3.20. Still, this bohemian spot is far better than the chains. *Babies and children admitted. Tables outdoors (5, pavement). Takeaway service.* **Map 17 C4.**

Nordic Bakery

14 Golden Square, W1F 9JF (3230 1077/ www.nordicbakery.com). Piccadilly Circus tube. **Open** 8am-8pm Mon-Fri; 11am-7pm Sat; 11am-6pm Sun. **Main courses** £3.20-£4. **Credit** MC, V.

The simple monochrome signage on media-savvy Golden Square is a clue that here is a haven of über-stylish Fenno-Scandinavian cool. Baskets, tea towels, denim aprons and a nature-inspired wall rug stop the hip warehouse-style interior getting too frosty, and for warmth you can rely on the charming staff and fat, tactile mugs of steaming coffee. At the counter, all is fresh and wholesome, with cute rye rolls filled with salmon tartar and pickled herring, though the karelian pies – hand-shaped rye pastry filled with rice and topped with egg butter, a Finnish favourite – should be tried at least once. Sweets include huge own-made sticky, syrupy cinnamon buns, a choice of Scandinavian cakes, and fresh fruit. Rather bizarrely, you can also get Japanese Asahi super dry beer. Customers at the neat black glass tables include Virgin Radio workers and comfort-seeking Finns. *Babies and children admitted. Takeaway service.* **Map 17 A4.**

Sacred

13 Ganton Street, W1F 9BL (7734 1415/ www.sacredcafe.co.uk). Oxford Circus tube. **Open** 7.30am-8.30pm Mon-Wed, Fri; 7.30am-9pm Thur; 10am-8pm Sat; 10am-6pm Sun. **Main courses** £5-£5.50. **Credit** (over £5) AmEx, MC, V.

Conveniently situated just off bustling Carnaby Street, this Antipodean café's mission is 'making the perfect coffee' according to the blurb. Hence the coffee machine stands aloft on a stylish wooden pulpit and the blend is produced in-house. Sacred's appeal is to those who prefer their food ethical: fair-trade coffee, free-range eggs, organic ingredients. We went straight for the coffee (try the Down Under favourite, flat white) and, from the small range of light meals, scrambled eggs with spring onions and feta on wholemeal toast (£4.60) – a delicious take on an old staple. There's a daily quiche and decent panini too. The cakes were less impressive and, at the time of our visit, not made on the premises. An organic carrot cake was dry and crumbly, and the salads behind the counter looked a bit haggard. Best to stick to the savouries, and the superb coffee. *Babies and children welcome: nappy-changing facilities. Separate room for parties, seats 40. Tables outside (2, pavement). Takeaway service.* **Map 17 A4.**

Yauatcha

15 Broadwick Street, W1F 0DL (7494 8888). Leicester Square, Oxford Circus, Piccadilly Circus or Tottenham Court Road tube. **Tea room Tea/snacks served** 11am-11.45pm Mon-Sat; 11am-10.45pm Sun. **Dim sum served** noon-11.45pm Mon-Sat; noon-10.45pm Sun. **Set tea** £22.50-£31.50. **Dim sum** £3.50-£7. **Main courses** £7.80-£38. **Credit** AmEx, MC, V.

It may seem slightly incongruous to sample French-style pastries in an establishment better known for its dim sum, but at Yauatcha, the combination invariably works. The ground-floor tea room is a vision of creamy blues and turquoise, with low leather seating prettily embellished with flowers. The cakes and pastries counter glows with colourful confections ranging from miniature mousses to plump macaroons in psychedelic hues. Such creations are sure to set any pastry-lover's heart racing; the flavour combinations and presentations have no bounds, in an impressive show of French technique melded with oriental flavours and aesthetics. Enticing selections include a blue tea and blackberry gateau: delicate enough to let the aromas of the tea shine through, while contrasting with the tart berries. The oriental afternoon set tea allows diners to sample a variety of cakes, as well as three classic dim sum and warm, fluffy green-tea and coconut scones. We wish tea leaves were left in the pot for future infusions; our osmanthus oolong hadn't been brewed long enough to release its peachy aroma. Service seems more attentive during the quieter tea-time hours, to our great relief. *Babies and children admitted. Booking advisable. Disabled: lift; toilet. Takeaway service (tea room).* **Map 17 B3.**

South Kensington

Hummingbird Bakery

47 Old Brompton Road, SW7 3JP (7584 0055/ www.hummingbirdbakery.com). South Kensington tube. **Open** 10.30am-7pm daily. **Main courses** £1.55-£3.75. **Credit** AmEx, MC, V.

This NY-style bakery-cum-café, done out in pink, black and brown tones, and with ruby-red velvet chairs and stools, is a popular South Ken spot for a slice of home-baked Americana. As evidenced by the pop art-like pictures on the walls, the Hummingbird is renowned for cupcakes, all of which come with an extra thick layer of frosting. Other sweet treats include the deliciously zingy key lime pie, proper American brownies, pecan pie and muesli bars, as well as a selection of tempting large cakes displayed on traditional stands. Aside from the cupcakes, pluses here include decent Illy coffee and outside tables; less impressive were the easily confused (though pleasant) staff, and a toilet that opens to clear view of the small café space. It's best to avoid Saturday afternoons, when the place is awash with screaming (posh) kids and frenetic energy: perhaps caused by overdosing on sugar. On such occasions, takeaway is the answer to your sweet cravings. *Babies and children admitted. Tables outdoors (4, pavement). Takeaway service; delivery service (1-6pm Mon-Fri, over £12.95 within zones 1 & 2).* **Map 14 D10.**

For branch see index.

St James's

5th View

5th floor, Waterstone's, 203-206 Piccadilly, W1J 9HA (7851 2468/www.5thview.co.uk). Piccadilly Circus tube. **Lunch served** noon-3pm Mon-Fri; noon-4pm Sat, Sun. **Tapas served** 5-9pm Mon-Sat. **Main courses** £9.50-£14. **Tapas** £3.50-£9.50. **Credit** AmEx, DC, MC, V.

The large Waterstone's in which 5th View is housed is a temple for bookworms. There's a hushed air about it, with customers quietly perusing the shelves, but as you make your way up the spiralling staircases towards the top floor café-bar, the magic is broken. Excited chatter and

Cake Boy

the clang of cutlery reverberate off the walls; but then we came to eat, not to pray. For lunch, 5th View offers a hearty selection of freshly prepared tarts, soups and salads that provides much-needed sustenance for the room of intellectuals, office workers and well-off students (making notes on Foucault while chowing down). Our peppery rocket salad with smoked chicken, juicy cherry tomatoes and black olives was simple in description, but the use of top-notch fresh produce shone through. At night, the place transforms into a chic after-work watering hole, serving inspired cocktails (watermelon and basil with tequila, vodka espresso). Food and drink are the attractions here – not the view, which is mainly of rooftops. *Babies and children welcome (until 5pm): high chairs. Disabled: lift; toilet. Separate room for parties, seats 60.* **Map 17 A5.**

West

Ladbroke Grove

Books for Cooks
4 Blenheim Crescent, W11 1NN (7221 1992/ www.booksforcooks.com). Ladbroke Grove tube. **Open** 10am-6pm, **lunch served** noon-1.30pm Tue-Sat. **Set lunch** £5 2 courses, £7 3 courses. **Credit** MC, V.
The back of this renowned bookstore – brimming with all the cookbooks any food-lover could want – houses a tiny sky-lit 'test kitchen' where scrumptious, home-style dishes are conjured up every day from noon. It has started to wear on our nerves, however, that the (well-earned) popularity of this café means that a visit requires perfect timing. We turned up 15 minutes before the start, but were met by the smug and triumphant faces of those who had staked out the dozen-or-so seats much earlier. Come any later, and you risk the chance of food running out. Lunch includes a three-course set menu (using recipes from the shop's cookery books) at a bargain £7. On our visit, dishes gave a nod to Latin America: a mexican green salad with corn relish and chilli peanut dressing; and an ancho chilli and garlic roast chicken with 'green' (spinach) rice. Both were flavourful and perfect examples of the kitchen's culinary skill. Luckily we still had room to savour the delicious cakes (chocolate, whiskey and apple, or berries and peaches); best of all, if you can't decide, you can ask for half servings of each.
Bookings not accepted. Disabled: toilet. **Map 19 B3.**

Westbourne Grove

Tea Palace
2008 RUNNER-UP BEST TEA ROOM
175 Westbourne Grove, W11 2SB (7727 2600/ www.teapalace.co.uk). Bayswater or Notting Hill Gate tube. **Open** 10am-7pm daily. **Tea served** 3-7pm daily. **Main courses** £8-£13. **Set tea** £17-£23.50. **Credit** AmEx, MC, V.
Sharing a street with fashionable boutiques and spas, Tea Palace attracts the pampered as well as the tea aficionados from across London. If you want to take some tea home, choose from around 160 varieties sold in attractive plum-coloured caddies. Decor in the seating area has a retro-chic vibe; a swirly purple carpet and tiered cake stands contrast tastefully with oriental wind chimes, quirky doily-effect patterns on walls, and soft leather banquettes. Besides common blends like darjeeling, assam and builders' brew, the 16-page list includes such exotica as cherry blossom black tea, lavender grey (earl grey blended with flowers from Provence) and green tea made with puffed rice. A dinky-sized portion of leaves is brought to the table for inspection, making the transformation into a fragrant brew all the more memorable. Surprisingly unstuffy, the atmosphere is laid-back and kids are welcomed. On our visit, the darjeeling first flush didn't live up to its promise, having slightly stewed notes – an unfortunate yet basic glitch in an otherwise enjoyable afternoon.
Babies and children welcome: high chairs; nappy-changing facilities. Booking advisable. Disabled: toilet. **Map 19 C3.**

Tom's Delicatessen
226 Westbourne Grove, W11 2RH (7221 8818/ www.tomsdelilondon.co.uk). Notting Hill Gate tube. **Open** 8am-7.30pm Mon-Fri; 8am-6.30pm Sat; 9am-6.30pm Sun. **Main courses** £7.95-£11.95. **Credit** MC, V.
Grammar pedants, look away: the singular possessive apostrophe is missing on both the sign and the awning. Tom's fans appear not to mind a jot, and come here in droves. The place is enormously popular with beautifully coiffed locals, who use it as a weekend brunch spot and do not have to worry about the generally high prices. They step carefully over Nelly the black cat and make for the rear courtyard, or grab a prized table on the small balcony. Weather's not smiling? There are numerous booths inside, under the framed vintage grocery packaging. The cake display and cute jars of old-school sweets greet customers as they enter. All-day breakfasts stream out of the kitchen at weekends (until midday) and include healthier choices such as muesli (assembled in-house) alongside the full english. The rest of the menu features rather pricey pizzas and salads. An antipasti platter (ingredients from the well-stocked basement deli) was generous and heaven-sent: feta-stuffed green peppers, pickled onions, chunky houmous, sweet garlic, and pungent capers. Service was friendly yet efficient, aiding the happy illusion that you've just spent the afternoon in Tom's (sorry, Toms) boho west London pad.
Babies and children welcome: high chairs. Tables outdoors (6, garden; 2, terrace). Takeaway service. **Map 7 A6.**

South West

Barnes

★ Orange Pekoe
2008 WINNER BEST TEA ROOM
3 White Hart Lane, SW13 0PX (8876 6070/ www.orangepekoeteas.com). Barnes Bridge rail/209 bus. **Open** 7.30am-5.30pm Mon-Fri; 9am-5.30pm Sat, Sun. **Main courses** £4.50-£8. **Credit** AmEx, DC, MC, V.
A riverside gem favoured by young families as well as tea experts, the Orange Pekoe tea room enjoys a broad following. Fans are attracted by its villagey charm, homely cooking and fabulous teas. It's a cosy, welcoming place with a food counter at the front leading to rustic-style tables towards the back. Wild flowers in alcoves, teatime trinkets and blackboard menus add to the homespun appeal. At the entrance, rows of black tea caddies are filled with around 50 special varieties. The house blend is especially invigorating – a carefully honed mix of darjeeling tea, underpinned by the rounded character of ceylon. Just as outstanding, silver-tipped jasmine deserves accolades for its deep, mellow, sweet fragrance. Knowledgeable, on-the-ball staff are happy to suggest and advise. Although we're tempted by the big, beautiful cakes, hearty sandwiches and cold lunch platters, it's the cream teas and pots of tea that keep us coming back. On sunny days, bag a table outside for a languorous afternoon clinking china and savouring the brew.
Babies and children welcome: crayons; high chairs; nappy-changing facilities. Tables outdoors (4, pavement). Takeaway service.

Southfields

Cake Boy NEW
Kingfisher House, Battersea Reach (off York Road), Juniper Drive, SW18 1TX (7978 5555/ www.cake-boy.com). Wandsworth Town rail. **Open** 8am-7pm Mon-Fri; 9am-6pm Sun. **Main courses** £3.80-£4.80. **Credit** MC, V.
This venture from UK-based Frenchman Eric Lanlard, cake-maker to the stars, finds its home in the spanking-new Battersea Reach riverside development. Seating areas are split in two: a clinical teaching kitchen full of counters and stools makes up one end; a contrastingly rich, decorative lounge with blossom-pink and ochre leather armchairs and encased chandeliers forms the other. A small number of largely uninspired but

fresh and well-produced sandwiches (salami and tomato on sesame-seed bagels, for instance) and rich, delicate savoury tarts (salmon and cress, smoked bacon) make for a decent light lunch. Most customers, though – many on business chats or suburban-gossip missions – are drawn in by the cakes, sweet muffins and pastries. An eye-catching layered chocolate cake was moist and rich, while the medley of creamy tartlets topped with colourful fruit combos (such as strawberry and kiwi fruit) demanded to be devoured. The choice isn't extensive, but the quality makes up for it.
Babies and children admitted. Café available for hire. Tables outdoors (10, terrace). Takeaway service. **Map 21 A3.**

South

Balham

Munchkin Lane
83 Nightingale Lane, SW12 8NX (8772 6800). Clapham South tube/Wandsworth Common rail. **Open** 8am-6pm Mon-Fri; 9am-5pm Sat. **Main courses** £3-£7. **Credit** MC, V.
The bright uncluttered space on Munchkin Lane's ground floor doesn't shriek 'family-friendly', so needn't frighten the grown-ups. Everything going on below stairs – a cheerful little play area with den; Cbeebies on a screen; lots of picture books; and a timetable of storytelling, puppet shows and toddler rhymes – draws in the pram posse. There's room for all in this reasonably priced and amiable café. We've had consistently reliable lunches here: piles of buttery scrambled eggs, served with ham and cheese; bacon and beans; crisp salads served in big bowls (greek, chicken caesar, tuna with egg and new potatoes, spinach and walnut); filled bagels, baked potatoes, and imaginative pasta dishes. The menu sticks to simple daytime staples, prepared to order and served with bonhomie. There's usually an irresistible own-made cake (moist carrot cake on our last visit), and good, strong coffee. For the little ones, there are babycinos, warm chocolate with marshmallows, gingerbread men and nursery stalwarts (macaroni cheese, shepherd's pie, fish pie and veg): all sensibly priced.
Babies and children welcome: children's menu; high chairs; nappy-changing facilities; toys. Separate room for parties, seats 30. Tables outdoors (2, pavement). ●

Battersea

Crumpet
66 Northcote Road, SW11 6QL (7924 1117/ www.crumpet.biz). Clapham Junction rail. **Open** 8.30am-5.30pm Mon-Sat; 10am-5.30pm Sun. **Set tea** £5 (2-4pm). **Main courses** £4.20-£7.50. **Credit** AmEx, MC, V.
Proper teas – with scones, cakes, hefty sandwiches and a range of blends from a Blackfriars-based merchant – are a major priority at Crumpet. It is, delightfully, a 'margarine-free zone', serves high-quality artisan-made bread, and has cakes baked by locals. The other priority here is children (always a good wheeze in this area), which means there are buggies and babes-in-arms everywhere. Families tend to sit in the light, airy back room, where there's a play area. The menu covers all infant tastes, from toasty fingers, crudités and a babycino on the side, to whimsical dishes called, for example, Rosy Posy pasta and Dylan's scrumptious chicken: all organic and free range where relevant. Visiting without children, we enjoyed a sedate light lunch of goat's cheese and walnut salad, and a lovely welsh rarebit accompanied by one of Crumpet's speciality Smooteas (a tall glass of green tea and grape: a bit insipid). This was followed by a big creamy cappuccino and a nice pot of formosa oolong with a large wedge of luscious lemon cake. Everything is presented with great care, in generous portions, and the high quality of ingredients shines through.
Babies and children welcome: children's menu; high chairs; nappy-changing facilities; play area; toys. Tables outdoors (2, pavement). Takeaway service. **Map 21 C5.**

CHEAP EATS

Brand values

London's collection of chain bakeries and patisseries is expanding faster than a choc-chip cookie on a hot oven tray. Here's our guide to the notable names.

Baker & Spice

54-56 Elizabeth Street, SW1W 9PB (7730 3033/www.bakerandspice.com). Sloane Square tube. **Open** 7am-7pm Mon-Sat; 8am-5pm Sun. **Main courses** £8-£15. **Credit** MC, V.

'Good animal husbandry comes at a price to all of us,' says the blackboard on the wall, reminding everyone that all of Baker & Spice's chicken is organic, and sourced from small free-range flocks. But like the other messages from the management dotted around this bakery, takeaway and café, the tone is unfortunately imperious. Staff are sweet, however, and the food is generally good, if pricey (a plate of four salads is £15). Large glasses of water are poured unbidden and the pâtisserie section overflows with scrumptious things – pecan slices, rugelach, macaroons, chocolate fudge cake, muffins and more. **Take home:** Catford honey and a loaf of sweet, golden crusted pain de mie. *Babies and children admitted. Bookings not accepted. Tables outdoors (5, pavement). Takeaway service.* **Map 15 G10**.

Konditor & Cook

30 St Mary Axe, EC3A 8BF (0845 262 3030/www.konditorandcook.co.uk). Liverpool Street tube/rail. **Open** 7.30am-6.30pm Mon-Fri. **Main courses** £4-£8. **Credit** AmEx, MC, V.

Larger than most branches of this cake-making café, the Gherkin outlet opened in late 2007. Anyone hoping for views over London will be disappointed; it's on the ground floor of the building. Still, you don't forget where you are – the interior is airy and modern, and slats satisfyingly criss-cross the large windows. City workers clearly love the place; it's packed with suits on weekday lunchtimes. Customers can choose from the daily changing hot meals (our melanza parmigiana was naughtily cheesy, but delicious) and ready-made salads and sandwiches from the cold counter. This wouldn't be Konditor & Cook without a fabulous display of cakes. They're all laid out to tempt you as you pay for your food and order coffee at the till. **Take home:** bags of star-shaped cookies and flirty gingerbread people. *Babies and children admitted. Tables outdoors (7, patio). Takeaway service.* **Map 12 R6**. **For branches see index**.

Ladurée

Harrods, entrance on Hans Road, SW1X 7XL (7893 8293/www.laduree.com). Knightsbridge tube. **Open** *Shop* 9am-9pm Mon-Sat; 11.30am-6pm Sun. **Breakfast served** 9-11.30am daily. **Lunch served** 11.30am-3.30pm Mon-Sat; noon-3.30pm Sun. **Tea served** 3.30-6.30pm Mon-Sat; 3.30-6pm Sun. **Dinner served** 6.30-8pm Mon-Sat. **Main courses** £15-£27.50. **Set meal** £29 2 courses, £34 3 courses. **Set tea** £21. **Credit** AmEx, DC, MC, V.

London now holds two branches of these ornate Parisian tea rooms – a large one in Harrods and a smaller outlet in the Burlington Arcade. The company has also spread to Monaco, Geneva and Berlin. Expect row after row of pastries and cakes, and shelves prettily stacked with pastel gift boxes. At £21, the afternoon tea is not great value for money. Ours included two finger sandwiches wrapped in waxed paper; they tasted little better than budget airline fare. And staff not refilling the teapot was simply mean. We liked the croissants, though, and the raspberry tart was a perfect mix of confectioner's custard, fruit and sweet pastry. **Take home:** light, airy macaroons (the rose-petal version is particularly good). *Babies and children welcome: high chairs. Bookings not accepted (tea). Disabled: toilet. Separate room for parties, seats 20. Tables outdoors (20, pavement).* **Map 14 E10**. **For branch see index**.

Le Pain Quotidien

72-75 Marylebone High Street, W1U 5JW (7486 6154/www.lepainquotidien.com). Baker Street or Bond Street tube. **Open** 7am-9pm Mon-Fri; 8am-9pm Sat; 8am-8pm Sun. **Main courses** £5.75-£7.95. **Credit** AmEx, MC, V.

A fast-expanding, rustically styled chain, Le Pain Quotidien was opened nearly two decades ago by Alain Coumount in Brussels. Bread remains the speciality. The farmhouse-style communal tables are relentlessly packed at weekends with bourgeois locals nibbling at sourdough loaves, or picking at charcuterie platters and fresh, inspired salads while sipping tea or coffee. Tartines (open-faced sandwiches) are the main draw, and there are plenty of creative toppings from which to choose, but our pork loin and artichoke hearts was pedestrian at best and didn't justify the £8.50 charge. Curiously, the eat-in and takeaway tartine options differ. **Take home:** harissa and wild capers in sea salt from the Mahjoub range.

Pâtisserie Valerie

44 Old Compton Street, W1D 5JX (7437 3466/www.patisserie-valerie.co.uk). Leicester Square, Piccadilly Circus or Tottenham Court Road tube. **Open** 7.30am-8.30pm Mon, Tue; 7.30am-11pm Wed-Sat; 9.30am-8pm Sun. **Main courses** £3.75-£8.25. **Credit** (over £5) AmEx, MC, V.

Now with over 15 outlets, including two gelaterias and branches in Bromley and Bristol, this popular Soho fixture has an old-fashioned decor with murals and Formica tables. We find the ground floor rather hemmed-in; head upstairs to the lighter first floor for a window table handy for people-watching. The menu offers a simple selection of soup, omelettes, pastas, salads and quiche; the quiche has never disappointed, with delicious pastry and plenty of the featured ingredients. All-day breakfasts run from a full english or eggs benedict to brioche french toast with maple syrup. **Take home:** a birthday gateau. *Babies and children welcome: high chairs. Takeaway service.* **Map 17 C4**. **For branches see index**.

Paul

29 Bedford Street, WC2E 9ED (7836 5321/www.paul-uk.com). Covent Garden tube. **Open** 7.30am-9pm Mon-Thur; 7.30-10pm Fri; 9am-10pm Sat; 9am-8.30pm Sun. **Main courses** £4-£8. **Credit** MC, V.

This French bakery has spread obscenely all over London, yet it just takes a visit to the Covent Garden flagship (launched a century after the first Paul opened its doors in tiny Croix, near Lille) to remind us of its appeal. The shop sells an array of freshly made baguettes – the sesame and camembert creation is inspired – alongside golden pastries, fruity tarts and boxed salads for eaters-on-the-go. Further back is the dining area, which we love for its old-fashioned continental charm. The place is clearly a hit with the tourists found here every day. Staff serve hot food such as quiches, soups, savoury crêpes and perfectly done omelettes. They can be harried and forgetful during lunchtimes, so best go for a relaxing breakfast or afternoon tea. **Take home:** breakfast tea and apricot jam. *Babies and children welcome: high chair. Disabled: toilet. Takeaway service.* **Map 18 D5**. **For branches see index**.

Babies and children welcome: high chairs. Disabled: toilet. Tables outdoors (7, pavement). Takeaway service. **Map 9 G5**. **For branches see index**.

Clapham

★ Breads Etcetera (100)

2008 RUNNER-UP BEST BREAKFAST

127 Clapham High Street, SW4 7SS (7720 3601/ www.breadsetcetera.com). Clapham Common or Clapham North tube. **Open** 10am-2pm Mon; 10am-6pm Tue-Thur, Sun; 10am-10pm Fri, Sat. **Main courses** £3.55-£15.50. **Credit** MC, V.

The well-run café with this artisan bakery was suitably packed with groups of thirtysomethings on our Sunday morning visit, with punters drawn by the flavoursome sourdough bread. The interior has a whiff of the NYC brunch spot about it (brick walls, maroon and cream striped textiles, shelving units), evoking a vibe that's both homely and 'urban'. Breads – choose from six-seed, walnut, white, wholemeal, olive and herb, and rye – are made from high-quality organic ingredients and form the basis of most dishes. Novelty is provided by the 'DIY toast' option, with Dualit toasters on tables. All-day brunch choices (£7-£8) run the gamut from greasy ('cowboy': fried egg in white sourdough, spicy sausage, onion, baked beans, dry-cured bacon) through to sweet ('sweet sensation': grilled banana bread with honey, seasonal fruit and cream) to healthy ('scandinavian': boiled egg, fish roe, ham, cheese, fresh cucumber, peppers and tomato). Sandwiches are also available, as are brownies, Luscombe juices and Monmouth coffee. *Babies and children admitted. Tables outdoors (2, pavement). Takeaway service.* **Map 22 B2**.

★ Macaron (100)

22 The Pavement, SW4 0HY (7498 2636). Clapham Common tube. **Open** 7.30am-8pm Mon-Fri; 9am-8pm Sat, Sun. **Main courses** £2.95-£4.20. **No credit cards.**

Don't search for 'Macaron' – this pâtisserie's name is nowhere on the signage – look for the giant pink ice-cream cone by the front door. Nab a small table on the pavement, gaze out over Clapham Common, and nod to the young locals popping in for a long baguette and coffee. It wouldn't take a large glass of wine to imagine you've been teleported to 1930s Paris. It's forever sunny inside this tea room; the ceiling is painted blue with fluffy clouds and fat cherubs. The saccharine extends to the crockery: old Royal Albert bone china, flowery with gold edging. On the menu, there's a varied selection of Chinese tea; a pot of nettle tea came full of fresh leaves thanks to the friendly waitresses. The display of freshly made baguettes and sandwiches on rye was tempting, though we opted for a creamy, moist leek tart (for which a side salad would have been appreciated). You'd expect the macaroons to be fabulous here – and you'd be right. There are rows and rows of pretty double-deckers (two pressed together with flavoured sweet cream), plus traditional varieties such as vanilla and pistachio; it's also worth trying the tropical flavours like lychee.
Babies and children admitted. Tables outdoors (3, pavement). Takeaway service. **Map 22 A2**.

South East
Deptford

Deptford Project [NEW]
121-123 Deptford High Street, SE8 4NS (07525 351 656/www.thedeptfordproject.com). Deptford rail/Deptford Bridge DLR. **Open** 8am-7pm Mon-Fri; 8am-6pm Sat; 10am-4pm Sun. **Main courses** £1.95-£4.95. **No credit cards**.
Not your typical eaterie, The Deptford Project is housed in a converted 1960s train carriage. The loos had a previous life as a garden shed, a brightly painted table spans the length of the interior, and cheery decking out front adds to the laid-back, arty vibe of the joint (the café is part of a regeneration plan for the area that includes a creative industries market and art galleries). The food on offer is unpretentious and homely – lunch options include the likes of a light potato salad accompanied by crunchy green salad, or satisfyingly spiced curry on a bed of turmeric-spiked basmati. If visiting for breakfast or afternoon tea, try the excellent muffins made with eggs from the company's own free-range chickens. There is a commitment to sourcing ingredients locally, and the coffee is sustainably farmed. Locals, from Goldsmiths students to young families, should find this a pleasant spot to chill and recharge.
Babies and children welcome: high chairs. Disabled: toilet. Tables outdoors (7, terrace).

Dulwich

Blue Mountain Café
18 North Cross Road, SE22 9EU (8299 6953/ www.bluemo.co.uk). East Dulwich rail. **Open** 9am-6pm Mon; 9am-10pm Tue-Sat; 10am-6pm Sun. **Main courses** £3.95-£7.95. **Set breakfast** £7.50 incl tea or coffee. **Credit** AmEx, MC, V.
Fashionable well before East Dulwich was, Blue Mountain has expanded its range over the years from caffeine and pastry fixes to a full-scale all-day eating experience. So now, groups of media mothers and their progeny can sit down to typically topical dishes such as butternut squash risotto with rocket, or pan-fried steak with steamed veg in a coconut curry sauce. Fried plantain and jerk chicken give a nod to this wealthy area's once-cosmopolitan vibe. Blue Mountain Café hasn't lost its slightly hippy dippy air, however. The eye-catching broken crockery mosaic in the outdoor seating areas and the quirky look of the back rooms remain. Service is friendly and efficient – the young staff are more than adept at ingratiating themselves with babycino-demanding sprogs and lunching Lordship Lane ladies. Our light lunch of buttery mushrooms and tofu in a soft baguette was delicious, even though the salad with it was a bit limp and bag-tasting. Still, the cafe's coffee and cakes are as delightful as ever; we were most impressed with the brownies.

Babies and children welcome: children's menu; high chairs; nappy-changing facilities. Separate room for parties, seats 10. Tables outdoors (5, garden; 5, terrace). **Map 23 C4**.

Jack's Tea & Coffee House
85 Pellatt Road, SE22 9JD (8693 0011). North Dulwich rail. **Open** 10am-5pm Mon-Fri; 10am-3pm Sat. **Main courses** £1.95-£5.95. **No credit cards**.
Wander off the well-trodden paths of Lordship Lane and you might be lucky enough to stumble across this charming family-run café, where chef James Hoffman and baker Fi Sweeney turn out superior grub to be enjoyed in the cosy premises. Friendly service and hearty café fare is what gives Jack's so much soul (character is added by its slightly dishevelled decor and old-fashioned till). The signature swedish meatballs and beetroot mayonnaise (the latter a whimsical Dr Seuss-like magenta) hits the spot every time; the tangy chunks of beetroot cutting through the rich and savoury meatballs, all encased in a wonderfully fluffy fresh baguette. Other temptations include own-made chicken liver pâté with toast and cornichons, and on a hot day, the watermelon, rocket and prosciutto salad, or Jack's special ice-cream sundae. Seasonal produce is on show in wooden crates in front of the bar. Come springtime, a tiny but well-looked-after garden patio hidden in the back is alive with flowers.
Babies and children welcome: high chairs; nappy-changing facilities; toys. Tables outdoors (3, garden; 3, pavement). Takeaway service. **Map 23 C5**.

Peckham

Petitou
63 Choumert Road, SE15 4AR (7639 2613). Peckham Rye rail. **Open** 9am-5.30pm Tue-Sat; 10am-5.30pm Sun. **Main courses** £6.55-£6.95. **Credit** AmEx, DC, MC, V.
Petitou appeared in the leafy backstreets of Peckham's bohemian quarter a few years ago, to a chorus of hallelujahs from locals who'd prayed for a respite from the burger and fried chicken joints of the high street. Many of the area's creative types continue to worship here regularly, basking in the light, arty and informal atmosphere. Devotees pay homage to the excellent coffee, nourishing lunches and daily changing menu of delicious cakes made by a team of hand-picked local domestic goddesses. Despite increased competition, Petitou is still the mainstay of this area's freelance community – not to mention the many lunching mums with toddlers. It achieves this thanks to a consistent attention to detail, a commitment to fresh and locally sourced produce (organic where possible), generous portions, fabulous pastries, fresh juices and assorted teas, but primarily due to the quietly civilised and mellow atmosphere generated by its owners.
Babies and children welcome: high chairs. Tables outdoors (6, patio). Takeaway service. **Map 23 C3**.

East
Docklands

Mudchute Kitchen
Mudchute Park & Farm, Pier Street, Isle of Dogs, E14 3HP (7515 5901/www.mudchutekitchen.org). Mudchute DLR. **Open** *Summer* 9am-5pm daily. *Winter* 9am-5pm Tue-Sun. **Main courses** £3-£8. **Credit** MC, V.
Mudchute City Farm's café is very much a family zone, complete with wipe-clean tablecloths and a toy-strewn kiddie corner. Order at the counter, where you'll see staff preparing snacks in the kitchen, and eat indoors to the soundtrack of toddlers bashing on a xylophone. Alternatively, perch on one of several outdoor benches next to the stable yard. The changing menu of weekday lunches could include Mudchute Farm Oxford Down lamb stew; farm egg and mayo salad; or fusilli with garlic shoots, cream and parmesan. Weekend breakfast feasts feature the likes of black pudding with bubble and squeak. Fairy cakes are on hand for kids hankering after a sugar high,

Interview
WILLIAM CURLEY

Who are you?
Pâtissier and chocolatier, and owner of **William Curley** outlets in Richmond (*see p313*), and John Lewis Foodhall on Oxford Street.
What's the best thing about running a café and shop in London?
I like being my own boss and this job gives me the opportunity to express myself. Also, it means I can work with my wife Suzue, who's also a pastry chef. We'd never spend time together otherwise. Not many people would put up with a chef's lifestyle and habits unless they understood them themselves – chefs are a special breed.
What's the worst thing?
Rent and rates. Rates are going up higher than the rate of inflation, yet you have to wonder what they are for as we still have to pay for things like getting our rubbish collected.
Which are your favourite London restaurants?
I'm not one for going out every day, I'd rather go somewhere really nice every two months. I like **Galvin at Windows** (*see p141*) for the views in particular, and **The Capital** (*see p139*), which also serves wonderful food in great surroundings. I use John Lewis Foodhall and Selfridges a lot too, and really like Selfridges' salt beef bar.
How green are you?
It's something that all businesses, large or small, are having to take seriously. We separate food and packaging, and recycle, and we are currently looking to change our company van from diesel to electric.
What is missing from London's restaurant scene?
I think it's exciting times, and it has been here for many years. London is so cosmopolitan it's hard to think of what's missing. How about a dessert restaurant!

CHEAP EATS

while parents might prefer more adult tea-time treats such as coffee and cardamom cake dotted with pomegranate seeds. A smokehouse has recently been built (staff have already smoked cheeses, geese, ducks, butter, garlic and eggs in it) and a wood-fired oven is due to be completed in the summer of 2008 – both of which should widen the choice of appetising dishes to accompany your day on this lively Docklands farm.
Babies and children welcome: children's menu; high chairs; nappy-changing facilities (farm); play area; toys. Tables outdoors (15, courtyard). **Map 24 C4.**

Shoreditch

Frizzante@City Farm
Hackney City Farm, 1A Goldsmith's Row, E2 8QA (7739 2266/www.frizzanteltd.co.uk). Bus 26, 48, 55. **Open** 10am-4.30pm Tue-Sun. **Main courses** £5.45-£10. **Credit** AmEx MC, V.
Arrive early enough at the weekend and you can enjoy a peaceful, supremely laid-back breakfast before, come late-morning, groups of young Hackneyites become penned in by herds of baby buggies. Even then, escape is easy. Just wander out into the yard and you'll see why the kids are beside themselves with excitement at the sight of ducks, rabbits, chinchillas and grumpy pigs at petting distance. The café is cosy and fittingly rustic – colanders and cheese graters make fun lampshades, there are Astroturf seats for kids to play on, and in warmer weather you can take your meal into the garden. For breakfast, try the addictive sweet-and-savoury combo of maple syrup-doused waffles with bacon, or a vegetarian plate of farm eggs, roasted tomatoes and hash browns, all chased down with bargain 85p tea. A changing blackboard menu offers hearty Italian main courses such as pappardelle with pheasant ragù, and the easy-on-the-palate children's menu includes the likes of pasta with cheese and tomato sauce. Save room for a scoop or two of gelato and you'll leave content as a calf in clover.
Babies and children welcome: children's menu; high chairs. Disabled: toilet. Separate room for parties, seats 40. Tables outdoors (12, garden). Takeaway service. Vegan dishes. **Map 6 S3. For branch see index.**

Jones Dairy Café
23 Ezra Street, E2 7RH (7739 5372/ www.jonesdairy.co.uk). Bus 26, 48, 55. **Open** 9am-3pm Fri, Sat; 8am-3pm Sun. **Main courses** £2-£6.50. **No credit cards.**

When the hubbub of Sunday's Columbia Road Flower Market gets too much, take a turn at the eastern end, down this cobbled lane. You'll find overhanging ivy, rickety tables and a very lovely, very small café. Expect a queue out of the door on market day – and some chess-like moves for soon-to-be-vacated tables – and something entirely more leisurely on Fridays and Saturdays. You enter through a set of bright-green barn doors. It's akin to walking into a welcoming farm kitchen, what with the floor of old terracotta tiles, white painted brick walls and an elderly Thomas stove in the corner. Half a dozen prized stools line three walls. Behind the counter, the open shelves are full of teapots and mixing bowls. The menu changes weekly and might include big bowls of asparagus soup or pizzas (baked in-house). The own-made lemonade was a dream on a hot day, and the wedge of carrot cake as good as any we've had. Service could have been more helpful, but regulars wouldn't have it any other way. Around the corner is Jones Dairy's shop, which features an array of artisan-made breads and farmhouse cheeses.
Babies and children welcome: high chair. Tables outdoors (2, pavement). Takeaway service. **Map 6 S3.**

Tea Smith NEW
2008 RUNNER-UP BEST TEA ROOM
8 Lamb Street, E1 6EA (7247 1333/www.tea smith.co.uk). Liverpool Street tube/rail. **Open** 11am-6pm daily. **Credit** MC, V.
Sleekly appointed with oriental-style furnishings, Tea Smith is a thoroughly modern set-up with a friendly, relaxed atmosphere. A bar counter at the front of the shop has room for a couple of high stools: a great perch to view the art of making the finest brews. The business is owned by a married couple, John Kennedy and Tomoko Kawase, who also run weekly masterclasses and a shop that sells all the props. The filtered water is temperature controlled; making tea involves a succession of metal spouts, tea infusers and jug juggling. For something unusual, check out: 'sparrow's tongue', a Korean green variety prized for its fresh flavour; 'thistle blossom' for its floral notes; or romantically entitled 'snow jewel', redolent of delicate fruits. Our gold star went to chilled green jasmine tea, infused overnight with cold water to bring out its clean-tasting aromatic qualities. Sweets from William Curley (*see p313*) include miniature green-tea cakes and lush chocolate nibbles.
Babies and children admitted. Takeaway service. **Map 12 R5.**

Mudchute Kitchen. See p311.

North East
Clapton

Venetia
55 Chatsworth Road, E5 0LH (8986 1642). Homerton rail/242, 308 bus. **Open** 8.30am-5pm Tue-Fri; 8am-5.30pm Sat; 9am-5pm Sun. **Main courses** £2.20-£3.95. **No credit cards.**
A homely charm radiates from this modest, welcoming café, which has been enthusiastically embraced by locals since opening in 2007. Standing out from the drabness of the surrounding shops, Venetia's brand of shabby chic – washed out, New England-style wood-panelled walls adorned with antique mirrors and vintage advertising prints – attracts families in search of tea and cakes (the staff are good with kids), neighbours in for Saturday coffee and a friendly chat, and weekday customers grabbing an almond croissant on the hoof. Sandwich fillings are pretty pedestrian (cheese salad, bacon and egg), but the bread is excellent. There's also soup and tasty salads such as herby and delicious chickpea, feta and sweet roasted pepper. Add a languorous soundtrack of jazzy blues and a couple of staff members (all the compact café needs) who greet customers by name, and you have a laid-back local drawing in a steady stream of caffeine-seeking Claptonites.
Babies and children welcome: high chairs; nappy-changing facilities; toys. Tables outdoors (2, pavement). Takeaway service.

North
Muswell Hill

Feast on the Hill
46 Fortis Green Road, N10 3HN (8444 4957). East Finchley tube or Highgate tube, then 43, 134 bus. **Open** 8am-5pm Mon-Sat; 9am-5pm Sun. **Main courses** £5.95-£9.95. **Credit** AmEx, MC, V.
This Muswell Hill institution, previously know as Café on the Hill, now features the logo from Feast, the long-associated deli next door. Fortunately, the format remains largely the same: all-day breakfasts, plus a short lunch menu served from noon to 4pm. The new kids' menu is a nod to the Muswell Hill muffia and their broods, though portions are pretty small. Breakfasts include several of the classics as well as new ideas such as olive and chorizo frittata with herb salad. Lunch dishes like our fish pie were a little ordinary by comparison. The drinks list caters to all: half a dozen red and white wines available by the glass or bottle, with smoothies for children and a wide range of teas and coffees for grandparents. Finish with a tasty fruit crumble or baked cheesecake, and browse through the papers provided. The decor is simple – wooden tables and chairs, fairly closely squeezed, and Jack Vettriano prints. Staff remain smiley despite the constant full house.
Babies and children welcome: children's menu; high chairs. Tables outdoors (4, pavement).

Newington Green

That Place on the Corner NEW
1-3 Green Lanes, N16 9BS (7704 0079/ www.thatplaceonthecorner.co.uk). Bus 73. **Open** 10.30am-6.30pm Mon-Sat; 10.30-3pm Sun. **Main courses** £4.85-£8.95. **Credit** MC, V.
Catering to the needs of sophisticated N16 parents and the contents of their Maclarens is a challenge. Too much IKEA plastic ware, or the very mention of a chicken nugget, raises a sneer. At the same time, an overly adult atmosphere risks alienating sociable families. That Place on the Corner appears to have the balance right. It's big enough for all the playroom paraphernalia to be laid out at one end, and huge windows emphasise the glorious spaciousness. The menu sticks sensibly to the tried and trusted pasta, panini and big-breakfast formula, with brasserie staples such as own-made burgers and fish cakes to bring further comfort. The coffee is of a high standard, and cakes and pastries come from a local bakery. Children can choose own-made shepherd's pie, spag bol and

CHEAP EATS

other pasta favourites, smaller burgers, and plaice or chicken goujons. They also have the option of mash, rice or chips and various vegetables to go alongside. Staff were overseeing a tastefully decorated party table at the playful end of the café when we visited, but we received unflustered, efficient attention and were struck by the proprietor's obvious fondness for children.
Babies and children welcome: children's menu; high chairs; nappy-changing facilities; toys. Disabled: toilet.

North West
Kensal Green

Brilliant Kids Café
8 Station Terrace, NW10 5RT (8964 4120/ www.brilliantkids.co.uk). Kensal Green tube/ Kensal Rise rail. **Open** 8am-6pm Mon-Fri; 9am-5pm Sat; 10am-4pm Sun. **Main courses** £5.50-£6.50. **Credit** MC, V.
Even though we equipped ourselves with a child to visit the splendid Brilliant, there was no need. Plenty of sprogless customers were at the front end of the café, away from the tot-friendly living room at back. Many come for the substantial all-day breakfast, with its thick bacon rashers and sausage; others know, as we do, that the daily special hot lunch is usually pretty special (chicken pie, shepherd's pie, curry), and made with meat from Devon Rose organics. You'll also get a mean cappuccino here, and the pastry goods are out of this world (especially the rough-hewn, individual quiches). What's more, the salads and fillings for the fresh bagels and loaves are imaginative and wonderfully fresh. There's a pleasant generosity about the café. Everything chalked up on the board can be scaled down for children's portions. Tiny rainbow-sprinkled fairy cakes and proper sausage rolls rarely fail to stimulate small appetites. Both the high-quality food, and the arty workshops for children held in the studio next door (£5 per hour), represent brilliant value for money.
Babies and children welcome: children's portions; high chairs; play area; supervised activities; crèche. Disabled: toilet. Restaurant available for hire. Tables outdoors (2, pavement; 2, garden). Takeaway service.

Gracelands
118 College Road, NW10 5HD (8964 9161/ www.gracelandscafe.com). Kensal Green tube. **Open** 8.30am-5pm Mon-Wed; 8.30-10pm Thur, Fri; 9am-10pm Sat; 9.30am-3pm Sun. **Main courses** £5.95-£12.95. **Credit** AmEx, MC, V.
A deeply fecund vibe prevails at this convivial café. Tow-haired toddlers and bouncing babies smeared with organic sweet potato greet you at the front door. More of them play in the tastefully appointed home corner, presided over by mamas nursing large cappuccinos, infants, mobile phones and laptops. If all this seems a mite too familial, be reassured: the affable women who run the café are conscientious about letting the child-free eat and drink in a quieter corner, often in the Eulabee shop next door. Food is own-made with care, served in generous portions. Breakfasts include big fry-ups, eggs benedict or pastries. Lunchtime specials follow on: the likes of chicken or lentil stew, or lighter choices such as our delicious buttery and garlicky mushrooms on toast. Quiches (goat's cheese and sweet potato is a favourite combination) are served with chunky salads of puy lentils, tomatoes and basil, and roasted veg. Creative workshops are run in the community rooms.
Babies and children welcome: children's menu; high chairs; nappy-changing facilities; toys. Tables outdoors (5, pavement; 4, garden). Takeaway service.

Hampstead

Chaiwalla NEW
2008 RUNNER-UP BEST TEA ROOM
4A-5A Perrins Court, NW3 1QS (7435 2151/ www.chaiwalla.info). Hampstead tube. **Open** 9am-6.30pm daily. **Main courses** £2.50-£5. **Credit** MC, V.

Inspired by tea (*chai*) stalls in Kolkata, West Bengal – on railway platforms, roadside corners and bazaars – Neil Sanyal has taken the tradition of serving spiced tea in clay pots and brought it to leafy Hampstead. Chaiwalla is no spit-and-sawdust caff. Modern styling gives it an urban appeal, with low seating, Indian inlay work, and images of Asian street scenes across the walls. Its earthenware tumblers, made in West Bengal, are disposable in India, but customers here are encouraged to take them home. Even though there's a small selection of specialist brews, it's the masala chai that scores top marks. Spiked with ginger and hints of cinnamon, it has just the right balance of milk and tastes all the better for being served in a clay pot. Lunches and sweetmeats are available, but we recommend samosas for the classic Indian afternoon-tea experience. Choose from six generously proportioned varieties – all baked rather than deep-fried. Our favourites were the chicken and paneer samosas because of their lively ginger, garlic and chilli spicing.
Babies and children admitted. Café available for hire. Tables outdoors (3, alleyway). **Map 28 B2**.

Outer London
Richmond, Surrey

★ William Curley
10 Paved Court, Richmond, Surrey TW9 1LZ (8332 3002/www.williamcurley.co.uk). Richmond tube/rail. **Open** 9.30am-8.30pm Mon-Sat; 10.30am-6.30pm Sun. **Main courses** £4.50-£5.30. **Credit** (over £8) MC, V.
This fine pâtisserie and chocolatier's can seem a bit severe, but the desserts and chocolates simply overflow with warmth and creativity. Playful French and Japanese influences are discernible in the treats – William Curley's Japanese-born wife Suzue is also an accomplished pâtissier and has a key role in this operation. We loved the freshly made pastries – a seasonal fruit tart with pretty curls of dark chocolate and a silky custard base – although, 'seasonal' was a loose term considering it was spring as we dug into figs and blackberries nestled among more timely offerings. Matcha and earl grey tea truffles had just the right balance of flavours and textures, but best were the hot chocolates: rich, but not cloying. Our spiced version was made with quality dark Toscano Black (from the Italian producer, Amedei), infused with whispers of cinnamon, nutmeg, ginger and honey. Positively decadent. Alternatively there are fine teas from Tea Smith (*see p312*) to sip. William Curley also sells sophisticated ice-creams in flavours such as green tea, red bean, yoghurt and orange and, of course, chocolate. All can be enjoyed at pavement tables on this charming pedestrianised shopping street tucked behind Richmond's main drag. Don't forget to buy some goodies to take home, such as a box of the award-winning house truffles, or bags of sweet miso and walnut cookies.
Babies and children admitted. Tables outdoors (2, pavement). Takeaway service.

PARK CAFÉS

Central
Marylebone

Garden Café
Inner Circle, Regents Park, NW1 4NU (7935 5729/ www.thegardencafe.co.uk). Baker Street or Regents Park tube. **Open** 9am-dusk daily. **Breakfast served** 9-11am, **lunch served** noon-4pm, **dinner served** (summer) 5-8pm daily. **Set lunch/dinner** £15 2 courses, £18.50 3 courses. **Main courses** £8.50-£12.50. **Credit** MC, V.
This café has a site adjacent to Queen Mary's rose garden, and English cottage-garden surrounds. It's run by Company of Cooks, who also run celebrated eateries and snack spots at Kenwood (*see p314*), Hyde Park Lido, Royal Festival Hall's Riverside Terrace, and RHS Garden Wisley. It is a

prime location for afternoon tea or, in summer, an early supper. Visitors are corralled in one direction or the other depending on whether they want counter or table service. The proudly British, and occasionally local, menu notes some esteemed suppliers, while the wine list favours France and includes a suitably light provençal rosé for alfresco drinking in hot weather. Baby gem and parmesan salad was a twist on the ubiquitous caesar, with croûtons and a warm, creamy cheese goo dolloped over the crisp leaves – very successful. Our ribeye steak with garlic and herb butter was a fine cut beautifully cooked, accompanied by plentiful (if lukewarm) skin-on fries. Herb roast chicken also impressed, though its accompanying new potatoes were overcooked. Staff are fairly swift (on our visit they seemed ratehr too keen to get home) so you may have time to wolf down a delicious cranachan or gooseberry syllabub before the show starts at the nearby open-air theatre.
Babies and children welcome: children's menu; high chairs. Booking advisable. Disabled: toilet. Restaurant available for hire (autumn and winter only). Tables outdoors (38, garden). Takeaway service. **Map 3 G3**.

West
Kensington

Kensington Palace Orangery
The Orangery, Kensington Palace, Kensington Gardens, W8 4PX (7376 0239/www.digbytrout. co.uk). High Street Kensington or Queensway tube. **Open** Mar-Oct 10am-6pm daily. Nov-Feb 10am-5pm daily. **Main courses** £8.95-£9.95. **Set tea** £12.50-£24.95. **Credit** AmEx, MC, V.
As far as afternoon teas go, this stunning 18th-century building offers a quintessentially English experience. Formidable white Corinthian pillars and marble statues lend the room a certain grandeur, but the piles of tempting own-made cakes, chirpy regulars and tourists basking in the beams of natural light chisel away some of the severity. If only they could have melted the frostiness of the waiting staff too. Still, we enjoyed the signature Orangery cake: a creamy orange cake with lashings of frosting, offering a burst of citrus and sunshine in every bite. Less stellar was the lemon meringue pie, which tasted as unappealing as it looked – the crust stale and the curd lacking zing. Most visitors opt for tea and cake, but the lunch menu is a compendium of tempting soups, salads and mains. The list of teas includes all the favourites, but also unusual brews such as quality leaves from England's first tea plantation, Tregothnan Estate, and Indian tulsi mint.
Babies and children welcome: children's menu; high chairs; nappy-changing facilities. Disabled: toilet. Tables outdoors (14, terrace). **Map 7 C8**.

South West
Fulham

The Lawn
Fulham Palace, Bishop's Avenue, SW6 6EA (7610 7160/www.thelawnrestaurant.co.uk). Putney Bridge tube. **Lunch served** noon-3pm, **tea served** 3-5pm, **dinner served** 6-10.30pm daily. **Breakfast served** 9-10.30am Sat, Sun. **Main courses** £9.50-£18.50. **Credit** AmEx, DC, MC, V.
A highly civilised addition to London's park café scene, whether you're taking tea in the old bishop's drawing room of Fulham Palace, or enjoying the sunshine outside on one of the luxuriously padded garden seats. Both locations provide quintessential views of clipped lawns and designer deckchairs. Indeed, like all Oliver Peyton venues, thought and money have been devoted to providing a stylish setting. The menu is more elegant than you'll find at similar set-ups, with the likes of garlic-and-thyme marinated spatchcock spring chicken with jersey royals, and steak tartare of rare-breed Ballindalloch beef. Our barbecued black bream was pleasingly crisp and smoky, but let down by the accompanying fennel salad which contained acrid slices of onion that made it memorable for

all the wrong reasons. Still, the lime and coriander-seed dressing showed promise. Best was the chocolate nut sundae, which contained three different choc ices plus whole hazelnuts and big chunks of walnut. Afternoon tea can be a simple scone or chelsea bun with Jersey clotted cream, Peyton & Byrne jams and a pot of tea or coffee (£5), or the more indulgent £12 affair including sandwiches and pastries.
Babies and children welcome: high chairs; nappy-changing facilities. Booking advisable weekends. Disabled: toilet. Tables outdoors (25, terrace). Takeaway service.

Wandsworth

Common Ground
Wandsworth Common, off Dorlcote Road, SW18 3RT (8874 9386). Wandsworth Common rail. **Open** 9am-5.30pm Mon-Fri; 10am-5.30pm Sat, Sun. **Main courses** £3.95-£9. **Credit** MC, V.
There's a pristine bowling green on one side, cricket pitches on another and a brand-new toddler's playground to the rear. A nature centre backs on to the front patio, which is spread with weathered garden tables and some kind of portable coffee shack in the shade of a large, healthy oak tree. The near-perfect setting explains why this converted park lodge teems with local Wandsworth parents and their many, many children at weekends (even in gloomiest February). When the weather's rough, they head indoors (one room is a conservatory, the other is lived-in comfortable with deep sofas, local art, papers and buckets of toys for the weekday mother and toddler groups). The coffee is good, as are the cakes and the ice-cream, but in general the catering is no better than it needs to be (and on the pricey side). Choose from a familiar roster of soups (three-bean was good on our most recent visit), quiches, baked potatoes, bacon sarnies (they need more bacon!), meat loaf and burgers. Even on slow days, the service is deeply daffy.
Babies and children welcome: children's menu; high chairs; nappy-changing facilities. Café available for hire. Tables outside (15, patio). Takeaway service.

South East
Dulwich

Pavilion Café
Dulwich Park, off College Road, SE21 7BQ (8299 1383/www.pavilioncafedulwich.co.uk). West Dulwich rail/P4 bus. **Open** *Summer* 9am-5.30pm Mon-Thur; 9am-6.30pm Fri-Sun. *Winter* 8.30am-3.30pm Mon-Fri; 9am-3.30pm Sat, Sun. **Main courses** £1.90-£6.95. **Credit** MC, V.
On a quiet weekday, it is bliss to take breakfast, lunch or tea in this light and airy, modern park café overlooking the green lawns and rhododendrons of Dulwich Park. In contrast, midday on a sunny weekend is definitely a bad time to go looking for food for hungry children. After 40 minutes queuing, we urgently needed one of the 'special Sunday bloody mary' cocktails. Most folk persevere, because the offer and the setting is so attractive. The all-day full breakfast is great value, the cakes are own-made and the specials are always interesting (moroccan lamb soup with pitta on the last outing). Hell, you can even get wine here. Staff mean well, with their organic and seasonal commitment, and new additions regularly appear on the menu (rum hot chocolate, or a Baileys latte, anyone?), but service is painfully slow. This would be the perfect park café, if only they could find a way of coping with the weekend rush.
Babies and children welcome: children's menu; high chairs; nappy-changing facilities; toys. Disabled: toilet. Tables outdoors (12, park). Takeaway service.

Greenwich

Pavilion Tea House
Greenwich Park, Blackheath Gate, SE10 8QY (8858 9695/www.companyofcooks.com). Blackheath rail/Greenwich rail/DLR. **Open** *Summer* 9am-6pm daily. *Winter* 9am-4pm daily. **Main courses** £3.25-£7.50. **Credit** MC, V.

It was chilly on our visit to this inviting hexagonal café at the business end of the park, which precluded a meal at one of the many outdoor tables surrounded by chestnut trees. Indoors, it is bright, clean and busy – expect lengthy queues and marauding children at weekend lunchtimes. Limited space means parents are requested to leave push-chairs outside; irritatingly, many still sneak them in. The menu contains several hearty dishes: perfect for when you've scaled the heights of this hilly park. We plumped for scrambled eggs with smoked salmon; the portion was big enough for two, served on generously buttered toast made with thick-sliced proper bread. Mixed bean casserole was warming and tomatoey, but needed some grated cheese or extra herbs to add interest. Sandwiches are prodigiously filled, but cakes were a mixed bunch. We didn't like the look of the industrial-sized cream scone so chose a nicely flavoured chocolate cake to mask the flavour of the sadly rather indifferent coffee.
Babies and children welcome: high chairs; nappy-changing facilities. Disabled: toilet. Tables outdoors (20, garden). Takeaway service.

East
Victoria Park

Pavilion Café NEW
Victoria Park, Crown Gate West, E9 5DU (8980 0030/www.the-pavilion-cafe.com). Bethnal Green tube/rail/Hackney Wick rail/26, 277 bus. **Open** *Summer* 8.30-5pm daily. *Winter* 8.30am-4pm daily. **Main courses** £4-£9.50. **No credit cards.**
In August 2007, tea merchant Rob Green and Australian chef Brett Redman transformed this park café overlooking Victoria Park's lake. It now serves a menu of organic produce, rare-breed meats and artisanal food to the park's many strollers; pushchairs and toddlers frequently fill the place. Fry-ups are the core of the menu, with moist black pudding and sensational sausages from the Ginger Pig among the highlights, but try and save room for the cakes (lemon drizzle, brownies and the like). Tea lovers will be delighted by the award-winning organic earl grey tea and the excellent orange pekoe (Rob imports these directly from Sri Lanka). The coffees are excellent too, using Monmouth coffee and Ivy House Farm organic milk. Prices are fair, and the café has a very friendly, happy buzz to it. Green and Redman are also committed to greening their business, from cutting waste to sourcing line-caught fish of 'safe' species from near Brighton.
Babies and children welcome: high chairs; nappy-changing facilites. Disabled: toilet. Tables outdoors (20, park). Takeaway service.

North
Highgate

Pavilion Café
Highgate Wood, Muswell Hill Road, N10 3JN (8444 4777). Highgate tube. **Open** *Summer* 9am-9pm daily. *Winter* 9am-4pm daily. **Main courses** £3.50-£10. **Credit** AmEx, MC, V.
With all the wisteria and rose bushes, it's hard to believe the A1000 is so close – such is the Pavilion's bucolic setting at the heart of Highgate Wood. Friendly, dedicated staff try to place each group of diners at their preferred table, and impressed us by pointing out that the freshly squeezed orange juice had run out (so many others would just bring the long-life stuff instead). The printed menu, supplemented by a few blackboard specials, has a Mediterranean slant, with big bowls of pasta and dishes such as pan-fried salmon on puy lentils. We opted for meze: fresh, warm falafel, grilled chorizo, and a dip of butternut squash and hazelnuts (there were plenty more to choose from), all served with lovely warm, spongy pitta bread. Kids have their own short menu of goujons, pasta and the like. The wide choice of sweet things runs from wheat-free lemon and polenta cake to a big dark chocolate brownie crowned with a huge scoop of ice-cream. Organic ingredients are used often,

and drinkers won't be disappointed when there's a choice of beers from Pitfield Brewery (EKG was the perfect summery choice) and Westons cider. There's a kiosk at the side for quick purchase of ice-creams and other refreshments to enjoy on the move or while sun-bathing by the sports field.
Babies and children welcome: children's menu; high chairs; nappy-changing facilities. Entertainment: jazz 6-8.30pm, Fri (summer). Tables outdoors (30, terrace; 8, veranda). Takeaway service.

Stamford Hill

Springfield Park Café
White Lodge Mansion, Springfield Park, E5 9EF (8806 0444/www.sparkcafe.co.uk). Stamford Hill or Stoke Newington rail/253, 254, 393 bus. **Open** *Apr-Oct* 10am-6pm daily. *Nov-Mar* 10am-4pm daily. **Main courses** £3.90-£5.90. **No credit cards.**
This child-friendly park café has a certain homely charm about it and appropriately attracts legions of families with their toddlers and pets. The Grade-II listed White Lodge Mansion, which houses the café, is a magnificent building best enjoyed while sitting outdoors at the plastic tables in the garden (connecting to the rest of Springfield Park). A focus on fresh, healthy foods means you won't find any artery-clogging burgers and chips here; instead, opt for freshly prepared hot and cold sandwiches, and the thoroughly delicious meze platters of scrumptious variety. Our summer platter came forth bursting with a three-bean and chickpea salad, tabouleh and houmous; the Absolute Med plate contained fresh stuffed vine leaves, falafels and a summery tomato salad. Own-made carrot cake, while pleasantly spiced, was slightly too sweet, but the banana cake trumped those we've had at other establishments. Staff are accommodating and mellow, as we'd expect from such a relaxing eaterie. As they say, 'a tranquil atmosphere is conducive to good digestion.'
Babies and children welcome: children's menu; high chairs. Disabled: toilet. Tables outdoors (20, garden; 6, pavement). Takeaway service.

North West
Hampstead

★ Brew House (100)
Kenwood, Hampstead Lane, NW3 7JR (8341 5384/www.companyofcooks.com). Archway or Golders Green tube then 210 bus. **Open** *Apr-Sept* 9am-6pm (9pm on concert nights) daily. *Oct-Mar* 9am-dusk daily. **Main courses** £4.25-£10.95. **Credit** MC, V.
Peak times at this much-loved Kenwood institution may seem chaotic, but that's just the customers. Look carefully and you'll see tight working like a well-oiled machine. It's an impressive set-up. The daily changing – albeit firmly structured – menu will feature some sort of gourmet sausages (and for once they are) served with gravy and roast veg, plus a hot dish (maybe lamb shanks) and something quichey. Locals frequently opt for the wholesome package deal on soup (say white bean and tomato) with bread, apple and a piece of cheese. Look in the self-serve cabinets for plump sandwiches that put the West End chains to shame: think superior ham with honey and caper mayonnaise, coronation chicken, egg and cress. Sweets cover everything from breakfast pastries too boozy indulgences such as our rather jammy sherry trifle. We've enjoyed the creamy papaya and rhubarb fools here on other visits too. To drink there's Marston's beer, small bottles of wine, San Pellegrino soft drinks, Union coffee and (over by the window) big jugs of water for everyone to help themselves. Come early for the legendary cooked breakfasts featuring those fabulous sausages, lush grilled mushrooms, roast tomatoes, admirably creamy scrambled eggs and wholesome toast.
Babies and children welcome: children's menu; high chairs; nappy-changing facilities. Disabled: toilet. Restaurant available for hire (evenings only). Separate room for parties, seats 120. Tables outdoors (200, garden and terrace). Takeaway service. Vegetarian menu. **Map 28 C1.**

Fish & Chips

Strange, really, that fish and chips has become Britain's national takeaway dish. For a start it can only be traced back a century and a half: a piffling blink of an eye when compared to, say, mince pies. Second, it scarcely springs from yeomanly olde England. Batter-fried fish is most likely a borrowing from Jewish cuisine, while fried chipped potatoes are probably a French creation. Fish and chips shares a similar history to pie and mash: shops sprang up to feed the industrial working classes, who wanted something tasty, cheap and filling. Which brings us to another oddity. The meal is meant to be devoured within minutes of being served. Fine to eat it out of a paper bag, fresh from the counter, but to wrap it up, then take it home to consume half an hour later results in a flaccid, soggy aberration. Best of all is to eat fish and chips on site, in a chippie.

Choose wisely, though: only a small proportion of London's fish and chip shops get it right. Below we list the best, and this year we particularly recommend **Two Brothers**, **Seashell** and **Nautilus**. Praise too, to the chip shops offering alternatives to over-fished species. Take a bow, **Sea Cow** (coley) and **Toff's** (halibut, trout), among others. For advice on which species are endangered, consult www.fishonline.org. For restaurants offering a wider range of piscine cuisine, *see* **Fish**, starting on p91.

Central

Barbican

Fish Central
149-155 Central Street, EC1V 8AP (7253 4970).
Old Street tube/rail/55 bus. **Lunch served** 11am-2.30pm Mon-Thur; 5-11pm Fri, Sat. **Main courses** £7.95-£14.50. **Credit** MC, V.
In 1968, when Fish Central opened, this corner of the city was hardly residential and the chippie took a unit in the shopping precinct. Now it spans four units – rather stylishly, with etched glass and pale tones of white and mint – and attracts an enthusiastic stream of locals: from media and financial bigwigs to students and residents of the nearby estates. Aside from chargrilled swordfish with paella, and new-season English lamb steaks, Fish Central's raison d'être is simple fish and seafood. Whole grilled Cornish plaice was crossed off the specials board as we arrived, but there was still deep-fried hake with tartare sauce to supplement the cod, haddock, plaice, skate and rock salmon that are the core of the printed menu. Italian white and red kick off the drinks list at £9.95; there's also draught IPA and Stella. Desserts are homely yet adventurous: fruit salad coming with banana leaf and mango sorbet, no less. Our bread and butter pudding had a great texture, but needed more fruit. The first-floor room is a good setting for parties and functions, for which the kitchen produces an impressive range of canapés. *Babies and children welcome: children's portions; high chairs. Booking advisable. Separate room for parties, seats 70. Takeaway service.* **Map 5 P3.**

Bloomsbury

North Sea Fish Restaurant
7-8 Leigh Street, WC1H 9EW (7387 5892).
Russell Square tube/King's Cross tube/rail/68, 168 bus. **Lunch served** noon-2.30pm, **dinner served** 5.30-10.30pm Mon-Sat. **Main courses** £8.90-£18.95. **Credit** MC, V.
A fish supper on a Friday night is clearly not yet out of fashion. On our visit, the decidedly old-school North Sea was packed with groups of pensioners and tourists tucking into huge (or gargantuan – there's a choice of two sizes) portions of fish and chips. The place has that slightly eerie feel of a chippie in a post-war seaside town (velvet-padded chairs, Artexed-white walls and all), but the prices are definitely 21st century; fish and chips starts at £9.95. The menu veers slightly from the standard repertoire. There's tuna with spicy chilli sauce, goujons or grilled chicken, for example. Nevertheless, we reckon it's best to stick to the classics: battered haddock, cod and, naturally, mountains of chips. This wasn't the best meal of the genre that we've sampled, but the chips are crunchy and the fish fresh. Desserts include a range of traditional English puds, and a fabulous cheesecake. *Babies and children welcome: high chairs. Booking essential weekends. Separate room for parties, seats 40. Takeaway service (until 11pm).* **Map 4 L4.**

Covent Garden

Rock & Sole Plaice
47 Endell Street, WC2H 9AJ (7836 3785).
Covent Garden tube. **Meals served** 11.30am-11pm Mon-Sat; noon-10pm Sun. **Main courses** £10-£14. **Credit** MC, V.
Operating as a fish and chip shop since 1874, this Covent Garden fixture is now run by a friendly Greek family. They serve classic English grub to tourists, local workers and anyone who knows their chips. The walls are covered in West End theatre posters, and the vibe is busy. On the ground floor, all tables are frequently taken (remember to check if there are seats available in the basement dining room), and the outside seating is popular in summer. At times, the fish could be fresher, but it comes perfectly fried in well-seasoned, crunchy

batter and is served with fantastic, chunky chips. There's a small selection of starters including calamares, houmous, and chilli king prawn rolls. For those not after traditional fish main courses, a choice of savelovs, chicken nuggets and pies awaits. English desserts, including a steaming hot sticky-toffee pudding, come with ice-cream or a dollop of bright-yellow custard. Takeaways are fairly priced; eating-in carries a surcharge. *Babies and children admitted. Booking advisable (over 4 people). Separate room for parties, seats 38. Tables outdoors (7, pavement). Takeaway service.* **Map 18 D3.**

Holborn

Fryer's Delight
19 Theobald's Road, WC1X 8SL (7405 4114).
Holborn tube/19, 38, 55 bus. **Meals served** noon-10pm Mon-Sat. **Main courses** £5.40-£6.70. **Unlicensed. Corkage** no charge. **No credit cards.**
This old-school Bloomsbury chippie has long been a cabbies' favourite. On our visit, dispiritingly true to form, there was a pair discussing the hopes of the BNP candidate in the local elections, while the hard-working family of Italian immigrants behind the counter waited on them. Don't let this put you off. Fryer's Delight is virtually unchanged since opening in 1962, and is decked out in a variety of retro caff styles (false ceiling, one mirrored wall, booth seating, pink and pale-blue Formica). 'The freshest fish available', says the leaping salmon on the cheery sign outside and, sure enough, our haddock was dipped in batter and deep-fried in beef dripping to order. Portions are big, but the plates are curiously small; you may have to rummage under your fish for extra chips, and you'll be grateful for the side plate that holds your generous helping of two pickled onions. The 'no-frills' ethos extends to the menu – there's nothing so fancy as mushy peas, only processed – but who cares when the basics are done just right? *Babies and children admitted. Takeaway service (until 11pm).* **Map 4 M5.**

Marylebone

Golden Hind (100)
73 Marylebone Lane, W1U 2PN (7486 3644).
Bond Street tube. **Dinner served** 6-10pm Mon-Sat. **Main courses** £5-£10.70. **Minimum** (dinner) £5. **Unlicensed. Corkage** no charge. **Credit** AmEx, MC, V.
Bet you've never seen a contraption like the pastel-hued art deco fryer at this marvellous chip shop. Sadly, it's only used to store menus these days (the cooking's done in a kitchen at the back), but the Golden Hind still oozes local character, entirely in keeping with its mazy Marylebone Lane location. On a busy late-Thursday lunchtime, we tucked into firm fillets of haddock in light batter, fluffy fish cakes spiked with black pepper and parsley, reliably gnarly chips, an elaborately fanned pickled onion, and the mandatory thin white sliced bread and butter – all accompanied by ginger beer. The Greek owners and staff really make a fuss over you, especially if you're with children (they earned their tips by kindly stashing and retrieving our pushchair). You can tell they've seen years of repeat business. Posher nosh like prawns and whitebait is available, and you can also bring your own wine. But on a lunch hour, or taking time out from a shopping trip to nearby Oxford Street, proper fish and chips like this really hits the spot. *Babies and children welcome: children's portions. Booking advisable. Takeaway service.* **Map 9 G5.**

★ Sea Shell
49-51 Lisson Grove, NW1 6UH (7224 9000/ www.seashellrestaurant.co.uk). Marylebone tube/rail. **Lunch served** noon-2.30pm Mon-Fri; noon-5pm Sun. **Dinner served** 5-10.30pm Mon-Fri. **Meals served** noon-10.30pm Sat. **Main courses** £12.75-£24.50. **Set meal** (lunch, 5-7pm Mon-Thur) £12.50 2 courses, £14.50 3 courses. **Credit** AmEx, DC, MC, V.

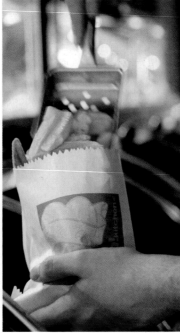

Driving down Lisson Grove, you may not realise that behind this long-established and highly popular takeaway lies an extensive restaurant, with bistro seating and walls covered in cheerful prints. Black-clad waitresses with all the elegance of Dior models bring plates of first-rate fish to the tables. Although the choice of species is not as wide as at some chippies, the menu also takes in main-course salads such as fresh tuna niçoise, and an excellent platter of chargrilled fish (monkfish, halibut, salmon and cod) with chilli and tartare sauces. Perfectly grease-free chips and thick, full-flavoured mushy peas are essential add-ons, and we happily made room for the own-made desserts of apple and almond cake and gooey bread and butter pudding. Draught beers are available, and the pleasing wine list starts at £11.95 with a choice of three house wines; for not much more you can have a bottle of lush South African bubbly. Class. *Babies and children welcome: children's menu; high chairs. Booking advisable Fri-Sat. Disabled: toilet. Separate room for parties, seats 25. Takeaway service.* **Map 2 F4**.

Victoria

Seafresh Fish Restaurant
80-81 Wilton Road, SW1V 1DL (7828 0747). Victoria tube/rail/24 bus. **Lunch served** noon-3pm, **dinner served** 5-10.30pm Mon-Fri. **Meals served** noon-10.30pm Sat. **Main courses** £6.25-£22. **Set lunch** £10.75-£11.50 2 courses. **Credit** AmEx, MC, V.
It may have been around for donkey's years, but Seafresh is still dishing out top-notch fish suppers. A large front window lets light stream into the clean, unfussy interior of pine panelling on white walls. A leather banquette runs down one side. Elderly regulars call in and are greeted cheerfully by the attentive staff. Well-to-do gents check the markets in the paper, and Japanese tourists come for a chat. Stick to the standards and you won't be disappointed. A dish of tangy taramasalata with pitta bread was thick enough to hold a spoon upright. Light, fluffy cod fillet had no excess grease in its crispy batter, nor did the chips – delicious with a large dollop of tartare sauce. We also tried the creamy fisherman's pie, which was substantial enough to satisfy the hungriest sea-dog's appetite. Dover sole, king prawns and a generous seafood platter are also available for those prepared to spend a bit more, or there's the takeaway section next door, if you're economically minded.

Babies and children welcome: high chairs. Booking advisable. Restaurant available for hire. Takeaway service. **Map 15 J10**.

West

Bayswater

Mr Fish
9 Porchester Road, W2 5DP (7229 4161/ www.mrfish.uk.com). Bayswater, Queensway or Royal Oak tube. **Meals served** 11am-11pm daily. **Main courses** £6.25-£12.95. **Set lunch** (11am-3pm) £6.75 cod & chips incl soft drink, tea or coffee. **Credit** AmEx, MC, V.
'One taste and you'll be hooked' is the subtitle. Mr Fish swims between genres. At first glance it's a simple modern fast-food joint, with takeaway counter at the front, bright caff behind (plastic chairs, tiled floor), laminated menus and breezy staff in baseball caps. Then you notice the 1950s-diner details (monochrome prints of classic cars and film stars, a neon sign, a loudish soundtrack), and even a touch of the New England seaside restaurant (turquoise wood-panelled walls, a well-stocked bar, a model boat). Food also varies in style, though our advice would be to paddle past the burgers, swerve round the seafood 'chowder' (homogeneous and bland, if only £2.40), and set course for the fish. This comes poached, grilled, or coated in matzo meal or breadcrumbs, as well as battered, in species from cod to sea bass. Lemon sole was beautifully fresh and delicate, the batter the brittle side of perfect; chips were big and soft within, mushy peas suitably thick. A bottle of London Pride was a fitting accompaniment. Finish, perhaps, with spotted dick. In all, well-priced and satisfying.
Babies and children welcome: children's menu; high chair. Takeaway service (until midnight). **Map 7 C5**.
For branch see index.

Notting Hill

Costas Fish Restaurant
18 Hillgate Street, W8 7SR (7727 4310). Notting Hill Gate tube. **Lunch served** noon-2.30pm, **dinner served** 5.30-10.30pm Tue-Sat. **Main courses** £5.20-£8. **No credit cards**.
An antidote to Notting Hill flummery, this no-nonsense chippie has been deep-frying since 1981. It is cunningly disguised as a common-or-garden

takeaway, but if you march past the gleaming fryer, you'll enter a gratifyingly simple dining room furnished with caff-style wooden tables and chairs and red leatherette banquettes. There's a Hellenic accent to the menu – the restaurant is sibling to the neighbouring Greek Cypriot Costas Grill – as evidenced by houmous in the starters, calamares among the mains, and retsina and palatable Keo lager on the drinks list. To start, a mound of pink, oniony taramasalata with toasted pitta (that could easily be shared by two) was surpassed by cod's roe clothed in the most fragile of batters. Still more pleasing were main courses of meaty rock salmon and delicate lemon sole, as were the golden brown chips (fried in vegetable oil), bowlful of mushy peas and pickled onion (presented Damien Hirst-style in six slices by the cheerful waitress). Desserts include baklava. Local families, ravenous toddlers in tow, were tucking in with abandon: and not a media darling in sight.
Babies and children admitted. Booking advisable dinner. Tables outdoors (2, pavement). Takeaway service. **Map 7 A7**.

South West

Chelsea

Tom's Place NEW
2008 RUNNER-UP BEST SUSTAINABLE RESTAURANT
1 Cale Street, SW3 3QP (7351 1806/ www.tomsplace.org.uk). South Kensington tube. **Meals served** noon-11pm Mon-Wed; noon-11.30pm Thur-Sat; noon-10.30pm Sun. **Main courses** £7.50-£18. **Credit** MC, V.
Tom Aikens' chippie has had a torrent of publicity on the back of the admirable policy of purchasing only sustainable fish. It's green in many other ways too, though some of this seems token; the all-English wine list may appear to have fewer 'food miles', but English wines rarely have a lower carbon footprint than those from the Continent. Whatever, on our visit the waitresses were cheerfully recommending wines not on the list – French wines – over the English ones. Prices are high even by Chelsea standards (£11.50 for a fish and chips takeaway) yet dish standards are not as consistently good as you'd hope. A starter of deep-fried squid with a dressing of lime and fresh coriander was mostly scraps of batter, with little squid; disappointing. Much better was a whole

fish! kitchen. See p318.

grilled megrim sole, simply served with lemon, capers and parsley butter. A starter of grilled Cornish sardines with a shallot chutney included excellent quality fish. Stop press: Tom's Place closed suddenly at the end of August 2008, after a dispute with neighbours about unpleasant smells and the council's environmental health officers starting legal proceedings against the restaurant. *Babies and children welcome: booster seats. Bookings not accepted. Takeaway service.* **Map 14 E11.**

Wandsworth

Brady's
513 Old York Road, SW18 1TF (8877 9599). Wandsworth Town rail/28, 44 bus. **Lunch served** 12.30-2.30pm Mon-Sat. **Dinner served** 6.30-10pm Mon-Wed, Sat; 6.30-10.30pm Thur, Fri. **Main courses** £7.55-£10.25. **Credit** MC, V.
The advertising at Brady's depicts a gentleman with a battered cod for a tie. All around are hastily scribbled menus depicting the haul of the day, and the prices. We sampled perfectly punchy potted shrimps as a starter but, on our visit, half-pints of prawns, calamares, anchovies, sardines and cockles were all available. Mismatched wooden chairs and tables give the dining room a homely atmosphere. Mermaids painted on the mirrors, and fish-theme borders, feel more Westcliff-on-Sea than Wandsworth. The lunch special of fun-sized fish, chips and sweet mushy peas for under a fiver is great value, the full-price option with chips as an extra perhaps less so. We'd like to have been able to report on the own-made honeycomb ice-cream which was going down a storm on the other tables, as well as apple crumble and bread and butter pudding, but the kitchen was abruptly closed without us being offered the chance to order any. *Babies and children welcome: children's portions; high chair. Bookings not accepted. Takeaway service.* **Map 21 A4.**

South

Battersea

Fish Club (100)
189 St John's Hill, SW11 1TH (7978 7115/ www.thefishclub.com). **Meals served** noon-10pm Tue-Sun. **Main courses** £5.95-£12. **Set meal** £25 per person (minimum 4) taster menu. **Credit** AmEx, MC, V.

You know you're not in a standard chippie the second you step through the door of Fish Club – straight on to a fish tank set in the floor. The live fish look only marginally fresher than the ones on ice behind the counter. Though you can have battered fish, chips and mushy peas, you can also savour more exotic repasts, such as prawn and chorizo skewers, grilled royal sea bream or red onion tart for the vegetarians. The more health-conscious can also swap chips for mash, salad or purple sprouting broccoli. There's a takeaway up front, with stools and newspapers to use while you wait. Two large bench tables at the back make this a restaurant of sorts; there's even a (very) small alfresco dining area. The service certainly gives the place a restaurant vibe; staff are attentive and knowledgeable, and you don't have to return to the counter to order the decadent desserts or get another beer. Fish Club is perfect if you're in the mood for fish and chips (they're delicious and straightforward – no mint in the mushy peas), but your partner is feeling a bit more adventurous. *Babies and children welcome: children's menu; high chair. Bookings not accepted. Disabled: toilet. Tables outdoors (3, courtyard; 2, pavement). Takeaway service.* **Map 21 B4.**
For branch see index.

Waterloo

Masters Super Fish
191 Waterloo Road, SE1 8UX (7928 6924). Waterloo tube/rail. **Lunch served** noon-3pm Tue-Sat. **Dinner served** 5.30-10.30pm Mon; 4.30-10.30pm Tue-Thur, Sat; 4.30-11pm Fri. **Main courses** £7.25-£12.50. **Set lunch** £7 1 course incl drink, tea or coffee. **Credit** MC, V.
This 'proper' chippie may not immediately impress, but beyond the initial impresssion created by mint-green paintwork, exposed new-brick walls and peach faux-marble tables, elements of character begin to appear. These include framed portraits of the original Maltese owners, signed photos of old-school celebs (Mark Curry and 'Lovejoy' among them) and personal and attentive service. It's the food that's the draw, though. Fresh fish is bought daily from Billingsgate, portions are huge and there are pleasing complimentary extras (three prawns per customer and a basket of sliced baguette to start; gherkins, pickled onions and the full range of condiments to complement the mains). Our battered cod was a generous, meaty fillet. The plaice equivalent didn't quite measure up; although clearly fresh it was rather wet and overwhelmed by an oversized cloak of batter. Chips were agreeably fat. Several grilled fish dishes are also available. Custom is diverse, with a number of tourists and couples sharing the rather hushed space with lone cabbies and local red-faced businessmen. If you're opting for a takeaway, order in the entrance area 'decorated' with hundreds of football match tickets. *Babies and children welcome: high chair. Booking advisable Fri, Sat. Takeaway service.* **Map 11 N9.**

South East

Dulwich

Sea Cow
37 Lordship Lane, SE22 8EW (8693 3111). East Dulwich rail/176, 196 bus. **Meals served** noon-11pm Tue-Sat; noon-8.30pm Sun. **Main courses** £7-£10. **Credit** MC, V.
The Sea Cow is the very essence of what a contemporary fish and chip shop should be. Unfussy but quietly cool decor – wooden slab tables, tiled floor, steel pendant lamps, putty-coloured walls and a smattering of beach-hut pictures – sets the scene. Friendly but no-frills service concentrates on dishing up the fried fish cooked to order. Tender chunks of coley, haddock or cod in crisp, mouth-watering batter; a heap of tiny whitebait, all fragrant crunch and mineral saltiness; fishy grilled thai fish cakes (just fish, garlic, lemongrass, coriander, and mayo to bind) – everything can be accompanied by dense, chunky chips and freshly cooked mushy peas. There's also

a small but well-priced wine list and decent beers (Adnams and Peroni). In the evening, Sea Cow morphs seamlessly from providing family suppers to catering for a more buzzy, urbane throng. The only thing lacking is pudding; a few single-serving tubs of ice-cream in the freezer wouldn't go amiss. *Babies and children welcome: children's menu; high chairs. Takeaway service.* **Map 23 C4.**

Herne Hill

★ Olley's
65-69 Norwood Road, SE24 9AA (8671 8259/ www.olleys.info). Herne Hill rail/3, 68, 196 bus. **Lunch served** noon-3pm Tue-Sun. **Dinner served** 5-10.30pm daily. **Set lunch** £7 1 course. **Main courses** £11.70-£22.30. **Credit** AmEx, MC, V.
Olley's has a decent claim to the crown of south London's best fish and chip restaurant, the main challenger being Masters in Waterloo (*see above*). This place is best known for its slightly cheesy 'specials', named after local celebs and restaurant critics – so the James Nesbitt Experience offers haddock, chips and peas, while the Guy Dimond Experience, named after *Time Out* magazine's food editor, and reassuringly expensive at just shy of a tenner, is another way of saying lemon sole with chips. Although most custom comes from takeaways, the mid-sized restaurant is also popular. The various fish (cod and haddock, of course, but also hake, halibut, monkfish, skate and others) come fried in an ace batter, grilled, steamed or with tomato and herb sauce. Chips are about as good as London can offer, and the mushy peas have a little more texture than your usual paste. Service can be sketchy, but is always friendly, and children are very welcome. *Babies and children welcome: children's menu; high chairs; nappy-changing facilities. Disabled: toilet. Separate room for parties, seats 25. Tables outdoors (6, pavement). Takeaway service.* **Map 23 A5.**

Lewisham

Something Fishy
117-119 Lewisham High Street, SE13 6AT (8852 7075). Lewisham rail/DLR. **Meals served** 9am-6pm Mon-Sat. **Main courses** £3.75-£6.65. **No credit cards.**
You can't really have a fish supper at Something Fishy, because last orders is 5.30pm – earlier if all the fish has been eaten. Most people pile into the bright blue canteen, with its workaday plastic seating and wipe-clean tables, at dinner time (traditional dinner: about 12.30pm). That's when the fish is at its freshest and there's a high chip turnover to ensure just-fried crispness. Before this, punters tend to choose the all-day breakfast over cod or haddock in batter. Whenever you eat, make sure you're hungry. The portions of fish are so large their battered ends spill over the plate. The flesh is firm and flaky, and the golden crisp, bubbled coating pleasantly light. Modest-sized versions of the meal of the day are available for smaller appetites. Those wanting to indulge in afters can choose knickerbocker glory or spotted dick and custard. We can't imagine coming here for anything other than fish and chips, but there are savelovs, rather pasty fish cakes and pies, as well as the option of steamed fish, mash and liquor for those trying to avoid fat. *Babies and children welcome: children's menu; high chairs. Tables outdoors (5, pavement). Takeaway service.*

East

Victoria Park

Fish House
126-128 Lauriston Road, E9 7LH (8533 3327). Mile End tube then 277 bus. **Meals served** noon-10pm daily. **Main courses** £9.50-£12.95. **Credit** AmEx, MC, V.
The Fish House formula of retro-stylish takeaway chippie juxtaposed with table-service restaurant is mostly successful. The two elements are kept

separate, physically and by way of menus. Takeaway customers are assigned two bench-tables at which to wait for (or eat) their battered cod, haddock, plaice, rock or scampi and chips. On the Sunday evening of our visit, there were copies of the *Observer* spread across these. Restaurant customers sit in a clinically stylish area to enjoy the likes of lobster bisque with bread and butter, grilled lemon sole with french fries and garlic butter, and king prawns with aïoli, as well as a range of English puds. Our cod and haddock were as fresh as the batter was crispy, while the chips achieved the crunchy-outside, fluffy-inside consistency with aplomb. Customers complaining about slack service passed us from the restaurant, suggesting things might not always be as smooth on that side of the fence. Italian ice-cream is available by the scoop.
Babies and children welcome: children's menu; high chairs; toys. Booking advisable weekends. Takeaway service.

North East
Dalston

Faulkners
424-426 Kingsland Road, E8 4AA (7254 6152/ www.faulkners.uk.com). Dalston Kingsland rail/67, 76, 149, 242, 243 bus. **Lunch served** noon-2.30pm Mon-Fri. **Dinner served** 5-10pm Mon-Thur; 4.30-10pm Fri. **Meals served** 11.30am-10pm Sat; noon-9pm Sun. **Main courses** £10.50-£18. **Set meal** £15.90-£19.90 4 courses (minimum 2). **Credit** MC, V.
It's clear that the more recent Turkish owners of Faulkners are attempting to appeal to old-school East Enders – this chippie's original patrons – rather than the area's newer, more youthful middle-class. Decorations consist of net curtains, photos of London past, a fish tank, a flat-screen TV and white linen tablecloths (with fake tulips upon them). The brightly lit space contained just two or three couples on the evening we visited. This was unsurprising; the atmosphere is a bit incongruous for fish'n'chips, with formal service and a rather tired vibe. On the plus side, our huge portion of haddock was bright white, perfectly flaky and covered with crisp, tasty batter. Less impressive were the soft, pale, thick-cut chips, while the mushy peas were flavoursome yet alarmingly bright-green. If you've room for more and like traditional English desserts, scan the pudding menu.
Babies and children welcome: children's menu; high chairs. Bookings advisable weekends. Disabled: toilet. Separate room for parties, seats 25. Takeaway service. **Map 6 R1.**

North
Finchley

★ Two Brothers Fish Restaurant
297-303 Regent's Park Road, N3 1DP (8346 0469/www.twobrothers.co.uk). Finchley Central tube. **Lunch served** noon-2.30pm, **dinner served** 5.30-10.15pm Tue-Sat. **Main courses** £9-£21.50. **Minimum** £10.95. **Credit** AmEx, MC, V.
Since Leon and Tony Manzi's retirement in January 2008, Two Brothers has been run by two other brothers, Mal and Nari Atwul, and our research has found no drop in standards. Swish compared to the average chippie, Two Brothers has a designer logo, colour-coordinated banquette seating, a coat room full of luxury brands, and a queue of smartly dressed locals just inside the door. Fortunately, friendly staff take and bring orders briskly. Blackboards advertise specials – perhaps a sweet potato and aubergine soup or a lime, ginger and mango brûlée tart – that may inspire a detour from a traditional fish supper. It was from here that we chose grilled black cod with tomato and caramelised pepper sauce. Bowls piled with mussels from Ireland were a popular order, as were the chocolate sundae and good-looking profiteroles. Maris Pipers are used for the glistening chips, fried in groundnut oil, and sauces such as the creamy

tartare are own-made. The choice of house wines includes two from the former owners' vineyard in the Côtes de Duras (neighbouring Bordeaux); the red has strong, sweet berry flavours.
Babies and children welcome: high chairs. Bookings accepted lunch only. Takeaway service (until 10pm).

Muswell Hill

Toff's
38 Muswell Hill Broadway, N10 3RT (8883 8656). Highgate tube then 43, 134 bus. **Meals served** 11.30am-10pm Mon-Sat. **Main courses** £6.95-£22.50. **Set meal** (11.30am-5pm) £5.95-£7.95 1 course incl tea or coffee. **Credit** AmEx, DC, MC, V.
Run by a family of Cypriot heritage, Toff's has a loyal following for its fish and chips, with customers determinedly queuing for both takeaways and tables in the convivial restaurant. We were eventually led upstairs (some in the queue insisted on waiting for ground-floor tables) to a wood-panelled dining room with sepia pictures of the fish trade, and white paper cloths on the tables. Kudos to Toff's for the blackboard promoting alternatives to cod, including trout, halibut, scampi and calamares. Honest-to-goodness coleslaw, made in-house, outshone the big, bright but bland mushy peas. Our fish cake starter was crisply crumbed, the interior a fine paste generously flavoured with parsley. Battered haddock and rock were beautifully fresh (matzo and grilled options are alternatives), but the chips were greasy. Old-school puddings come in huge portions. Service is similarly effusive, and kind. Finish with Greek-style coffee or refreshing mint tea.
Babies and children welcome: children's menu; colouring books; high chairs; party bags. Separate room for parties, seats 24. Takeaway service.

North West
Golders Green

Sam's
68-70 Golders Green Road, NW11 8LM (8455 9898/7171). Golders Green tube. **Meals served** noon-10pm daily. **Main courses** £8.45-£13.75. **Set lunch** (noon-4pm) £7.95 2 courses incl tea or coffee. **Credit** MC, V.
Set across two shop units, Sam's restaurant and takeaway stands out on Golders Green Road for its capacious dimensions, homely atmosphere and high-quality cooking. Fish comes fried, grilled or steamed, as well as in generous Mediterranean-style dishes such as our moist, herby fish kebab with tomato sauce and rice – great with the Turkish beer. Chippie staples such as mushy peas are nicely done too. Refreshing salads arrive just before the main courses, making starters superfluous, but that leaves some welcome room for dessert. The admirably light lockshen pudding (a Jewish speciality of noodles, eggs and raisins) had a well-judged cinnamon edge sweetly offset by vanilla ice-cream; rice pudding was creamily delicious. Staff were kind and gracious, and notably good with inquisitive children. Otherwise, the crowd tended to be an older set. The lunchtime meal deals are a favourite with local pensioners.
Babies and children welcome: children's menu; high chairs. Booking advisable. Disabled: toilet. Restaurant available for hire. Takeaway service.

Mill Hill

★ Booba's NEW
151 Hale Lane, HA8 9QW (8959 6002). Edgware tube/Mill Hill Broadway rail. **Meals served** noon-10pm Tue-Sun. **Main courses** £8-£15. **Credit** MC, V.
This local Turkish and (unsupervised) Jewish takeaway and restaurant, named after a Yiddish grandma, serves no shellfish and, instead of batter, they dip the fish in matzo meal before frying. The decor is old-fashioned and plain, with fishy collages on the wall. Service is cheerful, though a bit stretched (the owner-waiter also seemed to be helping in the kitchen on our visit). Starters include houmous and taramasalata with warm pitta, but

there's also whitebait or avocado. For mains, eight types of fish are offered – either grilled or fried, with chips or boiled potatoes and salad. Haddock was crisp and flaky, while grilled dover sole arrived cheerfully charred and as fresh as might be expected on a post-Bank Holiday visit. Portions are generous, and we like the chips, but the iceberg lettuce salad was a bit tired. To end, there's Turkish coffee or cappuccino to accompany own-made apple pie and the kind of ice-cream that reminds you of seaside holidays. We'd visit Booba's again, to try the halibut or trout; at these prices it won't break the bank.
Babies and children admitted. Booking advisable (Fri, Sat). Takeaway service.

West Hampstead

★ Nautilus
27-29 Fortune Green Road, NW6 1DT (7435 2532). West Hampstead tube/rail then 328 bus. **Lunch served** 11.30am-2.30pm, **dinner served** 4.30-10pm Mon-Sat. **Main courses** £9.50-£19.50. **Credit** MC, V.
A humble local takeaway and adjacent restaurant that's popular with young groups and older couples, Nautilus makes little effort to attract custom by its decor (though elsewhere the fruit-illustrated condiment trays would be fashionably kitsch). Instead, this pristine, family-run outfit successfully relies on friendly service and quality cooking. The menu extends from chicken and scampi to dover sole: fillets and cutlets, fried in matzo or grilled. The prices may shock at first, yet portions are gigantic and prime fish are handled with aplomb. A plaice fillet stretched across the plate, so there was barely room for the token wedge of tomato and torn lettuce. For our other choice, we cut open the crisp orange-brown crust of piping-hot haddock to reveal steaming moist white flesh beneath – quite glorious. Add a bowl of houmous or taramasalata to start, accompany with pickles and coleslaw and you'll have no room for the ready-made desserts from Disotto's (Nautilus knows to stick to what it does best). Carafes of wine are shaped like vinegar bottles, and the irony wasn't lost on us. We'll return though, for the warmth of the welcome and excellent fried fish.
Babies and children welcome: high chairs. Booking advisable. Takeaway service. **Map 28 A1.**

Outer London
Kingston, Surrey

fish! kitchen
58 Coombe Road, Kingston, Surrey KT2 7AF (8546 2886/www.fishkitchen.com). Norbiton rail/57, 85, 213 bus. **Meals served** noon-10pm Tue-Sat. **Main courses** £9.95-£23.95. **Credit** AmEx, MC, V.
Walk past the hot glass of the takeaway counter and you're in a shiny-tiled, retro tribute to fish and chip cafés of the past. Nevertheless, plenty about Kingston's fish!kitchen feels modern, from the swordfish club sandwiches to the red pepper salsa with the daily grills. When owner Tony Allan's adjacent fishmonger Jarvis is open, you can choose something from the counter. Otherwise the grills are chalked up on a blackboard, and from this a good, fresh tuna steak was a success. Ironically, fish and chips (£9.95 to £13.95), the mainstay of the menu and what attracts the majority of the after-work crowd, came up short on our visit. Tartare sauce was insufficiently astringent and had developed a skin in its little pot, and the beer batter on some otherwise commendable haddock was thick, podgy and soft. There was also a chip problem; staff informed us that the potatoes had too high a sugar content, leading to burnt exteriors, undercooked interiors. This was handled deftly (knocking the chips off the bill) by the friendly young team, who clearly play a part in maintaining fish!kitchen's status as a neighbourhood favourite, despite there being clear room for improvement.
Babies and children welcome: children's menu; high chairs. Disabled: toilet. Tables outdoors (20, terrace). Takeaway service.

Pizza & Pasta

Quick, cheap and cheerful, the popularity of pizza and pasta joints shows no sign of diminishing, even as the sector continues its gourmet trajectory and some venues are no longer as cheap as might be expected. We've rounded the chains up into a box to make it easy for you to compare what each has to offer. If you're after a more individual dining out experience, there are plenty of independent operations where they take real pride in what they are doing and in the quality of their ingredients. You'll find traditional family-run and family-friendly trattorias, such as **Donna Margherita**, as well as enthusiastic entrepreneurial ventures including **Giusto** and our Cheap Eats award-winner this year, **Franco Manca**, plus a couple of chains-in-waiting, such as the fun **Rossopomodoro** and buffalo-themed **Fratelli la Bufala**. For more restaurants that serve pasta and pizza, see **Italian** (starting on p177) and **The Americas** (p37).

Marylebone

★ Giusto NEW
43 Blandford Street, W1U 7HF (7486 7340).
Bond Street or Baker Street tube. **Lunch served** noon-3pm, **dinner served** 6.30-10.30pm Mon-Sat. **Main courses** £11.50-£13. **Credit** AmEx, MC, V.
On the small ground-floor shop-front is a bar-cum-takeaway for Italian favourites such as lasagne. But descend to the terracotta-tiled basement restaurant and you'll find a large, friendly pizzeria with imposing white wood-fired oven. The staff's enthusiasm is palpable and no doubt helps explain the notable list of pizzas and rib-sticking rustic dishes such as porchetta and roast potatoes. There are good Italian wines to be had at low mark-ups, but ice-cold Peroni, served in smart etched glasses, seemed the correct choice with pizzas such as the Allegro, featuring scamorza (a smoked semi-soft cheese), mozzarella, Italian sausage and cime di rapa. The signature folded pizza was a roll rather than calzone-style, filled with taleggio cheese and courgette, and decked with speck and salad. Sides of roast asparagus (a little mean) and a vibrant salad of beetroot and fennel, transformed the cheesy fast food into a nutritious midweek meal.
Babies and children welcome: high-chairs. Booking advisable. Separate room for parties, seats 16. Tables outdoors (3, pavement). Takeaway service. **Map 9 G5**.

Central

Clerkenwell & Farringdon

Santoré
59-61 Exmouth Market, EC1R 4QL (7812 1488).
Farringdon tube/rail/19, 38, 341 bus. **Lunch served** noon-3pm, **dinner served** 5.30-11pm Mon-Sat. **Main courses** £7.95-£15.95. **Set lunch** £9.95 2 courses. **Set meal** (5.30-7.30pm) £12.95 2 courses. **Credit** AmEx, MC, V.
Located in a dining hotspot, this pizza and pasta joint is competing well. The spacious dining room with large windows has an outdoors-in feel (and can get chilly). During our visit, it wasn't full and service was great – friendly, helpful and not intrusive. The food is pretty good too. Their antipasti selection is not the usual mixture of olives and hams, but includes things like a tasty omelette and two tarts: one crab and one tomato. Pizzas are delicious too, spun in the open kitchen at the rear. Choices range from the classics (funghi,

margharita) to speciality Neapolitan numbers. Of the meat and fish dishes, we loved the fish stew: a tomato broth crammed with fresh mussels, clams and prawns. All this was accompanied by an enjoyable house red from the varied wine list.
Babies and children welcome: high chairs. Takeaway and delivery service (£8 minimum, within 3-mile radius). Tables outdoors (10, pavement). **Map 5 N4**.

Euston

Pasta Plus
62 Eversholt Street, NW1 1DA (7383 4943/ www.pastaplus.co.uk). Euston tube/rail. **Lunch served** noon-2.30pm Mon-Fri. **Dinner served** 5.30-10.30pm Mon-Sat. **Main courses** £6.50-£15.50. **Credit** AmEx, DC, MC, V.
On a road known for saunas and strip clubs, Pasta Plus might raise a few eyebrows as to what its 'Plus' signifies. Yet, location aside, this family-run Italian is far from suspect, attracting a lunchtime crowd of local business people with its good-value dishes and swift service. Part of the restaurant is in a conservatory, which brings plenty of natural light to the rear of the room. Functional furniture and minimal decor of black and white prints create a simple, stylish look. We skipped starters, taking advantage of complimentary bruschetta. There's a wide range of main courses including fish, meat and several pasta dishes (all with own-made pasta), but notably no pizza. We went for the spaghetti pescatore and crab ravioli. The first dish arrived piled high with clams, mussels, king prawns and crab claws, and was thoroughly tasty. The ravioli also had a generous amount of crab meat, but the pasta pockets were thick and chewy. Portions are substantial, but it's worth eating up as the desserts aren't worth saving space for.
Babies and children welcome: high chairs. Tables outdoors (26, conservatory). Takeaway service. **Map 4 K3**.

Knightsbridge

Frankie's Italian Bar & Grill
3 Yeomans Row, off Brompton Road, SW3 2AL (7590 9999/www.frankiesitalianbarandgrill.com). Knightsbridge or South Kensington tube. **Lunch served** noon-2.30pm, **dinner served** 5.30-10.30pm Mon-Sat. **Meals served** noon-11pm Sat; noon-10pm Sun. **Main courses** £7.50-£14.40. **Credit** AmEx, MC, V.
Since its Piccadilly Circus restaurant closed down, the only West End branch of this small cod-Italian-

American chain is a space in Selfridges' basement (though their outlets in Putney, Chiswick and Knightsbridge do have other moneyed districts covered). Unremarkable both in design and cuisine, Frankie's is an attempt to mimic a New Jersey trattoria, and is the result of a rather peculiar arrangement between Frankie Dettori and Marco Pierre White. While its other branches market themselves as family restaurants, the Selfridges restaurant is markedly less kid-orientated. The menu offers fairly standard and not particularly inspiring Italian-American favourites, such as the pizza with mushroom and salami that we ordered. Pasta dishes were sauce-heavy and filling, while a chocolate mousse dessert had been overpowered by cream. Service seemed lethargic; we knew we'd been waiting too long when Frankie Valli came round on the soundtrack for the third time.
Babies and children welcome: high chairs. Takeaway service (pizza only). **Map 14 E10**. **For branches see index.**

Rocket
4-6 Lancashire Court, off New Bond Street, W1Y 9AD (7629 2889/www.rocketrestaurants.co.uk). Bond Street or Oxford Circus tube.
Bar **Open** noon-11pm, **meals served** noon-6pm Mon-Sat. **Main courses** £9-£12.
Restaurant **Lunch served** noon-3pm, **dinner served** 6-11pm Mon-Sat. **Main courses** £9-£15.
Both **Credit** AmEx, MC, V.
Lancashire Court is a small oasis in busy Mayfair and the perfect location for an eaterie such as Rocket. The first-floor restaurant specialises in creative pizzas (smoked chicken with red onion marmalade and rocket; goat's cheese and honey with mixed herbs, pine nuts and cherry tomatoes) and other modern international dishes. At lunchtime it quickly fills with a business crowd, but it's still possible to find a perch at the ground-floor bar area, which on warm days extends outdoors into the attractive courtyard. The lunch menu includes platters (around £13) and large salads, which can be shared as a snack or eaten as a main course. The hearty sandwiches come with thick-cut, well-seasoned fries. A zesty chicken, mustard and coriander burger was unhappily paired with a stale, white supermarket-style bun. Gravadlax with cucumber and lemon crème fraîche on wholemeal bread was a much fresher choice. The fish and chip salad with rocket looked enticing, but without tartare sauce the fish was almost tasteless. Rocket has branches in the City and by the river in Putney.
Babies and children welcome: high chairs. Booking advisable. Separate rooms for parties, seating 10 and 25. **Map 9 H6**.
For branches (Rocket, Rocket Riverside) see index.

Soho

Italian Graffiti
163-165 Wardour Street, W1F 8WN (7439 4668/www.italiangraffiti.co.uk). Oxford Circus tube. **Lunch served** noon-3pm, **dinner served** 5.30-11.30pm Mon-Fri. **Meals served** noon-11.30pm Sat. **Main courses** £7-£14. **Credit** AmEx, DC, MC, V.
Travel back in time to a 1980s trattoria, complete with pastel chairs, a mix of bare-brick and peach-sponged walls, marble-topped tables, '80s fabric banquettes and hanging baskets. The place is a strange U-shape, with open fires on either side of the restaurant adding to the cosiness. Italian Graffiti is a throwback in the nicest possible way, and that includes the menu. Salads were the only low point (unripe tomatoes and run-of-the-mill oil and vinegar for DIY dressings). To start, insalata tricolore was a decent version of the classic; to finish, panna cotta was a-wobble with creamy goodness. In between came gnocchi, a molten cheese-fest of comfort food; spaghetti puttanesca, punchily flavoured, just as it should be; and star of the show, the pizzas. These ooze quality: thin crispy bases, loaded with ingredients, and overhanging the plate. We were very happy with speck, tomato and provola cheese, but there are

Rossopomodoro. See p322.

more than ten options, including quattro formaggi, napoletana and capricciosa. Add charming service, and the picture of the family-run local in the centre of town is complete.
Babies and children welcome: booster seat; children's portions. Booking advisable. Takeaway service. **Map 17 B3**.

Kettners

29 Romilly Street, W1D 5HP (7734 6112/ www.kettners.com). Leicester Square or Piccadilly Circus tube. **Meals served** noon-midnight Mon-Wed, Sun; noon-1am Thur-Sat. **Main courses** £9.15-£19.90. **Credit** AmEx, MC, V.
This Soho institution has been around since 1867, but while retaining many elements of an elegant past, today's Kettners is sadly more than a little downmarket. Interestingly, as we went to press, Ilse Crawford's design studio (her work includes the High Road Brasserie) had been commissioned to help make changes. Kettners has the exterior and decor of a smart London hotel – along with a swanky champagne bar, formal service and a pianist at the grand piano – but a glance at the lengthy menu quickly reveals that the food is tailored more to families and tourists than to the sophisticates that you might expect to find in such surroundings. The list offers everything from pizzas and pasta to grilled meats and a few fish dishes, though the inclusion of pub grub such as burgers, fish and chips, and an all-day breakfast,

comes as a surprise. The tempting-sounding starters, mainly incorporating fish and seafood, were disappointing. Fried squid with garlic and Pernod mayonnaise was poorly seasoned, and king scallops wrapped in bacon were unremarkable. Pizzas are the best option; you can find better elsewhere in Soho, but Kettners' are generously topped with tasty ingredients. The wine list is interesting, but expensive; bottles start at £15.85.
Babies and children welcome: high chairs. Entertainment: pianist (1-3.30pm, 7-10.30pm Mon-Wed, Sun; 1-3.30pm, 6pm-midnight Thur-Sat). Separate rooms for parties, seating 12-85. **Map 17 C4**.

Spiga

84-86 Wardour Street, W1F 3LF (7734 3444/ www.vpmg.net). Leicester Square, Piccadilly Circus or Tottenham Court Road tube. **Lunch served** noon-3pm, **dinner served** 6-11pm 11pm Mon-Thur. **Meals served** noon-midnight Fri, Sat. **Main courses** £13.50-£16.50. **Set meal** (noon-3pm, 6-7pm daily) £13.95 2 courses, £15.95 3 courses. **Credit** AmEx, MC, V.
Spiga makes a refreshing change from the common or garden pizza chains, distinguished by its array of interesting dishes created from super-fresh ingredients. Simple starters – marinated sardines, grilled asparagus with quails' eggs, and plates of antipasti to share – show off the quality of the produce. To follow, the pizzas here are nothing less

than delicious: crisp bases covered with fresh, zingy tomato sauce. Try the pizza bufala, with creamy, uncooked buffalo mozzarella and sweet cherry tomatoes. Generous plates of classic Italian pasta dishes, including linguine with lobster and garlic, and aubergine and taleggio ravioli, are also tempting, as is the array of meat and fish dishes. Decorated with mirrored walls and Italian movie posters, Spiga is packed most nights of the week. The vibe is buzzy (bordering on noisy), but the staff keep on top of things.
Babies and children welcome: high chairs. Booking advisable. Disabled: toilet. Restaurant available for hire. Takeaway service. **Map 17 B4**.

West

Maida Vale

Red Pepper

8 Formosa Street, W9 1EE (7266 2708). Warwick Avenue tube. **Dinner served** 6.30-11pm Mon-Sat; 6.30-10pm Sun. **Lunch served** noon-3.30pm Sat, Sun. **Main courses** £8-£17. **Credit** MC, V.
Even on week nights, this neighbourhood Italian does a roaring trade. Tables, cheerfully crammed into the small, red-painted dining room, fill quickly, and a steady stream of locals flows in for takeaway pizzas. Service, as a result, is of the no-nonsense school (our quite polite request to move tables was

Chain gang

Think one pizza chain is much like any other? Think again. Here's the lowdown on the strengths and weaknesses of the main London chains.

★ ASK
160-162 Victoria Street, SW1E 5LB (7630 8228/www.askcentral.co.uk). Victoria tube/rail. **Meals served** noon-11.30pm Mon-Sat; noon-11pm Sun. **Main courses** £5.95-£11.95. **Credit** AmEx, DC, MC, V.

It's hard not to compare ASK with its sister chain Zizzi, and wonder exactly what separates them. Similar pizza, a choice of pastas and some safe salads make the quest difficult on face value, but it's the surroundings where ASK stands out; many of its restaurants are situated in prime positions or in restored listed buildings. The Victoria branch is certainly impressive, with a swirling staircase. The pizza, though admirably adventurous in its toppings, can be hit and miss. Yet on our visit, seafood ravioli was fresh and flavoursome, substantial salads spot-on, and service quick and attentive.
Babies and children welcome: children's menu; high chairs. Booking advisable. Takeaway service. **Map 15 H10.**
For branches see index.

★ Pizza Express
Benbow House, 24 New Globe Walk, SE1 9DS (7401 3977/www.pizza express.com). London Bridge tube/rail. **Meals served** noon-11pm Mon-Sat;

noon-10.30pm Sun. **Main courses** £5.45-£8.95. **Credit** AmEx, DC, MC, V.

Is a high street really a high street if it doesn't have Pizza Express? It's doubtful. This super-successful chain (owned, along with ASK and Zizzi, by Gondola Holdings) has established itself as a modern icon. Its perfectly palatable dough balls and popular pizzas are as familiar and comforting as anything Pizza Hut served up in the 1980s. Reliable, unintimidating and pleasant on the eye: if it were a partner it would be perfect marriage material. We're pleased to see the firm isn't resting on its enviable laurels though, with new pizzas and interesting additions to the wine list. An ever-evolving menu (bigging up tomatoes on our visit) means that as well as the dependable old favourites, there's something seasonal to keep the interest – and the taste buds – piqued.
Babies and children welcome: high chairs; nappy-changing facilities. Disabled: toilet. Tables outdoors (10, pavement). Takeaway service. **Map 11 P7.**
For branches see index.

Pizza Paradiso
61 The Cut, SE1 8LL (7261 1221/ www.pizzaparadiso.co.uk). Southwark tube/Waterloo tube/rail. **Meals served** noon-midnight Mon-Sat; noon-11pm Sun. **Main courses** £11.95-£17.95. **Credit** AmEx, DC, MC, V.

The restaurant, formerly known as Ristorante Olivetti, may have gone

mainstream with its name, and expanded from being a one-off Soho stalwart to a six-restaurant chain, but it still has enough individuality and charm to knock the socks off most of its chain rivals. The small Southwark branch has the atmosphere of a traditional Italian trattoria (buzzy, with tightly packed tables and slightly frazzled staff), yet it's the food that's really authentic. Appealing seafood and meat mains prove there's more to cheap Italian fare than pizza and pasta – though these are memorable too, with options going beyond (but including) the reliable favourites. Every neighbourhood should have one.
Babies and children welcome: high chairs. Booking advisable Wed-Fri. Tables outdoors (5, pavement). Takeaway service. **Map 11 N8.**
For branches see index.

★ La Porchetta
33 Boswell Street, WC1N 3BP (7242 2434). Holborn or Russell Square tube. **Lunch served** noon-3pm Mon-Fri. **Dinner served** 5-11pm Mon-Sat. **Main courses** £5.90-£9.90. **Credit** MC, V.

Members of this four-strong group feel more like local trattorias than part of a chain – and are all the better for it. The homely Holborn branch seems full with only a few diners. Tables are quite close together and waiting staff need to be on the svelte side to do their thing. La Porchetta prides itself on having a child-friendly vibe, and the casual but

dismissed with a cursory shake of the head from the higher powers), and the dishes arrive with unfailing alacrity. Unless you manage to nab a table by the window, Red Pepper is no place for lingering tête-à-tête. The focus is on the food: simple but enticing own-made pastas (pappardelle with organic chicken livers and sage, say, or fresh artichoke and king prawn ravioli), a daily-changing list of specials, and enormous thin-crust pizzas. Everything we sampled was exemplary: from a piping-hot pizza parmigiana, laden with mozzarella and aubergine, to a plate of perfectly grilled squid, sea bream and luscious king prawns. Regulars rhapsodise about the tiramisu, but the delicious dark chocolate tart (intense in flavour but light in texture) gets our vote every time.
Babies and children admitted. Booking advisable. Separate room for parties, seats 25. Tables outdoors (5, pavement). Takeaway service. **Map 1 C4.**

Westbourne Grove

Mulberry Street
84 Westbourne Grove, W2 5RT (7313 6789/ www.mulberrystreet.co.uk). Bayswater or Queensway tube.. **Breakfast served** 9am-1pm Sat, Sun. **Meals served** noon-midnight daily. **Main courses** £7.50-£10. **Credit** AmEx, MC, V.
Mulberry Street bills itself as London's only authentic New York-style pizza joint – and you have to give it points for trying. Everything's in place: the cosy booth seating, the dark lights, the early Madonna videos booming from behind the bar, and even the waitresses waltzing around in mini skirts. But does the food match the mood? Certainly the portions are authentically supersized. Pizzas are all 20in (51cm) and big enough for two or three hungry diners, though toppings were disappointingly bland: even on the self-proclaimed 'hot' variety. Starter-sized portions of pasta are huge too; spaghetti and meatballs might have been

heavy on the stodge but was too tasty for us not to scoff the lot. The cheery staff are happy to proffer a doggie bag, yet there's never any urgency to finish a meal quickly. Open until midnight every night, this is a great place to kick back, eat pizza, or watch a match, New York style. The kitchen also does weekend diner brunches, pancakes, waffles and eggs any way you want them. Just be sure to leave your calorie consciousness at the door.
Babies and children welcome: high chairs. Booking advisable. Separate room for parties, seats 30. Takeaway service; delivery service (over £20, within 5-mile radius). **Map 7 B6.**

South West

Fulham

Napulé
585 Fulham Road, SW6 5UA (7381 1122/ www.madeinitalygroup.co.uk). Fulham Broadway tube. **Lunch served** noon-3.30pm Sat, Sun. **Dinner served** 6-11.30pm Mon-Sat; 6-10.30pm Sun. **Main courses** £6.95-£14.50. **Credit** MC, V.
Napulé is deceptively small from the outside but spacious within. We were greeted warmly and led past appealing platters of antipasti and fresh bread to a bright, airy split-level room with a conservatory on the back (which is worth requesting when the weather's sunny and the roof is pulled back). The shared antipasti platter was as good as it looked on the way in: a rustic wooden board crammed with old favourites (mozzarella, bruschetta, parma ham) and a few new ones (grilled courgette, aubergine, and fennel among them). Pizza by the metre (compulsory for orders of two or more) impressed too, baked in the traditional Neapolitan-style in a wood-fired oven, and presented on a stand that makes it all feel rather special. Non-pizza lovers are well-catered for with a tempting range of meat, fish and pasta dishes. The basement room is handy for groups.

Babies and children welcome: high chairs. Booking advisable. Separate room for parties, seats 20. Takeaway service. **Map 13 A13.**
For branches (Luna Rossa, Made in Italy, Marechiaro, Regina Margherita, Santa Lucia) see index.

Rossopomodoro
214 Fulham Road, SW10 9NB (7352 7677). South Kensington tube then 14 bus. **Lunch served** noon-3pm, **dinner served** 6pm-midnight Mon-Fri. **Meals served** noon-midnight Sat, Sun. **Main courses** £7-£16. **Set lunch** £6.99-7.99 1 course incl drink **Credit** AmEx, MC, V.
The colour red represents fire, passion, and in Rossopomodoro's case, tomatoes, and plenty of them. Tins are stacked around the room to create an eye-catching installation of which Andy Warhol would be proud. This vibrant restaurant is good fun from the word go. Thanks to friendly staff and an upbeat soundtrack, it has a tangible buzz even when empty early in the evening. The Fulham Road branch is part of a chain originating in Italy that has recently expanded to Covent Garden and Notting Hill. Yet the place still feels fresh, not formulaic, with its bright, modern room, a mix of high and low tables, and an adventurous menu. Pizza-makers do their thing in full view of diners. They clearly know their craft, expertly executing everything from a simple napoli to the vesuvius: double-layered and bursting with cheese, salami and, of course, tomatoes. Starters were just as successful; a thoughtful waitress warned us that our Italian-style tortilla would take 20 minutes – it was worth the wait. Diners vary from dough-eyed couples to groups of families and friends – all revelling in this vivacious venue.
Babies and children welcome: high chairs. Booking advisable. Separate room for parties, seats 40. Takeaway service. **Map 13 C12.**
For branches see index.

CHEAP EATS

slightly chaotic atmosphere makes this branch a good family option in an area distinctly short on them. Foodwise, there's much to choose from: an appealing range of no-frills pizza and pastas that look and taste distinctly homemade. Service can be a little slow, but that just gives you more time to watch the drama unfold around you. The basement area is ideal for groups. *Babies and children welcome: high chairs. Booking advisable (5 or more people). Takeaway service.* **Map 10 L5**. **For branches see index**.

★ Prezzo

17 Hertford Street, W1J 7RS (7499 4690/www.prezzoplc.co.uk). Green Park or Hyde Park Corner tube. **Meals served** noon-11.30pm Mon-Sat; noon-11pm Sun. **Main courses** £5.75-£8.95. **Credit** AmEx, MC, V.

The Mayfair branch of this pizza chain looks more like an upmarket English pub than an Italian restaurant – all dark panelled wood and moody lighting, with tables thoughtfully spaced for a crowd consisting largely of trysting couples and map-toting tourists. Unfortunately the food isn't especially Italian either. While the silky mozzarella, tomato and basil starter raised hopes, these quickly sank along with the dough of an undercooked pizza, meagrely topped and light on the love. Pasta was better, and inexpensive, but the dish was delivered to the table with more of a slam than a smile. With

a few tweaks, Prezzo could challenge the big boys, but for now this branch has little more than a salubrious setting and low prices to recommend it. *Babies and children welcome: high chairs. Booking advisable. Takeaway service.* **Map 9 H8**. **For branches see index**.

Strada

31 Marylebone High Street, W1U 4PP (7935 1004/www.strada.co.uk). Baker Street or Bond Street tube. **Meals served** 11.30am-11pm Mon-Sat; 11.30am-10.30pm Sun. **Main courses** £7.25-£19.50. **Set meal** (noon-5pm Mon-Fri) £8.50 1 course incl drink. **Credit** AmEx, MC, V.

Strada may like to bill itself as stylish and contemporary, but in reality it's more moccasin than stiletto. Like the decor, the menu sits on the safe side: neutral, reliable yet never going to win any awards for innovation. Food is notorious for being a bit hit and miss, but on our visit the Marylebone branch delivered – for the most part. Seafood pasta was generously packed with juicy prawns, pizza arrived soggy in the centre, and refreshingly, the tiramisu didn't taste of fridge: nor did the tap water, which is presented to each table without a hint of a frown. Tightly packed tables mean canoodling is generally out of the question, but for group gatherings Strada is a popular option. A pleasant, if not particularly memorable, chain.

Babies and children welcome: children's portions; high chairs. Booking advisable. Disabled: toilet. Separate rooms for parties, seating 12 and 20. Takeaway service. **Map 3 G5**. **For branches see index**.

Zizzi

20 Bow Street, WC2E 7AW (7836 6101/ www.zizzi.co.uk). **Meals served** noon-11.30pm Mon-Sat; noon-11pm Sun. **Main courses** £6.95-£11.95. **Credit** AmEx, DC, MC, V.

An instant sense of warmth overcomes you when you walk into the Covent Garden branch of Zizzi. Perhaps it's the massive wood-fired oven stoked high to keep the pizzas cranking out, or maybe it's body heat generated by pre-theatre diners crammed into closely packed tables. It's probably not because of the brusque service, but that's not why people flock to this slightly more refined older sister of the ASK chain. It's more to do with the food: simple Italian dishes to suit most taste buds, at a price that won't break the bank. Our antipasti starter was predictable but perfectly pleasant to pick at; bruschetta seemed more like mashed tomato on toast; pizza and pasta were passable but hardly memorable.

Babies and children welcome: children's menu; high chairs. Booking advisable. Disabled: toilet. Tables outdoors (6, pavement). Takeaway service. **Map 18 E4**. **For branches see index**.

South

Balham

★ Ciullo's

31 Balham High Road, SW12 9AL (8675 3072). Clapham South tube/Balham tube/rail. **Dinner served** 6-11pm Mon-Thur; 6-11.30pm Fri, Sat; 5-10.30pm Sun. **Main courses** £5.50-£12.50. **Credit** MC, V.

Family-run Ciullo's passed the authenticity test on our last visit when two Tuscan ladies walked in somewhat warily off the street and were swept up in a tide of Italian exclamation and embrace. Staff are justifiably proud of this charming ristorante and their enthusiasm is infectious. The bright-orange walls, dodgy art and bar lined with dusty bottles of limoncello won't win any style awards, but who cares when food so cheap (pizza and pasta start at £6.50) tastes so good? The cooking is honest and traditional, ingredients market-fresh, portions generous, and the wine list decent and modestly priced. Pastas are reliably al dente and might include a spicy arrabbiata, or – our choice from the specials board – pappardelle in a flavourful ragù of minced venison and dried porcini. Pizzas are perfectly thin and crisp, but bear in mind that bruschetta also comes on a pizza base – we were glad of the contrast in our (nicely plump) fresh sardine starter. Our Tuscan friends seemed content with their grilled tuna too. Old-fashioned Ciullo's continues to set the standard in Balham. *Babies and children welcome: high chairs. Booking advisable. Tables outdoors (3, terrace).*

Battersea

★ Donna Margherita

183 Lavender Hill, SW11 5TE (7228 2660/ www.donna-margherita.com). Clapham Junction rail. **Lunch served** noon-3pm Fri. **Dinner**

served 6-10.30pm Mon-Thur; 6-11pm Fri. **Meals served** 12.30-11pm Sat; 12.30-10.30pm Sun. **Main courses** £6.50-£18.50. **Credit** AmEx, DC, MC, V.

The trattoria styling – open brickwork, mural, strings of garlic and display of antipasti – is so outdated it feels fresh, but perfect pizza never goes out of fashion, and here are some of the best puffy-yet-crisp pizza bases you'll find. Look on the specials sheet for wine bargains, such as Chiaretto rosé from Bardolino in the Veneto. The menu lists around 20 pizzas, plus half-and-half combo plates, though you may be diverted by the tempting pasta and gnocchi dishes made on the premises. We were impressed by the freshness and accurate cooking of the seafood, both in a starter of herb-crusted wood-roasted squid, and the garlicky pizza frutta di mare. Own-made desserts such as tiramisu and a white-chocolate-coated sponge shell filled with chocolate ice-cream are fine, but not worth saving room for. Surprisingly, Donna Margherita wasn't busy on our Sunday lunchtime visit, when it seems the perfect spot for young families. Staff are friendly, easy-going and in no hurry to see us leave. *Babies and children welcome: children's portions; high chairs. Booking advisable. Separate room for parties, seats 18. Tables outdoors (6, terrace). Takeaway service; delivery service (over £10 within 1-mile radius).* **Map 21 C3**.

Pizza Metro

64 Battersea Rise, SW11 1EQ (7228 3812/ www.pizzametropizza.com). Clapham Junction rail. **Dinner served** 6-11pm Tue-Fri. **Meals served** noon-11pm Sat; noon-10.30pm Sun. **Main courses** £8.50-£18.50. **Set meal** £16 2 courses. **Credit** MC, V.

After whispers of recent wobbles, Pizza Metro seems firmly back on top of its game. Parties of pizza-eaters were queuing out of the door at 9.30pm on a Thursday. The restaurant is packed with Neapolitan gusto, with its quirky murals and

determinedly cheery service. Our waiter produced glasses of prosecco while we were delayed just three minutes waiting for a table. Authentic, fully flavoured starters include bruschetta (bursting with fresh tomato), and a griddled vegetable plate dressed liberally in nice peppery olive oil. But the main event is their pizza, made the proper Italian way – simple, with a thin, crisp base, tomato sauce, mozzarella and one or two toppings: salty prosciutto, say, with peppery rocket; or the patented special of their meatballs, aubergine and fresh basil. All arrive as great belt-popping oblong tranches, served on table-width metal trays that rise to eye-level. The pasta dishes on offer are equally appealing. Rigatoni in an almost meaty sauce of aubergine, mozzarella, parmesan and fresh basil was as good as any we've tasted. Chirpy and charming, Pizza Metro is reason enough never again to resort to eating at a high-street chain. *Babies and children welcome: children's menu; high chairs. Booking advisable. Tables outdoors (10, pavement). Takeaway service: delivery service (over £15 within 2-mile radius).* **Map 21 C4**.

Brixton

★ ★ Franco Manca NEW (100)

2008 WINNER BEST CHEAP EATS
4 Market Row, Electric Lane, SW9 8LD (7738 3021/www.francomanca.com). Brixton tube/rail. **Meals served** noon-5pm Mon-Thur, Sun; noon-9.30pm Fri. **Main courses** £3.90-£5.60. **Credit** MC, V.

Brixton market couldn't be further removed from the sun-dappled piazzas of Naples, but its West Indian food stalls, wandering preachers and humid reggae soundtrack make a similarly colourful backdrop against which to indulge in a perfect pizza – and we do mean perfect. Franco Manca may seem spartan (a handful of café tables and a couple of shared pews beneath the peeling ceiling of the market hall), but this is a thinking punter's

pizzeria. Sourdough for the bases is left to rise 20 hours before baking; ingredients are largely organic (the owners flew in a cheesemaker from Sorrento to train their Somerset supplier in the fine art of mozzarella making); and the 500°C/930°F brick oven crisps up the crust without drying it out, while sealing the flavours of the toppings. Of the six pizzas offered on the menu, we plumped for one that mixed organic Brindisa chorizo with mozzarella: the peppery kick of the sausage meat contrasting with the smoothness of Somerset's finest. We also ordered a calzone that paired crumbling buffalo ricotta with a generous helping of delicious organic pork. The first was served with a smile, the second with a song. Proof that just a little Italy goes a long way in even the unlikeliest of places.
Babies and children admitted. Disabled: toilet. Tables outdoors (6, pavement). Takeaway service. Vegan dishes. **Map 22 E2.**

Clapham

Eco
162 Clapham High Street, SW4 7UG (7978 1108/www.ecorestaurants.com). Clapham Common tube. **Lunch served** noon-4pm, **dinner served** 6-11pm Mon-Fri. **Meals served** noon-11.30pm Sat; noon-11pm Sun. **Main courses** £6.95-£13.90. **Credit** AmEx, MC, V.
From its prime location at the Common end of the High Street, Eco has been feeding Clapham for over a decade. Yet while punters keep piling-in (arrive promptly, especially at weekends), it's clear from the outmoded 1990s interior – featuring an abundance of wavy plywood – that the renovators have stayed away. Tables, especially at the front, are crammed together; music is cranked so high that the only way to make yourself heard is to shout. Still, service is pleasant, if perfunctory, and the open kitchen turns out plates laden with reasonably priced food. A starter of pancetta-wrapped asparagus worked well, although another of artichoke and buffalo mozzarella seemed measly with the artichoke. Our pasta followed in a nicely truffle-oiled, creamy wine sauce, but was light on the porcini and pancetta. While locals swear by the vast pizzas (big enough to share), we would have preferred our fiorentina with a runnier egg and lighter crust. Eco keeps on buzzing, though, and it's worth noting that you can stock up at deli-next-door, Esca, until 8pm.
Babies and children welcome: high chair. Booking advisable; essential weekends. Tables outdoors (4, pavement). Takeaway service. **Map 22 B2.** **For branch see index.**

South East

Peckham

The Gowlett
62 Gowlett Road, SE15 4HY (7635 7048/ www.thegowlett.com). East Dulwich or Peckham Rye rail/12, 37, 40, 63, 176, 185, 484 bus. **Open** noon-midnight Mon-Thur; noon-1am Fri, Sat; noon-11.30pm Sun. **Lunch served** 12.30-2.30pm, **dinner served** 6.30-10.30pm Mon-Fri. **Meals served** 12.30-10.30pm Sat; 12.30-9pm Sun. **Main courses** £7.50-£8.50. **Credit** AmEx, DC, MC, V.
The smoking ban has been good to this hip neighbourhood pub and pizza dive. Now, instead of stale beer and fag ash, the wooden floor and leather-sofa setting is scented with stone-baked dough and home cooking. A larger food-aware customer base (and more families) is the result. Thin and crispy discs of garlic or tuscan anchovy bread are a perfect complement to a pint of the house beer (Adnams) or any of the other regularly changing real ales from this CAMRA award-winning joint (recently, Titanic Stout, White Adder and Shropshire's own Quaff were on the pumps). A seasonally changing 'special' pizza (a succulent chorizo, mixed pepper and white onion blend on our visit) has been added to the menu of half a dozen pizza choices, though bestsellers Gowlettini (mozzarella, goat's cheese, pine nuts, rocket and prosciutto – or sun-dried tomatoes for vegetarians)

and American Hot (spicy salami dripping with chilli oil) are hard to beat. New 'Lucky 7' night on Thursdays kicks off the weekend early as local musos drop in to spin their beloved 7-inch discs while knocking back a bottle or several of the keenly priced organic wines.
Babies and children admitted (until 9pm): nappy-changing facilities. Disabled: toilet. Entertainment: DJs 6.30pm Sun; jazz band last Wed of month 8.30pm; quiz 8.30pm Mon. Tables outdoors (3, heated terrace; 4, pavement).

East

Shoreditch

Furnace
1 Rufus Street, N1 6PE (7613 0598/ www.hoxtonfurnace.com). Old Street tube/rail. **Lunch served** noon-3pm Mon-Fri. **Dinner served** 6-11pm Mon-Sat. **Main courses** £6.85-£13. **Credit** MC, V.
Pizzerias probably outnumber phone boxes in London these days. Furnace opened in 1999 and seems to have been busy every night since. The restaurant attracts local professionals who treat it as a pitstop en route to somewhere else. It's an attractive place with high ceilings, lots of exposed brickwork, modern paintings and boxes of Barilla pasta decoratively arranged on shelves. Though daily pasta dishes are available, as well as meat and fish specials, customers come for the pizza. The open kitchen means you can watch your dough being flung around before it goes into the substantial wood-burning stone oven. The bases are thin and crisp and the toppings generous and inventive. The menu has changed little in the past

decade, but why come up with novelties when you've got toppings such as suckling pig with sour cream, or gorgonzola with poached pears? We tried a margharita and another one topped with goat's cheese, roasted peppers and rocket. The tomato sauce on both tasted beautifully fresh, and the goat's cheese and peppers worked wonderfully together. Although there's a varied Italian wine list, most customers stick with bottles of Moretti. After all, they're not stopping.
Babies and children admitted. Takeaway service. Separate room for parties, seats 40. **Map 6 R4.**

★ StringRay Globe Café Bar & Pizzeria
109 Columbia Road, E2 7RL (7613 1141/ www.stringraycafe.co.uk). Bus 26, 48, 55. **Meals served** 11am-11pm daily. **Main courses** £5-£11. **Credit** MC, V.
When the flower market fills Columbia Road on Sundays, an impressive queue snakes out of StringRay. Granted, the prices are low for such decent food, but the biggest draw is the café's trendy status among east London's fashion folk. Aviator sunglasses and leg-warmers are standard attire. A big wooden bar in the centre of the room limits the dining space, yet adds to the cosy atmosphere, along with small tables and low lighting from Tiffany lampshades. We visited on a Monday night to be met with a half-hour wait on a table for two. In deference to the student regulars, the menu offers breakfasts until 5pm, but the popular choice is for thin-crust pizzas. We opted for a fiorentina (from 19 varieties) and a dish of pork medallions topped with spinach, roasted red peppers and mozzarella. The oversized pizza

Franco Manca. See p323.

arrived steaming with garlicky spinach and was a mouth-watering success. The pork was an even bigger hit, the peppers adding sweetness to the meat. Skipping the unappetising-looking desserts, we completed the east London experience by walking down to Pollard Street to see Banksy's double yellow line flower.

Babies and children welcome: children's menu; high chairs. Booking essential. Tables outdoors (7, pavement). Takeaway service. **Map 6 S3**. **For branches see index.**

Wapping

★ Il Bordello

81 Wapping High Street, E1W 2YN (7481 9950). Tower Hill tube/DLR then 100 bus. **Lunch served** noon-3pm Mon-Fri. **Dinner served** 6-11pm Mon-Sat. **Meals served** 1-10.30pm Sun. **Main courses** £7.75-£22.95. **Credit** AmEx, DC, MC, V.

Bordello is Italian for brothel, although it's also used colloquially as a description of chaos. This neighbourhood Italian place is certainly chaotic, but in a way that's cheerily boisterous, exciting and big on atmosphere. The efficient and very friendly staff jolly along a throng of raucous, good-time customers. Copper panelling and large art deco Lempicka prints adorn the classy interior. The menu is similarly sophisticated, comprising an impressive range of fresh fish, seafood and good cuts of meat, as well as the expected pizza and pasta. We went for two pasta dishes: the tagliatelle special with scallops, langoustines and monkfish; and orecchiette with broccoli, anchovies and chilli.

At first all eyes were on their gimmicky electric cheese grater, but the focus soon turned to the enormous portions of wonderfully aromatic food. The pasta tasted fresh and the combination of flavours was superb. Should you make it through to dessert, we can thoroughly recommend the bold and boozy tiramisu.

Babies and children welcome: high chairs. Booking advisable. Disabled: toilet. Takeaway service. **For branch (La Figa) see index.**

North East
Stoke Newington

★ Il Bacio

61 Stoke Newington Church Street, N16 0AR (7249 3833). Stoke Newington rail/73 bus. **Dinner served** 6-11.15pm Mon-Fri. **Meals served** noon-11.15pm Sat, Sun. **Main courses** £5.50-£15.95. **Credit** MC, V.

The staff of Il Bacio welcome customers like old friends. Smiles and back-patting are followed by complimentary herbed olives and a basket of paper-thin Sardinian bread. The place is larger than it looks from the front, with two dining areas divided by a semi-open kitchen. On warmer days, the waiters open the french doors and put a couple of tables on the pavement – simultaneously treating passers-by to the likes of Dean Martin's 'That's Amore'. The kind service and sensible prices make the restaurant a hit with young families and, while there's no separate children's menu, the kitchen will make half portions of most main courses. The menu has a list of standard

Italian pizzas and pastas, as well as such Sardinian home-style specials as slow-cooked lamb. The wood-fired pizzas are absolutely enormous, and leftovers are put in a takeaway box without prompting. We avoided the chip-topped pizza, instead choosing goat's cheese and parma ham options. Both were very salty, but our water jug was topped up throughout. Desserts include Sardinian favourite sebadas (sweet ravioli) and a heavenly tiramisu.

Babies and children welcome: high chairs. Booking advisable. Separate room for parties, seats 50. Tables outdoors (3, pavement). Takeaway service; delivery service (over £10, within 2-mile radius). **Map 25 B1**. **For branches (Il Bacio Express, Il Bacio Highbury) see index.**

North West
Hampstead

Fratelli la Bufala

45A South End Road, NW3 2QB (7435 7814/ www.fratellilabufala.com). Belsize Park tube/ Hampstead Heath rail. **Lunch served** noon-3pm Tue-Fri. **Dinner served** 6-11pm Mon-Fri. **Meals served** noon-11pm Sat, Sun. **Main courses** £7.90-£16. **Set lunch** (Mon-Fri) £10 2 courses. **Credit** MC, V.

Mimmo, manager of this branch of the Italian buffalo-meat and mozzarella specialist, cuts an imposing figure as he welcomes customers into his restaurant: a great besuited giant beaming and bantering like a less follicularly challenged Artie Bucco from *The Sopranos*. Not that Fratelli la

Bufala is a patch on Vesuvio, even during its fifth-season decline. The overwhelming brightness and starchy aesthetic emptiness could be forgiven – as could the general air of rude bemusement among staff – if only the food were better. Starters, in fairness, can be decent: salciccia vesuvio comprises slices of smoky buffalo sausage arranged around a baked goat's cheese and served with a palate-confusing tapenade, sun-dried tomato paste and mayonnaise. But main courses on a recent trip were poor: a £16 sea bream special overcooked and served with bitter, rubbery aubergine slices; a dish of penne with buffalo sausage and broccoli arriving without the aforementioned sausage and replaced only grudgingly. All this and house wines weighing in at almost £14. Charismatic front-men aside, Fratelli can feel like a far-from homely and less-than capable local eaterie.

Babies and children welcome: high chairs. Booking advisable evenings. Separate room for parties, seats 20. Tables outdoors (2, pavement). Takeaway service. **Map 28 C3**. **For branch see index**.

Kilburn

Osteria del Ponte

77 Kilburn High Road, NW6 6HY (7624 5793). Kilburn Park tube. **Open** 4-11pm Mon-Fri; noon-11pm Sat, Sun. **Lunch served** noon-3.30pm Sat, Sun. **Dinner served** 5.30-10.30pm daily. **Main courses** £9-£12. **Credit** MC, V.

It seems that the Kilburn Park locals still haven't realised quite what a true gem they have right on their doorsteps in the Osteria del Ponte. The

oversized dining room was practically empty on our midweek visit. Perhaps it's the location on one of Kilburn High Road's less salubrious stretches; maybe people are too busy frequenting all the swanky pubs in Brondesbury to notice its existence. Either way, they are really missing out on a cracker. The erstwhile pub interior has been refurbished to accommodate a smart cocktail bar, a corner featuring cosy sofas and a projection screen, and – at the centre of all the action – a traditional wood-fired oven turning out top-notch pizzas. We plumped for a really superb fiorentina featuring raw spinach, enormous flakes of parmesan and a perfectly runny egg; we also sampled the 'Osteria special' with its abundance of spicy sausage, roasted peppers and fresh pungent rocket leaves. There's quite a wide range of traditional pasta dishes as well, and a list of specials that encompasses dishes as varied as monkfish wrapped in parma ham, as well as suckling pig with all the trimmings. The desserts on offer include a panna cotta with orange zest that perfectly balances the innate creaminess with a very subtle citrus bite.

Babies and children welcome: high chairs. Booking advisable. Restaurant available for hire. Tables outdoors (5, pavement). **Map 1 B1**.

West Hampstead

La Brocca

273 West End Lane, NW6 1QS (7433 1989). West Hampstead tube/rail/139, C11 bus. *Bar* **Open** noon-11pm Mon-Thur; noon-1am Fri;

11am-1am Sat; noon-midnight Sun. **Lunch served** noon-4pm Mon-Fri; noon-4.30pm Sat, Sun. **Main courses** £6-£14. *Restaurant* **Dinner served** 6-11pm daily. **Main courses** £10-£20. *Both* **Credit** AmEx, MC, V.

A local institution in West Hampstead for some considerable time, La Brocca has all the hallmarks of a quintessential family Italian restaurant. Its ground-floor and dimly lit cavernous basement premises are plastered with jolly prints of old Italy and cluttered with tables sporting red-checked tablecloths – it's all quite romantic in a distinctly *Lady and the Tramp* sort of way. The generous owner has a fondness for bringing out the shots, and there's a separate bar area for pre-prandial drinks. With few of the dishes costing less than £10, the restaurant is definitely pitching itself as more than a typical local pizza and pasta joint. Sometimes it does manage to succeed: a shared starter of garlic bread pizza with artichokes, goat's cheese, rocket and parma ham may have been rather let down by two unsightly and over-garlicky prawns, but tearing into the dish across the table did prove to be a real ice breaker. A special of perfectly pink duck breast with nicely textured saffron risotto, mangetout and red berry jus just about justified its fairly hefty price tag. Some of the other dishes we tried, including veal ravioli in a bland tomato and basil sauce, were decidedly disappointing. But the staff are always amiable, and the general atmosphere is jovial enough to make it well worth giving La Brocca a try.

Babies and children welcome: high chairs. Booking advisable. **Map 28 A2**.

The Gowlett. See p325.

Sarastro **Restaurant**
"The Show After The Show"

A sumptuous treasure trove hidden within a Grade II listed Victorian townhouse, Sarastro is perfectly located in the heart of London's Theatreland. A wide selection of delicious Mediterranean dishes are served with theatrical flair and passion against the elaborate backdrop of golden drapes and decorative frescoed walls.

Every Sunday matinee and Sunday and Monday evenings there are live performances from up and coming stars of the Royal and National Opera houses and from all over the world. Sarastro is perfect for red carpet parties and celebrations and ideal for pre- and post- theatre dining with a menu available at £12.50. Also available for lunch Monday - Saturday. A private function room is available for corporate and red carpet occasions (for up to 300 guests).

126 Drury Lane, London WC2 | Tel: 020 7836 0101 Fax: 020 7379 4666
www.sarastro-restaurant.com | E: reservations@sarastro-restaurant.com

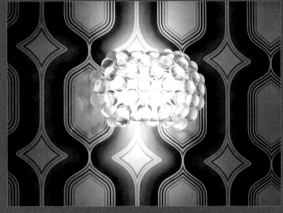

Drinking

Bars

No longer do you have to head into the West End for an excellent cocktail, or pay swanky hotel prices. Over the past three years every one of the Best Bar winners at the Time Out Eating & Drinking Awards has been located (gasp!) south of the river. Congratulations to the **Loft** in Clapham for nabbing this year's prize – and we still like **Lost Society**, not so far away, for its excellent drinks and fantasy country-house party decor. If hotel bars are your thing, a visit to the new **Coburg** at the reconceived Connaught hotel is a must, so too the revamped martini specialist **Dukes Hotel**, now overseen by the team behind One Aldwych, whose **Lobby Bar** is still super. We've included reviews of several favourite restaurant bars here, but others we like include those at **Christopher's** (see p37), **Medcalf** (see p57), **Pearl** (see p136), **St John** (see p55) and, when a spectacular view is an essential part of the order, **Galvin at Windows** (see p141).

For hundreds and hundreds of drinking options across the capital, consult the annual *Time Out Bars, Pubs & Clubs* guide.

Central

Aldwych

Lobby Bar (100)

One Aldwych, WC2B 4RH (7300 1070/ www.onealdwych.com). Covent Garden or Temple tube. **Open** 8am-11.30pm Mon-Sat; 8am-10.30pm Sun. **Food served** noon-5pm, 5.30-11pm Mon-Sat; noon-5pm, 5.30-10.30pm Sun. **Credit** AmEx, DC, MC, V.
Range and quality are the watchwords for cocktails at the main bar of swish hotel One Aldwych, to be enjoyed in its glamorous double-height space. Select your own martini spirit if none of the 20 listed martinis (£9.95), such as a Gazpacho with lemon-infused Tanqueray, green pepper, Midori and elderflower cordial, grabs you. A Number One from the 'One Aldwych Selection' (£9.95-£12.75) of Wyborowa, raspberry liqueur, passion fruit and champagne also stands out. Various sandwiches (£9), sushi, meze and working lunch plates (beef carpaccio, £11.95) make classy accompaniments.
Babies and children admitted. Disabled: toilet. Function room (capacity 100). **Map 18 F4**.

City

Hawksmoor (100)

157 Commercial Street, E1 6BJ (7247 7392/ www.thehawksmoor.com). Liverpool Street tube/rail. **Open** noon-1am Mon-Sat. **Food served** noon-3pm, 6.30-10.30pm Mon-Fri; 6.30-10.30pm Sat. **Credit** AmEx, DC, MC, V.
Hawksmoor's bar is stuck at one side of its rather unprepossessing restaurant space (see p37) and has no dedicated seating of its own beyond a few barstools. Still those stools are among London's finest ringside seats, for Hawksmoor's laid-back bartenders are cocktail intellectuals. The list tracks classics such as juleps and 'aromatic cocktails' from their inception: Gin and Pine (conceived in 1862) came in a cold glass of perfect proportion; Scoff Law (1924; whisky, Noilly Prat, pomegranate and lemon) was a smooth, unfussy blend. Purist means neither severe – there are also more frivolous daquiris, tikis and punches – nor expensive, with much at £6.50. American beers (Anchor Steam, Brooklyn Lager) and well-chosen international wines provide further options.

Babies and children admitted. Bar available for hire. Disabled: toilet. Function room (capacity 30). **Map 6 R5**.

Fitzrovia

Crazy Bear

26-28 Whitfield Street, W1T 2RG (7631 0088/ www.crazybeargroup.co.uk). Goodge Street tube. **Open/food served** noon-10.45pm Mon-Fri; 6-10.45pm Sat. **Credit** AmEx, DC, MC, V.
This low-lit, Lilliputian basement bar is the London outpost of an upmarket Oxfordshire hotel and pub group. A charming hostess leads you to its padded alcoves, swivel cowhide stools and low-slung leather armchairs. Swanky cocktails are mixed to perfection and include classics with a twist (lychee mojitos, strawberry and basil mules) and quirky originals. If mixed drinks don't appeal, there are three champagnes (Gaillimard, Pol Roger Reserve and Billecart-Salmon) available by the glass, as are a dozen wines. A level of sobriety is required for the incredibly glam but disorienting loos (the doors are hidden in the walls and everything is mirrored). Bar snacks include dim sum, spring rolls and satays. *See also p252.*
Babies and children admitted (lunch). Bar available for hire (Mon-Wed). **Map 17 B1**.

Market Place

11-13 Market Place, W1W 8AH (7079 2020/ www.marketplace-london.com). Oxford Circus tube. **Open** 11am-midnight Mon-Wed; 11am-1am Thur, Fri; noon-1am Sat; 1-11pm Sun. **Food served** 11am-3.30pm, 6.30pm-midnight Mon-Wed; 11am-3.30pm, 6.30pm-1am Thur, Fri; noon-1am Sat; 1-11pm Sun. **Admission** £7 after 11pm Fri, Sat. **Credit** AmEx, MC, V.
Still going strong, Market Place, just off Oxford Street, is packed with a loyal crowd who spill out on to the pedestrianised thoroughfare throughout the year, hungry for Spanish tapas, gourmet burgers, Latin street food and eclectic beats. The cool decor is all of natural materials – exposed bricks, stone and wood panelling. There's a decent DJ line-up in the basement, with occasional bands. The energetic bar staff serve a selection of well-made cocktails using fresh fruit purées and spirits that include Don Fulano Reposado tequila and Green Mark vodka. There are bottled beers

from all over Europe, as well as Amstel, Budvar and König Ludwig Hefe-Weizen on tap.
Disabled: toilet. Music (DJs 8pm nightly). Tables outdoors (8, terrace). **Map 9 J6**.

Hakkasan (100)

8 Hanway Place, W1T 1HD (7907 1888). Tottenham Court Road tube. **Open** noon-12.30am Mon-Wed; noon-1.30am Thur-Sat; noon-midnight Sun. **Food served** noon-3pm, 6-11.30pm Mon-Wed; noon-3pm, 6pm-12.30am Thur, Fri; noon-4pm, 6pm-12.30am Sat; noon-4pm, 6-11.30pm Sun. **Credit** AmEx, MC, V.
This thin, aquamarine sliver of a cocktail bar is as renowned as the upmarket Chinese eaterie (see p75) that surrounds it. Hakkasan is another world of beautifully lit oriental sophistication. Drinkers must negotiate the dining room's interlocking booth dividers to get to the long, back-lit bar; then it's simply a case of sitting (or standing) pretty and soaking up the glamour. Some 15 martinis and 26 long drinks are made with spirits such as 'Nikka whisky from the barrel' and 'Ciroc grape distilled vodka'. The signature Hakkatini mixes Campari, Belvedere Pomarancza, Grand Marnier, fresh apple and orange bitters; a Hakka is saké, Ketel One, lychee juice, passion fruit and coconut cream. Saké is a key ingredient and sold separately in cold and hot varieties (Kubota Manju and Kenbishi) too.
Babies and children admitted (until 7.30pm). Disabled: toilet. Function room (capacity 65). Music (DJs 9pm nightly; free). Restaurant (available for hire, capacity 150). **Map 17 C2**.

Long Bar

The Sanderson, 50 Berners Street, W1T 3NG (7300 1400/www.sandersonlondon.com). Oxford Circus or Tottenham Court Road tube. **Open/food served** 11.30am-2am Mon-Wed; 11.30am-3am Thur-Sat; noon-10.30pm Sun. **Credit** AmEx, DC, MC, V.
These days the Long Bar's clientele is more civilian than celebrity, but there's still easy glamour for the taking. The long bar in question is a thin onyx affair, though nabbing one of the eyeball-backed stools is an unlikely prospect. A better bet is the lovely courtyard, where table service, candlelight and watery features make a much nicer setting for cocktails. And, really, it would be wrong to order anything else, with a list of enticing flutes, long drinks and martinis to choose from: try a Santa Rosa (Stoli raspberry, crème de framboise and pêche, fresh raspberries and Laurent Perrier) or a Vesuvio martini (Ketel One Citron, lychee liqueur, lemongrass cordial and a dab of fresh chilli). Bar snacks are priced high (BLT for £14, burger for £16), though this is unlikely to be a problem for most of the punters.
Babies and children admitted (terrace). Disabled: toilet (in hotel). Function room (capacity 80). Music (DJ 10.30pm Fri; free). Tables outdoors (20, terrace). **Map 17 A2**.

Shochu Lounge

Basement, Roka, 37 Charlotte Street, W1T 1RR (7580 9666/www.shochulounge.com). Goodge Street or Tottenham Court Road tube. **Open** 5pm-midnight Mon, Sat; noon-midnight Tue-Fri; 6pm-midnight Sun. **Food served** 5.30-11.30pm Mon, Sat; noon-3.30pm, 5.30-11.30pm Tue-Fri; 6-10.30pm Sun. **Credit** AmEx, DC, MC, V.
The basement bar of contemporary Japanese restaurant Roka (see p193) is a buzzy, evening-only spot whose approach is part 21st-century cosmopolitan, part feudal Japan. It is named after the vodka-like spirit made from grains such as barley on which it bases many of its tonics and cocktails, the former (£6.90) a 75ml measure in an unusual range of flavours (rhubarb, blood orange, sharon fruit) adored by health-conscious celebs. The jasmine variety 'produces feelings of optimism and euphoria'. This may also be said of the cocktails (£8), such as the combination of shochu and saké with cucumber garnish in a Noshino martini. Food from the award-winning kitchens upstairs is available, including sushi, sashimi and robotayaki (chargrilled) dishes.
Music (DJ 8.30pm Thur-Sat; free). **Map 17 B1**.

Social

5 Little Portland Street, W1W 7JD (7636 4992/ www.thesocial.com). Oxford Circus tube. **Open/ food served** noon-midnight Mon-Wed; noon-1am Thur-Sat; 6pm-midnight occasional Sun. **Credit** AmEx, MC, V.

Proper cocktails, decent beers, a great jukebox, cutting-edge DJs and beans on toast remain the guiding stars of the much-loved Social's mission to the masses. Cocktails are around £6: classics (cosmopolitans with Ketel One Citron) and a few inventions (the 'Social' is a mix of Frangelico, Teichenné Butterscotch, cream and chocolate sprinkles). Shooters (£3, three for £7.50) suit the buzz in the cavernous basement DJ bar better than the more sedate, five-table affair upstairs. Beers (draught San Miguel to bottled Tsing Tao) offer a global view, and the handful of wines sets the tone for the menu, a staunchly bedsit approach to dining. Where else could you order spaghetti hoops on toast (£3.70) – grated cheese optional – or fish finger salad (£4)? The handmade pies are notable. *Babies and children admitted (until 5pm). Jukebox. Music (DJs/bands 7pm Mon-Sat, occasional Sun; free-£5).* **Map 9 J5.**

King's Cross

Big Chill House

257-259 Pentonville Road, N1 9NL (7427 2540/ www.bigchill.net). King's Cross tube/rail. **Open** noon-midnight Mon-Thur, Sun; noon-3am Fri, Sat. **Food served** noon-11pm daily. **Admission** £5 after 10pm Fri, Sat. **Credit** MC, V.

The multi-faceted Big Chill festival and music bar operation has made an impressive N1 splash a few doors down from the King's Cross Thameslink station. Easy-to-share dishes, platters, sandwiches and burgers are consumed by a music-savvy daytime crowd, as are Tiger, Budvar and Leffe by the bottle. Wines run from a house Oléa de Comté (£3.25/£12.50) to a £24.50 Sancerre. After dark, cocktails appear, including house varieties by the glass or jug (Big Chill Punch with Finlandia and white peach purée, £6.50/£19.50), accompanying an adventurous live music programme. Above the main bar area is an upstairs bar and terrace. *Babies and children admitted (until 6pm). Disabled: toilet, access ramp. Games (board games). Music (DJs/bands daily). Tables outdoors (12, terrace).* **Map 4 L3.**

Knightsbridge

Blue Bar (100)

The Berkeley, Wilton Place, SW1X 7RL (7235 6000/www.the-berkeley.co.uk). Hyde Park Corner tube. **Open/food served** 4pm-1am Mon-Sat; 4-11pm Sun. **Credit** AmEx, DC, MC, V.

The Blue Bar's colourful cocktail list is pricey, but the terrific drinks live up to their promise. Good basics include an impressive whisky sour, and in addition there are inventions such as the Amber Manhattan that we tried – essentially a perfect manhattan made with Macallan ten-year and titivated with maple and pecan liqueur, vanilla, Cointreau and orange bitters. The tapas have a distinct Asian fusion feel, with dishes such as queen scallops with wasabi and lime vinaigrette. Designer David Collins' handsome, cosy room is made lovelier by some low lighting – yet the crowd is very see-and-be-seen. It's nice to see the staff don't greet the celebs with the complacency they probably deserve. *Disabled: toilet (in hotel). Dress: smart casual.* **Map 9 G9.**

Mandarin Bar

Mandarin Oriental Hyde Park, 66 Knightsbridge, SW1X 7LA (7235 2000/www.mandarin oriental.com). Knightsbridge tube. **Open/food served** 10.30am-1.30am Mon-Sat; 10.30am-11.30pm Sun. **Admission** £5 after 10.30pm Mon-Sat. **Credit** AmEx, DC, MC, V.

The Mandarin Bar is hardly the best place for a quiet chat. It's not that the music is too loud – though there are small bands here nightly – and it's not that the acoustics are unforgiving. It's simply that the open spaces, the crowds of well-heeled revellers and the bright lighting prevent any sort of intimacy from developing. Despite the slick decor, the atmosphere is halfway between nightclub and business-class airport lounge. The drinks are perfectly OK, although for £14, we'd expect at least to be offered egg white for our whisky sour, and for it to be made as requested (we asked for it straight up; it was served on the rocks). There is an oriental flavour to the food, with dim sum and duck spring rolls, but other western favourites are available. *Disabled: toilet (in hotel). Music (jazz trio 9pm Mon-Sat, 8pm Sun).* **Map 8 F9.**

Zuma

5 Raphael Street, SW7 1DL (7584 1010/ www.zumarestaurant.com). Knightsbridge tube. **Open** noon-11pm Mon-Fri; 12.30-11pm Sat; noon-10pm Sun. **Food served** noon-2.15pm, 6-10.45pm Mon-Thur; noon-2.45pm, 6-10.45pm Fri; 12.30-3.15pm, 6-10.45pm Sat; 12.30-3.15pm, 6-10.15pm Sun. **Credit** AmEx, DC, MC, V.

This capacious, Japan-themed bar-restaurant (*see also p194*) has an open-plan design that one suspects would make the place terribly sad and terribly dated if there were no one in it. It's a good thing, then, that Zuma is always packed: at 10pm on a Monday night in February, the bar and the restaurant were both absolutely rammed. In spite of the crowds of eager customers, the impressive and knowledgeable staff took plenty of time over our drinks: a gentle old-fashioned made with a Japanese single malt, and a saketini that blended Tanqueray Ten with Tosatsuru Azure saké to potent effect. If you can bag a couple of stools, the people-watching is terrific. *Babies and children welcome: high chairs. Disabled: toilet. Function rooms (capacity 14). Restaurant. Tables outdoors (4, garden).* **Map 8 F9.**

Marylebone

★ Artesian

Langham Hotel, 1C Portland Place, W1B 1JA (7636 1000/www.artesian-bar.co.uk). Oxford Circus tube. **Open/food served** 5pm-1.30am daily. **Admission** (non-guests) £5 after 11pm Mon-Thur, Sun; £7 after 11pm Fri, Sat. **Credit** AmEx, DC, MC, V.

Breathtaking is the word for Artesian's list of cocktails: order any three, add service, and you won't get much change from £50. At least you'll be drinking them in some style. David Collins has done a fine job regenerating this high-ceilinged room at the Langham: lit by huge hanging lamps, the back bar is immeasurably dramatic; the chairs and tables are less eye-catching but still very handsome. The drinks almost live up to the setting. Our Essence of Shinjuku, rooted in Nigori saké and Yamazaki 18-year-old malt whisky, was a bit too subtle for its own good; the Cobbled Toddy, a tall mix of Monkey Shoulder whisky with orange, honey and a suspicion of port, was inspired. As well as the standard bar fare of

DRINKING

The Establishment. See p335.

omelettes and burgers, they offer sharing antipasti, meze and Chinese platters (£19 each). *Babies and children admitted (until 8pm). Disabled: toilet (in hotel). Games (dominoes).* **Map 9 H5.**

Mayfair

★ Coburg NEW (100)

2008 RUNNER-UP BEST BAR

The Connaught, Carlos Place, W1K 2AL (7499 7070/www.the-connaught.co.uk). Bond Street or Green Park tube. **Open** noon-1am daily. **Credit** AmEx, MC, V.

Luxurious, elegant and discreet, this is everything a good hotel bar should be. From the criminally comfortable, grey velvet, wing-backed chairs and chic, black glass tables, to the tiny skewer of iced fruit on a silver dish alongside each cocktail as a palate cleanser, every detail is considered. The champagne and wine selection is good, if showy, but it's the cocktails that are really worth coming for: an extensive list of expertly made classics, from creamy 19th-century flips to aromatic negronis and fruity champagne cobblers. The knowledgeable staff are worth consulting, as the spirits include several lesser-known treasures, particularly among Italian vermouths, bitters and gins. And while there's a short list of bar snacks – tuna, asparagus, tiger prawns all from £9 – the seemingly unending supply of complimentary nibbles should keep the wolf from the door. Prices are inevitably stiff, with cocktails starting at £12. *Disabled: toilet (hotel). Dress code: no jeans or trainers.* **Map 9 H7.**

Donovan Bar

Brown's Hotel, 33-34 Albemarle Street, W1S 4BP (7493 6020/www.roccofortehotels.com). Green Park tube. **Open/food served** 11am-1am Mon-Sat; noon-midnight Sun. **Credit** AmEx, DC, MC, V.

A smart, cosy little room can be found beyond the much less prepossessing main piano bar at Brown's. Lined with lovely black-and-white shots by the eponymous Swinging Sixties snapper, the Donovan mixes sophistication and buzz in more or less equal measures. Traditional cocktails are flawlessly executed (mojitos and manhattans, for example, cost £13.50), and the extravagantly long drinks menu offers some interesting contemporary variations on the classics (including the Appletini), and a wide range of non-alcoholic 'mocktails'. The free finger-food is imaginative and frequently replenished, and the staff are solicitous without being over-attentive. *Disabled: toilet (hotel). Music (jazz 9pm Mon-Sat; free).* **Map 9 J7.**

★ Library

Lanesborough Hotel, 1 Lanesborough Place, Hyde Park Corner, SW1X 7TA (7259 5599/ www.lanesborough.com). Hyde Park Corner tube. **Open** 11am-1am Mon-Sat; noon-10.30pm Sun. **Food served** noon-midnight Mon-Sat; noon-10.30pm Sun. **Credit** AmEx, DC, MC, V.

Whereas the bars at other high-end hotels in the Knightsbridge area are dressed to the nines and draw a younger, more boisterous crowd, the Library remains true to its name. The mood is gentle and mellow long into the night, helped along by deep leather wing chairs, a tinkling pianist, roaring fireplace and perpetually low lighting. Those books on the shelves are real, too. Attentive staff offer an extensive choice of vintage cognacs and above-par cocktails. Shame they can't supply pipe and slippers as well. *Disabled: toilet. Function rooms (capacity 180). Music (pianist 6.30pm daily; free).* **Map 9 G8.**

Mahiki

1 Dover Street, W1S 4LD (7493 9529/ www.mahiki.com). Green Park tube. **Open** 5.30pm-3.30am Mon-Fri; 7.30pm-3.30am Sat. **Food served** 5.30-10.30pm Mon-Fri; 7.30-10.30pm Sat. **Admission** £10 after 9.30pm Mon, Tue; £15 after 9.30pm Wed-Sat. **Credit** MC, V. The much-publicised popularity of Mahiki with junior members of the royal family means that you'll probably need to queue to get in, even

midweek; though once inside this Mayfair basement, you're as likely to end up sharing a booth with thirtysomething IT contractors on expenses as with rock star brats or blue bloods. Still, there's a nicely unbuttoned, relaxed feel to the place (encouraged by the faux-Hawaiiana, which extends to the grass-skirted bar staff), and the cocktails are excellent. Our zombie wasn't cheap (£12), but worth it for the dash of absinthe added to the rum and grapefruit juice. Zany TV chef Nancy Lam orchestrates the oriental bar snacks, and often provides the entertainment. *Bar available for hire. Music (DJs 10.30pm nightly).* **Map 9 J7.**

Polo Bar

Westbury Hotel, New Bond Street, W1S 2YF (7629 7755/www.westburymayfair.com). Bond Street or Oxford Circus tube. **Open** 11am-midnight Mon-Sat; noon-midnight Sun. **Food served** 11am-10.30pm daily. **Credit** AmEx, DC, MC, V.

Gorgeous art deco fittings that are just the right side of opulent characterise the Polo's individual statement of design intent; that's one reason it's such a hit with after-work revellers as well as discerning solo drinkers. Another is the cocktails: the barman here will knock you up a flawless version of one of the classics – in our case, a perfect Moscow Mule – or something a little more idiosyncratic: our De Vigne (£11) was a heady confection of vodka, lime and champagne. There's superior (and reasonably priced) bar food too: spring rolls, tapas, the usual club sandwiches and caesar salads, as well as pasta platters. *Babies and children admitted (until 6pm). Bar available for hire. Disabled: toilet (hotel).* **Map 9 H7.**

Piccadilly

Brumus Bar

Haymarket Hotel, 1 Suffolk Place, SW1Y 4BP (7470 4000/www.firmdale.com). Piccadilly Circus tube. **Open/food served** 11am-midnight daily. **Credit** AmEx, MC, DC, V.

A handsome fellow is Brumus, as you might expect at London's most talked-about new hotel. More surprisingly, he isn't a bit snobbish – in fact, on a Saturday night, at least half the attendees were decidedly unhip, somewhat elderly after-theatre types, lolling on the comfy mini furniture (think low easy chair rather than sloppy couch), fully accessorised by a horse made of cogs and delicious standing tea-light chandeliers. The pricey cocktails are imaginative, and we expected more bite from an intriguing Blazing Apple martini (Feijoa and red chilli, Feijoa vodka, Apple Sourz, lychee juice). There are good wines and, although not explicitly mentioned on the list, bottled beers such as Peroni. Food mostly comes in the form of platters (seafood, garden) at around £9, plus there are pre- and post-theatre dinners at £14.95 for 2 courses and £19.95 for three. *Babies and children admitted. Disabled: toilet. Entertainment (cabaret, 6pm Fri; free). Function rooms (capacity 50). Restaurant. Tables outdoors (5, pavement).* **Map 10 K7.**

St James's

★ Dukes Hotel (100)

35 St James's Place, SW1A 1NY (7491 4840/ www.dukeshotel.co.uk). Green Park tube. **Open** noon-11pm Mon-Sat; noon-10.30pm Sun. **Food served** noon-5pm daily. **Credit** AmEx, DC, MC, V.

Renovated top to bottom by hotelier Campbell Gray (of One Aldwych fame) and designer Mary Fox Linton, Dukes' discreet, highly regarded but old-fashioned bar has metamorphosed into a swish landmark destination for connoisseurs of life's good things. Ian Fleming was a regular and it's believed that Dukes' martinis, flamboyantly made at guests' tables, may have been the prototype for Commander Bond's favourite drink. You can get the Vesper martini here, but Dukes' own versions are stirred, not shaken. Choose from frozen Potocki vodka (a Polish rye variety) or Plymouth gin. The extra-dry vermouth is spritzed

into the chilled glasses with a perfume-style atomiser and there's a veritable rumba of lemon peel over the rims. With the expert barmen performing theatrically for each group of customers, there's a definite buzz about the place. And though the bill at the end of the night may well be best approached with your eyes closed, the payload is probably the best martini in the world. Trendy flavours (balsamic vinegar, chocolate, passion fruit, rose petal) and other such concoctions are available. The bar food has a distinctly traditional feeling, with clubby classics like salmon fish cakes, potted shrimps and welsh rarebit. *Dress: smart casual. Tables outdoors (4, garden).* **Map 9 J8.**

Soho

Floridita

100 Wardour Street, W1F 0TN (7314 4000/ www.floriditalondon.com). Tottenham Court Road tube. **Open** 5.30pm-2am Mon-Wed; (members/ guest list/doorman's discretion) 5.30pm-3am Thur-Sat. **Food served** 5.30pm-1am Mon-Wed; 5.30pm-1.30am Thur-Sat. **Admission** (after 7pm Thur-Sat) £15. **Credit** AmEx, DC, MC, V.

For a proper night out in the heart of Soho, take your beloved to Floridita, named after the famous Hemingway haunt in Havana: this glitzy but tasteful basement strives to get the drinks and entertainment just right. In the cavernous bar space, down the stunning staircase, the cocktail menu is categorised in Spanish. Most involve Havana Club Anejo Blanco expertly shaken with fresh mint, fresh lime, sugars and various dashes. The Hemingway Special also contains fresh grapefruit and Maraschino; the Presidente sweet vermouth and orange Curaçao; and the Chicago Flip, one of 14 *nuevo cubano* choices, vintage port shaken with egg yolk. Bar snacks such as deep-fried suckling pig with bacon are reasonable, the mains less so, and live music comes courtesy of Salsa Unica every evening. *See also p46. Babies and children admitted. Booking advisable. Disabled: toilet. Music (DJ & Cuban band 7.30pm Mon-Sat). Function rooms (capacity 60-80).* **Map 17 B3.**

LAB (100)

12 Old Compton Street, W1D 4TQ (7437 7820/ www.lab-townhouse.com). Leicester Square or Tottenham Court Road tube. **Open** 4pm-midnight Mon-Sat; 4-10.30pm Sun. **Food served** 6-11pm Mon-Sat; 6-10.30pm Sun. **Credit** AmEx, MC, V.

Keeping a happily mixed crowd of Sohoites well fuelled at this small, two-floor bar are some accomplished talents of the LAB (London Academy of Bartending) school. Graduates are aided by colleagues of considerable global experience, and can fix some 30 original cocktails (most around £7) or 50 classics, using high-end spirits and fresh ingredients. A Sri Thai menu (royal thai platter for two, £13.95) and fish cakes or marinated chicken wrapped in pandan leaves (both at £5.95) are offered by the well-known restaurant next door. *Bar available for hire. Dress: no ties. Music (DJs 8pm Mon-Sat).* **Map 17 C3.**

★ Milk & Honey (100)

61 Poland Street, W1F 7NU (7292 9949/ www.mlkhny.com). Oxford Circus tube. **Open** Non-members 6-11pm Mon-Fri; 7-11pm Sat. Members 6pm-3am Mon-Fri; 7pm-3am Sat. **Food served** 6pm-2am Mon-Sat. **Credit** AmEx, DC, MC, V.

'No name-dropping, no star fucking. No hooting, hollering, shouting or other loud behaviour' are some of the house rules here. This admirable restraint continues in the low-key speakeasy-style decor and in the lighting – so dim that you may have trouble reading the menu – but who cares, everyone looks fantastic. Milk & Honey is a members-only bar that is also open to all-comers at certain times, and it's worth reserving a table here for the cocktails alone. Staff know their business, and drinks (a long list includes sours, swizzles, punches and fizzes) are first rate and not

GATE

The Gate Restaurant, Bar and Club form the hub of Notting Hill's social scene. Spread over two venues dominating the junction at the very heart of Notting Hill, the Gate offers everything one could need for a great night out.

The establishment comprises a restaurant, bar, lounge, club and private rooms with many options available for private hire. Enjoy a light bite, a full dinner or delicious canapés with a wine list that compliments the food perfectly and an extensive cocktail selection. With a different DJ every night of the week offering up everything from R&B, Hip Hop and Funky House to Salsa, Soul and Pop classics, the party never ends at the Gate...

Gate Restaurant, Bar and Club

Gate Bar and Private Rooms, 90 Notting Hill Gate W11 3HP
Gate Bar and Lounge, 87 Notting Hill Gate W11 3JZ
Gate Restaurant and Club, 87 Notting Hill Gate W11 3JZ

Website: www.gaterestaurant.co.uk

For restaurant reservations, guestlist, party bookings and private hire
contact Chloe Campbell on 020 7727 9007
Email: general@gaterestaurant.co.uk

greedily priced (most cost £7.50). As well as crudité, cheese and cured meat platters, bar food also includes breast of Gressingham duck with honey and roasted potatoes (£14) and sides like edamame and shoestring potatoes (£3 each). A grown-up place and all the better for it.
Booking essential for non-members. Dress: smart casual; no sportswear. Function rooms (capacity 25). **Map 17 A3.**

South Kensington

190 Queensgate

The Gore Hotel, 190 Queensgate, SW7 5EX (7584 6601/www.gorehotel.co.uk). Gloucester Road or South Kensington tube. **Open/food served** noon-1am Mon-Wed, Sun; noon-2am Thur-Sat. **Credit** AmEx, MC, V.
The bar at the Gore Hotel groans with heavy, mahogany-panelled walls and oil paintings of grand old dukes, in strange contrast to the Euro-dance soundtrack, DJ nights and hip young bartenders showing off their knowledge of the 53-strong cocktail menu (£9.50 upwards). It's a mix that's thoroughly enjoyed by an eclectic clientele of hotel guests, concert-goers, businessmen and local students. Vodka lovers will be in heaven with 28 varieties to choose from, including six flavours of Stolichnaya (£6-£11); ditto whisky aficionados. The food menu features nicely executed twists on such standard bar favourites as tortilla filled with duck confit, mixed charcuterie, olives, pickles and sourdough to share and chargrilled rib-eye steak with mushroom, vein tomatoes and hand-cut fries. A velvet-draped 'Cinderella's Carriage' alcove at the back can be hired by those seeking further inebriated pomp and circumstance.
Music (DJs 10pm Sat; free). Function room (capacity 100). **Map 8 D9.**

West

Ladbroke Grove

Montgomery Place

31 Kensington Park Road, W11 2EU (7792 3921/www.montgomeryplace.co.uk). Ladbroke Grove tube. **Open** 5pm-midnight Mon-Fri, Sun; 2pm-midnight Sat. **Food served** 6-11pm daily. **Credit** AmEx, MC, V.
Any bar that takes its inspiration from the likes of the Rat Pack and Ernest Hemingway (with a soundtrack to match) is setting the standard pretty high, but the cocktails at this dark, slinky spot pass with flying colours. A watermelon fizz was a fabulously long and refreshing non-alcoholic option, while a Rio Bravo (fresh ginger mashed with almond syrup and shaken with lime and Sagatiba Pura cachaça, plus a lick of orange, £8) sorted the men from the boys. Substantial snacks have more than a hint of the Middle East and the Orient in dishes such as pan-fried duck with honey on a bed of ginger-infused wild rice, and shashlick of lamb. Staff may look trendier-than-thou, but are friendly and professional.
Babies and children admitted (afternoon Sat). Music (percussion 8pm Sun; free). Tables outdoors (2, pavement). **Map 19 B3.**

Trailer Happiness

177 Portobello Road, W11 2DY (7727 2700/ www.trailerhappiness.com). Ladbroke Grove or Notting Hill Gate tube. **Open** 5-11pm Mon-Fri; 6-11pm Sat. **Food served** 5-10.30pm Tue-Fri; 6pm-10.30pm Sat. **Credit** AmEx, MC, V.
A riot of oranges and browns, with '60s furniture, huge smoked-glass mirrors and Tretchikoff prints all over the walls, the bar takes pride of place in this basement and glows with a huge array of backlit bottles (many of them rum). Clued-up staff mix tikis and other rum cocktails, plus a number of house favourites such as the luscious grapefruit julep (Wyborowa vodka shaken with pink grapefruit, lime and pomegranate juices and a drizzle of honey over crushed ice) and the zingy Stone Pole (Zubrówka bison grass vodka with fresh lime, apple and ginger juices, plus ginger beer). Cocktails start at £6.50, and can be accompanied by snacks ('TV dinners') with a Deep

Coburg. See p330.

South accent, such as jerk chicken sandwich or Uncle Leroy's lamb and lemon racks.
Music (DJs 8pm Thur-Sat). Tables outdoors (4, pavement). **Map 19 B3.**

Westbourne Grove

Westbourne House NEW

2008 RUNNER-UP BEST BAR
65 Westbourne Grove, W2 4UJ (7229 2233/ www.westbournehouse.net). Bayswater or Royal Oak tube. **Open** 11am-11.30pm Mon-Thur; 11am-12.30am Fri, Sat; 11am-11pm Sun. **Food served** 11am-3pm, 5-11pm Mon-Fri; 11am-4.30pm, 5-11pm Sat, Sun. **Credit** AmEx, DC, MC, V.
Once a big old boozer, Westbourne House has swept up the fag ash and stale beer and replaced it with enough gilt mirrors, fairy lights and twinkly surfaces to keep Liberace happy. And this is a bar that's very much about showing off: the fag-smoking terrace out front teems with young professionals and people watching, or being watched. Inside, the twinkling gloom is shattered by pounding house music, perfect for the busy weekend crowd, but somewhat incongruous on a half-empty weeknight. The bar, however, makes a valiant effort to take drinks seriously, with a lengthy cocktail list that includes a section devoted to hard-core martinis, including an imposing gin and absinthe number, fruity options such as the gin, lemon and blackberry liqueur Bramble (both £7.50 plus 12.5% service), as well as just about every other classic under the sun, all very well made and served up in deliciously icy glassware.
Babies and children admitted (until 5pm). Bar available for hire. Function rooms (capacity 45). Tables outdoors (4, pavement). **Map 7 B6.**

★ Lonsdale

44-48 Lonsdale Road, W11 2DE (7727 4080/ www.thelonsdale.co.uk). Ladbroke Grove or Notting Hill Gate tube. **Open** 6pm-midnight Mon-Thur; 6pm-1am Fri, Sat; 6-11.30pm Sun. **Food served** 6-10.30pm daily. **Credit** AmEx, MC, V.
Top mixologist Dick Bradsell no longer tends bar at this beautifully over-designed 1970s sci-funk spot, but his spirits live on. The 18-page drinks menu is an historical tour of England's love affair with the mixed drink, from claret cups to sangarees to sours. Staff are proud of this heritage and it shows in a real desire to make sure you enjoy a great drink, be it a vintage classic or something from London's cocktail renaissance. The food is well judged, with classics such as bacon cheese burgers, and melon with parma ham, but given nice extra touches like onion marmalade with the burger and grapefruit and mint with the melon.
Babies and children admitted (until 8.30pm). Disabled: toilet. Function room (capacity 60).

Magician (9pm Wed; free). Music (DJs 9pm Fri, Sat; 8pm Sun; free). Tables outdoors (5, terrace). **Map 19 C3.**

South West

Fulham

Mokssh

222-224 Fulham Road, SW10 9NB (7352 6548/ www.mokssh.com). Fulham Broadway tube. **Open** noon-midnight Tue-Thur; noon-1am Fri, Sat; noon-10pm Sun. **Food served** noon-11pm Tue-Thur; noon-midnight Fri, Sat; noon-9.30pm Sun. **Credit** AmEx, DC, MC, V.
Lovers of lip-tingling cocktails and tempting Indian tapas will enjoy the bright pinks and reds of the decor, which lights up a depressing stretch of Fulham Road, even if some of the decorative touches tip into kitsch. If you're eating, perhaps opt for one of the Indian lagers or a robust red wine, as the fiery Indian tapas (around a fiver each for the likes of chicken hazari kebab – or push the boat out with tandoori scallops at £7.50) may zap any real appreciation of the flavoursome (lots of ginger and vanilla) cocktails.
Bar available for hire. **Map 13 C12.**

Parsons Green

The Establishment NEW

2008 RUNNER-UP BEST BAR
45-47 Parsons Green Lane, SW6 4HH (7384 2418/www.theestablishment.com). Parsons Green tube. **Open** 11am-midnight Mon-Sat; 11am-10.30pm Sun. **Food served** noon-10.30pm daily.
Bang opposite Parsons Green station, this stylish bar and restaurant (*see p243*) has already become a fixture for the well-heeled professionals of south-west London. Light and airy, with some eye-popping '60s geometric prints on the wall and tan leather upholstery, it's playful but casually sophisticated, an attitude that's also reflected in the drinks list, which nods to punches and cocktails of the past, but isn't afraid to stick the result in an outrageous tiki glass. British and seasonal ingredients are a recurrent theme in a fruity cocktail list (from £7) that includes a wide choice of gin (and genevers, gin's Dutch ancestor), lovage and nettle cordials, apples, mint and even several types of mead. A huge and varied wine list ranging from acclaimed English winery Chapel Down to New Zealand pinot noir also includes 40 or so by the glass (from £3.50 for a glass of Italian Trebbiano) as well as wine 'flights' (£15) featuring three 125ml wines assembled on different themes.
Babies and children admitted (until 5pm). Disabled: toilet. Function room (capacity 25). Restaurant (available for hire, capacity 55). Tables outdoors (6, courtyard).

DRINKING

South

Battersea

Dusk

339 Battersea Park Road, SW11 4LF (7622 2112/www.duskbar.co.uk). Battersea Park rail. **Open** 6pm-12.30am Tue, Wed; 6pm-1.30am Thur; 6pm-2am Fri, Sat. **Food served** 6-10.30pm Tue-Sat. **Credit** AmEx, MC, V.
Glossy furniture and fittings (leather cube stools, black wood tables, banquettes) attract a clubby, up-for-it crowd to this Battersea bar. It's not the place for a quiet drink to wind down after the working week from hell – but if letting it all hang loose with door-vetted dolly birds is your bag then Dusk delivers. Cocktails are a big thing, with a list of more than 60 on offer, among them classy favourites like the mint julep and look-what-we-can-do contemporary numbers like the Bloody Mary Soup containing chilli and garlic infusions and served with a side of toast. Food comes on sharing platters, more for soaking up booze than feasting on, covering corners from chicken yakitori to spinach and feta pies.
Bar available for hire. Dress: smart casual. Function room (capacity 100). Music (DJs 9pm Thur-Sat; free). Tables outdoors (10, terrace).

Frieda B

46 Battersea Rise, SW11 1EE (7228 7676/ www.frieda-b.co.uk). Clapham Junction rail/35, 37 bus. **Open** 5pm-midnight Mon-Thur, Sun; 5pm-2am Fri, Sat. **Credit** AmEx, MC, V.
The basement area of this small, two-floor bar works far better than the slightly awkward ground-level space. The latter offers comfy couches to sink into and an inbuilt DJ booth from which mix masters spin tunes at the weekend. Monthly wine tasting and mixology classes seek to draw in Clapham-ites looking for midweek entertainment, but otherwise this is more of a weekend spot. Friendly staff are a big plus, and new management

took over in 2008 with the aim of broadening the appeal of this admirably non-chainy venue, which offers a more intimate alternative to nearby bars.
Bar available for hire (Mon-Thur). Music (guitarist and singer 9pm Tue; DJs 10pm Fri, Sat; free). **Map 21 C4.**

Clapham

★ The Loft NEW

2008 WINNER BEST BAR
67 Clapham High St, SW4 7TG (7627 0792/ www.theloft-clapham.co.uk). Clapham North/ Clapham South tube. **Open** 6pm-midnight Mon-Thur; 5pm-1.30am Fri; noon-1.30am Sat; noon-midnight Sun. **Food served** 6-10pm Mon-Thur; 5-10pm Fri; noon-9pm Sat; noon-7pm Sun. **Credit** AmEx, MC, V.
This Clapham bar and restaurant offers punters pleasing views through a picture window spanning two sides of the venue. Food options are a notch up from gastropub favourites of the Moroccan lamb shank, plaice goujons, sea bass and asparagus risotto style. Cocktails are the stars of the extensive drinks menu, covering classics-with-a-twist (mojito with apple and pear juice), unusual creations (licorice whiskey sour), and seasonal specials using UK-sourced fruits where possible. Broadening the list of usual suspects on the draught taps is a range of less common bottled beers such as the Mexican Negra Modelo and American Anchor Steam. Weeknights are for lounging with serious cocktail in hand; weekends welcome DJs to up the ante with a roster of hip-shaking beats.
Babies and children admitted. Disabled: toilet. Music (DJs 9.30pm Fri, Sat; 4.30pm Sun; free). Restaurant (available for hire, capacity 50). **Map 22 B1.**

Lost Society

697 Wandsworth Road, SW8 3JF (7652 6526/ www.lostsociety.co.uk). Clapham Common tube/ Wandsworth Road rail/77, 77A bus. **Open**

5pm-1am Tue-Thur; 4pm-2am Fri; 11am-2am Sat; 11am-1am Sun. **Food served** 5-10pm Tue-Sun. **Admission** £5 after 9pm Fri, Sat. **Credit** AmEx, MC, V.
We're fans of Lost Society, former winner of the Time Out Best Bar award, and we're not the only ones – it's packed every weekend. Spanning six rooms, this behemoth bundles up sophisticated art deco decor with an aristo country-house party vibe to create a winning atmosphere of louche decadence. The extensive drinks list doesn't disappoint: from interesting bottled beers to bygone-era cocktails, plus whole bottles of spirits (Rip Van Winkle bourbon, £95 including mixers), they're all here. Meals comprise the temptingly simple likes of roast chicken with emmental mash, or pork fillet with rösti potatoes, followed by vanilla and saffron crème brûlée. Special events – Tuesday night cocktail classes, 1980s-themed fondue parties – tempt midweek party-goers.
Bar available for hire. Music (DJs 7pm Thur; 9pm Fri, Sat). Tables outdoors (20, garden). **Map 22 A1.**

South East

Blackheath

Zerodegrees

29-31 Montpelier Vale, SE3 0TJ (8852 5619/ www.zerodegrees.co.uk). Blackheath rail. **Open** noon-midnight Mon-Sat; noon-11.30pm Sun. **Food served** noon-11pm Mon-Sat; noon-10.30pm Sun. **Credit** AmEx, MC, V.
Food, or more accurately drink, miles are non-existent at this popular Blackheath bar and restaurant serving beers brewed on the premises. The microbrewery produces its own pilsner, pale ale, black lager and wheat ale, plus a changing choice of speciality or seasonal brews. If you're particularly taken with your pint you can buy some to take home, in anything from a four-pinter (£9.80) to a 50-litre keg (£95). Superior woodfired pizzas are the main belly-fillers on the menu, with

The Loft

umpteen number of topping combos: how about steak and salsa; salmon and mascarpone; or pear and gorgonzola. You could also opt for mussels cooked six different ways (thermidor, thai green curry or, of course, marinière), or bangers and mash – perfect with a pint.

Babies and children welcome: high chairs. Restaurant (available for hire, capacity 180). Tables outdoors (10, terrace).

Greenwich

Inc Bar

7A College Approach, SE10 9HY (8858 6721/ www.incbar.com). Cutty Sark DLR. **Open** 6pm-1.30am Wed, Thur; 7pm-3am Fri, Sat; 5pm-midnight Sun. **Credit** MC, V.

The longest cocktail list in south-east London offers nearly three dozen tempting variations. Eight martinis include apple and lychee versions made with heavenly Zubrówka, plus tequila- and rum-based ones that stretch the definition of a martini. If you need to impress, several champagne cocktails are on hand to help, or you could splash out on a £45 bottle of Montmains chablis. Located in Greenwich Market, Inc Bar is one of several drinking dens and eateries run by the same company in the local area, including Inc Brasserie in the fairly new O2 Arena at the former Dome. This outpost verges on the kitsch, with gumdrop-coloured lamps and decorative carnival masks lurking about.

Bar available for hire. Function rooms (capacity 50). Music (DJs 10pm Thur, Fri; 11pm Sat; free-£5).

London Bridge & Borough

Hide Bar

39-45 Bermondsey Street, SE1 3XF (7403 6655/www.thehidebar.com). London Bridge tube/rail. **Open** 10am-midnight Mon, Tue;

10am-1am Wed, Thur; 10am-2am Fri, Sat. **Food served** noon-4pm, 5.30-10pm Mon-Sat. **Credit** AmEx, MC, V.

The cocktail is king at this relaxed, unpretentious shrine to alcohol in its many forms. The staff are so enthused they will make you anything that catches your eye in the selection of vintage cocktail books kept close to hand. The grape and the grain aren't far behind, however, with a selection of 150 wines and a changing roster of draught beers from Greenwich Meantime Brewery. The food menu is also modified daily, and features the likes of Neal's Yard cheese platters, augmented by burgers, salads (chicken ceasar with chorizo, say, or bacon and avocado), as well as more substantial offerings, such as globe-spanning English lamb served with couscous and tzatziki. Feel like hiding from the word? The mellow, muted interior and eminently comfortable sofas make it easy.

Babies and children admitted. Bar available for hire. Drink tasting (7pm Tue; free). Function room (capacity 50). **Map 12 Q9.**

East

Bethnal Green

Bistrotheque
Napoleon Bar (100)

23-27 Wadeson Street, E2 9DR (8983 7900/ www.bistrotheque.com). Bethnal Green tube/ Cambridge Heath rail/55 bus. **Open** 6pm-midnight Mon-Sat; 4pm-11pm Sun. **Credit** AmEx, MC, V.

Off a rather unprepossessing street in Hackney, its entrance marked only by a planter and some smoking tables, this narrow ground-floor bar is sombre and a little austere in decor (warehouse bricks painted gunmetal grey, black and grey striped carpet). It's grown-up in attitude (wood panels and a Courvoisier Napoleon mirror behind

the bar, chandeliers in front, a bossa 'Blue Monday' on the stereo). There's a list of familiar beers, but it's better to explore the 30-strong wine list and two dozen cocktails. The Dark 'n' Stormy (Goslings dark rum, ginger ale, lime, bitters) was unimpeachable; a slightly underpowered Lemon Drop (Ketel Citron, lemon juice, lemon bitters) delivered an impressively nostalgic hit of 1980s sweetshop. *See also p108.*

Babies and children admitted. Disabled: toilet. Music (cabaret dates vary, ticket only). Function room (capacity 64). Restaurant.

Shoreditch

Green & Red

51 Bethnal Green Road, E1 6LA (7749 9670/ www.greenred.co.uk). Liverpool Street tube/rail/ 8, 26, 48 bus. **Open** 5.30pm-midnight Mon-Thur; 5.30pm-1am Fri, Sat; 5.30-10.30pm Sun. **Food served** 6-11pm Mon-Sat; 6-10.30pm Sun. **Credit** AmEx, MC, V.

This Mexican bar/cantina (*see also p47*) is as comfortable dishing out litre-jug cocktail options to Friday night tables of after-work carousers as talking you through the niceties of a £50 shot of aged tequila. Dressed in appropriate bar-shack distressed wood and generic Latin American propaganda posters, it is the place to drop in for a hangover-straightening Michelada with a 'brunch' of Jaliscan bar snacks – say, pan-fried chorizo and 'yam bean' salad with cucumber and peanuts. The unparalleled selection of premium tequilas is best encountered as a 'tasting flight' of three shots (£12 to £59.40). Quality cocktails include a tall Diablo (tequila, lime juice, ginger ale, crème de cassis) and pomegranate margarita.

Babies and children welcome: high chair. Disabled: toilet. Music (DJs 9pm Fri, Sat; free). Restaurant. Tables outdoors (6, terrace). **Map 6 S4.**

Sosho

Charlie Wright's
International Bar
45 Pitfield Street, N1 6DA (7490 8345).
Old Street tube/rail. **Open** noon-1am Mon-Wed;
noon-4am Thur, Fri; 5pm-4am Sat; 5pm-2am
Sun. **Food served** noon-3pm, 5-10pm Mon-Fri;
5-10pm Sat, Sun. **Admission** £4 after 10pm
Fri, Sat; £3 Sun. **Credit** MC, V.
Located just beyond the main Hoxton drag, this
decidedly unpretentious watering hole shares none
of its neighbouring area's airs and graces. During
the day you can fill up on perfectly passable Thai
food for a fiver, or pass the time watching football
on the big screen, playing pool or trying your hand
at darts. A late licence at weekends and regular
jazz nights bring in the night-time revellers, who
care less about posing than letting the good times
roll. Cocktails just wouldn't fit in with the vibe of
the joint, but the bottled beer and spirits on offer
fit the bill for accompanying the general, laid-back
vibe of the place.
Games (darts, fruit machine, pool tables).
Music (DJs 8pm Thur-Sun). Restaurant.
Map 6 Q3.

Loungelover (100)
1 Whitby Street, E1 6JU (7012 1234/www.
loungelover.co.uk). Liverpool Street tube/rail.
Open 6pm-midnight Mon-Thur, Sun; 5.30pm-
1am Fri; 6pm-1am Sat. **Food served** 6-11.30pm
Mon-Fri, Sun; 7-11.30pm Sat. **Credit** AmEx, DC,
MC, V.
Eclectic is a description that could have been
coined for Loungelover, the East End bar owned
by the same gang who run Annexe Trois in the
West End and Les Trois Garçons restaurant (*see*
p109) on the next block. Flaming torches greet
visitors, and matters never step down a notch from
there: the interior decoration manages to
accommodate stuffed animal heads, outsize
champagne glasses filled with flowers,
mismatched chairs, opulent chandeliers and more
hot-pink and cherry-red than should be allowed in
one room. The overriding impression is of class
not clutter, however, which makes Loungelover a
sure bet if you're on the lookout for a venue that'll
make you look good by association. An impressive
cocktail list (watch out for the 12.5% service
charge added to your bill) includes the wasabi-
spiked Zatoichi, and light bites are in a Japanese
vein – salmon tartare, breadcrumb and miso-
encrusted pork, tuna sashimi salad.

Booking advisable. Disabled: toilet. Music
(DJs 7pm Fri, Sat; live music: cabaret/soul
Sun, call for details). **Map 6 S4.**

Sosho
2 Tabernacle Street, EC2A 4LU (7920 0701/
www.sosho3am.com). Moorgate or Old Street
tube/rail. **Open** noon-midnight Tue; noon-1am
Wed, Thur; noon-3am Fri; 7pm-4am Sat; 9pm-
6am Sun. **Food served** noon-10.30pm Tue-Fri;
7-11pm Sat. **Admission** £5-£12 after 9pm Fri-
Sun. **Credit** AmEx, DC, MC, V.
If it's well-executed cocktails you're after, this east
London outpost of the Match bar empire delivers
the goods. Fruity concoctions include the Space
Gin Smash with muddled grapes and elderflower,
while darker creations include the lethal-sounding
Zombie containing five different rums and, it's
stipulated, 'Strictly limited to two per person per
night.' Match's own wines and a handful of beers
are also available. To line the stomach, there are
snacky bites such as quesadillas and prawn
skewers, as well as the filling likes of beer-battered
fish and chips, or jerk chicken sandwich with
mango salsa. Sosho is a DJ bar with a dedicated
dancefloor that moves it into clubbing territory,
and tends to attract a clientele from the City rather
than Shoreditch side of the tracks.
Babies and children admitted (until 6pm).
Disabled: toilet. Function room (capacity 100).
Music (DJs 8pm Wed-Fri; 9pm Sat, Sun).
Map 6 Q4.

North
Camden Town
& Chalk Farm

Gilgamesh
Stables Market, Chalk Farm Road, NW1 8AH
(7482 5757/www.gilgameshbar.com). Chalk Farm
tube. **Open** noon-3pm, 6pm-2.30am Mon-Fri;
noon-2.30am Sat, Sun. **Food served** noon-
3pm, 6-11pm daily. **Credit** AmEx, MC, V.
Gilgamesh is a Babylonian theme bar and
restaurant so screamingly over the top that it
makes Kubla Khan's pleasure dome look like a
bouncy castle. Accessed by escalator from the
market, the carved interior is reputed to have taken
600 sculptors six months to create – and that's not
hard to believe. Every surface is embellished to a
disorienting degree: bronze walls depict ancient

battles, pillars are inlaid with polished stones, and
ceilings shape-shift in the coloured spotlights. By
the time you've weaved a path to the lapis lazuli
bar you'll probably be prepared for the cocktail
menu: original recipe drinks are expertly mixed
and rich in eastern promise. The Ziggurat is fresh
watermelon juice, 42 Below vodka and chilli; the
Anu muddles Absolut Apeach, Plymouth gin,
peach purée and cucumber. Prophets of doom still
wail at the gates, but there's no sign of this
Babylon falling in the near future.
Babies and children admitted. Function room
(capacity 250). Music (DJs 8pm Fri, Sat; free).
Map 27 C1.

Islington

Elk in the Woods
39 Camden Passage, N1 8EA (7226 3535/
www.the-elk-in-the-woods.co.uk). Angel tube.
Open 10.30am-11pm daily. **Food served** noon-
10pm Mon; 10.30am-10.30pm Tue-Sat; 10.30am-
9.30pm Sun. **Credit** MC, V.
A decidedly grown-up drinking hole on pretty
Camden Passage, where you can look forward to a
proper seat and waiter service while you indulge
your inner sophisticate. Reservations are essential
from Thursday onwards and advisable the rest of
the week. The decor is laid-back boho, with a
sturdy concrete bar, roughed-up wooden tables, a
wall of ornate mirrors and a large stag's head –
the perfect lounging ground for a well-to-do N1
crowd. Classy bar snacks include the likes of
grilled risotto cakes with leek, thyme and taleggio,
and salt and pepper calamari served with a chilli
and palm sugar sauce. The concise wine list starts
at £14.50, cocktails from £7.
Babies and children admitted. Booking advisable.
Tables outdoors (4, pavement). **Map 5 O2.**

25 Canonbury Lane
25 Canonbury Lane, N1 2AS (7226 0955).
Highbury & Islington tube/rail. **Open** 5pm-
midnight Mon-Thur; 4pm-1am Fri; noon-1am
Sat; 1pm-12.30am Sun. **Food served** 6-10pm
Mon-Thur; 1-6pm Sun. **Credit** MC, V.
It's out with the Tiffany blue and in with a new
(slightly less appealing) brown and gold scheme.
And where once there were tapas to go with your
tom collins, there's now Thai food (red curry,
£5.95). This bar still has merit, though: cosy
dimensions, atmospheric lighting, bare boards and
chandeliers. Book the small conservatory at the
back for a snug soirée or sink into one of the low-
slung sofas by the big window in the front.
Cocktails (caipirinhas, whisky sours) are a
reasonable £6.50, though the crowd is more of a
wine-drinking, in-for-the-long-haul bunch. Decent
reds and whites start at £14 a bottle.
Babies and children admitted (until 7pm).

North West
Hampstead

Roebuck
15 Pond Street, NW3 2PN (7433 6871). Belsize
Park tube. **Open** noon-11pm Mon-Thur; noon-
midnight Fri, Sat; noon-10.30pm Sun. **Food**
served noon-3pm, 5-10pm Mon-Fri; noon-10pm
Sat; noon-9pm Sun. **Credit** AmEx, MC, V.
In stark contrast to the grey monster of a hospital
that towers above this place, the Roebuck is a
stylish and airy spot that is as well suited to a
quick cuppa as a raucous party in the basement
bar. It's a relative of the Eagle (*see p111*) in
Farringdon, so it's no surprise to find the food is
an adventurous take on pub grub – the halloumi
burger is a consistent favourite. There is a good
range of beers on tap too, from Früli to
Staropramen, as well as guest beers. Venture into
the terrific garden in summer and you'll find
many a medic nursing a pint. A good spot to meet
up before venturing to some of the more
pretentious places in Hampstead and Belsize
villages – or you could just decide to stay put.
Babies and children admitted (until 7pm).
Disabled: toilet. Function room (capacity 100).
Games (board games). Quiz (7pm Tue; £2).
Tables outdoors (16, garden). **Map 28 C3.**

Pubs

Organic bitter and cider from Suffolk, extra stout from Yorkshire, traditional London porter from Chiswick, and coffee beer from New Charlton – the range of brews available from the pubs on these pages is eclectic even before you start exploring the Belgian, German, Californian and Japanese options available on tap in the capital. The hostelries recommended here also provide a vital atmospheric antidote to the soulless chains that threaten but still haven't quite managed to engulf Britain. As such they deserve your support. These gems make ideal venues for meeting up before a meal out; for pubs where food is a large part of the offer, see the **Gastropubs** chapter (starting on p111). And for many more fabulous London pubs, grab a copy of the latest *Time Out Bars, Pubs & Clubs Guide*.

Central
Bloomsbury

Duke
7 Roger Street, WC1N 2PB (7242 7230/ www.dukepub.co.uk). Chancery Lane, Holborn or Russell Square tube. **Open** noon-11pm Mon-Sat; noon-10.30pm Sun. **Food served** noon-10pm Mon-Sat; noon-9.30pm Sun. **Credit** MC, V.
Like the Duke himself (of York that is), the one who marched his men to the top of the hill only to march them down again, this place has its quirks. Seating in the tiny main bar is a mix of vintage wooden booths and brightly coloured, Formica-topped tables dotted around on scuffed parquet. A shiny red piano beckons from one side, though you'd have to know your chops, since cool jazz is the music of choice. Portraits of vintage film starlets sets the 1930s to '50s mood. Food is served in a wood-lined dining room. For beer, Adnams and Greene King are on tap. *Babies and children admitted. Restaurant. Tables outdoors (3, pavement).* **Map 4 M4.**

★ **Lamb**
94 Lamb's Conduit Street, WC1N 3LZ (7405 0713). Holborn or Russell Square tube. **Open** 11am-midnight Mon-Sat; noon-10.30pm Sun. **Food served** noon-9pm daily. **Credit** AmEx, MC, V.

Redolent of the days when ales were real, men were men, and a pub was a pub, the Lamb does at least have the advantage of having been established in 1729. It found fame as a theatrical haunt when the A-list included Sir Henry Irving and stars of music hall; they're commemorated in vintage photos, surrounded by well-worn seats, much polished wood and a few elderly knick-knacks. In summer there's a patio at the back, and year-round punters range from discerning students to Gray's Inn barristers, though on our last visit we chatted to a pair of fur-coated old dears three sheets to the wind and happy as Larry (Olivier, perhaps). *Function room (capacity 40). No piped music or jukebox. Tables outdoors (3, patio; 3, pavement).* **Map 4 M4.**

Chancery Lane

Seven Stars
53 Carey Street, WC2A 2JB (7242 8521). Chancery Lane or Holborn tube. **Open** 11am-11pm Mon-Fri; noon-11pm Sat; noon-10.30pm Sun. **Food served** noon-3pm, 5-10pm Mon-Fri; 1-9pm Sat, Sun. **Credit** AmEx, MC, V.
People pile down here on weekday evenings, knowing full well they'll probably be forced to drink on the pavement outside – but they don't care. It's a fantastic social hub for London characters, from eccentric lawyers to burlesque babes. If you can squeeze into the small but perfectly proportioned interior, you'll get a slice of low-rent, bohemian London: archive film posters, checked tablecloths and an antique dumb waiter bringing food down from the tiny kitchen upstairs. The grub is unpretentious; there are no extensive menus to browse, just a few words chalked on the blackboard. It's one of the few London pubs where you're happy to pay £6 for a large glass of burgundy because you know you aren't being ripped off; the beers are also wonderfully kept, and the house martini a must-try. *No piped music or jukebox.* **Map 10 M6.**

Clerkenwell & Farringdon

★ **Fox & Anchor**
115 Charterhouse Street, EC1M 6AA (7250 1300/www.foxandanchor.com). Barbican or Farringdon tube/rail. **Open** 8am-11pm Mon-Fri; noon-11pm Sat. **Food served** 8am-11pm Mon-Fri. **Credit** AmEx, MC, V.
The Malmaison hotel chain recently restored and updated the beautiful interior of this old Smithfield meatpackers' favourite. The long bar is still there (now with a pewter top), as are the wood fixtures, the lovely snugs and the 8am weekday opening (try the full English at £8.95). Aside from the six hotel rooms upstairs, the most eye-catching change is the addition of a TV in a spot not central enough to be of much use, but visible enough to be a distraction. However, with an array of rarely seen bottled beers supplemented by six cask ales, the Fox is a beer-drinker's paradise. *Babies and children admitted (until 7pm). Disabled: toilet.* **Map 5 O5.**

Jerusalem Tavern (100)
55 Britton Street, EC1M 5UQ (7490 4281/ www.stpetersbrewery.co.uk). Farringdon tube/ rail. **Open** 11am-11pm Mon-Fri. **Food served** noon-3pm Mon, Fri; noon-3pm, 5-9.30pm Tue-Thur. **Credit** AmEx, MC, V.
The only pub to belong to the small St Peter's brewery at Bungay in Suffolk, the cosily tatty JT serves their sought-after ales in creeky, wood-panelled comfort. Behind the bar, seemingly hidden amid the timber divides and occasional raised seating, is a row of barrels, above which a board lists beers and their ABVs: Suffolk Gold, Grapefruit, Cinnamon & Apple, Organic, the whole range. In winter, a homely fireside encourages the desire for warm sustenance. Fabulous haddock and salmon fish cakes and various sausages (especially on Tuesdays) fit the bill nicely. *Bar available for hire (weekends only). No piped music or jukebox. Tables outdoors (2, pavement).* **Map 5 O4.**

Seven Stars

Nightingale. See p342.

Covent Garden

Lamb & Flag
33 Rose Street, WC2E 9EB (7497 9504). Covent Garden tube. **Open** 11am-11pm Mon-Sat; noon-10.30pm Sun. **Food served** noon-3pm Mon-Fri, Sun; noon-4.30pm Sat. **Credit** MC, V.
Defiantly traditional, the Lamb & Flag is always a squeeze – as it has been for the last 300 years – but no one seems to mind. Character is now in short supply around Covent Garden, and this place has the stuff in spades. On tap are draught Young's, Greene King and Courage Best, bottled Budvar and Peroni, and a daily menu usually including a ploughman's with a choice of eight cheeses. The afternoon-only bar upstairs is 'ye olde' to a fault. Pictures of passed-on regulars – 'Barnsey', Corporal Bill West et al – testify to its neighbourhood feel.
Babies and children admitted (lunch only). Music (jazz 7.30pm Sun; free). No piped music or jukebox. **Map 18 D4**.

Fitzrovia

Green Man
36 Riding House Street, W1W 7ES (7580 9087). Goodge Street or Oxford Circus tube. **Open** noon-11pm Mon-Sat; noon-10.30pm Sun. **Food served** noon-10pm Mon-Sat; noon-9.30pm Sun. **Credit** AmEx, MC, V.
The Green Man's USP is draught ciders: five on our visit, with several in bottles, a couple of ales

and ice-cold Sierra Nevada on tap. Aided by matey staff and a busy yet not noisy vibe, it's also a fine place for a drink and a chat. And if the incongruous '80s-indie soundtrack isn't quite up your alley, you might find the darker, sleeker upstairs bar a more mellow spot. This is one place were modernisation has worked.
Function room (capacity 70). Music (DJ/bands 7pm Thur, Fri; free). Tables outdoors (3, pavement). **Map 9 J5**.

Holborn

Princess Louise
208-209 High Holborn, WC1V 7BW (7405 8816). Holborn tube. **Open** 11am-11pm Mon-Fri; noon-11pm Sat; noon-10.30pm Sun. **Food served** noon-2.30pm, 6-8.30pm Mon-Thur; noon-2.30pm Fri, Sat. **Credit** AmEx MC, V.
The decorated tiles, stained-glass windows, finely cut mirrors and ornate plasterwork in the Princess Louis have all recently been carefully refurbished. The Victorian wood partitions create a rather confusing warren of snugs and alcoves; and the lavish lavs and Corinthian columns are especially impressive. The beer is all from Samuel Smith and sold for around £2 a pint: astonishing, given the fancy furnishings and central location. If on form, the Old Brewery Bitter can be a top drop; the bottled cherry beer, when poured in with the Extra Stout, is the nearest you'll get to liquid black forest gateau.
No piped music or jukebox. **Map 18 E2**.

Knightsbridge

Swag & Tails
10-11 Fairholt Street, SW7 1EG (7584 6926/ www.swagandtails.com). Knightsbridge tube. **Open** 11am-11pm Mon-Fri. **Food served** noon-3pm, 6-10pm Mon-Fri. **Credit** AmEx, MC, V.
The Swag & Tails feels like a cosy village local in the Surrey Stockbroker Belt, such is its setting, deep in an exceptionally exclusive warren of mews houses. The stripped pine and heavy curtains are plummy, and the ostentatious displays of champagne make it practically a period piece. Still, despite its dated feel and the inevitably too-high prices (burgers are £11.25), the welcome is usually warm, the music hand-picked (Dylan's last album when we visited) and the beer decent.
Babies and children admitted (restaurant only). Restaurant available for hire (Sat, Sun; capacity 34). Tables outdoors (6, conservatory). **Map 8 E9**.

Marylebone

Windsor Castle
27-29 Crawford Place, W1H 4LJ (7723 4371). Edgware Road tube. **Open** 11am-11pm Mon-Thur; 11am-midnight Fri, Sat; noon-10.30pm Sun. **Food served** noon-3pm, 6-10pm Mon-Fri, Sun; 6-10pm Sat. **Credit** MC, V.
A host of minor celebrities (think the likes of Joe Brown, Keith Chegwin and Dennis Waterman) may, or may not, have seen the laughably bad portrait of Prince Charles with a huge poppy and decided to dish out their autographs here. Landlord Michael Tierney's fixation with all things British and royal takes pub kitsch to absurd and wonderful lengths. Beers (Bombardier, Wadworth 6X, Adnams) have an unsurprisingly British bent, though the food is pub Thai and there's a German Blue Max Liebfraumilch (£3.30/£12) on the wine list. The fantastic Handlebar [moustache] Club has its monthly meeting here.
Babies and children admitted. Restaurant (available for hire, capacity 24). Tables outdoors (5, pavement). **Map 8 F5**.

Soho

Crown & Two Chairmen
31 Dean Street, W1D 3SB (7437 8192). Tottenham Court Road tube. **Open** noon-11pm Mon-Thur; noon-11.30pm Fri, Sat; noon-10.30pm Sun. **Food served** noon-10pm Mon-Sat; noon-9pm Sun. **Credit** AmEx, MC, V.
An array of global beers ('19 and counting') draws huge and happy crowds to the Mitchell Brothers' successful overhaul of this Soho institution. The colourful continental taps – Belle-Vue Kriek, Paulaner, Maredsous Blonde, Schneider Weisse, Küppers Kölsch and even Budvar Dark – stand in line with more familiar ones for Wadworth 6X and Guinness. Such variety comes in a more downbeat, open-plan interior, with plenty of space for you to tuck into your West Country Casterbridge beef burger with chips (£6.90). For intimacy, head to the refurbished space upstairs.
Babies and children admitted (until 5pm). **Map 17 B3**.

South Kensington

Anglesea Arms
15 Selwood Terrace, SW7 3QG (7373 7960/ www.capitalpubcompany.com). South Kensington tube. **Open** 11am-11pm Mon-Sat; noon-10.30pm Sun. **Food served** noon-3pm, 6.30-10pm Mon-Fri; noon-5pm, 6-10pm Sat; noon-5pm, 6-9.30pm Sun. **Credit** AmEx, MC, V.
DH Lawrence's local (a photograph on the wall shows him in Selwood Terrace on his wedding day in 1914), the Anglesea Arms was also once frequented by Dickens, and hosted the plotting of the Great Train Robbery. The ghost of a rather mysterious woman called Fifi, depicted in naked splendour in a painting on the wall, apparently roams the basement at night. Plenty of aristocratic etchings and late 19th-century London photos adorn the dark, panelled wood walls, adding to

the feel of a place lost in time. Real ales are the speciality here – Brakspear Oxford Gold, Hogs Back and Adnams among them – but there's Kirin and San Miguel on draught for the young 'uns. *Babies and children admitted. No piped music or jukebox. Restaurant (available for hire). Tables outdoors (12, terrace).* **Map 4 D11.**

West

Hammersmith

★ Dove

19 Upper Mall, W6 9TA (8748 9474). Hammersmith or Ravenscourt Park tube. **Open** 11am-11pm Mon-Sat; noon-10.30pm Sun. **Food served** noon-3pm, 5-10pm Mon-Fri; noon-4pm, 5-9pm Sat; noon-5pm Sun. **Credit** AmEx, MC, V.
Bang on the river near Hammersmith Bridge, the Dove can be cosy and romantic on a chilly winter's night (the perfect place for a date, in fact), but in the summer, it gets packed out. The pub is divided into four distinct areas: a decent-sized riverside garden/terrace, a low-ceilinged lounge bar, a gorgeous conservatory area with vine leaves and fairy lights snaking across the ceiling, and the tiny front bar, which merits an entry in Guinness World Records. Real ales including London Pride, ESB and Chiswick are very well kept. The 17th-century building is also steeped in history: 'Rule Britannia' was penned in an upstairs room, and Charles II and Nell Gwynne once caroused here.
No piped music or jukebox. Tables outdoors (8, riverside terrace). **Map 20 A4.**

Holland Park

Ladbroke Arms

54 Ladbroke Road, W11 3NW (7727 6648/ www.capitalpubcompany.com/ladbroke). Holland Park tube. **Open** 11am-11pm Mon-Sat; noon-10.30pm Sun. **Food served** noon-2.30pm, 7-9.30pm Mon-Fri; 12.30-3pm, 7-9.30pm Sat, Sun. **Credit** AmEx, MC, V.
The police station over the road once provided much of the Ladbroke's clientele. Now this gastropub is better known for its floral displays (the beer garden at the front is wildly colourful). Despite the smart dining section at the rear (and a wine list to match), the place does still draw in low-key middle-aged locals to enjoy a pint – Doom Bar from Cornwall's Sharp's brewery, perhaps, or Adnams Broadside. The well-upholstered, carpeted interior and efficient air-conditioning add to the sense of grown-up quality.
Babies and children admitted (dining only). No piped music or jukebox. Tables outdoors (12, terrace). **Map 7 A7.**

Maida Vale

★ Prince Alfred & Formosa Dining Rooms

5A Formosa Street, W9 1EE (7286 3287). Warwick Avenue tube. **Open** noon-11pm daily. **Food served** noon-3pm, 6.30-10pm Mon-Sat; noon-4pm, 7-10pm Sun. **Credit** MC, V.
The layout of this beautifully preserved 19th-century pub reflects Victorian society: a series of partitions around the magnificent central bar creates separate snugs originally intended to keep the classes and the sexes apart. Nowadays, though you can move between snugs via waist-height hatchways, these cramped compartments can be a slightly awkward environment for socialising. They're best for small groups, but may deter late arrivals who might feel they are intruding on a private party. The locals haven't been deterred from flocking here, however, for pints of Erdinger, Bombardier, Staropramen or Peroni.
Babies and children admitted. Disabled: toilet. Restaurant (available for hire). Tables outdoors (3, pavement). **Map 1 C4.**

South West

Barons Court

Colton Arms

187 Greyhound Road, W14 9SD (7385 6956). Barons Court tube. **Open** noon-3pm, 5.30-11.30pm Mon-Thur; noon-3pm, 5.30pm-midnight Fri; noon-4pm, 6.30pm-midnight Sat; noon-4pm, 6.30-11pm Sun. **Credit** MC, V.
A proper boozer, this, which, depending on your outlook, might be just the sort of ale-soaked cubbyhole you've been thirsting for, or the last place you'd hope to find yourself on a Friday night (last time we did, there were only five of us in the place, including the dear old landlord). With its tiny, trinket-adorned front bar, dark oak furniture and gentle refusal to refurb, the effect is somewhere between a *Life on Mars* '70s time warp and 'Barons Court does bucolic' (signs above the toilets read 'wenches' and 'sires'). Come to sup on London Pride, Timothy Taylor Landlord and Old Speckled Hen, served up in dimpled beer mugs. There's also a garden out back, perfect for June's Stella Artois Wimbledon warm-up at the nearby Queen's Club.
Children admitted (garden). Tables outdoors (4, garden).

Colliers Wood

★ Sultan

78 Norman Road, SW19 1BT (8542 4532). Colliers Wood or South Wimbledon tube. **Open** noon-11pm Mon-Thur, Sun; noon-midnight Fri, Sat.* **Credit** MC, V.

An ale drinker's nirvana, named after the famed 1830s racehorse, the Sultan is a much-loved locals' boozer and the only London pub owned by Wiltshire's Hop Back Brewery; on the weekly beer club evenings, chattering middle-aged customers enjoy the delights of GFB, Entire Stout, Summer Lightning and Quad Hop for the princely sum of just £1.90 a pint (carryouts are also available). The saloon bar is named after the beer-loving Ted Higgins, an actor from the original cast of Radio 4's *The Archers*; a smaller public bar shares its decor of cream walls and green panelling.
Beer club (6-9pm Wed; free). Disabled: toilet. Quiz (8.30pm Tue, Sept-June). Tables outdoors (8, garden).

Parsons Green

★ White Horse (100)

1-3 Parsons Green, SW6 4UL (7736 2115/ www.whitehorsesw6.com). Parsons Green tube. **Open** 9.30-am-11.30pm Mon-Wed, Sun; 9.30am-midnight Thur-Sat. **Food served** 10am-10.30pm daily. **Credit** AmEx, MC, V.
A stupendously popular SW6 stalwart – never mind the tired 'Sloaney Pony' nickname – does what it does best exceptionally well: namely, the fantastic (and somewhat mind-boggling) array of beers. There are 60 (count 'em) available at any one time, including 30 on draught, eight of which are cask ales (the likes of Harveys Sussex Best, Adnams Broadside and a rotating array of guest beers). There's always a cask mild, stout and porter on offer too, so it'll come as no surprise to hear that the pub hosts regular beer festivals. Punters are a generally well-to-do and decidedly loud lunch – off-duty chinos and air-kissing feature heavily.
Babies and children admitted. Disabled: toilet. Function room (capacity 90). No piped music or jukebox. Restaurant. Tables outdoors (30, garden).

Putney

Bricklayer's Arms

32 Waterman Street, SW15 1DD (8789 0222/ www.bricklayers-arms.co.uk). Putney Bridge tube/Putney rail. **Open** noon-11pm Mon-Sat; noon-10.30pm Sun. **Food served** 5-10pm Mon-Sat; 1-10pm Sun. **Credit** MC, V.
Close to the river, tucked down an unprepossessing cul-de-sac opposite a red-brick housing estate, is this plain and staggeringly simple pub, which celebrates real ale with much gusto and shows little consideration for anything else. Dating back to 1826, the oldest boozer in Putney has bona-fide bric-a-brac adorning the walls, wobbly pine tables on a threadbare floor and a real coal fire rumbling away beneath a pair

DRINKING

Palm Tree. See p343.

of headless antlers. Named 'Greater London Pub of the Year 2007' by CAMRA, this is the only London pub to serve Taylor's lesser-known gems on hand-pull: Golden Pride, Dark Mild, Ram Tam and Best Bitter. The regulars are beer boffins, flat-capped proprietors of free bus passes, and clued-up locals who can keep a secret.
Babies and children admitted (until 7pm). Tables outdoors (7, garden).

Wandsworth Common

Nightingale
97 Nightingale Lane, SW12 8NX (8673 1637). Clapham South tube/Wandsworth Common rail. **Open** 11am-midnight Mon-Sat; noon-midnight Sun. **Food served** noon-10pm daily. **Credit** AmEx, DC, MC, V.
At this great community local, the prodigious fundraising activities and home-produced newsletter are testament to the Nightingale's reputation. The pub was built in 1853 by Thomas Wallis; the exterior features green and brown glazed tiles, and hanging baskets fronting an attractive cobblestone street. The decor within is as boisterous and homely as the atmosphere, with the battle between patterned carpets and reupholstered tartan banquettes mollified by the warmth of a modern open fire. Smart and accommodating bar staff serve excellent pints of Young's Special and Bitter or Well's Bombardier to a harmonious mixture of friendly, cheery locals, businessmen and doting couples.
Babies and children admitted (until 9pm). Tables outdoors (12, garden).

South

Clapham

Bread & Roses
68 Clapham Manor Street, SW4 6DZ (7498 1779/www.breadandrosespub.com). Clapham Common or Clapham North tube. **Open** 4-11pm Mon-Thur; noon-midnight Fri, Sat; noon-10.30pm Sun. **Food served** 6-9.30pm Mon-Thur; noon-3pm, 6-9.30pm Fri; noon-4pm, 6-9.30pm Sat; noon-6pm Sun. **Credit** MC, V.
The Workers Beer Company is a funding organisation for trade unions and other campaigns which has been running festival beer tents for over 20 years. This WBC-run pub, which takes its name from a James Oppenheim poem associated with a textile strike ('Hearts starve as well as bodies, give us bread but give us roses'), is proud to sport its socialist credentials. Popular with local families for its world street food, it can lack atmosphere in the evenings, though that's being rectified by an unlikely move into burlesque with monthly Clapham or Bust nights. There are also regular reggae and world music DJs at weekends.
Babies and children admitted (until 9.30pm). Disabled: toilet. Entertainment (burlesque monthly; check website). Function room (capacity 100). Music (band monthly; check website). Tables outdoors (15, garden; 8, conservatory; 8, patio). **Map 22 B1.**

Stockwell

Priory Arms
83 Lansdowne Way, SW8 2PB (7622 1884). Stockwell tube. **Open** 11am-11pm Mon-Sat; noon-10.30pm Sun. **Food served** noon-2.30pm, 6.30-9.30pm Mon-Fri; noon-9.30pm Sat; 1-6pm Sun. **Credit** MC, V.
The Priory Arms feels less like a pub than a club house thanks to its cricket team, weekly quiz night and dizzying respect for real ale. The bar is lined with hundreds of labels provided by guest ales that have been pumped here down the years. It remains heaving with Harveys, Adnams and two guests, a vast selection of Belgian fruit beers and 16 country fruit wines, ranging from parsnip to dandelion. The gastro and Thai dishes are wolfed down by a packed house on any day of the week. A select drinker's heaven.
Children admitted (Sun lunch only). Function room (capacity 60). Quiz (8.30pm Sun; £1). Tables outdoors (4, patio).

South East

Deptford

Dog & Bell
116 Prince Street, SE8 3JD (8692 5664/ www.thedogandbell.com). New Cross tube/rail/ Deptford rail. **Open** noon-11pm Mon-Sat; noon-10.30pm Sun. **Food served** noon-2pm, 6-10pm Mon-Fri; noon-10pm Sat; noon-7pm Sun. **Credit** AmEx, MC, V.
Deptford's best bar is dark, foreboding and located in no man's land, which is all clearly quite irrelevant to the many regulars who beat a path to its door for a cherry-picked selection of real ales, and Beck's at less than £3 a pint. More than that, they come for the communal atmosphere. The bar billiards table stands neglected as everyday folk and Deptford's boho crowd mingle, usually in the side room now dominated by Fred Aylward's striking punk art. Proper meals (liver and bacon, chicken masala) are served too.
Babies and children admitted. Bar available for hire. Disabled: toilet. Quiz (9pm Sun; £1). Tables outdoors (4, garden).

Greenwich

Greenwich Union
56 Royal Hill, SE10 8RT (8692 6258/ www.greenwichunion.com). Greenwich rail/DLR. **Open** noon-11pm Mon-Sat; 11.30am-10.30pm Sun. **Food served** noon-10pm Mon-Fri, Sun; 11am-9pm Sat. **Credit** MC, V.
The Meantime Brewery's flagship is based on the training and recipes that founder Alistair Hook gleaned at age-old institutions in Germany. London Stout, Pale Ale, Helles, Kölner, Union, Strawberry and Raspberry varieties are brewed in nearby New Charlton and sold here on draught at reasonable prices. Hook has also been at pains to provide a global selection by the bottle: rare Cantillon Gueuze from Anderlecht, Brussels, Aecht Schlenkerla Marzen smoked beer from Bamberg, and so on. Wines, starting at £3.15 a glass, include a Spy Valley sauvignon blanc and Punto Alto pinot noir. Throw in proper cheeses, steak and stout pies and it's no wonder the Union is reliably busy.
Babies and children admitted (until 9pm). Tables outdoors (12, garden).

Herne Hill

Commercial
210-212 Railton Road, SE24 0JT (7501 9051). Herne Hill rail. **Open** noon-midnight daily. **Food served** noon-10pm Mon-Thur; noon-11pm Fri, Sat; noon-9.30pm Sun. **Credit** MC, V.
If four different types of chandelier, blue fairy lights, Shaker-style panelling and exposed brickwork make the pub look as if it's trying too hard, you should see the dressy, too-cool-for-school regulars. Still, there's a lot to like amid the noise (aural and visual), not least the most interesting selection of beers and spirits in the area including Budvar Dark, Paulaner and guest ales such as Pedigree served in dimply retro pint mugs.
Babies and children admitted. Disabled: toilet. Tables outdoors (5, garden). **Map 23 A5.**

London Bridge & Borough

Charles Dickens
160 Union Street, SE1 0LH (7401 3744/ www.thecharlesdickens.co.uk). Southwark tube. **Open** noon-11pm Mon-Fri; noon-6pm Sat, Sun. **Food served** noon-2.30pm, 6-8.30pm Mon-Fri; noon-5pm Sat, Sun. **Credit** MC, V.
Not somewhere that you're likely to stumble across unawares, near the mainline railway out of London Bridge, the Dickens has a scuffed-wood interior and few frills. Further inspection, though, will reveal a thoroughly Dickensian clientele enjoying the likes of Sharp's Eden Ale, Harveys Best, Slater's Queen Bee, Wettergate Essex Bomber and Dirty Dick and Golden Arrow. Bitburger and San Miguel are available on tap, and there's a choice of a dozen wines that make ideal accompaniments to the hearty mains (lamb shank, £8.25).

Babies and children admitted (until 7pm). Bar available for hire. Quiz (8.30pm Wed; free). Tables outdoors (3, pavement). **Map 11 O8.**

Gladstone Arms
64 Lant Street, SE1 1QN (7407 3962). Borough tube. **Open** noon-11pm Mon-Fri; noon-midnight Sat; noon-10.30pm Sun. **Food served** noon-3pm daily. **Credit** MC, V.
This may just be the coolest little pub in south-east London. The landlord has form, having run the equally bijou (and largely undiscovered) Smersh in Shoreditch and the famously debauched Islington 'whiskey café' Filthy McNasty's. The living-room sized Glad – visible from Borough High Street thanks to its garish mural – has become a second home for indie-folk types the Moon Music Orchestra, and has hosted many other hip shindigs. But it works equally well as a local pub.
Babies and children admitted (until 7pm). Music (bands 8pm Sat, Sun; free). **Map 11 P9.**

★ Rake
14 Winchester Walk, SE1 9AG (7407 0557). London Bridge tube/rail. **Open** noon-11pm Mon-Fri; 10am-11pm Sat. **Credit** (over £10) AmEx, MC, V.
We awarded this compact drinking den the Best Bar prize in the Time Out Eating and Drinking Awards 2007, and we're still taken by the mind-boggling array of beers sourced and sold. The layout consists solely of a small, unremarkable room and a heated patio, attesting to the fact that this bar doesn't pretend to be much more than a comfortable extension of the Utobeer stall in nearby Borough Market. Six taps are connected to a different draft each week and there are more than 100 bottled beers to pontificate over. Wines and cocktails aren't the thing here; snacks run to crisps and pork pies.
Babies and children admitted. Disabled: toilet. Tables outdoors (7, patio). **Map 11 P8.**

★ Royal Oak (100)
44 Tabard Street, SE1 4JU (7357 7173). Borough tube. **Open** 11am-11pm Mon-Fri; 6-11pm Sat; noon-6pm Sun. **Food served** noon-3pm, 5-9.45pm Mon-Fri; 6-9.45pm Sat; noon-4.45pm Sun. **Credit** MC, V.
True to its name, the Royal Oak seems wonderfully trapped in time. A pub for luvvies and lovers of Lewes brewery Harveys, the ales – Mild, Pale, Old, Best and Armada – are all under £3, keg cider includes Thatcher's Heritage and Weston's Stowford Press, while a felt-tipped menu boasts classics such as game pie, rabbit casserole, Lancashire hotpot and braised lamb shank. Music hall stars Harry Ray and Flanagan & Allen, here celebrated in framed, hand-bill form, would have tucked into the same decades ago. These days there's wine too. Nevertheless, an unused hatch for off sales remains, as do the shell-effect washbasins in the lavatory.
Disabled: toilet. No piped music or jukebox. Function room (capacity 40). **Map 11 P9.**

East

Brick Lane

Carpenter's Arms
73 Cheshire Street, E2 6EG (7739 6342). Liverpool Street tube/rail. **Open** noon-11.30pm Mon-Thur; noon-12.30am Fri, Sat; noon-11.30pm Sun. **Credit** MC, V.
Bought by the Kray twins in 1967 for their dear old mum, Violet, and used as a safe spot for a swift half, it was here that Ronnie tanked up on dutch courage before murdering Jack 'The Hat' McVitie. In short, it wasn't the sort of pub where you'd want to spill someone's pint. Today, the chunky tables, swaths of dark wood and historic windows make for a cosy place in which to hunker down with a pint to plan a bank job. There's also an intimate back room and a heated back garden. Tap talent includes four Dorothy Goodbody ales from Hereford's wonderful Wye Valley Brewery and a pair of Adnams bitters on draught. They pour alongside Germany's Licher Weizen and Früli fruit

DRINKING

beer. These days, the regulars are more Thompson Twins than Kray Twins: Hoxtonites, fashionistas, the odd ironic moustache and a few ambitious hats. *Babies and children admitted. Tables outdoors (6, garden).*

Pride of Spitalfields
3 Heneage Street, E1 5LJ (7247 8933). Aldgate East tube. **Open** 11am-11pm Mon-Sat; noon-10.30pm Sun. **Food served** noon-2.30pm Mon-Fri; 1-5pm Sun. **Credit** MC, V.
The Pride walks its own time-honoured path, hidden down a sidestreet and treating decks and the £20 pub roast as figments of a fetid imagination. Excellently kept real ale (Fuller's Pride and ESB, Brewers Gold) is the focus, with a bottle of Dubonnet telling the rest of the story. All around are archive photos and maroon upholstered seating that clashes magnificently with the bright red carpet. And as if that wasn't enough suburban 1980s, our visit also saw a punter strike up 'Ebony and Ivory' on the piano. The clientele remains a jolly blend of Japanese hipsters and old codgers. *Babies and children admitted. Tables outdoors (2, pavement).* **Map 12 S5**.

Limehouse

Grapes
76 Narrow Street, E14 8BP (7987 4396). Westferry DLR. **Open** noon-3pm, 5.30-11pm Mon-Thur; noon-11pm Fri, Sat; noon-10.30pm Sun. **Food served** noon-2pm, 7-9pm Mon-Fri; noon-2.30pm, 7-9pm Sat; noon-3.30pm Sun. **Credit** AmEx, MC, V.
Take a pew at one of the wonky wooden tables after a bracing Thames walk or join the blokey after-work crowd for banter at the bar – the Grapes is as old school as they come with its creaky wood-panelled interior, open fire and quirky memorabilia galore. There's plenty of good drinking on offer too: Brakspear Oxford Gold, Timothy Taylor Landlord and Adnams are among the many alternatives to standard draughts (the likes of Carlsberg, Stella, Guinness). There's no music to distract you from the pint-supping task at hand, and there's no need to leave Fido shivering on the pavement either – there's a rather thoughtful water bowl provided for him by the door. *No piped music or jukebox.*

Mile End

Palm Tree
127 Grove Road, E3 5BH (8980 2918). Mile End tube/8, 25 bus. **Open** noon-midnight Mon-Thur; noon-2am Fri, Sat; noon-1am Sun (last admission 10.45pm). **No credit cards**.
Gastro nothing, fancy cocktails nowhere (although there are half a dozen single malts we'd not noticed before), here's a place to get a fine pint of one of two cask ales (Batemans XB and Piddler on the Roof for our last visit), wine from a Stowells dispenser or generic liquor out of an optic. You'll also receive that pearl beyond price: atmosphere. There's the wonderful bronze glow of the wallpaper, a maroon pelmet around the curved central bar that adds a theatrical spin to the old photos of cabaret nonebrities (Paul Wood? Maxine Daniels?), a shelf of porcelain plates and dried hops hung above the drum kit. Any fears this is becoming a hollow heritage experience are soon allayed by the crammed music nights. *Music (jazz 9.45pm Fri-Sun; free). Tables outdoors (4, park).*

Shoreditch

Wenlock Arms
26 Wenlock Road, N1 7TA (7608 3406/ www.wenlock-arms.co.uk). Old Street tube/rail. **Open** noon-midnight Mon-Wed, Sun; noon-1am Thur-Sat. **Food served** noon-9pm daily. **No credit cards**.
A boxy old room of a place that hasn't been modified much in many years, thank heavens, the Wenlock attracts a unique mix of people. On any given night, you might find yourself sitting next to a table of beer-bellied ale-hunters going through the excellent and ever-changing range of beers served across eight handpumps, a group of art

Holly Bush. See p344.

students slumming it for the night away from their usual Hoxton haunts, or, of course, the ever-talkative regulars. This is, first and foremost, a local pub for local people, though your welcome will be far warmer here than in Royston Vasey. It's at its best for Thursday's popular quiz and for the weekend music, when veteran jazzers set up in the corner and start a session that almost invariably dissolves into a singalong.
Babies and children admitted (until 9pm). Function room (capacity 25). Music (blues/jazz 9pm Fri, Sat; 3pm Sun; free). Quiz (9pm Thur; free). **Map 5 P3.**

Stratford

King Edward VII
47 Broadway, E15 4BQ (8534 2313/ www.kingeddie.co.uk). Stratford tube/rail/DLR. **Open** noon-11pm Mon-Wed; noon-midnight Thur-Sat; noon-11.30pm Sun. **Food served** noon-3pm, 5-10pm Mon-Fri; noon-10pm Sat, Sun. **Credit** MC, V.
Amid the handsome etched glass and dark wood, gorgeous bright green tiles along a side corridor really stand out, but this pub is no museum piece: a mix of campus renegades and collared locals, with a nearly rowdy guitar-band soundtrack, keeps thing lively. There were four real ales – Nelson Brewery's Trafalgar Bitter and Nethergate's Suffolk County the rarities – and ten wines, all by glass and bottle, but no menus in evidence at 8.30pm. Has King Eddie scaled back the gastro ambitions? We hope not.
Babies and children admitted (upstairs only). Function room (capacity 100). Music (acoustic/ open mic 9pm Thur; free). Quiz (8.30pm Sun; free). Tables outdoors (5, yard).

North East
Dalston

Prince George
40 Parkholme Road, E8 3AG (7254 6060). Dalston Kingsland rail/30, 38, 56, 242, 277 bus. **Open** 5pm-midnight Mon-Thur; noon-1am Fri, Sat; noon-11.30pm Sun. **Credit** MC, V.
Wall-to-wall ironic outfits can be spied here of a Saturday night. We saw beauties (and a few beasties) sporting ocelot, sequins, space invader jumpers and – for some reason we couldn't fathom – a lot of unusual scarves as they supped Czech beer and real ale (Pride, Brakspear Bitter, Woodforde's Wherry). There are plenty of good wines by the glass too (from £3.40). Another draw is one of the best, free jukeboxes in London: Martha & the Muffins, Dolly Parton and the Temptations. Sadly, prices seem to have risen with the pub's profile: a pint of Guinness at £3.40 – in Dalston! *Babies and children admitted (until 8.30pm). Jukebox. Quiz (9pm Mon; £2). Tables outdoors (8, heated forecourt).* **Map 25 C5.**

North
Archway

Swimmer at the Grafton Arms
13 Eburne Road, N7 6AR (7281 4632). Holloway Road tube/Finsbury Park tube/rail. **Open** 5-11pm Mon; noon-3pm, 5-11pm Tue-Thur; noon-11pm Fri, Sat; noon-10.30pm Sun. **Food served** 5-9.30pm Mon; noon-3pm, 5-9.30pm Tue-Thur; noon-9.30pm Fri-Sun. **Credit** MC, V.
Walk into the Swimmer and you might think you'd found a genuine historic artefact, with battered wooden floors, panelling and pew seating. A while back, though, it was another kind of Victorian local, all plush, carpet and brass. No matter, for now it has a real buzz, helped by a funky, full-of-nice-surprises jukebox and events like the esteemed Monday night quizzes. Drinkers have Fuller's ales, a well above average range of draught lagers (Leffe, Litovel), and speciality beers (strawberry-tinged Belgian Früli). There are free papers and Wi-Fi. Another plus is a plant-lined terrace at the front.
Jukebox. Quiz (8.30pm Mon; £2). Tables outdoors (15, garden). Wireless internet (free).

Camden Town & Chalk Farm

Quinn's
65 Kentish Town Road, NW1 8NY (7267 8240). Camden Town tube. **Open/meals served** 11am-midnight Mon-Wed, Sun; 11am-2am Thur-Sat. **Credit** AmEx, MC, V.
Beyond Quinn's garish yellow exterior, few square inches inside are spared the trappings of the traditional pub treatment, from shelves of pretty plates to walls plastered with vintage prints; but with Miles Davis on the stereo and a stream of banter from two generations of Quinns behind the bar, it manages to feel like a real sanctuary from the outside world. There's a rotating selection of guest ales and one of the longest lists of Belgian and German bottled beers you'll find in the capital.
Babies and children admitted (until 7pm). Tables outdoors (7, garden). **Map 27 D1.**

Harringay

Salisbury Hotel
1 Grand Parade, Green Lanes, N4 1JX (8800 9617). Manor House tube then 29 bus. **Open** 5pm-midnight Mon-Wed; 5pm-1am Thur; 5pm-2am Fri; noon-2am Sat; noon-11pm Sun. **Food served** 6-10.30pm Mon-Fri; noon-11pm Sat; 1-7pm Sun. **Credit** MC, V.
Harringay's most imposing building, this Victorian beer palace has been spruced up rather than made over, the better to show off the vast, high-ceilinged rooms, glorious wooden bar, stained glass, statues and other fancies, without alienating the geezers who rub shoulders with the grungey-ish newer punters. Beers are mainly from Fuller's, with Litovel lagers on draught and many more in bottles; food is quality pub-grub. Live acts, in another spacious room, are a staple: bands, comedy and more.
Babies and children admitted. Disabled: toilet. Function room (capacity 120). Music (bands alternate Fri, Sat). Quiz (8.45pm Mon; £1).

Islington

Island Queen
87 Noel Road, N1 8HD (7704 7631). Angel tube. **Open** noon-11pm Mon, Sun; noon-11.30pm Tue, Wed; noon-midnight Thur-Sat. **Food served** noon-3pm, 6-10pm Mon-Thur; noon-4pm, 6-10pm Fri; noon-10pm Sat, Sun. **Credit** MC, V.
With its high, rust-coloured ceilings, Victorian wood panels, stunning cut-glass lamps, beautiful etched mirrors and ceiling fans, the Island Queen is architecturally striking and commands a strong local following. At the curved wooden bar, the taps dispense a good pick of continental beers – Leffe Blonde, Küppers Kölsch, Paulaner München, Franziskaner Weissbier and Früli – and British stuff like London Pride, Addlestones and Weston's cider. Duvel, Chimay White, Peroni, Pacifico Clara and Bierra Moretti are available by the bottle; the wine list tends towards the New World.
Babies and children admitted (until 7pm). Function room (capacity 60). Quiz (8pm Tue; £1). Tables outdoors (4, pavement). **Map 5 O2.**

North West
Hampstead

Holly Bush
22 Holly Mount, NW3 6SG (7435 2892/ www.hollybushpub.com). Hampstead tube/ Hampstead Heath rail. **Open** noon-11pm Mon-Sat; noon-10.30pm Sun. **Food served** noon-10pm daily. **Credit** (over £5) MC, V.
Hampstead may have become part of London in 1888, but no one seems to have told the Holly Bush. As the trend for gutting old pubs claims yet more NW3 boozers, this place becomes ever more popular. It's as picturesque as they come, tucked away on a quiet, gas-lit back street and delivering on all fronts: friendly staff, ancient interior and fine, reasonably priced food (from spruced-up sarnies to lamb shank in beer). Though the upstairs restaurant does a roaring trade, it's really all about getting the pints

in and perching by the fire or in one of the wooden booths. Our only complaint is that the backroom's glaring refurb could have been more sympathetic.
Babies and children admitted. Restaurant available for hire (60 capacity). **Map 28 B2.**

Spaniards Inn
Spaniards Road, NW3 7JJ (8731 6571). Hampstead tube/210 bus. **Open** 11am-11pm Mon-Fri; 10am-11pm Sat, Sun. **Food served** 11.30am-10pm Mon-Fri; noon-10pm Sat, Sun. **Credit** AmEx, MC, V.
While it may or may not be true that Dick Turpin hung out here (where there's been a boozer since 1580), the fact that there's a 'doggy wash' (a car wash for mucky mutts) says rather more about the place today. The pub's relative inaccessibility at the side of the Heath is also its chief advantage. In winter folk stop off mid-walk and warm up on the splendid pub grub before settling in a booth with one of the 24 draughts – perhaps an Adnams, Marston's Pedigree or Roosters Special, say.
Babies and children admitted. Entertainment (poetry 8pm Tue; free). Function room (capacity 50). Tables outdoors (80, garden).

St John's Wood

Clifton
96 Clifton Hill, NW8 0JT (7372 3427). St John's Wood tube. **Open** noon-11pm Mon-Sat; noon-10.30pm Sun. **Food served** noon-3pm, 6-9.30pm Mon-Sat; noon-4pm, 6.30-9pm Sun. **Credit** AmEx, MC, V.
A couple of hundred years old, and everyone's secret spot, the Clifton is long on atmosphere and blissfully short on hubbub. Borrow a board game or toast yourself at the roaring fire in the snug. Wood panelling abounds, perfectly in harmony with the unobtrusive murals and groovy chandeliers in each room. Outdoor types colonise the leafy terrace at the front, warmed in winter by gas heaters. The line-up of real ales includes Timothy Taylor Landlord, Black Sheep and Everards, and there's a good selection of wines available by the glass and bottle.
Babies and children admitted (until 7pm). Quiz (Wed 8.30pm; £2). Tables outdoors (12, garden). **Map 2 D1.**

Outer London
Richmond, Surrey

Cricketers
The Green, Richmond, Surrey TW9 1LX (8940 4372). Richmond tube/rail. **Open** noon-11pm Mon-Sat; noon-10.30pm Sun. **Food served** noon-7pm daily. **Credit** AmEx, MC, V.
Having Richmond Green as a beer garden is an obvious pull; the crack of leather on willow is the soundtrack for alfresco drinkers in summer. Despite creaky floorboards, this is a modern pub – there's a fruit machine and Sky Sports. Head upstairs for a wonderful view over the Green. Draught beers include Greene King IPA and Ruddles County, and the 18 types of burger that once graced the menu have been edged out by an arguably more fashionable list of pies.
Babies and children admitted. Function room (capacity 60). Tables outdoors (3, pavement).

Twickenham, Middlesex

Eel Pie
9-11 Church Street, Twickenham, Middx TW1 3NJ (8891 1717). Twickenham rail. **Open** 11am-11pm Mon-Wed; 11am-midnight Thur-Sat; noon-10.30pm Sun. **Food served** noon-3.30pm daily. **Credit** MC, V.
This pub slots nicely into what you think a Twickenham boozer ought to be: a little bit rugby, a little bit river, a little bit rock 'n' roll. Well, not really much rock 'n' roll, more 'the Spinners at Christmas'. The Eel does everything well: beer is supplied by Dorset's multi-award-winning Badger Brewery, with Best at £2.50 a pint and Tanglefoot at £2.75. In summer this pretty street is closed to traffic from Friday evening to Monday morning, so you can enjoy this pub from the outside as well as the inside.
Babies and children admitted (until 7pm). Quiz (9pm Thur; £1).

Wine Bars

The big story of the past 12 months has been the rise of the champagne bar. Unhindered by threat of an economic downturn, seeing a wide-open gap in the market for decent bubbly, operators have opened a number of exciting new venues. **St Pancras** has received acres of newsprint for its modish take on the genre in the remarkable new Eurostar conversion, while the owners behind **Amuse Bouche** have gone about their business more quietly, opening a second branch in Soho. Meanwhile, the bankers' bubbly bar, **Dion**, launched its third branch in Canary Wharf, and haute cuisine restaurant **Texture** (*see p140*) opened on Portman Square with a bright, airy and unpretentious champagne bar featuring nigh-on 100 bins.

In comparison, wine bars specialising in non-fizzy drinks have had a quiet time. Following the outstanding openings of **Green & Blue**, **Vinoteca** and **Vivat Bacchus** in recent years, things have settled down with just a few tweaks here and there. The much-underrated **Albertine** in Shepherd's Bush added shelving to display its stock and began selling wine at cheaper, shop prices. This is the formula that has proved so successful in other London wine bars – which offer the choice of drinking in or buying a bottle to take away. Selfridges was banned from serving smaller measures at its **Wonder Bar**: such a shame as this gave people the chance to try expensive wines for little outlay. But the place is still packed with people keen to learn, many of whom stop at the store's next-door wine department to find out more.

Overall, London's wine bars have improved dramatically in the past three years, approaching at last the level of those in Melbourne, San Francisco and Paris. The New World and up-and-coming areas in France, Italy and Spain now fill shelves that were once the refuge for tired, thin claret and port. The upward curve looks set to continue; look out soon for more new openings from Dion and Amuse Bouche.

Central

Belgravia

Ebury Wine Bar & Restaurant
139 Ebury Street, SW1W 9QU (7730 5447/ www.eburywinebar.co.uk). Sloane Square tube/ Victoria tube/rail.
Bar **Open** 11am-11pm Mon-Sat; 6-10pm Sun. *Restaurant* **Lunch served** noon-2.45pm Mon-Sat. **Dinner served** 6-10.15pm Mon-Sat; 6-9.45pm Sun. **Main courses** £10-£19.50. **Set meal** (noon-2.45pm, 6-8pm) £15.50 2 courses, £18.50 3 courses.
Both **House wine** £13.50 bottle, £3.60 glass. **Credit** AmEx, MC, V.
Not to be confused with the Ebury gastropub in nearby Pimlico, this slick, continental-style place has charms aplenty. Chief among these is the well-made dishes – a rabbit terrine, say, with chunky pieces of dark, flavoursome meat; a succulent rack of lamb with garlic and thyme sauce; and a fluffy, steaming spotted dick with custard. Such food is best enjoyed in the garish, theatre-set rear dining room with its great, swirling frescoes covering the ceiling and stealing down the walls. The 100-strong wine list impresses too, offering nearly half the bins, and every dessert wine, by the glass. Look out for the good Italian whites, such as Adelasia from Piedmont, made from the little known cortese grape. *Booking advisable.* **Map 15 H10**.

Bloomsbury

Vats Wine Bar & Restaurant
51 Lamb's Conduit Street, WC1N 3NB (7242 8963). Holborn or Russell Square tube.
Open noon-11pm Mon-Fri. **Lunch served** noon-2.30pm, **dinner served** 6-9.30pm Mon-Fri. **Main courses** £9.50-£17. **House wine** £15 bottle, £4.25 glass. **Credit** AmEx, DC, MC, V.
A proper, old-fashioned wine bar, Vats is a regular lunchtime haunt for Lincoln's Inn barristers and various other characters in the neighbourhood. The backroom restaurant gets lively and raucous come lunchtime, while a separate bar at the front is more sedate, and warmed by a fire in winter. Here, the tables are closely set, and full-length windows front on to the pleasant, villagey Lamb's Conduit Street. The wine list isn't likely to win any awards, with superior mainstream labels such as Tyrell's and Hennessy sharing space alongside Louis Latour. Latour's light, minerally Château de Blagny Meursault is the pick, showing slight peach and pineapple aromas, and good intensity from 2002. You'll often find folks whiling the afternoon away here, the dessert wine selection (including 1997 Château Coutet from Barsac, and a waxy, spicy, dried-apricot 2005 Muscat de Beaumes de Venise) offering a good excuse to linger. The food is pretty sound. A fish pie was filled with generous chunks of salmon and monkfish, as well as prawns and mussels; it was served with fondant potatoes and beans. *Babies and children admitted. Booking advisable. Separate room for parties, seats 50. Tables outdoors (4, pavement).* **Map 4 M5**.

City

El Vino
47 Fleet Street, EC4Y 1BJ (7353 6786/ www.elvino.co.uk). Chancery Lane or Temple tube/Blackfriars tube/rail. **Open** 8.30am-9pm Mon; 8.30am-10pm Tue-Fri. **Breakfast served** 8.30-11am, **meals served** noon-9pm Mon-Fri. **Main courses** £8.75-£12.95. **House wine** £16.30 bottle, £4.10 glass. **Credit** AmEx, DC, MC, V.
The ultimate old-fashioned wine bar, in the heart of London legal land. Many a barrister finds a way here from the Courts of Justice opposite, and you'll hear plenty of conversations about second homes in Tuscany. But despite the patrician air (enhanced since the journalists moved out of Fleet Street), this place has charm aplenty, with old, brass-tacked sofas, dark wood panelling and nicotine-stained walls. The staff, who are mainly Australian or from continental Europe, are young and willing. Barrels of port and sherry offer a cheap glass, and there is a decent selection of good Australian wines, including the delicate stone and lime flavours of Brian Barry's 2002 Clare Valley riesling. The food is appropriately simple and British. We enjoyed the crunchy, puffy beer batter on the fish, and calf's liver was nicely pink in the middle, yet charred on the outside. There's more to this place than meets the eye; other El Vinos are dotted near Blackfriars, Cannon Street and London Wall, and the company has a large mail-order business specialising in Bordeaux and Burgundy. *Separate room for parties, seats 50. Tables outdoors (8, courtyard).* **Map 11 N6**. **For branches see index.**

Clerkenwell & Farringdon

Bleeding Heart Tavern
Bleeding Heart Yard, 19 Greville Street, EC1N 8SJ (7404 0333/www.bleedingheart.co.uk). Farringdon tube/rail.
Tavern **Open** 7am-11pm Mon-Fri. **Lunch served** noon-3pm, **snacks served** 3-6pm, **dinner served** 6-10.30pm Mon-Fri. **Main courses** £8.45-£14.45.
Bistro **Lunch served** noon-3pm, **dinner served** 6-10.30pm Mon-Fri. **Main courses** £8.45-£15.50.
Restaurant **Lunch served** noon-2.30pm, **dinner served** 6-10.30pm Mon-Fri. **Main courses** £12.95-£24.50.
All **House wine** £16.95 bottle, £4.50 glass. **Credit** AmEx, DC, MC, V.
Exposed brick, dark Victorian-style furnishings and wooden stair-rails give the feel of a kind of upmarket Wetherspoon's experience to the Bleeding Heart. Punters pack into the small main room, gents in suits leaning against the bar along with a younger crowd from Clerkenwell design firms. In essence this is a pub with knobs on. There's a good selection of ales, but also plenty of wine thanks to proprietors Robert and Robyn Wilson (who run a restaurant next door and another in the City) also having a share in property in Hawke's Bay on New Zealand's North Island. From Hawke's Bay comes a tasty, not-overdone chardonnay 2006 with notable peach, melon and honeysuckle scents. Other wines on the list include Daniel Dampt's 2006 Chablis: lean but not mean, with stony, lime fruit and apples. Or there's the excellent-value 2006 Quinto do Crasto from the Douro valley in Portugal – rich, with blackcurrant fruit, cassis and spice. Food includes a good Anglo-French combo of blade of beef with portobello mushrooms, garlic and salted potatoes. *Booking advisable. Dress: smart; no shorts, jeans or trainers (restaurant). Separate rooms for parties, seating 30-40. Tables outdoors (10, terrace).* **Map 11 N5**.

★ Cellar Gascon

59 West Smithfield, EC1A 9DS (7600 7561/ 7796 0600/www.cellargascon.com). Barbican tube/Farringdon tube/rail. **Open** noon-midnight Mon-Fri. **Tapas served** noon-11.30pm Mon-Fri. **Tapas** £3.50-£8. **House wine** £16 bottle, £5 glass. **Credit** AmEx, MC, V.
If you fancy a trip to southern France without leaving London, head to Smithfields and settle into a table at Cellar Gascon, the attractive wine-focused annex to the celebrated Club Gascon (*see p101*). The leather banquettes of the popular bar are regularly packed with suited men and elegantly dressed women from nearby offices. Refreshingly free of pinot grigio and Aussie chardonnay, the expertly chosen wine list centres on France's south-west, a diverse region with some weird and wonderful grape varieties, including loin de l'oeil and tannat. As these wines are often ignored by UK wholesalers, the Gascon group imports nearly half of its cellar directly from small producers, and employs helpful and well-informed staff to assist in navigating the list. From fresh sharp whites to structured dark reds, you'll find something to work with the rich food that fills the menu. Tempting plates of charcuterie, including some fine Gascon black ham carved to order from a leg in front of you at the bar, proves very popular with the after-work crowd.
Babies and children admitted. Bar available for hire. Tables outdoors (3, pavement). Wine tasting: last Sat of mth; £20. **Map 11 O5.**

★ Vinoteca (100)

7 St John Street, EC1M 4AA (7253 8786/ www.vinoteca.co.uk). Farringdon tube/rail. **Open** noon-midnight Mon-Sat. **Lunch served** noon-2.45pm Mon-Fri. **Dinner served** 6.30-10pm Mon-Sat. **Main courses** £8.50-£13. **House wine** £12.95 bottle, £2.95 glass. **Credit** MC, V.
Vinoteca is much more than a 'wine bar'. Yes, you can come in and savour one of the 15 or so wines by the glass, but you can also buy a bottle or a case from the excellent 250-plus wine list, or treat yourself to excellent Iberian and Moorish-inflected cooking from the daily-changing menu. There were many flavours in our roast spatchcock of marinated quail, merguez sausage, herb fregola and harissa dressing, but they were perfectly judged. 'Perfectly judged' could also describe the wine list, which lists top producers from established and up-and-coming regions of Europe (mainly France, Spain, Portugal and Italy) and the New World (especially Australia, New Zealand and South America). By-the-glass offerings might

include an unusual white from Spain's Valdeorras region, made by the dynamic young Telmo Rodriguez from the rarely seen godello grape, or an impressively structured yet fruity Kiwi pinot noir from the Delta Vineyards in Marlborough. Vinoteca is constantly busy, but it has a distinctly laid-back vibe, thanks to friendly, knowledgeable staff and the low-key, rustic interior. It hosts a regular wine school taught by Tim Atkin MW, plus several other wine-related events in the downstairs private room. In all, it is a haven for in-the-know wine-lovers.
Babies and children admitted. Bookings not accepted dinner. Off-licence. Separate room for parties, seats 30. Tables outdoors (4, pavement). **Map 5 O5.**

★ Vivat Bacchus

47 Farringdon Street, EC4A 4LL (7353 2648/ www.vivatbacchus.co.uk). Chancery Lane tube/ Farringdon tube/rail.
Bar **Open/snacks served** noon-10.30pm Mon-Fri. **Snacks** £4-£12.
Restaurant **Lunch served** noon-2.30pm, **dinner served** 6.30-9.30pm Mon-Fri. **Main courses** £14.50-£35. **Set meal** £15.50 2 courses, £17.50 3 courses.
Both **House wine** £15.50-£19.95 bottle, £4.90-£6.90 glass. **Credit** AmEx, DC, MC, V.
What is it about quotations and wine bars? Scrawled throughout this rambling venue you'll find 'Champagne is a way of life, a state of mind, and better than Prozac' and more of such unalloyed praise. It's as if the love of the grape isn't made clear enough by a cellar of 20,000 bottles, and maps of world wine regions covering the walls. No one could help but notice, however, that South African-owned Vivat Bacchus is the place to drink good wine. Rarely can you find such a selection of South African bottles that includes the spice-edged, silky and strawberry-like 2004 Hamilton Russell pinot noir: something that competes with mid-range Burgundy. Bubbly is taking an ever-increasing role here and the list has expanded to include examples from the rest of the wine world too – Ca del Solo's 2005 Malvasia Blanco being an unusual, smoky, honey and peach-stone-filled wine from California. The interior decor of the whole place is somewhat odd and rather distracting throughout: exposed, unpolished wood beams; cardboard boxes full of wine above the bar; and air-con ducts circling above the punters' heads.
Bar available for hire. Booking advisable. Disabled: toilet. Off-licence. Wine club (7pm Mon; £25). **Map 11 N5.**

Covent Garden

Bedford & Strand

1A Bedford Street, WC2E 9HH (7836 3033/ www.bedford-strand.com). Covent Garden tube/Charing Cross tube/rail. **Open** noon-midnight Mon-Fri; 5pm-midnight Sat. **Lunch served** noon-3pm Mon-Fri. **Dinner served** 5.30-11pm Mon-Sat. **House wine** £13.25 bottle, £3.70 glass. **Credit** AmEx, MC, V.
With its glass-topped wood dividers, B&S looks more like a Yates's wine lodge than a hip bar, but it's one of the few non-touristy places in this part of town and buzzes even on a Monday night. Local lawyers sip and chomp at wine and food served promptly and well. Steak tartare arrived with a dull salad, but the steak, mixed with vinegar, a few capers and a quail's egg, was delicious. Sharp chive cream and a melting poached egg improved the soft, floppy fish cakes. Wines are euphemistically divided into 'Honest', 'Decent', 'Good' and 'Staff Picks', which effectively means 'Cheap', 'Average', 'Better' and 'Properly Chosen'. It's quite a task to find an enjoyable drop in the 'Honest' category. The likes of Gran Sasso's Montepulciano d'Abruzzo and Ribolla Gialla from Colli Orientali show it pays to head for 'Good'. Overall, the list needs pruning of larger brands and less interesting choices.
Babies and children admitted. Bar available for hire. Booking advisable. Wine club (5.30pm 1st Mon of mth; £10-£15). Wireless internet (free). **Map 18 E5.**

Café des Amis

11-14 Hanover Place, WC2E 9JP (7379 3444/ www.cafedesamis.co.uk). Covent Garden tube.
Bar **Open** 11.30am-1am Mon-Sat. **Meals served** 11.30am-11.30pm Mon-Sat. **Main courses** £12-£20.50.
Restaurant **Meals served** noon-3pm, 5-11.30pm Mon-Sat. **Main courses** £12.50-£21.50. **Set meal** (noon-3pm, 5-7pm, 10-11.30pm Mon-Sat) £14.50 2 courses, £16.50 3 courses.
Both **House wine** £15.75 bottle, £4.50 glass.
Both **Credit** AmEx, DC, MC, V.
Some still miss the former incarnation of this Covent Garden bar, with wires and exposed heating pipes aplenty. Now it's more like a hotel venue, with red alcove seating, dinky chandeliers and zinc bar, although head barman Jean-Luc is still there, patient and charming in equal measure. You can face him at the bar or recline in chairs by the wall, but seats fill quickly with opera- and ballet-goers. A new late licence to 1am means there

The Champagne Bar at St Pancras

can now be some proper post-curtain sessions too. Wines are fairly French-dominated, Leon Beyer gewürztraminer from 2005 providing interest. The classic French nomenclature 'Etrangers' is used to list wines outside France. Ondarre's 2001 Rioja Reserva shows what good value northern Spain provides in its most famous region: age, and vanilla, bold strawberry flavours emerging from time in the barrel. French-themed snacks include onion soup with toasted gruyère and croûtons, and steak tartare which comes with fashionably triple-cooked chips in its large version.
Babies and children admitted. Bar available for hire. Booking advisable. Entertainment: pianist 7pm Tue. Separate room for parties, seats 80. Tables outdoors (20, terrace). Wireless internet (free). **Map 18 E4.**

King's Cross

The Champagne Bar at St Pancras NEW
St Pancras International Station, Pancras Road, NW1 2QP (3006 1552/www.searcystpancras. co.uk). King's Cross tube/rail. **Open** 8am-11pm daily. **Breakfast served** 8-11am, **meals/ snacks served** noon-10pm daily. **Main courses** £5.75-£17.50. **Champagne** from £42 bottle, £7.50 glass. **Credit** AmEx, MC, V.
Don't let fatuous claims about this being the longest bar in Europe spoil what is a lovely pre-travel experience: glass of champagne in hand and tickets at the ready. Underneath William Barlow's vast curving roof, a wonder of the Victorian age, the station has been painted in original egg-shell blue, offset by equally delightful decorated brickwork. Given such a setting, it must have been difficult to build a bar to fit into it, but operators Searcy's have plumped for unobtrusive dark wood and banquettes, giving an urban restaurant look that just about works. Champagne is the thing, emphasised by a vast and laudable list of over 100 wines. It includes unusual bottles from some top houses, such as Pommery's rich, red fruit-scented Wintertime Blanc de Noirs, and the light, fresh and zesty Jean-Paul Deville at the cheaper end. One quibble is that smaller champagne houses, or even grower champagnes – made by the people who grow the grapes – aren't included. As for food, crunchy granola contrasted well with soft, slippery poached fruit and yoghurt, but tough slices of bacon came on overdone toast. In winter you'll need a big coat; there's powerful heating under every seat, but cold air swirls around this large railway shed.
Babies and children admitted. **Map 4 L3.**

Smithy's
15-17 Leeke Street, WC1X 9HY (7278 5949/ www.smithyslondon.com). King's Cross tube/rail. **Open** 11am-11pm Mon-Wed; 11am-midnight Thur; 11am-1am Fri, Sat; 11am-9pm Sun. **Lunch served** noon-3pm, **dinner served** 6-10.30pm Mon-Sat. **Meals served** 11am-5pm Sun. **Main courses** £9.50-£17. **House wine** £12.95 bottle, £3.30 glass. **Credit** AmEx, MC, V.
Rough, ready and perfect for the nine-to-five crowd, this solid, masculine venue is in one of the more unlikely locations for a quaint cobbled street: near King's Cross Thameslink railway station. The main room carries the bricked-up road theme into the bar, so watch for high heels getting caught and the occasional tumble. A wood-panelled second space next door resembles a youth club but is filled with office workers. The wine list doesn't set the world alight, but has a forte in mid-priced bottles such as the tasty, full-bodied, yet delicate and minerally pinot blanc Reserve Particulière 2005 from André Scherer. Domaine Cret des Garanches 2005 from Brouilly in Beaujolais was a nice light, raspberry-scented drop with soft tannins: drinkable even with white meat such as a juicy roast poussin with cocotte potatoes and tarragon sauce. Food is generally punchy, with well-cooked lamb's sweetbreads served with a rich partner of chicken and button onion terrine, as well as toasted brioche. Smithy's bills itself as one of King's Cross's best kept secrets – with everything else that goes on around here, that's doubtful.

Babies and children admitted. Booking advisable. Bar areas available for parties, seating 60 and 120. **Map 4 M3.**

Leicester Square

Cork & Bottle
44-46 Cranbourn Street, WC2H 7AN (7734 7807/www.corkandbottle.net). Leicester Square tube. **Open/meals served** 11am-11.30pm Mon-Sat; noon-10.30pm Sun. **Main courses** £11-£13.50. **House wine** £15.95 bottle, £4 glass. **Credit** AmEx, MC, V.
A cosy, tucked-away place for those in-the-know, this basement bar is one of the few independent establishments left around Leicester Square. A Mumm Champagne window display, sandwiched between cinemas and pizza joints, gives little idea of the delights below. Head downstairs and you'll see the appeal: lots of small rooms and alcoves perfect to hide away with a bottle. You can chomp on caesar salad and sizeable steak burgers to line the stomach in readiness for the long list of notable bottles (including many from the New World). Wine obsessive Don Hewitson has built up relationships with major growers over the 40 years of running the Cork & Bottle, and they're listed prominently. Some you'll like, such as Yves Chéron from the Rhône. Some you might not, such as the hefty shiraz of Grant Burge from Barossa in Australia. But you can't ignore 2000 Château D'Arvigny from Bordeaux – a great year for the region – and the fact that Hewitson's idiosyncratic choice is a relief in a world of standardised dross.
Babies and children admitted. Booking advisable (bookings not accepted after 6.30pm). **Map 18 C5.**

Marble Arch

★ Wonder Bar
Selfridges, 400 Oxford Street, W1A 2LR (0800 123400/www.selfridges.com). Bond Street or Marble Arch tube. **Open/meals served** 9.30am-8pm Mon-Wed, Fri, Sat; 9.30am-9pm Thur; noon-6pm Sun. **Main courses** £7.50-£19.95. **House wine** £18.99-£340, £3.25-£60 glass. **Credit** AmEx, DC, MC, V.
Anyone who professes to not liking wine is liable to be converted here. Selfridges Wonder Bar, overseen by their sommelier and wine buyer Dawn Davies, is one of London's best venues for sampling what the grape has to offer. Wrapped on a mezzanine around the store's wine shop, the red and blond wood space fills up rapidly with couples sharing a bottle at the bar, and groups of friends at the tail end of a shopping spree settling at the tables by the window. Sit back and enjoy the table service, or buy a card and pour your own wine in 125ml or 175ml measures from the 'jukebox'-style dispenser along one wall. This holds 52 regularly updated wines at £3 to £100 a glass. Among our recent favourites were Alvaro Palacios's 2004 Petalos del Bierzo, SC Pannell 2006 shiraz, and the rich, dense, spicy Vieux Télégraphe's 2003. As befits its position adjacent to the famous food hall, Wonder Bar has a menu sourced from artisan producers, including platters such as pata negra ham with celeriac rémoulade; a British cheese board with bread, biscuits, pears and quince paste; and organic beech-smoked salmon with salad and soda bread.
Babies and children admitted: high chair. Bar available for hire. Disabled: lift; toilet. **Map 9 G6.**

Piccadilly

★ 1707
Lower ground floor, Fortnum & Mason, 181 Piccadilly, W1A 1ER (7734 8040/ www.fortnumandmason.com). Piccadilly Circus tube.
Bar **Open** noon-11pm Mon-Sat; noon-7pm Sun. **Corkage** £5 half bottle, £10 bottle.
Restaurant **Meals served** noon-11pm Mon-Sat; noon-7pm Sun. **Main courses** £6-£26.
Both **House wine** £19.75-£25 bottle, £5-£5.25 glass. **Credit** AmEx, MC, V.
The revamp at Fortnum's, that most traditional of department stores, has created a bar that wouldn't

see left

Interview
DAWN DAVIES

Who are you?
Head sommelier at Selfridges, and in charge of the **Wonder Bar** (*see left*).
What's the best thing about running a restaurant in London?
London is a vibrant and fast-moving city where people are constantly looking for the latest trend or fashion. This makes the restaurant scene very dynamic as you are constantly able to challenge people with new wines and foods.
What's the worst thing?
Staffing is a huge problem; in London there is a general lack of good staff. People tend to see restaurants and bars as a stop-gap job. They do not realise that to serve people well is an art that is hard to achieve and takes skill and dedication.
Which are your favourite London bars and restaurants?
There are so many places in London that are great, but if I have to choose I absolutely love all Nigel Platts Martin's restaurants, not because I worked at the **Ledbury** (*see p105*) but because I genuinely believe that the service and food are second to none. **Vinoteca** (*see p346*) is another favourite as it is a great place to meet friends and get a fabulous bottle from the shop.
How green are you?
One of the most positive steps restaurants have taken this year is to push tap water. And with regards to wine, I am always keen to work with winemakers who employ organic or biodynamic growing methods.
What is missing from London's bar and restaurant scene?
Service is the biggest gripe I have. We need to take a long hard look at how we interact with customers. It is not just the food that people remember, but also the first instance they walk into a restaurant, and the very last moments of a meal. That is where you win or lose a customer and that is often forgotten.

DRINKING

The big four

There are four main wine bar chains in London, together responsible for around 100 outlets, many in the City. For venue details, check each chain's website; we also list all branches in the indexes at the back of this guide.

Davy's

www.davy.co.uk
Although this chain of wine bars was launched in the 1960s, many of its sites look as old as the founding date of Davy's wine merchants: 1870. Now owned by the fifth generation of the Davy family, most of the 40 outlets are in central London, with some in the suburbs. They all look similar: dark, often basement interiors, with prints on the walls, wood panelling, sawdust on the floor, and people in suits. Davy's venues are particularly good for large groups as the drinking area is spacious and big tables are to be had – and there's no VIP ropes or guest list in sight. Don't expect to find the latest cocktail or tunes, but enjoy the generally relaxed air nonetheless. Food is a classic array of sandwiches, pâtés and cheeses.

Pick of the bunch Davy's at Plantation Place (off Mincing Lane, EC3) has a modern, spruced-up eating area with room for 100, plus a fine wine selection that includes the wonderful Vosne Romanée Les Suchots, 2001, from Denis Mugneret. The list is well-chosen, with many old vintages, such as 1963 Cockburn's vintage port.

Best flavours Bordeaux is the heartland, with a good spread of vintages going back 40 years, which means you can opt for some under-priced, underrated years if you so wish: 1999 Château Cantemerle, for example, or 2001 Chadenne from the Fronsac sub-region, or Château d'Angludet. The company's Burgundy selection is almost as strong, with growers of the calibre of Etienne Sauzet and Pierre Morey.

Buy the case Davy's has spruced up its website retail arm, davywine.co.uk, with offers around the firm's classic French region heartland. The accompanying notes about the history of each wine are great, though rather less so when it comes to explaining the actual flavours. 'Huge texture and concentrated fruit flavours' is written under 1998 Château Calon-Ségur from Bordeaux, but it could apply to any of the 100-plus bottles on the list. Generally there are some real bargains to be found in an excellent claret selection.

Balls Brothers

www.ballsbrothers.co.uk
Though Balls Brothers could be seen as a more modern version of Davy's, its wine bars are also dominated by hunting prints, brass rails and plenty of Burgundy and claret. The company is family-owned too, by Richard Balls, but it has more West End branches, with 15 wine bars overall including those in the capital's financial district. There's also Gow's, a restaurant and oyster bar near Liverpool Street station, and an Irish-themed venue, Mulligans of Mayfair. Food tends to be classic bar fare (skewers, fish cakes), but there are tastier main course options such as beer-battered haddock with chips and pea purée. A set of seven new, minimalist, banquette-filled bars called Lewis + Clarke has been recently rolled-out too – evidence that the owners are aware of recent bar trends.

Pick of the bunch Balls Brothers in Victoria (on Buckingham Palace Road, SW1) has pleasant outdoor seating overlooking Grosvenor Gardens on a corner site. The interior is light-filled, the walls are largely unadorned and there's a sizeable back bar. It's bustling rather than rammed in the evenings, and is a fine early evening drinks spot in an area largely devoid of attractive options.

Best flavours It's rare to find good claret under, or around, £20 a bottle, but here there's a selection of Bordeaux at that price, such as 2002 Château Moulin de Pez, St Estèphe. That's the best feature of the selection, along with white Burgundy in a similar price-band, including 2005 Mâcon-Clessé, by Guillemot-Michel. The same list is replicated at every bar.

Buy the case All wines in the bars can be ordered by the case, but there's a larger selection of over 400 to order by phone or online, plus a team of advisers to help you choose what to buy. The website provides decent tasting notes and background on many wines too. It's worth using these: the company buys early and stores well. It is selling 2003 Bordeaux now, with Sociando-Mallet a fine cru bourgeois option from that

look out of place in Melbourne or San Francisco. As with the upstairs ice-cream parlour (see p306), the smart decor with slatted wood surrounds comes courtesy of David Collins. From the temperature-controlled walk-in wine cellar, Grosset's Polish Hill 2007 riesling from Australia and Santa Maria pinot noir from Au Bon Climat in California are highlights of the impressive by-the-glass choice of New World wines. Esteemed chef Shaun Hill has been brought in to shake up the menus. A salmon plate featured mild London-cure smoked salmon, along with beetroot-cured and gravadlax varieties – an excellent array of subtle flavours. Duck and cherry pie and scotch egg were meaty and rich, although potted shrimp lacked mace and overdid the butter. Nevertheless, there are more hits than misses at this stylish venue. *Babies and children admitted. Bar available for hire. Booking advisable. Disabled: toilet. Off-licence. Wireless internet (free).* **Map 9 J7.**

Soho

Amuse Bouche [NEW]

2008 RUNNER-UP BEST BAR
21-22 Poland Street, W1F 8QQ (7287 1661). Oxford Circus tube. **Open** noon-11.30pm Mon-Thur; noon-midnight Fri; 5pm-midnight Sat. **Lunch served** noon-3pm Mon-Fri. **Dinner served** 5-10pm Mon-Sat. **Main courses** £5-£8. **House wine** £23.50-£250 bottle, £5-£6 glass. Credit MC, V. **No credit cards.**
An offshoot of the popular champagne bar in Parsons Green, this Soho branch of Amuse Bouche continues the remit of providing quality fizz at low prices. The neutral, contemporary surroundings, not unlike an All Bar One, make it friendly and casual, although some might find having the football on downstairs (in the basement function room) and the smell of chips incompatible with a bottle of Bollinger. Starting with house champagne Bouché Père et Fils Brut NV at £5 per glass (plus 12.5% service), the 50-strong list then rises up through the ranks of big-name brands. Pretty much all cost under £50 a bottle, though some great vintages – notably Pol Roger Cuvée Winston Churchill '96 (£130) and Krug '96 (£200) – rise into the stratosphere, where you'll also find Cristal magnums (£750). Most commendable is the effort to include several lesser-known houses, a few at under £8.50 a glass, meaning it's possible to experiment without financial ruin. Champagne cocktails (from £5) are crisp and fruity. Staff are friendly and keen to help, even if they don't always know their stuff. It doesn't seem to bother the chattering girls and suits who love this place. *Babies and children admitted. Separate room for parties, seats 30. Wireless internet (free).* **Map 17 A3.**
For branch see index.

Shampers

4 Kingly Street, W1B 5PE (7437 1692/ www.shampers.net). Oxford Circus or Piccadilly Circus tube. **Open** 11am-11pm Mon-Sat (Aug closed Sat). **Meals served** noon-11pm Mon-Sat. **Main courses** £8.95-£16. **House wine** £12.95 bottle, £3.75 glass. Credit AmEx, DC, MC, V.
While many of the kids around Carnaby Street opt for the Puma shoes shop and assorted style bars, those with more experience drop into Shampers. Pinstripe suits and cardigans from the advertising and publishing worlds pack the place, and staff have trouble keeping up, serving quickly to a rammed bar and dining room. There's good British food such as potted Morecambe Bay prawns with sourdough toast, and smoked Rannoch venison with pickled fig to match some well-priced wines. The juicy, fruit-laden 2005 Ochoa tempranillo-garnacha blend from Spain comes in at under £4 a glass. Many wine bars mark-up the more well-known regions, but here you can drink them at a fair price. For instance, Sancerre and Chablis usually command a higher tag because owners know punters will pay more to drink them, but at Shampers Claude Fournier's Loire white and Daniel Dampt's northern Burgundy both fit in the £20 per bottle bracket – amazing. *Babies and children admitted. Bar available for hire. Booking advisable. Separate room for parties, seats 45. Tables outdoors (3, courtyard). Wireless internet (free).* **Map 17 A4.**

Strand

Gordon's

47 Villiers Street, WC2N 6NE (7930 1408/ www.gordonswinebar.com). Embankment tube/Charing Cross tube/rail. **Open** 11am-11pm Mon-Sat; noon-10pm Sun. **Meals served** noon-10pm Mon-Sat; noon-9pm Sun. **Main courses** £7.95-£11.95. **House wine** £13.50 bottle, £3.70 glass. Credit AmEx, MC, V.
One of London's oldest bars, Gordon's is adorned with sweaty, stained alcoves and cobwebs. Surprisingly this appeals to a young, trendy crowd, but you're still likely to find port-quaffing suits in the main bar. Food is served buffet-style, with salad. We found the tasty, crumbly pastry and rich, meaty filling of the pork pie superior to the likes of poached or smoked salmon, spinach and potato

year, or the merlot-dominated Ducluzeau from the outstanding 2000 vintage. Underrated Listrac appellation is another good choice.

Corney & Barrow
www.corney-barrow.co.uk
More famous once for its wine merchant arm, Corney & Barrow launched its wine bar business during the style bar whim of the 1990s. The bars have become firmly established since, while keeping much of the minimalist style of that period. Big glass windows and stark concrete lit by spotlights produce something of a jet-setting, international-airport feel, very much in contrast to the typical City wine bar. Roll-out plans were halted by an abortive move into the West End, so the directors have stuck to what they know in the City and Canary Wharf, with 11 bars in all. Many branches offer breakfast menus from 7.30am to fit in with the local working crowd. The website gives an excellent idea of what to expect at each venue. Food is served all day, but in the evening is restricted to bar snacks such as tempura prawns with chilli sauce. At lunch, there's a large choice, including chunky 28-day hung sirloin steak with chips, mushrooms, spinach and tomato.
Pick of the bunch A nightclub vibe permeates the interior of the Paternoster Square, EC4, bar, but the outside area – looking over the recent Paternoster development, and with St Paul's looming in the background – is a delight. With people to-ing and fro-ing, it's almost European in feel.

Best flavours The best thing about Corney & Barrow is the choice of 70 wines by the glass, meaning that if you mess up and choose something you don't like, it's not a complete disaster. Opt for something more unusual, then, such as Crozes-Hermitage Millepertuis from Guyot in the Rhône, or 2005 or 2001 Laguna de la Nava Reserva from Valdepeñas in Spain. These wines are contained in the 'other varietals' section, which is the strongest part of the list.
Buy the case With a separate web address – corney-barrow.com, rather than corney-barrow.co uk – the merchant and shop arm has the best selection of the competition. Choices are clearly laid out on the internet, with a guide to the main wine-producing regions, and helpfully it provides VAT-included by-the-case prices, as well as what it costs in bond (for storing in the UK, minus VAT and duty). Unlike the other chains, the New World is well-represented too, with rich Vavasour chardonnay from New Zealand by the case, plus 1998 and 1999 vintages of d'Arenberg The Dead Arm shiraz.

Jamies
www.jamiesbars.co.uk
Jamies has recently revamped its Bishopsgate branch to make it sleeker, and the Mayfair outpost to give it a townhouse feel. Jamies venues have less of a try-hard style bar atmosphere now, and the wine list has greatly improved over the past year thanks to a new buyer joining the company. The New World dominates in all venues, and there's an extensive by-the-glass

selection totalling 26 wines. Food is a hotchpotch of trad-British, Italian and pub styles.
Pick of the bunch The branch at Fleet Place, EC4, in a new office development close to Holborn Viaduct, has an attractive main room with unfussy surrounds, large, elegant lampshades, and a neat outside terrace. It can be hired for parties of up to 220 people.
Best flavours It's not often you find good-value drinking from California, Spain or Italy, but there's a bottle apiece from all three on the main Jamies list: Delicato old vine zinfandel from 2005; 2006 Barbera d'Asti La Caplana; and Dominio de Valdepusa's cabernet sauvignon 2003 from Toledo – all lovely choices.
Buy the case Unlike the other major chains, Jamies only offers a selection of wines from its bar and restaurant lists by the case, and just ten wines in total. They're delivered via its major supplier, wine merchant Bibendum. All are well-made and tasty, particularly the apricot, minerally 2006 A20 albariño from Spain, and the ripe, rich Knappstein 2004 cabernet sauvignon-merlot from Australia.
Stop press Just before we went to press, the Food & Drink Group, which owned the Jamies brand, including 31 venues in London and a further 17 franchised outside town, went into administration. The new owner is meant to be keeping 16 of the London sites under the Jamies name, with minimal changes, but it's too early to say what will happen to the other sites.

gratin – and to the pâté. A hazelnut-flavoured white verdejo from Portada in Portugal is a notable addition to the improved wine list, but specialities of the house are the assorted ports, sherries and Madeira. A drier style of the latter, sercial from Blandy's, was a glorious sweet and sour mix of dried prunes and hazelnuts, with biting acidity. Like Gordon's itself, it is a mix of seemingly apparent opposites that somehow works.
Babies and children admitted. Bookings not accepted. Tables outdoors (20, terrace). **Map 10 L7**.

West
Shepherd's Bush

Albertine
1 Wood Lane, W12 7DP (8743 9593/ www.gonumber.com/albertine). Shepherd's Bush tube. **Open** 10am-11pm Mon-Thur; 10am-midnight Fri; 6.30pm-midnight Sat. **Meals served** noon-10.30pm Mon-Fri; 6.30-10.30pm Sat. **Main courses** £5.90-£10.30. **Credit** MC, V.
In business over 20 years, Albertine nevertheless keeps up with market trends, recently installing shiny pine shelving to show off bottles to take away at lower prices. Still, it's worth taking a seat, for the atmosphere is cosy, with melting candles and dark wooden furniture. Fleur de Garrigues 2004 Les Auzines from Corbières and Giovanni Blason's 2004 cabernet franc from Friuli offer the kind of contrasting flavours in which Albertine's well-thought-out list specialises: on the one hand spice and rich blackcurrant fruit from the south of

France; on the other tight, light, controlled red fruits and acidity. Food is regulation wine bar fare: smoked mackerel pâté was agreeably sharp and creamy; french onion tart featured good, crumbly pastry; and chunky pork and leek sausages came with a steaming mound of mash.
Bar available for hire. Bookings not accepted evenings. Off-licence. Separate room for parties, seats 25. Wireless internet (free). **Map 20 B2**.

Westbourne Grove

Negozio Classica
283 Westbourne Grove, W11 2QA (7034 0005/ www.negozioclassica.co.uk). Ladbroke Grove or Notting Hill Gate tube. **Open** May-Sept 3.30pm-midnight Mon; 11.30am-midnight Tue-Fri, Sun; 9am-midnight Sat. Oct-Apr 3.30pm-midnight Mon-Fri, Sun; 9am-midnight Sat. **Meals served** noon-10.30pm Mon-Thur, Sun; noon-11.30pm Fri, Sat. **Main courses** £7-£15.99. **House wine** £6.99 bottle, £3.25 glass. **Corkage** £6.50. **Credit** AmEx, MC, V.
Negozio Classica is fashioned after an Italian enoteca. Therefore you can buy wine to take away or drink-in (there's a corkage charge of £6.50 per bottle), and enjoy a glass on its own or with a plate or two of food. Pull up a stool at the stainless-steel bar or sit at one of the small tables squeezed into the tiny floor space. In warmer months, there are a few tables outside, great for observing the Notting Hill habitat. Wines are primarily Italian, with Tuscany and Piedmont claiming the lion's share, plus bottles from the northern Trentino Alto Adige region (the lush, plummy lagrein from the producer Castelfeder is a great introduction to this relatively rare grape variety). There's also a

smattering of wines from the south, a range from Slovenia, and an excellent choice of grappas. About 20 wines are available by the 125ml and 175ml glass. Food tends to be compositions of cold meats and cheeses. Papa al pomodoro, a thick blend of ripe tomatoes, stale bread and top-quality olive oil, tasted rustically, properly Italian. There's a range of Italian salumi, olive oils and balsamic vinegars to buy too.
Babies and children admitted. Off-licence. Separate room for parties, seats 13. Tables outdoors (3, pavement). **Map 7 A6**.

South West
Putney

Putney Station
94-98 Upper Richmond Road, SW15 2SP (8780 0242/www.brinkleys.com). East Putney tube.
Bar **Open** 11.30am-midnight Mon-Sat; 11am-11pm Sun.
Restaurant **Meals served** noon-11.30pm Mon-Fri; 11am-11.30pm Sat, Sun. **Main courses** £5-£17.
Both **House wine** £7.50 bottle, £3 glass. **Credit** AmEx, MC, V.
Part of a group that includes the Wine Gallery in Chelsea and Union Café in Marylebone, this particular outpost of the Brinkley's chain is straight out of the *Neighbours* TV series: perfect for the Aussies who live in Putney, with its pot plants, venetian blinds and framed black and white prints 1980s-style. The main room is pleasant, light-filled, with cheery young staff behind a large, steel bar. Although wine

Vinoteca. See p346.

knowledge wasn't high on the service agenda when we visited, the list itself is well-chosen and, for London, remarkably priced. The tasty, aromatic Viña Sol from Spanish producer Torres is seen in many wine bars, but rarely at just £10 a bottle for this 2006 version. Further up the list there's evidence that Australian chardonnay can be refined as well as weighty, with Petaluma's version from 2005. The menu has been shaken up to give a global spread: lemon and rosemary chicken with new potatoes and harissa mayonnaise working well after vegetable spring rolls or baked buffalo mozzarella.
Babies and children welcome: high chairs; nappy-changing. Disabled: toilet. Separate room for parties, seats 40. Tables outdoors (3, pavement; 12, garden). Wireless internet (free).

South
Clapham

★ Green & Blue NEW
20-26 Bedford Road, SW4 7HJ (7498 9648/ www.greenandbluewines.com). Clapham North tube. **Open/meals served** 7am-11pm Mon-Thur; 7am-1am Fri, Sat; 10.30am-10pm Sun. **Main courses** £5.50-£7.75. **House wine** £5.75 bottle, £3.40 glass. **Credit** MC, V.

The newer, but smaller of Green & Blue's two sites, this Clapham wine bar is squeezed behind the railway lines. Large framed metallic windows in an elongated room produce a slightly temporary feel that belies owner Kate Thal's long-term aim to provide greater wine choice on London's high streets. As at the East Dulwich branch, you can buy wine to drink on site, or pay less and take away. It sounds like a recipe for empty dining rooms, but on our visit the place was full of people with their laptops, having a drink while typing. Franconia from Franken, 2005, showed clearly that dry, fresh, citrussy examples can be produced in Germany, albeit with a touch of richness. Also much underrated are red wines from the Loire region of France, so try the slightly cherry-stone, supple, raspberryish Chinon Les Gravières from Domaine Couly-Dutheil. The food is simple, consisting of various platters: a fish version with smoked mackerel, rich, juicy brown crab meat and gravadlax being the pick. Thal spends time choosing her wines, has bucket-loads of knowledge, and it shows.
Babies and children welcome (before 7pm): high chairs, nappy-changing. Disabled: toilet. Separate room for parties, seats 25. Wine-tasting: call for details; from £15. **Map 22 C1**.
For branch see index.

South East
London Bridge & Borough

Wine Wharf
Stoney Street, SE1 9AD (7940 8335/www. winewharf.com). London Bridge tube/rail. **Open** noon-11pm Mon-Sat. **Meals served** noon-10pm Mon-Sat. **Main courses** £4.50-£9. **House wine** £17 bottle, £4 glass. **Credit** AmEx, DC, MC, V.

Wine Wharf is housed in a beautifully renovated warehouse that is all exposed bricks, high ceilings and big windows, creating an airy and stylish space that is packed on week nights with the after-work crowd. The extensive geographical spread of the list offers an excellent opportunity to sample wines from around the world, including serious bubbly like Taittinger's Comtes de Champagne and the ultra-classy Salon 1990. With nearly half the well-kept wines available by the glass, a visit here is a good chance to try something new; we pitched a sleek Austrian grüner veltliner against a fruitier torrontés from Argentina. A blackboard with wine flavour profiles (an apparent attempt to reflect the educational vibe from Vinopolis next door) was unnecessary – the staff are knowledgeable and generously offered us samples of wines prior to ordering. Like the wine list, the 'bar bites' hail from all over the map (suggesting a lack of personality); you'll find thai fish cakes next to a chicken mayo sandwich, and a sharing platter with the worrying combination of duck spring rolls, chips and chicken kebabs.
Babies and children welcome (before 8pm): high chairs. Bar available for hire. Booking advisable. Disabled: toilet. Entertainment: jazz 7.30pm Mon. Off-licence. **Map 11 P8**.

East
Docklands

Dion Canary Wharf NEW
Port East Building, West India Quay, Hertsmere Road, E14 4AF (7987 0001/www.dionlondon. co.uk). West India Quay DLR. **Open** noon-11pm Mon-Fri. **Lunch served** noon-3pm, **meals/ snacks served** 3-11pm Mon-Fri. **Credit** AmEx, MC, V.

Dion has made the capital's financial districts its target. The latest branch, with nightclub-style tiling and exposed brick, is set in a converted warehouse at the foot of Docklands' towering office blocks. Expect parties of business people flashing their credit cards and talking loudly. Comfort food classics feature on the lunchtime menu, and tend to be superior to more ambitious dishes. Opt for caesar salad, or a juicy sirloin steak sandwich with tomato salsa, big chips and aïoli,

rather than red mullet with flageolet beans and anchovy paste. The array of champagne draws many, with Jacquart Brut Mosaïque one of the more affordable and drinkable options: rich, balanced and superior to the better-known Veuve Clicquot NV at the top of the list. Dion's efforts to direct customers towards more imaginative champagnes through the use of such headings as 'Unsung Heroes' is to be applauded.
Babies and children welcome (lunch): high chairs. Booking advisable. Disabled toilet. Separate rooms for hire, seating 40-100. Tables outdoors (40, terrace). **Map 24 B1**.
For branches see index.

North
Camden Town & Chalk Farm

BOD NEW
30 Hawley Crescent, NW1 8NP (7482 5937). Camden Town tube. **Open/tapas served** noon-5pm Mon, Sun; noon-11pm Tue-Sat. **Tapas** £3-£5. **House wine** £12.50 bottle, £3.25 glass. **Credit** AmEx, DC, MC, V.

Just off Camden Market's main thoroughfare, this Spanish wine bar – full name Bodega de Tapas – has approaching 50 excellent Spanish wines, many of them chosen from the new, emerging wine regions or from top producers. Oddly, the choice of sherries is very limited, though one PX dessert sherry, with its distinctive rum and raisin smell, is available by the glass. There's a selection of tapas to fill any gaps, but these can be variable; we found the morcilla moist and unctuous, but a bean stew dry and disappointing. The unlikely location, in an area mostly patronised by twentysomethings, may explain the lack of custom on the evening of our visit; but this can be a plus-point if you want the cavernous, two-storey room all to yourselves (that's if you don't count the two Spanish waitresses).
Babies and children admitted. Disabled: toilets. Entertainment: flamenco music 6pm Wed, Fri. Separate room for parties, seats 40. Wireless internet (free). **Map 27 C2**.

BEST WINE BARS

Home or away?
Sample wine in the bar, or take a bottle home at **1707** (*see p347*), **Albertine** (*see p349*), **Green & Blue** (*see left*), **Negozio Classica** (*see p349*), **Vinoteca** (*see p346*) and **Wonder Bar** (*see p347*).

Vin extraordinaire
Wines out of the ordinary at **Albertine** (*see p349*), **Green & Blue** (*see left*), **Vinoteca** (*see p346*) and **Wonder Bar** (*see p347*).

A perfect match?
Mouth-watering food with wine is de rigueur at **Cellar Gascon** (*see p346*), **Ebury Wine Bar & Restaurant** (*see p345*), **Negozio Classica** (*see p349*), **Putney Station** (*see p349*) and **Vinoteca** (*see p346*).

Bubbling over
Great champagne lists in the new **St Pancras** (*see p347*), **Amuse Bouche** (*see p348*) and **Dion** (*see left*).

Fresh and zesty
Take a glass with the young crowd at **Bedford & Strand** (*see p346*), **Putney Station** (*see p349*), **Smithy's** (*see p347*) and **Wonder Bar** (*see p347*).

A fine vintage
Tradition holds sway at **Cork & Bottle** (*see p347*), **El Vino** (*see p345*), **Gordon's** (*see p348*) and **Shampers** (*see p348*).

Eating & Entertainment

Burlesque

Brickhouse
152C Brick Lane, E1 6RU (7247 0005/
www.thebrickhouse.co.uk). Liverpool Street tube/rail.
Open noon-2am Tue-Fri; 6pm-2am Sat. **Lunch**
served noon-3pm Tue-Fri. **Dinner served**
6.30-10.30pm Sat. **Set lunch** £20 2 courses, £24
3 courses. **Set dinner** £32.50-£39.50 3 courses,
£50 5 courses. **Credit** AmEx, MC, V.
This supper club is home to burlesque bombshells,
cabaret stars and magic performers most nights of
the week. A flavoursome Modern European menu
offers the choice between three courses or a longer
grazing option – evidence that dining here is a
whole evening affair. Two mezzanine levels tower
over a small performing area on the ground floor;
grab a table there for some tassel-twirling action
as the performers strut around the tables.
Babies and children admitted. Booking advisable
(Fri, Sat). Disabled: toilet. Entertainment: house
band 9pm-1am Tue; various artists Wed-Sat, call
for details. Separate room for parties, seats 24.
Map 6 S5.

Volupté
7-9 Norwich Street, EC4A 1EJ (7831 1622/
www.volupte-lounge.com). Chancery Lane tube.
Open 11.30am-1am Tue-Wed; 11.30am-3am
Thur, Fri; 2pm-3am Sat. **Lunch served** 11.30am-
4pm Tue-Fri. **Tea served** 2.30-5pm Sat. **Dinner**
served 6-10pm Tue-Sat. **Main courses** £5.95-
£17. **Set lunch** £14.50 2 courses, £16.50
3 courses. **Set dinner** £25 2 courses, £30
3 courses. **Credit** MC, V.
Volupté offers everything from jazz/rock bands and
cabaret crooners to 1920s flapper dancers and table
magicians. Food is international and organic; the
menu changes monthly. Decently priced and well-
made retro cocktails are served in the upstairs bar,
warming up a louche crowd before they move
downstairs for a glittery show in the Moulin
Rouge-style stage room. Afternoon Tease takes
place on selected Saturdays and includes entry, a
table for the afternoon, live entertainment and a
traditional tea including lovely sandwiches,
scones, pastries and champagne. Blue n Buns (on
alternate Saturdays) is a similar affair.
Booking essential. Dress: smart casual.
Entertainment: cabaret 6pm Wed, Fri; 2.30pm,
7pm, 10pm Sat. Restaurant available for hire.
Map 11 N5.

Comedy

It's difficult to find a comedy venue that
serves food and laughs of equal standard.
There are, however, a few places in the
capital that offer dishes of a higher quality
than standard old-style pub grub. In south-
east London, **Up the Creek** (302 Creek
Road, SE10 9SW, 8858 4581, www.up-the-
creek.com) is well worth a visit. Over in
Maida Vale there's the **Canal Café Theatre**
(first floor, The Bridge House, on the corner
of Westbourne Terrace Road and Delamere
Terrace, W2 6ND, 7289 6056, www.canal
cafetheatre.com; map 1 C5), while in
Shoreditch there's the **Comedy Café** (66-
68 Rivington Street, EC2A 3AY, 7739 5706,
www.comedycafe.co.uk; map 6 R4).

The best-known comedy club in London is
probably Leicester Square's **Comedy Store**
(1A Oxendon Street, SW1 4EE, bookings
Ticketmaster 0870 060 2340, www.the
comedystore.co.uk; map 17 B5). Another
favourite is **Jongleurs Camden Lock** (11
East Yard, Camden Lock, Chalk Farm Road,
NW1 8AB, 0870 787 0707, www.jongleurs.
com; map 27 C1) – which has two other
London branches, in Battersea and Bow.

For up-to-date information on the capital's
comedy clubs, see the Comedy section in
the weekly *Time Out* magazine.

Dining afloat

Vessels for hire include canal cruisers from
the **Floating Boater** (Waterside, Little Venice,
Warwick Crescent, W2 6NE, 7266 1066,
www.floatingboater.co.uk; map 1 C5); the
Leven is Strijd (West India Quay, Hertsmere
Road, West India Docks, E14 4AE, 7987
4002, www.theleven.co.uk), a classic Dutch
barge, for views of Canary Wharf; and the
Elizabethan (8780 1562, www.thamesluxury
charters.co.uk), which is a replica of a 19th-
century Mississippi paddle steamer that
cruises from Putney eastwards to beyond the
Thames Barrier.

The **RS Hispaniola** next to Hungerford
Bridge (Victoria Embankment, WC2N 5DJ,
7839 3011, www.hispaniola.co.uk; map 10
L8) is a popular party venue with tapas bar,
cocktail lounge and a large restaurant.

DIY

Blue Hawaii
2 Richmond Road, Kingston upon Thames, Surrey
KT2 5EB (8549 6989/www.bluehawaii.co.uk).
Kingston rail. **Dinner served** 6pm-1am Mon-Sat.
Meals served noon-1am Sun. **Set meal** £11.95
unlimited barbecue. **Set dinner** £15 2 courses,
£19.50 3 courses. **Credit** AmEx, DC, MC, V.
Every night is party night at Blue Hawaii. Surrey's
own slice of the Big Island sees flower-garbed
waiting staff serve cocktails to bolshie birthday
groups and after-work parties in a restaurant-cum-
beach-hut setting. Ingredients are cooked to order
on a big teppanyaki grill at the front: choose from
a selection of vegetables, meat and seafood, mix in
own-made Hawaiian sauces, select some spices and
you're away. Cocktails are reasonably priced at
around £4. Saturday nights play host to resident
Elvis impersonator Matt King, while Sundays are
more family-oriented.
Babies and children welcome: children's menu; high
chairs; nappy-changing facilities; supervised play
area (noon-5pm Sun). Booking essential weekends.
Entertainment: musicians 10pm Fri, Sat.

Dogs' dinners

Wimbledon Stadium
Plough Lane, SW17 0BL (8946 8000/
www.lovethedogs.co.uk). Tooting Broadway
tube/Earlsfield rail/44, 270, 272 bus. **Dinner**
served 7-9.30pm Tue, Fri, Sat. **Set meal**
£20-£25 3 courses. **Admission** £5 grandstand.
Credit MC, V.

A night at the dogs entails an awful lot of whiling
away time in between very brief races – and, of
course, a lot of time spent betting. Dinner in one
of the grandstands is a good alternative way to
pass the time and need not mean soggy hotdogs
and plastic cups. There are three main places to
eat; one a fast-food takeaway, the other two proper
dining areas complete with waitress service. For
some events, there's a black tie dress code in the
smartest of the two dining areas, Star Attraction,
which has tiered seating overlooking the track. The
menu is surprisingly sophisticated, comprising
modern, French-accented food from a three-choice
prix fixe menu. Broadway suits more sociable,
intimate occasions, with tables of four or six
arranged so diners are facing one other, and races
shown on monitors. Bookings in either eaterie
include admission, race card and a three-course
meal, starting at a very reasonable £20. Bookable
extras to add to your night include tote vouchers,
champers, race sponsorship and a pre-paid bar tab.
Babies and children welcome: high chairs;
nappy-changing facilities. Booking essential.
Disabled: lift; toilet. Separate rooms for parties,
seating 28-120.

Jazz & soul

Dover Street
8-10 Dover Street, W1S 4LQ (7629 9813/
www.doverstreet.co.uk). Green Park or Piccadilly
Circus tube. **Open** 5.30pm-3am Mon-Sat.
Dinner served 6-10pm Mon-Thur; 7-11pm Fri,
Sat. **Music** Bands 9.30pm Mon; 7.30pm Tue-Sat.
DJs until 3am Mon-Sat. **Main courses** £13.95-
£21.95. **Set dinner** £24.95-£45 3 courses.
Admission £6 after 10pm Mon; £7 after 10pm
Tue; £8 after 10pm Wed; £12 after 10pm Thur;
diners only until 10pm, then £15 Fri, Sat. **Credit**
AmEx, DC, MC, V.
Dover Street is a fine London jazz venue and classy
restaurant rolled into one. Enjoy early evening
cocktails at one of two elegant bars, admiring the
black-and-white fashion and jazz prints that adorn
the walls, then dine from a Modern European
menu created by ex-L'Aventure chef Laurent
Pichaureaux while a lounge jazz trio tootle away.
After dinner, guests are invited on to the dancefloor
to work off their desserts, with live music and
dancing until 3am. An ongoing refurb of the
interior was taking place as we went to press.
Booking advisable, essential weekends. Dress:
smart casual. Separate rooms for parties, seating
20-100. **Map 9 J7**.

Green Note
106 Parkway, NW1 7AN (7485 9899/
www.greennote.co.uk). Camden Town tube.
Dinner served 7-10pm Wed, Thur, Sun;
7-10.30pm Fri, Sat. **Music** 9-11pm daily. **Tapas**
£2.25-£4.95. **Main courses** £7.95-£9.95.
Admission £4-£15. **Credit** MC, V.
Paintings of folk icons Joni Mitchell and Bob
Dylan adorn the walls of this relaxed Greenwich
Village-style hangout for Camden's beatniks. Eat
in the café/restaurant area out front or the music
venue in the back, which offers live acts ranging
from folk and blues to jazz and world music. The
fully vegetarian menu offers international tapas,
daily specials, and larger sharing plates, all
reasonably priced. There is also an extensive
cocktail list.
Babies and children admitted: high chair. Booking
advisable. Vegan dishes. **Map 27 C3**.

Jazz After Dark
9 Greek Street, W1D 4DQ (7734 0545/
www.jazzafterdark.co.uk). Leicester Square or
Tottenham Court Road tube. **Open** 2pm-2am
Mon-Thur; 2pm-3am Fri, Sat. **Meals served**
2pm-midnight Mon-Thur. **Music** 9pm Mon-Thur;
10.30pm Fri, Sat. **Main courses** £8.50-£10.95.
Set menu £10.95 3 courses. **Admission** £5
Mon-Thur; £10 diners, £15 non-diners Fri, Sat.
Credit AmEx, DC, MC, V.
Jazz After Dark is a late-night cocktail bar,
restaurant and jazz club of the old school: small,
low-lit and laid-back. The young, after-work crowd
takes in unsigned bands as well as seasoned

professionals, playing a range of jazz, blues, funk and Latin; some nights see impromptu sets from regulars Pete Doherty and Amy Winehouse. The cuisine is international, ranging from tapas to Tex-Mex, and there is a sizeable cocktail list.
Booking essential Fri, Sat. Dress: smart casual; no trainers. Restaurant available for hire. Tables outdoors (2, pavement). **Map 17 C3.**

Jazz Café
5-7 Parkway, NW1 7PG (7485 6834/ www.jazzcafelive.com). Camden Town tube.
Open 7pm-midnight Mon-Thur; 7pm-2am Fri, Sat; 7pm-midnight Sun. **Meals served** 7.30-9.30pm daily. **Music** daily; call for times. **Main courses** £16.50. **Set meal** £26.50 3 courses. **Admission** varies; call for details. **Credit** MC, V.
The balcony restaurant at this well-established venue has tables overlooking the stage, where a classy mix of soul, R&B, jazz and acoustic rock acts strut their stuff. Acts range from Martha Reeves and the Vandellas to New York hip-hop star Pharoahe Monch. The line-up often attracts a slightly more mature music fan, though things liven up on weekend club nights when diners descend on to the dancefloor. Check the website to see who's playing when. To eat, there's the likes of deep-fried prawns wrapped in filo, spicy chicken with rice and peas, and caramelised figs with vanilla ice-cream.
Booking advisable. Disabled: toilet. **Map 27 D2.**

Pizza Express Jazz Club
10 Dean Street, W1D 3RW (7439 8722/ www.pizzaexpresslive.com). Tottenham Court Road tube.
Restaurant **Meals served** noon-midnight daily.
Club **Meals served** 7.30-11pm daily. **Music** 9-11pm daily. **Admission** £15-£22.
Both **Main courses** £4.95-£8.25. **Credit** AmEx, DC, MC, V.
Crowds have been loyally flocking to the basement club of this pizzeria since it opened in 1965. Musicians have ranged from Van Morrison to Amy Winehouse; up-and-coming stars often make the line-up, as do stalwarts of the London jazz scene such as Ian Shaw and Barb Jungr. Pizza Express culinary standards make the eating part of this equation pleasant. The atmosphere is friendly too. Musicians play seven nights a week; check the website for details.
Babies and children welcome: high chairs. Booking advisable. Disabled: toilet. Takeaway service. **Map 17 B3.**

Le Quecum Bar
42-44 Battersea High Street, SW11 3HX (7787 2227/www.quecumbar.co.uk). Clapham Junction rail. **Open** 7pm-midnight Mon-Thur; 6pm-1am Fri, Sat; 6pm-midnight Sun. **Dinner served** 7-10pm Mon-Thur; 6-10pm Fri, Sat; 6-8pm Sun. **Music** 7pm-midnight Mon-Thur; 6pm-midnight Fri, Sat; occasional Sun. **Main courses** £8-£14. **Admission** (non-members) £5 Fri, Sat. **Membership** £65/yr. **Credit** AmEx, MC, V.
Pre-war France meets Django Reinhardt-style gypsy jazz at this original wine bar with live music almost every night. Brasserie food (french onion soup, frogs' legs, pâté, escargots) is served until 10pm; patrons are invited to linger a while in the luxurious bar or exotic tropical patio. If you don't fancy wine, there is Kronenberg and Amstell on tap, bottled beers including Leffe, chocolate martinis, and plenty of non-alcoholic options for anyone driving.
Booking advisable (Tue, Fri, Sat). Dress: smart. **Map 21 B2.**

Ronnie Scott's
47 Frith Street, W1D 4HT (7439 0747/ www.ronniescotts.co.uk). Leicester Square or Tottenham Court Road tube. **Open/music** 6pm-late daily. **Meals served** 6pm-1am Mon-Sat; 6-11pm Sun. **Main courses** £9-£29.50. **Set meal** £23 2 courses. **Admission** (non-members) £20-£36. **Membership** £165/yr. **Credit** AmEx, DC, MC, V.
Opened in 1959, Ronnie Scott's is one of the UK's oldest and best-known jazz venues. The likes of Tony Bennett still occasionally perform in this intimate setting; local stars such as Clare Martin

make regular appearances, and on Tuesday nights young musicians rip it up at a past-midnight jam session. The international menu features the likes of grilled squid with mango and chilli salsa, stuffed corn-fed chicken with garlic mousse and sage polenta, and sticky toffee pudding. The website offers details of forthcoming acts, online booking and a jazz podcast.
Bar available for hire. Booking advisable. Disabled: toilet. Dress: no shorts. Takeaway service. **Map 17 C3.**

606 Club
90 Lots Road, SW10 0QD (7352 5953/ www.606 club.co.uk). Earl's Court tube.
Open/meals served 7.30-11.45pm Mon; 7pm-12.30am Tue, Wed; 7pm-midnight Thur; 8pm-1.30am Fri, Sat; 7-11pm Sun. **Music** 9pm Mon; 7.30pm Tue, Wed; 8pm Thur; 9.30pm Fri, Sat; 8.30pm Sun. **Main courses** £8.95-£18.45. **Admission** (non-members) £8 Mon-Thur; £12 Fri, Sat; £10 Sun. **Membership** £95 first yr; £60 subsequent yrs. **Credit** AmEx, MC, V.

Steve Rubie's candle-lit, Parisian-style basement jazz club has been chilling out jazz aficionados both here on Lots Road and at its former location (606 King's Road) for over 30 years. There's music every night – ten bands a week – and the number of musicians that hang out after work give it some serious muso credibility. Diners can choose from a menu that changes regularly, but typically includes such dishes as salmon teriyaki, wild boar sausages with herb mash, and nachos. Note that if you're not a member, you have to dine.
Babies and children admitted. Booking advisable weekends. **Map 13 C13.**

Latin

Nueva Costa Dorada
47-55 Hanway Street, W1T 1UX (7631 5117/ www.costadoradarestaurant.co.uk). Tottenham Court Road tube. **Open/meals served** 5pm-3am Tue-Sat. **Main courses** £11.95-£16.50. **Credit** AmEx, DC, MC, V.

Salsa! See p354.

Evolving into an increasingly classy establishment in recent years, Nueva Costa Dorada allows guests to enjoy traditional Spanish fare alongside live nightly flamenco shows. It has a warm, cosy cocktail-bar feel and a great party atmosphere, with the dining tables arranged around the stage for optimum viewing. There's plenty of space for large groups, so it's a very popular venue for office and birthday parties. To eat, there is a mixture of tapas, such as tortilla and calamari, and a solid à la carte menu including dishes such as paella (£21-£28) and swordfish (£14.50). A Spanish-heavy wine list, small cocktail selection and bar nibbles are also available.
Babies and children admitted (until 11pm). Entertainment: flamenco shows 9.30pm Tue-Thur, 10pm Fri, Sat; DJ 11pm Thur-Sat. Restaurant available for hire. **Map 17 B2**.

Salsa!

96 Charing Cross Road, WC2H 0JG (7379 3277/www.barsalsa.info). *Leicester Square or Tottenham Court Road tube.*
Bar Open 5.30pm-2am Mon-Sat; 6pm-1am Sun.
Café **Open** 9am-5.30pm Mon-Sat. **Snacks served** noon-5.30pm Mon-Sat. **Set buffet** (noon-6pm Mon-Sat) 99p/kilo.
Restaurant **Meals served** 5.30-11pm daily. **Main courses** £4.75-£11.50.
Bar & Restaurant **Admission** £4 after 9pm Mon-Thur; £2 after 7pm, £4 after 8pm, £8 after 9pm, £10 after 11pm Fri, Sat; £3 after 7pm, £4 after 8pm Sun.
All **Credit** AmEx, MC, V.
There's rarely a quiet night at Salsa!, a restaurant, café, bar and dance club all rolled in to one. Dance classes suitable for complete beginners through to salsa pros are held in the bar six nights a week, costing £5 (£3 for diners). On Fridays there is a free two-hour introduction to Latin dance, including salsa, merengue and lambada, which is well worth checking out. Latin-themed drink promotions help lubricate your dancefloor performance, such as £2 caipirinhas all night Tuesday and two-for-one mojitos on Thursday. Food in the restaurant is a mixture of tapas and larger dishes such as fajitas and chargrilled steaks. Also worth a look is the Brazilian buffet in the café, costing 99p per kilo.
Booking advisable; essential weekends. Dress: smart casual. Entertainment: DJs 9.30pm daily; dance classes 7pm Mon, Wed-Sun; bands 9.30pm Tue, Thur-Sat. Tables outdoors (10, pavement). Takeaway service (café). **Map 17 C3**.

Music & dancing

Pigalle Club

215-217 Piccadilly, W1J 9HN (7734 8142/www.thepigalleclub.com). *Piccadilly Circus tube.*
Open 7pm-2am Mon-Wed; 7pm-3am Thur-Sat.
Dinner served 7-11.30pm Mon-Sat. **Set meal** £45 3 courses. **Admission** £10 after 10pm Mon-Thur; £10 after 7pm, £15 after 10.30pm Fri, Sat.
Credit AmEx, DC, MC, V.
This sleek, chic, basement supper club (part of the Vince Power stable) is all about 1940s-style glamour: low lighting, olive green carpets, antique fittings and diamond-shaped mirrors. Tables for diners are clustered around the stage, where jazz, jive and cabaret crooners serenade an appreciative audience. The Modern European food is pricey (£45 for three courses), but non-diners are welcome, so head for the bar and make like you're Sinatra.
Entertainment: live music 9pm daily. **Map 17 B5**.

Roadhouse

35 The Piazza, WC2E 8BE (7240 6001/www.roadhouse.co.uk). *Covent Garden tube.*
Open 5.30pm-3am Mon-Sat; 5.30pm-midnight Sun. **Meals served** 5.30pm-1.30am Mon-Sat; 5.30pm-midnight Sun. **Main courses** £8.25-£17. **Admission** £5 after 10.30pm Mon-Wed; £7 after 10pm Thur; £10 after 9pm Fri; £5 after 7pm, £12 after 9pm Sat; £5 after 7pm Sun.
Credit AmEx, MC, V.
The Roadhouse is a prime target for beery lads and riotous hen bashes (stag parties, however, are now banned), attracted by the happy-hour promotions, DJs and rock/pop bands on stage every night.

You'll find comfort food such as chicken wings, steaks and nachos on the American diner-style menu, while the bar staff will guide you through a 60-strong cocktail list.
Booking advisable. Dress: smart casual. Entertainment: bands/DJs 7pm daily. **Map 18 E4**.

Tiroler Hut

27 Westbourne Grove, W2 4UA (7727 3981/www.tirolerhut.co.uk). *Bayswater or Queensway tube.* **Open** 6.30pm-1am Tue-Sat; 6.30pm-midnight Sun. **Dinner served** 6.30pm-12.30am Tue-Sat; 6.30-11.30pm Sun. **Main courses** £12.90-£25. **Set meal** (Tue-Thur, Sun) £22.50 3 courses; (Fri, Sat) £25.50 3 courses. **Credit** AmEx, DC, MC, V.
Counting Kate Moss and Stella McCartney among its customers, this kitsch, family-run basement restaurant is decorated to resemble a traditional alpine ski lodge. Staff are clad in lederhosen and dirndls, while Tirolean music performances, ranging from accordions to cowbells, get diners on their feet; the occasional sing-a-long means this is not a place for the easily embarrassed. More serious is the good selection of German and Austrian beers and wines. To eat, expect sausages, spätzle, sauerkraut and strudel; vegetarians are well catered for with crumbed mushrooms, asparagus pasta and cheese fondue.
Babies and children admitted. Booking essential. Entertainment: cowbell show 9pm Tue-Sun. Restaurant available for hire. Vegan dishes. **Map 7 B6**.

One-offs

Dans Le Noir

30-31 Clerkenwell Green, EC1R 0DU (7253 1100/www.danslenoir.com/london). *Farringdon tube/rail.* **Lunch served** by appointment. **Dinner served** (fixed sittings) 7-7.30pm, 9-9.30pm Mon-Thur; 7-7.30pm, 9.15-9.45pm Fri, Sat. **Set dinner** £29 2 courses, £37 3 courses. **Credit** AmEx, MC, V.
For a colourful night out, try this pitch black restaurant where customers are served and guided around the room by blind staff – and no one is allowed to move around the room without the assistance of their guide. Guests order their food in the lit bar 20 minutes before dining, choosing from four 'surprise' menus. Expect Modern European fare; menus are regularly updated for variety and include vegetarian and meat- and seafood-free options. A 'dark bar' is open for wine, cocktails and tapas on a Friday (5.30-6.30pm) and for networking evenings on Mondays. There is also the opportunity to cook your own three-course menu under the guidance of the head chef and then invite a group of friends to enjoy your culinary creations in the dark.
Booking essential. Disabled: toilet. Separate room for parties, seats 60. **Map 5 N4**.

Lucky Voice

52 Poland Street, W1F 7NH (7439 3660/www.luckyvoice.co.uk). *Oxford Circus tube.* **Open/snacks served** 6pm-1am Mon-Thur; 3pm-1am Fri, Sat; 3-10.30pm Sun. **Credit** AmEx, MC, V.
This cute, Japanese-style karaoke bar offers nine well-designed private karaoke pods of varying sizes. Props such as hats, wigs and percussion are available; you can also create your own playlist ahead of visiting using the huge song database on the website. The cocktail list (all £7) includes tipples such as a Kimono (shochu mixed with lychee, guava, peach and lime) or a Sunshine 60 (gin, saké, apricot purée and pomegranate juice). Warm and cold saké is sold by the bottle (£24-£28). To assuage hunger, there are a few stonebaked pizzas (all £8), including a wasabi margherita.
Entertainment: karaoke pods for hire, £5-£10/hr. Over-21s only. **Map 17 A3**.
For branch see index.

Rainforest Café

20 Shaftesbury Avenue, W1D 7EU (7434 3111/www.therainforestcafe.co.uk). *Leicester Square or Piccadilly Circus tube.* **Meals served** noon-10pm Mon-Thur, Sun; noon-7.30pm Fri,

Sat. **Main courses** £10.90-£18. **Credit** AmEx, DC, MC, V.
London's largest family restaurant, the Rainforest Café is an extravagant tropical hideaway inhabited by animatronic apes and elephants, and complete with tropical storms and cascading waterfalls. It is extremely popular for kids' parties: for £13.90 each child get a main course, dessert, drink, party bag and free birthday cake. Food is colourful, fun and aimed at a younger palate, with several healthy options. Adults also have plenty of choice, all in keeping with the rainforest theme: try a 'leaping lizard meze' (£7.90), followed by 'sea bass samba' (£15.30). The real challenge, however, is getting your offspring seated without giving in to their demands for soft toys and T-shirts from the shop on the way in.
Babies and children welcome: bottle-warmers; children's menu; crayons; high chairs; nappy-changing facilities. Separate rooms for parties, seating 11-100. **Map 17 B5**.

Troubadour

263-267 Old Brompton Road, SW5 9JA (7370 1434/www.troubadour.co.uk). *West Brompton tube/rail.*
Café **Open** 9am-midnight daily. **Meals served** 9-11pm daily. **Main courses** £8-£18.
Wine bar/shop **Open** noon-10pm daily.
Club **Open** 8pm-midnight Mon-Wed, Sun; 8pm-2am Thur-Sat. **Meals served** 8-11pm daily. **Main courses** £8.25-£16.50.
All **Credit** AmEx, MC, V.
This café-bar, part folk club, part tearoom, was a key player in London's 1950s bohemian café movement. Bob Dylan played his first London gig here; it was also incubator to *Private Eye*, and the friendship between Ken Russell and Oliver Reed. The café offers made-to-order sandwiches and bistro-style dishes (omelettes, burgers, salads, fish and chips) while the basement club hosts music, poetry readings and stand-up comedy (check the website for more details). As we went to press the deli was being transformed into a wine shop-cum-wine bar. The art gallery above is available to hire for exhibitions or private parties, and the attic floor offers funky, quite luxurious accommodation for up to four people.
Babies and children welcome: children's portions; high chairs. Separate room for parties, seats 32. Club available for hire. Tables outdoors (8, garden). **Map 13 B11**.

Twelfth House

35 Pembridge Road, W11 3HG (7727 9620/www.twelfth-house.co.uk). *Notting Hill Gate tube.* **Open/meals served** noon-11pm Mon-Fri; 10am-11pm Sat; 10am-10.30pm Sun. **Main courses** £6.50-£13. **Credit** MC, V.
Reviving the 18th-century tradition of coffeeshop fortune-telling, this mystical, magical-themed bar offers 'astrological chart sessions' with owner Priscilla for £30. You can also have your basic chart printed for £5, or select a 'tarot card of the day' for £3. The restaurant that was once here has closed, to be replaced by two bars serving snacks. There's also a new range of astrologically themed tipples. They take their coffee seriously too.
Booking advisable. Tables outdoors (4, garden). **Map 7 A7**.

Opera

Sarastro

126 Drury Lane, WC2B 5QG (7836 0101/www.sarastro-restaurant.com). *Covent Garden or Holborn tube.* **Meals served** noon-11.30pm daily. **Main courses** £7.50-£15.50. **Set lunch** (noon-6.30pm Mon-Sat) £12.50 2 courses. **Set meal** £23.50 3 courses incl coffee. **Credit** AmEx, DC, MC, V.
Named after a character from Mozart's *The Magic Flute*, this flamboyant restaurant continues the operatic theme with ten individually styled opera boxes, velvet drapes, theatrical props and other colourful frippery. Food is Mediterranean-Turkish (cheese borek, grilled fish, kofte with rice, lemon tart), while the wine list starts at £13.50 for French house wines and hits the high notes with a good choice of champagnes. Established singers and up-

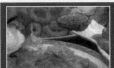

Elbow Room

and-coming stars from nearby opera houses sing at the cabaret every Monday and Sunday.
Babies and children welcome: high chairs. Booking advisable. Disabled: toilet. Entertainment: opera, string quartet 1.30pm, 8.30pm Mon, 8.30pm Sun. **Map 18 F3**.

Sports bars

All Star Lanes

Victoria House, Bloomsbury Place, WC1B 4DA (7025 2676/www.allstarlanes.co.uk). Holborn tube. **Open** 5-11.30pm Mon-Wed; 5pm-midnight Thur; noon-2am Fri, Sat; noon-11pm Sun. **Meals served** 6-11.30pm Mon-Wed; 6pm-midnight Thur; noon-2am Fri, Sat; noon-11pm Sun. **Main courses** £7.95-£24. **Bowling** (per person per game) £7.50 before 5pm, £8.50 after 5pm. **Credit** AmEx, MC, V.
Of Bloomsbury's two subterranean bowling dens, this is the one with aspirations. Taking inspiration from Stateside 'boutique' bowling alleys, there are four lanes (plus two private lanes upstairs) and diner-style booths at which to enjoy burgers, steaks and the spectacle of players bowling gutterballs. In the comfortable, subdued side bar you'll find classy red furnishings, glitterballs and an impressive selection of well-made cocktails. There's a sister branch in Bayswater and another scheduled to open on Brick Lane in late 2008. Be sure to book ahead.
Babies and children admitted (until 6pm). Booking advisable. Disabled: toilet. Separate room for parties, seats 30-75. **Map 18 E1**. **For branch see index**.

Bloomsbury Bowling Lanes

Basement, Tavistock Hotel, Bedford Way, WC1H 9EU (7691 2610/www.bloomsburylive.com). Russell Square tube. **Open** noon-midnight Mon-Wed; noon-1am Thur; noon-3am Fri, Sat; 1-10pm Sun. **Meals served** noon-10pm daily. **Main courses** £6.95-£7.95. **Bowling** from £36/hr 1 lane (maximum 6 people); £3 (per person per game) Mon-Wed until 4pm. **Credit** AmEx, MC, V.
While near-neighbour All Star Lanes makes a good stab at sophistication, BBL knows it's a big kids' playground. As well as the eight lanes, there's pool by the hour, table football, private karaoke booths and, next to the entrance, a small cinema. The American diner-styled restaurant serves burgers and NewYork-style pizzas. Laneside snacks are also available. A new Kingpin suite opened in 2008: a private bowling room complete with its own entrance, full-service cocktail bar and DJ booth. There are also plans for a 'hot tub' private karaoke room. Big kids indeed.
Booking essential. Disabled: toilet. No under-18s after 4pm. **Map 4 K4**.

Elbow Room

89-91 Chapel Market, N1 9EX (7278 3244/ www.theelbowroom.co.uk). Angel tube. **Open** 5pm-2am Mon; noon-2am Tue-Thur; noon-3am Fri, Sat; noon-1am Sun. **Meals served** 5-10pm Mon; noon-10pm Tue-Sun. **Main courses** £5-£8. **Pool** £6-£10/hr. **Credit** MC, V.
Part of the chain of bar-cum-pool halls, this is a well-designed, welcoming spot. The front third of the long L-shaped space is given over to a bar boasting a mix of comfortable private booths and high tables. The (bookable) pool playing area is surprisingly stylish: red curtains hang elegantly between tables while the walls are adorned with fetching rippled wood. The lighting is just right too, as is the level of the music. Bottles of wine start at £13, classic cocktails from £6.25 and a hustler-friendly menu of burgers, wraps, salads and meze costs £6-£10.
Booking advisable weekends. Disabled: toilet. Entertainment: DJs 7pm Thur-Fri, 9pm Sat, Sun. Separate room for parties, seats 30. **For branches see index**.

Sports Café

80 Haymarket, SW1Y 4TE (7839 8300/ www.thesportscafe.com). Piccadilly Circus tube/ Charing Cross tube/rail. **Open** noon-3am daily. **Meals served** noon-10pm daily. **Main courses** £7.95-£16.95. **Admission** £5 after 10pm Mon, Tue, Fri, Sat. **Credit** AmEx, MC, V.
You like sports? Grab a beer and pick any one of the 100 screens beaming out all things sports-related, from football and rugby league to Formula One and tennis. The key American sports are shown for the noticeable expat and tourist contingent, but this is also the London home of the England cricket team's Barmy Army. It's cramped and noisy for the big matches, but you can escape to shoot some pool (there are 11 tables), or grab a bite (buffalo wings, nachos, wraps, burgers, ribs, steaks) in the dining areas. DJs play chart hits from 10pm most nights.
Children admitted (until 9pm, dining only). Disabled: toilet. Music (DJs 10pm Mon, Tue, Fri, Sat). Restaurant available for hire. **Map 10 K7**.

24-hour eats

Tinseltown

44-46 St John Street, EC1M 4DT (7689 2424/ www.tinseltown.co.uk). Farringdon tube/rail. **Open** 24hrs daily. **Main courses** £6-£13. **Set lunch** (noon-5pm Mon-Fri) £5.50 2 courses incl soft drink. **No alcohol allowed. Credit** DC, MC, V.
Portraits of stars such as Travolta and De Niro line the walls of this Hollywood-themed diner and milkshake bar that attracts late-night clubbers, cabbies and insomniacs. Food (burgers, baguettes, burritos, breakfast) comes in American-sized portions, and various shakes are made with well-known branded chocolates (Ferrero Rocher, Creme Egg, Bounty). A sister restaurant in Hampstead is open until 3am on Friday and Saturday nights only.
Babies and children welcome: children's menu; high chair. Takeaway service. **Map 5 O5**. **For branches see index**.

Vingt-Quatre

325 Fulham Road, SW10 9QL (7376 7224/ www.vingtquatre.co.uk). South Kensington tube. **Open** 24hrs daily. **Main courses** £7.25-£14.75. **Credit** AmEx, MC, V.
Vingt-Quatre caters for a posh post-club Kensington and Chelsea crowd, fresh out of the high-class hotspots nearby, and thirsty for more champers. A half-bottle of Krug will set you back £75 after 10pm – in fact, all prices, particularly those of drink, shoot up after this hour. Alternatively, wind down with the range of therapeutic teas (£3.50). A small full english breakfast (with organic, free-range eggs) starts at £6.95 (£9.95 in the wee hours); the menu also features fish and chips, steak, club sandwiches with fries, omelettes and a few more adventurous options such as kimchee dumplings.
Babies and children admitted. Tables outdoors (2, pavement). **Map 14 D12**.

Views & victuals

Vertigo 42 Champagne Bar

Tower 42, 25 Old Broad Street, EC2N 1HQ (7877 7842/www.vertigo42.co.uk). Bank tube/ DLR/Liverpool Street tube/rail. **Open** noon-3pm, 5-11pm Mon-Fri. **Lunch served** noon-2.15pm, **dinner served** 5-9.30pm Mon-Fri. **Main courses** £5.50-£19. **Credit** AmEx, DC, MC, V.
Don't let prior booking, clearance from security and strictly enforced admission times put you off: this bar at the top of Tower 42 gives truly breathtaking views. Seats are arranged so that everyone can enjoy the panorama. Redecorated a couple of years ago in a soothing purple colour-scheme, it offers a selection of dishes from the menu of Rhodes Twenty Four restaurant (*see p54*), some 18 floors down (a plate of canapés; steak with grilled blue cheese mushrooms and watercress; pear and cinnamon tart). Champagne starts at £46 for a bottle of Veuve Delaroy Brut and rises to a blinging £795.50 for a magnum of Krug. There are also still wines (Provençal rosé £7.50 per glass) and cocktails (Pimm's royale £11.50).
Bar available for hire. Booking essential. Disabled: toilet; lift. Dress: smart casual. **Map 12 Q6**.

Maps

The following maps highlight London's key restaurant areas: the districts with the highest density of good places to eat and drink. They show precisely where each restaurant is located, as well as major landmarks and tube stations.

Queen's Park & Maida Vale

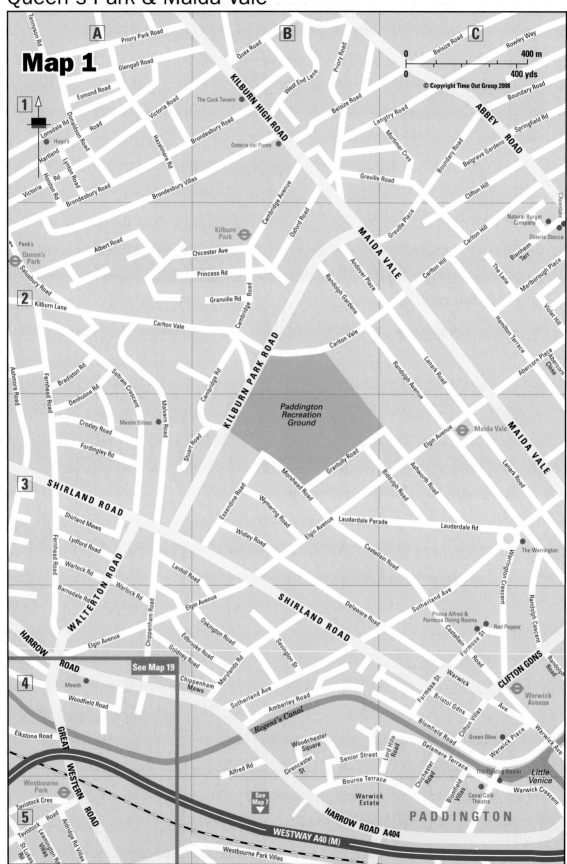

Map 1

A

B

C

Tennyson Rd
Priory Park Road
Quex Road
West End Lane
Priory Road
Belsize Road
Rowley Way

Glengall Road
The Cock Tavern
Belsize Road
Langtry Road
Springfield Rd
Boundary Road

Esmond Road
Victoria Road
Brondesbury Road
Osteria del Ponte
Mortimer Cres
Boundary Road
Belgrave Gardens

Lonsdale Rd
Donaldson Road
Road
Hazelmere Rd
Greville Road
Clifton Hill
L'Aventure

Hugo's
Hartland
Greville Place
Carlton Hill
Natural Burger Company

Lynton Road
Brondesbury Villas
Oxford Road
Greville Road
The Lane
Osteria Stecca

Honiton Rd
Cambridge Avenue
Carlton Hill
Blenheim Terr

Victoria
Kilburn Park
Chicester Ave
Andover Place
Carlton Hill
Marlborough Place
Violet Hill

Penk's
Albert Road
Princess Rd
Randolph Gardens
Hamilton Terrace
Abercorn Place
Abercorn Close

Queen's Park
Granville Rd
Cambridge Road
Carlton Vale
Randolph Avenue
Lanark Road

Salusbury Road
Carlton Vale
Paddington Recreation Ground
Elgin Avenue
Maida Vale

Kilburn Lane
Cambridge Rd
Grantully Road
Ashworth Road
Lanark Road

Ashmore Road
Bradiston Rd
Saltram Crescent
Malvern Road
Morshead Road
Biddulph Road

Fernhead Road
Denholme Rd
Mesón Bilbao
Wymering Road
The Warrington

Croxley Road
Fordingley Rd
Essendine Road
Widley Road
Elgin Avenue
Lauderdale Parade
Lauderdale Rd

SHIRLAND ROAD
Shirland Mews
Lydford Road
Stuart Road
Castellain Road
Warrington Crescent

Fernhead Road
Warlock Rd
Lanhill Road
Delaware Road
Sutherland Ave
Randolph Crescent

Barnsdale Rd
Warlock Rd
Chippenham Road
Elgin Avenue
SHIRLAND ROAD
Prince Alfred & Formosa Dining Rooms
Red Pepper

WALTERTON ROAD
Oakington Road
Edbrooke Road
Sevington St
Castellain Road
Formosa St
CLIFTON GDNS

Elgin Avenue
Goldney Road
Marylands Rd
Sutherland Ave
Formosa St
Warwick
Warwick Avenue

HARROW ROAD
See Map 19
Chippenham Mews
Amberley Road
Bristol Gdns
Clifton Villas
Warwick Ave

Mosob
Sutherland Ave
Regent's Canal
Blomfield Road
Green Olive
Warwick Place
Warwick Ave

Woodfield Road
Woodchester Square
Senior Street
Lord Hills Road
Delamere Terrace
The Floating Boater
Little Venice

Elkstone Road
Alfred Rd
Cirencester St
Chichester Road
Canal Café Theatre
Warwick Crescent

GREAT WESTERN ROAD
Bourne Terrace
Blomfield Villas

Westbourne Park
Tavistock Cres
Warwick Estate
PADDINGTON

Tavistock Road
Leamington Rd Villas
Aldridge Rd Villas
St Lukes Rd
See Map 7
HARROW ROAD A404
WESTWAY A40 (M)
Westbourne Park Villas

KILBURN HIGH ROAD
MAIDA VALE
KILBURN PARK ROAD
ABBEY ROAD
MAIDA VALE

1
2
3
4
5

0   400 m
0   400 yds
© Copyright Time Out Group 2008

MAPS

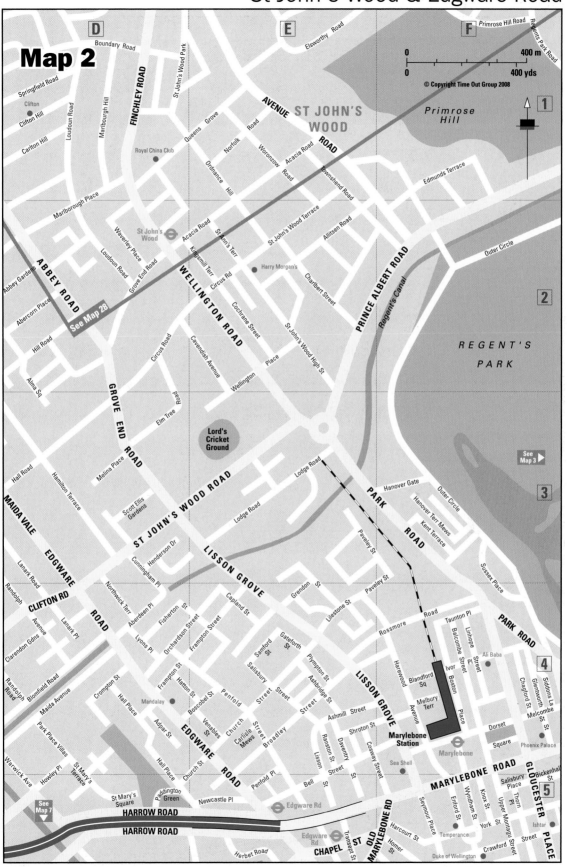

Map 2

MAPS

Camden Town & Marylebone

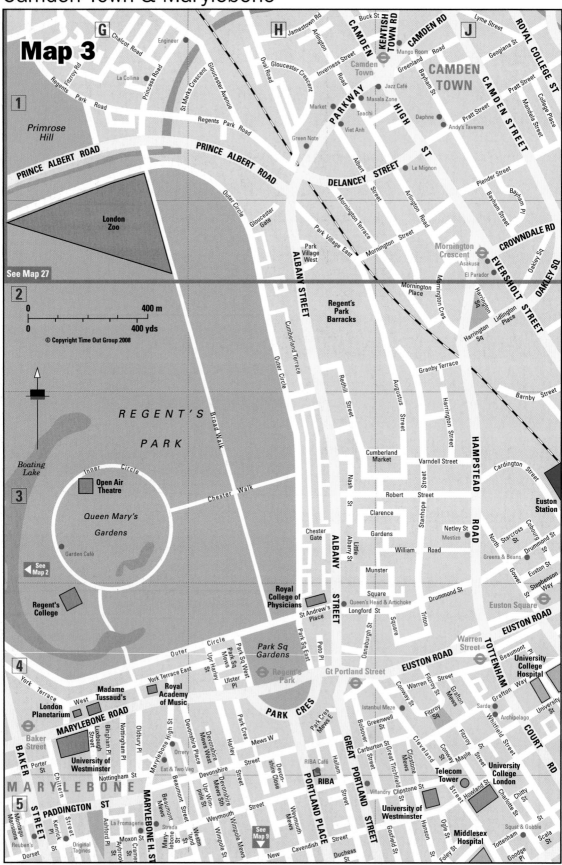

Map 3

See Map 27

0   400 m
0   400 yds
© Copyright Time Out Group 2008

MAPS

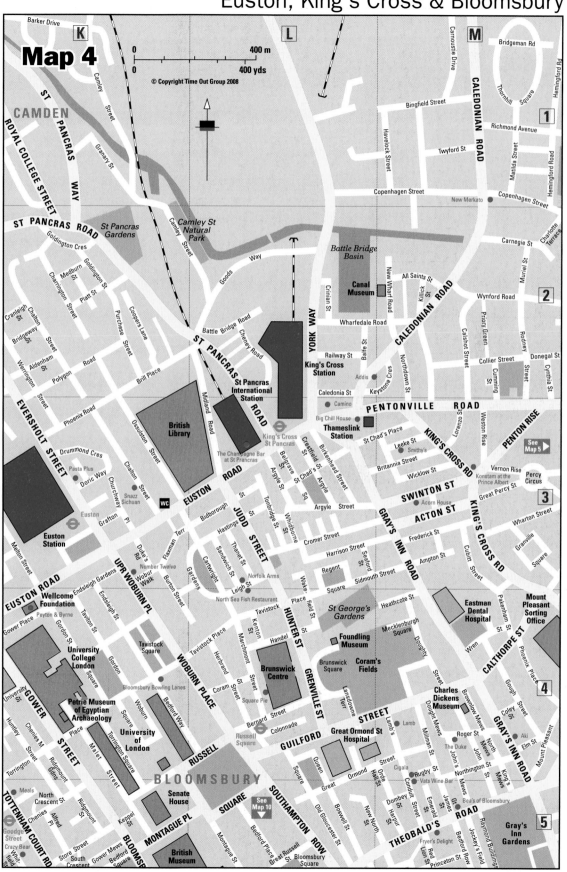

Map 4

Islington, Clerkenwell & Farringdon

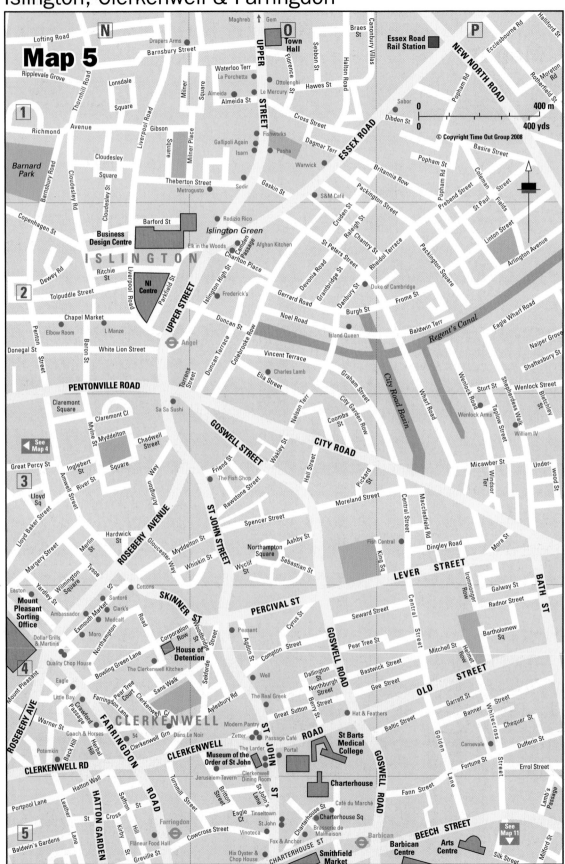

MAPS

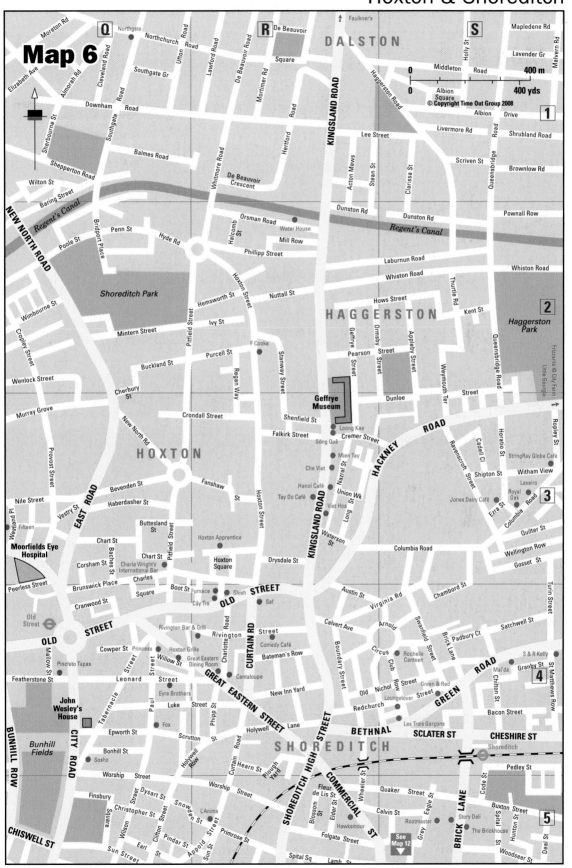

Notting Hill, Bayswater & Kensington

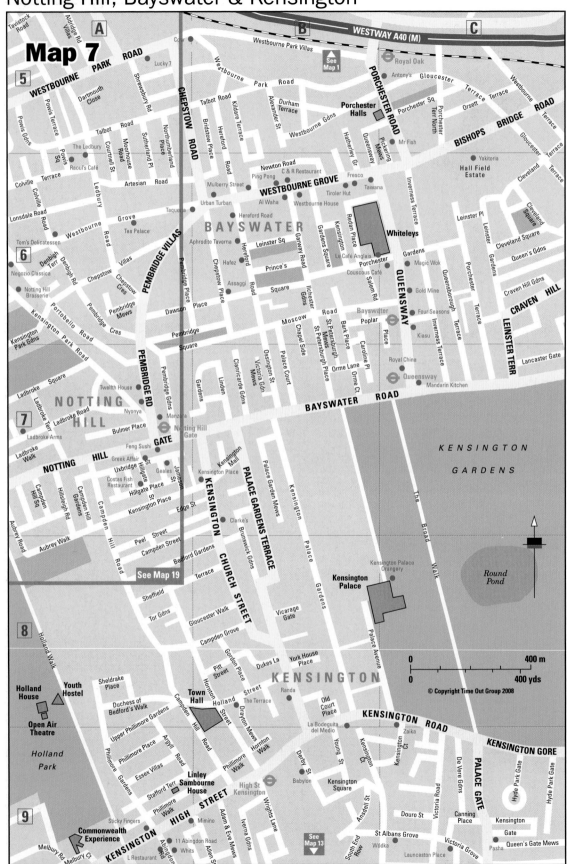

MAPS

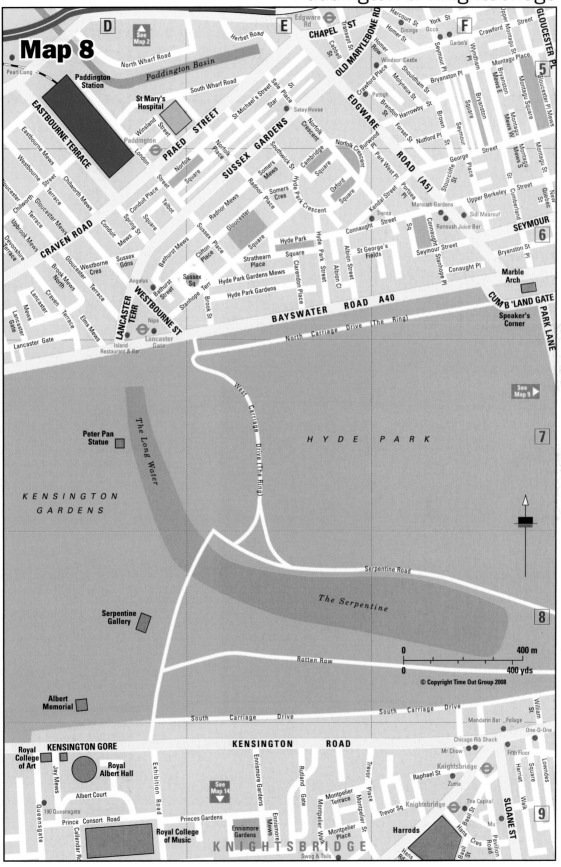

Map 8

Marylebone, Fitzrovia, Mayfair & St James's

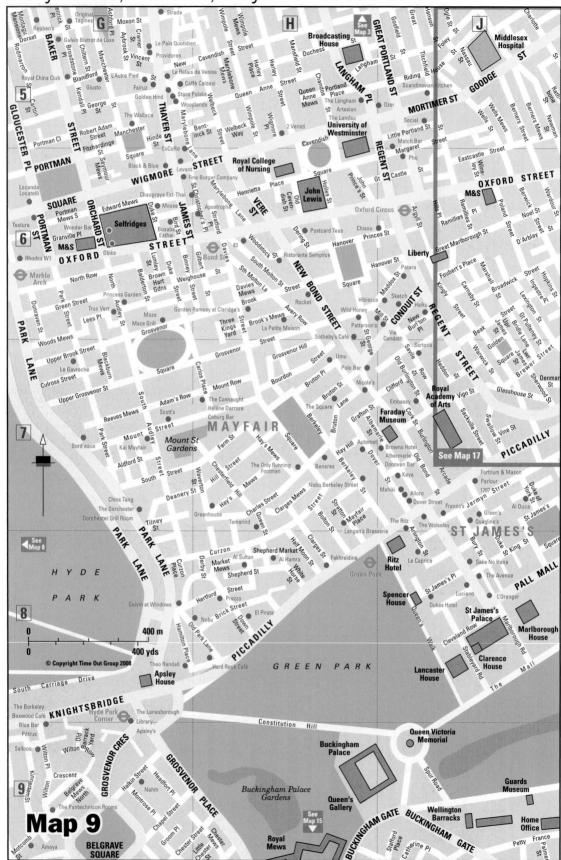

Map 9

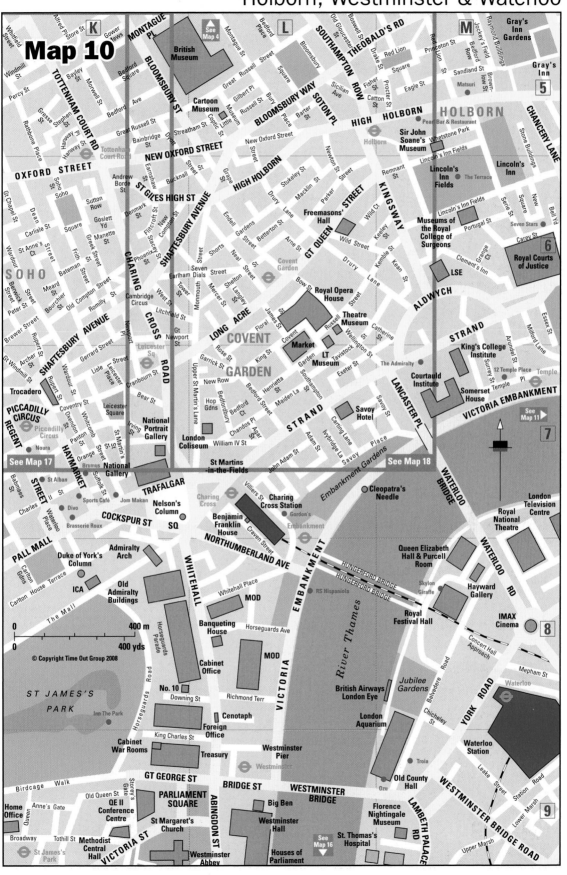

MAPS

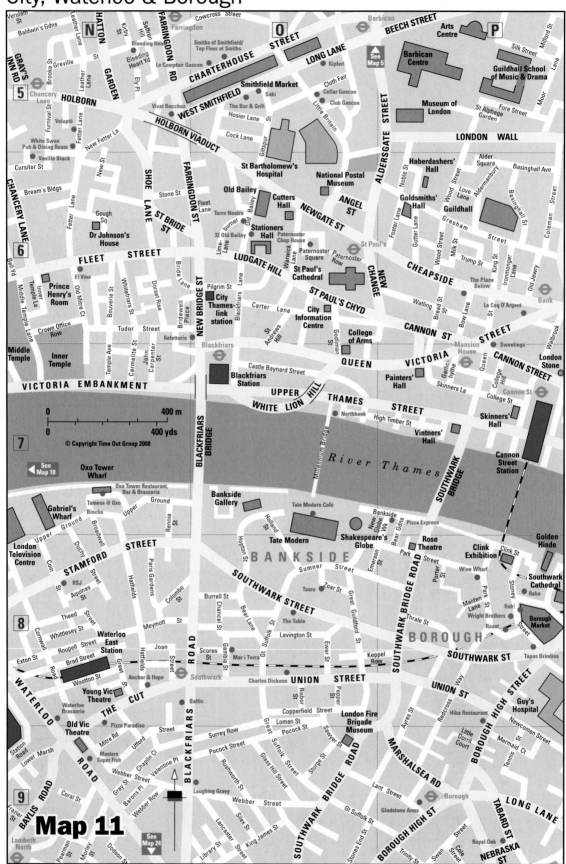

Map 11

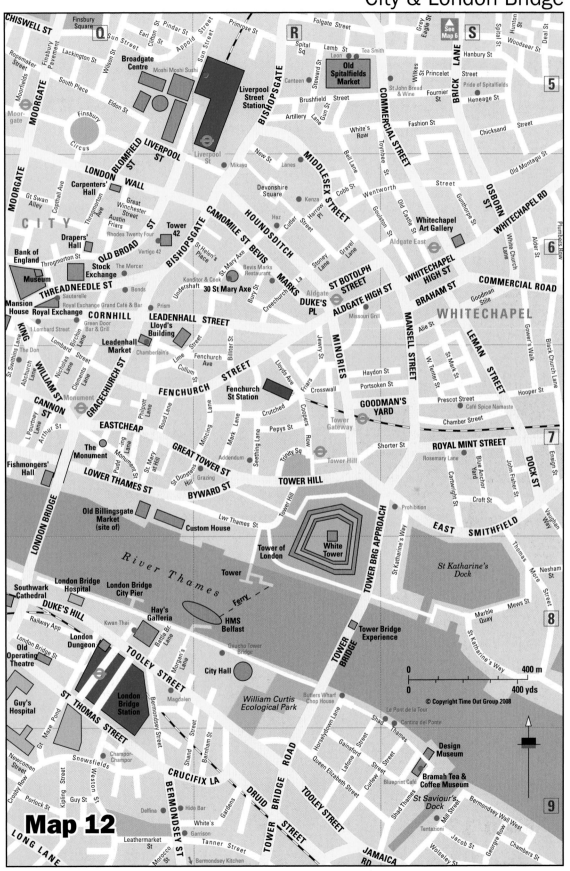

See Map 6

Map 12

Earl's Court, Gloucester Road & Fulham

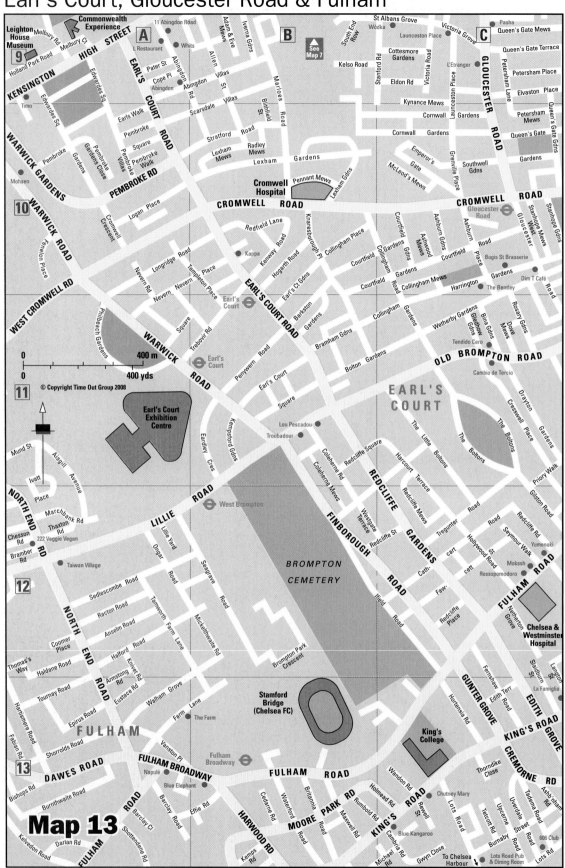

MAPS

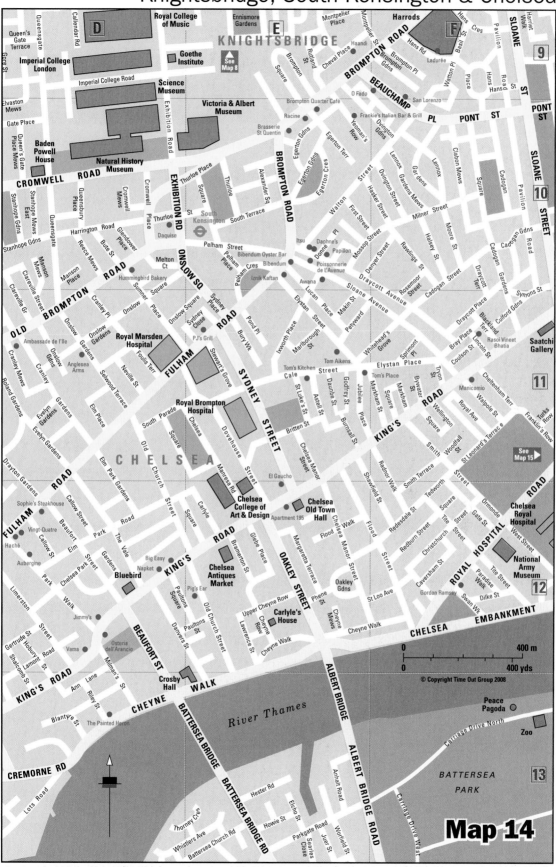

MAPS

Map 14

Belgravia, Victoria & Pimlico

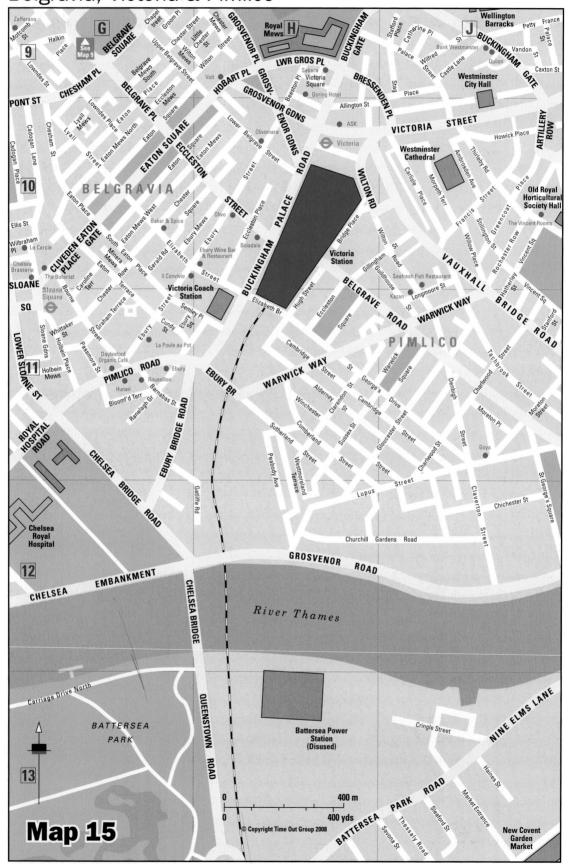

MAPS

Map 15

© Copyright Time Out Group 2008

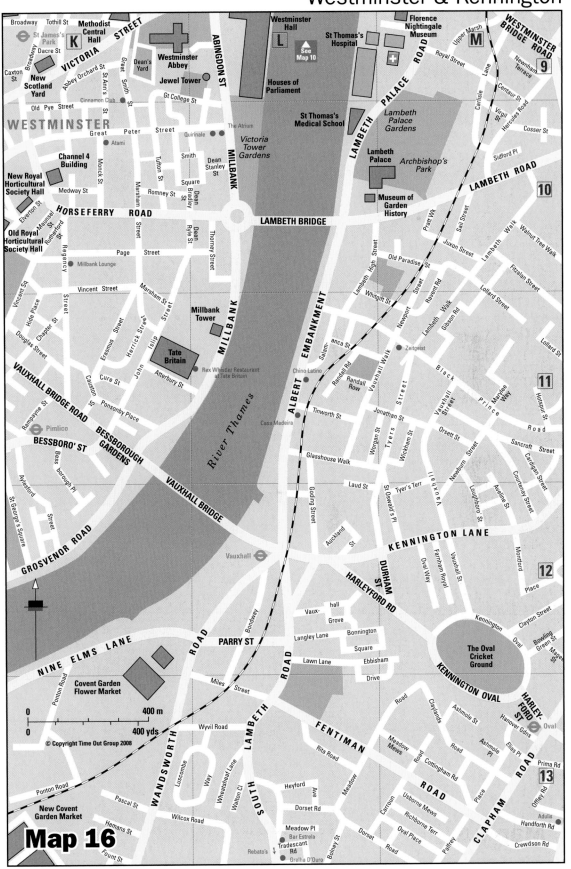

Map 16

Fitzrovia, Soho & Chinatown

Map 17

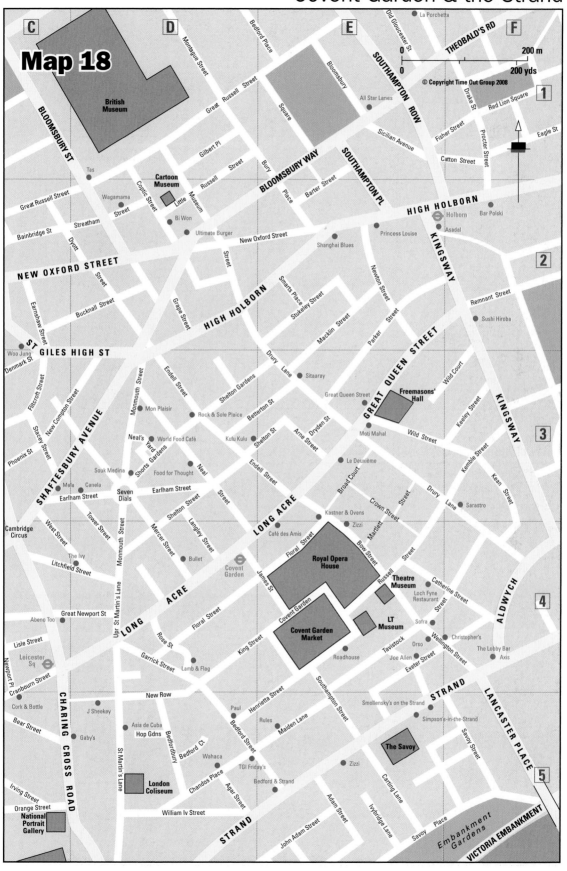

Map 18

Hammersmith & Shepherd's Bush

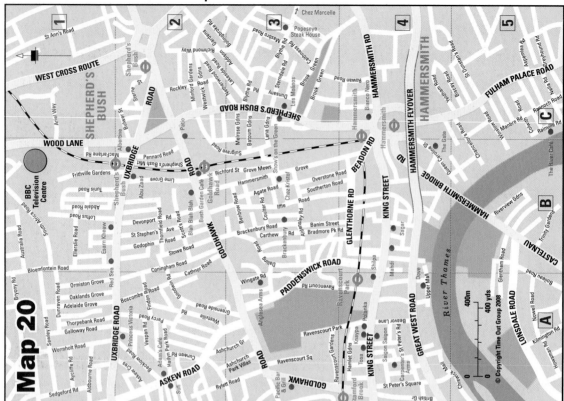

Notting Hill & Ladbroke Grove

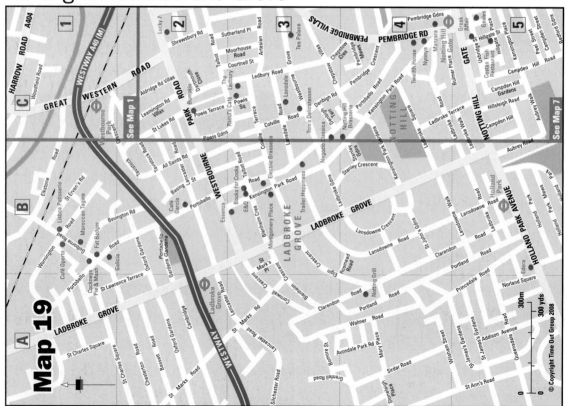

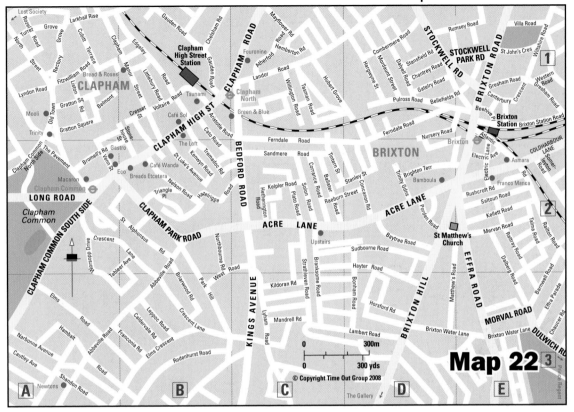

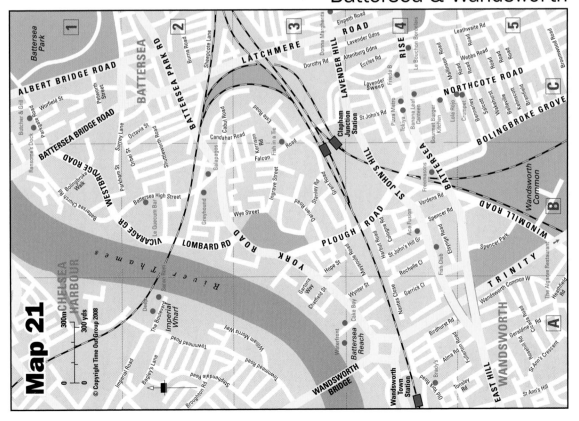

MAPS

Docklands

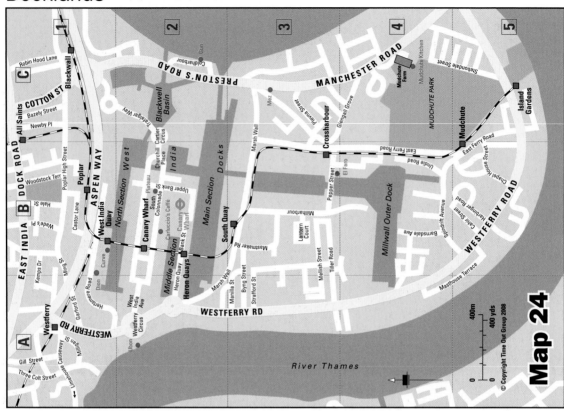

Map 24

Camberwell & Dulwich

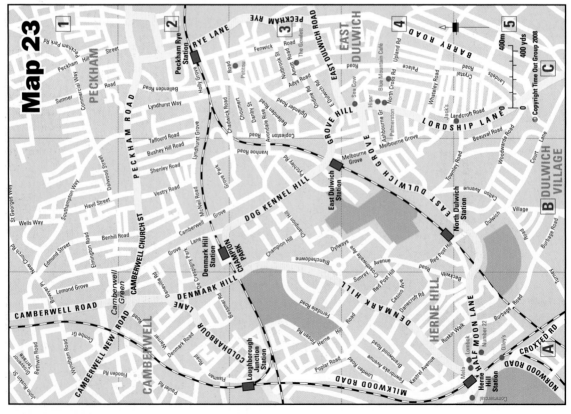

Map 23

MAPS

Kentish Town & Archway

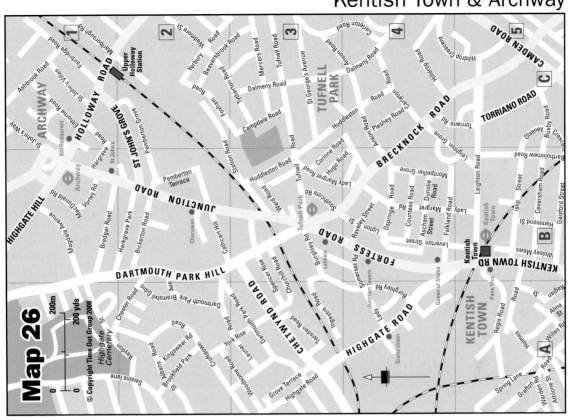

Dalston & Stoke Newington

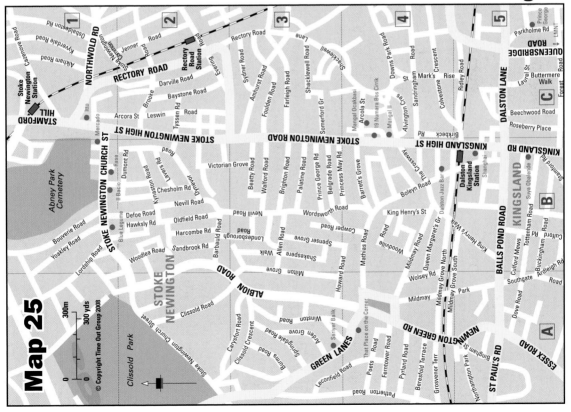

Hampstead & St John's Wood

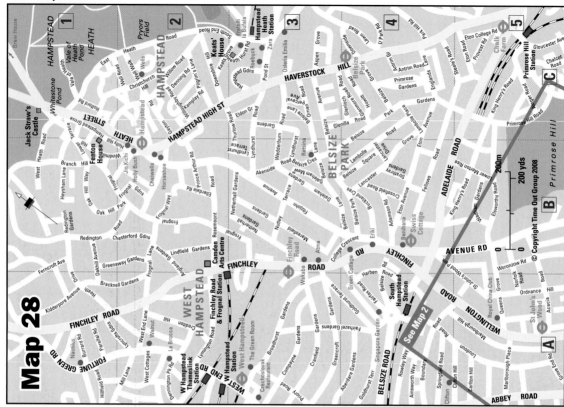

Camden Town & Chalk Farm

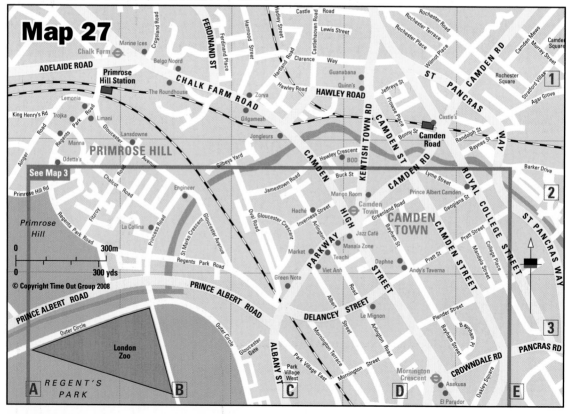

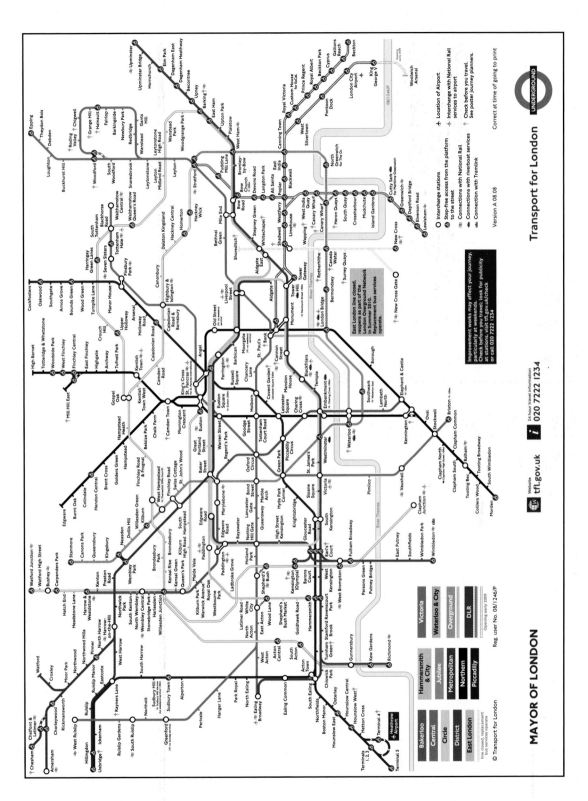

MAPS

MAYOR OF LONDON

Transport for London

Street Index

Grid references not allocated to a specific map can be found on Maps 1-16, which are contiguous and cover central London. Maps 17-28 cover individual areas, most of them outside the centre. The areas covered by all the maps are shown on p357.

A

Abbeville Road - Map 22 A3/B2/3
Abbey Gardens - C2/D2
Abbey Orchard Street - K9
Abbey Road - B1/C1/D2; Map 28 A5
Abbey Street - R10/S10
Abchurch Lane - Q7
Abdale Road - Map 20 B1
Abercorn Close - C2/D2
Abercorn Place - C2/D2
Aberdare Gardens - Map 28 A3/4
Aberdeen Place - D4
Abingdon Road - A9/B10
Abingdon Street - L9
Abingdon Villas - A9/B9
Acacia Road - D2/E1/2; Map 28 A5/B5
Acre Lane - Map 22 C2/D2
Acton Mews - R1
Acton Street - M3
Adam & Eve Mews - B9
Adam Street - L7; Map 18 E5
Adam's Row - L7
Adamson Road - Map 28 B4
Addison Avenue - Map 19 A5
Addison Gardens - Map 20 C2/3
Adelaide Grove - Map 20 A1
Adelaide Road - Map 27 A1; Map 28 B4/5/C5
Adpar Street - D4
Adys Road - Map 23 C3
Agar Grove - Map 27 E1
Agar Street - L7; Map 18 D5
Agate Road - Map 20 B3
Agdon Street - O4
Ainger Road - Map 27 A1/2; Map 28 C5
Ainsworth Way - C1; Map 28 A4
Air Street - J7; Map 17 A5
Aisgill Avenue - A11/12
Akenside Road - Map 28 B3
Albany Street - H2/3; Map 27 C3
Albemarle Street - H7/J7
Albert Bridge - E12/13
Albert Bridge Road - E13; Map 21 C1/2
Albert Court - D9
Albert Embankment - L10/11
Albert Road - A2
Albert Street - H1/J2; Map 27 C3/D3
Albion Close - E6
Albion Drive - S1
Albion Road - Map 25 A2/3/B2
Albion Square - S1
Albion Street - E6
Aldbourne Road - Map 20 A1
Aldenham Street - K2
Aldensley Road - Map 20 B3
Alder Square - P6
Alder Street - S6
Aldermanb'y - P6
Alderney Street - H11
Aldersgate Street - O6/P5/6
Aldford Street - G7
Aldgate High Street - R6
Aldridge Road Villas - Map 19 C2; A5
Aldwych - M6; Map 18 F4
Alexander Square - E10
Alexander Street - B5
Alfred Place - K5; Map 17 B1
Alfred Road - B4

Alice Street - Q10
Alie Street - S6
Alkham Road - Map 25 C1
All Saints Road - Map 19 B2
All Saints Street - M2
Allen Road - Map 25 B3
Allen Street - B9/10
Allington Street - H10
Alma Road - Map 21 A4/5
Alma Square - D2/3
Alma Street - Map 26 A5
Almeide Street - O1
Almorah Road - Q1
Alscot Road - R10/S10
Altenburg Gardens - Map 21 C4
Alvington Crescent - Map 25 C4
Amberley Road - B4
Ambrosden Avenue - J10
Amhurst Road - Map 25 C3
Amott Road - Map 23 C3
Ampton Street - M3
Amwell Street - N3
Andover Place - B2
Andrew Borde Street - K6; Map 17 C2
Angel Street - O6
Angland Gardens - Map 28 B2
Anhalt Road - E13
Ann Lane - D13
Ansdell Street - B9
Anselm Road - A12
Anson Road - Map 26 C3/4
Antrim Grove - Map 28 C4
Antrim Road - Map 28 C4
Appleby Street - S2
Appold Street - Q5/R5
Aquinas Street - N8
Archer Street - K7; Map 17 B4
Arcola Street - Map 25 A4
Arcora St - Map 25 C1/2
Arden Grove - Map 25 A3
Ardleigh Road - Map 25 A5/B5
Argyle Square - L3
Argyle Street - L3
Argyll Road - A9/3 A9/B9
Ariel Way - Map 20 C1
Aristotle Road - Map 22 B1
Arlington Avenue - P2
Arlington Road - H1/ J1/2; Map 27 C2/D3
Arlington Street - J8
Arlington Way - N3
Armstong Road - A12
Arne Street - L6; Map 18 E3
Arnold Circus - R4/S4
Artesian Road - Map 19 C3; A6
Arthur Street - Q7
Artillery Lane - R5
Artington Way - N3
Arundel Street - M6/7
Aryll Street - J6
Ascham Street - Map 26 B4
Ashbourne Grove - Map 23 C4
Ashbridge Street - E4
Ashbrook Road - Map 26 C1
Ashburn Gardens - C10
Ashburn Place - C10
Ashburnham Road - C13/14; D13
Ashby Street - O3
Ashchurch Grove - Map 20 A2/3
Ashchurch Park Villas - Map 20 A2/3
Ashmill Street - E4
Ashmole Place - M13
Ashmole Street - M13
Ashmore Road - A2/3
Ashwood Mews - C10
Ashworth Road - C3
Askew Crescent - Map 20 A1
Askew Road - Map 20 A2
Aspenlea Road - Map 20 C5
Aspen Grove - Map 28 C3

Aspen Way - Map 24 A1/B1/C1
Astell Street - E11
Atherfold Road - Map 22 C1
Athlone Street - Map 26 A5
Atlantic Road - Map 22 E1/2
Atterbury Street - K11
Aubrey Road - Map 19 B5/C5; A7/8
Aubrey Walk - Map 19 C5; A7/8
Auckland Street - L12
Augustus Street - J2/3
Austin Friars - Q6
Australia Road - Map 20 B1
Aveline Street - M11/12
Avenue Road - E1; Map 28 B5
Avery Row - H6
Avondale Park Road - Map 19 A3
Avondale Rise - Map 23 B3/C3
Aybrook Street - G5
Aycliffe Road; Map 20 A1
Ayers Street - P8/9
Aylesbury Road - O4
Aylesford Street - K11/12

B

Babmaes Street - K7
Baches Street - Q3
Back Church Lane - S6/7
Back Hill - N4
Bacon Street - S4
Bagley's Lane - Map 21 A2
Bainbridge Street - K5; Map 17 C2; Map 18 C2
Baker Street - G4/5
Balcombe Street - F4
Balderton Street - G6
Baldwin Terrace - P2
Baldwin's Gardens - N5
Balfe Street - L2
Ballater Road - Map 22 C2
Balls Pond Road - Map 25 A5/B5
Balmes Road - Q1
Baltic Street - P4
Banim Street - Map 20 B3
Bank Street - Map 24 B2
Bankside - P7
Banner Street - P4
Barbauld Road - Map 25 B2
Barclay Close - A13
Barclay Road - A13
Barford Street - N2
Baring Street - Q1/2
Bark Place - B6/7
Barker Drive - K1; Map 27 E2
Barkston Gardens - B11
Barnaby Street - J3
Barnham Street - Q9
Barnsbury Road - N1/2
Barnsbury Street - N1/O1
Barnsdale Avenue - Map 24 B4
Barnsdale Road - A3/4
Barnwell Road - Map 22 E2/3
Baron Street - N2
Barons Place - N9
Barrett's Grove - Map 25 B4
Barry Road - Map 23 C4/5
Barter Street - L5; Map 18 E1/2
Bartholomew Square - P4
Bartholomew Road - Map 26 B5
Basil Street - F9
Basing Street - Map 19 B2
Basinghall Avenue - P6
Basinghall Street - P6
Basire Street - P1
Bassett Road - Map 19 A2
Bastwick Street - O4/P4
Bateman Street - K6; Map 17 C3
Bateman's Row - R4

Bath Street - P3/4
Bathurst Mews - D6
Bathurst Street - D6
Batoum Gardens - Map 20 B3/C3
Battersea Bridge - E13
Battersea Bridge Road - E13; Map 21 B1/C1/2
Battersea Church Road - E13; Map 21 B1
Battersea High Street - Map 21 B2
Battersea Park Road - H13/J13; Map 21 C2
Battersea Rise - Map 21 B4/C4
Battle Bridge Lane - Q8
Battle Bridge Road - L2
Bayham Street - J1/2; Map 27 D3/E3
Bayley Street - K5; Map 17 C1
Baylis Road- N9
Baynes Street - Map 27 E1/2
Baynham Place - J1/2; Map 27 E3
Baystone Road - Map 25 C2
Bayswater Road - B7/C7/D7/E6/F6
Baytree Road - Map 22 D2
Bazely Street - Map 24 C1
Beadon Road - Map 20 B4
Beak Street - J6; Map 17 A4
Bear Gardens - P7/8
Bear Lane - O8
Bear Street - K7; Map 17 C5; Map 18 C5
Beatty Road - Map 25 B3
Beauchamp Place - F9/10
Beaufort Street - D12
Beaumont Mews - G5
Beaumont Place - J4
Beaumont Street - G5
Beauval Road - Map 23 B5/C5
Beaversbrook Road - Map 26 C2/3
Beavor Lane - Map 20 A4
Becklow Road - Map 20 A2
Beckwith Road - Map 23 A4/5/B4
Bedford Avenue - K5; Map 17 C2
Bedford Court - L7; Map 18 D5
Bedford Gardens - Map 19 C5; A8/B8
Bedford Place - L5; Map 18 D1/E1
Bedford Road - Map 22 C1/2
Bedford Row - M5
Bedford Square - K5; Map 17 C1
Bedford Street - L7; Map 18 D5/E5
Bedford Way - K4
Bedfordbury - L7; Map 18 D5
Beech Street - P5
Beechwood Road - Map 25 C5
Beehive Place - Map 22 E1
Beeston Place - H9
Belgrade Road - Map 25 B3
Belgrave Gardens - C1
Belgrave Mews North - G9
Belgrave Mews South - G9
Belgrave Place - G10
Belgrave Road - H10/J11
Belgrave Square - G9
Belgrave Street - L3
Bell Lane - R6
Bell Street - E4/5
Bell Yard - M6
Bellefields Road - Map 22 D1
Bellenden Road - Map 23 C2
Belleville Road - Map 21 C5
Belmont Close - Map 22 A1
Belsize Avenue - Map 28 C3
Belsize Crescent - Map 28 B3
Belsize Grove - Map 28 C4
Belsize Lane - Map 28 B3/4/C3
Belsize Park - Map 28 B4
Belsize Park Gardens - Map 28 C4
Belsize Road - B1/C1; Map 28 A4/B4
Belsize Square - Map 28 B4
Belvedere Road - M8/9
Benbow Road - Map 20 B3

Benhill Road - Map 23 B1/2
Bennerley Road - Map 21 C5
Bentinck Street - H5
Beresfold Terrace - Map 25 A4
Berkeley Square - H7
Berkeley Street - H7
Bermondsey Street - Q8/9/10
Bermondsey Wall West - S9
Bernard Street - L4
Berners Mews - J5; Map 17 A1/2/B2
Berners Street - J5/6; Map 17 A1/2
Berry Street - O4
Berwick Street - J6/6 K6; Map 17 B3/4
Bessborough Gardens - K11
Bessborough Place - K11/12
Bessborough Street - K11
Bessmer Road - Map 23 A2/3
Bethnal Green Road - R4/S4
Bethwin Road - Map 23 A1
Betterton Street - L6; Map 18 D3/E3
Bevenden Street - Q3
Bevington Road - Map 19 B1/2
Bevis Marks - R6
Bickenhall Street - F5
Bickerton Road - Map 26 B2
Bidborough Street - L3
Biddulph Road - B3/C3
Billiter Street - R6/7
Bina Gardens - C11
Bingfield Street - M1
Bingham Place - G4
Bingham Street - Map 25 A5
Binney Street - G6
Birchin Lane - Q6
Bird Street - G6
Birdcage Walk - K9
Birdhurst Road - Map 21 A4
Birkbeck Road - Map 25 C4/5
Birkenhead Street - L3
Biscay Road - Map 20 C4/5
Bishops Bridge Road - C5/D5
Bishops Road - A13
Bishopsgate - Q6/R5/6
Black Prince Street - L11/M11
Blackfriars Bridge - O7
Blackfriars Lane - O6
Blackfriars Road - N8/O8
Blackland Terrace - F11
Blanchedowne - Map 23 B3
Blandford Square - F4
Blandford Street - G5
Blantyre Street - D13
Bleeding Heart Yd - N5
Blenheim Crescent - Map 19 A3/B3
Blenheim Terrace - C2
Bletchley Street - P3
Blithfield Street - B10
Blkbrne's Mews - G7
Bloemfontein Road - Map 20 B1
Blomfield Road - C4/D4
Blomfield Street - Q5/6
Blomfield Villas - C5
Bloomfield Terrace - G11
Bloomsbury Square - L5; Map 18 E1
Bloomsbury Street - K5; Map 17 C1; Map 18 C1/D1/2
Bloomsbury Way - L5; Map 18 D2/E1/2
Blossom Street - R5
Blue Anchor Yard - S7
Blythe Road - Map 20 C3
Boileau Road - Map 20 A5/B5
Boleyn Road - Map 25 B4/5
Bolingbroke Grove - Map 21 B5/C5
Bolingbroke Road - Map 20 C2/3
Bolingbroke Walk - Map 21 B1
Bolney Street - L13
Bolsover Street - H4/J5
Bolton Gardens - B11/C11
Bolton Street - H7/8
Boltons, The - C11
Bomore Street - Map 19 A3
Bondway - L12

STREET INDEX

STREET INDEX

STREET INDEX

STREET INDEX

Advertiser's Index

Please refer to relevant sections for addresses / telephone numbers

Subject Index

SUBJECT INDEX

SUBJECT INDEX

SUBJECT INDEX

Area Index

AREA INDEX

Feng Shui Inn p70
4-6 Gerrard Street, W1D 5PG
(7734 6778/www.fengshuiinn.co.uk)
Golden Dragon p70
28-29 Gerrard Street, W1D 6JW
(7734 2763)
Haozhan p70
8 Gerrard Street, W1D 5PJ
(7434 3838/www.haozhan.co.uk)
Hing Loon p72
25 Lisle Street, WC2H 7BA
(7437 3602)
HK Diner p72
22 Wardour Street, W1D 6QQ
(7434 9544)
Imperial China p70
White Bear Yard, 25A Lisle Street,
WC2H 7BA (7734 3388/
www.imperial-china.co.uk)
Jen Café p73
4-8 Newport Place, WC2H 7JP
Joy King Lau p70
3 Leicester Street, WC2H 7BL
(7437 1132)
Laureate p72
64 Shaftesbury Avenue, W1D 6LU
(7437 5046)
Leong's Legends p72
4 Macclesfield Street, W1D 6AX
(7287 0288)
Little Lamb p72
72 Shaftesbury Avenue, W1D 6NA
(7287 8078)
London Hong Kong p73
6-7 Lisle Street, WC2H 7BG (7287
0352/www.london-hk.co.uk)
Mr Kong p73
21 Lisle Street, WC2H 7BA (7437 7341/
9679/www.mrkongrestaurant.com)
New Mayflower p73
68-70 Shaftesbury Avenue, W1D 6LY
(7734 9207)
New World p74
1 Gerrard Place, W1D 5PA
(7734 0396)
Royal Dragon p74
30 Gerrard Street, W1D 6JS
(7734 1388)

Japanese
Tokyo Diner p196
2 Newport Place, WC2H 7JP
(7287 8777/www.tokyodiner.com)
Zipangu p197
8 Little Newport Street, WC2H 7JJ
(7437 5042)

Korean
Corean Chilli p214
51 Charing Cross Road, WC2H 0NE
(7734 6737)

Chingford
Branches
Pizza Express
45-47 Old Church Road, E4 6SJ
(8529 7866)

Chiswick
Branches
Balans
214 Chiswick High Road, W4 1PD
(8742 1435)
Carluccio's Caffè
344 Chiswick High Road, W4 5TA
(8995 8073)
Eco
144 Chiswick High Road, W4 1PU
(8747 4822)
FishWorks
6 Turnham Green Terrace, W4 1QP
(8994 0086)
Frankie's Italian Bar & Grill
68 Chiswick High Road, W4 1CU
(8987 9988)
Giraffe
270 Chiswick High Road, W4 1PD
(8995 2100)
Gourmet Burger Kitchen
131 Chiswick High Road, W4 2ED
(8995 4548)
Nando's
187-189 Chiswick High Road, W4 2DR
(8995 7533)
Pizza Express
252 High Road, W4 1PD (8747 0193)
Strada
156 Chiswick High Road, W4 1PR
(8995 0004)
Tootsies Grill
148 Chiswick High Road, W4 1PR
(8747 1869)
Woodlands
12-14 Chiswick High Road, W4 1TH
(8994 9333)
Zizzi
231 Chiswick High Road, W4 2DL
(8747 9400)

Brasseries
High Road Brasserie p50
162-166 Chiswick High Road,
W4 1PR (8742 7474/
www.highroadhouse.co.uk)
Budget
Ground p304
217-221 Chiswick High Road,
W4 2DW (8747 9113/
www.groundrestaurants.com)
Fish
Fish Hook p95
8 Elliott Road, W4 1PE (8742 0766/
www.fishhook.co.uk)
French
La Trompette p105
5-7 Devonshire Road, W4 2EU
(8747 1836/www.latrompette.co.uk)
Le Vacherin p105
76-77 South Parade, W4 5LF
(8742 2121/www.levacherin.co.uk)
Gastropubs
Devonshire p115
126 Devonshire Road, W4 2JJ
(7592 7962/www.gordonramsay.com)
Duke of Sussex p115
75 South Parade, W4 5LF (8742 8801)
Roebuck p115
122 Chiswick High Road,
W4 1PU (8995 4392/
www.theroebuckchiswick.co.uk)
Modern European
Sam's Brasserie & Bar p238
11 Barley Mow Passage, W4 4PH
(8987 0555/www.samsbrasserie.co.uk)

City
The Americas
Green Door Bar & Grill p37
33 Cornhill, EC3 (7929 1378/
www.greendoorsteakhouse.co.uk)
Hawksmoor p37
157 Commercial Street, E1 6BJ
(7247 7392/www.thehawksmoor.com)
Missouri Grill p37
76 Aldgate High Street, EC3N 1BD
(7481 4010/www.missourigrill.com)
Bars
Hawksmoor p330
157 Commercial Street, E1 6BJ
(7247 7392/www.thehawksmoor.com)
Branches
Apostle (branch of Jamies)
34 Ludgate Hill, EC4M 7DE
(7489 1938)
Assembly (branch of Balls Brothers)
14-15 Seething Lane, EC3N 4AX
(7626 3360)
Balls Brothers
11 Blomfield Street, EC2M 1PS
(7588 4643)
Balls Brothers
158 Bishopsgate, EC2M 4LN
(7426 0567)
Balls Brothers
5-6 Carey Lane, EC2V 8AE (7600 2720)
Balls Brothers
Bury Court, 38 St Mary Axe, EC3A 8EX
(7929 6660)
Balls Brothers
52 Lime Street, EC3M 7BS (7283 0841)
Balls Brothers
Mark Lane, EC3R 7BB (7623 2923)
Balls Brothers
Minster Pavement, Mincing Lane,
EC3R 7PP (7283 2838)
Balls Brothers
2 St Mary at Hill, EC3R 8EE (7626 0321)
Bangers (branch of Davy's)
Eldon House, 2-12 Wilson Street,
EC2M 2TE (7377 6326)
Bangers Too (branch of Davy's)
1 St Mary at Hill, EC3R 8EE
(7283 4443)
Bishop of Norwich (branch of Davy's)
91-93 Moorgate, EC2M 6SJ
(7920 0857)
Bodean's
16 Byward Street, EC3R 5BA
(7488 3883)
Boisdale of Bishopsgate
Swedeland Court, 202 Bishopsgate,
EC2M 4NR (7283 1763)
Cellar (branch of Balls Brothers)
25 Moorgate, EC2R 6AR (7330 0969)
City Boot (branch of Davy's)
7 Moorfields High Walk, EC2Y 9DP
(7588 4766)
City Flogger (branch of Davy's)
Fen Court, 120 Fenchurch Street,
EC3M 5BA (7623 3251)
City FOB (branch of Davy's)
Lower Thames Street, EC3R 6DJ
(7621 0619)

City Pipe (branch of Davy's)
33 Foster Lane, off Cheapside,
EC2V 6HD (7606 2110)
Corney & Barrow
5 Exchange Square, EC2A 2EH
(7628 4367)
Corney & Barrow
19 Broadgate Circle, EC2M 2QS
(7628 1251)
Corney & Barrow
111 Old Broad Street, EC2N 1AP
(7638 9308)
Corney & Barrow
12 Mason's Avenue, EC2V 5BT
(7726 6030)
Corney & Barrow
1 Ropemaker Street, EC2Y 9HT
(7382 0606)
Corney & Barrow
2B Eastcheap, EC3M 1AB (7929 3220)
Corney & Barrow
23 Fenchurch Street, EC3M 7DQ
(7398 5870)
Corney & Barrow
1 Leadenhall Place, EC3M 7DX
(7621 9201)
Corney & Barrow
37A Jewry Street, EC3N 2EX
(7680 8550)
Corney & Barrow
3 Fleet Place, EC4M 7RD (7329 3141)
Davy's at Creed Lane
10 Creed Lane, EC4M 8SH (7236 5317)
Davy's at Exchange Square
2 Exchange Square, EC2A 2EH
(7256 5962)
Dion City
52-56 Leadenhall Street, EC3A 2BJ
(7702 9111)
Dion St Paul's
Paternoster House, 65 St Paul's
Churchyard, EC4M 8AB
(0871 223 6186)
Gable (branch of Balls Brothers)
1st floor, 25 Moorgate, EC2R 6AR
(7330 0950)
Gallery (branch of Balls Brothers)
10-11 Austin Friars, EC2N 2HG
(7496 9900)
Gaucho Broadgate
5 Finsbury Avenue, EC2M 2PG
(7392 7652)
Gaucho City
1 Bell Inn Yard, off Gracechurch Street,
EC3V 0BL (7626 5180)
Giraffe
Unit 1, Crispin Place, off Brushfield
Street, E1 6DW (3116 2000)
Gourmet Burger Kitchen
Tower Place, EC3R 5BU (7929 2222)
Gourmet Burger Kitchen
Condor House, St Paul's, EC4M 8AL
(7248 9199)
**Gow's Restaurant & Oyster Bar
(branch of Balls Brothers)**
81 Old Broad Street, EC2M 1PR
(7920 9645)
Habit (branch of Davy's)
Friday Court, Crutched Friars,
EC3 2ND (7481 1131)
Haz
6 Mincing Lane, EC3M 3BD
7929 3173)
Jamies
155 Bishopsgate, EC2A 2AA
(7256 7279)
Jamies
119-121 The Minories, EC3N 1DR
(7709 9900)
Jamies
5 Groveland Court, EC4M 9EH
(7248 5551)
Kazan
34-36 Houndsditch, EC3A 7DB
(7626 2222)
Last (branch of Balls Brothers)
73 Shoe Lane, EC4A 3BQ
(7583 8602)
Leon
12 Ludgate Circus, EC4M 7LQ
(7489 1580)
Leon
86 Cannon Street, EC4N 6HT
(7623 9699)
Manicomio
6 Gutter Lane, EC2V 7AD (7726 5010)
Missouri Angel
America Square, 14 Crosswall,
EC3N 2LJ (7481 8422)
Number 25 (branch of Jamies)
25 Birchin Lane, EC3V 9DJ
(7623 2505)
Le Pain Quotidien
Bow Bells House, 1 Bread Street,
EC4M 9BE (7486 6154)
Paul
New Armouries Building, Tower
of London, EC3N 4AB (7709 7300)

Paul
61 Leadenhall Market, EC3V 1LT
(7929 2100)
Paul
147 Fleet Street, EC4A 2BU
(7353 5874)
Paul
New Street Square, EC4A 3BF
(7353 3648)
Paul
Paternoster Lodge, Paternoster
Square, EC4M 7DX (7329 4705)
Paul
6 Bow Lane, EC4M 9EB
(7489 7925)
Pavilion (branch of Jamies)
Finsbury Circus Gardens, EC2M 7AB
(7628 8224)
Pizza Express
232-238 Bishopsgate, EC2M 4QD
(7247 2838)
Pizza Express
125 Alban Gate, London Wall,
EC2Y 5AS (7600 8880)
Pizza Express
Salisbury House, 150 London Wall,
EC2Y 5HN (7588 7262)
Pizza Express
1 Byward Street, EC3R 7QN
(7626 5025)
Pizza Express
20-22 Leadenhall Market, EC3V 1LR
(7283 5113)
Pizza Express
1 New Fetter Lane, EC4A 1AN
(7583 8880)
Pizza Express
7-9 St Bride Street, EC4A 4AS
(7583 5126)
Pizza Express
10 St Paul's Churchyard, Condor
House, EC4M 8AY (7248 9464)
Prophet (branch of Balls Brothers)
5-11 Worship Street, EC2A 2BH
(7588 8835)
Rocket
6 Adams Court, Old Broad Street,
EC2N 1DX (7628 0808)
Ruskins (branch of El Vino)
60 Mark Lane, EC3R 7ND
(7680 1234)
S&M Café
28 Leadenhall Market, EC3V 1LR
(7626 6646)
Saint (branch of Jamies)
1 Rose Street, Paternoster Square,
EC4M 7DQ (7600 5500)
Sterling
30 St Mary Axe, EC2A 8BF
(7929 3641)
Strada
88-90 Commercial Street, E1 6LY
(7247 4117)
Strada
4 St Paul's Churchyard, EC4M 8AY
(7248 7178)
Thai Hut
4 Burgon Street, EC4V 5BR
(7213 9884)
Thai Square
136-138 Minories, EC3N 1NT
(7680 1111)
Thai Square
1-7 Great St Thomas Apostle,
EC4V 2BH (7329 0001)
El Vino
3 Bastion High Walk, 125 London Wall,
EC2Y 5AP (7600 6377)
El Vino
30 New Bridge Street, EC4V 6BJ
(7236 4534)
El Vino
6 Martin Lane, off Cannon Street,
EC4R 0DP (7626 6876)
Wagamama
22 Old Broad Street, EC2N 1HQ
(7256 9992)
Wagamama
1 Ropemaker Street, EC2Y 9AW
(7588 2688)
Wagamama
Tower Place, off Lower Thames Street,
EC3N 4EE (7283 5897)
Wagamama
109 Fleet Street, EC4A 2AB
(7583 7889)
Wagamama
4 Great St Thomas Apostle, off Garlick
Hill, EC4V 2BH (7248 5766)
Willy's Wine Bar (branch of Jamies)
107 Fenchurch Street, EC3M 5JF
(7480 7289)
Wine Tun (branch of Davy's)
2-6 Cannon Street, EC4M 6XX
(7248 3371)
Yo! Sushi
Condor House, 5-14 St Paul's
Churchyard, EC4M 8AY (7248 8726)

AREA INDEX

AREA INDEX

AREA INDEX

AREA INDEX

Pizza & Pasta

Il Bordello p326
81 Wapping High Street, E1W 2YN
(7481 9950)

Waterloo

Branches

Canteen
Royal Festival Hall, Belvedere Road,
SE1 8XX (0845 686 1122)
EV Restaurant, Bar & Delicatessen
The Arches, 97-99 Isabella Street,
SE1 8DA (7620 6191)
Feng Sushi
Festival Terrace, Royal Festival Hall,
Belvedere Road, SE1 8XX (7261 0001)
Konditor & Cook
22 Cornwall Road, SE1 8TW
(7261 0456)
Le Pain Quotidien
Upper Festival Walk, Royal Festival
Hall, Belvedere Road, SE1 8XX
(7486 6154)
Paul
Waterloo Station, Mepham Street,
SE1 8SW (7261 9172)
Ping Pong
Festival Terrace, Southbank Centre,
Belvedere Road, SE1 8XX (7960 4160)
Pizza Express
The White House, 9C Belvedere Road,
SE1 8YP (7928 4091)
Strada
Riverside, Royal Festival Hall,
6 Belvedere Road, SE1 8XX
(7401 9126/www.strada.co.uk)
Tas
33 The Cut, SE1 8LF (7928 2111)
Wagamama
Riverside level, Royal Festival Hall,
SE1 8XX (7021 0877)
Yo! Sushi
County Hall, Belvedere Road, SE1 7GP
(7928 8871)

Brasseries

Giraffe p51
Riverside Level 1, Royal Festival
Hall, Belvedere Road, SE1 8XX
(7928 2004/www.giraffe.net)
Tamesa@oxo p52
2nd floor, Oxo Tower Wharf, Barge
House Street, SE1 9PH (7633 0088/
www.oxotower.co.uk)

East European

Baltic p87
74 Blackfriars Road, SE1 8HA (7928
1111/www.balticrestaurant.co.uk)

Fish & Chips

Masters Super Fish p317
191 Waterloo Road, SE1 8UX
(7928 6924)

French

RSJ p108
33 Coin Street, SE1 9NR (7928 4554/
www.rsj.uk.com)
Waterloo Brasserie p108
119 Waterloo Road, SE1 8UL (7960
0202/www.waterloobrasserie.co.uk)

Gastropubs

Anchor & Hope p119
36 The Cut, SE1 8LP (7928 9898)

International

Laughing Gravy p174
154 Blackfriars Road, SE1 8EN
(7721 7055/www.thelaughing
gravy.co.uk)

Japanese

Bincho p206
2nd floor, Oxo Tower Wharf, Barge
House Street, SE1 9PH (7803 0858/
www.bincho.co.uk)
Ozu p206
County Hall, Westminster Bridge
Road, SE1 7PB (7928 7766/
www.ozulondon.com)

Modern European

**Oxo Tower Restaurant,
Bar & Brasserie** p245
Eighth floor, Oxo Tower Wharf, Barge
House Street, SE1 9PH (7803 3888/
www.harveynichols.com)
Skylon p245
Royal Festival Hall, Belvedere Road,
SE1 8XX (7654 7800/
www.danddlondon.com)

Pizza & Pasta

Pizza Paradiso p322
61 The Cut, SE1 8LL (7261 1221/
www.pizzaparadiso.co.uk)

Spanish

Mar i Terra p265
14 Gambia Street, SE1 0XH
(7928 7628/www.mariterra.co.uk)

Turkish

Troia p279
3F Belvedere Road, SE1 7GQ
(7633 9309)

Wembley Middlesex

Branches

Nando's
420-422 High Road, Wembley, Middx
HA9 6AH (8795 3564)

Indian

Karahi King p172
213 East Lane, North Wembley, Middx
HA0 3NG (8904 2760)
Sakonis p172
129 Ealing Road, Wembley, Middx
HA0 4BP (8903 9601)
Sanghamam p172
531-533 High Road, Wembley, Middx
HA0 2DJ (8900 0777)

Middle Eastern

Mesopotamia p228
115 Wembley Park Drive, Wembley,
Middx HA9 8HG (8453 5555/
www.mesopotamia.ltd.uk)

West Hampstead

Branches

Banana Tree Canteen
237-239 West End Lane, NW6 1XN
(7431 7808)
Gourmet Burger Kitchen
331 West End Lane, NW6 1RS
(7794 5455)
Nando's
252-254 West End Lane, NW6 1LU
(7794 1331)
Pizza Express
319 West End Lane, NW6 1RP
(7431 8229)
Strada
291 West End Lane, NW6 1RD
(7431 8678)

East European

Czechoslovak Restaurant p86
Czech & Slovak House, 74 West End
Lane, NW6 2LX (7372 1193/
www.czechoslovak-restaurant.co.uk)

Fish & Chips

Nautilus p318
27-29 Fortune Green Road, NW6 1DT
(7435 2532)

Modern European

The Green Room p248
182 Broadhurst Gardens, NW6 3AY
(7372 8188/www.thegreenroom
nw6.com)
Walnut p248
280 West End Lane, NW6 1LJ
(7794 7772/www.walnutwalnut.com)

Pizza & Pasta

La Brocca p327
273 West End Lane, NW6 1QS
(7433 1989)

West Kensington

Branches

Best Mangal II
66 North End Road, W14 9EP
(7602 0212)

Turkish

Best Mangal p279
104 North End Road, W14 9EX
(7610 1050)

Vegetarian

222 Veggie Vegan p290
222 North End Road, W14 9NU (7381
2322/www.222veggievegan.com)

Westbourne Grove

Bars

Lonsdale p335
44-48 Lonsdale Road, W11 2DE
(7727 4080/www.thelonsdale.co.uk)
Westbourne House p335
65 Westbourne Grove, W2 4UJ
(7229 2233/www.westbourne
house.net)

Branches

Bodean's
57 Westbourne Grove, W2 4UA
(7727 9503)
Carluccio's Caffè
Westbourne Corner, 108 Westbourne
Grove, W2 5RU (7243 8164)
Elbow Room
103 Westbourne Grove, W2 4UW
(7221 5211)

Brasseries

Raoul's Café p50
105-107 Talbot Road, W11 2AT
(7229 2400/www.raoulsgourmet.com)

Cafés

Tea Palace p309
175 Westbourne Grove, W11 2SB
(7727 2600/www.teapalace.co.uk)
Tom's Delicatessen p309
226 Westbourne Grove, W11 2RH
(7221 8818/www.tomsdeli
london.co.uk)

French

The Ledbury p105
127 Ledbury Road, W11 2AQ
(7792 9090/www.theledbury.com)

Gastropubs

Cow p116
89 Westbourne Park Road, W2 5QH
(7221 0021/www.thecowlondon.co.uk)

Malaysian, Indonesian &
Singaporean

C&R Restaurant p222
52 Westbourne Grove, W2 5SH
(7221 7979)

Pizza & Pasta

Mulberry Street p322
84 Westbourne Grove, W2 5RT
(7313 6789/www.mulberry
street.co.uk)

Wine Bars

Negozio Classica p349
283 Westbourne Grove, W11 2QA
(7034 0005/www.negozioclassica.
co.uk)

Westbourne Park

African

Mosob p34
339 Harrow Road, W9 3RB
(7266 2012/www.mosob.co.uk)

The Americas

Lucky 7 p43
127 Westbourne Park Road, W2 5QL
(7727 6771/www.lucky7london.co.uk)

Westminster

Budget

Vincent Rooms p300
Victoria Centre, Vincent Square, SW1P
2PD (7802 8391/www.westking.ac.uk)

Indian

Cinnamon Club p153
The Old Westminster Library,
30-32 Great Smith Street, SW1P 3BU
(7222 2555/www.cinnamonclub.com)

International

The Atrium p174
4 Millbank, SW1P 3JA (7233 0032/
www.atriumrestaurant.com)

Italian

Quirinale p185
North Court, 1 Great Peter Street,
SW1P 3LL (7222 7080/
www.quirinale.co.uk)

Japanese

Atami p200
37 Monck Street, SW1P 2BL (7222
2218/www.atamirestaurant.co.uk)

Modern European

Bank Westminster p237
45 Buckingham Gate, SW1E 6BS
(7379 9797/www.bankrestaurants.
com)

Whetstone

Branches

ASK
1257 High Road, N20 0EW
(8492 0033)
Pizza Express
1264 High Road, N20 9HH
(8446 8800)

Whitechapel

Branches

Grapeshots (branch of Davy's)
2-3 Artillery Passage, E1 7LJ
(7247 8215)

Budget

Nando's p302
9-25 Mile End Road, E1 4TW
(7791 2720/www.nandos.com)

Indian

Café Spice Namaste p163
16 Prescot Street, E1 8AZ
(7488 9242/www.cafespice.co.uk)
Kolapata p165
222 Whitechapel Road, E1 1BJ
(7377 1200)
Lahore Kebab House p165
2 Umberston Street, E1 1PY
(7488 2551/www.lahore-kebab
house.com)

Tayyabs p165
83 Fieldgate Street, E1 1JU
(7247 9543/www.tayyabs.co.uk)

Willesden

Branches

Shish
2-6 Station Parade, NW2 4NH
(8208 9292)

Japanese

Sushi-Say p208
33B Walm Lane, NW2 5SH
(8459 2971)

Wimbledon

The Americas

Tootsies Grill p43
48 High Street, SW19 5AX
(8946 4135/www.tootsies
restaurants.com)

Branches

Butcher & Grill
33 High Street, SW19 5BY
(8944 8269)
Common Room (branch of Jamies)
18 High Street, SW19 5DX
(8944 1909)
Giraffe
21 High Street, SW19 5DX
(8946 0544)
Gourmet Burger Kitchen
88 The Broadway, SW19 1RH
(8540 3300)
Nando's
1 Russell Road, SW19 1QN
(8545 0909)
Le Pain Quotidien
4-5 High Street, SW19 5DX
(7486 6154)
Pizza Express
104 The Broadway, SW19 1RH
(8543 1010)
Pizza Express
84 High Street, SW19 5EG
(8946 6027)
San Lorenzo
38 Wimbledon Hill Road, SW19 7PA
(8946 8463)
Strada
91 High Street, SW19 5EG
(8946 4363)
Sukho
29 Wimbledon Hill Road, SW19 7NE
(8947 9199)
Tinseltown
Centre Court Shopping Centre,
4 Queens Road, SW19 8YA
(8605 2424)
Wagamama
46-48 Wimbledon Hill Road, SW19 7PA
(8879 7280)

Eating & Entertainment

Wimbledon Stadium p351
Plough Lane, SW17 0BL (8946 8000/
www.lovethedogs.co.uk)

French

Côte p107
8 High Street, SW19 5DX (8947 7100/
www.cote-restaurants.co.uk)

Gastropubs

Earl Spencer p118
260-262 Merton Road, SW18 5JL
(8870 9244/www.theearlspencer.co.uk)

Japanese

Kushi-Tei p205
264 The Broadway, SW19 1SB
(8543 1188/www.kushi-tei.com)

Winchmore Hill

Branches

Pizza Express
701 Green Lanes, N21 3RS
(8364 2992)

Wood Green

Branches

Nando's
Hollywood Green, Redvers Road,
N22 6EN (8889 2936)

Greek

Vrisaki p135
73 Myddleton Road, N22 8LZ
(8889 8760)

Woodford

Branches

Pizza Express
76-78 High Road, E18 2NA
(8924 4488)
Prezzo
8 Johnson Road, Woodford Green,
Essex IG8 0XA (8505 2400)

A-Z Index